# Eastern Europe

D0064406

ISBN 0-86442-116-8

9 780864 421166

Australia RRP $29.95
USA $21.95
UK £13.95
Canada $27.95
Singapore $39.95

2nd Edition

# Eastern Europe
## on a shoestring

**David Stanley**

**Eastern Europe on a shoestring**

**2nd edition**

**Published by**
    **Lonely Planet Publications**
    Head Office: PO Box 617, Hawthorn, Vic 3122, Australia
    Branches: PO Box 2001A, Berkeley, CA 94702, USA, and London, UK

**Printed by**
    Global Com Ltd, Singapore

**Front cover**
    Prague's St Nicholas Cathedral (Tom Owen Edmunds), The Image Bank

**First Published**
    April 1989

**This Edition**
    December 1991

Although the authors and publisher have tried to make the information as accurate as possible, they accept no responsibility for any loss, injury or inconvenience sustained by any person using this book.

National Library of Australia Cataloguing in Publication Data

Stanley, David
    Eastern Europe on a shoestring.

    2nd ed.
    Includes index.
    ISBN 0 86442 116 8.

    1. Europe, Eastern – Description and travel – Guide-books.
    I. Title.

914.704

## David Stanley

A quarter of a century ago, David's right thumb carried him out of Toronto, Canada, and onto a journey which has so far wound through 144 countries and territories, including a three-year trip from Tokyo to Kabul. His travel guidebooks for the South Pacific, Micronesia and Eastern Europe helped open those areas to budget travellers.

During the late 1960s Stanley got involved in Mexican culture by spending a year in several small towns near Guanajuato. Later he studied at the universities of Barcelona and Florence before settling down to get an honours degree (with distinction) in Spanish literature from the University of Guelph, Canada. This landed him a job as a tour guide in Fidel Castro's Cuba where Stanley developed an interest in 'socialist tourism'. Since then he's visited the countries covered in this book many times.

Having had the rare opportunity to spend long periods in Eastern Europe researching this book in the years immediately before and after 1989, Stanley is a keen observer of the changes presently taking place. From his base in Amsterdam he makes frequent trips to Eastern Europe, jammed between journeys to the areas worldwide he still hasn't visited. In travel writing Stanley has found a perfect outlet for his wanderlust.

## From the Author

Many people and organisations helped me compile this edition. The nationalities of those listed below are identified by the international automobile identification signs which follow their names.

Special thanks to Gerhard Visser (NL) and Bill Weir (USA) for getting my computer operational, to Erik van Eijk and Rianne Kielen for the loan of their beautiful home in Diemen (NL) where much of the book was written, to WG/unterm Dach at Wedding (D) for their kind hospitality, to David Crawford (USA) for inspiring the 1st edition of this book and sharing his intimate knowledge of Berlin during preparation of the 2nd edition, to Stefan Loose (D), Renate (D) and Jamie Walker (USA) for their kind advice, to

Adrian Grigorescu (RO) for showing me around Bucharest, to Fred Clements (NZ) for help in researching the Albania chapter, to Isidre Hernandez (E) and Rosa Molina (E) for information on Romania, to Jeff Bishop (USA) for his thoughts on the political situation in Eastern Europe, to the UNESCO Centrum Amsterdam (NL) for information on 'Biosphere Reserves' and 'World Heritage' sites, and to Musiques du Monde, Singel 281, Amsterdam (NL), for providing the dozens of CDs used to prepare the music sections. Without the constant support of Ria de Vos (NL) who spent hundreds of hours doing library research, keeping communications open between Amsterdam and Australia and solving all kinds of problems, this book might never have been finished.

The language sections were prepared with the assistance of Fred G Clements (NZ), Daniel Condratov (RO), Marek Faryna (PL), Sarah Gillman (AUS), Jorgj Harallamki (NZ), Jacek Herman-Izycki (PL), R Jankovic (YU), Slatina Kantschewa (BG), Koronczi Katalin (H), Dr J Kozubek (CS), Jan Larecki (PL), Joanna Mikolajczak (PL), Renata Novak-Pintarec (YU), Boris Petkov (BG), Jitka Pislovi (CS), Andonov Saso (YU), Udo Schwark (D), Anton Simko (CS),

Marzenna Smyczyńska (PL), Imre Ugrai (H), Fl Vasiliu (RO), Martina Veverková (CS) and Bill Wouters (NL).

Thanks to all these readers of the 1st edition who wrote in with their comments: Palita Abeywickrema (AUS), Trygve Anderson (USA), J Atkinson (GB), David Baird (E), Alan and Roz Bamber (GB), Sara Banaszak (USA), Jonathan Barlow (AUS), Marcel Bartos (AUS), Dianne Bennett (USA), Garrett P Bennett (USA), Thor Andre Berg (N), JCT Bishop (GB), Martin Bohnstedt (A), Roger Bielec (AUS), Daniel Bodis (NZ), Bill Bracewell (GB), Pat Browne (GB), Irene Braykovich (CDN), C H Brownlee (GB), Bob Buckie (CDN), Paula Bush (USA), Ester Cejas Romera (E), Marisha Chamberlain (USA), Eric Connor (GB), Philip J Crohn (AUS), Jeni Croome (GB), Carl R Curtis (USA), Saskia Derksen (NL), J T Dunlop (GB), Dolan H Eargle, Jr (USA), Ken Elliott (GB), Philip Elliott (AUS), Tony English (GB), A A Fearuley (GB), Mike Fee (NZ), Andrew Fraser-Urquhart (GB), Michael J Frost (GB), Daniel Gabriel (USA), Carrie J Galbraith (USA), Frank Gardiner (AUS), Frank Gardner (GB), David Goldman (USA), Doug Graham (USA), Nadyne A Gray (USA), Ed Green (AUS), Jerry Green (USA), Paul Greening (GB), Mark Gregg (AUS), Ron Haering (AUS), Bo Hakansson (S), Debbie Handley (AUS), C Robert Harberson (USA), Lance Hartland (GB), George Heath (USA), Mike Heppler (USA), Helene Hillenaar (NL), Len Houwers (NZ), R Jankovic (YU), Petra Kansy (D), Nick Kelleher (GB), P B Kempe (NL), Donna Kirkland (USA), Hank Krawczyk (CDN), Oliver Krug (NL), Steve Lantos (USA), Carrie Leana (USA), J Lerner (B), Sam Lipson (USA), Steve Ludington (USA), Hugh Macindoe (AUS), Hank Obermayer (USA), Matthew O'Brien (AUS), P Patterson (USA), Tas Pinther (USA), K I Porter (NZ), Andrew Rhodes (AUS), Robin Saltmarsh (AUS), Ebba Sass (D), Robert Sattler (USA), Benny Shanon (IL), Jack Shulman (USA), Lítězslav Šikýř (CS), Robert Sims (GB), Sarah Slover (USA), David Smith (GB), Lionel D Smith (CDN), Fran Snider (USA), Werenfried Spit (NL), Kerstin Sucher (D), R J Symons (GB), Glenn Tasky (USA), Montserrat Tresens (E), Deborah Turner (AUS), Murilo Vieira (B), Peter Vingerhoets (DK), Jenny Visser (NZ), Andrew Warmington (GB), Gael Wealleans (GB), Paul Welstone (USA), Hella and Horst Weiss (ZA), Megan Whilden (USA), Judith Wolford (USA), Colin Woodard (USA) and Susan Zance (CDN).

A (Austria), AUS (Australia), B (Belgium), BG (Bulgaria) CDN (Canada), CS (Czechoslovakia), D (Germany), DK (Denmark), E (Spain), GB (Great Britain), H (Hungary), IL (Israel), N (Norway), NL (Netherlands), NZ (New Zealand), PL (Poland), RO (Romania), S (Sweden), USA (United States), YU (Yugoslavia) and ZA (South Africa).

## From the Publisher

This edition of Eastern Europe on a Shoestring was edited at the Lonely Planet headquarters in Melbourne, Australia, by Adrienne Costanzo and Rob van Driesum. The maps were drawn or updated by Valerie Tellini with help from Jane Hart, based on material provided by the author. Margaret Jung designed the cover, produced the illustrations and was responsible for layout. Sharon Wertheim helped with the indexing. Krzysztof Dydynski and Richard Nebesky inserted some of the Slavic accents, and special thanks are due to Lonely Planet's computer whiz, Dan Levin, for getting the accents to boogie.

## Warning & Request

Things change – prices go up, schedules alter, good places go bad, bad places go bankrupt – nothing stays the same. So if you find things better or worse, recently opened or long since closed, please write and tell us, so we can make the next edition better!

Your letters will be used to help update future editions, and where possible, important changes will also be included as a Stop Press section in reprints.

All information is greatly appreciated, with the best letters receiving a free copy of the next edition, or any other Lonely Planet book of your choice.

# Contents

INTRODUCTION .................................................................................11

FACTS ABOUT THE REGION ..........................................................16

History .................16          Economy ....................20          Religion..........................22
People ..................20          Geography ..................21          Language........................22

FACTS FOR THE VISITOR ................................................................24

Planning ..............24          Time ...........................32          Information Offices........36
Visas....................26          Books .........................32          Accommodation.............37
Documents...........28          Health.........................33          Food .............................39
Money..................29          Film & Photography ...34          Entertainment...............40
Electricity ............31          Activities.....................35          Things to Buy...............40
Post ....................31          Work...........................36

GETTING THERE & AWAY ...............................................................42

Air .......................42          Land ...........................44          Package Tours ..............45
Train....................43          Sea.............................45          Warning........................45

GETTING AROUND............................................................................46

Air .......................46          Car & Motorbike .........47          Boat .............................50
Bus......................46          Bicycle .......................49          Local Transport.............50
Train....................46          Hitchhiking .................49

EASTERN GERMANY.......................................................................53

**Facts about the Country ...54**    Film & Photography ..................76    Meissen ............................140
History .........................54    Work..........................................76    Leipzig ..............................141
Geography ....................60    Activities....................................76    **Thuringia ........................ 147**
Government...................61    Highlights..................................77    Weimar..............................147
Economy.......................61    Accommodation ........................78    Erfurt.................................151
Population & People.......63    Food ........................................78    Eisenach ...........................153
Arts .............................64    Drinks ......................................79    Nordhausen .......................155
Religion........................67    Things to Buy ...........................79    **Saxony-Anhalt ................. 156**
Language ......................67    **Getting There & Away ....... 80**    Wernigerode.......................156
**Facts for the Visitor ..........71**    Air.............................................80    Quedlinburg .......................157
Visas & Embassies ........71    Land..........................................80    Magdeburg.........................158
Money...........................71    Sea............................................83    Halle..................................159
Climate & When to Go.....72    **Getting Around ................. 83**    Naumburg ..........................162
Tourist Offices ...............72    Bus............................................83    Freyburg.............................162
Business Hours & Holidays ......73    Train..........................................83    Lutherstadt Wittenberg ........162
Cultural Events...............73    Car & Motorbike .........................85    **Mecklenburg-Pomerania. 165**
Post & Telecommunications......73    Boat...........................................86    Schwerin ...........................165
Time .............................75    Local Transport...........................86    Wismar ..............................168
Laundry.........................75    **Berlin................................ 86**    Rostock ..............................170
Weights & Measures .......75    **Brandenburg.................... 126**    Warnemünde.......................171
Books & Maps ...............75    Potsdam.....................................127    Stralsund ...........................172
Media ...........................75    **Saxony.............................. 132**    Hiddensee Island ...............175
Health ..........................76    Dresden .....................................133    Rügen Island ......................175
Dangers & Annoyances..........76    Moritzburg .................................139

POLAND ..............................................................................................177

**Facts about the Country . 177**    Geography .................................183    Population & People..............184
History .........................177    Economy....................................183    Arts ...................................185

Culture ...........................186
Religion ..........................186
Language .........................187
**Facts for the Visitor ......... 190**
Visas & Embassies .................190
Money...............................192
Climate & When to Go............194
Tourist Offices .....................194
Business Hours & Holidays ....195
Cultural Events ....................196
Post & Telecommunications....196
Time...............................197
Weights & Measures ..............197
Books & Maps.....................197
Media..............................198
Health .............................198
Women Travellers...................198
Dangers & Annoyances...........198
Activities...........................199
Highlights of Poland...............199
Accommodation ....................200
Food ...............................201
Drinks .............................203
Entertainment .....................203
Things to Buy......................204
**Getting There & Away...... 204**
Air.................................204
Land ...............................205
Sea ................................207

**Getting Around ............... 207**
Air.................................207
Bus ................................207
Train...............................207
Car & Motorbike ..................210
Hitchhiking ........................212
Boat ...............................212
Local Transport....................212
Tours ..............................212
**Warsaw ......................... 213**
**Małopolska...................... 224**
Lublin..............................224
Kazimierz Dolny ..................228
Zamość.............................228
Przemyśl ...........................230
The Bieszczady Mountains .... 232
Łańcut .............................232
Rzeszów ...........................233
Nowy Sącz.........................234
Stary Sącz .........................236
The Tatra Mountains &
Zakopane..........................236
Kraków ............................244
Oświęcim ..........................252
Częstochowa ......................254
**Silesia ........................... 257**
Opole..............................257
Wrocław ...........................259
**Wielkopolska................... 265**

Poznań.............................265
Gniezno ...........................271
Toruń ..............................272
Bydgoszcz .........................275
**Pomerania...................... 276**
History.............................276
Information ........................277
Szczecin ...........................277
Świnoujście .......................280
Międzyzdroje ......................282
Kołobrzeg..........................283
Łeba ...............................283
Gdynia.............................285
Hel ................................286
Sopot ..............................288
Gdańsk ............................289
**Mazuria ......................... 294**
History.............................294
Malbork............................294
Olsztyn ............................295
The Elbląg Canal ..................298
Grunwald..........................298
Lidzbark Warmiński...............299
Frombork...........................299
The Great Mazurian Lakes .....300
Giżycko ............................302
Wilczy Szaniec.....................303
Mikołajki...........................303
Ruciane-Nida ......................305

**CZECHOSLOVAKIA............................................................................................... 307**

**Facts about the Country . 307**
History ............................307
Geography ........................311
Government .......................313
Economy...........................313
Population & People...............314
Arts ...............................314
Language ..........................315
**Facts for the Visitor ......... 318**
Visas & Embassies .................318
Money..............................319
Climate & When to Go...........321
Tourist Offices .....................321
Business Hours & Holidays ....322
Cultural Events ......................322
Post & Telecommunications....323
Time...............................323
Weights & Measures ..............323
Books & Maps.....................323
Media..............................324
Health .............................324
Activities...........................325
Highlights .........................325
Accommodation ....................326
Food ...............................327
Drinks .............................328

Entertainment......................328
Things to Buy......................329
**Getting There & Away .... 329**
Air.................................329
Land ...............................330
**Getting Around ............... 334**
Air.................................334
Bus ................................334
Train...............................334
Car & Motorbike ..................335
Bicycle ............................336
Local Transport....................336
Tours ..............................336
**Prague ........................... 336**
**Central Bohemia............. 356**
Karlštejn...........................357
Konopiště .........................357
Kutná Hora .......................357
Kolín ..............................360
**West Bohemia................. 360**
Karlovy Vary ......................360
Cheb ..............................364
Františkovy Lázně ...............366
Mariánské Lázně ................367
Plzeň...............................370
**South Bohemia ............... 372**

České Budějovice..................373
Český Krumlov ...................375
Tábor..............................376
**Moravia......................... 378**
Telč ...............................379
Znojmo............................380
Brno...............................382
Břeclav ............................386
**Bratislava ...................... 386**
**West & Central Slovakia . 394**
Trenčín ............................394
Žilina ..............................396
The Malá Fatra....................397
Banská Bystrica ...................399
**East Slovakia ................. 403**
The Vysoké Tatry .................403
Poprad-Tatry ......................407
Dunajec Gorge ....................408
Spišská Nová Ves..................408
Levoča.............................409
Spišské Podhradie .................410
Prešov .............................412
Bardejov...........................414
Bardejovské Kúpele ...............415
Košice .............................415

# HUNGARY .................................................................419

**Facts about the Country . 420**
History .................................................420
Geography ...........................................424
Economy..............................................425
Population & People.............................426
Arts ....................................................426
Language ............................................427
**Facts for the Visitor ........ 431**
Visas & Embassies ..................................431
Money.................................................432
Climate & When to Go...........433
What to Bring.......................................433
Tourist Offices ....................................433
Business Hours & Holidays ....434
Cultural Events ....................................434
Post & Telecommunications...435
Time....................................................435
Weights & Measures ...........................435
Books & Maps.....................................435
Media..................................................436
Health .................................................436
Film & Photography.............................436
Activities.............................................436
Highlights ...........................................437
Accommodation ..................................438
Food ...................................................440
Drinks .................................................441
Entertainment .....................................441

Things to Buy ......................441
**Getting There & Away ..... 442**
Air.......................................................442
Land ...................................................442
River ...................................................445
**Getting Around ............... 445**
Bus......................................................445
Train....................................................445
Car & Motorbike ....................448
Boat.....................................................448
Local Transport...................448
Tours...................................................449
**Budapest ........................ 449**
**The Danube Bend........... 472**
Getting There & Away...........472
Szentendre ..........................................472
Vác......................................................475
Visegrád ...............................................477
Esztergom ...........................................480
**Western Transdanubia ... 483**
Getting There & Away ........ 483
Tata.....................................................483
Komárom .............................................485
Győr ....................................................486
Pannonhalma .......................................489
Sopron ................................................490
Fertőd .................................................495
Kőszeg ................................................495

Szombathely.........................497
**Balaton Lake .................. 500**
Getting There & Away ..........500
Getting Around ...................500
Székesfehérvár ....................................500
Siófok ..................................................502
Balatonfüred.........................................505
Tihany ..................................................507
Veszprém .............................................509
Badacsony ...........................................510
Keszthely .............................................512
Hévíz...................................................515
**Southern Transdanubia .. 516**
Kaposvár..............................................516
Pécs ....................................................518
Szigetvár ..............................................523
Siklós ..................................................524
**The Great Plain.............. 524**
Kecskemét............................................525
Bugac ..................................................527
Szeged ................................................527
Debrecen .............................................530
Hortobágy ............................................533
**Northern Hungary........... 533**
Eger ....................................................533
Aggtelek ...............................................537
Tokaj....................................................537
Sárospatak ...........................................538

# ROMANIA ...............................................................541

**Facts about the Country . 542**
History .................................................542
Geography ...........................................549
Economy..............................................549
Population & People.............551
Arts ....................................................551
Language .............................................552
**Facts for the Visitor ........ 555**
Visas & Embassies ...............555
Money.................................................555
Climate & When to Go...........557
What to Bring.......................................557
Tourist Offices ....................................558
Business Hours & Holidays ....559
Cultural Events ....................................559
Post & Telecommunications...559
Time....................................................559
Weights & Measures ...........................560
Books & Maps.....................................560
Media..................................................560
Health .................................................560
Dangers & Annoyances...........560
Activities.............................................560
Highlights ...........................................561
Accommodation ..................................562
Food ...................................................563
Drinks .................................................564

Entertainment......................564
Things to Buy ......................564
**Getting There & Away ..... 565**
Air.......................................................565
Land ...................................................565
River ...................................................567
**Getting Around ............... 567**
Air.......................................................567
Bus......................................................567
Train....................................................567
Car & Motorbike ....................570
Hitchhiking ..........................................570
Boat.....................................................570
Local Transport...................571
Tours...................................................571
**Bucharest ....................... 571**
**Wallachia ....................... 584**
Snagov ................................................584
Curtea de Argeş....................585
Count Dracula's Castle ........585
Horezu.................................................586
Tîrgu Jiu...............................................586
Drobeta-Turnu Severin ........587
The Iron Gate ......................................588
**Dobruja .......................... 588**
Danube Canal .....................................589
Getting Around ...................................589

Mangalia ..............................589
Neptun-Olimp ......................591
Eforie Nord ..........................................591
Constanţa .............................................592
Mamaia ...............................................596
Histria .................................................597
**The Danube Delta .......... 597**
Getting Around ...................597
Tulcea..................................................598
On the Danube ....................................600
Sulina ..................................................601
Upriver from Tulcea ............601
Brăila ..................................................601
**Moldavia ........................ 603**
Iaşi......................................................603
**Bukovina ........................ 607**
Suceava ...............................................608
Putna ..................................................610
Rădăuţi ................................................610
Suceviţa ...............................................610
Moldoviţa .............................................611
Gura Humorului ...................611
**Transylvania................... 612**
Sinaia ..................................................613
Rîşnov & Bran ......................616
Braşov .................................................617
Sighişoara.............................................620

| | | |
|---|---|---|
| Sibiu....................622 | Hunedoara...............632 | Oradea....................638 |
| The Făgăraş Mountains.........625 | **Maramures...............634** | Băile Felix................640 |
| Cluj-Napoca.............626 | Baia Mare...............634 | Arad.......................641 |
| Alba Iulia................629 | Sighetu Marmaţiei.........636 | Timişoara.................643 |
| Deva....................632 | **Crişana & Banat............638** | |

## BULGARIA...................................................................................647

| | | |
|---|---|---|
| **Facts about the Country . 647** | Entertainment............669 | Getting Around............696 |
| History..................647 | Things to Buy.............669 | Burgas...................696 |
| Geography...............651 | **Getting There & Away.... 669** | Sozopol..................699 |
| Economy................652 | Air.......................669 | Coastal Camping Grounds......700 |
| Population & People..........652 | Land....................669 | Sunny Beach..............701 |
| Arts.....................653 | River....................672 | Nesebâr..................701 |
| Language................655 | Package Tours............672 | Varna....................703 |
| **Facts for the Visitor.........660** | **Getting Around.............672** | Golden Sands.............707 |
| Visas & Embassies..........660 | Air......................672 | Balchik...................708 |
| Money..................661 | Bus.....................672 | **Northern Bulgaria............ 708** |
| Climate & When to Go..........663 | Train....................672 | Vidin....................709 |
| Tourist Offices............663 | Car & Motorbike...........674 | Pleven...................710 |
| Business Hours & Holidays....663 | Boat....................674 | The Stara Planina.........713 |
| Cultural Events............663 | Local Transport...........674 | Troyan...................713 |
| Post & Telecommunications....664 | **Sofia....................... 675** | Karlovo..................714 |
| Time....................664 | **Western Bulgaria............ 684** | Kazanlâk.................714 |
| Weights & Measures.........665 | Bankya..................684 | Shipka...................715 |
| Books & Maps.............665 | The Rila Mountains.........685 | Etâr.....................715 |
| Media...................665 | Rila Monastery...........687 | Veliko Târnovo............715 |
| Health...................665 | **Thrace.....................688** | Ruse.....................719 |
| Activities.................665 | Koprivshtitsa.............688 | Shumen..................722 |
| Highlights................666 | Hisarya..................691 | Preslav..................723 |
| Accommodation............666 | Plovdiv..................693 | Madara..................724 |
| Food....................668 | Bachkovo Monastery........695 | Pliska....................724 |
| Drinks...................668 | **The Black Sea Coast....... 696** | |

## YUGOSLAVIA...............................................................................727

| | | |
|---|---|---|
| **Facts about the Country . 727** | Highlights................746 | Julian Alps................763 |
| History..................727 | Accommodation...........746 | Bled.....................763 |
| Geography...............733 | Food....................748 | Bohinj...................766 |
| Economy................733 | Drinks...................749 | Trekking Mt Triglav...........766 |
| Population & People..........734 | Entertainment............749 | Bohinjska Bistrica..........768 |
| Arts.....................735 | Things to Buy.............750 | Nova Gorica..............768 |
| Language................735 | **Getting There & Away..... 750** | **Croatia.................... 769** |
| **Facts for the Visitor.......... 739** | Air......................750 | Zagreb...................769 |
| Visas & Embassies..........739 | Land....................750 | Kumrovec................776 |
| Money..................740 | Sea.....................752 | Plitvice National Park........776 |
| Climate & When to Go..........742 | Package Tours............754 | Osijek...................779 |
| Tourist Offices............742 | **Getting Around.............754** | **Istria...................... 781** |
| Business Hours & Holidays....743 | Air......................754 | Getting Around............781 |
| Cultural Events............743 | Bus.....................754 | Koper....................781 |
| Post & Telecommunications....743 | Train....................755 | Izola.....................783 |
| Time....................744 | Car & Motorbike...........756 | Portorož..................783 |
| Weights & Measures.........744 | Hitchhiking...............757 | Piran.....................785 |
| Books & Maps.............744 | Boat....................757 | Poreč....................787 |
| Media...................744 | Local Transport...........757 | Rovinj...................789 |
| Health...................744 | **Slovenia....................758** | Pula.....................791 |
| Dangers & Annoyances..........745 | Ljubljana.................758 | Brioni...................793 |
| Film & Photography...........745 | Postojna..................762 | **Gulf Of Kvarner............ 794** |
| Activities.................745 | Škocjan Caves.............762 | Rijeka...................794 |

Opatija .................................798
Mali Lošinj .........................798
Krk......................................799
Baška .................................799
Rab.....................................800
Lopar..................................802
**Dalmatia**.............................**802**
History ................................803
Paklenica National Park .........803
Zadar..................................803
Šibenik................................806
Krka National Park.................808
Trogir .................................808
Split....................................809
Salona ................................815
Hvar ...................................816
Starigrad ............................819
Korčula ...............................820
Lumbarda............................822

Vela Luka ...........................822
Orebić ................................822
Mljet Island ........................823
**Dubrovnik**...........................**824**
**Montenegro**......................**829**
History ................................829
Getting Around ...................830
Kotor ..................................831
Cetinje ...............................831
Budva.................................832
Bar.....................................833
Ulcinj .................................833
Biogradska Gora National
    Park .............................834
Durmitor National Park .........834
**Bosnia-Hercegovina**.......**835**
History ................................835
Mostar ...............................836
Međugorje..........................838

Sarajevo.............................839
Travnik................................842
Jajce...................................843
**Vojvodina** .........................**844**
Novi Sad.............................844
Subotica..............................846
**Serbia**................................**846**
History.................................846
Belgrade .............................847
Southern Serbia...................853
**Kosovo** .............................**853**
Getting There & Away ..........854
Pejë....................................854
Prizren................................855
**Macedonia**.......................**856**
Skopje.................................857
Ohrid   ................................860
Bitola ..................................863

## ALBANIA ................................................................................867

**Facts about the Country . 867**
History ................................867
Geography ..........................872
Economy .............................873
Population & People...............873
Arts ....................................874
Religion ..............................875
Language ............................875
**Facts for the Visitor ......... 878**
Visas & Embassies ...............878
Customs..............................879
Money.................................879
Climate & When to Go...........880
Tourist Offices .....................880
Business Hours & Holidays ....880
Cultural Events ....................881
Post & Telecommunications....881
Time....................................881

Weights & Measures...............881
Books & Maps .....................881
Media .................................881
Health.................................882
Film & Photography ..............882
Highlights ...........................882
Accommodation ..................882
Food ..................................882
Drinks .................................883
Entertainment......................883
Things to Buy ......................883
**Getting There & Away ..... 883**
Air ......................................883
Land ...................................883
Package Tours .....................883
**Getting Around ................ 885**
Train....................................885
Other ..................................885

Local Transport.....................885
**Tiranë**................................**886**
Durrës.................................889
**Southern Albania**.............**890**
Fier & Apolonia ....................890
Gjirokastër ..........................891
Sarandë...............................892
Butrint ................................892
Berat ..................................892
Elbasan ..............................893
Pogradec.............................894
Korçë..................................894
**Northern Albania** ............**895**
Krujë ..................................895
Lezhë .................................896
Shkodër ..............................896

## ALTERNATIVE PLACE NAMES ......................................................898

## INTERNATIONAL AUTOMOBILE SIGNS............................................901

## INDEX ......................................................................................902

Maps ..............................902   Text ...............................903

# Map Legend

## BOUNDARIES

| | |
|---|---|
| — · — · — · — | ........ International Boundary |
| — · · — · · — | ................ Internal Boundary |
| ++++++++++++ | .... National Park or Reserve |
| – – – – – – – | ........................... The Equator |
| ················ | ........................... The Tropics |

## SYMBOLS

| | |
|---|---|
| ◉ NEW DELHI | ........................ National Capital |
| ● BOMBAY | ......... Provincial or State Capital |
| ● Pune | .............................. Major Town |
| • Borsi | .............................. Minor Town |
| ■ | ......................... Places to Stay |
| ▼ | ......................... Places to Eat |
| ≜ | ............................... Post Office |
| ✈ | ..................................... Airport |
| i | ..................... Tourist Information |
| ⊖ | ............. Bus Station or Terminal |
| 66 | ............. Highway Route Number |
| ☾ ✝ ♪ | ...... Mosque, Church, Cathedral |
| ∴ | ......................... Temple or Ruin |
| ✚ | .................................... Hospital |
| ※ | .................................... Lookout |
| ▲ | ............................ Camping Area |
| ⊓ | ............................... Picnic Area |
| ⌂ | ............................ Hut or Chalet |
| ▲ | ........................ Mountain or Hill |
| | ........................ Railway Station |
| | .............................. Road Bridge |
| | ........................... Railway Bridge |
| | ................................ Road Tunnel |
| | ............................. Railway Tunnel |
| | ................... Escarpment or Cliff |
| | ........................................... Pass |
| | ............ Ancient or Historic Wall |

## ROUTES

| | |
|---|---|
| | ........ Major Road or Highway |
| – – – – – | ......... Unsealed Major Road |
| | ........................ Sealed Road |
| – – – – – | ..... Unsealed Road or Track |
| | ........................... City Street |
| ++++++++++ | ............................... Railway |
| ─●─ | ................................. Subway |
| ················ | .................... Walking Track |
| – – – – – | ........................ Ferry Route |
| +++++++++ | ........ Cable Car or Chair Lift |

## HYDROGRAPHIC FEATURES

| | |
|---|---|
| | .................... River or Creek |
| | .............. Intermittent Stream |
| | ........ Lake, Intermittent Lake |
| | ........................... Coast Line |
| | ..................................... Spring |
| | ................................. Waterfall |
| | ................................... Swamp |
| | ............... Salt Lake or Reef |
| | ................................. Glacier |

## OTHER FEATURES

| | |
|---|---|
| | Park, Garden or National Park |
| | ....................... Built Up Area |
| | ... Market or Pedestrian Mall |
| | ......... Plaza or Town Square |
| | ............................. Cemetery |

Note: not all symbols displayed above appear in this book

# Introduction

Since the 1st edition of this book in April 1989, Eastern Europe has undergone kaleidoscopic changes. Political structures have been shaken or turned upside down, bureaucratic controls have been lifted, and one country (the German Democratic Republic) even ceased to exist! As a result, this book has had to be totally rewritten.

Eastern Europe isn't the same place any more! The many rules and regulations of socialist central planners have largely been scrapped and replaced by free competition. For visitors, careful advance preparations are now less important than being on the lookout for the good deals once there. Spontaneous trips are now fairly routine but you have to be on your toes to dodge rising prices. That's where we try to help.

Despite the new accessibility, Eastern Europe is still the 'last frontier' of tourism in Europe. From the Baltic to the Balkans a treasure-trove of history and natural beauty awaits you. Central Europe has been the source of much of our Western culture, especially in literature and music, and this volatile region has shaped world history. This century alone, both world wars began here and the recent democratic revolutions have laid low the East-West Cold War. Aside from this legacy there are vast forests, rugged mountains, quiet lakes and mighty rivers just waiting to be discovered.

The many museums, churches and castles of Eastern Europe equal those of Western Europe in every respect, except that they're less publicised, less crowded and more

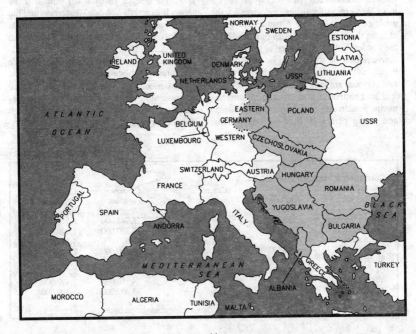

accessible. And you won't be discouraged by the admission fees. The theatres and concert halls are less expensive, and prices in general are lower. The people are friendlier than along the beaten tourist trails of the West. Many locals are curious to meet visitors and contact is now much more relaxed.

The Eastern European countries are not all alike. Romania and Czechoslovakia are as different as Sicily and Scandinavia. To understand the region you'll need to visit several countries. Don't spend all your time in the capitals as you'll usually find it's cheaper and much less crowded in provincial towns. Those who feel they've seen Czechoslovakia and Hungary after visiting Prague and Budapest are the equivalent of tourists who think that all there is to the USA and Australia is New York, Los Angeles and Sydney.

Independent budget travel is possible all year throughout the region and only Albania still makes you book in advance. Many countries have abolished visa requirements for most Western nationalities, and visas for the other countries (except Albania) are available on the spot at consulates or (usually) at the border. You'll be amazed at the ease and convenience of travel. Public transport is highly developed, and food, entertainment and services are inexpensive.

The reintroduction of capitalism has meant double and even triple-digit inflation and rising prices in hard-currency terms.

Sometimes, however, the cost for foreigners may actually go down as national currencies are devalued, thus it's difficult to predict how much things will cost in future. It's possible that the prices listed herein will have increased substantially in Poland and Czechoslovakia, but not as much in Hungary and only a little in Yugoslavia and Berlin. Romania and Bulgaria are variables. If you can, visit one of the more expensive countries, Germany and Yugoslavia, first. That way you'll appreciate the others all the more.

In this book we've quoted all prices in US dollars or German Marks (Deutschmarks). This was done by converting local currency prices at the official bank rate in force at the time. In some cases prices will have gone up but within individual chapters accommodation prices should remain relative to one another, so you'll soon be able to judge how much you'll need to spend.

One thing is certain: travel in Eastern Europe will never be nicer than it is right now. The longer you put off your trip the larger the crowds of other Westerners and the more you'll have to pay. The Communists subsidised many of the things most needed by visitors: public transport, cultural facilities (museums, theatres, etc), self-service restaurants, publications, etc. Only at regular tourist hotels did you have to pay a price equivalent to real costs. Private entrepreneurs are unlikely to be as generous, though the service will probably get better.

**Countries & Populations**

| Country | Area (sq km) | Capital | Country Population | Capital Population |
|---|---|---|---|---|
| Eastern Germany | 108,813 | Berlin | 18,748,000 | 3,500,000 |
| Poland | 312,683 | Warsaw | 37,780,000 | 1,649,000 |
| Czechoslovakia | 127,889 | Prague | 15,620,000 | 1,211,000 |
| Hungary | 93,032 | Budapest | 10,590,000 | 2,115,000 |
| Romania | 237,500 | Bucharest | 23,000,000 | 2,298,000 |
| Bulgaria | 110,994 | Sofia | 8,970,000 | 1,208,000 |
| Yugoslavia | 255,804 | Belgrade | 24,110,000 | 1,470,000 |
| Albania | 28,748 | Tiranë | 3,200,000 | 300,000 |

A final warning is in order regarding street name changes. Some municipal authorities have been more enthusiastic about removing the old street signs from streets than about putting up new ones. In other cases the names of streets have been officially changed back to what they were before 1945 but no-one has bothered to change the street signs at all. Maps printed before 1991 may now be out of date. This situation is bound to cause confusion for several years and changes are still being made, so don't be alarmed if Marx Engels Platz or Lenin utca seem to have vanished from the face of the earth!

**STOP PRESS**

While this book was being printed, the fighting and chaos in Yugoslavia were getting worse by the day. Many governments were strongly advising their citizens to defer nonessential travel until things quieten down. We suggest you heed their advice for the time being, and that you find out the latest news before making any decision to travel to Yugoslavia. ■

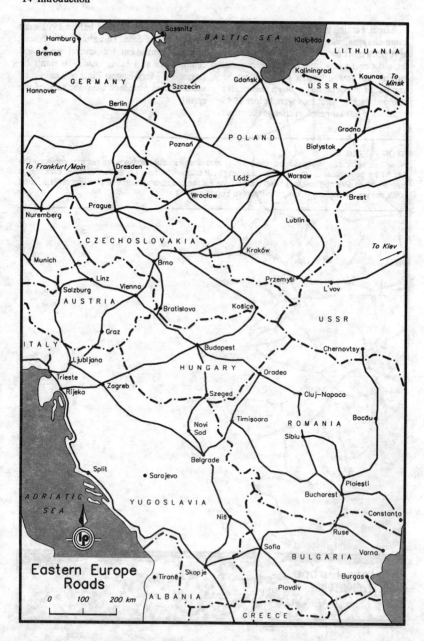

Eastern Europe
Roads

0     100     200 km

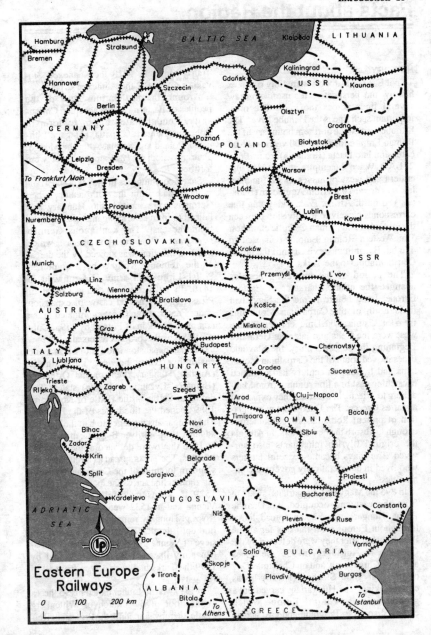

**Eastern Europe Railways**

0     100     200 km

# Facts about the Region

## HISTORY

To put Eastern Europe's incredibly complex history into perspective it's useful to draw several lines across the map. The most important such line is the Danube River. The Danube formed the northern boundary of the Roman Empire for about 500 years, with an extension into Dacia (Romania) from 106 to 271 AD. When the empire was divided into eastern and western halves in 395, another line was drawn south from Aquincum (Budapest) to north Africa. Even today this line corresponds closely to the division between the Orthodox and Roman Catholic churches. The Western Roman Empire collapsed in 476 but Byzantium survived until the fall of Constantinople to the Turks in 1453.

The period of the migrating peoples changed the ethnic character of Eastern Europe. Long before Rome the Slavs had lived north of the Carpathian Mountains from the Vistula to the Dnieper rivers. To the west were the Celts and later the Germans. Beginning in the 6th century, the Slavonic tribes moved south of the Carpathian Mountains and by the 9th century had occupied everything east of a line running from Magdeburg to Trieste. In the south they expanded as far as Greece. The Daco-Roman population of present Romania proved numerous enough to absorb the newcomers. In Albania the original Illyrian inhabitants also survived. The Slavs became peaceful farmers who lived in democratically governed communities.

In 896 the Magyars (Hungarians) swept in from the east and occupied the Danube Basin. Hungarian horsemen spread terror throughout Europe with raids as far as the Pyrenees, but after they were defeated by the Germans at Augsburg in 955 the tribes accepted Christianity, and on Christmas Day of the year 1000 Stephen (István) I was crowned king. The Hungarians carved out a great empire in central Europe which extended south to Belgrade and east across Transylvania. In 1018 they annexed Slovakia and in 1102 they annexed Croatia.

Around the millennium most of the peoples of Eastern Europe accepted Christianity. Feudal states began to form in Bohemia, Bulgaria, Croatia, Hungary, Lithuania, Poland and Serbia. After the Mongol Tatar invasion of 1241, many cities were fortified.

Saxon communities in Slovakia and Transylvania date from the 13th century when Germans were invited into Hungary and Poland to form a buffer against fresh attacks from the east. The continuous German *Drang nach Osten* (drive to the east) which began at this time was slowed by the defeat of the Teutonic Knights by a combined Polish-Lithuanian army at Grunwald in 1410. In 1701 Berlin became capital of Prussia and a renewed eastward expansion under Frederick the Great culminated in the complete partition of Poland by 1795. Only in 1945 was this process reversed.

Turkish expansion into Europe was made easier by rivalry between the Catholic (Austria, Hungary, Venice) and Orthodox (Bulgaria, Byzantium, Serbia) states. The defeat of Serbia at the Battle of Kosovo in 1389 opened the floodgates of the Balkans. The Hungarians managed to halt the Turkish advance temporarily at Belgrade in 1456, but in 1526 they were defeated at the Battle of Mohács. The Turks spread as far north as the southern foothills of the Carpathians, drawing another line across the map of Europe. In 1529 they unsuccessfully laid siege to Vienna and in 1532 were stopped again at Kőszeg. Hungary remained under Ottoman rule until the defeat of the second Turkish siege of Vienna in 1683. A combined Christian army liberated Buda in 1686 and by 1699 the Turks had been driven from all of Hungary.

In 1517 Martin Luther nailed his 95 theses to the door of the church of Wittenberg Castle, thereby launching the Protestant Reformation. This soon took hold in northern Germany, and from 1618 to 1648 the Thirty Years' War between Protestants and Catholics devastated much of northern Europe. A dispute between Poland and Sweden in the mid-17th century added to the destruction in central Europe. Plague columns still recall the pestilence and war which halved the populations of some countries.

The rise of the Austrian Habsburg dynasty accompanied these wars. After the fall of Hungary to the Turks, the Habsburgs assumed the thrones of Hungary, Bohemia and Croatia. In 1620 the Catholic Habsburgs tightened their grip on Bohemia, and then expanded into Hungary and the Balkans in the wake of the declining Ottoman Empire. From 1703 to 1711 Hungarians led by the Transylvanian prince Ferenc Rákóczi II fought an unsuccessful war of independence against the Habsburgs. During the 18th and 19th centuries the Habsburgs controlled a vast empire from Prague to Belgrade and east into Transylvania. In 1867 Austria and Hungary agreed to share control of the region through a dual Austro-Hungarian monarchy.

Poland was wiped off the map of Europe by the partitions of 1722, 1793 and 1795. Prussia and Russia took most of Poland for themselves, with Austria receiving a small slice in the south. It's not hard to understand why the Poles sided with Napoleon, whose entry into Eastern Europe in 1806 marked the beginning of the transition from feudal autocracy to modern, bourgeois capitalism. Napoleon's final defeat in 1815 allowed the Prussians and Habsburgs to reimpose their rule. In 1848 there were unsuccessful liberal-democratic revolutions throughout central Europe against the prevailing absolutism.

In the Balkans the uprisings and wars against Ottoman oppression continued into the 20th century. In 1876 the Bulgarians rose against the Turks, leading to the Russo-Turkish War of 1877 and Bulgarian autonomy in 1878. Bulgarian independence followed in 1908. Romania and Serbia declared complete independence from the Turks in 1878 and the Habsburgs occupied

Bosnia-Hercegovina (in present-day Yugoslavia) that same year, annexing it outright in 1908. Macedonia and Albania remained under Turkey until the First Balkan War (1912). After the Second Balkan War (1913), Serbia and Greece divided Macedonia between themselves. Bulgarian dissatisfaction with this result led to further fighting during both world wars.

In 1914 Habsburg and tsarist imperial ambitions clashed in the Balkans and all of Europe was drawn into a catastrophic war. By November 1918, war weariness led to the collapse of the autocracies in Russia, Austria-Hungary, Bulgaria and Germany as sailors mutinied and troops abandoned the fronts. In 1919 there were socialist revolutions in Germany and Hungary, but they were put down by right-wing militarists. Had the revolutions succeeded, the history of the 20th century would have been totally different.

The end of WW I saw the restoration of Poland and the creation of Czechoslovakia and Yugoslavia. Although the new borders were supposed to follow ethnic boundaries, Northern and Western Bohemia went to Czechoslovakia despite the largely German population. Similarly, the Hungarians of Slovakia, Transylvania and Vojvodina, the Albanians of Kosovo and the Ukrainians of south-east Poland all became homogeneous majorities in foreign countries next to their motherlands. This situation and the socioeconomic conditions in Germany were largely responsible for the rise of Hitler and the outbreak of WW II.

The history of Eastern Europe after 1933 is one of constant Nazi aggression backed by threats and violence. In September 1938, Britain and France sold out Czechoslovakia at the Munich Conference, ending the possibility of any effective military resistance to the Nazis in the east. Bulgaria, Hungary and Romania soon fell in line behind Germany. Uncertain of Western backing after Munich, the Soviet Union signed a nonaggression pact with Germany on 23 August 1939 to buy time. When Poland resisted Hitler's demands it was promptly invaded, touching off WW II. Yugoslavia and the USSR shared this fate in 1941.

Hitler's programme of military expansion led to the destruction of Germany. In February 1943 the German 6th Army capitulated at Stalingrad, and by May 1945 the Soviet army had captured Berlin. At the Yalta Conference in February 1945, Churchill, Roosevelt and Stalin agreed on 'spheres of influence' in Europe. The Potsdam Conference of August 1945 divided Germany and Berlin into four occupation zones. The borders of Poland and the USSR moved west and those Germans who had not already fled East Prussia, Pomerania and Silesia were deported.

## Post WW II

With the arrival of Soviet troops in Bulgaria, Communist-led governments took over from Nazi or monarcho-fascist regimes East Germany, Hungary and Romania. Communist partisans took control in Yugoslavia and Albania. Czechoslovakia continued as a democratic coalition until the Communist Party took full control during a political crisis in March 1948.

The events in Czechoslovakia set off a chain reaction as the frustrated Western allies decided it was time to consolidate the areas under their control against further Communist advances. In June 1948, a new currency linked to the US dollar was introduced into the three western sectors of Berlin, allegedly to facilitate postwar reconstruction.

This created a tremendous problem for Communist officials in East Germany where nationalisation of the economy was not yet complete. Rather than face an uncontrollable black market which would have bled them white, the Soviet army closed the surface transit routes from West Germany to West Berlin a few days later. The air routes remained open and for 11 months the 'Berlin Airlift' supplied the western zones of the city. This crisis may be seen as the beginning of the 'Cold War'.

The lines were drawn even more clearly when NATO formed in April 1949. The Federal Republic of Germany was created in September, the German Democratic Republic in October. The Council for Mutual Economic Aid (Comecon), the dominant economic planning body in Eastern Europe until 1990, was also created in 1949. The Warsaw Pact was not signed until May 1955, when West Germany was admitted to NATO.

A second Berlin crisis occurred in August 1961 when East Germany built a wall around West Berlin to stem the flow of refugees. The 1971 Quadripartite Agreement on Berlin, signed by the USA, the USSR, the UK and France, normalised the de facto situation in the city. After the 1975 Helsinki Conference on Security & Cooperation in Europe (CSCE), at which 35 governments accepted the status quo in Europe, tensions relaxed considerably.

Between 1945 and 1989, the Communist governments throughout Eastern Europe emphasised heavy industry, central planning and social justice. Agriculture was collectivised in all of the countries except Poland and Yugoslavia. Yet there were wide variations in approach and in later years Bulgaria, Czechoslovakia, East Germany and Hungary attained respectable levels of development, while the inhabitants of Poland, Romania and the USSR suffered prolonged hardship. Well before the 1989 Communist breakdown, there were popular upheavals in East Germany (1953), Hungary (1956), Czechoslovakia (1968), Poland (1956, 1970, 1976, 1981) and Romania (1987), but these were suppressed by military force.

By the late 1980s the Soviet Union had adopted a policy of nonintervention towards Eastern Europe, and local Communist governments could no longer count on Soviet military support to remain in power. The first crack in the Eastern bloc appeared in Poland in April 1989, when the Communist regime agreed to legalise Solidarity and allow partially free elections. The Solidarity election victory in June 1989 and the appointment of non-Communist Tadeusz Mazowiecki as prime minister in August were unprecedented events watched all across Eastern Europe.

Gradual reform was also taking place in Hungary, which began dismantling its border controls with Austria in May 1989 and opened its borders in September. In October the Hungarian Communists relinquished their monopoly on power.

The event which really signalled the end of Eastern European Communism, however, was the crumbling of the Berlin Wall on 9 November 1989. East Germans had begun flowing to the West through Hungary at the rate of 5000 a week in the summer of 1989. When the Soviet Union failed to order Hungary to halt the flow, antigovernment demonstrations began in Leipzig in September and these grew until hardliner Erich Honecker was forced to resign as East Germany's leader on 9 October. After a demonstration in East Berlin on 5 November attended by one million people, the Communists dramatically opened the Wall. On 1 July the two Germanys formed an economic union and on 3 October the country was formally reunited.

The fall of the Wall had sudden repercussions in Czechoslovakia where student demonstrations began on 17 November 1989 culminating in the resignation of the Communist government 10 days later. On 10 November 1989 hardliner Todor Zhivkov, who had headed the Bulgarian government for the previous 35 years, was sacked. Aside from the opening of the Berlin Wall, the political event which captured world attention most dramatically was the violent overthrow of the Ceauşescu regime in Romania in December 1989, complete with the execution of Nicolai and Elena Ceauşescu by firing squad.

Between 18 March and 17 June 1990, six Eastern European countries held their first free elections in 50 years. An electorate of 90 million chose the new teams which would carry them through the transition from planned to market economies. In the northern countries (Eastern Germany, Poland, Czechoslovakia and Hungary), centralist parties and coalitions that favoured a rapid transition to a free market system were successful. In the southern countries (Romania and Bulgaria), leftist parties advocating a more gradual switch to the free market carried the day. Socialists also won the free elections in Serbia in December 1990 and Albania in March 1991. Despite this, the left-wing governments in the Balkan countries began enacting economic reforms as far-reaching as any introduced by the right-wing parties farther north.

The free elections were a setback for the participation of women in politics, however. During the 1990 elections the percentage of women in the Romanian parliament dropped from 34.3% to 3.5%, in Czechoslovakia from 29.5% to 6% and in Hungary from 20.9% to 7%.

The crumbling of the Soviet empire gave rise to a resurgence of nationalism. Ethnic passions long held in check in Slovakia, Slovenia and Croatia now threatened to fragment Czechoslovakia and Yugoslavia. The Albanian minority in Yugoslavia, the Hungarian minority in Romania and the Turkish minority in Bulgaria have had to fight for their survival. In Serbia neo-Communists have used anti-Albanian sentiments to strengthen their political position, and in Romania popular hatred of the Gypsy minority is on the rise. Only Hungary and Poland with their largely homogeneous populations are untouched by virulent nationalism, although Hungary continues to be haunted by the territories lost after WW I, and anti-Semitism has managed to raise its head in Poland and several other countries.

The events of 1989 seemed to demonstrate that state socialism had run its course. The booming prosperity of Western Europe made the collapse of uncompetitive Eastern Europe almost inevitable as economic paralysis led Eastern European consumers to revolt. The bureaucratic command system had worked fine for rebuilding heavy industry after WW II, but technologically the region was falling far behind and there was a real possibility of being economically marginalised after the final integration of the European Community in 1992. Without the two essential ingredients of a modern society – parliamentary democracy and a market economy – further progress would have been difficult.

The fall of Communism was also a result of the arms race. With their stable economies, strong national currencies and high rate of economic growth, Western countries were able to increase military expenditures and modernise their forces at a rate the socialist countries could only match by curtailing consumer production. At some point Mikhail Gorbachev decided that the surest way to get the sweeping arms reductions and unconditional Western support he needed was to sacrifice Eastern Europe. Unilateral Soviet tank and troop reductions in 1989 were followed by a Conventional Forces in Europe (CFE) agreement in 1990 and the disbanding of the Warsaw Pact itself in 1991. By the end of 1991 all Soviet troops had been withdrawn from Czechoslovakia and Hungary and by mid-1994 they had to be out of Eastern Germany and Poland. NATO military strength, on the other hand, has remained intact and economic conditions in the USSR have only got worse.

Goethe once wrote, 'Grey, dear friend, is all theory and green is the golden tree of life.' The relatively quiet disappearance of Eastern European Communism will be commented upon for many years to come. Meanwhile, reader Bob Buckie of Amherstburg, Ontario, Canada, put it this way:

All in all, it's an interesting and exciting time to visit Eastern Europe while it goes through a transition stage. People on the street and in trains are very eager to talk about what is happening, but it will take a few years before they can recover from the previous regimes. Unfortunately, I think that no-one over 40 will ever completely recover.

## PEOPLE

While Western Europe is dominated by five large nations, Eastern Europe is fragmented into some 15 nationalities. The Slavs are by far the most numerous ethnic group in Eastern Europe. There are three distinct groups of Slavs: the West Slavs (Czechs, Poles, Slovaks and Sorbs), the South Slavs (Bulgarians, Croats, Macedonians, Montenegrins, Serbs and Slovenes) and the East

Slavs (Belorussians, Russians and Ukrainians). The Albanians, Germans, Hungarians, Romanians, Gypsies and the Baltic peoples are non-Slavic groups. Hungary's 60,000-member Jewish community is the largest in Eastern Europe.

The English term 'Gypsy' reflects an early belief that these people came from Egypt, though it is now known that they originated in northern India. Their westward migration began before the 10th century, and by the 15th century some groups had reached Western Europe. A second wave of Gypsy migration began in the early 19th century and continues today, mostly Romanian Gypsies bound for Austria or Germany. Some 250,000 Gypsies live in Hungary, 80,000 in Slovakia, 20,000 in Bohemia and Moravia, and 15,000 in Poland. Without land to support themselves, many Gypsies were forced into irregular activities to stay alive, leading to their expulsion from many countries. Some Gypsies turned to music as a livelihood, usually developing the popular music of the country in which they happened to live.

## ECONOMY

Until 1990 the economic activities of Eastern Europe and the USSR were coordinated by the Council for Mutual Economic Assistance (CMEA or Comecon), founded in 1949. The concept was that each country would specialise in producing whatever suited it best, though in practice the Soviet Union provided Eastern Europe with raw materials such as oil, natural gas, iron ore, cotton, timber and mineral ores, receiving manufactured goods like machinery, textiles and footwear in return.

Long-term contracts were intended to make economic planning easier, but the lack of competition and 40 years of trade focused only on supplying the Soviet Union have left Eastern Europe with outdated industries uncompetitive on the world market. Trade within the group was originally conducted in 'accounting roubles', but this proved unworkable and in its final decade nearly all Comecon trade was done on a barter basis.

The crash of the administrative command systems in 1989 made the 'coordination of economic plans' obsolete and in 1990 the Comecon was dissolved. Since January 1991 all regional trade has been conducted in hard currency and Eastern Europe has been hard hit by sharp cutbacks in deliveries of Soviet gas and oil.

In 1990 the economies of all of the countries contracted as inefficient production was phased out and excess workers were allowed to become unemployed. Women have been most affected by the lay-offs and the scrapping of childcare facilities. Some factories have even adopted a policy of hiring only men for the next generation of jobs. Linked to this are campaigns to make abortion illegal and put women back in the home. Women returning from maternity leave no longer automatically get their jobs back.

As prices seek market levels, double-digit inflation has become a way of life. The privatisation of state assets and foreign investment should spark an economic revival in the long run, but meanwhile the vast majority of workers earning the equivalent of US$100 to US$150 a month are having difficulty making ends meet, and the huge apartment block complexes of Eastern Europe may yet become havens for drug dealing and crime.

Environmental problems, especially acid rain from the burning of brown coal, call for urgent attention. In 1990 there were 22 nuclear plants based on discredited Soviet technology in operation in Czechoslovakia, East Germany, Hungary and Bulgaria. In 1976 a Soviet-made VVER reactor at Greifswald near Stralsund came within one hour of melting down when 11 of its 12 cooling pumps failed simultaneously, an incident hushed up by the East German government until 1990. Construction of further nuclear power plants has been halted in Czechoslovakia and Poland, including one huge VVER reactor at Temelín just 100 km north of Linz, Austria. Now billions of dollars are required to bring the Eastern European plants up to Western safety standards.

Although all of the countries are now headed towards some form of market economy, the playing field is far from even. Poland is burdened by a massive US$46 billion hard-currency debt and Hungary's US$20 billion debt is just as serious considering the country's smaller size. Yugoslavia is also heavily indebted. (East Germany owed about the same as Hungary until West Germany picked up the tab.) The foreign debts of Czechoslovakia and Bulgaria, on the other hand, are manageable and Albania and Romania have almost no debts at all, largely because of the extreme paranoia of their former Communist rulers.

European Community membership seems out of the question for most of Eastern Europe for the foreseeable future, and it could be a decade or more before living standards in even relatively developed Czechoslovakia and Hungary approach those of the West. In 1989 and early 1990 there was talk of a 'new Marshall Plan' for Eastern Europe, but with West German attention diverted towards East Germany and the USA absorbed in the Gulf War, interest declined and Western aid has been rather meagre. The European Community, for example, has kept its doors shut to Eastern Europe's most exportable products, especially steel, textiles and agricultural produce.

As hope fades, many Eastern Europeans have sought a solution by moving West, especially from the poorer areas like Albania, Poland, Romania and the USSR. The exodus from Eastern Germany to Western Germany continues unabated and Soviet Jews, ethnic Germans, Romanian Gypsies and a hundred thousand others are at the gate. In 1989 some 1.3 million Easterners moved West – the greatest population shift since WW II. In panic the governments of Germany, Austria and Italy have had to erect an Iron Curtain of their own to limit the flood of economic refugees from the east. The border between the two Europes is as real as ever.

## GEOGRAPHY

The pivotal mountain range of central Europe is the Carpathian Mountains, which swing round from Romania into Czechoslovakia. There's excellent hiking in this range, especially in Romania's Făgăraş Mountains and the Tatra Mountains of Czechoslovakia and Poland. The Balkan Mountains are shared by Albania, Bulgaria, Greece and Yugoslavia. Musala Peak (2925 metres) in Bulgaria's Rila Massif is the highest in Eastern Europe. North-west of Ljubljana, Yugoslavia, are the Julian Alps.

One of the scenic highlights of Eastern Europe is the Dalmatian Coast of Yugoslavia. Here the mountains dip into the Adriatic to form a broken coastline with countless islands of Grecian beauty. The best beaches in the region are those along the Black Sea in Bulgaria and Romania. The Baltic coast of Germany and Poland has a beauty all its own. The most popular lake in Eastern Europe is Hungary's Balaton Lake.

Another great geographical feature of Eastern Europe is the Danube River, the second-largest river in Europe after the Volga. Napoleon called the Danube the 'king of the rivers of Europe'. The 2850-km-long Danube flows through eight countries, past three capitals, 1075 km of it in Romania. To see the Danube at its best, tour the Danube Bend in Hungary or Romania's Danube Delta. The greatest river north of the Carpathians is Poland's Vistula, which passes Kraków, Warsaw and Toruń. Other famous rivers are the Elbe (at Dresden) and the Vltava (at Prague).

## RELIGION

Protestants predominate in Eastern Germany, with Protestant minorities in Hungary and Romania. Catholicism is the main religion in Czechoslovakia, Hungary, Poland and northern Yugoslavia. Muslims constitute a majority only in Albania.

In 1054 the pope excommunicated the Church of Constantinople and all Orthodox churches which refused to accept papal infallibility. Nowadays the Orthodox faith is prevalent in Bulgaria, Romania and eastern Yugoslavia with patriarchs in Belgrade, Bucharest, and Sofia, and metropolitans in Prague and Warsaw. There have been many attempts to reunify the Orthodox and Roman Catholic churches. Orthodox churches that have accepted papal supremacy while retaining the Orthodox Eastern rite are known as Uniates or Greek Catholics.

## LANGUAGE

Here in *Mitteleuropa*, German is probably the best international language to know. German is widely understood by the older people in Czechoslovakia, Hungary and Transylvania (Romania). It's also helpful along the Adriatic and Black Sea coasts, where German tourists prevail, in Poland and, of course, in Eastern Germany. If you know French, Italian or Spanish you won't understand spoken Romanian, but you'll pick up isolated words and the meaning of simple texts.

Russian was taught in the schools after 1945, but since 1989 English has been far more common and there's always someone at major hotels and travel agencies who knows it. Many students and young professionals speak good English and are often happy to have the chance to talk to Western visitors. In Bulgaria, Romania and Serbia people sometimes learn French at school.

It's always easier to make yourself understood if you write your message down using numbers instead of words. For instance, when buying tickets, write down the time according to the 24-hour clock and the date using a Roman numeral for the month. If you want to know about reservations, write down a large capital R with a box around it and a question mark. To ascertain a price, repeat the name of the local currency in a questioning way (złoty? forint? etc), offering a pen and paper on which your informant can write the answer. A surprising amount of information can be communicated in this way, if you're imaginative.

Twelve major languages are spoken in the countries covered in this book. Eight of these (Bulgarian, Czech, Macedonian, Polish, Serbo-Croatian, Slovak, Slovene and Sorbian) are Slavonic languages. These languages are closely related in grammar and vocabulary and if you pick up a few words in one you'll be surprised how the corresponding phrases in the others are almost identical. The other major languages you'll encounter are Albanian, German, Hungarian and Romanian.

In 863 the missionaries Sts Cyril and Methodius created the Cyrillic alphabet that is now used in Bulgaria, the USSR and parts of Yugoslavia. Cyrillic script was used in Romania until the mid-19th century. The Slavs have a tremendous respect for the Cyrillic alphabet which helped them resist cultural assimilation by dominant neighbours and renders their languages more precisely (notice all the accents which must be used when a Slavonic language is written in Latin characters). It only takes a few hours to learn this alphabet, so make the effort if you'll be visiting these countries.

# Facts for the Visitor

## PLANNING
### When, How Much & How Long?
Spring (April to mid-June) is the best time to come as the days are long and the tourist masses still haven't arrived. Summer (mid-June to early September) is the time for hiking and camping, the peak season for budget travellers and just about everyone else. September is a good month along the Adriatic coast, but in October the camping grounds close down and the days become shorter. October to March can be rather cold and dark with smog from coal-burning furnaces, though this is the peak theatre and concert season in the cities.

This book is designed for the budget traveller who intends to stay at B-category (2nd-class) hotels or in private rooms, take lunch at self-services and dinner at moderate full-service restaurants, go to a concert or the theatre a couple of nights a week, sightsee independently on foot or by public transport and travel 2nd class by train or bus. With a little care it should be fairly easy to do all that on under US$25 a day in Czechoslovakia, Hungary or Poland, on under US$45 a day in Eastern Germany and Yugoslavia. In Romania and Bulgaria prices vary greatly and although US$30 a day should get you by, Romanian hotel bills can add up. Two people travelling together can save about 35% on accommodation costs, and tent campers will spend even less.

To cover all of the areas described in this book you'll need a month each for Poland and Yugoslavia, and three weeks each for Bulgaria, Czechoslovakia, Eastern Germany, Hungary and Romania. Of course, not everyone has six months for holidays and a week in each country still adds up to almost two months, so you'll have to pick and choose. Try to avoid hopping from capital to capital.

### What to Bring
Bring an internal-frame backpack which converts into a canvas suitcase by zipping the straps into the back. Big external-frame backpacks are fine for mountain climbing but don't fit into coin lockers and are a real nuisance on public transport. A day pack or shoulder bag will also be required. A neck pouch or money belt worn under your clothing is the safest way to carry money and documents (never pack such things in your luggage). If you want to camp you'll need a tent and sleeping bag, otherwise forget the tent and you won't really need the sleeping bag either. Clothing which can be added in layers according to the climate is much better than a bulky coat.

Bring photos of your home, family, place of employment, etc, as conversation pieces. Take chocolate bars and canned food to Romania, though Romanian customs officials may relieve you of some of it if they're particularly hungry that day. Shaving cream and tampons are poor quality or unavailable in Eastern Europe and you should also bring your own toilet paper. A rubber sink plug and a pocket calculator with clock and alarm functions will come in handy, and a small pocket compass can prove invaluable in orienting yourself when you first arrive in a town. Insect repellent is useful near wooded areas. A personal notebook in which to record tips from other travellers is always handy.

While there's no problem bringing in the type of personal effects most people travel with, be aware that antiques, books printed before 1945, crystal glass, gemstones, lottery tickets, philatelic stamps, precious metals (gold, silver, platinum), securities and valuable works of art must sometimes be declared in writing. To bring a video camera or personal computer into some countries, you may need the original purchase receipt. Don't carry letters or parcels on behalf of third parties. Entry with banknotes of any Eastern European country may also be restricted. If in doubt ask about customs regulations when you apply for your visa. Throughout the region customs checks are pretty cursory these days and you probably won't even have to open your bags, just be aware of the restrictions.

## Appearances & Conduct

Though high heels and ties won't be required, Eastern Europeans are more conservative dressers than North Americans. You'll usually be admitted to 1st-class restaurants, opera houses, concert halls, discos, hotel bars and the like even in jeans, but you'll feel more comfortable if you dress up a little. Shorts or miniskirts are not the best attire for visiting churches.

Although Eastern Europeans routinely shake hands, a man should wait for the woman to extend her hand first. In polite greetings use the person's title (Professor, Doctor, etc) before the surname. People only address friends, relatives and those much younger than themselves by their first names.

If you're invited for dinner at a local home take flowers for the hostess (but not red roses which have romantic implications) and a bottle of wine or brandy for the host. As most people get up early to go to work, evening visits usually end by 11 pm. In most of Europe people hold the knife in the right hand, the fork in the left, and keep both hands above the table during the meal.

## The Top 10

According to the author the 10 highlights of Eastern Europe are:

- Baščaršija bazar, Sarajevo Yugoslavia
- Danube Bend, Hungary
- Diocletian's Palace, Split, Yugoslavia
- Dubrovnik city walls, Yugoslavia
- Jasna Góra Monastery, Częstochowa, Poland
- Rila Mountains, Bulgaria
- Sanssouci Park, Potsdam, Germany
- Sibiu, Romania

- Tatra Mountains, Czechoslovakia/Poland
- Veliko Târnovo, Bulgaria

## The Bottom 10

The author rates these as the 10 worst attractions of the region:

- Count Dracula's Castle, Bran, Romania
- Dubrovnik Cathedral treasury, Yugoslavia
- Europa Centre, Berlin, Germany
- Hitler's Bunker, Wilczy Szaniec, Poland
- House of the People, Bucharest, Romania
- Hunedoara Castle, Romania
- Međugorje pilgrimage area, Yugoslavia
- Postojna Caves, Yugoslavia
- Siófok, Hungary
- Sveti Stefan village, Yugoslavia

## The World Heritage List

UNESCO keeps a list of 'cultural and natural treasures of the world's heritage' including these in Eastern Europe:

Bulgaria
- Boyana Church near Sofia
- Ivanovo rock-hewn churches near Ruse
- Kazanlâk Thracian Tomb
- Madara Horseman
- Nesebâr (old city)
- Pirin National Park
- Rila Monastery
- Srebarna Nature Reserve
- Thracian Tomb of Svechtari

Eastern Germany
- Palaces and Parks of Potsdam and Berlin

Hungary
- Budapest (banks of the Danube with the district of Buda Castle)
- Hollókő (traditional village)

Poland
- Auschwitz Concentration Camp
- Bialowieza National Park
- Kraków historic centre
- Warsaw historic centre
- Wieliczka salt mine near Kraków

Yugoslavia
* Dubrovnik (old city)
* Durmitor National Park
* Kotor and its gulf
* Ohrid and its lake
* Plitvice Lakes National Park
* Škocjan Caves near Ljubljana
* Split (historic centre with Diocletian Palace)
* Stari Ras and Sopoćani
* Studenica Monastery

## Biosphere Reserves

The UNESCO 'Man and the Biosphere Programme' lists 285 areas with unique natural values in 72 countries. Within Eastern Europe these are:

Bulgaria
* Alibotouch Reserve (Pirin Massif)
* Bistrichko Branichté Reserve (on Mount Vitosha)
* Boatine Reserve (Stara Planina)
* Djendema Reserve (Stara Planina)
* Doupkata Reserve (Rodopi Mountains)
* Doupki-Djindjiritza Reserve (Pirin Massif)
* Kamchiya Reserve (coast south of Varna)
* Koupena Reserve (Rodopi Mountains)
* Mantaritza Reserve (Rodopi Mountains)
* Maritchini ezera Reserve (Rila Mountains)
* Ouzounboudjak Reserve (Strandzha Planina)
* Parangalitza Reserve (Rila Mountains)
* Srébarna Reserve (west of Silistra)
* Steneto National Park (Stara Planina)
* Tchervenata sténa Reserve (near Bachkovo Monastery)
* Tchoupréné Reserve (Stara Planina)
* Tsaritchina Reserve (Stara Planina)

Czechoslovakia
* Křivoklátsko Protected Landscape Area (between Prague and Plzeň)
* Slovenský Kras Protected Landscape Area (near Rožnava)
* Třeboň Basin Protected Landscape Area (around Třeboň)
* Palava Protected Landscape Area (around Mikulov)
* Polana Reserve (south-east of Banská Bystrica)
* Šumava Mountains Protected Landscape Area (south-west of České Budějovice)

Eastern Germany
* Steckby-Loedderitz Forest Nature Reserve (Elbe River near Aken)
* Vessertal Nature Reserve (near Suhl)

Hungary
* Aggtelek Reserve
* Hortobágy National Park
* Kiskunság Reserve (south-west of Kecskemét)
* Lake Fertő Reserve (east of Sopron)
* Pilis Reserve (near Visegrád)

Poland
* Babia Góra National Park (south-west of Kraków)
* Białowieża National Park
* Lukajno Lake Reserve (near Mikołajki)
* Slowinski National Park (west of Łeba)

Romania
* Pietrosul Mare Nature Reserve (Maramureş)
* Retezat National Park (north-west of Tîrgu Jiu)
* Rosca-Letea Reserve (Danube Delta)

Yugoslavia
* Tara Canyon Ecological Reserve (Durmitor National Park)
* Velebit Mountains (between Senj and Zadar)

## VISAS

You will need a passport that is valid for at least another six months to travel through Eastern Europe. Bulgaria and Romania still require visas of everyone, but Czechoslovakia, Hungary and Poland are now granting visa-free status to an increasing number of Western nationalities. Citizens of almost all Western countries need no visa to enter Germany or Yugoslavia. Albanian visas must be arranged in advance through a tour operator or travel agency.

Visas are usually issued immediately by consulates in Eastern Europe, though Bulgarian and Polish consulates levy a 50% to 100% surcharge for prompt 'express visa service'. Otherwise Bulgarian consulates make you wait seven working days for your tourist visa! Those still requiring a Czechoslovak, Hungarian or Polish visa are advised to get it at a consulate and not to rely on it being available at the border. Bulgarian and Romanian visas, on the other hand, are usually easily obtained at the border.

Consulates are generally open weekday mornings (if there's both an embassy and a consulate, you want the consulate). Consulates in countries not next to the one you want to visit are less crowded (for example, get your Polish visa in Bucharest, your Hungarian visa in Sofia or Warsaw, etc).

Take your own pen with you and be sure to have a good supply of passport photos which actually look like you. Never list a sensitive occupation such as journalist, minister of religion, policeman or soldier on visa applications. If you're one of those, put down teacher, truck driver, sales clerk, or something similar. Consulates never check.

You can also apply for a visa from a consulate in your home country by registered mail, though this takes about two weeks unless you request 'express' service for an additional fee. First you must request an application form and enclose a stamped, self-addressed envelope. In the USA you can obtain your visas for an additional fee of US$27.50 per visa through Visa Services (☎ 202-387 0300), 1519 Connecticut Ave North-West, Suite 300, Washington DC 20036.

Visa fees (US$8 to US$30 per entry) must be paid in cash hard currency (no travellers' cheques). Most countries will issue double-entry visas upon request for double the normal fee. Most visas may be used any time within three to six months from the date of issue but Albanian visas are for specific dates. You're usually allowed to spend a month in a country.

Decide in advance if it's a tourist or transit visa you want. Transit visas are often cheaper and issued sooner, but it's usually not possible to extend a transit visa or change it to a tourist visa.

The visa form may instruct you to report to police within 48 hours of arrival. If you're staying at a hotel or other official accommodation (camping ground, youth hostel, private room arranged by a travel agency, etc) this will be taken care of for you by the travel agency or the hotel or camping ground reception. The hotel or camping ground will stamp the back of your visa form to prove that you were registered, and immigration will look at the stamps as you're leaving the country. If too many nights are unaccounted for, you could have some explaining to do.

If you're staying with friends or in a private room arranged on the street, you're supposed to register with the police. Again, if it's only for a couple of nights during a two-week stay, immigration probably won't make a fuss about the missing stamps, although technically you're breaking the law. No such stamps are necessary in Romania or Yugoslavia – it's mainly in Bulgaria, Hungary and Poland that you need the stamps. During the Communist era these regulations were strictly enforced but things are pretty casual these days.

You're required to have your passport with you at all times and you'll have to show it when checking into hotels, changing money, etc. If you stay 30 days or less in a country you don't need to apply for an exit permit but if you're staying for a longer period ask about this at a tourist office. If you lose your passport or visa and are issued a replacement, then you *do* have to apply to the police for an exit permit before you will be permitted to leave the country. These formalities can take several days so try not to lose your passport or visa in the first place.

For a visa extension, go to the official government travel agency (such as Ibusz, Balkantourist, Čedok, ONT, Orbis) and ask them how to go about it. You'll probably have to report to the police in person. Office hours are short and the lines long, so don't leave it till the last minute. Try to avoid this inconvenience by asking for enough time when you collect your visa in the first place.

If you were born in an Eastern European country, be sure to check with its embassy in your present country of residence about any special regulations which might apply to you. Unless you've formally renounced your original citizenship and the petition has been accepted by the country in question, you may still be considered one of its citizens and could have difficulty leaving once inside. You might have to serve in the local army for a year or two! This could even be the case if your parents emigrated when you were an infant or if you married a national of the Eastern European country in question. If you do find yourself in such a situation, there's

**Visa Requirements**

| Country | US Citizens | Australians & New Zealanders | British | Canadians |
| --- | --- | --- | --- | --- |
| Albania | required | required | required | required |
| Bulgaria | required | required | required | required |
| Czechoslovakia | none | required | none | none |
| Germany | none | none | none | none |
| Hungary | none | required | none | none |
| Poland | none | required | required | required |
| Romania | required | required | required | required |
| Yugoslavia | none | none | none | none |

not much the consul of your adopted land will be able to do to rescue you.

The many rules and regulations described here and throughout this book aren't really as complicated as they may at first appear. In practice you'll easily be able to comply with them. Keep in mind that the requirements can change overnight and the trend is towards making things easier. You may be pleasantly surprised.

The chart above shows which nationalities require visas in Eastern Europe.

### Consulates in Greece

Greece is a major southern gateway to the region and most of the Eastern European consulates are in the suburb of Paleo Psihiko, north-east of central Athens. Get there on bus No 603 from Akadimias Street. Paleo Psihiko has a confusing network of circular streets and the bus drivers don't speak English, so have someone write out the address you want in Greek. Get off at Psihiko Town Hall for the Bulgarian Consulate, 33 Stratigou Kalari St (open weekdays from 10 am to noon), and the Romanian Consulate, 7 Em Benaki St (open Monday and Wednesday from 4.30 to 6.30 pm, Tuesday, Thursday and Friday from 10 am to noon). Ask directions.

For the Hungarian Consulate, 16 Kalvou St (open weekdays from 9 am to noon), stay on bus No 603 to the corner of Diamandidou and Kalvou streets. The Czechoslovak Consulate, 6 G Seferi St (open weekdays from 9 to 11 am), is near the Hungarian one; the

Polish Consulate, 22 Chryssanthemon St (open weekdays from 8.30 to 11.30 am except Wednesday 11 am to 7 pm) is five blocks west of these.

The Yugoslav Consulate, 25 Evrou St (open weekdays from 8.30 to 11 am) is between Paleo Psihiko and Athens (get off bus No 603 when you see the US Embassy).

### DOCUMENTS

The only document you'll need is a passport that is valid for at least six months. You can pick up most required visas upon arrival in Europe but have about 10 passport-size photos ready when you apply. Carry a photocopy of your passport identification page, driver's licence, credit cards, travellers' cheques, purchase receipts, camera identification number, airline tickets, railway pass, etc, in a secure place separate from the originals and leave another copy at home.

A Youth Hostel Association (YHA) membership card could save you money in several Eastern European countries. If you're a student bring along a current International Student Identity Card (ISIC) or purchase one at a student travel agency first chance you get (proof of student status required). Nonstudents under 26 years of age can obtain a Youth International Educational Exchange (YIEE) card from most offices issuing the ISIC and receive many of the same reductions. If you're a member of an automobile club, bring along your membership card (or a 'Card of Introduction') as this could entitle you to free breakdown service, maps and legal advice from sister clubs in Eastern Europe.

## MONEY

Except in Germany, US dollars are the preferred hard currency. Bring half your money in cash US dollars or Deutschmarks (DM) in small denominations and the rest in American Express travellers' cheques in a variety of denominations. It's worth having plenty of small-denomination banknotes as it's often impossible to get change in hard currency. Failure to pay attention to this small detail can lead to tremendous problems once inside Eastern Europe. If you have only large bills you may be forced to take change in local currency at a bad rate.

Almost everywhere in Eastern Europe cash is preferred over travellers' cheques. In Poland it's extremely difficult to cash a travellers' cheque as only a few banks will do it. Cheques are all right in the other countries, but in all of Europe travellers' cheques are becoming less and less attractive as commissions go steadily up: you pay far more than the original 1% for the safety that goes with these cheques! Ask the exchange office what commission it deducts before signing your cheque as there are some real rip-offs (Chequepoint in Prague is an example). In Yugoslavia travellers' cheques are widely accepted at a slightly better rate than cash.

Thomas Cook travellers' cheques are not recommended as Thomas Cook offices charge 1% commission to cash their own cheques! American Express offices charge no commission to cash their own cheques but both they and Thomas Cook give rates worse than banks. (A cheeky little sign posted at American Express offices reads: 'There's no reason for it: *it's just our policy.*') If you're changing over US$20, you're usually better off going to a post office or bank and paying the standard 1% to 2% commission to change there.

Keep a record of which cheques you've cashed in case the remaining cheques are stolen and you have to make a claim. To report stolen American Express travellers' cheques, ring 273-571 600 in England (country code 44) reverse charges from anywhere in Eastern Europe (if you can't call reverse charges, quickly give your number and ask them to call you right back).

American Express offices in Western

Europe will break large American Express travellers' cheques down into smaller denominations at no charge. It used to be impossible to do this in Eastern Europe (or to receive cash advances on credit cards) but American Express offices recently opened in Budapest and Warsaw, joining the well-established American Express facilities in Athens, Berlin and Vienna, so things seem to be getting easier. Credit cards are only useful in Eastern Europe if you're staying at five-star hotels.

Banks and American Express offices in Eastern Europe charge 6% to 15% commission to convert dollar travellers' cheques into dollars cash, if they will do it at all. You can change your travellers' cheques into cash DM in Germany but German banks often charge high commissions on dollar cheques (up to DM 10) and give lousy rates. It's well worth having a few travellers' cheques in DM which can be cashed in Germany without commission. You can easily obtain cash advances on credit cards at banks in Berlin.

International transportation tickets must usually be paid cash in hard currency. You'll also need Western cash at consulates, duty-free shops and hard-currency bars in hotels. Occasionally hotel bills and sightseeing tours must be paid for directly in hard currency and some hotels give discounts to those paying with cash US dollars or Deutschmarks. One-dollar bills make excellent tips, while US$5 and US$10 notes are seldom refused when offered as gifts! Even 50 or 100 US$1 bills wouldn't be too many to take, as you can use them to pay for almost anything when you first arrive in a country and they're also very handy should you temporarily run out of local currency.

You can change money at travel agencies, post offices, banks and exchange offices. Most of the countries have a standard official rate you receive wherever you change. Travel agencies are faster and more efficient than banks though their commission is often slightly higher. In Hungary post offices are good places to change, while in Czechoslovakia and Yugoslavia banks are preferred. In

Poland (as yet the only country where the foreign currency market is completely free) private exchange offices (kantors) are very efficient and offer excellent rates, but only for cash. In Bulgaria travel agencies actually give a *higher* rate than banks. On weekends and evenings you can usually change money at the luxury hotels for the same rate as at travel agencies, but check.

Some countries such as Albania and Poland ask you to fill in a currency declaration upon arrival listing all Western currency in your possession. Don't lose the form or all your money could be subject to confiscation! It's OK to leave with less money than you declared but not more. Compulsory currency exchange has been abolished throughout the region.

### Black Market

Only Romania still has a thriving black market offering up to five times the official rate. In Bulgaria, Czechoslovakia and Hungary the black market only pays 10% to 25% more than the banks – not enough to make it worth involving yourself in this dangerous, illegal activity. In Poland and Yugoslavia the black market no longer exists (though thieves eager to get their hands on your money may pretend it does).

Changing money on the black market is still illegal, but since 1989 the main danger has shifted from the police (who are now low profile) to the black marketeers themselves. Many of the people who ask you to change money on the street are thieves who will try to cheat you of most or all of your cash.

If you do decide to deal with them, hang onto your cash until you have the offered money in your hand, then count it one more time before putting it in your pocket. Beware of the age-old trick of banknotes folded in two to make them look more numerous. If during an exchange the marketeer takes the local currency back from you after you've counted it, break off contact immediately as a rip-off is definitely intended. In that circumstance, the money you have counted will disappear in a sleight-of-hand trick and you'll end up with a much smaller amount.

Never change with two men together. If a second man appears while you're negotiating, split. Don't be pressured into changing more than you originally intended. Thieves will always insist that you change a large amount – one way of recognising them. Know what the local currency looks like and don't be in a hurry. Beware of receiving obsolete Polish or Yugoslav currency.

If you meet someone reliable and are able to do the act in private, change enough to cover your entire remaining stay, to avoid having to take this serious risk a second time. Camping grounds, private rooms, restaurants and taxi cabs are often good places to change since you know with whom you're dealing. Vendors at street markets selling any kind of imported goods will want hard currency. Just pose an innocent question like, 'excuse me sir, can you tell me where I can change cash dollars?' If they're interested they'll let you know. Waiters at fancy restaurants sometimes suggest it about the time they bring you the bill.

Exchange offices in Berlin, Poland and Vienna often sell the Eastern currencies at bargain rates, but it's usually illegal to take this money back into the countries of origin because the import and export of all Eastern European currencies is prohibited. Small change is no problem, however, and excess local currency may be deposited at the border against a receipt allowing you to pick the money up again next visit. Customs checks are pretty lax these days and if you just say you don't have any local currency (if asked) the officers probably won't pursue the matter. Keep in mind, however, that the Eastern European currencies are almost worthless outside the region and it's usually impossible to reconvert soft currency into hard currency. Only change what you need, and go on a spending spree on your last few days if there's anything left.

### Tipping

Throughout Eastern Europe you tip by rounding up restaurant bills, taxi fares, etc to the next even figure as you're paying. In some countries such as Germany, restaurants will already have added a service charge to your bill so you needn't round it up much, while in others like Hungary 10% is standard if you feel you have been well attended. Never leave tips on restaurant tables as this is not the custom anywhere – the waiter will just assume you don't intend to tip and someone else may pocket the coins.

Restaurant cloakroom and public toilet attendants may expect a small tip unless a standard fee is posted. A couple of your smallest coins in the empty plate on the counter should be sufficient.

Unconventional tips such as small Western banknotes and packets of Western cigarettes will have more impact than their equivalent value in local currency. Never give money, sweets or pens to children on the street as this creates a real nuisance. In general, do as you would at home, but don't overtip.

### ELECTRICITY

In all of Eastern Europe the electric current is 220 volts AC, 50 Hz, and plugs have two round prongs. The availability of electric outlets depends on the category of the accommodation.

### POST

If you wish to receive mail you can have it sent care of your consulate, American Express or poste restante (general delivery) at a main post office. Obtain a current list of the addresses of your country's diplomatic missions from a passport office or public library before you leave home, though the consulates of many countries will no longer hold mail for tourists and virtually none will accept parcels.

American Express offices and representatives which will hold 'clients' mail' are listed in the booklets *Guide to Travel Service Offices* and *Traveler's Companion* available free at American Express offices. You can pick up your mail and telegrams without charge if you have American Express travellers' cheques or their credit card and they'll forward mail for a flat fee of about US$5. What American Express won't do is

accept parcels or registered letters, answer telephone enquiries about mail or hold mail longer than 30 days.

If you're using poste restante, tell your correspondents to put the number 1 after the city name to ensure that the letter goes to the main post office in that city. You should also have them underline your last name, as letters are often misfiled under first names. Some post offices (such as those in Yugoslavia) charge a small fee for each letter picked up.

When deciding on your mail pick-up points, don't choose too many or you'll sacrifice the flexibility of being able to change your plans after arrival. Try to pick a central location you'll be transiting several times during office hours.

To send a parcel from Eastern Europe you must take it unwrapped to a main post office. Have the paper, string and tape ready. They'll sometimes ask to see your passport and note the number on the form. If you don't have a return address within the country just put your name care of any large tourist hotel. Air mail isn't that much more expensive than surface mail, so be sure to use it. Occasionally you'll have to pay duty in hard currency on souvenirs mailed from the country, but once a parcel is accepted it will probably reach its destination.

Postage is cheap in Poland, Czechoslovakia, Romania, Bulgaria and Albania so mail lots of postcards from there. As in all countries, if you put favourable comments on the back of postcards they won't be 'lost'.

## TIME

Most of the places covered in this book are on Central European Time (GMT/UTC plus one hour), the same time used from Spain to Poland. Romania, Bulgaria and Greece are on East European Time (GMT plus two hours). If it's 6 pm in Warsaw and Madrid, it will be 7 pm in Bucharest and Sofia, 8 pm in Moscow, 5 pm in London, noon in New York, 9 am in California and 3 am the next morning in Melbourne, Australia.

Daylight-saving time runs from April to September (clocks everywhere are turned an hour ahead these months). If you're travelling in Eastern Europe at this time, you'll get a bonus hour of daylight every afternoon! Just make sure you don't get caught out with timetables on the 'change-over' days.

## BOOKS

The classic series of guidebooks to the individual Eastern European countries is *Nagel's Encyclopedia-Guides*, published in Switzerland (Nagel Publishers, 7 rue de l'Orangerie, CH-1211 Geneva 7) in English, French and German editions. Although they provide a fair number of maps, good history and description, there's little practical information and they're expensive and hard to find. Nagel is highly recommended if you'll be spending a long time in one country.

*The Rough Guide to Eastern Europe* (Harrap-Columbus, London, UK) is something of a misnomer as only Hungary, Romania and Bulgaria are included. Written in a lively contemporary style with lots of interesting background material, it's worth buying for the last two countries though *The Rough Guide to Hungary* is preferable for the first. There are also individual Rough Guides to Berlin, Czechoslovakia, Poland, and Yugoslavia. In the USA the series goes under the banner 'The Real Guide' and is published by Prentice Hall.

If you can read German, *Osteuropa* by Norbert Ropers (Anders Reisen, Rowohlt Taschenbuch Verlag GmbH, Hamburg) contains worthwhile background information on recent trends, although it really isn't a practical guidebook.

Schedules for the main Eastern European railway and ferry routes are given in the monthly *Thomas Cook Continental Timetable*. Thomas Cook travel agencies often sell single copies, and you'll find yourself referring to the Eastern Europe pages constantly.

Volume One of *The Guide to Budget Accommodation* published by the International Youth Hostel Federation lists IYHF youth hostels in all of the Eastern European countries except Albania and Romania. The Bartholomew *World Travel Map, Eastern Europe* (1:2,500,000) is also useful. *Let's Go: Europe* by Harvard Student Agencies (St Martin's Press, New York) is worth considering for budget travellers who will be passing through Western Europe.

Among the most intriguing travel books about Eastern Europe are *A Time of Gifts* (Penguin Books, 1979) and *Between the Woods and the Water* (Penguin Books, 1987) by Patrick Leigh Fermor. In December 1933 Fermor set out on a year-and-a-half walk from Holland to Turkey with a budget of £1 a week. The first volume covers the stretch from Rotterdam to the Danube, the second Hungary and Romania. Though the style of travel Fermor describes is now possible only in a few Third World countries where life is still simple, his books would make wonderful companions for anyone curious enough to retrace his steps.

*Black Lambs & Grey Falcons, Women Travellers in the Balkans*, edited by John B Allcock & Antonia Young (Bradford University Research Ltd, 10 Hey St, Bradford BD7 1DQ, England), is a collection of 14 essays on notable English-speaking women who have visited and written about the Balkan Peninsula since the mid-19th century.

*Eastern Europe Since Stalin*, edited by Jonathan Steele (David & Charles, Newton Abbot, 1974), is a readable survey of the period 1953 to 1973. The texts of newspaper and magazine articles published in the East, plus landmark speeches by Communist leaders, are reprinted between blocks of even-handed editorial comment. This book not only covers the power shifts within the various Communist parties, but gives a feel for the perplexing problems that pre-1989 Eastern European reformers faced.

*Eastern Europe and Communist Rule* by J F Brown (Duke University Press, Durham, 1988) is a readable political history of Eastern Europe's four decades of Communism with special attention to the 1970s and 1980s. Published just prior to the collapse of Communism, Brown's book presents a unique picture unclouded by current revisionism.

For detailed information on the politics, economics and societies of the individual countries, the series 'Marxist Regimes' (Pinter Publishers, London and New York) edited by Bogdan Szajkowski is indispensable. Published titles include *Bulgaria* by Robert J McIntyre, *German Democratic Republic* by Mike Dennis, *Hungary* by Hans-Georg Heinrich, *Romania* by Michael Shafir and *Yugoslavia* by Bruce McFarlane.

The Central & East European Publishing Project (☎ 0865-31 0793), St Anthony's College Annexe, Belsyre Court, 57 Woodstock Rd, Oxford OX2 6HQ, England, is a charitable foundation which assists Eastern European publishers and supports and promotes translation of works by Eastern European authors. Books in English published with the CEEPP's help include *Politics in Hungary* by János Kis, *The Ontolgy of Socialism* by Jadwiga Staniszkis, *Selected Poems* by Ana Blandiana and *My Childhood at the Gate of Unrest* by Paul Goma.

## HEALTH

Eastern Europe is a fairly healthy place in which to travel. Tap water is usually safe to drink although standards do vary, so it's always best to ask advice locally. If you decide not to drink tap water, then you shouldn't use ice cubes either as even luxury hotels often make their ice from tap water. In these cases also avoid leafy vegetables which will have been washed in tap water, and take care with raw or undercooked eggs which can cause intestinal illnesses. Air pollution is worst in winter when coal is universally used for heating, but heavy cigarette smoking is a much bigger nuisance and nonsmokers can expect to receive little or no consideration.

No vaccinations are required unless you arrive directly from an infected area outside Europe. An injection of gamma globulin against infectious hepatitis A spread by contaminated food or water is probably the best shot to get, but wait until you're just about to leave as the protection period is only six months. If you need any injections when you're inside Eastern Europe, make sure that the needle or syringe has not been used before.

Medical care is readily available, although not always up to Western standards. Embassies, tourist information, international hotels and offices can often supply the name of an English-speaking doctor or dentist. Private practice is still far less common in these countries than it is in the West and you might have to attend a government clinic. Sometimes you can arrange special medical attention for direct payment in hard currency, officially or unofficially.

In emergencies you should resort to the casualty ward of any large general hospital. Hospital emergency departments in Eastern Europe can cope with most medical problems and the fees they ask (if any) will be a lot less than a foreigner would pay in a Western country. Most hospital doctors are eager to practise their English and will be very helpful, though in many cases the facilities are overcrowded.

If your problem isn't that serious try asking for advice at a pharmacy (chemist). Locally produced drugs and medicines are inexpensive and there's often someone there who understands a little English, German or at least sign language. Drug stores also sell multivitamins (ask for the 'forte' variety), bottled medicinal water and even herbal tea. For diarrhoea get carbon tablets (generic name: *carbo activatus*) such as Norit. Western brand names are expensive in the East, so bring along any medicines you cannot do without, including something for headaches, common colds and an upset stomach. Pre-scriptions must be expressed in generic terminology.

Health resorts and spas are common in Bulgaria, Czechoslovakia, Hungary, Romania and Yugoslavia, offering complete medical programmes against payment in hard currency. In Bratislava, Budapest and Prague there are special offices booking spa treatment from around US$80 a day including room and board. Hungary is especially famous for its hot springs which are accessible to everyone for a couple of dollars a visit, and massages and other health services are available at these. Less known but similar are the thermal baths of Bulgaria. In Czechoslovakia these baths are usually reserved for patients under medical supervision.

### Health Insurance

Some European countries such as Britain have mutual agreements allowing free medical treatment for each other's nationals. Sometimes they require an official form or document proving that the traveller is insured in his/her home country. If you're one of the lucky ones, get this before you leave home. Otherwise you'll have to pay for medical care in some countries, although in others it's free for everyone. Hospital bed charges are levied everywhere but the rates are usually much lower than in Western countries.

If you decide to buy a special travel accident insurance policy, make sure it covers emergency medical evacuation to your home country and (if possible) baggage insurance. These policies usually only cover charges above and beyond what your national health insurance will pay and only prove useful if you have a really serious accident. Some policies specifically exclude 'dangerous activities' such as skiing, motorcycling or mountaineering, which would make the insurance pretty useless if you intended to do such things.

### FILM & PHOTOGRAPHY

Serious photographers should bring with them enough film and batteries. Kodak film is often hard to obtain, though you can usually find it in Hungary and Yugoslavia. Germany is a good place to stock up on film. Some Eastern European colour films cannot be developed outside the originating country because of the different technological processes involved. Soviet-made cameras and B&W film are very cheap in Hungary.

It's prohibited to take pictures of anything that might be considered of strategic value, such as bridges, tunnels, harbours, docks, reservoirs, dams, railway stations, airports, government buildings, radio or TV stations, power plants, factories, laboratories, mines, border crossings, military installations, local soldiers or police. It's also forbidden to take photos through the window of an aircraft, but aside from this you may photograph anything you like. Ask permission before taking close-up photos of people.

## ACTIVITIES
### Canoeing & Kayaking
Those with folding kayaks will want to launch them on the Krutynia River in Poland's Great Mazurian Lakes district or on the Danube, Rába and Tisza rivers in Hungary. Special canoeing tours are offered in both these countries, as well as Yugoslavia. One of the world's great kayaking adventures is the Tour International Danubien (TID) on the Danube River in July and August (see the general Getting Around section for more information).

### Cycling
For information on this activity or means of transport see the Bicycle section under Getting Around.

### Hiking
There's excellent hiking in Eastern Europe with numerous well-marked trails through forests, mountains and the various national parks. Public transport will often bring you to the trailheads, and chalets or mountain 'huts' provide shelter and perhaps a hot bowl of soup. In this book we provide detailed information on hiking through the Tatra Mountains of Poland and Czechoslovakia, the Mala Fatra of Czechoslovakia, the

Bucegi and Făgăraş ranges in Romania's Carpathian Mountains, the Rila Mountains of Bulgaria and Yugoslavia's Julian Alps, but there are many other less well-known hiking areas. The best months are from June to September, especially late August and early September when the snow and crowds will have melted.

### Horse Riding
Though horse riding can be arranged in all the countries, it's best developed in Hungary. See the Activities section in the Facts for the Visitor section of the Hungary chapter.

### Sailing & Yachting
Eastern Europe's most famous yachting area is the passage between the long rugged islands off Yugoslavia's Dalmatian Coast. Yacht tours and rentals are available there, though you certainly won't be able to do it 'on a shoestring'. If your means are limited, the Great Mazurian Lakes of north-east Poland are a better choice as small groups can rent sailing boats by the day for very reasonable rates. Hungary's Balaton Lake is also popular among sailing enthusiasts.

### Skiing
Eastern Europe's premier skiing areas are the Tatra Mountains of Poland and Czechoslovakia, the Romanian Carpathians near Braşov, Mount Vitosha and Borovets near Sofia, Bulgaria, and Slovenia's Julian Alps. The season runs from mid-December to March and serious skiers with limited time should look into an all-inclusive package tour. It's also possible to do it on your own if you don't mind competing for facilities with lots of locals.

### White-Water Rafting
This exciting activity is offered in summer on three of Eastern Europe's wildest rivers: the Dunajec River along the border of Poland and Czechoslovakia, the Tara River in Montenegro and the Soča River in Slovenia. Prices are much higher in Yugoslavia than in the other two countries, though raft trips there are much better organised.

## Courses

**Language** Although a few summer schools do exist (see Debrecen in the Hungary chapter, for example), regular language schools for foreigners are rare. It's always possible, however, to find local tutors willing to instruct you in their language for a reasonable amount. Ask at special schools teaching English to local residents or ask a tourist office or your consulate to recommend someone. If this is your intention, bring a good textbook and bilingual dictionary as books for teaching Eastern European languages to English speakers can be hard to find.

## WORK

English teaching is a growth industry in Eastern Europe and probably the best avenue to explore if you don't have a lot of money. Though you should be able to find work teaching English, local wage levels average just US$100 to US$150 a month, so you probably won't get rich doing it.

One church-connected group, the International Cultural Foundation (☎ 071-723 0721, fax 071-724 2262), 42 Lancaster Gate, London W2 3NA, England, runs summer language schools in Bulgaria, Czechoslovakia, Hungary and Poland in July and August. Volunteer teachers receive full board, accommodation and pocket money during the six weeks of classes (25 hours a week) and in certain cases transport from Britain to Eastern Europe is also paid. No experience is required.

## INFORMATION OFFICES

Each of the Eastern European countries has an official government travel agency organising tourism within the country. These are the Europäisches Reisebüro (Eastern Germany), Orbis (Poland), Čedok (Czechoslovakia), Ibusz (Hungary), the Oficiul Naţionál de Turism (Romania), Balkantourist (Bulgaria), and Albturist (Albania). In Hungary there are many other travel agencies (Cooptourist, Volántourist, Dunatours, etc) in addition to Ibusz. In Yugoslavia tourism is also decentralised.

All of these agencies have branches in nearly every city and town within their own country and foreign offices around the world. The addresses of offices abroad are listed in the Facts for the Visitor section of each chapter. These offices are primarily travel agencies which reserve hotel rooms, sell transport tickets, sightseeing tours, etc. In most cases they also provide general tourist information though this is not their main function.

Each country also has a student travel bureau which you should patronise if you have a student card or an IYHF youth hostel card. The bureaus are Jugendtourist (Eastern Germany), Almatur (Poland), the CKM (Czechoslovakia), Express (Hungary), the BTT (Romania), Orbita (Bulgaria) and Ferijalni Savez Jugoslavije (Yugoslavia). Their primary task is to organise excursions for youth groups within the country, but often they assist foreign youth as well. Youth hostel accommodation and discount international train tickets to Western Europe at student rates are sometimes available from them.

Large cities often maintain municipal information offices which are excellent sources of information on local attractions, theatres, events, etc, but do not make travel arrangements. The national railway companies usually have a central ticket office in each major city within their respective countries. Go to these for tickets and reservations rather than struggling with the throng at the railway station. The railway offices and some of the travel agencies are packed around mid-afternoon, so check the hours and go early.

Railway information counters in train stations aren't usually equipped to provide tourist information, and the clerks at ticket windows will often refuse to give train times if you could have got them from the information counter. Tourist information offices are sometimes not the best sources of train or bus information, so double-check what they tell you. Always try to use the correct information office for the sort of thing you want to know as some clerks can get downright nasty if you don't.

If you have serious legal or medical problems, you can always ask your country's consul for advice (don't ask to speak to the ambassador unless you're an accredited diplomat yourself). Consuls are usually friendly and happy to talk to a fellow citizen far from home, but they do not provide the services of a travel agency. Students from Third World countries are an information source not to be overlooked. Most speak English or French and are quite friendly.

Throughout this book we've tried to list the most effective information offices. The service at these often varies, improving if you're both courteous and persistent. If it becomes obvious that an office is no more interested in helping you than you are in paying top dollar, leave quietly and make your own arrangements. Each chapter explains how this can be done.

## ACCOMMODATION
### Hotels
If you want to stay at a standard high-rise tourist hotel, you'll find one in every city. In this book, however, we've concentrated on the older, 2nd-class hotels. There are still quite a few 'grand hotels' around, overflowing with old-fashioned Victorian elegance. Throughout the region, hotels are graded as five-star (deluxe-category), four-star (A* category), three-star (A category), two-star (B category), or one-star (C category).

Rooms at one and two-star hotels begin around US$15/25 single/double. Sometimes the price difference between a single and a double isn't very much. The cheapest rooms have a sink but shared bath which means you'll have to go down the corridor to use the toilet or shower. Sometimes the communal showers are locked and you're charged extra every time you get the key. If you do find a good inexpensive hotel, be sure to book a room for your entire stay upon arrival. Otherwise you could find it's been reserved by someone else when you try to extend your stay.

Hungarian, Romanian and Yugoslav hotels are a lot more expensive than camping and private rooms, so you probably won't want to use them often. Czechoslovak and Polish hotels can be quite affordable. In Bulgaria hotel bills must be paid directly in hard currency and in Albania there isn't much choice about where you can stay. Both Bulgaria and Romania have special deals offering big discounts on two and three-star hotels if you pay in advance at a travel agency (see the Facts for the Visitor section of those two chapters).

In most of the Eastern European countries except Hungary, nationals of the country get a lower rate at hotels. This explains why all those really expensive hotels are full. This is justified in a way because wages in the West are much higher than those in the East. If everyone paid the same it would either be ridiculously cheap for us or not affordable for locals. With privatisation, prices are likely to float up to whatever the market will bear.

### Private Rooms
In all of Eastern Europe except Albania, travel agencies arrange private-room accommodation in local homes. In Hungary you can get a private room almost anywhere but in the other countries only the main tourist centres have them. Some 1st-class rooms are like mini-apartments with cooking facilities and private bathrooms for the use of guests alone. Prices vary from US$5 to US$20 per person but there's often a 50% surcharge if you stay less than three or four nights. Still, these rooms can be excellent value and are almost always cheaper than a hotel, so ask for them as your first accommodation preference.

Sometimes you'll be offered a *sobe* (private room) by a proprietor on the street. The price may be cheaper than what the agencies charge but quality control will be lacking. Along the Adriatic coast of Yugoslavia this is a common practice. You can also knock on the doors of houses bearing *sobe* or *zimmer frei* signs and ask if they have a room for you. If the price asked is too high, try bargaining.

In large cities the rooms are often in distant suburbs, but public transport is good and the agency arranging the room should be able to sell you a detailed city map. In Hungary the rooms are often in high-rise complexes and arriving after dark is confusing, though you usually cannot occupy the room until 5 pm. Aside from having a place to stay, you'll get to experience a slice of local life. Though not essential, take flowers if you really want to impress your landlady upon arrival.

## Pensions

Since the opening up of Eastern Europe in 1989, small private pensions have proliferated. Priced somewhere between hotels and private rooms, pensions usually have less than 10 rooms and the resident proprietors often make a good portion of their income from a small restaurant on the premises. You'll get a lot more personal attention than you would at a hotel at the cost of a wee bit of your privacy. If you arrive at night or on a weekend when the travel agencies assigning private rooms are closed, pensions are well worth a try, though they could be full. Call ahead to check prices and ask about reservations – German is almost always spoken, as is, increasingly, English.

## Camping

The cheapest way to go is camping (US$2 to US$10 per person). There are numerous camping grounds in all of the countries except Albania. Most are large 'autocamps' intended mainly for motorists though they're often easily accessible on public transport and there's almost always space for backpackers with tents. Many camping grounds rent small on-site bungalows for double or triple the regular camping fee. In the most popular resorts all the bungalows may be full in July and August, but ask.

Quality varies from one country to the next. It's abysmal in Romania, unreliable in Bulgaria, crowded in Hungary, good in Germany, and variable in Poland. Only coastal Yugoslavia has nudist camping grounds (marked FKK) which are actually excellent places to stay because of their secluded locations. A camping carnet (available from your local automobile or camping club) gets you a 5% to 10% discount at many camping grounds and often serves as a guarantee so you don't have to leave your passport at reception.

The camping grounds may be open from April to October, May to September, or perhaps only June to August, depending on the category of the facility and demand. You can't always go by what travel agencies tell you about camping grounds because they may not know or would rather see you staying at a hotel. Freelance camping is often prohibited, so before you pitch your tent on a beach or in an open field observe what others are doing. If in doubt keep out of sight of the road – good policy regardless.

## Hostels

Youth Hostels affiliated to the International Youth Hostel Federation (IYHF) are found in all of the countries except Albania and Romania. A youth hostel card is not essential to stay at most of the hostels, although you usually get a small discount if you have one.

The hostels in Poland and Yugoslavia are similar to those in Western Europe and easily used. Polish hostels are extremely basic but inexpensive (US$2) and friendly, while Yugoslav hostels are crowded and overpriced (US$10 to US$15). The hostels in Bulgaria are sometimes difficult to use as the wardens of hostels off the beaten track are unaccustomed to receiving Western members; it's always best to have a 'Pirin' Travel Agency call ahead to announce your arrival.

In Czechoslovakia the hostels are actually fairly luxurious 'junior' hotels with double rooms often fully occupied by groups. Most of the Hungarian hostels are regular student dormitories only open to travellers for six or seven weeks in midsummer. The hostels of Eastern Germany used to require reservations a month or more in advance but now they're freely open to everyone.

Many Czechoslovak and Hungarian cities have dormitories known as 'tourist hostels' which are not connected with the IYHF and have no rules (mixed dorms, no curfew, smoking and drinking in the room, etc).

These are intended for local visitors and you'll have to be persistent to use them (US$1 to US$3 per person). Ask the local tourist office for a referral.

Student dormitories cost just US$4 and up for students, though they're often available to all ages and even families. They only open to travellers during the summer holidays but courses sometimes don't begin until October. Student travel agencies such as Almatur (Poland) will have information about these. In Berlin there are many private student hostels, some of them former youth hostels.

### Mountain Huts

In the mountain areas of Bulgaria, Czechoslovakia, Poland, Romania and Yugoslavia there are mountain 'huts' or chalets offering dormitory accommodation (under US$10 per person) and basic meals to hikers. It's usually not possible to reserve a bed at a hut, although in Bulgaria the huts and the IYHF youth hostels are the same thing. Weather conditions will probably limit your use of the huts to summer, although some are open all year. Huts near roads or cable cars fill up fast, as do those in popular areas such as the Tatra Mountains. The huts are excellent places to meet Eastern European students.

### Waiting Rooms & Trains

Another place to stay at a pinch are railway station waiting rooms. So long as you have a ticket this is no problem. In midsummer the floors at Budapest's railway stations are lined with sleeping bags and there's even a rude 'wake up' service at 5.30 am. In Romania waiting rooms are one of the few cheap places to stay outside the camping season. Always put your luggage in a coin locker or cloakroom before dozing off.

Also compare the price of a hotel to that of a 2nd-class couchette or a 1st-class sleeper (US$3 to US$6) on an overnight train. Couchettes are very practical in Bulgaria, Czechoslovakia, Poland, Romania and Yugoslavia, so use your creativity to figure something out. The catch is that it's often hard to get a couchette or sleeper reservation, so don't leave it too late.

### FOOD

There are cheap self-service cafeterias *(buffet express)* in almost every Eastern European town. You usually pay at the end of the line, but sometimes (especially in Poland) you pay at the beginning of the line and get a ticket. Cashiers tend to be indulgent with tourists who can't speak the language, so just point at something acceptable that someone else is eating. Otherwise ask the person in line behind you what a certain dish is called. Some self-services offer genuine local dishes at surprisingly low prices and you can usually get a beer with the meal (but seldom in Poland).

Self-services tend to close around 7 pm weekdays, at 1 pm on Saturday and all day Sunday. For busy sightseers they're just the place for breakfast or lunch. Even cheaper and faster places for a snack are outdoor kiosks where hot dogs, pizza or ice cream are sold. These are common and impossible to list in a book. Regular table-service restaurants have longer opening hours than the self-services. Hotel restaurants keep the longest hours and are usually receptive to foreign tourists, so try there if everything else is closed. The hotel restaurants of Bulgaria, Czechoslovakia and Poland offer fine food properly served at very reasonable prices. The more pretentious establishments sometimes insist on advance reservations.

Throughout Eastern Europe restaurant menus are translated into German but only occasionally into English. Always insist on being shown a menu even if it's only in the local language to get an idea of the price range. Waiters who resist bringing the menu probably intend to overcharge. Not everything on the menu will be available, so as you enter the restaurant observe what others are eating and if the menu is incomprehensible or useless just point at somebody else's plate when the waiter returns.

Two sure signs of a good restaurant are a price list posted outside and a crowd of local people eating inside. It's worth trying the folklore restaurants where regional cuisine is offered. These are known as *csárdas* in Hungary or *mehanas* in Bulgaria. In Czechoslovakia and Hungary there are excellent wine restaurants *(vinárna* or *söröző)* and beer halls *(pivnice* or *borozó)*. Czech beer is about the best in the world and the wines of Bulgaria, Hungary, Romania, Slovakia and Yugoslavia are excellent. Budapest and Bohemia are famous for their pastries served at cafés *(kavárna)*.

There's no such thing as a private table in most Eastern European restaurants. You must share with whoever shows up, which can be a problem if you're a nonsmoker. Men dressed in shorts are not admitted to better restaurants and in winter everyone must check their coat. After Western Europe you'll find food is cheap in Eastern Europe – there's no double pricing as there is for hotel rooms, and a little extra money goes a long way here, so splash out now and then.

It's standard practice to round up restaurant bills to the next higher unit or 10% to 15% maximum. If you're dissatisfied with the food or service or feel you have been overcharged, you can convey the message by paying the exact amount. Give tips directly to the waiter as you pay. Don't wait to leave money on the table as the person serving you will simply assume you don't intend to tip and someone else may pocket the coins.

## ENTERTAINMENT

If you enjoy music and theatre you can see first-rate performances at extremely low prices in Eastern Europe. Every large city has an opera house and a separate theatre for operettas and musicals. There will be a concert hall (filharmonia) plus dramatic, satirical and puppet theatres, and sometimes a permanent circus. Jazz clubs are found in Czechoslovakia, Hungary and Poland.

Apart from the capitals many provincial towns such as Bratislava, Brno, Dresden, Győr, Pécs and Wrocław are important musical centres. Municipal information offices are your best source of information about cultural events. All performances are listed in the daily papers, and although you may not know the language, enough information will be comprehensible in the listings to enable you to locate the theatre and try for tickets.

There are theatrical ticket offices in Berlin, Budapest and Prague, but you'll get better seats by going directly to the theatre box office *(kassa)* itself. If this fails try for a ticket at the door half an hour before showtime. If the box office still doesn't have any, make a little sign with the words 'I'm looking for a ticket' in the local language and stand outside holding it. Often people have extra tickets. Except in Prague you probably won't have to go to this bother and will get tickets directly from the box office. In places where tickets are in high demand by both tourists and locals (such as in Dresden and Prague), government travel agencies may be able to obtain a ticket for you against payment in hard currency, though this jacks up the price considerably. In Prague scalpers sell opera tickets for hard currency.

Most theatres close for a six-week holiday during the summer. Instead look for performances by visiting companies at open-air theatres or on public squares. Folklore programmes are often offered and there are summer festivals. Most Eastern European towns have a Cultural Centre which publishes a monthly list of regular events. Cinemas are cheap and usually show movies in the original language though since 1989 sex and violence are the standard fare. Latecomers are not admitted and it's rude to walk out in the middle of a film. Smoking is not allowed in cinemas. Discos and nightclubs stay open late everywhere and are good places to make local contacts, though you'll have to be neatly dressed.

## THINGS TO BUY

Many Eastern European countries are critically short of consumer goods. When something especially good comes on the market it sells out fast. Thus it's important to buy things when you see them! Books and records are good value, as are musical and scientific instruments. High-quality art books are produced in Czechoslovakia,

Hungary and Poland. Footwear and clothing are cheap in Czechoslovakia and Bulgaria. Eyeglasses are inexpensive everywhere, so get an extra pair if you know your prescription. If you want newspapers and magazines in English, go to the boutique in the most luxurious hotel in town.

When you enter a supermarket and certain sections in department stores, you must pick up a shopping basket at the entrance. Stores use this system as a means of controlling the number of people inside: if the baskets are all taken you must wait at the cash register until you can get one from somebody who's leaving. If you enter without a basket you'll have an unnecessary argument with the sales staff. Many grocery shops do not provide plastic bags in which to carry away your purchases, so bring your own or an empty day pack.

Hard-currency shops in all the countries sell imported goods and top-quality local products. These shops are often located in luxury hotels and the prices are fairly reason-able. The company names to watch for are Comturist (Romania), Corecom (Bulgaria), Intourist (Hungary), Pewex (Poland) and Tuzex (Czechoslovakia). Always save the receipts for major purchases made with Western currency as this will allow you to take the items out of the country without paying an export tax.

Goods purchased with local currency over a certain value are subject to tax. Customs officials get strict about this if it looks like you're trying to make a business of it by exporting too many of the same item. Duty is charged on valuable things like fur or leather coats, gold jewellery and antique watches, unless you have receipts to prove that you paid in hard currency. If you have such things with you on arrival in Eastern Europe ask if you need to declare them. Some of the export restrictions are listed in the various chapters of this book, though since 1989 things are a lot more relaxed than they were.

# Getting There & Away

## AIR

Surprisingly, airfares to/from Eastern Europe are usually expensive. If you're coming from North America, Australia or New Zealand, your best bet is to buy the cheapest possible ticket to Western Europe and proceed from there. Look for a discount ticket to London, Amsterdam, Vienna, Athens, Istanbul or anywhere in Germany. Vienna is a perfect gateway as Czechoslovakia and Hungary are both just hours away.

Emphasise that you want the cheapest possible fare whenever dealing with travel agencies or airlines, and compare prices at several offices before deciding. You may be able to save money by advancing or delaying your trip slightly to take advantage of a lower seasonal fare. Start enquiring well ahead as some low fares have advance purchase requirements. Some round-trip excursion fares with fixed dates are cheaper but there are big penalties for subsequent changes or cancellations.

### To/From the USA

Icelandair flies from Baltimore, New York and Orlando to Amsterdam, Copenhagen, Frankfurt/Main, London, Luxembourg, Salzburg and Vienna, with free onward bus connections available in Luxembourg to Düsseldorf, Frankfurt/Main and Stuttgart (bus reservations required). In the USA call Icelandair toll-free on 800-223 5500 to ask about off-season and 'last minute' one-way fares.

It's possible to get cheaper one-way fares to Europe from 'bucket shops' in New York City. These agencies purchase blocks of 'empty' seats from airlines at a fraction of their value and pass the savings on to you. For example, TFI Tours (☎ 212-736 1140 or 800-223 6363), 34 West 32nd St, 12th floor, New York, NY 10001, promises 'daily departures with guaranteed reservations on scheduled airlines'. The Sunday travel sections of the *Boston Globe, Chicago Sun Times, Dallas Morning News, Los Angeles Times, Miami Herald* and *New York Times* carry ads from many such companies.

TAROM Romanian Air Transport (☎ 212-687 6013) sometimes offers stand-by flights from New York to Vienna for as little as US$225 one-way, while LOT-Polish Airlines (☎ 800-223 0593) has stand-bys from Chicago or New York to Warsaw for US$299 one-way.

### To/From Canada

Just get the cheapest return ticket to London (around C$400), Amsterdam (C$500) or a closer gateway and proceed to Eastern Europe by bus.

### To/From Australia & New Zealand

Garuda Indonesia flies from Melbourne to Amsterdam, Frankfurt, London, Paris or Rome for A$1790 to A$2265 return, depending on the season, but its flights tend to be disorganised. Malaysian Airlines will get you to Athens for A$1780 return.

Lauda Air offers Adelaide-Sydney-Bangkok-Vienna (or London) for A$2072 to A$2750 return, depending on the season. Stopovers in Bangkok are one week maximum but there are no other restrictions and Lauda uses modern aircraft with lots of legroom. The Lauda flight arrives in Vienna in the morning, allowing you to continue to Hungary or Czechoslovakia on the same day.

Aeroflot is a couple of hundred dollars cheaper but it has old equipment, theoretical schedules, and there's a long delay changing planes in Moscow. However, Aeroflot will enable you to fly to Eastern Europe without going through Western Europe first, and depending on how you look at it, a stopover in Moscow could be an added bonus.

### To/From the UK

Regular one-way fares from Britain to Eastern Europe are expensive though tickets to Berlin are often cheaper than the train. If you're going to the Balkans compare the price of a cheap package tour booked on a 'last minute' basis as this may be no more than the flight alone. Check the London weeklies *Time Out* and *TNT* for ads from bucket shops offering cheap flights.

STA Travel (☎ 071-937 9921) in London sells an 'open jaw' return trip routing London-Berlin (£75) and Bucharest-London (£100) which allows you to traverse the countries of your choice without having to return to your starting point.

### To/From Africa

Bucket shops in Nairobi, Kenya, sell Egypt Air tickets to Athens for US$310 one-way with a free stop in Cairo. From Greece there are buses to Bulgaria and trains or ferries to Yugoslavia.

### To/From Asia

From South-East Asia the very cheapest fares to Western Europe are offered by the Eastern European carriers. Ironically, these fares usually don't apply if you wish to end up in Eastern Europe itself, though you can often get a free stopover, which amounts to the same thing. The Aeroflot route from Singapore or Bangkok via Moscow is particularly popular. On flights with Balkan Bulgarian Airlines, Czechoslovak Airlines (ČSA), LOT-Polish Airlines, TAROM Romanian Air Transport and Yugoslav Airlines (JAT) you'll transit an Eastern European capital.

### TRAIN
#### International Tickets

There are three levels of railway fares in Eastern Europe. The most expensive are tickets between Western and Eastern Europe. Only buy these as far as your first possible stop within the region. Tickets between individual Eastern European countries are less expensive, and cheaper still are domestic tickets within a single country. From Amsterdam a one-way, 2nd-class train ticket will cost US$76 to Berlin, US$125 to Poznań (Poland), US$135 to Cheb (Czecho-slovakia), US$185 to Budapest and US$160 to Ljubljana (Yugoslavia).

Until 1991 train fares between the seven Warsaw Pact countries were based on 'accounting roubles'. The rouble fare would be converted into the local currency (złoty, crowns, forint, etc) and you paid the equivalent in whichever Western currency you chose. MÁV Hungarian Railways gave foreigners a 50% discount on these already low fares if they paid in hard currency. At this rate you could go from Budapest to Prague for only US$8, 1st class. On 1 January 1991 the USSR cut off cheap oil supplies to Eastern Europe and henceforth all international trade, transport included, had to be settled in hard currency. This has led to rising prices, so check fares carefully once you get there.

Tickets between Eastern European countries are valid for two months outbound or four months for a return trip and you may stop over as often as you wish. In all the Eastern European countries, international train tickets should be purchased at a travel agency, not in the railway station. If you have a student card, you're eligible for a discount on international railway tickets between Eastern European countries.

#### Railway Passes

The Interrail pass (sold to European residents aged 25 and under) is valid for unlimited 2nd-class railway travel in all of Eastern Europe except Albania. Interrail costs about US$325 for one month and, although not valid within the country of purchase, it does get you a 50% reduction on one return-trip journey to the border.

A new Interrail pass for people aged 26 and over was introduced in Britain in May 1991. It's now possible to travel through 24 countries by train for one month for £235, or through 21 countries (but not Spain, Portugal or Morocco) for 15 days for £175. The ferry from Brindisi, Italy, to Patras, Greece, and all trains in Eastern Europe (except Albania) are included. Information is available at British Rail offices, but the ticket is not valid in the UK, and proof of six months' residence in the UK is required.

In 1989 Hungary became the first Eastern European country to accept the Eurail pass, followed in 1991 by Eastern Germany. Czechoslovakia-bound, your Eurail pass will take you to Schirnding (Germany) near Cheb. Vienna is a convenient gateway to Czechoslovakia and Hungary with frequent bus, boat and rail connections (US$15 and two hours to Sopron or Bratislava, US$30 and four hours to Budapest or Prague by train). If you begin or end your Eurail pass in Vienna, you won't have to count the days spent touring the Austrian capital. Eurail travellers will find Trieste, Italy, the best gateway to Yugoslavia with 17 buses a day to nearby Koper and a boat to Istria.

Keep in mind that in 1991 the Eurail pass was still not valid in Czechoslovakia and Yugoslavia. Unless this situation has changed, remember that if you want to go from Hungary to Italy or Germany you must go via Austria, otherwise you'll have to pay the fare to the Czechoslovak or Yugoslav conductor on the train and it won't be cheap! When you buy your pass, check carefully to determine which countries are now included.

The Eurail pass is not good value for touring Eastern Europe as very little of the region is included as yet and the alternative means of travel are much cheaper, so only buy one with the intention of using it mostly in Western Europe.

### Trans-Siberian/Mongolian

Through trains link China to Moscow in five or six days with onward connections in Moscow to all Eastern European capitals. It used to be very cheap to travel from Budapest to Beijing on these trains, but in 1991 ticket prices in Hungary increased 500% on this route! Now you'll pay around US$1000 one-way – more than it would cost you to fly. Westbound travel from China to Europe still costs only US$307, so this is now more of a way of getting to Eastern Europe than it is of getting away. There have also been recent reports of cheap tickets to China still being obtained through Orbis in Warsaw.

Westbound, wait till you get to Beijing to buy your ticket, as tickets sold in Western countries are much more expensive. The China International Travel Service (CITS) in Beijing and Shanghai books sleepers to Moscow, but not over a month nor less than five days in advance. Reservations between China and Moscow are tight in June, July and August and 10 days are required to arrange Soviet and Mongolian transit visas in Beijing. You can't make your onward train reservation from Moscow to Eastern Europe until you get to Moscow. There you can do it at the Intourist office in the railway station from which you'll be departing if you want to leave the same day, or at the Central Travel Bureau, ulitsa Petrovska 15 (Metro: Marx Prospekt) for subsequent days.

## LAND
### To/From the UK

The cheapest way to go from London to Eastern Europe is to take a bus to Berlin. You have to change buses in Amsterdam but there are immediate connections and a through ticket is sold at London's Victoria Coach Terminal (☎ 071-730 0202).

If you're bound for Yugoslavia, Romania or Bulgaria, take a chance on a 'magic' bus to Belgrade, as advertised in the weekly entertainment papers *Time Out* and *LAM*. Most of the buses bound for Greece will drop you off in Yugoslavia. During winter, trans-European bus service is greatly reduced and sometimes even suspended, so check schedules carefully. A through train ticket from Britain to any Eastern European capital costs much more than you would pay for these buses.

### To/From Western Europe

Numerous railway lines link the two Europes but buses are usually much cheaper than trains. Budget Bus (☎ 627 5151), Rokin 10, Amsterdam, has buses to Berlin, Prague, Budapest and Zagreb throughout the year. For more information see the Getting There & Away section in the respective chapters. For information on ride services *(Mitfahrzentralen)*, see the Berlin section of this book.

For Czechoslovakia take a train from Linz

(Austria) to České Budějovice, a bus from Vienna to Brno or Bratislava, or a train from Vienna to Bratislava or Břeclav. For Hungary there are buses from Vienna to Sopron and Budapest, as well as trains. Otherwise you can take the train from Graz, Austria, to Szombathely, Hungary. In summer the Danube hydrofoil glides expensively from Vienna to Budapest (US$60 one-way).

There are many ways to reach Yugoslavia. Several railway lines converge on Ljubljana from Austria and Italy. The main line from Munich to Athens runs via Ljubljana and Belgrade. There are several trains a day between Thessaloniki and Skopje. If you have plenty of time and want to save a few dollars, there's a secondary line from Florina, Greece, to Bitola, Yugoslavia.

From Greece to Bulgaria a bus will be half the price of the train. Athens travel agencies selling tickets are listed in the Getting There & Away section of the Bulgaria chapter. The main railway line from Istanbul to Belgrade passes through Sofia and there are also cheap buses from Istanbul to Bucharest.

## SEA

There are ferries to Swinoujście and Gdańsk, Poland, from Copenhagen (Denmark), Ystad (Sweden), Nynäshamn (Sweden) and Helsinki (Finland). Ferries also connect Denmark and Sweden to Eastern Germany. There are ferries from Corfu (Greece) to Dubrovnik (Yugoslavia), as well as numerous lines across the Adriatic from Italy to Yugoslavia.

The cheapest way to go from Sweden to Czechoslovakia or Hungary is to take the ferry from Trelleborg to Sassnitz, Germany (US$16 one-way). In Sassnitz buy a train ticket across Eastern Germany to Děčín, Czechoslovakia, where you'll be able to pick up a domestic ticket across Czechoslovakia. Don't buy a through ticket in Sweden itself as this will be much more expensive.

## PACKAGE TOURS

A package tour is not the best way to see Eastern Europe and only worth considering if your time is very limited or you have a special interest such as skiing, canoeing, sailing, spa treatment, etc. Some package tours to beach resorts in Bulgaria, Romania and Yugoslavia are cheaper than a return airfare, and transport, accommodation, food and organised sightseeing are included. A package tour is still the cheapest way to visit Albania, though this could change. Check the Albania chapter in this book for details.

Most tour prices are for double occupancy, which means singles have to share a double room with a stranger of the same sex or pay a healthy single supplement for a single room. Your guide will speak the language of the originating country of the group – German if you join a tour in Berlin, Greek if you sign up in Athens. Tours from Britain with an English-speaking guide are slightly more expensive because of higher transport costs, though they are still competitive.

Seven-day Danube cruises from Vienna to Ruse on large Bulgarian riverboats are the cream of the Eastern European packages, but prices begin around US$1700 including a flight back to Vienna. Twelve-day Danube cruises on Soviet ships from Vienna to Istanbul and Yalta run US$2200 and up. Any travel agent will be able to book these trips.

## WARNING

This chapter is particularly vulnerable to change – prices for international travel are volatile, routes are introduced and cancelled, schedules change, special deals come and go, and rules and visa requirements are amended. Airlines and governments seem to take a perverse pleasure in making price structures and regulations as complicated as possible. You should check directly with the airline or travel agent to make sure you understand how a fare (and ticket you may buy) works. In addition, the travel industry is highly competitive and there are many lurks and perks. The upshot of this is that you should get opinions, quotes and advice from as many airlines and travel agents as possible before you part with your hard-earned cash. The details given in this chapter should be regarded as pointers and are not a substitute for careful, up-to-date research.

# Getting Around

## AIR

Considering the cheapness of train and bus travel within Eastern Europe, air travel is a real luxury. Aside from the speed, however, a plane trip can save you a bit of money on transit visas, for example from Warsaw to Belgrade (US$144 one-way), a trip which could require transit visas for Czechoslovakia and Hungary if you went by train. If you like flying for fun, domestic fares within Bulgaria, Czechoslovakia, Poland and Romania are reasonable, although still much more than the train. In Yugoslavia they're fairly expensive because foreigners pay about double what a Yugoslav would pay. There are no domestic flights in Hungary. Only Yugoslavia has airport taxes, which are only a couple of dollars. All the other airports are 'free'.

## BUS

Buses are slightly more expensive than trains. In most Eastern European countries buses complement the railways rather than duplicate their routes, but in Czechoslovakia and Hungary you have a choice of either. In these two countries you're better off taking buses for short trips and express trains for long journeys.

The ticketing system varies in each country, but to be safe always try to buy a ticket in advance at the station. If this is not possible you'll be told so. In Czechoslovakia the ČSAD bus system is computerised. Hungary and Yugoslavia also have good bus services. Occasionally you'll be charged extra for baggage (in Yugoslavia, always).

American traveller Sarah Slover, who travelled all over Hungary and Czechoslovakia, sent us these comments:

My travels went very smoothly. I was on a *lot* of buses and trains and not a single one left late or broke down and I always got a seat, usually immediately. I enjoyed my trip and found travelling alone to be safe and easy. People definitely noticed I was foreign but didn't stare or make comments like in Latin America.

## TRAIN

You'll do most of your travelling within Eastern Europe by train. All of the countries have well-developed railway networks similar to those of Western Europe. You'll have a choice between local trains which stop at every station, and express trains. Both have advantages. The local trains are only half the cost of the express trains but they never have reserved seats. Once you find a place to sit it's yours for the trip, and since passengers are constantly coming and going you eventually get a place even on a full train. First-class travel by local train costs about the same as 2nd class on an express and is quite comfortable, so long as you're in no hurry. First-class compartments have six seats, 2nd class eight seats.

If you choose an express be sure to get an express ticket and ask if there are compulsory seat reservations. It's sometimes a hassle getting these tickets, so don't leave it too late. Express trains are often marked in red on posted timetables, local trains in black. The symbol R with a box around it means reservations are mandatory. The boards listing departures are usually yellow, and those for arrivals are white.

Tickets for express trains are best purchased at the central railway ticket office a day before. On overnight trains always try to book a 2nd-class couchette or a 1st-class sleeper a few days in advance. Make sure your ticketing is all in order before you board the train. If you have to arrange a reservation, buy a ticket or upgrade a local ticket to express on a moving train, you'll pay a healthy supplement.

### Luggage

Almost every railway station in Eastern Europe has a luggage room where you can deposit your luggage as soon as you arrive.

In Poland this can be expensive as you're charged 1% of the declared value of your luggage but elsewhere it's fairly cheap. In main stations the left-luggage office is open around the clock.

Many railway stations also have complicated coin lockers. You compose a four-digit number on the inside of the door, insert a coin and close the locker. To open it again you arrange the same number on the outside and with luck the door will open. Don't forget the number or the location of your locker!

## CAR & MOTORBIKE

To drive a car into most Eastern European countries you'll need the car registration papers and liability insurance (the 'green card'), although a carnet is not required. If you're not the car owner, you must have notarised written permission (or the rental agreement) to be in possession of it. Details of the car, boat or other vehicle will be written into your passport. If you're driving a camper van or caravan, you may be asked to provide an inventory of the equipment carried inside. The vehicle must bear a country identification sticker.

Although not always required, you should bring an international driver's licence. If you're renting you'll have to tell the agency exactly which countries you plan to visit so it can make sure the insurance is in order. Many German agencies refuse to allow their cars to be taken to Eastern Europe because of an increasing incidence of car theft. If you have a new car, a steering-wheel lock may save it from being stolen. Park in well-travelled areas, lock the car and consider removing the windshield wipers at night.

Driving at night can be dangerous as roads are often narrow and winding, and horse-drawn vehicles, bicycles, pedestrians and even domestic animals may be encountered at any time. In case of an accident you're supposed to notify the police and file an insurance claim. Never sign any documents you cannot read – insist on a translation and sign that if it's acceptable. If your car has significant body damage from a previous accident, point this out to customs upon arrival and have it noted somewhere, as damaged vehicles are only allowed to leave the country with police permission.

Many cities don't allow private cars in the centre of town and finding parking space is difficult, so it's often best to find a place to stay at the edge of town and commute by public transport.

Travel by private car often allows you to get off the beaten track and to avoid overpriced accommodation by simply moving on. With public transport prices going up fast, it could even be cheaper if there are a few of you.

### Fuel

To stop border jumpers from Austria and Germany from filling up cheaply, fuel must sometimes be purchased using coupons paid for with hard currency at the border or tourist offices. The farther you are from the Austrian or German border, the less likely the attendants are to enforce this rule which does make the price considerably higher. Once purchased, the coupons are not refundable though they sometimes have the advantage of allowing you to cut in front of horrendous queues at petrol stations.

Unleaded fuel (Bleifrei in German) is hard to find in Eastern Europe, so bring a 20-litre can in which to carry an extra supply, especially if your car is fitted with a catalytic converter, as this expensive component can be ruined by leaded fuel. Check your car's octane requirement: if it's a modern model designed for unleaded fuel but without a converter, it'll run quite happily on regular (sometimes called 'normal') 92/94 octane leaded. If in doubt, however, only use premium (super) fuel with an octane rating of around 98, particularly if your Western car is an older model. Don't use the 86 octane 'normal' which many of the locals use in their vehicles because it'll make your high-compression Western engine ping like mad. The tank opening of cars burning unleaded fuel may be too small for the type of fuel nozzle used with leaded fuel, so you'll need a funnel. Modern motorcycles are all set up for unleaded fuel but don't have catalytic converters, which means they'll have no trouble with 92/94 octane leaded; however, stick to 98 octane super on older models.

## Road Rules

Standard international road signs are used throughout Eastern Europe. Everywhere you drive on the right side of the road and overtake on the left. Keep right except when overtaking, and use your turn signals for any change of lane and when pulling away from the kerb. You're not allowed to pass a whole line of cars whether they are moving or stopped. Speed limits are posted, and are generally 110 km/h on motorways (freeways), 90 km/h on the open road and 60 km/h in built-up areas. Motorcycles are usually limited to 90 km/h on motorways, and vehicles with trailers to 80 km/h. In towns you may only honk the horn to avoid an accident. The use of seat belts is mandatory outside built-up areas and motorcyclists must wear a helmet. Children under 12 and intoxicated passengers are not permitted in the front seat. Driving after drinking even the smallest amount of alcohol or beer is a serious offence.

Throughout Europe, when two roads of equal importance intersect, the vehicle coming from the right has the right of way. In many countries this also applies to cyclists, so take care. On roundabouts (traffic circles) vehicles already in the roundabout have the right of way. Public transport vehicles pulling out from a stop also have right of way. Stay out of lanes marked 'bus' except when you're making a right-hand turn. Pedestrians have the right of way at marked crossings and whenever you're making a turn. In Europe it's prohibited to turn right against a red light even after coming to a stop.

It's usually illegal to stop or stand at the top of slopes, in front of pedestrian crossings, at bus or tram stops, on bridges or level crossings or within three metres of a car filling up at a petrol station. You must use a red reflector warning triangle when parking on a highway (in an emergency). If you don't use the triangle and another vehicle hits you

from behind, you will be held responsible. You must use headlights when driving through heavy fog during the day.

Beware of trams (streetcars) as these have priority at crossroads and when turning right (provided they signal the turn). Don't pass a tram which is stopping to let off passengers until everyone is out and the tram doors have closed again (unless, of course, there's a safety island). Never pass a tram on the left or stop within one metre of tram tracks. A police officer who sees you blocking a tram route by waiting to turn left will flag you over. Traffic police administer fines on the spot (always ask for a receipt).

## Rental

Car rentals in Eastern Europe aren't cheap. As a rough guide, for a minimum three-day rental of the cheapest car with unlimited mileage, including collision insurance and tax, Europcar/National Car Rental charges US$216 in Czechoslovakia, US$248 in Germany, US$233 in Hungary, US$154 in Poland and US$120 in Yugoslavia.

If you're coming from North America, Australia or New Zealand, ask your airline if it has any special deals for rental cars in Europe, or check the ads in the weekend travel sections of major newspapers. Europe-By-Car (not Europcar) in New York City rents new Citroën cars available in Amsterdam at US$699 for 32 days, including insurance and unlimited mileage, but you must book ahead from the USA. Check first whether there are restrictions on taking the car into certain Eastern European countries. Another US company, Kemwel Car Rental (☎ 800-678 0678), offers unlimited-mileage rentals in Hungary at US$149 a week. This is much less than you would pay in Europe.

It's better to resist the temptation to rent the most luxurious model, as it will stand out and could be a target for theft, vandalism or occasional harassment by traffic police. Finding unleaded fuel in Eastern Europe is problematic and petrol pumps of any kind are few and far between, so ask for a car that burns leaded fuel and is easy on fuel consumption.

## Purchase

Since 1990, Eastern Europeans have flooded Western Europe on car-buying expeditions – a good indication that what's available back home isn't competitive. For more information, see the Berlin section in this book.

## BICYCLE

Cycling is a cheap, convenient, healthy, environmentally sound and, above all, *fun* way of getting around. Because of the flat terrain and lack of heavy traffic, the best areas for bicycle touring are the northern halves of Eastern Germany and Poland and the Hungarian Great Plain. Quality bicycles can be purchased in Berlin, and a natural route from there would be north to the Baltic coast, west to the Mazurian Lakes and south through east Slovakia to Hungary. Having experienced all that, you should be ready for Romania and Bulgaria. Those with less time could simply rent a bicycle in Berlin and use it to tour the area north of Berlin.

Reader Len Houwers of Levin, New Zealand, sent us this letter:

My girlfriend and I have been travelling through Europe and Asia for over a year now on pedal power: two mountain bikes, rear carrier bags, sleeping bags and tent. Having spent five months cycling through Europe we can recommend the bike as a totally independent vehicle for travellers which allows you to get really close to the countryside and people, provided it stays dry and you're not in a hurry. We averaged about 400 km a week, which was four days cycling and three rest days to cover various city sights. At most hotels the reception allowed us to park our bikes in our room or found a spare lockable room free of charge. International travel by train is a hassle as they usually separate you from your bike which gets sent ahead. To avoid this separation, travel to border towns by train, cross the border by bike, then catch another train on the other side.

Readers Jenny Visser and Mike Fee of Wellington, New Zealand, sent the following letter:

We cycled and camped through Czechoslovakia, Poland, Hungary, Bulgaria and a little of Yugoslavia in the summer months of 1990, covering approximately 4000 km in over eight weeks. We would like to point out just how ideal much of Eastern Europe is for cycling. Eastern European roads were of surprisingly good quality (although when they did deteriorate they were nearly always quiet. This allowed us to relax and enjoy the cycling, a luxury not often available on busier northern and southern European roads. The negative side was the disgusting exhaust put out by all Eastern European vehicles, especially buses and trucks. Often we would be left gasping in a cloud of blue or black smoke as these vehicles lumbered along the road. We had thought that signposting outside the main centres might produce some difficulty for navigation, but again we were pleasantly surprised by its availability.

One final note for cyclists contemplating including any of these countries in their itinerary: take plenty of spares. Before you leave the West go over your bike with a fine-tooth comb and fill your repair kit with every imaginable spare (spokes, tyres, inner tubes, bearings, cones, grease, derailleurs, etc). We had to make a 300-km detour back into Germany to buy a new front derailleur. The man in the 'specialist' bicycle shop in Prague just laughed at us when we inquired about a replacement.

## HITCHHIKING

As long as public transport remains cheap, hitchhiking is more for the adventure than the transport. In many countries drivers expect riders to pay the equivalent of a bus fare. The best hitchhiking is in Eastern Germany and the worst is in Yugoslavia. In Romania traffic is light and probably not going far and everywhere you'll be up against small, full vehicles. Most of the big Western cars you see are driven by tourists who never stop. This said, just make yourself a small cardboard destination sign and give it a try. City buses will usually take you to the edge of town. Before hitchhiking on a motorway (freeway) make sure it's not prohibited. If you look like a Westerner your chances of getting a ride will be much better.

Women will find hitchhiking safer than in Western Europe, but standard precautions should be taken: never accept a ride with two men, don't let your pack be put in the boot (trunk), only sit next to a door you can open, ask the driver where he/she is going before you say where you're going, etc. Don't hesitate to refuse a ride if you feel at all uncomfortable, and insist on being let out at the first sign of trouble. Best of all, try to find a travelling companion (although three people will almost never get a ride).

## BOAT

A number of interesting boat trips are possible. One of the most unforgettable is the journey on the big Jadrolinija car ferry down the Dalmatian Coast of Yugoslavia from Split to Dubrovnik. The best river trips are through the Danube Delta from Braila to Sulina and up the Elbe River from Dresden to Bad Schandau. A hydrofoil along Bulgaria's Black Sea coast or up the Danube from Ruse to Vidin can be memorable. Other classic trips include the slow boats from Budapest to Esztergom or across Balaton Lake in Hungary. In Poland some cities on the Vistula offer river trips in their vicinity, and excursion boats ply the Mazurian Lakes in north-east Poland. The Weisse Flotte is active around Berlin and on the Baltic. Most services operate from April to October only, sometimes for shorter periods.

### Canoe or Kayak

Every summer since 1955, up to 1000 people have paddled themselves down the Danube from Ingoldstadt in Germany to Silistra in Bulgaria, under the banner of the Tour International Danubien (TID) organised by the German Canoe Club. This is not a race! The world's longest annual canoe cruise covers 2084 km in daily laps of 40 to 75 km spread over two months. It's possible to sign up for only a portion of the trip, and boat and bus transfers to/from Germany are arranged. Participants sleep in camps beside the river and combine sightseeing with travel. You must provide your own canoe or kayak and camping gear, as the German Canoe Club does not rent sporting boats of any kind. Applications close on 31 March and the trip itself lasts from the last Sunday in June to the last Saturday in August each year.

For more information on the TID, send a self-addressed, stamped envelope or an International Postal Reply Coupon to any of the following people:

- Rolf Kunze, Deutscher Kanu-Verband, Friedrich-Breuer-Strasse 42, D-5300 Bonn 3, Germany (☎ 0228-47 2040).
- Rodney Baker, 11 Holt Fen, Little Thetford, Ely CB6 3HB, England (☎ 0353-64 8802).
- Walter Danner, 29 Kawartha Dr, Pontiac, Quebec J0X 2G0, Canada (☎ 819-682 5041).
- Frank and Doreen Whitebrook, 10 Ridgeland Close, Richmond Hill, Lismore, NSW 2480, Australia (☎ 066-24 2077).

## LOCAL TRANSPORT

Public transport in Eastern Europe is cheap and the low price has no effect whatsoever on the service, which is generally first rate. In most cities, buses and trams begin moving at 5 am or earlier and continue until around 10.30 or 11.30 pm. There are metro (subway or underground) lines in Berlin, Bucharest, Budapest and Prague. The Warsaw metro has been under construction for years and is still not open.

For all forms of public transport you must buy tickets in advance at a kiosk or from a machine. Information windows in bus and railway stations sometimes have tickets for local transport. Once aboard you validate your own ticket by using a punch machine positioned near the door. Watch how the

locals do it. Different tickets are sometimes required for buses, trolley buses, trams (streetcars) and the metro, but at other times they're all the same. If all the kiosks selling tickets are closed, ask another passenger to sell you a ticket. There are no conductors and tickets are seldom checked, but you'll be fined if an inspector catches you without a valid ticket.

Karl-Friedrich Schinkel's sculpture in East Berlin glorifying Frederick the Great; the shield held up by the victory goddess puts him alongside Alexander the Great and Julius Caesar

# Eastern Germany

When the Berlin Wall crumbled on 9 November 1989, the rationale which had held the German Democratic Republic (GDR) together since 1961 ceased to exist. With the floodgates open to economic competition from the West, East Germany's political identity soon became redundant. On 1 July 1990 the Deutschmark replaced the wobbly Ostmark as legal tender in the east and on 3 October 1990 the two Germanys were formally reunited. A 45-year hangover from WW II had ended and the 'Cold War' was over.

These events drastically altered the landscape for anyone wishing to visit what are now the six north-easternmost states of the Federal Republic of Germany (FRG). Onerous regulations requiring visas, advance hotel reservations, compulsory currency exchange, police registration and limiting freedom of movement have been abolished. These improved circumstances are balanced by overcrowding and fast-rising prices. Previously you had to be rather adventurous to travel around the GDR on your own but now it's easy for anyone to go.

Yet this intriguing land of Bach, Brecht, Cranach, Goethe, Händel, Hegel, Humboldt, Luther, Schiller and Schumann still has a tremendous amount to offer. Museum lovers will never finish perusing the local collections and the musical life remains rich. Communism sheltered East Germany from the crass commercialism and overdevelopment of the West. While West Germany became Americanised after WW II, there was no comparable Russianisation of East Germany. Travelling between the two is like stepping back in history 25 years, and small towns like Bautzen, Colditz, Meissen, Naumburg, Quedlinburg, Stralsund and Wernigerode still have a timeless medieval air.

Eastern Germany's stormy recent history is best experienced in Berlin where Hitler lived and died and the infamous Wall rose

and fell. German governments seated at Berlin have catastrophically collapsed four times this century, in 1918, 1933, 1945 and 1989. Nazis and Communists alike were heirs to Prussian puritanism and discipline, and it's no coincidence that both monumental cities of Frederick the Great, Berlin and Potsdam, are here.

Farther south in Dresden there's the softer Saxon heritage of Augustus the Strong, at Weimar the holy shrines of classical German literature, and elsewhere both the pilgrimage places associated with Martin Luther: Wittenberg where he launched the Reformation and Eisenach where he took refuge and translated the Bible. Accessible hiking trails penetrate Eastern Germany's low mountain ranges while the northern coastline and lakes beckon active travellers and also those who only want somewhere quiet to rest. Come now before too many people find out about it.

# Facts about the Country

## HISTORY

Never part of the Roman Empire, this region was occupied by the West Slavs around the end of the 6th century. German merchants settled among them. In the 10th century the Saxons began pushing east and by the millennium the border between Germany and Poland was along the Oder River, about where it is today. The subjugated Slavonic tribes intermingled with their conquerors and the Slavonic language disappeared, except in tiny Sorbian pockets between Bautzen and Cottbus.

Market towns like Berlin, Erfurt, Magdeburg and Leipzig developed between the 10th and 13th centuries. Trade was first by river and sea, then by road. Wars with Poland continued through the Middle Ages as the Germans expanded east along the Baltic coast. In the 13th century the German knightly orders gained control of East Prussia, Latvia and Estonia.

In the 14th and 15th centuries the Hanseatic League developed a remarkable trading network from the Baltic Sea to the North Sea. Independent city states such as Reval (Estonia), Riga (Latvia), Danzig (Gdańsk), Stralsund, Rostock, Wismar, Lübeck, Hamburg, Bremen, Bergen (Norway) and Bruges (Belgium) flourished. Much of the medieval architecture we now admire in those ports was built in those days.

The towns of the German interior were in a perpetual state of feud with the landed gentry. In 1412 Frederick of Nuremberg from the house of the Hohenzollern acquired the Mark Brandenburg. He subdued the gentry, then conquered the previously independent towns. In 1470 the elector of Brandenburg established his residence at Berlin.

In the early 16th century the Protestant Reformation took hold in the nascent feudal states of north Germany – Brandenburg, Mecklenburg, Pomerania and Saxony. The Thirty Years' War (1618-48) between the Protestant north Germans and the Habsburg-Spanish Catholic forces led to unparalleled destruction. A half to two-thirds of the population died in this part of Germany.

In 1660 Frederick William (the 'Great Elector') obtained East Prussian independence from Polish suzerainty. Elector Frederick I had himself crowned king of Prussia in 1701 and his son, Frederick William I, built Prussia into one of the strongest military forces in Europe with an efficient bureaucracy. The next king, Frederick II (the Great), took Silesia from Austria in 1742 and annexed East Prussia in 1772. By 1795 three partitions had wiped Poland off the map.

Prussia itself was defeated by Napoleon in 1806 and occupied by French troops. Heavy taxes were extorted from the occupied lands, but a few democratic reforms were also introduced, such as the emancipation of the serfs in 1807 and the founding of Humboldt University in 1809. Napoleonic control sparked an upsurge of nationalism throughout Europe, and the Prussian army was transformed from a mercenary force into a modern national army. In 1813 the combined armies of Austria, Prussia, Russia and Sweden defeated Napoleon at Leipzig.

After this War of Independence against French domination, the development of industry led to the creation of an urban working class. After a strike in 1844 the Prussian semi-absolutist regime prohibited further strikes and in 1847 a 'potato revolt' in Berlin was suppressed. About the same time, the 'United Assembly' denied funds to the king unless he produced a constitution and allowed representative government. When this was not forthcoming an unsuccessful liberal-democratic revolution broke out in 1848. In Berlin workers and students battled at over 200 barricades against disciplined Prussian troops.

Chancellor Otto von Bismarck consolidated Prussia's position as head of a confederation of north German states, and the Franco-Prussian War of 1870 resulted from French fears of a powerful, unified Germany. After the Prussian victory the

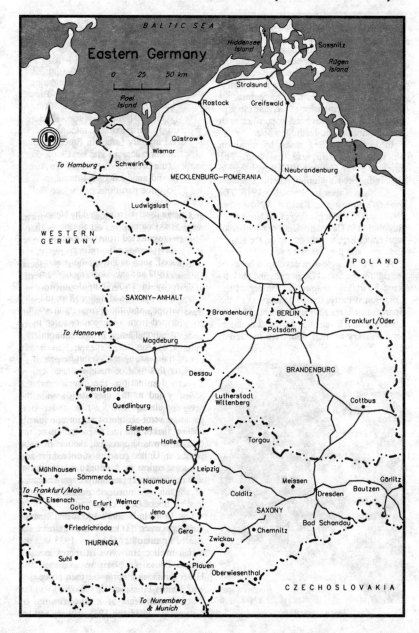

Prussian king, William (Wilhelm) I, was proclaimed German Emperor *(Kaiser)* in the Hall of Mirrors at Versailles on 18 January 1871. The military despotism promoted the rapid development of a capitalist economy. The transition from capitalism to imperialism took place at the turn of the century, but the aggressive expansion of German monopolies eventually provoked a conflict with British imperialism, leading to war.

In January 1918 a strike by munition workers in Berlin was thwarted. The example of the October 1917 Revolution in Russia inspired a similar rebellion against the German Kaiser in November 1918. The seamen's uprising in Kiel on 3 November 1918 marked the beginning of the November Revolution in Germany. On 9 November all workers in Berlin went on strike, the Kaiser abdicated and the war was over.

A power struggle then developed between the right-wing Social Democrats and the left-wing Spartakus League, forerunner of the Communist Party. On 15 January 1919 the Spartakus leaders Karl Liebknecht and Rosa Luxemburg fell into the hands of counter-revolutionary soldiers and were murdered,

Ernst Thälmann

and in March 1919 thousands of workers were killed or imprisoned by the military. The strength of the Berlin workers' movement is illustrated by the fact that the constituent assembly, dominated by Social Democrats, met in Weimar instead of Berlin to draft Germany's republican constitution.

The world economic crisis of 1929 led to massive unemployment, strikes and demonstrations. The German Communist Party under Ernst Thälmann gained strength. The monopolies and financial capital saw a way out of the crisis in the establishment of an open, terroristic dictatorship. Flick, Krupp, Thyssen, the IG-Farbenindustrie, and the Siemens and AEG trusts were among the main supporters of Hitler. Later these companies made huge profits from armaments orders, the murderous exploitation of the German working class and the use of slave labour from the concentration camps and occupied countries. A united antifascist front was not formed in Germany largely because of the anti-Communist paranoia of the leading Social Democrats.

On 30 January 1933 President Hindenburg appointed Hitler chancellor, and the Reichstag fire of 27 February 1933 was the signal for a brutal wave of repression. All opposition to the Nazis was crushed and Hitler's vicious programme then proceeded with deadly efficiency. In October 1933 the fascists withdrew from the League of Nations and in March 1935 military service

Rosa Luxemburg

was reintroduced. In 1936 and 1937 anti-Communist pacts were signed with Japan and Italy, the demilitarised Rhineland was reoccupied in March 1936 and fascist troops were sent to Spain from 1936 to 1939. Austria was annexed in March 1938, in October 1938 it was Czechoslovakia's turn and finally, in September 1939, Hitler invaded Poland, leading to war with Britain and France.

Throughout the Nazi period, underground groups of the German Communist Party maintained a heroic resistance which cost many of them their lives. A National Committee for a Free Germany was set up in the USSR in 1943 by emigrants and German prisoners of war, while the German officers who attempted to assassinate Hitler in 1944 preserved the honour of their nation.

In February 1945 it was decided at Yalta which parts of Germany would be occupied by the various Allies, and Anglo-American bombings of Germany intensified. On 23 April 1945 advance detachments of the 5th Soviet Guards made contact with the US 1st Army at Torgau on the Elbe River, 50 km north-east of Leipzig, and on 8 May 1945 the German High Command surrendered at Berlin-Karlshorst.

## The Communist Era

After the war Germany suffered the fate of many of its victims. Pomerania, Silesia and East Prussia were annexed by Poland and the USSR, and about 6,500,000 Germans were returned to Germany from Czechoslovakia, Hungary, Poland and Yugoslavia. The Oder-Neisse Line became the new eastern border. According to the Yalta Agreement, Germany was divided into four zones and Berlin was occupied by the four victorious powers pending the reunification of Germany.

In April 1946 the Social Democratic Party in the Soviet zone was united with the Communist Party to form the Socialist Unity Party (SED), which won the elections later that year. It began nationalising industry and, by 1948, 61% of production in the Soviet zone came from the public sector. A two-year

development plan was drawn up in 1948, followed by a five-year plan in 1951.

On 20 June 1948 a new currency linked to the dollar was introduced in the Western sectors of Berlin, setting the stage for a 42-year division of Germany. Four days later the USSR interrupted land traffic between the western zones and West Berlin. The Western allies countered this with a military airlift operation which supplied West Berlin by plane. Late in 1948 all trusts, banks and insurance companies in East Berlin were expropriated, and with these reforms in place the Soviet Union lifted the blockade in May 1949. In September 1949 the Federal Republic of Germany (FRG) was created out of the three western zones; in response the German Democratic Republic (GDR) was founded in the Soviet zone on 7 October 1949 with Berlin as capital.

In March 1952 Washington and Bonn rejected an offer from Stalin of a united Germany on the basis of strict political and military neutrality. That such an option was indeed possible way back then is proved by the implementation of the Austrian State Treaty of May 1955 which terminated the occupation of Austria through neutrality.

From 1945 to 1955 West Germany received US$4 billion in Marshall Plan aid from the USA, while East Germany had to pay US$10 billion in war reparations to the Soviet Union. Whole factories and railway lines were dismantled and sent east. East Germany had to shoulder the full burden of responsibility for the wartime misdeeds of both Germanys. The strain on the GDR's economy reached breaking point on 17 June 1953, three months after Stalin's death, when East German workers went on strike over increased work norms. After the disturbances were put down by GDR police and Soviet troops, the workload was reduced and on 1 January 1954 the USSR cancelled all outstanding reparations and debts.

A fifth of the population (3,500,000 people) left East Germany before 1961, most of them for economic reasons. While causing economic havoc in the east, the influx of skilled labour was a windfall worth billions to West Germany. Until May 1952 the GDR border with West Germany was fairly open. Then a five-km restricted area was created and border controls tightened. Potential refugees switched to defecting while on legal 'holiday' trips to the west. In 1956 travel authorisations became much more difficult to obtain and the tide of migration shifted to Berlin. There anyone could enter West Berlin simply by boarding the U-Bahn or crossing the street. In 1960 a reckless 'economic main programme' of rapid industrialisation and collectivisation in East Germany turned the flow of refugees into a flood.

On 13 August 1961 thousands of East German troops, police and workers militia suddenly appeared in East Berlin, took up positions at major intersections and strung barbed wire along the border with West Berlin. Passengers arriving in the city by train were put back on board and told to go home. The temporary barrier was soon replaced by a high concrete wall.

The building of the Berlin Wall must be seen against the background of the Bay of Pigs invasion of Cuba on 17 April 1961. International tensions were at the breaking point and West Berlin was as much a bone in the throat of the GDR and USSR as Cuba appeared to be to the USA. The real seriousness of the situation is illustrated by a promise from Khrushchev to take West Berlin if the US invaded Cuba.

Construction of the Wall allowed the GDR to proceed with its development without further influence from the West. The Wall served its purpose well and the subsequent economic revival of the GDR would have been impossible without it. While blackening the GDR's image in Western eyes, the Wall brought stability to the country. In 1964 the GDR's economy began to blossom.

West Germany had been unwilling to accept the establishment of the GDR, desiring reunification on its own terms and even the return of territories annexed by Poland and the USSR in 1945. Until the early 1970s the Federal Republic was able to prevent the Democratic Republic from being recognised in the West. This policy changed with the far-sighted *Ostpolitik* of Willy Brandt, who replaced hardliner Konrad Adenauer as West German chancellor in 1969. In 1970 West Germany signed a treaty with the USSR recognising the territorial integrity of all the states of Europe within their existing boundaries.

In 1971, with détente in full swing, a Quadripartite Agreement was signed by the Soviet Union, the USA, Britain and France normalising the status quo in Berlin. With this agreement in place, many Western countries recognised the GDR and established diplomatic relations. In 1972 the FRG and the GDR agreed on a Basic Law to govern their bilateral affairs, although full recognition was prevented by the West German constitution. In 1973 the GDR was admitted to the United Nations.

## Recent History

In May 1971 the GDR's postwar leader, Walter Ulbricht, a 'Moscow' Communist who had spent WW II in the USSR, was removed from power for opposing détente. Ulbricht was replaced by Erich Honecker, a 'national' Communist imprisoned by the Nazis from 1935 to 1945. Honecker emphasised consumer production, yet, despite living standards far better than those of any other Eastern European country, the GDR only attained levels half as high as West Germany. With European unity just over the horizon and the Western technological lead increasing, the country seemed likely to fall even further behind. After March 1985, when Gorbachev took over in the USSR, the East German Communists no longer had full Soviet backing.

The GDR's identity as the first German socialist state was undermined by West German TV programmes accessible to 85% of East Germans. These created consumer attitudes and the Communist regime failed to communicate effectively, leading to increasing alienation between people and state. Accusations that the results of the local elections of 7 May 1989 were falsified gave people the feeling of being unrepresented in government.

Meanwhile the West German government was offering instant citizenship and emergency benefits to any East German who made it across the border, and many took the first opportunity to 'escape'. Most of the 340,000 East Germans who eventually left in 1989 were well-educated young people aged between 20 and 30, the very group West Germany needed most. In a capitalist society where everyone had to rely on their own efforts, these people were likely to do far better than in a socialist state where economic equality was an ideal. Of course this was what had forced the GDR to restrict foreign travel in the first place.

In May 1989 Hungary began dismantling its border controls, creating a gap in the security net which had held the Eastern bloc together for 40 years. By August, 5000 East Germans a week were reaching West Germany via Hungary, and when the Hungarian government opened its border with Austria on 10 September, 12,000 East Germans crossed within 72 hours.

The failure of the Soviet Union to intervene at this point and oblige the Hungarians to respect their treaties, sent the East German public the signal that Soviet troops would not be used to prop up the Communist regime, and on 25 September mass demonstrations against the government began in Leipzig.

The protesters were also encouraged by political changes elsewhere in Eastern Europe. In August 1989 a non-Communist government had taken office in Poland and moves towards reform were well advanced in Hungary. An informal opposition had already existed in the GDR for several years in the form of a 'peace movement' centred around the Lutheran Church. The East German government countered by prohibiting travel to Hungary, so would-be defectors began taking refuge in the West German Embassy in Prague where 5000 were soon camped.

On 7 October 1989 Mikhail Gorbachev visited East Berlin for the 40th anniversary celebrations of the foundation of the GDR. Gorbachev urged the ruling Politburo to take the lead in reform, a course strongly resisted by Honecker who feared destabilisation. (West Germany had promised Gorbachev DM 10 billion in economic aid if he didn't try to prop up East Germany's Communist government.) Monday-evening demonstrations continued in Leipzig throughout October, with the number of participants doubling each time and the unrest spreading to other cities.

On 9 October Honecker ordered a crackdown on the Leipzig protesters but his internal security chief, Egon Krenz, wavered and cancelled the order. As things slipped out of control, Honecker resigned on 18 October and was replaced by Krenz, who was unpopular because of his long association with the regime. On 5 November 1989 a million people gathered in Berlin's Alexander Platz to demand change. In a desperate bid to keep pace with events Krenz reshuffled the Politburo, promised free elections and, on 9 November 1989, opened the Berlin Wall. (The choice of that particular date, the 51st anniversary of Kristallnacht 1938, when the Nazis conducted a notorious pogrom against German Jews, was a brilliant final ploy by the Communists which has prevented the day from being celebrated as a German national holiday.)

Krenz had gambled that giving East Germans the freedom to travel to the West (a major demand of the protesters) would convince most of them to stay home, but the opening of the wall only increased the mass emigration and by early 1990 as many as 2000 a day were departing. After televised revelations of the lavish perks enjoyed by the Communist leadership, Krenz and his Politburo resigned on 3 December 1989. Hans Modrow, the reformist Dresden party leader, took over from Krenz.

New Forum, the original opposition group founded in September 1989, and others such as Democracy Now, United Left and Democratic Awakening contained a strong leftist element interested in 'democratic dialogue' with the regime and preserving 'the real and successful socialist achievements of the GDR' (wording from the draft programme of Democracy Now). The Social Democratic

Party, re-established in the GDR on 7 October 1989, also favoured gradual change.

On 28 November 1989 West German chancellor Helmut Kohl entered the fray with a 10-point plan for German reunification and the popular mood began swinging away from mere reform. After a meeting with Gorbachev in February 1990 even Modrow came out in favour of reunification.

Elections were scheduled for 18 March 1990, and only two weeks before them the Social Democratic Party (Sozialdemokratische Partei Deutschlands, or SPD) was leading the polls with a programme of gradual change and preserving positive elements of East Germany's identity. Then Kohl intervened again by campaigning for quick reunification and a one-for-one currency exchange (at this time one Deutschmark was trading for 10 Ostmarks on the black market). At an Erfurt election rally the crowd chanted, 'Helmut, take us by the hand, lead us to the miracle land.' At another election rally in Leipzig, Kohl declared, 'No-one will be worse off and many will be better off.'

Bundesbank president Karl Otto Pöhl warned that a one-for-one exchange rate would lead to economic collapse in the east (which subsequently proved true) but Kohl claimed the mass emigration (120,000 East Germans left the GDR in the first two months of 1990) made gradual change impossible and played on the long-standing desire for reunification on both sides of the border. Kohl reassured West German voters that taxes would not have to be increased to pay for reunification.

Kohl's generous promises swung the election in favour of his Christian Democratic Union (CDU) which received 41% of the popular vote. The Social Democrats got 22% and the Socialists (ex-Communists) just 16%. The groups which had spearheaded the November 1989 'revolution' were completely sidelined. Christian Democrat Lothar de Maziere became prime minister and formed a conservative alliance which implemented the economic and monetary union of the two Germanys on 1 July 1990. East Germans were given one week to convert 4000 Ostmarks each into Deutschmarks at the one-to-one rate. The rest of their savings and debts were converted at a two-to-one rate. Prices and wages were also converted one-to-one, dooming the inefficient East German industries to certain bankruptcy.

On 12 September 1990 representatives of the two Germanys and the four wartime Allies signed the 'Two-Plus-Four Treaty' at Moscow, ending the postwar system of occupation zones; on 3 October 1990 the East German parliament voted itself out of existence and the GDR became part of West Germany. Reunification had nothing to do with a negotiated merger of the two states: West Germany simply annexed East Germany. The *Anschluss* complete, Kohl's CDU easily won the all-German elections of 2 December 1990.

## GEOGRAPHY

Eastern Germany is a rectangle 500 km long and 350 km wide in north-east Germany. It extends over two geographical zones, the North European Plain in the north and the mountain chain of the Mittelgebirge in the south, covering 108,333 sq km (compared to 248,706 sq km in Western Germany).

There's a great deal of variety in a small area. The tideless Baltic coast features fine sandy beaches in wooded surroundings. Behind this are the many lakes of Brandenburg and Mecklenburg-Pomerania. The Spreewald north-west of Cottbus is a marshy area where rural residents reach their homes by boat.

The Harz around Wernigerode in Saxony-Anhalt is a hilly area known for its old traditions and scenic beauty. Picturesque Thuringia (Thüringen), the 'Green Heart of Germany', with its soft, rolling hills and valleys, is a magnificent hiking area. Eastern Germany's highest peak is Fichtelberg (1214 metres) at Oberwiesenthal in the Erzgebirge almost on the Czech border. In the Sächsische Schweiz (Saxon Switzerland) along the Elbe River between Dresden and Bad Schandau are picturesque rocks *(Steine)* and gorges, sandstone cliffs and bizarre landforms.

## GOVERNMENT

From 1952 to 1990 what was then the GDR consisted of 14 districts *(Bezirke)*: Berlin, Cottbus, Dresden, Frankfurt, Gera, Halle, Karl-Marx-Stadt, Leipzig, Magdeburg, Neubrandenburg, Potsdam, Rostock, Schwerin and Suhl. With reunification these were scrapped and regional government was reorganised on the basis of six federal states, or *Länder*, as it had been prior to 1952: Berlin, Brandenburg, Mecklenburg-Vorpommern (Mecklenburg-Pomerania), Sachsen (Saxony), Sachsen-Anhalt and Thüringen (Thuringia).

As a city state, Berlin has a status in Germany similar to that of Bremen or Hamburg. Half the Berlin budget was previously supplied by the federal government but this has been discontinued. There's a popularly elected parliament *(Abgeordnetenhaus)* which in turn appoints a mayor and senators who act as government ministers. The main political parties in Berlin are the Christian Democratic Union (CDU, conservatives), the Social Democratic Party (SPD, moderate socialists), the German Socialist Party (PDS, the former Communists), the Alternative List (environmentalists), the Free Democratic Party (liberals) and the Republican Party (far right). Berlin is divided into 23 independently run districts.

In June 1991 the German parliament voted to move the seat of government from Bonn to Berlin. It will take a decade to move all government ministries and employees east, though the chancellor and parliament must be in Berlin within four years. The German senate will remain in Bonn.

## ECONOMY

Eastern Germany's only abundant natural resource is soft brown coal (lignite), obtained from open-pit mines in the Cottbus area. The burning of this coal to generate electricity has caused serious environmental problems, such as deforestation from acid rain, and wastes from the coal-based chemical industry have been dumped into rivers.

The region also has the most important reserves of uranium in Europe outside the USSR, and potash is mined around Stassfurt south of Magdeburg. In general, however, Eastern Germany has far fewer natural resources and less industry than Western Germany. The Ruhr region always produced 90% of Germany's hard coal and steel.

East Berlin was the largest industrial centre in East Germany, especially in electronics, machinery, textiles and chemicals. Industry was also concentrated around Halle, Leipzig and Chemnitz (formerly Karl Marx Stadt). Synthetic oil was produced from lignite by hydrogenation at Leuna between Halle and Leipzig. In the 1960s the Communists built a modern steel mill at Eisenhüttenstadt near the Oder River which used Soviet ore and Polish or local coke. The southern hills of Saxony and Thuringia featured skilled industries developed from traditional handicrafts. The Carl Zeiss works at Jena, which produced cameras and optical equipment, and the Meissen porcelain factory were good examples. Rostock was the major port. The future of all of these is now in doubt.

### The Economy Under Communism

While the West German 'economic miracle' received wide publicity, East Germany's recovery in the 1960s was even more remarkable considering the wartime destruction, postwar reparations, loss of skilled labour and isolation from Western markets. Before the war, industry in what was then central Germany was light to medium industry dependent on raw materials (hard coal, coke, steel, etc) and semifinished products from the West. The GDR had to start from scratch. Despite the lack of raw materials, careful economic planning built the GDR into the largest industrial and trading nation in Eastern Europe and one of the world's 10 most industrialised nations. By the end of the 1960s, East Germany was the Soviet Union's most important economic partner.

After the war, metallurgy, electric power, chemicals and general and electrical engineering were developed in East Germany, producing synthetic rubber and gas, plastics, fertilisers, ships, machinery, textiles, radios, TVs, household appliances, precision instruments, optical equipment, cameras and film. Industry accounted for 48% of the gross national product, services 41% and agriculture only 11%.

The oil price increases of the mid-1970s and a worldwide economic slowdown caused the GDR's external debt to grow from US$1.4 billion to US$14.2 billion between 1971 and 1981. Trade was balanced with US$27.9 billion in exports against US$27.6 billion in imports (1986) with 65.9% of trade with other socialist countries, 30.7% with the developed West and 3.4% with developing countries. Imports included 2.1 million tonnes of garbage shipped from West Germany to East Germany in 1988.

In 1986, 37.7% of the workforce was employed in industry, 21% in services, 10.8% in agriculture and forestry, 10.3% in commerce, 7.3% in transportation and communications, 6.7% in construction, 3.1% in handicrafts and 3.1% in other occupations. Some 87.7% belonged to official trade unions. Not only was there full employment and job security, but according to government statistics 99% of women of working age were employed (in Western Europe barely a third have jobs). Women comprised 48.3% of the workforce in East Germany as opposed to only 37% in West Germany. Salaries were much lower than in West Germany but housing, food and transportation were heavily subsidised and medical care and education free.

Problem areas included a shortage of fruit and vegetables and long waiting periods to buy a car or obtain low-rent housing. The old Ostmarks weren't backed up by goods or services and there wasn't much on which to spend them, thus the long lines at restaurants, ticket offices, amusements, etc, and the constant search for something worthwhile to buy.

Because of the Communist policy of full employment, most Eastern industries were 30% overstaffed. Another Communist theory of the 'international division of labour'

meant that there was no competition between the Comecon countries, each of which specialised in something and had a monopoly on it. Workers gained no experience with individual initiative, the spontaneous nature of which was discouraged. Communist accounting methods made no allowance for reinvestment or depreciation and all profits were taken by the state. Thus too, there were no taxes. During the 1980s, 14 billion Ostmarks were invested in the four-megabit computer chip to circumvent a NATO ban on the export of high technology to the East. East Germany had hoped to become the Japan of Eastern Europe, but the Robotron computer is now as obsolete as the two-stroke Trabant automobile.

Before WW II much of Prussia was divided into 3000 huge landed estates. The land reform of 1945 divided all farms larger than 100 hectares among 544,000 farm workers, smallholders and refugees. In the 1950s there was a migration away from the farm to jobs in industry in the cities and in the early 1960s agriculture was collectivised. The much larger size of the fields is still immediately apparent as you travel from Western Germany into Eastern Germany. This rationalised and increased production through the use of modern equipment and fertilisers, while providing better security for the individual farmer. Compared to West Germany, however, productivity was low: only 40% as high per person or 75% per hectare. The main crops are wheat, rye, potatoes and sugar beets, with cattle and pigs the common livestock.

## The Economy Under Capitalism

As part of the Federal Republic of Germany the region obtained membership in the European Community through the back door. Yet less than a year after reunification the euphoria seemed to be turning sour. By mid-1991 Eastern Germany was facing a severe economic crisis with 50% unemployment and stagnant industry. Things seemed worse than during the Great Depression of the 1930s. The Eastern German gross domestic product dropped 10% in 1990, and another 20% in 1991. Industrial production dropped 53%.

New investment was reduced to a mere trickle with most of it related to marketing Western products in the East rather than producing anything there. Western German companies preferred to let Eastern German companies go bankrupt and then buy up their assets cheaply, rather than having to assume responsibility for the old employees. Many Western German retail chains even required Eastern German shops to sign contracts promising not to sell any Eastern German products at all before they would agree to stock their shops! Eastern Germany had gone from Stalinist Communism to Thatcherite capitalism in one jump.

After 31 December 1990, exports from Eastern Germany to the USSR had to be paid in hard currency rather than the old 'accounting roubles', so the orders suddenly ceased. With exports paralysed, bankruptcy became inevitable and even blue chips such as Interflug, Carl Zeiss, Wartburg, Trabant and the shipbuilding industry were being liquidated. Over a million claims filed on property confiscated by the Communists inhibited anyone from purchasing property in the East. The one-to-one exchange rate doomed Eastern German industry to bankruptcy from the start. A two-to-one exchange rate would have given East German companies a chance of competing by offering their lower quality products at much lower prices.

Western Germans were staggered by the cost of modernising Eastern Germany, estimated to be DM 1 trillion over the next decade. In early 1991 the soaring costs forced steep increases in taxes on incomes and petrol despite Kohl's election promise not to do so. As Western Germany struggled under the strain of providing social benefits to its new citizens in the east, some 20,000 a month continued to move west, as high as ever. In March 1991 *Der Spiegel* magazine estimated that 750,000 Eastern Germans were considering moving west.

Eastern Germany's present position is something like that of Ireland where the older people lose their jobs and the young leave. Many East Germans thought that by becoming part of West Germany they would immediately get all the consumer goods they saw on TV. Many bought cars on credit and then lost them together with their jobs. Eastern Germans seem to have become the poor relations in a capitalist Germany, citizens of a second-class state within a state.

Yet a better analogy may perhaps be found in Germany itself. Until WW II, northern Germany was the richest part of the country, but after the war Germany's wealth moved south, with the big auto makers (Mercedes and BMW), electronics (IBM) and the armaments industries all based there. The same thing may eventually happen in the east (market economists swear it will) but it could take a decade or more and the generation which made the changes possible may be sacrificed somewhere along the way.

A failure by Eastern Germany to adapt to the 'market economy' despite all the advantages of Western German subsidies and EC membership casts a pall over the efforts of the other Eastern European countries to adapt to capitalism. Distracted by the Gulf War, the USA and Western Europe have largely abandoned Eastern Europe to its own devices. After reunification all GDR police and army officers were fired. Some have been prosecuted for allegedly abetting terrorists, while the rest got greatly reduced pensions. This example has contributed to a stiffening by hardliners in the USSR who aren't eager to share their fate. In Eastern Germany the wheels of history are spinning quickly and it's a fascinating time to be there.

## POPULATION & PEOPLE
There are 16,680,000 people in Eastern Germany, compared to 61,240,000 in Western Germany. Unlike Western Germany which has 4,400,000 foreign residents, Eastern Germany's population consists for 99.7% of Prussians and Saxons, with a small Slavonic minority, the Sorbs and Wends, in the south-east corner. The southern half of Eastern Germany is much more densely populated and industrialised than the north. In all, 75% of the population live in urban areas.

Berlin is the largest city in Germany and one of the ten biggest cities in Europe. West Berlin with 2.2 million inhabitants occupies 480 sq km, and 1.3 million people live in East Berlin (403 sq km). By the year 2005 the population of reunified Berlin could double to about six million. Prior to the building of the Wall some 60,000 East Berlin workers held jobs in West Berlin and crossed the border daily. Once the border was closed their places were taken by immigrants. There are 250,000 non-German residents in West Berlin, about half of them Turkish. The others are mostly Yugoslavs, Poles, Greeks and Italians. More than a quarter of the population of Kreuzberg is foreign.

Tens of thousands of foreign troops are still present in Eastern Germany though the occupation system was suspended on 3 October 1990. The withdrawal of 12,000 US, British and French troops and dependants from West Berlin, as well as a much larger number of Soviet troops from the rest of Eastern Germany, is to be completed by 1994.

Eastern Germans are socially more conservative than Western Germans, though the only place you really have to wear a tie is to a wedding or funeral. Nude bathing is very common in Eastern Germany – in fact, it's one of the few freedoms these people were formerly allowed. Nude beaches are marked FKK.

## ARTS

Germany has always been one of the pillars of European civilisation and the eastern part of the country has supplied its full share of famous names. Cultural pilgrims on the trail of familiar textbook figures will find plenty to keep them busy here.

Probably the most renowned visual artist with roots in these parts is Lucas Cranach the Elder (1472-1553), who was appointed court painter to the prince-elector of Saxony at Lutherstadt Wittenberg in 1505. During his 45 years in Wittenberg, Cranach's studio turned out hundreds of paintings and woodcuts. Though best known for his portraits,

Cranach initiated the Lutheran school of painting. After a Protestant defeat in 1547 Cranach joined the elector in exile at Augsburg in 1550, returning with him to the new electoral court at Weimar in 1552. Cranach died there the following year.

Cranach was a close personal friend of religious reformer Martin Luther (1483-1546), and his paintings provide our visual image of Luther and associates. Born in Eisleben, 32 km west of Halle, Luther was educated at the University of Erfurt, and in 1505 he entered the Augustine monastery at Erfurt as a monk. Ordained a priest in 1507, Luther began teaching at Wittenberg University the next year, holding the chair of biblical theology from 1512. The excessive selling of indulgences led Luther to nail his 95 theses to the church door at Wittenberg Castle on 31 October 1517. Luther's rejection of ecclesiastical hypocrisy soon enmeshed with national resentment against Rome, and the German princes defended Luther from papal excommunication in January 1521.

In April 1521 Luther defied the Diet (national assembly) of Worms with the words, 'Here I stand. I can do no other.' Although the Diet banned his person and works from the empire, Luther had become a hero to a section of the nobility and until March 1522 he was given refuge at Wartburg Castle outside Eisenach. During this time he translated the New Testament from Greek into German, thus setting the language in its present form. (In 1534 he translated the Old Testament from Hebrew.)

Despite his role as father of the Protestant Reformation, Luther deplored violence and taught obedience to the civil authorities, a doctrine that partly explains the many Luther museums and memorials which enjoyed full state support during the recent Communist period. According to Luther, idols exist only in the hearts of men and when the hearts are changed the idols are forgotten. After 1532 Luther left the leadership of the movement to his colleague and neighbour in Wittenberg, the educator Philip Melanchthon (1497-1560).

During the 18th century Enlightenment, the court at Weimar attracted figures of European stature. Though born in Frankfurt/Main and educated at Leipzig, Johann Wolfgang von Goethe (1749-1832) moved to Weimar in 1775, spending the rest of his life there despite an invitation from Napoleon to resettle in Paris. Arguably the greatest of German writers, Goethe the poet, dramatist, novelist, critic, painter, statesman, teacher, scientist and philosopher was perhaps the last European to achieve the Renaissance ideal of excellence in many fields. Inspired successively by the spirituality of Gothic architecture, the balanced order of Classicism and the passion of Romanticism, Goethe also recognised world literature as a vehicle of international respect and understanding, as exemplified by his critical writings on Serbian poetry. His greatest work, the drama *Faust,* is a masterful compendium of all that went before him as the archetypical Western man strives relentlessly for meaning. Goethe characterised his literary works as 'fragments of a great confession'.

Goethe's closest friend was the poet, dramatist and novelist Friedrich Schiller (1759-1805). As a youth, Schiller was forced into a military academy by the tyrannical duke of Württemberg. When Schiller's first play dealt with a young noble forced to become an outlaw because of corruption, the duke forbade him to write any others, whereupon Schiller deserted and, after a period in Leipzig, settled in Weimar in 1787. Schiller's most famous work is the dramatic cycle *Wallenstein* (translated by Samuel Taylor Coleridge), based on the life of a treacherous Thirty Years' War general who plotted to make himself arbiter of the empire until his murder in 1634. If *Wallenstein* demonstrated the corrupting effects of power, Schiller's other great play, *William Tell*, dealt with the right of the oppressed to rise against tyranny. Large museums to both Schiller and Goethe exist in Weimar today.

Berlin too produced remarkable individuals like Alexander von Humboldt (1769-1859), a precursor of modern environmentalism through his studies of the relationship of plants and animals to their physical surroundings. Son of an important Berlin family, Humboldt set out in 1799 on a five-year exploration of Latin America, including a three-month journey on foot through the Amazon rainforest and the ascent of Andean peaks around Quito. He was among the first to connect geological faults with volcanoes and earthquakes. His fortune depleted by the cost of the expedition and the publication of 30 volumes of results, Humboldt entered the service of Prussia's king in 1827 as tutor to the crown prince. In addition he lectured on physical geography at Berlin University, organised one of the first international scientific conferences ever and led an expedition to Siberia in 1829. The rest of his life he devoted to his book *Kosmos,* a popularised five-volume survey of the complete scientific knowledge of his time.

Humboldt's contemporary, Georg Wilhelm Friedrich Hegel (1770-1831), came to Berlin in 1818 to occupy the chair of philosophy at Berlin University, becoming rector in 1830 just prior to his death from cholera. Hegel created an all-embracing classical philosophy that is still influential today. His dialectical system in which thesis and antithesis are resolved by a higher synthesis inspired existentialists, Marxists and positivists alike.

In the 20th century the State Bauhaus in Weimar (1919-25), Dessau (1925-32) and Berlin (1932-33) shattered the 200-year-old supremacy of the French École des Beaux-Arts and laid the foundations for modern architecture. The school of design established by Walter Gropius (1883-1969) in 1919 taught architects to consider only immediate needs, materials and technical possibilities with no reference to previous styles. The Bauhaus school building (1926) a few blocks west of Dessau-Hauptbahnhof, is an early example of this new international style. The Nazis closed the school and Gropius emigrated to Cambridge, Massachusetts, becoming the chairman of Harvard University's department of architecture. Other Bauhaus directors were Ludwig Mies van der Rohe, who established the department of architecture at the Illinois Institute of Technology, and László Moholy-Nagy, who founded the Chicago Institute of Design.

In the 1920s Berlin was the theatrical capital of Germany and its most famous practitioner was poet and playwright Bertolt Brecht (1898-1956). Brecht moved to Berlin from Munich in 1924 and was here converted from cynical anarchism to the didactic Marxism of his mature period. Brecht's experience in WW I made him a lifelong pacifist, and in Marxism he thought he had found a scientific alternative to the moral dilemmas of a mass society and capitalist selfishness. Yet it was the poetic simplicity of his moral parables, the precise language and sharp characterisations which lifted his work above dogmatic concerns. Brecht revolutionised the theatre by detaching the spectators from what was happening on stage to permit them to observe and judge without illusion or involvement. Viewed from the 1990s Brecht's works are a stirring rebuttal to fascism and war, woven with music and song which make even German-language productions appealing to non-German speakers.

In 1933 Brecht fled the Nazis to Denmark, and then to Sweden in 1939. Always one step ahead of disaster, in May 1941, just days before Hitler's invasion of the USSR, he took the Trans-Siberian Railway from Finland to Vladivostok. Brecht settled at Santa Monica, California, and attempted to write for Hollywood, until 30 October 1947 when he was compelled to appear before the notorious Committee on Un-American Activities of the US Congress. The next day Brecht sailed for Europe and after a time in Switzerland accepted the directorship of the Berliner Ensemble in East Berlin in 1949 where his work has been performed ever since. He died of a heart attack in 1956.

Eastern Germany's leading contemporary novelist, Christa Wolf (1929- ) maintained her independence while living and publishing in the GDR. Her *Der geteilte Himmel* (1963), or 'Divided Heaven', is the story of a young woman whose fiancé abandons her for life in the West. In *Nachdenken über Christa* (1968), or 'Thinking About Christa', based on the early death of a female friend, Wolf ponders individual self-realisation in a collective society. Her novel *Kindheitsmuster* (1976), or 'Patterns of Childhood', traces her own childhood under fascism and poses the question, 'How have we become the way we are?'

Wolf's preoccupation with the role of women in history and society found its highest expression in *Kassandra* (1983) in which she creates a utopic female counterpart for the aggressive thought/action male model. The incapacity of humanity to prevent nuclear self-destruction is the theme of *Störfall* (1986), Wolf's literary response to Chernobyl. Long before 1989 Wolf bridged the gap between the two Germanys and won high esteem on both sides of the Wall.

## Music

It's significant indeed that the two greatest Baroque composers should have been born in Saxony on the same year. Johann Sebastian Bach (1685-1750) was born at Eisenach into a prominent family of musicians. From 1708 to 1717 he served as court organist at Weimar, moving to Leipzig in 1723 where he spent his remaining 27 years as city musical director. Bach's duties at Leipzig involved conducting services at St Thomas and St Nikolai, supplying music and training boys to sing in the Thomas Choir. During his life Bach produced some 200 cantatas, plus masses, oratorios, passions and other elaborate music for the Lutheran service, and sonatas, concertos, preludes and fugues for secular use. Though regarded as a conservative by his contemporaries, the Bach revival which began 50 years after his death continues today.

At the age of 18 George Frederick Händel (1685-1759) left his native Halle for Hamburg. During his three years in Italy he mastered the Italian opera. Händel's first visit to England was in 1710 and the highly successful performance of his opera *Rinaldo* there the next year encouraged him to spend most of the rest of his life in that country. Händel composed 40 operas before the public lost interest in the genre in 1741. At this Händel switched to oratorios – his *Messiah* (1742) is still regularly performed. Händel democratised court music by performing before a large public in churches, parks and gardens, an aspect of lasting influence. The birthplaces of both Händel and Bach are now large museums.

In the 19th century the musical traditions of Saxony continued unabated with the songwriter Robert Schumann (1810-56), born at Zwickau. In 1843 Schumann opened a music school at Leipzig in collaboration with composer Felix Mendelssohn (1809-47), director of Leipzig's famous Gewandhaus Orchestra. From 1848 to 1861 the famous Hungarian composer and piano virtuoso Franz Liszt (1811-86) lived at Weimar where he wrote his *Dante* and *Faust* symphonies, a piano sonata, two piano concertos, the *Totentanz* and other illustrious works. In 1869 the Grand Duke invited Liszt to return to Weimar to found a music school, which still exists today.

The musical traditions mentioned above continue to thrive: the Dresden Opera and Leipzig Orchestra are known around the world. Electronic synthesiser music became the rage in Eastern Germany after the first electronic concert in East Berlin's Palast der Republik on 31 January 1980. The first LP devoted entirely to electronic music came out in 1982 and from 1986 a weekly 'electronics' programme was broadcast over Jugendradio DT64. An annual 'electronics live' festival has been held in East Berlin since 1988. Synthesiser music with its elements of fluid, nonrhythmic New Age music and 'space music' is a modern genre that is gaining increasing popularity in Eastern Europe.

## RELIGION

Theoretically, Protestants make up 80% of the population, Catholics 8%. In practice less than 5% of the Protestants and 25% of the Catholics are active churchgoers. The Protestant church played a major role in the overthrow of German Communism by providing a gathering place for antigovernment protesters, and some of the leaders of the first opposition groups were Protestant pastors.

Sixty per cent of West Berliners are Lutherans and 12.5% of them are Catholics. Most Turkish Berliners are Muslim and some 17% of West Berliners profess no religion. In 1933 there were 160,000 Jews living in Berlin. Some 6500 live in West Berlin today.

## LANGUAGE

Having been shielded from most contact with foreigners until very recently, far fewer people speak English in Eastern Germany than in Western Germany. English will get you by in West Berlin, and elsewhere things are well enough organised to make it fairly easy to get around without knowing much of the language. When you do need help there's almost always someone nearby who speaks a little English. Even a few words of broken German makes initial contact easier, however, and don't worry about making mistakes as any attempt to speak German will be appreciated.

Written German is more or less phonetic, so pronunciation is easier than you'd think once you break long German words up into syllables. (In German you can often indicate exactly what you mean by joining two or more words together to form a new word.) The vowels with umlaut accents are ä (or 'ae') pronounced as the ai in fair, ö (or 'oe') as the e in her, and ü (or 'ue') as the ue in glue. The diphthongs are ai pronounced as the i in like, au as the ou in mouse and eu as the oy in boy.

To assist English speakers in recognising German place names quickly, we've separated the words *Strasse* and *Platz* from the names of streets and squares. The commonly abbreviated -*str* has been spelled out. While German books and signs would always read Kurfürstenstr and Alexanderplatz, we put Kurfürsten Strasse and Alexander Platz. It's worth knowing the difference between the

German words *Burg* ('boork', castle) and *Berg* ('bairk', mountain) which you'll often find stuck to place names. A classic example is the word for castle hill/mound: *Burgberg*.

In reading German texts be aware of the German 'capital B' with a tail ( ß ) which is often used in the middle or at the end of a word to represent 'ss'. Nouns always have a capital letter.

## Greetings & Civilities

hello
  *hallo/guten Tag*
goodbye
  *auf Wiedersehen*
good morning
  *guten Morgen*
good evening
  *guten Abend*
please
  *bitte*
thank you
  *danke*
I am sorry/forgive me
  *Es tut mir leid/Verzeihen Sie*
Excuse me.
  *Entschuldigung.*
You are very kind.
  *Das ist sehr nett von Ihnen.*
yes
  *ja*
no
  *nein*

## Small Talk

Do you speak English?
  *Sprechen Sie Englisch?*
I don't understand.
  *Ich verstehe nicht*
Could you write it down?
  *Könnten Sie das aufschreiben?*
Where do you live?
  *Wo wohnen Sie?*
What work do you do?
  *Welchen Beruf haben Sie?*
I am a student.
  *Ich bin Student*
I am very happy.
  *Ich bin sehr glücklich*

## Accommodation

youth hostel
  *Jugendherberge*
camping ground
  *Zeltplatz*
private room
  *Privatzimmer*
How much is it?
  *Wieviel kostet das?*
Is that the price per person?
  *Ist das der Preis pro Person?*
Is that the total price?
  *Ist das der Gesamtpreis?*
Are there any extra charges?
  *Kommen da noch Kosten hinzu?*
Where is there a cheaper hotel?
  *Wo gibt es ein preiswerteres Hotel?*
Should I make a reservation?
  *Ist eine Reservierung notwendig?*
single/double room
  *Einzel-/Doppelzimmer*
It is very noisy.
  *Es ist sehr laut*
Where is the toilet?
  *Wo ist die Toilette?*

## Getting Around

What time does it leave?
  *Wann fährt es ab?*
When is the first bus?
  *Wann fährt der erste Bus?*
When is the last bus?
  *Wann fährt der letzte Bus?*
When is the next bus?
  *Wann fährt der nächste Bus?*
That's too soon.
  *Das ist zu bald*
When is the next one after that?
  *Wann fährt der übernächste?*
How long does the trip take?
  *Wie lange dauert die Fahrt?*
arrival
  *Ankunft*
departure
  *Abfahrt*
timetable
  *Fahrplan*
Where is the bus stop?
  *Wo ist die Bushaltestelle?*

Where is the railway station?
*Wo ist der Bahnhof?*
Where is the taxi stand?
*Wo ist der nächste Taxistand?*
Where is the left-luggage room?
*Wo ist die Gepäckaufbewahrung?*

## Around Town

Just a minute.
*Einen Augenblick.*
Where is...?
*Wo ist...?*
the bank
*die Bank*
the post office
*das Postamt*
the telephone centre
*die Telefonvermittlung*
the tourist information office
*das Fremdenverkehrsamt*
the museum
*das Museum*
the palace
*der Palast*
the castle
*die Burg*
the concert hall
*die Konzerthalle*
the opera house
*das Opernhaus*
the musical theatre
*das Musiktheater*
Where are you going?
*Wohin gehen Sie?*
I am going to...
*Ich gehe nach...*
Where is it?
*Wo ist es?*
I can't find it.
*Ich kann es nicht finden*
Is it far?
*Ist es weit?*
Please show me on the map.
*Zeigen Sie mir das bitte auf der Karte.*
left
*links*
right
*rechts*
straight ahead
*geradeaus*

I want...
*Ich möchte...*
Do I need permission?
*Benötige ich eine Genehmigung?*
May I?
*Darf ich?*

## Entertainment

Where can I hear live music?
*Wo wird live-Musik gespielt?*
Where can I buy a ticket?
*Wo kann ich eine Karte kaufen?*
I'm looking for a ticket.
*Ich möchte eine Karte haben*
I want to refund this ticket.
*Ich möchte diese Karte zurückerstattet haben*
Is this a good seat?
*Ist das ein guter Platz?*
at the front
*vorne*
ticket
*Karte*

## Food

I am hungry.
*Ich bin hungrig*
I do not eat meat.
*Ich esse kein Fleisch*
self-service cafeteria
*Cafeteria mit Selbstbedienung*
grocery store
*Lebensmittelladen*
fish
*Fisch*
soup
*Suppe*
salad
*Salat*
fresh vegetables
*frisches Gemüse*
milk
*Milch*
bread
*Brot*
sugar
*Zucker*
ice cream
*Eiscreme*

hot coffee
  *heisser Kaffee*
mineral water
  *Mineralwasser*
beer
  *Bier*
wine
  *Wein*

## Shopping

Where can I buy one?
  *Wo kann ich das kaufen?*
How much does it cost?
  *Wieviel kostet das?*
That's (much) too expensive.
  *Das ist (viel) zu teuer*
Is there a cheaper one?
  *Gibt es noch etwas preiswerteres?*

## Time & Dates

today
  *heute*
tonight
  *heute abend*
tomorrow
  *morgen*
the day after tomorrow
  *übermorgen*
What time does it open?
  *Wann wird geöffnet?*
What time does it close?
  *Wann wird geschlossen?*
open
  *geöffnet*
closed
  *geschlossen*
in the morning
  *morgens*
in the evening
  *abends*
every day
  *täglich*
At what time?
  *Um wieviel Uhr?*
when?
  *wann?*

| | |
|---|---|
| Monday | *Montag* |
| Tuesday | *Dienstag* |
| Wednesday | *Mittwoch* |
| Thursday | *Donnerstag* |
| Friday | *Freitag* |
| Saturday | *Samstag* |
| Sunday | *Sonntag* |

| | |
|---|---|
| January | *Januar* |
| February | *Februar* |
| March | *März* |
| April | *April* |
| May | *Mai* |
| June | *Juni* |
| July | *Juli* |
| August | *August* |
| September | *September* |
| October | *Oktober* |
| November | *November* |
| December | *Dezember* |

## Numbers

| | |
|---|---|
| 1 | *eins* |
| 2 | *zwei* |
| 3 | *drei* |
| 4 | *vier* |
| 5 | *fünf* |
| 6 | *sechs* |
| 7 | *sieben* |
| 8 | *acht* |
| 9 | *neun* |
| 10 | *zehn* |
| 11 | *elf* |
| 12 | *zwölf* |
| 13 | *dreizehn* |
| 14 | *vierzehn* |
| 15 | *fünfzehn* |
| 16 | *sechzehn* |
| 17 | *siebzehn* |
| 18 | *achtzehn* |
| 19 | *neunzehn* |
| 20 | *zwanzig* |
| 21 | *einundzwanzig* |
| 22 | *zweiundzwanzig* |
| 23 | *dreiundzwanzig* |
| 30 | *dreissig* |
| 40 | *vierzig* |
| 50 | *fünfzig* |
| 60 | *sechzig* |
| 70 | *siebzig* |
| 80 | *achtzig* |
| 90 | *neunzig* |
| 100 | *(ein)hundert* |

# Facts for the Visitor

### VISAS & EMBASSIES
Most readers of this book – Australians, New Zealanders and Japanese included – require no visa to enter Germany. Unless you're a citizen of a Third World country you can probably stay up to three months. Many documents will be required if you decide to get married, otherwise your passport will suffice.

### MONEY
The currency is the German Mark, or Deutschmark (DM), which in Germany is usually referred to as the Mark. One Mark is divided into 100 Pfennig (Pf). There are banknotes of DM 5, DM 10, DM 20, DM 50, DM 100, DM 200, DM 500 and DM 1000. In 1989 new banknotes were issued though the larger 1980 series is still widely circulated. Beware of confusing the old DM 5 and DM 20 banknotes which are the same colour and have similar designs, although the DM 20 note is larger, and watch out for counterfeit banknotes made on colour photocopy machines!

Credit cards are not widely used and cash is the preferred means of payment. It's fairly easy to get cash advances at banks, however. The most popular credit cards are Eurocard (MasterCard), American Express, Visa and Diner's Club. There are no restrictions on the import or export of cash or travellers' cheques.

A commission of DM 3 to DM 10 (ask first!) is charged every time you change foreign currency into Deutschmarks. If you know for sure you'll be visiting Germany, buy some travellers' cheques expressed in Deutschmarks before you leave home. You don't have to worry about currency fluctuations and no commission is charged to cash a DM travellers' cheque. The banking system is still rather primitive in Eastern Germany and DM travellers' cheques are much easier to cash than dollar cheques.

If you'll be going on into Eastern Europe, you'll need a supply of cash dollars or Deutschmarks in small bills to cover petty expenditures which must be paid in Western currency. A couple of hundred Deutschmarks in 10s and 20s should suffice. Don't neglect to take care of this as travellers' cheques are usually not accepted to pay for visas, international railway tickets, duty free goods, etc.

## Currency
At last report the exchange rate was about US$1 = DM 1.69.

## Costs
Although considerably more expensive than any of the other countries included in this book (except perhaps Yugoslavia), Eastern Germany is still a bit cheaper than Western Germany. It's good value if you're coming from Western Europe, but be prepared if you're arriving from Poland, Hungary or Czechoslovakia. This is sure to change over the next few years, especially as Eastern Germany adopts the transportation tariffs of Western Germany. Museum admissions have already been raised to Western levels.

## CLIMATE & WHEN TO GO
Eastern Germany lies in a transition zone between the temperate maritime climate of Western Europe and the rougher continental climate of Eastern Europe. Continental and Atlantic air masses meet here. The mean annual temperature in Berlin is 11.1°C, the average range of temperatures varying from -0.7°C in January to 18°C in July. The average annual precipitation is 585 mm and there is no special rainy season. The camping season is from May to September.

## TOURIST OFFICES
Municipal information offices in the towns and cities sell maps and brochures, answer questions, handle local sightseeing tours, rent private rooms and have theatre tickets. They're especially knowledgeable about local events. Receptionists at large hotels will answer questions when they're not too busy.

Apart from the regular information office, each town has a branch of the Europäisches Reisebüro, the former government travel agency. The division of this company serving Germans wishing to travel abroad is called Reise Welt but it's the same thing. The Reisebüro der DDR (the old name) used to have a monopoly on all travel arrangements for foreign tourists but now it's only useful for buying international train tickets and sometimes for private rooms or hotel reservations.

## Representatives Abroad
The Europäisches Reisebüro has a number of offices and representatives abroad which may be worth checking:

Bulgaria
    Reisebüro, Bulevard Stambolijski 37,
    BG-1000 Sofia (☎ 873 526)
Czechoslovakia
    Reisebüro, Pářížská 7,
    CS-11001 Prague 1 (☎ 26 2292)
Hungary
    Reisebüro, Fovam tér 2-3,
    H-1056 Budapest V (☎ 18 1963)
Japan
    Reisebüro, 107 Aoyama Dai-ichi, Mansion 303,
    4-14 Akasaka, 8-chome, Minato-ku, Tokyo 107
    (☎ 405 1981)
Poland
    Reisebüro, ulica Krucza 46,
    PL-00-509 Warsaw (☎ 28 3472)
UK
    Berolina Travel Ltd, 22 Conduit St,
    London W1R 9TB (☎ 071-629 1664)

## Information on Berlin
For advance tourist information on Berlin and hotel reservations write to: Verkehrsamt Berlin, Europa Centre, D-1000 Berlin 30. Information on the political status of Berlin and a copy of *Berlin for Young People* is available from: Informations zentrum Berlin, D-1000 Berlin 12, Hardenberg Strasse 20. For festival tickets write to: Berliner Festspiele GmbH, D-1000 Berlin 30, Budapester Strasse 48. If you want information on exhibitions, trade fairs and congresses write to: Ausstellungs

Messe Kongress GmbH, Messedamm 22, D-1000 Berlin 19.

## BUSINESS HOURS & HOLIDAYS

Because of a German law governing business hours, shopping hours are very limited compared to Britain or the USA. Department stores are generally open from 9 am to 6 pm weekdays and from 9 am to 2 pm Saturday, although most stay open until 4 pm the first Saturday of each month. In many cities shops stay open until 7 or 8 pm on Thursdays. On Saturday mornings only department stores and large shops are open.

Banking hours are weekdays from 9 am to 1 pm. Most banks also open two afternoons a week but the days and times vary from bank to bank. Post offices are open weekdays from 8 am to 6 pm, Saturday from 8 am to 1 pm.

Museums may open as early as 9 am and close at 6 pm, although 10 am to 4 pm is more common. Many museums, monuments and theatres close on Mondays. Admission to museums ranges anywhere from DM 1 to DM 6 though students usually get a 50% discount.

The main restaurants are open from 10 am to midnight with varying closing days. The cheaper restaurants are closed on Saturday afternoon and Sundays, although places in the railway stations and fast-food stands open daily. Night bars are open from 9 pm to 4 am.

Public holidays include New Year's Day (1 January), Good Friday (March or April), Easter Monday (April), Labour Day (1 May), Ascension Day (the 40th day after Easter), Pentecost or Whitsunday (the seventh Sunday after Easter), Whitmonday (the day after Pentecost), Reunification Day (3 October), Cemetery Day (the Wednesday after the third Sunday in November) and Christmas (25 and 26 December).

## CULTURAL EVENTS

Eastern Germany is a music lover's paradise. Aside from the regular concerts there are music festivals of international repute throughout the year. They include the Thuringian Bach Festival in the second half

of March; the Vogtland Festival of Music in May; the Dresden Music Festival in the last week of May and first week of June; the Dresden International Dixieland Jazz Festival also in May; the Händel Festival in Halle in June; the Sanssouci Park Festival in Potsdam in June; the International Music Seminar in Weimar in July; the Berlin Festival of Music and Drama in the last week of September and first two weeks of October; and the Gewandhaus Festival in Leipzig in October.

On a Sunday in March the Sommergewinn Festival in Eisenach celebrates the driving out of winter with a km-long procession. For this event, which dates back to 1286, the town is decorated with the traditional symbols of a pretzel, a hen and an egg. The Leipzig Fair in March and September is one of Eastern Europe's main trade fairs. There's a large Christmas Fair off Alexander Platz in Berlin in the last week of November and the first three weeks of December (daily from 1 to 8 pm).

West Berlin organises festivals with a vengeance. In February or March there's the International Film Festival, followed by the Theatre Meeting in May. Then there's the Berlin Festival Weeks in September and the Jazz Fest in October or November. Tickets to these events sell out fast so write to the Berliner Festspiele GmbH (☎ 030-25 4890), Budapester Strasse 50, 1000 Berlin 30, a couple of months in advance if it's important to you to attend. If you're in Berlin in early March, don't miss the International Tourism Exchange (ITB) at the Fairgrounds where you can learn about worldwide travel possibilities (though every bed in Berlin will be booked this week). Summertime district street fairs and festivals are announced in the fortnightly Berlin entertainment magazines *Tip* and *Zitty*.

## POST & TELECOMMUNICATIONS

Postal rates are uniform throughout Germany but mail-sorting facilities are still hopelessly antiquated in Eastern Germany, so wait to do all of your mailing in West

Berlin. Letters mailed in East Berlin take a week longer to arrive. Post offices in West Berlin and Western Germany, on the other hand, are among the fastest and most efficient in Europe, so patronise them.

### Postal Rates

Airmail letter rates are DM 1 (20 grams) within Europe, DM 1.65 (five grams) to North America and DM 1.85 (five grams) to Australia. Ten-gram letters are DM 1.90 to North America and DM 2.30 to Australia. Postcards take 60 Pfennig within Europe, DM 1.05 to North America and DM 1.25 to Australia. Aerogrammes take DM 1.65 to anywhere but you have to buy them in stationery shops.

### Receiving Mail

If you'd like to receive mail in Berlin, have it sent c/o Poste Restante, Postamt Bahnhof Zoo, D-1000 Berlin 12, Germany. Such mail can be picked up at counter No 9 in the Zoo Station post office (open 24 hours a day), but you'll have to show your passport. There's no charge to pick up letters.

Otherwise you can have it addressed c/o American Express Travel Service, Kurfürstendamm 11, D-1000 Berlin 15, Germany. The American Express office holding such 'client's mail' is on Breitscheid Platz near Zoo Station (weekdays from 9 am to 5 pm, Saturday from 9 am to noon). It holds mail for 30 days but won't accept registered mail or parcels. This service is free if you have American Express travellers' cheques or one of its credit cards, otherwise it's DM 2 each time you come in. Mail will be forwarded for a flat DM 8 fee.

### Telephones

To telephone Eastern Germany from Western Europe dial the international access code (varies from country to country), 37 (the country code for Eastern Germany), the area code and the number. Some important area codes are 2 (East Berlin), 33 (Potsdam), 41 (Leipzig), 46 (Halle), 51 (Dresden), 53 (Meissen), 61 (Erfurt), 81 (Rostock), 84 (Schwerin), 91 (Magdeburg), 451 (Wittenberg), 455 (Quedlinburg), 621 (Weimar), 623 (Eisenach), 821 (Stralsund), 824 (Wismar) and 927 (Wernigerode).

To call West Berlin from Western Europe dial the international access code, 49 (the country code for Western Germany), 30 (the West Berlin area code) and the number. Public telephones in West Berlin take 30 Pfennig for six minutes and work well. To call East Berlin from West Berlin (30 Pfennig) add the prefix 9 to the number. From East Berlin to West Berlin the prefix is 849.

The telephone infrastructure in Eastern Germany is decades behind that of Western Germany and even placing a call from West Berlin to East Berlin or vice-versa is extremely difficult. Usually all you'll get is a busy signal. If you have any international calls to make, do so in West Berlin. All post offices have public telephones.

Bear in mind that the Eastern German telephone system is being completely rebuilt and that the area codes and numbers throughout this chapter could change. If your call doesn't go through, try dialling local information.

If you want to talk to friends in North America, just call them from a pay phone and quickly give them your number so they can call you right back. This is much cheaper than calling reverse charges (collect).

Most pay phones in Germany accept telephone cards, not coins. Even if you do locate a coin-operated phone it will probably be in use with a few people waiting to get in while the adjacent card phone may be free! As these cards (available at any post office) can be used throughout the country, they're a good investment if you'll be making many calls. The DM 20 card only gets you DM 20 worth of calls but the DM 50 card is good for DM 60 worth of calls.

## TIME
Germany is on Central European Time (GMT/UTC plus one hour), the same time used from Madrid to Warsaw. Daylight-saving time comes into effect at the end of March when clocks are turned one hour forward. At the end of September they're turned an hour back again.

## LAUNDRY
Laudromats are fairly common in West Berlin so wait to do your laundry there.

## WEIGHTS & MEASURES
The electric current is 220 volts AC, 50 Hz. Germany uses the metric system.

## BOOKS & MAPS
*Guide to East Germany* by Stephen Baister and Chris Patrick (Bradt Publications, England, 1990) is a complete sightseeing guide researched in mid-1989. As the authors candidly admit, 'at that time the German Democratic Republic still seemed firmly established and there was little or nothing to hint at the events that were to come later that year.' Unlike most other titles in the Bradt series, this one hardly mentions hiking and practical information is sadly lacking.

The most complete German guidebook to the region is *Baedeker's Deutschland – Ost* (Verlag Karl Baedeker, 1991). Though good on culture it also ignores the needs of the flesh.

*The Real Guide: Berlin* by Jack London (Prentice Hall Press, New York, 1990)

covers the entire city in admirable detail – all you need for an unforgettable couple of months in Berlin. In Britain it's called *The Rough Guide: Berlin*. If your German is adequate you may prefer *Berlin ein Handbuch* by Loose, Mlyneck and Ramp (Michael Muller Verlag, Erlangen, 1988).

The best map of Berlin is the indexed *Falkplan Berlin mit Potsdam* which covers the entire city in admirable detail. Pick one up at a good bookshop before your arrival as it will prove invaluable.

*The Berlin Diaries 1940-1945 of Marie 'Missie' Vassiltchikov* (Chatto & Windus, London, 1985) is one woman's daily record of the war years as seen from the inside. Missie's contacts in the diplomatic community and among the old nobility provided many insights, and she knew some of the people involved in the fumbled 1944 coup attempt. As a personal account of the changing mood of the time, Missie's diaries are unmatched.

*The Other Germany* by John Dornberg (Doubleday, New York, 1968) is a readable examination of life in East Germany during the period following construction of the Wall in 1961.

*The German Democratic Republic since 1945* by Martin McCauley (Macmillan Press, London, 1983) is a thorough political history of the workings of a vanished state.

*Zoo Station, Adventures in East & West Berlin* by Ian Walker (Atlantic Monthly Press, New York, 1987) is one man's account of a city still split by the Wall. Walker explores West Berlin's hip westie demimonde and East Berlin's dissident mood in a fascinating glimpse of the counterculture scene.

It's often difficult in Germany to obtain reading material of any kind in English, so bring some with you.

## MEDIA
There are 15 daily German-language newspapers published in Berlin, the most independent of which is *Die Tageszeitung* (the 'taz'), a national newspaper. The Thursday edition of this paper contains a complete

weekly calendar of events. The *Berliner Zeitung* is an established East Berlin paper now controlled by *Stern* magazine, while *Neues Deutschland* is owned by the German Socialist Party (ex-Communists).

The Berlin newspaper *Zweite Hand* (Second Hand) comes out three times a week and carries classified listings of jobs *(Arbeit & Mehr)*, vehicles for sale *(Fahrzeuge & Zubehör)*, apartments for rent *(Wohnen & Immobilien)*, lonely hearts *(Ich & Andere)*, etc. Throughout the paper the word *'biete'* lists things being offered while *'suche'* indicates ads placed by people looking for something.

Of special interest to visitors are the fortnightly magazines *Tip* and *Zitty* which cover virtually everything that's happening on the entertainment scene, both alternative and mainstream, in Berlin. The magazines come out on alternate weeks so one or the other should suffice for your stay. The monthly *Berlin Programm Magazin* is also literally jammed with useful information. Although in German, these publications are fairly easy to follow.

Surprisingly, no English newspaper or magazine is published in Berlin.

## HEALTH

No vaccinations are required to visit Germany. South of Berlin the tap water may taste terrible but there's no particular health problem with it. In the north the water tastes fine and in Berlin the water is also OK.

If you require medical treatment in Eastern Germany go to any general hospital *(Krankenhaus)* and ask for the emergency department *(Rettungstelle)*. You'll get different reactions at different hospitals and can never be sure how much you'll be charged. Emergency treatment could well be free, as it is at hospitals in Western Germany.

## DANGERS & ANNOYANCES

Theft is still relatively rare in Eastern Germany and people generally leave you alone, but be careful in crowded Berlin railway stations where (foreign) pickpockets are often active.

Don't allow others to help you put your luggage in a coin locker, especially at West Berlin's Zoo Station. They may switch keys as they're closing the locker and later come back to pick up your things.

If you're Black or Asian you may encounter racial prejudice, such as not getting served in a restaurant. People in Eastern Germany are not familiar with foreigners and can be rather xenophobic.

## FILM & PHOTOGRAPHY

Stock up on film in Germany, especially if you have any special needs. Kodak film is hard to find in Eastern Europe, so buy it here. It's also relatively cheap to have your film processed in Berlin. A roll of Kodachrome 64 film (36 exposures) will cost DM 10 and another DM 3 with development.

## WORK

Legally, only European Community citizens may work in Eastern Germany and temporary work permits are not available. With unemployment running at about 50%, this is not a prime job-hunting area. The average income in Eastern Germany is around DM 1200 a month, less than half that in Western Germany. Busking and hawking are widespread in the cities and nobody really cares if you do it, though strictly speaking it's not legal. Hawkers are supposed to have a permit, though few do.

To get an idea of the sort of jobs available in Berlin check the *'Stellenmarkt'* (Employment Market) section in the classified newspaper *Zweite Hand*. Many of the positions offered are for unskilled work, and the sort of advertisers appearing here are mainly interested in finding cheap labour and not overly concerned whether you're legally authorised to work in Germany. Jobs are offered under the heading *'biete'* while people looking for work advertise themselves under *'suche'*.

## ACTIVITIES
### Cycling

Until 1990, visitors were prohibited to enter Eastern Germany on a bicycle or moped but these restrictions no longer exist. The region has much to offer cyclists in the way of a well-developed hostel network and lightly travelled back roads, especially in the flat, less populated north. Offshore islands like Poel and Rügen are ready made for pedal-powered travellers. Rügen Island has the added advantage of varied scenery and a wealth of protected bays and inlets that are ideal for sailing, although this sport is still undeveloped in Eastern Germany.

If you don't have a bicycle, you can easily buy or rent one at any of the numerous bike shops in West Berlin. Most Berlin bike shops also sell detailed cycling maps, and after you become acclimatised it's clear pedalling north. Get a good lock for your bike.

### Hiking
The Rennsteig, a ridge path through the Thuringian Forest (Thüringer Wald), stretches 168 km with youth hostels spaced out along the way (Tabarz, Tambach-Dietharz, Oberhof). The 'Hohe Sonne' restaurant near Eisenach is the trailhead.

Other fine hiking areas are the Sächsische Schweiz, south-east of Dresden, and the Harz Mountains, south of Wernigerode. There are many other possibilities.

## HIGHLIGHTS
### Museums & Galleries
Eastern Germany has dozens of illustrious museums, such as the Dahlem and Pergamon museums in Berlin and the Neue Meister Gallery in Dresden. Less well-known are the excellent special-interest museums, two of which are the Oceanic Museum and Aquarium in Stralsund and the Indianer Museum in Dresden. Otto Nagel House is a small Berlin gallery that exhibits proletarian art. Among the many historical museums, the Georgi Dimitroff Museum in Leipzig focuses on the Reichstag fire trial, while the Soviet Army Museum in Karlshorst (East Berlin) deals with WW II. The Nationale Mahn- und Gedenkstätte at Sachsenhausen concentration camp (near Berlin) recalls Nazi atrocities.

### Castles & Palaces
Eastern Germany has castles from every epoch, including medieval Königstein and Wartburg castles, Renaissance Wittenberg Castle, Baroque Jagdschloss Moritzburg and Romantic Wernigerode Castle.

Among the many palaces, Potsdam's imposing 18th century Schloss Sanssouci and the Neues Palais (also at Potsdam) stand out. Berlin's 17th century Schloss Charlottenburg and Dresden's 18th century Schloss Pillnitz are also fine. An older surviving palace is the 15th century Albrechtsburg at Meissen, while Schloss Schwerin is an example of 19th century Romanticism.

### Historic Towns
There are many historic towns among which Meissen and Quedlinburg have a fairy-tale air, Stralsund has a salty taste of the sea, Weimar is *the* repository of German culture and Berlin is a historic city of European stature.

### Hotels & Restaurants
The hotel scene is changing fast as privatisation proceeds, but the church-operated Christliches Hospiz in East Berlin and Marthahaus Christliches Hospiz in Halle will remain good. The Touristenhaus Grünau in East Berlin is a privatised youth hostel, now an excellent youth hotel. The Hotel am Ring in Erfurt is a former workers' residence which now accommodates tourists, while Quedlinburg's Hotel Zum Bär is just the old German inn you expected.

The restaurants are changing even faster as some go broke and others scramble to upgrade their service and food to Western standards. Café Prag Speise Bar and Radeberger Keller, both in Dresden, should make it, and Auerbach's Keller is such a Leipzig institution that things wouldn't be the same without it. The Kreuzberg's Rathaus Casino and Schwarzes Café are two West Berlin eateries you'll enjoy.

## ACCOMMODATION
## Camping

Excepting those in Dresden and Leipzig, all of the Intercampings are remote. Previously only the Intercampings were allowed to accept foreigners, but now all camping grounds in Eastern Germany are available, giving travellers many more possibilities. Most rent small bungalows – convenient if it's raining. However, if you want to make camping your main form of accommodation, you'll probably need your own transport.

## Hostels

Youth hostels in Eastern Germany cost DM 13 to DM 15 for 'juniors' 26 and under, and DM 15 to DM 18 for 'seniors' 27 and over, depending on the category of the hostel (the West Berlin hostels are more expensive). Camping at a hostel (where permitted) is half-price. If you don't have a youth hostel sleeping sheet, it's DM 6 extra to rent one, though some hostels insist you rent one even if you do have one. Breakfast is included in the overnight price and you usually get a pot of tea (a pot of coffee is DM 2 extra). Dinner could cost anything from DM 4.50 to DM 8.

You can only check in after 3 or 4 pm (variable) and must be out by 9 am. Always leave the room key at the reception when you go out. You don't need to do chores at the hostels and there are few rules and no curfew. There's no maximum age limit and you can probably get in without a YHA card. The hostels are often used by cyclists and are open all year.

One of the few travel agencies willing to book youth hostel beds for trips around Eastern Germany is German International Travel (☎ 22324), Allee nach Sanssouci 2, Potsdam 1570 (DM 10 service charge). Drop in to talk to them when you're in Potsdam or write ahead if you want to find out about their canoe and bicycle trips. They specialise in arranging package tours for incoming youth groups.

The addresses of the state offices of the Deutsches Jugendherbergswerk (DJH) controlling youth hostels in Eastern Germany are:

Berlin & Brandenburg
  Tempelhofer Ufer 32, 1000 Berlin 61
  (☎ 030-262 9529)
Saxony
  Kleinolbersdorfer Strasse 61, 9063 Chemnitz
  (☎ 071-64 3027)
Thuringia
  Jacob Strasse 1, 5300 Weimar (☎ 0621-4143)
Sachsen-Anhalt
  Grosse Nikolai Strasse 6, 4020 Halle
  (☎ 046-29875)
Mecklenburg-Vorpommern
  Postfach 19, 2510 Rostock 5 (☎ 081-37 8743)

## Private Rooms

Municipal information offices rent private rooms at around DM 25 per person without breakfast. Single rooms are in short supply and you must arrive during office hours to get a room. This is also a good way to meet a German family, but beware of rooms in distant suburbs.

## Cheap Hotels

There's no shortage of older hotels but the least expensive places are often full. The cheapest hotels only have rooms with shared bath. Before 1990 it was hard to convince a cheap hotel to take you but now they're all eager for your business. Hotel rooms often include breakfast (bread, butter, marmalade, sliced meats and cheeses, coffee or tea), but ask first.

## Expensive Hotels

Hotels are graded from one to five stars. The Interhotels of Berlin, Chemnitz, Dresden, Erfurt, Gera, Halle, Leipzig, Magdeburg, Oberhof, Potsdam, Rostock, Suhl and Weimar are Eastern Germany's high-profile accommodation. They charge from DM 100, usually including breakfast. Reservations for these can be made without difficulty at travel agencies worldwide, at the Europäisches Reisebüro in Berlin or at any other Interhotel.

## FOOD

Restaurants always post their menu outside (in German) with prices listed, though drink prices are often *not* listed and these can add up. Watch for daily specials chalked onto blackboards. Beware of early closing hours and always use the cloakroom if there is one (the waiter/waitress will send you back if you don't). Tipping is not necessary although you should round up the bill as you're paying. Lunch is the main meal of the day in Germany.

A *Gaststätte* is somewhat less formal than a 'restaurant' while a *Weinkeller* (wine cellar) or *Bierkeller* (beer cellar) would be fine for a lighter meal. Most town halls in Eastern Germany have an atmospheric restaurant, or *Ratskeller*, in the basement which serves traditional German dishes. The 'Gastmahl des Meeres' chain specialises in seafood. If you're on a low budget you can get German sausages and beer at stand-up food stalls or *Imbiss* in all the towns. Some self-service restaurants and bars collect a cash deposit (*Pfand*) on the cutlery or beer mugs. A *Konditorei*, or café, is the place to indulge in that sinful German habit of coffee and cakes.

A good German breakfast usually includes hearty bread and rolls, butter, marmalade, cheese, several types of sliced meat, a hard-boiled egg and lemon tea (or coffee).

Some German stand-bys include *Bockwurst* (a type of sausage), *Kartoffelpuffer* (potato fritter), *Klossen* (dumplings), *Rippenspeer* (spare ribs), *Rotwurst* (black pudding), *Rostbratl* (grilled meat), *Wiener Schnitzel* (breaded veal cutlet) and *Würstchen* (small sausages).

The most famous traditional Berlin dish is *Eisbein mit Sauerkraut*, a huge, fatty knuckle of pork with pickled cabbage. *Boulette*, a big meatball containing breadcrumbs which you literally drown in mustard, was introduced by Huguenot immigrants in the 17th century. You might also enjoy trying Berlin liver cooked with onions and apple. Everywhere pork and chicken are far more common than beef.

The food in Eastern Germany can be rather boring. If you enjoy exotic cuisines you'll find them all in West Berlin but elsewhere be prepared for quite a few bland, lukewarm meals, casually served.

## DRINKS

German beer is famous and a German speciality is *Weizenbier* which is made with wheat instead of hops and served in a tall, half-litre glass with a slice of lemon. *Berliner Weisse*, or 'white beer', is a foaming, low-alcohol wheat beer with red or green fruit-juice syrup added.

Eastern Germany's best beers hail from Saxony, especially Radeberger Pils from near Dresden and Wernesgrüner from the Erzgebirge on the Czech border. In East Berlin, Berliner Pilsner is the local brew whereas Schultheiss is brewed in West Berlin.

## THINGS TO BUY

Art reproductions, books, posters, catalogues and magazines are sold in museums and special shops. All the stores are bulging with shiny consumer goods made in Western Germany – you won't find much made here. Prices are high so wait to do your shopping elsewhere. Previously Poles came to Eastern Germany to shop but since the day Ostmarks were swapped for Deutschmarks it's been the other way around.

People from countries outside the European Community are eligible for a refund of value-added taxes (VAT) up to 11.5% on luxury goods purchased at certain participating shops. The shops provide customers with a 'tax-free cheque' equivalent to the amount of tax collected and this (with the original sales receipt attached) must be stamped by German customs as you're leaving the country. You're not allowed to use the items purchased until you're out of Germany. In West Berlin participating shops are listed in the booklet *Shopping in Berlin* available at the tourist office for DM 2, but the sort of gear they sell isn't cheap with or without the tax refund. Of course the people who dreamed up this system assumed you'd be travelling by car or plane. Bus drivers and railway conductors aren't likely to want to wait at the border while you're getting your cheques stamped. If you're leaving by air, have the cheques stamped at the airport before you check in (you have to show the articles). In Czechoslovakia and Hungary, Čedok and Ibusz travel agencies are supposed to cash the tax-refund cheques.

# Getting There & Away

## AIR

Until 1990 only US, British and French carriers such as Pan Am, British Airways and Air France were allowed to fly into West Berlin, but the city is now served by dozens of carriers (though not Interflug, the former East German state airline, which went bankrupt in 1990).

Regular flights from Western Europe to Berlin are usually more expensive than the train or bus but not always, so check with a budget travel agency. To/from London a flight could be less than a full-fare train ticket. For information on cheap flights to far places see the listings of travel agencies under Orientation in the Berlin section, below.

Individuals offering plane tickets they no longer require, at very cheap prices, advertise in the *'Urlaub & Reisen' (biete)* section of the classified Berlin paper *Zweite Hand*.

## Departure Tax

The departure tax from Berlin's Tegel Airport is DM 3.50 but it's usually included in the price of the ticket. The departure tax for charter flights is DM 5 and it must be paid at check-in.

## LAND
## Bus

**To/From Western Germany** It's cheaper to go to Berlin by bus from Western Germany than by train. Regular buses operate to Berlin's Funkturm Bus Station all year from Bremen (eight hours, DM 79, daily), Düsseldorf (10 hours, DM 104, daily), Frankfurt/Main (11 hours, DM 99, twice a week), Goslar (five hours, DM 57, daily), Hamburg (3½ hours, DM 65, daily), Hanno-

ver (four hours, DM 58, daily), Kiel (six hours, DM 76, daily), Lübeck (four hours, DM 61, daily), Munich (nine hours, DM 123, daily), Nuremberg (seven hours, DM 92, daily) and many intermediate points. The Bremen and Frankfurt/Main buses will drop off or pick up passengers in Magdeburg and Potsdam, the Düsseldorf buses only in Magdeburg.

For bus information in Hannover contact the Cebu Reise-Centre (☎ 0511-32 1777), Bahnhof Strasse 1. In Munich contact Bayern Express (☎ 089-55 3074), Arnulf Strasse 16-18, and in Nuremberg contact Amtliches Bayerisches Reisebüro (☎ 0911-22 4791), Hallplatz 11-15. Advance reservations may be necessary and any German travel agency should be able to tell you where to go for them. A convenient West Berlin travel agency handling bus tickets is Reisebüro Zoo, Hardenberg Platz 2 opposite Zoo Station.

Return fares are notably cheaper than two one-ways. Those under 27 and over 60 get a 40% discount and seats can be reserved a month in advance. Checked baggage is DM 2 extra per piece. Some of the coaches are quite luxurious with WC, air-con, steward and snack bar.

**To/From Western Europe** There's a bus twice a week all year between Amsterdam and Berlin (686 km, 10 hours, US$55 one-way, US$90 return trip). People aged under 26 or over 60 and card-carrying students get a 15% discount. For those boarding in Berlin baggage is sometimes DM 2 extra, whereas in Amsterdam the first two bags are free. In midsummer this bus runs four times a week and there are connections in Amsterdam with buses to/from London (871 km, 24 hours to/from Berlin, US$105 one-way) and Paris (1115 km, 21 hours to/from Berlin).

Advance reservations should be made at Bayern Express (☎ 830 0960), Mannheimer Strasse 33, West Berlin; Budget Bus (☎ 627 5151), Rokin 10, Amsterdam; Eurolines (☎ 071-730 8235), 52 Grosvenor Garden, Victoria, London; or Eurolines (☎ 4038 9393), bus station Porte de la Villette, Paris

Nord. Though cheaper than the train, these long bus rides can be tedious so bring along a good book.

**To/From Yugoslavia** Luxury buses run all year between West Berlin's Funkturm Bus Station and Belgrade (twice a week, DM 155), Ljubljana (twice a week, DM 119), Rijeka (weekly, DM 130), Split (weekly, DM 152) and Zagreb (five a week, DM 130). Return trips are about 25% cheaper and students get 10% off. Baggage is DM 3 per piece extra. Most of these buses leave at 8.15 am, although a few to Zagreb leave at 4 pm. Advance reservations are suggested.

**Train**

Train tickets from Berlin to Western Europe are expensive: DM 43 to Hannover, DM 81 to Frankfurt/Main, DM 117 to Munich, DM 122 to Amsterdam, DM 252 to London. Those under 26 years of age qualify for a Wasteels ticket at a considerable discount (Frankfurt/Main DM 58, Amsterdam DM 90, London DM 177). Check the Berlin section for travel agencies handling Wasteels. While more expensive than the buses, trains are far more frequent and you can save on accommodation by arriving or departing on an overnight train (almost all of the buses run during the day).

International tickets are valid for two months from the date of issue. If you can afford the price of a train ticket, be sure to also get a seat reservation (DM 3.50 extra) as the trains sometimes fill up. Seat reservations must be made six hours or more prior to departure.

Both the European railway passes, the Interrail pass (available to residents of Europe aged 25 and under) and, since 1991, the Eurail pass are valid in Eastern Germany. Don't buy a Eurail pass if your main intention is to visit Eastern Europe, as the only other country that is included is Hungary and individual tickets will work out much cheaper. Railway fares to Berlin are much cheaper from Eastern European cities than from Western Europe.

Train tickets to Berlin from the Eastern European countries are valid for all railway stations in Berlin *(Stadtbahn)*. This means that if you have a ticket to Berlin from Czechoslovakia you can take the S-Bahn from Berlin-Lichtenberg to Alexander Platz or Zoo stations on the same ticket. In the opposite direction, take the S-Bahn to Berlin-Lichtenberg and your train. You cannot use the Berlin U-Bahn in this way, however.

**To/From Western Germany** The main rail routes from Western Germany to Berlin are from Hamburg (369 km, four hours), Hannover (284 km, 3½ hours) via Magdeburg, Frankfurt/Main (557 km, eight hours) via Erfurt, and Munich (690 km, 10 hours) via Leipzig. Service from Nuremberg to Leipzig (363 km, five hours) is every couple of hours.

The reunification of Germany has allowed several smaller railway lines across the former GDR border to reopen. Nine trains a day now run from Lübeck to Bad Kleinen (62 km, one hour) with some carrying on to Rostock. Another minor route is Kassel to Halle (216 km, four hours) via Nordhausen.

**To/From Western Europe** The daily Nord-West Express takes 12 hours from Hoek van Holland Haven to Berlin Zoo (742 km). Ferry connections to/from Britain (1052 km from Berlin) are available in Hoek, and Amsterdam passengers join the train at Amersfoort. A one-way 2nd-class ticket from Amsterdam to Berlin is US$80.

The Ost-West Express leaves London's Victoria Station daily for Berlin (1192 km, 22 hours) via Oostende, Brussels and Cologne. A Paris portion of the same train takes 15 hours between Paris Nord and Berlin (1117 km). A discount flight from Berlin to London is usually cheaper than a full-fare train ticket.

**To/From Scandinavia** The two daily boat trains to/from Copenhagen via Warnemünde, the Neptun and Ostsee expresses, arrive/depart Berlin-Lichtenberg Station

(483 km, 11 hours). To/from Sweden via Sassnitz there's the Sassnitz Express from Stockholm to Berlin-Lichtenberg (1029 km, 17 hours) and the Berlinaren Express from Malmö (439 km, 12 hours) to Berlin Zoo.

From Sweden you'll save money by only purchasing a train ticket as far as the port (Gedser or Trelleborg) and buying a separate ferry ticket to Germany there. Through tickets sold in Sweden are much more expensive.

**To/From Czechoslovakia & Beyond** All trains between Czechoslovakia and Berlin terminate and begin at Berlin-Lichtenberg Station. Daily trains from Berlin-Lichtenberg to Prague and Budapest include the Pannonia, Metropol, Meridian, Balt-Orient and Hungaria expresses. The Meridian runs overnight (383 km, seven hours) to/from Prague. The morning Vindobona and afternoon Primator also link Berlin-Lichtenberg to Prague (six hours). Several of these trains continue as far as Romania, Bulgaria and Yugoslavia.

To/from Leipzig you can catch the daily Karlex Express to Karlovy Vary (240 km, five hours) and Monday to Saturday a local 2nd-class train runs between Plauen, Germany, and Karlovy Vary (118 km, three hours). Local trains between Bad Schandau, Germany, and Děčín (22 km) are fairly frequent.

A ticket from Berlin to Budapest will cost DM 132 in 1st class or DM 88 in 2nd class. Sleepers to Budapest are DM 71 (1st class) or DM 47 (2nd class).

**To/From Poland** Many trains from Warsaw to Berlin call at Berlin-Zoo Station and continue to Western Germany. Service between Berlin and Warsaw (578 km, nine hours) via Frankfurt/Oder and Poznan operates several times a day. The nightly 'Gedania' Express to/from Gdańsk (515 km, 10 hours) via Szczecin arrives/departs Berlin-Lichtenberg Station.

A train ticket from Berlin to Poznań will be DM 31 1st class, DM 26 2nd class. If you're on a low budget only buy a ticket to Rzepin (DM 17), the first major junction in Poland. Before leaving Berlin pick up some Polish currency at a bank to allow you to purchase a cheap onward ticket from Rzepin to Szczecin, Poznań, Wrocław or Kraków. It might also be cheaper to pay the Polish conductor the difference.

Several trains a day run from Leipzig to Wrocław (280 km, eight hours) via Dresden, Görlitz and Zgorzelec, most of them going on to Warsaw. If the timing is inconvenient, take any train to Görlitz, cross the bridge to Zgorzelec on foot and pick up a local Polish train there.

### Car & Motorbike

Some highway border crossings between Eastern Germany, Poland and Czechoslovakia are only open to citizens of those countries, though the crossings mentioned here are open to everyone. In each case the name of the German border post is provided.

The main highway border crossings into Poland are Pomellen (20 km west of Szczecin), Frankfurt/Oder (on the autoroute south of the city), Forst (24 km east of Cottbus) and Görlitz. From Eastern Germany to Czechosklovakia you have a choice of only Schönberg (six km north of Františkovy Lázně) and Zinnwald (48 km south of Dresden).

### On Foot

If you want to walk out of or into Germany to/from Czechoslovakia, take a bus or train to Děčín, and then a bus to the tiny Czech village of Hřensko which is in a lovely valley right on the German border. The first German village, Schmilka, is a 30-minute walk away. If the Elbe steamers are operating, you can cruise downriver to Dresden, otherwise cross the Elbe by ferry and catch a train from Schmilka-Hirschmühle Station to Dresden. Don't worry if you get stuck waiting a couple of hours as the scenery around here is great and there are hiking trails up into the hills.

To/from Poland the easiest place to walk across is the bridge over the Neisse River which links central Görlitz to Zgorzelec. Local railway stations are within walking distance from the border on each side and you won't need to hassle about international tickets.

### Ride Services

Aside from hitchhiking, the cheapest way to get to Berlin from Western Europe is as a paying passenger in a private car. Such rides are arranged by the *Mitfahrzentrale* in all Western German cities. You pay a reservation fee to the agency and your share of petrol to the driver. The local tourist information office will be able to direct you to a couple of such offices.

Eurostop operates a chain of 70 lift centres in seven different countries, including the following: Amsterdam (Nieuwezijds Voorburgwal 256, ☎ 622 4342), Barcelona (Pintor Fortuny 21/1, ☎ 318 2731), Brussels (rue du Marché aux Herbes 27, ☎ 512 1015), Copenhagen (Vesterbrogade 54a, ☎ 23 2440), Florence (Borgo dei Greci, ☎ 28 0626), Paris (84 Passage Brady, ☎ 4246 0066 or 4770 4670), Zürich (Fierzgasse 16, ☎ 42 2300), Vienna (Daungasse 1a, ☎ 408 2210) and Milan (Via Col di Lana 14, ☎ 832 0543), among others.

### SEA

There are five large car ferries in each direction daily all year between Trelleborg, Sweden, and Sassnitz Hafen near Stralsund (DM 27 one-way from Sunday to Thursday, DM 34 on Friday and Saturday, four hours). Trelleborg is just south of Malmö, Sweden, near Copenhagen in Denmark.

From April to October ferries also run several times a week between the Danish island of Bornholm and Sassnitz Hafen (DM 30 one-way from Monday to Thursday, DM 36 from Friday to Sunday, 3½ hours).

Car ferry service is also good from Gedser, Denmark, to Warnemünde near Rostock (DM 15 one-way, two hours, all year). For information in West Berlin contact the Schwedisches Reisebüro, Joachimstaler Strasse 10, 1000 Berlin 15.

# Getting Around

### BUS

Bus routes complement but rarely duplicate the railway services. Schedules are usually posted in the railway stations.

From mid-April to October luxury double-decker coaches run north from West Berlin's Funkturm Bus Station daily at 6.30 am to Schwerin (DM 33), Wismar (DM 38), Rostock (DM 41), Warnemünde (DM 43), Stralsund (DM 39) and Sassnitz (DM 47). There's a 25% discount for people over 60, a 50% discount for those 26 and under. Baggage is DM 3 apiece. In Berlin reservations are available from Sonnenschein Reisen (☎ 456 6044), Waldersee Strasse 23-24 (U-Bahn: Franz Neumann Platz) or at the bus station.

### TRAIN

Eastern Germany has a dense rail network with 14,226 km of track. Railway travel is punctual, efficient, inexpensive and less crowded than in most other European countries. All the cities described in this chapter are connected by frequent fast trains. In mid-1991, fares were 11 Pfennig per km in 2nd class, 16 Pfennig per km in 1st class, though these may be much increased in 1992 as prices are brought up to Western levels. Supplements for travel on fast (D) and express trains are DM 3 or DM 6 on Eurocity and Intercity trains. Make sure you have the right ticket, otherwise you'll pay an additional supplement to the conductor.

If you want to make a long trip by train ask about the 'Super-Spar-Tarif' which allows a return trip by train anywhere within Germany for DM 130 (2nd class). These tickets are only valid for 10 days and you must spend the weekend at your destination before beginning the return journey, but stopovers along the way are allowed. Travel is restricted to certain days.

It's usually no problem buying a ticket and even international tickets are easily purchased at main railway stations. Return-trip

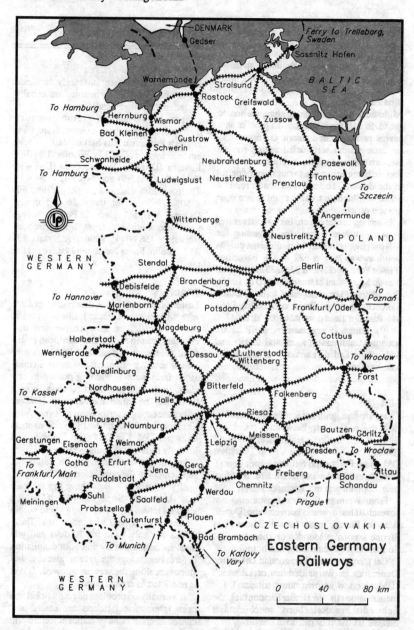

**Eastern Germany Railways**

0    40    80 km

tickets purchased at railway station ticket windows cost the same as two one-ways. International tickets with a 40% discount for those 26 and under are available at some Jugendtourist offices. Card-carrying students get a 25% discount on train tickets at station ticket windows. A *Netzkarte* valid for unlimited train travel in Eastern Germany costs DM 340 for 30 days.

Train stations in Eastern Germany are very convenient with left-luggage rooms *(Gepäckaufbewahrung)*, restaurants and boards listing arrivals *(Ankunft)* and departures *(Abfahrt)*. The trains shown in red are expresses. Watch for the symbol R in a box which indicates that you must make a computerised seat reservation. Be aware that the fee at left-luggage rooms is per *calendar* day so if your bag is in there past midnight you'll pay for two days!

The most common types of trains are *Schnellzug*, or 'fast' train (marked D on time-tables), *Eilzug*, or 'semi-fast' train (E), and *Personenzug*, or local train (P). The supplement on a D train is double that on an E train. No supplement is payable on local P trains so always use them for journeys of less than an hour or so and have a couple of beers with your savings. On international services an additional supplement is payable to use TEE (Trans-Europ-Express) or IC (Intercity) trains. These supplements are always higher if paid on the train instead of at a ticket window.

### Routes

There are several main railway routes worth knowing about. An important line is from Berlin-Lichtenberg or Berlin-Schöneweide to Halle, Weimar, Erfurt and (sometimes) Eisenach. This operates almost hourly and all of the Berlin trains call at Schönefeld Airport, a good place to pick them up. At Schönefeld you can also catch trains to Potsdam, Magdeburg, Leipzig and Dresden. Trains from Berlin to Dresden or Leipzig, and Dresden to Leipzig, are frequent. Two other main routes are Berlin-Lichtenberg to Stralsund or Rostock.

Also very useful is the main line down the west side of Eastern Germany from Rostock to Schwerin, Magdeburg, Halle and Leipzig with a through train every couple of hours. One of these services goes to Erfurt instead of Leipzig. Across the bottom of Eastern Germany there are through trains running Dresden-Chemnitz-Gera-Jena-Weimar-Erfurt.

Journey times from Berlin are one hour to Potsdam, about 2½ hours to Dresden, Halle and Leipzig, 3½ hours to Rostock and Schwerin and four hours to Erfurt.

### CAR & MOTORBIKE

There are 1913 km of Autobahn or limited access roads in Eastern Germany, many of them dating from the Hitler years. The former transit corridors between Western Germany and Berlin were maintained with Western money even prior to 1990 and the whole system is now being upgraded. The roughness of the roads was previously compensated for by a lack of traffic, but flocks of big Western vehicles have now joined the dirty little Trabants and Wartburgs. As you're being shaken by the cobbled streets found in most towns, just keep thinking how quaint it is!

You must have the green insurance card to drive a car into Germany. If you have an accident and your vehicle is rendered inoperable, the police or garage may advise you to rent a car because the costs will be paid for by the insurance. Be aware, however, that if the other party is not guilty you will have to pay the costs yourself.

### Road Rules

Speed limits are 50 km/h in built up areas, 80 km/h on the open road and 100 km/h on motorways (also in West Berlin). This is less than in Western Germany because of the poor condition of the roads. Unlike Austria, which levies heavy tolls on most north-south highways, in Germany the roads are free.

Drivers must use their signals when changing lanes, for example, to pass another vehicle, or when leaving a parked position. Turn-offs from main highways are rather abrupt, creating a serious hazard in rainy weather. At traffic lights a yellow light indicates both a change to a red light *and* a change to a green light. Unlike in Western Germany, in Eastern Germany you can turn right against a red light so long as a green arrow is posted.

### Rental

There's 14% tax on car rentals but it's usually included in the quoted price. All the international chains are represented in Berlin but all of their cars are often reserved in advance. Only Hertz allows its vehicles to be driven into Poland, but this may have changed.

### Purchase

Berlin is one of the best places in Eastern Europe to pick up a cheap used car. The classified newspaper *Zweite Hand* has a section listing cars available for less than DM 500 *(PKW bis 500,- biete)*. You may be able to snap up a Trabant for as little as DM 100! A Czech-made Škoda or Soviet-made Lada would be ideal, as servicing for these is readily available throughout Eastern Europe. Motorcycles for sale are listed under *'Motorräder – biete'*. Beware of ads including the words *'ohne TÜV'* as these are for vehicles that cannot be registered, and before agreeing to anything make sure the ownership can be legally transferred to you.

You can often buy a car with the registration (TÜV) just about to expire for an incredibly low price, and this may be no problem if you're able to drive it out of Germany (and the EC) before the dealine (officials in Poland or Czechoslovakia may not scrutinise the registration papers that closely). What you *will* require is insurance, and agencies arranging it are listed in the yellow pages of the phone book under *'Auto Versicherung'*. If you have a German friend who will help with all this, so much the better.

In West Berlin, Sipo GmbH, Bülow Strasse 99 (U-Bahn: Nollendorf Platz), has good used cars beginning around DM 8000, all with a 12-month guarantee.

If you want to buy a moped or motorcycle, try Zwei-Rad Zillmer, Brüsseler Strasse 45 (U-Bahn: See Strasse). Prices for new bikes

begin around DM 1500 and go up to DM 5000. The place does not rent motorcycles.

### BOAT

From April to October Weisse Flotte excursion boats ply the lakes, rivers and coastline of Eastern Germany – an excellent, inexpensive way of seeing the country as you get around. In the north, trips on the Baltic are possible, and the big paddle-wheel steamers operating out of Dresden are a fine way to tour the Elbe and see much of the area around Dresden. The Weisse Flotte is also very active at Berlin, Potsdam, Rostock, Schwerin, Stralsund, Warnemünde and Wismar.

### LOCAL TRANSPORT

All city buses and trams require tickets purchased at kiosks. Always buy bus and tram tickets before boarding and validate your ticket once aboard.

### Taxi

If your taxi doesn't have a meter, ask the price in advance. Fares may be higher at night. There are usually taxi stands at the main railway stations or you can telephone the taxi dispatcher and have one sent to you. You must pay for the taxi's return trip, and trips out of town are double fare.

# Berlin

Berlin, the largest city in Germany, has more to offer visitors than almost any city in Europe. Sliced in half by a 162-km-long Wall until as recently as mid-1990, East and West Berlin retain their individual characters despite a common city-wide government. Berliners on both sides of the former divide still speak in terms of East Berlin and West Berlin and it will be years before the wounds of the Cold War are fully healed.

You'll find East Berlin far less commercialised, less crowded and often friendlier than West Berlin, though the service at bars, restaurants and offices is not

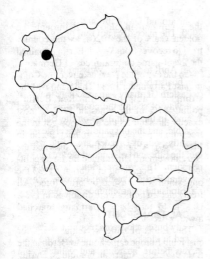

and Lenin, all of whom visited Berlin many times. The philosopher Hegel taught at the University of Berlin from 1818 to 1831, only one of the remarkable individuals who helped make this great city what it is today. Frederick II 'the Great', who reigned from 1740 to 1786, commissioned many of the massive Baroque-Rococo buildings along Unter den Linden to symbolise his growing power. His favourite architect was Georg Wenzeslaus von Knobelsdorff who designed the Opera House and Humboldt University in Berlin, and the Sanssouci Palace in Potsdam. Even more striking is the adapted Greek architecture of the neoclassical architect Karl Friedrich Schinkel (1781-1841), who built the Schauspielhaus, Neue Wache and Altes Museum in Berlin, plus the Nikolaikirche and Charlottenhof Palace in Potsdam. These sights will keep you busy.

There's so much happening in Berlin and so much to see that you'll only scratch the surface. The list of museums, monuments, memorials, art galleries and exhibitions is endless. Keep in mind that this city is more appealing on the inside than on the outside. To really understand what it's all about takes time. While two weeks is enough to get the feel of Berlin, it won't seem long enough.

as smooth. The individual attention often makes up for the inefficiency, however, and it's still more of an adventure to be in 'the East'.

For decades capitalism and socialism competed side by side in Berlin and a tremendous infrastructure of things to see and do has been built up. Berlin now has three major opera houses, two operetta theatres, two national galleries, two universities, two state libraries, two zoos, two major excursion boat fleets and scores of world-class museums. Though the city lost its number one tourist attraction when the Wall was knocked down, the new easy access to all parts of the city and previously off-limits areas in the surrounding countryside more than compensate.

Berlin today is like a reckless adolescent looking for his/her place in the world. Everything – the arts, entertainment, festivals, politics – throbs with youthful energy. Many of the 3.5 million Berliners have found safe roles as consumers, but there's also a large counterculture community and the political struggles continue. Though the prices will shock you, the best things in Berlin are free.

As you travel through the city you'll be following in the footsteps of Marx, Engels

## History

The first recorded settlement on the site was a place named Kölln (1237) on present Museum Island. Medieval Berlin developed on the opposite bank of the Spree River near St Nicholas Church and spread north-east to Alexander Platz. In 1432 these minor Hanseatic trading centres on the route from Magdeburg to Poznań were merged.

In 1442 and 1448 elector Frederick II of Brandenburg conquered the previously independent town and established the rule of the Hohenzollern dynasty, which lasted until 1918. Berlin's importance increased in 1470 when the elector moved his residence here from Brandenburg and built a palace where the Palace of the Republic is today. Courtiers replaced merchants as the dominant social class. In 1539 the Protestant Reformation took hold. During the devastating Thirty

Years' War (1618-48) Berlin lost half its population, but this was partly made up for by thousands of Huguenot refugees fleeing religious persecution in France. Strong fortifications were erected between 1658 and 1683 and a canal built linking the Spree to the Oder. This waterway made Berlin the trading crossroads of northern Germany.

Throughout the 17th and 18th centuries Prussia expanded eastward at the expense of Poland. In 1701 Frederick I made Berlin capital of the kingdom. Between 1648 and 1800 the population jumped from 6000 to 150,000. By 1734 the city had grown so large that the city walls had to be razed. The imposing restored palaces along Unter den Linden went up in the 18th century as Frederick II embellished Berlin.

The 19th century began badly with a French occupation from 1806 to 1813. In 1848 a democratic revolution was suppressed, stifling political development. Capitalism flourished under the reactionary regime which followed and Berlin grew into the 'largest tenement city in the world'. From 1850 to 1870 the population doubled as the Industrial Revolution took hold. In 1871 Bismarck united Germany into the Second Reich under Kaiser Wilhelm I, making Berlin an imperial city, and the population continued to soar. By 1890 the population was 1,600,000 and passed two million in 1905. The masses of immigrant workers lived under the worst conditions imaginable.

The years leading up to WW I saw Berlin become an industrial giant, but power was concentrated in the hands of an autocracy which blundered into WW I. The senseless wartime violence and the example of the Russian Revolution led to revolt throughout Germany. On 9 November 1918 Philipp Scheidemann, leader of the Social Democrats, proclaimed the German Republic from a balcony of the Reichstag. A few hours later Karl Liebknecht proclaimed a Free Socialist Republic from a balcony of the Berlin City Palace. In January 1919 the Berlin Spartakists Karl Liebknecht and Rosa Luxemburg were murdered by remnants of the old imperial army which entered the city and drowned the revolution in blood. All through the golden years of the 1920s, as the country tried to recover from WW I, Berlin remained the avant-garde cultural focus of Germany.

On the eve of the Nazi takeover, the Communist Party under Ernst Thälmann was the strongest single party in 'Red Berlin', polling 31% of the votes in 1932 (almost exactly the same as the 30% they got in the free municipal elections in East Berlin in May 1990). Although Munich spawned the Nazi movement, Hitler made Berlin its political centre. Beginning in February 1933 the opposition was crushed by brute force. All freely elected bodies were dissolved in 1934. Unable to turn back, Germany marched towards disaster.

The results of Hitler's vicious plans for enslaving Europe came home to Berlin in the form of Anglo-American bombings. During the 'Battle of Berlin', from November 1943 to March 1944, British bombers made 35 major attacks on the city. Most of the buildings you see today along Unter den Linden had to be reconstructed from empty shells. Berlin was also a centre of anti-Nazi resistance. A valiant attempt by German officers to overthrow the dictatorship on 20 July 1944 failed and between 180 and 200 of those involved were executed by the Nazis, 89 of them at the Plotzensee prison in Berlin. The 18,500 Soviet soldiers buried in Berlin remind us of the last terrible battle which raged in the city until 2 May 1945, when the Soviet army took Berlin by storm, bringing the fascist madness and WW II abruptly to an end.

In August 1945, the Potsdam Conference sealed the fate of the city by agreeing that each power would occupy a separate zone. In June 1948 the city was split in two when the three Western Allies introduced West German currency and established a separate administration in the western sectors. The Soviets blockaded West Berlin because of this, but an airlift kept the city in the Western camp.

In October 1949 East Berlin became the capital of the GDR and an integral part of East Germany. Construction of the Wall in

August 1961 was almost inevitable as East Germany could no longer support the drain of skilled labour lured west by higher wages. Between 1945 and 1961 some three million East Germans left.

When Hungary decided to breach the Iron Curtain in May 1989, the East German government was back where it had been in 1961, this time without Soviet backing. On 9 November 1989 the Wall opened, but border controls continued until 1 July 1990 when West German currency was adopted in what was then still East Germany.

The Unification Treaty between the two Germanys designated Berlin the official capital of Germany, and in June 1991 the German parliament *(Bundestag)* voted to move the seat of government from Bonn to Berlin over the next decade at a cost of DM 60 to DM 80 billion. This is certainly to the advantage of the Eastern German states which could have been all too easily ignored by faraway Bonn, and from Berlin Germany will exert much more influence on the Europe of the 21st century than it would have if the government had remained at Bonn.

## Orientation

Berlin, in the centre of Europe, halfway between Amsterdam and Warsaw, sits on the great plain of the northern German lowlands. Roughly a third of Berlin is made up of parks, forests, lakes and rivers. There are more trees here than in Paris and more bridges than in Venice. Much of this natural beauty of rolling hills and quiet shorelines is on the south-eastern and south-western sides of the city.

The Spree River winds across the city for over 30 km from the Grosser Müggelsee to Spandau, where it joins the Havel River. North and south of Spandau the Havel widens into a series of lakes from Tegel to Potsdam. The lakes were gouged out by glaciers during the last ice age, the surrounding hills being formed from the moraines. From Potsdam the Havel flows on into the Elbe and past Hamburg before reaching the North Sea. A dense network of canals links the

other waterways and there are beautiful walks along some of them.

The area that presently comprises Berlin was only amalgamated in 1920 when eight towns, 59 villages and 27 landed estates were joined to form a single municipality. Towns like Charlottenburg, Dahlem, Friedrichshagen, Grünau, Kladow, Köpenick, Schöneberg, Schmöckwitz, Spandau, Tegel and Wannsee have maintained their separate identities until today. Crowded Kreuzberg is a countercultural centre and Turkish ghetto, while the spacious suburbs out towards the Grünewald forest are strictly upper class.

The tourists' haunt centres on Unter den Linden, the fashionable avenue of aristocratic Berlin. Together with its continuation, Karl Liebknecht Strasse, they extend east from the Brandenburg Gate to Alexander Platz, one-time heart of socialist Germany. Between these two are some of Berlin's finest museums, on an island in the Spree River. The theatre district revolves around Friedrich Strasse, which crosses Unter den Linden just south of Friedrich Strasse Railway Station.

The ruin of Kaiser Wilhelm Memorial Church on Breitscheid Platz, a block away from Zoo Station, is your best central reference point in West Berlin. The tourist office and hundreds of shops are in the Europa Centre at the end of the square farthest away from the station. Kurfürsten Damm (Ku'-damm), West Berlin's most fashionable avenue, runs 3.5 km south-west from Breitscheid Platz. North-east between Breitscheid Platz and the Brandenburg Gate is Tiergarten, a vast city park which was once a royal hunting domain.

While in Berlin keep in mind that the street numbers usually (but not always) go up one side of the street and down the other. Also, there's often more than one street with the same name, which is why we always include the nearest mass transit station in addresses.

Be aware too that a continuous street may change names several times as it goes along. Around the end of 1991 some 300 East Berlin street names may be changed for political reasons, so be prepared. Also watch out for speeding cycles on bike routes down the pavement (sidewalk) and canine excrement everywhere – there are more dogs than people in Berlin!

## Information

The Berlin-Information tourist office below the TV tower near Alexander Platz Railway Station is open daily from 8 am to 8 pm. The helpful, patient staff can give you a map and answer questions. The scale model of Berlin in this office will help you find your bearings.

The more crowded Berlin Tourist Information Office (Verkehrsamt Berlin), at Budapester Strasse 45 by the Europa Centre in West Berlin, is open daily from 8 am to 10.30 pm. In addition to supplying brochures and answering questions, they book hotel rooms for a DM 3 commission, though seldom at the cheaper places mentioned in this book. Don't believe them if they tell you everything is full.

Also near Zoo Station is the Informationszentrum Berlin, 2nd floor, Hardenberg Strasse 20 behind the Deutsche Bundesbahn ticket office (open weekdays from 8 am to 7 pm, Saturday from 8 am to 4 pm). It's less oriented towards consumer tourism and supplies two excellent free booklets in English: *Berlin for Young People* and *Berlin – Outlook.*

If you want to make contact with Berlin's political counterculture, try the café (closed Saturday) in the rear courtyard at Mehringhof, Gneisenau Strasse 2 (U-Bahn: Mehring Damm). Many alternative groups meet in this building as the posters plastered everywhere attest.

**Other Tourist Offices** Tourist information on the other Eastern European countries is available from Balkantourist (Bulgaria), Unter den Linden 40; Čedok (Czechoslovakia), Strausberger Platz 8 (U-Bahn: Strausberger Platz); Ibusz (Hungary), Karl Liebknecht Strasse 9 (S-Bahn: Alexander Platz); and Orbis (Poland), Warschauer Strasse 5 (U-Bahn: Frankfurter Tor).

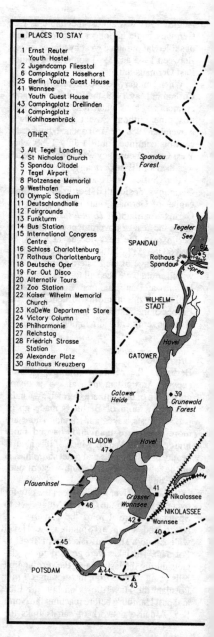

■ PLACES TO STAY

1 Ernst Reuter Youth Hostel
2 Jugendcamp Fliesstal
6 Campingplatz Haselhorst
25 Berlin Youth Guest House
41 Wannsee Youth Guest House
43 Campingplatz Dreilinden
44 Campingplatz Kohlhasenbrück

OTHER

3 Alt Tegel Landing
4 St Nicholas Church
5 Spandau Citadel
7 Tegel Airport
8 Plotzensee Memorial
9 Westhafen
10 Olympic Stadium
11 Deutschlandhalle
12 Fairgrounds
13 Funkturm
14 Bus Station
15 International Congress Centre
16 Schloss Charlottenburg
17 Rathaus Charlottenburg
18 Deutsche Oper
19 Far Out Disco
20 Alternativ Tours
21 Zoo Station
22 Kaiser Wilhelm Memorial Church
23 KaDeWe Department Store
24 Victory Column
26 Philharmonie
27 Reichstag
28 Friedrich Strasse Station
29 Alexander Platz
30 Rathaus Kreuzberg

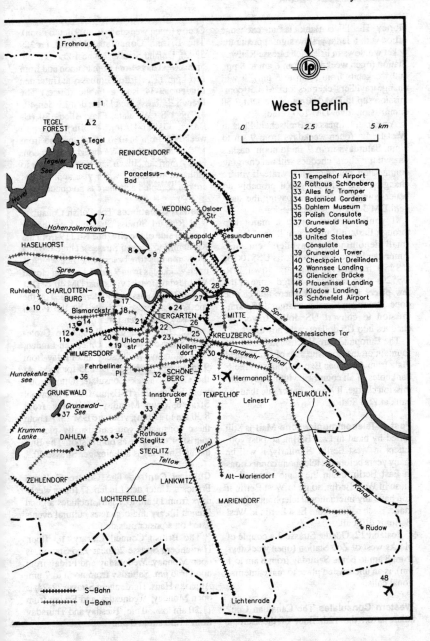

**West Berlin**

0        2.5        5 km

31 Tempelhof Airport
32 Rathaus Schöneberg
33 Alles für Tramper
34 Botanical Gardens
35 Dahlem Museum
36 Polish Consulate
37 Grunewald Hunting Lodge
38 United States Consulate
39 Grunewald Tower
40 Checkpoint Dreilinden
42 Wannsee Landing
45 Glienicker Brücke
46 Pfaueninsel Landing
47 Kladow Landing
48 Schönefeld Airport

+++++++  S-Bahn
+++++++  U-Bahn

**Money** The DVB Bank has an exchange office with a large yellow sign opposite the ticket windows in Friedrich Strasse Railway Station (open weekdays from 8 am to 8 pm, and weekends from 9 am to 5 pm). It will change travellers' cheques for DM 3.50 commission (up to DM 100 value) or DM 7.50 commission (over DM 100 value).

American Express on Breitscheid Platz in West Berlin (open weekdays from 9 am to 5 pm, Saturdays from 9 am to noon) cashes its own travellers' cheques without charging commission, but gives a lousy rate. If you're changing over US$20, you'll probably do better going to a bank and paying the standard DM 3 to DM 10 commission.

If you're embarking on a major trip through Eastern Europe, you'll need lots of small denomination travellers' cheques. American Express will break its US$100 or US$50 travellers' cheques down into US$20s at no additional charge – one of the few places in the region where this can be done. American Express charges 10% commission to convert US dollar travellers' cheques into US dollars cash, however!

The Europa Centre Wechselstube, by the fountain on the opposite side of Breitscheid Platz from American Express, buys and sells banknotes of all countries without any commission charge. It gives a better rate than the bank at Zoo Station.

**Post & Telecommunications** Mail is still sorted by hand in East Berlin, so post your letters in West Berlin. Similarly, it will be many years before the telephone connections in East Berlin attain the same standard as those in West Berlin, so go to West Berlin if you have any international telephone calls to make. Even calling from East Berlin to West Berlin is difficult.

Postamt 12, Goethe Strasse 3 a couple of blocks west of Zoo Station (open weekdays from 8 am to 6 pm, Saturday from 8 am to 1 pm), is an uncrowded place to make international calls.

**Western Consulates** The Canadian Consulate is on the 12th floor of the Europa Centre (open weekdays from 9 am to noon). The British Consulate General (☎ 309 5292), Uhland Strasse 7-8 near Zoo Station, opens weekdays from 9 am to noon and from 2 to 4 pm. (The British Embassy at Unter den Linden 32-34 isn't a public office.) The French Embassy is at Unter den Linden 40.

The US Consulate, Clay Allee 170 (U-Bahn: Oskar-Helene-Heim), is open weekdays from 8.30 to 11.30 am, and from 1.30 to 3 pm, closed Wednesday afternoon. For 'American citizen services' it's better to go in the afternoon when visa applications are not accepted and there is no queue.

**Eastern Consulates** The Polish Consulate is at Richard Strauss Strasse 11 on the far western side of the city (bus No 119 from the Ku'damm to Lassen Strasse). Huge crowds press into this tiny basement office which is open weekdays from 9 am to 1 pm but closed Wednesday (tourist visas cost DM 40, or DM 50 for British passport holders, issued on the spot). Visas are not issued by the Polish Embassy, Unter den Linden 72.

The Hungarian Consulate, Otto Grotewohl Strasse 6 (S-Bahn: Unter den Linden, open Monday, Wednesday and Friday from 9 am to 1 pm), charges DM 35 for visas. At the Czechoslovak Consulate, Otto Grotewohl Strasse 21 (U-Bahn: Otto Grotewohl Strasse, open Monday to Friday from 8.30 am to 11 pm), visas are DM 13. At both these consulates you can usually pick up tourist or transit visas on the spot. The Bulgarian Embassy is at Leipziger Strasse 20.

**Cultural Centres** The Centre Culturel Français, Unter den Linden 37 (open weekdays from 11 am to 7 pm), includes a good French library and organises cultural events listed on a poster outside.

The British Council Library, 1st floor, Hardenberg Strasse 20 near Zoo Station, is open Monday, Wednesday and Friday from noon to 6 pm, Saturday from noon to 7 pm. Amerika Haus, Hardenberg Strasse 22-24, is open Monday, Wednesday and Friday from 11.30 am to 5.30 pm, Tuesday and Thursday from 11.30 am to 8 pm.

**Travel Agencies** The Europäisches Reisebüro, in the tall building on the east side of Alexander Platz, is a large travel agency (open Monday to Saturday) offering a variety of services. At Berlin-Tourist downstairs you can make room reservations, book local sightseeing tours and buy theatre tickets. Counter No 5 in the back office makes train reservations, while the adjacent counter No 6 sells international railway tickets.

Reise Welt, Charlotten Strasse 45 just off Unter den Linden, is a good place to buy international train tickets or make reservations as it's not too crowded. Youth-fare international train tickets are available from 'Jugendtourist', Friedrich Strasse 79a (open weekdays from 10 am to 6 pm, Saturday from 9 am to noon).

If you want a regular return railway ticket, check with the Deutsches Reisebüro (DER), Kurfürsten Damm 17 near Zoo Station, which will tell you about special discount offers the railway station ticket office won't bother to mention.

SRS Studenten Reise Service, Marien Strasse 23 (U-Bahn and S-Bahn: Friedrich Strasse), offers flights at student (age 34 or less) or youth (age 25 or less) fares. A cheap flight to London will cost about DM 226 one-way (available to everyone). Wasteels discount youth train tickets (age 25 and under) are also available. SRS sells the FIYTO youth and ISIC student cards (DM 10 and one photo) and can answer questions about travel around Eastern Germany. The staff is very helpful.

Reisebüro Zoo, Hardenberg Platz 2 opposite Zoo Station, sells bus tickets to Western Germany, Holland, Britain, etc.

Travel agencies offering cheap flights advertise in the *Reisen* classified section of *Zitty*. The best of these is Alternativ Tours (☎ 881 2089), Wilmersdorfer Strasse 94 (U-Bahn: Adenauer Platz). It specialises in unpublished, discounted tickets to anywhere in the world.

**Laundry** The Wasch Center, Wex Strasse 34 (U-Bahn: Bundesplatz), is a self-service laundromat which charges DM 6 to wash six kilos, soap included. Drying is DM 1 for 15 minutes. It's open from 6 am to midnight daily. The Bio-wasch Center, Uhland Strasse 53 (U-Bahn: Hohenzollern Platz, open from 6 am to 11 pm), is similar.

**Bookshops** For paperbacks in English try the Marga Schoeller Bücherstube, Knesebeck Strasse 33-34. It carries mostly fiction. A better selection of books in English, both new and second-hand, is at Wordsworth Books, Goethe Strasse 69 (say hello to Robin from Adelaide when you go in). Both of these should have something in English by local writer Christa Wolf.

East Berlin's biggest bookshop is Das Internationale Buch Bouvier, Spandauer Strasse 4 (S-Bahn: Marx-Engels-Platz), which has glossy art books, German travel guidebooks and some maps, but only cheap novels in English.

There are two travel bookshops in West Berlin: Kiepert, Knesebeck Strasse 2 at Hardenberg Strasse (U-Bahn: Ernst Reuter Platz), and Schropp, Potsdamer Strasse 100 (U-Bahn: Kurfürsten Strasse). They have maps and German guidebooks to almost everywhere.

**Health** If you need to see a doctor, go to the emergency department of Charité Hospital (*Rettungstelle der Charité*) on Hermann Matern Strasse a couple of blocks from Friedrich Strasse Railway Station. As you come from the station, look for an unmarked driveway where a couple of ambulances are parked on the right, just beyond the underpass that is below the main high-rise building.

This Humboldt University-operated facility is open 24 hours a day but the basic consultation fee varies: it's DM 6 weekdays, DM 18 weekends, and DM 25 between 7 pm and 8 am. Under the Communists such attention was free, and as prices are still in flux, you could be charged something different or perhaps nothing at all. This was the best medical facility of the former GDR and is just as good as anything in West Berlin,

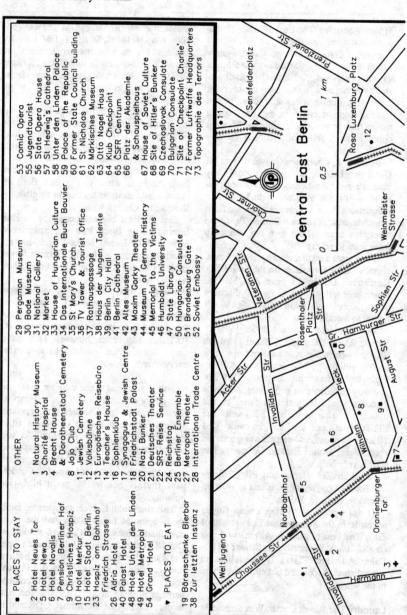

PLACES TO STAY
- 2 Hotel Neues Tor
- 5 Hotel Newa
- 6 Hotel Novalis
- 7 Pension Berliner Hof
- 9 Christliches Hospiz
- 10 Hotel Merkur
- 15 Hotel Stadt Berlin
- 23 Hospiz am Bahnhof Friedrich Strasse
- 26 Adria Hotel
- 40 Palast Hotel
- 48 Hotel Unter den Linden
- 49 Hotel Metropol
- 54 Grand Hotel

▶ PLACES TO EAT
- 19 Bärenschenke Bierbar
- 38 Zur letzten Instanz

OTHER
- 1 Natural History Museum
- 3 Charité Hospital
- 4 Brecht House
- 8 Das Internationale Buch Bouvier & Dorotheenstadt Cemetery
- 8 Jojo Club
- 11 Jewish Cemetery
- 12 Volksbühne
- 13 Europäisches Reisebüro
- 14 Teacher's House
- 16 Sophienklub
- 17 Synagogue & Jewish Centre
- 18 Friedrichstadt Palast
- 20 Nazi Bunker
- 21 Deutsches Theater
- 22 SRS Reise Service
- 24 Reichstag
- 25 Berliner Ensemble
- 27 Metropol Theater
- 28 International Trade Centre
- 29 Pergamon Museum
- 30 Bode Museum
- 31 National Gallery
- 32 Market
- 33 House of Hungarian Culture
- 34 St Mary's Church
- 36 TV Tower & Tourist Office
- 37 Rathauspassage
- 38 Haus der Jungen Talente
- 39 Berlin City Hall
- 41 Berlin Cathedral
- 42 Altes Museum
- 43 Maxim Gorky Theater
- 44 Museum of German History
- 45 Memorial to the Victims
- 46 Humboldt University
- 47 State Library
- 50 Hungarian Consulate
- 51 Brandenburg Gate
- 52 Soviet Embassy
- 53 Comic Opera
- 55 Jugendtourist
- 56 State Opera House
- 57 St Hedwig's Cathedral
- 58 Unter den Linden Palace
- 59 Palace of the Republic
- 60 Former State Council building
- 61 St Nicholas Church
- 62 Märkisches Museum
- 63 Otto Nagel Haus
- 64 Klub Checkpoint
- 65 CSFR Centrum
- 66 Platz der Akademie & Schauspielhaus
- 67 House of Soviet Culture
- 68 Site of Hitler's Bunker
- 69 Czechoslovak Consulate
- 70 Bulgarian Consulate
- 71 Site of 'Checkpoint Charlie'
- 72 Former Luftwaffe Headquarters
- 73 Topographie des Terrors

Central East Berlin

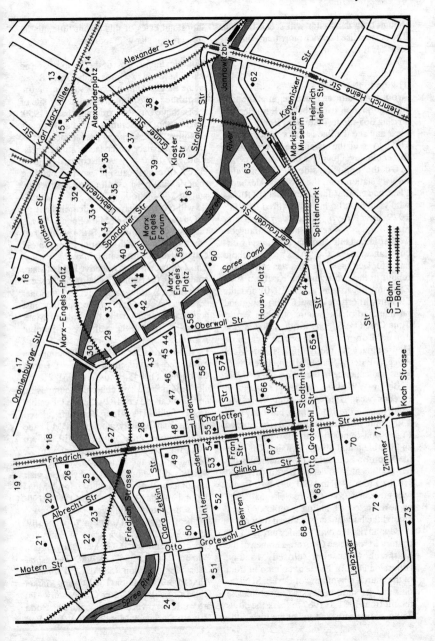

though only the doctor will speak English. The personalised service more than compensates for this.

## Things to See

**Around Alexander Platz** Begin at the tourist information office below East Berlin's soaring 365-metre **TV tower** (1969). If it's a clear day and the line isn't too long, pay the DM 3 to go up the tower. The Telecafé at the 207-metre level revolves once an hour.

On the opposite side of the elevated railway station from the tower is Alexander Platz, named after Tsar Alexander I of Russia who visited Berlin in 1805. Alfred Döblin's 1929 novel *Berlin Alexanderplatz* (later made into a TV serial) about a transport worker forced into criminal activities by circumstance made the 'Alex' a household name for Germans. The area was completely rebuilt in the 1960s and the **Kauf am Alex Zentrum** department store (1970) and the 39-storey **Interhotel Stadt Berlin** now stand on one side of the square, and the **World Time Clock** (1969) on the other. Beyond the domed **Congress Hall** beside Teacher's House stretches orderly, lifeless Karl Marx Allee (formerly Stalin Allee), faced with glass and concrete in the 1950s.

Before WW II the vast open square that extends west from Alexander Platz was solidly packed with buildings, but today only 13th century **St Mary's Church** (free, closed Friday and Sunday) with its organ (1721) and marble pulpit (1703) remains. Opposite the **Neptune Fountain** (1891) nearby is the red-brick central tower of **Berlin City Hall** (1870). From 1948 to 1990 only East Berlin was governed from the 'red city hall' (the name refers to the building's colour). A frieze around the building depicts local history.

Beyond rise the twin Gothic spires of 13th century **St Nicholas Church**, a branch of the Märkisches Museum (closed Monday, admission DM 2). The bear column in front of the church is symbolic of Berlin. St Nicholas and its surroundings were completely rebuilt from 1981 to 1987 to mark the city's 750th anniversary, and today the twee little

shops and cafés of this quaint little quarter are very popular with tourists.

**Museum Island** West of the TV tower, on an island between two arms of the Spree River, is the sleek, contemporary **Palace of the Republic** (1976) which occupies the site of the Baroque City Palace demolished in 1950. During the Communist era the People's Chamber *(Volkskammer)* used to meet in this showpiece palace which faces Marx-Engels-Platz. In 1990 it was discovered that an excess of cancer-causing asbestos building material had been used in the construction, and the 180-metre-long Palace of the Republic will probably have to be demolished!

On the south side of Marx Engels Platz is the former **Council of State** *(Staatsrat)* building (1964) with a portal from the old City Palace incorporated into the façade. This body acted as a collective head of state, controlling the Supreme Court, the Prosecutor General, foreign policy and national security. The modern white building just across the canal on the east side of Marx Engels Platz was the Ministry of Foreign Affairs.

North across the busy avenue looms the great neo-Renaissance dome of **Berlin Cathedral** (1904, admission DM 2), the city's main Protestant church. The imposing neoclassical edifice (1829) beside the cathedral is Schinkel's **Altes Museum** (closed Monday and Tuesday, admission DM 1), the oldest public museum in Berlin, where changing art exhibitions are presented. Behind this is the Neues Museum (1855), which is still being rebuilt, but you can visit the adjacent **National Gallery** (closed Monday and Tuesday, admission DM 1) with 19th and 20th century paintings.

The **Pergamon Museum** (open daily, admission DM 2) is a feast of antiquity, especially classical Greek, Babylonian, Roman, Islamic and Oriental. The Ishtar Gate from Babylon (580 BC), Pergamon Altar from Asia Minor (160 BC) and Market Gate from Miletus, Greece (2nd century AD) are world-renowned monuments. The **Bode Museum** (closed Monday and Tuesday) houses sculpture, paintings, coins and Egyptian art, although not all sections are open every day. There's a good café upstairs in this museum.

**Along Unter den Linden** A stroll west down Unter den Linden takes in the greatest surviving monuments of the former Prussian capital. All the captions may be in German at the **Museum of German History** in the former Armoury (1706) opposite the Unter den Linden Palace (1732), but the extensive collection of objects, maps and photos is fascinating. Be sure to see the building's interior courtyard with its 22 heads of dying warriors by Andreas Schlüter.

Next to this museum is Schinkel's **Neue Wache** (1818), now the Memorial to the Victims of Fascism & Militarism. **Humboldt University** (1753), the next building west, was originally a palace of the brother of Frederick II, and was converted to a university in 1810. Beside this is the massive **State Library** (1914). An equestrian statue of Frederick II stands in the middle of the avenue in front of the university.

Across the street from the university, beside the Old Library (1780) with its curving Baroque façade, is Knobelsdorff's **German State Opera** (1743). On Bebel Platz, the square between these buildings, the Nazis staged a notorious book burning on 10 May 1933. A decade later in scores of concentration camps they fulfilled Heinrich Heine's terrible prophecy: 'Where books are burned, people too are burned in the end.' Behind this site is Catholic **St Hedwigs Cathedral** (1773), modelled on the Pantheon in Rome.

Detour south-west two blocks to Platz der Akademie to see the twin French and German cathedrals in perfect neoclassical harmony. The cathedrals are copies of similar buildings on Piazza del Popolo in Rome. Today the French Cathedral (1780) is the **Huguenot Museum** (closed Monday and Friday). Some 20,000 French Huguenots settled in Berlin-Brandenburg after 1685. Between the cathedrals is the **Concert Hall** (Schauspielhaus), built by Schinkel in 1821, bombed by the British in 1944 and reopened in 1986 after being completely reconstructed in the original style.

A block west at Friedrich Strasse 176-179 is the **House of Soviet Culture** (closed Sunday) with art and photography exhibitions, a Russian bookshop (open weekdays) and soft lounge chairs for a break. Stadtmitte U-Bahn Station is nearby.

**Around Tiergarten** At the west end of Unter den Linden (S-Bahn: Unter den Linden) is the **Brandenburg Gate** (1791), a symbol of Berlin and once the boundary between East and West Berlin. The route of the Wall south from here to Potsdamer Platz is plain to see. The winged victory and four-horse quadriga atop the gate was taken to Paris by Napoleon as a spoil of war, only to be returned to Berlin by the victorious Prussians a few years later. At the open-air flea market around the gate you can buy East German and Soviet military caps, belts, helmets, binoculars, army manuals, hammer & sickle emblems, flags, painted pieces of the Wall, Soviet pocket watches, etc. Compare prices before buying anything and bargain.

Beside the Spree River just north of the Brandenburg Gate is the **Reichstag** (1894), the German parliament until it was burned by the Nazis on the night of 27-28 February 1933 as a pretext for rounding up their opponents. At midnight on the night of 2-3 October 1990 the reunification of Germany was enacted here. The restored Reichstag contains an excellent exhibition covering German history from 1800 to the present (closed Monday, admission free). All of the captions are in German only but a kiosk upstairs near the entrance to the exhibition rents a Walkman with a 45-minute guided tour in English, French or German for DM 2. Downstairs, there's a good café for a coffee, and a cafeteria with goulash soup and Bockwurst. Between the Reichstag and the river is a small memorial to some of the 191 people who died trying to cross the Wall.

Berlin's huge inner-city park, **Tiergarten**, stretches west from here towards Zoo Station. Once a private hunting ground of the

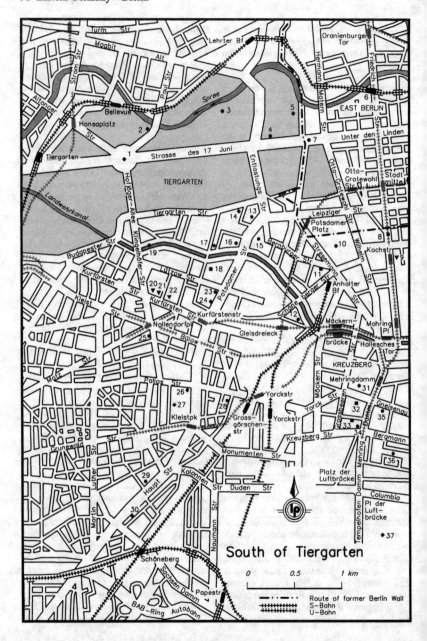

South of Tiergarten

0        0.5        1 km

— · — · —   Route of former Berlin Wall
+++++++++   S-Bahn
+++++++++   U-Bahn

■ PLACES TO STAY

11 Jugendhotel International
18 Berlin Youth Guest House
32 Riehmers Hofgarten Hotel
33 Hotel Transit

▼ PLACES TO EAT

9 Unemployment Office
20 Zum Ambrosius Restaurant
21 Café Einstein
22 Spatz Steakhouse

OTHER

1 Victory Column
2 Schloss Bellevue
3 Kongresshalle & Spreefahrt
4 Soviet War Memorial
5 Reichstag
6 Friedrich Strasse Station
7 Brandenburg Gate
8 Site of Checkpoint Charlie
10 Martin Gropius Bau
12 Youth Hostel Association
13 Philharmonie
14 Museum of Arts & Crafts
15 State Library
16 New National Gallery
17 Bewag
19 Bauhaus Museum for Design
23 Schropp Bookstore
24 Made in Berlin Clothing
25 Metropol Disco
26 Pallas Bunker
27 Supreme Court
28 E & M Leydicke Bar
29 Madhouse Ecstasy Disco
30 Odeon Theatre
31 Rathaus Kreuzberg
34 Mitwohnzentrale Kreuzberg
35 Mehringhof
36 Chamisso Platz
37 Tempelhof Airport

prince electors, it became a park in the 18th century and from 1833 to 1838 it was landscaped with streams and lakes. Strasse des 17 Juni which leads west from the Brandenburg Gate through the park was known as the East-West Axis during the Nazi era, Hitler's showplace entrance to Berlin. On the north side of this street, just west of the gate, is a **Soviet War Memorial** flanked by the first Russian tanks to enter the city in 1945. German police with dogs defend the memorial against desecration by neo-Nazi skinheads.

Turn left (south) on Entlastungs Strasse just beyond the memorial and continue straight ahead till you see the **Philharmonie** (1963), designed by Hans Scharoun, diagonally across the street. This striking modern concert hall is unique in that the orchestra is completely surrounded by rows of seats. The **Musical Instruments Museum** (1984), Tiergarten Strasse 1 beside the Philharmonie (closed Monday, admission free), has a rich collection that is beautifully displayed. In the café downstairs is a 1920 Leipzig Orchestrion (antique jukebox) which will serenade you as you have your coffee if you insert a DM 1 coin. The **Museum of Arts & Crafts** (1985), Tiergarten Strasse 6 on the opposite side of the Philharmonie (closed Monday, admission free), houses precious objects from medieval times to 1930s Art Deco.

Red-brick **St Matthew Church** (1846) stands just south of the above buildings in the centre of Berlin's new 'Kulturforum', and beyond it is the **New National Gallery**, Potsdamer Strasse 50 (closed Monday, permanent collection downstairs free, special exhibitions DM 6), with 19th and 20th century paintings. This sleek, ultramodern gallery (1968) is a creation of the famous architect Mies van der Rohe. The **State Library** (1976) across the street contains reading, periodical and exhibition rooms (closed Sunday).

From the New National Gallery walk west along the Landwehrkanal (without crossing it) past the Bewag building, or 'Shell House', (1932) to the **Museum for Design**, Klingelhofer Strasse 13-14 (closed Tuesday, admission DM 3.50, free on Monday). This museum dedicated to the Bauhaus school (1919-33), which laid the basis for much contemporary architecture, is housed in a building designed by its founder, Walter Gropius.

North up Hofjäger Allee from this museum is the **Victory Column** (1873), topped by a gilded statue of the Roman victory goddess, Victoria, visible from much of Tiergarten, which commemorates 19th century Prussian military adventures. Just north-east is **Schloss Bellevue** (1785), built for Prince Ferdinand, brother of Frederick II the Great and now an official residence of the President of Germany.

East along the Spree River is the **Kongresshalle** (1957), nicknamed the 'pregnant oyster' for its shape. The arched roof collapsed in 1980 but has since been rebuilt. The photo and art exhibits (often with Third World themes) inside are worth a look (closed Monday, admission free) but the main attraction are the soft seats where you can take a rest. You can board an excursion boat behind the building.

**Along the U6 U-Bahn Line** The house at Chaussee Strasse 125 (U-Bahn: Nordbahnhof or Oranienburger Tor), where the famous playwright **Bertolt Brecht** lived from 1953 until his death in 1956, can be visited Tuesday to Friday from 10 to 11.30 am, Thursday from 5 to 6.30 pm and Saturday from 9.30 am to 1 pm in groups of eight people maximum with a German-speaking guide (admission free). Go into the rear courtyard and up the stairs to the right. The entrance is upstairs.

Next to Brecht House is **Dorotheenstadt Cemetery** (1762) with tombs of the illustrious, such as the architect Schinkel, the philosopher Hegel, the poet Johannes R Becher and Brecht himself. There are two adjacent cemeteries here: you want the one closer to Brecht's house. The **Natural History Museum** (1810) nearby at Invaliden Strasse 43 (closed Monday, U-Bahn: Nordbahnhof) has a good collection of dinosaurs and minerals, plus an interesting exhibit on Charles Darwin.

All of the stations along the U6 U-Bahn line from Stadion der Weltjugend south to Stadtmitte (excepting Friedrich Strasse) were below East Berlin and tightly sealed until mid-1990, although U6 still rumbled through. Nothing remains of the famous

**Checkpoint Charlie,** but if you want to see where it stood get off at Koch Strasse Station and walk north on Friedrich Strasse. The abandoned multi-million-dollar structure at Friedrich Strasse 207-208 was, until 1990, the headquarters of all Western intelligence organisations in Berlin and from here, or from the now-removed Allied guard trailer in the middle of the street nearby, photos were taken of everyone crossing the border. The Cold War rhetoric of this period is perpetuated across the street in the Haus am Checkpoint Charlie, a commercial museum charging DM 5 admission (open daily from 9 am to 10 pm).

Just west on Zimmer Strasse is the site of the former SS/Gestapo headquarters where the **Topographie des Terrors** exhibition (open daily) documents Nazi crimes. A platform atop a high mound of rubble from the ruined buildings provides of good view of this desolate area. The Wall used to run along the north side of Zimmer Strasse, and sections of it may still remain. The adjacent **Martin Gropius Bau** (1881) is the venue of major exhibitions relating to some aspect of life in Berlin (open daily, admission DM 8).

The massive grey government office block at the north-west corner of Zimmer Strasse and Otto Grotewohl Strasse used to be the headquarters of Hermann Göring's Luftwaffe. Diagonally opposite the Czechoslovak Consulate just north on the corner of Otto Grotewohl Strasse and Voss Strasse is the site of **Hitler's bunker.** The Chancellery built here by Albert Speer in 1938 was demolished after the war and the bunker below it (where Hitler shot himself on 30 April 1945) was completely effaced in the late 1980s when the Communists built the apartment complex which presently occupies the site.

Reboard U6 at Stadtmitte (make sure you get on the right line!) and ride south to Platz der Luftbrücke to savour the sombre lines of **Tempelhof Airport**, now a US Air Force base, domestic airport and police headquarters, which constitutes the largest surviving architectural monument from the Nazi period. Seldom used today, before WW II this was the largest airport in Germany. An imperial parade ground occupied this site until the Wright brothers introduced aviation here in 1908. In the late 1930s Albert Speer erected the sinister grey buildings emblazoned with white stone eagles which overpower the square today, a vivid reminder of the Nazi destruction of humanity. Lest anyone forget this history, the US Air Force placed a Nazi eagle's head (1940) on a pedestal in front of their base in 1985. Even the soaring **Airlift Monument** in the park fails to subdue the sense of evil.

Double-decker bus No 119 begins at Platz der Luftbrücke and runs right through West Berlin, including a drive all the way down **Kurfürsten Damm**. If you board here you should get the top front seats for a great scenic trip. Stay on all the way to Hagen Platz, the other end of the line, which is within walking distance of Grunewald S-Bahn Station.

**West Berlin** The stark ruins of neo-Romanesque **Kaiser Wilhelm Memorial Church** (1895) in Breitscheid Platz (S-Bahn and U-Bahn: Zoologischer Garten), engulfed in the roaring commercialism all round, marks the heart of rebuilt West Berlin. The British bombing attack of 22 November 1943 left standing only the broken west tower. The former entry hall below the tower and the modern church (1961) may be visited. (As you're standing beside the church, look west across the street and you'll see a yellow Eduscho sign at Tauentzien Strasse 13. On weekdays you can get a nice cup of coffee in there for DM 1.10.)

By the **Globe Fountain** (1983) next to the tower, assorted street artists and musicians play to the crowd. Just beyond rises the gleaming **Europa Centre** (1965) with a rotating Mercedes symbol on top. You can pay DM 3 to stand on the 20th floor observation deck but you can get a view almost as good for free from the 18th floor. North-east of the Europa Centre on Budapester Strasse is the elephant gate to West Berlin's **aquarium and zoo**, but it's a stiff DM 12 to see

both (open daily). This first zoo in Germany opened in 1844.

**KaDeWe Department Store** (1907) or Kaufhaus des Westens on Wittenberg Platz a few blocks south has been the main temple to German consumerism since the turn of the century and it's still the largest department store in Europe.

**Along the Wall** At Wittenberg Platz or Zoo Station board the U1 U-Bahn line towards Schlesisches Tor. The movie, *Linie 1*, was made about this line and you'll get some great views of Berlin after the U1 escapes from its tunnel east of Kurfüsten Strasse Station and carries you up onto an elevated trestleway. Your fellow passengers will be as colourful as those who appeared in the film because the U1 rolls right through counter-culture **Kreuzberg**. Stay on to Schlesisches Tor, heart of the largest Turkish community outside Turkey, then follow the overhead U-Bahn line east a block to the Spree River. The longest surviving stretch of the **Berlin Wall** is just across the bridge.

As the Wall was being demolished in mid-1990, this 300-metre section was turned over to artists who created a permanent open-air art gallery along the side facing Mühlen Strasse (the side facing the river is sprayed with graffiti). Walk along the median strip as far as Berlin-Hauptbahnhof Railway Station where you can pick up the S-Bahn.

The Wall only existed for two-thirds of the life of the German Democratic Republic – from 1945 to 1961 there was no Wall. It's hard to visualise the Wall from this isolated fragment, but Ian Walker captures the mood in his fascinating book, *Zoo Station:*

The Wall was epic, beautiful in its way, the white concrete, the metal crosses, the watchtowers standing like toy soldiers. We had loved that snowy night when we scaled the wooden watchtower in Spandau.

**Retracing the GDR** Several interesting sights are accessible on East Berlin's two U-Bahn lines, which intersect at Alexander Platz. Take a train to Märkisches Museum Station. The collection of the **Märkisches**

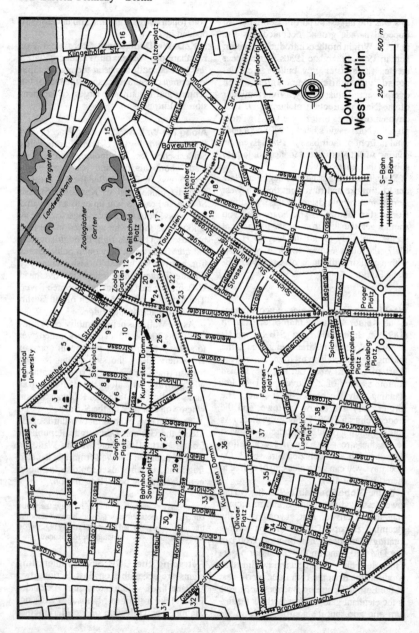

Downtown
West Berlin

LP

0    250    500 m

S–Bahn
U–Bahn

■ PLACES TO STAY

3   Jugendgästehaus am Zoo
15  Inter-Continental Hotel

▼ PLACES TO EAT

6   Dicke Wirtin Pub
7   Schwarzes Café
24  Pizzeria Amigo
25  Café Kranzler
27  Café Bleibtreu
31  Café Extra Dry
33  Beiz Restaurant
34  Schalander Café
37  Loretta's Biergarten

OTHER

1   Wordsworth Books
2   Kiepert Bookshop
4   Postamt 12
5   School of Art Concert Hall
8   British Consulate
9   Informationszentrum Berlin
10  Theater des Westens/Quasimodo
11  Zoo Station
12  Filmzentrum Zoo Palast
13  Berliner Festspiele
14  Zoo & Aquarium
16  Bauhaus Museum for Design
17  Europa Centre & Tourist Office
18  KaDeWe Department Store
19  Djungel Club
20  American Express
21  Kaiser Wilhelm Memorial Church
22  Wertheim Department Store
23  Ku'damm Eck
26  Jewish Community Centre
28  Marga Schoeller Bucherstube
29  Go in Pub
30  Salsa Pub
32  Kurbel Cinema
35  Madow Pub
36  Big Eden Disco
38  Bio-wasch Centre

**Museum** (closed Monday and Tuesday) is intended to illustrate the history of Berlin, and special features include a scale model of Berlin in 1750 and drawings by Heinrich Zille. Bears housed in a pit in the park behind the museum are the official mascots of the city.

**Otto Nagel Haus**, Märkisches Ufer 16-18 on the Spree Canal nearby (closed Friday and Saturday, admission 50 Pfennig), exhibits the work of Berlin painter Otto Nagel (1894-1967) and his contemporaries. Many of the paintings here have social themes popular under the old regime. The good little café inside serves beer and liqueurs produced in Eastern Germany.

Get back on the U-Bahn to Alexander Platz where you change to the U-Bahn line towards Hönow. Get out at Frankfurter Tor Station to take in a little early 1950s Joe Stalin chic at the point where Karl Marx Allee becomes Frankfurter Allee.

Continue by U-Bahn in the direction of Hönow to Magdalenen Strasse Station and the former headquarters of the East German Stasi (secret police). In Haus 1 at Rusche Strasse 59 (from the station around the corner to the right) is **Antistalinistische Aktion**, a museum of GDR memorabilia housed in the former executive suite of Erich Mielke, the Minister of State Security (open Wednesday to Sunday from 2 to 5 pm, admission DM 5). On the evening of 15 January 1990 some 50,000 demonstrators gathered outside this complex to protest ongoing Stasi activities. As they entered the compound, the crowd was attracted to the modern building with the gold-coloured windows near Haus 1, the only brightly lit building at the time. Stasi agents incited the mob to break into the building by throwing thousands of old currency declaration forms collected from tourists out the upper windows. Inside the demonstrators found stocks of imported liquor and cigarettes, the Stasi bowling alley and recreational facilities, etc. Meanwhile Stasi officers in the foreign intelligence centre, the tall, well-protected buildings directly above the U-Bahn station, had time to destroy their documents. There isn't a lot to see in the museum but it's fun to wander around this complex, until recently one of the most tightly guarded of its kind in the world.

Continue east on the same U-Bahn line to

Berlin-Lichtenberg. The **Socialists' Memorial** (Gedenkstätte der Sozialisten) at Friedrichsfelde Cemetery is a couple of blocks north-east of the station up Gudrun Strasse. Here Rosa Luxemburg, Karl Liebknecht, Ernst Thälmann, Wilhelm Pieck, Walter Ulbricht and many other leading socialist revolutionaries are buried. This memorial was first created in 1926, destroyed by the Nazis in 1933 and rebuilt in 1951.

When you return from the cemetery, go into Berlin-Lichtenberg Railway Station and take the S-Bahn (not the U-Bahn) to Ahrensfelde and back to see **Marzahn**, the vast housing development built by the Communists in the 1980s. The huge apartment blocks separated by wide, lifeless roads flank this railway line for km after km – an impressive example of socialist living! What you won't notice from the train are the thin walls which allow the 170,000 residents to keep in close touch with their neighbours on all sides.

**Karlshorst to Köpenick** Take the S-Bahn in the direction of Erkner to Karlshorst Station to visit Berlin's most striking museum, housed in the building where the German high command signed the unconditional surrender on 8 May 1945. The **Soviet Army Museum** (open Tuesday to Friday from 9 am to 1 pm and 3 to 6 pm, Saturday from 9 am to 4 pm, Sunday from 9 am to 2 pm, closed the last Saturday of each month, admission free) is at the end of Fritz Schmenkel Strasse, about one km from the station. The captions are all in Russian, although German labels are sometimes tacked on below. Gruesome photos of executed Nazi war criminals culminate this amazingly explicit exhibition. The museum buffet downstairs is good. Don't be surprised if the Soviet soldiers on guard duty here offer to sell you part of their uniform! This fascinating museum may disappear in 1994 when the surrounding Soviet military base is to be closed, so see it while you can.

Reboard the S-Bahn at Karlshorst and ride four stops east to Berlin-Friedrichshagen.

Walk or take a tram three stops south on picturesque Bölsche Strasse to Seebad Friedrichshagen behind the Berliner Bürger Brau brewery (ask directions). From the excursion boat landing on the north-west side of the **Grosser Müggelsee**, Weisse Flotte ferries cross the lake to Rübezahl once or twice an hour from May to September (DM 2). If you'd rather walk there's a tunnel under the Müggelspree River at Seebad Friedrichshagen and a footpath along the lakeshore right around to Rübezahl where you'll find a large beer garden.

From Rübezahl walk south through the forest to the **Müggelturm**, a 30-metre-high tower (1961) you may climb for DM 1 for a sweeping view of forests, rivers and lakes – the best view in Berlin. This tower is on Kleiner Müggelberg (82 metres); Berlin's highest natural hill, Grosser Müggelberg (115 metres), is to the east.

Backtrack to Müggelheimer Damm, the busy highway you crossed near Rübezahl, and take bus No 169 north-west to Schloss Platz, Köpenick. The nearby **Applied Arts Museum**, or Kunstgewerbemuseum (closed Monday and Tuesday, admission DM 1), is housed in a Baroque palace built by the Dutch architect Rutger von Langerfeld between 1678 and 1688. This attractive museum near the junction of the Spree and Dahme rivers features a silver buffet service of 1698 from the Knights' Hall of the former Berlin City Palace.

Some souvenir shops around Berlin sell miniature Captain of Köpenick (Hauptmann von Köpenick) dolls based on local shoemaker Wilhelm Voigt, who, on the afternoon of 16 October 1906, dressed in a captain's uniform borrowed from a used-clothing shop and ordered a few soldiers to accompany him to Köpenick Town Hall. There Voigt arrested the mayor and forced the treasurer to turn over his cash holdings. The incident ended in failure as Voigt was unable to find the passport forms and official stamp that these authorities had previously refused him on the grounds that he was not eligible to work in Prussia. Ten days later Voigt was arrested and eventually sentenced to four

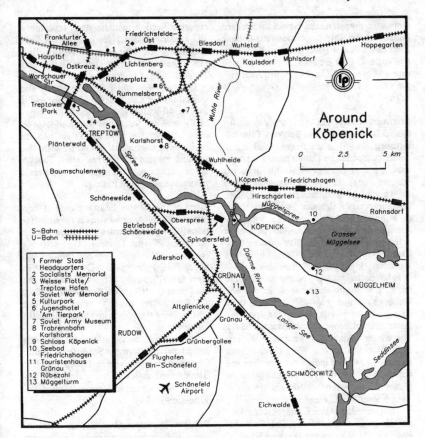

Around
Köpenick

S–Bahn ++++++++
U–Bahn ++++++++

1 Former Stasi
   Headquarters
2 Socialists' Memorial
3 Weisse Flotte/
   Treptow Hafen
4 Soviet War Memorial
5 Kulturpark
6 Jugendhotel
   'Am Tierpark'
7 Soviet Army Museum
8 Trabrennbahn
   Karlshorst
9 Schloss Köpenick
10 Seebad
   Friedrichshagen
11 Touristenhaus
   Grünau
12 Rübezahl
13 Müggelturm

years in jail, but this was later commuted to two years, and after his release the Hauptmann spent the rest of his life playing himself at circuses and fairs. He died in the city of Luxembourg in 1922. In the neo-Gothic **Köpenick Town Hall** (1904), the huge, red-brick building on Alt Köpenick a block from Schloss Köpenick, is a memorial room dedicated to the Hauptmann with the original safe and strongbox he raided. Ask the town-hall doorkeeper to let you in.

A few blocks west of Schloss Platz on Oberspree Strasse is Berlin-Spindlersfeld S-Bahn Station where you can board a train to Treptower Park. From the elevated S-Bahn station you'll see the long line of **Weisse Flotte** excursion boats docked along the riverside. A trip on one of these boats is an essential part of any visit to Berlin, so check them out and come back later if you don't go now (for more information on the Weisse Flotte, see the Activities section).

**Treptower Park** stretches south-east from the station. Its main feature is the **Soviet War Memorial** (1949). To get there walk up the river past all the boats till you see a large triumphal arch across the park beyond the busy highway on the right. This leads to the memorial. Five thousand Soviet soldiers are buried around this huge monument, built from the stones of Hitler's chancellery. The **Kulturpark**, East Berlin's amusement park (open May to mid-October from 11 am to 7 pm daily except Monday and Tuesday), is beyond.

**Charlottenburg** Built as a country estate for Queen Sophie Charlotte, **Schloss Charlottenburg** (1699) is an exquisite Baroque palace on Spandauer Damm three km northwest of Zoo Station (U-Bahn: Richard Wagner Platz). The palace was bombed in 1943 but has been completely rebuilt. Before the entrance is a Baroque equestrian statue of Sophie's husband, Frederick I (1700). Along the River Spree behind the palace are extensive French and English gardens (free admission), while inside the many buildings are an important group of museums.

In the central building below the dome are the former living quarters of Sophie and Frederick, which may only be seen on a 45-minute tour with a German-speaking guide (closed Monday, admission DM 7). The winter chambers of Frederick William II, upstairs in the New Wing (1746) to the east, may be visited individually on the same ticket. The **Romantic Art Collection** of the National Gallery is housed downstairs in this wing (closed Monday, admission free).

The combined palace ticket includes three buildings in the gardens. The **Schinkel Pavilion** (1825) was the summer house of Frederick William III. Farther back by the river is the **Belvedere** (1790), a Rococo teahouse which now houses a collection of Berlin porcelain. The neoclassical **Mausoleum** (1810) on the other side of the gardens contains the tombs of several kings and queens (closed in winter).

In addition to these sights, three branches of the State Museum at Charlottenburg should not be missed (all closed Friday and free admission). The **Museum of Prehistory** occupies the west wing of the palace. Across the street at the beginning of Schloss Strasse are the Egyptian and Antiquities museums. The **Egyptian Museum** has a superb collection, including the 14th century BC bust of Queen Nefertiti from Tell el-Amarna. The **Museum of Antiquities** (1859) has objects from ancient Greece and Rome displayed on four floors.

Huge crowds are often waiting for the guided tour of Charlottenburg Palace and it may be difficult to get a ticket. This is especially true on weekends and holidays so come another day. If you can't get into the main palace content yourself with the façades, gardens and free museums. Though the all-inclusive ticket is good value there's plenty to see without paying.

**West of the Centre** Four km west of Zoo Station at a major crossroads is the **International Congress Centre** on Messe Damm (U-Bahn: Kaiser Damm). This striking complex nicknamed *Das Superding* (The Super Thing) cost a billion Deutschmarks to erect in 1979. In the fairgrounds across the road from the ICC is the **Funkturm** (1926), a 138-metre-high tower you may ascend for DM 5. Only the police and taxi radios still use this tower.

Three stops west on the U1 towards Ruhleben is the **Olympic Stadium** (U-Bahn: Olympia-Stadion) where Hitler watched Black American Jesse Owens steal the show at the 1936 Olympic Games (open daily, admission DM 1).

**Dahlem Museum** One Berlin museum worth all the others combined is the **Dahlem Museum**, Lans Strasse 8 (U-Bahn: Dahlem-Dorf, closed Monday, admission free). Here is kept the better part of the former Prussian art collections amassed by Frederick the Great, evacuated from Museum Island during WW II and never returned to East Berlin. This fantastic museum full of old master paintings, sculpture, ethnographical exhibits, and Indian, Oriental and Islamic art will knock you over. Arrive early in the morning and plan to spend the day there. There's a cafeteria downstairs in the museum, or you can have a picnic lunch on the grass outside.

A couple of blocks away is the **Botanical**

**Garden**, Konigin Luise Strasse 6-8 (open daily, DM 2.50 admission), which opened in 1903. The **Botanical Museum** (closed Monday, admission free) is just outside the garden.

**Spandau to Wannsee** Take the U7 U-Bahn in the direction of Rathaus Spandau to Zitadelle. There's no charge to enter the grounds of **Spandau Citadel** (1594), one-time Askanian castle and Prussian fortress, which once guarded the junction of the Havel and Spree rivers, still important trade routes. Tickets (DM 1.50) are required to visit the museum (closed Monday) in the gatehouse and climb the 154 steps of Julius Tower (1160).

Cross the Havel just west of the citadel and explore **Spandau village** which manages to retain a medieval air despite the trendy shops and department stores. **St Nicholas Church**, where elector Joachim II consented to the first Lutheran communion in 1539, is just north of Markt square.

The Linden Ufer/Spandau landing below the bridge over the Havel, three blocks south-east of Markt, is an important departure point for tour boats to Tegel, Pfaueninsel, Wannsee (DM 7) and Potsdam. The main shipping route from Western Germany to Poland passes this point and you'll see many large Polish cargo boats tied up waiting to go through the locks. The Oder-Havel Canal was built from 1905 to 1914.

From Rathaus Spandau at the south-west end of the village take bus No 134 (towards Gutshof Glienicke) south to Kladow. Halfway down you pass **Helle Berge** on the right, a good hiking area. Get off at Ritterfeld Damm a few stops beyond the British air base – ask the bus driver for the *BVG-Personenschiffahrt*. The Kladow ferry landing is at the bottom of the hill below the old church (ask).

The passenger ferry to Wannsee leaves Brücke III at Kladow hourly at 31 minutes past the hour all year and the fare is a regular BVG transit ticket, with transfers possible (all transit passes accepted). The 15-minute

trip across the **Havel River** is quite beautiful with small sailing boats all around. You pass a large bathing establishment by the shore. **Wannsee** is West Berlin's smartest summer resort, the departure point for many excursion boats (S-Bahn: Wannsee).

Take double-decker bus No 116 west from Wannsee to Glienicker Brücke. Here you can cross the ironically named **Brücke der Einheit** (Bridge of Unity) into Potsdam. The two Germanys once exchanged captured spies on this iron bridge erected in 1909. Overlooking the bridge is **Schloss Glienicke** (closed Monday), the summer residence of Prince Carl von Preussen from 1824 until his death in 1883 and the finest artistic ensemble of Berlin classicism and romanticism in West Berlin. Admission is charged to the palace but the enchanting wooded park is free.

There's a lovely walk along the Havel from the bridge to **Pfaueninsel** and beyond. Opportunities to lose yourself in the wooded hills here are many. All bus lines in this area run to Bahnhof Wannsee where you can catch the S-Bahn back to central Berlin.

From Glienicker Brücke you could walk to Potsdam's Cecilienhof Palace in only 10 minutes (take a sharp right after the bridge and continue straight ahead beside the lake).

**Death Camp** A visit to at least one Nazi concentration camp should be included in any trip to Europe, and Sachsenhausen (closed Monday, open all year, admission free) near Berlin is among the most convenient. The S-Bahn runs to Oranienburg from Ostkreuz Station every 20 minutes and it's only a 15-minute walk from Oranienburg Station to the camp. A map is posted outside the station or just ask anyone for the **Nationale Mahn- und Gedenkstätte**. All Berlin transit tickets and passes are valid for this 45-minute train ride north from Berlin.

Sachsenhausen was an SS training camp where personnel for some 2000 other Nazi concentration camps around Europe was trained. This 'mother camp' opened in 1933, the same year the Nazis took power. Of the 200,000 people held at Sachsenhausen, over

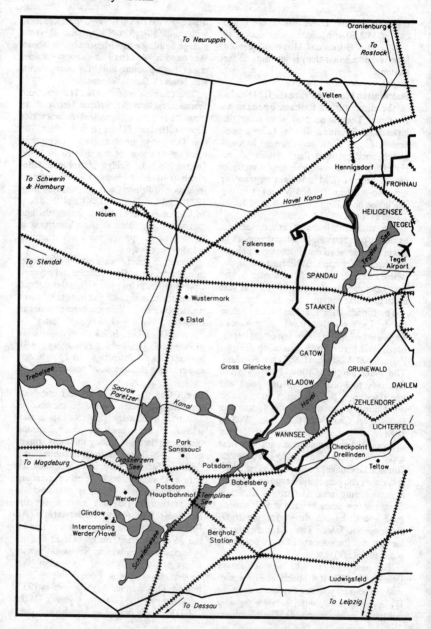

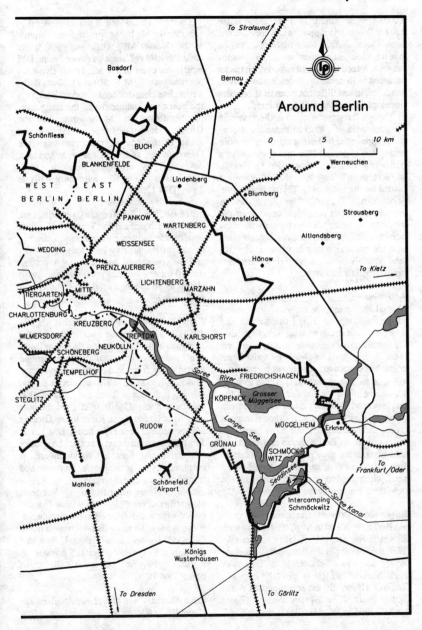

Around Berlin

100,000 were killed. In 1941 alone some 18,000 Soviet prisoners of war were executed here. One bizarre feature of Sachsenhausen was the 'shoe-testing track' where 150 prisoners were forced to walk 40 km a day on tracks surfaced with cement, cinder, stone, gravel, sand, etc, to test different types of shoe soles developed by a 'research institution'.

Though the gas chambers and crematoria are preserved, it's hard to sense the barbarism represented by Sachsenhaussen without seeing the historical film that is shown in a hall here several times a day (DM 1). Though in German, it's easy to follow – times are posted on the entry gate. There are also two photo exhibits, one on the Resistance in various European countries, another on the history of the camp. Unfortunately the captions are only in German. A souvenir shop near the entrance sells a brochure in English (and possibly some leftover GDR commemorative medals and stamps).

## Activities

Central Berlin may be crowded with roads, office buildings and apartments but the south-east and south-west sections of the city are surprisingly green with forests, rivers and lakes. From April to October tourist boats cruise the waterways, calling at picturesque villages, parks and castles. If you're looking for an organised tour of Berlin, skip all the bus tours (which aren't much different from those offered in dozens of other European cities) and board one of the many excursion boats unique to Berlin. Food and drink are sold aboard but they're moderately expensive, so take along something to nibble or sip. Tickets used to be difficult to obtain but now there's no problem.

**Spree River Cruises** The Spree River crosses Berlin from east to west, connecting with an extensive network of lakes and canals. Take the S-Bahn in the direction of Königs-Wusterhausen or Schönefeld to Treptower Park Station, which is directly opposite Treptow Hafen, six km south-east of Alexander Platz. The Berlin Weisse Flotte (☎ 265-3266 in West Berlin) is based here.

Daily at 11 am and 3 pm from April to October the big boats operate from Treptow to the Grosser Müggelsee and back, a trip called the *Müggelseefahrt* (three hours, DM 8.50). An even better trip is the five-hour *Seerundfahrt* (DM 12.50) at 11.30 am daily, a complete circuit of south-eastern Berlin via the Spree and Dahme rivers, the Langersee, the Seddinsee, the Müggelspree and the Grosser Müggelsee. One of the prettiest areas is the Müggelspree between the Dämeritz-See and the Grosser Müggelsee, covered during this trip. There's also a four-hour return trip to Charlottenburg daily at 2 pm (DM 12.50).

Same day tickets are sold at the ticket office labelled 'Tagesverkauf' (offerings are listed on a board). The 'Vorverkauf' ticket windows sell advance tickets only. These big excursion boats carry hundreds of passengers so you should have no trouble getting on. All these trips are a great introduction to Berlin as you lounge on deck – highly recommended.

**Canal & River Boats** 'Spreefahrt' (☎ 394 4954), in a kiosk by the riverside behind the Kongresshalle in Tiergarten (S-Bahn: Unter den Linden), offers circular cruises around Berlin daily from mid-April to September. The morning cruise at 9.30 am circles central Berlin via the Spree River and Landwehrkanal (three hours, DM 10). At 1 pm the boat sails right up the Spree River to the Grosser Müggelsee and back (four hours, DM 12). A 1½-hour evening trip at 6 pm (DM 8) passes Westhafen and Schloss Charlottenburg. A commentary is provided in German and refreshments are sold on board.

Similar trips are offered by Reederei Heinz Riedel (☎ 693 4646) whose kiosk is just downstream from the Kongresshalle. From April to October its boat travels down the Spree to the Landwehrkanal, then east through a lock and 'under the bridges' to Kreuzberg two or three times daily (three hours, DM 10).

**Lake Boats** From Tegel to Potsdam the Havel River widens between the forests into a picturesque series of lakes. Most of the large tour boats are based at Wannsee (S-Bahn: Wannsee) and Tegel (U-Bahn: Tegel), although it's also possible to board at Kladow, Spandau and Potsdam.

The Stern und Kreisschiffahrt (☎ 81 0004) operates three lines several times daily all summer. Line 1 runs from Wannsee to Potsdam via Pfaueninsel and Glienicker Brücke from April to October (one hour, DM 6.50). Line 2 operates from April to October from Wannsee on a seven-lake return trip (two hours, DM 9). Line three is a grand tour between Tegel and Wannsee (from mid-April to September, two hours, DM 8.50).

Other companies such as Reederverband (☎ 331 5017), Reederei Bruno Winkler (☎ 391 7010) and Reederei Triebler (☎ 331 5414) also operate on these routes and their schedules and prices are sometimes more convenient, so check.

## Places to Stay

**Camping** The camping facilities in Berlin are not good. There are several camping grounds in West Berlin charging DM 6.40 per person plus DM 5 per tent but they're far from the centre, crowded with caravans and often full. They cater almost exclusively to permanent residents who live in their caravans all year, and although you may be admitted if you're polite and persistent, they aren't really set up to receive casual tourists. For more information call the German Camping Club (☎ 030-24 6071) during business hours.

The only camping ground convenient to public transport is *Campingplatz Kohlhasenbrück* on Stubenrauch Strasse in a peaceful location overlooking the Griebnitzsee in the far south-west corner of Berlin. Bus No 118 from Wannsee S-Bahn Station runs directly there. If the gate is locked when you arrive, just hang around until someone with a key arrives, then search for the manager in the caravan near the gate.

If Kohlhasenbrück is full you'll have to walk two km east along the Teltowkanal to *Campingplatz Dreilinden* at Albrechts-Teerofen.

*Campingplatz Haselhorst* is near Spandau two km north-west of Haselhorst U-Bahn Station. Walk north on Daum Strasse to Pulvermuhlen Weg and then west to the canal.

At last report the *Krossin Lake Intercamping*, two km beyond Schmöckwitz in the far south-east corner of East Berlin, had gone bankrupt, so check with the tourist office below the TV tower before heading out there.

The best camping around Berlin is at Potsdam, so turn to that section if you're keen to unroll the tent.

**Hostels – East Berlin** The two youth hostels in East Berlin are now privately run and no longer connected with the IYHF, but their prices are about the same as those charged by the hostels in West Berlin, and your chances of getting a bed without reserving weeks in advance are infinitely better. You don't need a YHA card and everyone is welcome. For an advance reservation at either of the two write to: Jugend-, Touristik- und Sport-Hotel GmbH, Franz-Mett-Strasse 7, 1136 Berlin (☎ 510 0114, fax 512 4040).

The 747-bed *Jugendhotel 'Am Tierpark'* (☎ 512 0032), Franz-Mett-Strasse 7 (U-Bahn: Tierpark), offers rooms at DM 45/60 single/double without bath, DM 60/90 with bath, or DM 30 per person in a four-bed dormitory, breakfast included. Lunch and dinner are available for DM 7 each. It's open all year and usually has free beds. Across the street is the East Berlin zoo.

One of the nicest places to stay in Berlin is the *Touristenhaus Grünau* (☎ 681 4422), Dahme Strasse 6 in a quiet, attractive location beside the Dahme River in the quaint little town of Grünau. Take the S-Bahn to Berlin-Grünau, then any tram two stops towards Köpenick. It offers 150 beds in two, three, four and five-bed rooms at DM 25 per person including breakfast. Though on the far south-east side of Berlin, transport to the city centre from here is good and there are hiking possibilities in the nearby Berlin City Forest (Berliner Stadtwald). There's usually space, though groups occasionally book out the whole place, so try calling first.

**Hostels – West Berlin** The three youth hostels in West Berlin fill up fast on weekends and all summer, so call before going out. Until early July the hostels are often fully booked by noisy school groups. Although the hostels are open to anyone, priority is given to those under 27 years of age. If you aren't already a YHA member you'll have to buy an International Guest Card for a one-off payment of DM 30 (it can also be paid in six daily instalments of DM 5). These cards are sold at the hostels. None of the hostels offers cooking facilities but breakfast is included in the overnight charge; lunch is DM 5.90, dinner DM 7.50. The hostels stay open all day throughout the year.

The only hostel within walking distance of the city centre is the 364-bed *Berlin Youth Guest House* (☎ 261 1097), Kluck Strasse 3 (U-Bahn: Kurfürsten Strasse), which costs DM 22 for juniors, DM 25 for seniors.

The ultramodern 264-bed *Wannsee Youth Guest House* (☎ 803 2034), Bade Weg 1 on the corner of Kronprinzessinen Weg, is in a pleasant lake-front location on Grosse Wannsee near the beach. Although 15 km south-west of the centre, this hostel is only an eight-minute walk from Nikolassee S-Bahn Station, with fast commuter trains to Zoo Station and Friedrich Strasse. It's also DM 22 for juniors, DM 25 for seniors, and a DM 20 key deposit is required.

The *Ernst Reuter Youth Hostel* (☎ 404 1610), Hermsdorfer Damm 48, is in the far north of West Berlin. Take the U-Bahn to Tegel, then bus No 125 right to the door. The 110 beds are DM 17.90 for juniors, DM 20.90 for seniors. Try here first if you're arriving without a reservation.

The only sure way of getting into one of the West Berlin hostels is to write to the Deutsches Jugend-Herbergswerk (☎ 030-262 3024), Tempelhofer Ufer 32, 1000 Berlin 61, several weeks in advance. State precisely which nights you'll be in Berlin and enclose an International Postal Reply Coupon (available at any post office) so they can send back confirmation. You must give an address where the confirmation can be sent to. Otherwise you could just try calling a hostel to ask if they'll reserve a place for you.

The *Jugendgästehaus am Zoo* (☎ 312 9410), Hardenberg Strasse 9a three blocks from Zoo Station, charges DM 40/70 single/double, DM 26 dormitory, DM 6 extra for breakfast. It's limited to people under 27 but the location is great if you get in.

The *Jugendhotel International* (☎ 262 3081), Bernburger Strasse 28 (S-Bahn: Anhalter Bahnhof), has rooms at DM 45/80 single/double including breakfast. When things are busy you could have to share a three, four or five-bed room at about DM 36 per person. It's often fully booked by school groups.

*Hotel Transit* (☎ 785 5051), Hagelberger Strasse 53-54 (U-Bahn: Mehring Damm), a youth hotel crowded with young travellers, offers 120 beds at DM 55/85 single/double or DM 30 per person in a six-bed dorm, a big breakfast included. All rooms have a shower. The Transit sometimes fills up with school groups from March to May and in September and October, but in the other months it should have free beds.

The *Studenthotel Berlin* (☎ 784 6720), Meininger Strasse 10 (U-Bahn: Schöneberg), operates like a youth hostel but you don't need a card. Bed and breakfast is DM 31 per person in a double, DM 29 per person in a quad. Call first as it's often full.

From mid-July to mid-September you can sleep in a big tent at the *International Jugendcamp Fliesstal* (☎ 433 8640) in northern West Berlin. From U-Bahn Tegel take bus No 222 (towards Lübers) four stops to the corner of Ziekow Strasse and Waldmannsluster Damm. The tents are behind the Jugendgästehaus Tegel, a huge red-brick building opposite the bus stop. Beds in large communal tents are DM 7 per person (blankets and foam mattresses provided) and check-in is after 5 pm (no curfew). Officially this place is only for those aged 14 to 23, but they don't turn away foreigners who are a little older. The maximum stay is three nights. Food can be purchased at the camp and a cheap breakfast is sold in the morning. Sit around the campfire at night.

If all else fails there's the *Bahnhofsmission* at Zoo Station which provides dorm beds for DM 15 (no breakfast). The office is on Jebens Strasse below the train tracks just outside the station. It's there mostly to help down-and-outs. Ring the bell beside the door.

**Private Rooms** Your best bet for private rooms is the *'Zimmervermittlung'* counter at Berlin-Tourist (open weekdays from 10 am to 6 pm, Saturdays from 10 am to 5 pm) in the Europäisches Reisebüro on Alexander Platz. It has rooms in East Berlin for DM 15 to DM 25 per person and can also reserve hotel rooms throughout Eastern Germany.

Berlin-Information at the TV tower (U-Bahn and S-Bahn: Alexander Platz) sometimes has private rooms at DM 30 per person, though they're often full.

The Verkehrsamt Berlin tourist office in the Europa Centre (U-Bahn and S-Bahn: Zoologischer Garten) will find you a private room for DM 45 per person (minimum stay two nights) plus DM 3 commission.

If these fail, you can turn to one of the *Mitwohnzentrale* listed in the following section, which will always be able to arrange a private room for you.

**Long-Term Rentals** If you'd like to spend some time in Berlin, look for someone willing to sublet their apartment. Many Berliners take off for extended holidays and are only too happy to have the bills paid while they're gone. Check the *Wohnungen* classified section in *Zitty* or *Zweite Hand*, or visit one of the agencies called *Mitwohnzentrale* which arrange private subrentals for periods as short as a day, week or month. They charge 10% of the monthly rental rate or DM 3 per person per day for short stays. If you're staying for under a month, you'll end up sharing a flat with others, a good way to meet people.

Take the escalator up to the *Mitwohnzentrale* (☎ 88 3051) on the 2nd floor of the Ku'damm-Eck shopping arcade at Kurfürsten Damm 227 near Zoo Station. It has apartments which cost DM 35/60/80 single/double/triple per day, plus longer-term, cheaper rooms.

*Mitwohnzentrale Charlottenburg* (☎ 324 3031), Sybel Strasse 53 (U-Bahn: Adenauer Platz), has rooms for DM 35 a day per person (minimum stay two nights) or DM 500 a month. It's open Monday from 9 am to 8 pm, Tuesday to Friday from 9 am to 7 pm and Saturday from 10 am to 6 pm.

*Mitwohnzentrale Kreuzberg* (☎ 786 2003), 3rd floor, Mehring Damm 72 (U-Bahn: Platz der Luftbrücke), has rooms for DM 15 to DM 30 daily per person. The monthly rate for a room in a shared flat is DM 200 to DM 500 per person. Whole flats are harder to locate (up to DM 500 plus 20%). It's open weekdays from 10 am to 7 pm, Saturday from 11 am to 4 pm.

**Cheaper Hotels – East Berlin** There's a cluster of relatively inexpensive hotels on the streets just north of Friedrich Strasse Railway Station. It's usually easier to get a room at these than at similar establishments in West Berlin and the location is great, just minutes on foot from the theatres and museums around Unter den Linden.

The friendly *Christliches Hospiz* (☎ 280 5145), August Strasse 82, has 70 rooms at DM 50/80 single/double without bath, DM 70/100 with bath, breakfast included. This clean, five-storey hotel run by the Verband Christlicher Hospize of the Protestant church is perhaps the nicest in East Berlin, if you get a room.

Part of the same chain is the 110-room *Hospiz am Bahnhof Friedrich Strasse* (☎ 280 5162), Albrecht Strasse 8, which is also DM 50/80 single/double with shared bath, breakfast included.

The 70-room *Adria Hotel* (☎ 282 5451), Friedrich Strasse 134, charges DM 70/120 single/double, breakfast included. This old, six-storey hotel has only rooms with shared bath.

The family-operated, nine-room *Hotel Merkur* (☎ 282 8297), at Wilhelm Pieck

Strasse 156, is DM 78/114 single/double with bath and breakfast. It's a little overpriced but should have rooms.

A good medium-priced choice is the 57-room *Hotel Newa* (☎ 282 5461), Invaliden Strasse 115, which costs DM 65/120 single/double with shared bath, DM 150 double with bath, breakfast included.

Other places to try include: the *Hotel Neues Tor* (☎ 229 7090), Invaliden Strasse 102 (U-Bahn: Nordbahnhof); *Hotel Novalis* (☎ 282 4008), Novalis Strasse 5 off Wilhelm Pieck Strasse; *Hotel-Pension Berliner Hof* (☎ 282 7478), Friedrich Strasse 113a at Oranienburger Strasse; and *Hotel Märkischer Hof* (☎ 282 7155), directly across the square from the Berliner Hof.

If you're staying in this area you can get a good stand-up breakfast weekdays at the *Bäckerei Jürgen Lange*, Linien Strasse 130 (U-Bahn: Oranienburger Tor).

Though rather out of the way, *Gästehaus 19, ARWOGE*, Storkower Strasse 14 (S-Bahn to Ernst Thälmann Park, then walk 10 minutes), is a modern, eight-storey tourist hotel with 128 rooms that cost DM 50/80 single/double including breakfast. The toilet and shower are shared by each cluster of four rooms in this former workers' residence. For reservations call 436 5387 during business hours or 439 4103 at other times. The tourist office below the TV tower can book you in here.

**Cheaper Hotels – West Berlin** Inexpensive *Hotel Pensionen* do exist in West Berlin but they're all small, plain and uncommercial, so expect no luxury and try calling first. Prices begin around DM 50/80 single/double for a room with shared bath. Breakfast is usually DM 8 to DM 15 extra, although a light breakfast of tea or coffee, bread, butter and jam is sometimes included in the rate. The tourist office in the Europa Center will refuse to book any of the places mentioned here, so you'll just have to start calling or walking.

There are several budget places west of Zoo Station and north of the Ku'damm: *Pension Knesebeck* (☎ 31 7255), Knesebeck Strasse 86-87 just off Savigny Platz; *Pension Centrum* (☎ 31 6153), Kant Strasse 31; *Pension Niebuhr* (☎ 324 9595), Niebuhr Strasse 74; *Hotel Pension Derby* (☎ 324 3418), Wieland Strasse 18; *Pension Alt-Lietzow*, Mommsen Strasse 11; *Pension Bachmann* (☎ 324 4488), Mommsen Strasse 27; and *Hotel Pension Majesty* (☎ 323 2061), Mommsen Strasse 55.

The *Hotel Charlottenburger Hof* (☎ 324 4819), Stuttgarter Platz 14 above Café Voltaire (open 24 hours) outside Charlottenburg S-Bahn Station, is larger and farther away and thus more likely to have space.

Two similar hotels south of the Ku'damm are *Hotelpension Pariser Eck* (☎ 881 2145), Pariser Strasse 19, and *Pension Elton* (☎ 883 6155), Pariser Strasse 9.

There are five budget pensions in the building at Lietzenburger Strasse 76 on the corner of Uhland Strasse. These establishments have no connection with the sordid sex clubs downstairs. *Hotel-Pension May* on the 4th floor is well above the action.

Three places just south of Breitscheid Platz are *Pension Riga* (☎ 211 1223), Ranke Strasse 23, *Hotelpension Nürnberger Eck* (☎ 24 5371), Nürnberger Strasse 24a, and *Pension Fischer* in the same building as the Nürnberger Eck.

If you'd rather stay out in Kreuzberg (U-Bahn: Mehring Damm), try *Hotelpension Südwest* (☎ 785 8033), Yorck Strasse 80, or *Pension Kreuzberg* (☎ 251 1362), Grossbeeren Strasse 64.

**Expensive Hotels** If you want a luxury hotel you'll do better at one of the Interhotels in East Berlin which are closer to the museums, theatres, and mass transit. If you don't mind socialist-modern architecture, their prices are also lower than those asked at Western chain hotels such as West Berlin's Inter-Continental.

The 305-room *Hotel Unter den Linden* (☎ 220 0311), near Friedrich Strasse Railway Station, charges DM 150/240 single/double, while the 880-room *Hotel Stadt Berlin* (☎ 219 4333) on Alexander Platz – the largest hotel in Berlin – is DM 150/225 single/double. The 346-room *Hotel Berolina*

(☎ 210 9541), at Karl Marx Allee 31 (U-Bahn: Schilling Strasse), charges DM 140/155 single/double for a small room, DM 235 double for a large room. This three-star hotel is less comfortable and convenient than the other two (both four-stars). Prices at all these include bath and breakfast.

One up-market West Berlin hotel deserves special attention. The 22 rooms at *Riehmers Hofgarten* (☎ 78 1011), Yorck Strasse 83 in Kreuzberg (U-Bahn: Mehring Damm), cost DM 156/196 single/double, including a big breakfast. Bus No 119 from the Ku'damm passes the door. This elegant, eclectic edifice erected in 1892 will delight romantics and it's a fun area in which to stay.

### Places to Eat

There's a restaurant for every cuisine under the sun in Berlin – literally thousands of them. Greek, Yugoslav and Italian restaurants serve good food at reasonable prices. Most restaurants post their menu outside and daily specials are listed on a blackboard. A cooked lunch or dinner at an unpretentious restaurant will cost DM 17 if you order carefully. The price includes tax and service. Tipping is not obligatory although you can round your bill up to the next Deutschmark. Do this as you pay rather than leave money on the table.

At those prices it's unlikely you'll wish to sit down to a meal more than once a day. Substantial snacks are available at the many *schnell Imbiss* stands around the city. In addition to German stand-bys like *Rostbratwurst* and *Currywurst*, most *Imbiss* also have *döner kebap*, a filling Turkish sandwich of lamb cut from a vertical spit and stuffed into a big piece of pita bread with lots of salad (DM 4). Many *Imbiss* also offer half barbecued chickens (DM 5).

One Berlin treat to get acquainted with right away is a hot cup of DM 1.10 coffee dispensed by a coin-operated machine at many Eduscho and Tchibo outlets around Berlin. You have to drink standing up and this deal isn't offered on evenings or weekends (even though the shop itself may be open), but the throngs of local people tell you

you're onto something good. You'll soon learn to recognise the Eduscho and Tchibo trademarks from afar, but not all outlets offer this service.

**Breakfast** Breakfast cafés are a Berlin institution catering to the city's late risers. In addition to canned music in a genteel setting you can get a filling brunch of yoghurt, eggs, meat, cheese, bread, butter and jam for around DM 10.50 (coffee extra). Some of the breakfasts are huge, so consider sharing one between two people. They also make a good lunch.

Typical of the genre are *Café Bleibtreu*, Bleibtreu Strasse 45 (S-Bahn: Savigny Platz; breakfast from 9.30 am to 2 pm), and *Schalander*, Olivaer Platz 4 (U-Bahn: Adenauer Platz; breakfast until 5 pm). The *Zillemarkt*, Bleibtreu Strasse 48, also does breakfasts and has a special lunch menu from noon to 1 pm on weekdays.

*Schwarzes Café*, Kant Strasse 148 near Zoo Station, serves breakfast any time and is open around the clock from 11 am Wednesday until 3 am Monday. This is one place to get off the street if you happen to roll into Berlin in the middle of the night.

On weekdays from 7 to 11 am you can get breakfast at the *Kleine Konditorei am Metropol Theater* opposite the exit from Friedrich Strasse Railway Station.

**Eating Cheap** There are lots of places to eat near Alexander Platz. Next to the tourist office below the TV tower is a basic cafeteria (open daily from 7 am to 6 pm). Better meals with regular table service can be had at *Gaststätte Alextreff* (daily from 11 am to 4 pm), upstairs between the elevated tracks and the Rathauspassage. There are many places to consume a quick snack standing up below the Rathauspassage.

Substantial, inexpensive meals are consumed in the food halls of the large West Berlin department stores, KaDeWe and Wertheim. At KaDeWe (U-Bahn: Wittenberg Platz) the top floor is the 'gourmet floor'. At the *Club Culinar* in the basement at Wertheim, Kurfürsten Damm 232 near the

Ku'damm-Eck, you can get a good bowl of soup or half a chicken for a lower-than-average price. There's also a supermarket, café and a small wine bar with half a dozen Berliners in very good spirits down there.

*Pizzeria Amigo*, Joachimstaler Strasse 39-40 near Zoo Station (open daily from 11 am to 1 am), serves a wicked plate of spaghetti Napoli or a pizza Margherita for only DM 5. It's self-service but the food is good and there's a fine place to sit down.

The *Athener Grill*, Kurfürsten Damm 156 (U-Bahn: Adenauer Platz), has spaghetti, pizza, steaks, salads, Greek dishes and big mugs of draught beer at the lowest prices in town. It's also self-service but there are plenty of tables. It's open daily from 11 am to 4 am.

**Subsidised Meals** If even these cheap places are too expensive, you can enjoy a hot subsidised meal (DM 5 to DM 10) in a government cafeteria. They're open weekdays only and you clear your own table.

If you have a valid student card there's the *Mensa* of Technical University, Hardenberg Strasse 34 three blocks from Zoo Station (open weekdays from 8 am to 5 pm).

The *Kantine* downstairs in Rathaus Charlottenburg, Otto-Suhr-Allee 100 close to Schloss Charlottenburg (U-Bahn: Richard Wagner Platz), serves nonemployees from 2 to 2.30 pm only. It's in the basement inside the building, not the expensive Ratskeller outside. What's available is written on a blackboard at the far end of the counter. This is a good place to have lunch after seeing Schloss Charlottenburg.

The *Rathaus Casino* on the 10th floor of Rathaus Kreuzberg, Yorck Strasse 4-11 (U-Bahn: Mehring Damm; open weekdays from 7.30 am to 3 pm), offers cheap lunch specials and great views. Everyone is welcome. (Nearby at Yorck Strasse 14 is an Eduscho outlet dispensing cheap coffee on weekdays.)

Also good is the *Kantine* in the unemployment insurance office *(Arbeitsamt)* at Charlotten Strasse 90 (U-Bahn: Koch Strasse; open weekdays from 9 am to 1 pm).

Just walk straight in and take the lift on the left up to the 5th floor.

Another unemployment office with a *Kantine* on the 5th floor (open weekdays from 8.30 am to 12.30 pm) is at Müller Strasse 16 just outside Wedding U-Bahn Station. (In fact, almost any Arbeitsamt you see in West Berlin will have a cheap *Kantine*.)

The cafeteria in the *State Library* (closed Sunday) opposite the New National Gallery in Tiergarten offers soup, salad and sandwiches, plus hot specials. You have to check your bag (free) to get in.

There's a reasonable self-service restaurant straight back inside the office building at Unter den Linden 38 (open weekdays from 8 am to 2 pm) – convenient for sightseers.

**East Berlin** One of the easiest places to experience a typical German meal is the *Ratskeller* (daily 11 am to 1 am) below Berlin City Hall just south of the TV tower (S-Bahn and U-Bahn: Alexander Platz). Prices are reasonable but the service tends to be slow.

More expensive is the *Gastmahl des Meeres*, on the corner of Spandauer Strasse and Karl Liebknecht Strasse (S-Bahn: Marx-Engels-Platz), which specialises in seafood such as whole trout (charged by weight) and eel.

*Zur letzten Instanz*, Waisen Strasse 14-16 (U-Bahn: Kloster Strasse), is a typical Berlin tavern (built in 1525) on a backstreet behind the Haus der jungen Talente south-east of Alexander Platz. Meals are served. The place got its present name 150 years ago when a newly divorced couple came in from the nearby courthouse with their witnesses for a few drinks. By the time they were ready to leave they'd made up and decided to remarry the next day, at which one of those present exclaimed, 'This is the court of last resort!'

The *Bärenschenke Bierbar*, Friedrich Strasse 124 (U-Bahn: Oranienburger Tor), is an unpretentious local pub serving meals from 10 am to 11 pm (closed Monday). Specialities include *Schlachteplatte mit Blut und Leberwurst* (a mixed meat plate typical of Berlin), *Wildsuppe* (venison soup) and *Gebackener Camembert* (fried cheese). There's a nice long bar here where you can chat with Berliners as you swill your beer.

**West Berlin** Since most West Berlin restaurants offer exotic cuisine, finding authentic German fare takes a little doing. *Beiz*, Schlüter Strasse 38 off the Ku'damm (open daily from 6 pm to 2 am), is rather expensive. *Dicke Wirtin*, Carmer Strasse 9 off Savigny Platz, is an old German pub offering goulash soup and beer. In summer make for *Loretta's Biergarten*, Lietzenburger Strasse 89 behind the ferris wheel. Stein of pils in hand at a long wooden table out the back, you'd swear you were in Bavaria.

More out of the way but full of atmosphere is *Zum Ambrosius*, Einem Strasse 14 (U-Bahn: Nollendorf Platz). The specials are marked on blackboards outside this rustic pub/restaurant. If Zum Ambrosius fails to please, try *Spatz*, a block away at Kurfürsten Strasse 56, a basement pub and steakhouse (opens at 6.30 pm daily except Sunday). There's a second Zum Ambrosius at Kurfürsten Strasse 40 just outside Kurfürsten Strasse U-Bahn Station.

**Cafés** *The* place for coffee and cakes is *Café Kranzler* (open daily till midnight), on the corner of Kurfürsten Damm and Joachimstaler Strasse near Zoo Station. Look for the circular pavilion up on the roof.

Berlin's most elegant literary café is *Café Einstein*, Kurfürsten Strasse 58 (U-Bahn: Kurfürsten Strasse; open daily from 10 am to 2 am). This is a good place to go with friends if you want to talk.

The *Café zum Trichler*, Schiffbauer Damm 7 around the corner from the Berliner Ensemble (U-Bahn and S-Bahn: Friedrich Strasse), is a favourite hang-out for actors and the literary crowd. It opens at 5 pm.

A café for women only is *Extra Dry*, Mommsen Strasse 34 off Lewisham Strasse (U-Bahn: Adenauer Platz).

A counterculture café with real earthy atmosphere is *Seifen und Kosmetik*, Schliemann Strasse 21 (S-Bahn: Prenzlauer Allee).

A late-evening place to visit is *Café 'Arkade'*, Französische Strasse 25 near Platz der Akademie (U-Bahn: Französische Strasse), which stays open until midnight daily. Here you can get excellent Viennese coffee, ice cream or drinks in a pleasant relaxed atmosphere.

### Entertainment
**Musical Theatres** East Berlin beats West Berlin hands down as far as opera and operetta go and the best theatres are conveniently clustered near Friedrich Strasse Railway Station. The productions are lavish with huge casts, and the best seats cost less than half the same tickets in West Berlin. Some theatres (such as the Metropol) give students and pensioners a 50% discount on unsold tickets 30 minutes before the performance. All performances are listed in the monthly *Berlin Programm Magazin*, available at newsstands, hotels and tourist offices. Tickets to special events are available from the Festspielgalerie, Budapester Strasse 48 across from the Kaiser Wilhelm Memorial Church (open daily from noon to 7 pm). Many of the theatres take Monday evening off and close from mid-July to late August.

Good seats for performances on the same evening are usually obtainable, and unclaimed tickets are made available an hour before the performance. The best way to get in is simply to start making the rounds of the box offices at about 6 pm. If there's a big crowd of people waiting at one theatre, hurry on to the next. You're allowed to move to unoccupied, better seats just as the curtain is going up. Berlin's not stuffy so you can attend theatre and cultural events dressed as you please.

East Berlin's two opera houses are the *State Opera House*, Unter den Linden 7 (the box office is open Monday to Saturday from noon to 6 pm, Sunday from 2 to 6 pm), and the *Comic Opera* (Komische Oper), Behren Strasse 55-57 at the corner of Glinka Strasse (U-Bahn: Französische Strasse; the box office across the street opens Tuesday to Saturday from noon to 6 pm, tickets DM 3 to DM 45).

West Berlin's *Deutsche Oper* (1961), Bismarck Strasse 35 (U-Bahn: Deutsche Oper), is all glass and steel. Its box office opens Monday to Saturday from 11.30 am to 5.30 pm, Sunday from 10 am to 2 pm (tickets DM 10 to DM 125).

Musicals and operettas are presented at the *Metropol Theater*, Friedrich Strasse 101-102 directly in front of Friedrich Strasse Railway Station (box office opens Monday to Saturday from 10 am to 6 pm). It's not as famous as the State Opera or Comic Opera so tickets are easier to obtain – highly recommended! (Don't confuse this Metropol theatre with the Metropol disco in West Berlin.)

Seats are much more expensive at West Berlin's *Theater des Westens*, Kant Strasse 12 near Zoo Station (the box office across the street is open Tuesday to Saturday from noon to 6 pm, Sunday from 3 to 6 pm), which also features musicals, though this beautiful old theatre (1896) has style. It's hard to see from the cheap seats.

The new *Friedrichstadt Palast* (1984), Friedrich Strasse 107, offers vaudeville musical revues but it's often sold out (box office opens Tuesday to Saturday from noon to 3.30 pm and from 4 to 6.30 pm).

**Concert Halls** East Berlin's wonderfully restored *Schauspielhaus* is on Platz der Akademie (U-Bahn: Stadtmitte; box office opens Tuesday to Saturday from 2 to 6 pm).

All seats at West Berlin's *Philharmonie*, Matthaikirch Strasse 1 (U-Bahn: Kurfürsten Strasse, then bus No 148), are excellent, so just take the cheapest. Do try to hear at least one concert at the Philharmonie.

Other musical programmes are offered at the *School of Art Concert Hall*, Hardenberg Strasse 33 near Zoo Station (tickets sold Tuesday to Friday from 3 to 6.30 pm, Saturday from 11 am to 2 pm).

**Other Theatres** Even if your German is nonexistent, the *Berliner Ensemble*, Bertolt Brecht's original theatre, near the Friedrich Strasse Railway Station (box office opens Tuesday to Saturday from 11 am to 3.30 pm and from 4 to 6.30 pm), is worth attending for both the architecture and classic Brecht plays. Most of Brecht's works include music. *The Threepenny Opera*, Brecht's first great popular success, premiered here in 1928.

Share the joys and fantasies of childhood at the *Puppentheater*, Greifswalder Strasse 81-84 just outside Ernst Thälmann Park S-Bahn Station. Performances are often held on weekdays at 10 am and 3 pm, but check. Tickets are usually available at the door.

East Berlin's ultramodern *Zeiss Grossplanetarium* near Prenzlauer Allee S-Bahn Station offers programmes daily from Wednesday to Sunday at 3.30, 5 and 6.30 pm (admission DM 4).

**Cinemas** If you want to see a movie, go on Wednesday ('Cinema Day', or *Kinotag)* when tickets are half-price (DM 6). The *Filmzentrum Zoo Palast*, Hardenberg Strasse 29a near Zoo Station, contains nine cinemas (the film festival is held here) and there are many other movie houses along Kurfürsten Damm, but foreign films are dubbed into German. (If the film is being shown in the original language with German subtitles it will say 'O.m.U.' on the advertisement. If it's in English the ad will be marked 'engl. OF'.)

See movies in the original English at the *Odeon Theatre* (☎ 781 5667), Haupt Strasse 116 (U-Bahn: Innsbrucker Platz, or S-Bahn: Schöneberg). There are three shows daily.

The *Kurbel Cinema* (☎ 883 5325), Giesebrecht Strasse 4 off Kurfürsten Damm (U-Bahn: Adenauer Platz), also usually has at least one film in English.

The Original Version, Sesenheimer Strasse 17 (U-Bahn: Deutsche Oper), hires out movie videos in English if you have access to a viewer.

**Youth Centres** The nightlife scene in East Berlin is less slick but more authentic than that in West Berlin. Your best bet is the various youth cultural centres which offer a variety of entertainment possibilities under one roof. All are good places to meet people

and they're relatively drug-free compared to West Berlin.

The *Haus der jungen Talente*, Kloster Strasse 68/70 south-east of Alexander Platz (U-Bahn: Kloster Strasse), offers films (at 7 pm, DM 3), pantomime (at 7 pm, DM 3), folk dancing (at 7 pm, DM 5), cabaret (at 8 pm, DM 10), jazz (at 9 pm, DM 8), blues (at 9 pm, DM 5), a disco (at 9 pm, DM 3), café entertainment, etc. What's on varies daily so pick up a copy of the monthly programme at the door.

A more counterculture place is *Jojo* (☎ 282 4656), Wilhelm Pieck Strasse 216 (U-Bahn: Oranienburger Tor), which includes a cinema, bookshop, theatre, music room, bar, disco and café. The DM 5 entry price admits you to everything, but it's only open in the evening and things don't start moving until 11 pm.

*Checkpoint*, Leipziger Strasse 55 (U-Bahn: Spittelmarkt), puts on a nightly programme of video, jazz, disco, cinema, theatre, dance, art gallery, bar, café and live music. Not everything is offered every night so check the programme.

**Discos** West Berlin has a reputation for its nightlife and nothing happens until 10 pm. That's the time to stroll down the Ku'damm amid all the glitter. A disco tout will hand you an invitation to *Big Eden*. Before you get sucked into any of the tourist joints along the strip, take a look up Bleibtreu Strasse and around Savigny Platz where the locals go.

West Berlin discos are wild and you have to put a big effort into keeping up with the scene. The favourite tourist disco is *Big Eden*, Kurfürsten Damm 202 (open daily from 7 pm). Other than Friday and Saturday nights there's no cover charge, but they make up for it in the price of the drinks. *Society*, Budapester Strasse 42 opposite the Europa Centre, is similar.

If you'd rather dance with Berliners it's *Far Out*, Kurfürsten Damm 156 (U-Bahn: Adenauer Platz). The entrance to this Bhagwan disco is beneath the bowling alley around the side of the building. It's open from 10 pm, closed Monday, with a DM 10 cover charge on Friday and Saturday, DM 5 other nights. Drinks are normally priced.

For a slightly offbeat trip try the *Metropol*, Nollendorf Platz 5 (U-Bahn: Nollendorf Platz), popular with gays and straights. The big disco operates Friday and Saturday nights from 10 pm, the small disco Sunday to Thursday from 10 pm. Rock concerts unroll at the Metropol (☎ 216 4122) around 7 pm, but they're often sold out.

One disco with live 'independent underground' music (hard rock or punk) is *Madhouse Ecstasy*, Haupt Strasse 30 in Schöneberg (U-Bahn: Eisenacher Strasse). It has top bands playing from 9 pm to dawn every Friday and Saturday night (DM 10 to DM 20 cover charge depending on the fame of the group, student discounts available). On other nights you can dance in its Madhouse or Funhouse discos (DM 5 cover charge) after 10 pm. For information on what's happening in Ecstasy call its business office at ☎ 781 1865 weekdays from noon to 4 pm or direct to the disco at ☎ 782 0649 other times (they speak English). Fascist skinheads are not admitted.

In East Berlin try the disco below the TV tower (S-Bahn or U-Bahn: Alexander Platz) which opens at 8 pm Friday and Saturday. Entry is free but there's a DM 10 minimum consumption charge. It's upstairs above the tourist office.

The music scene in Berlin is constantly changing and for up-to-date information it's best to check the fortnightly magazines *Zitty* and *Tip* which carry complete listings of what's happening.

**Pubs** There are thousands of pubs, or *Kneipen*, in Berlin, and in the absence of licensing hours they're open day and night (usually from 7 pm to 4 am). Many pubs offer live music and food. A cover charge of DM 4 to DM 15 may be asked if there's live music, although some places only charge admission on Friday and Saturday nights.

The *Sophienklub*, Sophien Strasse 6 off Rosenthaler Strasse (S-Bahn: Weinmeister Strasse), has jazz nightly from 9 pm with a special programme on Tuesday and Saturday nights.

*Quasimodo*, Kant Strasse 12a near Zoo Station (open from 9 pm, music from 10 pm), is a Jazzkeller with live jazz, blues or rock every night.

For folk music try *Go In*, Bleibtreu Strasse 17 (S-Bahn: Savigny Platz; open daily from 8 pm). *Salsa*, Wieland Strasse 13, features Latin American and Caribbean music. It opens at 8 pm, has live music from 10.30 pm and offers free admission Sunday to Thursday. *Madow*, at Pariser Strasse 23-24 (open Wednesday, Friday, Saturday and Sunday from 10 pm), features music from the 1970s. There's a DM 4 cover charge and you can dance.

The *Djungel Club*, Nürnberger Strasse 56 (U-Bahn: Wittenberg Platz), is a late-night place for the super cool (closed Tuesday). If you're too old, fat, poorly dressed or not with it you won't get past the doorkeeper. It's such an insiders scene they don't even have a sign outside, but look for the tropical vegetation in the window of the place next to the Alles für den Hund canine paraphernalia shop. If they see this book in your hand there's no way you'll be admitted.

A typical Berlin pub is *E & M Leydicke*, Manstein Strasse 4 (S or U-Bahn: Yorck Strasse). This oldest pub in Berlin (founded 1877) bottles its own liqueurs on the premises. Open daily from 4 pm to midnight, it's more of a drinking place than anything else.

**Contacts** Bored in Berlin? Check the *'Ein-, Zwei-, Mehrsamkeit'* (Lonely Hearts) section in the newspaper *Zweite Hand*. The ads are classified under *'Er sucht Sie'* (he

looking for her), *'Sie sucht Ihn'* (she looking for him), *'Sie sucht Sie'* (she looking for her), *'Er sucht Ihn'* (he looking for him) and *'Suche'* (just looking). There's no charge to advertise yourself (☎ 26 9261 in West Berlin).

**Spectator Sports** There's trotting at *Trabrennbahn Karlshorst* (Karlshorst Race Track) near Karlshorst S-Bahn Station after 6 pm Tuesdays and 2 pm Saturdays throughout the year (admission DM 2). Even if you're not a regular horse racing fan, this is a wonderfully informal place to see local people enjoying themselves. Buy the programme (DM 2) at the gate if you intend to wager. There are dozens of stands here dispensing cheap food and drink so come hungry and thirsty.

From September to June you can see soccer (European football) every other Saturday at 3 pm at the *Friedrich Ludwig Jahn Sportpark* (U-Bahn: Dimitroff Strasse) or the *Olympic Stadium* (U-Bahn: Olympia-Stadion). The matches alternate between the two stadiums on successive weeks, so check.

On weekends you're welcome to join in soccer and volleyball games in the field in front of the Reichstag.

### Things to Buy

Tauentzien Strasse is the main shopping street for affluent West Berlin consumers. At the Wittenberg Platz end of this street is KaDeWe (Kaufhaus des Westens), an amazing six-storey, turn-of-the-century department store which sells just about everything you can name. Wertheim, Kurfürsten Damm 232, West Berlin's second department store, is less pretentious and less expensive.

Shops selling discount cameras are along Augsburger Strasse near the Ku'damm.

The largest camping goods store in West Berlin with a good selection of top quality tents and backpacks is Alles für Tramper, Bundesallee 88 (U-Bahn: Walther Schreiber Platz).

Good, inexpensive, second-hand clothes of all descriptions may be had at Made in

Berlin, Potsdamer Strasse 106 (U-Bahn: Kurfürsten Strasse). You can find some pretty funky attire there!

The Kunstsalon, Unter den Linden 41, has German art books, reproductions, sheet music, records and cassettes. Meissner Porzellan, Unter den Linden 39, sells the famous Meissen porcelain.

There's an open-air flea market (Trödelmarkt) every Saturday and Sunday morning on Strasse des 17 Juni at Tiergarten S-Bahn Station. Don't buy any GDR paraphernalia here as you can get it much cheaper at the street market around the Brandenburg Gate.

**Eastern European Products** Several countries have cultural centres in Berlin (open weekdays) which sell their books, maps, records, handicrafts and souvenirs. The House of Hungarian Culture, Karl Liebknecht Strasse 9, and the Polish Cultural Centre, Karl Liebknecht Strasse 7, are opposite St Mary's Church near Alexander Platz. The Bulgarian Cultural Centre is at Unter den Linden 10, and the Czechoslovak Cultural Centre (ČSFR Centrum) is at Leipziger Strasse 60.

### Getting There & Away

**Bus** The Funkturm Bus Station (U-Bahn: Kaiser Damm) is open from 5.30 am to 10 pm. Westkreuz S-Bahn Station is within walking distance from this bus station.

Bayern Express (☎ 87 0181) has buses to Amsterdam, Frankfurt/Main, Hannover, Munich, Nuremberg and many points in southern Germany. Sperling GmbH (☎ 33 1031) has service to Bremen, Düsseldorf, Goslar, Hamburg, Kiel, Lübeck and other cities in northern Germany. Tickets are available from most travel agencies in West Berlin. For more information on bus services between Berlin and Western Europe see the Getting There & Away section in the introduction to this chapter.

**Train** For information on international trains to/from Berlin see the chapter introduction. Information on all railway services in Eastern Europe is available from counters No 5 & 6 downstairs in the back office of the Europäisches Reisebüro on Alexander Platz. They sell international train tickets and make reservations for the same price as the counters in the railway stations but without the queues. The ticket and reservation offices at Berlin-Friedrich Strasse, Berlin-Alexander Platz, Berlin-Hauptbahnhof and Berlin-Lichtenberg railway stations are also far less congested than the one in Berlin-Zoo Station.

**Railway Stations** East Berlin's main railway station is Bahnhof Berlin-Lichtenberg, with trains to all parts of Eastern Germany and Eastern Europe. This station is easily reached by S-Bahn (direction Wartenberg, Ahrensfelde or Strausberg Nord) or on the Hönow U-Bahn line. The reservation office opens on weekdays from 6 am to 8 pm, on weekends from 8 am to 6 pm, and international tickets are easily purchased. The helpful attendants in the station information office speak good English and there's no crowd! The left-luggage room is open nonstop (DM 2 per piece per *calendar* day) and there are plenty of coin lockers.

Trains to Poland and the USSR depart Berlin-Hauptbahnhof as well as Berlin-Lichtenberg. The left-luggage office at the Hauptbahnhof only closes from 1.30 to 3 am.

Many trains to Dresden, Leipzig, Halle, Chemnitz, Gera, Erfurt and Magdeburg also leave from Bahnhof Berlin-Schöneweide. All trains travelling to the south and west of Eastern Germany stop at Flughafen Berlin-Schönefeld.

Bahnhof Berlin-Zoologischer Garten (Zoo Station) on Hardenberg Platz is the main railway station in West Berlin, although some trains to/from Western Germany also stop at Berlin-Wannsee or Berlin-Spandau. This overcrowded station features plenty of coin lockers (DM 2.50), a reservation office (long, slow queue), a railway information office (*Zugauskunft*), a 24-hour post office with public telephones opposite and a tourist information office (*Verkehrsamt*) which makes (expensive) hotel reservations for DM 3 commission.

The currency exchange office of the Deutsche Verkehrs-Kredit Bank (open until 9 pm Monday to Saturday, and 6 pm Sunday) is just outside.

Trains between Poland and Western Europe pass through West Berlin so you can get on or off at Zoo Station. Trains to Berlin from Czechoslovakia and Hungary, however, terminate at Lichtenberg Railway Station in East Berlin. From there you can take the S-Bahn to Alexander Platz or Berlin-Zoo.

Train tickets to/from Berlin are valid for all railway stations in the city *(Stadtbahn)* which means that on arrival or departure you may use the S-Bahn network (but not the U-Bahn) to proceed to your destination or go to the station on the same ticket. It's always best to board trains leaving Berlin at the originating station.

**Hitchhiking** You can hitchhike to Dresden, Hannover, Leipzig, Munich, Nuremberg and beyond from Checkpoint Dreilinden at Wannsee, the entrance to the main highway between Berlin and Western Germany. Take the S-Bahn to Wannsee, then walk less than a km up Potsdamer Chausee and follow the signs to Raststätte Dreilinden. There's always a bunch of hitchhikers here but everyone gets a ride eventually. Bring a small sign stating your destination and consider waiting until you find a car going right where you want to go.

**Ride Services** Next to hitchhiking, the cheapest way to get from Berlin to Western Germany is as a paying passenger in a private car. There are numerous *Mitfahrzentralen* (ride agencies) in West Berlin arranging such rides. As a passenger you pay a DM 10 to DM 17 commission to the agency, plus petrol money to the driver.

One office is on the platform of the U1 U-Bahn line towards Schlesisches Tor at Zoologischer Garten underground station (☎ 31 0331, open daily from 8 am to 9 pm). Another office (☎ 882 7604, also open daily from 8 am to 9 pm) is on the 2nd-floor shopping arcade at Kurfürsten Damm 227

(Ku'damm-Eck). Other Mitfahrzentralen are listed in the 'Mitfahrer' classified section of *Zitty*. The people answering the phone in these offices always speak good English, so don't hesitate to call around.

If you arrange a ride a few days in advance, be sure to call the driver back the night before and again on departure morning to make sure he/she is still going.

### Getting Around

**To/From the Airport** Most Eastern European and Third World carriers fly from Berlin-Schönefeld Airport (SXF), next to Flughafen Berlin-Schönefeld Railway Station just outside the southern city limits, 25 km south-east of Alexander Platz. The S-Bahn from Zoo Station and Alexander Platz runs to Schönefeld every 20 minutes from 4 am to 1 am. Otherwise take bus No 171 to/from U-Bahn Rudow direct to/from the terminal, also every 20 minutes.

Flughafen Tegel (TXL), West Berlin's main commercial airport, six km north-west of Zoo Station, receives most flights from Western Europe. Regular BVG transit buses run to gate No 8 upstairs at the terminal – bus No 128 from Kurt Schumacher Platz U-Bahn Station, and bus No 109 from the Inter-Continental Hotel via Zoo Station. These buses operate every 15 minutes from 5 am to midnight. Near the tourist office in the main hall at Tegel is a baggage storage office (open from 5.30 am to 10 pm) and a bank.

Tempelhof Airport (THF) receives mostly domestic and American military flights (U-Bahn: Platz der Luftbrücke). Flugplatz Gatow west of the Havel River is a British air-force base.

**Public Transport** The Berliner Verkehrs-Betriebe (BVG) operates an efficient suburban railway (S-Bahn), underground (U-Bahn), ferry and bus system which reaches every corner of Berlin and the surrounding area. Trams exist only in East Berlin. The BVG ferry from Kladow to Wannsee operates hourly all year (except when there's ice or fog) with regular tickets, passes and transfers accepted. System maps are posted in all stations and most vehicles and are available free from all ticket or information windows. You'll find the whole system easy to use.

A single DM 2.70 ticket allows unlimited transfers on all forms of public transport within two hours, and return trips are allowed. A four-ride *Sammelkarte* works out slightly cheaper at DM 9.20. You validate your own ticket in a red automat *(Entwerter)* at the entrances to the S and U-Bahn stations. There's no ticket control but if you're caught by an inspector without a valid ticket there's a DM 60 fine (no excuses accepted). The S-Bahn (but not the U-Bahn) is part of the German railway system so Eurail and Interrail passes are valid on it.

You can carry a bicycle in specially marked cars on the S-Bahn or U-Bahn, but a second half-fare must be paid. Daily, weekly and monthly tickets allow you to take a bicycle with you free. You're not allowed, however, to take a bike on the West Berlin U-Bahn weekdays from 2 to 5.30 pm or on the East Berlin S-Bahn weekdays from 6 to 7.30 am and 3.30 to 6 pm.

Since 1990 the public transportation systems in East and West Berlin have been unified and West Berlin tickets are valid throughout the network, even as far as Potsdam and Oranienburg – a bargain. In mid-1991 single tickets in East Berlin still cost only 20 Pfennig (!) but they will definitely have increased by the time you get there, and as long as a price difference remains, East Berlin tickets will not be valid in West Berlin. However, if you don't buy a transit pass and are travelling strictly within East Berlin (the boundary is still marked on posted maps), check prices as it may still be a little cheaper.

The S-Bahn differs from the U-Bahn in that more than one line uses the same track. Destination indicators on the platforms tell you where the next train is going. All trains from Friedrich Strasse run to Alexander Platz. For Treptow Park you want a train going to Schönefeld or Königs Wusterhausen. For Karlshorst or Köpenick look for the Erkner train. To go to Bahnhof Berlin-Lichtenberg you want the Ahrensfelde or Strausberg trains. The Oranienburg and Bernau trains go north through Pankow. The system is easy to use and route maps are posted in all carriages, but you have to pay attention.

The double-decker buses offer great views from the upstairs front seats. One of the most popular double-decker routes is bus No 119 which runs from Grunewald to Kreuzberg via the Ku'damm. It's fun just to get on it in either direction and trace your route from above with the help of a good map. The bus numbers of all Berlin city buses changed on 2 June 1991. In this book we give the new numbers but be aware that older publications may still have the former numbers.

The S and U-Bahn lines close down between 1 and 4 am, but night buses run every 30 minutes all night from Zoo Station to key points such as Rathaus Spandau, Alt Tegel, Hermann Platz, Rathaus Steglitz, Mexiko Platz, etc. Regular fares apply.

**Special Tickets** The best transportation deal in Berlin is a seven-day (DM 28) ticket which entitles you to use the whole BVG network during any seven-day period. A slight variation on this is the Monday to Saturday *6-Tage-Wertmarke* ticket (DM 26) and the 24-hour unlimited travel Berlin Ticket (DM 9). Since the latter is good for 24 hours, it will overlap the morning or evening of another day, allowing an extra ride. A monthly ticket, *Monatswertmarke Umweltkarte* ('environment ticket'), is DM 65. All

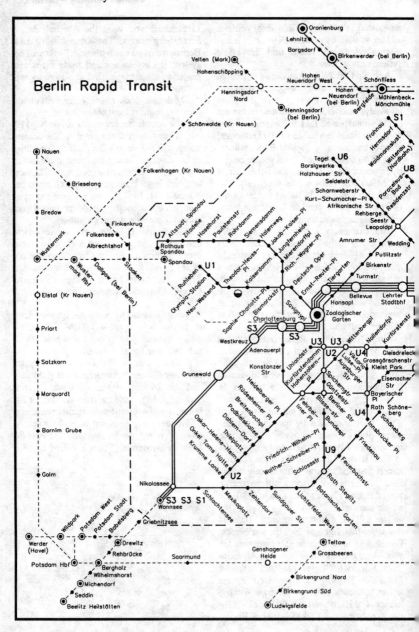

Berlin Rapid Transit

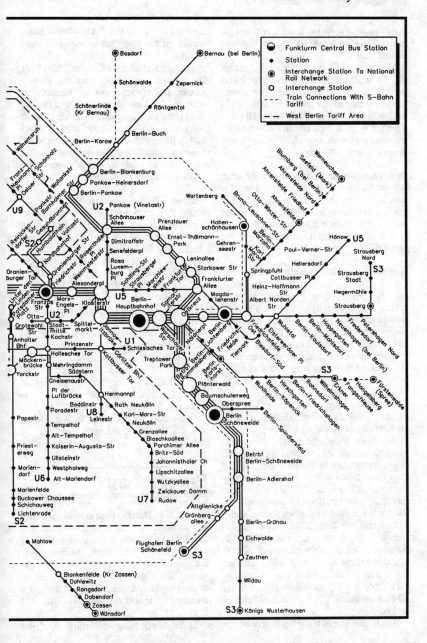

transit passes except the seven-day ticket are transferable and can be shared between several people.

Bus drivers sell single tickets, but multiple, 24-hour, seven-day or monthly tickets must be purchased in advance. The seven-day ticket can only be purchased at the BVG Information kiosk (open daily from 10 am to 6 pm) in front of West Berlin's Zoo Station; the other passes are available from automats in mass transit stations.

**Taxi** There's a taxi stand beside all main railway stations. The basic flag-fall tariff is DM 3.40, then an additional DM 1.70 per km. Sunday and holidays it's DM 1 extra and oversized luggage is 50 Pfennig apiece. All taxis have meters and it's no more expensive in the middle of the night.

**Rentals – Car & Motorcycle** All of the large car rental chains are represented in Berlin and their rates for the cheapest car begin around DM 175 daily or DM 850 weekly with unlimited mileage. Collision insurance begins at DM 26 a day extra. Rental cars are often fully booked in Berlin so advance reservations are advisable, and you may even get a better rate by booking from abroad.

Among the large chains only Hertz (☎ 261 1053), Budapester Strasse 39 at the Europa Center, allows its cars to be driven into Poland (check first), but only if you hire a steering-wheel lock at DM 5 daily.

A good independent car rental company is Minibus Service, Zieten Strasse 1 (U-Bahn: Nollendorf Platz). Its cheapest cars are DM 59 a day including 100 km, DM 119 a day including 800 km or DM 145 a weekend including 1500 km. It's open weekdays from 9 am to 6 pm, Saturdays from 9 am to 1 pm.

Eurorent (☎ 2096 2175), Clara Zetkin Strasse 30 (U-Bahn and S-Bahn: Friedrich Strasse), offers a 'super spar Tarif' of DM 102 day or DM 374 weekly with unlimited mileage for the cheapest car (collision insurance DM 25 a day extra) but may demand DM 4000 deposit! It has a branch at Schönefeld Airport.

Small companies offering discount car

rentals advertise in the *'PKW – Vermietung'* section of the classified newspaper *Zweite Hand.*

Budget/Sixt Rent-a-Car (☎ 261 1357), Budapester Strasse 18 near the Europa Center, has Harley-Davidson motorcycles such as the Low Rider Custom (DM 77 daily), the Heritage Softail Classic (DM 88 daily) and the Electra Glide Classic (DM 99 daily). Rates include 70 km, and weekly and monthly rentals are possible, but reservations must be made well in advance as the bikes are usually all taken.

**Rentals – Bicycle** Zweirad Bahrdt (☎ 323 8129), Kant Strasse 89 (S-Bahn: Charlottenburg), rents bicycles at DM 15 a day, DM 10 a day for three days or more, DM 40 for two weeks, DM 60 for three weeks or DM 80 a month. A deposit of DM 100 must be paid and they'll want to see your passport. Do use the lock provided with the cycle. This is also a good place to buy a bicycle. It's open weekdays from 9 am to 6 pm, Saturdays from 9 am to 1 pm.

Bicycles can also be rented at the Fahrrad Büro-Berlin (☎ 784 5562), Haupt Strasse 146 (U-Bahn: Kleist Park). They charge DM 12 a day, DM 60 a week, DM 50 deposit, and open Monday to Wednesday and Friday from 10 am to 6 pm, Thursday from noon to 7 pm and Saturday from 10 am to 2 pm.

Most other bicycle shops in West Berlin will also rent bikes, but not for less than 24 hours.

# Brandenburg

The State of Brandenburg surrounds Berlin and includes the former districts of Potsdam, Frankfurt and Cottbus. It's a watery region of lakes, marshes and rivers, and canals connecting the rivers Oder and Elbe utilise the Havel and Spree rivers which meet at Spandau in Berlin. The Spreewald, a marshy area near Cottbus, was inhabited by Slavonic Sorbs right up until WW II.

Brandenburg was the birthplace of the

Kingdom of Prussia which dominated the German Empire after 1871. In 929 the German king Henry I the Fowler captured the Slavonic town in Brennaburg on the Havel River, and, although the Slavs retook the area in 983, by 1150 Brandenburg was firmly in the hands of the German margrave of the Nordmark (North March).

## POTSDAM

Potsdam, on the Havel River just beyond the south-west tip of Berlin, became important in the 17th century as the residence of the Elector of Brandenburg. Later, with the creation of the Kingdom of Prussia, Potsdam became a royal seat and garrison town, and in the mid-18th century Frederick the Great built many of the marvellous palaces in Sanssouci Park which visitors come to see today. Hitler exploited Potsdam's prestige by organising a lavish ceremony here on 21 March 1933 to proclaim to President Hindenburg 'the union between the symbols of the old greatness and the new strength'.

Twelve years later, on 14 April 1945, just a week before the war's end, British bombers devastated the historic centre of Potsdam, but fortunately most of the palaces escaped undamaged (only the City Palace was badly hit). To make a point of their victory over German militarism, the victorious allies chose the city for the Potsdam Conference of August 1945, which set the stage for the temporary division of Berlin and Germany into four occupation zones.

Though within easy commuting distance of Berlin, you'll need more than a day to enjoy the lovely parks, palaces and waterways of this German Versailles in a leisurely way. Accommodation is easy to arrange and the small-town ambience is pleasant, so consider staying at Potsdam and seeing Berlin as a day trip instead of the other way around!

## Orientation

If you arrive by S-Bahn from Berlin-Wannsee and you want to go directly to the centre of town, get out at Potsdam-Stadt Railway Station, just south-east across the Havel. The next stop after Potsdam-Stadt is Potsdam-West which is closer to Sanssouci Park; most trains also stop at Bahnhof Wildpark (ask), closer still. The Wannsee trains usually continue on to Potsdam-Hauptbahnhof Station, off Lenin Allee five km south-west of the centre of town. If you need a cloakroom for luggage storage (DM 2 per piece) you'll find one open from 8 am to 6 pm at Potsdam-Hauptbahnhof.

If you come by train from Berlin-Karlshorst or Schönefeld you'll arrive at Potsdam-Hauptbahnhof. Buy tram or bus tickets at a kiosk and catch a tram outside the station. If you want to go directly to Sanssouci Palace, get off the tram when you see the huge arch at Platz der Nationen. The trams continue through the city and run south across the bridge past the Interhotel Potsdam. For the Bassin Platz Bus Station leave the tram at Platz der Einheit. For the tourist office get out a stop later near the Nikolaikirche. Bus No 695 runs direct from Potsdam-Hauptbahnhof to Cecilienhof Palace via the Neues Palais and Sanssouci Park.

There are no luggage storage facilities at Bassin Platz Bus Station, only toilets and a few cheap places to get a snack. All buses from Berlin arrive here.

## Information

Potsdam-Information (☎ 33-21100), Friedrich Ebert Strasse 5 on Alter Markt next to the Nikolaikirche, sells a variety of maps and brochures but is incredibly crowded in summer (open daily from 9 am to 6 pm). If it's closed try the reception of the nearby Interhotel Potsdam.

German Travel International (☎ 22324), Allee nach Sanssouci 2 off Platz der Nationen (open weekdays from 8 am to 4 pm), will book youth hostel beds all around Eastern Germany for a flat DM 10 fee.

## Things to See

**Sanssouci Park** This large park is open round the clock with no admission charge, but the various palaces and galleries scattered through it cost DM 2 to DM 6 each to enter. Begin with Knobelsdorff's **Schloss**

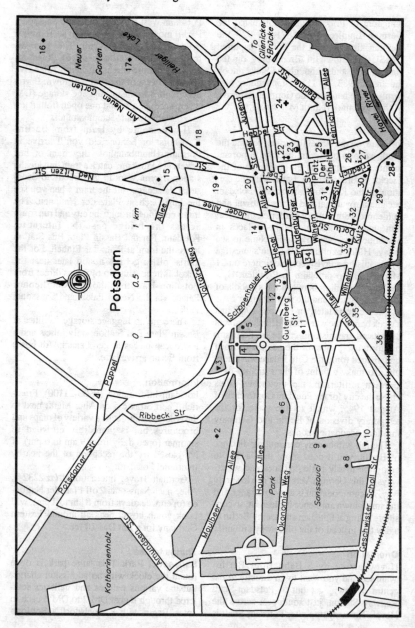

■ PLACES TO STAY

14  Hotel am Jägertor
18  Youth Hostel
28  Interhotel Potsdam

▼ PLACES TO EAT

3  Brolier Beer Garden
10  Gaststätte Charlottenhof
32  Cafeteria

OTHER

1  Neues Palais
2  Orangerie
4  Schloss Sanssouci
5  Bildergalerie
6  Chinese Teahouse
7  Bahnhof Potsdam-West
8  Schloss Charlottenhof
9  Roman Baths
11  Hans Otto Theatre
12  German Travel International
13  Cabaret am Obelisk
15  Russian Colony
16  Cecilienhof Palace
17  Marble Palace
19  Town Hall
20  Nauener Tor
21  Schwarzer Adler Pub
22  Sts Peter & Paul Church
23  Bassin Platz Bus Station
24  Hospital
25  Post Office
26  Nikolaikirche
27  Potsdam-Information
28  Weisse Flotte
29  Stadium
30  Film Museum
31  Europäisches Reisebüro
33  Potsdam Museum
34  Platz der Nationen
35  Mosque
36  Bahnhof Wildpark

**Sanssouci** (1747), a famous Rococo palace with glorious interiors (open daily all year, closed the first and third Mondays of the month). Tickets (DM 6) are sold at a small window behind the palace and since visitors are only admitted in groups at periodic intervals with a German-speaking guide, it's important to arrive early if you want a ticket for that day. Weekends and holidays are especially busy. If you do get in don't miss the room with the golden spider's web motif on the ceiling.

While you're waiting for your assigned tour to begin, visit the **Bildergalerie** (open daily from May to October) on the east side of Sanssouci or the small picture gallery (closed Monday and Tuesday) at the west end of the palace. The **Orangerie** (1862) west of Sanssouci Palace is also worth seeing, both for the copies of 47 Raphael frescoes inside and the view of all Potsdam from the tower (open daily from May to October). The **Chinese Teahouse** (1757) is south-east of here in the middle of the park.

The late-Baroque **Neues Palais** (1769), summer residence of the royal family, is by far the largest and most imposing building in the park, and the one to see if your time is limited. Visitors are admitted individually as they arrive, so you shouldn't have trouble getting in (open daily all year, closed the second and fourth Monday of the month, admission DM 6). Avoid coming from 12.45 to 1.15 pm when the ticket seller takes off for lunch.

Schinkel's **Schloss Charlottenhof** (1826) must also be visited on a German-language tour, but don't wait around too long if the crowds are immense. The exterior of this Italian-style mansion is more interesting than the interior (open daily from May to October, DM 4).

**Central Potsdam** The Baroque **Brandenburg Gate** on Platz der Nationen bears the date 1770. From this square a pleasant pedestrian street, Brandenburger Strasse, runs directly east to **Sts Peter & Paul Church** (1868). The Bassin Platz Bus Station is next to this church. From near here Friedrich Ebert Strasse runs north to **Nauener Tor** (1755), another monumental arch.

Follow Friedrich Ebert Strasse south and you'll come to the great neoclassical dome of Schinkel's **Nikolaikirche** (1849, open daily from 2 to 5 pm) on Alter Markt. In front of the Nikolaikirche is an obelisk behind which stood the Potsdam City Palace, badly damaged in WW II and later demolished. The site is now occupied by a partly completed theatre, begun by the Communists and scrapped after reunification. To the left of the Nikolaikirche is the **Hans Marchwitza Kulturhaus** in Potsdam's old town hall (1755), which today contains several art galleries upstairs (open daily, free) and two elegant restaurants in the cellar. The **Film Museum** (closed Monday) housed in the royal stables (1685), the high-rise Interhotel Potsdam (1969) and the Weisse Flotte are across the street from Alter Markt.

**Neuer Garten** This winding park along the west side of Heiliger Lake is a fine place to relax after all the high art in Park Sanssouci. The **Marble Palace** (1792) is right on the lake.

Farther north is **Cecilienhof Palace**, an English-style country manor built in 1913-16 for Princess Cecilie, a daughter of Kaiser Wilhelm II. It's quite a contrast to the Rococo palaces and pavilions in Sanssouci Park. Cecilienhof is remembered as the site of the 1945 Potsdam Conference and large photos of the participants Stalin, Truman and Churchill are displayed inside (open daily all year, closed the second and fourth Monday of each month, admission DM 3). Part of the building has been made into a luxury hotel.

You can walk from Cecilienhof Palace to Glienicker Brücke (and bus No 116 back to Wannsee) in about 10 minutes.

### Activities
**Excursion Boats** Weisse Flotte excursion boats operate on the lakes around Potsdam, departing from the dock below the soaring Interhotel Potsdam regularly between 9 am and 5.30 pm from April to September. There are frequent boats to Wannsee (DM 6.50) with some boats continuing on to Tegel (DM 10 from Potsdam). Other frequent trips are to Werder.

The *Romantische Schlossrundfahrt* is a scenic four-hour loop right around Potsdam passing a number of outlying palaces (operates daily from May to September, DM 12).

Saturday at 8.30 am (from mid-May to mid-September) there's a boat down the Havel all the way to the town of Brandenburg (DM 20 single or return, four hours). From Brandenburg it would be easy to return to Potsdam or Berlin by train.

**Organised Tours** Potsdam-Information, Friedrich Ebert Strasse 5 (open daily from 9 am to 6 pm), offers three-hour city sightseeing tours daily in summer. The 10 am tour (DM 20) visits Cecilienhof while the 2 pm tour (DM 34) visits Sanssouci.

### Places to Stay
**Camping** *Intercamping D-139 Werder/ Havel*, Riegelspitze, is eight km south-west of Potsdam. There are small bungalows, but they're booked solid in July and August. The snack bar near the middle of the camping ground has a pleasant terrace overlooking the lake. Enquire there if the camping ground office is closed when you arrive. A small grocery store is opposite the snack bar. The Glindowsee almost surrounds the camping ground and in summer you can swim there. Bus No D-31 Werder from platform No 2 at Potsdam's Bassin Platz Bus Station passes within a five-minute walk of this camping ground every couple of hours. One bus departs from Bassin Platz daily at 6 pm. The bus goes down Lenin Allee within a few hundred metres of Potsdam-Hauptbahnhof but doesn't stop right in front of the station, so make certain you're waiting at the right bus stop.

There's also the *Gaisberg-Geltow D-125 Campground* right on the Templiner Lake, two km from Potsdam-Hauptbahnhof along a pleasant road through the forest. Open from April to October, it's DM 4.50 per person (students DM 2), plus DM 1 to DM 6 per tent (depending on size). It also has 13 bungalows for DM 20 to DM 25 plus DM 5.50 per person for bedding, but the bungalows are often full. Tent space is always available and for those without a car this is the most convenient place to camp around Berlin.

**Hostel** The 48-bed *Am Neuen Garten Youth*

*Hostel* (☎ 22515), Eisenhard Strasse 5 between central Potsdam and the Neuer Garten, is in a large mansion between Neuer Garten and the centre. It's DM 14 for juniors, DM 17 for seniors, plus DM 7 for sheets (compulsory) and DM 4 for breakfast (tea).

**Private Rooms** The Zimmernachweis office in Potsdam-Information, Friedrich Ebert Strasse 5 (open in summer on week-days from 1 to 8 pm, weekends and holidays from 9 am to 6 pm), arranges private rooms in Potsdam at DM 20 to DM 35 per person. If you can get a room near the centre this is your best bet.

**Hotels** The 222-bed *Am Schwielochsee Tourist Hotel* (☎ 2850), Am Schwielochsee 110, is in a modern, three-storey building by Schwielow Lake, not far from Intercamping D-139 listed earlier (same bus to get there). This former youth hostel has only rooms with shared bath so it's fairly reasonable (DM 30 to DM 40 per person), but the remote location makes it convenient only if you have your own transport.

The functional, 25-room *Hotel Am Jägertor* (☎ 21834), Hegel Allee 11 in the centre, is overpriced at DM 80/130 single/double with shared bath, DM 110/140 with private bath. The breakfast buffet is DM 15 extra.

The 187-room, five-star *Interhotel Potsdam* (☎ 4631), Lange Brücke, is the place to stay if you have money (DM 175/225 single/double, bath and breakfast included).

The 42 rooms at the three-star *Hotel Schloss Cecilienhof* (☎ 23141) in the Neuer Garten begin at DM 130/250 single/double with bath and breakfast and you get to sleep in one of Potsdam's most famous buildings. If you don't mind the price, have a travel agent book your room well in advance.

**Places to Eat**

The cheapest self-service in town is *Schnell Sicher Rationell Cafeteria* at the DV Zentrum Potsdam, the building with the mosaics on the wall at the corner of Wilhelm Kutz Strasse and Dortu Strasse. It serves breakfast from 8 to 9.30 am and lunch from 11.30 am to 1 pm, weekdays only.

Just behind the triumphal arch on Platz der Nationen is the *Gastmahl des Meeres* which specialises in seafood.

The *Klosterkeller*, Friedrich Ebert Strasse 94 on the corner of Gutenberg Strasse, includes a grill bar (open weekdays from 8 am to 9 pm, weekends from 8 am to 3 pm), a regular restaurant (daily 11.30 am to midnight), a beer garden (May to September) and a night bar (Tuesday to Saturday 9 pm to 3 am, erotic show at midnight, cover charge for men). Prices are moderate and the place combines modern German décor with a traditional menu.

The *Badische Weinstube*, Gutenberg Strasse 90, often has good weekday lunch specials as advertised in the window.

Getting something to eat while touring Sanssouci Park can be problematic, so consider taking a picnic lunch. Otherwise try the large beer garden directly behind and to the north-west of Sanssouci Palace. You can't see it from the palace and there's only one tiny sign reading 'Zum Broiler', so look around or just follow the crowd. There are different counters selling beer, cakes, ice cream, chicken and other hot meals.

The *Gaststätte Charlottenhof* just outside the park near Schloss Charlottenhof offers much more elegant dining in this area, if you have time.

For afternoon coffee and cakes *Café Heider*, Friedrich Ebert Strasse 28 just across from the Nauener Tor, is good.

**Entertainment**

The Besucherservice, Brandenburger Strasse 18 (closed Sunday and Monday) has tickets for performances at the *Hans Otto Theater*, Zimmer Strasse 10, and the *Schlosstheater* in the Neues Palais. Wednesdays at 7.30 pm from July to mid-September there are organ concerts at various churches in Potsdam. Potsdam-Information, Friedrich Ebert Strasse 5, will know which churches.

The Film Museum opposite Interhotel Potsdam shows films for children in the morning and afternoon, quality films for adults in the evening.

The *Potsdamer Kabarett am Obelisk*, Schopenhauer Strasse 27, presents drama (in German) on contemporary themes at 8 pm from Wednesday to Sunday. Its ticket office (open weekdays from 8 am to 4.30 pm) is in the rear courtyard.

A local pub with a real earthy atmosphere is the *Schwarzer Adler*, Gutenberg Strasse 91 (closed Tuesday).

### Getting There & Away

Potsdam's Bassin Platz Bus Station is accessible from West Berlin on bus No 138 from Rathaus Spandau (hourly from 6 am to 8 pm) and bus No 113 from Wannsee (every 20 minutes from 5 am to 1 am).

Bus No 113 takes a roundabout route through Babelsberg, so if you're headed for Cecilienhof Palace it would be much faster to take bus No 116 from Wannsee to the Glienicker Brücke and walk from there.

Hourly S-Bahn trains run from Berlin-Wannsee to Potsdam-Stadt, Potsdam-West and Potsdam-Hauptbahnhof, the most direct route by rail.

You can also come on the double-decker S-Bahn from Berlin-Karlshorst Station to Potsdam-Hauptbahnhof every hour. It's possible to pick this train up at Flughafen Berlin-Schönefeld – look for a local train to Werder (Havel) or Brandenburg on platform D. The S-Bahn takes only 50 minutes to travel from Schönefeld to Potsdam. Remember to punch your S-Bahn ticket before boarding the train. All Berlin transit passes are valid for the trip to Potsdam by either S-Bahn or BVG transit bus and for local trams and buses around Potsdam.

From April to October large excursion boats ply between Wannsee and Potsdam (DM 6.50 one-way). This service operates six times a day from April to October, 11 times a day from May to mid-September.

All fast trains between Berlin-Karlshorst and Magdeburg stop at Potsdam-Hauptbahnhof. Trains between Hannover and Berlin-Zoo also stop at Potsdam-Stadt.

For Schwerin take a train from Potsdam-Hauptbahnhof to Stendal.

Rail connections from Potsdam south to Leipzig or Dresden are poor. A couple of trains a day call at Potsdam-Hauptbahnhof between Rostock and Leipzig but they pass in the night. You may be able to pick up an infrequent train to Dessau by changing at Bergholz Station (check with the information office), but to travel between Potsdam and Saxony it's usually simpler to change at Berlin-Schönefeld.

Advance train tickets and times are available from the Reisebüro, Friedrich Ebert Strasse 115.

# Saxony

The Free State of Saxony (Sachsen) includes the former districts of Dresden, Leipzig and Chemnitz (until recently Karl Marx Stadt). The Germanic Saxon tribe originally occupied Niedersachsen and Holstein in north-western Germany, from whence groups migrated to England in the 5th century. In the late 8th century the Saxons were conquered by Charlemagne and converted to Christianity, and expanded south-eastward into the territory of the pagan Slavs in the 10th century.

The medieval history of the various Saxon duchies and dynasties is complex, but in the 13th century the duke of Saxony at Wittenberg obtained the right to participate in the election of Holy Roman emperors. Involvement in Poland weakened Saxony in the 18th century, and ill-fated alliances, first with Napoleon and then with Austria, led to the ascendance of Prussia over Saxony in the 19th century.

In the south, Saxony is separated from Bohemia by the Erzgebirge, Eastern Germany's highest mountain range. The Elbe River cuts north-west from the Czech border through a picturesque area known as the 'Saxon Switzerland' towards the old capital, Dresden. Leipzig, a great educational and commercial centre on the Weisse Elster

River, rivals Dresden in historic associations. Quaint little towns like Bautzen, Görlitz and Meissen punctuate this colourful, accessible corner of Germany. The illustrious 18th century organ builder Gottfried Silbermann was from Freiberg, between Dresden and Chemnitz, and two of his organs may be seen in Freiberg Cathedral. Colditz between Meissen and Leipzig is well-known in Britain for its 16th century castle where Allied prisoners were held during WW II and whose daring escapes later became the subject of a TV series.

## DRESDEN

In the 18th century the Saxon capital Dresden was famous throughout Europe as 'the Florence of the north'. During the reigns of Augustus the Strong (ruled 1694-1733) and his son Augustus III (ruled 1733-63) Italian artists, musicians, actors and master craftsmen, particularly from Venice, flocked to the Dresden court. Canaletto depicted the rich architecture of the time in many paintings which now hang in Dresden's Alte Meister Gallery alongside countless masterpieces purchased for Augustus III with income from the silver mines of Saxony. The great Baroque palaces with their priceless art treasures and the brilliant musical traditions survive today, despite devastation in 1945.

The Elbe River cuts a curving course between the low, rolling hills, and in spite of modern rebuilding in concrete and steel, Dresden holds visitors' affection. There are numerous museums, and with the many fine palaces and outstanding excursions, there is ample reason to spend some time in the area. Fortunately the facilities are good. Three nights are the bare minimum required to do Dresden justice.

### Orientation

There are two main railway stations: Dresden-Hauptbahnhof on the south side of town and Dresden-Neustadt on the north. Both stations have all facilities but the Hauptbahnhof is more convenient. Take tram No 11 (under the tracks beside the station) to get to Post Platz near the Zwinger.

Otherwise walk to town along Prager Strasse, the pedestrian mall directly in front of the station.

### Information

Dresden-Information (☎ 51-495 5025), at Prager Strasse 10-11 on the east side of the mall in front of the Hauptbahnhof, sells maps and theatre tickets and there's an accommodation service.

A branch of Dresden-Information is in the underpass below the Goldener Reiter statue in Neustadt, but it only sells maps and souvenirs.

### Things to See

**Dresden Altstadt** A 10-minute walk north along Prager Strasse from the Hauptbahnhof brings you into the Altmarkt area, the historic hub of Dresden until the 1945 bombing. On the right you'll see the rebuilt **Kreuzkirche** (1792), famous for its boys' choir, and behind it the **Neues Rathaus** (1912).

Cross busy König Johann Strasse to the **City Historical Museum** (closed Friday) in a building erected in 1776. North-west up Landhaus Strasse is Neumarkt and the massive ruins of the **Frauenkirche** (1738), once Germany's greatest Protestant church, a reminder of the February 1945 Anglo-American bombings ordered by Churchill. Some 35,000 people died in this atrocity which happened at a time when the city was jammed with refugees and the war almost over. The figure of Martin Luther keeps watch. On this same square is the interesting **Transportation Museum** (closed Monday, DM 4).

Leading north-west from Neumarkt is Augustus Strasse with a 102-metre-long 'Procession of Princes' depicted on the outer wall of the old royal stables. This street brings you directly to the Catholic **Hofkirche** (1755) where the organ is played each Saturday at 4 pm from May to October. The ruins of the Renaissance **Royal Palace** directly behind the cathedral are slowly being restored as part of a long-term programme.

Most of Dresden's priceless art treasures

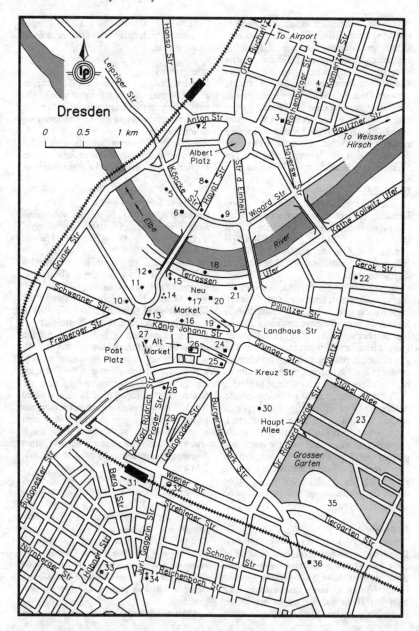

Dresden

0   0.5   1 km

■ PLACES TO STAY

3  Hotel Rothenburger Hof
4  Hotel Stadt Rendsburg
6  Hotel Bellevue
20 Hotel Dresdner Hof
24 Hotel Gewandhaus
33 'Rudi Arndt' Youth Hostel
36 Hotel Astoria

▼ PLACES TO EAT

2  Alt Dresden Winzer Stube
13 Restaurant Am Zwinger
27 Gaststätte Wallterrasse

OTHER

1  Dresden-Neustadt
5  Japanisches Palais
7  Goldener Reiter
8  Romantic Museum
9  Museum für Volkskunst
10 Staatsschauspiel
11 Zwinger
12 Semperoper
14 Palace Ruins
15 Catholic Hofkirche
16 Palace of Culture
17 Transportation Museum
18 Weisse Flotte
19 City Historical Museum
21 Albertinum
22 Kupferstichkabinett
23 Botanical Gardens
25 Neues Rathaus
26 Kreuzkirche
28 Centrum Department Store
29 Tourist Office
30 Hygienemuseum
31 Dresden-Hauptbahnhof
32 Bus Station
34 Russian Church
35 Zoo

are in two large buildings, the Zwinger and the Albertinum, about three blocks apart below a majestic bend of the Elbe. To reach the **Albertinum** on Brühlsche Garten just off Terrassen Ufer, stroll east along the terrace overlooking the river. Here you'll find the **Neue Meister Gallery** with renowned 19th and 20th century paintings (closed Monday,

DM 5) and the **Grünes Gewölbe** or 'Green Vault', one of the world's finest collections of jewel-studded precious objects (closed Thursday). The Grünes Gewölbe is entered through a door on the west side of the building down some stairs, but the ticket office is inside the main entrance. Both the Albertinum museums are free on Tuesdays after 2 pm.

On the west side of the Hofkirche is Theater Platz with Dresden's glorious opera house, the neo-Renaissance **Semperoper**. The first opera house on the site opened in 1841 but burned down in 1869. Rebuilt in 1878, it was again destroyed in 1945 and only reopened in 1985 after the Communists invested millions in the restorations. The Dresden opera has a tradition going back 350 years and many works by Richard Strauss, Carl Maria von Weber and Richard Wagner premiered here.

The south side of Theater Platz is filled by the Baroque **Zwinger** (1728) with no less than five major museums. The most important are the **Alte Meister Gallery**, with old master paintings including Raphael's *Sistine Madonna* (closed Monday), and the **Historisches Museum** with a fantastic collection of ceremonial weapons (closed Wednesday). There's also the **Mathematics Saloon** with old instruments and timepieces (closed Thursday), the **Museum für Tierkunde** with natural history (closed Thursday and Friday) and the **Porcelain Collection** (closed Friday), all housed in opposite corners of the complex with separate entrances. The grey porcelain bells of the clock on the courtyard's east gate chime hourly on the hour (you'll see the crowd waiting). However, the Zwinger is presently undergoing extensive renovations and several of its museums could still be closed.

**Dresden Neustadt** At the north end of the Augustus Bridge, the **Goldener Reiter** statue (1736) of Augustus the Strong beckons us to visit Neustadt. The Haupt Strasse beyond the statue is a pleasant pedestrian mall with the **Romantic Museum** (closed Monday and Tuesday) at No 13. In

Albert Platz at its north end there's an evocative marble monument to the poet Schiller.

Other museums in the vicinity of the Goldener Reiter include the **Museum für Volkskunst** (closed Monday), with a folk art collection at Köpcke Strasse 1, and the **Japanisches Palais** (1737), Palais Platz, with Dresden's famous ethnological museum (closed Friday).

**Farther Afield** Dresden's most surprising attraction is the **Indianer Museum**, Hölderlin Strasse 15 (closed Monday) in Radebeul, eight km north-west of Dresden-Neustadt (trams No 4 or 5). The museum was founded by adventure writer Karl May (1842-1912), whose tales of the Wild West such as *The Treasure of Silver Lake* and *Old Surehand* captured the imagination of several generations of young Germans. Here you'll see a huge collection of authentic North American Indian clothing and artifacts kept in an oversized log cabin! If you liked *Dances with Wolves* you'll enjoy this museum.

**Afternoon Side Trip East** From 1765 to 1918 **Pillnitz Palace** on the Elbe east of Dresden was the summer residence of the kings and queens of Saxony. The most romantic way to get there is by Weisse Flotte excursion boat from near Dresden's Augustus Bridge. Otherwise take tram No 14 from König Johann Strasse or tram No 9 from in front of the Hauptbahnhof east to the end of the line, then walk a few blocks down to the riverside and cross the Elbe on a small ferry operating throughout the year. The museum at Pillnitz (open from May to mid-October) closes at 5 pm but the gardens and palace exterior with its oriental motifs are far more interesting than anything inside (which must be visited on a boring German-language tour), so don't worry if you arrive too late to get in. In summer the Dresden Philharmonic Orchestra sometimes holds concerts here.

After enjoying the gardens (which stay open till 8 pm), take bus No 85 from the loop at the west end of the park back along the right bank of the Elbe to Körner Platz at Loschwitz near the north end of the Elbe

Bridge just east of Dresden. Here you'll find an extremely interesting **funicular railway**, or 'Bergbahn' (the entrance is hidden – ask), which climbs to the Luisenhof Restaurant, a café on an enclosed terrace with a fantastic view of the Elbe and Dresden. From the café follow Plattleite north a few blocks through Weisser Hirsch to the tram line (tram No 11), which you will take west back to Dresden.

**Museum Tickets** The ticket office at the Albertinum sells a season ticket to many Dresden art museums for DM 8 (students DM 4) for one day or DM 10 (students DM 7.50) for one year. This not only saves you money but allows you to bypass the long ticket queues. The museums which accept it are listed on the back of the ticket.

**Activities**
**On the Elbe** From mid-April to mid-October the Weisse Flotte (White Fleet) runs daily paddlewheel steamers upriver from Dresden to Schmilka in the Sächsische Schweiz (Saxon Switzerland) near the Czech border. Shorter trips terminate at Pirna and Bad Schandau. The boats are big and departures frequent, so you shouldn't have difficulty getting a ticket even in midsummer. Local trains return to Dresden from Schmilka-Hirschmühle opposite Schmilka about once an hour until late in the evening with stops all along the river.

Between Pirna and Bad Schandau the scenery climaxes at medieval **Königstein Castle** (1241) on a hilltop to the west. Here the Elbe River has cut a deep valley through the hills with striking sandstone formations protruding from the banks. Two such rock pinnacles are Lilienstein (415 metres) and Pfaffenstein (427 metres), north and south of Königstein, and there's also Bastei (305 metres) downstream near Rathen. All can be climbed.

**Bad Schandau**, a quaint resort town on the river's right bank 40 km south-east of Dresden, is the starting point for the Kirnitzschtalbahn eight km to Lichtenhainer Waterfall. From May to mid-October this narrow-gauge railway runs hourly, the rest of the year every couple of hours on school days only. Hiking trails lead south from the falls up onto the ridge above the river, then west back to Bad Schandau through the Schrammsteine, a lovely walk of a couple of hours.

## Places to Stay

**Camping** There are two Intercampings near Dresden. The closest is *Dresden-Mockritz Camping* just south of the city. Take bus No 76 towards Mockritz from behind Dresden Hauptbahnhof (frequent). This will take you directly there. There are bungalows but they're often full and in summer this camping ground can be very crowded.

A more appealing and distant possibility is *Moritzburg Camping* on Mittel Teich, a 10-minute walk beyond Schloss Moritzburg (take the Moritzburg bus from Dresden Hauptbahnhof Bus Station). The camping ground is spacious, and there's a restaurant and even small caravans (camping trailers – often full). The lake is too murky for swimming but rowing boats are available and the nearby park offers hours of restful walks – recommended.

**Hostels** The 62-bed *'Rudi Arndt' Youth Hostel* (☎ 47 0667), Hübner Strasse 11, is a nine-minute walk from the south exit of the Hauptbahnhof. The overnight charge is DM 14.50 for juniors, DM 17.50 for seniors.

An excellent alternative is the 72-bed *'Wilhelm Dieckmann' Youth Hostel* (☎ 74786), Weintrauben Strasse 12, Radebeul. This hostel is 10 km north-west of Dresden, but access is easy as Radebeul-Weintraube Station on the S-Bahn line from Dresden to Meissen (hourly service or better) is only a few minutes' walk away. You can also get there on trams No 4 and 5 from central Dresden but it's easier to come by train the first time. The hostel has its own bar, but the best feature is the double rooms available at normal YHA prices (DM 14 juniors, DM 17 seniors). The breakfast is good here.

**Private Rooms** Dresden-Information, Prager Strasse 10, has private rooms at DM 25 to DM 40 per person. It also keeps a list of inexpensive pensions (DM 21 to DM 80), but none are in the city centre, so be sure to have the staff there phone before trekking out somewhere.

**Cheaper Hotels** Two inexpensive old hotels within walking distance of Bahnhof Dresden-Neustadt survive in a picturesque old quarter of Dresden unaffected by the wartime bombings, though both are usually full. The 33-room *Hotel Rothenburger Hof*, Rothenburger Strasse 17, is DM 45/75 single/double with shared bath and breakfast. The 20-room *Hotel Stadt Rendsburg* (erected in 1884), Kamenzer Strasse 1, is DM 23/57 single/double with shared bath but without breakfast.

If the two hotels above are not available, take an eastbound tram No 11 up Bautzner Strasse as far as the 54-room *Park Hotel*, Bautzner Land Strasse 7, a 10-minute ride. The Park is an excellent place to stay (DM 55 double), although noise from the downstairs disco late at night and trams in the very early morning can be a problem. The hotel restaurant is unpretentious and colourful. Unfortunately the Park is often full.

Nearby Weisser Hirsch, a suburb east of Dresden and north of the Elbe, is full of small pensions but most have *besetzt* (full) notices on the door and the others don't answer. Plattleite is the street running towards the river just where you get off tram No 11 opposite the Park Hotel. Try the 15-room *Hotel-Pension Haus Sonneneck*, Plattleite 43, and nine-room *Pension Steiner*, Plattleite 49. A few blocks east of Plattleite are the eight-room *Hotel Felsenburg*, Riss Weg 68, and seven-room *Pension Christine Kunath*, Hietzig Strasse 8. If you're told they're full, always ask if they know anyone in the neighbourhood who rents private rooms (*privat Zimmer*). This would be a great area in which to spend a few days if you manage to find something.

**Expensive Hotels** Of the four gleaming, 300-room Interhotels on Prager Strasse near the Hauptbahnhof, the cheapest is the *Hotel*

*Bastei* (DM 90/105 single/double including breakfast) next to the flashy *Interhotel Newa* (DM 161/199 single/double, including breakfast). The *Hotel Königstein* has singles/doubles with bath from DM 104/114, though breakfast is DM 12 per person extra. *Hotel Lilienstein* charges DM 119/143 for singles/doubles with breakfast.

A step down in price but not necessarily in quality is the 99-room *Hotel Gewandhaus*, at Ring Strasse 1 beside the Rathaus (DM 65/100 single/double without bath, DM 80/127 with bath, breakfast included). For character and location you can't beat it.

The spanking new *Hotel Dresden Hof* next to the Frauenkirche ruins, a six-storey blend of architecture old and new, charges DM 240/345 single/double including breakfast and use of the fitness club. Bourgeois decadence is also catered for at the five-star *Interhotel Bellevue* (DM 220/320 single/double facing the street, DM 280/380 facing the river, breakfast included) on Köpcke Strasse near the Goldener Reiter.

Dresden's most interesting up-market hotel by far is the *Schloss Eckberg Hotel*, Bautzner Strasse 134 between Dresden Neustadt and Weisser Hirsch (tram No 11). This romantic castle (1861) in a lovely park overlooking the Elbe has rooms for DM 105 to DM 120 single, DM 120 to DM 178 double, breakfast included. Be aware that many of the rooms are in a modern annexe called 'Haus Eckberg', so if you want to stay in the castle itself be sure to ask for a room in the *'Schloss'*. Under the Communists the Eckberg was a youth hostel and the castle was restored by young volunteers in their spare time, though there's nothing spartan about it today.

## Places to Eat

A quick, easy place to snatch a bite between museums is the big cafeteria (open daily till 7 pm) at street level in the modern *Restaurant Am Zwinger* on Post Platz, the large square on the south side of the Zwinger. The *Radeberger Keller* (open daily till midnight) downstairs in the same building offers good, reasonably priced meals and isn't much more expensive than the cafeteria, so it's far preferable if you have time.

The Restaurant Am Zwinger caters mostly to tourists. A much cheaper self-service favoured by local people is the *Gaststätte Wallterrasse* (closed Saturday afternoon and Sunday), downstairs at Wall Strasse 11, half a block south of the Am Zwinger. The portions are large and there's plenty of draught beer.

The *Café Prag Speise Bar* (open daily from 10 am to 10 pm) on Altmarkt, just across the square from the Kreuzkirche, offers inexpensive meals served informally at the counter or to your table.

Good inexpensive meals with full service are available at *Gaststätte Am Gewandhaus* (open daily till 10 pm) in a separate building behind the Hotel Gewandhaus.

For something special dine at the *Kügelgen Haus Restaurant* (open from 11 am to 11 pm daily), Haupt Strasse 13 below the Romantic Museum in Neustadt. There's a beer cellar (open from 5 pm to 11 pm daily) below the restaurant.

## Entertainment

Dresden's two largest theatres, the *Semperoper* and *Staatsschauspiel*, stand on opposite sides of the Zwinger. The *Staatsoperette*, Pirnaer Land Strasse 131, is in the far east suburbs of the city (trams No 6, 9, 12, 14). Tickets for all three theatres may be had at the Zentrale Vorverkaufskasse in the Altstadler Wache, the stone building on Theater Platz opposite the Semperoper between the equestrian statue and the palace ruins (closed Wednesday, Saturday and Sunday). All theatres close for holidays from mid-July to the end of August.

Elbe Tourist, Kreuz Strasse 2, often has Semperoper tickets for DM 30 and up. You can always make a last try for Semperoper tickets at the 'Abendkasse' in the theatre itself an hour before the performance, or stand outside the door with a small sign reading *Ich möchte eine Karte haben* (I'd like to have a ticket). If you do get a chance for tickets to the Semperoper, take them with profuse thanks, for the performances are brilliant and the opera house is Dresden's architectural highlight. Note that the opera restaurant is rather hidden in the basement below the cloakrooms.

A variety of musical events are presented in the Palace of Culture with a change of programmes daily (admission DM 10 to DM 40).

The *Tonne Jazz Club* on Tzschirner Platz behind the Albertinum often offers live jazz Friday and Saturday at 8.30 pm. Tickets are available at Dresden-Information.

### Getting There & Away

Dresden is just over two hours south of Berlin-Lichtenberg Railway Station by fast train (189km). The Leipzig-Riesa-Dresden service (120 km, 1½ hours) operates hourly. Trains from Erfurt (253 km, five hours) travel via Chemnitz and Gera. The double-decker S-Bahn runs 27 km north-west to Meissen every half-hour.

Direct trains go to/from Prague (194 km, four hours), Nuremberg (391 km, six hours), Munich (542 km, 8½ hours), Stuttgart (581 km, 9½ hours) and Wrocław (160 km, four hours). All trains between Berlin and Prague

stop here. A slightly adventurous way to go to Poland is to take a local train to Görlitz (106 km), then walk across the Neisse River bridge to Zgorzelec, where you'll find onward Polish trains to Jelenia Góra (76 km) and Wrocław (163 km). For advance train tickets and information try the Reisebüro, König Johann Strasse 22.

### Getting Around

Buy a strip of six bus and tram tickets at a kiosk as soon as you arrive. Remember that baggage costs another fare. One of the most useful trams is No 11 which runs between the two railway stations via Post Platz and on to Weisser Hirsch in the far north-eastern suburbs.

### MORITZBURG

Like a French Renaissance chateau, **Jagd-schloss Moritzburg** rises impressively from its lake 14 km north-west of Dresden. Erected as a hunting lodge for the duke of Saxony in 1546, the palace was completely rebuilt in Baroque style in 1730. Try to come during visiting hours (closed December and January, closed Tuesday in November and

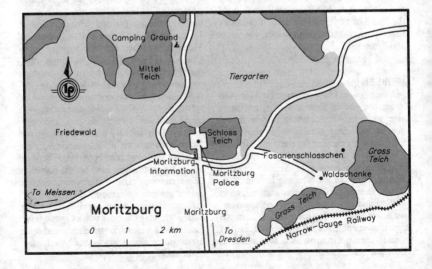

February, closed Monday all year) as the interior is impressive. The *Schlosscafé* (closed Monday and Tuesday) to the right as you enter the palace serves traditional Saxon meals. Be prepared for unbelievable quantities of meat.

Behind the palace a huge park stretches out, and a walk through the woods is just the thing to clear a travel-weary head. Get a map from the information office (open in summer only) near the palace entrance and hike to **Fasanenschlosschen** (1782), a former hunting villa which is now a natural history museum (open daily from mid-March to October). Then backtrack through the forest to the camping ground on Mittel Teich where you can rent a rowing boat to tour the lake.

### Getting There & Away

Bus service between Dresden and Moritzburg is fairly good. Check platform No 4 at the bus station beside Dresden Hauptbahnhof.

An interesting if slow way to get to the palace is by narrow-gauge steam train. Take the Dresden-Meissen S-Bahn to Radebeul Ost, then catch the infrequent Schmalspurbahn (narrow-gauge railway) to Radeburg and get out at the Moritzburg village stop. At the speed of a cycling grandma, it follows a marvellous course through woods, vineyards and lakes.

### MEISSEN

Meissen is a perfectly preserved old German town, the site of Europe's most northerly vineyards. In Albrechtsburg, the medieval quarter crowning a ridge high above the Elbe, is the former ducal palace and Meissen Cathedral, a magnificent Gothic structure. Augustus the Strong of Saxony created Europe's first porcelain factory here in 1710. Unlike Dresden, Meissen was undamaged in WW II and the winding, cobbled streets of the lower town are fun to explore. You might consider spending a night here instead of simply seeing the town as a stop between Dresden and Leipzig.

### Orientation & Information

The bus station is behind the train station, a five-minute walk from the old town. There's a left-luggage office in the railway station. As you leave the train station, turn left and you'll soon see the Elbe River bridge and the old town. Elb Strasse straight ahead from the bridge soon leads into Markt.

Meissen-Information (☎ 53-4470), An der Frauenkirche 3, is in the old Brauhaus (1571) just off Markt.

### Things to See

On Markt Platz are the **Rathaus** (1472) and the 15th century **Frauenkirche** (open from 2 to 5 pm, closed Monday). You can climb the church tower (1549) and by the door is the schedule of the tower's porcelain carillon. The **Town Museum** (closed Friday) is nearby at Heinrichs Platz 3.

The way up to **Albrechtsburg** begins beside the Vincenz Richter Restaurant on Markt Platz. Albrechtsburg's towering 13th century Gothic **cathedral** is visible from afar, but unfortunately the only way to visit it and see the Lucas Cranach the Elder altarpiece is with a boring German-speaking guide (open daily, DM 2). The Renaissance **palace** (1471) beside the cathedral is now a major museum (closed Monday and in January, DM 3). Below Albrechtsburg all Meissen stretches out like a painting by Cranach himself, the old buildings completely unmarred by the block concrete edifices which now dominate Dresden.

Meissen has long been famous around the world for its 'White Gold' chinaware with the blue crossed swords insignia. The original **porcelain factory** was in the castle, and the present factory, at Tal Strasse 9, a km south-west of town, can be visited. There are often impossibly long lines for the porcelain demonstrations (DM 3) but you should be able to get into the museum (DM 3) without difficulty (open from April to October, closed Monday). Unless you're really interested, don't waste your time on it and settle for the porcelain display you can see for free in the shop at Markt 8.

## Places to Stay

*Intercamping 'Rehbockschänke'* is three km south-east of Meissen, at Scharfenberg on the main road to Dresden.

The 54-bed *youth hostel* (☎ 3065) is at Wilsdruffer Strasse 28 just south of town. It's DM 13 for juniors, DM 15.50 for seniors.

Meissen can easily be seen as a day trip from Dresden or as a stop on the way to Leipzig, though the abundance of inexpensive accommodation in Meissen makes it worth considering using the town as a base. Meissen-Information, An der Frauenkirche 3, has private rooms at DM 25 per person.

The 16-room *Hotel Mitropa* right inside Meissen Railway Station itself (through the restaurant) is DM 44/75 single/double with shared bath. The old *Hotel Ross* (1898) across the street from the station has been closed for years but check to see if it has reopened. A block behind the railway station is the 19-room *Hamburger Hof Hotel*, Dresdner Strasse 9, with Meissen's cheapest hotel rooms: DM 30/57 single/double without bath or breakfast.

The 11-room *Hotel Goldener Löwe*, Heinrichs Platz 6 off Elb Strasse, is DM 40/70 single/double for a bathless room with breakfast. An apartment here with all facilities is DM 160 double. Look for the golden lion on the side of this fine old hotel in the middle of the lower town.

## Places to Eat

The *Mitropa Restaurant* in Meissen Railway Station is reasonable.

Check the stand-up buffet in the middle of Kleinmarkt, a square just down from Markt Platz. If it's operating you'll get a very nice snack for a low price. Otherwise try the *Schnellgaststätte Zentrum*, Gerbergasse 14 just a block farther down Marktgasse (closed Saturday and Sunday).

*Vincenz Richter*, an expensive tourist restaurant in a wood-beamed house built in 1523 beside the Frauenkirche on Markt, has a very short menu but the wine list is many pages long. It opens Wednesday to Saturday from 3 to 11 pm, Sunday from 10 am to 3 pm.

There used to be a good self-service on the back terrace of the *Burgkeller* opposite Albrechtsburg Cathedral, though this could have changed. Even if it has, you'll always get a panoramic view of Meissen by visiting the place.

## Entertainment

If you're in Meissen on a Friday, Saturday or Sunday night, check for programmes at the Stadttheatre, an old building dated 1545 on Theater Platz. There's often a disco here on Fridays and Saturdays at 9 pm.

## Getting There & Away

Meissen is easily accessible as a half-day trip from Dresden by riverboat (mid-May to September) or train. Meissen is on the railway line from Dresden to Leipzig via Döbeln, less than an hour from Dresden by double-decker S-Bahn (the regular express trains are faster but several times more expensive). Train service Leipzig-Meissen (107 km) is far less frequent than Dresden-Meissen (27 km). Train tickets and times can be checked at the Reisebüro at Leipziger Strasse 1 off Elb Strasse.

A direct bus runs from Meissen to Moritzburg but it sometimes leaves from stand No 1 at the bus station, and other times from stand No 7 on Bahnhof Strasse near the railway station, so ask. The hours are posted in the railway station and at the nearby bus terminal.

## LEIPZIG

Leipzig, Eastern Germany's second-largest city, is right in the middle of the southern half of the region. This, together with the musical traditions and the city's role as host to some of Germany's most important trade fairs, puts Leipzig on most German itineraries. Aside from its business-oriented present, Leipzig is a city with a past. Here Bach worked from 1723 until his death in 1750, Napoleon met with defeat in 1813 and Georgi Dimitroff stood up to the Nazis in 1933. Leipzig was always a major publishing and library centre, today hosting one of Europe's most important annual book design exhibitions. The city's Deutsche Bücherei

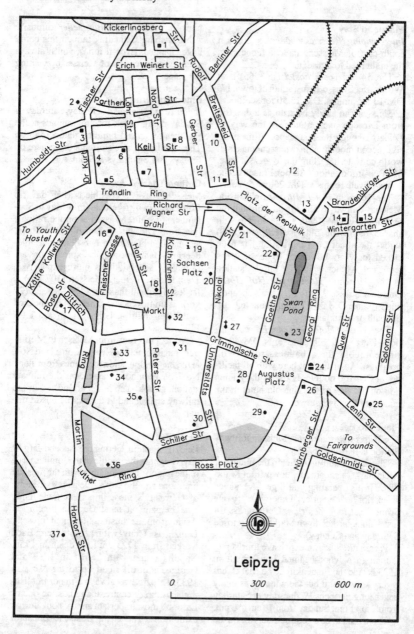

**Leipzig**

0      300      600 m

**■ PLACES TO STAY**

1 Haus Ingeborg
3 Pension am Zoo
5 Hotel International
6 Pension Norddeutscher Hof
7 Hotel Norddeutscher Hof
8 Interhotel Merkur
10 Hotel Vier Jahreszeiten
11 Hotel Astoria
14 Hotel Continental
15 Hotel Bayrisher Hof
16 Hotel Bürgerhof
21 Park Hotel
22 Hotel Stadt Leipzig
26 Hotel Deutschland

**▼ PLACES TO EAT**

4 Cafeteria Restaurant
31 Auerbachs Keller

**OTHER**

2 Zoo
9 Café Vis a Vis & Jugendtourist
12 Leipzig-Hauptbahnhof
13 Reisebüro Private Room Service
17 Schauspielhaus
18 Reise Welt
19 Leipzig-Information
20 Orion Night Club
23 Opera House
24 Post Office
25 Grassimuseum
27 St Nikolai Church
28 University
29 Gewandhaus Concert Hall
30 Egyptian Museum
32 Old Town Hall (Altes Rathaus)
33 St Thomas Church
34 Bach's House
35 Eden Tanzbar
36 New Town Hall (Neues Rathaus)
37 Georgi Dimitroff Museum

## Orientation

Leipzig-Hauptbahnhof (1915) with 26 platforms is the largest terminal station in Europe. The main baggage room at Leipzig Hauptbahnhof won't accept backpacks and the coin lockers are often full. Instead take your pack to the oversized-baggage room just inside the far west exit from the station, beside the stairs going down.

To enter the city centre next to the station, use the underpass to cross wide Platz der Republik. Most of Leipzig's tram lines stop in the centre of this square, and historic Markt with the old town hall is just a couple of blocks south-west. Here you'll find museums and churches, inviting restaurants and cafés. The rings around the old city centre follow the lines of the former city walls.

Giant Augustus Platz (formerly Karl Marx Platz), three blocks east of Markt, is ex-socialist Leipzig, the space-age lines of the university (1975) and concert hall (1983) juxtaposed against the functional opera house (1960). Leipzig's famous International Fairgrounds are about three km south-east along Lenin Strasse. The massive Battle of Nations Monument looms just beyond.

## Information

Leipzig-Information (☎ 41-79590, open from 9 am to 7 pm weekdays, and from 9.30 am to 2 pm Saturday) is at Sachsen Platz 1 between the Hauptbahnhof and old town hall. Bear right after going through the underpass. They give away free city maps and sell theatre tickets.

Bavaria Studentenreisebüro (☎ 719 2267), in the tall university building at Augustus Platz 9, sells youth/student train and plane tickets and is a generally useful travel agency.

If you came for the Leipzig Fair and don't have a Fair Card, you can buy one at Messetourist, Katharinen Strasse 3.

## Things to See

**Old Leipzig** The Renaissance **old town hall** (1556) on Markt, one of Germany's largest,

houses almost seven million volumes, including every book published in German since 1913. Leipzig was never as badly bombed as Dresden, so a lot of old buildings and hotels remain in the city centre. The Intercamping is convenient and a full day can be spent doing the round of museums.

houses the City History Museum (closed Monday). Behind it is the **Alte Börse** (1687) with a monument to Goethe (1903) in front. Goethe, who studied law at Leipzig University, called the town a 'little Paris' in his drama *Faust*. **St Nikolai Church** (1165) between Markt and Augustus Platz has a remarkable interior.

Just west of Markt is **St Thomas Church** (1212) with the tomb of composer Johann Sebastian Bach in front of the altar. The Thomas Choir which Bach led is still going strong. Beside the church at Thomaskirchhof 16 is **Bach's house**, now a museum (closed Monday, DM 2).

Follow the tram line that passes St Thomas south a few blocks to reach the **Georgi Dimitroff Museum**, housed in the former Supreme Court of the Reich (1888). This important museum has an excellent collection of old master paintings downstairs, but don't miss the **Reichstag Fire Museum** upstairs (the entrance is obscure, so ask). Here you'll see the original courtroom where Dimitroff made a fool of Hermann Göring in 1933 and listen to a recording in English describing the proceedings (ask the attendant to put it on). The Dimitroff Museum closes at 2 pm on weekends, though the art gallery stays open until 5 pm. Both museums are closed Monday and open till 9.30 pm on Wednesday.

**Other Sights** Leipzig has many other museums but more impressive is the **Battle of Nations Monument** on Lenin Strasse, beyond the fairgrounds about five km south-east of the railway station (trams No 15 or 20). To get there from the Dimitroff Museum catch tram No 21 beside the Neues Rathaus. This tremendous structure was erected in 1913 to commemorate a victory by combined Prussian, Austrian, Swedish and Russian armies during the Napoleonic wars. After his defeat at Leipzig, Napoleon abdicated and was exiled to Elba. Climb up on top of the monument for the view (open daily until 4 pm).

An afternoon visit to Leipzig's **zoo** (DM 3) is a good way to top off a busy day. The zoo is renowned for its breeding of lions and tigers. The entrance is off Dr Kurt Fischer Strasse beside the old Kongresshalle, a short walk north-west from the station or the old town. In summer the zoo stays open until 6.30 pm.

### Places to Stay

**Camping** *Intercamping Leipzig-Nord*, Am Auensee, is in a pleasant, wooded location near the city (take trams No 10 or 28 to the end of the line at Wahren, then walk eight minutes). On-site A-frame bungalows are DM 20 double but they're often full. Regular bungalows are DM 30/40 double/triple, DM 50 for five people. Camping is DM 4 per person plus DM 3 per tent. Even if the sign outside says 'closed', ask at the office anyway – they may take you.

**Hostels** The 104-bed *'George Schumann'* Youth Tourist Hotel (☎ 40530) at Käthe Kollwitz Strasse 64-66 is in the western section of the city. This large, prewar mansion with a pleasant garden at the back offers accommodation in three-bed rooms. Make advance reservations in summer as it fills quickly. Get there on tram No 2 from the railway station. Beds are DM 14 for juniors, DM 17 for seniors.

There's also the 36-bed *Alfred Frank Youth Hostel* (☎ 57189), Gustav Esche Strasse 4 on Auen Lake, a five-minute walk from the Intercamping. It's a Mark cheaper.

**Private Rooms** Leipzig-Information, Sachsen Platz 5, rents private rooms at DM 25 per person. The Reisebüro has a poorly marked 'Zimmernachweis' office in the east corner of the railway station (entry from the parking lot) with private rooms at DM 27/31 single/double (open Monday to Thursday from 9 am to 6 pm, Friday from 9 am to 7 pm, Saturday from 9 am to noon).

**Cheaper Hotels** There are many inexpensive hotels within walking distance of the railway station, for example, the 21-room *Hotel Vier Jahreszeiten*, Rudolf Breitscheid Strasse 23. At last report rooms without bath or breakfast were priced at DM 29/49/69 single/double/triple, and although these prices are sure to have increased it will probably still be Leipzig's best buy.

The *Haus Ingeborg* hotel, Nord Strasse 58 a couple of blocks north of the Interhotel Merkur, has 10 simple rooms with shared bath at DM 50 to DM 70 double. If they don't answer downstairs, ring the door marked 'Feldmann' up on the 3rd floor. *Pension Am Zoo*, Dr Kurt Fischer Strasse 23, is similar at DM 45 double.

Also try *Pension Norddeutscher Hof*, Löhr Strasse 15. The 57-room *Hotel Norddeutscher Hof*, Löhr Strasse 4, used to be inexpensive but recent renovations have boosted prices.

The 27-room *Hotel Bürgerhof*, above the expensive Vietnamese restaurant at Grosse Fleischergasse 4, is DM 40/65 single/double with breakfast (shared bath), but the six singles are usually all taken.

Moving up in price there's the 174-room *Park Hotel*, Richard Wagner Strasse 7, at DM 65/100 single/double without bath but including breakfast. *Hotel Continental*, Georgi Ring 14 opposite the east side of the railway station, is DM 97/143 single/double with bath and breakfast (55 rooms). The nearby 45-room *Hotel Bayrischer Hof*, Wintergarten Strasse 13, is somewhat cheaper at DM 65/100 single/double with shared bath.

**Expensive Hotels** As a major trade fair city, Leipzig has no less than six big Interhotels. The soaring five-star *Interhotel Merkur*, Gerber Strasse 15 near the station, is top of the line at DM 220/295 single/double with breakfast. This palatial, Japanese-built hotel throws in a buffet breakfast and use of the fitness club with the room.

All of Leipzig's other deluxe hotels face noisy tram lines. The overpriced *Astoria Hotel*, Platz der Republik 2 (DM 145/250 single/double with bath and breakfast), is right beside the station. The three-star *Hotel Zum Löwen* (108 rooms), on Rudolf Breitscheid Strasse behind the Astoria, is DM 113/184 single/double with bath and breakfast.

Opposite the station is the four-star *Hotel Stadt Leipzig*, Richard Wagner Strasse 1-5, at DM 120/230 single/double with bath and breakfast. The *Hotel Deutschland* (formerly Hotel Am Ring) on Augustus Platz is DM 115/205 single/double.

The most elegant of the luxury hotels is the 100-room, three-star *Hotel International* on Tröndlin Ring. This Baroque palace erected in 1771 and converted into a hotel in 1889 includes lots of class in the price: DM 110/195 single/double with bath and breakfast.

## Places to Eat

Since 1525 Leipzig's most famous eatery has been *Auerbach's Keller*, downstairs in the Mädler-Passage just south of the Rathaus. Look for the statues depicting scenes from Goethe's *Faust* near the entrance. (After carousing with students at Auerbach's Keller, Mephistopheles and Faust left riding on a barrel.)

The nearby *Naschmarkt Buffet*, Grimmaische Strasse 10, is a cheap cafeteria which closes at 6 pm on weekdays, 1 pm Saturdays. The upstairs dining room at the *Burgkeller* across the street is a lot less expensive than the restaurant downstairs but it's closed weekends.

The cheapest lunches are served on weekdays at the *Cafeteria Restaurant*, Dr Kurt Fischer Strasse 4-10. Two large *Mitropa* restaurants are at platform level in the railway station: *Restaurant West* is a cheap self-service while *Restaurant Ost* offers full service.

If you're staying at the youth hostel, a great little pub nearby is the *Am Johanna Park*, Sebastian Bach Strasse 13. The beer is on tap, they serve good meals and even have a pool table and dartboard.

## Entertainment

Ask Leipzig-Information about tickets to the *Opernhaus* and ultramodern *Gewandhaus*

*Concert Hall*, both of which are on Augustus Platz. Established in 1743, the Gewandhaus Orchestra is Europe's oldest – in fact, the composer Mendelssohn was once its conductor. The *Schauspielhaus*, at Bose Strasse 1, is a few blocks west of Markt. All of the theatres close for holidays during July and August.

Leipzig's *Musical Comedy Theater*, Dreilinder Strasse 30-32, is on the far west side of the city (take trams No 15, 17, 27 or 57 from Platz der Republik to Wilhelm Liebknecht Platz, then ask).

*Eden Tanzbar*, Peter Strasse 34, is a disco (open from 8 pm to 3 am, closed Monday and Tuesday, DM 4 admission).

For late-evening entertainment try the *Orion Night Club*, Nikolai Strasse 39-45 north of St Nikolai Church, which opens from 10 pm to 4 am Tuesday to Saturday.

*Café Vis a Vis*, Rudolf Breitscheid Strasse 33, a block north of the west exit from the Hauptbahnhof, is a great little bar/café with a friendly young clientele (open from 11 am to 3 am Tuesday to Friday, 2 pm to 3 am Saturday).

If you're staying at the Intercamping, check *Haus Auensee* across the street. It has a disco (DM 4) on Wednesday, Friday, Saturday and Sunday nights. Other times there's a pleasant terrace restaurant overlooking the lake.

**Leipzig Fair** The Leipzig Fair, a major vehicle of East-West trade, is the only medieval fair to survive into our times. The tradition goes back to medieval markets at the crossing of the Via Regia from Western Europe to Poland and the Via Imperii from the Baltic to Nuremberg. In the 16th century, spices, wines and metal goods from the south were traded for wool, canvas and hides from the north. Chartered in 1165, the original fair was held on the market square in front of the Rathaus.

Today, the spring trade fair in mid-March features engineering, electrical engineering, electronics and instrumentation, while the autumn trade fair in early September emphasises chemicals, motor vehicles, textile machinery, printing and paper-making equipment. Consumer goods are shown at both fairs with sporting equipment displayed at the autumn fair. A separate book fair takes place in late April. For more information write to the Leipzig Fair Agency (☎ 0375-39 1122), Queensgate Centre, Orsett Rd, Grays, Essex RMI7 5DJ, England. The Fair Card costs £16 and should be ordered from this agency two months in advance. During the Leipzig Fair all hotel rooms are full and restaurants hike their prices, so avoid Leipzig at this time unless it's the fair you're interested in.

### Getting There & Away

Fast trains connect Leipzig to Berlin-Lichtenberg (182 km, 2½ hours) via Lutherstadt Wittenberg (83 km from Leipzig). Service between Leipzig and Dresden (120 km, two hours) via Riesa is frequent. Other fast trains run from Leipzig to Chemnitz (81 km, 1½ hours), Gera (72 km, 1½ hours), Halle (38 km, 40 minutes) and Weimar (82 km, 1½ hours). A major express line leads north from Leipzig to Rostock (405 km) via Halle, Magdeburg and Schwerin. An overnight train with sleepers is available to Rostock via Potsdam.

Long-distance trains run direct from Leipzig to Cologne (nine hours), Frankfurt/Main (375 km, six hours), Karlovy Vary (240 km, five hours), Munich (487 km, 7½ hours), Nuremberg (336 km, five hours), Stuttgart (526 km, eight hours) and Warsaw (704 km, 14 hours).

For advance international railway tickets go to Reise Welt, Katharinen Strasse 1-3, or the Reisebüro, nearby at Reichs Strasse 18. Jugendtourist, Rudolf Breitscheid Strasse 39, offers cheap international train tickets for those aged 26 and under.

### Getting Around

Leipzig's city transport system is based on trams; buy a strip of tickets at a kiosk as soon as you arrive. Validate your ticket yourself once aboard.

# Thuringia

The State of Thuringia (Thüringen) occupies a basin cutting into the heart of Germany between the Harz Mountains and the hilly Thuringian Forest. The Germanic Thuringians were conquered by the Franks in 531 and converted to Christianity by St Boniface in the 8th century. The duke of Saxony seized the area in 908 and for the next thousand years the region belonged to one German principality or another. Only in 1920 was Thuringia reconstituted as a state with something approaching its original borders. Under the Communists the state was split into the districts of Erfurt, Suhl and Gera but since 1990 it's a single unit once again.

## WEIMAR

Not a monumental city nor a medieval one, Weimar appeals to more refined tastes. As a respository of German humanistic traditions it's unrivalled, but these can be difficult to assimilate by a foreign visitor in a rush. The parks and small museums are meant to be savoured, not downed in one gulp.

Many famous men lived and worked here, including Lucas Cranach the Elder, Johann Sebastian Bach, Christoph Martin Wieland, Friedrich Schiller, Johann Gottfried von Herder, Johann Wolfgang von Goethe, Franz Liszt, Walter Gropius, Lyonel Feininger, Vasili Kandinsky, Gerhard Marcks and Paul Klee. The State Bauhaus, which laid the foundations of modern architecture, functioned in the city from 1919 to 1925.

Weimar is best known abroad as the place where the German constituent assembly drafted a republican constitution after WW I. As a result, the German republic which preceded the rise of fascism was known as the Weimar Republic (1919-33), although you won't see much reference to it here. The horrors of Buchenwald concentration camp are well remembered, however. You'll need two full days to see Weimar and its surroundings.

## Orientation

The centre of town is just west of the Ilm River, a 20-minute walk south of the railway station. Buses run fairly frequently between the station and Goethe Platz, from whence you'll wend your way east along small streets to Herder Platz or Markt.

## Information

There are two information offices in Weimar. Weimar-Information (☎ 621 2173), Markt Strasse 4 across the square from the Elephant Hotel, is open weekdays and Saturday mornings. Ask about tickets to cultural events here.

The Museum Ticket Office, Frauentor Strasse 4, sells a ticket valid for eight of Weimar's museums (DM 8 for students, DM 12 for others). Entry tickets to the Goethe Museum *must* be purchased here.

## Things to See

**City Centre** A good place to begin your visit is on Herder Platz. The **parish church** (1500) in the centre of the square has an altarpiece (1555) finished by Lucas Cranach the Younger which features a portrait of his father, Lucas Cranach the Elder. In front of this church is a statue of the philosopher and writer Johann Gottfried von Herder (1744-1803) who settled here in 1776.

A block east of Herder Platz towards the Ilm River is Weimar's major art museum, the **Schlossmuseum** (closed Monday) on Burg Platz. This large collection, with masterpieces by Cranach, Dürer and others, occupies three floors of the former residence of the elector of the Duchy of Saxony-Weimar.

Platz der Demokratie with the renowned music school founded in 1872 by Franz Liszt is up the street running south from the castle. This square spills over into Markt Platz, where you'll find the neo-Gothic **Rathaus** (1841) and the house in which Lucas Cranach the Elder spent his last two years and died (in 1553).

West of Markt via some narrow lanes is Theater Platz with statues (1857) of Goethe and Schiller and the **German National**

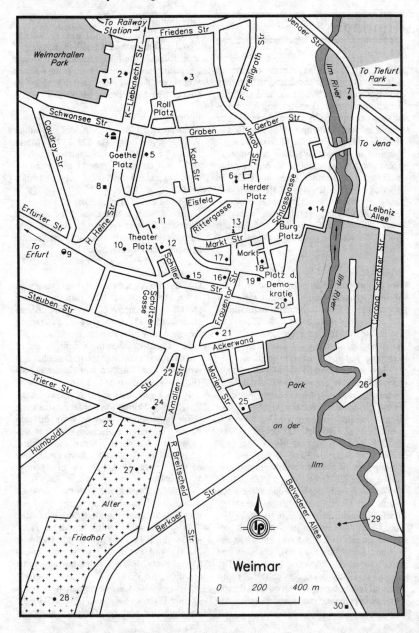

Weimar

0    200    400 m

■ PLACES TO STAY

8   Hotel Russischer Hof
19  Interhotel Elephant
22  Christliches Hospiz
23  'am Poseckschen Garten' Youth
    Hostel
30  Interhotel Belvedere

▼ PLACES TO EAT

1   Gaststätte Weimarhalle

    OTHER

2   City Historical Museum
3   Jacobskirchhof
4   Post Office
5   Students' Club 'Kasseturm'
6   Parish Church
7   Goethe-Schiller Archive
9   Bus Station
10  German National Theatre
11  Kunsthalle
12  Wittums Palace
13  Weimar-Information
14  Schlossmuseum
15  Schiller Haus
16  Museum Ticket Office
17  Rathaus
18  Lucas Cranach's House
20  Franz Liszt Music School
21  Goethe Museum
24  Museum of Prehistory
25  Liszt House
26  Goethe's Cottage
27  Goethe-Schiller Mausoleum
28  Märzgefallenen Monument
29  Römisches Haus

**Famous Men** From Theater Platz, Schiller Strasse curves around to **Schiller Haus** (closed Tuesday, DM 5) at No 12, now newly restored. Schiller lived in Weimar from 1799 to 1805, a contemporary of Goethe who spent the years 1775 to 1832 here. The **Goethe Museum** (closed Monday, DM 5) is a block ahead and right, by far the most important of the many home museums of illustrious former residents. There are two parts to this museum: to the right the personal quarters where Goethe resided, and upstairs an exhibition on his life and times. The

Goethe

**Theatre**, where the constituent assembly, escaping the revolutionary climate in Berlin, drafted the constitution of the German republic in 1919. Also on this square is the **Kunsthalle** (closed Monday) and **Wittums Palace** (closed Monday and Tuesday, DM 3), now a major museum dedicated to the poet Christoph Martin Wieland (1733-1813). Wieland, who moved to Weimar in 1772, was the first to translate Shakespeare's complete works into German.

immortal work *Faust* was written here. The nice little café in the museum is a bonus.

**Liszt House** (closed Monday, DM 3) is south on Marien Strasse by the edge of Park an der Ilm. Liszt resided in Weimar in 1848 and from 1869 to 1886, and here he wrote his *Hungarian Rhapsody* and *Faust Symphony*. The yellow complex next to Liszt House is the original **Bauhaus** where Walter Gropius laid the groundwork for all modern architecture. The buildings themselves were erected by the famous architect Henry van de Velde from 1904 to 1911.

The tombs of Goethe and Schiller lie side by side in a neoclassical crypt (closed Tuesday) in the **Alter Friedhof**, two blocks west of Liszt House. Behind the mausoleum is an onion-domed Russian Orthodox church (1862). Continue south through the cemetery, past a church and over a small bridge. Here you'll find the **monument 'Den Märzgefallenen 1920'**, designed in 1922 by Walter Gropius, destroyed by the Nazis in 1933 and re-erected in 1945. The monument honours workers murdered by the military during the November 1918 revolution.

**Parks & Palaces** Weimar boasts three large parks, each replete with monuments, museums and attractions. Most accessible is **Park an der Ilm** which runs right along the east side of Weimar and contains Goethe's cottage (DM 3). Goethe himself landscaped the park.

A km or two farther south is **Belvedere Park** with a Baroque palace (open from May to September, Wednesday to Sunday), orangerie, viewpoints, etc. Schloss Belvedere itself may be closed for renovations but the main attractions here are the beautiful gardens and park which could absorb hours. To get to Belvedere take bus No 11 from Goethe Platz towards 'Ehringsdorf' as far as Café Hainfels, then walk 15 minutes. Coming back, get on the bus going in the same direction as the one that brought you here – bus No 11 makes a big circle.

**Tiefurt Park**, a few km east of the railway station, is similar but smaller (palace closed on Monday and Tuesday, admission DM 3). Duchess Anne Amalia organised famous intellectual 'round-table gatherings' here in the late 18th century. Get there on bus No 3 from Goethe Platz hourly.

**Buchenwald** The Buchenwald museum and memorial are on Ettersberg Hill, beyond a large Soviet military base 10 km north-west of Weimar. You first pass the memorial (open at any time) with mass graves of some of the 56,500 victims from 18 nations. The concen-

tration camp and museum (closed Monday and after 4 pm other days) are a km beyond. German antifascists, Soviet and Polish prisoners of war and many others were held at Buchenwald for slave-labour purposes in nearby underground armaments factories. On 11 April 1945, as US troops approached, the prisoners rose in armed rebellion, overcame the SS guards and liberated themselves. Many prominent German Communists and Social Democrats, Ernst Thälmann and Rudolf Breitscheid among them, were murdered here.

Buses run to Buchenwald from Weimar Hauptbahnhof (bus platform No 31) every hour or so. Pay the driver.

### Places to Stay

**Camping** The closest *Intercamping* is at Weissensee, Am Terrassebad, seven km north-west of Sömmerda. Take a direct bus to Sömmerda from stop No 25 in front of Weimar Station or a train from Erfurt to Sömmerda, then another bus to Weissensee, then walk 20 minutes.

**Hostels** Weimar's three city youth hostels are no longer connected with the Deutsches Jugendherbergswerk since they have been privatised, so for current information ask at Weimar-Information. All are in the southern section of the city a couple of km away from the railway station. The closest is the 81-bed *'Am Poseckschen Garten' Youth Hostel* (☎ 4021) at Humboldt Strasse 17 near the Alter Friedhof.

Rather than stopping at the 'Am Poseckschen Garten' it's worth the five-minute walk a couple of blocks south-west to the less crowded 56-bed *'ErnstThälmann' Youth Hostel* (☎ 2076) at Windmühlen Strasse 16, a continuation of Humboldt Strasse (bus No 6 from the station).

The 51-bed *'Maxim Gorki' Youth Tourist Hotel* (☎ 3471) is on the opposite side of the Alter Friedhof at Zum wilden Graben 12 (bus No 5 from the station).

The 80-bed *'Albert Kuntz' Youth Hostel* (☎ 67216) at Buchenwald is still an official hostel.

**Private Rooms** The Gästezimmer Vermittlung office on Kauf Strasse opposite Weimar-Information has private rooms (open weekdays from 1.30 to 6.30 pm, Saturdays from 8.30 am to 1 pm).

**Hotels** There are two reasonably priced hotels on the square in front of the railway station, the 24-room *Thüringen* (DM 60/90 single/double with breakfast) and the 47-room *International* (from DM 45/65 single/double). Both are all right although the taps in the Thüringen give off a terrible screech.

The *Hotel Russischer Hof* on Goethe Platz has rooms with bath and breakfast from DM 85/135 single/double.

The 115-room, three-star *Interhotel Elephant*, Markt 19, charges DM 160/255 single/double. Actually, it's a characterful old building quite appropriate for Weimar, fine if you can afford it.

Not far away is the recently renovated 41-room *Christliches Hospiz* (☎ 2711), Amalien Strasse 2 near Goethehaus.

The luxurious *Interhotel Belvedere* on Belvedere Allee south of town opened in 1991.

## Places to Eat

The buffet at Herder Platz 3 is a cheap self-service with pleasant tables to sit at, but it's only open weekdays from 7.30 am to 4.30 pm. The *Gastmahl des Meeres*, Herder Platz 16 (open daily), serves seafood at reasonable prices in a Renaissance house dating back to 1566.

The *Ratskeller* below the Reisebüro at Markt 10 (closed Sunday and Monday) is less expensive than most of the other fancy restaurants around here.

The *Gaststätte Weimarhalle* back by the park off Karl Liebknecht Strasse (open daily from 9 am to 11 pm, Tuesday and Wednesday from 9 am to 3 pm) is inexpensive and has a large dining room overlooking a pond.

The hotel restaurants in the Thüringen and International hotels in front of the railway station are unpretentious, accessible, inexpensive and good.

**Cafés** The poorly marked *Goethe Café*, Wieland Strasse 4 between Goethe Platz and Theater Platz, is the place for afternoon coffee and cakes (daily). There's also *Café Esplanade*, Schiller Strasse 18.

## Entertainment

The *German National Theatre* on Theater Platz is the city's main theatre. To buy tickets to this theatre and other events, try the Besucherabteilung office in the adjacent street.

Organ music is performed in the Herder Church every Sunday at 6 pm from June to mid-September (DM 4).

Weekends there's sometimes a disco at the *Students' Club 'Kasseturm'* in the round tower on Goethe Platz.

## Getting There & Away

There are direct trains to Weimar from Berlin-Lichtenberg (264 km, 3½ hours), Eisenach (78 km, 1½ hours), Frankfurt/Main (293 km, five hours), Halle (86 km, 1½ hours) and Leipzig (82 km, 1½ hours). Trains from Dresden (232 km, five hours) arrive via Chemnitz and Jena. There's frequent service between Erfurt and Weimar, a 22-km, 20-minute trip. For practical travel arrangements go to the Reisebüro, Markt 10.

## ERFURT

This trading and university centre, founded as a bishop's residence by St Boniface in 742, is the capital of Thuringia. Erfurt University, dating back to 1392, counted Martin Luther among its students. Undamaged during the war, Erfurt is a town of towers and flowers with colourful burgher mansions gracing the well-preserved medieval quarter. Fortunately industry has kept to the modern suburbs. Each summer the International Horticultural Exhibition (IGA) takes place in the western section of Erfurt.

## Orientation

As you come out of the railway station turn left, then right and walk straight up Bahnhof Strasse. In a few minutes you'll reach the Anger, a large square at the city's heart.

Continue straight ahead and follow the tram tracks along Schlösser Strasse past the Rathaus till you come to Dom Platz, Erfurt's most impressive sight.

## Information

Erfurt-Information (☎ 61-26267) is at the corner of Bahnhof Strasse and Juri Gagarin Ring, halfway between the station and the Anger.

Jugendtourist is at Fischmarkt 6 and Schlösser Strasse 17 (two offices).

## Things to See

Begin by visiting the **Anger Museum** (closed Monday and Tuesday), Anger 18 on the corner of Bahnhof Strasse, then cross Dom Platz and take Markt Strasse east to Fischmarkt, the medieval city centre. Historical buildings such as the **Rathaus** (1873), **Haus Zum Breiten Herd** (1584) and the **House of the Red Ox** (1562) surround this square.

The 13th century Gothic **Dom of St Mary** and adjacent **Severikirche** (closed) crown a hilltop just west of the old town. The wooden stools (1350) and stained glass (1410) in the choir, and figures on the portals, make the Dom one of the richest medieval churches in Germany (open until 5 pm Monday to Saturday, 4 pm Sunday).

The eastbound street beside the Rathaus leads to the medieval **Krämerbrücke** (1325), now completely restored and lined on each side with timber-framed shops. This is the only such bridge north of the Alps!

Continue east on Futter Strasse for a block till it terminates at Johannes Strasse with the **City Historical Museum** (closed Friday and Saturday) around the corner at number 169. From the historical museum go south on Johannes Strasse to a large church, on the opposite side of which is Anger.

## Places to Stay

**Hostels & Private Rooms** The 80-bed *'Karl Reimann' Youth Hostel* (☎ 26705), Hochheimer Strasse 12, is on the western side of the city (tram No 5 southbound to the terminus). It's DM 14 for juniors, DM 17 for seniors.

Erfurt-Information has private rooms but the singles are usually all taken.

**Hotels** The 163-room, four-star *Interhotel Erfurter Hof* in front of the train station has great atmosphere but you pay for it (from DM 120/190 single/double, breakfast included).

A much cheaper possibility is the 118-room *Hotel Bürgerhof*, Bahnhof Strasse 35-36 beside Erfurt-Information. This older hotel near the station charges DM 41/81 single/double with shared bath, breakfast included.

Atmosphere is sadly lacking in the 319-room, three-star *Interhotel Kosmos*, Juri Gagarin Ring 126-127 a few blocks away. Its soaring, out-of-place silhouette is reflected in its prices (DM 110/170 single/double).

The high-rise *Hotel am Ring*, Juri Gagarin Ring 148 a little north of the Kosmos, has two-bedroom apartments accommodating up to four people for DM 80 (DM 4 per person extra for breakfast). One room in an apartment is DM 40/50 single/double. This former workers' residence is likely to have rooms.

Nearby at Juri Gagarin Ring 154-156 is the *Thüringen Hotel* (☎ 69028) where singles/doubles/triples with bath and breakfast are DM 57/73/89. This former youth tourist hotel now operates as a regular hotel.

## Getting There & Away

Erfurt is well connected by train to Eisenach (56 km, one hour), Dresden (253 km, five hours), Leipzig (104 km, 1½ hours), Nordhausen (80 km, 1½ hours), Sömmerda (25 km, 30 minutes), Suhl (65 km, 1½ hours), Weimar (22 km, 20 minutes) and most other cities in Eastern Germany.

Erfurt is midway between Berlin and Frankfurt/Main and the main line from Berlin-Lichtenberg (286 km, four hours) reaches Erfurt via Halle. To/from the Baltic coast you may have to change at Magdeburg although some trains run straight through. The Reisebüro at Anger 62 will have train tickets and times.

## EISENACH

Eisenach is a picturesque medieval town in the south-west corner of Eastern Germany on the edge of the Thuringian Forest. From Romanesque Wartburg Castle overlooking Eisenach the landgraves ruled medieval Thuringia. Richard Wagner based his opera *Tannhäuser* on a minstrel's contest which took place in Wartburg Castle in 1206-07. Martin Luther was kept in protective custody here by the elector under the assumed name 'Junker Jörg' after being excommunicated and put under the ban of the empire by the pope.

More recently the first country-wide proletarian party, the Social Democratic Workers' Party, was founded at Eisenach by August Bebel and Wilhelm Liebknecht in 1869. Another first was the first automobile produced in Eisenach in 1898. The sturdy little Wartburg cars formerly assembled in the local factory are still seen all over Eastern Europe.

### Orientation

Eisenach is the westernmost town in Eastern Europe. The railway station and medieval Wartburg are on opposite sides of town. If time is short take a bus or taxi to the Wartburg and walk back through the forest. To walk to the castle from the station follow Bahnhof Strasse west under the arch, cross the square and continue west on Karl Strasse to Markt. Two blocks west of Markt is Schlossberg with the Predigerkirche Museum (closed Monday) on the corner. Follow Schlossberg directly south-west (another two km uphill) and you'll come to Wartburg.

### Information

Eisenach-Information (☎ 623 6161) is at Bahnhof Strasse 3 near the station.

### Things to See

Most tourists come to Eisenach to see the old fortress of **Wartburg** on a hilltop overlooking the Thuringian forests and hills. Martin Luther translated the New Testament from Greek into German while in hiding here in 1521-22, thus making an immense contribu-

tion to the development of a uniform written German language. In summer huge crowds line up for tours of Wartburg's palace and its Romanesque great hall, so count on waiting a while unless you arrive early. The view from Wartburg's tower (no queue) alone is worth the trip. You pay DM 1 to enter the complex and climb the tower, another DM 3 to tour the castle with a German-speaking guide.

In town the **Thuringian Museum** (closed Monday, admission DM 2) in the former town palace (1751), Markt 24, has a collection of ceramics and paintings of local interest. The interior of the **Georgenkirche** (rebuilt in 1676) on Markt has three balconies which run all the way around, plus a glorious organ and pulpit. Four members of the Bach family served as organists here between 1665 and 1797.

Up the hill from the Georgenkirche is **Lutherhaus** (open daily, admission DM 3), the future reformer's home from 1498 to 1501. The late-Gothic architecture is far more interesting than the exhibits. Don't miss **Bachhaus** (closed Wednesday, DM 4) on Frauenplan, where the composer was born in 1685. After a look around the museum go down into a room where Bach's music is played.

The composer Wagner rates a small display in the **Reuter-Wagner Museum** (closed Monday) on the back way up to Wartburg. The **Gedenkstätte Parteitag 1869** (closed Monday) nearby at Marien Strasse 57 has a fascinating exhibit on the 19th century workers' movements in Germany. The adjacent **Kartausgarten** with its 1825 teahouse (open May to September Tuesdays 9.30 am to 12.30 pm, Thursdays 1.30 to 5 pm, Saturdays 1.30 to 4 pm) is a relaxing contrast to it all.

### Places to Stay

**Hostels & Private Rooms** Try the 52-bed *'Erich Honstein' Youth Hostel* (☎ 2012), Born Strasse 7 (DM 13 for juniors, DM 15.50 for seniors), or the 105-bed *'Artur Becker' Youth Hostel* (☎ 3613), Mariental

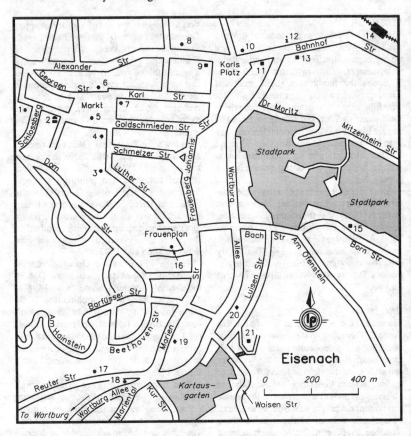

Eisenach

0    200    400 m

24 in the valley below Wartburg (DM 14 for juniors, DM 17 for seniors).

The Zimmernachweis office at Eisenach-Information, Bahnhof Strasse 3 (open weekdays from 2 to 7 pm, Saturdays from 1 to 6 pm), has private rooms.

**Hotels** Eisenach has long been a tourist centre of note, so hotel accommodation is not lacking. The 29-room *Bahnhofs Hotel* near the station is cheap at DM 30/45 single/double and rooms are usually available, but be prepared as there's no shower in the entire hotel!

The 42-room *Park Hotel*, Wartburg Allee 2 nearby, has a shower on each floor but is DM 45/75 single/double with breakfast. If you're willing to pay that, consider walking a block farther west to the quieter, 45-room *Thüringer Hof Hotel* just behind the statue of Martin Luther beyond the old gate, which charges exactly the same.

A step up in class and elevation is the 54-room *Stadt Eisenach Hotel* (DM 45/80 single/double), Luisen Strasse 11-13 overlooking the Kartausgarten above the Automotive Museum, or stay at the 29-room *Hotel Auf der Wartburg* which costs DM

1 Predigerkirche Museum
2 Post Office
3 Lutherhaus
4 Residenzhaus
5 Georgenkirche
6 Thuringian Museum
7 Rathaus
8 Konzertbüro
9 Thüringer Hof Hotel
10 Nikolaikirche
11 Park Hotel
12 Eisenach-Information
13 Bahnhofs Hotel
14 Railway Station
15 'Erich Honstein' Youth Hostel
16 Bachhaus
17 Reuter-Wagner Museum
18 'Wartburg Express'
19 Gedenkstätte Parteitag 1869
20 Automotive Museum
21 Stadt Eisenach Hotel

65/90 single/double, up beside the castle, a place for romantics and lesser tourists.

**Places to Eat**
A good place for a quick chicken, chips and Wartburg pils is the *Broiler Stübchen Bar*, Frauenberg Johannis Strasse 5 (open weekdays from 11 am to 6 pm, Sundays from 11 am to 2 pm).

The *Zwinger Restaurant* downstairs in the Park Hotel is very reasonable and open from 7 am to 11 pm daily.

**Entertainment**
If you want to buy theatre tickets, try the Konzertbüro, Alexander Strasse 85 (open Tuesday to Friday).

For spicier tastes there's an erotic dance show called 'Happy Legs' at the *Nacht Bar* of the *Stadt Café*, Karl Strasse 33-35 (open Tuesday to Saturday 9 pm to 4 am). During the day this café serves coffee, ice cream and beer at its outdoor tables.

**Getting There & Away**
Train connections to Erfurt (56 km) are good, and through trains running between

Frankfurt/Main and Berlin-Lichtenberg also call here. Reise Welt, Bahnhof Strasse 5 next to Eisenach-Information, has train tickets and information.

**Getting Around**
The Wartburg Express, a couple of wagons pulled by a jeep, shuttles up Wartburg Allee to the castle for DM 2.50 each way.

## NORDHAUSEN
Nordhausen, a large railway junction just south of the Harz Mountains, is interesting primarily as the southern terminus of the narrow-gauge railway over the forested hills to/from Wernigerode (60 km, three hours, four trains a day). There's an old town centre a little over a km from the station if you get stuck here.

**Places to Stay & Eat**
The *Hotel Handelshof* directly in front of the railway station charges DM 40/56 for singles/doubles with shared bath and breakfast (70 rooms), but the 28 singles are often all taken. If they're full, try the 12-room *Gaststätte 'Zur Sonne'*, at Hallesche Strasse 8, which is about one km away (ask directions).

If you don't like those prices, take the toy train 11 km to Ilfeld where there are cheaper pensions and a forest where you could camp freelance. In fact, almost any of the stations between Ilfeld and Wernigerode offer good hiking and unofficial camping possibilities.

The nearest Intercamping is Kelbra-Kyffhäuser on Kelbra Dam, five km southwest of Berga-Kelbra Railway Station (17 km east of Nordhausen on the line to Halle).

**Getting There & Away**
The narrow-gauge station adjoins the main railway station where connections are available to/from Halle (97 km, 2½ hours by local train), Erfurt (80 km, 1½ hours) and Kassel (119 km, 2½ hours).

# Saxony-Anhalt

The State of Saxony-Anhalt (Sachsen-Anhalt) comprises the former East German districts of Magdeburg and Halle. Originally part of the duchy of Saxony, medieval Anhalt was split into smaller units as the sons of various princes divided the region among themselves. The plethora of minor dukes made it easy for Prussia to dominate the area from the 17th century onwards. In 1863 Leopold IV of Anhalt-Dessau united the three existing duchies and in 1871 his realm was made a state of the German Reich.

The mighty Elbe River flows north-west across Saxony-Anhalt past Lutherstadt Wittenberg, Dessau and Magdeburg on its way to the North Sea at Hamburg. Wittenberg is a charming small town full of history, and Magdeburg would also be a fascinating city had it not been bombed out in WW II. On the Saale River south of Magdeburg is Halle, a dynamic industrial city with enough sights to justify a visit, and farther south, the Romanesque cathedral of Naumburg.

The Harz Mountains fill the south-west corner of Saxony-Anhalt, with Mt Brocken (1142 metres) as the highest peak. Quaint little towns like Quedlinburg and Wernigerode hug the gentle, wooded slopes while a network of narrow-gauge railways makes getting into the back country fun. Genuine steam locomotives puff their way up, around and over the Harz Mountains, climbing from 234 metres at Wernigerode to 540 metres at Drei Annen Hohne, 14 km south. The wood-framed Berghotel overlooks Drei Annen Hohne Station, and from here hiking trails lead north to Ottofels (600 metres) and the Steinerne Renne waterfalls on the way back to Wernigerode.

## WERNIGERODE

Surrounded by verdant hills, Wernigerode is a quaint little town at the very foot of the Harz Mountains. A romantic ducal castle rises above the medieval town centre. Here you find the northern terminus of the steam-operated, narrow-gauge Harzquerbahn which has chugged 60 km south to Nordhausen for almost a century. In summer this is a busy tourist centre attracting large throngs of German holiday-makers. Nevertheless Wernigerode is still well worth a visit.

### Orientation & Information

The bus and railway stations are adjacent on the north side of town. A large map is posted in front of the train station. If you follow Rudolf Breitscheid Strasse and Bahnhof Strasse south-east a couple of blocks you'll reach Breite Strasse which runs straight south-west into Markt Platz.

Wernigerode-Information (☎ 927 3035) is at Breite Strasse 12.

### Things to See

Wander through the streets admiring the medieval brick and wood houses. The **town hall** (1544) on Markt Platz with its pair of pointed black-slate towers is a focal point, and the **Harz Museum** (closed Sunday) on Klint Strasse a block behind features local history and natural history.

On Markt Strasse south of the town hall you can get in a string of wagons towed by a tractor (DM 2.50 one-way) and ride up to Wernigerode's fairy-tale neo-Gothic **castle**, though it's also easy to walk (the castle is visible from most parts of town – follow the crowd). Built from 1862 to 1885 by Graf Otto of Stolberg-Wernigerode, the castle's Schloss Museum (closed Monday, entry DM 5) is worth visiting to see the chapel and great hall. You don't need to go around with a guide so you shouldn't have to wait too long to get in. The views of all Wernigerode from the castle terrace are free.

### Places to Stay

Wernigerode-Information, Breite Strasse 12, arranges private rooms. Private rooms can also be rented at Harz Tourist Service, Burgberg 9b on the road up to the castle (open weekdays from 2 to 5 pm, weekends from 10 am to 3 pm).

Your first choice for a hotel room should be the 16-room *Hotel Weisser Hirsch*, Markt

Platz 5, at DM 35/50 single/double with shared bath, breakfast included. The adjacent *Gotisches Haus Hotel* was recently rebuilt and is very expensive.

The 11-room *Hotel Zum Post*, Markt Strasse 17, is also good at DM 30 per person with breakfast (less DM 5 if you stay two nights). The 18-room *Hotel Schlossblick*, Burg Strasse at Schöne Ecke, is also DM 30 per person. If all these are full try the 11-room *Hotel Zur Tanne*, Breite Strasse 59 (closed Wednesday and Thursday).

### Places to Eat

The 'in' place to eat is the *Ratskeller* in the basement of the town hall on Markt Platz. Another typical German restaurant is the *Zur bunten Stadt*, Breite Strasse 49 (open from 10 am to 8 pm, closed Monday). Cheaper meals are served at the *Gaststätte Zur Sonne*, Johannis Strasse 27 on Neuer Markt between the railway station and town (open weekdays from 9 am to 11 pm, weekends 9 am to 3 pm).

### Getting There & Away

There are four buses daily from Wernigerode to Bad Harzburg (22 km) where you can connect with trains to Goslar, Hannover and other cities in Western Germany.

Wernigerode is on a dead-end railway line 24 km south-west of Halberstadt. In Halberstadt connect for Quedlinburg, Magdeburg or Berlin-Schöneweide, though some trains run straight through. The Reisebüro, Breite Strasse 39, has train tickets and information.

The narrow-gauge railway runs south from Wernigerode to Nordhausen (60 km, three hours) about four times daily all year. Tickets are available at the station and normal railway tariffs apply.

### QUEDLINBURG

Unspoiled Quedlinburg, a medieval German town at the edge of the Harz Mountains, is so quaint you expect to meet Hansel and Gretel around every corner. Almost all the buildings in the centre are of timber-framed brick, street after cobbled street of them. It's a little farther away from Western Germany than Wernigerode and slightly off the beaten track, so Quedlinburg gets far fewer tourists than its neighbour.

### Orientation & Information

The centre of the old town is a 10-minute walk from the train station. Go straight ahead on Kurt Dillge Strasse and follow the signs once you pass the post office.

Quedlinburg-Information (☎ 455 2866) is at Markt 12.

### Things to See

A statue of the medieval epic hero Roland (1427) stands before Quedlinburg's Renaissance **town hall** (1615) on Markt, the main square.

On a rocky hill just south-west is the old castle district, Schlossberg, containing the Romanesque **Church of St Servatii** (1129), or 'Dom' (closed Monday, DM 1). The crypt dates back to the 10th century. In 1938 the Nazi SS confiscated the Dom to use it for their meetings as a 'Germanic solemn shrine'. This profanation ended in 1945. The adjacent **Schloss Museum** (closed Monday, admission DM 2.50) in the 16th century castle has a good historical collection. The view of Quedlinburg from the castle is one of the most evocative in Germany.

To get in some hiking, take a bus or train 10 km south-west to Thale at the mouth of the lovely **Bode Valley** in the Harz Mountains south of Quedlinburg. Here you'll find a cable car (closed Monday in winter) to Hexentanzplatz (the 'Witch's Dancing Ground' mentioned in Goethe's *Faust*), a trail up the valley and several caves.

### Places to Stay

Quedlinburg-Information, Markt 12, has ample private rooms and is eager to rent you one.

There are only two hotels. The 30-room *Hotel Zum Bär*, Markt 8 (DM 32/62 single/double), is in an old building right in the centre of town. If you'd rather be near the train station, the 42-room *Hotel Quedlinburger Hof* (DM 30/50 single/double) is a hundred metres to the left as you leave the station. Both hotels have only rooms with shared bath, and breakfast is not included.

### Getting There & Away

Quedlinburg is connected to Halberstadt (19 km) by rail, with connections there for Wernigerode and Magdeburg. For Halle (95 km) change at Wegeleben. For tickets and times ask at the Reisebüro, Steinbrücke 9.

## MAGDEBURG

Magdeburg, by the Elbe River at a strategic crossing of transportation routes from Thuringia to the Baltic and Western Europe to Berlin, was severely damaged by wartime bombing. It was rebuilt in steel and concrete and only merits a brief visit. Before 1989 Magdeburg was a bulwark of Eastern Europe and large numbers of Soviet soldiers and civilians were stationed here. Now it's the capital of Saxony-Anhalt.

Train connections with Western Germany are good, and although Magdeburg works fine as a gateway city to the region, it's better to have only a quick look around and then continue to Quedlinburg or Wernigerode, picturesque towns in the Harz Mountains south-west of Magdeburg where there are cheaper hotels and a nicer atmosphere.

### Orientation

From the broad square in front of the station, Wilhelm Pieck Allee leads east to a bridge over the Elbe with Alter Markt a block back on the left.

### Information

Magdeburg-Information (☎ 91-31667) is at Alter Markt 9. No free maps are offered although a perusal of the one posted in the office should suffice.

### Things to See

The centre of the old town is Alter Markt with a copy of the bronze 'Magdeburg Rider' figure (1240) of King Otto the Great facing the **Rathaus** (1698). Behind the Rathaus are the ruins of the 15th century **Johannis-kirche** (closed Monday and Tuesday, open from mid-April to mid-October) with a fas-

cinating collection of photos of Magdeburg before WW II. For your DM 1 admission you may climb the tower for a sweeping view of the rebuilt city.

South two blocks is the 12th century Romanesque convent **Unser Lieben Frauen**, now a museum (closed Monday, DM 2). On some evenings concerts are given here. South again is the soaring 13th century Gothic **Dom** with its fine sculptures. Entry to the Dom is from the cloister. The **Historical Museum** (closed Monday) is on Otto von Guericke Strasse at the corner of Danz Strasse, just west of the Dom. The original 'Rider' statue is kept here.

### Places to Stay

There's no Intercamping nearby but you can get a private room through Magdeburg-Information, Markt 9.

The 44-room *Hotel Grüner Baum*, Wilhelm Pieck Allee 40 on the north side of the square in front of the railway station, to the left as you exit, offers Magdeburg's least expensive hotel rooms (DM 45/88 for a single/double with shared bath, breakfast included).

The 355-room, four-star *Interhotel International*, Otto von Guericke Strasse 87 directly across the square from the station, has rooms with private bath and breakfast from DM 75 per person.

Around the corner from the Interhotel, at Leiter Strasse 10, is a fairly luxurious *Youth Tourist Hotel* (☎ 33881, DM 51/74 for a single/double without breakfast). A YHA card may net you a DM 3 discount here!

The 113-room *Hotel Zur Ratswaage*, Julius Bremer Strasse 1 a block behind Markt, is overpriced at DM 82/109 single/double with bath and breakfast.

### Getting There & Away

Most trains between Hannover and Berlin-Zoo call at Magdeburg. Between Magdeburg and Berlin-Zoo (139 km) these trains stop at Potsdam-Stadt. Trains from Cologne (470 km, seven hours) are frequent. Trains from East Berlin leave from a variety of stations but all pass Schönefeld Airport and Potsdam-

Hauptbahnhof, carrying on to Halberstadt (58 km).

Magdeburg is on the main route of trains from Rostock and Schwerin to Leipzig or Erfurt. Trains from Leipzig to Magdeburg run via either Halle or Dessau. The Reisebüro at Wilhelm Pieck Allee 14 has train times and tickets.

## HALLE

Halle, a pleasant, untouristed town 40 km north-east of Leipzig, is the chemical capital of Eastern Germany. Despite this, a few churches and museums in the old town justify a brief visit. During the last years of Communism many new apartments were built in the historic centre of Halle near the Händel Museum, and the tasteful way this was done demonstrates how far the science of city planning has come since Berlin and Dresden were rebuilt. Many Halle residents live in Halle Neustadt on the west side of the Saale River, a planned city built by the Communists from 1964 to 1980.

### Orientation

Trams in Halle follow a roundabout route, so to get to the centre from the Hauptbahnhof walk through the underpass and straight down the shopping mall, Leipziger Strasse, past the 15th century Leipziger Turm to Markt.

### Information

Halle-Information (☎ 46-23340), Kleinschmieden 6 on the corner of Grosse Stein Strasse a block north of Markt, can answer questions.

Jugendtourist is at Leipziger Strasse 27, behind the Leipziger Turm.

SRS Studenten Reiseservice, Francke Platz 1, sells student/youth train and plane tickets and is a good budget travel agency if you need help making arrangements. It also sells ISIC student cards.

### Things to See

In the centre of Markt, Halle's central square, is a statue (1859) of the great composer George Frederick Händel. You can't miss

**Markt Kirche** (1529) with its four tall towers dominating the square. A small bridge links two of the towers. It's worth going inside to see the exquisitely decorated Gothic interior. The main altar, pulpit, organ and vaulting in this church are quite wonderful. Friedemann Bach, the eldest son of Johann Sebastian Bach, once served as organist here for 20 years.

Also on Markt is the **Roter Turm** (1506), a great red tower which is now an art gallery, and just south at Grosse Marker Strasse 10 is the **City Historical Museum** (closed Friday).

Composer George Frederick Händel was born in Halle in 1685, and his home at Grosse Nikolai Strasse 5 has been converted into a major museum (closed Monday) with a large collection of musical instruments. Händel left Halle in 1703 and, after stays in Hamburg, Italy and Hannover, spent the years 1712 to 1759 in London where he achieved great fame. Mementos of the period make the museum worth visiting and it offers the added attraction of a pleasant coffee shop.

On Friedemann Bach Platz a few blocks

George Frederick Händel

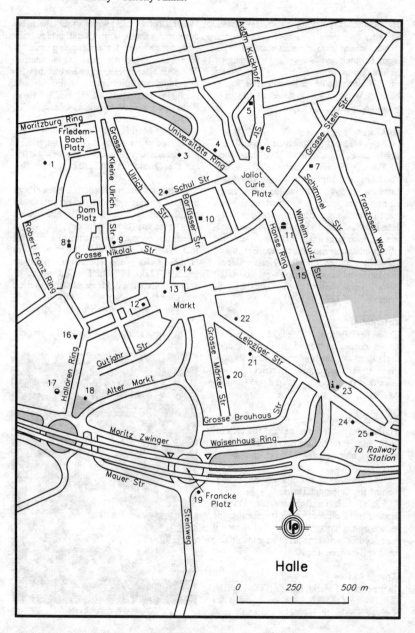

Halle

0        250        500 m

| | |
|---|---|
| 1 | Moritzburg Castle |
| 2 | Neues Theater |
| 3 | Martin Luther University |
| 4 | Theater des Friedens |
| 5 | Martha-Haus Christliches Hospiz |
| 6 | Gaststätte Martha-Klause |
| 7 | Hotel Weltfrieden |
| 8 | Dom (old cathedral) |
| 9 | Händel Museum |
| 10 | Hotel Pilsner Urquell |
| 11 | Post Office |
| 12 | Markt Kirche |
| 13 | Roter Turm |
| 14 | Halle-Information |
| 15 | Red Flag Monument |
| 16 | Gaststätte zum Würzburger |
| 17 | Bus Station |
| 18 | Moritzkirche |
| 19 | Studenten Reiseservice |
| 20 | City Historical Museum |
| 21 | Konzerthalle (ex-church) |
| 22 | Reise Welt |
| 23 | Leipziger Turm & Jugendtourist |
| 24 | Theaterkasse |
| 25 | Hotel 'Rotes Ross' |

beyond Händel Haus is 15th century **Moritzburg Castle** with its art museum and Gothic chapel.

## Places to Stay

**Camping** The closest Intercamping is at Seeburg on the northern shore of the Süsser See, 20 km west of Halle (last bus from Halle at 8.30 pm). The Seeburg bus departs from stand No 7 at the bus station near the Moritzkirche in the centre of Halle, not the Hauptbahnhof. It's an additional 15-minute walk from the bus stop to the camping ground. A good alternative is the Intercamping at Bad Bibra (see the Naumburg section that follows).

**Hotels** Halle-Information, Kleinschmieden 6, provides private rooms.

The 345-room, four-star *Interhotel Stadt Halle*, Ernst Thälmann Platz 17 near the Haupbahnhof, is expensive at DM 150/250 single/double.

A better bet price-wise, location-wise and atmosphere-wise is the older, 47-room *Hotel 'Rotes Ross'*, Leipziger Strasse 76 between the station and centre of town (DM 70/100 single/double with shared bath, breakfast included).

The very friendly 21-room *Martha-Haus Christliches Hospiz* (☎ 24411), Adam Kuckhoff Strasse 5-8, is DM 35/67 single/double without bath or breakfast.

If Martha-Haus is full, *Hotel Weltfrieden*, Grosse Stein Strasse 64-65, has 29 basic double rooms with shared facilities from DM 61 (no singles).

At last report the *Hotel Pilsner Urquell*, Barfüsser Strasse 20, was closed for extensive renovations.

## Places to Eat

The *Gaststätte Zum Würzburger* (open weekdays from 11 am to 8 pm) on Hallorenring is inexpensive. An up-market place to eat is the *Ratsgaststätte* upstairs in the old town hall (1892) on Markt. The restaurant in the *Hotel Weltfrieden* is not too expensive and open daily.

## Entertainment

You can find out what's happening in Halle at the Theaterkasse, Leipziger Strasse 82. The *Theater des Friedens* on Joliot Curie Platz is Halle's main stage, but there's also the *Neues Theater* at Grosse Ulrich Strasse 51. Concerts are sometimes held at the Händel Haus.

The best little bar in town is *Gaststätte Martha-Klause*, Martha Strasse 28 near Theater des Friedens (open Monday to Friday from 3 to 11 pm). It's the perfect place to go after the show.

## Getting There & Away

Halle is on the route of fast trains from Rostock and Magdeburg to Leipzig or Erfurt, and also from Berlin-Lichtenberg or Berlin-Schöneweide to Erfurt and Eisenach. If you're coming from Dresden, you may have to change at Leipzig. Between Lutherstadt Wittenberg and Halle you may have to take a local train (68 km, one hour). For train tickets and times try Reise Welt, Leipziger Strasse 6.

## NAUMBURG

Naumburg is one of those pretty little medieval towns that Germany is famous for. It is strategically located between Halle/Leipzig and Weimar with frequent trains. There are two youth hostels in the area and an Intercamping at Bad Bibra, all of which makes this town well worth including in a German itinerary.

### Orientation & Information

The railway station is two km north-west of the old town, but there are frequent trams. Platz der Einheit is a good place to get off the tram (ask). If you'd rather walk just follow the tram tracks into town.

Naumburg Information (☎ 2514) is at Lindenring 38.

### Things to See

Naumburg is picturesque, its **old town hall** (1528) and Gothic **St Wenzel Church** (built 1218-1523) rising above the central marketplace. The **City Historical Museum** (closed Monday) is beyond the polyclinic on the east side of Naumburg at Grochlitzer Strasse 49-51.

In the ancient western quarter of the town stands the magnificent Romanesque **Cathedral of Sts Peter & Paul** (DM 3.50) with the famous 13th century statues of Uta and Ekkehard in the west choir. The cloister, crypt, sculpture and four tall towers of this great medieval complex are unique. Unfortunately the cathedral *(Dom)* can only be visited on a boring German-language tour (DM 3.50).

### Places to Stay

Ask Naumburg-Information, Lindenring 38, about private rooms. The old *Hotel Goldener Löwe*, Salz Strasse 15-16 near the centre, is only DM 15 per person, so of course the 17 rooms are always full. Give it a try on your way to the youth hostel.

The only other place to stay is the 161-bed *'Werner Lamberz' Youth Tourist Hotel* (☎ 5316) at Am Tennis Platz 9, four km on the opposite side of Naumburg from the train station.

There's an *Intercamping* at Bad Bibra, Am Waldschwimmbad, 19 km north-west of Naumburg (last bus from Naumburg Railway Station at 7.30 pm). The closest railway station to Bad Bibra is Laucha, five km east of the camping ground.

### Getting There & Away

There are fast trains to Naumburg from Halle (45 km, one hour), Leipzig (54 km, one hour), Jena (37 km, 45 minutes) and Weimar (42 km, 45 minutes), and a local line to Artern via Laucha and Freyburg. Reise Welt, Markt 6, will have train tickets and times.

## FREYBURG

Freyburg, eight km north-west of Naumburg and easily accessible by train or bus, is picturesquely situated in the Unstrut Valley with a large medieval castle on the wooded hilltop directly above. The castle will be closed for restoration for many years to come, but the adjacent tower (closed Monday) may be visited for its splendid view.

### Places to Stay & Eat

There's one small hotel in Freyburg, the *Zur Neuenburg* at Wasser Strasse 27, but the 43-bed *'Friedrich Ludwig Jahn' Youth Hostel* (☎ 295), Schloss Strasse 21a on the road up to the castle, is a better bet (DM 14.50 for juniors, DM 17.50 for seniors). The bus to Bad Bibra Intercamping passes Freyburg.

## LUTHERSTADT WITTENBERG

Wittenberg is best known as the home of Martin Luther, but the Renaissance painter Lucas Cranach the Elder also lived here for 45 years. Wittenberg was a famous university town and seat of Electoral Saxony until 1547, when the Protestant princes were defeated by Catholic emperor Charles V and the elector moved to Weimar. Frederick the

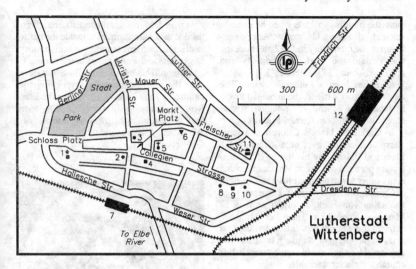

Lutherstadt
Wittenberg

1  Wittenberg Castle & Youth Hostel
2  Lucas Cranach's House
3  Old Town Hall
4  Hotel Goldener Ring
5  St Mary's Church
6  Bierstuben
7  Bahnhof Wittenberg-Elbtor
8  Melanchthon Museum
9  Hotel Wittenberg Hof
10  Lutherhaus
11  Post Office
12  Bahnhof Lutherstadt Wittenberg

Wise of Saxony founded Wittenberg University in 1502, and Shakespeare had Hamlet and Horatio studying here; in 1817 it merged with Halle University. It was at Wittenberg Castle in 1517 that Luther launched the Reformation, an act of the greatest cultural importance to all of Europe.

Today the unspoiled town centre contains many artistic monuments and museums connected with those events. You can see most of Wittenberg during a three-hour stopover, though it's also a nice place to spend the night.

### Orientation

There are two railway stations. You'll probably arrive at Bahnhof Lutherstadt Wittenberg on the main line from Berlin to Leipzig/Halle. Bahnhof Wittenberg-Elbtor is a minor stop on a secondary line from Dessau. The main station is a pleasant 10-minute walk from the centre of town. From the station exit, walk straight ahead between the two railway lines and then go right under the tracks. Continue straight up on the street that cuts across the park into Collegien Strasse. This will bring you to the Lutherhaus.

### Information

Wittenberg-Information (☎ 451 2537) is at Collegien Strasse 8.

Check for cultural events and tickets at the Theatre Service office, Markt 10 (closed weekends).

### Things to See

The **Lutherhaus**, at Collegien Strasse 54 (closed Monday, admission DM 4, Sunday free), contains an original room furnished by Luther in 1535. Luther moved into this monastic building in 1508 when he came to teach at Wittenberg University. After dissolution of the monastery in 1522, the building was considered Luther's property and remained so until his death in 1546. Since 1883 it has been a Luther Museum. The home of Luther's friend, the humanist Philip Melanchthon, nearby at Collegien Strasse 60, is also a museum (closed Friday).

In Gothic **St Mary's Church** is a large altarpiece, begun by Lucas Cranach the Elder and finished by his son in 1555, containing portraits of Luther, Melanchthon and many other townspeople, plus a self-portrait of Cranach the Elder himself. Luther married Katherina von Bora, a former nun, in St Mary's in June 1525 and often preached here. In this church was celebrated the first mass in the German language in 1526. The baptismal font and marble tombstones in this church are also remarkable.

Imposing monuments to Luther and Melanchthon stand in front of the impressive **old town hall** (1535) nearby. Over the town hall's Renaissance portico (1570) is Justitia with sword and scales, for it was from the portico balcony that sentences were passed and executions carried out.

On one corner of Markt is the **House of Lucas Cranach the Elder**, Schloss Strasse 1, with a picturesque courtyard you may enter. Cranach purchased the building in 1513, a year after his marriage, and resided here until 1550. The property carried with it the lucrative privilege of selling wine and Cranach eventually became one of the richest men in Wittenberg. Aside from his prodigious studio which employed as many as 10 artists, Cranach also owned a nearby pharmacy, a printing press and a bookshop.

At the west end of town is **Wittenberg Castle** (1499) with its huge rebuilt Gothic church (closed Monday). Luther nailed his Ninety-five Theses to the door of this church on 31 October 1517, but in 1858 a bronze door replaced the wooden door of Luther's time. His tomb may be viewed below the pulpit and Melanchthon's tomb is opposite. From Wednesday to Sunday you may climb the 289 steps of the 88-metre-high church

tower for DM 1. Organ concerts are advertised at the church entrance. Inside the castle itself are two museums: natural history downstairs and a city museum upstairs.

If you still have some time, the **Stadt Park** near the castle contains a very enjoyable children's zoo. If you want to see the Elbe River, walk south a short distance on the road that goes under the railway tracks near Wittenberg-Elbtor Station.

Martin Luther

### Places to Stay

There's no camping ground near Wittenberg. Wittenberg-Information, Collegien Strasse 8, has private rooms at DM 25 per person (closed weekends). The 104-bed *'Otto Plättner' Youth Hostel* (☎ 3255) is housed in Wittenberg Castle (DM 13.50 for juniors, DM 16 for seniors).

There are two attractive hotels. The 20-room *Hotel Wittenberger Hof*, Collegien Strasse 56 beside the Lutherhalle, used to be the cheapest place but after renovations in 1990 it became much more expensive.

The 40-room *Hotel Goldener Adler*, Markt 7, is DM 37/50 single/double without bath, DM 70 double with bath, breakfast not included.

### Places to Eat

For a simple German meal try the *Bierstuben*, Jüden Strasse 27 (closed weekends). It's just far enough off the beaten track to cater mostly to locals.

The *Schlosskeller* (closed Monday and Tuesday) in the castle basement is worth a look if you want to splash out a little.

### Getting There & Away

Wittenberg is on the main line to Leipzig and Halle – less than two hours south of Berlin-Lichtenberg (99 km) by fast train. All the Berlin trains stop at Schönefeld Airport. There's a restaurant and left-luggage room at Wittenberg Station. For train tickets and times ask at the Reisebüro, Markt 12.

# Mecklenburg-Pomerania

The State of Mecklenburg-Pomerania (Mecklenburg-Vorpommern) comprises the former East German districts of Schwerin, Rostock and Neubrandenburg. This low-lying, postglacial region of lakes, meadows, forests and Baltic beaches stretches across northern Germany from Schleswig-Holstein to Poland, just south of Denmark and Sweden. Most of the state is historic Mecklenburg, and only Rügen Island and the area from Stralsund to the Polish border traditionally belong to Western Pomerania, or Vorpommern. The rest of Pomerania went to Poland in 1945.

By the 7th century Slavonic tribes had displaced the original Germanic inhabitants of Mecklenburg, but in 1160 the duke of Saxony, Henry the Lion, conquered the region under the guise of introducing Christianity and made the local Polish princes his vassals. Germanisation gradually reduced the Slavonic element and in 1348 the dukes of Mecklenburg became princes of the Holy Roman Empire. Tall red-brick churches remain from the medieval period when the towns were members of the Hanseatic trading league. In the 16th century Lutheranism was adopted. Sweden became involved in the area during the Thirty Years' War and held Wismar and environs from 1648 to 1803 and Stralsund and Rügen from 1648 to 1815. In 1867 the whole region joined the North German Confederation and in 1871 the German Reich.

Bismarck once remarked that when the world came to an end he would move to Mecklenburg because everything was 20 years behind the times there. That about sums up the atmosphere here even today, and since Eastern Germans now have a much wider choice of summer holiday destinations it's far less crowded than it used to be. Dazzled by the attractions in adjacent areas, few English-speakers venture this way, which is unfortunate as Germany's Baltic coast has a lot to offer. The offshore islands of Poel, Hiddensee and Rügen are still undiscovered paradises for outdoors people. Just keep in mind the very short swimming season (July and August only, unless you're a member of the Polar Bears Club). Spring and autumn can be cold.

## SCHWERIN

Almost surrounded by lakes, Schwerin is perhaps the most picturesque town in Eastern Germany. The town gets its name from a Slavonic castle known as 'Zaurin' (animal pasture) on the site of the present Schloss. This former seat of the Grand Duchy of Mecklenburg and contemporary capital of Mecklenburg-Pomerania is an interesting mix of medieval and 19th century architecture. It's small enough to get around and packed with attractions – an OK place to stop on the way north to the Baltic coast.

### Orientation & Information

As you come out of the railway station you'll see a large hotel on your right. Go towards it, then down the hill to Pfaffen Teich, a lake where you turn right again. The city centre focuses on Markt beyond the south end of this lake. Farther south, around Schlossinsel

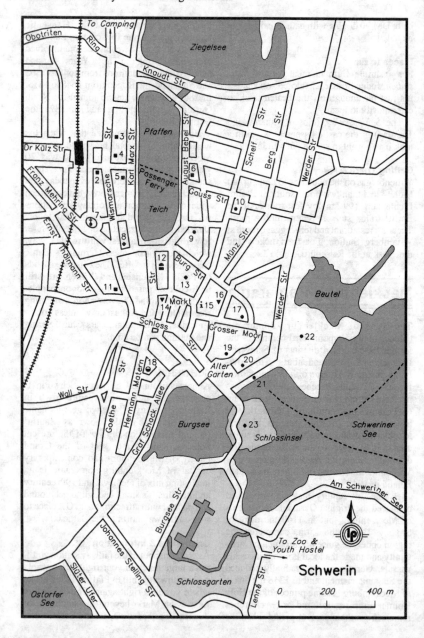

Schwerin

0        200        400 m

1 Railway Station
2 Hotel Stadt Schwerin
3 Hotel Polonia
4 Bahnhofshotel
5 Niederländischer Hof Hotel
6 Hospiz am Pfaffenteich
7 St Paul's Church
8 Arsenal
9 Stadttourist
10 Schelfkirche
11 Hotel Wendenhof
12 Post Office
13 Dom
14 Schweriner Café
15 Schwerin-Information
16 Alt Schweriner Schankstuben
17 Historical Museum
18 Bus Station
19 Mecklenburg State Theatre
20 State Museum
21 Weisse Flotte
22 Marstall
23 Schloss

on the Schweriner See, are the museums, parks and tour boats which will keep you entertained.

Schwerin-Information (☎ 84-86 4509) is at Am Markt 11.

### Things to See

Above Markt rises the tall 14th century Gothic **Dom**, a superb example of north German red-brick architecture. On Wednesdays in summer there are organ concerts at 8 pm in the Dom. Climb the 19th century church tower (DM 1) for the view. The winding medieval streets of the old town complement well the verdant parks and gardens along the lakes.

Schwerin's neo-Gothic **Schloss** (closed Monday) is on an island connected to the lakeside promenades by causeways. At the end of the causeway on the city side is the **State Museum** (closed Monday) with an excellent collection of old Dutch masters including Frans Hals, Rembrandt, Rubens and Breughel. The other causeway leads to the 18th century **Schlossgarten**. Schwe-

rin's **zoo** (daily 8 am to 7 pm) is three km south-east of here.

### Activities

**On the Lakes** From May to September Weisse Flotte excursion boats operate on the **Schweriner See** from Schlossbucht, the landing beside the museum opposite the castle. The cruises depart daily in season at 10 am and 2 pm (DM 6). A ferry trip south from the same landing to Zippendorf, a lakeside resort near the zoo, runs six times daily in midsummer. Departure times are posted.

### Places to Stay

**Camping** *Seehof Intercamping*, 10 km north of Schwerin on the west shore of the Schweriner See, is easily accessible on bus No 8 from the bus station, or take any northbound tram from the railway station to the end of the line at KGW (Klement Gottwald Werk) and catch bus No 8 there. Buses run hourly as late as 10.30 pm daily. There aren't any bungalows and in summer it's crowded, but there's a snack bar that stays open till 9 pm and of course the lake for swimming and rowing.

**Hostel** Schwerin's 63-bed *'Kurt Bürger' Youth Hostel* (☎ 21 3005) is on Waldschulen Weg just opposite the entrance to the zoo, about four km south of the city centre (bus No 15 from the bus station on Hermann Matern Strasse). It's DM 13.50 for juniors, DM 16 for seniors.

**Private Rooms** Schwerin-Information, Am Markt 11, has private rooms. Stadt Tourist, Körner Strasse 18, also rents private rooms (open daily after 4 pm).

**Hotels** The cheapest hotels are the 24-room *Polonia* (DM 25/35 single/double) and the 23-room *Bahnhofshotel* (DM 21/37), both without private bath or breakfast, opposite the railway station.

If you would like a room with a private bath, the seven-storey, 166-room *Hotel Stadt*

*Schwerin,* also in front of the station, can supply it (from DM 87/124 single/double including breakfast).

Others worth a look are the 16-room *Hotel Wendenhof,* Wismarsche Strasse 104 a couple of blocks south of the station, and the 12-room *Hospiz am Pfaffenteich,* Gauss Strasse 19 near the far landing of the small ferry which crosses Pfaffen Teich from near the station. They're worth trying though usually closed or full.

Best of all, try for one of the 27 rooms at the tasteful old *Niederländischer Hof Hotel,* Karl Marx Strasse 13-14 right on Pfaffen Teich, a block down from the Hotel Stadt Schwerin. At DM 30/50 single/double with breakfast but only shared bath this is Schwerin's best bargain and it's also free of the tram noise you get in the places along Wismarsche Strasse.

### Places to Eat

*Zum Goldbroiler,* Wismarsche Strasse 104, serves half and quarter barbecued chickens. The *Grill Station* fast-food place across the street has the same for less if you're in a hurry and don't need table service. For seafood it's the *Gastmahl des Meeres,* Grosser Moor 5 (expensive).

The moderately expensive *Alt Schweriner Schankstuben* on the Schlachtermarkt behind Schwerin-Information in the old town serves meals till 10 pm and wine till midnight. The *Schweriner Café,* Busch Strasse 7 just off Markt, is a great place to get a coffee during the day and a drink at night.

### Getting There & Away

Fast trains arrive regularly from Rostock (87 km, 1½ hours), Magdeburg (194 km, three hours), Halle (280 km, 4½ hours), Leipzig (318 km, five hours) and Berlin-Lichtenberg (238 km, 3½ hours). From Weimar and Erfurt you may have to change at Magdeburg. From Wismar it's often faster to change trains in Bad Kleinen than to wait for a through service. Trains from Hamburg and Lübeck travel via Bad Kleinen. For train

tickets and times ask at the Reisebüro, Grosser Moor 9.

Reservations for the afternoon Sonnenschein Reisen coach to West Berlin (mid-April to October, DM 33) are available from Reisebüro Schwerin Plus, Schmiede Strasse 21. People aged 26 and under get a 50% discount.

## WISMAR

Wismar, about halfway between Rostock and Lübeck, became a Hanseatic trading city in the 13th century. For centuries Wismar belonged to Sweden and traces of Scandinavian rule can still be seen. It's less hectic than Rostock or Stralsund, a pretty little town worth seeing for itself and also the gateway to Poel Island.

### Information

Wismar-Information (☎ 824 2958) at Bohr Strasse 5a has maps, brochures, stickers, etc.

### Things to See

Like many other German cities, Wismar was a target for Anglo-American bombers just a few weeks prior to the end of the war. Of the three great red-brick churches that once rose above the rooftops, only **St Nikolai** (closed Sunday and Monday) is intact. The massive red shell of **St George's** has been left as a reminder of the April 1945 raids. Cars now park where 13th century **St Mary's Church** once stood, although the great brick steeple (1339) still towers above.

Apart from this it's hard to believe that Wismar's gabled houses were seriously bombed. Nearby in a corner of Markt are the graceful old **Waterworks** (1602) and the **Rathaus** (1819). The **City Historical Museum** (closed Monday) at Schweinsbrücke 8 near St Nikolai has many interesting exhibits.

### Activities

To get out onto the Baltic, board a Weisse Flotte or private excursion boat to Kirchdorf on **Poel Island,** a very popular summer bathing resort for Germans. The trips operate

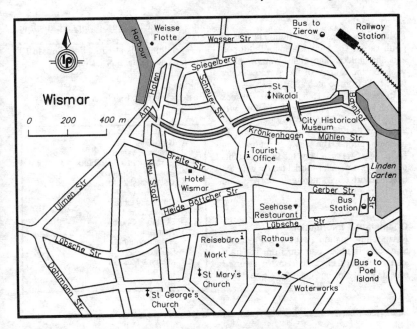

from May to September (one hour, DM 6). You can also get to Poel by bus several times a day from the bus station near the corner of Lübsche and Bahnhof Strasse. Otherwise the Weisse Flotte offers 90-minute cruises (DM 7) out to sea from Wismar three times a day.

## Places to Stay

*Zierow Intercamping* is on the coast eight km north-west of Wismar. Bus service to Zierow from beside Wismar Railway Station finishes at 5 pm, after which you'll either have to take a taxi (just under DM 20) or a highway bus to Gägelow from whence it's a four-km walk downhill to Zierow. There's a shop at Zierow but no bungalows.

Wismar-Information, Bohr Strasse 5a, arranges private rooms.

The only hotel is the picturesque 18-room *Hotel Wismar* at Breite Strasse 10, erected in 1896. Singles/doubles are DM 28/38, but the reception doesn't open until 2 pm and they could be full.

## Places to Eat

For some local seafood try the *Fischrestaurant 'Seehase'*, at Altböter Strasse 6 (open weekdays from 10.30 am to 8 pm).

## Getting There & Away

Trains arrive from Rostock (57 km, 1½ hours) every couple of hours and from Berlin-Lichtenberg (270 km, 5½ hours) twice a day. Between Schwerin and Wismar (32 km) it's often quicker to change trains at Bad Kleinen than to wait for a through service. Trains to/from Lübeck and Hamburg travel via Bad Kleinen. For train tickets and times try the Reisebüro, An der Hegede 1 on the corner of Lübsche Strasse.

There are daily buses to/from Lübeck, Kiel, Rendsburg and Hamburg from beside the railway station (hours posted).

Large motor vessels and hydrofoils link Wismar to Neustadt in Schleswig-Holstein (DM 10 one-way).

## ROSTOCK

Rostock, the largest city in lightly populated north-eastern Germany, is a major Baltic port and shipbuilder. The giant Warnow shipyards on the estuary of the Warnow River were built from scratch after 1957.

In the 14th and 15th centuries Rostock was an important Hanseatic city trading with Riga, Bergen and Bruges. Rostock University, founded in 1419, was the first in northern Europe. The salty city centre along Kröpeliner Strasse retains the flavour of this period. It's a popular tourist centre with the beach resort of Warnemünde only 12 km north.

### Orientation & Information

Rostock-Information (☎ 81-22619), Lange Strasse 5, is about two km from the train station. To get there take tram No 11 or 12 outside the station and get off at the next stop after the Rathaus and St Mary's Church in the centre of town.

Jugendtourist is at Kröpeliner Strasse 10 (upstairs above the fabric shop).

### Things to See

Rostock's greatest sight is 13th century **St**

| | |
|---|---|
| 1 | Kröpeliner Tor |
| 2 | Interhotel Warnow |
| 3 | Europäisches Reisebüro |
| 4 | Rostock-Information |
| 5 | Ostseegaststätte |
| 6 | 'Zum Heiligen Kreuz' Museum |
| 7 | University Library |
| 8 | Jugendtourist |
| 9 | St Mary's Church |
| 10 | Rathaus |
| 11 | Hotel Nordland |
| 12 | Steintor |
| 13 | Maritime Museum |

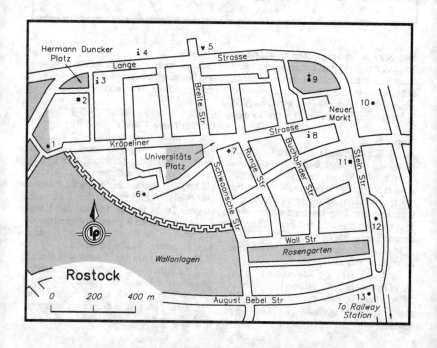

Mary's Church (closed Monday) which survived the war unscathed. This great medieval brick edifice contains a functioning astronomical clock (1472), a Gothic bronze baptismal font (1290), a Renaissance pulpit (1574) and a Baroque organ (1770) – all artistic treasures. Ascend the 207 steps of the 50-metre-high church tower for the view.

Kröpeliner Strasse, a broad pedestrian mall lined with 15th and 16th century burgher houses, runs west from the Rathaus on Neuer Markt to the 14th century Kröpeliner Tor (closed Thursday) on the city walls. Halfway along, off the south-west corner of Universitäts Platz, is the Kloster 'zum Heiligen Kreuz' Museum (closed Monday) in an old convent (1270).

Rostock also has a good Maritime Museum (closed Friday) on August Bebel Strasse opposite the tower at the entrance to town from the railway station.

If you've got a little spare time, Rostock's zoo on the south-west side of town (tram No 11) is pleasant and there's a large beer garden opposite the entrance.

### Places to Stay

The 85-bed *'Traditionsschiff' Youth Tourist Hotel* (☎ 71 6202) is in a converted freighter on the harbour at Schmarl-Dorf between Rostock and Warnemünde (S-Bahn to Lütten Klein Station, then walk 25 minutes). The closest Intercampings are at Wismar and Stralsund.

Rostock Information, Lange Strasse 5, does not rent private rooms. For these you must go to Reisebüro Zwerg (☎ 22386), Am Alter Markt 13 a few blocks east of the Rathaus (open weekdays from 8 am to 10 pm, Saturdays 8 am to 8 pm, Sundays 8 am to 2 pm).

Of the hotels the, eight-storey, 82-room *Hotel am Bahnhof* opposite the train station is overpriced at DM 82/134 single/double for a room with shared bath and breakfast. Even more expensive is the nine-storey, four-star *Interhotel Warnow*, Hermann Duncker Platz 4, at DM 120/190 single/double with bath and breakfast. Instead try the *Hotel Nordland*, Stein Strasse 7 beside the post office

on Neuer Markt, with 35 rooms from DM 35/40 single/double without bath or breakfast.

### Places to Eat

The plush *Ostseegaststätte*, Lange Strasse 9 near Rostock-Information, specialises in seafood in the upstairs dining room and there's a pizzeria downstairs. The service is good but it's not the cheapest place in town.

The *Gastmahl des Meeres* opposite the Maritime Museum on August Bebel Strasse also specialises in seafood and is equally expensive.

### Getting There & Away

There are direct trains to Rostock from Berlin-Lichtenberg (231 km, three hours), Schwerin (87 km, 1½ hours), Magdeburg (281 km, four hours), Erfurt (475 km, seven hours) and Leipzig (via Halle 407 km, 6½ hours). Trains run to Stralsund, Rostock, Wismar and Schwerin every couple of hours. Overnight trains with sleepers are available to/from Leipzig via Potsdam. The Reisebüro at Hermann Duncker Platz 2 in front of Hotel Warnow sells train tickets and books sleepers.

There are two car-ferry trains a day between Berlin-Zoo Station and Copenhagen via Rostock. These trains connect with the international ferry service from Warnemünde to Gedser, Denmark. The ferry terminal is a few minutes' walk from Warnemünde Railway Station and the crossing takes only two hours.

Reservations for the afternoon luxury coach to West Berlin (mid-April to October, DM 41) can be made at Reisebüro Zwerg, Alter Markt 13. People aged 26 and under get 50% off.

### WARNEMÜNDE

Warnemünde, at the mouth of the Warnow River on the Baltic Sea (Ostsee) just north of Rostock, is Eastern Germany's most popular beach resort. Trying to find a room here in midsummer used to be a hopeless task, but now that Eastern Germans are able to spend their holidays wherever they like it's not nearly as crowded as it used to be. Regular commuter trains connect Warnemünde to Rostock every 15 minutes and the town can easily be used as a base for day trips to Rostock, Wismar, Stralsund and even Schwerin. It's a good choice if you want to enjoy the comforts of city life while staying at what is ostensibly a small fishing village on the beach.

### Things to See

From the railway station turn left and cross the small bridge over **Alter Strom**, the old harbour. This picturesque inlet is still lined with quaint fishermen's cottages, one of which has been converted into a **museum** (open daily except Wednesday and Sunday, or Monday in July and August, DM 2). It's next to the *Imbiss* straight ahead from the bridge, a block back from Alter Strom.

After a brief visit, return to Alter Strom and follow the crowded promenade north to the sea where German tourists congregate. Warnemünde's broad sandy beach stretches west from the lighthouse (1898), chock-a-block with bathers on a hot summer's day.

### Activities

From May to October Weisse Flotte boats depart from near the mouth of Alter Strom on harbour cruises. Numerous private fishing boats tied up along Am Alter Strom also offer one-hour harbour cruises for DM 10 per person. The Weisse Flotte is cheaper (DM 6 for one hour, DM 10 for two hours) so check its office at the north end of Am Alter Strom before deciding which trip to take. It used to be hard to get on the Weisse Flotte boats, but now with so many private vessels competing for your business you should have no problem.

### Places to Stay & Eat

The 65-bed *Erwin Fischer Youth Hostel* (☎ 52303), Park Strasse 31, is DM 13.50 for juniors, DM 16 for seniors.

For a private room in Warnemünde go to the 'Kurverwaltung' or 'Urlauberanmeldung' office on the corner of Wachtler and Heinrich Heine streets, three blocks back from the Strand Hotel. The sign outside the building says 'Kur- und Erholungswesen' – it's in a corner of the park not far from the Kaufhalle supermarket. Not only are the name and location confusing but the office hours are capricious: Monday, Thursday and Friday from 8.30 to 11.30 am and 2 to 3.30 pm, Tuesday 8.30 to 11.30 am and 2 to 6 pm, and Wednesday 8.30 to 11.30 am only. You enter through a back door. Good luck!

The functional, 24-room *Promenade Hotel*, See Strasse 5, is DM 82 double without bath or DM 92 with private bath (no singles). A better bet is the cheerful, 48-room *Strand Hotel*, See Strasse 12, with rooms beginning at DM 43/76 single/double with shared bath, breakfast included. Both have a nice seaside atmosphere.

The 15-storey, 350-room *Neptune Hotel* overlooking the beach at Warnemünde is DM 180/270 single/double with private bath and breakfast, fine for those with five-star wallets and Sheraton tastes.

### Getting There & Away

It's easy to get to Warnemünde on the double-decker S-Bahn. Trains depart every 15 minutes from Rostock Station. The 20-minute trip takes you past row after row of modern apartment blocks to the Baltic coast.

## STRALSUND

Stralsund, an enjoyable city on the Baltic north of Berlin, is nearly surrounded by lakes and the sea, which once contributed to its defence. A Hanseatic city in the Middle Ages, Stralsund later formed part of the Duchy of Pommern-Wolgast. From 1648 to 1815 Stralsund was under Swedish control. Today it's an attractive old town with fine museums and buildings, pleasant walks and a restful, uncluttered waterfront. Rügen Island is just across the Strelasund and the ferry to Hiddensee leaves from here.

### Orientation & Information

From the main railway station cross the causeway to the right and you're in the old town. Continue up Tribseer Strasse to Neuer Markt and you'll have St Mary's Church on

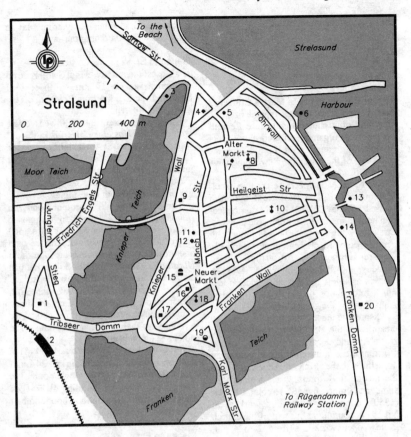

## Stralsund

0    200    400 m

1   Hotel Am Bahnhof
2   Railway Station
3   Rowboat Rentals
4   Stralsund Theatre
5   Kniepertor
6   Weisse Flotte
7   Rathaus
8   St Nikolai's Church
9   'Grete Walter' Youth Hostel
10  St Jacob's Church
11  Oceanic Museum & Aquarium
12  Historical Museum
13  Fish Market
14  Heilgeistkirche
15  Post Office
16  Hotel Schweriner Hof
17  Nordland Hotel
18  St Mary's Church
19  Bus Station
20  Hotel Baltic

the right and the museums of Mönch Strasse on the left.

Stralsund Information (☎ 821 2439) is at Alter Markt 15.

## Things to See

First visit 14th century **St Mary's Church**, a massive red-brick edifice typical of north German Gothic church architecture. Recitals on the 1659 organ are offered every other Wednesday in summer at 8 pm. Climb the 345 steps of the tower for a sweeping view of all of Stralsund.

Nearby on Mönch Strasse are two excellent museums. The **Historical Museum** (closed Monday, DM 2) has a large collection housed in the cloister of an old convent. Stralsund's highlight is the adjoining 13th century convent church, now a fantastic **Oceanic Museum & Aquarium** (closed Monday and Tuesday in winter, DM 2). There's a large natural history section and much information on the fishing industry. Aquariums on the ground floor contain tropical fish while those in the basement display creatures of the Baltic Sea, North Sea and North Atlantic Ocean.

From these museums make your way north through the old city to Alter Markt with the medieval **Rathaus**, itself a delightful sight, and impressive **St Nikolai Church** (1350). Long-term restoration work at St Nikolai is continuing but part of the church is now open weekdays from 2 to 4 pm, Saturday from 9 to 11 am and Sunday from 11 am to noon.

There are many gabled Baltic houses on the small streets just north of Alter Markt, and the old harbour is close by. You'll want to stroll out along the sea wall, then walk west along the waterfront park for a great view of Stralsund's skyline.

## Activities

From May to September Weisse Flotte ships depart from the old harbour for **Hiddensee Island** (DM 20 return trip). Alternatively, consider just taking the regular ferry across the Strelasund to Altefähr on **Rügen Island**.

It operates eight times a day from May to early October (50 Pfennig one-way).

## Places to Stay

The closest *Intercamping* is at Stahlbrode on the coast, about 19 km south-east of Stralsund and four km from Reinberg off the main road to Berlin.

Stralsund's excellent 180-bed *'Grete Walter' Youth Hostel* (☎ 2160) is in the old waterworks (1690) at Am Kütertor 1 near the Oceanographic Museum. It's DM 14 for juniors, DM 17 for seniors.

Stralsund-Information, Alter Markt 15, has private rooms but few singles.

The functional old 41-room *Hotel Am Bahnhof*, Tribseer Damm 4 right opposite the train station, is your best bet for a hotel room (DM 32 per person with shared bath and breakfast). Cheaper yet is the nine-room *Nordland Hotel* on Platz der Solidarität just across the causeway, but it's usually full.

The 40-room *Hotel Schweriner Hof*, Neuer Markt 2-3 beside St Mary's Church, is rather expensive at DM 50 per person for a room with shared bath and breakfast. The hotel restaurant is good.

Stralsund doesn't have an Interhotel so the best on offer is the rather grim, 34-room *Hotel Baltic* (DM 54/108 single/double), a monolithic, Stalin-era building at Franken Damm 17 in an ugly neighbourhood south of the harbour.

## Places to Eat

The *Ratskeller* below the town hall on Alter Markt is open daily from 9 am to 10 pm. The *Ratscafé*, Alter Markt 9, is a great place for a cup of tea or coffee and its meal prices are lower than those of many other local restaurants (closed Monday).

## Getting There & Away

Express trains arrive from Rostock (73 km, 1½ hours), Magdeburg (354 km, 5½ hours), Leipzig (429 km, 5½ hours) and Berlin-Lichtenberg (247 km, three hours). Some of the Berlin trains run straight through from Leipzig to Stralsund.

International trains between Berlin-Zoo

and Stockholm or Oslo use the car ferry between Sassnitz Hafen and Trelleborg, Sweden. Some trains to/from Sassnitz Hafen don't stop at Stralsund's main railway station but instead call at Stralsund-Rügendamm, another station on the south-east side of the city.

For train tickets and times try the Reisebüro, Alter Markt 10 next to the Rathaus.

From mid-March to September there are daily buses to Kiel (DM 40 one-way) and Hamburg from Stralsund Bus Station. For reservations for the afternoon luxury coach to Berlin (mid-April to October, DM 39) contact Reisebüro Zwerg, Ossenreyer Strasse 23. People aged 26 and under get 50% off but baggage is DM 3 apiece.

In summer enquire at the Weisse Flotte office about ships from Sassnitz to Świnoujście (Swinemünde), Poland, which generally leave at 8.30 am from Wednesday to Saturday at 8.30 (DM 25 return).

## HIDDENSEE ISLAND

Hiddensee is a narrow island about 17 km long off Rügen's west coast north of Stralsund. No cars are allowed on Hiddensee. At last report there were no camping grounds, youth hostels or hotels either, only a couple of tiny guesthouses, so check the latest accommodation situation with Stralsund Information before planning an overnight trip.

The Weisse Flotte runs regular passenger boats from Stralsund to Neuendorf, Vitte or Kloster villages on Hiddensee several times a day from May to September. In winter this service also operates on most days. If you want to take a bicycle on this boat, check beforehand as it may not be allowed.

## RÜGEN ISLAND

Rügen Island, just north-east of Stralsund and connected by causeway, is Germany's largest island. At Stubnitz, six km north of Sassnitz, is the highest point on the island (118 metres) and steep chalk cliffs tower above the sea. The main resort area is around Binz, Sellin and Göhren on a peninsula on Rügen's east side.

### Places to Stay

None of the 16 camping grounds of Rügen was allowed to accept Western tourists until 1990. The largest concentration of them is at Göhren.

There's a 108-bed youth hostel at Strandpromenade 35, Binz (☎ 2423). It's DM 14.50 for juniors, DM 17.50 for seniors.

Several small hotels exist, such as the 15-room *Gaststätte Zentralhotel*, Haupt Strasse 13, Binz, the 19-room *Gaststätte Mecklenburger Hof*, Bahnhof Strasse 67, Bergen, and the 10-room *Hotel Am Markt*, Am Markt, Putbus. The only place you'll be reasonably certain of finding a room is at the 116-room, four-star *Rügenhotel*, See Strasse 1, Sassnitz.

### Getting There & Away

Local trains run every couple of hours from Stralsund to Sassnitz (52 km) or Binz (52 km) on Rügen's north-east side. Both services pass Lietzow, 13 km before Sassnitz, where you may have to change trains (ask). From Binz a narrow-gauge railway continues to Göhren (14 km) at Rügen's east tip. Everyone arriving in Germany by ferry from Trelleborg, Sweden, disembarks at Sassnitz.

Tickets for the luxury afternoon coach from Sassnitz to West Berlin (mid-April to October, DM 47) are handled by Reisebüro Rügentourist, Haupt Strasse 50, Sassnitz. People aged 26 and under get 50% off.

Wawel Castle in Kraków, home to Polish royalty
for many centuries

# Poland

By far the largest country in Eastern Europe, Poland has had a tumultuous past. The weight of history is on Kraków, the illustrious royal city; Gdańsk (Danzig), the former Hanseatic trading town where WW II began; Auschwitz, a reminder of the depths to which humanity can descend; and rebuilt Warsaw, symbol of the resilient Polish spirit. In 1939 Poland displayed great courage in being first to say 'no' to Hitler and half a century later it again changed the course of history by becoming the first European state to break free of Communism.

In 1944 Stalin commented that fitting Communism to Poland was like putting a saddle on a cow. Now that the saddle has finally been removed, the pace of economic change goes faster here than anywhere else in Eastern Europe as the Poles struggle desperately to pull their country up by the bootstraps. Though the full benefits of the changes are still far in the future, Poland has already taken on new life as goods reappear in the shops and small Polish businesspeople spread their wares in the streets. The psychological change is tremendous.

Aside from the historical and cultural sides to this subtle land of Chopin and Copernicus, there's the gentle beauty of Baltic beaches, quiet north-eastern lakes and forests, and the majestic mountains in the south, all requiring time to be appreciated. Each of the separate regions of Poland has its own character: Mazovia (around Warsaw), Małopolska ('Little Poland', in the south-east), Silesia (in the south-west), Wielkopolska ('Big Poland', in the west), Pomerania (in the north-west) and Mazuria (in the north-east). Palpable differences remain between the areas once controlled by Austria, Germany and Russia; yet bound together by Catholicism, language, nationality and a common experience, Poland has a unity few other nations in the region can match.

Poland today is a peaceful, safe place to

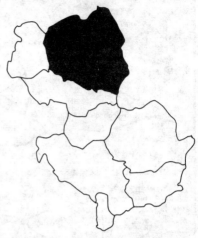

visit. Once you have a visa there are few additional hassles. Even the visa requirements have the advantage of keeping down the number of visitors. It's an exciting time to be in Poland and, for those with hard currency to spend, it's the right time. You'll find the Poles eager to meet you and you'll share the frustrations of their everyday life. It's an experience you won't easily forget.

# Facts about the Country

### HISTORY
In the 6th and 7th centuries AD the West Slavs pushed north and west and occupied most of what is now Poland. By the 10th century the leaders of the Polanian tribe in western Poland were uniting other Slavonic tribes under their rule. Mieszko I adopted Christianity in 966, a date considered to mark the formation of the first Polish state, and in the year 1000 the Gniezno Archbishopric was founded. Boleslav the Brave took the title of king in 1025 and his descendant, Boleslav the Bold, consolidated the power of

Poland

0      50      100 km

the Piast dynasty over a territory very similar to the Poland of today.

There was constant pressure from the west as the Germans pushed into Pomerania and Silesia, so, to be less vulnerable, from the 11th century onwards Polish kings were no longer crowned in Poznań but in Kraków. In the mid-12th century the country was divided into four principalities and a weakened Poland soon fell prey to invaders. In 1226 the Teutonic Knights, a Germanic military and religious order, were invited to come to Poland by the Prince of Mazovia to subdue the restive Prussians of the northeast. Once the knights had subjugated the Baltic tribes they turned their attention to the Poles. The order set up a state in the lower Vistula area east of Gdańsk/Toruń, ruled from their castle at Malbork. Tatar invasions devastated southern Poland in 1241 and 1259. Though Poland was reunified in 1320, the knights held onto Pomerania and Prussia.

From the 14th to 17th centuries Poland was a great power. It's said that the 14th century king, Casimir III the Great, last of the Piast dynasty, 'found a Poland made of wood and left one made of masonry.' His administrative reforms increased the significance of towns like Kraków, Lublin and Poznań. When Casimir died without an heir, the throne passed to the daughter of the King of Hungary, Princess Jadwiga, who in 1386 married the Duke of Lithuania, uniting the two countries under the Jagiello dynasty.

In 1410 the combined Polish, Lithuanian and Ruthenian (Ukrainian) forces under Ladislaus Jagiello defeated the Teutonic Knights at Grunwald south of Olsztyn. After the Thirteen Years' War (1454-66) the Teutonic order was broken up and in 1525 the secular Duchy of Prussia became a fiefdom of the Polish Crown. In 1490 King Casimir IV of Poland also assumed the Hungarian throne.

The early 16th century monarch Sigismund I the Old brought the Renaissance to Poland and in 1543 Nicolaus Copernicus published his immortal treatise *De Revolutionibus Orbium Coelestium*. At a time when much of Europe was being torn apart by religious wars and persecutions, there was relative peace and tolerance in Poland. Lithuania and Poland were formally united as one country in 1569 to oppose Russian expansion, and the Polish-Lithuanian Commonwealth became the largest country in Europe, stretching from the Black Sea to the Baltic Sea.

After the death of Sigismund Augustus in 1572, the Jagiello dynasty became extinct and the Sejm (parliament) decided future kings would be elected by the entire gentry (about 10% of the total population), a system which greatly increased the power of the feudal nobility. In the early 17th century Sigismund III, an elected king from the Swedish Vasa line, moved the capital from Kraków to Warsaw. Sigismund III also embroiled Poland in Swedish dynastic wars and, though the country successfully held off Sweden and Moscow for a time, in 1655 a Swedish invasion ('the Deluge') devastated Poland's towns. King Jan III Sobieski, builder of Warsaw's Wilanów Palace, led a crusade against the Turks which resulted in their removal from Hungary after 1683.

Weak leadership, constant wars and the domination of the gentry over the middle class led to the decline of Poland in the 18th century. Poland's last king, Stanislaus Poniatowski, tried to reverse the situation with reforms, but the powerful magnates resisted strongly, leading to civil war and a pretext for foreign intervention. In the first partition of Poland in 1772, Russia, Prussia and Austria took 29% of the national territory. In 1791 the king granted Poland a democratic constitution (the second in the world) but the magnates again revolted, leading to a second partition in 1793. A year later Tadeusz Kościuszko, a veteran of the American Revolution, led a war of independence against the invaders but was defeated in 1795. A subsequent third partition that year wiped Poland right off the map of Europe until 1918.

The oppressed Poles supported Napoleon, who set up a Duchy of Warsaw in 1807 from where he led his Grand Army to Moscow in 1812 (the beginning of a special Franco-Polish relationship which has continued until today). After 1815 Poland again came under tsarist Russia. There were unsuccessful uprisings against this in 1831, 1848 and 1864 with Poland's position worsening after each one. A Russification and Germanisation policy was enforced in the areas controlled by those powers; Poles were permitted to maintain their identity only in the Austrian-occupied part around Kraków.

## The 20th Century

Poland was completely overrun by the Germans during WW I, but in 1919 a Polish state was again established by the Treaty of Versailles. Then the Polish military struck east and took big chunks of Lithuania, Belorussia and the Ukraine, inhabited by non-Polish majorities, from a weakened Soviet Union. In 1926 Marshal Józef Piłsudski, ex-commander of the Polish Legions which had fought alongside Austria in WW I, staged a military coup and set himself up as dictator. Poland gained a measure of prosperity under Piłsudski, but by the time of his death in 1935 Poland had been ruined by the depression and soon fell victim to Hitler.

WW II began in Gdańsk (at that time the Free City of Danzig) where 182 Poles at Westerplatte held out for a week against the battleship *Schleswig Holstein*, Stuka dive bombers and thousands of German troops. To the west the Polish Pomorska Brigade of mounted cavalry met General Guderian's tanks – medieval lances against modern armour – in a final suicidal charge. Polish resistance continued for almost a month and German losses during the campaign were as great as subsequent losses during the 1940-41 invasions of Western Europe, the Balkans and North Africa combined. As these events took place in the west, the Soviet Union invaded from the east and took back the territories lost in the 1919-21 Polish-Soviet War. Poland had been partitioned for the fourth time.

During WW II Poland was the only country in Europe which never produced any quislings (collaborators). The Nazi governor general, Hans Frank, ruled those areas not directly incorporated into the Reich. Poles resident in the areas which had been annexed by Germany were deported east. Yet two resistance groups, the London-directed Armia Krajowa (Home Army) and the Communist Gwardia Ludowa (People's Guard), later the People's Army, fought on inside Poland. In July 1944 the Red Army liberated Lublin and set up a Communist-led provisional government.

Six million Poles – a fifth of the population – died during the Nazi terror, half of them Jews. During the Warsaw Ghetto uprising of 1943, some 70,000 poorly armed, starving Jews led by Mordechai Anielewicz held out against the full weight of the Nazi army for 27 days. The Warsaw uprising was begun on 1 August 1944 by the Home Army as Soviet forces approached the right bank of the Vistula River. The intention was to evict the retreating Germans from Warsaw and have a non-Communist force in place to greet the Soviet army, but the uprising was premature. The Nazis brought up reserves to halt the Red Army in Praga across the river, then engaged the 50,000 Polish irregulars in house-to-house combat.

By 2 October, when the remaining partisans surrendered with honour, some 250,000 Poles had died, many of them civilians slaughtered en masse by SS troops. All the remaining inhabitants were then expelled from the city and German demolition teams levelled Warsaw street by street. The Soviet armies which entered the city three months later encountered only desolation. Ironically the Germans set the stage for a post-war Communist Poland by physically eliminating the bulk of the non-Communist resistance within the country.

At the Teheran Conference in November 1943, Churchill, Roosevelt and Stalin decided that everything east of the Odra (Oder) and Nysa (Neisse) rivers – which meant Silesia, Pomerania and Mazuria – was to be returned to Poland after centuries of German control. At the same time the Soviet Union was to get the eastern territories, reducing Poland's land area to four-fifths of the prewar size. Millions of people were dislocated by these changes which brought Poland's borders back to where they had been eight centuries earlier. Poland's postwar borders were guaranteed by the creation of the Warsaw Pact in 1955, and in 1970 Chancellor Willy Brandt signed a treaty accepting the Oder-Neisse border.

## Recent History

After the war a Soviet-style Communist system was installed in Poland and the country was run according to five and six-year plans with little relation to economic reality. Though shortages of consumer goods persisted, the *nomenklatura* of party bureaucrats enjoyed many privileges. Intellectual freedom was curtailed by the security apparatus and individual initiative stifled. In 1956, when Nikita Khrushchev denounced Stalin at the Soviet 20th Party Congress, Bolesław Bierut, the Stalinist party chief in Poland, died of a heart attack!

In June 1956 workers in Poznań rioted over low wages, and in October, Władysław Gomułka, an ex-political prisoner of the Stalin era, took over as party first secretary. Gomułka introduced a series of superficial reforms reducing Soviet domination of Poland and freeing political prisoners, but the basic system continued unchanged. After the Arab-Israeli War of 1967, party hardliners used an 'anti-Zionist' purge to enforce discipline, but by December 1970 living conditions had declined to the point where workers in northern Poland went on strike over food price increases. When 300 of them were shot down during demonstrations, Edward Gierek replaced Gomułka as party leader and persuaded the strikers to return to work by promising sweeping changes.

Gierek launched Poland on a reckless programme of industrial expansion to produce exports which could be sold on world markets. Money to finance this was supplied by 17 capitalist governments and 501 banks, and by 1981 the country had run up a hard-currency debt of US$27 billion. Many of the ill-founded heavy industry schemes ended in failure as a recession in the West shrank the markets for Polish exports at the end of the 1970s.

This decade of mismanagement left Poland bankrupt. Living standards fell sharply as Poland was forced to divert goods to export from domestic consumption, to earn hard currency with which to service the debt. The election of a Pole to the papacy in October 1978, and the visit to Poland by John Paul II in June 1979, also changed the atmosphere in a country where the party was supposed to play the 'leading role'.

In 1980 a wave of strikes over sharp price increases forced Gierek out and marked the emergence of Lech Wałęsa's Solidarity trade union which soon had 10 million members (a million of them also Communist Party members). Solidarity said all it wanted was self-management of the factories by workers' councils instead of central planning. At first the Polish government was conciliatory, recognising Solidarity in November 1980, and conceding to a five-day work week. In September 1981, many of Solidarity's demands for reduced central planning and greater worker control over enterprises were met.

Things soon got out of hand as union militants challenged government authority. Strikes and obstruction threatened Poland with economic collapse and a Soviet military intervention which could have led to a bloody civil war. On 13 December 1981 martial law was declared by General Wojciech Jaruzelski, who had become prime minister in February 1981, and thousands were interned as the government broke up the union. In October 1982 Solidarity was dissolved by the courts and by July 1983 martial law could be lifted.

A year after the imposition of martial law, General Jaruzelski introduced economic reforms of his own based on greater autonomy for state corporations. In April 1986, the government set in motion 'second stage' reforms providing for decentralisation, worker control of companies, greater competition, incentives, a market economy and some political pluralism. These initiatives lacked public support, and in a November 1987 referendum Poles cast a vote of no confidence in the Communist government.

Meanwhile Solidarity had been biding its time, and in 1988 fresh strikes followed government attempts to remove food subsidies. The big pay increases won by the striking workers clearly revealed government weakness, and officials agreed to meet with Solidarity to discuss reform, realising that without a compromise Poland would explode.

In April 1989, nine weeks of round-table talks between Solidarity and the Communists ended in an accord which legalised Solidarity and the other opposition groups. A 100-seat senate was to be created, giving Poland a two-house parliament for the first time since 1946. Both the senate and the new president would have veto power over a 460-seat Sejm, though these vetoes could be overridden by a two-thirds majority vote in the lower house. The Polish United Workers Party and allied parties were guaranteed 65% of the seats in the lower house, while the other 35% of the Sejm and the entire senate were to be chosen in Eastern Europe's first Western-style elections.

The sweeping Solidarity victory in the June 1989 elections soon caused the Communist coalition to fall apart and in August 1989 Tadeusz Mazowiecki was picked to head a Solidarity-led coalition, thus becoming the first non-Communist prime minister of an Eastern European country in over four decades. Though General Jaruzelski was elected by parliament in July 1989 to serve as a transitional president, the Communist era in Poland had come to an end, and the two-million-member Polish United Workers

Party dissolved itself at its congress in February 1990.

The Mazowiecki government adopted a 'shock therapy' economic programme to switch Poland from a planned to a free-market economy. On 1 January 1990 price and currency exchange controls were removed, allowing both to find their real levels. During the first month, prices jumped 79% but the markets suddenly filled with products. Inflation was eventually brought under control as the złoty stabilised against Western currencies, though at the cost of wages losing 30% of their purchasing power in 1990 and industrial production falling by 45%. The Mazowiecki team also prepared for privatisation by cutting subsidies to inefficient state industries, thereby sending unemployment up from zero to 7.5% in 1990.

Though Mazowiecki's achievements in just over a year had earned high marks, Lech Wałęsa (who had participated in the round-table talks and was still leader of Solidarity) felt the reforms weren't moving fast enough and that he could change that by becoming president himself. In September 1990 General Jaruzelski graciously offered to step down as president even though he only was in the second year of his six-year term, and in December 1990 the Gdańsk electrician was elected president. Two political parties emerged from the ranks of the old Solidarity: Wałęsa's populist Centre Alliance and Mazowiecki's more moderate Democratic Union.

## GEOGRAPHY

Stretching 650 km from north to south and 690 km from east to west, 312,683-sq-km Poland is the seventh-largest nation in Europe, just a little smaller than reunified Germany (357,519 sq km). It's a low country with all of the mountains in the south. The Sudeten Mountains south of Jelenia Góra in Silesia are 280 km long and 50 km wide, with a medium height of 1200 metres culminating in Śnieżka (1605 metres). The Beskidy and Pieniny mountains in the Western Carpathians run along the Slovak border north of the Tatras. The Bieszczady Mountains in the Eastern Carpathians are open grassy peaks which reach 1346 metres at Tarnica.

Poland's highest mountains are the rocky Tatras, a section of the Carpathian range that Poland shares with Slovakia. The Polish Tatras (150 sq km) are 50 km long and rise to Rysy (2499 metres), and the Slovak Tatras (600 sq km) culminate in Gerlachovský Štít (2654 metres). Poland's lowest point is actually 1.8 metres below sea level in the Vistula delta.

Lowland predominates in central Poland, a land of great north-flowing rivers such as the Vistula, Odra, Warta and Bug. The entire drainage area of the 1047-km Vistula, the mother river of Poland, lies within Poland's boundaries and most of the rest of the country is drained by the Odra. Poland has more post-glacial lakes than any country in Europe except Finland. West of the Vistula is the Pomeranian lake district, and east are the picturesque Mazurian Lakes. The coastal plain along the broad, sandy, 524-km Baltic coast is spotted with sand dunes, bays and lakes, separated from the sea by narrow sand bars.

## ECONOMY

After WW II, Poland was a patchwork of small farms with 38% of the economy in ruins. In the rebuilding process the emphasis was placed on heavy industry, leading to serious shortages of consumer goods. Industry, services and agriculture each contribute about a third to the gross national product. Poland's workforce of nearly 20 million is employed in industry and commerce (44%), agriculture (30%), services (11%) and government (8%). With privatisation, employment in services is expected to increase sharply as industry declines.

Heavy industries include steel mills (at Warsaw, Kraków and Katowice), shipbuilding (at Gdańsk), mining machinery and chemicals, while among the light industries are textiles (at Łódź), food products, beverages, paper, timber and glass. In 1986, 17.1 million metric tons of crude steel were produced. Poland is the fourth-largest producer of hard bituminous coal in the world, most of it from Silesia. Brown coal is burned for electricity. Sulphur and copper are extracted in southern Poland.

These activities have created tremendous environmental problems. Untreated sewage and industrial wastes are released into the Vistula River which carries them down to the Gulf of Gdańsk. The six nations bordering the Baltic Sea dump thousands and millions of tonnes of heavy metals, nitrogen, phosphorous, oil and highly toxic chloride compounds (PCBs) into the water every year, causing fish catches to plummet. In the south the steel mills at Nowa Huta and Katowice and other industries in Upper Silesia have caused severe air pollution, including the acid rain which is dissolving Kraków's medieval monuments. In 1990 Poland halted construction of its first nuclear power plant which was being built near Gdańsk using outmoded Soviet technology.

Poland is the world's second-largest producer of rye. Barley, oats, oilseed, potatoes, sugar beets and wheat are also important. Though an exporter of livestock and sugar, Poland still imports grain. The land use breakdown is 48% arable land, 1% permanent crops, 13% meadows and pastures, 29% forest and woodland and 9% other uses. Throughout the Communist period Poland was unique in Eastern Europe in that 83% of agricultural land was privately farmed by small holders, while 15% was owned by the state and only 2% by cooperatives.

Tourism is growing fast, as evidenced by the 42-storey, 521-room Marriott Hotel operating in Warsaw since October 1989. The hotel is a joint venture between LOT Polish Airlines (the building's owner), Marriott Corporation (which manages the hotel) and Ilbau Construction of Austria (which built it). The Inter-Continental and Holiday Inn chains also have modern hotels in Warsaw, and Hilton, Hyatt and Sheraton seem soon to follow. A new terminal building at Warsaw Airport is underway.

Until recently machinery, coal, transportation equipment and chemicals were exported to other Communist countries, particularly the USSR which supplied Poland with raw materials such as metals and phosphates for industry, plus 80% of Poland's crude oil. Trading patterns changed rapidly after 1 January 1991 when Poland began to accept only hard currencies (not 'accounting roubles') for its exports. With the USSR collapsing, Poland is looking more and more to the West. In 1990 Poland had an encouraging US$3.4 billion trade surplus with the West and a 4.4-billion-rouble surplus with the East.

Poland has hard-currency debts of over US$46 billion. The mountain of debt is growing: even without any new credits, Polish indebtedness will double over the next seven years while the economy will only expand by 50% at best. This indebtedness is discouraging foreign investment.

## POPULATION & PEOPLE

Over half the 38 million inhabitants of Poland live in towns and cities, the six largest of which are Warsaw, Lódź, Kraków, Wrocław, Poznań and Gdańsk. The southwest is the most densely populated part, especially the area around Lódź and Katowice, while the north-east is the least populated. There's a serious housing shortage forcing many young families to live with in-laws. Literacy is 98%.

At the end of WW II millions of Germans were evicted from East Prussia, Pomerania and Silesia, their places taken by further millions of Poles from the Ľvov region of the Ukraine. Half a million Ukrainians, Belorussians and Lithuanians were resettled in the USSR. In the 18th century a third of the world's Jews lived in Poland but tragically few of Poland's 3.5 million prewar Jews survived the Nazis.

These forced migrations and exterminations created a homogeneous population. Before the war, minorities accounted for 30% of the population of Poland. Today only 1.5% are minorities, mostly Ukrainians and Belorussians. Though only five or six thousand Jews remain in Poland, this hasn't prevented some demented elements from using anti-Semitism as a political tool. (It's estimated that 31% of Poles are anti-Semitic to one degree or another.) Ten million Poles live abroad in North America, the Soviet Union, France and Brazil. Poles refer to the overseas Polish community as 'Polonia' and overseas Poles as 'Polonians'.

## ARTS

Poland is a land of remarkable individuals, so many in fact that visitors often lose their way among the unfamiliar names. Aside from Copernicus and Chopin one soon becomes acquainted with Jan Matejko (1838-93) whose monumental historical paintings hang in galleries all around Poland. By creating dramatic visual images of decisive moments in Polish history, Matejko inspired his compatriots at a time when Poland was under foreign yokes.

A kindred spirit was the Romantic poet Adam Mickiewicz (1798-1855) who sought the lost motherland in his writings. Mickiewicz explored the ethical and moral problems of a Poland subject to Russia and held out the hope of eventual redemption, in the same way that Christ was resurrected.

Henryk Sienkiewicz (1846-1916) wrote historical novels which gave Poles a new sense of national identity and won the author a Nobel Prize. His book *The Knights of the Teutonic Order* published in 1900 makes fascinating reading in light of the Nazi attack on Poland four decades later.

One contemporary novelist, the ex-Socialist Realist Tadeusz Konwicki (born 1926), started out as a Stalinist but after Stalin's crimes were revealed in 1956 turned to depicting Polish life under a hollow system. Recent Konwicki works such as *The Polish Complex* (1982) and *Moonrise, Moonrise* (1987), both translated into English, again explore the theme summed up in the 1797 Polish national anthem: *Jeszcze Polska nie zginęła póki my żyjemy* (Poland has not yet perished as long as we live).

### Music & Dance

Polish folk music dates back far beyond the first written records of mid-16th century mazurka rhythms. The *krakowiak* is an old folk dance from the Kraków region, while the mazurka, a spirited Mazovian folk dance similar to a polka, originated in central Poland. Danced by a circle of couples in three-four time with much improvisation, mazurkas were originally accompanied by bagpipes.

The *polonaise* is a dignified ceremonial dance that originated as a formal march in the 16th century. During the 17th and 18th centuries the polonaise was used to open functions at the royal court. Arrayed according to their social station, the couples would promenade around the ballroom in three-four time, knees bending slightly on every third gliding step.

The romantic composer Frédéric Chopin (in Polish, Fryderyk Szopen) (1810-49) raised this dance music (mazurkas, polonaises and waltzes) to the level of concert pieces. Written at a time when central Poland was under Russian domination, Chopin's music displays the melancholy and nostalgia which became hallmarks of the Polish national style.

Frédéric Chopin

Stanisław Moniuszko (1819-72) 'nationalised' 19th century Italian opera music by introducing folk songs and dances onto the stage. His *Halka* (1858) about a peasant girl abandoned by a young noble was the first Polish national opera, and many of Moniuszko's operatic characters now belong to Polish national 'mythology'. Together Chopin and Moniuszko were the creators of the Polish national school of music.

The 20th century composer Karol Szymanowski (1882-1937) strove to merge the traditions of Polish music with those of Europe. His ballet *Harnasie*, based on the folklore of the *Górale*, the Highlanders of the Tatra Mountains, employed modern technical devices also used by the Russian Igor Stravinsky.

## CULTURE

Poles greet each other by shaking hands much more than is done in the English speaking world. Men also shake hands with women, though it's customary for the woman to extend her hand first. Poles bump into each other a lot and never apologise. They're not being rude, it's just what they're accustomed to.

If a Polish family befriends you, you'll be smothered with hospitality, in which case just submit and feel right at home going along with their suggestions. When the time comes, propose a toast to the health of the hostess, and be sure to take flowers and perhaps chocolates for the lady of the house whenever you're invited for dinner at a Polish home. Never arrive early for a dinner engagement, preferably a little late, and be prepared to stay later than you'd planned. At the end of a meal always say *dziękuję* (thank you) as you get up, even in restaurants when sharing a table with strangers.

In this strongly Catholic country Easter is just as important as Christmas, and the most remarkable Easter event is the seven-day Passion Play at Kalwaria Zebrzydowska, 23 km south-west of Kraków. A re-enactment of Christ's entry into Jerusalem on Palm Sunday is followed by a crucifixion on Good Friday and a resurrection on Easter Sunday witnessed by hundreds of thousands of people. At times the crowd has become so excited that it has attempted to rescue Christ from the 'Roman soldiers'! Forty-two calvary chapels representing the Stages of the Cross have been set up on this hilly site near the 17th century Bernardine monastery. Of the few mystery cycles still performed in Europe, this is the oldest and most renowned – don't miss it if you're in Kraków around Easter.

On All Souls' Day (November 1) people visit the cemeteries and adorn the graves with candles and flowers. In the mid-19th century, Poles adopted the custom of the Christmas tree from Western Europe. Before Christmas Eve dinner, hay is put under the tablecloth. When everyone is seated, each pulls out a blade of hay at random. To get a long blade signifies a long life, while a shorter one indicates a more complicated future. Traditionally an extra place is set at the table for an unexpected guest. There will be 12 courses, one for each of the 12 apostles. At midnight on Christmas Eve, a special mass is celebrated in all churches, while New Year's Eve is marked by formal balls.

## RELIGION

In 966 AD Poland became the easternmost Roman Catholic country in Europe while Russia and most of the Balkan countries converted to Eastern Orthodox Christianity. Archbishops are seated at Kraków, Poznań, Warsaw and Wrocław. The Polish Church often had a distant relationship with Rome until 1978, when a Pole was elected Pope. Today the overwhelming majority of Poles are fervent Catholics and on Sundays every church is full to overflowing. The Catholic university in Lublin (founded in 1918) and the Academy of Catholic Theology in Warsaw are leading church-controlled institutions. Częstochowa with its Black Madonna is one of the most important pilgrimage centres in Europe.

The narrow line between church and state has always been difficult to define in Poland. The lives of two Catholic priests, Father Maximilian Kolbe, executed at Auschwitz in 1941, and Father Jerzy Popiełuszko, murdered by the secret police in 1984, symbolise the close relationship between church and people. The church openly encouraged Solidarity throughout the years when it was banned, and the overthrow of Communism was as much a victory for Catholicism as it was for democracy. It's no coincidence that Catholic religious instruction was reintroduced in the public schools just as the teaching of Marxist ideology was dropped. Though religion classes are voluntary, children who choose not to attend must sit out in the corridor. The church has also campaigned for an anti-abortion law.

## LANGUAGE

German is widely understood in Poland, and increasingly, English. While trying to make yourself understood you'll greatly increase comprehension by writing the word or message down on a piece of paper. A pocket English-Polish dictionary will come in handy; consider bringing one with you as they're often hard to find in Poland. *Polish for Travellers* by Berlitz is a useful language guide. Best of all, check out a set of 'learn Polish' language tapes or records from your local library and listen to them a couple of times before leaving home.

Some of the 32 letters in the Polish alphabet are pronounced quite differently than they are in English. As a very rough way of making oneself understood, pronounce the Polish c as the English ts, ch as kh; ć, ci (before a vowel) and cz as ch; dź, dzi (before a vowel) and dż as the j in jelly (but dz as in English); j as y; ł as w; ń as the ny in canyon; ś, si (before a vowel) and sz as sh (but s as in English); w as v; y as the i in sit; and ż, rz, ź and zi (before a vowel) as the s in pleasure (but z as in English). The ogonek below ą and ę makes those vowels nasal. The vowels a, e, i, o and u are pronounced as in Italian or Spanish and r is always trilled. There are many refinements to the above which would take several pages to outline. In almost all Polish words, the stress falls on the next-to-last syllable.

When consulting indexes in Polish books or maps be aware that letters with acute, ogonek and overdot accents are considered distinct from the same letter without an accent, so if you don't find the word immediately, check further down the column. The nine accented letters are ą, ć, ę, ł, ń, ó, ś, ź and ż.

The first words a visitor to Poland should learn are *proszę* (please) and *dziękuję* (thank you). Also be aware of *tak* (yes), *nie* (no), *dzień dobry* (good morning), *do widzenia* (goodbye) and *nieczynne* (closed). You'll quickly learn *remont* which means something like 'under repair'. You'll see this word posted frequently on museums, hotels and restaurants which close for extended renovations. Another common word is *nie ma* which means something like 'nothing' or 'not available'.

Public toilets (or 'WC') are marked with a circle for women and a triangle for men. When holding up fingers to indicate numbers in Poland, remember to begin with the thumb, otherwise you'll get one more item than you want.

## Greetings & Civilities

hello
  *cześć* (very informal)
hello/good morning
  *dzień dobry*
good evening
  *dobry wieczór*
goodbye
  *do widzenia*
please
  *proszę*
thank you
  *dziękuję*
excuse me/forgive me
  *przepraszam*
You are very kind.
  *Jest pan bardzo uprzejmy.* (to males)
  *Jest pani bardzo uprzejma.* (to females)
yes
  *tak*
no
  *nie*

## Small Talk

Do you speak English?
  *Czy mówisz po angielsku?*

I don't understand.
*Nie rozumiem.*
Could you write it down?
*Czy mógł byś to zapisać?*
Where do you live?
*Gdzie mieszkasz?*
What work do you do?
*Jaką wykonujesz pracę?*
I am a student.
*Jestem studentem.*
I am very happy.
*Jest mi bardzo przyjemnie.*

## Accommodation

youth hostel
*schronisko młodzieży*
camping ground
*kemping*
private room
*kwatera prywatna*
How much is it?
*Ile to kosztuje?*
Is that the price per person?
*Czy to jest cena od osoby?*
Is that the total price?
*Czy to jest ostateczna cena?*
Are there any extra charges?
*Czy są jakieś dodatkowe opłaty?*
Can I pay with local currency?
*Czy mogę płacić w lokalnej walucie?*
Where is there a cheaper hotel?
*Gdzie jest tańszy hotel?*
Should I make a reservation?
*Czy mam zrobić rezerwację?*
single room
*pokój jednoosobowy*
double room
*pokój dwuosobowy*
It is very noisy.
*Jest bardzo głośny.*
Where is the toilet?
*Gdzie jest ustępy?*

## Getting Around

What time does it leave?
*O której odjezdza?*
When is the first bus?
*O której jest pierwszy autobus?*
When is the last bus?
*O której jest ostatni autobus?*

When is the next bus?
*O której jest następny autobus?*
That's too soon.
*To za wcześnie.*
When is the next one after that?
*O której jest następny po nim?*
How long does the trip take?
*Jak długo trwa podróż?*
arrival
*przyjazdy*
departure
*odjazdy*
timetable
*rozkład jazdy*
Where is the bus stop?
*Gdzie jest przystanek autobusowy?*
Where is the railway station?
*Gdzie jest stacja kolejowa?*
Where is the taxi stand?
*Gdzie jest postój taksówek?*
Where is the left-luggage room?
*Gdzie jest przechowalnia bagazu?*

## Around Town

Just a minute.
*Chwileczkę.*
Where is...?
*Gdzie jest...?*
the bank
*bank*
the post office
*poczta*
the telephone centre
*urząd telefoniczny*
the tourist information office
*informacja turystyczna*
the museum
*muzeum*
the palace
*pałac*
the castle
*zamek*
the concert hall
*sala koncertowa*
the opera house
*opera*
the musical theatre
*teatr muzyczny*
Where are you going?
*Dokąd idziesz?*

I am going to...
*Idę do...*
Where is it?
*Gdzie to jest?*
I can't find it.
*Nie mogę (tego) znaleźć.*
Is it far?
*Czy to daleko?*
Please show me on the map.
*Proszę pokazać mi to na mapie.*
left
*lewo*
right
*prawo*
straight ahead
*prosto*
I want...
*chcę...*
Do I need permission?
*Czy potrzebuję pozowolenie?*
May I?
*Czy wolno?*

## Entertainment

Where can I hear live music?
*Gdzie mogę iść na koncert?*
Where can I buy a ticket?
*Gdzie mogę kupić bilet?*
I'm looking for a ticket.
*Szukam biletu.*
Where can I refund this ticket?
*Gdzie mogę zwrócić ten bilet?*
Is this a good seat?
*Czy to jest dobre miejsce?*
at the front
*z przodu*
ticket
*bilet*

## Food

I am hungry.
*Jestem głodny.* (male)
*Jestem głodna.* (female)
I do not eat meat.
*Nie jadam mięsa.*
self-service cafeteria
*bar samoobsługowy*
grocery store
*sklep warzywniczy*

fish
*ryba*
soup
*zupa*
salad
*sałatka*
fresh vegetables
*świeża jażyna*
milk
*mleko*
bread
*chleb*
sugar
*cukier*
ice cream
*lody*
hot coffee
*gorąca kawa*
mineral water
*woda mineralna*
beer
*piwo*
wine
*wino*

## Shopping

Where can I buy one?
*Gdzie mogę kupić?*
How much does it cost?
*Ile to kosztuje?*
That's (much) too expensive.
*To jest zbyt drogie.*
Is there a cheaper one?
*Czy jest coś tańszego?*

## Time & Dates

today
*dzisiaj*
tonight
*dzisiaj wieczorem*
tomorrow
*jutro*
the day after tomorrow
*pojutrze*
What time does it open?
*O której jest otwarte?*
What time does it close?
*O której jest zamknięte?*

open
  *otwarto*
closed
  *zamknięto*
in the morning
  *rano*
in the evening
  *wieczorem*
every day
  *codziennie*
At what time?
  *O której godzinie?*
when?
  *kiedy?*

| Monday | *poniedziałek* |
| Tuesday | *wtorek* |
| Wednesday | *środa* |
| Thursday | *czwartek* |
| Friday | *piątek* |
| Saturday | *sobota* |
| Sunday | *niedziela* |

| January | *styczeń* |
| February | *luty* |
| March | *marzec* |
| April | *kwiecień* |
| May | *maj* |
| June | *czerwiec* |
| July | *lipiec* |
| August | *sierpień* |
| September | *wrzesień* |
| October | *październik* |
| November | *listopad* |
| December | *grudzień* |

**Numbers**

| 1 | *jeden* |
| 2 | *dwa* |
| 3 | *trzy* |
| 4 | *cztery* |
| 5 | *pięć* |
| 6 | *sześć* |
| 7 | *siedem* |
| 8 | *osiem* |
| 9 | *dziewięć* |
| 10 | *dziesięć* |
| 11 | *jedenaście* |
| 12 | *dwanaście* |
| 13 | *trzynaście* |
| 14 | *czternaście* |
| 15 | *piętnaście* |
| 16 | *szesnaście* |
| 17 | *siedemnaście* |
| 18 | *osiemnaście* |
| 19 | *dziewiętnaście* |
| 20 | *dwadzieścia* |
| 21 | *dwadzieścia jeden* |
| 22 | *dwadzieścia dwa* |
| 23 | *dwadzieścia trzy* |
| 30 | *trzydzieści* |
| 40 | *czterdzieści* |
| 50 | *pięćdziesiąt* |
| 60 | *sześćdziesiąt* |
| 70 | *siedemdziesiąt* |
| 80 | *osiemdziesiąt* |
| 90 | *dziewięćdziesiąt* |
| 100 | *sto* |

# Facts for the Visitor

## VISAS & EMBASSIES

You must have a passport and in some cases a visa to enter Poland. Visas are as a rule not issued at the border. Your passport must be valid six months after the expiry of the visa. Citizens of Austria, Belgium, Finland, France, Germany, Italy, Luxembourg, the Netherlands, Sweden and the USA do not require visas, and soon many other nationals may also be able to enter Poland without a visa. Check with one of the Polish consulates listed in this section or at any LOT Polish Airlines office. By phone it's much easier to get through to LOT than to a consulate and they'll have the latest information in their computer.

Polish tourist visas cost about US$25 (or US$35 for citizens of the UK) and two photos are required. In Eastern Europe visas are generally issued in 24 hours, with an express one-hour visa service available if you pay 50% more. A multiple-entry visa valid for up to four entries costs US$33. A reduced visa fee is available to students who are 23 years of age and under.

If you apply to the consulate in your home country by registered mail it could be several weeks before you get your passport back. Ask about express service when you write in for the application forms. The Polish consulates at Belgrade, Berlin, Bratislava, Bucharest, Budapest, Ostrava, Prague, Sofia, Varna and Zagreb are generally open weekday mornings. Otherwise call one of the consulates listed below. Some consulates are tremendously overcrowded or charge unusually high fees, so get your visa well in advance, allowing yourself the opportunity to try elsewhere if need be.

If you're asked how long you wish to stay in Poland when you apply for the visa, say one month even if you plan to stay less. That way you won't have to worry about visa extensions should you decide to stay a little longer. Since you must personally register with the police if you stay over a month, it's best to limit your stay to 30 days maximum. You can get a regular visa for a stay of up to 90 days, however. The first and last days of your stay in Poland are not counted against the duration of stay noted on the visa.

Polish visas may be used any time within three or six months from the date of issue. A cheaper, 48-hour transit visa is also available (onward visa required). If you have to extend your tourist visa within Poland, go to the local passport office *(biuro paszportowe)* on a weekday morning. Any tourist office will have the address.

The visa form says that you must register with the police within 48 hours of crossing the border. This regulation is primarily aimed at visitors who stay with Polish friends or relatives. If you're staying in any type of official accommodation (hotel, youth hostel, camping ground, etc) this formality will be taken care of for you. Places where you stay will stamp your visa form to show that you were properly registered. This system is a hangover from the former Communist regime which is gradually being ignored.

## Polish Consulates

Polish consulates abroad include:

Australia
    7 Turrana St, Yarralumla, ACT 2600 (Canberra) (☎ 73 1208)
    10 Trelawney St, Woollahra, NSW 2025 (Sydney) (☎ 32 9816)
Austria
    Hietzinger Hauptstrasse 42c, 1130 Vienna XIII (☎ 82 3272)
Belgium
    28 rue des Francs, 1040 Brussels (☎ 733 7748)
    Plantijn Moretuslei 130, 1ste Verdien, 2000 Antwerp (☎ 235 6334)
Canada
    1500 Avenue des Pins Ouest, Montreal, PQ H3G 1B4 (☎ 514-937 9481)
    2603 Lakeshore Blvd West, Toronto, ON M8V 1G5 (☎ 416-252 5471)
Denmark
    Richelieus Alle 10, Copenhagen – 2900 Hellerup (☎ 62 7244)
Finland
    Armas Lindgrenintie 21, 00570 Helsinki 57 (☎ 68 3077)
France
    5 rue de Talleyrand, 75007 Paris (☎ 4551 6080)
    45 Boulevard Carne, 59000 Lille Nord (☎ 2006 5030)
    79 rue Crillon, 69458 Lyon (☎ 7893-14-85)
Germany
    Leyboldstrasse 74, 5000 Cologne 51 Marienburg (☎ 38 7013)
    Lasenstrasse 19/21, 1000 Berlin 33 (☎ 826 2046)
    Poetenweg 51, 7022 Leipzig (☎ 52763)
    Stephanstrasse 16, 2500 Rostock 1 (☎ 23878)
Greece
    22 Chrissenthemon, GR-15452 Athens – Paleo Psychico (☎ 671 6917)
Italy
    Via Rubens 20, Monti Parioli, 00197 Rome (☎ 360 9695)
    Via Sporting Mirasole 2, 20090 Noverasco di Opera, Milan (☎ 524 2241)
Japan
    13, 5 Mita 2-chome, Meguro-ku, Tokyo 153 (☎ 711 5224)
Netherlands
    Alexanderstraat 25, 2514 JM The Hague (☎ 360 2806)
Norway
    Olaf Kyrres Plass 1  0-273 Oslo 2 (☎ 44 8639)
Portugal
    Avda das Descobertas, 1400 Lisbon (☎ 61 2350)
Spain
    Calle Guisando 23 bis, 28035 Madrid – 35 (☎ 216 1365)
Sweden
    Praestgardsgatan 5, S-17232 Sundbyberg (Stockholm) (☎ 29 7018)
    Adolf Fredriksgaten 13, S-21774 Malmö (☎ 67416)

Switzerland
   Elfenstrasse 20a (Postfach 30), 3006 Berne
   (☎ 44 0452)
UK
   19 Weymouth St, London W1N 3AG
   (☎ 71-580 0476)
   2 Kinnear Rd, Edinburgh EH355 PE
   (☎ 55 20301)
USA
   2224 Wyoming Ave NW, Washington DC 20008
   (☎ 202-234 3800)
   1530 North Lake Shore Dr, Chicago IL 60610
   (☎ 312-337 8166)
   233 Madison Ave, New York NY 10016
   (☎ 212-889 8360)

## MONEY

The fiscal climate in Poland is freeing up so
quickly that some of the following information could be out of date by the time you visit
Poland. Check with a Polish consulate or
LOT office for the latest state of affairs with
currency declaration forms, etc.

One of the successes of the Mazowiecki
government was the establishment of the
złoty (zł) as a convertible currency. By
legalising private currency trading (the
former 'black market') in 1990 and allowing

the country's currency to find its own value
on the open market, Poland took a giant step
along the road to economic reform.

Upon arrival, only change enough money
for the first day or two as the rates vary
between exchange offices and banks. You'll
usually get the best rates at private exchange
offices known as 'kantory', but they only
take cash (no travellers' cheques). In Poland
the dollar is still the preferred hard currency
and its value against the złoty is slightly
better than other currencies such as the
Deutschmark or British pound.

Travellers' cheques are not liked in
Poland. Only a few main banks will accept
them and commissions of up to 3% with a
US$10 minimum have been reported! The
Polska Kasa Opieki (PKO) bank usually
charges a standard US$1.25 commission to
cash a travellers' cheque; but you have to
search for a branch willing to do it, line up
and wait while they complete the paperwork.
After that you'll get a rate lower that you'd
have got in seconds without commission for
cash at a private kantor. Some inefficient
state banks simply refuse to change travellers' cheques at all, so bring cash if you can.

Credit cards are only accepted in Orbis hotels and expensive restaurants and shops which cater mostly to tourists. The best known cards are American Express, Visa, Diners Club, Eurocard and Access/Mastercard. In late 1990 a new American Express office opened in Warsaw at ulica Bracka 16, on the corner of Aleje Jerozolimskie.

In Poland you pay for everything (except visas, duty-free goods and international transportation tickets) directly in Polish złoty. The import and export of Polish currency is still prohibited though there's no reason for you to do either. Before you leave it's no problem changing złoty back into hard currency at exchange houses. Be sure to do so as the złoty is still not widely recognised outside Poland. No receipts are required to change excess złoty back into another currency, nor are they given when you change cash.

Private exchange offices in Poland will sell you Romanian lei at a rate better than you'd get on the black market in Romania itself. They also have Czechoslovak, Hungarian and Bulgarian currency but the rates for these are only slightly better than the official rates in those countries. However, it's always a good idea to pick up a small amount to ease your entry.

If you change money with someone on the street, you're likely to get *less* than you would at a kantor and run the risk of being ripped off. A British reader sent us this:

We were approached in the pedestrian subway near Warsaw Central Station by two men wanting to change money. They offered a good rate (2000 złoty more than the bank rate for DM). We are not green when it comes to dealing on the black market, but these guys were slick! We watched them count out our money (1,500,000 złoty for DM 200) and they handed it to us. No problem, until we reached our dormitory room and realised that under the new 100,000 złoty note on top was a pile of completely worthless 100 złoty notes. Later we heard many stories about violence being used on tourists in black market transactions.

## Currency Declaration

Upon arrival in Poland, the customs officer will ask you to fill out a currency declaration specifying precisely how much money you have with you. Each different currency must be listed, with cash and travellers' cheques separated on different lines, so have these figures ready. Gold jewellery must also be declared on the form. This regulation was invented by the Communists as a way of controlling the former black market, and even though it doesn't serve much purpose anymore it's still being enforced.

Officially you're not allowed to take out more foreign currency than you listed on the form, but when you leave Poland the customs officer will probably take the form back from you without even looking at it. Keep everybody happy by not losing your declaration. If on entry or departure you're carrying banknotes from Poland or any other Eastern European country, be aware of the fact that it may still be prohibited to have them with you (another vestige of Communism).

## Currency

Poland may have a greater variety of banknotes in circulation than any other country. Depicted on the banknotes are the commander in chief of the International Brigades during the Spanish Civil War, Karol Świerczewski (50 złoty); 19th century socialist activist Ludwik Waryński (100 złoty); Paris Commune Commander in Chief Jarosław Dąbrowski (200 złoty); 18th century patriot Tadeusz Kościuszko (500 złoty); 16th century astronomer Mikołaj Kopernik (1000 złoty); 10th century king Mieszko I (2000 złoty); 19th century composer Frédéric Chopin (5000 złoty); early 20th century artist Stanisław Wyspiański (10,000 złoty); radium co-discoverer Maria Skłodowska-Curie (20,000 złoty); 18th century geologist Stanisław Staszic (50,000 złoty); 19th century opera composer Stanisław Moniuszko (100,000 złoty); the Polish national emblem (200,000 złoty); and Nobel Prize-winning author Henryk Sienkiewicz (500,000 złoty).

When you first arrive, study Poland's banknotes carefully as the high denominations and great variety of bills can be confusing. The similar colour and appearance of the 200 and 20,000 and the 1000 and 100,000 notes doesn't help either! Złoty banknotes printed before 1975 are worthless.

### Exchange Rate

Poland used to be caught in the grip of inflation. In 1981 one US dollar was worth 34 złoty; in 1986, 160 złoty; in November 1987, 310 złoty; in May 1989, 3750 złoty; and in July 1989, 6000 złoty. By late 1990 it was relatively stable at 9000 to the dollar, but by late 1991 it had devalued a bit further to 11,114 to the dollar. We list all prices in this chapter in US dollars to make them more meaningful to foreigners, not out of fear that the złoty will swing out of control again.

There's only one market exchange rate now, which is somewhere between what the old official and black market rates would have been. This makes accommodation a lot cheaper while all other prices are still very manageable in hard currency terms.

### Costs

You should be able to see Poland in relative comfort following the recommendations in this book for under US$20 per person per day. That includes a room at a medium-priced hotel, at least one meal a day at a good restaurant, admissions and 1st-class transportation by train. Couples, families and small groups will spend less, and if you camp or sleep in youth hostels, go 2nd class on the train, and eat only at self-services you might end up spending under US$10 per person per day. Before congratulating yourself on how cheap it is, remember that Polish workers only make the equivalent of about US$100 a month.

Aside from being a bonanza for budgeteers, the low prices open other possibilities. If you're tired of travelling and want to hang out somewhere for a while, you can live very well in Poland for US$15 a day, provided you stay in one place. Ask any tourist office to find you a Polish language teacher, then just pass your time reading, writing, studying, painting or whatever. The friends you make during that time could end up being friends for life.

### CLIMATE & WHEN TO GO

Poland has a moderate continental climate with considerable maritime influence along the Baltic coast, which makes conditions variable from year to year. Spring is a time of warm days and chilly nights, while summer (June to August) can be hot. Autumn (September to November) brings some rain and there can be snow from December to March. In the mountains the snow lingers until mid-April. From late October to February it gets dark around 5 pm.

The sea coast is the sunniest part of the country in summer; the Carpathian Mountains are sunnier in winter. July is the hottest month, February the coolest. Warsaw has average daily temperatures above 14°C from May to September, above 8°C in April and October and below freezing from December to February. Expect Poland to be cooler and rainier than Western Europe.

In the mountains the ski season runs from December to mid-March, though between Christmas and New Year all the facilities will be packed. Spring (April and May) is a good time for sightseeing. Mountain hiking and camping are good and uncrowded in June and September; late August and early September are a relatively dry, sunny time to tour the Great Mazurian Lakes. To swim in the Baltic you'll have to come in July and August. The cities are visitable all year, and winter is sometimes even preferable as most theatres and concert halls are closed throughout summer.

### TOURIST OFFICES

Orbis is the government travel agency organising tourism in Poland with 180 offices in cities and towns around the country. Like western travel agencies, its main functions are to make reservations, sell transportation tickets and book rooms at luxury hotels. Its staff will also give information if they're not too busy, and in most offices there's somebody who speaks English. Orbis offices abroad (listed in this section) tend to be more cooperative than those within Poland.

The Polish Tourists & Country-Lovers' Association (PTTK) has offices in towns and resort areas which often know about accommodation in city dormitories, camping grounds and mountain huts, and even have information on hitchhiking *(autostop)*. But English is seldom spoken, and what the staff tell you about facilities outside their immediate area may be unreliable. They often sell excellent indexed city or hiking maps of both their own and other areas, so always have a look inside whenever you see the letters PTTK.

Most cities also have local tourist offices, such as Syrena in Warsaw and Wawel Tourist in Kraków, usually identified by the letters IT *(Informacja Turystyczna)* on the door. These are better sources of information but have fewer tickets. Sometimes they offer private room accommodation. Gromada, Juventur, Sports-Tourist and Turysta are tourism cooperatives catering exclusively to the domestic market. They don't usually arrange accommodation, sell train tickets or speak English.

### Student Travel

Almatur is the Travel & Tourism Bureau of the Union of Polish Students. Its offices issue student cards (US$4) and know about student accommodation in July and August. They are also excellent sources of general information.

Both the western ISIC (International Student Identity Card) and eastern IUS (International Union of Students) cards are valid in Poland for student discounts on museum admissions and train or ferry tickets, though some older officials still insist on the IUS version. We've even heard of travellers who were fined by a conductor on a moving train because they couldn't produce an IUS card to go with their discount train ticket!

Almatur organises excellent weekly horse riding and sailing holidays which foreign students may join. In July and August there are Almatur International Camps of Labour in which participants work 46 hours a week as construction, agricultural, or forest labourers. After work there are excursions, sporting and cultural events, etc. Get details from Orbis offices abroad.

### Orbis Offices Abroad

Orbis offices outside Poland include:

Austria
    Orbis, Schwedenplatz 5, 1010 Vienna
    (☎ 63 0810)
Bulgaria
    Orbis, Bulevard Stambolijski 29, Sofia
    (☎ 87 3051)
Czechoslovakia
    Orbis, Parizska 18, 11000 Prague (☎ 231 8195)
Finland
    Orbis, Fredrikinkatu 81 B 12, 00100 Helsinki
    (☎ 44 5448)
France
    Orbis, 49 Avenue de l'Opéra, 75002 Paris
    (☎ 4742 0742)
Germany
    Polorbis, Hohenzollernring 99-101,
    5000 Cologne 1 (☎ 52 0025)
    Polorbis, Glockengiesserwall 3, 2000 Hamburg
    1 (☎ 33 7686)
    Orbis, Warschauerstrasse 5, 1034 Berlin
    (☎ 589 4530)
Hungary
    Orbis, Vorosmarty ter 6, Budapest V (☎ 17 0532)
Italy
    Orbis, Via Veneto 54a, Rome (☎ 475 1060)
Netherlands
    Orbis, Leidsestraat 64 (upstairs)
    1017 PD Amsterdam (☎ 625-3570)
Sweden
    Orbis, Birger Jarlsgatan 71, 11356 Stockholm
    (☎ 23 5348)
UK
    Polorbis, 82 Mortimer St, London W1N 7DE
    (☎ 01-637 4971)
USA
    Orbis, 333 North Michigan Ave, Chicago,
    IL 60601 (☎ 312-236 9013)
    Orbis, 500 Fifth Ave, Suite 1428, New York,
    NY 10036 (☎ 212-391 0844)
USSR
    Gorkovo 56/86, Moscow (☎ 250 1780)

## BUSINESS HOURS & HOLIDAYS

Banking hours are weekdays 8 am to 12.30 pm. Stores are generally open weekdays from 10 am to 6 pm, although this can vary an hour or two either way. Grocery stores open earlier and work Saturday until 1 pm. Most businesses post their hours on the door.

Milk bars tend to open between 6 and 8 am and close between 5 and 7 pm. Restaurants sometimes stay open later, but only some first class restaurants are open as late as 10 pm. Many milk bars and some restaurants are closed Saturday afternoon and Sunday, although enough stay open to make finding something to eat no problem. With privatisation and increased competition, businesses keep longer hours than they did.

Museums usually open at 9 or 10 am and close anywhere from 3 to 6 pm, with slightly shorter hours in winter. Most museums close on Mondays, although a few maverick institutions close on Tuesdays and occasionally both days. Most are also closed on days following public holidays. Most live theatres are closed on Mondays and from the end of June to the end of September.

Public holidays in Poland include 1 January (New Year), Easter Monday (March or April), 1 May (Labour Day), Corpus Christi (a Thursday in May or June), 15 August (Assumption Day), 1 November (All Souls' Day), 11 November (Independence Day), 25 and 26 December (Christmas). Independence Day commemorates 11 November 1918 when Poland reappeared on the map of Europe.

As many as a dozen trade fairs and exhibitions a year are held in Poznań, the largest of which are the International Technical Fair in June and the Consumer Goods Fair in September. For information about the fairs contact: Poznań International Fair (☎ 69 2592, fax 66 5827), Głogowska 14, 60-734 Poznań. An International Book Fair is held in Warsaw in May.

## CULTURAL EVENTS

Poland's many annual festivals provide the opportunity to experience the best in music, film and folklore amid an exciting cultural milieu. All the annual events referred to below are listed in the city sections under 'entertainment'; also ask at local tourist information offices.

Old music festivals are held in Łańcut

(May), Stary Sącz (June), Toruń (September) and Wrocław (December), while contemporary music festivals are held at Wrocław (February), Poznań (March), Warsaw (September and October) and Kraków (November). For organ music it's Kraków (April) and Gdańsk (July and August). Singing can be heard at Kraków (April), Opole (June), Gdańsk (June to August), Sopot (July and August) and Wrocław (September).

Jazz festivals are held at Warsaw (January and October), Wrocław (March) and Kraków (October). Poland's leading folk festivals are those of Kazimierz Dolny (July), Żywiec (August) and Zakopane (September). Film festivals are held at Kraków (May and June) and Gdańsk (September). Annual street fairs take place in Poznań (June or July) and Gdańsk (June and August).

## POST & TELECOMMUNICATIONS

You're better off receiving mail care of your embassy in Warsaw rather than poste restante which is unreliable. Most mail boxes

are red. In large cities there are green mail boxes for local mail, steel-blue boxes for airmail and red boxes for long-distance mail Always use airmail, even for parcels. Main post offices are open from 8 am to 8 pm weekdays. In large cities one post office stays open around the clock.

New technology has made placing international telephone calls from Poland to other European countries much easier, though problems still exist in placing domestic calls within Poland itself. Trying to make calls from Poland to North America or Australia is almost hopeless. You'll wait around for hours and hours without success. A far better idea is to send a telegram to your party with a time and telephone number where you can be reached, since incoming calls go right through. The price of telephone calls placed from hotels is much higher than what you'd pay to call from a main post office.

To call Poland, dial the international access code (different from each country), then 48 (the country code for Poland), the area code (without the initial zero) and the number. From North America the international access code is 011. Important area codes include 2 (with seven-digit phone numbers in Warsaw), 22 (with six-digit numbers in Warsaw), 12 (Kraków), 58 (Gdańsk), 61 (Poznań), 71 (Wrocław) and 91 (Szczecin). When transmitting telex messages from North America, the country code 867 must precede the telex number.

## TIME
GMT/UTC plus one hour. Poland goes on summer time at the end of March when clocks are turned an hour forward. At the end of September they're turned an hour back.

## WEIGHTS & MEASURES
The electric current is 220 volts AC, 50 Hz.

## BOOKS & MAPS
Bookshops and tourist offices in Poland sell excellent city and regional maps, often complete with indexes. Tram and bus routes are shown on the maps, which is handy. Usually a particular bookshop or tourist office will only have two or three different maps available, so to get a complete collection for all the cities on your itinerary you'll have to keep trying as you go along. The *Samochodowa Mapa Polski* is the best map of the country.

*The Polish Way* by Adam Zamoyski (John Murray, London, 1987) is a superb cultural history of Poland full of maps and illustrations which bring the past 1000 years to life. This book reads as smoothly as a novel though it's 100% factual.

*The Struggles for Poland* by Neal Ascherson (Michael Joseph, London, 1987) developed from a television series on Polish history in the 20th century. Ascherson provides much information on the formative 1930s and 1940s when the physical shape of modern Poland was decided.

*Mad Dreams, Saving Graces* by Michael T Kaufman (Random House, New York, 1989) is a fascinating insider's look at Poland from the imposition of martial law in 1981 to the eve of the fall of Polish Communism in 1988. Kaufman, the *New York Times* correspondent in Warsaw those years, really brings Father Jerzy Popiełuszko, Marek Edelman (the only surviving leader of the Warsaw Ghetto Uprising), government movers and Solidarity shakers to life.

*The Captive Mind* (Random House, New York, 1981) is a collection of essays by Nobel Prize-winning Polish poet and novelist Czesław Miłosz, who left Poland in 1951 and now lives in California.

*Poland, A Novel* by James A Michener (Ballantine Books, New York, 1983) is a most readable dramatisation of the history of Poland.

As far as travel guidebooks go, *Poland* by Marc E Heine (Hippocrene Books, New York, 1987) might be useful for anyone planning a trip around south-east Poland from Warsaw by rental car. The rest of Poland is only briefly covered and no practical information is provided. Heine is strong on art and history, with much on churches and palaces in small towns that foreign tourists seldom visit. Another guide of the same name,

*Poland* by Tim Sharman (Columbus Books, London, 1988), is very similar to Heine though a wider area is covered.

*Nagel's Encyclopedia-Guide Poland* (Nagel Publishers, Geneva, 1986) is far more complete than either of the above, has good maps and detailed information on every corner of the country. It's highly recommended to anyone planning a long stay.

Poland's leading travel writer, Ryszard Kapuscinski, hasn't written much about Poland but his true accounts of war and revolution in Africa and other Third World areas have found an international audience. *The Soccer War,* based on an actual armed conflict between Honduras and El Salvador over a 1969 soccer match, was recently published in the USA by Knopf. Kapuscinski is now doing a book on the Soviet Union, a continent-sized country which seems to be decomposing the way Africa did in the 1960s.

## MEDIA
### Newspapers
The *Gazeta International*, formerly a semi-official organ of the Solidarity trade union but now independent, is published weekly in English by the *Gazeta Wyborcza*. To subscribe for one year (50 issues) send a cheque for US$45 to: Gazeta International, Dzielna 11a, m. 21, PL 01-023 Warszawa, Poland. In Poland you'll often find it at the reception counters of the luxury hotels.

Poland's other English language weekly is *The Warsaw Voice*, published by the Polish Interpress Agency. To subscribe for 26 weeks send US$50 to: The Warsaw Voice, ulica Bagatela 12, 00-585 Warszawa, Poland. The *Gazeta* is more politically committed than the *Voice*. Unfortunately both papers are hard to find outside Warsaw so grab them when you see them.

## HEALTH
Most foreigners have to pay for medical treatment although in emergencies it's often free. Citizens of the UK receive free treatment if they can prove coverage back home. In Warsaw call your consulate for the name of a private doctor experienced in treating foreigners. Speaking English often helps to jump hospital queues as Polish doctors are all keen to practise their English! Orbis offices abroad can arrange stays at Polish health spas.

## WOMEN TRAVELLERS
A 19-year old Canadian traveller sent us this:

Being female and alone I found it impossible to eat in peace in any of the local restaurants. Without exception in every local place I went there would be at least one table with a couple of guys at it who were completely drunk. And it would take about three minutes before one of them would sit down at my table and start slurring away at me in Polish. No matter what I did or how angry I got he'd just sit there with eyes half open swaying back and forth. Even if I had the waiter remove him he often came back. I never once felt the least bit threatened in Poland only irritated to death. As a result, which was really a shame, I was forced to eat only in Orbis hotel restaurants Poles can't afford or where they aren't allowed to go and get drunk.

Many women I met in Poland who travelled by themselves or with other women had even worse experiences than me. I met two very nice English girls who'd several times been asked 'how much?' – if you catch my drift. It seemed to me that Poland is like the Middle East in that if you dress conservatively you'll get less hassling from the men. These two didn't wear anything that was revealing or anything but they dressed as they would at home with leather jackets, etc, which made them stick out like sore thumbs. Anyway, I was perfectly safe in Poland but I found the men frustrating at times.

## DANGERS & ANNOYANCES
Many Poles are chain smokers, so choose your seating in restaurants, bars and trains with this in mind.

Since the fall of Communism, Poland has experienced increasing violent crime. While it's still a lot safer than most large American or Western European cities, be aware of your surroundings on lonely streets in big cities and watch out for pickpockets in crowded railway stations, especially in Warsaw. It's also unwise to leave money and valuables unattended in hotel rooms. Lock your luggage if you can. By removing the temptation you'll usually eliminate the danger.

Clerks in self-services and fast-food

outlets will sometimes cheat you out of small amounts (US$0.05, etc). Since you don't speak Polish and can't be 100% sure of the price, they're in a stronger position and know it. Defend yourself by asking the clerk to write down the amount due on a piece of paper before you produce any money (offer him/her a pen and paper). Often you'll be able to see the amount rung up on the cash register. When paying exact change to get rid of small bills, don't put any money on the counter until you have the entire sum ready. Otherwise the clerk may switch the banknotes already tendered for lower denominations while you're getting the small bills together.

## ACTIVITIES

Zakopane, Poland's premier southern mountain resort, features hiking in summer and skiing in winter. With a little advance planning you could also arrange white-water rafting on the Dunajec River from Zakopane. Hikers less interested in meeting their fellows along the trails should consider instead the Bieszczady Mountains south of Przemyśl.

Mikołajki in the Great Mazurian lake district of north-east Poland is a major yachting centre with boats available for rent. Canoeists and kayakers will be quite at home here, and this part of Poland is flat enough also to appeal to cyclists, as is most of northern Poland.

## HIGHLIGHTS OF POLAND
### Nature

Poland excels in mountains, lakes and coast. Those wishing to commune with the Baltic will find the beaches of Łeba unending and the sand dunes inspiring. Mikołajki is a fine place to begin exploring the 3000 Mazurian lakes, while Zakopane is the launching pad for hikes into the Tatras, Poland's most magnificent mountain range. The Białowieska Forest in the far east is home to the largest remaining herd of European bison and other wildlife. Each of these environments is distinct and equally worth experiencing.

## Museums & Galleries

Warsaw's National Museum holds Poland's largest and finest art collection, though Kraków's Czartoryski Art Museum has individual works which are unsurpassed. The Musical Instruments Museum in Poznań will delight music lovers, as will Chopin's birthplace at Żelazowa Wola, 50 km west of Warsaw. Finally, the Auschwitz Museum at Oświęcim is perhaps the most meaningful of them all.

## Castles

Malbork Castle, one-time seat of the Teutonic Knights, is perhaps the largest surviving medieval castle in Europe, while another 14th century castle at Lidzbark Warmiński is less known but equally impressive. For hundreds of years Kraków's Wawel Castle sheltered Polish royalty, most of whom are still buried in the adjacent cathedral. Lublin Castle intrigues us with its remoteness and memories of Nazi atrocities committed within its walls. True castle lovers will seek out Pieskowa Skała Castle and nearly a dozen others along the Eagles' Nests Route from Kraków to Częstochowa.

## Palaces

It's not surprising that Poland's capital, Warsaw, contains Poland's two most magnificent royal palaces: the 17th century Wilanów Palace and the 18th century Łazienki Palace. In the countryside feudal magnates built splendid Renaissance, Baroque and Rococo palaces such as the Branicki Palace at Białystok, the Rogalin Palace near Poznań, and Łańcut Palace.

## Historic Towns

Of all Poland's cities, only Kraków, the de facto capital till 1596, survived WW II relatively untouched. The historic cores of Poznań, Toruń and Gdańsk have been masterfully restored. All three grew rich from trade in the Middle Ages, as the homes of rich burghers around their central squares and the magnificent churches attest. Zamość in south-east Poland is unique as a perfectly preserved 16th century Renaissance settlement.

## Hotels

In a region where sterile high-rise hotels were erected according to plan, Toruń's Zajazd Staropolski Hotel merges with the medieval cityscape. Pensjonat 'Mikołajki' in Mikołajki is the way of the future, a small, privately owned pension offering lots of personalised service. The Hotel 'Zamkowy' in Łańcut Palace and the barge hotel in Gdańsk really let you experience your surroundings, while the church-run Dom Pielgrzyma in Częstochowa lets you be a real pilgrim. Other pilgrims will find the Auschwitz Museum Hotel at Oświęcim an excellent, inexpensive place to stay.

## Restaurants

Due to changing conditions it's unwise to recommend a restaurant in Poland, so those selected here are mostly top end. Kraków's Wierzynek Restaurant, for instance, is probably the most renowned in Poland, with apologies to the Bazyliszek Restaurant in Warsaw. Poland's most famous seafood restaurant is Pod Łososiem in Gdańsk, though Szczecin's Chief Restaurant is also excellent and a lot less pretentious. Perhaps the nicest hotel restaurant in Poland is the one in the Panorama Hotel in Nowy Sącz.

## ACCOMMODATION
### Camping

There are hundreds of camping grounds in Poland, many offering small timber bungalows which are excellent value. IFCC card holders get a 10% discount on camping fees. Theoretically most camping grounds are open May to September, but they tend to close early if things are slow. The opening and closing dates listed in official brochures (and this book) are only approximate. The yellow *Polska Mapa Campingów* map lists most camping grounds.

### Hostels

Poland is the only country in Eastern Europe with youth hostels similar to those of Western Europe. Overnight fees are very low and persons without YHA membership cards can also use the hostels though they pay a little more. Although there's no maximum age limit, persons under 26 have priority. Children under age 10 cannot use the hostels. Groups larger than five persons must book a month in advance and Polish school groups crowd the hostels from mid-May to mid-June. Many hostels are open only in summer although the main ones operate all year. The hostels are closed from 10 am to 5 pm and you must arrive before 9 pm.

All 1500 IYHF hostels in Poland are run by the Polskie Towarzystwo Schronisk Młodzieżowych (PTSM) and have a green triangle over the entrance. A large percentage are located in school buildings. In cities where there's more than one youth hostel, if the first you visit is full they may be willing to call around to the others to find you a bed.

### International Student Hotels

In July and August the Polish student travel agency, Almatur, arranges accommodation in vacant student dormitories in 19 university towns. The addresses of these hotels change annually so you'll have to ask about them at local Almatur offices. You share a room of one to four beds and there are usually cooking facilities, cheap cafeterias and even disco clubs on the premises. Accommodation costs US$11 single, US$9 for a bed in a double or US$7 per person in a triple. If you take the triple rate you'll often have the room to yourself anyway.

Orbis offices abroad sell open vouchers for Almatur hotels costing US$10 per night for full-time students, US$15 per night for young people under 35. Persons over 35 are not accommodated. With such a voucher you're guaranteed bed and breakfast without reservations, provided you arrive by 2 pm. If you buy nine vouchers the 10th is free. Ask about Almatur 'Student Travel Vouchers' (STV) or 'Youth Travel Vouchers' (YTV) at Orbis offices abroad, as the vouchers must be purchased prior to your arrival in Poland. Before using a voucher, however, ask the price if you pay cash as it's sometimes cheaper. Unused vouchers are refunded in Polish currency.

## Private Rooms

It's possible to stay in private rooms (*prywatny pokóy*) in Poland, though they're less common than in Hungary or Yugoslavia. A few municipal tourist offices (*Biuro Zakwaterowań*) arrange private rooms but their prices are sometimes high, almost what you'd pay for a budget hotel. The agencies classify the rooms according to 1st, 2nd or 3rd category. Singles are scarce and during busy periods all their rooms could be full.

Sometimes you're offered a private room by an individual on the street outside a tourist office or private room agency. Their prices may be lower and open to bargaining. The trouble is, it's not strictly legal as you're supposed to register with the authorities in each new place you visit. As long as you stay in official accommodation this is done for you. But if you accept an unlicensed private room the householder will not register you, nor will he/she be happy to learn that you went in to the police and registered yourself, thereby providing clear evidence of their untaxed moonlighting. However, in some cities like crowded Kraków and Gdańsk these 'black' rooms are good places to stay, so it's up to you to decide whether it's worth the very slight risk of being caught unregistered. Beware of rooms far from the centre of town.

## Hotels

Hotels are graded from one to five stars, and foreign tourists are allowed to stay in all but the holiday homes owned by factories, trade unions, etc. Orbis hotels are all in the expensive, three and four-star category and a few hotels belonging to international chains such as Inter-Continental and Marriott are five-star. Municipal hotels are usually cheaper, and the PTTK has a chain of 'Dom Turysty' and 'Dom Wycieczkowy' wich have hotel rooms and dorm beds. A country inn is called a *zajazd* or *gościniec*.

Hotel prices vary according to the season and these are different in the various regions of Poland. At Zakopane the high ski season is from mid-December to March, while in Poznań hotel rates increase dramatically at trade fair time. The low season runs from October to April in northern Poland and Wrocław, or November to March in Kraków. In Warsaw hotel prices are the same throughout the year. Rooms booked from abroad through a travel agency or Orbis are much more expensive than what you'd pay locally.

Rates are usually posted on a board at hotel reception desks. Compare the price of a room with private bath to one with shared bath. Sometimes it's only a slight difference, other times it's a lot. If in doubt about the quality ask to *see* a room before checking in, in which case it's unlikely they'll give you their worst room. On arrival day, hotel rooms cannot be occupied until after noon, 2 pm or 4 pm, so leave your things at the station.

## FOOD

### Milk Bars

In Poland the word 'bar' is almost always used in the sense of snack bar or refreshment bar, and 'cocktail' means fruit cocktail or something similar. The cheapest places to eat in Poland are milk bars (*bar mleczny*). These are also good places to try local dishes not available at expensive restaurants. Never take the meat dishes at a milk bar, however. These are priced three or four times higher than anything else so most Poles avoid them, thus what you get will probably have been on display for quite a while. You could have had the same thing freshly prepared in a better restaurant for only a little more money.

Milk bars are self-service (*samoobsługa*). You either pay at the end of the line cafeteria-style or, more often, you pay first and get a receipt which you hand to the person dispensing the food. This can be confusing if you don't know the Polish name of whatever it is you want, but most cashiers are patient and will try to understand if you point to something someone else is eating. Try asking the person in line behind you what a particular dish is called. Sometimes you'll order the wrong thing, which adds to the excitement. Milk bar lines usually move quickly, so don't be put off.

Some milk bars close Saturday afternoons and all day Sunday. Keep in mind that the difference in price between a fast-food stand and a first-class restaurant is much less in Poland than it is in the west. Eat at self-service cafeterias to save time, not money. Whenever you have the time to enjoy a proper meal, go to one of the better restaurants listed herein or any top-end hotel, not a milk bar.

## Restaurants

Restaurants and coffee shops at the luxury Orbis hotels are open to everyone. Invariably they have the widest selection of dishes and the best service, although the atmosphere can be pretentious and even dull. Unlike hotel rooms which sometimes cost foreigners more than Poles, meals at hotel restaurants are the same price for everyone which makes them relatively cheap. These are the *only* places in Poland where you can get a good English breakfast of ham and eggs with juice (about US$3). Elsewhere you may have to settle for soup.

Always ask to see the menu and have a look at the prices. Waiters who speak English or German and simply tell you what's available will charge extra for the service. If a waiter wants to be helpful, ask him or her to translate the menu or tell you what's available, as very few Polish restaurants offer everything listed. Soup is *zupy* and a main course is *dania*. Watch for the *obiad firmowy* (recommended meal) on restaurant menus.

When ordering seafood keep in mind that you will be charged by weight, and the price on the menu may only be for 100 grams. Beware of accepting things you didn't order such as a sliced tomato salad as this could be a ploy to double your bill. In Polish restaurants it's customary to occupy any vacant seat, which can be a problem if you don't smoke. If you're wearing a coat you must deposit it at the coat check whenever there is one. It's also customary to round restaurant bills up to the next higher unit (but only in

places with table service, not milk bars). Write what you want to pay on the bill.

It may be cheap to eat in Poland (for tourists) but too often the quality reflects the price. Menus are usually only in Polish, occasionally in German and very seldom in English. Many things on the menu will not be available anyway, and even in hotel restaurants whole categories such as soups and desserts will be unavailable. Salads are almost never fresh but pickled, and fresh fruit and vegetables are rare. Almost every dish includes some meat, so vegetarians will have a problem. Salt and pepper are usually not on the table, so you must either catch the waiter's attention or get up and search the other tables.

The main meal in Poland is eaten at lunchtime. As a result, restaurants often close unexpectedly early, forcing you to dine on cake and ice cream if you left it too late. Many restaurants have live music and 'dancing' after 7 pm, which brings food service to an end. The political changes in Poland have at least made it easier to get a beer with your meal, but often only small cans or bottles of imported beer are stocked. Restaurant difficulties due to the poor supply situation may be understandable but the low level of service is not.

## Cafés & Bars

Few restaurants serve dessert, so for cake and ice cream go to a *kawiarnia* (café). Alcohol is also served at these. Polish cafés are social meeting places where people sit around and talk. A *winiaria* is a wine bar. There's a real shortage of cosy little western-style bars where you can just drop in for a drink in the evening. If that's what you had in mind, go to the biggest and most expensive hotel in town and patronise its lounge rather than conduct a futile search. There you won't have to contend with a lot of smoke, noise and drunks, and it stays open late.

## Polish Specialities

Poland is a land of hearty soups such as *botwinka* (beet greens soup), *kapuśniak* (cabbage soup), *krupnik* (potato soup), *zacierka* (noodle soup) and *żur* (sour cream soup). Many traditional Polish dishes originated farther east, including Russian borsch or *barszcz* (red beet soup), Lithuanian *chłodnik* (cold pink cream soup), *kołduny* (turnovers with meat) and *kulebiak* (cabbage and mushroom loaf). Two world-famous Polish dishes are *bigos* (sauerkraut and meat) and *pierogi* (dumplings served with potatoes and cheese or sauerkraut and mushrooms).

A few special Polish dishes to watch for on restaurant menus are roast duck *(kaczka)* or goose *(gęś)* with apples, pound steak *(zraz)* in cream sauce, breaded pork cutlet *(kotlet schabowy)*, pea puree with pig's leg *(golonka)* and sauerkraut, tripe *(flaki)* Polish style, and sauerkraut with sausage and potatoes. *Zawijasy słowiańskie* is a meat roll of spicy stuffing wrapped in ham and deep fried. Beefsteak tartar is raw minced meat with a raw egg, sardine, chopped onions and seasoning. Only sample this at a first-class establishment where you can be sure of the quality. A favourite Polish fast food is *zapiekanka,* a long bread roll baked with onions, cheese and mushrooms on top.

Mushrooms *(grzyby)* have always been great favourites in Poland, either boiled, pan-fried, stewed, sautéed, pickled or marinated. Cucumbers are served freshly sliced and seasoned with honey, pepper or cream as a salad *(mizeria)*. *Ćwikła* is a salad of red beetroot with horseradish. Potatoes are made into dumplings, patties or pancakes *(placki ziemniaczane)*. *Kopytka* is chunks of dough served with a semi-sweet sauce – good for breakfast at milk bars. *Pyzy* is similar to *kopytka* except that the chunks are stuffed with meat. A traditional Polish dessert is *mazurek* (shortcake). In early summer you can get fresh strawberries, raspberries or blueberries with cream. Hot chocolate is called *kakao*.

## DRINKS

Most restaurants serve alcohol only after 1 pm. You'll sometimes get a beer before 1 pm but never anything harder. It can also be difficult to get a beer after 10 pm. Some restaurants have certain rooms in which alcoholic drinks are not served at all (beware of signs reading *sala bezalkoholowa)*. Hard liquor is available by the bottle only in Monopolowy stores – alcoholism has long been a big problem in Poland and is getting bigger still.

Now that beer prices have been allowed to go up (still cheap by international standards) your favourite brew is much more readily available in Poland. When ordering beer at restaurants always ask for Polish beer, unless the price of imported beer is clearly indicated on the menu. Otherwise you could end up paying 50% more for German or Czech beer than you would for an acceptable Polish equivalent such as Żywiec or Leżajsk. If you want your beer cold you must say *zimne piwo* (pronounced 'jimne pivo') when ordering, otherwise you'll automatically get it at room temperature even in the best places.

Red and black currant juices are popular non-alcoholic drinks. All wine is imported so pay attention to the price which may be for a glass, not a bottle. Vodka (served chilled) is the national drink, which the Poles claim was invented here. Other notable drinks include *myśliwska* (vodka flavoured with juniper berries), *śliwowica* (plum brandy) and *winiak* (grape brandy). The favourite Polish toast is *na zdrowie* (to your health), sometimes followed by a rendition of *Sto lat,* a popular hymn which means 'may you live 100 years'.

## ENTERTAINMENT

A section near the back of the daily papers carries announcements of concerts, plays, etc, plus cinema times and even museum hours. It doesn't take any knowledge of Polish to understand these listings, as Handel is Handel and Schubert Schubert in any language. The name and address of the theatre are usually given, and a quick stop there to check the information and pick up tickets clinches the matter. When checking theatre listings it's important to check *both* local papers, as the list in one may be incomplete.

Discos are common in Poland, usually

opening around 9 pm from Thursday to Saturday. Also ask about jazz clubs, operetta, opera, concerts, special events and so on at your hotel reception or at local tourist offices.

### Cinemas

Movies are usually shown in the original language with Polish subtitles, and the admission is cheap. Most are films like *Cousins* and *Bagdad Café* that were around in the west a few years ago.

### THINGS TO BUY

Cepelia shops belonging to the Folk Art & Crafts Cooperatives Union sell authentic local handicrafts such as tapestries, rugs, embroidery, lace, hand-painted silks, sculptures in wood, pottery, paper cut-outs, folk toys, wrought iron objects, silver jewellery and amber necklaces. Jubiler stores sell jewellery and watches. Works by living professional artists are sold at Desa shops. Amber necklaces are an excellent portable souvenir typical of Poland, and a good one shouldn't be over US$20. If buying amber see the Malbork Castle exhibits first.

Imported goods and export-quality Polish products are sold in Pewex and Baltona hard currency shops. Western alcohol and cigarettes are cheaper at Pewex than they are in the west. Goods at Pewex are priced in US dollars; you can pay in złoty or DM but they'll calculate it at a lousy rate. Travellers' cheques are not accepted at Pewex. Since 1989 the retail trade in Poland has come out of the shops into the streets with thousands of small sidewalk vendors displaying wares they often purchased on 'tourist' trips to other countries.

Desa shops have complete information on complicated and changeable Polish export regulations, so check before making large purchases. A customs duty of 80% is charged on crystal. It's forbidden to take works of art and books produced before 9 May 1945 out of Poland. Only 30 postage stamps produced after 1970 can be exported at a time. Large quantities of amber could cause problems. Otherwise you're allowed to export from Poland goods up to a value of US$200 duty-free. Items purchased with hard currency may usually be freely exported provided you have official sales receipts.

# Getting There & Away

### AIR

The national carrier, LOT Polish Airlines, flies to Warsaw from New York, Chicago, Montreal, Melbourne, Singapore, Bangkok, Beijing, New Delhi, Cairo, Tel Aviv, Istanbul, Tunis and numerous European cities. Regular one-way fares to Warsaw are not cheap: US$475 from Frankfurt/Main, US$500 from Amsterdam, US$550 from Paris and US$620 from London. Ask travel agents about special charter and advance purchase excursion fares on LOT and note the restrictions. People aged 22 and under get a 25% discount on flights from Western Europe.

LOT has 'Super Saver' fares from New York to Warsaw ranging from US$719 return in the low season (November to March) to US$929 return in the high season (mid-June to September). The minimum stay is seven days, the maximum three months. One-way fares are US$499 to US$599. These prices are for midweek departures; weekend departures are about US$50 more per return ticket. In the USA call LOT for information at ☎ 800-223 0593 toll free (in Canada ☎ 800-361 9071).

Bucket shops in Europe and Asia sell LOT tickets at deep discounts. For example, Malibu Travel (☎ 626 2650), Damrak 30, 1012 LJ Amsterdam, Holland, offers Amsterdam or Brussels to Singapore for US$550 one-way, US$1000 return, with a free stopover in Warsaw. Ask around the budget travel agencies in Singapore, Penang and Bangkok for similar deals.

### To/From Neighbouring Countries

Yugoslav Airlines has direct flights from Warsaw to Belgrade for US$144 one-way.

This is a lot more expensive than the train but you'll save time and perhaps money on Czechoslovak and Hungarian transit visas (where required).

### Travel Agencies

Private Polish travel agencies such as Sawa Tour, ulica Wspólna 65a, Warsaw, can book cheap flights to anywhere departing from Berlin. It's probably cheaper to wait and buy your ticket after arrival in Berlin, Amsterdam or London, but the savings may be eaten up if you have to shop around and wait for a reservation. With a ticket from Sawa Tour you'll know exactly when your flight will depart and be able to plan accordingly.

### Departure Tax

Poland doesn't have an airport tax.

### LAND
### Bus

In summer and autumn, Coach Europe operates a luxury bus service based in Britain with weekly service from Glasgow and London to Warsaw. Tickets are available from Traveller's Check In, 35 Woburn Place, London WC1, the Buchananan Bus Station, Killermont St, Glasgow, and Orbis, ulica Bracka 16, Warsaw. Fares London-Warsaw are £69 one-way, £119 return. This is certainly less than a train or plane ticket.

Eurolines, Place de Brouckère 50, Brussels, has a bus from Brussels to Kraków (28 hours) every two weeks from March to December. From June to September another bus goes from Brussels to Warsaw (27 hours) once or twice a month. The fare on both these services is US$110 one-way, US$175 return. In Amsterdam, tickets and information are available from Budget Bus (☎ 627 5151), Rokin 10.

Polish buses leave regularly for Western European cities and they're much cheaper than the train. Advance bookings are required and Orbis offices can either sell tickets or direct you to an office that does. For example, Orbis, Puławska 43, Warsaw, sells bus tickets from Warsaw to Amsterdam (US$84), Brussels, Cologne, Copenhagen, Frankfurt/Main, Hamburg, London (US$128), Moscow, Oslo, Paris, Venice and many other Western European cities. Most services only operate from May to October. The window selling these tickets is open weekdays from 8 am to 3 pm.

The Syrena Tourist Office, ulica Krucza 16/22, Warsaw, sells tickets for a weekly Polish bus from Warsaw to Paris, France (US$95 one-way). The bus only operates from May to October.

A Hungarian Volanbus runs twice a week between Budapest and Zakopane (US$8, nine hours).

### Train

It's important to keep in mind that there are three price levels for tickets on Polish trains. The most expensive are tickets to Poland bought in Western Europe. Avoid these by breaking your journey in Czechoslovakia or Hungary, from where you pay the much cheaper rate for travel between Eastern European countries. Cheaper still are domestic fares within Poland itself. You can easily take advantage of these by breaking your journey at the first city inside Poland (Szczecin, Poznań, Wrocław, Katowice, Kraków, Nowy Sącz, etc). Holders of students cards get a 25% discount on train tickets for travel within the Eastern European countries. The Interrail pass (sold to European residents aged 25 and under) is valid in Poland.

**To/From Holland** The Nord-West Express runs daily from Hoek van Holland Haven (with ferry connections from Britain) to Moscow via Berlin, Poznań and Warsaw. Amsterdam passengers join the train at Amersfoort. Travelling times from Hoek van Holland are 12 hours to Berlin, 18 hours to Poznań and 22 hours to Warsaw. Only 2nd-class seats are available to Poland though the train also carries sleeping cars. A one-way 2nd-class ticket from Amsterdam to Poznań is US$125.

**To/From Britain & France** The Ost-West Express leaves London's Victoria Station daily for Warsaw (33 hours) via Oostende, Brussels, Cologne, Berlin and Poznań. A Paris portion of this train and the Nord-West Express mentioned earlier are linked to the Oostende train at Rzepin just inside Poland (Paris to Warsaw is 25 hours). At Rzepin you can change for Wrocław or Szczecin.

**To/From Germany** Many trains run between Berlin and Warsaw (nine hours) via Frankfurt/Oder and Poznań. If you really want to save money only get a ticket from Berlin to Rzepin, the first major junction inside Poland. There you could buy a cheap onward ticket with złoty and connect for Szczecin, Poznań, Wrocław or Kraków. Bring a little Polish currency with you if you plan to do this as it may be difficult to change at Rzepin.

The nightly Gedania Express with seats and sleeping cars runs from Berlin's Lichtenberg station to Gdańsk (10 hours) via Szczecin. Trains from Cologne to Kraków (24 hours) travel via Leipzig, Dresden and Wrocław. Another line goes from Frankfurt/Main to Warsaw (22 hours) via Leipzig, Dresden and Wrocław.

**To/From Czechoslovakia** The overnight Bohemia Express between Prague and Warsaw (13 hours) travels via Wrocław. Between Wrocław and Prague the journey takes about seven hours. The Silesia Express travels via Katowice between Prague and Warsaw. The Chopin Express from Vienna to Warsaw (13 hours) runs daily via Břeclav and Katowice. To go from Košice to Kraków see below.

**To/From Hungary & Beyond** From Budapest the Bathory Express travels daily to Warsaw (13 hours) via Komarno, Puchov and Katowice. This fast overnight train originates in Budapest. The Polonia Express from Belgrade goes via Budapest, Hatvan, Žilina and Katowice to Warsaw (16 hours from Budapest). Change at Katowice for Kraków.

The Cracovia Express travels direct from Budapest to Kraków (13 hours) via Kosice and Nowy Sącz daily all year. The Karpaty Express from Bucharest to Warsaw follows this same route but misses Budapest. The Varna Express from Sofia to Warsaw (mid-June to mid-October only) does likewise.

To western Poland there's the Bem Express from Budapest to Szczecin (17 hours) via Wrocław and Poznań. The Varsovia Express from Budapest to Gdynia (18 hours) runs via Bratislava, Katowice and Warsaw.

**To/From Romania** The daily Karpaty Express between Bucharest and Warsaw via Przemyśl avoids Czechoslovakia and Hungary by transiting the USSR. Sleeping cars are available to/from Warsaw. Check with a Soviet consulate to determine whether a transit visa is required.

### Car & Motorbike
The main highway border crossings into Poland from Germany are Kołbaskowo (20 km west of Szczecin), Świecko (at Frankfurt/Oder), Olszyna (24 km east of Cottbus) and Zgorzelec (at Görlitz). From Czechoslovakia you may cross at Jakuszyce (between Liberec and Jelenia Góra), Kudowa-Słone (43 km east of Kłodzko), Chałupki (12 km north of Ostrava), Cieszyn (31 km east of Ostrava), Chyżne (west of Zakopane), Łysa Polana (east of Zakopane), Piwniczna (31 km south of Nowy Sącz) and Barwinek (between Rzeszów and Prešov). The names above are those of the Polish border posts. Other highway border crossings may be restricted to local residents and closed to Western tourists, so check.

### On Foot
If you want to avoid the hassle or expense of getting an international train ticket, the easiest place to walk across the Polish/Czechoslovak border is between Cieszyn (Poland) and Český Těšín (Czechoslovakia), virtually one city cut in half by the Olza River. On the Czechoslovak side the onward train connections to Prague and Žilina are good.

From Germany you could walk across the bridge over the Neisse/Nysa River from Görlitz to Zgorzelec where there are onward railway services to Jelenia Góra (76 km) and Wrocław (163 km).

## SEA

### Freighters

The Polish Ocean Lines (PLO), ulica Długa 76, Gdańsk (weekdays 9 am to 1 pm), accepts passengers on its container ships sailing from Bremerhaven, Germany, to Halifax (US$910 one-way) and New York (US$1010 one-way) every week. There are three double cabins on the ships and sometimes one single cabin is available. The 'owner's cabin' costs 10% more. The complete routing is Bremerhaven, Halifax, New York, Baltimore, Wilmington, New York, Le Havre, Rotterdam, Bremerhaven.

The PLO is one of the last companies with a trans-Atlantic passenger-carrying freighter service, and a voyage on one of its ships would be a memorable way to begin or end your trip. If you buy a car in Europe and want to take it home with you on the ship, this can be arranged (additional charge). Agents abroad include:

Canada
McLean Kennedy Ltd, Box 1086, Montreal, Que, H2Y 2P5 (☎ 514-849 6111)
Germany
Hamburg Sud Reiseagentur GmbH, Postfach 1661, 2 Hamburg 11 (☎ 37051)
Netherlands
Nederlands Transport Bureau, Box 23068, 3016 DL Rotterdam (☎ 414 5611)
UK
Gdynia America Shipping Lines Ltd, 238 City Road, London EC1 V2LQ (☎ 071-251 3389)
USA
GAL Inc, 39 Broadway, 14th floor, New York, NY 10006 (☎ 212-952 1280)

### Ferries

Polferries offers regular year-round service to Świnoujście and Gdańsk from Denmark, Sweden and Finland.

Reservations are recommended for car or cabin accommodation although deck space is almost always available. An aeroplane-type seat costs extra. Return tickets (valid for six months) are 20% cheaper than two one-ways. Holders of ISIC student identity cards and pensioners receive a 10% discount on ferry tickets. Other reductions are available to families of three or more persons.

If you're going to Świnoujście, there are services from Copenhagen, Denmark, five times a week (260 Danish crowns one-way, 10 hours), and from Ystad, Sweden, twice a day (230 Swedish crowns one-way, eight hours). Ferries sail to Gdańsk from Oxelösund, Sweden (400 Swedish crowns one-way, 18 hours) weekly and from Helsinki, Finland (320 FIM one-way, 37 hours) twice a week.

# Getting Around

## AIR

LOT Polish Airlines operates domestic flights daily except Sunday from Warsaw to Rzeszów (US$40), Kraków (US$35), Wrocław (US$45), Poznań (US$35), Szczecin (US$45) and Gdańsk (US$35). These fares are one-way. Also ask about half-price student standby fares. You must check in at least an hour before international flights, 30 minutes before domestic flights. Passports must be shown when checking in for domestic flights.

## BUS

Long distances in Poland are more commonly covered by train (PKP) than by bus (PKS). Buses are used mostly in mountainous areas, such as around Zakopane. Seats on long-distance buses can and should be booked ahead. Baggage is carried free. When asking for the bus station, write PKS on a piece of paper; for the train station write PKP.

## TRAIN

Poland has 27,092 km of railway line allowing you to reach almost every town by rail. Express trains *(expresowy)* with seat reservations are the best way to travel. Direct trains

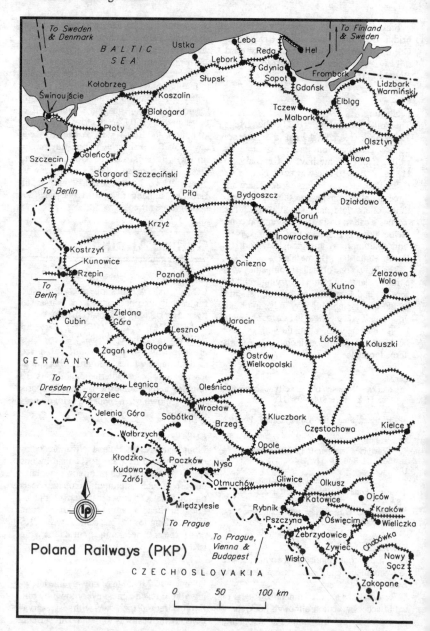

## Poland Railways (PKP)

0      50      100 km

(*pośpieszne*) are also fast and don't usually require reservations, but are much more crowded. Local trains (*osobowe* or *normalne*) are OK for short trips and never require reservations. Even 1st-class travel is inexpensive with more room, fewer drunks, less noise and less smoke.

The best trains are the 'name trains' which usually run to and from Warsaw. To use one of these express trains you must reserve a seat, but reservations are easily made up to two months in advance in main railway stations or at Orbis offices (US$0.50). On departure day, reservations can only be made at the railway station. The name trains have Wars dining cars and comfortable compartments – 1st class is quite luxurious. We list these trains throughout this chapter – be sure to take them whenever possible.

As in other European countries, train departures (*odjazdy*) are usually listed on a yellow board while arrivals (*przyjazdy*) are on a white board. Express trains are in red, local trains in black. Watch for the symbol R enclosed in a box, which indicates a fully reserved train. Departure boards also indicate whether a train offers both 1st and 2nd-class accommodation, plus the train number and departure track (*peron*). The Polish railway system goes on its summer timetable (with extra services) around 1 June.

Tickets for express trains are 50% more expensive than tickets for local stopping trains, so make sure you've got the correct ticket for your train (by writing your destination and the departure time on a piece of paper to show the cashier, for example). Otherwise the conductor will charge you a supplement. In large stations, tickets for different trains are sometimes sold at different windows. Check the train number over the window to make sure you're in the right line and ask information. If you're forced to get on a train without a ticket, find the conductor right away and he/she will sell you one with only a small supplement instead of the heavy fine you'd pay if he/she found you first. Tickets *are* checked on Polish trains. First class costs 50% more than 2nd class.

## Railway Pass

Like many European countries, Poland has instituted a national railway pass which is worth considering. The Polrailpass is valid on all trains in Poland including expresses and those with compulsory seat reservations. To use a train in which seat reservations are required, ask the ticket office in the station for a free seat reservation or, if this is not possible, just go to the conductor on the train itself and ask him/her for the free reservation. Whenever presenting your pass always tell the conductor your destination so he/she can advise you if you have to change somewhere or are on the wrong train.

Some reservation clerks will still try to charge you US$0.50 for a seat reservation, though this is supposed to be free with the pass. When you buy your Polrailpass ask for the brochure describing the pass in English, French, German and Polish, then just show the relevant section to the clerk if he/she asks you to pay a reservation fee. Couchettes and sleepers always cost extra.

The Polrailpass costs US$50/35 1st/2nd class for eight days, US$60/40 1st/2nd class for 15 days, US$67/45 1st/2nd class for 21 days and US$75/50 1st/2nd class for one month. It's really only worth buying the pass if you'll be staying at least two weeks and travelling extensively. You might as well take 1st class while you're at it. The Polrailpass won't save you any money (train fares are low in Poland) but you will avoid having to always line up to buy tickets, and the pass allows you to change plans at will.

The Polrailpass is sold at Orbis offices both in Poland and abroad. If you know the exact day you'll be arriving in Poland by train, buy the pass prior to arrival and you'll only need to get a train ticket as far as the Polish border.

## Couchettes & Sleepers

Overnight trains are a good way of saving money in Poland while getting to your destination. A 1st-class ticket and sleeper are often less than the price of a hotel, and you arrive in the next city early in the morning, saving a lot of time. The attendant in the sleeping car sells soft drinks and coffee and express trains often carry good stand-up dining cars. You can't beat a breakfast of *flaki* (tripe) and coffee (US$1.25).

Second-class couchettes (US$4) contain six beds to the compartment, three to a side. First-class sleepers (US$5) have only two beds. There's a third type called 'special' 2nd class which has three beds to the compartment (US$4.50). It used to be very hard to book these, involving over an hour in line at an Orbis office. Now that most railway stations are computerised, you can book your couchette or sleeper at the reservation window at any railway station in minutes. Orbis, the Polish travel agency, also books couchettes and sleepers for the same price and its staff is more likely to speak English.

## Railway Stations

Railway stations in Poland have good facilities: left-luggage rooms open round the clock, cafeterias, waiting rooms, newsstands, posted timetables, etc. There are public toilets in all railway stations (and in many other places) and you're expected to pay around US$0.05 to use them.

When you check your baggage at railway cloakrooms (*przechowalnia bagażu*) you must declare the value of the object in złoty and sign the form (have the amount written down on a piece of paper ready to show the clerk). You're charged 1% of the declared value which includes insurance. This makes it fairly expensive if you declare anything near the real value, though in small stations you can easily forgo the insurance and just pay the standard US$0.10 fee. We've never heard of anyone actually losing luggage properly checked at a Polish train station, though that's no guarantee. You pay the left-luggage charge when you pick the item up, not when you deposit it (useful to know if you arrive in the country with no Polish currency).

## CAR & MOTORBIKE

To drive a car into Poland you'll need your driver's licence, the car registration card and liability insurance (the 'green card'). If your insurance isn't valid for Poland you must buy an additional policy at the border. The car registration number will be entered in your passport.

Always use the octane rating 94 yellow petrol or octane 98 red (super), as the octane 86 green fuel can damage your engine. Unleaded octane 91 petrol *(benzyna bezołowiowa)* is hard to find, so pick up a list of the few stations carrying it at an Orbis office abroad or at the Polish Automobile Association office at the border. If your car only runs on unleaded, you'll have to carry plenty of jerry cans.

Lines for petrol can be several hundred metres long, though if you want unleaded you can often go ahead as not too many local cars can use that pump. Diesel is easier to obtain than regular petrol. Before joining a fuel queue, check the signs indicating what's available ('brak' means empty).

Petrol stations are few and far between, so plan ahead and expect queues, especially in the south where waiting times can be up to five hours. Most are open from 6 am to 10 pm (Sunday 7 am to 3 pm) though some work around the clock. You used to have to buy foreign-currency petrol coupons from Orbis to get fuel, but these have now been abolished. You're allowed to import or export fuel in a spare tank up to a maximum of 10 litres, though with luck the border guards might be a bit more lenient about unleaded petrol, which is hard to get in Poland.

When asking directions of people along the road, always write the place name on a piece of paper to avoid any misunderstanding. The Polski Związek Motorowy (Polish Automobile Association) offices in all large cities provide breakdown service *(pomoc drogowa)* and other assistance to motorists. If you're a member of an automobile club at home, bring along your membership card with an international letter of introduction, as this could entitle you to free breakdown service and legal advice from the PZM.

## Road Rules

Of Poland's 258,588 km of roads, 50% are classified as improved hard surface (asphalt, concrete or stone block), 9% unimproved hard surface (crushed stone or gravel), 39% earth and 2% other urban roads. The roads are narrow but in good condition and there isn't too much traffic. The speed limit is 110 km/h on expressways, 90 km/h on other open roads and 60 km/h in built-up areas. The police fine motorists frequently but the amount is usually small. You're not allowed to spend the night in a vehicle parked in a rest area by the road.

Cyclists are not allowed to ride two abreast on highways.

## Rental

You can rent a Polish-made Fiat 125, Polonez, or Ford Sierra for about US$310 a week with unlimited mileage, plus US$6 per day extra for compulsory insurance. The minimum period for unlimited mileage rentals is seven days; for shorter periods you must pay a minimum 100-km mileage charge. It's usually cheaper to prebook your car through an Orbis office abroad rather than just front up at an agency inside Poland. Rates are lower in the off season from November to March, and at last report there was no tax on car rentals. Unlimited mileage cars cannot be taken out of Poland, and you must be 21 or over.

Some of the cars are in pretty poor shape so check the vehicle carefully before you drive off. If the lights aren't in order, for example, you could be fined. Insist on exchanging the car at the next Orbis rental office if you discover that they've unloaded a lemon on you.

If you had thought of renting a car in Berlin and driving it into Poland, think again as most German car rental agencies will not allow their vehicles to be taken to Poland. This is because of a report circulated by the Federal Office of Criminal Investigations in Wiesbaden concerning 'criminal organisations which have specialised in stealing new vehicles'. At last report, only Hertz would let its cars be taken to Poland (check first as this may have changed), but only if you hired a steering-wheel lock at an additional DM 5 a day.

## HITCHHIKING

Hitchhiking is a practical way of getting around and even Polish women regularly travel 'autostop'. There's even an official 'autostop' card complete with coupons for drivers available from PTTK offices! It's mostly large commercial vehicles that pick up hitchhikers and they expect to be paid the equivalent of a bus fare. This considered, you'll probably want to hitchhike more for the adventure or when public transport is inadequate than to save money.

## BOAT
### Local Boats

A pleasant way to sightsee is from a ship, and local cruises on the Vistula River are offered at Kraków and Toruń. Other local river cruises are available at Bydgoszcz, Gdańsk, Szczecin and Wrocław. The day excursion from Gdańsk or Sopot to Hel across the Gulf of Gdańsk is recommended. Most of these trips operate only in summer. Local ferries of interest to visitors are found at Frombork and Świnoujście.

Enthusiasts for canal cruising by narrow boat won't want to miss a trip on the Elbląg Canal from Ostróda to Elbląg where the boats are carried up and down ramps on rail-mounted platforms. Also in north-east Poland, excursion boats of the Mazurian Shipping Company's White Fleet run daily from May to September between Giżycko, Mikołajki and Ruciane-Nida, while other tourist boats operate out of Augustów and Ostróda.

## LOCAL TRANSPORT

Local buses, trolley buses and trams cost about US$0.05 a ride, but tickets must be purchased in advance at kiosks or Ruch newsstands. Buy a bunch of them as drivers don't sell tickets. Tickets purchased in one Polish city may be used in another though ticket prices vary, so ask. You punch the ticket as you board. Public transport operates from 5.30 am to 11 pm. Express buses (pośpieszny) are double fare, night buses after 11 pm triple fare. Luggage is an extra

fare. Though tickets aren't checked often, you will receive a stiff fine if you're caught without one at a spot check.

### Taxi

Since the Polish złoty was made into a 'hard' currency, taxis are a lot easier to find. There are always regular taxi stands in front of railway stations and near markets, plus other strategic points around town. It's also possible to flag down taxis on the street. Beware of taxis waiting in front of the tourist hotels, and unmarked, unmetered 'pirate' taxis which will try to overcharge. Always insist that the meter be turned on and carry proper change. If there's no meter agree on the price beforehand.

Taxi meters have difficulty keeping up with inflation. At last report taxis charged 140-200 times the meter fare. This could change as the meters are adjusted, so check by asking your hotel receptionist or any Polish acquaintance. It doesn't hurt to round the fare up. Outside city limits and after 11 pm taxis charge double. Luggage and the number of passengers don't affect the fare. A short trip around town may cost US$1, while an hour-long search for a youth hostel including a 10-km drive out of town may reach US$6, tip included. If drivers are especially helpful in finding a cheap place to stay, tip them generously.

## TOURS

Of the package tours to Poland offered by Orbis offices abroad, the most interesting cater to special interests such as horse riding, skiing, yachting, health resorts, etc, which are hard to organise on your own. A two-week ski package from Amsterdam to Karpacz (near Jelenia Góra) or Zakopane will run about US$800 per person, double occupancy, all-inclusive. A 21-day stay at a Polish health resort during the high season (May to September) will run US$735/1260 single/double including accommodation with bath, meals and medical treatment.

Orbis offices inside Poland offer organised city sightseeing tours in Warsaw,

Kraków and other cities. The best of the Warsaw trips are to Wilanów Palace and Chopin's birthplace at Żelazowa Wola, while at Kraków you have the salt mines and Auschwitz-Birkenau to choose from. Most operate from mid-May to September only.

# Warsaw

Warsaw (Warszawa), a city of nearly two million inhabitants in the north-east corner of Eastern Europe, is almost equidistant from Berlin (579 km), Prague (625 km), Vienna (689 km) and Budapest (679 km). Viewed another way, Warsaw is almost the same distance from London (1432 km) and Sofia (1466 km). The Vistula (Wisła) River cuts a curving course across Poland, from the Carpathian Mountains in the south to the Baltic in the north, and halfway down sits Warsaw, off-centre now that the country's borders have moved west.

The strategic location in the centre of the Mazovian lowland led to the site being fortified in the 14th century, and in 1596 King Sigismund III Vasa had the capital transferred here from Kraków. Warsaw has long resisted foreign domination: by the Swedes in the 17th century, tsarist Russia in the 19th century and Nazi Germany and the Soviet Union in the 20th century.

Many of Warsaw's finest avenues, parks and palaces were built in the 18th century, whereas the 19th century was a period of decay with the city as a mere provincial centre of the Russian Empire. Yet this was nothing compared to WW II when hundreds of thousands of residents were killed and all the survivors finally expelled before the city was levelled block by block. Before WW II a third of the population of Warsaw was Jewish but only a handful of Jews remain today.

In a way, Warsaw reborn from wartime destruction epitomises the Polish nation. The masterful rebuilding of old Warsaw and its harmonious union with the new symbolise the determination of the Polish people to develop and build without sacrificing an identity which has always been their greatest strength. You'll witness that identity in the museums and churches, but more directly in the surprisingly candid people. Warsaw is a fascinating layer cake which you will need several days to digest.

## Orientation

If you're coming by train you'll probably arrive at Central Station beside the Palace of Culture & Science near the corner of Aleje Jerozolimskie and Marszałkowska. Dump your things in the baggage room and start hostel or hotel hunting using the listings in this section. If you arrived by plane, the airport transportation possibilities are described under Getting Around.

Warsaw has many focal points but you'll soon become acquainted with Plac Zamkowy, the gateway to old Warsaw, and the Royal Way, which runs 10 km south-east from this square to Wilanów Palace with changing names: Krakowskie Przedmieście, Nowy Świat, Aleje Ujazdowskie, Belwederska, Jana Sobieskiego and Aleja Wilanowska. Plan your sightseeing around this corridor.

## Information

**Tourist Offices** Tourist information is available from an information cum souvenir shop marked 'IT' at Plac Zamkowy 1 in the old town.

The information counter at Orbis, ulica Bracka 16, on the corner of Aleje Jerozolimskie, is also available, but this is a travel agency, not a tourist office, and it's usually very busy. Other Orbis offices are at Marszałkowska 142, on the corner of Królewska, and upstairs in the Metropol Hotel, Marszałkowska 99a.

Just opposite Central Station is the Polski Związek Motorowy (Polish Automobile Association), Aleje Jerozolimskie 63, where you should be able to buy a good indexed map of Warsaw.

**Other Information Offices** Student travel is handled by Almatur, ulica Kopernika 23, and

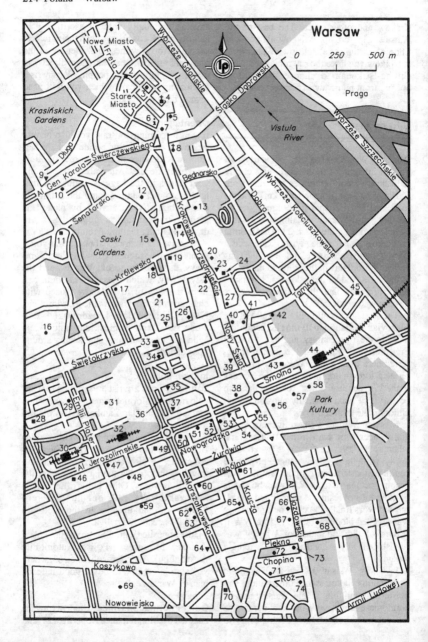

# Warsaw

0    250    500 m

Nowe Miasto

Stare Miasto

Krasińskich Gardens

Praga

Vistula River

Saski Gardens

Krakowskie Przedmieście

Park Kultury

Nowy Świat

Al Jerozolimskie

Marszałkowska

Koszykowa

Nowowiejska

Chopina

■ PLACES TO STAY

11  Saski Hotel
14  Hotel Europejski
19  Hotel Victoria Inter-Continental
24  PTTK Dom Turysty Hotel
28  Holiday Inn Hotel
43  Smolna Youth Hostel
45  Dom Nauczyciela ZNP Hotel
46  Marriott Hotel
49  Metropol & Polonia Hotels
50  Forum Hotel
61  Grand Hotel
70  MDM Hotel

▼ PLACES TO EAT

 9  Gruba Kaśka Cafeteria
23  Uniwersytecki Milk Bar
25  U Matysiaków Restaurant
35  Bar Hybrydy
37  Zodiak Bar
39  Familijny Milk Bar
54  Praha Bar
55  Rybka Bar
64  Złota Kurka Milk Bar

    OTHER

 1  New Town Square
 2  Barbican
 3  Old Town Square
 4  St John's Cathedral
 5  Royal Palace
 6  'IT' Tourist Information
 7  Plac Zamkowy
 8  St Anne's Church
10  Jewish Historical Institute
12  Wielki Opera House
13  Radziwiłł Palace
15  Tomb of the Unknown Soldier
16  Synagogue

17  Orbis (train tickets)
18  Zachęta Art Gallery
20  University of Warsaw
21  Ethnological Museum
22  Church of the Holy Cross
26  Antykwariat Warszawski
27  Academy of Sciences
29  Akwarium Club
30  Central Railway Station
31  Palace of Culture & Science
32  Śródmieście Railway Station
33  Main Post Office
34  Filharmonia Concert Hall
36  Department Stores
38  American Express & Orbis
40  Wagon-lits Travel
41  Almatur
42  Chopin Museum
44  Powiśle Railway Station
46  LOT Polish Airlines
47  Polish Automobile Association
48  Operetta Theatre
49  Orbis
51  Kasy Teatralne
52  Intourist
53  Europäisches Reisebüro
56  Former Party House
57  National Museum
58  Armed Forces Museum
59  Sawa Tour
60  Hungarian Cultural Centre
62  Balkantourist
63  Czechoslovak Cultural Centre
65  Syrena Travel Office
66  Bulgarian Consulate
67  American Embassy
68  Canadian Embassy
69  Politechnical University
71  Czechoslovak Consulate
72  Romanian Consulate
73  Hungarian & Yugoslav Consulates
74  British Embassy

they're generally helpful (weekdays 9 am to 3.30 pm). They'll be able to tell you about the International Student Hotels which are open in July and August only. Try to make bookings for other Polish cities. Also ask about one-week Almatur sailing and horse riding trips.

If you don't have the International Youth Hostel Handbook, a map listing all Polish youth hostels is available from PTSM (Polskie Towarzystwo Schronisk Młodzie-żowych), at ulica Chocimska 28 near Łazienkowski Park, 4th floor, suite 423 (weekdays 8 am to 3 pm).

**Useful Organisation** The Exploration Society, a Polish travel club, meets at the Dom Kultury Ochota, ulica Grójecka 75 (not far from Camping OST 'Gromada'), Fridays at 7 pm. Many of the members speak English so a visit would be a way of meeting some interesting local people.

**Money** To cash a travellers' cheque try the Bank Polska Kasa Opieki SA (PKO) at the corner of Aleje Jerozolimskie and Marszałkowska across the street from the Forum Hotel. The private exchange offices behind this bank are more efficient but only accept cash.

**Post** Poste restante is at window No 12 in the main post office, ulica Świętokrzyska 31-33.

**Foreign Embassies** Many of the embassies you'll want to visit to pick up visas or mail are located along Aleje Ujazdowskie between Aleje Jerozolimskie and Łazienki Park. The largest is the American Embassy (☎ 28 3041), Aleje Ujazdowskie 29/31 (mailing address: American Embassy Warsaw, c/o AmConGen (WAW), APO New York 09213, USA). The Canadian Embassy (☎ 29 8051) is just down the street opposite at ulica Matejki 1/5. The Swiss Embassy, Aleje Ujazdowskie 27, is next to the American Embassy.

The British Embassy is two blocks south of these, at the corner of Aleje Ujazdowskie and Aleje Róż, though only diplomatic business is dealt with there. British and New Zealand travellers must trek out to the British Consulate, ulica Wawelska 14 (weekdays 9 am to 2.30 pm) in an inconvenient southern suburb of Warsaw. The Australian Embassy (☎ 17 6081) is at ulica Estońska 3/5 on the east side of the Vistula (take any eastbound tram on Aleje Jerozolimskie and get off at the first stop across the river). The German Embassy, ulica Walecznych 10 (weekdays 9 am to 12.30 pm), is not far from the Australian Embassy. The Austrian Embassy, ulica Gagarina 34, is just south-east of Łazienki Park.

**Visas for Other Countries** The Eastern European embassies are all in the vicinity of the US Embassy. The Bulgarian Consulate, Aleje Ujazdowskie 35 (open Monday, Wednesday and Friday 10 am to noon), issues tourist visas valid three months from the date of issue for US$19 and one photo, but you

have to wait seven working days. If you want a tourist visa on the spot it's US$38. Thirty-hour transit visas are always issued on the spot: US$12 for one entry, US$18 for two entries (no photos required).

Visas for the other Eastern European countries are more easily obtained. The Yugoslav and Hungarian consulates are side by side on Aleje Ujazdowskie, a block south of the US Embassy, and both are open Monday, Wednesday and Friday from 9 am to noon. Hungarian visas cost US$20 and two photos for one entry, US$33 and four photos for two entries, and are issued at once. Be sure to get a tourist and not a transit visa. The Romanian Consulate, around the corner at ulica Chopina 10, keeps the same hours but is not as efficient about issuing visas.

Nearby at ulica Koszykowa 18, on the corner of Aleje Róż, is the Czechoslovak Consulate (Monday to Friday 8 to 11 am). You'll receive a tourist or transit visa right away upon payment of US$7 and two photos for one entry, US$22 and four photos for two entries, though some nationalities are charged more (such as British – US$40!). Arrive early as it can get crowded.

**Cultural Centres** The Czechoslovak Cultural Centre, Marszałkowska 81, provides tourist information and there's a Czech bookstore adjacent for maps and guides. Balkantourist, Marszałkowska 83, has information on Bulgaria. The Hungarian Cultural Centre, Marszałkowska 76/80, dispenses Hungarian travel information and books, and there's a Hungarian travel office (Ibusz) around the corner.

**Travel Agencies** Sawa Tour, ulica Wspólna 65a, can book cheap flights to anywhere departing from Berlin.

**Things To See**
**The Old Town** From Plac Zamkowy you enter the old city along ulica Świętojańska. You'll soon come to 14th century Gothic **St John's Cathedral**, and then the **Rynek Starego Miasta**, the old town square. If you're there at 10 am be sure to catch the film

at the **City Historical Museum**, Rynek Starego Miasta 33 (closed Monday), which unforgettably depicts the wartime destruction of the city. It's hard to believe that all the 17th and 18th century buildings around this square have been completely rebuilt from their foundations. Stroll around, visiting the shops, galleries and restaurants.

Continue north a block on ulica Nowomiejska to the **Barbican Gate** (1548), part of the medieval walled circuit around Warsaw. Walk towards the river inside the walls a bit to find the city's symbol, the **Warsaw Mermaid** (1855). (Once upon a time a mermaid, Syrena, rose from the river and told a fisherman, Wars, and his wife, Sawa, to found a city here.) Everything north of this wall is New Town (Nowe Miasto). Straight ahead on Freta, beyond several historic churches, is **Rynek Nowego Miasta** with more churches. The delightful streets and buildings in both Old and New towns are best explored casually on your own without a guidebook.

**The Royal Way** On a tall pillar (1644) in the centre of Plac Zamkowy is a statue of King Sigismund III. The **Royal Castle** (1619) on the east side of the square developed over the centuries as successive Polish kings added wings and redecorated the interior. In 1945 all that remained was a heap of rubble but from 1971 to 1974 the castle was carefully rebuilt. The ticket office is around on the north side on the building, but in summer demand far outstrips supply so arrive early and be prepared to wait (closed Monday, free Thursday).

On the south side of Plac Zamkowy is **St Anne's Church** (1454), one of the most beautiful churches in the city. If you have time it's worth walking out on the **Śląsko Dąbrowski Bridge** behind the Royal Castle for a view of Warsaw's skyline. The highway underpass below Plac Zamkowy dates from 1949.

Continue south on Krakowskie Przedmieście where there are many aristocratic residences, especially the **Radziwiłł Palace** (1643), on the left beside a church. The Warsaw Pact was signed in this building on 14 May 1955. Almost opposite this palace is the neoclassical **Europejski Hotel** (1877), behind which are Saski Gardens with the **Tomb of the Unknown Soldier** and its permanent honour guard occupying a fragment of an 18th century royal palace destroyed in WW II. The ceremonial changing of the guard here takes place Sundays at noon.

North of the square before the tomb is the massive **Wielki Opera House** (1965), while to the south is the modern Victoria Inter-Continental Hotel. On the west side of this hotel is the **Zachęta Art Gallery** (closed Monday) which often stages great art shows in summer. South a block beyond the circular **Evangelical Church** (1781) is the **Ethnological Museum** (closed Monday), ulica Kredytowa 1. This large museum has collections of tribal art from Africa, Oceania and Latin America, as well as Polish folklore.

From this museum follow ulica Traugutta east a block back to the Royal Way. Just around the corner on the right is the 17th century **Church of the Holy Cross**. The heart of Frédéric Chopin is preserved in the second pillar on the left-hand side of the main nave of this church (though Chopin left Warsaw at the age of 20 and died of tuberculosis in Paris when only 39, he was a Polish nationalist to the end).

In front of the 19th century **Academy of Sciences** (Staszic Palace) nearby stands the famous statue (1830) of Polish astronomer Nicolaus Copernicus by the Danish sculptor Bertel Thorvaldsen. Below the Academy towards the river is the **Chopin Museum**, ulica Tamka 41 (closed Sunday) with memorabilia such as Chopin's last piano and one of the best collections of Chopin manuscripts in the world. They'll play recordings of his music if you ask.

**More Museums** Return to the Royal Way and head south on Nowy Świat (New World Street), crossing Aleje Jerozolimskie (Jerusalem Avenue) to the former **Party House** (1951), where the Central Committee of the Polish United Workers' Party used to meet. The large building beside this on Aleje

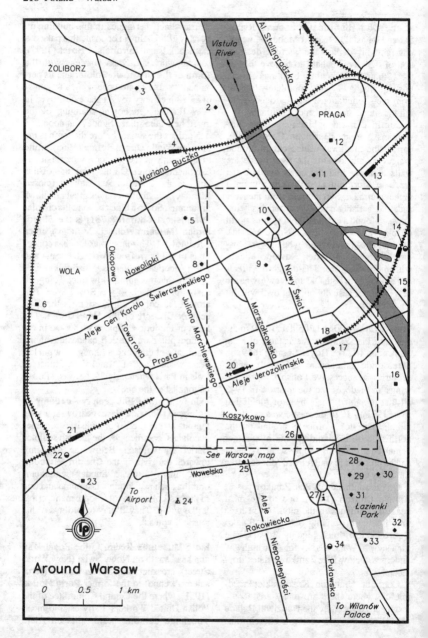

ŻOLIBORZ

Vistula River

Al Stalingradzka

PRAGA

3

2

4

Mariana Buczka

12

11

13

10

5

14

Okopowa

Nowolipki

8

9

Nowy Świat

15

WOLA

Aleje Gen Karola Świerczewskiego

Juliana Marchlewskiego

Marszałkowska

6

7

Towarowa

Prosta

18

19

17

20

Aleje Jerozolimskie

16

Koszykowa

21

26

22

See Warsaw map

28

29

30

23

Wawelska

25

31

To Airport

24

27

Łazienki Park

32

Aleje

33

Rakowiecka

34

Niepodległości

Puławska

**Around Warsaw**

0     0.5     1 km

To Wilanów Palace

■ PLACES TO STAY

6  Syrena Hotel
7  Karolkowa Youth Hostel
12  Nowa Praga Hotel
16  Solec Hotel
23  Orbis Vera Hotel
24  Camping OST 'Gromada'
26  MDM Hotel

OTHER

1  Praga Railway Station
2  Citadel
3  Św Stanisława Kostki
4  Gdańska Railway Station
5  Warsaw Ghetto Monument
8  Warsaw Chamber Opera
9  Wielki Opera House
10  Old Town Square (Rynek)
11  Zoo
13  Wileńska Railway Station
14  Stadion Bus & Railway Stations
15  Stadium
17  National Museum
18  Śródmieście Railway Station
19  Palace of Culture & Science
20  Central Railway Station
21  Zachodnia Railway Station
22  Central Bus Station
25  British Consulate
27  Youth Hostel Association Office
28  Orangerie
29  Chopin Monument
30  Łazienki Water Palace
31  Belvedere Palace
32  Austrian Embassy
33  PDK Universus Bookstore
34  Orbis (bus tickets)

Jerozolimskie is the **National Museum** (closed Monday) which has a magnificent collection of paintings. Be sure to see *The Battle of Grunwald* by Jan Matejko. During WW II this huge painting was evacuated to Lublin and secretly buried. The Nazis offered a reward of 10 million Reichsmarks for information leading to its discovery but no one accepted. After the war Matejko's work was uncovered and restored.

Towards the riverside next to the National Museum is the **Armed Forces Museum** (closed Monday and Tuesday) with a large assortment of old guns, tanks and planes on the terrace outside.

**The Royal Palaces** Southbound again on the Royal Way, walk down Aleje Ujazdowskie past many foreign embassies to **Łazienki Park** (it's a little far so take a bus or taxi if you can). The park is best known for its 18th century neoclassical **Water Palace** (closed Monday and during bad weather), summer residence of Stanislaus Augustus Poniatowski, the last king of Poland. This reform-minded monarch, who gave Poland the world's second written constitution in 1791, was deposed by a Russian army and a confederation of reactionary Polish magnates in 1792.

The **Orangerie** (1788) in the park is also well worth seeing for its theatre and gallery of sculpture (closed Monday). On summer afternoons concerts are often held in this gallery. The striking **Chopin Monument** (1926) is just off Aleje Ujazdowskie but still within the park. On summer Sundays at 12 noon and 5 pm excellent piano recitals are held here. Poland's Head of State resides in the neoclassical **Belvedere Palace** (1818), just south of the monument.

Six km farther south on bus No 193 is **Wilanów Palace** (1696), the Baroque summer residence of King John III Sobieski who defeated the Turks at Vienna in 1683, ending their threat to Central Europe forever. In summer it's hard to gain admission to the palace (closed Tuesday) due to large groups and limited capacity, but even the exterior and 18th century French-style park are worth the trip. Guided tours begin every 15 minutes from 9.30 am to 2.30 pm but only 35 people are admitted each time, and on weekdays tour groups often pre-book all the tickets. On Saturday, Sunday and holidays the palace is reserved for individuals so these are good days to come, but arrive early and be prepared to stand in line. Don't come on Tuesday or the day following a public holiday as not only the palace but also the park behind the palace will be locked. While you're at Wilanów the **Poster Museum** (Muzeum Plakatu) in the former royal stables beside the palace is worth a visit (closed Monday). There are two fancy restaurants between the bus stop and the palace where you could have lunch.

**Other Sights** Warsaw's **Palace of Culture** (1955) near the Central Station is a depressing Stalin-era building, although you may care to take the elevator up to the observation terrace on the 30th floor for the panoramic view. There's also a **Technical Museum** (closed Monday), several theatres and a congress hall in the palace. A large street market selling everything from imported beer to car tyres functions in the park around the palace.

Most of the **Citadel** (1834) on the north side of the city is still occupied by the military; however, part of it may be visited through the Brama Straceń, the large gate near the middle of the Citadel wall on the river side. This large fortress was built by the Russians after a Polish uprising in 1830. There's a museum (closed Sunday and Monday) and plaques recalling the Poles executed here by the tsarist forces a century or more ago. Buses No 118 and 185 stop near the Citadel entrance.

West of the citadel near Plac Komuny Paryskiej is the **Church of Sw Stanisława Kostki** with the red-granite tomb of Father Jerzy Popiełuszko in the yard. Prior to his murder by the secret police in October 1984 the 37-year-old priest had earned the enmity of Communist hardliners by giving sermons in support of Solidarity and providing those opposed to the regime with a rallying point. The government cooled the passions aroused by the crime by publicly trying and sentencing to long prison terms the four officers responsible. Don't miss the photo display on Father Popiełuszko's political activities inside behind the altar. Also in the churchyard is a moving memorial to those who died in Nazi death camps during WW II.

### Activities

**Organised Tours** The Orbis office at ulica Świętokrzyska 20 opposite the main post office books Orbis sightseeing tours, but this is more easily done at the reception desks of the Forum, Grand, Victoria, Holiday Inn or Europejski hotels. The tours cost anywhere from US$7 to US$14 per person and operate from June to September.

Five-hour city tours depart daily except Sunday, while the Wednesday tour to Wilanów Palace would ensure that you actually get inside. The Sunday trip to Chopin's family home at **Żelazowa Wola**, 50 km west of Warsaw, includes a live recital of his music by a leading pianist – recommended. (You can also go to the Chopin Museum on your own by train from Warszawa Śródmieście Station to Sochaczew, then bus No 6 hourly to Żelazowa Wola.)

No tourist excursion boats operate on the Warsaw reach of the Vistula River at the moment.

### Places to Stay

**Camping** From May to September one of the best places to stay in Warsaw is *Camping OST 'Gromada'* (**☎** 25 4391), ulica Żwirki i Wigury 32, south-east of town on the road in from the airport (bus No 175 from the airport to the gate). Tent space is US$2.50 per person and bungalows are US$8 double or US$14 for four persons. Rooms in a large pavilion on the grounds are available for the same price when all the bungalows are full. There's a large restaurant on the grounds and the atmosphere is informal and welcoming.

**Hostels** The *youth hostel* (**☎** 27 8952) at ulica Smolna 30 is on the top floor of a large concrete building a few minutes' walk from Warsaw Powiśle Railway Station in the centre of the city. Go in the entrance with the green triangle and up to the top of the stairs. There's no shower or hot water here, it's dusty, crowded and 108 steps up, but the charge will be under US$2. Stow your gear in a locker during the day. The curfew is 10.30 pm.

The ulica Karolkowa 53a *youth hostel* (**☎** 32 8829), just off Aleje Gen Karola Świerczewskiego, is less convenient. To get there catch a north or westbound tram No 1, 13, 20, 24, 26, 27 or 34. Get off at the 'Centrum-

Wola' department store, then walk back on the right and look for a three-storey building among the trees beyond *Bar Wenecja*.

**Private Rooms** The Syrena Travel Office (☎ 25 7201), ulica Krucza 17 across the street from the Syrena Tourist Office, arranges accommodation in private homes at US$8 single, US$11 double. Although the office stays open till 8 pm you should try to get there before 4 pm. You cannot occupy the room until 6 pm so leave your luggage at the station.

**Cheaper Hotels** A good place to stay in Warsaw is *Dom Nauczyciela ZNP* (☎ 27 9211), Wybrzeże Kościuszkowskie 31/33, on the Vistula Embankment – take a taxi to get there. This modern hotel is actually a school teachers' hostel but visitors are accommodated when rooms are available at US$6/8 single/double without bath, US$12/16 with bath. Some of the rooms on the upper floors have excellent views of the river.

The *PTTK Dom Turysty Hotel* (☎ 26 3011), Krakowskie Przedmieście 4/6 opposite the Academy of Sciences, has rooms at US$11/14 single/double without bath, US$17/24 with bath, or US$16 triple without bath. Be prepared for dirty public toilets if you didn't take a room with private facilities, and throngs of excited Polish schoolchildren running through the halls. The six-bed dorms here are reserved for them.

The *Hotel Saski* (☎ 20 4611), Plac Dzierżyńskiego 1, has rooms without bath at US$11/18 single/double. Showers are extra. This 141-bed hotel has real character and a fine location.

The *Hotel Syrena* (☎ 32 1257), ulica Syreny 23 off Górczewska, is larger than the Saski so you have a better chance of a room (US$10/12 single/double without bath or breakfast). A drawback is the location on the far west side of Warsaw, though there's a frequent bus service.

At a pinch you could also consider the *Nowa Praga Hotel* (☎ 19 5001), which is in a poor location east of the zoo on the far east side of the river. The Nowa Praga, a somewhat better place than the Hotel Syrena, charges US$9/18 for singles/doubles without bath, US$12/24 with bath, breakfast included.

**Expensive Hotels** All of Warsaw's other hotels are in the luxury tourist bracket. The *Polonia* (US$37/49 single/double with bath) and *Metropol Hotels* are right opposite the Palace of Culture, a block from Central Station, good for anyone who rolls in absolutely exhausted. The 751-room *Forum Hotel* nearby is exactly the same as any high-rise Hilton.

The sterile *Dom Chłopa, Marriott, Holiday Inn, Victoria-Inter-Continental* and *Grand* hotels are not far from the Forum, but the four-star *Europejski Hotel* (☎ 26 5051), Krakowskie Przedmieście 13, is your best bet for location, facilities and atmosphere. Erected in 1877 in the neo-Renaissance style, this was Warsaw's first modern hotel. Be prepared for rates beginning at US$44/66 single/double for a small room, US$83/123 for a large room, all with bath and breakfast included. The *Bristol Hotel* (1901) across the street has been closed for many years. It would be an excellent second choice if and when it were ever reopened.

*Hotel Warszawa*, a three-star, 17-storey Stalinist erection at Plac Powstańców Warszawy 9 near the centre of town, is US$23/29 single/double without bath, US$28/38 with bath, breakfast included.

Less well-known is the *MDM Hotel* (☎ 21 6211), at Plac Konstytucji 1, directly south down Marszałkowska from the Forum Hotel. Rooms begin at US$19 single without bath and US$30/38 single/double with bath. Although it is a little out of the way, transport from here is good. Plac Konstytucji is Warsaw's best example of an overpowering Stalinist square which makes the MDM fun, fun, fun.

**Places to Eat**
**In the Old Town** Warsaw's finest restaurants

are on Rynek Starego Miasta, the old town square. Most famous is the *Bazyliszek Restaurant*, Rynek Starego Miasta 5 (upstairs), where game dishes like wild boar and venison are served. Sloppy dressers are not welcome. The *Kamienne Schodki Restaurant*, Rynek Starego Miasta 26, specialises in roast duck with apples (menu in English and German).

The *Rycerska Restaurant*, ulica Szeroki Dunaj 11 just a block and a half from the old town square, has been gentrified and is now fairly upmarket (no shorts).

*Pod Barbakanen*, Mostowa 27/29 just north of the old town gate (Barbikan), is a cheap milk bar with blue chequered tablecloths. *Pod Samsonem*, ulica Freta 3, also serves inexpensive, unpretentious meals.

**Along the Royal Way** There are many places to eat at along this busy corridor. *Uniwersytecki Milk Bar*, at Krakowskie Przedmieście 20, and *Familijny Milk Bar*, Nowy Świat 39, are cheap. The elegant *Staropolska Restaurant*, Krakowskie Przedmieście 8 beside Dom Turysty, gives a taste of old Warsaw as you dine by candlelight (moderately expensive).

*U Matysiaków*, ulica Świętokrzyska 18, offers hearty, unpretentious meals with full table service.

Farther south near the National Museum are *Szwajcarski Milk Bar*, Nowy Świat 5, and the adjacent *Złota Rybka Restaurant*, Nowy Świat 7, which specialises in fish dishes. The Złota Rybka is often full of noisy drunks who contribute to the seafaring air and the food is good (though not cheap).

**In the City Centre** Two large cafeterias in the centre of town are the *Praha Bar*, in the middle of the block at Aleje Jerozolimskie 11/19, and the *Zodiak Bar*, behind Wars Centrum Department Store. The Zodiak is cheap and easy because you pay at the end of the line, though the food is heavy and unappetising.

*Bambino Milk Bar*, Krucza 21 beside Air France diagonally opposite the Grand Hotel,

offers typical Polish food at low prices. *Złota Kurka Milk Bar*, Marszałkowska 55/57, is down near the MDM Hotel on Plac Konstytucji.

The 42-storey *Marriott Hotel* opposite Central Station has a self-service buffet on the 2nd floor (enter through the main entrance and take the lift), just don't wear a backpack or grubby clothes in here – act as if you own the place.

**Bars & Cafés** *Winiarnia Fukier*, Rynek Starego Miasta 27, is an old wine shop with great atmosphere and good company. *Kawiarnia Gwiazdeczka*, ulica Piwna 40 a block from Rynek Starego Miasta, is informal, a good place to head for a drink if Fukier happens to be closed.

The *U Hopfera Wine Shop*, Krakowskie Przedmieście 53 near Plac Zamkowy, is similar to Fukier. *Bar Boruta*, ulica Freta 38 on the corner of Rynek Nowego Miasta, is also a good place to sit and chat over drinks in the evening.

**Entertainment**
You will find theatre, concert and cinema offerings in the daily newspapers. If you're after theatre tickets, go to Kasy Teatralne, Aleje Jerozolimskie 25, which has tickets for many events. The *Filharmonia* booking office is at ulica Sienkiewicza 12. If you're attending a concert in the smaller 'sala kameralna', enter by the ulica Moniuszki entrance on the other side of the building. Warsaw's National Philharmonic Orchestra is Poland's finest.

Tickets for the *Wielki Opera House*, Plac Teatralny, and the *Warsaw Operetta*, ulica Nowogrodzka 49 near Central Station, are sold at the theatres. The Wielki Opera is often sold out a few days in advance (logical: the best seats are only US$1!). You may have better luck at the smaller *Warsaw Chamber Opera*, at ulica Świerczewskiego 76b (in the back courtyard). The Kasy Teatralne handles its tickets.

Nightly at 8 pm from June to September

there's a folklore show accompanied by traditional Polish cuisine in the restaurant at the *Europejski Hotel* (about US$14 per person). Reservations should be made in advance at the Europejski reception.

The *Akwarium Club*, Emilii Plater 49 between the Palace of Culture and the Holiday Inn, is the place for hot jazz and local action. Before paying the US$2 cover charge to go upstairs, make sure the music is live and not only compact discs! Also ask when it's over or you may be charged only to catch the last 10 minutes. There's no cover to sit downstairs.

Friday and Saturday there's a student disco at *Bar Hybrydy*, ulica Kniewskiego 7/9 (downstairs) behind the department stores a block east of the Palace of Culture.

**Festivals** Annual events worth asking about include the 'Złota Tarka' (Golden Washboard) Jazz Festival in early spring, the Festival of Contemporary Music 'Warsaw Autumn' in September and October, and the 'Jazz Jamboree' in late October.

### Things to Buy

The best places to shop for souvenirs, amber jewellery, clothing, etc, are the boutiques in the ulica Krucza 23/31 block, directly across from the Orbis Grand Hotel. The high prices are justified by the quality.

For contemporary art try Desa, Nowy Świat 23, a gallery which displays current trends in painting. There are other shopping possibilities along Nowy Świat in this vicinity.

The department stores on the east side of the Palace of Culture are more public curiosities than places to shop. The store at ulica Nowomiejska 17 beside the Barbican Gate in the old town sells a great variety of Polish postcards. The Poles are noted graphic designers, and the poster shops on Rynek Starego Miasta offer real bargains.

### Getting There & Away

**Air** The LOT Polish Airlines office is in the Marriott Hotel building on Aleje Jerozolimskie opposite the central railway station.

Yugoslav Airlines, Nowogrodzka 31 near the Forum Hotel, has direct flights from Warsaw to Belgrade for US$144 one-way.

**Bus** Orbis, Puławska 43 (there's another Orbis office nearby – watch the number), sells advance PKS bus tickets to places all over Poland – essential! The Central Bus Station serving western and southern Poland is on the west side of the city near Warsaw Zachodnia Railway Station.

The Stadion Bus Station serving northeast Poland, including the Lake District, is on the east side of the Vistula. An easy way to get there is to take a commuter train from Warsaw Śródmieście Railway Station in front of the Palace of Culture east to Warsaw Stadion Railway Station which adjoins the bus terminal.

**Train** International trains depart Warsaw Central Station for Berlin Zoo, Bucharest, Budapest, Cologne, Paris, Frankfurt/Main, Holland, Leipzig, London, Prague and Vienna. These are described in the chapter introduction. Domestic expresses run to every part of Poland. For information on 'name train' expresses leaving Warsaw for cities around Poland turn to the section of this book dealing with the city you wish to reach. All these trains carry mandatory seat reservations.

*Train Tickets* Most express trains leaving Warsaw carry mandatory seat reservations. These seats, sleepers and couchettes can be reserved at Central Station or Orbis, ulica Bracka 16. You can also purchase international railway tickets between Eastern European countries at this Orbis office but payment must be made in Western currency.

Both domestic and international railway tickets can also be purchased at the smaller Orbis office in the Metropol Hotel, Marszałkowska 99a, but the international window closes at 2 pm. Orbis at Marszałkowska 142 also sells train tickets and it's sometimes less crowded.

Wagon-lits Travel, Nowy Świat 64, sells

train and air tickets to points outside Eastern Europe.

### Getting Around

**To/From the Airport** Bus No 175 goes to Okęcie International Airport (10 km) from outside Central Station opposite the LOT office (punch a regular ticket), while bus No 114 goes to the domestic airport. To get between the terminals (about three km) take either bus up ulica Żwirki i Wigury a few stops, cross the street and take the other bus back (or just grab a cab).

The 'linia specjalna' bus runs to Terminal 1 at the international airport from ulica Emilii Plater between Central Railway Station and the Palace of Culture, every 20 minutes from 4.30 am to 10.30 pm (pay the driver, US$0.30).

**Bus & Tram** In Warsaw, city buses of the 100, 200, 300, 400 and 500 series plus all trams and trolley buses require only a single US$0.05 ticket (punch both ends). Suburban buses of the 700 and 800 series and express buses with a letter instead of a number require two US$0.05 tickets, both punched at each end. Night buses of the 600 series operating between 11 pm and 5 am call for four US$0.05 tickets, all punched at both ends – a total of eight punches! Heavy baggage is an additional fare on all services.

You must purchase tickets at a newsstand (Ruch) before boarding the service, then validate them once aboard by punching them in a device near the door. Drivers don't sell tickets. You're liable for a US$5 fine if caught without a valid ticket during a spot check.

**Taxi** Many taxi drivers will try to overcharge you, yet cabs are often essential for getting around. Ask somebody by what figure the meter fare is multiplied (at last report by 140), then make sure it's switched on. Government taxis with 'radio taxi 919' on the side of the vehicle are the least likely to cause problems. Beware of taxis parked in front of luxury hotels.

**Car Rental** The Warsaw Hertz agent is Orbis, Nowogrodzka 27. See page 211 for more information on car rental.

# Małopolska

Much of south-eastern Poland still bears a gentle bucolic air. Here in Małopolska ('Little Poland') you'll see people working the fields as they have for centuries, and long wooden horse carts along the roads. Until 1918 the region was divided into two parts. Everything north of the Vistula and a line drawn east from Sandomierz (including Lublin and Zamość) came under Russian control in 1815. South of this was 'Galicia' under the Habsburgs of Austria. Kraków remained semi-independent until 1846 when it was annexed by Austria. After an abortive uprising in 1863-64 tsarist Russia suppressed Polish culture in the territory it occupied, while the southern areas enjoyed considerable autonomy under the Austro-Hungarian empire. In 1915 Germany evicted the Russians and in 1918 the whole area once again became Polish. The impact of this chequered history can still be seen.

While nearby industrial cities like Katowice and Łódź have little to offer the average visitor, nearly every foreign tourist makes it to Kraków, one of the great art centres of Europe. Some also join the hordes of Polish excursionists on their way to the mountains around Zakopane. There's much more to south-eastern Poland, however, such as the holy sanctuary of Jasna Góra at Częstochowa, perfectly preserved Renaissance Zamość, the superb Baroque palace at Łańcut, and the horrors of Auschwitz, Birkenau and Majdanek. It's easy to lose the crowds in the unspoiled mountains along the southern border. Here is Poland to be savoured.

### LUBLIN

Long a crossroads of trade, Lublin was an important point of contact between Poland and Lithuania. In 1569 a political union of

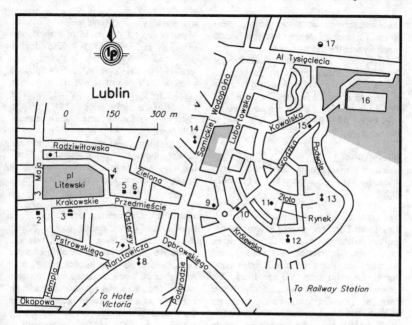

Lublin

| | |
|---|---|
| 1 | Radziwiłł Palace |
| 2 | Hotel Lublinianka |
| 3 | Post Office |
| 4 | Karczma Lubelska Restaurant |
| 5 | Dom Wycieczkowy |
| 6 | Orbis (train tickets) |
| 7 | J Osterwa Theatre & Filharmonia |
| 8 | Brigittine Church |
| 9 | New Town Hall |
| 10 | Kraków Gate |
| 11 | Old Tribunal |
| 12 | Cathedral |
| 13 | Dominican Church |
| 14 | Carmelite Church |
| 15 | Town Gate |
| 16 | Lublin Castle |
| 17 | Bus Station |

Russians and Germans, culminating in the Nazi death camp at Majdanek. For a time in 1944 Lublin was capital of liberated Poland.

Somehow the compact old town (Stare Miasto) retains the flavour of this turbulent past with its narrow crumbling streets, defensive towers and ominously isolated castle, long a prison. During the 19th century the city expanded west to Plac Litewski and under the Communists spectacular growth mushroomed in all directions. Many foreign students study at the Lublin Catholic University, Poland's oldest private university. Lublin is off the beaten track so people are interested to meet you, which is half the reason for coming.

## Orientation

The railway station with its architecture echoing Lublin Castle is several km south of the city centre so catch a trolley bus or taxi. Plac Łokietka in front of Kraków Gate marks

these kingdoms was signed here, creating the largest European state of the time. Beginning in the 17th century, Lublin saw repeated foreign invasions by Swedes, Austrians, the boundary between the old and new towns. Go through the gate and you'll soon reach Rynek, the old market square.

Krakowskie Przedmieście extends west from Kraków Gate, and most of Lublin's hotels, restaurants and large stores line this slightly decadent old avenue. The Orbis Unia Hotel, universities, parks and modern buildings are on Aleje Racławickie, its westward continuation.

## Information

The tourist office at ulica Krakowskie Przedmieście 78 sells good maps and is generally helpful.

## Things to See

**Old Town** The 14th century **Kraków Gate**, built to protect Lublin from Tatar invasions, is now the **City History Museum** (closed Monday and Tuesday). You'll get a good view of Lublin from the top floor. The entrance isn't obvious so look for it. Rather than enter the old town straight away, go south-east a block on ulica Królewska to reach the Baroque **cathedral** (1596). Beside the cathedral is the 19th century neo-Gothic **Trinitarian Tower** with a religious art museum and another 360° panorama of Lublin, and below, a passage into the old city.

Walk straight ahead to Market Square (Rynek) with the 16th century **Tribunal**, formerly the town hall, in the centre and many old town houses around. East of here at the end of ulica Złota is the beautiful **Dominican Church**, rebuilt after the fire of 1575. In the first chapel to the right of the entrance is a large historical painting, *The Lublin Fire of 1719*.

As you leave the church, turn right and continue north down the slope and through the Town Gate to **Lublin Castle**, which originated in the 14th century but assumed its present Neo-Gothic form in 1826. During the war it was a Gestapo jail and 450 prisoners were murdered here just hours before Lublin was liberated in July 1944. There's a good view from in front of the castle and an impressive museum inside (closed Monday

and Tuesday). One large painting by Jan Matejko depicts the union of Poland and Lithuania at Lublin in 1569. The 'devil's paw' *(czarcia łapa)* table in the museum recalls a legendary event at Lublin's Tribunal when a devil's court rendered a midnight verdict in favour of a poor widow. The Chapel of the Holy Trinity (1415) off the castle courtyard contains unique Byzantine-influenced frescoes but is usually closed.

A bustling street market fills the area between the castle and the bus station. From this bus station you can take a city bus or taxi to Majdanek concentration camp or an interurban bus to Kazimierz Dolny.

**Majdanek Concentration Camp** Just south-east of Lublin (buses No 23, 28, 153 and 156 pass the site), Majdanek was the second-largest Nazi death camp in Europe. Here, where 360,000 human beings perished, barbed wire and watchtowers, rows of wooden barracks and the crematoria have been left as a memorial to the dead and a warning to the living. An even more gripping memorial is the immense concrete dome covering the ashes of the victims. Poles often leave bunches of flowers here.

As you arrive you'll see a massive stone monument by the highway. There's a sweeping view of the camp from there. The museum (open from 8 am to 3 pm daily except Monday) is in the barracks to the right, outside the barbed wire fence on the west. Among the more gripping exhibits are two large buildings holding hundreds of thousands of pairs of shoes. The huge camp you see today is only a fraction of the facility the Nazis intended as part of their extermination programme. The Soviet army cut short their work.

## Places to Stay

**Camping** If you have a tent try the camping ground (open June to September) at ulica Sławinkowska 46 on the west side of the city, up beyond the Botanical Garden. Buses No 18 and 32 stop on a road behind the camping: find your way through a small woods, up a narrow lane and around the perimeter to the camping ground's main entrance. Simple, inexpensive bungalows are available, but they're often full.

**Hostels** Lublin's youth hostel is at ulica Długosza 6 opposite Miejski Park, not far from the Orbis Unia Hotel. It's difficult to locate the hostel as no sign faces the street, but just look for a low, yellow building between two large schools with a red letter box in front. The entrance is around the side – search.

*Dom Noclegowy*, ulica Akademicka 4 (☎ 38285) is close to the Orbis Unia Hotel beside the university (US$5/7 single/double shared bath). This neat, eight-storey student residence is cheap but often full.

Almatur, ulica Langiewicza 10, in the university district west of Dom Noclegowy, may be able to arrange accommodation in vacant student dormitories during July and August. If it's closed when you arrive, ask some passing student type to help you find that year's Almatur hostel.

**Hotels** The *PTTK Dom Wycieczkowy* (previously known as Hotel Europa), at ulica Krakowskie Przedmieście 29, offers double rooms at US$11 or a bed in a four-bed dormitory for US$3 – good value.

The old *Hotel Lublinianka*, at ulica Krakowskie Przedmieście 56, which opened in 1900, is slightly overpriced at US$14/23 single/double without bath, US$18/45 with bath.

Lublin has two high-rise hotels. The three-star *Victoria Hotel*, ulica Narutowicza 58, is US$23/32 single/double with bath. The four-star *Orbis Unia Hotel*, Aleje Racławickie 12 beside the Catholic University, is US$38/53 single/double with breakfast. Hotel prices are reduced from October to March.

**Places to Eat**
The *Ogrodowy Milk Bar*, ulica Krakowskie Przedmieście 57, and *Turystyczny Milk Bar*, ulica Krakowskie Przedmieście 29, are cheap. Another place in this vein is the *Staromiejski Milk Bar*, ulica Trybunalska 1 just inside the Kraków Gate in the old town.

The restaurant in the *Orbis Unia Hotel*, Aleje Racławickie 18, is the best in Lublin and the only place in town where you can be sure of a cold beer. Its menu is in English and French. The *Restauracja Karczma Słupska*, Aleje Racławickie 22 just west of the Orbis Unia Hotel, is a folkloric restaurant with live music in the evening (cover charge).

The *Powszechna Restaurant* in the Lublinianka Hotel serves filling meals accompanied by good white wine and, in the evening, live music. The *Karczma Lubelska Restaurant*, at Plac Litewski 2, is a local hang-out in the evening, sometimes with live music.

**Entertainment**
For Filharmonia tickets check the ticket office at ulica Osterwy 7. Concerts are most likely on Saturday nights. Opposite the Brigittine Church just around the corner is the ticket office of the *J Osterina Theatre* (1886). Although it presents mostly drama in Polish, you might attend until the first intermission to see the theatre and sample the acting.

*Teatr Muzyczny* tickets are available at its administrative office, ulica Krakowskie Przedmieście 21 in the centre of town. The operettas are performed at different locations, so ask. Check the daily papers which list performances at all these theatres.

**Getting There & Away**
**Bus** Buses run west to Kazimierz Dolny and Łódź, south-west to Kraków, Częstochowa, Rzeszów and Zakopane, south-east to Zamość and north-west to Warsaw. The bus to Kazimierz Dolny leaves about once an hour from platform No 3 at the bus station and takes 1½ hours (tickets inside at window No 5) – you want the 'Puławy' bus though not all of them pass Kazimierz Dolny.

**Train** Express trains connect Lublin to Warsaw (175 km, three hours). Local trains travel to Przemyśl (via Rozwadów) and Zamość. There's an overnight train with couchettes to and from Kraków. To reserve a seat on a train or book a couchette go to Orbis, ulica Krakowskie Przedmieście 29 beside Dom Wycieczkowy.

## KAZIMIERZ DOLNY

This charming old Polish town on the banks of the Vistula River is best done as a day trip from Lublin, 40 km east. Accommodation in Kazimierz is tight and everything can be seen in a couple of hours. In summer an excursion boat could take you 13 km downstream to Puławy where buses and trains back to Lublin are frequent.

In the 16th century, Kazimierz Dolny (or 'Lower Kazimierz' to distinguish it from another Kazimierz at Kraków) grew rich as a trading centre, sending salt and grain down the river to Gdańsk on rafts to exchange for salted herring. Legend tells how the town's founder, Casimir the Great, kept his Jewish mistress Esterka in a nearby castle connected to his residence by tunnel. Right up to WW II the population of Kazimierz Dolny was predominantly Jewish, but all were killed.

Everything in Kazimierz Dolny is within walking distance of the burgher houses on Rynek. The engaging interior of the Mannerist **parochial church** (1613) above the square shelters one of the oldest organs (1620) in Poland. From the nearby ruins of the 14th century **castle** built by Casimir the Great you get a panoramic view of the town, river and vicinity. There's a **museum** (closed Monday) on ulica Senatorska, but chances are you'll prefer a bottle of the local Warka beer at the beer garden below the church. Lots of Polish tourists visit Kazimierz Dolny each summer, and in July the Polish Festival of Folk Singers and Bands is held here.

## ZAMOŚĆ

Zamość hasn't changed much since the 16th century when its chessboard street pattern was laid down by the Italian architect Bernardo Morando. The intact town square has an almost Latin American flavour with its long arcades and pastel shades.

Jan Zamoyski, chancellor and commander in chief of Renaissance Poland, founded Zamość in 1580 as an ideal urban settlement and impregnable barrier against Cossack and Tatar raids from the east. Its position on a busy trade route midway between Lublin and Ľvov prompted merchants of many nationalities to settle here. Zamość's fortifications withstood Cossack and Swedish attacks in 1648 and 1656 but by the 18th century its military value had dwindled. Later it was used as a military prison.

The Nazis renamed Zamość 'Himmlerstadt' and expelled the Polish inhabitants from 292 nearby villages. Their places were taken by German colonists to create an eastern bulwark for the Third Reich. Surrounded by parks and totally unspoiled today, Zamość is unique in Eastern Europe. Zamość doesn't get a lot of Western visitors so expect a few stares.

### Orientation

The bus and train stations are on opposite sides of Zamość, each about two km from the centre. The marketplace is on the north edge of the old town along ulica Przyrynek.

### Information

The tourist office (☎ 71006), at ulica Łukasińskiego 5a, is behind Hotel Renesans and may know of private rooms. It's open weekdays from 7 am to 4 pm, Saturdays from 9 am to noon. Otherwise try Orbis, ulica Grodzka 18.

### Things to See

You'll want to begin on **Rynek Wielki**, surrounded by Italian-style arcaded dwelling houses once owned by wealthy Greek and Armenian traders. The curving exterior stairway was added to the 16th century **town hall** in 1768. The House 'Under the Angel' (1634), Ormiańska 26 on Rynek Wielki, is a **museum** (closed Monday) which presents the opportunity to see a good collection of historical paintings plus the interior of an Armenian merchant's house. Just off the south-west corner of this square, at ulica Staszica 37, the famous German revolutionary, Rosa Luxemburg, was born in 1870.

Continue west a bit to **St Thomas' Collegiate Church** (1598), a three-aisled Mannerist basilica. South-west of this church is the old

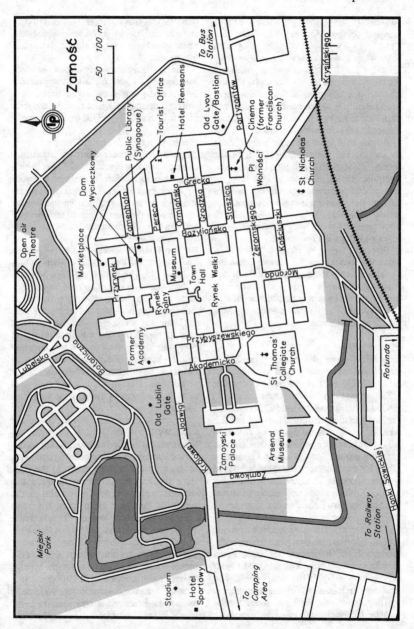

Zamość

0   50   100 m

To Bus Station

Krysińskiego

Public Library (Synagogue)
Tourist Office
Hotel Renesans
Old Lvov Gate/Bastion
Partyzantów
Cinema (former Franciscan Church)
Pl Wolności
Dom Wycieczkowy
St Nicholas' Church
Open air Theatre
Marketplace
Zamenhofa
Pereca
Ormiańska
Grodzka
Staszica
Grecka
Bazyliańska
Przyrynek
Żeromskiego
Kościuszki
Rynek Solny
Museum
Town Hall
Rynek Wielki
Moranda
Lubelska
Bolnicza
Former Academy
Przybyszewskiego
Akademicka
St Thomas' Collegiate Church
Old Lublin Gate
Jadwigi
Królowej
Zamoyski Palace
Arsenal Museum
Zamkowa
Rotunda
Miejski Park
Hanki Sawickiej
To Railway Station
To Camping Area
Stadium
Hotel Sportowy

Arsenal (1583), now a museum of old weapons (closed Monday). The **Zamoyski Palace** (1585) nearby lost much of its character when it was converted into a military hospital in 1831. North again on ulica Akademicka is the former **Academy** (1648). The fortifications opposite this building have been beautifully landscaped and made into a park extending east along the north side of Zamość to the **open-air theatre**.

Re-enter the town south from the theatre to see the old **synagogue** (1620) at the corner of Zamenhofa and Bazyliańska, now a public library. Do go inside. East on Zamenhofa you come again to the bastions of Zamość. Turn right and walk south towards **Lvov Gate** (1820) where you'll find a 16th century bastion with endless passageways which groups may enter.

Return to Rynek Wielki and follow ulica Moranda south from the square. Cross the park and go over the train tracks and a bridge till you get to the **Rotunda** (1831), a circular gun emplacement where the Nazis liquidated their victims. Today it's something of a Polish national shrine.

### Places to Stay

The *PTTK Dom Wycieczkowy* (☎ 2639), beside the old synagogue on ulica Zamenhofa, is US$2 per bed in a five-bed dorm or US$3 per bed in a four-bed dorm.

Other alternatives are the *PTTK Camping* (☎ 2499) on ulica Królowej Jadwigi, one km west of town, and the *Sportowy Hotel* (☎ 6011) behind the stadium between the camping ground and town (US$3 double or US$9 for an apartment, but usually booked by sports groups). The grey wooden building at ulica Królowej Jadwigi 7 across the street from the Sportowy operates as a youth hostel in July and August.

The tourist office may know of private rooms, otherwise the best place to stay is the modern *Hotel Renesans* (☎ 2001), ulica Grecka in the old city. A pleasant room with private bath is US$7/10 single/double. The hotel is often full so call first for reservations.

The three-storey, three-star *Hotel Jubilat* right beside the bus station is more expensive (US$9/14 single/double with bath), less convenient and rather dirty and unpleasant. These drawbacks mean it almost always has free rooms.

The *Hotel Pracowniczy No 4*, at ulica Młodzieżowa 6 just off ulica Partyzantów between the bus station and town, is a worker's dormitory which rents rooms with private bath and TV at US$4 per person.

### Places to Eat

Zamość's best is the *Hetmańska Restaurant*, ulica Staszica opposite Lvov Gate, which specialises in *żur* (cream soup with bits of meat) and pork roll à la Zamoyski. The atmosphere is jovial as shouts from the waiters mingle with the loud laughs of the clientele echoing from the domed ceilings.

### Getting There & Away

There are trains and buses between Lublin and Zamość. The train takes three hours to reach Zamość from Lublin on a roundabout route so you're better off coming by bus as these run every half-hour and are much faster.

Continuing south-east from Zamość is not easy as there's no direct train service and only a morning bus to Rzeszów (via Jarosław and Łańcut) and an afternoon bus to Jarosław. To or from Przemyśl you change at Jarosław. (Jarosław's bus and train stations are adjacent.) Book your ticket in advance.

### PRZEMYŚL

Przemyśl, on the Soviet border 80 km south-east of Rzeszów, has long been the boundary between Poland and the lands to the east. Here the San River curves between the wooded foothills of the Carpathians; on the slopes of the main town loom six huge churches and their towers. To guard the border area the Austrians fortified Przemyśl in 1873 by constructing gun emplacements and fortresses on the hilltops for a wide radius around the city, and fought bitterly against tsarist forces here in 1914-15.

Study a map of Eastern Europe and you'll realise that Przemyśl is very near the point where Poland, the USSR, Czechoslovakia,

Hungary and Romania meet, smack in the heart of the region. L'vov is only 92 km east and lots of Soviets sit around Przemyśl Railway Station waiting for their trains across the border amid huge piles of baggage. Przemyśl has something of the excitement of a border town – it would make the perfect setting for a post-Cold War novel (any romantics out there?).

Przemyśl is listed as the final destination of trains all over Poland, and a direct railway link from Romania via the USSR makes it a potential gateway to Poland. It's also a jumping-off point for the Bieszczady Mountains farther south. Be forewarned, there's nothing special to see here, but if you hang around long enough you may become a character in the novel yourself.

## Orientation

From Przemyśl Główny Railway Station go up the slope to ulica Mickiewicza, then right and straight ahead all the way into town. The bus station is on the opposite side of the railway tracks but between the two stations is an underpass.

## Information

Centrum Informacji 'San' is at ulica Dworskiego 2, on the corner of ulica Mickiewicza a block from the railway station.

## Things to See

Przemyśl is a city of churches and parks with Rynek at its heart. In the south-east corner of Rynek stands the Baroque **Franciscan Church** (1778), extraordinarily rich in paintings and decorative details. Just above this church is the **Muzeum Narodowe** (closed Monday) wich houses a good collection of Ukrainian folk costumes and icons. The **Carmelite Church** behind and above the museum is beautifully decorated and has a pulpit in the form of a fully rigged sailing

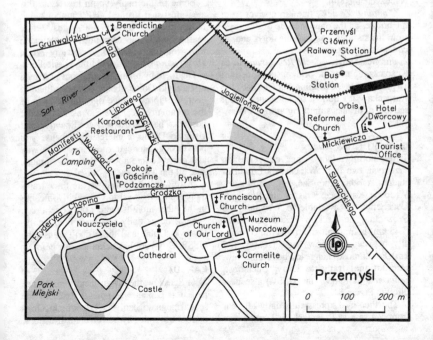

ship. Przemyśl's **cathedral** (1571) with its massive detached tower is to the west of here. There's a small **castle** on the wooded hilltop above the cathedral.

### Places to Stay & Eat

The old *Hotel Dworcowy*, also known as *Dom Wycieczkowy 'Przemysław'*, at ulica Dworskiego 4 opposite the railway station, offers large rooms at US$6/7 single/double with shared bath, but it's sometimes full.

*Dom Wycieczkowy 'Sportowy'*, Mickiewicza 30, a seven-minute walk from the station to the left, has rooms for US$5 double. The 'Sportowy' is large and clean, but you use the toilet down the hall.

Less conveniently accessible from the station but just on the edge of the old town is the teacher's hostel, *Dom Nauczyciela* (☎ 2768), 2nd floor, ulica Chopina 1, where rooms begin at US$3 per person. The *PTTK Pokoje Gościnne 'Podzamcze'*, nearby at ulica Waygarta 5, could be tried if Dom Nauczyciela is full.

*Camping 'Zamek'*, one km upriver from the bridge, on the opposite side of Przemyśl from the stations, has 15 bungalows and, of course, camping space.

For meals the *Karpacka Restaurant*, ulica Kościuszki 5 near the bridge, stays open till 10 pm daily. In the evening students pack the Karpacka – it's quite a social scene. You'll see lots of drunks stumbling around Przemyśl.

### Getting There & Away

Three main railway lines converge on Przemyśl, two from Warsaw via Lublin or Radom, another from Szczecin via Poznań, Wrocław, Katowice, Kraków and Rzeszów. Couchettes are available to Wrocław and Szczecin. The Kraków-Przemyśl service (245 km) is frequent and trains run continually between Rzeszów and Przemyśl (87 km). For Zamość change to a bus at Jarosław. International trains to L'vov, Bucharest, Sofia and Varna (via the USSR) also pass through Przemyśl.

The Pieniny Express runs daily all year from Warsaw to Przemyśl (542 km, seven

hours), departing from Warsaw in the afternoon, Przemyśl in the middle of the night. The train travels via Kraków Główny and Rzeszów and reservations are required.

Orbis, Plac Legionów 1 in front of the railway station, can answer complicated questions about trains, make reservations and book couchettes.

### THE BIESZCZADY MOUNTAINS

The enormous mountain pastures of this sparsely populated region in the south-east corner of Poland offer hiking in summer and cross-country skiing in winter. After WW II Ukrainian nationalists carried on a guerilla war here for several years to resist the region's final incorporation into Poland. In one 1947 incident they ambushed a Polish military convoy and killed the 2nd Army commander, General Karol Świerczewski, the renowned 'General Walter' who had led the International Brigades during the Spanish Civil War.

Some of the many youth hostels in this area are listed in the IYHF handbook, but most only open in July and August. Other tourist hostels and camping grounds exist; look for the 1:75,000 *Bieszczady Mapa Turystyczna* which lays out the possibilities.

Get there by taking a train from Przemyśl to Ustrzyki Dolne, then a bus from there to Ustrzyki Górne village right in the heart of the mountains near the Slovak and Soviet borders. The train trip between Przemyśl and Ustrzyki Dolne is interesting because you pass through Soviet territory most of the way and guards come aboard the train to make sure all the windows are closed.

In July and August there are three trains daily from Przemyśl to Ustrzyki Dolne, but in the other months there's only one a day. Several buses daily run from Przemyśl to Ustrzyki Dolne and these don't transit the USSR. Buy your bus ticket the day before.

### ŁAŃCUT

Near Rzeszów, the magnificent Renaissance palace at Łańcut was built in 1629 by the feudal magnate Stanisław Lubomirski. Originally surrounded by powerful fortifications, these were dismantled in the 18th century. Towards the end of the 19th century the Potocki family rebuilt the palace in French Baroque style.

In 1944, just a week before the arrival of the Soviet army, Count Alfred Potocki fled to Switzerland behind 11 railway cars loaded with artworks stripped from the palace. You wouldn't know it, however, from the rich furnishings in the present **Museum of Interior Decoration**. On the far side of the park is a pavilion where the antique **carriage collection** is kept.

Tickets to both museums must be purchased in a separate building outside the compound. Ask for the *kasy*. The palace closes at 2 pm some days and all day Monday and Tuesday, but the park is open daily till sunset. In May a Festival of Chamber Music is held in the palace.

At the other end of the block south from the kasy is an old Jewish **synagogue**, now a museum (it's the two-storey yellow building on the corner).

### Places to Stay & Eat

One wing of the palace is now the *Hotel 'Zamkowy'* (☎ 2671) with rooms for US$6 double/triple without bath, US$16/20 with bath (no singles) – a great place but often full. The *'Zamkowa' Restaurant* behind the hotel specialises in *żur słowiański* (cream soup with bits of meat) and *omlet z serem i sosem czekoladowym* (omelette with cream cheese and chocolate). Try the excellent Leżajsk beer brewed just north of Łańcut.

The *PTTK Dom Wycieczkowy* is at ulica Dominikańska 1 in a corner of Łańcut's main square (Rynek).

### Getting There & Away

Łańcut is on the main railway line between Przemyśl and Kraków. Buses run from Łańcut to Rzeszów several times an hour. The bus station adjoins the park but the railway station is about two km away (take a taxi). A town map is posted inside the bus station.

## RZESZÓW

Rzeszów could be useful as a base from which to visit the palace at Łańcut, 17 km east. The historic centre of Rzeszów is presently undergoing extensive restoration which will greatly enhance its appeal as a tourist centre in future years. The massive housing projects *(osiedle)* encircling Rzeszów have all been created since 1945, a dramatic example of what Communism did for a previously depressed area.

### Orientation

The bus and train stations are adjacent to one another on the north side of the old town. Plac Farny is Rzeszów's hub with Rynek, the main square, and ulica 3 Maja, the main street, nearby.

### Information

Informacja Turystyczna is at ulica Asnyka 10 near the stations. The PTTK Tourist Office, ulica Matejki 2, is beside the youth hostel on Rynek.

### Things to See

The **Bernardine Church** (1629) on ulica 1 Maja contains a fine late-Renaissance altar. From the **Parish Church** on Plac Farny follow ulica 3 Maja south to the **museum** (closed Monday) in the 17th century Piarist Monastery at No 19. Farther south beyond the **Lubomirskich Palace** is a large 17th century **fortress** used by the Austrians as a jail in the early 20th century.

Rzeszów's 16th century **town hall** (rebuilt in 1897) is in the centre of Rynek and nearby at Rynek 6 is an **Ethnological Museum**. Also on Rynek is a statue of Tadeusz Kościuszko who fought the Russians for Polish independence in 1795. Two old **synagogues** are on ulica Bożnicza just north of Rynek, one of which is now an Arts Centre, the other an archive.

### Places to Stay

The *Hotel PTTK*, at Plac Kilinskiego 6, is right in front of the stations and has simple singles/doubles with shared bath for US$4/6. Nearby *Hotel Polonia*, ulica Grottgera 16,

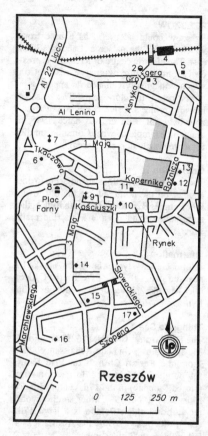

1 Hotel Rzeszów
2 Bus Station
3 Hotel Polonia
4 Railway Station
5 Hotel PTTK
6 National Theatre
7 Bernardine Church
8 Post Office
9 Parish Church
10 Old Town Hall
11 Youth Hostel
12 Old Town Synagogue
13 New Town Synagogue
14 Museum
15 Lubomirskich Palace
16 Fortress (former jail)
17 Filharmonia

Rzeszów

0    125    250 m

speciality such as roast goose. *Hortex,* ulica Słowackiego 18 behind the old town hall, is a great place to enjoy coffee, ice cream and cakes.

### Entertainment

Rzeszów's modern concert hall *(filharmonia),* ulica Szopena 30, is in the park near the fortress. Every three years a Festival of Polish Folk Groups Resident Abroad is held in Rzeszów.

### Getting There & Away

Rzeszów is on the main railway lines from Przemyśl to Warsaw and Kraków. For Lublin and Zamość take a bus. Orbis, Plac Wolności 2 beside the New Town Synagogue, will have train tickets and times.

### NOWY SĄCZ

Nowy Sącz (Neusandez), pronounced 'nove-sonch', sits in a wide valley among the low hills of the Beskid Range at the junction of the Dunajec and Kamienica rivers. Apple orchards fill the surrounding countryside. Founded in the 13th century on a medieval trade route from Hungary, Nowy Sącz became famous in the mid-15th century for its uniquely Polish school of Gothic painting. Today the town offers another chance to

has singles/doubles/triples for US$4/7/9 (shared bath). *Hotel Rzeszów,* Aleje 22 Lipca 2, an 11-storey high-rise across from a huge socialist monument, charges US$29/44 single/double with bath.

The youth hostel is at Rynek 25 above Alka Night Club, right in the heart of the old town.

### Places to Eat

The *Bar 'U Wojciecha'* milk bar is downstairs at the *Hotel PTTK,* but the entrance is around the corner. The *Rzeszowska Restaurant,* at ulica Kościuszki 9, serves local get off the beaten track and a good base for exploring the surrounding countryside. With direct train service to/from Czechoslovakia and Hungary it's a perfect gateway to Poland.

## Orientation

Nowy Sącz has two railway stations: the main station on the line from Budapest to Warsaw (via Tarnów) and the much smaller Nowy Sącz Miasto Station on the line from Zakopane (via Chabówka). If you want to leave your luggage you'll have to go to the main station but if you're arriving from Zakopane and want to go to the Panorama Hotel get out at Nowy Sącz Miasto.

The main railway station is two km south of the old town (Stare Miasto) but bus No 7 connects the two fairly frequently. Detailed city maps (with bus routes) are displayed at all city bus stops in Nowy Sącz.

## Information

Try the receptions of the Orbis-Beskid or Panorama hotels.

## Things to See

In the centre of Nowy Sącz's old town square, Rynek, is the 19th century **town hall**. The **Dom Gotycki Museum**, ulica Lwowska 3 near Rynek, has a collection of old Orthodox icons and other artworks (closed Monday). **St Margaret's Collegiate Church** (1446) is behind the museum. An old **synagogue** (1746) at ulica Berka Joselewicza 12 on the north side of the old town is now an art gallery (closed Monday and Tuesday).

An **Ethnographic Village Museum** or 'skansen' is about two km beyond the PTTK Hotel (buses No 14 or 15).

## Places to Stay

The eight-storey *Orbis-Beskid Hotel*, a block down from the railway station, is US$15/28 single/double with private bath and breakfast.

For cheaper accommodation try the *PTTK Hotel*, ulica Jamnicka 2, three km north-east of the railway station (US$7 single or double). Walk straight ahead from the station

to the Orbis-Beskid, turn right and follow ulica Limanowskiego and its continuation, ulica Królowej Jadwigi, east to a river which you cross on a footbridge. The hotel (open all year) is in a camping ground (open mid-May to September) just across the bridge. Buses No 14 and 15 from the station pass the hotel.

A more convenient place to stay, just off Rynek in the old town, is the *Hotel Panorama*, ulica Romanowskiego 4a overlooking the Dunajec River. Rooms with shower are US$8/10 single/double. The hotel reception also rents private rooms in town at US$2 per person.

## Places to Eat

Unlike most of Nowy Sącz's restaurants, which are stuffy, dark and full of smoke, the one in the Panorama Hotel is pleasant and airy. Its menu (in Polish only) is extensive and the food good. Try the *rosół*, a bouillon with little dumplings stuffed with meat.

The *Staropolska Restaurant*, Rynek 28, is an elegant place to dine. Near the railway station there's a cheap milk bar at ulica Batorego 81 between the Orbis-Beskid Hotel and the station.

## Getting There & Away

The Cracovia Express runs daily between Kraków and Budapest via Nowy Sącz, Presov and Kosice, departing from Nowy Sącz southbound in the evening and arriving in Nowy Sącz from Czechoslovakia in the very early morning. If you need to change money at that hour, try the nearby Orbis-Beskid Hotel. Tickets and reservations for this train are available from Orbis, ulica Długosza 10.

The Tatry Express departs Warsaw in the early morning reaching Nowy Sącz (464 km) six hours later. For the return the Tatry leaves Nowy Sącz in the afternoon. The Pieniny Express does the opposite, leaving Warsaw in the afternoon and Nowy Sącz in the very early morning. Both trains travel via Kraków, though the Tatry calls at Kraków Płaszów only, the Pieniny at Kraków

Główny as well. The Pieniny runs daily all year but the Tatry is seasonal, so check. Reservations are required.

To go from Nowy Sącz to Zakopane by train you must change at Chabówka. The train trip from Nowy Sącz to Chabówka is quite beautiful as you cross the green wooded hills through a patchwork of forests and fields. This train is often pulled by a steam locomotive.

## STARY SĄCZ

If you find Nowy Sącz too fast, a 15-minute train ride eight km south-west will bring you to Stary Sącz, a peaceful, unspoiled town of single-storey dwellings with high, sloping roofs lining the quiet, cobbled streets. In one corner of the central square peasants park their carts and tie up their horses beside a rustic open-air market. A low, forested hill provides a backdrop for sleepy little Stary Sącz.

### Things to See

Stary Sącz originated in 1257 when a Hungarian princess founded a **Convent of St Clare** here. The highlight of the present 18th century convent church is a pulpit (1671) surrounded by a carved tree growing from a reclining figure of Jesse. In the building opposite the church is an art gallery with recent paintings from the area. The Stary Sącz Festival of Old Music is held in the convent during the last week in June each year.

The only other specific sight in town is the **Regional Museum**, Rynek 6 (Tuesday to Sunday 10 am to 1 pm), with a dusty accumulation of old photos and local artifacts.

### Places to Stay & Eat

Other than a summertime youth hostel in a school beside the parish church, there's nowhere to stay so make it a day trip from Nowy Sącz. Lots of simple places to have lunch are found around the main square.

### Getting There & Away

You can come by train or frequent bus from Nowy Sącz. The buses arrive/depart Stary Sącz's central square. The railway station is a pleasant 10-minute walk from the centre.

## THE TATRA MOUNTAINS & ZAKOPANE

Poland is a flat, open land of lakes and rivers, but in the south the Sudeten and Carpathian mountain ranges break through the plains. The Tatra Mountains 100 km south of Kraków are the highest knot of these ranges with elevations averaging 2000 metres. Here, folded granite and limestone were shaped by glaciation to create a true Alpine environment. The Czechoslovak border runs along the ridges of these jagged Carpathian peaks.

The entire Polish portion of the range is included in Tatra National Park (217 sq km, entry free). Zakopane, the regional centre, is known as the winter capital of Poland due to its popularity as a ski resort. Because so many tourists come here, everything is very well organised and there are lots of facilities. For summer visitors it's a chance to do some hiking and meet the Poles in an unstructured environment. Many students come here on holidays, and your conversations with them may be as memorable as the rugged landscape itself.

### Orientation

Zakopane, at an altitude of 800 to 1000 metres, will be your base. The bus and railway stations are adjacent on the north-east edge of town. From the railway station, cross the street and take ulica Kościuszki past the bus station straight up into town. You'll pass the tourist office on the right, then Hotel Giewont before reaching the post office, your reference point in Zakopane.

Ulica Krupówki, Zakopane's pedestrian mall, is always jammed with throngs of parading Polish tourists attired in trendy ski or hiking gear. The cable car to Mt Kasprowy Wierch is at Kuźnice, four km south of the stations. 'Rondo', a roundabout midway between the railway station, or town, and Kuźnice, is another good reference point.

The left-luggage office in the railway station is open around the clock. If you want to leave your luggage somewhere in town,

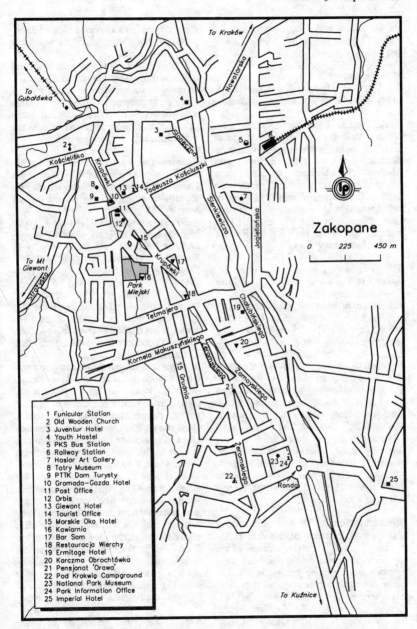

Zakopane

0    225    450 m

1  Funicular Station
2  Old Wooden Church
3  Juventur Hotel
4  Youth Hostel
5  PKS Bus Station
6  Railway Station
7  Hasior Art Gallery
8  Tatry Museum
9  PTTK Dom Turysty
10 Gromada–Gazda Hotel
11 Post Office
12 Orbis
13 Giewont Hotel
14 Tourist Office
15 Morskie Oko Hotel
16 Kawiarnia
17 Bar Sam
18 Restauracja Wierchy
19 Ermitage Hotel
20 Karczma Obrochtówka
21 Pensjonat 'Orawa'
22 Pod Krokwią Campground
23 National Park Museum
24 Park Information Office
25 Imperial Hotel

the cloakroom beside the restaurant in the PTTK Dom Turysty is open from 8 am to 6 pm.

## Information

The TPT 'Tatry' tourist information office is at ulica Kościuszki 7 on the way in from the stations.

The Cultural Information Centre, ulica Kościuszki 4, will know of any local events including the Festival of Highland Culture in September and the Karol Szymanowski Musical Days in October.

The Tatra National Park Information Office, ulica Chałubińskiego 42 at 'Rondo', sells good maps and can answer hiking questions, often in English. The national park museum among the trees just behind this office sells the same maps.

## Things to See & Do

**Zakopane** Founded in 1888, the **Tatra Museum** (closed Monday and Tuesday) is hidden among the trees behind Dom Turysty just down from the post office. Downstairs are displays on the folklore of the region including paintings on glass, peasant costumes, farm implements and dwelling interiors. Upstairs is natural history, including an excellent relief map of the Tatras. From here walk down ulica Krupówki and turn left on ulica Kościeliska to reach an old **wooden church** (1851) with a pioneer cemetery behind.

Return to the corner of ulica Krupówki and proceed west under the overpass to the **funicular railway** (built in 1938) up Mt Gubałówka (1123 metres). The last return trip is at 8 pm (US$0.65 return trip). There's a fine view from the top.

**Mountain Climbing** The best thing to do in Zakopane is to climb **Mt Giewont** (1909 metres). Walk or take a taxi a couple of km up ulica Strążyska to the trailhead, then follow a broad track up through the forest to some huts where there's a small tea shop. Here one goes right and circles around, climbing steeply to the shoulder of the mountain (red trail). From the cross atop

Giewont you get a sweeping view of Zakopane and the Tatras, a truly magnificent spectacle on a clear day.

Return to Zakopane along the blue trail down the Kondratowa Valley (easier going), finishing at the cable car terminus at Kuźnice. Refreshments are sold at the *Hala Kondratowa Hostel*. The whole circle trip can be done in about six hours without too much difficulty.

**Kuźnice** The work of Polish avant-garde artist Władysław Hasior can be seen at the **Hasior Art Gallery**, ulica Jagiellońska 7 up the hill from the railway station (closed Monday and Tuesday).

For an introduction to the natural history of this area visit the **Przyrodnicze Museum of Tatra National Park** (open Tuesday to Sunday 9 am to 2 pm) in the forest just below 'Rondo' on the road up to the Kuźnice cable car.

Since it opened in 1935, almost every Polish tourist has made the **cable-car trip** from Kuźnice to the summit of **Mt Kasprowy Wierch** (1985 metres) where you can stand with one foot in Poland and the other in Czechoslovakia. There's a great view from here, clouds permitting, and also a restaurant which opens at 9 am. Many people return to Zakopane on foot down the Gąsienicowa Valley, and the most intrepid walk the ridges all the way across to Morskie Oko Lake via Pięć Stawów, a very strenuous hike taking a full day in good weather.

In June, July and August the cable car operates from 7.30 am to 8 pm; other months it's more like 8 am to 5 pm. Tickets are US$3 return trip until 1 pm, US$2 after 1 pm. When you buy a return trip ticket you automatically get a reservation for a return two hours later. Advance cable car tickets are sold at Orbis, ulica Krupówki 22 beside the post office (3rd floor, room 6). You can also usually get one at the terminal itself, though you risk running into a long line and having to wait an hour or more to go up, so it's best to book through Orbis the day before.

**Morskie Oko** One of the highlights of a visit

to Zakopane is the bus trip to Morskie Oko Lake (the name means 'eye of the sea' from a legendary tunnel said to connect the lake to the Adriatic). It's best to book return tickets a few days in advance at the bus station, although tickets are often available on the bus itself (you want the 'Polana Palenica' bus). A couple of hours at the lake is enough.

From Polana Palenica it's still nine km (not steep) to the lake, though horse carts are available at US$1 each way. At Włosienica, 20 minutes before the lake, is a restaurant and behind it about 500 metres straight up to the left is a camping ground. At the lakeside itself is a large tea shop serving *bigos* (boiled cabbage).

A stone path runs around this mountain-girdled glacial lake – a lovely 40-minute stroll. You can climb to an upper lake, Czarny Staw, in another 20 minutes or so. **Mt Rysy**, the highest point in the Polish Tatras (2499 metres), rises directly above this upper lake. In late summer, when the snow has finally gone, you can climb it in about four hours from the tea shop. Lenin climbed Mt Rysy in 1913.

**Side Trip West** Take a bus (they depart frequently) west from Zakopane to **Chochołów**, a very interesting village with large log farmhouses along the roadside for quite a distance. It's like an open-air museum of traditional architecture, except that all the houses are inhabited and the farming people have retained their age-old ways. There's a small museum by the store opposite the church, and you can walk around the village.

On the way back to Zakopane get off at Kiry and walk up the Kościeliska Valley to the Hala Ornak Hostel. A broad stone road runs right up the valley. From the hostel you can climb the black trail to idyllic Smreczyński Lake in about 15 minutes. The orange trail connects Hala Ornak to the Chochołowska Valley, making a circle trip possible. Buses from Kiry back to Zakopane are frequent.

**Activities**

From May to September Orbis offers white-water rafting on the Dunajec River for US$7 per person, but this must be booked about a week in advance. Try doing this through an Orbis office in some other Polish city.

**Places to Stay**

**Camping** The camping ground *Pod Krokwią* (open June to September) on ulica Żeromskiego between town and Kuźnice has seven large bungalows, each containing several double and triple rooms (US$4 double without bath, US$5 double with bath), but they're often full.

**Hostels** Zakopane has a convenient year-round youth hostel at ulica Nowotarska 45 (☎ 66203). From the railway station walk straight up ulica Kościuszki to a bridge across a small stream. Here, turn right and follow ulica Sienkiewicza down to the corner of ulica Nowotarska, an easy 10-minute walk (the hostel is down the driveway in front of you – its sign is pointed the wrong way).

Alternatively the *Dom Wycieczkowy Kuźnice* in the back of the restaurant at the Kuźnice (lower) cable car station is US$4 double or US$2 for a bed in a three or four-bed dorm.

**Private Rooms** The cheapest option by far is a private room from the TPT 'Tatry' Biuro Zakwaterowań, ulica Kościuszki 7 (open daily 8 am to 8 pm). These rooms are US$2/3 single/double (1st category), but they only rent for stays of four nights or more. Often no singles are available. In a pinch, a taxi driver would probably be able to find you an unofficial room in a private home.

The Orbis office (3rd floor, room 6) beside the post office arranges room and board at small *pensjonaty* in Zakopane for about US$7 per person. The *Orbis Pensjonat 'Orawa'*, ulica Żeromskiego 23, towards town from the camping ground, controls rooms in several houses in this area. Some of the Orbis pensjonaty, such as those on ulica Wierchowa, are far from the centre and only worth considering if you have transport.

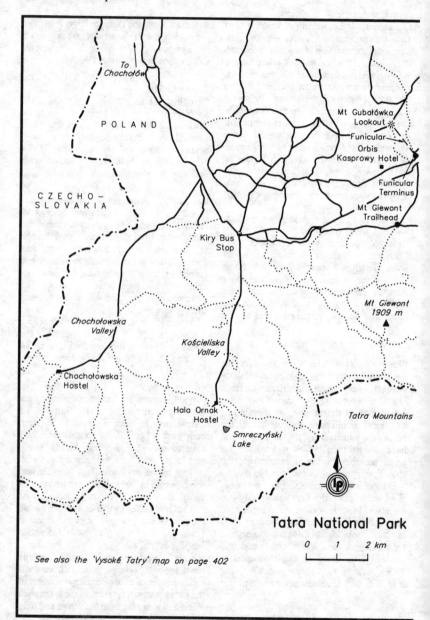

To Chochołów

POLAND

CZECHO-
SLOVAKIA

Mt Gubałówka
Lookout

Funicular

Orbis
Kasprowy Hotel

Funicular
Terminus

Mt Giewont
Trailhead

Kiry Bus
Stop

Mt Giewont
1909 m

Chochołowska
Valley

Kościeliska
Valley

Chochołowska
Hostel

Hala Ornak
Hostel

Smreczyński
Lake

Tatra Mountains

Tatra National Park

0    1    2 km

See also the 'Vysoké Tatry' map on page 402

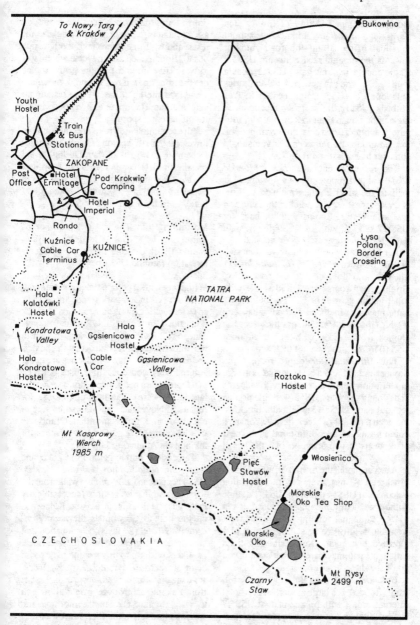

**Hotels** The *Dom Turysty PTTK*, ulica Gen Zaruskiego 5, is a few minutes' walk from the post office along the road running towards the mountains. Rooms are US$5/8 single/double without bath, US$11 double with bath, or you can get a bed in dormitories with four beds (US$3), eight beds (US$2) or 28 beds (US$1.50). There's a restaurant in the building open 8 am to 9.30 pm. Unfortunately Dom Turysty is so swamped by excited groups of pre-teens that you should consider it as a last resort only.

The recently renovated *Hotel Morskie Oko* on ulica Krupówki, just a few minutes' walk up the street from the main post office, is the cheapest regular hotel in the centre so it's usually full. Rooms without bath are US$4/7 single/double or US$9 double with bath. The hotel restaurant is overpriced.

For only a few dollars more you can stay at the modern *Hotel 'Gromada-Gazda'*, ulica Zaruskiego 6 next to the post office. Bright, clean rooms are US$8 single with toilet but no shower or US$14 double with bath, breakfast included – good value. The *'Orbis-Giewont' Hotel* across the street has singles from US$9 to 17, doubles from US$10 to 28, breakfast not included.

The *'Juventur-Słoneczny' Hotel*, ulica Słoneczna 2a off ulica Nowotarska, is a large modern hotel that caters mostly to students and young people (US$5/9 single/double without bath, US$8/13 with bath, breakfast included). It's only a block from Zakopane's youth hostel, so keep it in mind as the next place to try if you arrive to find the hostel full.

A private hotel, the *Ermitage*, ulica Chałubińskiego 8, has rooms with individual balconies at US$14 double or US$11 double without a balcony, breakfast included. It's in a large residential building a 15-minute walk from the post office or stations – sort of a glorified *pensjonat*. Downstairs is a good restaurant you may care to visit even if you don't stay here.

*Hotel Imperial*, ulica Balzera 1 up the hill from 'Rondo', is a large modern sports hotel offering rooms with private bath at US$5/7 single/double. It's such a good deal that Polish tour groups often pack the rooms, so ask a tourist office to help you call ahead for reservations. To get there take the Kuźnice bus to 'Rondo' then ask any local which way to walk (five minutes). Some of the rooms on the top floor have splendid mountain views and the hotel has a large restaurant, café and bar. The Imperial is a good choice if you have transport.

All accommodation rates are considerably lower in the off season, October to mid-December and April to May. During the ski season (mid-December to March) prices double. Zakopane is one of Poland's most popular tourist centres, so on weekends and holidays everything could be full.

**Mountain Huts** There are a number of 'mountain huts' (large hostels) in Tatra National Park offering inexpensive accommodation (around US$3 per person) for the hiker. All serve basic meals. The hostels are in high demand at certain times and camping isn't allowed in the park (there are bears!), so before setting out it's a good idea to check with the Biuro Obsługi Ruchu Turystycznego (PTTK), ulica Krupówki 12 next to the Tatra Museum. It controls all the hostels and will know for sure which ones are open. Alternatively you could just take pot luck that there'll be a bed for you (don't arrive too late in this case). The huts often close for repairs in November and May so be sure to check during those months. Otherwise they're open all year. The best weather for hiking is in August.

The easiest 'hut' to get to from Zakopane is the giant *Hala Kalatówki Hostel* (84 beds, US$4 per person), a 30-minute walk from the Kuźnice cable car station (accessible by local bus). Half an hour beyond Kalatówki on the trail to Giewont is the *Hala Kondratowa Hostel* (20 beds). For location and atmosphere it's great, but note the small size.

Hikers wishing to traverse the park could begin at the *Roztoka Hostel* (96 beds), accessible via the Morskie Oko bus. An early start from Zakopane, however, would allow you to visit Morskie Oko in the morning and continue through to the *Pięć Stawów Hostel*

(70 beds), a couple of hours' walk on the blue trail over a high pass from Morskie Oko. Pięć Stawów (Five Lakes) is by far the most scenically located hostel in the Polish Tatras.

A good day's walk west of Pięć Stawów is the *Hala Gąsienicowa Hostel* (100 beds), from which one can return to Zakopane. In the western part of the park are the *Ornak* (75 beds) and *Chochołowska* (161 beds) hostels, connected by trail.

## Places to Eat

Don't wait too late to eat: restaurants close early and after 7.30 pm all you may be able to find is ice cream. Decide beforehand where you're going to have dinner and check the closing time or reservation requirements. About the cheapest self-service is the *Sam Bar*, ulica Krupówki 71, but it's not recommended.

Zakopane's finest restaurant is in the *Hotel 'Orbis-Giewont'* diagonally across from the post office. The menu is in English and German and there's even cold beer. Try a dish with *bryndza* (sheep cheese). The café serves a good breakfast. Though theoretically it's open until 11.30 pm, the head waiter may deny you entry unless you have a reservation.

*Restauracja Wierchy,* ulica Tetmajera 2 at Krupówki, has regional dishes, though you must struggle with a Polish menu and they stop serving at 7 pm. It's a good enough place for lunch. From 8 pm to 2 am the Wierchy is a disco (US$2 admission plus US$2 consumption).

A folklore-style restaurant worth seeking out is the *Karczma Obrochtówka,* ulica Kraszewskiego 10, a small street running between Zamoyskiego and Chałubińskiego streets halfway between 'Rondo' and town (coming from town, turn left at ulica Zamoyskiego 13a). Traditional Polish dishes are served in the basement of a large log house (Tuesday to Sunday noon to 9 pm).

The upstairs dining room of the *Gubałówka Restaurant* beside the upper funicular station has a limited menu but it's formal and expensive enough to discourage the hordes of adolescents from entering. Crowd control is also exercised by the poorly marked entrance – just keep looking. A speciality here is *placek po zbójnicku* (two large potato pancakes topped with goulash). A 10% service charge is added to the menu prices.

**Cafés** The *Kawiarnia Kmicic* near City Park just off ulica Krupówki is a cozy little place for coffee, cakes and ice cream in the afternoon or a couple of drinks in the evening (open from 9 am to 9 pm). The warmed 'Tatrzańska Jesień' wine will do your heart good on a cold night. The menu is in English and German.

## Things to Buy

Street vendors in Zakopane sell woollen sweaters, caps, gloves and socks at very reasonable prices. Bargaining should get you 25% off the first price.

## Getting There & Away

The Sawa and Tatry express trains (reservations required) take just over six hours to cover the 444 km from Warsaw to Zakopane, departing Warsaw in the early morning, Zakopane in the afternoon. The Sawa passes Kraków Główny in the late morning on its way to Zakopane. Both trains are seasonal, so check to see if they're operating at the time you wish to travel.

From Kraków to Zakopane (147 km) it's faster to take a bus than the train, but try to book advance tickets at the bus station. Overnight trains arrive from Wrocław and Warsaw. Couchettes and sleepers to these cities are easily reserved at Orbis, ulica Krupówki 22 beside the post office, or at the railway station. Bus service is nonexistent from Zakopane to Częstochowa and the connections by train are bad (you arrive late at night from Zakopane).

There's a direct Volanbus twice a week from Zakopane to Budapest (US$8, nine hours) on Thursday and Sunday, an excellent way to get from Poland to Hungary (Czech transit visa required for some). Get your ticket from the driver (reservations not possible).

Pedestrians with onward visas may use the

Łysa Polana highway border crossing off the road to Morskie Oko. From Łysa Polana there's a road around to Tatranska Lomnica via Zdiar (30 km). In perfect summer weather, rugged backpackers with an early start could hike from the border over mountain passes well above 2000 metres to the Zbojnicka or Teryho chalets in Slovakia. However, for many reasons this route is probably more practical northbound than southbound. See the Vysoké Tatry section in the Czechoslovakia chapter of this book for details.

### Getting Around

There are buses to Kuźnice several times an hour from stand No 7 at the bus station. Buy your ticket inside the terminal. A taxi from the centre of Zakopane to Kuźnice will be about US$2.

## KRAKÓW

Kraków (population 800,000) is the third-largest city in Poland. Over a millennium ago Prince Krak founded a settlement on Wawel Hill, above a bend of the legendary Vistula River. Boleslav the Brave built a cathedral here in 1020 and transferred the capital here from Poznań shortly after. The kings of Poland ruled from Wawel Castle until 1596, but even afterwards Polish royalty continued to be crowned and buried in Wawel Cathedral.

At this crossing of trade routes from Western Europe to Byzantium and from Southern Europe to the Baltic, a large medieval city developed. Kraków was devastated during the 13th century Tatar invasions, but rebuilt. In January 1945 a sudden encircling manoeuvre by the Soviet army forced the Germans to quickly evacuate the city, and Kraków was saved from destruction. Today Stare Miasto, the old town, harbours world-class museums and towering churches while Kazimierz, the now silent Jewish quarter, tells of a sadder recent history, and Auschwitz is close by.

Kraków was a medieval students' town. Jagiellonian University, established at Kraków in 1364, is Poland's oldest; Copernicus studied here. It's still the second-largest university in Poland (after Warsaw) and 10% of the present population are higher education students. This is the one Polish city you simply cannot miss.

### Orientation

The main train and bus stations are next to one another just outside the north-east corner of the old town. Ulica Pawia, with the tourist office and several hotels, flanks the stations to the west. To walk into town follow the crowds into the underpass at the corner of Pawia and Lubicz, then bear slightly right and lose yourself in the old streets until you come out on Rynek Główny, Kraków's glorious Market Square.

Trains on the line Przemyśl-Wrocław usually call at Kraków Płaszów Railway Station south of the centre, not Kraków Główny. If there isn't a connecting train leaving immediately for the main station, take tram No 3 or 13 from ulica Wielicka, a few minutes' walk straight ahead from Kraków Płaszów, to 'Poczta Główna', the main post office on Westerplatte.

### Information

There's an excellent tourist information office at ulica Pawia 8, a few minutes' walk from the stations. They'll sell you maps and brochures, and direct you to the accommodation service next door.

**Consulates** There are three: the Austrian Consulate, ulica Św Jana 12, the US Consulate (☎ 22 9764), ulica Stolarska 9, and the French Consulate, ulica Stolarska 15.

### Things to See

**Around Market Square** You'll probably want to begin your visit on Rynek Główny, Kraków's wonderful Market Square, the largest medieval town square in Europe. It was here on 24 March 1794 that Tadeusz Kościuszko proclaimed a nationwide armed uprising to save Poland from partition. The 16th century Renaissance **Cloth Hall** (Sukiennice) dominates the square and there's a large craft market under the arches.

Upstairs is a museum (closed Monday and Tuesday) of 19th century paintings, including several well-known historical works by Jan Matejko.

The 14th century **Church of Our Lady** fills the north-east corner of Rynek Główny. The huge main altarpiece (1489) by Wit Stwosz (Veit Stoss) of Nuremberg is the finest sculptural work in Poland. The altar's wings are opened daily at noon. A trumpet call sounded hourly from one of the church towers recalls a 13th century trumpeter cut short by a Tatar arrow.

On the opposite side of the Cloth Hall is the 14th century **Town Hall Tower**, complete with a café serving hot honey wine *(miód)* in the cellar. The town hall itself was demolished in 1820. The nude photography shows at the **Muzeum Historii Fotografii**, Rynek Główny 17, attract big crowds.

Take ulica Św Anny (the street running west from the corner of the square closest to the tower) a block to the 15th century Collegium Maius, the oldest surviving part of **Jagiellonian University**. Enter the Gothic courtyard. Also visit the **City Historical Museum** at Rynek Główny 35 (closed Monday and Tuesday).

Go north from the Cloth Hall to the **art gallery** at ulica Św Jana 14 which specialises in pornographic comic books. Farther up at Św Jana 17 is the **Czartoryski Art Museum** (closed Wednesday and Thursday), the collection of a wealthy Polish family donated to Kraków over a century ago. The most famous works here are Leonardo da Vinci's *Lady with an Ermine* and Rembrandt's *Landscape with the Good Samaritan*. Raphael's *Portrait of a Young Man*, stolen from this museum during WW II, has never been recovered. Captions are provided in French.

**The Royal Way** Around the corner from the Czartoryski Museum on ulica Pijarska is a remaining stretch of the medieval city walls which once surrounded Kraków, where the greenbelt is today. Go through **St Florian's Gate** (1307) to the **Barbican**, a defensive bastion built in 1498. Kraków's **Royal Way** runs south from St Florian's Gate to Wawel Castle.

Re-enter the city and follow ulica Floriańska south to Rynek Główny, then south again on ulica Grodzka. At Plac Wszystkich Świętych, where the tram tracks cut across Grodzka, are two large 13th century **monastic churches**, Dominican on the east and Franciscan on the west. Cardinal Karol Wojtyła resided in the Episcopal Palace across the street from the Franciscan Church for a dozen years until he was elected Pope John Paul II in 1978. South on Grodzka is the 17th century Baroque Jesuit **Sts Peter & Paul Church**. The Romanesque **Church of St Andrew** (1086) alongside was the only building in Kraków which resisted the Tatar attack of 1241, and those who had taken refuge inside survived.

Continue south another block, then take the lane on the right (ulica Podzamcze) which leads to the ramp up to **Wawel Castle**, Poland's Kremlin. The huge equestrian statue of Tadeusz Kościuszko above this ramp was a donation of the people of Dresden to replace an earlier statue destroyed by the Nazis. **Wawel Cathedral** (1364) will be on your left as you enter. Before going inside, buy a ticket at the small office opposite (closed Sunday morning) to climb the bell tower and visit the main crypt. For four centuries this church served as the coronation and burial place of Polish royalty, and 100 kings and queens are interred in the crypt. The Sigismund Chapel (1539), the closed one on the south side with the gold dome, is considered to be the finest Renaissance construction in Poland.

The 16th century **main palace** (closed Monday) is behind the cathedral. The tickets you buy at the gate will admit you to the different museum departments arrayed around the great Italian Renaissance courtyard. Wawel is famous for its 16th century Flemish tapestry collection, but there is much else of interest including the crown jewels and armoury. The castle's greatest treasure is the 13th century Piast coronation sword, the 'Szczerbiec'. Many of the exhibits were evacuated to Canada in 1939 where

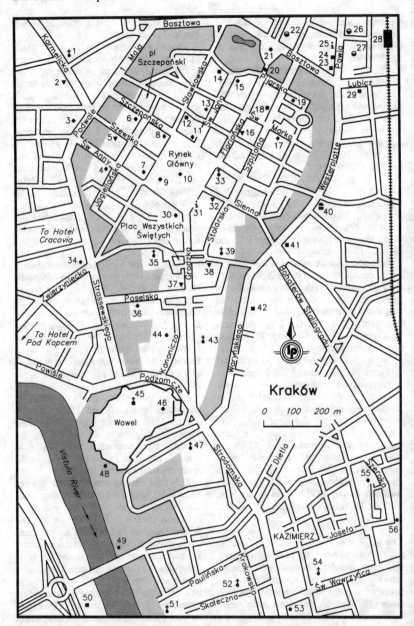

Kraków

0    100    200 m

■ **PLACES TO STAY**

12  Hotel Saski
14  Hotel Francuski
18  Hotel Pollera
23  Hotel Polonia
24  Hotel Warszawski
29  Hotel Europejski
41  PTTK Dom Turysty
42  Hotel Monopol
50  Forum Hotel

▼ **PLACES TO EAT**

 2  Bar Kapitański
 5  Piccolo Pizza
16  Żywiec Restaurant
32  Pionier Milk Bar
37  Balaton Restaurant
38  Grodzka Restaurant

**OTHER**

 1  Carmelite Church
 3  Dom Książki
 4  Collegium Maius
 6  Stary Teatr
 7  Cultural Centre (Pałac Pod Baranami)
 8  City Historical Museum
 9  Town Hall Tower
10  Cloth Hall (Sukiennice)
11  Orbis (train tickets)

13  Cartoon Gallery
15  Czartoryski Art Museum
17  Orbis (bus tickets)
19  Teatr Im J Słowackiego
20  St Florian's Gate
21  Barbican
22  Bus No 100
25  Tourist Office
26  Bus No 208
27  Bus Station
28  Kraków Główny Station
30  Museum Historii Fotografii
31  Almatur
33  Church of Our Lady
34  Filharmonia
35  Franciscan Church
36  Archaeological Museum
39  Dominican Church
40  Post Office
43  St Peter & Paul Church
44  Stanisława Wyspiańskiego Museum
45  Wawel Cathedral
46  Wawel Castle
47  Bernardine Church
48  Dragon Statue
49  Excursion Boats
51  Pauline Church
52  St Catherine's Church
53  Ethnographic Museum
54  Corpus Christi Church
55  Jewish Cemetery
56  Jewish Museum

they sat out the war. Hans Frank, the Nazi governor general of Poland (later condemned to death at Nuremberg), resided in the castle during WW II. Keep in mind that the castle closes at 3 pm and a limited number of tickets are sold each day, so try to arrive before noon.

Wind your way down the back of Wawel Hill to the park along the Vistula River. Once upon a time a legendary dragon dwelt in a cave below the hill near the river. This fearsome creature had the nasty habit of feeding on fair maidens until Prince Krak put an end to his depredations by throwing him a burning sheep soaked in pitch which the greedy dragon ate, terminating his existence. A modern **bronze dragon** now stands before the same cave breathing real fire, a creation of local sculptor Bronisław Chromy. Nearby you'll find the landing for **excursion boats** which operate on the Vistula River in summer, making scenic 1½ hour trips upriver to Bielany (US$1).

**Kazimierz** Founded in the 14th century by Casimir the Great, Kazimierz was settled by Jews a century later. To get there from the castle, walk south along the riverside and under the bridge to the 18th century **Pauline Church**, which you enter through a small door in the high wall around the complex. Visit the crypt and then go east on ulica Skałeczna past Gothic **St Catherine's Church** (1373) to ulica Krakowska where you again meet the tram tracks. Follow these south a block to the **Ethnographic Museum** (closed Tuesday). East on ulica Św Wawrzyńca is Gothic **Corpus Christi Church**.

Ulica Józefa, the next street north of Corpus Christi, ends eastbound at a 15th century synagogue, now the **Jewish Museum** (open daily May to September). The old **Jewish cemetery** at ulica Szeroka 40 is just north of here. East of the cemetery you'll encounter another tram route which will take you back to the city centre (take tram No 3 or 13).

**Nowa Huta** Just east of Kraków is the industrial community of Nowa Huta with its Lenin Steel Works, built by the Communists in the early 1950s to balance the clerical/aristocratic traditions of the old capital. Far from acting as a bulwark of the regime, a May 1988 strike by 20,000 steelworkers here contributed greatly to that government's eventual fall. Now tens of thousands of tonnes of carbon monoxide, sulphur dioxide and particulates emitted annually by the steel mill threaten to destroy Kraków's monuments.

**Wieliczka** The **salt mines** at Wieliczka, 13 km south-east of Kraków, can be reached by bus or train. From the railway station walk left/south about 10 minutes, under a bridge and into town. When you see the Kaviarna Restaurant on the left, turn right up the hill and continue about 100 metres. The mine is on the right. Try to arrive before 2 pm to be sure of getting on a tour (2½ hours, US$1); they open early every day.

You enter the mines down an elevator shaft, then follow a guide five km through the many chambers carved from solid salt. The mine's nine levels of galleries stretch 120 km – some 20 million tonnes of rock salt were extracted over 700 years. According to a local legend the deposits were discovered in the 13th century by a Hungarian princess named Kinga whose lost ring was found in a block of salt extracted here. Thus it's not surprising that the largest underground chamber should be the **St Kinga Chapel**; it took 30 years to carve, measures 54 by 17 metres and is 12 metres high.

Another feature of Wieliczka is a health resort 200 metres below the surface where patients under medical supervision are treated for allergies. It's certainly a change of pace from museums and churches!

**Back to Nature** In a picturesque forested valley sprinkled with sandstone cliffs and caves, 22 km north-west of Kraków, is **Ojców National Park**. Hiking trails fan out from the Ojców bus stop.

There's a museum in the large Renaissance courtyard at **Pieskowa Skała Castle**, nine km beyond Ojców, but only a small part of the castle may actually be visited. Huge tour groups are waiting to enter when the castle doors open at 10 am (closed Monday).

Both park and castle are easily accessible from Kraków on the Olkusz bus. The bus ticket is usually purchased on the bus itself, although try getting one in the station. There's no way to carry on from Olkusz directly to Auschwitz, so make it a day trip.

### Activities
**Organised Tours** The Orbis office in the Hotel Cracovia, Aleje Puszkina 1, offers city sightseeing tours (US$9, three hours, daily) plus day trips to the salt mines (US$12, five hours, four times a week) and Auschwitz-Birkenau (US$14, five hours, three times a week) from mid-May to September.

Consider hiring a personal guide (US$7) to show you around the cathedral. There's usually one waiting at the ticket office (ask). Guides are also available for Wawel Castle.

### Places to Stay
Kraków is Poland's premier tourist attraction and the city's hotels are more expensive than elsewhere, so if you can skip a night by arriving in the morning or leaving in the afternoon, so much the better. Kraków hotel prices are slightly lower from November to March.

**Camping** From June to September *Camping 'Krak'* at the junction of the highways arriving from Katowice and Częstochowa in the far north-west corner of Kraków, offers good camping facilities at US$3 per person (own tent). The traffic noise here is considerable.

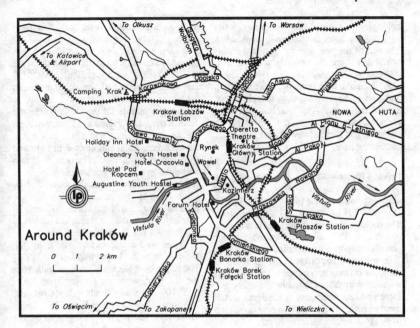

**Around Kraków**

0    1    2 km

The adjacent four-star motel is expensive (US$34/43 single/double with bath) but the motel bar is handy (bus No 208 from the airport or Kraków Railway Station).

**Youth Hostels** Both year-round youth hostels are west of the old town. The closest to the centre is in the functional concrete building at ulica Oleandry 4, beyond Hotel Cracovia. There are hot showers! Although this is the largest hostel in Poland it's often full in summer.

There's a second hostel behind the large Augustine Church at Tadeusza Kościuszki 88, just west of the city (trams No 1, 2, 6 or 21 direction 'Salwator' to the terminus). Members stay in a one-time convent overlooking the Vistula River.

Both charge US$6 per person in a double room or US$3 for a bed in an eight to 16-person dormitory. Those aged 26 and under pay US$5 per person double, US$2 per person dorm.

**Other Hostels** The easiest hotel-style accommodation is at the big, crowded *PTTK Dom Turysty*, ulica Westerplatte 15/17, an eight-minute walk from the stations. The singles/doubles are overpriced at US$14/18 and the only real reason to come here is if you're interested in a bed in one of the eight-bed dormitories which go for US$5 each. There's a large self-service restaurant downstairs. Dom Turysty is a sort of glorified youth hostel, so it's a good place to meet other travellers.

During July and August, visit Almatur, Rynek Główny 7 (in the arcade), to find out about International Student Hotels both here and in other cities, which are good, cheap places to stay. Those over age 35 cannot use these hotels.

The *'Kaczek' Student's Hotel*, Aleje 3 Maja 5 diagonally across the park from the Orbis Hotel Cracovia, is US$11 single, US$8 for a bed in a double, US$7 for a bed in a triple. This six-storey student residence belonging to Jagiellonian University is run as a regular hotel from July to September. The rest of the year you can still rent rooms but you'll share the building with resident students (prices slightly lower in winter). The 'Rotunda' disco is in the same building, and one of Kraków's youth hostels is just around the corner. The 'Kaczek' is a great place to stay if you want to meet Polish students, and there always seems to be a lot happening here.

**Private Rooms** At ulica Pawia 8, near the bus and train stations, is an office arranging stays in private homes for around US$12/15 single/double 1st class, US$10/14, 2nd class. The rooms are often far from the city centre, so ask first. This office or the one next door can also help you find a hotel.

You may also be offered a private room by someone on the street outside. The price will be similar to that charged in the office but there's no quality control by the agency. Ask them to point out the location on a good map of Kraków before agreeing to go.

**Cheaper Hotels** The *Hotel Warszawski*, ulica Pawia 6, is right next to this office, about US$16/19 single/double without bath. The more appealing *Hotel Polonia*, ulica Basztowa 23 just around the corner from the Warszawski, is also US$16/19 single/double without bath. Ask for a room facing the quieter back garden. The Polonia will give you a 20% discount if things are slow and you stay at least three nights. There's even an elevator that works!

Surprisingly the rather basic *Hotel Europejski*, ulica Lubicz 5 opposite the train station, is more expensive than the Warszawski and Polonia hotels: US$18/24 single/double with shared bath, so make this one your last choice. Beware of tram noise at these hotels.

The *Hotel Pollera*, ulica Szpitalna 30 in the old city, is US$16/21 single/double without bath, US$26 double with bath – quieter and good value. The four hotels above are all run by Wawel Tourist and the

lack of competition is reflected in their prices.

A step up from these is the *Hotel Saski*, ulica Sławkowska 3 just off Rynek Główny: US$23 single without bath, US$29/39 single/double with bath, breakfast included.

**Expensive Hotels** Of the Orbis hotels, the *Francuski*, ulica Pijarska 13, is the most elegant, convenient and least expensive. This 57-room hotel was erected in 1912 and fully renovated in 1991. The new tariff was still unknown as this book went to press. If it's too expensive, check the *Hotel Polski*, ulica Pijarska 17 nearby, which charges US$22 single without bath, US$28/29 single/double with bath, breakfast included. For couples this is an excellent choice.

If you need a modern high-rise hotel, the *Orbis Cracovia*, Aleje Puszkina 1 (US$67/108 single/double), is a 10-minute walk from the old town, while the *Orbis Forum Hotel* (US$109/129 single/double) is quieter but less convenient – south of Wawel Hill across the river. If you're on a package tour they'll probably put you in the *Holiday Inn* four km west of the centre.

By far the most unusual place to stay in Kraków is the *Hotel Pod Kopcem*, Aleje Waszyngtona (☎ 22055), located in a 19th century Austrian fortress on a hilltop overlooking the city. There's a cool forest surrounding the hotel, plus coffee shop and restaurant. Room rates begin at US$29 double without bath, US$36 double with bath. If you wanted to splurge once in Poland, this is it! Bus No 100 from Plac Matejki 3, opposite the Barbican, ends in front of the hotel (hourly). Ask the tourist office to call ahead to make sure there's room, but even if you're not staying, the Hotel Pod Kopcem merits a visit.

### Places to Eat
**Around Market Square** *Pionier Milk Bar*, ulica Sienna 1 just off Market Square, is a great cheap place for breakfast. It's a little hidden in the red brick building half way up the block. The colourful *Żywiec Restaurant*, ulica Floriańska 19, has a rough-and-ready

beer-hall atmosphere but the meals are substantial and inexpensive.

Kraków's most exclusive restaurant is the *Wierzynek*, Rynek Główny 15. Drop by beforehand for reservations if you want to be sure of a table that evening. Another upmarket place offering Polish *haute cuisine* is *Restauracja Staropolska*, ulica Sienna 4 just off Rynek Główny. You're expected to be neatly dressed at these two.

**West of Market Square** *Piccolo Pizza*, ulica Szewska 14, is self-service and the line is sometimes long. Other cheap places to eat in this vicinity include the *Ludowa Restaurant*, ulica Św Anny 7, or the *Restauracja 'Cechowa'*, ulica Jagiellońska 11 just around the corner. *Bar Kapitański* at ulica Karmelicka 16 farther west, dishes out huge pieces of fried fish to those in the line at the counter.

**South of Market Square** The *Grodzka Restaurant*, Plac Dominikański 6, offers tableservice meals in unpretentious surroundings. A more formal restaurant just across the square is the *Kurza Stopka*, Plac Wszystkich Świętych 10. For better Hungarian food than you'll get in Hungary try the highly recommended *Balaton Restaurant*, ulica Grodzka 37 (menu in Polish only).

**Near the Station** If you have some time to kill at the train station, or arrive late and want something to eat after checking into one of the nearby hotels, the *Restauracja Armenia*, ulica Lubicz 3 near Hotel Europejski, is relaxed and inexpensive (open until 10 pm).

**Cafés** *Jama Michalika*, ulica Floriańska 45, is the elegant turn-of-the-century café you'd expect to find in Kraków. Many famous artists and dramatists have sat in there on the forest green velvet couches surrounded by art deco chandeliers, stained glass and dark wood. Friday, Saturday and Monday nights there's a cabaret show at Jama Michalika.

For coffee and ice cream you can't beat *Kawiarnia 'Alvorada/Austropol'*, Rynek Główny 30. A less touristed place for coffee and cakes is *Kawiarnia U Zalipianek*, ulica

Szewska 24. In summer you can relax on its open terrace facing a park.

### Entertainment

Look at the listings in the daily papers. One of the first things to do in Kraków is visit the *Filharmonia* booking office (open weekdays 9 am to noon and 5 to 7 pm), ulica Zwierzyniecka 1, for tickets to any concerts which happen to coincide with your stay. Don't be fooled by the low price of the ticket, this orchestra ranks with the best in the world.

The newly renovated *Teatr Im J Słowackiego*, ulica Szpitalna, offers classical theatre, opera and ballet. The *Teatr Miniatura* is just behind and shares the same box office. Kraków's *Operetta Theatre*, ulica Lubicz 48, is a 10-minute walk east of the railway station. Lots of trams pass this theatre for the return trip.

In the evening there's sometimes jazz at the *Pod Jaszczurami Student Club*, Rynek Główny 8. Films and other events happen at the *Cultural Centre* (Pałac Pod Baranami), Rynek Główny 27. The *'Rotunda' Students' Cultural Centre*, ulica Oleandry 1 opposite the youth hostel near Hotel Cracovia, has a good disco at 8 pm on Wednesday, Friday, Saturday and Sunday.

*Maxime*, ulica Floriańska 32, is Kraków's most exclusive disco (dancing from 9.30 pm to 4 am).

**Festivals** Kraków has one of the richest cycles of annual events in all of Poland. Ask about the Organ Music Days and Student Song Festival in April, the Polish Festival of Short Feature Films in May or June, the 'Kraków Days' and wreath-letting on the Vistula River in June, 'Music in Old Kraków' in August, the Folk Art Fair in September, the 'Zaduszki Jazzowe' Jazz Festival and 'Polonez' dancing contest in October, the International Review of Modern Ballet in November, and the exhibition of Christmas scenes around Christmas.

During Easter week there's the famous week-long Passion Play at nearby Kalwaria Zebrzydowska; on Assumption (15 August)

a solemn procession in folk costumes is held in the same village. The 'Kraków Days' are opened on Corpus Christi (a Thursday in May or June) by the 'Lajkonik', a legendary figure disguised as a Tatar riding a hobby-horse!

### Getting There & Away

**Train** Kraków is on the main railway line between Przemyśl and Szczecin via Katowice, Opole, Wrocław and Poznań. Another important line through the city is Warsaw to Zakopane. The Cracovia Express arrives direct from Budapest via Kosice and Nowy Sącz. Coming from Prague or Vienna you usually change at Katowice, although in summer there's a daily train direct from Vienna. From Germany there are direct trains from Berlin, Cologne, Frankfurt/Main and Leipzig.

The Sawa express train departs Warsaw in the early morning, reaching Kraków Główny (302 km) about three hours later. The return trip is in the evening. The Krakus and Pieniny expresses do the opposite, leaving Warsaw in the late afternoon and Kraków in the early morning. Reservations are required on these excellent trains which ensure fast, easy transport between the two cities.

From mid-June to August the Lajkonik Express runs direct between Kraków Główny and Gdańsk (621 km, seven hours), leaving Kraków in the early morning and Gdańsk in the afternoon. This train also services Malbork, Sopot and Gdynia and reservations are required.

**Tickets** Train tickets, reservations and couchettes are available from Orbis on the north side of Market Square. The Orbis office at ulica Św Marka 25 sells long-distance bus tickets for the next or subsequent days. Expect long lines at both these offices.

### Getting Around

Trams and city buses use the same US$0.10 tickets, so buy a bunch as soon as you arrive. Most places in the centre are easily accessible on foot.

**To/From the Airport** Balice Airport is 18 km west of Kraków on the road to Katowice. Bus No 208 from the railway station runs directly there.

## OŚWIĘCIM

Auschwitz (Oświęcim) and Birkenau (Brzezinka), two deadly Nazi concentration camps 54 km west of Kraków, have been preserved as memorials to the four million people of 28 nationalities who perished here. From all Europe the fascists brought Jews and others for slave labour purposes in the nearby armaments factories. Aside from the main camps there were 40 subcamps scattered throughout the area. As one group of starving victims became too weak to continue, they were led into the gas chambers, their places taken by fresh arrivals off the trains.

It's difficult to conceive of the minds that could invent such a system. Children (especially twins) were held in the camps for medical experimentation. Father Maximilian Kolbe, who voluntarily took the place of another inmate sentenced to death in 1941, was declared a saint by Pope John Paul II in 1982. For us, a visit to these haunting memorials reveals the unimaginable brutality of war and warns of the danger in putting politics above people. These lessons more than justify the trip.

### Orientation

Today the main Auschwitz camp contains a museum (closed Monday, admission free), cinema, restaurant and hotel, while the Birkenau camp has been left more or less as it was found. Oświęcim Railway Station is about one km north of the Auschwitz Museum. Birkenau is three km north-west of Auschwitz or two km south-west of the train station.

There are no buses to Birkenau, so it's best to take a taxi from Oświęcim Railway Station to Birkenau first. Ask to be driven around to the monument at the back of the camp. Have the taxi wait so that you'll have a ride on to Auschwitz. There is frequent bus

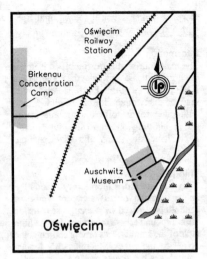

The camp could hold 200,000 inmates at a time.

**Auschwitz** Established in May 1940 in what used to be Polish army barracks, Auschwitz was the original extermination camp. The museum is in the various prison blocks, with different blocks dedicated to victims from different countries. You won't forget the thousands of individual ID photos of the dead. Finally there's a gas chamber and crematorium. Pick up the guidebook which contains maps of the sites, plus penetrating information and photos. The cinema shows a Soviet film taken just after the 1945 liberation. Ask when they'll be showing the English version to a group. If you buy 15 tickets they'll schedule an English showing just for you, although the film's message is clear in any language. Near the museum entrance is a flower shop if you'd like to leave a token.

service from the Auschwitz Museum back to the railway station.

(Several readers have written in to protest about the 'American tourist' approach recommended above. One suggested going to the museum first 'to do your homework' while another wrote that 'the bleak approach to Birkenau is definitely a different experience when made on foot rather than by taxi'. Perhaps you should decide how to handle it according to the weather that day.)

**Near Oświęcim** The Baroque palace at **Pszczyna**, 25 km west of Oświęcim, is now a museum (closed Monday). The palace, about one km from the station, is situated in a large park at one corner of the picturesque town square (several restaurants here). Get to Pszczyna by direct train from Katowice, or from Oświęcim with a change of trains at Czechowice.

### Places to Stay & Eat
The *hotel* (☎ 23217) at Auschwitz is located directly above the museum entrance. Clean, comfortable rooms with a sink inside but shared bath cost US$7/11 double/triple. There's a large cafeteria alongside (closes early).

### Things to See & Do
**Birkenau** The museum and film at Auschwitz tell the terrible tale eloquently, but to really grasp the full magnitude of the crime Birkenau simply *must* be seen. Birkenau surprises by its vast size. At the back of the camp is a monument flanked on each side by the sinister ruins of gas chambers and crematoriums, blown up by the retreating Nazis. Each gas chamber accommodated 2000 and there were electric lifts to raise the bodies to the ovens. From the monument you'll have a view of the railway lines which brought victims to the wooden barracks stretching out on each side, almost as far as you can see.

### Getting There & Away
Auschwitz is fairly easy to reach. Local trains run almost hourly to Oświęcim from Kraków and Katowice. There are also direct buses from Kraków to the Auschwitz camp gate, although some end at the station on the opposite side of town (buses No 1 and 2 from there to the train station should pass the

camp). If there are a few of you, consider hiring a taxi at Kraków Railway Station for the excursion to Auschwitz and Birkenau (US$10 should be enough).

## CZĘSTOCHOWA

Częstochowa (Tschenstochau) is the spiritual heart of Poland. Pilgrims from every corner of the country come to Jasna Góra (Luminous Mountain) Monastery to worship the image of the Black Madonna, Poland's holiest icon. The best time to arrive is at dawn when the churches are overflowing with nuns in silent prayer. This could be the most sacred place you'll ever visit.

### History

Częstochowa was first mentioned in 1220. In 1382 Duke Władysław of Opole invited the Paulites of Hungary to establish Jasna Góra Monastery. The famous icon of the Black Madonna was brought from the east in 1384. The story goes that it had been painted at Jerusalem long before. In 1430 the image was cut by invading Protestant Hussites. During restoration a scar from the sword blow was left on the Madonna's face as a reminder.

Early in the 17th century the monastery was fortified and subsequent Swedish (1655) and Russian (1770) sieges were resisted. Rebuilding took place after a fire in 1690, and centuries of patronage increased the richness of Jasna Góra. Industry developed at the end of the 19th century with the building of the railway from Warsaw to Vienna. Today Częstochowa has a steel works with 30,000 employees, plus clothing, chemical and paper industries. The Communists built Częstochowa into a major industrial centre to balance the clerical influence at Jasna Góra.

### Orientation

From the railway station, walk north a block to Aleje Najświętszej Marii Panny, locally known as Aleje NMP. Jasna Góra is on a low hill at the end of this important avenue, one km due west. If you're arriving in the early morning darkness you'll see a bright light high above the monastery.

### Information

The main tourist information office is in the underground passageway at the end of Aleje NMP beside the Orbis Patria Hotel. It sells maps of many other cities in Poland.

Another tourist office is upstairs in the office building above Restaurant Bristol, ulica Piłsudskiego 1 near the railway station.

### Things to See

Today **Jasna Góra Monastery** retains the appearance of a fortress, a vibrant symbol of Catholicism tossed in a secular sea. Inside the compound are two churches. On the high altar of the smaller, less ornate church is the image of the Black Madonna. It's hidden behind a silver curtain (1673) and only exposed during the frequent religious services. This makes it difficult to have a close

The Black Madonna

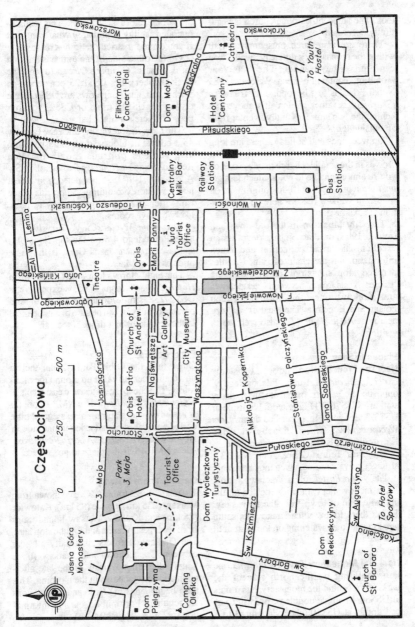

Częstochowa

Jasna Góra Monastery

Park 3 Maja

Dom Pielgrzyma

Camping Olejka

3 Maja

Jasnogórska

Orbis Patria Hotel

Tourist Office

Starucha

Al Najświętsze

Church of St Andrew

Theatre

Orbis

Marii Panny

'Juri' Tourist Office

Jana Kilińskiego

H Dąbrowskiego

Al W. Lenina

Al Tadeusza Kościuszki

Art Gallery

City Museum

Waszyngtona

Dom Wycieczkowy 'Turystyczny'

Pułaskiego

Mikołaja Kopernika

Z Modzelewskiego

F Nowowiejskiego

Stanisława Palczyńskiego

Jana Sobieskiego

Al Wolności

Bus Station

Railway Station

Centralny Milk Bar

Piłsudskiego

Hotel 'Centralny'

Dom Mały

Filharmonia Concert Hall

Wilsona

Warszawska

Katedralna

Cathedral

Krakowska

To Youth Hostel

Sw Kazimierza

Sw Barbary

Dom Rekolekcyjny

Kazimierza

Sw Augustyna

Kościelna

To Hotel Sportowy

Church of St Barbara

0   250   500 m

look. The adjacent Baroque church is beautifully decorated.

There are also three museums to visit within the monastery's defensive walls. You can't miss the **Arsenal**. The **600 Year Museum**, containing Lech Wałęsa's 1983 Nobel Prize, is just beyond. The **Treasury** *(Skarbiec)* is rather hidden. It's above and behind the two churches and you enter from an outside terrace.

On weekends and holidays there are long lines to enter all three museums, and the crowds in the smaller church may be so thick you're almost unable to enter, much less get near the icon. A great 10-day pilgrimage on foot from Warsaw reaches here on Assumption (15 August).

The **City Museum** in the old town hall (rebuilt 1908) on Plac Biegańskiego has an excellent historical collection and much information on the chain of ruined castles perched atop sandstone crags along the 'Eagles' Nests Route' between Częstochowa and Kraków, once the border between Poland and Bohemia. The local **art gallery** nearby at Aleje NMP 47 is also well worth visiting.

## Places to Stay
**Near the Train Station** The old three-storey *Hotel 'Centralny'*, at ulica Piłsudskiego 9, opposite the eastern exit from the railway station, is US$6/9/11 single/double/triple or US$3.50 for a bed in a four-bed dorm. *Dom Wycieczkowwy 'Mały'*, nearby at ulica Katedralna 18, is US$8/12 single/double.

The 'Jura' Tourist Office, Aleje NMP 37, arranges private rooms, when they have any.

The *youth hostel*, ulica Wacławy Marek 12, is inconvenient since it's located on the opposite side of town from the monastery. To get there follow ulica Krakowska south one km and keep watching on the right until you see it.

**Near the Monastery** *Dom Pielgrzyma*, the large building on the north side of the parking lot behind the monastery, has rooms at US$30/40 single/double or beds in four-bed dorms at US$10 (check-in from 3 to 8

pm, doors close at 10 pm). This church-operated facility is probably what you want if you came for strictly religious reasons.

On the other side of the tour bus parking lot is pleasant *Camping Oleńka* (open June to September). It's US$1.25 per person to pitch a tent, and bungalows are US$9 single or double, US$17 triple or US$23 for four people. There's a snack bar.

The *Dom Rekolekcyjny*, ulica Św Barbary 43 a couple of blocks south of Jasna Góra, also shelters pilgrims. South of Dom Rekolokcyjny is *Hotel Sportowy*, ulica Św Andrzeja 8/10 (US$6 per person) in a neat new two-storey building. Since this place isn't often used by pilgrims, they're more likely to have rooms.

The *Dom Wycieczkowy 'Turystyczny'*, ulica Pułaskiego 4/6 on the top floor of a sports centre near Jasna Góra, is the same price as Dom Mały.

The eight-storey, four-star *Orbis Patria Hotel*, also near Jasna Góra, is expensive at US$27/38 single/double with bath and breakfast, but you can be sure of a good meal in the restaurant or a drink at the bar.

## Places to Eat
Other than the Orbis Patria Hotel there's nowhere decent to eat at up around the monastery. The cheapest, fastest and easiest place is *Centralny Milk Bar*, Aleje NMP 19 not far from the railway station. There's a good little coffee-and-cakes bar attached to one side. If all you want is a beer, the *Astoria Restaurant*, Aleje NMP 46, is the place to go.

## Getting There & Away
There are direct trains to Częstochowa from Warsaw (235 km), Opole (95 km), Katowice (86 km) and Kraków. Warsaw-bound trains from Budapest, Vienna and Prague stop here. The Opolanin Express runs daily all year between Częstochowa and Warsaw (three hours), departing Warsaw in the late afternoon and Częstochowa in the morning. This train begins/ends in Opole and reservations are required. For train tickets and information try Orbis, Aleje NMP 40.

# Silesia

Silesia (Śląsk) in south-western Poland is the industrial heart of the country. Although Silesia accounts for only 6% of Poland's area, it provides a fifth of its wealth, including half its steel and 90% of its coal (8% of the world supply). The Upper Silesian Basin around Katowice, source of both the Vistula and Odra rivers, is densely developed, populated and polluted. Lower Silesia stretches north-west along the Odra past Wrocław. The fertile farming area between Opole and Wrocław is known as 'Green Silesia' while the coal-mining region of Upper Silesia is called 'Black Silesia'.

Silesia was originally inhabited by Slavonic tribes, the largest of which, known as the Ślęzanie, gave their name to the region. Medieval Silesia was autonomous under Piast princes. In 1335 Silesia was annexed to Bohemia and from 1526 to 1742 it was under Austria's Habsburgs. Frederick the Great took Silesia for Prussia in 1742. Throughout the German period the large Polish minority was subjected to 'Germanisation'. After WW I Polish nationalist uprisings resulted in most of Upper Silesia going to Poland while Lower Silesia remained part of Germany until 1945. That year the German population was expelled and Silesia returned to Poland after a lapse of six centuries.

While tourists may not be attracted to the industrial wonders of Katowice and vicinity, Wrocław is an old historic city with an intense cultural life. Opole is a convenient stop off the beaten track, while the Sudeten Mountains west of Kłodzko (the 'Góry Stołowe') and south of Jelenia Góra (Karkonoski Park Narodowy) lure hikers.

## OPOLE

Opole (Oppeln), a pleasant small town on the Odra River, gets so few tourists you'll be an object of curiosity if you stop there. It's a good place to wander around without being distracted by too many sights. The location midway between Kraków, Częstochowa and Wrocław couldn't be better. The town's only real claim to fame is the Festival of Polish Song, held in the open-air theatre on Pasieka Island during the second half of June.

Longtime home to the Opolanie tribe, by the end of the 12th century the town had become capital of the Opole duchy. With the extinction of the Opole Piast dynasty in 1532 the area passed to Bohemia and later Prussia. Despite the long period of German rule the Polish element remained strong here.

### Orientation

The main railway station (Opole Główne), main post office and bus station are adjacent on the south side of town. March straight up ulica Krakowska to Rynek, the central square. A few trains stop at Opole Wschodnie Station, just north-east of town along ulica Oleska.

### Information

The tourist information centre, ulica Książąt Opolskich 22, has a good selection of maps for sale. Also check the PTTK office, ulica Krakowska 15/17 near the centre of town.

### Things to See

The ugly Italianate **town hall** (1936) in the centre of Rynek is surrounded by beautiful, rebuilt, 18th century burgher houses. From the east corner of the square follow ulica Św Wojciecha two blocks to the **Opole Museum** (closed Monday) with a pictorial collection of local interest. **St Mary's Church** is just above.

Retrace your steps to the south corner of Rynek and the 14th century **Franciscan Church**. The tombs of the Opole Piasts are in the chapel on the south side. **Opole Cathedral** is north-west of Rynek.

Follow ulica Katedralna west to the Młynówka Canal and cross the bridge to Pasieka Island. A little south is a small lake in a very pleasant park with a rustic coffee shop (usually closed) to one side. The single **tower** overlooking the park is all that remains of the 14th century Piast castle.

There's considerable river traffic on the **Odra River**, mostly coal barges. You see it

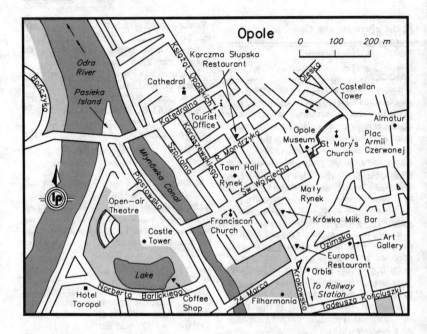

all on a stroll down the west side of Pasieka Island to the pedestrian bridge at the island's south end. Opole's **zoo** is in the large park over the bridge.

### Places to Stay

The nine-storey *Opole Hotel* in front of the railway station is expensive at US$23/28 single/double with bath and breakfast, while the *Hotel Toropol* upstairs in the sports centre at ulica Norberta Barlickiego 13 on Pasieka Island hesitates to give foreigners rooms.

Your best bet for a budget room is the *Hotel 'Remak'* (☎ 36429), ulica Kowalska 4 south of Opole Główne Station, across the bridge over the railway tracks. It's hidden behind a large athletic centre – ask for the *hala sportowa*. Open all year, rooms are US$8/12 single/double.

In July and August ask Almatur, Plac Armii Czerwonej 1, about the international student hotel in Opole. Opole is without camping facilities.

### Places to Eat

The *Krówka Milk Bar*, ulica Krakowska 13 a block from the main square, is cheap. The *Karczma Słupska Restaurant*, ulica Książąt Opolskich 6, is recommended for its folkloric flavour – *golonka pieczona* (pig's leg) is a speciality. Also check out the *Europa Restaurant* across the street from the Orbis office.

The place for coffee, cakes and ice cream is *Kawiarna Teatralna*, ulica Krakowska 35 beside Orbis.

### Getting There & Away

Opole is on the main railway line from Przemyśl to Szczecin via Kraków, Katowice, Brzeg, Wrocław and Poznań. There are also direct trains from Częstochowa (95 km), Nysa and Rzepin. Orbis, ulica Krakowska 31, reserves seats and couchettes.

The Opolanin Express travels daily throughout the year between Warsaw and Opole (330 km, five hours), leaving Warsaw in the afternoon and Opole in the early morning. This train calls at Częstochowa. Reservations are required.

## WROCŁAW

Wrocław, historic capital of Lower Silesia, was German Breslau from 1742 until 1945. In the 13th century Wrocław had been capital of a local Piast dynasty, then the town passed from Bohemia to the Habsburgs and finally Prussia. During the final phase of WW II, the Nazis fortified the area and though surrounded, the 40,000 German soldiers at 'Festung Breslau' held out from 15 February to 6 May, only surrendering after Berlin fell on 2 May 1945. In the course of this 81-day siege 70% of the city was destroyed.

Immediately after the war, any German residents who hadn't already fled were deported and the ruins were resettled by Poles from Ľvov in the Ukraine. People in Wrocław still have a sentimental attachment to Ľvov and you'll sometimes see historical displays on that city in the museums, or advertising for tourist trips to Ľvov. Even the local beer brewed in Wrocław is called 'piwo Lwów'!

Today this enjoyable big city by the Odra offers good museums, historic buildings, concert halls, theatres, parks and over 120 canals, plus a picturesque central square and a memorable cluster of churches by the river. Wrocław is a lively cultural centre, a students' city, and the clubs are packed if anything's happening. It's all conveniently located so you can do most of your sightseeing on foot.

## Orientation

Wrocław Główny Railway Station is convenient to most of the hotels. To walk to Rynek, the old market square, turn left on ulica Świerczewskiego and walk three blocks to ulica Świdnicka. Turn right and continue straight into town.

## Information

The 'Odra' tourist information office, ulica Świerczewskiego 98, is below Hotel Piast I diagonally opposite the railway station.

A second tourist office with a better selection of maps and brochures for sale is at ulica Kazimierza Wielkiego 39.

**Money** To change a travellers' cheque you must go to the PKO bank, Plac Solny 16.

## Things to See

**The Old Town** As you walk along ulica Świdnicka into town you'll pass **Corpus Christi Church** on the right and the neoclassical **Opera House** on the left. Next to the Monopol Hotel is **St Dorothy's Church**. When you reach the pedestrian underpass turn left a block to the Ethnographic and Archaeological **museums** (both are closed Monday and Tuesday). They have separate entrances but are in the same complex at ulica Kazimierza Wielkiego 34/35. Unfortunately only Polish captions are posted in the Archaeological Museum, making the exhibits rather meaningless to foreigners.

Continue west again in the same direction and turn right across the street first chance you get, then straight around into Plac Solny, the old salt market which is now a flower market and spills into Rynek, the medieval marketplace with its Renaissance and Baroque burgher houses. Wrocław's Gothic **Ratusz** (town hall), built between 1327 and 1504, is one of the most intricate in Poland and now contains a museum (closed Monday and Tuesday) in the arched interior. At the north-west corner of Rynek is 14th century **St Elizabeth's Church** with its 83-metre tower. The two small houses on the corner, connected by a gate, are known as Hansel and Gretel.

Walk east from this church along the north side of Rynek and continue due east on ulica Wita Stwosza, with a digression to visit the Gothic **Church of St Mary Magdalene** on the right. Note the 12th century Romanesque portal on the far side of the church.

**Museums & Churches** Keep straight on ulica Wita Stwosza till you reach the Orbis Panorama Hotel. The **Museum of Architecture** (closed Monday) in the 15th century convent across the street from the hotel has

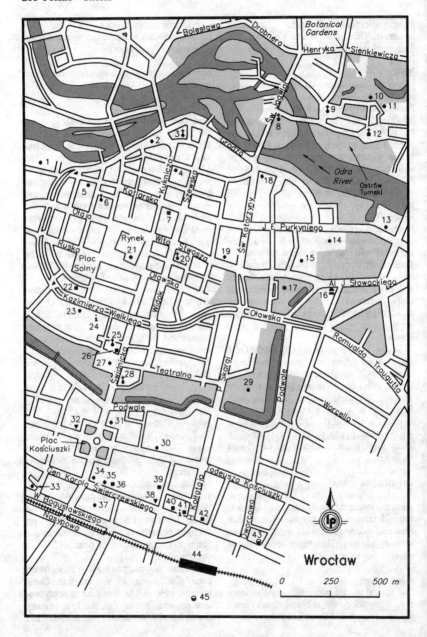

Wrocław

0    250    500 m

■ PLACES TO STAY

7   Teachers' Hostel
17  Orbis Panorama Hotel
22  PTTK Stacja Turystyczna
26  Monopol Hotel
36  Hotei Polonia
39  Hotel Piast II
40  Europejski Hotel
41  Hotel Piast I
42  Grand Hotel

▼ PLACES TO EAT

32  KDM Restaurant
38  Wzorcowy Milk Bar

OTHER

1   Arsenal (Military Museum)
2   Collegium Maximum
3   Jesuit Church
4   Kalambur Theatre
5   Rura Jazz Club
6   St Elizabeth's Church
8   Church of the Virgin Mary on the
    sands
9   Church of the Holy Cross

10  Botanical Gardens
11  Archdiocesan Museum
12  Cathedral
13  National Museum
14  Panorama Racławicka
15  Museum of Architecture
16  Post Office
18  Market
19  Art Gallery
20  Church of St Mary Magdalene
21  Ratusz (Town Hall)
23  Archaeological Museum
24  Tourist Office
25  St Dorothy's Church
27  Opera House
28  Corpus Christi Church
29  Bastion
30  Pałacyk Student Club & Almatur
31  Centrum Department Store
33  Polski Theatre
34  Orbis
35  Gambling Casino
37  Operetka Theatre
41  Tourist Office
43  Old Bus Station
44  Railway Station
45  New Bus Station

a scale model of Wrocław as it appeared in 1740.

In the park around behind this museum is the **Panorama Racławicka**, a huge 360° painting of the Battle of Racławice (1794) near Kraków during which the national hero, Tadeusz Kościuszko, led the Poles against Russian forces intent on partitioning Poland. Created in 1894 by Jan Styka and Wojciech Kossak, the painting is 120 metres long and 15 metres high. It was originally displayed at Ľvov and reopened at Wrocław in 1985. You're given headphones with an English or German commentary, but they screech and the story is difficult to follow.

You may have difficulty getting panorama tickets (admission US$1.50, students US$0.75, closed Wednesday) as visitors are only admitted 17 times a day in groups of 40 persons, and tour groups often book all the showings a couple of days in advance. If this is the situation when you arrive and the ticket clerk isn't helpful, go to the administrative office upstairs beyond the TV sets where groups with tickets for the next tours are waiting (if the door attendant tries to stop you, say you're going to the souvenir stand which is also up there). The people there will probably fix you up if you come on friendly and interested. Alternatively someone standing at the door may offer to sell you a ticket purchased earlier which they cannot use.

Just east beside the park is the **National Museum** (closed Monday and Tuesday) with a large collection of masterpieces of medieval Silesian art. Cross the bridge over the Odra beside the museum, taking a glance upstream at the **Most Grunwaldzki** (1910), the most graceful of Wrocław's 90 bridges.

On the north side of the river, turn left when the tram tracks bend right and walk west into Ostrów Tumski, an old quarter inhabited since the 9th century. In the 10th century the ducal palace was here. The chapels at the rear of the Gothic **Cathedral of St John the Baptist** deserve special attention. The **Archdiocesan Museum** (closed Monday) is at ulica Kanonia 12 between the cathedral and the Botanical **Gardens**. The gardens (established in 1811) are a lovely, restful corner of the city well worth seeking out.

West again from the cathedral is the two-storey Gothic **Church of the Holy Cross**. Keep straight and cross the small bridge to the 14th century **Church of the Virgin Mary on the Sands** which has a stunning Gothic interior.

Southbound now, follow the tram tracks across another small bridge to the huge, red-brick **city market** (1908). Then follow the riverbank downstream a block or two till you reach a large **Jesuit Church** (1755) with the **Collegium Maximum** (1741) just beyond. Inside this ornate Baroque building is the magnificent Aula Leopoldina, now used for formal university functions.

**Parks & Zoo** Take a taxi or trams No 1, 2, 4, 10, or 12 east to Wrocław's enjoyable **zoo**. In summer, **excursion boats** operate on a branch of the Odra several times a day from the landing beside the zoo.

Across the street from the zoo is a famous early work of modern architecture, **Centenary Hall** or 'Jahrhunderthalle', erected in 1913 by the famous German architect Max Berg to commemorate the defeat of Napoleon in 1813. Try to get inside to appreciate this great enclosed space (tip the guard). The steel needle beside the hall was the symbol of the 1948 Exhibition of the Regained Territories. The **Szczytnicki Park** beyond includes an attractive Japanese garden.

**Circle Trip** Provided there are no obstructions due to road works, tram No 0 makes a complete loop around Wrocław in about 45 minutes, the best city tour you'll ever get for US$0.10. You can pick it up in front of the railway station.

**Places to Stay**
**Camping** Wrocław's camping ground is near the Olympic Stadium across Szczytnicki Park from the zoo on the east side of the city

(trams No 9, 12, 16, and 17 pass the entrance). There's a row of simple, clean bungalows, and from 15 May to 30 September foreigners wishing to pitch a tent are *never* turned away. English and German are spoken.

**Hostels** The youth hostel at ulica Kołłotaja 20 is just behind the Grand Hotel, a few minutes' walk from the railway station. Only dorm beds are available but it's open all year. The receptionist will hold your luggage until they open at 5 pm.

The PTTK runs a *Stacja turystyczna* at ulica Szajnochy 11 (upstairs) just off Plac Solny in the old town. The hostel reception is only open from 5 to 9 pm and a bed in a six, 10, or 18-bed dormitory will be around US$3. The one double room is US$6. It's open all year.

The *Ośrodek Zakwaterowań Nauczycieli*, ulica Kotlarska 42 right in the middle of town, is a teachers' hostel with rooms at US$6 single or double, or US$3.50 for a bed in a three-bed room, US$3 for a bed in a four-bed room. This place is really intended for teachers only but it will take others if space is available.

**Private Rooms** Odra Tourist, ulica Świerczewskiego 98 opposite the railway station, can arrange private rooms at US$9/13 single/double in 2nd category, US$13/19 single/double in 1st category. None of the rooms is near the station.

**Cheaper Hotels** A whole row of relatively inexpensive hotels line ulica Świerczewskiego, to the left as you come out of the railway station. The *Grand Hotel*, ulica Świerczewskiego 102 right across from the station, is US$17/21 single/double without bath, US$21/26 with bath, breakfast included. *Hotel Piast I*, just west on the next corner, is US$8/12 single/double without bath, US$16 double with bath.

The *Hotel Europejski*, at ulica Świerczewskiego 94/96, charges US$12/16 single/double for a 2nd-class room, US$25/33 for a 1st-class room, private bath and breakfast

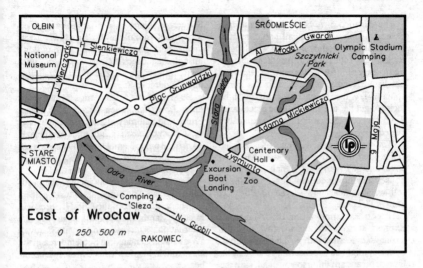

East of Wrocław

0    250  500 m

included in all. Better value is the *Piast II Hotel* (formerly the Hotel Odra) around the corner at ulica Stawowa 13 (US$8/12 single/double without bath, US$9/16 with bath, breakfast not included). No English is spoken here.

*Hotel Polonia*, ulica Świerczewskiego 66, is more expensive than any of the hotels just mentioned (US$26/34 single/double with bath and breakfast). Wrocław's gambling casino is beside the Polonia.

Rooms facing the street in the Grand, Piast I, Europejski and Polonia hotels get a lot of tram noise; the Piast II is on a quiet side street.

**Expensive Hotels** Of the four Orbis hotels the *Monopol Hotel* (erected in 1890) beside the Opera is the most colourful (from US$13/24 single/double without bath, US$38/50 with bath, breakfast included). Hitler stayed at a suite in the Monopol Hotel and addressed the crowds from the balcony whenever he visited Breslau. The *Panorama Hotel* (US$43/60 single/double with bath and breakfast) should be your choice if you want a fine modern hotel near the centre of town. Avoid the *Orbis-Novotel* and the

*Orbis-Wrocław*, both of which are way off in the southern suburbs. Prices at these hotels are lowest from October to April.

**Places to Eat**
**Near the Train Station** Wrocław doesn't shine in the food department, and there's no good middle-level place to eat near the railway station. The Europejski and Polonia hotels both have restaurants, but after struggling with the Polish/German menu for 10 minutes you'll be told that what you wanted isn't available. The *Cyganeria Restaurant,* ulica Kościuszki 31, looks bad at first, full of men drinking warm beer and vodka straight, but actually the food is quite good and the staff friendly.

Another place to fill your stomach is the *Wzorcowy Milk Bar*, ulica Świerczewskiego 86 a block from the station.

**In the Old Town** *Bar Ratuszowy*, Rynek Ratusz 27a on the corner of Sukiennice behind the old town hall, has cheap cafeterias upstairs and down. They often serve Polish peasant specialities. It's a green building, part of the block in the middle of the square – it's worth taking a few minutes to locate.

The *Piwnica Świdnicka Restaurant*, in a basement of the old town hall, serves reasonable meals in a medieval setting which dates back to the 14th century. Another subterranean eatery, the *Ratuszowa Restaurant* nearby at Rynek-Ratusz 2, also has atmosphere. Try the *golonka* soup! You'd be lucky to get fed in either of these places after 7 pm and sometimes both are inexplicably closed.

*Winiarnia Bachus*, Rynek 16, is a wine cellar open in the evening (closed Monday, cover charge). *Herbowa*, Rynek 19, is a teahouse serving excellent desserts. Cheap self-service meals are served at *Bar pod Złotym Dzbanem*, Rynek 23.

If you assumed from the American Express stickers in the window that the *Królewska Restaurant* at Dwór Wazów, Rynek 5, might be expensive, you'd be right. If price means anything to you at all, skip the meal and go upstairs to the very elegant café where you can get ice cream and a glass of wine for a more manageable price.

The passageway behind the Królewska leads straight back through the courtyard to another tourist trap (I mean, fine restaurant), the *Mieszczańska*, ulica Kiełbaśnicza 6/7, which comes with such typical Polish features as warm beer, pickled salad, a fanciful menu and a kitchen which closes at 8.30 pm. The 'miodosytnia' in the basement below this restaurant is OK for coffee, cakes and drinks.

The only place in Wrocław where you can be sure of a good meal, properly served, is the restaurant or coffee shop in the *Panorama Hotel*.

## Entertainment

Wrocław is a major cultural centre and during the winter season you'll have a lot to choose from. Check the listings in the morning papers, *Słowo Polskie* and *Gazeta Robotnicza*, or the evening paper, *Wieczór Wrocławia*.

At the *Operetka Theatre*, ulica Świerczewskiego 67, actors, actresses, costumes, music, scenery – everything is superb. The *Teatr Polski*, nearby at ulica Zapolskiej 3 off

Świerczewskiego, also offers excellent performances in Polish. If Wrocław's *mime theatre* performs here during your stay, don't miss it. Also check *Filharmonia Hall*, ulica Świerczewskiego 17, and the *Opera House*, ulica Świdnicka 35.

Be sure to attend any jam sessions at the *Rura Jazz Club*, ulica Łazienna 4. Great! Friday and Saturday nights there's a disco at the *Pałacyk Student Club*, ulica Kościuszki 34, from 8 pm to 3 am. Dance music is played for an older crowd at the *KDM Restaurant*, Plac Kościuszki 5/6, from 7 pm on.

Annual musical events include the Festival of Polish Contemporary Music held in February; the 'Jazz of the Odra' jazz festival in early March; the Flower Fair in July; the International Oratorio and Cantata Festival, 'Wratislavia Cantans', in September; and the Days of Old Masters' Music in early December.

## Things to Buy

Wrocław's shopping is concentrated around Plac Kościuszki and along ulica Świdnicka to Rynek. The largest of the department stores is Centrum, ulica Świdnicka 40 at Plac Kościuszki. Have a look around. There's an excellent Russian bookstore at Rynek 14 with many books in English or German. Other foreign books are available from the bookstore at Rynek 59.

## Getting There & Away

**Train** Main lines from Szczecin to Przemyśl (via Poznań and Kraków), and Warsaw to Jelenia Góra (via Lódź), cross at Wrocław. Other direct trains come from Gdynia or Gdańsk (via Poznań). There's service from Katowice (180 km), Poznań (165 km) and Rzepin (224 km) every couple of hours.

Several trains a day arrive from Berlin (via Rzepin) and Cologne, Frankfurt/Main and Hannover in Germany (via Dresden and Leipzig). The daily Bohemia Express to/from Prague arrives and departs in the middle of the night. Dresden and Prague are each about seven hours away. Orbis, at ulica Świerczewskiego 62, is where you go to buy international train tickets, reserve seats, couchettes, etc.

The Odra Express runs daily all year between Warsaw and Wrocław (390 km, five hours), departing Warsaw in the afternoon and Wrocław in the early morning. At certain times of year (ask) the Fredro Express does the opposite, leaving Warsaw in the early morning and Wrocław in the afternoon. Reservations are required for both trains.

# Wielkopolska

Western Poland, or Wielkopolska ('Great Poland'), was the cradle of the Polish nation. Here on a plateau along the Warta River lived the Polanians, a Slavonic tribe which gave their name to the whole country. In 966 Mieszko I, duke of the Polanians, was baptised at Gniezno. Mieszko's son, Boleslav the Brave, was crowned king in 1025, establishing the Piast dynasty which ruled Poland until 1370.

In 1253 Prince Przemysl I granted Poznań municipal rights and the city became a regional centre. Wars in the 18th century seriously weakened Poland, and in 1793 Western Poland was annexed to Prussia. After Bismarck set up the German Empire in 1871, Germanisation and German colonisation became intense. Returned to Poland in 1919, the area was seized by the Nazis in 1939 and devastated during the liberation battles of 1945.

Today the rebuilt regional capital Poznań is a great industrial, commercial and historical city, well worth a stop on the way to or from Berlin. Gniezno can easily be visited on the way to Toruń, an enchanting old riverside town by the Vistula. Though the German influence is still evident, western Poland is as Polish as you can get.

## POZNAŃ

Poznań (Posen), on the main east-west trade route halfway between Berlin and Warsaw, has long been a focal point of Polish history. A wooden fort stood on Ostrów Tumski (Cathedral Island) in the 9th century, and from 968 to 1039 Poznań was capital of Poland. In 1253 Stare Miasto (Old Town) was founded on the left bank of the Warta River and it continued to play a major role in the life of the country. By the 15th century Poznań was already famous for its fairs, and despite Swedish assaults in the 17th century the city remained an important trading centre. In 1815 the Congress of Vienna created the Grand Duchy of Poznań under Prussian suzerainty, but after 1849 the Germans took direct control. Part of Poland from 1918 to 1939, the 1945 battle to liberate the city lasted over a month.

A 1956 strike for higher wages by workers at the huge Cegielski Engineering Works was one of the first of its kind in Poland. The Works, founded by Hipolit Cegielski in 1846 and still the city's largest employer, manufactures railway rolling stock, diesel engines and machinery. Since 1925 Poznań has been the site of Poland's largest international trade fairs, although the good restaurants, historic places and varied museums draw visitors all year. Poznań's Żytnia rye vodka is Poland's best.

Polmos
POZNAŃ
Extra
ŻYTNIA
Vodka
100 PER CENT NEUTRAL
SPIRITS DISTILLED FROM RYE
40% obj.        0,5 dm³
PRODUCE OF POLAND

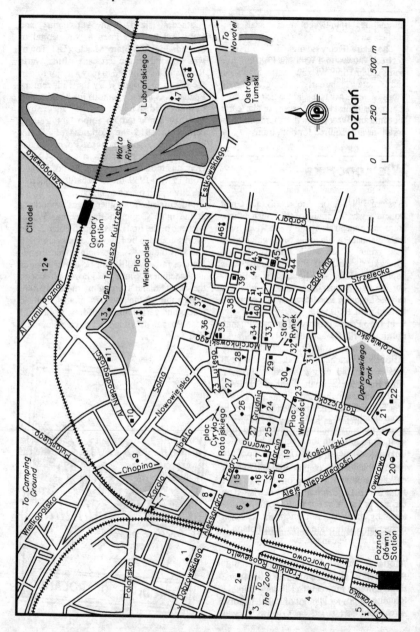

Poznań

■ PLACES TO STAY

2   Orbis Mercury Hotel
10  Niepodległości Youth Hostel
11  Orbis Polonez Hotel
17  Lech Hotel
19  Wielkopolska Hotel
22  Orbis Poznań Hotel
29  Poznański Hotel
33  Orbis Bazar Hotel
39  Dom Turysty PTTK

▼ PLACES TO EAT

7   Myśliwska Restaurant
24  Smakosz Restaurant
27  Pod Arkadami Milk Bar
28  Bistro Piccolo
30  Przynęta Restaurant
36  Astoria Restaurant

    OTHER

1   World Computer Travel
3   Solidarity Headquarters
4   International Fairgrounds
5   Biuro Zakwaterowania
6   Solidarity Monument

8   Opera House
9   US Consulate
12  Commonwealth War Cemetery
13  Polish War Memorial
14  Carmelite Church
15  Almatur
16  Palace of Culture
18  Filharmonia
20  PKS Bus Station
21  Musical Theatre
23  Orbis (domestic train tickets)
25  Moulin Rouge Night Club
26  Polski Theatre 'Naród Sobie'
31  St Martin's Church
32  Sawa Tour
34  National Museum
35  Post Office
37  Vegetable Market
38  Decorative Arts Museum
40  Franciscan Church
41  Tourist Office
42  Old Town Hall
43  Musical Instruments Museum
44  Parish Church
45  Archaeological Museum
46  Dominican Church
47  Archdiocesan Museum
48  Cathedral

## Orientation

Poznań Główny Railway Station is a 20-minute walk from the centre of the city. Left-luggage is upstairs in the main hall between tracks one and four. Exit the station from this hall and walk north to the second street, ulica Św Marcin, which you follow east. Turn left with the tram tracks at Aleje Marcinkowskiego, then right at the Bazar Hotel and straight ahead to Stary Rynek, the old town square.

## Information

The tourist office at Stary Rynek 77 is extremely helpful and sells maps.

**Money** If you arrive on a weekend or at night and need to change money, try the nearby Hotel Mercury (cash only). Touts wishing to change money or take you to their taxi may greet you at the train station. You don't really need their assistance and will pay extra if you accept it.

**Consulate** The US Consulate (☎ 59586) is at ulica Chopina 4.

## Things to See

**Museums** There are half a dozen museums in the historic buildings on or near Stary Rynek. Begin with the one in the Renaissance **old town hall** (closed Saturday) which will envelop you in Poznań's medieval past. The coffered ceiling in the vestibule dates from 1555. Every day at noon a bugle sounds and butting heraldic goats appear above the clock on the town hall façade opposite Proserpina's fountain (1766). The **Musical Instruments Museum** (closed Monday), Stary Rynek 45, is one of the best of its kind in Europe.

Nearby at the south-eastern corner of the square is the **Archaeological Museum** (closed Monday) in a 16th century Renaissance palace. Make a side trip to the end of ulica Świętosławska from beside this museum to visit the Baroque **parish church**, originally a Jesuit church. There's a peculiar **Military Museum** (closed Monday) full of little lead soldiers in one of the modern buildings in the very centre of Stary Rynek itself. Notice the art gallery opposite. There are two more museums, one political (Stary Rynek 3) and the other literary (Stary Rynek 84), on the west side of the square near the tourist office.

Go up ulica Franciszkańska near the tourist office to the beautiful 17th century **Franciscan Church**. In the Castle of Przemyśl on the hill opposite is the **Decorative Arts Museum** (closed Monday and Tuesday). Go around the church and west on ulica Paderewskiego to the Bazar Hotel. The **National Museum** (closed Monday), with Poland's best collection of Dutch and Spanish paintings, is in the large building across the street on the hotel's north side.

**Other Sights** The historic centre of Poznań has a lot more to offer than just museums, most of which you'll be able to discover for yourself without a guidebook. However, a few sights just outside the centre deserve your attention.

Walk north from the Bazar Hotel to the end of Aleje Marcinkowskiego, then turn right, then left on ulica Działowa, the first street. You'll pass two old churches before reaching the striking **Polish War Memorial**. Pass it and continue north on Aleje Niepodległości to the 19th century Prussian **citadel**. Though Poznań fell to the Soviet army in January 1945, 20,000 German troops held out inside this fortress for another two months and the city was badly damaged by artillery fire. There's much to see around the citadel, including a couple of war museums (closed Monday) and monuments to the Soviet liberators. The **Commonwealth War Cemetery** here is a moving sight for English-speaking visitors.

Poznań's towering red-brick Gothic **cathedral** is at Ostrów Tumski on the east side of the Warta River. Any eastbound tram from the north side of town will take you there. The Byzantine-style Golden Chapel (1841), mausoleum of Mieszko I and Boleslav the Brave, is behind the main altar. The **Archdiocesan Museum** (closed at present) at the north end of ulica Lubrańskiego near the cathedral is surprisingly rich.

Poznań's most compelling sight is the large bronze **monument** in the park beside the Palace of Culture, which you may have noticed on your way in from the railway station. Erected in 1981 by supporters of the trade union Solidarity, the monument commemorates 'Black Thursday', 28 June 1956, when rioting by workers demanding higher wages was put down by force with as many as 70 killed and hundreds injured. The two huge crosses, bound together, symbolise the struggle of Polish workers for 'bread and freedom' and the dates recall various popular upheavals: 1956 (Poznań), 1968 (Warsaw), 1970 (Gdańsk), 1976 (Radom), 1980 (Gdańsk). Next to the monument is a statue of the Romantic poet Adam Mickiewcz.

**Kórnik & Rogalin** Each of these small towns 20 km south of Poznań boasts a large palace of the landed nobility in expansive parks. The two are similar, so unless you've got plenty of time or your own transport, one might be representative of the other. Kórnik is the easiest to reach with frequent bus service from Poznań. Buses between Kórnik and Rogalin are only a couple of times a day, but maybe you'll be lucky! There's a bus from Rogalin directly back to Poznań every couple of hours.

The 19th century English-style country manor at Kórnik (closed Monday) was rebuilt on the site of an earlier palace by the famous Berlin architect Karl Friedrich Schinkel. A highlight at Rogalin is the small art gallery (closed Monday and Tuesday) hidden behind the 18th century Rococo palace. Its collection of 19th century German and Polish paintings is quite good. Some of the oak trees in the surrounding park are almost nine metres around and 1000 years old. The three largest trees are named for the legendary brothers Lech, Czech and Rus who founded Poland, Bohemia and Russia. It's possible to stay in Rogalin Palace for US$50 double with bath.

## Places to Stay

Hotel prices go up 75% during the eight annual trade fairs, and during the main trade fair in June all accommodation will be fully booked, so check the dates carefully before heading this way. The price increases are also in effect a few days before and after the fairs.

The tourist office, Stary Rynek 77, knows of workers' dormitories offering tourists accommodation at very low rates (around US$3 per person). All are in distant suburbs but easily accessible on public transport and well worth considering if you'll be staying a couple of days.

**Camping** *Poznań-Strzeszynek Camping*, at ulica Koszalińska 15, is on the far north-west edge of Poznań (bus No 106). It's open June to September.

**Hostels** Of Poznań's youth hostels the closest to Poznań Główny Railway Station is at ulica Berwińskiego 2/3 (☎ 63680), the tall yellow building opposite Kasprzaka Park. To get there leave the station by the west exit and go left along ulica Głogowska till you come to the park (five minutes).

Closer to the old town, but a 20-minute walk from the train station, is the youth hostel at Aleje Niepodległości 32/40 (☎ 56706). If your train happens to stop at Poznań Garbary Railway Station it's closer. The hostel is hidden down a corridor up on the top floor of this huge institutional building.

The youth hostel at ulica Głuszyna 127 is 10 km south-east of Poznań but it's smaller, with a friendly management. There's no phone so you'll just have to take a chance going out there: take bus No 58 from Poznań Starołęka Railway Station (accessible by local train or tram).

These hostels are supposed to be open all year but seldom are. Just make the rounds

after the opening hour (5 pm) until you find a bed.

Almatur, ulica Aleksandra Fredry 7 behind the Palace of Culture, will have information on International Student Hotels (open July and August).

**Private Rooms** The Biuro Zakwaterowania, ulica Głogowska 16 at the end of the long white building across from the west exit from the railway station, can arrange accommodation in private homes at US$10/14 single/ double. The Biuro is open extra long hours at fair time and is probably your best bet then (normal hours are weekdays 9 am to 7 pm, Saturday 9 am to 3 pm).

The Orbis Biuro Obsługi Cudzoziemców (BOC) office downstairs in the Orbis Poznań Hotel also has private rooms at US$12/15 single/double.

**Cheaper Hotels** The *Lech Hotel*, ulica Św Marcin 74 between the railway station and town, is US$17/25 single/double with bath and breakfast. The *Wielkopolska Hotel* across Św Marcin from the Lech charges US$12/ 22 single/double without bath, US$17/25 with bath, breakfast included.

Marginally cheaper is the *Poznański Hotel*, Aleje Marcinkowskiego 22, charging US$10/17 single/double without bath, US$17/25 with bath. The rooms facing the street are noisy. The price includes a cooked breakfast but you can't take it until 8 am, spoiling your plans for an early departure!

*Dom Turysty PTTK* at Stary Rynek 91, a 19th century building right on Poznań's main square, has beds in seven-bed dormitories for US$6 per person, and rooms with bath for US$14/22 single/double (no breakfast). The location can't be beaten.

**Expensive Hotels** There are a number of high-rise luxury hotels in Poznań. They all have about the same to offer, so you can choose by location alone. The *Orbis Mercury* (US$22/ 29 single/double with bath and breakfast) is closest to the international fairgrounds and railway station, whereas the 14-storey *Orbis Polonez*, Aleje Niepodległości

54/68 (US$19/34 single/double with bath and breakfast), is quieter and nearer the sightseeing attractions. The more upmarket *Orbis Poznań* (US$28/40 single/double with bath and breakfast) is in a poor location near the bus station, while the *Orbis Novotel* is out on the highway east of Poznań and convenient to nothing but your car.

Far better value than any of these is the historic, recently renovated *Orbis Bazar Hotel*, Aleje Marcinkowskiego 10 opposite the Poznański, just off Plac Wolności. The Bazar (opened 1842) was a centre of Polish nationalism during the late 19th and early 20th centuries, as a display in the lobby proclaims. Closed for renovations in 1991, the Bazar should have reopened by the time you arrive.

## Places to Eat

**Old Town** A self-service buffet at Stary Rynek 76 serves tasty platefuls of spaghetti but there's always a long line. The *Ratuszowa Wine Cellar*, Stary Rynek 55, is for real: you go down into the cellar to get wine. Draught beer is served at *Pod Piwoszem*, ulica Wrocławska 12 just south off Stary Rynek.

**West of the Old Town** There are many good places to eat in the streets and squares west of the old town, beginning with the *Bazar Hotel* which boasts one of the best hotel restaurants in Poland. Try the Polish dishes like boiled knuckle, tripe, *kołduny* (meat turnovers) and veal *zraziki* (escalopes). The atmosphere is great!

Just two blocks west of here is the *Smakosz Restaurant*, ulica 27 Grudnia 9, which is open till 11 pm and serves excellent food. The *Mewa Milk Bar*, Plac Wolności 1 below Hotel Poznański, is good for breakfast. At *Bistro Piccolo*, Plac Wolności 17, you get a good plate of spaghetti and a glass of hot tea for under a dollar (open daily).

The *Astoria Restaurant*, ulica 23 Lutego 29 opposite the main post office, is a good local restaurant with table service. The *Pod Arkadami Milk Bar*, Plac Cyryla Ratajskiego 10, is great for a snack.

The *Przynęta Restaurant*, ulica Św Marcin 34 (closed Sunday), specialises in fish dishes, while the *Dietetyczna Restaurant* next door is cheaper but also good.

**Cafés** When it's time for coffee, cakes and ice cream, stop at *Sukiennicza*, Stary Rynek 100. *Miodosytnia u Rajców*, Stary Rynek 93, specialises in a sweet honey wine known as *miód* (mead).

## Entertainment

The *Opera House*, ulica Aleksandra Fredry 9, is in the park behind the Solidarity monument. Poznań's symphony orchestra plays at the *Filharmonia*, ulica Św Marcin 81 opposite the Palace of Culture. Check there for performances by the famous Poznań Boys' & Men's Philharmonic Choir which specialises in old music. Also check the *Polski Theatre 'Naród Sobie'*, ulica 27 Grudnia, which sometimes has good programmes. The *Musical Theatre* next to the Orbis Poznań Hotel features Broadway shows like *My Fair Lady* and *Me and My Girl*.

Counter No 2 at Orbis, ulica Św Marcin 33, sells theatre and concert tickets. St John's Fair in June or July and the Poznań Musical Spring in March are annual events to enquire about.

The *Moulin Rouge Night Club*, ulica Kantaka 8/9, offers more basic entertainment in the form of a midnight floor show which includes striptease. There's a cover charge and minimum consumption.

## Things to Buy

There's an Antykwariat (second-hand) bookstore at Stary Rynek 54, and Desa, Stary Rynek 48, has antiques plus old jewellery and paintings. Keep in mind that books and works of art produced before 1945 cannot be exported. Jubiler, Stary Rynek 40, has contemporary Polish jewellery but the best pieces of amber have already been picked out by others. Cepelia, Stary Rynek 49, sells handicraft items including folk costumes. Another Cepelia shop at Stary Rynek 86 has sweaters, some clothing and dolls in folk costumes.

Księgarnia, ulica Gwarna 10 at 27 Grudna near the Lech Hotel, has a large selection of LP records. Also visit the large flower and vegetable market in Plac Wielkopolski in the old town.

The Solidarity Headquarters, ulica Zwierzyniecka 15 between Hotel Mercury and the zoo, has a small store downstairs (open Monday noon to 7 pm, Tuesday to Friday 10 am to 5 pm) selling distinctive Solidarność pins, stickers, postcards and flags.

### Getting There & Away

**Air** World Computer Travel, at ulica J Dąbrowskiego 5a, has return flights to North America (US$725) and Melbourne, Australia (US$1275), usually departing from Berlin or Amsterdam. It also sells cheap bus tickets to western Germany, though you may be told they're only for Poles. Sawa Tour, ulica Podgórna 6, offers discounted air tickets and currency exchange at good rates.

**Bus** Buses to Kórnik and Rogalin leave frequently from the PKS bus station but from a different platform every time, so ask at the Informacja window opposite Kasa No 1 inside the station, then buy your ticket at Kasa No 8.

Every Friday, Saturday and Sunday an afternoon bus (US$2) runs from Poznań to Słubice which is connected to Frankfurt/Oder, Germany, by two bridges. In the past, western tourists were not allowed to use the bridge in the centre of town but had to cross at Świecko on the autoroute just south of Słubice. With the reunification of Germany this most probably has changed.

**Train** Direct trains arrive at Poznań from Berlin, Copenhagen, Hoek van Holland, Kiev, Moscow and Paris abroad, and Ełk, Gdynia/Gdańsk, Kraków, Olsztyn, Rzepin, Szczecin, Toruń, Warsaw and Wrocław in Poland. As you see, it's quite a crossroads! If you're arriving in Poland from Western Europe via Berlin, stop here instead of going straight through to Warsaw.

Book domestic train tickets and couchettes at Orbis, ulica Św Marcin 33. The Orbis office at aleja Karola Marcinkowskiego 21, next to the Poznański Hotel, sells international train tickets and has the Polrailpass.

The Warta and Lech express trains run daily all year between Warsaw and Poznań (311 km, 3½ hours). The Warta departs Warsaw in the morning and Poznań in the late afternoon, whereas the Lech does the opposite. Reservations are required on both trains.

### GNIEZNO

Gniezno (Gnesen), a small town 50 km east of Poznań, was the birthplace of the Polish nation. Here the legendary hero Lech found the white eagle now represented on the Polish flag. Already in the 8th century the Polanian tribe had their main fortified settlement at Gniezno, and in the 10th century, when Mieszko I converted to Christianity, a kingdom was established here. In the year 1000 Boleslav the Brave and the German emperor Otto III had a historic meeting at Gniezno.

A large museum and imposing cathedral bring these events to life for those who make it a day trip from Poznań or stop off for a few hours on the way to Toruń.

### Things to See & Do

**The Museum of the Origin of the Polish State** (closed Monday) at Jelonek Lake on the west side of Gniezno offers a unique audiovisual presentation of the early history of Poland downstairs. Ask if they can put it on for you in English. Upstairs is a historical portrait gallery with English captions. Many of the exhibits are replicas but these are clearly marked 'kopia'.

In the centre of town is the 14th century Gothic **cathedral** with the silver sarcophagus (1662) of St Adalbertus on the main altar. The life story of this saint appears on the cathedral's famous Romanesque bronze doors (1170), inside below the tower. The Bohemian monk Adalbertus arrived at Gniezno in 996 on his way to the lands east

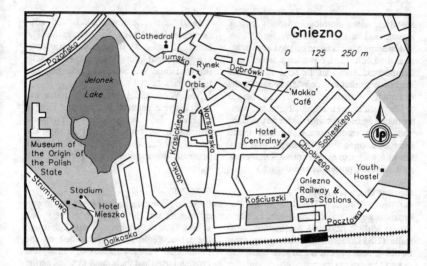

of the mouth of the Vistula River where he intended to convert the heathen Prussians. Instead the tribesmen killed the monk, whose remains were bought back by Boleslav the Brave for their weight in gold. Pope Sylvester canonised Adalbertus in 999, elevating Gniezno to an archbishopric at the same time.

### Places to Stay & Eat

The youth hostel is in a large red school building at ulica Pocztowa 11 near the adjacent bus and train stations. Also near the stations is the *Hotel Centralny*, ulica Chrobrego 32 beside the theatre, but at last report it was closed for renovations.

The newer *Hotel Mieszko* on ulica Strumykowa overlooking Gniezno's sports stadium is US$14/22 single/double with private bath but no breakfast.

The *'Mokka' Café*, ulica Chrobrego 7 between stations and cathedral, is good for a morning snack. The *Restauracja Gwarna*, ulica Mieszka 1, specialises in *żur polski* (sour cream soup).

### Getting There & Away

Gniezno is on the main railway line from Wrocław to Gdynia via Poznań, Inowrocław and Bydgoszcz. Through trains from Poznań to Olsztyn via Toruń and Iława also pass here. Otherwise to go from Gniezno to Toruń you must change at Inowrocław. Local trains to/from Poznań (52 km) are frequent and these stop at Poznań-Garbary Station as well as Poznań Główny.

## TORUŃ

Toruń (Thorn), halfway between Poznań or Warsaw and Gdańsk, was founded by the Teutonic Knights in 1233. Its position on the Vistula River at a crossing of trade routes made it an important member of the medieval Hanseatic League. The wealth this brought is reflected in Toruń's three towering Gothic churches. Two are near Rynek Staromiejski, the old town square in the merchants' quarter, while the third adjoins Rynek Nowomiejski, the new town square in the craftsmen's quarter. The ruins of the knights' castle can still be seen by the river between these two districts.

Fortunately medieval Toruń, still enclosed in surviving sections of the city walls, was not seriously damaged in WW II. It offers a chance to step briefly back in history without a lot of other tourists on your heels. Look for gingerbread, a local speciality made with honey using 18th century moulds.

## Orientation

There are several railway stations in Toruń. Although Toruń Miasto is closer to the centre of town, most trains stop at Toruń Główny, the main station on the south side of the river. Catch a bus in front of the station and get off at the first stop across the bridge. Walk east from the stop and within minutes you'll be on Rynek Staromiejski, the old town square. The main bus station is near the northern edge of town, an easy walk.

## Information

The PTTK Tourist Office is at the west end of ulica Różana just by the passage into the old town.

## Things to See

**The Old Town** A showcase in front of the old town hall on Rynek Staromiejski lists the opening hours of Toruń's six museums. Begin with the **historical museum** (closed Monday and Tuesday) in the 14th century old town hall itself, one of the largest of its kind in the Baltic states. The statue of Copernicus beside the town hall was erected in 1853. Don't miss the nearby **Oriental Art Museum** (closed Wednesday and Thursday) in 15th century Pod Gwiazdą house at Rynek Staromiejski 35, featuring a hanging wooden staircase dated 1697.

Just off the north-west corner of the square is 14th century **St Mary's Church**, a typical Gothic hall church with all naves of equal height – but what a height! The presbytery, stained glass windows, organ (1609) and decoration of this church are fine.

Gothic **St John's Church**, on ulica Żeglarska south of Rynek Staromiejski, is remarkable for its soaring white interior and the richness of its altars. West at ulica Kopernika 17 from this church is the birthplace (in 1473) of astronomer **Nicolaus Copernicus**, now a museum dedicated to the man who moved the earth and stopped the sun (closed Wednesday and Thursday).

Copernicus stayed in Toruń until his 17th birthday when he left to study in Kraków.

Go around the corner beyond the museum and walk straight down to the riverside. Here you'll see the **medieval walls and gates** which once defended Toruń. Walk east along the river past the castle ruins. To reach the ruins turn left, then left again on ulica Przedzamcze. The **Castle of the Teutonic Knights** was destroyed in 1454 but its massive foundations are visible. Early 14th century **St James Church** is off Rynek Nowomiejski in the north-east section of the old town. The flying buttresses on this church are rare in Poland.

## Places to Stay

**Camping** *Camping 'Tramp'* (open May to September), near the south end of the highway bridge over the Vistula River, is a five-minute walk from Toruń Główny Railway Station. There are four-bed bungalows (US$12 for the unit), camping space (US$3 per person) and a restaurant open till midnight. A hotel-style room in the building adjoining the restaurant is US$7 single or double. The camping ground restaurant is OK for a beer but avoid eating there as they will deliberately bring you things you didn't order just to jack up the bill.

**Hostel & Private Rooms** Toruń's *youth hostel* (☎ 27242) is at ulica Rudacka 15, across the river east of Toruń Główny Railway Station (bus No 13).

For a private room try the Biuro Zakwaterowan, Rynek Staromiejski 20 (weekdays 7 am to 3 pm).

**Hotels** The *Hotel Pod Trzema Koronami*, Rynek Staromiejski 21, is cheap and basic at US$3/5 single/double without bath or breakfast, though the location is great, right on the old town square. It's not very pleasant, but what do you expect at those prices?

The *Pod Orłem Hotel*, ulica Mostowa 15 (US$4/7 single/double without bath or breakfast, US$8 double with bath), is still cheap but nicer, as is the *Polonia Hotel* opposite the municipal theatre.

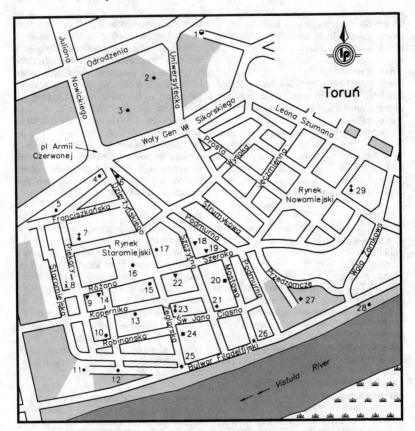

Toruń

The *PTTK Dom Wycieczkowy*, ulica Zjednoczenia 24 several blocks north of the bus station, has double rooms at US$6, or a bed in a four-bed dormitory for US$3.

For a mild splurge consider the *Zajazd Staropolski*, ulica Żeglarska 14, a tasteful small hotel two blocks from the old town square. Back rooms with bath (but no breakfast) are US$8/9 single/double or US$16 for a double with a street view. The hotel restaurant has a nice open atmosphere and the menu is clearly written in German (Żywiec beer available!).

Two Orbis hotels, the *Helios* and *Kosmos*,

grace the park just west of the old town but don't bother with either of them as they charge nonsense prices (from US$56/78 single/double).

### Places to Eat

*Pod Arkadami Milk Bar*, ulica Różana 1 just off Rynek Staromiejski, is an excellent place to sample genuine Polish dishes at low prices. Observe what the local people are eating, then point so the cashier can ring up your order. There's a good pizza place at ulica Różana 5 nearby.

For more sedate dining with proper table

1 Bus Station
2 Ethnographic Park
3 Ethnographical Museum
4 Municipal Theatre
5 Copernicus University
6 Polonia Hotel
7 St Mary's Church
8 PTTK Tourist Office
9 Pizzeria
10 Kawiarna Pod 'Atlantem'
11 Crooked Tower
12 Monastery Gate
13 Copernicus Museum
14 Pod Arkadami Milk Bar
15 Orbis (train tickets)
16 Old Town Hall
17 Oriental Art Museum
18 Staromiejska Restaurant
19 Bar Express
20 Pod Orłem Hotel
21 Archaeological Museum
22 Pod Gołębiem Restaurant
23 St John's Church
24 Hotel Zajazd Staropolski
25 Sailor's Gate
26 Bridge Gate
27 Castle Ruins
28 Excursion Boat Landing
29 St James' Church

service try *Pod Gołębiem*, ulica Szeroka 37. *Bar Express*, ulica Szeroka 24, is a self-service cafeteria where you pay for what you choose. The *Staromiejska Restaurant*, at ulica Szczytna 2, around the corner from Express, is a popular full-service restaurant (beer!).

**Cafés** *Kawiarnia Pod 'Atlantem'*, Ducha Św 3 near the Copernicus Museum, is a nice informal place for coffee and cakes in plush surroundings.

### Entertainment
The *Municipal Theatre* is on Plac Armii Czerwonej at the north entrance to the old town. Every second Friday at 7 pm there's a concert in the old town hall. In September the International Old Music Festival is held in Toruń.

### Getting There & Away
There are direct services from Gdańsk, Malbork, Olsztyn (via Iława), Poznań and Warsaw. Most trains to Warsaw carry mandatory seat reservations, so ask. Services between Gdańsk and Poznań require Toruń passengers to change trains, southbound at Bydgoszcz, northbound at Inowrocław. Seat reservations can be made at Orbis at ulica Żeglarska 31 on Rynek Staromiejski or at Toruń Główny station.

The Kujawiak Express runs daily all year between Warsaw and Toruń (242 km, three hours), departing Warsaw in the afternoon and Toruń in the morning. This train also services Bydgoszcz and reservations are required.

### BYDGOSZCZ
Bydgoszcz (Bromberg) is an untouristed Polish town 47 km west of Toruń, worth a half-day side trip by train or a stop of a couple of hours. The town is near the outlet of the Brda River into the Vistula and the Bydgoszcz Canal links the Vistula to the Odra via the Brda, Noteć and Watra rivers.

Bydgoszcz has the distinction of being the site of the first mass executions of civilians by Nazi *Einsatzgruppen* (death squads) during WW II. Days after the outbreak of war, some fanatical German residents opened fire on retreating Polish troops here, leading to Polish reprisals against German civilians. After the German army captured the city, the SS rounded up and shot some 20,000 Poles, many of them up on Bydgoszcz's main square. By 1945 a quarter of the population of the town had been killed.

### Information & Orientation
Just outside the station is a helpful tourist information office. From the station take a tram or walk straight down ulica Dworcowa to Aleje 1 Maja. At the foot of this avenue is a pedestrian bridge over the Brda River to Stary Rynek, the main square.

### Things to See & Do
There are two museums (both closed Monday) near the bridge. The **District Art**

**Museum**, Aleje 1 Maja 4, exhibits contemporary Polish painting upstairs. In room 19 of the museum in the old **riverside granaries** are some striking photos of the Nazi occupation of Bydgoszcz, though unfortunately no explanation is provided in English or German.

From May to September **excursion boats** offer cruises on the Brda River from Bydgoszcz. The ticket office is in the red brick building just downstream from the granaries museum.

A striking **monument** to the Polish victims of WW II stands in the centre of Stary Rynek, with Bydgoszcz's Gothic **parochial church** (1502) a little behind. A lovely 16th century painting of the Virgin with a rose graces the high altar of this church. The **Galeria Sztuki Współczesnej** in a corner of Stary Rynek sells contemporary Polish works of art.

### Places to Stay & Eat

The *Hotel Centralny,* Dworcowa 85 near the railway station, has rooms without bath at US$5/8 single/double. The Biuro Zakwaterowań in this hotel can find you a private room. More luxurious accommodation is available at the high-rise *Hotel Brda,* Dworcowa 94, which charges US$28/45 single/double.

Also close to the railway station is the youth hostel, ulica Sowińskiego 5, in a school behind a large red brick church a block and a half from the Brda Hotel.

More memorable accommodation in the centre of town is available at the *Orbis Pod Orłem Hotel,* Aleje 1 Maja 14, which was built in 1898 and closed for renovations in 1990. Perhaps the best place of all is the old *Hotel Ratuszowy,* at ulica Długa 37 (US$6/10 single/double without bath or breakfast).

*Ratuszowy Milk Bar*, ulica Długa 28 just up from Stary Rynek, offers basic meals.

### Getting There & Away

Bydgoszcz is on the main line from Wrocław to Gdynia via Poznań and Gniezno. There's also direct service to Warsaw via Toruń.

# Pomerania

The Polish Baltic coast stretches 524 km from Germany to the USSR, a region of rugged natural beauty where endless beaches and shifting dunes alternate with vast bays, lagoons and coastal lakes. Most of Pomerania (north-western Poland between the Vistula and Odra rivers) was part of Germany until 1945, though the area from Bydgoszcz to Gdynia belonged to Poland from 1918 on.

Here Baltic beach resorts such as Świnoujście, Kołobrzeg, Ustka, Łeba, Hel and Sopot join historic cities such as Szczecin and Gdańsk to put Pomerania on most Polish itineraries. Areas of special interest to naturalists include Wolin National Park near Międzyzdroje and Slovincian National Park west of Łeba. By land, Szczecin is the western gateway to the Baltic coast, while Świnoujście and Gdańsk are terminals of ferries from Denmark, Sweden and Finland.

## HISTORY

Northern Poland has long been a battleground between Poles and Germans. Poland never really controlled the Slavonic tribes of western Pomerania, and beginning in the 12th century the area was absorbed by the margraves of Brandenburg. In eastern Pomerania the Germanic Teutonic Knights, invited here in 1226 to help subdue the restive Prussian tribes, played a similar role. From their castles at Malbork and Toruń, the knights defied the king of Poland until their defeat in the 15th century by combined Polish and Lithuanian forces. Although the Duchy of Prussia was a vassal of Poland in the 16th century, wars with Sweden and internal dissent weakened Poland's position in the 17th century.

In 1720 the Kingdom of Prussia reoccupied all of western Pomerania, and the first partition of Poland (1772) brought everything south as far as Toruń under Prussian control (Toruń itself wasn't annexed by

Prussia until 1793). After the Congress of Vienna in 1815, Poland south-east of Toruń came under tsarist Russia, a situation that persisted until WW I. In 1919 the Treaty of Versailles granted Poland a narrow corridor to the sea, separating East Prussia from Pomerania. Since the Free City of Danzig (Gdańsk) was populated mostly by Germans, the Polish government built Gdynia from scratch after 1922.

In 1939 Hitler's demand for a German-controlled road and rail route across Polish territory to East Prussia and the incorporation of Danzig into the Third Reich sparked WW II. In 1945 the German inhabitants were expelled from Pomerania and East Prussia. Poland got Pomerania and the southern half of East Prussia (Mazuria) while the Soviet Union took the northern half of East Prussia including the capital Königsberg (Kaliningrad). Today there's no tourism to that corner of the Russian Federation, while northern Poland is open to view.

## INFORMATION

The 1:400,000 'Pobrzeże Bałtyku' map of north-western Poland available at bookshops and tourist offices is well worth having.

## SZCZECIN

Szczecin (Stettin), pronounced 'shtechin', one-time capital of the Duchy of West Pomerania, was captured by the Swedes in 1630. They sold it to Prussia for two million thalers in 1720 and until 1945 it was part of Germany. Lovers of trivia might like to know that Empress Catherine the Great of Russia was born at Szczecin as duchess Sophia Augusta Anhalt-Zerbst in 1729. After the first partition of Poland in 1772, this town near the mouth of the Odra River became the main port of Berlin, to which it was connected by canal.

Destroyed in WW II, Szczecin wasn't rebuilt as carefully as were Gdańsk, Warsaw, Poznań and Wrocław, with the result that this thoroughly Polish city near the German border is now more of a gateway to Poland or the Baltic coast than a destination in itself. There are ferries to and from Scandinavia from nearby Świnoujście, a daily train to and from Berlin, and good railway connections to the rest of Poland. Half a day is enough to see the scattered red brick remnants of Gothic and neo-Gothic Szczecin.

## Orientation

You'll probably arrive at Szczecin Główny Railway Station near the river on the south edge of the city centre. You'll see a pedestrian walkway over the tracks and up into the city. If you leave this way, you'll soon reach Aleje 3 Maja with the city centre to the right, the shortest way to go if you wish to walk to your hotel.

If on the other hand you go through the underpass into the main station building itself, you'll find taxis waiting at the exit facing the river. To walk from there, go past the bus station just north and follow the tram tracks north-west to the Harbour Gate at the east end of Plac Zwycięstwa, a 10-minute walk away.

## Information

The Pomerania Biuro Turystyki (tourist office), Aleje Jedności Narodowej 50, is of little help. Try the PTTK office nearby on Plac Lotników for maps.

For information on ferries from Świnoujście to Denmark and Sweden, go to Polferries, ulica Wyszyńskiego 28.

## Things to See

In 1725 the Prussians erected the **Harbour Gate** (off Plac Zwycięstwa) to mark the purchase of this area from the Swedes for two million thalers. Today, the gate houses a shop that has a good selection of Polish handicrafts. The old city was between here and the river.

Walk north on Aleje Niepodległości two blocks and turn right onto Plac Żołnierza Polskiego to the **National Museum** (closed Monday). This museum and its annexe across the street have a collection of paintings and artefacts of local interest.

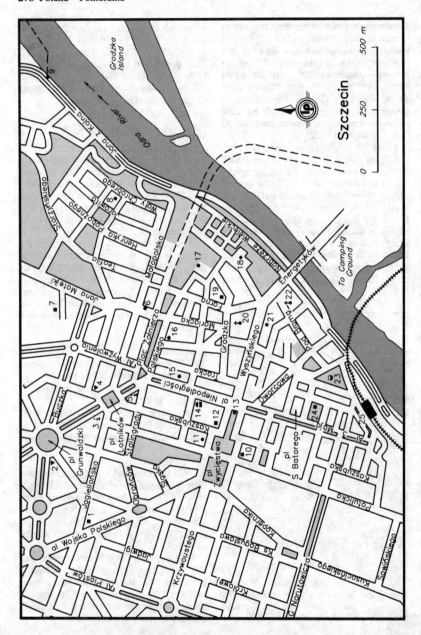

Szczecin

1 Gryf Hotel
2 Chief Restaurant
3 PTTK Tourist Office
4 Balaton Restaurant
5 Pomerania Biuro Turystyki
6 Gate of Prussian Homage
7 Orbis Neptun Hotel
8 Museum
9 Dworzec Morski Hydrofoil Landing
10 Piast Hotel
11 Orbis
12 Pomorski Hotel
13 Harbour Gate
14 Post Office
15 Milk Bar Extra
16 National Museum
17 Castle of the Dukes of Pomerania
18 City Museum
19 Summertime Youth Hostel
20 St James' Church
21 Polferries
22 St John's Church
23 Bus Station
24 Dom Turysty PTTK
25 Szczecin Główny Railway Station

Continue east towards the river to the 16th century **Castle of the Dukes of Pomerania**, a fine Renaissance building with a lookout tower you can climb, café, art gallery, theatre and some faculties of the university. Musical events are often held here during the day, so check early enough to have time to come back. Opera and operetta are also performed in the castle.

The **City Museum** (closed Monday) in the rebuilt 15th century town hall, near the Orbis Arkona Hotel between castle and river, has many interesting old maps and paintings. These show vividly how much of the old quarter around the now isolated old town hall was lost. The *Miodosytnia U Wyszaka* in the town hall's basement serves hot honey wine (*miód*). On your way back into town you'll pass the late Gothic **St James Church** – impressive with its soaring interior, now fully restored.

**Excursion Boats** North-east along the riverside from here, beyond the ugly concrete overpass, is **Dworzec Morski**, a landing for harbour tour boats (last departure at 1 pm). The commuter ferry to Plaza Mieleńska, a nearby beach, also allows a fair glimpse of the harbour.

On Wały Chrobrego, the high embankment above Dworzec Morski, stand monumental buildings erected just before WW I. The middle one at the top of the stairs is a maritime museum and theatre. There's an excellent view of the river and port from here.

### Places to Stay

**Camping** The *PTTK Camping* (☎ 61 3264) at Dąbie, a few km east of Szczecin, is easily accessible on public transport. Take tram No 2, 7 or 8 to the end of the line, then bus No 56, 62 or 72 till you see the sign on the left. Szczecin Dąbie Railway Station is closer to the camping ground than the main station. Bungalows are available. It's open May till September and English is spoken.

**Hostels** The youth hostel, ulica Unisławy 26, is up Aleje Wyzwolenia north of the centre, on the top floor of a large school just off Plac J Kilińskiego (trams No 2 and 3). Look for the green triangles over the door and go up to the top of the stairs (registration 5 to 8 pm only). In July and August there's a summer youth hostel at ulica Grodzka 22 in the old town.

**Hotels** Closest to the stations is the *Dom Turysty PTTK*, Plac S Batorego 2, which charges US$5/11 single/double for a plain room without sink or toilet. It's often crowded with noisy adolescents but at least it's free of tram noise.

Of the two older hotels on bustling Plac Zwycięstwa, the less appealing is the *Pomorski* at US$12/14 single/double without bath or breakfast. The *Piast Hotel* nearby (US$9/16 without bath, breakfast included) has a better atmosphere and is farther from the noisy tram lines.

Similarly priced but more pleasant than

any of these is the *Gryf Hotel*, Aleje Wojska Polskiego 49. The attractively decorated rooms are US$9/17 single/double without bath, US$13/20 with bath, breakfast included.

### Places to Eat

*Milk Bar Extra*, Aleje Niepodległości 5 diagonally opposite the main post office, serves cheap, cafeteria-style meals (closed Sundays). The *Balaton Restaurant* on Plac Lotników offers Hungarian food. Many evenings a dance band plays at the Balaton and food service is suspended.

The *Chief Restaurant* on Plac Grunwaldzki is a seafood specialist as the goldfish swimming in several aquariums in the dining room suggest. Try the *szaszłyk bałtycki* (Baltic *shashlik*), a shish kebab of fish and meat served with rice and fried mushrooms. The kitchen is open from 11 am to 9 pm daily and the menu is in German. Chief manages to be unpretentious and the service is excellent – recommended.

### Getting There & Away

**Train** A main line runs from Szczecin to Przemyśl in south-eastern Poland via Poznań, Wrocław, Opole and Kraków. Other trains to Wrocław go via Rzepin. Trains from Warsaw arrive via Poznań. The Gedania Express calls at Szczecin daily between Gdynia and Berlin-Lichtenberg. Local service to Szczecin from Gdańsk (374 km) or Poznań (214 km) is frequent. Local trains operate between Świnoujście and Szczecin Główny via Szczecin Dąbie.

The Chrobry Express runs daily all year between Warsaw and Szczecin (522 km, six hours), departing from Warsaw in the afternoon and Szczecin in the early morning. At certain times of year (ask) the Błękitna Fala Express does the opposite, departing Warsaw in the early morning and Szczecin in the afternoon. Reservations are required on both trains.

Couchettes are available from Szczecin to Gdynia, Warsaw, Wrocław, Kraków and Przemyśl. Orbis, Plac Zwycięstwa 1, makes reservations, sells international train tickets and books couchettes.

### ŚWINOUJŚCIE

This fishing port at the mouth of the Świna River is a popular Baltic beach resort. Świnoujście (Swinemünde), pronounced 'shwino-UESHT-yeh', is an important Polish naval base with an active commercial port. International ferries arrive regularly from Scandinavia and there are good train connections to Szczecin (64 km) and beyond. Theoretically a hydrofoil service also exists to/from Szczecin but it's often out of service.

Świnoujście is a busy little town just far enough away from the beach to have a life of its own and not be a nuisance. A large park lies between town and the beach and there's lots of inexpensive accommodation. The location right on the German border is also very interesting. In July the 'Fama' Student Artistic Festival is held here.

### Orientation

The train from Szczecin crosses the Dziwna River at Wolin and passes Międzyzdroje on Wolin Island before reaching the railway station at Świnoujście Port on the right (east) bank of the Świna River. The international ferry terminal is a five-minute walk from the railway station.

Right beside the adjacent train and bus stations is a car ferry (every 15 minutes, free for pedestrians) across the river to Świnoujście town on the left (west) bank of the river, a 20-minute walk from the beach. Świnoujście is situated on Uznam, a coastal island bounded by the Świna River, the Szczecin Lagoon, the Gulf of Pomerania and the Peenestrom in Germany.

### Information

The Pomerania Tourist Office, ulica Armii Krajowej 14a (weekdays 7 am to 3 pm), doesn't have many maps and nobody speaks English, so you may find the PTTK, ulica Paderewskiego 24, a better information source.

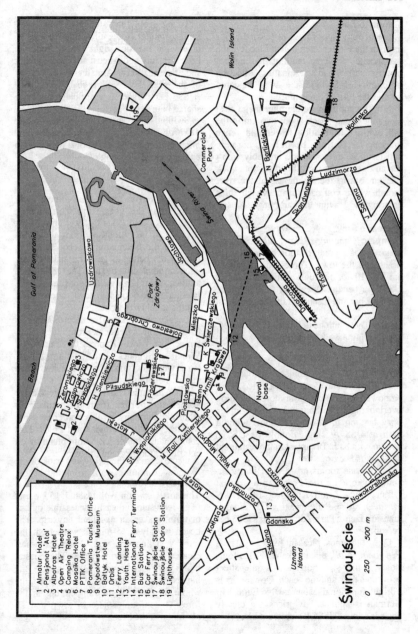

## Świnoujście

1 Almatur Hotel
2 Pensjonat 'Atol'
3 Albatros Hotel
4 Open Air Theatre
5 Camping 'Relax'
6 Mosolka Hotel
7 PTTK Office
8 Pomerania Tourist Office
9 Rybołówstwa Museum
10 Bałtyk Hotel
11 Orbis
12 Ferry Landing
13 Youth Hostel
14 International Ferry Terminal
15 Bus Station
16 Car Ferry
17 Świnoujście Station
18 Świnoujście Odra Station
19 Lighthouse

0    250    500 m

## Things to See

The **Muzeum Rybołówstwa** (closed Monday), in the former town hall at Plac Rybaka 1 opposite the ferry landing, has natural history exhibits and a fascinating collection of photos of Świnoujście as it appeared around the turn of the century.

You'll want to make the pilgrimage west along the broad beach about two km to the tall, white observation tower and fence marking the **German border**. It's not very sinister these days and you probably won't see any guards. In the other direction, walk one km out to the lighthouse at the river mouth where you can sit and watch ships entering and leaving the harbour.

## Places to Stay

**Camping** *Camping 'Relax'*, ulica Słowackiego 1, has a great location between park, beach and the town. Three-bed bungalows are US$10 for the unit while camping is US$1 per person. Open May to September, there's a bar and restaurant on the premises.

**Hostel** The youth hostel, ulica Gdyńska 26, is a 15-minute walk west from the port (open in summer only).

**Hotels** Most of Świnoujście's hotels are open all year. The *Hotel Bałtyk*, ulica Armii Krajowej 5, an older, four-storey building overlooking the harbour just across from the ferry landing in town, has rooms without bath at US$7/9 single/double or US$16 double with bath. Breakfast in the restaurant downstairs is extra.

For private rooms go to the Biuro Zakwaterowania in the Pomerania Tourist Office, ulica Armii Krajowej 14a. *Hotel Mozaika*, ulica Paderewskiego 1, a large mansion facing Park Zdrojowy, is US$5 per person.

One of the most pleasant places to stay is *Pensjonat 'Atol'*, ulica Orkana 3. This four-storey, family-style hotel is on a quiet street between a park and the beach. Downstairs is a bright, functional restaurant. No English or German is spoken but prices are clearly posted: around US$6/9 single/double.

Young people and students should head for the *Almatur Hotel*, ulica Żeromskiego 17 in a large mansion right across from the beach. In July and August advance booking should be made at an Almatur office. The rest of the year there will probably be space (US$3 per person in a double room with shared bath).

Świnoujście's top-end hotel is the two-star *Albatros Hotel*, ulica Kasprowicza 2 a few minutes from the beach. Rooms with private bath are US$10/15 single/double.

## Getting There & Away

Large car ferries arrive here almost daily throughout the year from Copenhagen (Denmark) and Ystad (Sweden). Ferry tickets can be purchased from the Orbis office at the International Ferry Terminal, though it's better to get your tickets elsewhere in advance to be sure. The Orbis office at ulica Armii Krajowej 2 opposite the ferry landing in Świnoujście town doesn't sell international ferry tickets.

Local train service to Szczecin (97 km) via Międzyzdroje is frequent. From June to September the Wawel Express to Kraków via Wrocław originates here. Also summer only is an overnight train to/from Warsaw which carries sleeping cars.

In the past it has not been possible to drive across the border from Świnoujście to Ahlbeck, Germany, as this border crossing was reserved for Germans and Poles. This could change but check before planning on entering/exiting Poland this way.

## MIĘDZYZDROJE

This small town on Wolin Island, 15 km east of Świnoujście and easily accessible by bus or train, makes an excellent day trip. The beach is only a 15-minute walk from the railway station and you'll find the water clearer than at Świnoujście. The coastal bluffs just east of town reach 95 metres, the highest on the Polish coast. Give yourself the whole day here: a morning hiking in the forest, lunch somewhere in town and an afternoon at the beach.

## Things to See & Do

Huddled right up along the east side of Międzyzdroje is **Wolin National Park**, a thick deciduous forest covering the low hills between the Szczecin Lagoon (Zalew Szczeciński) and the Gulf of Pomerania. The rare European bison, sea eagle and mute swan abide here. Hiking trails penetrate the forest from the edge of town.

Pick up a hiking map at the PTTK, ulica Paderewskiego 24, Świnoujście, or at the coffee shop in Dom Kultury in the beach park in the middle of Międzyzdroje. The **Muzeum Przyrodnicze** of Wolin National Park is between the railway station and the beach.

## Places to Stay

There are lots of places to stay in Międzyzdroje but all of them are owned by Polish trade unions, factories and mass organisations and do not admit paying customers. The Pomerania Tourist Office, ulica Światowida 19 (weekdays from 7 am to 3 pm), is supposed to arrange private rooms, but they're worse than useless and their standard response to every request is *nie ma*. It's possible that this will change as some of these outfits go bankrupt or begin to recognise the value of money, but for now you'll have to make Międzyzdroje a day trip.

## Getting There & Away

All trains between Szczecin and Świnoujście stop here.

## KOŁOBRZEG

Kołobrzeg (Kolberg), on the Baltic at the mouth of the Parsęta River, was an important member of the 14th century Hanseatic League. Though a Polish bishop had been present here since the early 12th century, the region was ruled by Piast princes subject to the German Holy Roman Emperor rather than the Polish king. The town was developed as a seaside resort and spa in the 19th century, but in 1945 it became a stronghold in the defensive 'Pomerania Line' and was 90% devastated during 10 days of fighting between German and Polish troops.

Today much of Kołobrzeg consists of rectangular apartment blocks, and about the only thing still worth seeing in the old town is a five-naved, red-brick Gothic **collegiate church**. A long **pier** stretches out into the sea from the crowded sands of Kołobrzeg's wide Baltic beach. The brine springs and radioactive mud baths of Kołobrzeg are used to treat circulatory system diseases and diabetes under medical supervision. A Salt Fair is held here in July.

## Places to Stay

The modern eight-storey *Hotel Skanpol*, on ulica Dworcowa overlooking a park two blocks from the railway station, is US$20/30 single/double with bath and breakfast. In July and August the rate is higher.

The 'Baltywia' Tourist Bureau (weekdays 7 am to 3 pm) at ulica Wojska Polskiego 5 behind Hotel Skanpol has private rooms at US$3 per person. You may have difficulty making yourself understood here.

The camping ground is on the east side of town opposite the Orbis Solny Hotel, between the railway tracks and the beach. All the large hotels you see along the waterfront park are holiday homes for Polish workers and not open to the public.

## Getting There & Away

Kołobrzeg is connected to Szczecin (138 km) every couple of hours by local train. To go east towards Lębork and Gdynia, you usually have to change at Koszalin.

## ŁEBA

If you're looking for a Baltic beach resort you won't have to share with thousands of holidaying Polish workers and their families, where the small town ambience still prevails and the surrounding nature is relatively undisturbed, you won't go wrong by choosing Łeba (pronounced 'wemba'). The beach here stretches in both directions as far as the eye can see, and only one old mansion breaks through the forest crowning the beachside sand dunes. Unlike the polluted waters around Gdańsk, you can swim in the open Baltic here.

## Orientation

Trains and buses from Lębork terminate at Łeba Railway Station two blocks west of ulica Kościuszki, Łeba's main drag. This shopping street runs north a few hundred metres, crosses a canal, and ends in a park which you walk through to reach the sea.

## Things to See

Łeba is on a brief stretch of the Łeba River which joins Łebsko Lake to the sea. Just before dusk, people head down to the river mouth to join the fishers in watching the sunset. The river divides Łeba's beach in two. The town is nestled back out of the way behind the eastern beach, while the beach on the west side of the river is far less crowded. The broad white sands of this western beach stretch back 75 metres to the dunes – one of the best beaches on the entire Baltic.

Further west of town and the river, a sand bar of white pine-covered dunes separates shallow Lake Łebsko from the Baltic. Here one finds **Słowiński National Park**, where the largest shifting sand dunes in Eastern Europe create a striking desert landscape. During WW II, Rommel's Afrika Korps trained in this desert, and a small Polish military base is still hidden among the dunes. V-1 rockets were fired at England from here, and you can still find what appear to be the old concrete launching pads.

The road into the park runs along the north shore of Lake Łebsko for 2.5 km to the Rabka park entry gate (pedestrians free, cars US$1.25, gate closed from October to April), then another 4.5 km to Wydmy Ruchome where vehicular traffic ends. In July and August there are buses from Łeba to Wydmy Ruchome (7 km) every two hours. From the end of the road it's a two-km walk to a magnificent, 42-metre-high sand dune which simply must be climbed for a sweeping view of desert, lake, beach, sea and forest. You can return to Łeba on foot along the beach with perhaps a stop for a swim – something you can't do in the Sahara!

## Places to Stay

*Dom Wycieczkowy PTTK,* ulica 1-go Maja 6 on the corner of ulica Kościuszki, just two blocks from the railway station, is the place to try first. Rooms with private bath (but no hot water) are US$5 single or double. If the PTTK doesn't work out there's the three-storey *Hotel Morska* beside the cinema between town and the beach (US$7 single or double).

The *Intercamp,* a five-minute walk west from the railway station (signposted), has camping space at US$1.25 per person or rooms in a central building for US$5 (up to three persons). In 1984 the International Camping and Caravanning Jamboree was held here.

There are two more camping grounds a few hundred metres west of the Intercamp (to the right), and these have more shade and are closer to the beach. The first is *Camping 'Przymorze' No 21* which also operates the local Biuro Zakwaterowań (private rooms). The second is run by the PTTK and has lots of pretty little three-bed wooden cabins among the pine trees which go for US$4 per unit. All these camping grounds are open from mid-May to mid-September. On a hot summer weekend every bed at Łeba will be occupied by people from the Tri-City area, so have your tent ready.

## Places to Eat

The *Restaurant Morska,* in the hotel of the same name, is about the best place to eat. There's nowhere to get breakfast before 9 am in Łeba, so it's best to buy something the night before.

## Getting There & Away

To get to Łeba by train you'll have to change at Lębork on the main railway line from Szczecin to Gdańsk. Trains only run from Lębork to Łeba every three or four hours. If you're unlucky, check the bus station across the street from Lębork Railway Station where there are buses to Łeba (US$0.50) every hour or more. There are a couple of buses a day from Gdynia direct to Łeba (59 km).

The Posejdon and Słupia express trains run daily all year between Warsaw and

Lębork (413 km, five hours). The Posejdon leaves Warsaw in the early morning and Lębork in the late afternoon, while the Słupia does the opposite. Both trains travel via Gdynia/Gdańsk/Malbork and reservations are required.

## GDYNIA

The Tri-City conurbation, Gdynia-Sopot-Gdańsk, stretches 30 km along the west side of the Gulf of Gdańsk on the Baltic Sea. Gdynia (Gdingen), the northernmost of the three, is the base for much of Poland's merchant and fishing fleet. Unlike Gdańsk which is on a river, Gdynia is a real Baltic port looking out onto the open sea, with sailors on the streets and seagulls flying above.

In 1922 the Polish parliament decided to build a port on the site of a small village here to give Poland an outlet to the sea at a time when Gdańsk was still the Free City of Danzig. With the help of French capital, Gdynia had become one of the largest ports on the Baltic by the outbreak of WW II. Unlike most other towns along the north coast which are German in origin, Gdynia is Polish through and through.

### Things to See

Sightseeing centres around Gdynia's broad main pier, Nabrzeże Pomorskie, pointing out into the Gulf of Gdańsk. Along it runs an attractive walkway past museum ships, ferry terminals, an aquarium and finally a monument to the writer Joseph Conrad. In summer you can catch an excursion boat to Hel from here.

Two historic **museum ships** (closed Monday) are stationed on this pier. The *Błyskawica*, a WW II warship, is permanently moored at the pier. The *Dar Pomorza*, a three-masted sailing vessel built at Hamburg in 1909, was christened the *Prinzess Eitel*. In 1919 France got the ship for reparations and it was purchased by Poland as a naval training ship in 1929. The *Dar Pomorza* spent the war years in Stockholm. It's still an active training ship and often travels abroad to show the flag, so

there's no assurance it will be there when you are.

### Places to Stay

**Private Rooms** There's a Biuro Zakwaterowań at ulica Dworcowa 7 near Gdynia Główna Railway Station which arranges accommodation in private homes for US$8 double for two nights. They don't rent rooms for one night and there are no singles.

**Hotels** The *Bristol Hotel*, an old-style hotel conveniently located at ulica Starowiejska 1, is US$9 per person with shared bath. The price includes a revolting breakfast of cold fish covered with chilli sauce. It's the kind of place a seaman would appreciate on coming ashore after a long voyage, though the earthy atmosphere will appeal to any rough-and-ready traveller looking to get off the beaten track.

Rooms at the shiny 12-storey *Orbis Gdynia Hotel* begin as low as US$12/17 single/double, though most accommodation there is much more expensive.

### Places to Eat

The restaurant at the *Bristol Hotel*, ulica Starowiejska 1, serves good meals (breakfast excluded) and there's a bar attached. Nearby at ulica Świętojańska 16 between the Bristol and the pier is *Milk Bar Ekspres* which offers cheap cafeteria food.

### Entertainment

The *Musical Theatre*, Plac Grunwaldzki 1, is near the Orbis Gdynia Hotel.

### Getting There & Away

All long-distance trains arriving in the Tri-City area call at Gdynia, Sopot and Gdańsk. Southbound trains usually originate in Gdynia while trains to Szczecin begin in Gdańsk. For information about some of these and the local electric commuter trains, see the Gdańsk section.

The bus station is in front of Gdynia Railway Station. Bus tickets are sold at the 'kasy PKS' near the train reservation windows inside the railway station. Buses of

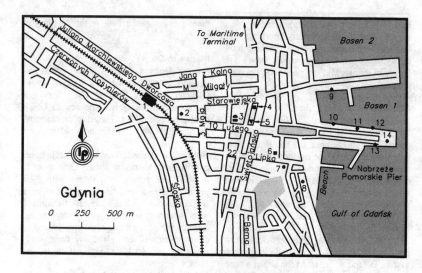

Gdynia

0    250    500 m

1   Gdynia-Główna Railway Station
2   Biuro Zakwaterowań
3   Post Office
4   Bristol Hotel
5   Milk Bar Ekspres
6   Orbis Gdynia Hotel
7   Musical Theatre
8   Naval Museum
9   Fishing Boats
10  Museum Ship 'Błyskawica'
11  Ferry Terminal
12  Museum Ship 'Dar Pomorza'
13  Oceanographic Museum & Aquarium
14  Joseph Conrad Monument

possible use to visitors include those to Hel, Łeba and Świnoujście (runs overnight).

The Marine Terminal (Dworzec Morski) where some international ferries tie up, is a couple of km north-east of the railway station (take a taxi).

### HEL

Hel, a real Baltic fishing village near the tip of the narrow peninsula separating the Gulf of Gdańsk from the sea, is the favourite day-trip destination for Tri-City area visitors.

### Things to See & Do

The local **Fishing Museum** is in the old red church opposite the harbour. There's a beach on the bay just west of the harbour, or walk a little over one km across the peninsula to the sea beach.

### Places to Stay & Eat

There are no hotels at Hel, though the PTTK Tourist Office, Generała Waltera 80 near the harbour, might be able to suggest a place to stay. Next to the PTTK is the *Kaszubska Bar* with big mugs of draught beer.

### Getting There & Away

On summer mornings excursion boats to Hel leave from the end of the long wooden pier at Sopot, and less frequently from Gdańsk and Gdynia. In Gdańsk buy tickets at ulica Wartka 4 on the waterfront. Upon arrival in Hel, buy your return ticket at the kiosk ashore right away as it closes as soon as the ship's capacity has been reached. There's a small bar aboard where you can get coffee or a beer. The open deck at the back makes for a very pleasant trip.

It's nice to take the boat over but they only allow 1½ hours at Hel, enough for a walk

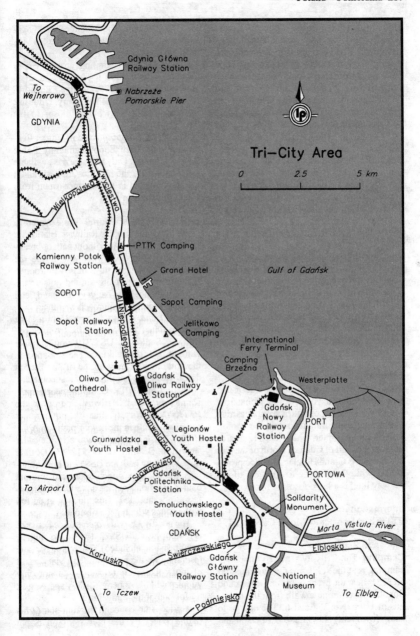

around town and a drink. If you want more time to enjoy the beach you'll have to get a train back. This is no problem as local trains run Hel-Gdynia about four times a day, while the service from Hel to Reda (where there are immediate connections for Gdynia and Gdańsk) is seven times a day. The train trip to/from Gdynia takes over two hours while the boat needs only one.

## SOPOT

Sopot (Zoppot), south of Gdynia by electric train, has been Poland's most fashionable seaside resort since Napoleon's former doctor, Jean Haffner, erected baths here in 1823. During the interwar period, Sopot belonged to the Free City of Danzig, only fully joining Poland in 1945. Sopot has a much greater abundance of budget accommodation than either Gdańsk or Gdynia, and the resort atmosphere makes for a pleasant stay. Several expensive resort hotels line the wide and white sandy shores stretching north from Jelitkowo, but budget accommodation is also available. Unfortunately the Vistula River flushes thousands of tonnes of pollutants into the Gulf of Gdańsk every year, so swimming here is not recommended.

### Orientation

Turn left as you leave the railway station and in a few minutes you'll reach Bohaterów Monte Cassino, Sopot's attractive pedestrian mall which leads straight down to the 'molo', Poland's longest pier, which juts 512 metres out into the Gulf of Gdańsk. North of the pier and the Orbis Grand Hotel is a seaside promenade, while behind the town, west of the railway line, is a large forest.

### Information

PTTK is at Bohaterów Monte Cassino 31.

### Places to Stay

**Camping** The Tri-City's most convenient camping is at the *Jelitkowo Campground* (☎ 53 2731) near the beach between Gdańsk and Sopot, a seven-minute walk from the terminus of trams No 2, 4 and 6. The charge to camp (own tent) is US$2.50 per person and

US$1.50 per tent. The 25 three-bed bungalows go for US$16 triple. It's open from May to September.

There's another camping ground, *Sopot Camping*, open June to August, at ulica Bitwy pod Płowcami 79, about one km north of Jelitkowo on the main highway. It doesn't have any bungalows but is closer to the beach.

The *PTTK Camping* is a convenient five-minute walk from Sopot-Kamienny Potok Railway Station. Only tent space is available (no bungalows), the facilities are basic and it can get crowded in the summer (open from June to September).

**Hotels & Private Rooms** The *Dworcowy Hotel* near the Sopot Railway Station is US$5/8 single/double without bath or breakfast. The Biuro Zakwaterowań beside the Dworcowy arranges stays in private rooms. If they can't help, hang around outside the office looking lost, baggage in hand, and wait until someone approaches you.

*Hotel Irena*, ulica Chopina 36 in a large mansion just down the hill from Sopot Railway Station, is US$7/10 single/double without bath or breakfast. The sex shop in the hotel may or may not be of interest but don't worry, the hotel itself is respectable.

Behind the PTTK Camping near Sopot-Kamienny Potok Railway Station is the *PTTK Dom Turysty*, but it's no bargain: rooms with bath in the newer 'pavilion A' are US$17/27 single/double while in the older 'pavilion B' they're US$12/23. Double rooms without bath are US$12 in both buildings and there is one single room without bath in pavilion A which costs US$7. Breakfast is not included. This place is often full with groups which get a discount rate.

The nearby *Maryla Hotel* at ulica Sepia 22 is rather plush at US$23 double (no singles, breakfast not included). There's a bar and restaurant on the premises. The Maryla sort of looks like a country club but not only yuppies will like it here – in July and August try for one of the bungalows.

If price is no concern, the four-star *Orbis Grand Hotel* by the pier right on Sopot

Beach should be your choice. This 118-room, neo-Baroque resort hotel built in 1926 is a 10-minute walk from Sopot Railway Station. Singles/doubles begin at US$10/14 with breakfast and go up to US$89 double for a suite overlooking the sea. During July and August these prices double. There's a gambling casino in the hotel, and the Grand is the sort of place where you expect to rub shoulders with the cream of European society, though you're more likely to be engulfed in a group of packaged Americans these days.

### Places to Eat

The *Zdrojowy Milk Bar* on Plac Konstytucji 3 Maja, not far from the Sopot Railway Station, is easy because you pick up the food before paying. The nearby *Albatros Restaurant* in the Dworcowy Hotel is a world better and not that much more expensive. The elegant restaurant in the *Orbis Grand Hotel* by the pier offers grilled salmon, smoked eel and tenderloin *zrazy* (pound steak) in a loaf of bread. Sopot lives off tourism, so expect to be cheated slightly in bars and restaurants.

### Entertainment

Summer activities centre around the open-air *Opera Leśna* in the forest, 15 minutes' walk straight west from Bohaterów Monte Cassino. The Opera and Musical Theatre Festival is held here in July and the International Song Festival in the last 10 days of August. Rock groups appear on the programme of the latter.

For tickets to the Opera Leśna check with the Bałtycka Agencja Artystyczna (BART), ulica Kościuszki 61 a couple of blocks south of Sopot Railway Station.

### Getting There & Away

All long-distance trains stop here. For train times and sleeper, couchette or seat reservations try Orbis, Bohaterów Monte Cassino 49.

### GDAŃSK

Gdańsk (Danzig) on the Motława River, a stagnant arm of the Vistula, about four km from the sea, is Poland's largest port, a major

shipbuilding centre, and the birthplace of Solidarity. Though in existence as early as the 9th century, the beautiful historic centre dates from the Hanseatic period when medieval Gdańsk was one of the richest ports in Europe providing access to the Baltic for much of Central Europe.

From 1454 to 1793 Gdańsk belonged to the Polish crown, and the largely German population was pacified by the autonomy and many privileges granted by Poland's kings. A famous 17th century resident was astronomer Jan Hevelius, after whom the local beer is named. Physicist Daniel Fahrenheit and philosopher Arthur Schopenhauer also hailed from here.

After WW I, the Treaty of Versailles created the Free City of Danzig, with Poland administering essential services such as the port, post and railways, and the German residents dominating municipal government. What could have developed into a profitable commercial relationship for both sides was soured by petty nationalism.

At 4.45 am on 1 September 1939 the first shots of WW II were fired as the battleship *Schleswig-Holstein* opened up on a Polish military depot at Westerplatte near Gdańsk. Gdańsk was 55% destroyed during the war and the entire historic core had to be rebuilt, but you'd hardly know it today, so well was the job done. Now, with industrialisation and billowing smokestacks, central Gdańsk has a serious pollution problem.

### Orientation

Gdańsk Główny Railway Station is a 10-minute walk from the centre. Go through the underpass in front of the station, then follow the tram tracks about three blocks south till you see an old stone gate on the left. Turn left there and walk straight down ulica Długa into Długi Targ, the old market square. The bus station is in the opposite direction, west through the main tunnel from the railway station.

International ferries from Germany, Sweden and Finland arrive at the Polferries terminal, ulica Przemysłowa 1 at Nowy Port right opposite the Westerplatte Monument.

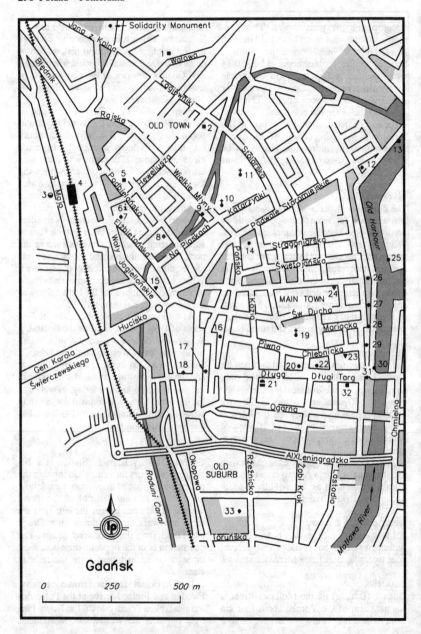

Solidarity Monument
Jana z Kolna
Wałowa 1
Łagiewniki
Błednik
Rajska
OLD TOWN 2
Heweliusza
Wielkie Młyny
Podbielańska 5
Podwale Staromiejskie
Stolarska
11
Katarzynki 10
9
3 Maja 4
3
6
7
Elżbietańska
Na Piaskach
8
Wały Jagiellońskie
15
Pańska
Stragoniarska
14
Świętojańska
13
Old Harbour
12
MAIN TOWN 24
Św Ducha
Koza
16
19
Mariacka
25
26
27
28
29
30
Hucisko
Gen Karola Świerczewskiego
17
18
Piwna
Chlebnicka
23
20
22
31
Długa
21
Długi Targ
32
Ogarna
Okopowa
OLD SUBURB
Rzeźnicka
Żabi Kruk
Łastadia
AIXLeningradzka
Raduni Canal
33
Motława River
Chmielna
Toruńska

# Gdańsk

0        250        500 m

---

■ PLACES TO STAY

1 Wałowa Youth Hostel
2 Orbis Hevelius Hotel
5 Hotel Monopol
13 Floating Hotel Boat
32 Jantar Hotel

▼ PLACES TO EAT

15 Ruczaj Milk Bar
23 Kawiarnia Flisak
24 Pod Łososiem Restaurant

OTHER

3 Bus Station
4 Gdańsk Główny Railway Station
5 Orbis
6 Tourist Office
7 Biuro Zakwaterowań
8 Old Town Hall

9 Great Mill
10 St Catherine's Church
11 St Bridget's Church
12 Ferry to Sopot & Hel
14 Hala Targowa Market
16 Armoury
17 Golden Gate
18 High Gate
19 Church of Our Lady
20 Main Town Hall
21 Post Office
22 Artus Mansion
25 Museum Ship 'Soldek'
26 Big Crane & Maritime Museum
27 Holy Ghost Gate
28 Mariacka Gate & Archaeological
    Museum
29 Chlebnicka Gate
30 Excursion Boats
31 Green Gate
32 Almatur
33 National Museum

---

Get there by electric train to Gdańsk Brzeźno Station, the station before Nowy Port Station. Trams No 7 and 15 from Oliwa also stop at Gdańsk Brzeźno. If you're arriving by ferry it might be better to take a taxi into town as no tram or train tickets are sold at Gdańsk Brzeźno. Otherwise walk one km east to Gdańsk Nowy Port Station.

### Information
The tourist office is at ulica Heweliusza 8 opposite the railway station.

### Things to See
Medieval Gdańsk was comprised of three quarters: the Old Town (Stare Miasto), the Main Town (Główne Miasto) and the Old Suburb (Stare Przedmieście). The principal streets of the Main Town run perpendicular to the port, which is reached through a series of gates. During their annual visits Polish kings entered the Main Town through the adjacent **High Gate** (1588) and **Golden Gate** (1614) and proceeded east along ulica Długa, the **Royal Way**.

Długi Targ (Long Market), the historic town square, is the very heart of old Gdańsk. The towering 15th century main **town hall**

on the corner of this square contains a good **Historical Museum** (closed Monday) in the buildings' coffered Gothic chambers and a great view from the tower. Behind Neptune's Fountain (1613) stands the **Artus Mansion** where local merchants once met. The Renaissance **Green Gate** (1568) at the east end of the square gives access to the old harbour on the Motława River. The excursion boats departing from the landing near the gate are highly recommended (see the Excursion Boats section that follows).

Two blocks north along the harbour is the Mariacka Gate with the **Archaeological Museum** (closed Monday) and through this gate is ulica Mariacka, the most picturesque in Gdańsk, lined with 17th century burgher houses. Follow it west to the Gothic **Church of Our Lady**, the largest brick church in Poland. You may climb the 78-metre tower for US$0.20.

Continue west on ulica Piwna (Beer Street!) to the Dutch Renaissance **Armoury** (1609), and take the street running north straight to Gothic **St Catherine's Church** in the Old Town. Opposite this church is the 14th century **Great Mill**. Just behind St Catherine's is **St Bridget's Church** (1514),

Lech Wałęsa's place of worship. You can sometimes catch a glimpse of him at mass on Sunday at 11 am. At the back of the church are some Solidarity mementos including a memorial to Father Jerzy Popiełuszko.

**Near Gdańsk** On the north side of Gdańsk at the entrance to the **Lenin Shipyards**, just north-east of Gdańsk Główny Railway Station, is a tall **monument** with three steel crosses and anchors to 45 workers killed during a December 1970 strike. The monument, erected in 1980, stood here throughout the period of martial law. Nearby at Wały Piastowskie 24 is the **Solidarity headquarters** with a kiosk in the entrance hall selling Solidarność stickers, pins, caps and even umbrellas.

At Oliwa between Gdańsk and Sopot is a soaring 13th century **Cistercian cathedral** in a park, with a museum (closed Monday) in the adjacent monastery. The cathedral's Rococo organ (1788) is one of the best in Europe – ask about organ concerts (often on Tuesdays in July and August). Get there on trams No 6, 12 and 15, or by electric train to Gdańsk Oliwa Station.

From the post office on ulica Długa walk south four blocks to the former Franciscan monastery (1514) in the Old Suburb, south of the Main Town. The monastery now houses the **National Museum** (closed Monday), ulica Toruńska 1 at Rzeźnicka, with porcelain and paintings. The highlight of this large collection is Hans Memling's *Last Judgement*.

**Excursion Boats** From April to October excursion boats to Westerplatte (US$1) depart several times daily from the landing near Gdańsk's Green Gate. This is one of the best trips of its kind in Poland, allowing a fine cross-section view of Gdańsk's harbour. At **Westerplatte** a towering monument (1968) with sweeping views commemorates the heroic resistance of the Polish naval garrison here which held out for a week against ferocious attacks in September 1939. Bus No 106 also connects Gdańsk to Westerplatte.

From mid-May to September there are boats across the Baltic from Gdańsk to the fishing village of **Hel** on the Hel Peninsula (US$2 one-way). From June to August, boats go to Gdynia. Alternatively, take a boat from Gdańsk to Hel, then a second from Hel to Gdynia or Sopot. Be sure to get out on the water if you're in the area in season.

### Places to Stay
**Camping** If you arrive on the international ferry from Scandinavia, the closest camping ground to the wharf is *Camping Brzeźna*, ulica Karola Marksa 234 (tram No 7 or 15 from the wharf).

**Hostels** There are four youth hostels in the Gdańsk area, open all year. Most convenient is the hostel at ulica Wałowa 21, a large red-brick building set back from the road, only a five-minute walk from Gdańsk Główny Railway Station. There are no showers, however.

The other three hostels are between Gdańsk and Sopot, too far to walk. First is the hostel at ulica Smoluchowskiego 11 (trams No 2, 9, 12, and 13 pass nearby).

For the hostel in the large red school building at aleja Legionów 11 take trams No 2, 4, 7 or 8 which stop outside.

The friendly Aleje Grunwaldzka 238/240 hostel is in a small sports complex near Oliwa. Take tram No 6, 12 or 15 to 'Abrahama' – ask someone where to get off.

The student travel agency Almatur, Długi Targ 11, is the place to enquire about the international student hotels open during July and August.

**Private Rooms** Private rooms (US$4/7 single/double) are arranged by the Biuro Zakwaterowań at the beginning of ulica Elżbietańska near the Gdańsk Główny Railway Station (open daily from 7.30 am to 7 pm in summer). None of the rooms is in the centre of town and singles are often not available. Freelancers on the street outside this office may have an unofficial private room to offer you, perhaps in the centre, but their prices are about double those inside.

**Hotels** About the only medium-range hotel in Gdańsk is the old *Jantar Hotel*, Długi Targ 19, with singles/doubles at US$6/9 without bath or breakfast, US$10 double with bath. You couldn't ask for a more central location – if you get in there you're lucky.

Poland's most unique accommodation is offered on the blue and white *barge* permanently moored on ulica Wartka on Gdańsk's old harbour at the point where the Raduni Canal joins the Motława River. They rent cabins to visitors at US$7 per person.

The functional, commercial *Mesa Hotel*, ulica Wały Jagiellońskie 38 near the station, is way overpriced at US$34/45 single/double with private bath but no breakfast. An even more pretentious place is the 20-floor *Orbis Hevelius Hotel* (US$54/75 single/double). Hotel prices in the Tri-City area are lowest from October to April.

### Places to Eat

The *Neptun Milk Bar*, ulica Długa 32-34, serves hearty cheap meals cafeteria-style. The *Itaca Bar*, ulica Długa 18, has grilled meats like gyros, shish kebabs, hamburgers and cheeseburgers dispensed self-service at the bar. The *Gedania Restaurant*, ulica Długa 75, has table service, beer (!) and live music after 8 pm.

The restaurant downstairs in the *Jantar Hotel*, Długi Targ 19, serves unpretentious, filling meals. There's a great *pizzeria* (spaghetti available!) at ulica Piwna 51, just up the street from the Church of Our Lady.

*Pod Łososiem*, ulica Szeroka 52, is Gdańsk's most famous restaurant and seafood is the speciality, as the picture of the salmon in the window suggests. Dress up and try to reserve.

The *Ruczaj Milk Bar*, ulica Wały Jagiellońskie 8 not far from the train station, is a good place for breakfast. The dumplings and mushrooms are good – watch what the locals take.

**Cafés** *Palowa Coffee House* in the basement of the main town hall on Długi Targ is a good place to sit and read, or eat cakes and ice cream. *Kawiarnia Flisak*, at ulica Chleb-

nicka 10/11, Gdańsk, offers reasonable drink prices, and there are friendly locals (open daily from 2 pm to 2 am).

### Entertainment

Check the local papers and ask tourist information about events. The *Wybrzeże Theatre*, ulica Św Ducha 2, is behind the armoury in the Main Town. The *State Baltic Opera and Concert Hall*, Aleje Zwycięstwa 15, is near Gdańsk Politechnika Railway Station.

Annual events to ask about include the Gdańsk Days in June, the International Choral Meetings from June to August, the International Festival of Organ and Chamber Music in July and August, the Dominican Fair in early August and the Festival of Polish Feature Films in September.

### Getting There & Away

**Train** Direct trains arrive at Gdynia/Gdańsk from Berlin-Lichtenberg (via Szczecin), Poznań, Szczecin, Wrocław, Warsaw (via Malbork) and Olsztyn (also via Malbork). Couchettes are available to Prague, Warsaw, Szczecin and Berlin. Couchettes must be booked at the Orbis office in the Hotel Monopol near the train station.

The Neptun and Kaszub express trains run from Warsaw to Gdańsk (333 km, 3½ hours) daily all year, with the Neptun departing from Warsaw in the morning and Gdańsk in the evening. The Kaszub does the opposite, leaving Gdańsk in the morning and Warsaw in the late afternoon. From mid-June to August the Lajkonik Express runs direct between Kraków Główny and Gdańsk (621 km, seven hours), leaving Kraków in the early morning and Gdańsk in the afternoon. All these trains also service Sopot and Gdynia, and reservations are required.

**Ferry** Large car ferries arrive at Gdańsk once or twice a week throughout the year from Oxelösund, Sweden, and Helsinki, Finland. International ferry tickets are available at the Orbis office in Hotel Monopol.

### Getting Around

**Tram & Train** Transport around the area is

easy. Tram lines carry you north from Gdańsk to Oliwa and Jelitkowo. To go to Westerplatte you can take a bus or boat. Cheap commuter trains run constantly between Gdańsk, Sopot, Gdynia and Wejherowo. At Reda change for Hel. Tickets are sold by automatic machines which you must punch before going onto the platform.

# Mazuria

Mazuria stretches from the Vistula to the Soviet border north of the Mazovian plain. Here the Scandinavian glacier left behind a typical postglacial landscape, and many of the 3000 lakes are linked by rivers and canals to create a system of waterways well favoured by yachtspeople. The winding shorelines with many peninsulas, inlets and small islands are surrounded by low hills and forests, making the picturesque lake districts around Olsztyn, Mikołajki and Suwałki of north-eastern Poland one of the most attractive and varied touring areas in the country. Add to this the many fascinating historical remains and the opportunity to venture into places which seldom see English speakers, and you'll have all the reasons you need to visit.

## HISTORY
The historic regions of Warmia and Mazuria were the southern half of German East Prussia until 1945 (the northern half is now part of the Russian Federation). Originally inhabited by heathen Prussian and Jatzvingian tribes, the area was conquered in the 13th century by the Germanic Teutonic Knights who had been invited in by the Polish Prince Conrad of Mazovia in 1225. The intention was that the knights would convert the Baltic tribes and depart, but instead they created a powerful religious state on the north-east border of Poland.

The Battle of Grunwald in 1410 turned out to be a pivotal showdown between the knights and the Polish Crown. The knights' defeat at the battle was followed by other

long wars which led to the Treaty of Toruń (1466) which gave Warmia (Ermeland), the area between Olsztyn and Frombork, to Poland for over three centuries. It was during this period that the famous Polish administrator and astronomer lived in Warmia, and today we can follow the Copernicus Trail from Olsztyn to Lidzbark Warmiński and Frombork. (Though born in Toruń and a student in Kraków, Copernicus spent the last 40 years of his life in Warmia.)

Mazuria came under the Hohenzollerns of Brandenburg in the 16th century and in 1772 Warmia was also annexed to the Kingdom of Prussia. In a 1918 plebiscite, Warmia and Mazuria voted to remain German while the area around Suwałki went to Poland. During WW II the Nazis militarised Mazuria, which became a base for Hitler's dreams of conquest. This policy brought seven centuries of German involvement in the area to an ignominious end. However, even today, Lutheran Protestantism is alive in central Mazuria whereas Warmia remains more stolidly Catholic.

## MALBORK
From 1309 to 1457 Malbork (Marienburg) was the headquarters of the Teutonic Knights and one of the largest medieval fortified castles in Europe. The Teutonic Knights with their white robes and black crosses originated during the Third Crusade (1198), and with the Templars and Hospitallers became one of the three great military/religious orders of the time. In 1271 Monfort Castle in Palestine was lost and the order began searching for a new headquarters.

Construction of Malbork Castle began in 1276 and in 1309 the order's capital was shifted here from Venice. Constant territorial disputes with Poland and Lithuania finally culminated in the Battle of Grunwald in 1410. The order was defeated at this battle but continued to hold the castle until 1457. From 1772 to 1945 Malbork was incorporated into Prussia and extensive restorations were carried out in the years prior to WW I when Malbork was viewed as a romantic symbol of the glory of medieval Germany.

After WW II the Polish authorities in turn continued the work to preserve this great monument of Gothic culture. The museum here was opened in 1960.

### Things to See & Do

**Malbork Castle**, overlooking the Nogat River, an eastern arm of the Vistula, was badly damaged during WW II but has now been largely restored. It consists of the service facilities of the 15th century Lower Castle (between the railway line and the main gate), the 14th century Middle Castle where the Grand Master lived and the 13th century High Castle.

The first courtyard features an outstanding museum of Polish amber. Three floors of exhibits are to be seen in the rooms around the second courtyard (High Castle). One hall contains a superb collection of inlaid antique weapons. In the far corner a passageway leads to the Gdanisko Tower. Yes, the gaping hole in the floor was the toilet!

At least four hours are required to explore this imposing monument (open from 8.30 am to 5 pm May to September, 9 am to 2.30 pm October to April, closed Mondays). You used to be allowed to wander around on your own, but a new regulation forces you to join a group with a Polish-speaking guide unless you're willing to pay US$10 for an English-speaking guide. If a boring two-hour monologue in Polish isn't your idea of fun, you should be able to 'lose' your guide once inside the castle.

The best view of Malbork Castle is from the train. Coming from Gdańsk it's on the right immediately after you cross the river; northbound towards Gdańsk it's on the left just beyond Malbork Station.

### Places to Stay & Eat

If you'd like to spend the night there's a camping ground (open from June to August) on ulica Portowa about two km beyond the castle, away from the station. The *Hotel Sportovy* (open all year) behind the camping ground has rooms, though the receptionist is unhelpful.

### Getting There & Away

Malbork can be seen as a stopover between Gdańsk and points south or east, or you can visit it as a day trip from Gdańsk (58 km). Most trains between Gdańsk and Warsaw or Olsztyn stop here. Sometimes to go between Malbork and Olsztyn (126 km) you must change trains at Elbląg or Bogaczewo or both. The castle is a 15-minute walk from the train station.

The Posejdon Express links Malbork to Warsaw (282 km, three hours), Gdańsk, Gdynia, Lębork and Koszalin, passing northbound in the morning and southbound in the evening. From mid-June to August the Lajkonik Express passes Malbork on its way between Kraków and Gdańsk/Gdynia, also northbound in the morning and southbound in the afternoon. Northbound you can combine the two to allow a 2½-hour stopover in Malbork between Warsaw and Gdańsk (also southbound, though the castle would be closed). Reservations are required.

## OLSZTYN

Olsztyn, 177 km south-east of Gdańsk, is the capital of Mazuria and a regional transportation hub. For travellers, Olsztyn is important as a jumping-off point for Lidzbark Warmiński, Grunwald, the Elbląg Canal and the Great Mazurian Lake District rather than as a destination in itself. Though the food and accommodation are good, you can see the city's historic sites in a couple of hours.

From 1466 to 1772 the town belonged to the Kingdom of Poland, and none other than Nicolaus Copernicus, administrator of Warmia, commanded Olsztyn Castle from 1516 to 1521. Here he made astronomical observations and began writing *On the Revolutions of Celestial Bodies*. With the first partition of Poland, Olsztyn became Prussian Allenstein and remained so until 1945.

### Orientation

Olsztyn Główny Railway Station and the bus station are adjacent on the north-east side of town, a 15-minute walk from the centre.

Walk south-west on ulica Partyzantów past Plac Gen Bema to Aleje Dąbrowszczaków on the left. When this street terminates in the city centre, cross the street and look for ulica 22 Lipca which takes you to High Gate and the old town. Olsztyn Zachodni Railway Station is just a short walk west of the castle.

## Information

The tourist office in the PTTK complex beside the High Gate is helpful in providing maps of the Mazurian Lakes and advice. It's open weekdays from 9 am to 4 pm, Saturday from 10 am to 2 pm.

## Things to See

**High Gate** is all that remains of the 14th century city walls. Just west, **Olsztyn Castle** contains a good museum (closed Monday) with some explanations posted in English, including much on Copernicus. The old market square nearby is surrounded by gabled burgher houses. Red-brick **St James Cathedral** just south-east dates from the 16th century.

## Places to Stay

Olsztyn has lots of large, inexpensive hotels, so don't worry if your train gets you there late – you'll find a room. Olsztyn's youth hostel is at ulica Kopernika 45 between the stations and town, an eight-minute walk from either.

Don't bother asking at high-rise *Hotel Kormoran* across the street from the railway station as it caters mostly to tour groups (US\$34/39 single/double).

The five-storey *Hotel Pracowniczy*, at ulica Kętrzyńskiego 5 just around the corner from the railway station, is a former workers' residence which now rents singles, doubles and triples at US\$4 per person. The main problem here is corridor noise from excited Polish neighbours, though it's still the best value in Olsztyn.

Singles/doubles/triples without bath or breakfast cost US\$7/8/10 at the functional three-storey *Dom Wycieczkowy 'Nad Łyną'*, Aleja Wojska Polskiego 14. It's only a 10-minute walk from the railway station via ulica Kolejowa (see the map).

The modern *Warmiński Hotel*, ulica Głowackiego 8 about a 10-minute walk from the station, is US\$10/14 single/double for a room with shared bath, US\$12/16 with shower.

If you'd like to be in the centre, the *PTTK Dom Wycieczkowy* in the High Gate, ulica Staromiejska 1, is US\$7/14 single/double with shared bath. If they don't have a single ask if they can rent you one bed in a double.

*Hotel Relaks,* ulica Żołnierska 13a beside a large sports centre, is a comfortable six-storey hotel with singles/doubles with private bath at US\$11/ 12. A few rooms with shared bath are US\$8 double.

The *PTTK Camping* on ulica Sielska above Lake Krzywe (Ukiel) is about five km west of town. Bus No 7 from the railway station passes the gate.

## Places to Eat

*Wars Self-Service,* Aleje Zwycięstwa 218 at the city end of Aleje Dąbrowszczaków, is cheap and has a place attached to get cakes and coffee. The *Liwa Milk Bar*, ulica Pieniężnego 18 just around the corner from the PTTK, has cheap cafeteria food. In the middle of the old town *Restauracja Eridu,* ulica Marchlewskiego 3-4, offers Islamic dishes.

*Pod Samowarem*, Aleje Dąbrowszczaków 26 between the stations and town, serves excellent inexpensive meals in its unpretentious dining room – it's also a good place to go if you only want a few drinks. Recommended. The *Bar Staromiejski* in the old town serves wine till 9 pm.

If you would like to dine in style, the *Restauracja Francuska,* on the corner of Dąbrowszczaków and Mickiewicza, should be your choice. The impeccably dressed waiters, sharp modern décor and French cuisine will add up to a bill several times higher than at any other restaurant listed here, but Poland being Poland you may still consider it cheap. The menu is posted outside.

## Getting There & Away

There are direct trains from Gdynia/Gdańsk (via Malbork), Poznań (via Ostróda, Iława

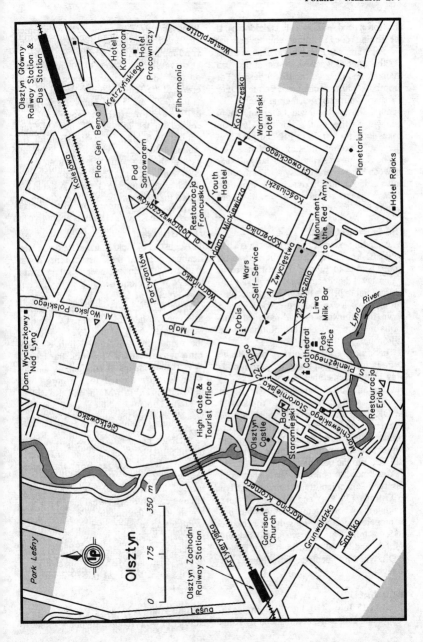

Park Leśny

Olsztyn

0    175    350 m

Olsztyn Główny
Railway Station &
Bus Station

Hotel Kormoran
Hotel Pracowniczy
Filharmonia
Westerplatte
Kołobrzeska
Warmiński Hotel
Głowackiego
Planetarium
Hotel Relaks
Kętrzyńskiego
Plac Gen Bema
Pod Samowarem
Restauracja Francuska
Youth Hostel
Kościuszki
Kopernika
Monument to the Red Army
Kolejowa
al Dąbrowszczaków
Adama Mickiewicza
Wars Self-Service
Al Zwycięstwa
22 Stycznia
Liwa Milk Bar
Lyna River
Partyzantów
Warmińska
1 Maja
Orbis
Cathedral
Post Office
S pieniężnego
Al Wojska Polskiego
Dom Wycieczkowy 'Nad Łyną'
22 Lipca
High Gate & Tourist Office
Staromiejski
Okopowa
Restauracja Eridu
Giełkowska
Olsztyn Castle
Bar
Zamkowa
Mrągowskiego Staromiejskie
Marcina Kromera
Garrison Church
Grunwaldzka
Stare kka
Leśna
al Jerycho
Olsztyn Zachodni
Railway Station

and Toruń) and Warsaw (via Działdowo). If the timing doesn't allow you to use the Gdańsk train, you may have to change trains at Elbląg and Bogaczewo to travel between Malbork and Olsztyn (no direct buses). For Frombork you must change at Braniewo. For Lidzbark Warmiński change at Czerwonka (though the bus is much faster and more frequent on this route). For the Mazurian Lakes look for a train to Ełk and get off at Giżycko, Mikołajki or Ruciane-Nida.

The Kormoran Express runs daily all year between Warsaw and Olsztyn (237 km, three hours), departing Olsztyn in the morning, Warsaw in the afternoon. Reservations are required.

## THE ELBLĄG CANAL

A fascinating excursion from Olsztyn is a trip on the 81-km Elbląg Canal built in 1848-60 from Ostróda to Elbląg. The difference in water level between these towns is 100 metres, and to bridge this gap the boats pass through two locks and are carried up and down five slipways on rail-mounted platforms or 'ramps', a technical solution unique in Europe!

Theoretically the excursion boats leave Ostróda for Elbląg at 8 am daily from mid-May to mid-September (11 hours, US$11) but captains often cancel the trip if not enough passengers are around. You should be OK from mid-June to August and on weekends, but be sure to check with Mazur-Tourist, ulica Staromiejska 6, Olsztyn, the day before to confirm that there definitely will be a trip the next day.

You'll need to get a very early start from Olsztyn. Convenient trains connect Olsztyn to Ostróda (39 km) and Elbląg (97 km), making the whole circuit quite feasible, but be prepared for a very long day. Check the 6.35 am train from Olsztyn to Gdańsk via Ostróda and the 9.14 pm train from Elbląg to Olsztyn, but remember, these times could change!

## GRUNWALD

Here, on 15 July 1410, the allied armies of Poland and Lithuania, commanded by King Władysław Jagiełło, met the heavily armed Teutonic Knights under Grand Master Ulrich von Jungingen in one of the largest battles of medieval Europe. Some 30,000 men fought on each side and the outcome broke the power of the Teutonic order forever.

In 1960, the 550th anniversary of the battle, a 30-metre-high monument was erected on the hilltop at Grunwald (Tannenberg) to mark the site. Behind the monument is a museum where a 20-minute excerpt from a feature film about the battle is shown to groups. The film is narrated in Polish with subtitles in German. A shield just inside the museum is inscribed 'Grunwald 1410, Berlin 1945'.

### Near Grunwald

In August 1914 Field Marshal Paul von Hindenburg defeated the Russian army at the Battle of Tannenberg near Olsztynek, and after WW I a monumental marble structure was erected at Sudwa, two km west of Olsztynek between Olsztyn and Grunwald, to commemorate this victory. On Hindenburg's death, on 2 August 1934, Hitler had the monument transformed into **Hindenburg's mausoleum**. Towards the end of WW II the remains of Hindenburg and his wife were transferred to Marburg/Lahn, between Frankfurt/Main and Kassel in western Germany, and the mausoleum itself was blown up by the advancing Soviet army in 1945.

All that remains now are overgrown foundations in the forest behind an elderly people's home not far from the *Zajazd 'Mazurski' Zaprasza Hotel*. The ruins are not marked, but look for what was once a large circular enclosure with what may have been a wall across the middle. It's certainly not worth trying to come here by public transport, but if you have a car you might stop for a meal at the excellent hotel restaurant (whole fried lake fish is a speciality) or perhaps even the night (US$9 double, no singles).

### Getting There & Away

Buses run every couple of hours direct to

Grunwald from Olsztyn via Olsztynek. It's not too hard to hitchhike back to Olsztyn if the return connection is inconvenient.

## LIDZBARK WARMIŃSKI

Lidzbark Warmiński (Heilsberg) is best known as the episcopal seat of the bishops who ruled the Duchy of Warmia from 1466 to 1772 under the Polish Crown. In the 14th century a strong castle was built here which the Polish bishops later adopted as their residence, adding a neoclassical palace to the complex in the 17th century. The most famous resident was Nicolaus Copernicus who worked here from 1503 to 1510 as an advisor to his uncle, Bishop Łukasz Watzenrode.

### Things to See & Do

The huge 14th century red-brick **castle** in Lidzbark Warmiński is a memorable medieval monument. The vaulted chambers of the castle interior now house the world-class **Museum of Warmia** (closed Monday, captions in English and German) with Gothic sculpture and painting in the grand refectory downstairs, a large art gallery and exhibition on the restoration of historic monuments upstairs. Also to be seen are a gilded chapel, old weapons in the cellars and a splendid arcaded interior courtyard.

In the middle of town is a large 14th century northern German red-brick church. The **High Gate** on the way from the stations dates from the same period.

### Places to Stay & Eat

The *Dom Wycieczkowy PTTK* in the medieval High Gate (Wysoka Brama), between the adjacent bus and train stations and the castle, provides accommodation. Just outside Wysoka Brama on the way back to the stations is *Bar 'Smak'* with coffee, cakes and meals.

### Getting There & Away

Frequent buses cover the 46 km between Olsztyn and Lidzbark Warmiński, making it an easy day trip. Onward trains and buses from Lidzbark Warmiński to other places of interest in this area are infrequent and seldom direct; if you want to come from Olsztyn by train you must change at Czerwonka.

## FROMBORK

Frombork (Frawenburg), on the south-east shore of the Vistula Lagoon (Zalew Wiślany) between Lidzbark Warmiński and Gdańsk, was founded by colonists from Lübeck, Germany, in the 13th century. From 1466 to 1772 this area was under the Polish Crown, which explains all the old Polish monuments in Frombork's 14th century cathedral. It was during this period that the famous astronomer Nicolaus Copernicus lived and worked on Cathedral Hill (from 1512 to 1516, and from 1522 until his death in 1543). Eighty per cent of the lower town was destroyed during WW II fighting, but luckily Cathedral Hill was less affected. The medieval walls, towers and gates surrounding the hill still protect Frombork's main monuments.

### Orientation

The train, bus and ferry terminals are all adjacent in Frombork, a five-minute walk from the centre of town.

### Things to See & Do

Frombork's red-brick Gothic **cathedral** (erected in 1388) contains Copernicus' unmarked grave, beneath the aisle by the second pillar on the right as you stand below the organ. On the opposite side of this pillar is a statue of the astronomer. In summer, recitals are given on the cathedral's Baroque organ (1683). The former bishop's palace next to the cathedral is a **Copernicus Museum** (closed Monday). On the other side of the cathedral is the **Radziejowski Tower** (1685) with a small planetarium, a Foucault pendulum and an art gallery. The gallery atop the tower gives a superb view of the town and Vistula Lagoon.

Just below Cathedral Hill is a tall statue of Copernicus which makes him look rather like Chairman Mao. A more offbeat attraction is the 14th century **Church of St Nicholas**, now the town's coal-burning thermal power plant.

## Places to Stay & Eat

There's a camping ground at ulica Braniewska 14, one km east of Frombork. The youth hostel, ulica Elbląska 11, is a couple of blocks west of the centre of town.

The *PTTK Dom Wycieczkowy* in the park just west of Cathedral Hill is not cheap at US$20 double or US$12 for a bed in a four-bed dorm. Meals in its restaurant are more reasonable, so plan on having lunch there. The receptionist at Dom Wycieczkowy should be able to provide the address of someone renting less expensive private rooms.

The modern two-storey *Hotel Słoneczny* near the centre of town is grossly overpriced at US$28/45 single/double. One traveller who stayed here reported that the rooms were dirty. The whole town closes down around 4 pm so be prepared for a *quiet* evening.

## Getting There & Away

Frombork is on the railway line from Elbląg to Braniewo via Tolkmicko. Getting to Frombork from Gdańsk by train involves a change at Elbląg and there's often a wait of several hours for connections. Coming from Olsztyn you must change trains at Braniewo. The easiest way to get to Frombork is by bus from Gdańsk.

Another way to come is via Krynica Morska on the Amber Coast, a sandy strip running east from Gdańsk to the USSR. Buses connect Gdańsk to Krynica Morska, and a passenger ferry (no cars) should cross the Vistula Lagoon from Krynica Morska to Frombork (US$1). Check ferry times at the tourist office in Gdańsk before setting out this way.

## THE GREAT MAZURIAN LAKES

The Great Mazurian Lake District north-east of Olsztyn is a verdant land of rolling hills interspersed with glacial lakes, healthy little farms, scattered tracts of forest and many small towns. There are literally thousands of postglacial lakes to the north and south of Mikołajki. A fifth of the surface of this area is covered by water and another 30% by forest. Lake Śniardwy (110 sq km) is the largest lake in Poland, and Lake Mamry and adjacent waters total an additional 102 sq km. The large, clean lakes and abundant forests are an irresistible beacon for boaters, anglers and nature lovers. Polish tourists also arrive in great numbers though it's much less crowded after 15 August.

## Orientation & Information

Pick up the 1:60,000 *Jezioro Śniardwy* map or the 1:120,000 *Wielkie jeziora mazurskie* map at a bookstore before you come. These maps can be frustratingly difficult to find in the area itself.

## Activities

The Great Mazurian Lakes are well connected by canals, rivers and streams, making this a paradise for canoeists and kayakers. Established kayak routes follow the Krutynia River near Ruciane-Nida, and the Czarna Hańcza River in the Augustów area. People arriving by train with folding kayaks could get on the Krutynia River Kayak Trail near Spychowo Railway Station between Olsztyn and Ruciane-Nida. There's a waterside hostel *(stanica wodna)* at ulica Juranda 30, Spychowo. Check with the PTTK in Olsztyn to make sure it's open and ask about other such riverside hostels at Krutyń, Ukta and Nowy Most. Otherwise begin at Sorkwity on the railway line between Olsztyn and Mrągowo or at Ruciane-Nida itself.

Yachtspeople will want to sail on the larger lakes, and boats with or without captains can usually be hired at the yacht harbours in Giżycko, Mikołajki, Ruciane-Nida and Węgorzewo. If you have difficulty making the arrangements, ask your hotel or pension manager for help or go to a tourist office.

## Getting There & Away

Communications are good, with three different west-east railway lines running across the region from Olsztyn (the gateway city) to Ełk via Giżycko, Mikołajki or Ruciane-Nida. Frequent buses link the settlements on north-south routes, so getting around is easy.

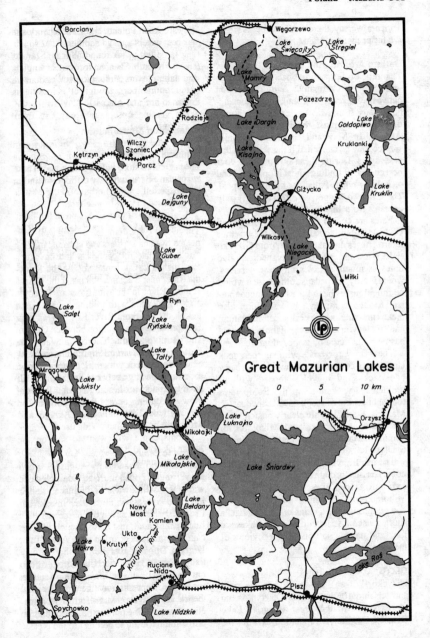

Great Mazurian Lakes

To/from Warsaw there are direct buses which are faster than the train.

## Getting Around the Lakes

Theoretically, excursion boats of the Mazurian Shipping Company's White Fleet run between Giżycko, Mikołajki and Ruciane-Nida daily from May to September, though the service is most reliable from June to August. In May and September a daily service may be cancelled if there are too few passengers. During these slow months your best chance of finding a boat is on a weekend or holiday when Polish tour groups appear. The Giżycko-Węgorzewo trip (US$5) only operates from June to August.

Fares are US$7 Giżycko to Mikołajki and US$8 Mikołajki to Ruciane-Nida. Two-hour return cruises on Lake Kisajno from Giżycko (US$5) are also offered. Foreigners pay five times as much as Poles on these services, which is only fair because otherwise it would be ridiculously cheap for us and uneconomical for the company. This situation also means the captains are very accommodating, and will let you aboard even if the whole boat has been chartered by a special group.

These are large boats with an open deck above and a coffee shop below; you can carry backpacks and bicycles aboard without problems. The same company also operates tourist boats out of Augustów, farther east in Mazuria. Schedules are clearly posted at the lake ports in Giżycko and Mikołajki, or enquire at Mazur-Tourist, ulica Staromiejska 6, Olsztyn.

The trip from Giżycko to Mikołajki (four hours) passes through several canals with an extension to Lake Śniardwy. Between Mikołajki and Ruciane-Nida (three hours) you go through the Guzianka Lock and get a short cruise on Lake Nidzkie. The lakes are long and narrow so you get good views of the shorelines.

## GIŻYCKO

Giżycko (Lötzen), between lakes Niegocin and Kisajno 105 km east of Olsztyn, is the tourist centre of the Great Mazurian Lake District. Despite its reputation as a resort,

Giżycko is not an especially attractive town and it's useful mostly as a base from which to visit Hitler's bunker at Wilczy Szaniec (see the Wilczy Szaniec section) or to pick up a lake boat to Mikołajki or Węgorzewo (Angerburg). Węgorzewo itself is lacking in things to see and places to stay, so it's not worth visiting except as a day trip from Giżycko by boat.

## Orientation & Information

The port on Lake Niegocin (26 sq km) is near the centre of town with the railway station on the east and the yacht harbour on the west, a few hundred metres from either.

A large map of Giżycko is posted in front of the adjacent bus and train stations on Plac Dworcowy. Head up ulica Armii Krajowej to ulica Dąbrowskiego. The staff at Orbis, ulica Dąbrowskiego 3, can answer questions and perhaps provide a map. Continue west on ulica Warszawska to Plac Grunwaldzki, the centre of town.

## Things to See

There's nothing much to see in Giżycko except perhaps a large 19th century **fortress** on the west side of town which once guarded the narrow passage between the lakes. If you have time it's worth going beyond this fortress and cutting across the isthmus to the shore of Lake Kisajno near the Almatur and Sport hotels.

## Places to Stay

**Camping** In July and early August Giżycko is overrun by Polish tourists, although those with a tent will always find a place to pitch it. If you go west on ulica Olsztyńska from Plac Grunwaldzki you'll reach the Łuczański Canal, just across which are two camping grounds near the lake. At the first, *Wigry Camping*, just before the railway tracks, there's a small harbour where you can rent a sailing boat. The *Yacht Club Camping*, next to the Mazurski Yacht Club just beyond the tracks, rents rooms in a former workers' dormitory at US$4 per person, in addition to providing camping space.

**Hotels** Rooms at the modern, four-storey *Hotel Wodnik*, ulica 3 Maja 2 just off Plac Grunwaldzki in the centre of town, cost US$13/20 single/double with bath (breakfast US$4 extra). Foreign bus tour groups always stay at the Wodnik – it's their kind of place. The Biuro Zakwaterowania, renting private rooms, is inside Hotel Wodnik.

The *PTTK Dom Wycieczkowy* is between the train tracks and the lake right beside the Łuczański Canal, but on the town side across the canal from the camping grounds.

Just beyond the bridge over the canal is *Motel Zamek*, ulica Moniuszki 1, with rooms with bath at US$23 double. When it's cold outside, a log fire will be burning in the small bar at the reception. If the price is right for you, this is Giżycko's most pleasant hotel.

Farther west a km or two is the stadium where a road leads off to the right towards Lake Kisajno and two hotels. The *Sport Hotel*, ulica Moniuszki 22, has rooms at US$5 single without bath or US$9 double with bath (higher prices in July and August). You can also camp here (bungalows available) and it's a quieter site than the two just mentioned. The *Almatur Hotel* is nearby. In the off season the receptions of both hotels close early so don't expect to get a room if you arrive late. Boat rentals are possible.

### Places to Eat
The *Omega Bar*, ulica Olsztyńska 4, is a self-service. In the centre of town is the full-service *Mazurska Restaurant*, ulica Warszawska 6. The food, though OK, is not that great and the portions are small. In the evening there's often live music here.

### WILCZY SZANIEC
World War II buffs will certainly want to visit **Hitler's wartime headquarters**, the *Wolfschanze* or Wolf's Lair (Wilczy Szaniec in Polish), at Gierłóż, 30 km west of Giżycko or 10 km east of Kętrzyn. Hitler spent most of his time here from 24 June 1941 to 20 November 1944. The base had its own railway station and airfield surrounded by minefields, anti-aircraft guns and camouflaging.

The Germans blew up the Wolfschanze on 24 January 1945 and only cracked concrete bunkers remain, but it's significant as the site of the 20 July 1944 assassination attempt by Colonel Claus von Stauffenberg. Tragically, a heavy wooden table saved the dictator and as many people died and as much property was destroyed in the last year of war as during the first five combined.

### Things to See & Do
Over 70 reinforced bunkers are scattered through the forest. A large map of the site is posted at the entrance and all the bunkers are clearly numbered: Bormann No 11, Hitler No 13, Göring No 16, etc. The roofs of the eight most important are eight metres thick! Bring along a torch (flashlight) if you want to explore inside the bunkers (although large signs warn you that it is dangerous to do so). It's somehow fitting that these sinister remains should be the most tangible personal mementos left behind by the dictator.

A film about Hitler is shown in the cinema (*kino*) at the site but only for groups (buy 20 tickets for US$6 total and they'll gladly run the film for you alone).

### Places to Stay & Eat
The *Dom Wycieczkowy* at the site is US$6/9 single/double. The *Restaurant 'Leśna'* behind the Dom serves reasonably good food. A basic camping ground is nearby.

### Getting There & Away
Kętrzyn (Rastenburg), a large town on the railway line from Olsztyn to Ełk via Giżycko, is the starting point for most visits to Wilczy Szaniec. Trains from Kętrzyn to Węgorzewo pass right through the site but only stop at Parcz, two km east – walk back along the paved highway towards Kętrzyn. Buses on the route from Kętrzyn to Węgorzewo via Radzieje stop right at the gate. You can see Goering's bunker (No 16) from both the train and the road.

### MIKOŁAJKI
During summer the best gateway to the lakes for hikers and campers is Mikołajki

(Nikolaiken), 86 km east of Olsztyn on a railway line to Ełk. Perched on a picturesque narrows crossed by three bridges, there are scenic views on all sides of this pearl of Mazuria. The red-roofed houses of Mikołajki stretch along the shore of narrow Lake Mikołajskie just north of the Mazurian Landscape Park and Lake Śniardwy. Wild horses are in the forests to the south. Lakes Ryńskie, Tałty, Mikołajskie and Bełdany together fill a postglacial gully 35 km long.

## Orientation & Information

The bus station is beside a large Evangelical church near the bridge in the centre of town. The train station is several blocks east down ulica Kolejowa.

The SMPT 'Wigry' Tourist Office is on ulica Kolejowa near the bus station. In late July ask about the International Festival of Country Music, or 'Country Picnic', in nearby Mrągowo.

## Things to See

Europe's largest surviving community of **wild swans** is at nearby Lake Łuknajno. The 1200 to 2000 swans nest in April and May but stay at the lake all summer. The young birds are brown, the adults white. The 'Rezerwat Łuknajno' is about four km east of Mikołajki, beyond the Osiedle 'Łabędzia' suburb. Several observation towers beside the lake make viewing possible.

## Activities

Mikołajki is an important yachting centre with a new Schronisko Żeglarskie (waterside hostel) overlooking the yacht harbour. The rental office next to the Schronisko rents boats capable of carrying up to four people from around US$14 daily.

## Places to Stay

**Camping** Camping 'Wagabunda', ulica Leśna 2, is across the bridge and two km west of town. In addition to camping space there are lots of neat little four-bed bungalows beginning at US$6 for the unit.

**Private Rooms** The Biuro Zakwaterowania (for private rooms) is at the 'Wigry' Tourist Office. Ask here about accommodation at the Schronisko Żeglarskie (waterside hostel) overlooking the yacht harbour.

**Pensions** The cheapest pension is Pensjonat 'Mazury', ulica Ogrodowa 1, a large house two blocks from the railway station (US$4/8 single/double). It's open all year.

Pensjonat 'Mikołajki' (☎ 16437), ulica Kajki 18 near the centre of town, is Mikołajki's newest pension (US$8/14 single/double). The double rooms have private bath. A big breakfast is US$3 per person extra and other meals are available, perhaps the best home cooking you'll get in Poland. The rooms are often fully booked but the owner speaks perfect English so call him up for reservations (open from April to mid-October only).

Pensjonat 'Na Skarpie', ulica Kajki 96, is one km beyond Pensjonat 'Mikołajki'. Some rooms have excellent lake views.

If you have transport and don't mind spending more, Pensjonat 'Wodnik', ulica Kajki 130 about three km from central Mikołajki, has a beautiful location behind a dairy farm right on Lake Mikołajskie. Swim off the floating dock or hire a small boat and row yourself around the lake. The 12 rooms go for US$25 per person including breakfast, or you may also camp. The Wodnik is open from June to September only.

In July and August all room prices in Mikołajki are doubled.

## Places to Eat

All the tour groups eat at the Restaurant Portowa just above the lake-boat landing. The food is nothing special but prices are reasonable.

## Getting There & Away

There's no bus to Ruciane-Nida but there is an hourly bus service to Mrągowo and several buses a day to Giżycko. Trains run to Olsztyn and Ełk.

## RUCIANE-NIDA

Hiking trails lead 23 km south from Mikołajki through the forest past many lakeside camping grounds to Ruciane-Nida (Rudschanny), in the heart of the Pisz Forest between picturesque Bełdany and Nidzkie lakes. Lake Nidzkie (18.3 sq km) is considered the most beautiful of the Mazurian lakes for its small forested islands. Ruciane-Nida is the right place to end a trip through the lake district by excursion boat, yacht, bicycle or foot as train service back to Olsztyn is good.

### Orientation & Information

The adjacent bus and train stations are a five-minute walk from the lake-boat landing.

### Places to Stay

Places to stay include the *PTTK Dom Wycieczkowy,* ulica Mazurska 16, and *Pensjonat 'Bełdan',* both north of the railway station, and the more expensive *Orbis Pensjonat 'Kowaljik'* across the bridge. The 'Kowaljik' looks south down Lake Nidzkie. The *PTTK camping ground* is on Lake Nidzkie, a 20-minute walk south-west of the railway station.

### Getting There & Away

Train service to Olsztyn and Ełk is every couple of hours. There's a bus to Mikołajki via Ukta.

Fountain statue in the wonderful old town square
of Telč

# Czechoslovakia

Czechoslovakia, a medium-sized country in the heart of Europe, is rich in history and natural beauty. The rugged mountains of Slovakia and the historic towns of Bohemia and Moravia are unsurpassed. The medieval cores of some 40 towns have been preserved and about 4000 fairy-tale castles, chateaux, manors and ruins are scattered around the countryside. A total of 500 museums and 50,000 artistic monuments is concentrated in the towns and cities. There's so much to see that you could make repeated visits to this appealing land.

Czechoslovakia is doubly inviting for its cultured, friendly people and excellent facilities. The hotels and restaurants and the transportation network are equalled only in Western Europe. Ninety per cent of English-speaking visitors limit themselves to Prague and occasionally Bratislava. The clever few who escape the hordes in the capitals soon experience how helpful the Czechoslovak people can be, for everything outside Prague and Bratislava is still off the beaten track.

Early in 1990 Czechoslovakia changed its name officially to the Czech and Slovak Federative Republic (ČSFR), which is a federation of the Czech Republic (ČR) and the Slovak Republic (SR). It will, however, take some time for this change to filter through to common usage.

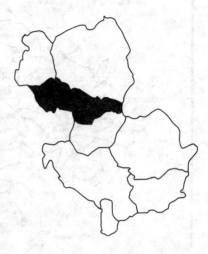

# Facts about the Country

## HISTORY

In antiquity this area was inhabited by the Celts and was never part of the classical Roman Empire. The Celtic Boii tribe which inhabited the Bohemian basin gave the region its present name. Germanic tribes conquered the Celts in the 4th century AD, and between the 5th and 10th centuries the West Slavs settled here. From 830 to 907 the Slavonic tribes united into the Great Moravian Empire and adopted Christianity.

Towards the end of the 9th century, the Czechs seceded from the Great Moravian Empire and formed an independent state. In 995 the Czech lands were united under the native Přemysl dynasty as the principality of Bohemia. The Czech state became a kingdom in the 12th century and reached its peak under Přemysl Otakar II from 1253 to 1278. Many towns were founded at this time.

The Přemysls died out in 1306 and, in 1310, John of Luxembourg gained the Bohemian throne through marriage and annexed the kingdom to the German empire. His son, Charles IV, became King of the Germans in 1346 and Holy Roman Emperor in 1355. Inclusion in this medieval empire led to a blossoming of trade and culture. The capital, Prague, was made an archbishopric in 1344 and in 1348 Charles University was founded. These kings were able to keep the feudal nobility in check, but under Wenceslas IV (1378-1419) the strength of the monarchy declined. The church became the largest landowner.

In 1415 the religious reformer Jan Hus, rector of Charles University, was burnt at the stake in Constance. His ideas inspired the nationalistic Hussite movement which swept Bohemia from 1419 to 1434. After the defeat of the Hussites, the Jagiello dynasty occupied the Bohemian throne. Vladislav Jagiello merged the Bohemian and Hungarian states in 1490.

With the death of Ludovic Jagiello at the Battle of Mohács in 1526, the Austrian Habsburg dynasty ascended to the thrones of Bohemia and Hungary. Thus Bohemia, which was strongly affected by the Protestant Reformation, became subject to the Catholic Counter-Reformation backed by the Habsburgs. The Thirty Years' War, which wracked Europe from 1618 to 1648, began in Prague, and the defeat of the uprising of the Czech Estates at the Battle of White Mountain in 1620 marked the beginning of a long period of forced re-Catholicisation, Germanisation and oppression.

Yet, under the Habsburgs, Czech culture was never as totally suppressed as was Polish culture under the Russian tsars, for example,

and during the early 19th century a National Revival Movement rediscovered the linguistic and cultural roots of the Czechs and Slovaks. Despite the defeat of the democratic revolution of 1848, the industrial revolution took firm hold in the Czech lands as a middle class emerged.

Slovakia had a somewhat different history from Bohemia. In the first half of the 10th century, the Magyars invaded Slovakia and, in 1018, annexed it to Hungary. Slovakia remained part of Hungary until 1918, although the Spis region of East Slovakia belonged to Poland from 1412 to 1772.

When the Turks overran Hungary in the 16th century, the Hungarian capital moved from Buda to Bratislava. The creation of the Austro-Hungarian empire in 1867 brought all of present Czechoslovakia under one rule.

In 1914 Austro-Hungarian expansionism in the Balkans led to war, but no fighting took place in what is now Czechoslovakia. On 29 October 1918 the Czechoslovak Republic, a common state of the Czechs and Slovaks, was proclaimed. The first president was Tomáš Masaryk, followed in 1935 by Eduard Beneš, who later headed a government-in-exile in London. Three-quarters of the

Austro-Hungarian monarchy's industrial potential fell within Czechoslovakia, as did three million Germans.

After annexing Austria in the Anschluss of March 1938, Hitler turned his attention to Czechoslovakia. By the infamous Munich diktat of 30 September 1938, Britain and France surrendered the border regions of the republic to Nazi Germany, and in March 1939 the Germans occupied the rest of the country. The Czech lands were converted into the so-called 'Protectorate of Bohemia and Moravia' while a clero-fascist puppet state headed by Monsignor Josef Tiso (later executed as a war criminal) was set up in Slovakia.

On 29 May 1942 the acting Nazi Reichs-Protector, Reinhard 'Hangman' Heydrich, was assassinated by two Czechs who had been parachuted in from London for the purpose. As a reprisal, the Nazis surrounded the peaceful village of Lidice, 25 km north-west of Prague, shot all the males and deported all the females to concentration camps. Czechs and Slovaks fought with the Allied forces on all fronts, and the antifascist resistance within the country culminated in the Slovak National Uprising (SNP) in August 1944. Although the Slovaks easily overthrew the local fascist regime, the Germans sent in forces which crushed the uprising. Fighting continued, however, until late October. After the German surrender in May 1945, the Soviet army occupied the country (West Bohemia was liberated by the US troops). Unlike Germany and Poland which were devastated during WW II, Czechoslovakia was largely undamaged.

## Post WW II

After liberation, a National Front was set up from the parties which had taken part in the antifascist struggle. In April 1945, even before the rest of the country had been freed, a meeting of the Front at Košice laid down a programme for national and democratic revolution. A power struggle then developed between the socialists and those who favoured capitalism. After the Munich sell-out, resentment against the West was rife and

the strength of the Communist Party grew. In the Constituent National Assembly elections of May 1946, the Communists won 38% of the votes and the Social Democrats 15.6%, forming a National Front majority. Communist Party chairman Klement Gottwald became prime minister.

In February 1948 the Social Democrats withdrew from the coalition in an attempt to overthrow Gottwald. Demonstrations and a general strike convinced President Beneš to accept the resignations of the 12 government ministers involved and appoint Communist replacements. The new Communist-led government then revised the constitution and voting system so that in fresh elections in May it received 86% of votes. Beneš resigned in June (and died in August) and, in July, Klement Gottwald became president. These events took place at a time when there were no Soviet troops in the country.

In March 1948 the new government approved a land-reform bill limiting property ownership to 50 hectares. All businesses with over 50 employees were nationalised. Socialist reconstruction continued through the 1950s and agriculture was reorganised on a large-scale cooperative basis. Gottwald died in 1953, after catching pneumonia at Stalin's funeral, and was succeeded by Antonín Zápotocký, and later by Antonín Novotný, who was president until March 1968.

In April 1968, the new first secretary of the Communist Party, Alexander Dubček, introduced lionising reforms. Censorship ended, political prisoners were released and rapid decentralisation of the economy began. Dubček refused to bow to pressure from Moscow to withdraw the reforms, and this led to a political crisis.

On the night of 20 August 1968 the 'Prague Spring' came to an end as Czechoslovakia was occupied by 250,000 Soviet soldiers backed by token contingents from some of the other Warsaw Pact countries. The Czechs and Slovaks met the invaders with the same passive resistance they had previously applied to the Austro-Hungarians and Germans. The 'revisionists' were removed from office and conservative orthodoxy was re-established. One enduring reform of 1968 was the federative system, which established equal Czech and Slovak republics.

In 1969 the 'realist' Dr Gustav Husák was elected first secretary and in 1975 president. Husák led Czechoslovakia through two decades of centralised socialist development. Yet opponents of the regime were marginalised and the population as a whole had to endure bureaucratic inconveniences, such as waiting 30 hours in line to get an exit visa simply to travel abroad.

In 1977 the trial of the rock music group 'The Plastic People of the Universe' inspired the formation of the human rights group Charter 77. (The puritanical Communist establishment saw in the nonconformism of the young musicians a threat to the status quo, while those disenchanted with the regime viewed the trial as part of a pervasive assault on the human spirit.) Made up of a small assortment of Prague intellectuals, Charter 77 functioned as an underground opposition throughout the 1980s.

By 1989 Gorbachev's *perestroika* was sending shock waves through the region and the fall of the Berlin Wall on 9 November raised expectations that changes in Czechoslovakia were imminent. On Friday 17 November 1989 a student march up Prague's Národní ulice towards Wenceslas Square (Václavské náměstí) was broken up by police. The next Monday 250,000 people gathered in Wenceslas Square to protest against the violence used against the students. The protests widened with a general strike on 27 November 1989, culminating in the resignation of the Communist Party's Politburo. The 'velvet revolution' was over.

Civic Forum, a coalition of opposition groups formed after the 17 November violence, was led by playwright-philosopher Václav Havel, Prague's best known 'dissident' and ex-political prisoner. Havel took over as the country's interim president by popular demand – in the free elections of June 1990, Civic Forum and its counterpart in Slovakia, Society against Violence, were

successful. The Communist Party, which suffered a drop in membership from 1,700,000 in 1987 to 800,000 in 1990, still won 47 seats in the 300-seat Federal Parliament.

Havel rejected the idea of reprisals against the Communists and called for national reconciliation. Friction between Slovakia and Prague is, however, on the increase, with several separatist parties calling for Slovak independence from the Czechoslovak federation. In December 1990 the Federal Parliament approved a constitutional amendment granting the Czech and Slovak republics greater autonomy in economic matters, with the Federal Government retaining control of defence and foreign affairs. The disputed oil pipeline from the Soviet Union was turned over to a special federal state corporation. In February 1991 the Civic Forum split into two factions: the social democrats favoured by Havel, and Thatcherite conservative elements led by the Finance Minister, Vaclav Klaus. Privatisation and the slashing of state subsidies have hit Slovakia hardest as the Communists concentrated much of the country's heavy industry there. More autonomy for the Czech and Slovak republics is on the cards.

## GEOGRAPHY

Czechoslovakia is a landlocked country of 127,889 sq km, with 78,864 sq km of it in Bohemia and Moravia, and 49,025 sq km in Slovakia. Approximately 33% of Czechoslovakia lies 500 metres above sea level and 3% of it is over 1000 metres above sea level. This hilly country is a clear physical barrier between the northern European Plain and the Danube Basin. About 40% of the land is arable, 13% is meadows and pastures, and the rest is largely mountain and forest. In Bohemia the forests have been devastated by acid rain resulting from the burning of coal. As yet, the Slovakian forests have been less affected.

The plains of East Slovakia are a transition to the steppes of the Ukraine, and southern Slovakia is a fertile lowland stretching down to the Danube. The 120-sq-km Moravian

Karst north of Brno features limestone caves, subterranean lakes and the Macocha Abyss, which is 128 metres deep. The Slovak Paradise (Slovenský raj) near Spišská Nová Ves is another fantastic karst area. There are thousands of small fish ponds in South Bohemia, many of them dating from the Middle Ages.

The Morava River flows out of Moravia and enters the Danube (Dunaj in Czech) just west of Bratislava. The Váh River of Slovakia joins the Danube at Komárno. The Danube itself forms the border with Hungary from Bratislava to Štúrovo/Esztergom. Bohemia's most famous river is the Vltava (Moldau in German), which originates near the Austrian border and flows north through Český Krumlov, České Budějovice and Prague. It eventually joins the Labe, which becomes the Elbe in Germany. The Vltava and Labe rivers drain 40% of the country and flow into the North Sea, while the Danube and its tributaries drain another 54% of the

country and flow into the Black Sea. The Baltic-bound Odra (Oder) River originates in Czechoslovakia near Ostrava but soon enters Poland.

Czechoslovakia consists of two geologically distinct mountain systems: the old Bohemian Massif west of a line drawn from Znojmo to Ostrava, and the younger Carpathians to the east of that line. The broad, flat mountain ranges of Bohemia and Moravia are quite different from the pronounced valleys, steep slopes, deep canyons and wild rivers of Slovakia. In general the mountains of Slovakia are higher and much more sharply defined than those of the Czech lands.

Bohemia nestles between the Šumava Mountains along the Bavarian border, the Ore Mountains (Krušné Hory) along the eastern German border and the Giant Mountains (Krkonoše) along the Polish border east of Liberec. Žilina is caught between the Beskydy of Moravia and the Malá Fatra

(Little Fatra) of Slovakia, and to the east are the Vysoké Tatry (High Tatra). Gerlachovský štít (Gerlach in German) at 2655 metres is the highest of the mighty peaks in this spectacular alpine range which Czechoslovakia shares with Poland. The Nízke Tatry (Low Tatra) are between Poprad-Tatry and Banská Bystrica.

The opportunities for hiking are almost endless, especially in the Carpathian Mountains where the Tatra of Slovakia exceed 2000 metres. There are six national parks: Krkonoše (east of Liberec), Malá Fatra (east of Žilina), Nízke Tatry (between Banská Bystrica and Poprad-Tatry), Vysoké Tatry and Pieniny (both north of Poprad-Tatry) and Slovenský raj (near Spišská Nová Ves).

## GOVERNMENT

Czechoslovakia is one state, two nations and three historic lands. Within the Czech Republic (ČR) are Bohemia and Moravia, while the Slovak Republic (SR) corresponds to Slovakia.

## ECONOMY

From 1948 to 1989 Czechoslovakia had a centrally planned economy with industry

producing 70% of the national income. Before WW II, industry was concentrated in the Czech lands, but under the Communists heavy industry was developed throughout the country, with Slovakia being industrialised almost from scratch. The famous Škoda Works at Plzeň were balanced by the oil refineries at Bratislava, cement works at Banská Bystrica and an iron mill at Košice. There's a major industrial area around Ostrava in North Moravia with coal mining, chemicals, a steel mill and car production. Bratislava and Prague are also important industrial centres.

Engineering is the most important industry. Every fourth engineering project is for export. Electrical engineering, metallurgy, chemicals and rubber are also important. Czechoslovakia has abundant sources of power. Over 120 million tonnes of coal are extracted annually and there are nuclear generating stations at Třebíč (between Telč and Brno) and Trnava (north-east of Bratislava). The most important fields of consumer production are textiles (North Bohemia), leather, glass (Karlovy Vary), porcelain and ceramics. Bata shoes originated at Zlín, east of Brno.

The collectivisation of agriculture made possible the use of modern farm machinery. Czechoslovakia's workforce declined to a third of its prewar size (only 12.3% of the workforce is now engaged in agriculture). Cooperatives account for about three-quarters of agricultural land and state farms for the rest. Barley, corn, oats, potatoes, rye, sugar beets and wheat are cultivated, and cattle, hogs and horses are the main livestock.

Leading exports are machinery, industrial and transportation equipment, electrical goods, iron and steel, power plants, complete factories and refineries. Oil, natural gas and raw materials comprise almost half of the country's imports. Machinery and equipment are also imported. Before 1989, 80% of foreign trade was with the Warsaw Pact countries. Unlike Poland, which is burdened with a massive foreign debt, the amount owed to Western bankers by Czechoslovakia

Czechoslovak National Coat of Arms

is relatively small, which gives the country an edge over Hungary and Poland in future development. A stable economy and a high standard of living are other positive factors.

## POPULATION & PEOPLE

Two West Slavonic peoples, the Czechs and the Slovaks, inhabit the country. Czechs account for 64.3% of the population, Slovaks for 30.5%. After WW II most of the German inhabitants were evicted although about 60,000 still remain. In addition there are Hungarians (3.8%), Poles (0.4%), Ukrainians (0.3%) and other minorities, including Gypsies. The 600,000 ethnic Hungarians in Slovakia are by far the largest minority.

Some 55% of the people are Catholic and 10% are Protestant. There's a saying that it took 40 years of Communism to make good Catholics of the Czechs!

Czechoslovakia has 16,661,000 inhabitants. The major cities and their populations are Prague (1,211,000), Bratislava (380,000), Brno (372,000), Ostrava (325,500), Košice (203,000) and Plzeň (170,000).

## ARTS

Czechoslovak culture has a long and distinguished history. Prague University, the oldest in Central Europe, was founded in 1348, about the time that the Gothic architect Peter Parler was directing the construction of St Vitus Cathedral and other magnificent works. The 16th century sculptor Master Pavol of Levoča left masterpieces in remote East Slovakia.

In the early 17th century, the region was torn by the Thirty Years' War, and the educational reformer Jan Ámos Comenius (1592-1670) was forced to flee Moravia. In exile Comenius (Komensky in Czech) produced a series of textbooks that were to be used throughout Europe for two centuries. His *The Visible World in Pictures*, featuring woodcuts made at Nuremberg, was the forerunner of today's illustrated schoolbook.

The national revival period of the early 19th century saw the re-emergence of the Czech and Slovak languages as vehicles of culture. Late 19th century romanticism is exemplified in the historical novels of Alois Jirasek (1851-1930), whose works chronicled the entire history of the Czechs. His finest was *Temno* (Darkness) (1915), which dealt with the period of national decline. Karel Čapek (1890-1938) brought the Czech word *robot* (imitation human being) into international usage through a 1920 play featuring a human-like machine that almost manages to enslave humanity. Čapek's novel *The War with the Newts* (1936) was an allegory of the totalitarianism of the time.

### Music

Czechoslovakia is often referred to as the 'conservatoire of Europe'. In many families, at least one member plays an instrument and each village and town has its own band or orchestra. You will be deeply impressed by the musical performances put on here.

During the 17th century, when Bohemia and Moravia came under Austrian domination and German was the official language, Czech culture survived in folk music. In Slovakia folk songs helped to preserve the Slovak language during the millennium of Hungarian control. The songs tell of love, lament, anticipation and celebration as vigourous dancing overcomes the uncertainty of life. Today it is in East Slovakia that the ancient folk traditions are best preserved.

The works of Czechoslovakia's foremost composers, Bedřich Smetana (1824-84) and Antonín Dvořák (1841-1904), express the nostalgia, melancholy and joy which are part of the Czech personality. In his operas Smetana used popular songs that display the innate peasant wisdom of the people to capture the nationalist sentiments of his time. Smetana's symphonic cycle *Má Vlast* (My Country) is a musical history of the country. Dvořák attracted world attention to Czech music through his use of native folk materials in works such as *Slavonic Dances* (1878).

The opera composer Leoš Janáček (1854-1928) shared Dvořák's intense interest in folk music and created an original national style by combining the scales and melodies of folk songs with the inflections of the

Czech language. His best known works are *Jenufa* (1904) and *Příhody Lišky Bystroušky*, or The Cunning Little Vixen (1924).

## Dance

Bohemia's greatest contribution to dance floors is the polka, a lively folk dance in which courting couples rapidly circle the floor in three-four time with three quick steps and a hop. Since its appearance in Paris in 1843, the form has been popular worldwide. Smetana used the polka in his opera *The Bartered Bride* (1866).

## LANGUAGE

German is widely understood, especially in western Czechoslovakia. Under the Communists everybody learned Russian at school but this is now being replaced by English. In rural Slovakia very few people speak anything other than Slovak.

Czech and Slovak are two closely related, mutually comprehensible Slavonic languages which evolved from the same mother tongue during the 1000-year separation of these peoples. Czech is a strange and convoluted language with a great aversion to the liberal use of vowels. Many words contain nothing that we could identify as a vowel. One famous tongue twister goes *strč prst skrz krk* which means 'stick your finger through your throat' and is pronounced just as it's spelt!

On the positive side, many Czech letters sound about the same as they do in English. You'll be understood once you learn to pronounce c as ts, č as ch, ch as in loch, ď as in duty, ě as ye, j as the y in yet, ň as the first n in onion, ř as rzh, š as sh, ť as the first t in student and ž as the s in pleasure. An accent lengthens a vowel and the stress is always on the first syllable. When consulting indexes on Czech or Slovak maps, be aware that 'ch' comes after 'h'. An English-Czech phrasebook will prove invaluable, but it can be hard to find one here so consider bringing one with you. Some useful Czech words that are frequently used in this chapter are: náměstí (square), nádraží (station), ulice (street) and

most (bridge). In Slovak, ulica is the word for street and námestie that for square.

## Greetings & Civilities

hello
*ahoj, nazdar*
goodbye
*na shledanou*
good morning
*dobré jitro*
good evening
*dobrý večer*
please
*prosím*
thank you
*děkuji*
I am sorry/Forgive me.
*promiňte*
You are very kind.
*Jste velmi laskav.*
yes
*ano*
no
*ne*

## Small Talk

Do you speak English?
*Mluvíte anglicky?*
I don't understand.
*nerozumím*
Could you write it down?
*Můžete to napsat?*
Where do you live?
*Kde bydlíte?*
What work do you do?
*Jakou práci děláte?*
I am a student.
*Jsem student.*
I am very happy.
*Jsem velmi šťastný.*

## Accommodation

youth hostel
*mládežnická noclehárna*
camping ground
*kemping*
private room
*soukromý pokoj*
How much is it?
*Kolik je to?*

Is that the price per person?
*Je to cena za osobu?*
Is that the total price?
*Je to celková cena?*
Are there any extra charges?
*Jsou tu nějaké zvláštní poplatky?*
Can I pay with local currency?
*Mohu platit místní měnou?*
Where is there a cheaper hotel?
*Kde je levnější hotel?*
Should I make a reservation?
*Měl bych si zamluvit pokoj?*
single room
*jednolůžkový pokoj*
double room
*dvoulůžkový pokoj*
It is very noisy.
*Je velmi hlučný.*
Where is the toilet?
*Kde je záchod?*

## Getting Around

What time does it leave?
*V kolik hodin to odjíždí?*
When is the first bus?
*Kdy jede první autobus?*
When is the last bus?
*Kdy jede poslední autobus?*
When is the next bus?
*Kdy jede příští autobus?*
That's too soon.
*To je příliš brzy.*
When is the next one after that?
*Kdy jede příští potomhle?*
How long does the trip take?
*Jak dlouho trvá cesta?*
arrival
*příjezdy*
departure
*odjezdy*
timetable
*jízdní řád*
Where is the bus stop?
*Kde je autobusová zastávka ?*
Where is the railway station?
*Kde je nádraží?*
Where is the taxi stand?
*Kde je stanoviště taxiků?*
Where is the left-luggage room?
*Kde je úschovna zavazadel?*

## Around Town

Just a minute.
*okamžik*
Where is...?
*Kde je...?*
the bank
*banka*
the post office
*pošta*
the telephone centre
*telefonní ústředna*
the tourist information office
*cestovní kancelář*
the museum
*muzeum*
the palace
*palác*
the castle
*hrad, zámek*
the concert hall
*koncertní síň*
the opera house
*opera*
the musical theatre
*hudební divadlo*
Where are you going?
*Kam jdete?*
I am going to...
*Já jdu do...*
Where is it?
*Kde je to?*
I can't find it.
*Nemohu to najít.*
Is it far?
*Je to daleko?*
Please show me on the map.
*Prosím, ukažte mi to na mapě.*
left
*vlevo*
right
*vpravo*
straight ahead
*rovně*
I want...
*Já chci...*
Do I need permission?
*Potřebuji povolení?*
May I?
*Smím?*

## Entertainment

Where can I hear live music?
*Kde si mohu poslechnout živou hudbu?*
Where can I buy a ticket?
*Kde si mohu koupit lístek?*
I'm looking for a ticket.
*Hledám lístek.*
I want to refund this ticket.
*Chci vrátit ten lístek.*
Is this a good seat?
*Je to dobré místo?*
at the front
*vpředu*
ticket
*lístek, vstupenka*

## Food

I am hungry.
*Mám hlad.*
I do not eat meat.
*Nejím maso.*
self-service cafeteria
*samoobslužná restaurace*
grocery store
*obchod potravin*
fish
*ryba*
soup
*polévka*
salad
*salát*
fresh vegetables
*čerstvá zelenina*
milk
*mléko*
bread
*chléb*
sugar
*cukr*
ice cream
*zmrzlina*
hot coffee
*horká káva*
mineral water
*minerální voda*
beer
*pivo*
wine
*víno*

## Shopping

Where can I buy one?
*Kde si mohu jeden koupit?*
How much does it cost?
*Kolik to stojí?*
That's (much) too expensive.
*To je příliš drahé.*
Is there a cheaper one?
*Je něco levnější?*

## Time & Dates

today
*dnes*
tonight
*dnes večer*
tomorrow
*zítra*
the day after tomorrow
*pozítří*
What time does it open?
*Kdy se otevírá?*
What time does it close?
*Kdy se zavírá?*
open
*otevřeno*
closed
*zavřeno*
in the morning
*ráno*
in the evening
*večer*
every day
*každý den*
At what time?
*V kolik hodin?*
when?
*kdy?*

| | |
|---|---|
| Monday | *pondělí* |
| Tuesday | *úterý* |
| Wednesday | *středa* |
| Thursday | *čtvrtek* |
| Friday | *pátek* |
| Saturday | *sobota* |
| Sunday | *neděle* |
| | |
| January | *leden* |
| February | *únor* |
| March | *březen* |
| April | *duben* |

| May | *květen* |
| June | *červen* |
| July | *červenec* |
| August | *srpen* |
| September | *září* |
| October | *říjen* |
| November | *listopad* |
| December | *prosinec* |

## Numbers

| 1 | *jeden* |
| 2 | *dva* |
| 3 | *tři* |
| 4 | *čtyři* |
| 5 | *pět* |
| 6 | *šest* |
| 7 | *sedm* |
| 8 | *osm* |
| 9 | *devět* |
| 10 | *deset* |
| 11 | *jedenáct* |
| 12 | *dvanáct* |
| 13 | *třináct* |
| 14 | *čtrnáct* |
| 15 | *patnáct* |
| 16 | *šestnáct* |
| 17 | *sedmnáct* |
| 18 | *osmnáct* |
| 19 | *devatenáct* |
| 20 | *dvacet* |
| 21 | *dvacet jedna* |
| 22 | *dvacet dva* |
| 23 | *dvacet tři* |
| 30 | *třicet* |
| 40 | *čtyřicet* |
| 50 | *padesát* |
| 60 | *šedesát* |
| 70 | *sedmdesát* |
| 80 | *osmdesát* |
| 90 | *devadesát* |
| 100 | *sto* |

# Facts for the Visitor

## VISAS & EMBASSIES

A passport is required to enter Czechoslovakia. Since 1990 citizens of Canada, the USA and most Western European countries no longer require a visa to visit Czechoslovakia – if you're one of those, read no further. At last report, citizens of Australia, Greece, Japan, New Zealand and Portugal still needed a visa. This could change, so ask at a Czechoslovak consulate if you hold a passport from one of those countries.

### Visas, Compulsory Exchange & Stamps

The following information applies only to those who require a visa. If you don't need a visa, you will not be subject to the following Communist-era bureaucratic controls.

Czechoslovak tourist and transit visas are readily available at consulates throughout Europe at a cost of US$7 to US$30. You will need two photos per entry (maximum two entries per visa). To get a transit visa, you must have a visa (if one is required) for the next country on your route beyond Czechoslovakia. A transit visa is just that and cannot be changed to a tourist visa upon arrival.

Visas at the border are only available at the Czechoslovak border points with Germany and Austria. You can use your visa at any time within five months of the date of issue. Complete the application clearly and completely using block letters. Any irregularity, even changing pens halfway through, will mean that you will have to fill out another form and line up again.

You'll be asked how many days you wish to stay in Czechoslovakia, to a maximum of 30 days. This number will be written on your visa. A late report indicates that compulsory exchange has been abolished in Czechoslovakia and that everyone now receives the same standard bank rate. Confirm this when you apply for your visa.

Entry stamps into Czechoslovakia give the hour as well as the date of entry. For example, a stamp reading 23 10 1 – 2 indicates that you entered on 23 October 1991 at 2 am. The length of your stay is calculated in multiples of 24 hours, beginning with the hour of your arrival. In other words, the first and last days each count as one day. To allow for transit time, you are permitted to leave six hours after the completion of the last 24-hour period. So, if you entered at 2 pm on

23 October 1991 with a 25-day tourist visa, you would have to depart by 8 pm on 17 November 1991 (17 11 1 – 20).

The visa form bears a notice advising you to report to police within 48 hours of arrival, but this is aimed mostly at those who stay with relatives or friends. Police registration is only required if you needed a visa to enter the country. If you get an official stamp from the place where you're staying, you don't have to bother registering. If you do stay with the locals, they probably won't wish you to register your presence in their home with the police. If you're travelling around and have a lot of other stamps from hotels, the missing nights probably won't be noticed, but you may run the risk of being fined at the border if you don't get police registration.

These requirements may seem like a lot of red tape, but they are quite straightforward. You may enter the country at any time within five months of the date of issue of the visa, go wherever you want without further formalities (so long as you stay in official lodgings) and depart across any border you choose. You're even allowed to walk or ride a bicycle across highway border points.

### Czechoslovak Consulates & Embassies

Czechoslovak consulates and embassies around the world include the following:

Australia
    169 Military Rd, Dover Heights, Sydney NSW 2030 (☎ 371 8878)
Austria
    Penzingerstrasse 11-13, 1140 Vienna (☎ 894 3747)
Belgium
    152 Avenue A Buyl, 1050 Brussels (☎ 647 5898)
Canada
    1305 Avenue des Pins Ouest, Montreal, Quebec H3G 1B2 (☎ 514-849 4495)
Denmark
    Ryvangs Alle 14-16, 2100 Copenhagen (☎ 29 1888)
France
    18 rue Bonaparte, 75006 Paris (☎ 4329 4160)
Germany
    Ferdinandstrasse 27, 5300 Bonn 1 (☎ 28 5287)
Italy
    Via dei Colli della Farnesina, 144-Lotto VI, 00194 Rome (☎ 327 8741)

Netherlands
    Parkweg 1, 2585 JG The Hague (☎ 355 7566)
New Zealand
    12 Anne St, Wadestown, Wellington (☎ 72 3142)
Switzerland
    Muristrasse 53, 3006 Bern 16 (☎ 44 3645)
UK
    25 Kensington Palace Gardens, London W8 4QX (☎ 071-229 1255)
USA
    3900 Linnean Ave NW, Washington, DC 20008 (☎ 202-363 6319)

### Visa Extensions

You can extend your stay at police stations inside Czechoslovakia. Extensions cost US$5. If you wish to stay longer than 30 days, you will have to extend your visa once at least. Bratislava is a good place to do it and any Čedok (the official government travel agency) office will be able to advise you on the procedure. The offices handling these matters open for very short hours and have long lines, so don't leave it till the last day!

### MONEY

There are banknotes of 10, 20, 50, 100, 500 and 1000 Czechoslovak crowns or korun (Kčs); coins are of 5, 10, 20 and 50 heller (halířů) and 1, 2, 5 and 10 Kčs. Always have a few small coins in your pocket for use in public toilets and public transport machines. In late 1991 the official rate was US$1 = 29 Kčs. At the same time, the Prague black market was offering about 10% more.

Although many visitors succumb to the temptation of the black market, you should keep in mind that it's still illegal and that many of the people changing money on the street are professional thieves with years of experience in cheating tourists. They'll switch the bundle of banknotes after they've been counted for paper or small bills, or use some other trick, such as supplying worthless banknotes issued before the currency reform of 1953. Another favourite trick is to pay tourists with Polish 500 złoty notes instead of similar-looking 500 crown bills which are worth 500 times more! In an inexpensive country like Czechoslovakia it's foolish to risk large amounts of cash with potential criminals, though it's less risky if you are propositioned by someone who can't run away, such as a waiter, taxi driver or hotel receptionist.

If you change money at a Čedok office, you'll be charged 2% commission *(výlohy)*. Banks usually charge only 1% commission and give better rates, but their hours are shorter than Čedok's and they're slower and harder to find. Some exchange offices in heavily touristed areas advertise higher rates but then don't mention their sky-high commission – if in doubt, ask first. Changing money legally on a weekend is problematic, so be prepared.

However you change your money, once you have Czechoslovak money you'll have to spend it, as it's almost impossible to change it back into hard currency. The import or export of over 100 Kčs is prohibited, but you can deposit excess crowns with customs upon departure to be picked up within three years on your next visit. There's no advantage to importing crowns as the bank rate inside Czechoslovakia is as good as the rate outside the country, though you could bring the permitted 100 Kčs with you to cushion your arrival.

### Costs

When the 1st edition of this book came out in 1989 you got only 9 Kčs for US$1 at the official rate. Two years later banks were giving 30 Kčs to the dollar (the old black market rate), although prices remained about the same. At the beginning of 1991, prices went up by 100% to 300% and, although it's still cheap for foreigners, keep in mind that the average local worker only earns the equivalent of US$100 a month.

The hotel prices listed in this book are exactly what was being charged around the end of 1990, but don't count on them being that low by the time you get there. In fact, the longer you delay your trip, the higher prices are sure to be. In late 1990 you could live well on US$20 a day, eating at good restaurants, staying at medium hotels and travelling extensively by train. Today you may have trouble even finding a private

room in Prague or Bratislava for that money. Get out of the capitals and your costs will drop dramatically. As long as Czechoslovakia remains a bargain, it's smart to spend more to enjoy the luxuries you really can't afford back home (and Czechoslovaks can't afford here). There will always be time to go back to rock-bottom travel later.

## CLIMATE & WHEN TO GO

The climate is temperate – maritime in the west and continental in the east. Czechoslovakia enjoys warm summers and cool, humid winters with clearly defined spring and autumn seasons. Prague has average daily temperatures above 14°C from May to September, above 8°C in April and October, and below freezing in December and January. The eastern part of the country is cooler and drier than the west. In winter dense fogs (or smogs) can set in anywhere.

## TOURIST OFFICES

Čedok has 165 branch offices around the country which you can consult if you have questions, wish to change money, or want accommodation, travel or sightseeing arrangements made. It is, however, oriented towards the top end of the market. Čedok offices usually have someone on the staff who speaks English, French or German.

Czechoslovakia's youth travel bureau is CKM Student Travel (Cestovní Kancelář Mládeže) and has offices in most cities. They're a better source of information on money-saving arrangements than Čedok and also sell student cards.

Two organisations which arrange accommodation and treatment at health spas and mineral springs are Balnea, in the Czech Republic, and Slovakoterma, in the Slovak Republic.

There are municipal information offices in Prague and Bratislava. The staff are very knowledgeable about sightseeing, food and entertainment but don't make reservations or sell tickets. Receptionists in expensive hotels are usually helpful with information when they're not busy.

## Čedok Offices Abroad

Čedok offices in countries outside Czechoslovakia include:

Austria
    Parkring 12, Vienna 1 (☎ 52 0199)
Belgium
    19 rue d'Assaut, 1000 Brussels (☎ 511 6870)
Bulgaria
    Bulevard Stambolijski 27, Sofia (☎ 87 7713)
Denmark
    Vester Farigagsgade 6, 1605 Copenhagen V (☎ 12 0121)
France
    32 avenue de l'Opéra, Paris 2e (☎ 4742 8773)
Germany
    Kaiserstrasse 54, Frankfurt/Main (☎ 23 2975)
    Strausberger Platz 8/9, 1017 Berlin-Friedrichshain (☎ 439 4113)
Hungary
    Kossuth ter 18, 1055 Budapest (☎ 12 8233)
Italy
    Via Bissolati 33, 00187 Rome (☎ 46 2998)
Netherlands
    Leidsestraat 4, 1017 PA Amsterdam (☎ 622 0101)
Poland
    Ulica Nowogrodzka 31, 00 511 Warsaw (☎ 26 7076)
Romania
    Strada Visarion 9a, Bucharest (☎ 59 6860)
Sweden
    Sveavagen 9-11, 111 57 Stockholm (☎ 20 7290)
Switzerland
    Uraniastrasse 34/2, 8001 Zürich (☎ 211 4245)
UK
    17-18 Old Bond St, London W1X 3DA (☎ 071-629 6058)
USA
    10 East 40th St, Suite 1902, New York, NY 10016 (☎ 212-689 9720)
Yugoslavia
    Gundulicev venac 36, Belgrade (☎ 76 3191)

## BUSINESS HOURS & HOLIDAYS

Banking hours are weekdays from 9 am to 2 pm. On weekdays shops open at around 8 am and close at 6 pm. Some stay open until 7 pm on Thursdays. Bakeries and grocery stores open earlier. Many small shops, particularly in country areas, close for a long lunch, reopening by 3 pm at the latest. Other shops are closed on Monday mornings. Almost everything closes at around 1 pm on Saturday and all day Sunday. Hotel restaurants are open every day.

Most museums are closed on Mondays and the day following a public holiday. Many gardens, castles and historic sites in Czechoslovakia are closed from November to March and open on weekends only in April and October. In spring and autumn you may have to wait around for a group to form before being allowed in, so again it's better to go on weekends. In winter, before making a long trip out to some attraction in the countryside, be sure to check that it's open. Staff at some isolated sights take an hour off for lunch, and ticket offices often close at 4 pm, even if the building itself is open until later. The main town museums stay open all year. Students usually get 50% off the entry price at museums, galleries, theatres, cinemas, fairs, etc. Many churches remain closed except for services.

Public holidays include 1 January (New Year's Day), Easter Monday, 1 May (Labour Day), 9 May (Liberation Day – this will be 8 May as of 1992), 5 and 6 July (National Holidays), 28 October (Republic Day), 24 to 26 December (Christmas Days). Republic Day commemorates 28 October 1918, when the independent Czechoslovak Republic was proclaimed.

## CULTURAL EVENTS

Since 1946 the Prague Spring International Music Festival has taken place in the second half of May. The Bratislava Lyre in May or June features rock concerts. In June there's a festival of brass band music at Kolin. In August the Frédéric Chopin Music Festival occurs in Mariánské Lázně. Karlovy Vary comes back with the Dvořák Autumn Music Festival in September. The Bratislava Jazz Days are held in September and Prague's International Jazz Festival is held in October. Both Brno and Bratislava have music festivals in October.

Moravian folk art traditions culminate in late June at the Strážnice Folk Festival between Brno and Bratislava, and during the first week of July folk dancers from all over Slovakia meet at the Východná Folklore Festival, 32 km west of Poprad-Tatry. In mid-August the Chod Festival at Domažlice,

57 km south of Plzeň, affords a chance to witness the folk songs and dances of South and West Bohemia.

The Brno International Trade Fair of consumer goods unfolds every spring. In August or September agricultural exhibitions are held in Nitra and České Budějovice.

## POST & TELECOMMUNICATIONS

In Prague it's best to have your mail sent care of your embassy, where it will be held for a longer time and more reliably. Elsewhere, if you use poste restante, include the words 'Pošta 1' in the address. Postage is cheap so always use airmail. Most post offices are open from 8 am to 7 pm.

To send parcels abroad, you will need to go to a post office with a customs section. Although the main post offices often don't have a customs section, staff there will be able to tell you which post office you should go to. These post offices are usually open from 8 am to 3 pm.

## Telephones

You can make international telephone calls at main post offices and, within Europe, they usually go through right away. Telephone rates for three minutes are about US$2 to Austria, US$3 to Germany, US$4 to Britain or France and US$8 to North America. Check the rates with the clerk before placing your call and ask for a receipt.

To call Czechoslovakia from Western Europe, dial the international access code, 42 (the country code for Czechoslovakia), the area code and the number. Important area codes include 2 (Prague), 5 (Brno), 7 (Bratislava), 17 (Karlovy Vary) and 95 (Košice).

Public pay telephones are frustrating as the telephone system in Czechoslovakia has deteriorated over the years and you may have to dial several times for even local calls to go through. Many public telephones on the street don't work at all, though those in post offices are more reliable.

## TIME

GMT/UTC plus one hour. At the end of March Czechoslovakia goes on summer time and clocks are set forward an hour. At the end of September they're turned back an hour.

## WEIGHTS & MEASURES

The electric current is 220 volts, 50 Hz AC. The metric system is used in Czechoslovakia.

## BOOKS & MAPS

Unlike Poland, where English is now the second language for literature, far more books on Czechoslovakia are available in German than in English. If you do see a good book in English on the country, snap it up as there aren't many.

One famous Czech classic, *The Good Soldier Švejk* by satirist Jaroslav Hašek (1883-1923), pokes fun at the pettiness of the government and military service alike. In the book, a Prague dog-catcher is drafted into the Austrian Army before WW I, and by carrying out stupid orders to the letter he succeeds in completely disrupting military life.

*Nightfrost in Prague: the End of Humane Socialism* by Zdeněk Mlynář (Karz Publishers, New York, 1980) is an inside political view of the events of 1968 by a former secretary of the Central Committee of the Communist Party of Czechoslovakia.

Ludvík Vaculík gives an insight into the mood of dissident Prague writers during the 1980s in his collection of chronicles, *A Cup of Coffee with My Interrogator* (Readers International, London, 1987), which has an introduction by Václav Havel.

The collection of papers entitled *Václav Havel or Living in Truth* (Meulenhoff, Amsterdam, 1986), edited by Jan Vladislav, includes Havel's famous 1978 essay 'The power of the powerless'. Havel describes the conformism of those who simply accepted the 'post-totalitarian system' by 'living within the lie'. In contrast, 'dissidents' who dared say, 'The emperor is naked!' endured many difficulties but at least earned respect by 'living within the truth'.

After the 1968 Soviet invasion, Czech novelist Milan Kundera saw his early works, *The Joke* and *Laughable Loves*, removed from library shelves; in 1975, he settled in France. In 1979, in response to publication of *The Book of Laughter and Forgetting*, which combines eroticism with political satire, the Communist government revoked Kundera's Czech citizenship. His 1984 book, *The Unbearable Lightness of Being*, deals with a brain surgeon who is reluctantly cast as a dissident after the 1968 Soviet invasion.

As far as travel literature goes, *Guide to Czechoslovakia* by Simon Hayman (Bradt Publications, England) is a practical guidebook aimed at the independent budget traveller. There's much information on hiking and activities – a rarity in guides to Europe! It's distributed in the USA by Hippocrene Books.

A more substantial guide than this is *Nagel's Encyclopedia-Guide Czechoslovakia* (Nagel Publishers, Geneva, 1985). Its 480 pages of detailed descriptions and good maps cover the country exhaustively, though the practical information is simply tacked on at the end of the book in the form of lists.

Czechoslovak bookshops usually have *Czechoslovakia/Prague* (Olympia, Prague) by Marcel Ludvík & Otakar Mohyla, a handy, inexpensive guidebook with alphabetical listings. There's also a more detailed *Olympia Guide* by Michal Flegl to Prague if you're planning to live there. Both are useful for sightseeing only. A good indexed map of Czechoslovakia is the blue-coloured *Československo Automapa* 1:800,000.

## MEDIA
### Newspapers & Magazines
Over 100 newspapers and magazines are published in Czechoslovakia. You can often find *Time* and *Newsweek*. *Welcome to Czechoslovakia* is a quarterly tourist review.

The first issue of *Prognosis*, the monthly English-language newspaper, appeared in March 1991. Aside from the usual tourist information, this high-quality publication carries informative articles on the current economic changes in Czechoslovakia. To subscribe, send a postal (money) order for US$25 (for 10 issues) to Prognosis, Dlouha třída 12, 11000 Praha 1.

The *Neue Prager Presse* is a weekly newspaper in German published by Orbis, Vinohradska 46, CS-120 41 Prague 2.

## HEALTH
All health care is free to citizens of Czechoslovakia. First aid is provided free to visitors in case of an accident. Otherwise, foreigners must pay a fee, sometimes in hard currency. British nationals receive free medical attention.

### Thermal Baths
There are 900 curative mineral springs and 58 health spas in Czechoslovakia which use mineral waters, mud or peat. Most famous are the spas of West Bohemia (Františkovy Lázně, Karlovy Vary and Mariánské Lázně). Recommended Slovak health spas are Bardějovské Kupele and Trenčianske Teplice.

Unlike Hungary, where hot-spring waters are open to everyone, in Czechoslovakia spas are reserved for the medical treatment of patients. Public thermal swimming pools, however, are available at Karlovy Vary, Trenčianske Teplice and Komárno. All the spas have colonnades where you may join in the 'drinking cure', a social ritual that involves imbibing liberal quantities of warm spring water and then parading up and down. Admission is free but you need to bring your own cup.

Though the resorts are pleasant to visit, to receive medical treatment at a spa you must book in advance through Balnea, Pařížská 11, 110 01 Prague 1, if you're interested in going to a Czech spa, or Slovakoterma, Radlinského 13, 800 00 Bratislava, if you want a Slovak spa. The recommended stay is 21 days. Daily prices begin at US$40/60 for a single/double in the cheapest category in the winter season, and rise to US$95/160 in the top category during the main summer season. Accompanying people not taking a spa treatment get about a third off. From October to April prices are reduced. The price includes medical examination and care, spa curative treatment, room and board, and the spa tax. The clientele tends to be elderly. Čedok offices abroad will have full information about spa treatments.

## ACTIVITIES
### Skiing
The ski season runs from Christmas to March in the Krkonoše, Vysoké Tatry, Nízke Tatry and Malá Fatra. Quality ski gear is hard to rent in Czechoslovakia, so bring your own with you if you can. Waits at the ski lifts can be excruciatingly long.

### Hiking
Serious hikers should head east to Slovakia, especially to the Malá Fatra, Vysoké Tatry and Slovenský raj (near Spišská Nová Ves). The latter is a karst area that was designated as a national park in 1988. The better known Moravian Karst, north of Brno, is similar. A more remote hiking area is the Dunajec Gorge at Pieniny National Park in East Slovakia, where you may also be able to go white-water rafting and canoeing.

## HIGHLIGHTS
### Museums & Galleries

Prague's State Jewish Museum in the former ghetto is easily the largest and most authentic of its kind in Eastern Europe. The Slovak National Uprising Museum in Banská Bystrica, a 'political' museum built by the Communists, survives because of the crucial period it documents in Slovakia's history. The 'panorama' in Brno's Technological Museum lets you see the world as it was in 1890. Košice's Art History Museum is outstanding for its exhibition of works of art which are set alongside large colour photos of architectural monuments from the same periods. Finally, at the museum of the Tatra National Park at Tatranská Lomnica, you have the rare opportunity of stepping out the door and exploring the very things you saw in the exhibits.

### Castles

Holy Roman Emperor Charles IV's Karlštejn Castle looks like something out of Disneyland but it's genuine 14th century. Český Krumlov Castle has the same effect. Spišský hrad, in remote Spišské Podhradie, is the largest castle in the country, and Trenčín Castle is well known as having been perhaps the most strategic. Brno's 17th century Spilberk Castle remains a symbol of Habsburg and Nazi repression.

### Historic Towns

Czechoslovakia is a country of historic towns, and the five most authentic and picturesque are perhaps Bardějov, Kutná Hora, Levoča, Tábor and Telč (see the relevant sections later in this chapter).

### Hotels

The vast majority of the country's hotels are still government-owned, so the following choices have nothing to do with room prices, which may change completely from one day to the next. So, assuming that you have sufficient funds, the elegant Interhotel Paříž in Prague and the Grandhotel in Starý Smokovec are not the sort of places that you would associate with proletarian equality. The Zvon Hotel in České Budějovice harks back to the Renaissance or earlier, while Pension u Rudolfa in Bratislava is the way of the future. Telč's Hotel Pod Kaštany should satisfy those who are not attracted by the choices just mentioned: it's friendly, affordable and nice.

### Restaurants

Only an Australian guidebook would list beer halls among the best restaurants in Czechoslovakia and here they are: the Restaurace Prazdroj in Plzeň and the 'Masné Krámy' in České Budějovice (Pilsner or Budweiser anyone?). Bratislava's Slovenská Restaurant serves just the sort of ethnic cuisine you've been dreaming about! The Miskolc Hungarian Restaurant in Košice is better than most Hungarian restaurants in Hungary. One Prague restaurant where you won't be overcharged or treated as an intruder is the 'snack bar' in the Palace of Culture. It's much nicer than the name implies.

## ACCOMMODATION
### Camping

Camping is popular in Czechoslovakia. There are about 600 camping grounds, which are usually open from May to September. The camping grounds are primarily intended for motorists so you're often surrounded by noisy caravans and car campers. The camping grounds are open to everyone and are good places to meet people. They are often accessible on public transport, but there's usually no hot water. Most have a small snack bar where beer is sold and many have small bungalows for rent which are slightly cheaper than a hotel room. Pitching your own tent in these camping grounds is definitely the least expensive form of accommodation. Freelance camping is prohibited.

### Hostels

The International Youth Hostel Federation (IYHF) handbook shows an impressive network of youth hostels in Czechoslovakia, but when you try to use them, you often find that they're either full, closed or nonexistent. The major cities lack year-round Western-style hostels with dormitory beds, though in July and August many student dormitories are converted into temporary youth hostels.

Some of the places listed in the handbook are rather luxurious Juniorhotels with single and double rooms, especially those in Prague, Karlovy Vary, Mariánské Lázně, Bratislava, Harrachov (near Liberec), Banská Bystrica, Horný Smokovec (Vysoké Tatry) and Jasná pod Chopkom (Nízke Tatry). Though they're open all year, most are permanently full. Officially, the Juniorhotels are meant for people under 30 years of age, but this does not apply to foreigners with youth hostel cards.

Hostelling is controlled by CKM Student Travel, which has offices in all cities. To get into a hostel, it's best to go first to the CKM office and ask the staff to make a reservation for you. These offices keep very short business hours, sometimes opening only on weekday afternoons. If you go directly to the hostel itself, your chances vary. Occasionally CKM offices will agree to make advance bookings for you over the phone at hostels in other cities, if you offer to pay for the telephone charges. A YHA membership card is not always required to stay at CKM youth hostels, though it will get you a reduced rate.

There's another category of hostel not connected with the CKM. Tourist hostels (*Turistické ubytovny*) are intended for visitors from other Eastern European countries and provide very basic dormitory accommodation without the standards and controls associated with IYHF hostels (mixed dormitories, smoking in the room, no curfew, etc). They're very cheap, but you'll have to be persuasive and persistent to stay in them. Ask about tourist hostels at Čedok offices and watch for the letters TU on accommodation lists published in languages other than English.

Similarly the letters UH refer to an *Ubytovací hostinec*, which is a pub or inn offering basic rooms without private facilities.

## Private Rooms & Pensions

In contrast to Hungary, private rooms are not readily available to Western tourists. They do exist, however, so ask for them at the Čedok offices in Brno, Karlovy Vary, Mariánské Lázně and Plzeň or at Pragotur in Prague. Most have a three-night minimum-stay requirement.

In Prague many private travel agencies now offer private rooms and, though their charges are much higher than those of Čedok and Pragotur, the service is also better. Unlike the government agencies, which often act as if they're doing you a favour by finding you a room, the private agencies actually want your business! This is by far the easiest way to find accommodation in Prague if you don't mind paying at least US$18/25 for a single/double a night.

Until recently the government had a monopoly on hotel accommodation and competition was an antisocial activity. Now small, privately owned pensions are springing up which offer more personalised service than the hotels at lower rates, though the locations aren't as good. Look for these in Bratislava and watch out for *privat zimmer* signs, which announce the availability of private rooms.

## Hotels

Czechoslovakia has a good network of hotels covering the entire country, and almost all of the hotels (excluding holiday homes owned by unions and factories) will accept foreign guests. In Prague the cheaper hotels are permanently full, whereas hotels in smaller towns are always cheaper and more likely to have rooms. In places well off the beaten track, the police (VB) may be able to help you find a place where you can stay if all else fails.

There are five categories of hotels: A* deluxe (five stars), A* (four stars), B* (three stars), B (two stars) and C (one star). The B-category hotels usually offer reasonable comfort for about US$15/25 a single/double with shared bath or US$25/35 with private bath. In small towns and villages, there are sometimes also C-category hotels, but renovations have upgraded most of them to B-category in the cities. Čedok owns many of the top-end hotels.

Staff at Čedok and CKM offices around Czechoslovakia will telephone ahead to hotels in other cities to make room reservations for you (choose one of the places listed in the Places to Stay section under each city or town). You'll get more personalised service at Čedok offices in smaller towns. In Bratislava, Čedok will reserve your room if you agree to pay for the hotel price and telephone charges in advance. In Prague Čedok staff are so overwhelmed with Western tourists that they're only interested in booking rooms in really expensive hotels. Upon arrival in a place you'll usually do better to look around on your own. Rooms booked from abroad through Čedok are much more expensive than what you would pay locally at the same hotels.

Many hotels will not rent rooms till 2 pm, so leave your luggage at the station. If you have a room with shared bath, you may have to pay extra to use the communal shower and search for the cleaning staff to get the key. Hotel receptionists usually sell soft drinks and beer for just slightly more than shop prices but they're often kept under the counter, so ask.

Many upmarket hotels insist on payment in hard currency in cash – travellers' cheques are often not accepted, nor are crowns, even with a bank receipt.

Some of the hotels and restaurants listed in this chapter may be closed temporarily because of privatisation, so check before going out of your way to get there.

## FOOD

The food is good in Czechoslovakia. The cheapest places to eat at are the self-service restaurants (samoobsluha) which you'll find everywhere. Sometimes they have really tasty dishes like barbecued chicken or hot German sausage. Self-services are just right for a quick cooked lunch between sights. The cheapest meals are to be had in busy beer halls. If the place is crowded with locals, is noisy and looks chaotic, chances are it will have great lunch specials at ridiculously low prices.

In Bohemia make frequent visits to the great little pastry shops (kavárna or cukrárna), which offer cakes, puddings and coffee as good as anything you'll find in neighbouring Austria.

Lunches are generally bigger and cheaper than dinners. Dinner is eaten early and latecomers may have little to choose from. If a restaurant deigns to serve you after 8 pm, you're lucky and by 9 pm most will be closed. Seldom does a restaurant have everything that is on the menu, though this could change as more restaurants are being privatised.

You'll rarely have trouble finding a place to eat at, but when you do, try the dining room of any large hotel. Hotel restaurants in Czechoslovakia are cheap in hard-currency terms, though the atmosphere is often stuffy and formal. Check your coat before entering or the waiter will send you back to do so. The serving staff sometimes use a 'reservations requirement' as a way of keeping out undesirables. Occasionally, pretentious service aside, these places will have menus in English or German with fish dishes available, and even vegetarians should be able to find something suitable. You can usually get a good cooked breakfast at a hotel. Hotel restaurants stay open later and don't close on weekends, and there's less likelihood of 'mistakes' on your bill than there might be at an independent tourist restaurant.

Hotel restaurants are fairly standard so we don't devote a lot of space to them in this book. Just look at our hotel listings then go and check out the hotel restaurants for yourself. Don't expect to be served at any restaurant if you arrive within half an hour of closing time. Tipping is optional, though you're expected to round up the bill.

Always check the posted menu before entering a restaurant to get an idea of the price range. If no menu is displayed inside or out, insist on seeing one before ordering. It doesn't matter if it's only in Czech or Slovak (as is often the case). Studený jídlo means cold dishes, teplé jídlo means warm dishes and *polévka* means soup. The waiter may be able to translate a few dishes, otherwise just take pot luck. If you simply let the waiter tell you what's available without seeing a price list, you'll be overcharged every time. If the person serving you refuses to show you a written menu, you should just get up and walk out.

### Local Specialities

*Pražská šunka* (smoked Prague ham) is taken as an hors d'oeuvre with Znojmo gherkins, followed by a thick soup, such as *bramborová polévka* (potato soup) and *zeleninová polévka* (vegetable soup). The Czechs serve meat dishes with *knedlíky* (flat circular dumplings) or sauerkraut, whereas the Slovaks favour paprika and *halušky* (potato and flour gnocchi with grated cheese). Carp *(kapr)* from the Bohemian fish ponds can be breaded and fried or baked. Vegetarian dishes include *smažený sýr* (fried cheese) and *knedlíky s vejci* (scrambled eggs with dumplings). Czech fruit dumplings *(ovocné knedlíky)* come with melted butter or curd cheese and a whole fruit inside.

### DRINKS

Czechoslovakia is a beer drinker's paradise: where else could you get four or five big glasses of top quality Pilsner for under a dollar? Czech beer halls *(pivnice)* put Munich to shame and most also serve full meals. Bohemian beer *(pivo)* is about the best in the world and the most famous brands are Budvar (the original Budweiser) and Plzeňský Prazdroj (the original Pilsner). South Moravia and West Slovakia are famous for their wine, either red *(červený víno)* or white *(bílý víno)*. You can be sure of a good feed at a *vinárna* (wine restaurant).

Special things to try include Becherovka, an exquisite bittersweet Czech liqueur made at Karlovy Vary, *zubrovka* (vodka with herb extracts) and *slivovice* (plum brandy). Grog is rum with hot water and sugar – a great pick-me-up. *Limonáda* is a good nonalcoholic drink. Connoisseurs should visit the wine museum in Bratislava and the beer

museum in Plzeň, both of which are excellent.

### ENTERTAINMENT

Theatres and concert halls were heavily subsidised by the Communists so admission prices are still far below those in Western Europe and the programmes are first-rate. In Prague, unfortunately, the best theatre tickets are cornered by scalpers who demand payment in hard currency, but in smaller centres like Karlovy Vary, Plzeň, České Budějovice, Brno, Bratislava and Košice you can see top performances at minimal expense. Check the theatres listed in this section early in the day. Czechoslovakia is a very conservative country when it comes to social customs and you are expected to dress up when going to the theatre. Most theatres are closed in summer.

Outside Prague, Czechoslovakia's nightlife is rather limited, though after 9 pm there's usually a band playing in the bar of the best hotel in town (US$2 cover charge) and on weekends a disco will be pumping up somewhere – ask. You must often contend with overbearing door attendants and contemptuous waiters. Movies are always very cheap and usually shown in the original language with local subtitles.

### Spectator Sports

Ice hockey is the national sport, followed by soccer (football) and tennis. Among the best Czechoslovak hockey teams are Sparta (the Prague city club), the Dukla (military) clubs of Trenčín and Jihlava, and the VSZ club of Košice and the Poldi club of Kladno (near Prague), both of which are factory clubs. Outstanding soccer teams include Sparta and Bohemians (Prague city clubs), Inter and Slovan (Bratislava city clubs) and Baník from Ostrava (a factory club). Cross-country ski racing is popular in winter.

### THINGS TO BUY

You're supposed to pay an export duty if you export goods worth over 500 crowns, although customs checks are pretty lax these days. Officially, knitwear for adults, sporting equipment and musical instruments are subject to 300% export duty, and the export of leather or fur goods, shoes, bicycles and antiques is banned. Very cheap maps of other parts of Eastern Europe can be found in Czechoslovakia if you look out for them.

Clothing is good value but it's often hard to find anything in your size. You should also check the quality carefully. Classical records and colour-photography books are popular. Garnet jewellery has been a Bohemian speciality for over a century. The ancient Egyptians used this semiprecious gemstone as a kind of travel insurance that was guaranteed to protect the wearer from accidents. Outside Prague the largest department store chain is Prior. Some department stores have soft porn photos for sale in the same showcase as photos of the pope!

Tuzex hard-currency shops sell imported goods, china, Bohemian crystal, Jablonec costume jewellery, garnets, fancy leather goods, special textiles, lace, antiques and souvenirs. Be sure to keep the receipts for anything you purchase here as you may be required to prove that you paid hard currency to export the goods duty-free from Czechoslovakia.

In most shops and supermarkets the number of people inside is controlled by shopping carts or baskets. You cannot enter without one, so pick one up at the door or stand in line and wait for someone to leave. You must even pick up a shopping basket when you enter a bookshop!

# Getting There & Away

## AIR

The national carrier, Československé Aerolinie (ČSA), operates a fleet of Ilyushin and Tupolev aircraft to Prague from New York, Montreal, Jakarta, Singapore, Kuala Lumpur, Bangkok, Bombay, Abu Dhabi, Dubai, Damascus, Cairo, Larnaca, Tripoli, Tunis, and many European cities. Nonstop flights from New York to Prague operate twice a week and some continue to Bratislava. Fares are complicated and variable, so in the USA telephone 800-223 2365 toll-free for the latest information.

From Western Europe return excursion flights are actually cheaper than one-ways! For example, Amsterdam-Prague is US$425 one-way or US$330 return (with a minimum-stay requirement of one weekend, and a maximum-stay requirement of three months). London-Amsterdam is US$490 one-way and US$435 return. These cheaper tickets are nonrefundable once purchased and flight dates cannot be changed. All fares are seasonal, so check with your travel agent.

There's no airport departure tax on international flights leaving Czechoslovakia.

## LAND

### Bus

Bus service to/from Austria is cheaper than the train. There's a bus several times a day from Vienna (Mitte Busbahnhof) to Brno (129 km, three hours) and Bratislava (64 km, two hours). Several bus lines go from Hungary to Czechoslovakia, but none of them goes from Poland. Try to buy your ticket the day before. Sogia Ltd (☎ 323 4006), 12 Petraki St, Athens, Greece, has a direct bus from Athens to Prague every Saturday at 7 am (US$85 one-way, 36 hours). This bus travels via Austria so no Hungarian transit visa is required. In Prague enquire at Hotel Panorama for return services to Athens.

There's a weekly Eurolines bus service throughout the year from The Hague and Amsterdam to Prague (16 hours, US$85 one-way, US$140 return, with a 10% discount for those under 26 or over 60.) If you get off at Plzeň it's a little cheaper. In July and August, this bus runs twice weekly. For tickets contact Budget Bus, Rokin 10, Amsterdam, or the ČSAD, Sabaucka 2, Prague. This is much cheaper than the train, so you'll need to reserve far in advance.

Many of the long-distance international buses you see advertised in bus stations around Czechoslovakia are only for locals – foreigners are not accepted.

### Train

The easiest way to get to Czechoslovakia from Western Europe is by train. Keep in mind that railway fares within Czechoslovakia are much cheaper than tickets to/from Western Europe. For example, going from Amsterdam to Cheb is expensive at US$130 one-way 2nd class. When travelling between Western and Eastern Europe, pay as little of the Czech portion in hard currency as you can and use border towns such as Cheb, Plzeň, Břeclav and Bratislava as entry or exit points. In other words, buy tickets which terminate or begin in these towns. When leaving, you can buy a ticket as far as the border using Czechoslovak crowns.

In Czechoslovakia you should purchase international train tickets in advance from Čedok, but do this somewhere other than Prague, as the Čedok office there is mobbed. All international tickets must be paid for in hard currency and are valid for two months with unlimited stopovers. Students get a 25% discount on train tickets to other Eastern European countries. Fares to Berlin, Poland and Hungary used to be very cheap but are now being revised. Interrail passes are accepted in Czechoslovakia.

Most of the major trains listed here travel daily throughout the year and require compulsory seat reservations. First-class sleepers and 2nd-class couchettes are available on almost all of these trains. From mid-June to mid-September additional services are put on.

**To/From Western Europe** Prague is on the main line used by all direct trains from Berlin to Vienna and Budapest, so access from both of those cities is easy. The Pannonia, Metropol, Meridian, Balt-Orient and Hungaria express trains all travel daily between Berlin-Lichtenberg and Prague (the Meridian runs overnight, taking seven hours), continuing on to Budapest. The morning Vindobona and afternoon Primátor also link Berlin-Lichtenberg to Prague.

The Vindobona and Smetana express trains link Vienna to Prague via Tábor (six hours). It's also possible to travel north-west

from Vienna on local 2nd-class trains by changing at Gmünd and České Velenice, the border points.

Vienna (Südbahnhof) to Bratislava is only a short 64-km hop done twice a day (two hours). Alternatively, there are six trains from Vienna (Nordbahnhof or Süd) to Břeclav (1½ hours). Twice a day there's a service between Linz, Austria, and České Budějovice.

From Western Germany you'll probably transit Nuremberg and Cheb. The Západní Express travels daily between Paris and Prague via Frankfurt/Main, Nuremberg and Cheb (18 hours). Local railcars shuttle between Cheb and Schirnding, Germany, twice a day. Trains from Zürich and Munich go via Furth im Wald and Plzeň. Twice a day there's a local train from Furth im Wald, Germany, to Domažlice, Czechoslovakia.

Two lesser known routes between Eastern Germany and Czechoslovakia are Leipzig to Karlovy Vary (the Karlex Express, which takes five hours) and Zittau to Liberec (which takes one hour). From Monday to Saturday a local 2nd-class train links Plauen, Germany, to Karlovy Vary, taking three hours. Local trains between Bad Schandau, Germany, and Děčín are fairly frequent.

**To/From Eastern Europe** All express trains running between Budapest and Berlin-Lichtenberg pass through Bratislava, Brno and Prague. Of these, the Hungaria is a day train, and the Meridian, Balt-Orient, Pannónia and Metropol are night trains. Going south, the Meridian and Balt-Orient run during the day, the Hungaria during the evening and the Metropol and Pannónia overnight. The Amicus Express is especially convenient as it runs between Budapest and Prague (8½ hours), travelling overnight in both directions and originating in those cities.

From farther afield, the Pannónia originates in Sofia and travels via Romania, the Meridian originates in Sofia and travels via Yugoslavia, and the Balt-Orient originates in Bucharest.

Connections between Poland and Prague

will go through either Wrocław or Katowice. The Baltyk travels to/from Gdynia via Wrocław, and the Bohemia runs to/from Warsaw via Wrocław to/from Prague, taking 12 hours. Take the Silesia if you want to go to/from Warsaw via Katowice to/from Prague (11 hours).

Going to/from Warsaw and Katowice, the Polonia stops at Žilina and Banská Bystrica on its way to/from Budapest and Belgrade. The Bathory, which travels between Warsaw and Budapest via Katowice, can drop you off in Trenčín in the middle of night. The Bem to/from Szczecin via Poznan and Wrocław can also drop you off in Trenčín in the wee hours en route to Budapest. The Varsovia runs overnight to/from Gdynia and Warsaw to/from Bratislava.

Some trains between Poland and Hungary pass through Slovakia, an interesting back-door entry. The Cracovia, which travels between Kraków and Budapest, runs through Košice, the major gateway to eastern Czechoslovakia. To/from Warsaw and Nowy Sącz the Karpaty also stops at Košice on its way to/from Bucharest. Local trains run twice a day between Muszyna, Poland, and Plavec, Czechoslovakia (15 minutes). The Rakoczi shuttles daily between Budapest and Košice (4½ hours). Local 2nd-class trains connect Košice and Miskolc, Hungary, twice a day.

Both daily trains to/from Moscow, the Dukla to/from Prague and the Slovakia to/from Bratislava, pass through Košice.

## Car & Motorbike

Some highway border crossings are only open to citizens of Czechoslovakia, Poland and Hungary, though this could change. The following crossings (listed clockwise around the country) are open to everyone. In each case, the name of the Czechoslovak border post is provided.

From Poland, you can cross at Harrachov (between Liberec and Jelenia Góra); Náchod (43 km east of Kłodzko); Bohumín (12 km north of Ostrava); Český Těšín (31 km east of Ostrava); Trstená (west of Zakopane); Javorina (east of Zakopane); Mníšek nad Popradom (31 km south of Nowy Sącz); and Vyšný Komárnik (between Rzeszów and Prešov).

From the USSR, you can cross at Vyšné Nemecké (94 km east of Košice).

The border crossings to/from Hungary are at Slovenské Nové Mesto (opposite Sátoraljaújhely); Hraničná pri Hornáde (21 km south of Košice); Kráľ (45 km north-west of Miskolc); Šiatorská Bukovinka (just north of Salgotarjan); Slovenské Ďarmoty, Šahy (80 km north of Budapest); Komárno (opposite Komárom); Medveďov (13 km north of Győr); and Rusovce (16 km south-east of Bratislava).

From Austria, there are crossings at Petržalka (at Bratislava); Mikulov (24 km west of Břeclav); Hatě (10 km south of Znojmo); Nová Bystřice (18 km south of Jindřichův Hradec); Halámky (south-east of České Budějovice); České Velenice (opposite Gmünd); Horní Dvořiště (38 km south of České Budějovice); and Studánky (which is between Český Krumlov and Linz).

From Western Germany, you can enter at Strážný (66 km north of Passau); Železná Ruda (81 km south of Plzeň); Folmava (between Regensburg and Plzeň); Rozvadov (between Nuremberg and Plzeň); and Pomezí nad Ohří (eight km west of Cheb). From Eastern Germany you have a choice of only Vojtanov (six km north of Františkovy Lázně) and Cinovec (48 km south of Dresden).

## On Foot

If you want to avoid the hassle or expense of getting an international train ticket, consider walking across the border! Two easy places to do this are at Český Těšín, which is on the opposite side of the Olše (Olza) River from Cieszyn, Poland, and Komárno, which is just across the Danube from Komárom in Hungary. All of these places have good onward train services, making this a viable option for the slightly adventurous traveller.

In East Slovakia you could walk from Slovenské Nové Mesto Station (62 km south-east of Košice by local train) to Sátoraljaújhely in Hungary. The border crossing is very close to the Slovak railway station, and the Hungarian station is only two km away on the other side of Sátoraljaújhely; local trains also connect the two stations a couple of times a day. Hungarian train services south-west from Sátoraljaújhely to Sarospatak and Miskolc are frequent.

If you want to walk into Austria, an easy place to do it is from Mikulov, an unspoiled Moravian town with a large chateau on one hill and a church on another. Mikulov is on the railway line from Břeclav to Znojmo and the station is very close to the Austrian/Czechoslovak border point. You could easily cross on foot and then hitchhike the 77 km south to Vienna. It's also possible to walk into Austria from Bratislava, but this area is congested and less exciting.

# Getting Around

## AIR

For those who enjoy the excitement of flight, ČSA offers morning and afternoon flights daily from Prague to Bratislava (US$15), Poprad-Tatry (US$19) and Košice (US$20).

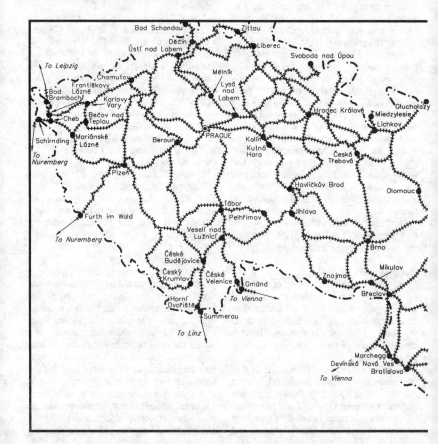

There are also flights from Bratislava to Košice (US$13). You pay in crowns and there's no airport departure tax on domestic flights.

## BUS

Within Czechoslovakia, ČSAD express buses are often faster and more convenient than the train. Buses are a little more expensive than trains, but, by European standards, both are cheap. Because of numerous footnotes, posted bus timetables are almost impossible to read, so patronise information. As more buses leave in the morning, it's better to get an early start. You sometimes have to pay a small additional charge for checked luggage.

Since bus ticketing is computerised at main stations like Prague and Karlovy Vary, you can sometimes book a seat ahead and be sure of a comfortable trip. At large stations, make sure you're in the right ticket line. Way stations are rarely computerised and you must just line up and pay the driver. Reservations can only be made in the originating station of the bus, and at peak periods you may have to stand part of the way if you don't have one.

All over Czechoslovakia, if you want to find a bus station or bus stop, write the letters ČSAD on a piece of paper and show it to someone. If you want to find a train station, write ČSD (which stands for Czechoslovak State Railways) on the paper.

Most bus and railway stations have a left-luggage room *(úschovna)*. There's a 15-kg maximum-weight limit for left luggage but it's not always enforced. If you lose the receipt, you'll have to pay a fine to recover your bag.

## TRAIN

The 13,114 km of track maintained by the Czechoslovak State Railways reaches every part of the country. Railway lines tend to run south towards Austria and Hungary, reflecting the country's political alignment in the late 19th century, when the tracks were laid down. Although a line was built east from Prague to Kiev as early as the 1880s, only in 1955 was this main route to the Soviet border reopened as a modern double-track line – at a cost of a billion crowns.

Using the Czechoslovak railway system successfully involves a little ingenuity. Some trains operate only on certain days, but the footnotes on the posted timetables are incomprehensible. The clerks at the information counters never speak English, not even in major stations, so, to get a departure time, try writing down your destination and the date you wish to travel, then point to your watch and pray.

You tell the ticket seller which type of train you want. On departure *(odjezdy)* notice boards in railway stations the *druh vlaku* column indicates the category of each train: Ex (express – these are often international trains and stop at fewer stations than fast trains); R *(rychlík –* fast trains, for which you always pay a surcharge); Sp *(spěšný –* trains to mountain areas); and Os *(osobní –* ordinary trains). The letter R inside a box or circle means that reservations are mandatory, while an R alone means that it's a fast train. Reservations are not possible on ordinary trains. In major cities, you usually have to make seat reservations at a different counter, so make sure you're standing in the right queue.

Express and rychlík trains are usually marked in red, and tickets for these often have a red strip across the middle. If you plan to travel on an express or rychlík train, make sure you get an express ticket, otherwise the conductor will levy a fine. Staff at ticket counters will happily sell you an invalid ticket and you'll have no recourse later. Most train tickets are valid for 48 hours, but check this when you buy your ticket. If you have to purchase a ticket or pay a supplement on the train for any reason, you'll have to pay extra charges to the conductor. First-class tickets cost 50% more than 2nd-class and nonsmoking compartments are available.

In many stations, the complete timetable is posted on notice boards. Look at the map and find the connection you want, then look for the table with the corresponding number. If you're going to be in Czechoslovakia for any length of time, it's a good idea to purchase the complete railway timetable book, the *Cestovný poriadok ČSD*. It can be hard to find but you can usually get one at Nadas, Hybernská 5, Prague (Metro: náměstí Republiky). With this book your mobility will be vastly enhanced.

One way to save on hotel bills while getting around is by using overnight trains. Cheap couchettes are available from Košice to Bratislava, Brno, Děčín, Karlovy Vary, Liberec, Prague and vice versa. Book these in advance at a Čedok office or a main railway station.

### Annoyances

Some Czechoslovak railway conductors try to intimidate foreigners by pretending that there's something wrong with their ticket, usually in the hope that the confused tourists will give them some money to get rid of them. Always make sure that you have the right ticket for your train and don't pay any 'fine' or 'supplement' unless you first get a written receipt. When you arrive at your destination, take your ticket and the receipt to a Čedok office and ask for an explanation. If the conductor refuses to provide an official receipt, refuse to pay any money at all, as this only encourages them to be more demanding with the next tourist they encounter.

One US reader sent us this letter:

I purchased a round-trip ticket to Prague in Budapest. On the train the conductor took my entire ticket and said he would give it back when we arrived in Prague (he took other people's tickets as well). Unfortunately, he did *not* give me back my ticket in Prague and I didn't remember it till later that day. I ended up having to buy another ticket back to Budapest and was later told that the conductor probably did good business on the black market with tickets such as mine.

The only circumstance in which a conductor has the right to hold your ticket is when you board a train on which you've reserved a couchette or sleeper, in which case the attendant will keep your ticket overnight so you don't have to be woken for ticket controls. Don't forget to ask for it back.

## CAR & MOTORBIKE

The types of petrol available are special (90 octane), unleaded (95 octane), super (96 octane) and diesel. Unleaded fuel may be called *olovnatých přísad, bez olova* or *natural.* You're supposed to purchase fuel using vouchers paid for with hard currency, although this regulation is not always enforced. When it is, simply drive on to another station. Be aware that fuel in containers is subject to a 300% export tax.

### Road Rules

Speed limits are 40 km/h or 60 km/h in built-up areas, 90 km/h on open roads and 110 km/h on motorways; motorcycles are limited to 90 km/h. Beware of speed traps on the autoroutes. Parking in the historic centre of Prague is restricted to vehicles with a permit and only people lodged in hotels on Wenceslas Square are allowed to drive there. The police single out foreign cars for traffic fines, so make sure you get a Škoda or Lada when you rent a car.

### Rental

The main agency handling car rentals in Prague is Pragocar (☎ 235 2809), Štepánská

42 off Wenceslas Square, which represents Avis, Budget, Europcar and InterRent. Pragocar also has counters at the airport and the Inter-Continental Hotel.

## BICYCLE

After a recent trip around Czechoslovakia by bicycle, Richard Nebesky of Melbourne, Australia, had this to report:

Czechoslovakia is small enough to be traversed on a bicycle. It is fairly safe for cyclists as most drivers will do their utmost to avoid them. Cyclists still should be careful as the roads are very narrow, potholed, and in towns the cobblestones and tram tracks can be a dangerous combination, especially when it has been raining. Theft is a problem especially in Prague, Brno, Bratislava and Plzeň, thus a good long chain and lock are a must.

A mountain bike or a sturdy touring bike with at least 18 gears is probably the best choice. Many parts of the country are hilly. Most major roads are in good condition, but the minor ones can be rough. There are many well-marked tracks (both dirt tracks and roads) in the forests to ride through, which are much more enjoyable than the roads full of vehicles blowing plumes of exhaust fumes.

Many locals use bicycles, so it's fairly easy to transport them on trains. First purchase your train ticket and then take it with your bicycle to the railway luggage office. There you fill out a card which will be attached to your bike; on the card you write your name, address, destination and departing station. You will be given a receipt that should include all the accessories that your bicycle has, such as lights and dynamo. You are not allowed to leave any luggage on the bicycle, and it is advisable to take off the pump and water bottles, as they could disappear along the way. The cost of transporting a bicycle is usually one-tenth of the train ticket. It is best to collect the bicycle from the goods carriage as soon as you arrive at your destination. You can also transport bicycles on most buses if they are not crowded and if the bus driver is willing.

## LOCAL TRANSPORT

Buses and trams within cities operate from 4.30 am to 11.30 pm daily. In Prague some main bus routes operate every 40 minutes all night. Tickets sold at newsstands must be validated once aboard as there are no conductors. Tickets are hard to find at night, on weekends and out in residential areas, so carry a good supply. Automats at Prague Metro stations sell tickets which can be used on all forms of public transport in Prague.

### Taxi

Taxis have meters and you pay what they show – just make sure the meter is switched on. There are always taxi stands near luxury hotels.

## TOURS

Čedok offices abroad offer package tours to Czechoslovakia and, as usual, the most interesting cater to special interests that are hard to organise on your own. Seven-night ski holidays offered from January to March are centred in Špindlerův Mlýn and Pec pod Sněžkou in Krkonoše National Park, north-west of Svoboda nad Upou along the Polish border. From December to April more expensive seven-night ski packages are available to the Vysoké Tatry resorts of Štrbské Pleso and Starý Smokovec. From May to October seven-night golf packages are offered to Mariánské Lázně and its 18-hole course. You can also arrange to stay at Czech and Slovak spas.

# Prague

Prague (Praha in Czech) is like a history lesson come true. As you walk among the long stone palaces or across the Karlův most (Charles Bridge), with Smetana's Vltava flowing below and pointed towers all around, you'll feel as if history had stopped somewhere back in the 18th century. Goethe called Prague the prettiest gem in the stone crown of the world. A millennium earlier in 965 the Arab-Jewish merchant Ibrahim Ibn Jacob described Prague as a town of 'stone and lime'.

This story-book city in the centre of Bohemia experienced two architectural golden ages: a Gothic period under Holy Roman Emperor Charles IV and then a Baroque period during the Habsburg Counter-Reformation. In the 18th century, Czech culture was suppressed, so it's not at all surprising that Prague's two greatest Baroque architects, Christopher and Kilian Dientzenhofer, were Germans.

Today Prague is the seat of the governments of both the ČR and ČSFR, the houses of the Federal Parliament, and the leading centre of much of the country's intellectual and cultural life. Unlike Warsaw, Budapest and Berlin, which were major battlefields during WW II, Prague escaped the war almost unscathed. Since the war, careful planning and preservation have prevented haphazard modern development.

Prague has so much to offer in the way of historic buildings and museums that you won't finish seeing it. Don't attempt to – get close to the city and leave it. Although everyone will want to spend a few days in this great European art centre, it's only in the little towns of Bohemia or the mountains of Slovakia that you'll learn what this country is really all about. You'll find later that your most treasured memories are of places the folks back home never heard of.

### Orientation

Almost exactly midway between Berlin and Vienna, Prague nestles in a picturesque valley, its high hills topped by castles and its river spanned by 17 bridges. This river, the Vltava (Moldau), swings through the centre of the city like a question mark, separating **Malá Strana** (Little Quarter), with the Baroque homes of the nobility, from **Staré Město** (Old Town), the early Gothic city centre. North of Malá Strana is **Hradčany**, the medieval castle district where royalty used to reside, while **Nové Město** (New Town) is a late Gothic extension of Staré Město to the south, almost as far as the old citadel, Vyšehrad. Only in 1784 did these four royal towns unite within a single system of fortifications.

Unforgettable features include Prague Castle, visible from almost everywhere in the city, and Wenceslas Square (Václavské náměstí), Prague's Champs Elysées, which points north-west to Staroměstské, the old town square. Between these two squares is Na příkopě, a busy pedestrian street where most of the information offices are found. Our maps of Prague are only for initial orientation – buy a detailed city map the first chance you get.

### Information

The best place to pick up brochures and ask questions is at the Prague Information Service (PIS), Na příkopě 20. The courteous, helpful workers are a relief, but they cannot find you a room nor sell you any tickets.

Čedok, Na příkopě 18, also has an information counter but staff there are less knowledgeable than at PIS.

If you want any information on motoring in Czechoslovakia, such as petrol, repairs, accidents, camping contact Autoturist, Ječná 40 (Metro: I P Pavlova).

**Student Travel** The CKM Student Travel Centre, Jindřišská 28, is helpful with information, but the staff cannot make reservations at hotels or youth hostels.

The Student Travel Agency Uniset, 28 října 9, just off Wenceslas Square towards Národní (Metro: Můstek), provides accommodation, personal guides, tours, sports and general information.

The travel office of the International Union of Students, Pařížská 25 (side door), sells IUS student identification cards. It is open on weekdays from 1 to 3 pm. These are handy for discounts in museums, etc, and the card also gets you a 25% discount on international train tickets in Eastern Europe.

**Money** Čedok, Na příkopě 18, is the easiest place to change money. If you don't mind waiting in line, the commission charge is slightly lower at the State Bank, Na příkopě 28. The Živnostenská Bank, Na příkopě 20,

gives a good rate and charges a standard US$1 commission. It's worth going in there just to admire the décor!

Some exchange offices around Prague have adopted tricky practices, such as posting the selling rates for foreign currencies on large boards outside, which are much higher than the buying rate they'll pay you, or advertising slightly higher rates without mentioning the high commission charges. Watch out for the small Chequepoint exchange offices along the tourist strips of Prague which charge US$3 commission for each transaction. One reader claimed he was able to bargain for a better rate at Chequepoint!

Beware of sleight-of-hand experts along Na příkopě and of pickpockets in restaurant queues. People who lean over to look at your menu are often more interested in your wallet. Several people have written in to report that they were cheated or robbed in this way.

**Post & Telecommunications** The main post office, Jindřišská 14, is open 24 hours a day, but poste restante is only available during business hours. You can make international telephone calls here.

**Foreign Embassies** Most of the foreign embassies are housed in magnificent Baroque palaces in Malá Strana, below the castle (Metro: Malostranská). The British Embassy, Thunovská 14, also serves Australians and New Zealanders. The Romanian Consulate, Nerudova 5 (open Monday, Wednesday and Friday from 9 am to noon) issues visas immediately for US$30.

A block over at Tržistě 15 is the US Embassy (☎ 53 6641). (The mailing address is: US Embassy Prague, c/o Amcongen (PRG), APO New York 09213 USA.) Nearby is the German Consulate (☎ 53 2351), Vlašská 19 (open Monday to Friday from 8.30 am to 12.30 pm, and Thursday from 2.15 to 4 pm. The Consulate of Yugoslavia, Mostecká 15 (open Monday, Wednesday and Friday from 9 am to noon), is also in this area.

The Hungarian Consulate, I V Mičurina 1

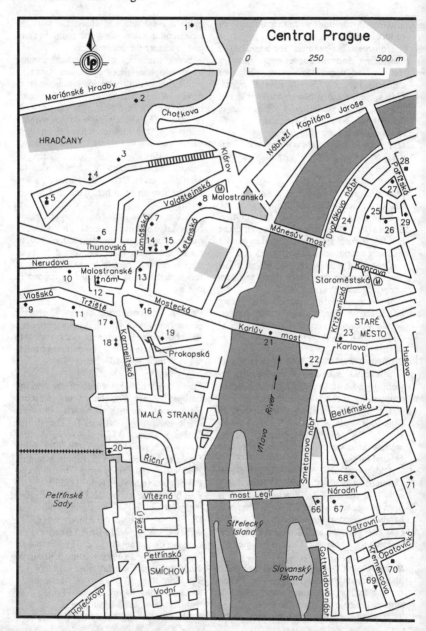

Central Prague

0      250      500 m

Mariánské Hradby

Chotkova

HRADČANY

Klárov

Valdštejnská

Malostranská

Nábřeží Kapitána Jaroše

Móneseův most

Dvořákovo nábř.

Pařížská

Tomášská

Letenská

Thunovská

Nerudova

Malostranské nám.

Vlašská

Tržiště

Mostecká

Karmelitská

Prokopská

Staroměstská

Karlův  most

Křižovnická

Karlova

STARÉ
MĚSTO

Kaprova

Husova

Betlémská

Vltava River

Smetanovo nábř.

MALÁ STRANA

Říční

Vítězná

Petřínské
Sady

Újezd

Petřínská

SMÍCHOV

Vodní

Holečkova

most Legií

Střelecký
Island

Slovanský
Island

Gottwaldovo nábř.

Národní

Ostrovní

Křemencova

Opatovická

Betlémská

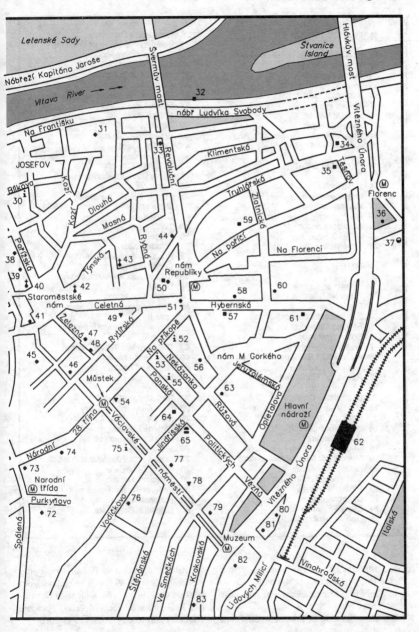

■ PLACES TO STAY

28  Inter-Continental Hotel
32  Albatros Botel
34  Opera Hotel
35  Merkur Hotel
50  Interhotel Paříž
57  Meteor Hotel
59  Atlantic Hotel
61  Hybernia Hotel
64  Palace Hotel
70  Koruna Hotel

▼ PLACES TO EAT

14  U Schnellu
15  U Svatého Tomáše Beer Hall
16  Vinárna Jadran
49  Restaurace u Supa
54  Automat Koruna
69  U Fleků Beer Hall
78  Kavárna Luxor

OTHER

1  Hungarian Consulate
2  Belveder Summer Palace
3  Golden Lane
4  Basilica of St George
5  St Vitus Cathedral
6  British Embassy
7  Wallenstein Palace
8  Wallenstein Gardens
9  German Consulate
10  Romanian Consulate
11  US Embassy
12  St Nicholas Church
13  Malostranská Beseda Theatre-
    Café
14  St Thomas Church
17  Vrtba Garden
18  Church of Our Lady Victorious
19  Museum of Musical Instruments
20  Funicular Railway
21  Statue of St John Nepomuk
22  Smetana Museum
23  Clementinum
24  Dvořák Concert Hall
25  Decorative Arts Museum

26  Old Jewish Cemetery
27  International Union of Students
29  Staronová Synagogue
30  Čedok (excursions office)
31  Convent of St Agnes
33  ČSA Office
36  Municipal Museum
37  Florenc Bus Station
38  Balnea
39  Balkantourist
40  St Nicholas Church
41  Old Town Hall
42  Týn Church
43  St James Church
44  Kotva Department Store
45  Narcis Vinárna
46  Former Klement Gottwald
    Museum
47  Carolinum
48  Tyl Theatre
50  Pragotur
51  Powder Gate
52  Prague Information Service
53  Čedok (train tickets)
55  Čedok (accommodation service)
56  Loutka Children's Theatre
58  Nadas Bookstore
60  Masarykovo nádraží (railway
    station)
62  Praha-Hlavní nádraží (railway
    station)
63  CKM Student Travel Centre
65  Main Post Office
66  National Theatre
67  New Stage
68  AR Tour
71  Reduta Jazz Club
72  Dům Slovenské Kultůry
73  Máj Department Store
74  Laterná Magika
75  Čedok (excursion office)
76  Varieté Praga
77  Institute for Educational Travels
79  Polish Consulate
80  Smetana Theatre
81  Federal Parliament
82  National Museum
83  Bulgarian Consulate

(open Monday, Tuesday, Wednesday and Friday from 10 am to 1 pm), and the Canadian Embassy, Mickiewiczova 6, are near Hradčanská Metro Station.

On the other side of town near Muzeum Metro Station are the Polish Consulate, Wenceslas Square 49 (open weekdays from 8.30 am to noon), and the Bulgarian Consulate, Krakovská 6 (open Monday, Tuesday, Thursday and Friday from 9 to 11 am).

**Travel Agencies** The tourist offices or airlines of most of the other Eastern European countries are along Pařížská, just off Staroměstské náměstí, including Bulgaria (No 3), Hungary (No 5), Eastern Germany (No 7), Poland (No 18), Yugoslavia (No 20) and Romania (No 20). The Hungarian travel office Ibusz is nearby at Kaprova 5.

Balnea, Pařížská 11, can arrange accommodation and treatment at Czech spas for at least US$70/120 single/double a night, all-inclusive (food, lodging, medical attention).

**Bookshops** Knihy Melantrich, Na příkopě 3, has a good selection of maps and local guidebooks. Prague's international bookshop is at Na příkopě 27. Nadas, Hybernská 5, sells railway timetables (Cestovný Poriadok ČSD).

The Knihkupectví Bookstore, at Staroměstské náměstí 16, has maps of towns and areas all around the country. Hungarian books, maps, records and folk art are available at Maďarská Kultura, Národní 22.

The Geologické Knihy a Mapy, Malostranské náměstí 19, has geological tomes in English and detailed geological maps of every part of the country. These aren't designed for hiking, but may be useful if you're very interested in a certain area.

## Things to See

**Hradčany** Prague's finest churches and museums are found in Hradčany, the wonderful castle district stretching along a hilltop west of the river. The easiest way to organise a visit is to take the metro to Malostranská, then tram No 22 up the hill around to the back of Hradčany as far as the 'Pamatník Písemnictví' tram stop in front of the Savoy Hotel. From here Pohořelec and Loretánská streets descend to the castle gate.

A passage at Pohořelec ulice 8 leads up to the **Museum of Czech Literature** in the Strahov Monastery, which was founded in 1140 but rebuilt in the 17th century. Before visiting the museum, find the separate entrance to the library (built in 1679), which opens for groups every half-hour. Buy a ticket in the museum, then wait at the library

door for a group to form. The church beside the library is beautifully decorated, and a lane leading east from the monastery gives you a good view of the city.

Nearby on Loretánské náměstí is the Baroque **Cěrnín Palace** (1687), now the Ministry of Foreign Affairs. The **Loreta Convent** (closed Monday), opposite the palace, shelters a fabulous treasure of diamonds, pearls and gold, and a replica (1631) of the Santa Casa in the Italian town of Loreto, said to be the Nazareth home of the Virgin Mary carried to Italy by angels in the 13th century! Unfortunately, the tour groups are so thick here that you'll have difficulty getting near the most striking objects in the convent museum. Consider coming back in the afternoon when the masses have vanished.

Loretánská soon opens onto Hradčanské náměstí, with the main gate to Prague Castle at its eastern end. At Hradčanské náměstí 2 is the **Military Historical Museum**, which is open from May to October (closed Monday), housed in the Renaissance Schwarzenberg-Lobkowitz Palace (1563).

Just across the square at number 15 is the 18th century Šternberský Palace which contains the **National Gallery**. This has the country's main collection of European paintings with whole rooms of Cranachs and Picassos. Luckily, the groups never have time to visit, so you can see it in relative peace. This and the many other branches of the National Gallery around Prague open Tuesday to Sunday from 10 am to 6 pm.

**Prague Castle** Prague Castle was founded in the 9th century, then rebuilt and extended many times. Always the centre of political power, it's still the official residence of the president. As you enter the castle compound under an arch dated 1614, you'll see the cathedral **treasury** in a chapel directly in front. On the north side of this courtyard is the **Castle Picture Gallery** with a good collection of Baroque paintings in what was once a stable.

The second courtyard is dominated by **St Vitus Cathedral**, a glorious French Gothic

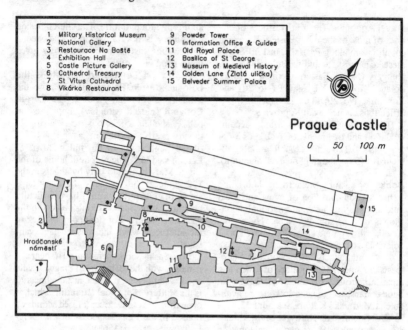

| | | | |
|---|---|---|---|
| 1 | Military Historical Museum | 9 | Powder Tower |
| 2 | National Gallery | 10 | Information Office & Guides |
| 3 | Restaurace Na Baště | 11 | Old Royal Palace |
| 4 | Exhibition Hall | 12 | Basilica of St George |
| 5 | Castle Picture Gallery | 13 | Museum of Medieval History |
| 6 | Cathedral Treasury | 14 | Golden Lane (Zlatá ulička) |
| 7 | St Vitus Cathedral | 15 | Belveder Summer Palace |
| 8 | Vikárka Restaurant | | |

**Prague Castle**

0    50    100 m

structure begun in 1344 by order of Emperor Charles IV and only completed in 1929. The stained-glass windows, frescoes and tombstones (including that of the founder in the crypt) merit careful attention. The 14th century chapel with the black imperial eagle on the door on the cathedral's south side contains the tomb of St Wenceslas, the 'Good King Wenceslas' of the Christmas carol. The small door beside the chapel windows leads to a chamber where the Bohemian crown jewels are kept; however, entry is not al-

PRAŽSKÝ HRAD

Prague Castle

lowed. Close to the back of the cathedral is the large silver tomb (1736) of St John Nepomuk, who was thrown to his death in the river in 1393 when he refused to tell King Wenceslas IV what the queen had confided to him at confession.

Adjacent to the clock tower, on the south side of the cathedral, is the entrance to the **Old Royal Palace** with its huge Vladislav Hall, built between 1486 and 1502. A ramp to one side allowed mounted horsemen to ride into the hall and conduct jousts indoors. On 23 May 1618 two Catholic councillors were thrown from the window of an adjacent chamber by irate Protestant nobles, an act that touched off the Thirty Years' War, which devastated Europe from 1618 to 1648.

As you leave the palace, the **Basilica of St George** (1142), a remarkable Romanesque church, will be directly in front of you. In the Benedictine convent next to the church is the National Gallery's collection of Czech art from the Middle Ages to the 18th century (closed Monday). There's a small bar in the museum where you can get a much needed cup of coffee and a piece of cake.

Behind this gallery, follow the crowd into **Golden Lane** (Zlatá ulička), a 16th century tradesman's quarter of tiny houses built into the castle walls. The novelist Franz Kafka, who was born in Prague in 1883, lived and wrote in the tiny house at No 22. On the right, just before the gate leading out of the castle, is **Lobkovický Palace**, Jirská 3, which houses a museum of medieval history containing a copy of the crown jewels. From the eastern end of the castle, a stairway leads back down towards Malostranská Metro Station.

**Malá Strana** From Malostranská Metro Station, follow Valdštejnská around to Valdštejnské náměstí, past many impressive palaces, especially the **Wallenstein Palace** (1630), now the Ministry of Culture, which fills the entire east side of the square. A famous figure in the Thirty Years' War, General Albrecht Wallenstein started out on the Protestant side then went over to the Catholics and built this palace with the expropriated wealth of his former colleagues. In 1634 the Habsburg emperor Ferdinand II learned that Wallenstein was about to switch sides once again and had him assassinated at Cheb. The palace gardens are accessible from May to September through a gate at Letenská ulice 10, a block away.

Continue south on Tomášská and round the corner to Letenská to reach **St Thomas Church**, a splendid Baroque edifice built in 1731. Behind Malostranské náměstí nearby is the formerly Jesuit **St Nicholas Church** (1755), the greatest Baroque building in Prague, its dome visible from afar. Malá Strana was built up in the 17th and 18th centuries, below the protective walls of Prague Castle, by the victorious Catholic clerics and nobility on the foundations of the Renaissance palaces of their Protestant predecessors.

After a wander around the square, follow the tram tracks south along Karmelitská. At the back of the courtyard at Karmelitská 25 is the **Vrtba Garden** (1720) with interesting statuary. Just beyond it, at Karmelitská 9, is the **Church of Our Lady Victorious** (1613) with the venerated wax Holy Infant of Prague (1628). Originally erected by Lutherans, this church was taken over by the Carmelite Order after the Catholic victory at the Battle of White Mountain (1620), depicted in a painting in the church choir.

Backtrack a little and take narrow Prokopská ulice towards the river. You'll soon reach a beautiful square surrounded by fine Baroque palaces. Continue on the left on Lazenská towards the massive stone towers of the **Church of Our Lady Below the Chain**. On the right, as you approach the church, is the **Museum of Musical Instruments** (closed Monday), Lazenská 2, in the one-time Palace of the Grand Order of the Maltese Falcon.

To the left of the church, Lazenská leads out to Mostecká with the **Karlův most** to the right. This enchanting bridge, built in 1357 and graced by thirty 18th century statues, was the only one in Prague until 1841. Take a leisurely stroll across it, but first climb the **tower** on the Malá Strana side for a great bird's-eye view. In the middle of the bridge is a bronze statue (1683) of St John Nepomuk.

Across on the Staré Město side of the bridge is the 17th century **Clementinum**, once a Jesuit college but now the State Library, which has over three million volumes. After Prague Castle this is the largest historic building in the city. To the right and around at the end of Novotného lávka is the **Smetana Museum** (closed on Tuesday), in a former waterworks building beside the river. Ask to hear a recording of the composer's music. The view from the terrace in front of the museum is the best in Prague.

**Staré Město** Beside the Clementinum, narrow Karlova ulice leads east towards Staroměstské náměstí, Prague's old town square and still the heart of the city. At its centre is a monument to the religious reformer Jan Hus, erected in 1915 on the

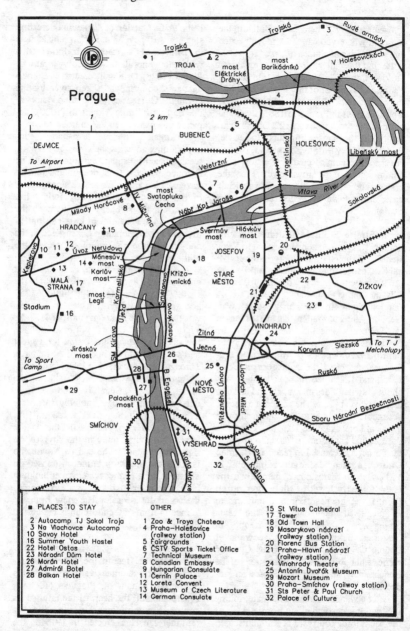

Prague

0       1       2 km

**PLACES TO STAY**
2 Autocamp TJ Sokol Troja
3 Na Vlachovce Autocamp
10 Savoy Hotel
16 Summer Youth Hostel
22 Hotel Ostas
23 Národní Dům Hotel
26 Morán Hotel
27 Admirál Botel
28 Balkan Hotel

**OTHER**
1 Zoo & Troya Chateau
4 Praha–Holešovice
  (railway station)
5 Fairgrounds
6 ČSTV Sports Ticket Office
7 Technical Museum
8 Canadian Embassy
9 Hungarian Consulate
10 Černín Palace
11 Loreta Convent
13 Museum of Czech Literature
14 German Consulate

15 St Vitus Cathedral
17 Tower
18 Old Town Hall
19 Masarykovo nádraží
   (railway station)
20 Florenc Bus Station
21 Praha–Hlavní nádraží
   (railway station)
24 Vinohrady Theatre
25 Antonín Dvořák Museum
29 Mozart Museum
30 Praha–Smíchov (railway station)
31 Sts Peter & Paul Church
32 Palace of Culture

500th anniversary of his death by fire at the stake. Below the clock tower of the **old town hall** is a Gothic horologe (1410) which entertains the throng with apostles, Christ, a skeleton and the cock every hour on the hour. Immediately after the show, a tour of the building, including the 15th century council chamber, begins inside. Do climb the tower for the view!

In another corner of the square is the Baroque **St Nicholas Church**, designed by Kilian Dientzenhofer. More striking is the Gothic **Týn Church** (1365) with its twin steeples. The tomb of the 16th century Danish astronomer Tycho Brahe is in front of the main altar and the church is extremely rich in artworks. Unfortunately, the Týn Church keeps capricious hours. If the main entrance is shut, check to see if the side door at Celetná 5 is open.

From a corner of Staroměstské náměstí near the horologe, take Železná ulice southeast to the **Carolinum**, Železná 9, the oldest remaining part of Prague University, founded by Charles IV in 1348. Next to this at Železná 11 is the neoclassical **Tyl Theatre** (1783), where the premier of Mozart's *Don Giovanni* took place on 29 October 1787 with the composer himself conducting.

Around the corner at Rytířská 29 is an ornate neo-Renaissance palace (1894), once the Klement Gottwald Museum and now a bank. From one corner of this building Na mustku leads into Wenceslas Square, Prague's fashionable boulevard where demonstrators gathered in 1968 and 1989 (Metro: Můstek).

Don't walk up the square just now, but go round the corner to the left into Na příkopě, a crowded pedestrian mall which leads to the **Powder Gate** (1474) on náměstí Republiky. Gunpowder was stored here in the 18th century and the gate only received its neo-Gothic appearance in 1886. From March to November you may climb the gate tower. Prague's Royal Way, followed by medieval Bohemian kings after their coronation, led through this gate and via Celetná and Karlova streets to the Karlův most, then up Nerudova to Prague Castle.

**Vyšehrad** Take the metro to Vyšehrad where the **Palace of Culture** (1981) and Forum Hotel rise above a deep ravine crossed by the Nuselský Bridge (formerly known as the Klement Gottwald Bridge). During the Communist era, unsmiling guards kept the public out of the palace unless they had business inside. Now the doors are wide open and you're free to explore at will.

From here the twin towers of the neo-Gothic **Sts Peter & Paul Church** are visible to the west. Walk towards them along Na Bučance and through the gates of the 17th century **Vyšehrad Citadel**, seat of the 11th century Přemysl princes of Bohemia. You pass the Romanesque **Rotunda of St Martin** before reaching **Slavín Cemetery**, right behind the Sts Peter & Paul Church. Many distinguished people are buried here, including the composers Smetana and Dvořák. The view of the Vltava Valley from the citadel battlements along the south side of the Vyšehrad ridge is superb.

**Monday Specials** In Prague on a Monday? Most museums and galleries will be closed, but the Prague Jewish Ghetto (closed Saturday) and the Mozart and National museums (both closed Tuesday) stay open.

The **Prague Ghetto**, Pařížská 19 (Metro: Staroměstská), includes a fascinating variety of monuments, now part of the **State Jewish Museum**. The early Gothic Staronová Synagogue (1270) is one of the oldest in Europe. All-inclusive tickets are sold in the museum across the lane from the synagogue, beside which is the pink Jewish Town Hall with its picturesque clock tower built in the 16th century. Follow the crowd down U Starého Hřbitova to the Klausen Synagogue (1694) and another section of the museum.

The collections of the State Jewish Museum have a remarkable origin. In 1942 the Nazis brought the objects here from 153 Jewish communities in Bohemia and Moravia for a planned 'museum of an extinct people' to be opened once their extermination programme was completed! The interior of one of the buildings bears the names of 77,297 Czech Jews and the names of the camps where they perished. (On the list are the three sisters of Franz Kafka.)

Behind the Klausen Synagogue is the **Old Jewish Cemetery** with 12,000 tombstones – an evocative sight. The oldest grave is dated 1439, and, by 1787, when the cemetery ceased to be used, the area had became so crowded that burials were carried out one on top of the other as many as 12 layers deep!

If you're into music there's the **Mozart Museum** in Villa Bertrámka, Mozartova 169 (Metro: Aňdel, then ask directions), where Mozart finished composing *Don Giovanni* in 1787. Czech film maker Miloš Forman's Oscar-winning movie *Amadeus* about the life of Mozart was shot mostly in Prague.

Looming above the south-eastern end of Wenceslas Square is the **National Museum** (Metro: Muzeum) with ho-hum collections on prehistory, 19th and early 20th century history, mineralogy and a herd of stuffed animals. The captions are only in Czech and the neo-Renaissance museum building (1890) itself is as interesting as what's on display.

**The Velvet Revolution** In front of the National Museum on Wenceslas Square stands an **equestrian statue** of the 10th century king Václav I or St Wenceslas, patron saint of Bohemia. Wenceslas' zeal in spreading Christianity and his submission to the German king Henry I led to his murder by his own brother, Boleslav I. Alarmed by reports of miracles at Wenceslas' grave, Boleslav had the remains reinterred in St Vitus Cathedral in 932, and the saint's tomb soon became a great pilgrimage site.

In the 20th century, the vast square in front of the statue has often been the scene of public protests. Just below the statue is a simple memorial with candles, photos and flowers dedicated to those who resisted Soviet tanks here in 1968. Also here on 16 January 1969 a Czech student named Jan Palach publicly burned himself to protest the Soviet invasion.

Stroll down Wenceslas Square past the majestic Art-Nouveau façades and turn left onto Národní to the **Albatros Theatre**, which is diagonally opposite the Máj Department Store. A film entitled *Velvet Revolution* is shown regularly here with the soundtrack in English or German at alternate showings. The film vividly portrays the inability of the Communist leadership to react effectively to student demonstrators in 1989 and their growing reliance on police force which eventually led to their downfall.

Nearby, under the arcade at Národní 16, is a simple plaque bearing the date 17 November 1989, which commemorates student demonstrators beaten here by police on this day. If after this tour you'd like to savour the subtle milieu behind Prague's 'velvet revolution', you can't beat the Art-Deco **Kavárna Slávie**, at Národní 1, right opposite the National Theatre, where dissident intellectuals and lesser conspirators have been meeting for decades.

**Nearby Palaces** The early Baroque **Troya Chateau** (1685), north of the Vltava River, was recently reopened after many years of restoration work. The 17th century frescoes on the ceilings are now fresh and on the chateau walls hangs a fine collection of 19th century painting. This impressive red and white building, surrounded by formal gardens and built for Count Václav Vojtěch of Šternberg, is open from May to October only (closed Monday). On a wooded hillside next to the chateau is Prague's **zoo**, which is open daily. Get there on bus No 112 from nádraží Holešovice Metro Station.

If the crowds in central Prague begin to get to you and you need a little peace, head for the **Hvězda Summer Palace** (closed Monday) which is in a large forest park west of the city. The Habsburgs built this Renaissance chateau in the 16th century as a summer residence and hunting lodge. The bloody final phase of the decisive Battle of White Mountain took place on the chateau grounds on 6 November 1620. The Catholic victory signified the reimposition of Habsburg rule on would-be Protestant Bohemia and the loss of national independence for exactly 300 years.

Today this place of national defeat functions as a **Museum of Czech Culture** especially dedicated to the novelist Alois Jirásek (ground floor) and the painter Mikoláš Aleš (upstairs). In the chateau basement is an exhibit on the battle. The name Hvězda means 'star' and the ground-floor stucco ceiling of this unique six-pointed building is one of the finest Renaissance artworks north of the Alps, yet the tour groups seldom visit. To get there, take the metro to Dejvická, then tram No 20 or 26 west to the end of the line. As you walk south on Libočka, you'll see the chateau's pointed roof rising out of the forest. Go under the railway tracks and turn left. A stairway up into the forest is just beyond the large church.

**One Last Museum** On your last afternoon in Prague, set aside a little time for the **Municipal Museum** (closed Monday), the large white neo-Renaissance building above Florenc Metro Station. Here you'll see maps and photos of the numerous monuments you've visited around town, plus interesting artifacts to put them in perspective. But the museum's crowning glory is a huge scale model of Prague created in 1834. Don't miss it!

**Organised Tours** The Čedok office at Bílkova 6, near the Inter-Continental Hotel, arranges bus excursions to historic sites in the environs, including castles and spas. Departures are only during the high season (15 May to 15 October) and prices range from US$26 to US$33. The tours are given in English and German only. You meet the bus at the Inter-Continental Hotel.

Čedok, Wenceslas Square 24, also books excursions to Karlštejn/Konopiště (US$26), Kutná Hora (US$24) and Plzeň (US$24), and boat trips on the Vltava River (US$18). A private travel agency, Top Tour, Rybná 3 near Pragotur, also offers excursions of this kind.

The Pražská Informační Služba, Pánská 4, offers three-hour bus tours of Prague in English and German (US$8) every afternoon throughout the year. At this office you can also hire a personal guide able to speak almost any major European language to show you around the city for US$8 (three hours) for one or two people, plus US$4 for each additional person.

### Places to Stay

**Camping** In summer the easiest thing to do is to pitch a tent. *Sport Camp TJ Vysoké Školy* (☎ 52 1632) off Plzeňská, west of the city, offers tent space (US$2 per person, plus US$2 per tent). You can also rent small bungalows for US$8 double, which are often full. There's a poor restaurant on the premises. Take tram No 4 or 9 from Anděl Metro Station to Poštovka, then walk a km up the hill. It's open from April to the end of October – recommended.

There's a much smaller camping ground (open from June to August) with nine bungalows at *TJ Sokol Troja* (☎ 84 2833), Trojská 171, near the zoo (bus No 112 from nádraží Holešovice Metro Station). A bungalow here will be US$4/8 single/double, but, of course, the place is always full. Also try the house at Trojská 157 and others on the street which sometimes have camping space in their back yards, but beware of overcrowding.

**Hostels** The IYHF handbook lists the *CKM Juniorhotel*, at Žitná 12 (Metro: Karlovo náměstí), as Prague's youth hostel, but you're invariably told it's full up with groups for the rest of the month. Trying to make an advance booking by mail is also a waste of time. Occasionally the staff will refer you to some other CKM hostel with vacant space, but don't count on it.

For information on other youth hostels, enquire at CKM Student Travel, Žitná 10, beside the Juniorhotel (open weekdays during business hours). They'll know about the summer youth hostel (open in July and August) at Koleje Strahov near Spartakiádní Stadión (stadium) (buses No 143, 149 and 217 from Dejvická Metro Station). You could also just go directly to this hostel. Ask too about the new *CKM Juniorhotel Vltava* near Roztyly Metro Station, south of the city, and the *Admira Hostel*, to the north.

The CKM runs a year-round youth hostel at *TJ Ubytovna*, U školské zahrady on the north side of Prague (take tram No 17 or 25 from nádraží Holešovice Metro Station to 'Střelničná'). Trouble is, if you just go there, you'll probably be told that it's full (with whom is a mystery as you're unlikely to meet any other travellers there). Ask CKM at Žitná 10 for a reference before heading out that way. If you do manage to get in, it's US$5 for bed and breakfast.

Actually, the people at Žitná 10 are much more interested in renting expensive private rooms than in helping you find the youth-hostel bed you came looking for. Their private rooms are expensive (US$35 double, no singles) and no better than the room you could have obtained much more easily at the train station. This CKM office may agree to make reservations at Juniorhotels in other cities around Czechoslovakia for those who know their exact itinerary.

At a pinch you could try the *TJ Dolní Mecholupy* (☎ 75 1262) at the end of Pod Hřištěm, in a suburb about 10 km east of Prague. Take the metro to Želivského, and then bus No 111, 228 or 229 to Dolno-mecholupská, but ask the staff at Pragotur to phone the hotel before you make the long trip out. Dorm beds cost US$7, breakfast is available, it's open all year and is often full.

If it's getting late and you still don't have a bed, consider spending the night at the *Turistická Ubytovna* on Malého ulice, a five-minute walk from Florenc Bus Station (Metro: Florenc). To get there, walk east along Křižíkova ulice past the Karlín Theatre and Florenc Hotel. Turn right on Pluku ulice just after the railway bridge. The hostel is just before the next railway bridge. The doors don't open until 6 pm and all you'll get is a dorm bed (US$4), but it beats the floor at Hlavní nádraží (railway station).

**Room-Finding Services** Your best bet for a private room is Pragotur, U Obecního domu 2 near the Powder Gate (Metro: náměstí Republiky). The accommodation window at Pragotur opens daily at 10 am and again at 5 pm (get in line 20 minutes before then). The staff can arrange private rooms at US$10/15 single/double, plus a US$1 daily registration fee, but there is a three-night minimum-stay requirement. All of the rooms are far from the centre but public transport is good. You cannot occupy the room until 5 pm, so leave your luggage at the station. Pragotur some-times also has hotel and dormitory space, but not every day. The staff will not accept advance reservations for a return trip later on. Rekrea at Pařížská 28, near the Inter-Continental Hotel (Metro: Staroměstská), rents private rooms at US$12 double (no singles). It's only open during regular busi-ness hours, but not many people know about this office, so there's no queue. The staff are willing to rent rooms for just one or two nights.

The big news on the Prague accommoda-tion scene is the many private travel agencies arranging private rooms and apartments. Their prices are higher but the service is better and *they always have rooms!*

AVE Limited (☎ 235 8389), with branches in all of Prague's main railway stations, rents private rooms at US$18/35 single/double or whole apartments from US$50 to US$70 double. Ask AVE about hostel accommoda-tion. It's open daily so look for it upon arrival, but don't change money there as you'll get a lousy rate. Co-op Tour at Hlavní nádraží sometimes has dorm beds for US$4.

Top Tour (☎ 232 1077), Rybná 3, just a block down from Pragotur, is also very good. First-category rooms (with private bath) are US$35/54 single/double and 2nd category rooms (with shared bath) are US$21/34. Apartments are also available (US$61 double, US$86 for four people, US$109 for eight people). Rooms are available in the city centre, and the office is open daily all year until 7 pm.

AR Tour at Karolíny Světlé 9, a side street leading down from Národní 13, not far from the National Theatre (Metro: Národní třída), rents private apartments around Prague for US$32/44 single/double. Though the prices are higher, there are no queues here and there are always rooms, usually of superior quality and close to the centre, too.

The harried staff at the Čedok Accommodation Service, Panská 5, will try to force you into an expensive hotel. The only reason to come here at all is to rent an unofficial private room from the eager householders who crowd the street outside looking for hard-currency guests. They'll ask about the same (US$18/35 single/double) as the agencies just listed – bargain if you think the price is too high and check the location on a good map before going. Be absolutely certain that you have understood the price correctly.

To reserve a private room over the phone, call Tomáš Vaculík (☎ 353 8923 weekdays or 74 90 66 Monday and Tuesday evenings) a few days in advance and he'll meet you at the station. He speaks English and German. If you arrive by plane, ask at the Čedok office in the airport about private rooms.

**A Special Tip** One of the strangest places you can stay at in Prague (if you get in!) is *Na Vlachovce Autocamp* (☎ 84 1290), Rudé armády 217, north of the city. Despite the name, there's no camping ground here. Instead you sleep in a small bungalow shaped like a Budvar beer keg (no joke!) for only US$10 double. The kegs are uncorked from April to October only, but there's a good folk restaurant open throughout the year. Walk straight through the restaurant to the hotel reception in the back yard. Get there on tram No 5, 17 or 25 from nádraží Holešovice Metro Station to 'Ke Stírce'.

**Hotels – Cheaper Hotels** There's an acute shortage of budget accommodation in Prague, and even during the off season finding a cheap hotel can be a frustrating, time-consuming experience. Hotel receptionists will invariably say that the rooms are all full unless you first lay US$5 or DM 10 on the desk. Such a 'gift' should inspire them to go through their books more carefully to 'discover' a room for you (keep one finger on the bill until they confirm a satisfactory vacancy). If you do get a room, book for your entire stay in Prague, otherwise you risk

having to go through this again. (Some sharp receptionists will want to give you a room for only one night in the hope of another gift.) Most Prague hotels charge US$2 extra for a shower if there's not one in the room. All hotel prices are expected to increase sharply over the next few years.

Here's a list of older B-category hotels in geographical sequence across the city: *Opera Hotel*, Těšnov 13 (Metro: Florenc); *Merkur Hotel*, Těšnov 9; *Hybernia Hotel*, Hybernská 24 (Metro: náměstí Republiky); *Meteor Hotel*, Hybernská 6; *Adria Hotel*, Wenceslas Square 26 (Metro: Můstek); *Hotel Křivan*, náměstí I P Pavlova 5 (Metro: I P Pavlova); *Hotel Luník*, Londýnská 50 (Metro: I P Pavlova); *Morán Hotel*, Na Moráni 15 (Metro: Karlovo náměstí); *Balkan Hotel*, Svornosti 28 (Metro: Anděl); and *Savoy Hotel*, Keplerova 6 (tram No 22). Singles/doubles in these hotels begin around US$14/22 with shared bath (the Morán Hotel has no single rooms).

Two C-category hotels in the Žižkov district of Prague just east of Hlavní nádraží are the *Hotel Národní dům*, Bořivojova 53 (take trams No 9, 10, 13 and 26 to 'Lipanská'), at US$8/12/18 single/double/triple with shared bath; and the *Hotel Ostas*, Orebitská 8, off Husitská, behind Hlavní nádraží, at US$12/22 single/double without bath, including breakfast and dinner.

**Medium Hotels** The B*-category *Grand Hotel Europa*, Wenceslas Square 25 (Metro: Můstek), is an Art-Nouveau extravaganza, brimming with old-world atmosphere for US$15 single without bath and US$21/31 single/double with bath, but it's 'always' full. The B*-category *Hotel Družba*, at Wenceslas Square 16, charges US$14/22 single/double without bath, US$30 double with bath.

The fashionable, A*-category *Atlantic Hotel*, at Na poříčí 9 (Metro: náměstí Republiky), is US$29/44 single/double with bath.

The A*-category *Koruna Hotel*, at Opatovická 16 (Metro: Národní třída), is US$21/32 single/double with colour TV and private bath, but it's full up with groups.

If a 20-minute metro ride doesn't deter you, consider the modern 23-storey *Hotel Kupa* (☎ 791 0041), Anežky Hodinové-Spurné 842, very close to Háje Metro Station. It's US$25/45 single/double, including breakfast, with each two rooms sharing a toilet and shower. Ask Top Tour (listed in the Room-Finding Services section) about this place.

**Expensive Hotels** One expensive hotel to know about is the *Interhotel Paříž*, at U Obecního domu 1 (Metro: náměstí Republiky), an eclectic *fin-de-siècle* edifice across the street from Pragotur. If you're going to let them sock it to you, you may as well go down in style. It costs US$80/120 single/double with bath and breakfast.

The newly renovated, deluxe *Palace Hotel*, Pánská 12, charges an incredible US$235/260 single/double with bath and breakfast. Of course, Prague's gambling casino is there!

The nine-storey *Inter-Continental Hotel*, at Pařížská on the corner of náměstí Curieových (Metro: Staroměstská), is US$140/170 single/double with bath. It was built in 1974.

Better value than any of these hotels are Prague's B*-category floating hotels, gigantic barges that are permanently moored along the Vltava. The *Admirál Botel*, Hořejší nábřeží (Metro: Anděl), is US$52 double with breakfast. The *Albatros Botel*, Nábřeží Svobody, is similar to the Admirál in price but much noisier because it is next to a highway. Both are usually booked out by German tour groups.

## Places to Eat

Filling your stomach in Prague is usually easier than finding a place to sleep, though most restaurants are closed by 9 pm and the service is often slow. Be aware that the serving staff in some Prague restaurants in the tourist centre shamelessly overcharge foreigners and about the only way to avoid this is to insist on seeing a menu, even a menu in Czech, to get an idea of the price range. Menus are often posted somewhere but if they're not, and the waiter refuses to show

you one listing prices, just get up and walk out.

**Self-Service** About the cheapest and quickest place in Prague to eat at is at *Automat Koruna*, on the corner of Wenceslas Square and Na příkopě above the Můstek Metro Station. You must eat standing up and there are queues for everything, but they move quickly. In one corner of Automat Koruna, beside the coffee stand, is a flash grill bar serving shish kebab and steaks.

The *Delicatesse Buffet* at the Palace Hotel, opposite the main post office, near the corner of Jindřišská and Panská, has a self-service salad bar!

**Staré Město** Cheap, basic food is dispensed self-service at *Vegetarka* (open weekdays from 11 am to 2.30 pm), upstairs at Celetná 3, beside Týn Church, just off Staroměstské náměstí. There's always a queue and, despite the name, most of the dishes contain meat, though a few vegetarian plates are listed at the top of the menu.

Farther up this street at Celetná 22 is *Restaurace u Supa*, a good place for a deep dark beer and a meal. Also try *U Prince*, Staroměstské náměstí 28, near the old town hall.

The *Jihočeské Pohostinství Restaurant*, Na příkopě 17, specialises in South Bohemian cuisine.

*U Pinkasu*, Jungmannovo náměstí 16, hidden at the back of the main square, opposite the Laterná Magika theatre, is a great little beer hall which also serves meals.

*Restaurace V Krakovské*, Krakovská 20, just off Wenceslas Square, is another typical Czech beer-hall-style restaurant.

For local dishes, try the restaurant in the *Dům Slovenské Kultůry*, Purkyňova 4, right beside Národní třída Metro Station.

**Malá Strana** About the only place in Malá Strana to get a quick snack is the Yugoslav-style *Vinárna Jadran* at Mostecká 21. *Restaurace Regent*, Karmelitská 20, is good for lunch or just a cold one.

*U Schnellu*, at Tomášská 2, just off

Malostranské náměstí, serves good food and cold beer, but you may have to wait to get in.

**Hradčany** The *Restaurace Na Baště* (closed Monday), just inside Prague Castle to the left, is an unpretentious place that serves decent meals but terrible coffee. The *Vikárka Restaurant* is right next to St Vitus Cathedral. The *Občerstvění Bufet*, in a corner of Golden Lane, is the only place in Hradčany where you can get fast sausages and beer.

Big mugs of draught beer and basic meals can be had at *U Černého Vola*, Loretánské náměstí 1, just up from the Loreta Convent.

**Others** *U Kalicha Restaurant*, Na bojišti 12 (Metro: I P Pavlova), serves excellent Czech meals and big mugs of beer; it's open daily from 11 am to 3 pm and from 5 to 11 pm. Menus in English and German are available. This place featured in the novel *The Good Soldier Švejk*.

The various modern restaurants in the *Palace of Culture* have menus in English and German. The *Snack Bar* (open daily from 9 am to 9 pm) on the ground floor is just the place for ice cream, a glass of wine or a pork chop and a beer. If you want something more formal, try the *Panoráma Restaurant* upstairs. There's also a night bar here, open Tuesday to Saturday from 9 pm to 4 am.

**Cafés** *Kavárna Luxor*, upstairs at Wenceslas Square 41, offers coffee and cakes in unpretentious elegance. Prague's oldest café (1708) is *U zlatého hada*, Karlova ulice 18, near the Clementinum. *Kavárna Slávie*, Národní 1, was mentioned earlier under the Velvet Revolution in the Things to See section in this chapter.

### Entertainment

Don't come to Prague for the music! To get opera tickets you almost have to be a local resident, as most tickets are sold weeks ahead. The same goes for Laterná Magika performances (see Lighter Fare later in this chapter) and all the best concerts. Look for the *vyprodáno* (sold out) notices before trying to figure out what's on. The official

price for the best seats at the National Theatre is only about US$3, which explains why they're all sold out.

Large blocks of tickets are reserved months in advance by regular subscribers and most of the rest are snapped up by scalpers who resell them to tourists for US$15 or more. You'll probably be approached at the ticket office by a slightly nervous person with just the ticket you want, asking for hard currency. Sometimes scalpers may end up with more black tickets than they can resell, giving you the opportunity to bargain for a lower price at the door just before the performance. The special hard-currency ticket offices listed here charge about the same as the scalpers.

**Ticket Agencies** Sluná in the Alfa Cinema Arcade, Wenceslas Square 28, sells tickets for concerts (including operettas at the Karlín Theatre) and many other events advertised on posters in the office. There's a second Sluná office in the arcade at Panská 4, opposite Čedok's accommodation service.

Concert tickets are available from the FOK Symfonický Orchestr office on U Prašné brány right between the Powder Gate and Pragotur (Metro: náměstí Republiky). They should have something, but from May to August the office is open on Monday, Wednesday and Friday only and Monday to Friday the rest of the year.

Tickets to sports events are available from ČSTV, Dukelských hrdinů 13 (Metro: Vltavská), but you must go at least one day before (open weekdays from 8am to noon and from 2 to 4 pm).

You can pay with crowns at all of these places, but the Institute for Educational Travels (IFB), Wenceslas Square 27, sells tickets for hard currency only: Laterná Magika (US$19), opera (US$24), National Theatre (US$32) and pantomime (US$9). The people there also do a three-hour city sightseeing tour Tuesday to Saturday at 10 am and 2 pm (US$7).

Čedok, Bílkova 6, sometimes has tickets for the Smetana Theatre (US$22) and other events, again for hard currency. Top Tour,

Rybná 3 near Pragotur, also arranges National Theatre (US$28) and Laterná Magika (US$25) tickets.

**Theatres** Opera and ballet are performed at the neo-Renaissance *National Theatre*, built in 1883, Národní 2 (Metro: Národní třída), while the ultramodern *New Stage*, built in 1983, Národní 4, specialises in serious theatre. Opera and ballet are also presented at the neo-Renaissance *Smetana Theatre* on Vítězného únóra (Metro: Muzeum).

The ticket offices for the New Stage (Nová Scéna) and National Theatre (Národní Divadlo) are both just inside the New Stage. The Smetana Theatre (Smetanovo Divadlo) has its own ticket office at the theatre, but all three are sold out weeks ahead.

For operettas and musicals go to the *Karlín Theatre of Music*, Křižíkova 10, near Florenc Bus Station (Metro: Florenc). Because it's a little out of the way and not as famous, tickets are often available – recommended.

**Concert Halls** Prague's main concert venue is the neo-Renaissance *Dvořák Hall*, náměstí Jana Palacha (Metro: Staroměstská), where the Prague Spring Music Festival is held in late May.

Prague's wonderful Art-Nouveau municipal concert hall, *Smetana Hall* (Obecního domu), náměstí Republiky 5, right next to the Powder Gate, is not used that often but when it is, tickets are available from FOK, which is around the corner, or at the box office inside, an hour before the performance.

Also check the *Palace of Culture* (Metro: Vyšehrad) for events. Concerts are held there regularly and tickets are usually available at the box office.

**Lighter Fare** The *Laterná Magika*, Národní 40 (Metro: Národní třída), offers a unique combination of theatre, dance and film. Tickets, however, are difficult to obtain.

*Video Disco Herna* is downstairs at Národní 25 and is open Tuesday to Saturday from 9 pm to 4 am.

For jazz, try *Reduta*, Národní 20. The club opens at 9 pm with music from 9.30 pm to midnight. Tickets (US$2 cover charge) are sold after 5 pm on weekdays or after 6 pm on Saturdays, and they *are* available. The latest addition to the Prague entertainment scene is the *porno cinema* next to Reduta.

If you want to delve deeper into Prague's lowlife, go to the *Narcis Vinárna* at Melantrichova 5, between Můstek and the old town hall (open from 8 pm to 3 am, US$1 cover charge), a Gypsy hang-out frequented by prostitutes. There's live music and dancing.

Also visit the *Loutka Children's Theatre*, náměstí Maxima Gorkého 28, which has performances at 9 am on weekdays, 10 am and 2 pm on Saturdays, and 2 and 4 pm on Sundays. This mix of puppets and pantomime is great fun (sit in the back row if the place is full of kids). The ticket office is open weekdays from 2 to 4 pm; on weekends you can usually get a ticket at the door just before the show.

The Jazz Art Club, Vinohradská 40, behind the National Museum, is less snobby than Reduta and there's a bar for those who want to socialise as well as listen to music. It's possible to buy records here. The owner, Milan Svoboda, is a well-known jazz musician who has toured Europe and the States. It's open from 9 pm to 2 am.

**Beer Halls** One Prague institution not to miss is *U Fleků*, Křemencova 11 (Metro: Národní třída), a genuine German-style beer garden where you can sit at a long communal table in the back courtyard or in one of the front halls during bad weather. Waiters circulate periodically with mugs of the excellent dark 13° ale that is brewed in-house and, less frequently, with plates of goulash and knedlíky. Next door is the *U Fleků Cabaret*, where the fun begins at around 7.30 pm and continues until 10.30 pm (US$1 cover charge). You should be able to squeeze into both the 991-seat beer hall (open daily from 8.30 am to 11 pm) and the cabaret (open Tuesday to Saturday from 6 to 11 pm) without difficulty.

**Malá Strana** *U Svatého Tomáše*, Letenská 12 (Metro: Malostranská), is a beer hall which also serves meals (daily from 11 am to 11 pm). During the day it can be fully reserved for groups (downstairs) or completely full up with people having lunch (upstairs), so it's better to try it at night (US$1 cover charge). The 12° Braník beer on tap has a better reputation than the food.

*Malostranská Beseda*, Malostranské náměstí 21 (Metro: Malostranská), presents jazz, folk, country, rock music, rock opera and so on nightly in their theatre-café; visitors are welcome.

**Night Clubs** The *Revue Alhambra Night Club* (open Tuesday to Sunday from 8.30 pm to 3 am) at the Ambassador Hotel, Wenceslas Square 5 (Metro: Můstek), presents a Las Vegas-style floorshow called 'Prague after Dark' nightly at 11 pm (US$3 cover charge). You can dance there before and after the show. Reservations can be made at the hotel reception. There's also a gambling casino at the Ambassador (open daily from 4 pm to 4 am).

A less touristy nightclub is the *Varieté Praga*, Vodičkova 30 just off Wenceslas Square, which has a two-hour floor show daily except Monday at 9.30 pm, then dancing from 11.30 pm to 2 am (US$3 cover charge).

**Free Entertainment** In the evening you can stroll along Na příkopě, where buskers play for the throng, or Wenceslas Square, where fast-food automats, cinemas and night bars stay open late. Můstek is thick with black-market hustlers after dark. The floodlit Staroměstské náměstí and the Karlův most are other magical attractions of nocturnal Prague.

**Things to Buy**
You'll find many interesting shops along Celetná, between Staroměstské náměstí and náměstí Republiky. The Kotva Department Store on náměstí Republiky is the largest in the country. There's also the Máj Department Store, Národní and Spálená.

**Getting There & Away**
**Air** ČSA (☎ 235 2671), Revoluční 5 (Metro: náměstí Republiky), books twice-daily flights from Prague to Bratislava (US$15), Poprad-Tatry (US$19) and Košice (US$20). With rocketing fuel costs, these fares may have increased.

**Bus** Buses to Karlovy Vary, Brno and most other towns in the western half of the country, and as far away as Bratislava, depart from the Florenc Bus Station, Křižíkova 4 (Metro: Florenc).

*Tickets* Reservations at Prague's Florenc Bus Station are computerised! To obtain a ticket, first determine the departure time *(odjezdy)* of your bus by looking at the posted timetable beside platform No 1 or asking at the information counter. Then get in line at any of the ticket counters. Make sure that your bus isn't on the sold-out *(vyprodáno)* list on the television screens here. If it is, pick another bus. The further ahead you book, the better your chances of getting the bus you want. Your bus ticket indicates the platform number *(stání)* and seat number *(sed)*. You may be charged extra for baggage. The coaches are quite comfortable (no standing) and fares are low.

**Train** Trains run from Berlin-Lichtenberg to Prague via Dresden (seven hours, 386 km) every three or four hours. Several of the trains arriving from Berlin continue on to Vienna. There's a service twice a day from Nuremberg via Cheb (6½ hours, 372 km) and daily from Linz, Austria via České Budějovice (292 km). Many trains arrive from Budapest via Brno and Bratislava (10 hours, 630 km). From Poland you have the choice of arriving via Wrocław or Katowice. There are overnight trains with sleepers to and from Košice (10 hours).

Čedok, Na příkopě 18, sells international train tickets but you have to pay in Western currency. It can take as long as three hours to buy an international ticket at the Prague Čedok office, so pick up your ticket in another town if at all possible.

**Railway Stations** Prague has four main railway stations. International trains between Berlin and Budapest often stop at Praha-Holešovice Railway Station (Metro: nádraží Holešovice) on the north side of the city. Other important trains terminate at Praha-Hlavní nádraží (Metro: Hlavní nádraží) or Masarykovo nádraží (Metro: náměstí Republiky), both of which are close to the city centre. Some local trains to the south-west depart from Praha-Smíchov Railway Station (Metro: Smíchovské nádraží). If you arrive at one of these in the very early morning without any local currency to buy metro tickets, just ask someone to change your smallest Western coin or banknote – anyone will do it.

Hlavní nádraží handles trains to Benešov (one hour, 49 km), České Budějovice (2½ hours express, 169 km), Cheb via Plzeň (220 km), Karlovy Vary via Chomutov (199 km), Košice (708 km), Mariánské Lázně (three

hours express, 190 km), Plzeň (114 km) and Tábor (1½ hours express, 103 km). Trains to Brno (3½ hours express, 257 km) and Bratislava (5½ hours express, 398 km) may leave from either Hlavní nádraží, Praha-Holešovice or Masarykovo nádraží. This is confusing, so study the timetables posted in one of the stations to determine which one you'll be using, then confirm the time at the information counter or at Čedok. To go to Kutná Hora (1½ hours, 73 km) you may use Praha-Holešovice or, more frequently, Masarykovo nádraží. Karlstejn trains always depart from Praha-Smíchov.

Hlavní nádraží is Prague's largest station and has several exchange offices and accommodation services upstairs, and a tourist information booth downstairs. The station restaurants on the top floor are unpleasant. The left-luggage office is in the basement, so drop your bags off upon arrival and stroll into town to look for a room or a meal.

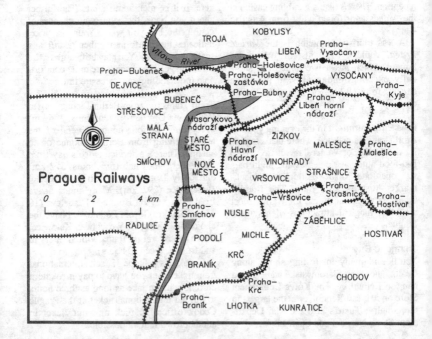

## Getting Around

**To/From the Airport** Ruzyně Airport is 17 km west of the city centre. Every half-hour an airport bus (under US$1) departs from the ČSA office, Revoluční 25 (Metro: náměstí Republiky). There's a left-luggage office in this terminal. You can also reach the airport on city bus No 119 from Dejvická Metro Station.

**Public Transport** All public transport in Prague costs the same flat fare. Tickets valid on trams, city buses and the metro are sold by automats at the entrance to all metro stations or by newspaper kiosks. Buy a good supply, then validate your ticket as you enter the vehicle or metro. Once validated, tickets are valid for 90 minutes. Three-day (US$2) and five-day (US$3) tourist tickets are now available which are valid on all forms of public transport. You can only buy these at I P Pavlova Metro Station. The recorded announcements on the trams and the metro are strangely reassuring.

**Underground** The first line of the Prague Metro, built by the Communists with Soviet assistance, opened on 9 May 1974. The metro operates from 5 am to midnight with three lines connecting all bus and railway stations, as well as many tourist attractions. You can change from one line to another without using another ticket. Spend a little time studying the system map in a station the first time you enter and don't get into the rear carriage, as station names are poorly displayed. In general, though, using the metro is easy.

Line A runs from the north-west side of the city at Dejvická to the east at Strašnická; line B runs from the south-west to Nové Butovice to the centre at Florenc; line C runs from the north at nádraží Holešovice to the south-east at Háje. Line A intersects line C at

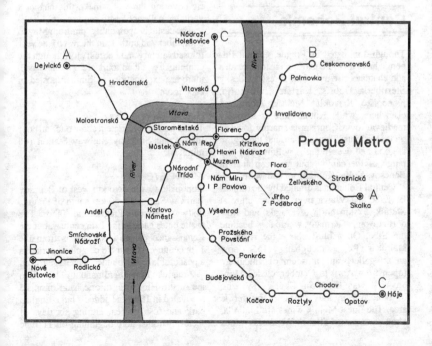

Muzeum; line B intersects line C at Florenc; line A intersects line B at Můstek.

**Taxi** Taxis are cheap, but only if the meter is turned on. If the driver won't turn on the meter, establish the price before you set out, otherwise you'll end up paying much more.

**Excursion Boats** Prague's riverboat terminal is on the right bank of the Vltava between Jiráskův most and Palackého most (Metro: Karlovo náměstí). In July and August there are cruises upriver to Štěchovice (three hours each way, 28 km) daily except Monday at 8 am and 9 am. In May, June and the first half of September, the boats only run on weekends and holidays. Shorter trips downriver to the Troja Zoo (1½ hours each way, 10 km) depart on the same days at 9.15 am and at 1.15 pm. Check at the wharf or telephone 29 8309 or 29 3803 in advance as all seats are sometimes booked for groups.

# Central Bohemia

Though dominated by Prague, Central Bohemia has a lot more to offer. Historic castles and chateaux rise out of the forests at Český Šternberk, Dobříš, Karlštejn, Kokořín, Konopiště, Křivoklát, Mělník, Žleby and elsewhere, while Kutná Hora is a lovely medieval town. Tourism is sharply focused on these sights. Transport around the region is good and everything is within a day-trip range of the capital, but you can stay in Benešov, Kolín, Kutná Hora and Mělník.

Central Bohemia is drained by the romantic Labe and Vltava rivers, which unite at Mělník, 32 km north of Prague, and flow north towards Germany, where they become the Elbe. On a bluff above the rivers at **Mělník** is a Renaissance chateau (1554), now an art gallery and museum of viticulture (open from April to October, closed Monday). It was Emperor Charles IV who introduced Burgundy vines to this fertile area. The finest Mělník wines are Ludmila, a red wine named after St Wenceslas' pious

grandmother, and Chateau Mělník, a sparkling red wine. (Direct trains go to Mělník from Kolín, but services from Praha-Vysočany Railway Station are poor, involving a change at Všetaty, so you're better off coming by bus.)

## KARLŠTEJN

It's an easy day trip from Prague to Karlštejn Castle, 33 km south-west. Erected by Emperor Charles IV in the mid-14th century, this towering, fairy-tale castle crowns a ridge above the village, a 20-minute walk from the railway station.

A highlight of Karlštejn Castle is the Church of Our Lady (1357) with its medieval frescoes. In a corner of this church is the private oratory of the king, the walls of which are covered with precious stones. Even more magnificent is the Chapel of the Holy Rood in the Big Tower, where the coronation jewels were kept until 1420. Some 128 painted panels by Master Theodoric covering the walls make this chapel a veritable gallery of 14th century art.

The castle is open until 5 pm from May to September and until 3 pm the rest of the year (closed January and February). Although the compulsory guided tours are only in Czech, there are explanations in English posted in each room.

### Getting There & Away

Trains leave for Karlštejn about once an hour from Praha-Smíchov Railway Station (40 minutes).

## KONOPIŠTĚ

Konopiště Castle, two km west of Benešov Railway Station, is 50 km south of Prague, midway between Prague and Tábor. The castle dates back to the 14th century, but the Renaissance palace it shelters is from the 17th century. The whole complex overlooks a peaceful lake surrounded by a large forest.

Archduke Franz Ferdinand d'Este, heir to the Austro-Hungarian throne, had Konopiště renovated in 1894 and added a large English park and rose garden. During six days of secret meetings here beginning on 11 June

1914, Archduke Ferdinand and Kaiser Wilhelm II of Germany tried to establish a common strategy for the impending world war. Ferdinand's huge collection of hunting trophies and weapons is still on display at the castle. On 28 June 1914 the hunter, however, became the hunted and his assassination at Sarajevo touched off the very war the gentlemen had discussed. (In fairness it should be noted that Ferdinand was against military action.)

Konopiště Castle is open from April to October (closed Monday) but you must arrive by 2 pm if you want to see both the state chambers and the palace collections. The castle may only be visited with a boring Czech-speaking guide, so ask for the typed summary in English. Huge tour groups are led through the castle one after another.

### Places to Stay & Eat

To see Konopiště Castle and the park at a more leisurely pace, spend the night at the old *Hotel Pošta*, Tyršova 162 on the square in Benešov (US$9/14 single/double with bath). The *Restaurace na Knížecí*, another of Czechoslovakia's amazing beer halls, is on the square, just minutes from the Pošta (post office).

In the park surrounding the castle is a *camping ground* (open from May to September) next to the expensive *Konopiště Motel*.

### Getting There & Away

Local trains leave Prague's Hlavní nádraží for Benešov (one hour, 49 km) about once an hour. Most trains to/from Tábor (54 km) and České Budějovice (120 km) also stop here. There are occasional buses from Benešov Railway Station to the castle.

## KUTNÁ HORA

In the 14th century, Kutná Hora, 66 km east of Prague, was the second-largest town in Bohemia after Prague. This was due to the rich veins of silver below the town itself. The silver *groschen* minted here was the hard currency of central Europe at the time. During the 16th century, Kutná Hora's boom burst and mining ceased in 1726, so the medieval townscape has come down to us basically unaltered.

### Orientation

The railway station is three km east of the centre whereas the bus station is more conveniently located just on the north-eastern edge of the old town.

The easiest way to visit Kutná Hora on a day trip is to arrive on the morning express train from Prague's Masarykovo nádraží, then take a 10-minute walk from Kutná Hora Railway Station to Sedlec to visit the ossuary (see the Things to See section that follows). From there it's another 15-minute walk or a five-minute bus ride to Kutná Hora Bus Station, where you can check the times of buses back to Kolín or Prague. From the bus station it's only a few minutes' walk into old Kutná Hora.

### Information

Čedok is next to the Mědínek Hotel on Palackého náměstí, a quaint square created when the Gothic town hall was demolished after a fire in 1770.

### Things to See

At Sedlec, only a km from the railway station on the way into town (turn right when you see a huge church), is a cemetery with a Gothic **ossuary** *(kostnice)* decorated with the bones of some 40,000 people. In 1870 František Rint, a local woodcarver, arranged the bones in the form of bells, a chandelier, monstrances and even the Schwarzenberg coat-of-arms – a truly macabre sight (closed Monday).

As you enter Kutná Hora from the bus station you'll pass the former **Ursuline convent** (1743), which houses an exhibition of antiques, and, if you go straight ahead, you'll see the **Stone House** (1485), Radnická 24, with jousting knights on the façade, now the local historical museum. Both are closed on Monday.

Rather than visit either of these straight away, just note their location and go on to the **Hrádek Mining Museum** (closed Monday), to the left down several narrow, winding

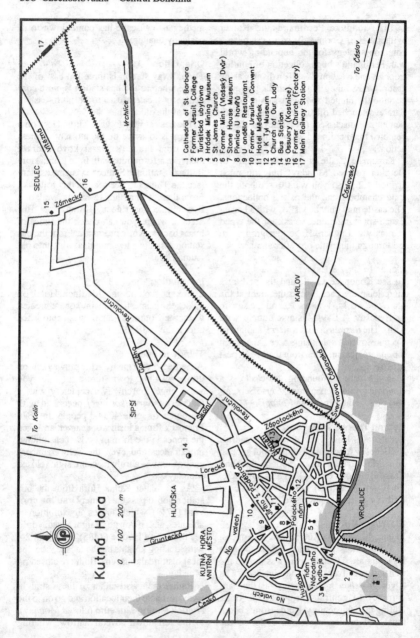

**Kutná Hora**

0   100   200 m

1 Cathedral of St Barbara
2 Former Jesuit College
3 Turistická ubytovna
4 Hrádek Mining Museum
5 St James Church
6 Former Mint (Vlašský Dvůr)
7 Stone House Museum
8 Pivnice U havířů
9 U anděla Restaurant
10 Former Ursuline Convent
11 Hotel Mědínek
12 J K Tyl Museum
13 Church of Our Lady
14 Bus Station
15 Ossuary (Kostnice)
16 Former Church (Factory)
17 Main Railway Station

streets from the Stone House (ask for the Hrádek). This 15th century palace contains an exhibit on the mining that made Kutná Hora wealthy, and a huge wooden device used in the Middle Ages to lift up to 1000 kg at a time from shafts that were 200 metres deep. This museum's real attraction, however, is the 45-minute guided tour through 500 metres of **medieval mine shafts** on one of the 20 levels below Kutná Hora. You don a white coat and helmet, and pick up a miner's lamp, but the tour only begins when a group of at least five people gathers, which is why you should come here first. If a tour isn't about to leave just as you happen to arrive, make your presence known and head off to visit the town's other monuments, checking back at intervals.

Just beyond the Hrádek is the 17th century former **Jesuit college** which has Baroque sculpture in front of it and a good view of the Vrchlice River Valley from the promenade. Nearby is Kutná Hora's greatest monument, the **Cathedral of St Barbara** (closed Monday), begun in 1388 by Peter Parler, the architect of St Vitus Cathedral in Prague, and finished in 1547. The exquisite net vault above the central nave is supported by double flying buttresses in the French high-Gothic style.

From the cathedral you'll see the tall tilting tower of the **St James Church** (1330), which is on the other side of the Hrádek. Just past St James is the Gothic Royal Mint, **Vlašský dvůr** or Italian Court, now occupied by city offices; however, it is possible to visit. Master craftsmen from Florence began stamping silver coins here in 1300.

### Places to Stay

The *Hotel Mědínek*, a modern four-storey hotel on Palackého náměstí, costs US$21 double with bath (no singles).

At a pinch you could also try the *Turistická ubytovna*, náměstí Národního odboje 56, a basic dormitory.

### Places to Eat

The *Pivnice Černý Kůň*, Kollárova 8, behind Hotel Mědínek, is a good place for a beer.

*U anděla*, Radnická 10, on the corner of náměstí 1 máje, is a decent place to eat. In front of the plague column nearby is *Pivnice U Havířů* (closed Monday) with a *vinárna* (closed Monday and Tuesday) at the back.

### Getting There & Away

Kutná Hora is on a main railway line between Prague and Brno. Trains arrive from Prague's Masarykovo nádraží (1½ hours, 73 km) via Kolín every couple of hours.

### KOLÍN

Kolín on the Labe River is an old town seldom visited by tourists. The Kmochův Festival of brass-band music is held here every June. The town centre is next to the river, a 15-minute walk from the adjacent bus and train stations.

### Things to See

Kolín has a picturesque central square with a Baroque Marian column (1682) and fountain (1780) in the middle. A block away is the towering Gothic **St Bartholomew Church** begun by Peter Parler.

### Places to Stay

The *Hotel Savoy*, Rubešová 61 just off the central square, is US$7/10 single/double without bath.

### Getting There & Away

Kolín is a major junction on the Prague-Košice main line, with frequent service to/from Prague (one hour, 62 km). All trains to/from Moravia, Slovakia and Poland stop here. Another important line through Kolín is Havlíčkův Brod to Děčín via Mělník. Buses run regularly from Kolín Bus Station to Kutná Hora, 14 km south by road.

# West Bohemia

Cheb and Plzeň are the western gateways to Czechoslovakia. All trains from Western Germany pass this way and the stately old Habsburg spas, Karlovy Vary, Františkovy

Lázně and Mariánské Lázně, are nearby. The proximity to Bavaria helps to explain the famous Pilsner beer which originated in Plzeň. South-west of Plzeň is Domažlice, centre of the Chod people, where folk festivals are held in August. In West Bohemia you can enjoy the charm of southern Germany at a fraction of the price.

## KARLOVY VARY

Karlovy Vary (Karlsbad) is the largest and oldest of Czechoslovakia's many spas. According to a local tradition, Emperor Charles IV discovered the hot springs by chance while hunting a stag. In 1358 he built a hunting lodge here and gave the town his name. Beginning in the 19th century, famous people such as Beethoven, Bismarck, Brahms, Chopin, Franz Josef I, Goethe, Liszt, Metternich, Paganini, Peter the Great, Schiller and Tolstoy came here to take the waters, and busts of a few of them grace the promenades. Karl Marx came to Karlovy Vary to take the cure in 1874, 1875 and 1876. Ludvík Moser began making glassware at Karlovy Vary in 1857 and today Bohemian crystal is prized around the world.

There are 12 hot springs here containing 40 chemical elements that are used in medical treatment of diseases of the digestive tract and metabolic disorders. If you have diarrhoea or constipation, this is the place to come. Mineral deposits from the springs form stone encrustations which are sold as souvenirs. Karlovy Vary's herbal Becherovka liqueur is known as the 13th spring.

Karlovy Vary still bears a definite Victorian air. The elegant colonnades and boulevards complement the many peaceful walks in the surrounding parks. The picturesque river valley winds between wooded hills, yet the spa offers all the facilities of a medium-sized town without the bother. After hustling around Prague this is just the place to relax. It's hard not to like Karlovy Vary.

## Orientation

Karlovy Vary has two railway stations. Express trains from Prague and Cheb use Karlovy Vary horní nádraží, across the Ohře River, just north of the city. Trains to/from Mariánské Lázně stop at Karlovy Vary dolní nádraží, which is opposite the main ČSAD bus station. The city bus station is in front of the market, three blocks east of dolní nádraží. T G Masaryka, the pedestrian mall in Karlovy Vary's city centre, runs east to the Teplá River. Upstream is the heart of the spa.

### Information

Čedok is on the corner of třída Jiřího Dimitrovova and Moskevská. A second Čedok office is at Tržiště 23 near the Yuri Gagarin Colonnade.

There's an administrative office in the Gagarin Colonnade where foreigners can arrange medical treatment at the spa. This costs at least US$70 per person a day, including room and board.

### Things to See

As you follow the riverside promenade south from the stations, you'll pass the modern Thermal Sanatorium (1976) and the neo-classical **Colonnade of Czechoslovak-Soviet Friendship**, formerly the Mill Colonnade (1881), designed by Josef Žitek. On a nearby hill is the **old castle tower** (1608) on the site of Charles IV's 1358 hunting lodge. Today it's a restaurant; it's open until 1 am and is closed on Monday and Tuesday. Down the hill from the castle is the **House of the Three Moors**, or Dagmar House, Tržiště 25, where Goethe stayed during his many visits to Karlovy Vary.

Opposite this building is a Čedok office and a bridge which leads to the pulsing heart of Karlovy Vary, the Vřídlo or Sprundel Spring in the **Yuri Gagarin Colonnade**. Here 2000 litres a minute of 72.2°C water shoot up 12 metres from a depth of 2500 metres. The colonnade, erected in 1975, is named after the world's first astronaut, who visited the spa in 1961 and 1966. Throngs of Czechoslovak tourists, funny little cups in hand, pace up and down the colonnade, taking the drinking cure. Bring a cup of your own for some piping hot liquid refreshment and maybe it'll even do you some good!

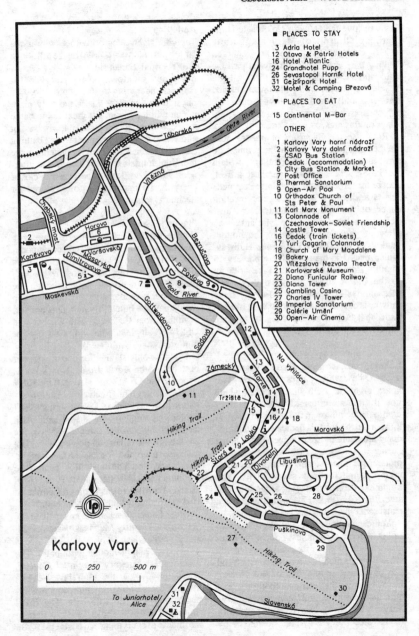

PLACES TO STAY

3 Adria Hotel
12 Otava & Patria Hotels
16 Hotel Atlantic
24 Grandhotel Pupp
26 Sevostopol Horník Hotel
31 Gejzírpark Hotel
32 Motel & Camping Březová

PLACES TO EAT

15 Continental M-Bar

OTHER

1 Karlovy Vary horní nádraží
2 Karlovy Vary dolní nádraží
4 ČSAD Bus Station
5 Čedok (accommodation)
6 City Bus Station & Market
7 Post Office
8 Thermal Sanatorium
9 Open-Air Pool
10 Orthodox Church of
   Sts Peter & Paul
11 Karl Marx Monument
13 Colonnade of
   Czechoslovak-Soviet Friendship
14 Castle Tower
16 Čedok (train tickets)
17 Yuri Gagarin Colonnade
18 Church of Mary Magdalene
19 Bakery
20 Vítězslava Nezvala Theatre
21 Karlovarské Museum
22 Diana Funicular Railway
23 Diana Tower
25 Gambling Casino
27 Charles IV Tower
28 Imperial Sanatorium
29 Galérie Umění
30 Open-Air Cinema

Karlovy Vary

0     250     500 m

Just above the Gagarin Colonnade is the Baroque **Church of Mary Magdalene** (1736) designed by Kilian Dientzenhofer. Follow the Teplá River south-west past the **Vítězslava Nezvala Theatre** (1886) till you reach the **Karlovarské Museum** (closed Monday and Tuesday), Nová Louka 23, which has history and natural history displays on this area.

Return to the Gagarin Colonnade, cross the bridge again and follow the promenade west along the river to the bakery at Stara Louka 52, where you can purchase a fresh box of the famous *oplatky* wafers. Beyond is the **Grandhotel Pupp**, a former meeting place of the European aristocracy. Just before the hotel you'll see Mariánská, an alley on the right leading to the bottom station of the **Diana Funicular Railway**, which rises 166 metres to the top every 15 minutes from 10 am to 6 pm. Take a ride up to the **Diana Tower** for great views and pleasant walks through the forest. If the railway is closed, follow the network of footpaths that begins near this station. A café adjoins the Diana Tower.

**Loket** If you have an afternoon to spare, take a ČSAD bus, which passes about every two hours, eight km south-west to Loket, where you'll find an impressive 13th century **castle** on the hilltop in the centre of town. A museum in the castle is dedicated to the china dishware made in Loket since 1815. On the façade of the Hotel Bílý Kůn, in Loket's picturesque town square, is a plaque commemorating Goethe's seven visits. You might even consider staying at the inexpensive *Bílý Kůn* (☎ 94171) which also has a restaurant where you can get lunch.

You can walk back to Karlovy Vary from Loket in about three hours. Follow the blue-and-white trail down the left bank of the Ohře River, which flows between Cheb and Karlovy Vary, to the **Svatošské Rocks**. Here you cross the river on a footbridge and take the road to Doubí (served by Karlovy Vary city bus No 6). This riverside path down the forested valley is lovely.

### Activities

Top your sightseeing off with a swim in the large **open-air pool** *(bazén)* on the hill above the Thermal Sanatorium. Karlovy Vary's numerous sanatoriums are reserved for patients undergoing treatment prescribed by physicians – in fact, this is the only place which will let you in. It's great fun to bathe to the beat of rock music, but you're not allowed to dive and you must wear a bathing cap. The bazén is reserved for patients in the morning; tourists are admitted in the afternoon from 2 to 9 pm. The bazén is closed every third Monday and is often closed for 'technical reasons'.

### Places to Stay

On weekends Karlovy Vary fills up with Germans on mini holidays and accommodation is tight. Čedok, on the corner of třída Jiřího Dimitrovova and Moskevská, will place you in a private home, though the US$17 per person charge is more than you would pay at a hotel! Private rooms are also available from Čedok, Tržiště 23, but cost US$14/18 single/double with a three-night minimum-stay requirement.

If you're only staying for one night, your best bet is the *Adria Hotel*, Koněvova 1, opposite the ČSAD bus station (US$10/14 single/double). The C-category *Hotel Turist*, Dimitrovova 18, near Čedok, costs US$7 double (no singles) with shared bath. Also try the *Hotel Národní Dům*, T G Masaryka 24, though it's rather run down and subject to noise from the Variete Orfeum nightclub/disco downstairs, which cannot be recommended. A better choice is the *Hotel Jizera*, Dimitrovova 7, near Čedok, at US$11/16 single/double without bath.

Other hotels closer to the spa include the *Sevastopol-Horník*, Mariánskolázeňská 27, and the rather flash *Otava Hotel*, I P Pavlova 4 (US$14/27 single/double with bath). The gracious B*-category *Interhotel Central*, Divadelní 17, near the Vítězslava Nezvala Theatre, costs US$21/33 single/double without bath, US$35/60 with bath. The *Hotel Atlantic*, Tržiště 23, above Čedok, is right in the middle of everything and costs US$22/33 single/double without bath, US$47 double with bath.

Karlovy Vary's premier address is the *Grandhotel Pupp*, Mírové náměstí 6, a stuffy 358-room hotel founded in 1701 and operated from 1773 to 1945 by the Pupp family. A room in the annexe with bath and breakfast will set you back US$60 to US$90 single, US$83 to US$125 double, or you can play the big shot for a lower price by dining at one of the hotel's pretentious restaurants.

**South of Town** There are several good places to stay at along Slovenská just south of the spa centre, which you can reach from the market on bus No 7 with the sign 'Březová'. The first place you come to is the friendly *Gejzírpark Hotel* beside the public tennis courts, a new building with simple rooms at US$5 single with shared bath, US$15 double with private bath. The hotel has free hot showers and, unlike those in many other hotels, they're not locked. You can use the 14 adjacent tennis courts – ask the hotel receptionist.

Not far from the Gejzírpark Hotel is the expensive *Motel Březová* (☎ 25101), Slovenská 9, with rooms with private bath at US$30 single or double, though they're often full. There's also an overcrowded camping ground here (US$8 double). There's only enough hot water for the first two campers in the morning queue. The motel is open from April to October and camping is from May to September only. There's a restaurant on the grounds.

For youth hostellers, the cheapest accommodation is the *Juniorhotel Alice* (☎ 017-24848), about four km south of town, not far from the motel. Here you can share a three-bed room; in summer the hostel could be full so try to reserve a place.

**Places to Eat**

The best place for breakfast is the *Continental M-Bar*, Tržiště 27, near the Yuri Gagarin Colonnade. There's a great little ice-cream parlour inside the M-Bar, and just up the hill at Tržiště 31 is a grill with greasy barbecued chicken and cold beer. Unless you're really starved, order only a quarter, as the chickens are huge and you'll be charged by weight.

The restaurant in the *Hotel Jizera*, at Dimitrovova 7, serves a good breakfast of bacon and eggs.

**Entertainment**

Karlovy Vary's main theatre is the *Divadlo Vítězslava Nezvala* on Leninovo náměstí, not far from the Yuri Gagarin Colonnade. The main ticket office *(předprodej)* for the theatre is open Tuesday to Saturday from 1.30 to 6 pm. Also notice the theatre's tiny ticket counter in the Gagarin Colonnade. From mid-May to mid-September concerts are held in the colonnade daily except Monday.

Among the many cultural events are the Jazz Festival in March, the Dvořák Singing Contest in June, the International Magicians Meeting in July, the Dvořák Autumn Festival in September and the International Festival of Touristic Films in September. Ask about these and other events at the Předprodej Vstupenek Oks (cultural office) in the Thermal Sanatorium.

**Getting There & Away**

**Bus** There are direct trains to Prague, but it's faster and easier to take one of the hourly buses (122 km). Also take a bus between Karlovy Vary and Mariánské Lázně, as the train takes twice as long. The only way to go directly to Plzeň (83 km) is by bus. Seats on express buses can and should be reserved in advance by computer at the ČSAD bus station.

An international bus links the spa to Vienna twice a week, which costs US$30 one-way. Get your ticket from Čedok, Tržiště 23.

**Train** The Karlex Express travels daily between Berlin-Lichtenberg and Karlovy Vary via Leipzig and Františkovy Lázně (reservations are required). Cheb (52 km) and Mariánské Lázně (two hours, 53 km) are connected to Karlovy Vary by local trains. Couchettes and sleepers are available to/from Košice (897 km) on the Thermal Express.

## Getting Around

Before boarding a city bus, buy some tickets from an automat (feed it small coins). A good service to know about is city bus No 11, which runs hourly from horní nádraží (railway station) to the city bus station at the market, then on over the hills to Leninovo náměstí and the Yuri Gagarin Colonnade. The more frequent city bus No 13 going to Trznice also runs to the market from horní nádraží.

## CHEB

This old medieval town on the Ohře River, near the western tip of Czechoslovakia, is an easy day trip by train from Karlovy Vary or Mariánské Lázně. Only a few km north of the Bavarian border, Cheb (formerly Eger) retains a strong German flavour. During the day the stores, cafés and restaurants of Cheb are literally jammed with Germans who pop across the border to enjoy Czechoslovakia's low prices. In the evening things quieten down a lot.

## Orientation & Information

Čedok is on the corner of třída 1 máje and třída Československo-Sovětského Přátelství (třída SČSP).

If you've just arrived from Germany, you can change money at Čedok. The nearby Hvězda Hotel will also change cash and there's a regular bank at the railway station. The railway station is open all night, so you can wait there if you arrive or depart at an ungodly hour.

The Cultural Information Office, náměstí Krále Jiřího 33, sells theatre and concert tickets.

## Things to See

Although the area around the railway station is ugly, only a few minutes' away up třída SČSP is the picturesque town square, with burgher houses that have sloping red-tile roofs. In the middle of this square is Špalíček, a lustre of 16th century Gothic houses which were once Jewish shops. Behind these is the Municipal Museum (closed Monday) which has an excellent his-

torical exhibition. The Thirty Years' War military commander Duke Albrecht Wallenstein was murdered here in 1634 and the museum devotes a room to him. Also on the square is the Baroque former new town hall (1728), now the city art gallery.

At the back of the Municipal Museum is St Nicholas Church, a massive Gothic structure with a sculpture-filled interior (closed Monday). Notice the portal (1270) and the Romanesque features, such as the twin towers. A few blocks away is Cheb Castle (open from April to October, closed Monday), erected in the 12th century by Friedrich I Barbarossa, leader of the Eastern Crusades. The Black Tower dates from 1222 but the exterior fortifications were built in the 17th century. The 12th century Romanesque chapel in the castle is a rare sight in Czechoslovakia.

## Places to Stay

There are a number of small hotels in Cheb. The cheapest is the *Hotel Chebský Dvůr*, třída SČSP 43 near the bus station (US$5/7 single/double). The *Slávie Hotel*, třída SČSP 32, is US$8/12 single/double. The friendly *Hradní Dvůr Hotel*, at Dlouhá 12, costs US$6/11 single/double. All three of these are often full.

Private rooms from Čedok are more expensive: US$13 double (no singles). The *Hvězda Hotel*, Krále Jiřího 4, is more expensive again at US$17 single, US$22 to US$50 double, but is pleasant, with some rooms overlooking the main square. They're also more likely to have rooms.

The nearest camping grounds are at Dřenice (☎ 31591) on Jesenice Lake, five km east of Cheb, and Lake Amerika, two km south-east of Františkovy Lázně. Both are open from mid-May to mid-September.

Because the hotels of Cheb are often used to house transient workers or tour groups, it may be easier and perhaps cheaper to find a room at nearby Františkovy Lázně.

## Places to Eat

Cheb's self-service *bufet* is at Svobody 18 near Čedok. The *Mléčná Jídelna* beside the

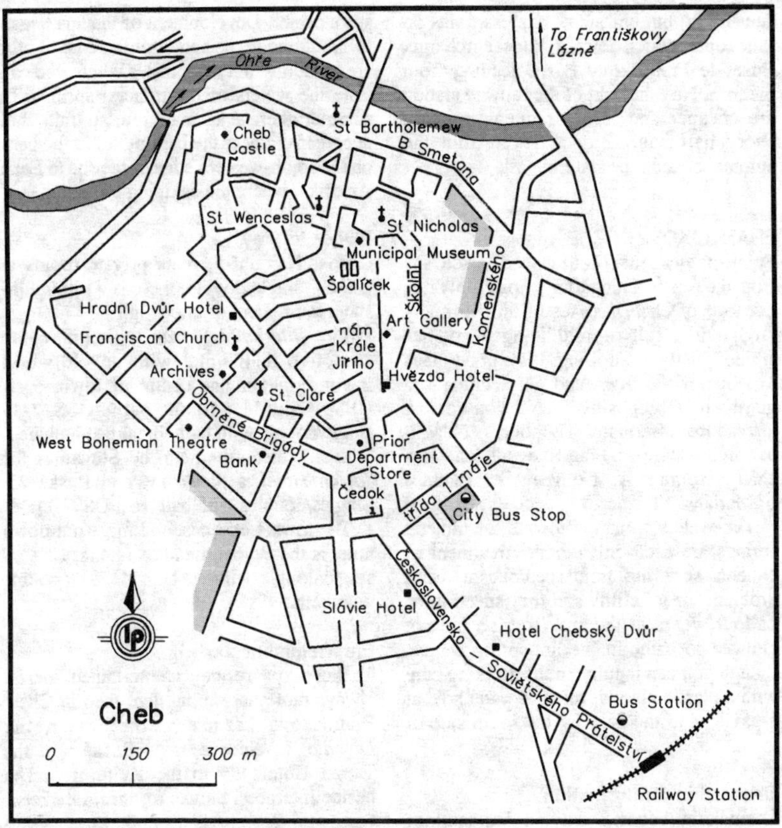

Cheb

0       150      300 m

Slávie Hotel is also fast and easy if you should find all the regular restaurants completely packed.

### Getting There & Away

Most trains arriving in Czechoslovakia from Nuremberg (three hours, 190 km) stop here, with express trains to/from Stuttgart (six hours, 342 km), Munich and Frankfurt/Main daily. The train from Berlin-Lichtenberg and Leipzig stops at nearby Františkovy Lázně, not Cheb. There are trains to Cheb from Prague (four hours express, 220 km) via Plzeň and Mariánské Lázně.

A railcar covers the 13 km from Cheb to Schirnding, Germany, twice a day. Tickets are available at the station (US$2 one-way, US$4 return, valid two months). To board an international train, enter through the door marked *zoll-douane* (customs) to one side of the main station entrance at least an hour before departure. If you miss the train to Schirnding and don't mind hitchhiking, you could take a city bus to Pomezí (every half-hour or so) which is near the border, eight km west of Cheb, and then cross into Germany on foot.

Local trains run to Františkovy Lázně

(seven km) but beware of express trains on this route which levy a huge surcharge. Buses to Františkovy Lázně leaving from platform No 8 in front of the railway station are cheaper and more frequent, running every half-hour. Buy a ticket from the automat outside the station – ask.

## FRANTIŠKOVY LÁZNĚ

Františkovy Lázně (Franzensbad), an old spa from the Austro-Hungarian empire, only five km north of Cheb, has a restful air with many large parks full of middle-aged couples sitting quietly or strolling. It's a good place to stop for the night and get acclimatised gently to Czechoslovakia if you've just arrived from Germany. The sober neoclassical architecture of Františkovy Lázně is a change from the Art-Nouveau extravagance of Mariánské Lázně.

The waters from the town's 24 mineral springs are used only for the treatment of patients suffering from rheumatism, heart problems or infertility and they spend three or four weeks at the spa. Tourists are not allowed to bathe in the hot-spring waters, though you can indulge in the drinking cure with a plastic glass of mineral water sold at a pavilion in the park on the south side of town.

### Orientation & Information

Františkovy Lázně is only six km south of Vojtanov, a highway border crossing from Eastern Germany. The main streets of town are Ruská and Národní, which intersect about halfway between the railway station (a few blocks north-east) and the spa centre (a few blocks south). If you arrive by bus, you'll probably get out on Leninova, a block west of the corner of Ruská and Národní streets.

Čedok, Národní 5, can answer questions.

### Things to See

A **Municipal Museum** is at Dr Pohořeckého 8, opposite the B Němcové Theatre (closed Saturday and Sunday). Národní ulice runs directly south to the **František Spring** at the spa's centre. Development of the spa began in 1792, and in the parks south and east of it are pavilions and colonnades where you can taste the waters of the mineral springs. In summer there's a small tourist train that departs from near the parking lot in the park on the south-western edge of the spa to Lake Amerika, where the camping ground is.

### Places to Stay

Čedok, Národní 5, rents private rooms at US$5/8 single/double (there is a minimum-stay requirement of three nights).

The *Interhotel Slovan*, Národní 6, an attractive mall hotel with an old-world flavour right in the centre of town, costs US$18 single without bath, US$23/35 single/double with bath, breakfast included.

Less pretentious than the Slovan is the *Tatran Hotel*, a block away at Ruská 25. Singles/doubles with bath cost US$7/11.

The town's cheapest and most run-down hotel is the *Bajkal*, Leninova 84, at US$6/9 single/double without bath, US$11 double with bath.

### Entertainment

To keep spa residents entertained there's always more happening here than in Cheb. Františkovy Lázně's main theatre, the *Divadlo B Němcové*, is on Ruská near the Tatran Hotel. Go to the Kulturní Služba beside Interhotel Slovan for theatre tickets.

### Getting There & Away

The Karlex Express arrives here from Berlin-Lichtenberg (eight hours, 372 km) daily. From Monday to Saturday, a local train also arrives from Plauen, Germany (two hours, 68 km). An overnight train with sleepers is available to Bratislava and Košice (reservations are required). For most other journeys it's better to connect at Cheb, which you can reach from Františkovy Lázně by bus.

## MARIÁNSKÉ LÁZNĚ

Small, provincial Mariánské Lázně (Marienbad) is Czechoslovakia's most famous spa, but in many ways it ranks second to the larger, more urbane Karlovy Vary. The resort developed quickly during the second half of the 19th century, but famous guests began arriving before then. The elderly Goethe wrote his *Marienbader Elegie* for young Ulrika von Levetzow here. The town's grand hotels, stately mansions, casinos, colonnades and gardens will delight 19th century romantics.

Mariánské Lázně boasts 140 mineral springs, all of which are closed to the public. Thirty-nine of these are used for treating diseases of the kidneys and of the urinary and respiratory tracts. The hillsides and open spaces around the massive Victorian bathhouses and hotels have been landscaped into parks with walks where overweight visitors can try to burn off some extra calories. The town's 628-metre elevation (compared with 447 metres elevation at Karlovy Vary) gives the spa a brisk climate which makes the pine-clad Bohemian hills to the north all the more inviting. You could even hike the green trail 35 km north to Loket in a very long day.

### Orientation & Information

The adjacent bus and train stations are three km south of the centre of town. Head north down Hlavní třída. Trolley bus No 5 follows this route from the railway station to the centre of town. Čedok is at Hlavní třída 46.

### Things to See

The **Maxim Gorky Colonnade** (1889) is the centre of Mariánské Lázně. Throngs of the faithful promenade back and forth here, holding a teapot of hot mineral water in their hands as a sign of devotion to the drinking cure. At one end of the colonnade is the **Pavilion of the Cross Spring** (1818), and at the other is a new musical fountain which puts on free shows for the crowd on the stroke of every odd hour. The canned music (Muzak) is sometimes a little off key, but that's Marienbad.

A shop facing the Pavilion of the Cross, opposite the Maxim Gorky Colonnade, sells the delicious *Lázeňské oplatky*, a large circular wafer filled with sugar or chocolate. You can peek through a side window to see them being made.

Above the Maxim Gorky Colonnade is the **Municipal Museum** on Goetha náměstí, where Goethe stayed in 1823. The museum can only be visited with a group from Monday to Friday at 9, 10 and 11 am or 2 and 3 pm. A recorded commentary is played during the visit (in English on Tuesday and Thursday at 1 pm only; in German on Monday and Wednesday at 1 pm only) but it's not that interesting, so only bother with it if you have extra time. Yellow-and-blue signs behind the museum lead to the **Geology Park**, where you can go for a pleasant walk among the stone structures and old trees while listening to incomprehensible explanations in Czech.

In front of the museum is the circular **Catholic church** (1848), and just south of it are **Rudolph's Pavilion** (1823), the former casino (now a social club), and the **New Baths** (1895).

In a park just north-west of the centre is the **Pavilion of the Forest Spring** (1869), with bronze statues of Goethe and Ulrika nearby. Down towards the railway you'll find **Ferdinand's Spring** and **Rudolph's Spring**.

### Places to Stay

There is plenty of accommodation in Mariánské Lázně but in midsummer everything will be taken. If so, visit Čedok, Hlavní třída 46, which has private rooms at US$5/8 single/double. You must, however, rent them for a minimum of five days.

On Plzeňská beside the stadium, only a five-minute walk from the stations, is *Motel Start*, which costs US$4 per person in the hotel section or US$5 double for a bungalow. Camping at the motel is US$1 per person. Motel Start is just a plain, prefabricated building without any of the character of the town's other hotels, but it is cheap.

Just south of Motel Start is *TJ Lokomotiva*, a sports centre with neat four-bed bungalows for US$2 per person. You must arrive and register during normal business hours.

*Autocamp Luxor* (☎ 3504) is a larger and

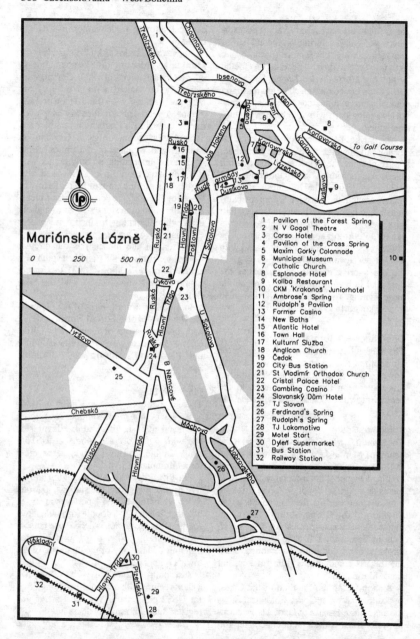

Mariánské Lázně

0    250    500 m

1   Pavilion of the Forest Spring
2   N V Gogol Theatre
3   Corso Hotel
4   Pavilion of the Cross Spring
5   Maxim Gorky Colonnade
6   Municipal Museum
7   Catholic Church
8   Esplanade Hotel
9   Koliba Restaurant
10  CKM 'Krakonoš' Juniorhotel
11  Ambrose's Spring
12  Rudolph's Pavilion
13  Former Casino
14  New Baths
15  Atlantic Hotel
16  Town Hall
17  Kulturní Služba
18  Anglican Church
19  Čedok
20  City Bus Station
21  St Vladimír Orthodox Church
22  Cristal Palace Hotel
23  Gambling Casino
24  Slovanský Dům Hotel
25  TJ Slovan
26  Ferdinand's Spring
27  Rudolph's Spring
28  TJ Lokomotiva
29  Motel Start
30  Dyleň Supermarket
31  Bus Station
32  Railway Station

To Golf Course

quieter camping ground at Velká Hleďsebe, four km south-west of the railway station by a roundabout route (take a taxi if you can). It's open from May to September.

The *CKM 'Krakonoš' Juniorhotel* (☎2624) is at the top of a toboggan run that is six km from the stations (take bus No 12 from the city bus station opposite Čedok) to the door. Most of the rooms are doubles.

**Hotels** Lots of fine old hotels line Hlavní třída on the way into town from the stations. The first you reach is the C-category *Slovanský Dům*, Hlavní třída 22, Mariánské Lázně's cheapest hotel. Unfortunately, it's always full.

The *Cristal Palace Hotel*, Hlavní třída 2, costs US$13/20/25 single/double/triple without bath, US$27 double with bath, breakfast included. The *Atlantic Hotel*, at Hlavní třída 26, is US$15/22 single/double without bath, US$19/31 with bath, and the *Corso Hotel*, Hlavní třída 16, charges US$14/21 single/double without bath, US$35 double with bath.

**Places to Eat**

The *Koliba*, on ulice Dušíkova at the northeastern edge of town, is an up-market, folk-style restaurant. The *Jalta Vinárna*, upstairs at Hlavní třída 42, serves good food. A block south past the Altantic Hotel is *Café Polonia*, which is good for coffee and cakes. You may find it hard to get a seat.

**Entertainment**

Check the *N V Gogol Theatre* (1868) for musical programmes. Many events are held at *Chopin Haus*, Hlavní třída 30. There's a disco called the American Night Club in the *Corso Hotel*, Hlavní třída 16.

The International Music Festival in May and July and the Chopin Festival in August are special events to ask about at the Kulturní Služba, Hlavní třída 38.

**Getting There & Away**

There are direct buses between Mariánské Lázně and Karlovy Vary (47 km) which take half the time of the local train. If you'd like

to stop off somewhere between the spas, choose Bečov nad Teplou, where you'll find a castle in a wooded valley.

Train services to Cheb (30 km) and Plzeň (76 km) are good. Most international express trains between Nuremberg and Prague stop at Mariánské Lázně.

## PLZEŇ

The city of Plzeň (Pilsen), midway between Prague and Nuremberg, is the capital of West Bohemia. Located at the confluence of four rivers, this town was once an active medieval trading centre. An ironworks was founded at Plzeň in 1859, which Emil Škoda purchased 10 years later. The Škoda Engineering Works became a producer of high-quality armaments which attracted heavy bombing at the end of WW II. The rebuilt Škoda Works now produces machinery, automobiles and locomotives.

Beer has been brewed at Plzeň for 700 years and the town is famous as the original home of Pilsner. The only genuine Pilsner trademark is Plzeňský Prazdroj, or Pilsner Urquell in its export variety. Although the emphasis is on industry, Plzeň has sights enough to keep you busy for a day. Devoted beer drinkers will not regret the pilgrimage.

### Orientation & Information

Plzeň has six bus stations, none of them near the two railway stations. The largest is the Central Autobus nádraží, Leninova ulice, opposite the Škoda Works and west of J K Tyla Theatre, with direct buses to Karlovy Vary, Mariánské Lázně, Prague and České Budějovice. The main train station, Hlavní nádraží, is on the east side of town. Between these is the old town, which is centred around náměstí Republiky.

Čedok is at Sedláčkova 12, just off náměstí Republiky.

### Things to See

The most convenient place to begin sightseeing is on náměstí Republiky, the old town square. Gothic **St Bartholomew Church** in the middle of the square has the highest

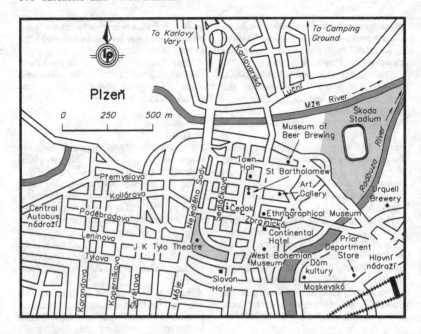

tower in Bohemia (103 metres). Inside the soaring 13th century structure are a Gothic Madonna (1390) on the high altar and fine stained-glass windows. Outstanding among the many gabled buildings around the square is the Renaissance **town hall** (1558).

An old town house on the east side of the square contains the extensive **Ethnographical Museum** (closed Monday). Just south on Františkanská is the 14th century **Franciscan church**. Behind this church, around the block, is the **West Bohemian Museum**, with natural history exhibits and paintings.

**Beer Lovers Only** Plzeň's most interesting sight by far is the **Museum of Beer Brewing** (closed Monday), Veleslavínova ulice 6, north-east of náměstí Republiky. Located in an authentic medieval malt house, the museum displays a fascinating collection of artifacts related to brewing. Ask for the typewritten explanatory text in English or German. If all that reading makes you thirsty,

visit the *Pivnice na Parkánu*, which is right beside (or behind) the beer museum.

Just around the corner at Perlova 6 is an entrance to one section of the nine km of medieval **underground corridors** below Plzeň. These were originally built as refuges during sieges, hence the numerous wells.

Some were later used to store kegs of beer. To enter you must wait for a group of at least five people to gather, then follow them on a boring Czech tour. The underground corridors are closed on Monday and Tuesday. The bottle shop right beside the entrance to the corridors sells takeaway Pilsner Urquell if you get tired of waiting.

The famous **Urquell Brewery** is only a 10-minute walk from here, a little north of Hlavní nádraží. Only groups organised by travel agencies are admitted to the brewery, but the twin-arched gate dated 1842-92, which appears on every genuine Pilsner label, is visible from the street. Beside the gate is the *Restaurace Prazdroj*, just the place for a one-litre mug (!) of that 12-proof brew.

### Places to Stay

Accommodation in Plzeň is on the expensive side. The B-category *Slovan Hotel*, Smetanovy sady 1, a fine old hotel with a magnificent central stairway, is US$16/25 single/double without bath, US$35 double with bath, breakfast included.

Also impressive is the *Continental Hotel*, Zbrojnická 8, at US$22/34 single/double without bath, US$31/46 with bath, breakfast included. This is also where you'll find Plzeň's gambling casino.

The modern seven-storey *Hotel Central*, náměstí Republiky, opposite St Bartholomew Church in the very centre of town, is expensive at US$26/40 single/double with bath and breakfast.

Čedok, Sedláčkova 12, has private rooms for US$6/12 single/double. They don't mind if you only stay a night or two, but the rooms are often full.

The two *camping grounds* (with bungalows) are at Bila Hora, five km north of the city (bus No 20). Both are open from May to mid-September.

### Places to Eat

The cheapest place to eat at is *Bufet Slávie* in the Čas Cinema Arcade on náměstí Republiky. Pilsner Urquell is on tap.

The *Restaurace Prazdroj*, next to Urquell

Brewery, serves excellent and inexpensive meals, so head that way when you get hungry. The enormous *fin-de-siècle* restaurant in Hlavní nádraží is also very good.

### Entertainment

For entertainment, try the *J K Tyla Theatre* (1902) or the ultramodern *Dům kultury* beside the river.

### Getting There & Away

All international trains from Munich (via Furth im Wald, 5½ hours, 330 km) and Nuremberg (via Cheb) stop at Plzeň. There are fast trains to České Budějovice (two hours, 136 km), Cheb (106 km) and Prague (114 km). Train services to Mariánské Lázně (76 km) are also good, but if you want to go to Karlovy Vary (83 km), take a bus.

# South Bohemia

South Bohemia is the most German-looking part of Czechoslovakia. The many quaint little towns have a Bavarian or Austrian flavour, enhanced by some 5000 medieval carp ponds in the surrounding countryside. On the Šumava ridge, south-west of Prachatice, is Mt Boubín (1362 metres) with its primeval forest of spruce, pine and beech trees. The Vltava River originates on this plateau.

After WW I, South Bohemia was given to Czechoslovakia on historical grounds, although over half of its population was German. Hitler's claims to the area nearly touched off war in 1938. After WW II the Germans had to leave and the region became Czech, though Germanic touches linger in the hearty food and drink. Well off the beaten track, South Bohemia is overflowing with history.

## ČESKÉ BUDĚJOVICE

České Budějovice (Budweis), the regional capital of South Bohemia, is a charming medieval city halfway between Plzeň and

Vienna. Here the Vltava River meets the Malše and flows north to Prague. Founded in 1265, České Budějovice controlled the importation of salt and wine from Austria and was a Catholic stronghold in the 15th century. Nearby silver mines made the town rich in the 16th century. After a fire in 1641 much was rebuilt in the Baroque style. In 1832 the first horse-drawn railway on the continent arrived here from Linz, Austria, which is directly south.

High-quality Koh-i-Noor pencils are made here but the city is more famous as the original home of Budweiser beer (Budvar to the Czechs). You are not allowed to visit the brewery. České Budějovice is a perfect base for day trips to dozens of nearby attractions, so settle in for a couple of days. Picturesque little Bohemian towns within easy commuting distance include Český Krumlov, Jindřichův Hradec, Písek, Prachatice, Tábor and Třeboň.

## Orientation & Information

It's a 10-minute walk west down třída Maršála Malinovského from the adjacent bus and railway stations to náměstí Jana Žižky, the centre of town.

Čedok is at náměstí Jana Žižky 39. CKM Student Travel is at Osvobození 14.

## Things to See

Náměstí Jana Žižky, a great square surrounded by 18th century arches, is one of the largest of its kind in Europe. At its centre is **Samson's Fountain** (1727), and to one side stands the Baroque **town hall** (1731). The allegorical figures on the town hall balustrade – Justice, Wisdom, Courage and Prudence – are matched by four bronze dragon gargoyles. Looming 72 metres above the opposite side of the square is the **Black Tower** (1553), with great views from the gallery (open from April to October, closed

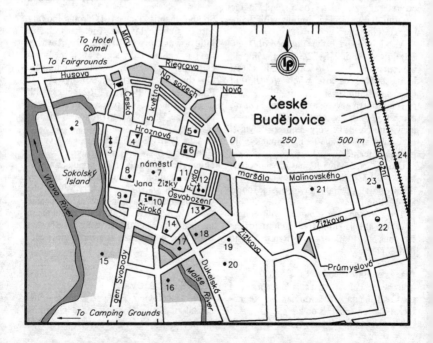

Monday). Beside this tower is **St Nicholas Cathedral**.

The backstreets of České Budějovice, especially Česká ulice, are lined with old burgher houses. West near the river is the former **Dominican monastery** (1265) with another tall tower. You enter the church from the Gothic cloister. Beside the church is a medieval warehouse where salt was kept

1  Rabenstein Tower
2  Sports Stadium
3  Dominican Monastery
4  Masné Krámy Beer Hall
5  Privat Tour
6  St Nicholas Cathedral
7  Samson's Fountain
8  Town Hall
9  Bishop's Residence
10 Slunce Hotel & Čedok
11 Zvon Hotel
12 St Anne's Church & Concert Hall
13 CKM Student Travel
14 Jihočeské Theatre
15 Open-Air Theatre
16 State Library
17 Městský Dům kultury
18 Museum of South Bohemia
19 Dům kultury
20 Divadelního Sálu DK
21 Prior Department Store
22 Bus Station
23 Malše Hotel
24 Railway Station

until it could be sent down the Vltava to Prague. Stroll south along the riverside behind the warehouse, past the remaining sections of the 16th century walls. The **Museum of South Bohemia** (closed Monday) is just south of the old town.

**Hluboká nad Vltavou** One side trip not to miss takes in the neo-Gothic Tudor palace at Hluboká nad Vltavou (Frauenberg), 10 km north, which is easily accessible by bus. There used to be a castle here that was built in the 13th century, but in the years 1841 to 1871 the landowning Schwarzenberg family rebuilt the edifice on a grand scale and laid out the extensive park. The palace's 144 rooms were inhabited right up to WW II.

The romantic palace interiors with their original furnishings are closed from November to March and every Monday, but the park is open any time. Also open throughout the year, in the former palace riding school, is the **Alšova Jihočeská Galérie**, an exceptional collection of Gothic painting and sculpture and Dutch painting.

**Places to Stay**
During the Agricultural Fair held here in late August or early September, hotel prices soar and rooms fill up, so check the dates if your visit falls around this time.

The old *Malše Hotel*, Nádražní 31, opposite the railway station, costs US$8/10 single/double without bath, US$14 double with bath. In the same block as the Malše is the recently renovated *Hotel Grand* at US$14/21 single/double without bath, US$16/25 with bath, breakfast included.

The *Zvon Hotel*, náměstí Jana Žižky 28, is good value at US$9/14 single/double without bath, US$21/32 with bath. In 1991 the *Slunce Hotel*, náměstí Jana Žižky 37, was closed for renovations but it may have reopened by the time you get there.

Privat Tour, Hroznová at the corner of Norbeta Fryda, rents private rooms, but check the price of a hotel room first. Ask at CKM, Osvobození 14, for summer youth hostels.

Also in summer consider camping at the

*Dlouhé Louce Autocamp* (☎ 38308), Stromovka 8, a 20-minute walk south-west of town (bus No 6). Tent space is available from May to September, and bungalows are available all year. The *Stromovka Autocamp* (☎ 28877) on Litvínovská, just beyond Dlouhé Louce Autocamp, is open from April to October. The showers are clean and the water hot, but beware of bar prices. There's a military airport in the area so expect to be rocked to sleep by jet engines.

### Places to Eat

About the best place in town for a colourful meal is the *'Masné Krámy' beer hall* in the old meat market (1560), on the corner of Hroznová and 5 května. There's another good beer hall on the ground floor at the back of the *Zvon Hotel*. Upstairs is a more sedate restaurant.

A third fine beer hall in this town of beer is the *Restaurace U Železné Panny*, on the corner of Biskupská and Široká streets, diagonally opposite the bishop's residence. All of these places serve meals.

### Entertainment

České Budějovice has two cultural centres, both near the Museum of South Bohemia. The old *Městský Dům kultury* is by the river, and another *Dům kultury* is on the square behind the museum. If you like opera, go to the *Divadelního Sálu DK* behind this newer Dům kultury.

The *Jihočeské Theatre*, by the river on ulice Dr Stejskala, also presents opera often. *St Anne's Church*, Norbeta Fryda 6, functions as České Budějovice's concert hall.

### Getting There & Away

Twice a day there's a train to/from Linz, Austria (three hours, 125 km). Connections with trains from Prague to Vienna are made at Veselí nad Lužnicí, 41 km north-east of České Budějovice. There are fast trains to Plzeň (two hours, 136 km), Tábor (one hour, 66 km), Prague (2½ hours, 169 km) and Jihlava (two hours, 132 km). For shorter distances you're better off travelling by bus. The bus to Brno (182 km) travels via Telč.

A bus to Vienna's Mitte Bahnhof (US$7) departs from České Budějovice Bus Station on Friday, and to Linz Post Office (US$3) on Wednesday and Saturday. Advance bookings may be necessary.

## ČESKÝ KRUMLOV

Český Krumlov (Krumau), a small medieval town 25 km south of České Budějovice, is one of the most picturesque towns in Europe, its appearance almost unchanged since the 18th century. Built on an S-shaped bend of the Vltava River, the 13th century castle occupies a ridge along the left bank. The old town centre sits on the high tongue of land on the right bank. South-west are the Šumava Mountains, which separate Bohemia from Austria and Bavaria.

Český Krumlov's Gothic border castle, rebuilt into a huge Renaissance chateau by 16th century Italian architects, is second only to Prague Castle as a fortified Bohemian palace and citadel. The Renaissance lords of Rožmberk (Rosenberg) seated here possessed the largest landed estate in Bohemia, which passed to the Eggenbergs in 1622 and to the Schwarzenbergs in 1719. Český Krumlov is a little out of the way but well worth the effort to visit. On summer weekends the town fills up with day-trippers from nearby Austria!

### Orientation & Information

Čedok is on náměstí Svornosti. If you're spending the night in town, you can buy tickets to local events from the office at Latran 15.

### Things to See

Get off the bus from České Budějovice at Český Krumlov Špičák, the first stop in town. Just above this stop is **Budějovická Gate** (1598), which leads directly into the old town. On the right, two blocks south, is the **castle** entrance. The oldest part of the castle is the lower section with its distinctive round tower, but it's the massive upper castle which contains the palace halls that are open to visitors. It is said that the castle is haunted by a White Lady who appears from time to time to forecast doom.

Just across the high bridge behind the palace is the unique Rococo **chateau theatre** (1767). Behind this, a ramp to the right leads up to the former **riding school**, now a dancing school and restaurant. Cherubs above the door offer the head and boots of a vanquished Turk. Above this are the Italian-style castle **gardens**. The **'Bellarie' summer pavilion** and a modern revolving open-air theatre are features of these gardens. The castle interiors are open from April to October only (visits are only conducted when a group forms), but you can walk through the courtyards and gardens almost any time.

On náměstí Svornosti across the river in the old town are the Gothic **town hall** and a Baroque plague column (1716). Just above the square is **St Vitus Church** (1439), a striking Gothic hall church. Nearby is the **Regional Museum** (closed Monday) with a surprisingly good collection housed in the old Jesuit seminary (1652). The scale model of Český Krumlov as it was in 1800 is a

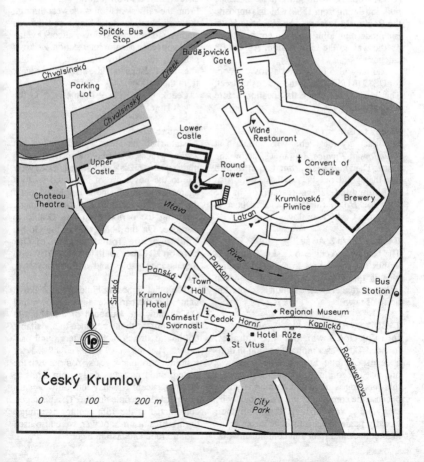

**Český Krumlov**

0    100    200 m

highlight. Continue in the same direction, turn left (ask directions) and you'll soon find the autobusové nádraží (bus station) and a bus back to České Budějovice. There's a great view of town from near this bus station.

## Places to Stay

Though Český Krumlov is an easy day trip from České Budějovice, there are several hotels if you would like to linger. The *Krumlov Hotel* on náměstí Svornosti (US$8/12 single/double without bath, US$10/18 with bath) has atmosphere, as does the *Hotel Růže* (US$13 double with bath), a Renaissance building dating from 1588, which is opposite the Regional Museum. The *Vyšehrad Hotel* is a modern building on a hill north of town on the way to the train station. All are B* category.

You may also be offered a private room for US$7 to US$10 by someone on the street. This is fine, but check the location before you set out.

## Places to Eat

For lunch try the 'Petra Voka' goulash at *Krumlovská Pivnice*, Latran 13, below the castle. The *Vídně Restaurant*, Latran 78, also has that good old beer-hall flavour. Also recommended is the restaurant in the *Krumlov Hotel*. Šumavský ležák beer is brewed in Český Krumlov.

## Getting There & Away

The best way to come to Český Krumlov is by bus and the service from České Budějovice is quite frequent. Intervals between trains are greater and the station is several km north of town.

## TÁBOR

In 1420 God's warriors, the Hussites, founded Tábor as a military bastion in defiance of Catholic Europe. The town was organised according to the biblical precept that 'nothing is mine and nothing is yours, because the community is owned equally by everyone'. New arrivals threw all their worldly possessions into large casks at the marketplace and joined in communal work.

This extreme nonconformism helped to give the word Bohemian the meaning we associate with it today.

Planned as a bulwark against Catholic reactionaries in České Budějovice and farther south, Tabor is a warren of narrow broken streets with protruding houses which were intended to weaken and shatter an enemy attack. Below ground, catacombs totalling 14 km provided a refuge for the defenders. This friendly old town, 100 km south of Prague, is well worth a brief stop.

## Orientation & Information

From the railway station walk west through the park between Hotel Slavia and the bus station. Continue west down ulice 9 května until you reach a major intersection. Žižkovo náměstí, the old town square, is straight ahead on Palackého třída, a 15-minute walk from the stations.

Čedok is on třída 9 května next to the Palcát Hotel.

## Things to See

A statue of the Hussite commander, Jan Žižka, graces Žižkovo náměstí, Tábor's main square. Žižka's military successes were due to the novel use of armoured wagons against crusading Catholic knights. Around the square are the homes of rich burghers, spanning the period from late Gothic to Baroque. On the north side is the Gothic **Church of the Transfiguration of Our Lord on Mt Tábor** (built in 1440-1512) with Renaissance gables and a Baroque tower (1677).

The other imposing building on Žižkovo náměstí is the early Renaissance town hall (1521), now the **Museum of the Hussite Movement**, with the entrance to a visitable 650-metre stretch of the underground passages. The museum has been closed for restoration for many years. You can visit the underground passages daily from April to October except Monday, but only when a group of 15 people forms. The passages, constructed in the 15th century as refuges during fires or times of war, were also used to store food and mature lager.

The arch at Žižkovo náměstí 22, beside the old town hall, leads into Mariánská ulice and then Klokotská ulice, which runs south-west to the **Bechyně Gate**, now a small historical museum. The captions are only in Czech and the museum is closed on Monday. Kotnov Castle, founded here in the 12th century, was destroyed by fire in 1532; in the 17th century the ruins were made into a brewery which is still operating. The castle's remaining 15th century round tower may be climbed from the Bechyně Gate museum for a sweeping view of Tábor, the Lužnice River and the surrounding area.

### Places to Stay

Though you can easily visit Tábor when you're travelling between Prague and České Budějovice or Jihlava, there are four hotels if you want to stay. Your best bet is the *Slavia Hotel*, Valdenská 591, opposite the adjacent bus and train stations, with singles/doubles without bath for US$8/11 or US$9/13 with bath. It's often full.

The other three hotels are on 9 května, between the stations and the town centre. You first come to the red-brick, neo-Gothic *Slovan Hotel*, ulice 9 května 678, which charges US$8/11/13 for single/double/triple with shared bath. Next is the modern *Palcát Hotel*, ulice 9 května 2471/2, a modern six-storey hotel where German tour groups always stay (US$17/23 single/double with bath). The undesirable *Jordán Hotel* (presently closed) is near the entrance to the old town.

### Places to Eat

The *Restaurace U zlatého lva* (upstairs) on Žižkovo náměstí, opposite the fountain, is a great place for a meal or a beer.

### Entertainment

Tábor's two theatres, the *Městské Divadlo* and *Divadla Oskara Nedbala*, are next to one another on Palackého třída.

### Getting There & Away

Tábor is on the main railway line between Prague and Vienna. The line from České Budějovice to Prague also passes through here. Local trains run to Pelhřimov. To go to Jihlava (74 km) or Plzeň (113 km) you're better off taking a bus.

# Moravia

Moravia, the third historic region of the ČSFR, is often overlooked by tourists visiting Bohemia and Slovakia. This is an attraction in itself, but Moravia also has its own history and natural beauties, such as the karst area north of Brno. The theatres and art galleries of Brno, the capital, are excellent, and quaint towns like Kroměříž, Mikulov, Telč and Znojmo await discovery. The Moravian Gate between Břeclav and Ostrava is a natural corridor between Poland and the Danube Basin. Heavy industry is concentrated in North Moravia, which is next to Polish Silesia, whereas fertile South Moravia produces excellent wines. Well placed in the geographical centre of the country, Moravia is a great place to explore.

## TELČ

Telč (Teltsch) was founded in the 14th century by the feudal lords of Hradec as a fortified settlement with a castle separated from the town by a strong wall. The artificial ponds on each side of Telč provided security and a sure supply of fish. After a fire in 1530, Lord Zachariáš, then governor of Moravia, ordered the town and castle rebuilt in Renaissance style by Italian masons. Profits from gold and silver mines allowed Lord and Lady Zachariáš to enjoy a regal lifestyle.

After the death of Zachariáš in 1589, building activity ceased and the complex you see today is largely as it was then. The main square of this loveliest of Czech towns is unmarred by modern constructions, and the fire hall at náměstí Zachariáše z hradce 28 is poignant evidence of local concern to keep it that way. Surprisingly few visitors frequent the narrow, cobbled streets of the fairy-tale town of Telč.

## Orientation

The bus and train stations are a few hundred metres apart on the east side of town, a 10-minute walk along ulice Masarykova towards náměstí Zachariáše z hradce, the old town square.

## Things to See

Telč's wonderful old town square is surrounded on three sides by 16th century Renaissance houses built on the ruins of their Gothic predecessors after the 1530 fire. This origin gave the square its basic unity with a covered arcade running almost all the way around it. Though from other eras, the 49-metre Romanesque **tower** east of the square and the Baroque **Marian column** (1717) in the square itself do not detract from the town's character.

Telč's greatest monument is the splendid Renaissance **water chateau** (1568) at the square's western end. You can only go on a tour of the chateau (closed Monday) with a Czech-speaking guide, so ask at the ticket office when the next group visit will begin and pick up the explanatory text in English

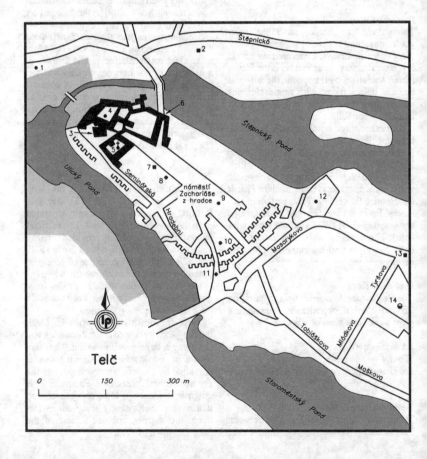

Telč

or German. While you're waiting for your guide to arrive, you can visit the local historical museum, which you can enter from the chateau courtyard, or the **Jan Zrzavý Art Gallery**, which is in a wing of the palace that faces the formal garden to the right. A scale model of Telč in the chateau museum dated 1895 shows that the town hasn't changed at all in the past century. The All Saints Chapel in the chateau houses the tombs of Zachariáš of Hradec and his wife, Catherine of Valdštejn.

The Baroque church (1655) of the former **Jesuit college** is at the western end of náměstí Zachariáše z hradce; **St James Church** (1372) beyond is Gothic. Go through the gate beside St James Church to the large English-style park surrounding the duck ponds, which were once the town's defensive moat. You can go on restful walks across the ponds to the medieval towers of the town while enjoying the gentle pastoral views.

### Places to Stay

You may get a room at the C-category *Hotel U Nádraží*, Nádraží 164 on the east side of town near the bus and train stations, but only if the 'chef' likes you. In any case, the U Nádraží (closed on Wednesday) is a good place for a beer and a basic meal.

The *Černý Orel Hotel*, náměstí Zachariáše z hradce 7, a Baroque building that has an

| | |
|---|---|
| 1 | Greenhouse |
| 2 | Hotel Pod Kaštany |
| 3 | St James Church |
| 4 | Water Chateau |
| 5 | Jesuit Church |
| 6 | Small Gate |
| 7 | Hotel Černý Orel |
| 8 | Town Hall |
| 9 | Marian Column |
| 10 | Romanesque Tower |
| 11 | Big Gate |
| 12 | Cemetery Chapel |
| 13 | Hotel U Nádraží |
| 14 | Bus Station |

outdoor terrace in summer, charges US$9/14 single/double with bath. Most rooms have a hot shower but the toilet is down the hall.

The friendly *Hotel Pod Kaštany* (☎ 066-96 2431), on ulice Stepnická just outside the old town, costs US$7/8 single/double with bath. This hotel tends to be partly occupied by school groups but four rooms are reserved for individuals. There's a good beer bar attached.

Private rooms are advertised at the house at náměstí Zachariáše z hradce 32.

### Places to Eat

The restaurant at the *Černý Orel Hotel* is the best in town (try the fresh carp or trout from the local fish ponds) but be aware that the menu prices haven't been updated for years – ask.

Morning coffee is available from the *Občerstvění* at náměstí Zachariáše z hradce (closed Monday).

### Getting There & Away

The railway line through Telč is pretty useless, as it stops at Slavonice on the Austrian border. Instead there are frequent buses from Telč to Jihlava. Buses going from České Budějovice to Brno and vice versa stop at Telč several times a day. To go from Telč to Znojmo you must change buses at Kasárna, as there is no direct service.

## ZNOJMO

High towers rise above the picturesque town of Znojmo (Znaim), the Dyje River winding through the deep valley below. In the 11th century Prince Břetislav I built a castle to control a busy trade route which passed through here, and Přemysl crown princes resided here in the 12th century. Early in the 19th century, promenades took the place of the demolished city walls. Today Znojmo is known for its gherkins and wines.

### Orientation & Information

The bus and train stations are next to each other just south-east of the old town. From the stations, follow 17 listopadu north to náměstí Vítězství, then turn left on Leninova to reach náměstí T G Masaryka, Znojmo's open-air market square. Čedok is at Obroková 1.

## Things to See

At the northern end of náměstí Masaryka is the old town hall, which was destroyed in WW II and has since been rebuilt in a modern style. In summer you may climb the pointed **town hall steeple** (1448). Kramařská, a narrow lane off Obroková ulice, opposite the tower, leads to the **medieval cellars** (*podzemí*) below Znojmo, which may be visited from mid-May to September daily except Monday. At the other end of the square rises **Wolf's Tower** and halfway down towards it is the **art gallery** (dům Umění), at náměstí Masaryka 11.

Proceed north-west across two squares to the **Museum of South Moravia** housed in the former Minorite monastery. Opposite the museum is a brewery; beyond it are **Znojmo Castle** and the 11th century **Rotunda of St Catherine** with its remarkable Romanesque wall paintings (1134) of the Přemysl rulers. The street in front of the museum ends abruptly at a ravine. A footpath below and to the left runs along the brewery's outer wall to the castle. If the gate is locked, ask the staff at the museum where they keep the key and sell tickets. The view from the castle grounds is superb, but the castle interior has been closed for long-term renovations. The exterior of the rotunda can be seen from the castle entrance, but as the rotunda lies within the brewery compound you cannot visit it (this may change, so ask). The trails here leading down into the forest are well worth following if you have time.

Visible to the south of the museum is the Gothic **Church of St Nicholas** in a quaint corner of old Znojmo. From the two-storey **Chapel of St Wenceslas** (1521) beside this

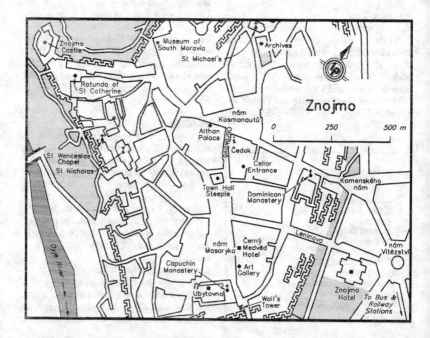

church you get an excellent view of the scenic valley and the dam on the Dyje River.

## Places to Stay & Eat

The *Znojmo Hotel* at Leninova 1, on the roundabout near the stations, is by far the largest hotel in town, though it was closed for renovations in 1991 and could still be.

The cheaper *Černý Medvěd Hotel*, at náměstí Masaryka 7, costs US$7 double (no singles) with shared bath, but as it's the only hotel at the moment, it's usually full. For some great ice cream, visit the shop at náměstí Kosmonautů 8.

The *TJ Znojmo Ubytovna*, in the Capuchin Monastery at the southern end of náměstí T G Masaryka, offers dormitory beds (reception is open from 6 to 10 pm). A recent report indicates that this building has been returned to the church and the hostel closed, so don't count on being able to stay there.

*Autocamp U Napoleonova dubu* (☎ 7438) is at Suchodrdly u Znojma, three km northeast of the railway station. It's open from mid-May to mid-September and bungalows are available.

Appeasing hunger pangs in Znojmo is difficult on Sundays or any evening, so plan ahead where you're going to eat. The situation should improve soon once private enterprise gets around to meeting the demand.

## Entertainment

The *South Moravian Theatre* is on náměstí Republiky south of Wolf's Tower.

## Getting There & Away

Train services to Jihlava (99 km) are infrequent. Local trains travel between Znojmo and Brno (two hours, 89 km) every couple of hours, though they follow a roundabout route. Trains are fairly direct to Břeclav though slow (two hours, 69 km), but for Brno, Jihlava and most other points the bus is much quicker than the train. To go to Bratislava, change trains at Břeclav.

Znojmo is on the main road from Vienna to Prague via Jihlava. There's a direct bus to Vienna (89 km) twice a week in summer, and

twice a day a local 2nd-class train covers the 18 km from Znojmo to Retz, Austria. If you want to hitchhike south, take the Břeclav train as far as Mikulov (45 km), walk across into Austria and stick out your thumb. You'll be in Vienna in a couple of hours.

## BRNO

Halfway between Budapest and Prague, Brno (Brünn) is the third-largest city in Czechoslovakia and has been the capital of Moravia since 1641. Its large fortress was an instrument of Habsburg domination. The botanist Gregor Mendel (1822-84), who formulated the modern theory of heredity, worked in Brno. After the Brno-Vienna railway was completed in 1839, Brno developed into a major industrial centre. The country's most important international trade fairs take place in the city in February, April, September and October.

This surprisingly untouristy city has a rich cultural life and its compact centre holds a variety of fascinating sights. Although you can visit Brno in a very busy day, stay longer and delve deeper. This is the sort of place you want to return to.

## Orientation & Information

Brno's main railway station is at the southern edge of the old town centre. Opposite the train station is the beginning of Masarykova, a main thoroughfare which trams and pedestrians follow into the triangular náměstí Svobody, the centre of town. The new autobusové nádraží (bus station) is 800 metres south of the railway station, beyond the Prior Department Store. To get to the bus station, go through the pedestrian tunnel under the train tracks, then follow the crowd along the elevated walkway.

Čedok is at Divadelní 3. CKM Student Travel is at Česká 11.

**Money** The State Bank is at Rooseveltova 18/20, near the Mahenovo Theatre.

**Post** The main post office is open 24 hours a day and is at the western end of the railway station.

## Things to See

As you enter the city on Masarykova, turn left into Kapucínské náměstí to reach the **Capuchin Monastery** (1651). In the ventilated crypt (closed Monday) below the church are the intact mummies of monks and local aristocrats deposited here before 1784. At the western end of Kapucínské náměstí is the recently restored Dietrichstein Palace (1760), with the **South Moravian Museum** (closed Monday).

The street in front of the monastery soon leads into Zelný trh and its colourful open-air market. Carp used to be sold from the waters of the Baroque Parnassus Fountain (1695) at Christmas. The **Reduta Theatre**, Zelný trh, is where Mozart performed in 1767. The operettas presented at the Reduta are excellent.

On ulice Radnická, just off the northern side of Zelný trh, is Brno's 13th century **old town hall**, which has a splendid Gothic portal (1511) below the tower. Inside the passage behind the portal are a stuffed crocodile, or 'dragon', and a wheel, traditional symbols of the city. Legend tells how the

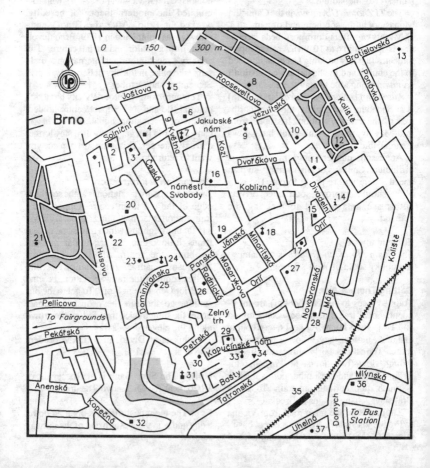

dragon once terrorised wayfarers approaching the nearby Svratka River; the wheel was supposedly made by a cartwright in league with the devil.

Continue north and take a sharp left to **St Michael's Church** (1679) and the former Dominican convent. At ulice Dominikánská 9, beside the church, is the Renaissance **House of the Squires of Kunštát** (closed Monday), where special art exhibitions are held. Facing the square on the other side of the church is the 16th century **new town hall** with its impressive courtyard, stairways and frescoes. Around the corner at ulice Husova 14 is the **Moravian Gallery of Applied Art** (closed Monday).

In the large park on the hill above this gallery is the sinister silhouette of **Špilberk Castle**, founded in the 13th century and converted into a citadel and prison during the 17th century. Until 1857 opponents of the Habsburgs were held here, including the Italian poet Silvio Pellico and other members of the Carbonari (an Italian secret political society who fought for the unification of Italy). Later, the Nazis tortured their victims in dungeons below Špilberk. Sections of the castle and the castle museum will be closed for restoration until 1994, but you should be able to get into the Gestapo casemates. You can enjoy a good view from the ramparts.

On Petrov Hill, where the city's original castle stood, is the neo-Gothic **Cathedral of Sts Peter & Paul**, rebuilt in the late 19th century on the site of an older basilica. The Renaissance **bishop's palace** adjoins the cathedral. In 1645 the Swedish general Torstensson who was besieging Brno declared that he would leave if his troops hadn't captured the city by noon. At 11 am the Swedes were about to scale the walls when the cathedral bell keeper suddenly rang noon. True to his word, the general broke off the attack; since that day the cathedral bells have always rung noon at 11 am.

From Petrov Hill descend Petrská into Zelný trh and turn right into ulice Orlí to get to the **Technological Museum** (closed Monday), another Brno curiosity. Buy a ticket for the Panorama, a rare apparatus

■ PLACES TO STAY

2 Slavia Hotel
4 Hotel Avion
6 Hotel U Jakuba
15 Astoria Hotel
19 Europa Hotel
20 International Hotel
28 Grand Hotel
32 Korso Hotel
36 Metropol Hotel

▼ PLACES TO EAT

34 Bufet Petrov

OTHER

1 Beseda Concert Hall
3 CKM Student Travel
5 St Thomas Church
7 St James Church
8 Janáček Theatre

9 Jesuit Church
10 Předprodej (theatre ticket office)
11 Mahenovo Theatre
12 City Art Gallery
13 Radost Puppet Theatre
14 Čedok
16 Ethnographical Museum
17 Měnín Gate
18 St John's Church
21 Špilberk Castle
22 Moravian Gallery of Applied Art
23 New Town Hall
24 St Michael's Church
25 House of the Squires of Kunštát
26 Old Town Hall
27 Technological Museum
29 Reduta Theatre
30 South Moravian Museum
31 Cathedral of Sts Peter & Paul
33 Capuchin Monastery
35 Main Railway Station
37 Prior Department Store

installed here in 1890 which offers continuous showings of the wonders of the world in 3-D. The programme is changed every couple of weeks so there are lots of regular visitors. Nearby on ulice Minoritská is **St John's Church** (rebuilt in 1733) with fine altarpieces, an organ and painted ceilings.

On nearby náměstí Svobody is a striking plague column (1680). At ulice Koblizna 1 in a corner of the square is the **Ethnographical Museum** (closed Monday) which has Moravian folk costumes and implements. Just north is the parish church, **St James** (1473), with a soaring nave in the purest Gothic style. This is Brno's most powerful church. **St Thomas Church** and the former **Augustinian monastery**, now an art gallery, are just north of St James.

Also worth seeing is the **City Art Gallery** (Dům umění), Malinovského náměstí 2, beside the Mahenovo Theatre. Excellent art exhibitions are sometimes staged in this gallery. **Villa Tugendhat** (1932), a classic work of modern architecture designed by Ludwig Mies van den Rohe, is at Černopolní 45 above Lužánky Park, a km north-east of St Thomas Church.

**Slavkov u Brna** On 2 December 1805 the famous 'Battle of the Three Emperors' took place in the open, rolling countryside between Brno and Slavkov u Brna (Austerlitz). Here Napoleon Bonaparte, a product of emerging bourgeois capitalism, defeated the combined armies of Emperor Franz I (Austria) and Tsar Alexander I (Russia), defenders of the aristocratic, feudal past. The battle was decided at Pracký Kopec, a hill 12 km west of Slavkov u Brna where a monument was erected in 1912. After the battle Napoleon spent four days concluding an armistice at the Baroque **chateau** (1705) in Slavkov u Brna.

Slavkov u Brna is 21 km east of Brno and is easily accessible by bus from Brno's autobusové nádraží (ask about times and platform numbers at the information counter. The chateau's historical exhibit on Napoleon's life is open Tuesday to Sunday from April to November. The decorated palace rooms and the gallery wing, which requires a separate ticket, are open daily from April to October. Unfortunately, Pracký Kopec is difficult to reach by public transport.

**Scenic Caves** The Moravský Kras (Moravian Karst), 20 km north of Brno, is formed by the underground Punkva River. There are a number of caves, chasms, canyons, lakes and the 128-metre-deep **Macocha Abyss**. At Punkevní, which is connected to Macocha, small boats carry tourists on the river into the deepest caves to see stalactites and stalagmites. Other caves to be visited include Kateřinská, Balčárka and Sloupsko-Sošuvské. Traces of prehistoric humans have been found in the caves.

To get there, take a bus to Jedovnice, four km south-east of Punkevní. From 20 May to 23 September, Čedok, Divadelní 3, Brno, organises bus tours to the caves (US$10 including lunch). Cave admissions are included in the price. The caves are open to the public all year; try to get there in the morning as the guides start to knock off around 2 pm. In summer there will be queues to get in.

**Places to Stay**

Čedok, Divadelní 3, arranges rooms in private homes for US$10 a night per person plus 15% commission (three-night minimum stay). All private rooms are far from the centre but easily accessible on public transport.

Before coming to Brno, check carefully that your visit does not coincide with one of the city's many trade fairs, as hotel rates double at this time and all public facilities become very overcrowded.

**Camping** *Autocamp Bobrava* (☎ 32 0110) is just beyond Modřice, 12 km south of the city. Take tram No 2, 14 or 17 to the end of the line, then walk the remaining three km. Otherwise take a train to Popovice Railway Station, 500 metres from the camping ground. There's no hot water but the restaurant is good (open from mid-April to mid-October). Bungalows are available.

**Hostels** CKM Student Travel, Česká 11, knows of accommodation for students and youth hostellers in disused student dormitories, but these are only open during July and August.

**Hotels** Brno has four B-category hotels. The *Korso Hotel*, Kopečná 10 (US$12/16 single/double without bath, US$21 double with bath), and *Metropol*, Dornych 5 (US$19/29 single/double without bath, US$23/35 with shower), are both near the railway station.

In the centre of town are the *Astoria Hotel*, Novobranská 3 (US$14/21 single/double without bath, US$17/30 with bath), and the *Europa Hotel*, Jánská 1/3 (US$14/19 single/double – no rooms with bath). A step up in price is the *Hotel U Jakuba*, Jakubské náměstí 6 (US$17/26 single/double with shower). The B*-category *Hotel Avion*, Česká 20, costs US$24 double without bath, US$19/28 single/double with bath. Beware of tram noise at all the hotels.

## Places to Eat
The cheapest and easiest place to eat at is the stand-up *Bufet Petrov* on the corner of Bašty and Masarykova streets, opposite the railway station. *Pipi Grill*, náměstí Svobody 11, offers roast chicken and beer, which you also consume standing up. *Bufet Sputnik* on Česká has strawberry milkshakes.

*Jídelna Samoobsluha*, Minoritská 2 opposite St John's Church, is a self-service where you can at least sit down. For much finer dining than any of these basic eateries offer, try the restaurants in either the *Grand* or *International* hotels.

## Entertainment
Opera and ballet are performed at the modern *Janáček Theatre* (Janáčkovo divadlo) (1965), Sady osvobozeni, named after composer Leoš Janáček, who spent much of his life in Brno. The nearby neo-Baroque *Mahenovo Theatre* (Mahenovo divadlo) (1882), designed by the famous Viennese theatrical architects Fellner and Hellmer, presents classical drama in Czech.

Try to see an operetta at the *Reduta*

*Theatre* (1760) on Zelný trh. The singing and dancing are excellent and the programmes enjoyable even if you don't understand Czech.

For tickets to the Janacek, Mahenovo and Reduta theatres, go to Předprodej, Dvořákova 11, a small booking office behind the Mahenovo Theatre (open weekdays from 12.30 to 5 pm, and Saturday from 9 am to noon). The staff are usually helpful to foreign visitors. In summer the regular theatres are closed.

Also check the *Beseda Concert Hall* next to the Slavia Hotel. This is possibly still closed for restorations.

If you're around on Sunday, don't miss the *Radost Puppet Theatre*, Bratislavská 32, which puts on shows at 10 am and 2.30 pm (Sunday only). It's kids' stuff but great fun if you haven't enjoyed puppets for a while.

## Getting There & Away
**Bus** There are two buses a day between Vienna (Mitte Bahnhof) and Brno. The bus to Vienna departs from platform No 20 at the bus station twice a day (170 Austrian schillings one-way).

For shorter trips buses are faster and more efficient than the trains. A bus is better if you're going to Znojmo or to/from South Bohemia or Kroměříž.

**Train** All trains between Budapest and Berlin stop at Brno. If you're going to/from Vienna, change trains at Břeclav. To go to/from Košice, change trains at Přerov. Direct trains from Bratislava (two hours express, 141 km) and Prague (three hours express, 257 km) are frequent.

## BŘECLAV
Břeclav, a major railway junction midway between Znojmo, Brno and Bratislava, is a useful stopping-off point or gateway to Czechoslovakia from Austria. There's an exchange office at the railway station.

Břeclav is the centre of the Podluží ethnic area and a major folk festival is held each June at Strážnice, 17 km north-east by bus.

## Places to Stay & Eat

Břeclav has two B-category hotels about a five-minute walk north of the railway station, across the park and straight ahead. The *Hotel Slavia*, at Leninova 20, costs US$8/11 single/double with bath, and the *Hotel Grand*, at Leninova 8, is similar. The restaurant at the Slavia is good. A night at either of these is a good way to avoid the hotel crunch in Brno and Bratislava, though both the Grand and Slavia are sometimes full.

Near the castle *(zámek)*, about a 10-minute walk beyond the hotels, is *Autocamp Pod zámkem* (☎ 20413), open from May to September. Bungalows are available.

The restaurant in Břeclav Railway Station is hidden. Look for the side door marked *jídelna* next to the snack bar inside the station.

## Getting There & Away

There's a direct train service from Vienna to Břeclav (91 km) six times a day. All express trains between Brno and Bratislava stop at Břeclav, though the international trains are often an hour late. The highway border crossing point into Austria is at Mikulov, 24 km west on the railway line to Znojmo.

# Bratislava

Bratislava (Pozsony in Hungarian, Pressburg in German) is the second-largest city in Czechoslovakia. Here the Carpathian Mountains, which begin at the Iron Gate of Romania, finally come to an end. As you arrive at the main railway station, you'll see vineyards on the slopes of the Little Carpathian Mountains which meet the Danube River here. The Austrian border is almost within sight of the city and Hungary is just 16 km away.

Founded in 907 AD, Bratislava was already a large city in the 12th century. Commerce developed in the 14th and 15th centuries and in 1467 the Hungarian Renaissance monarch Matthias Corvinus founded a university here, the Academia Istropolitana. The city became Hungary's capital in 1541 after the Turks captured Buda and remained so for nearly three centuries. Between 1563 and 1830, 11 Hungarian kings and seven queens were crowned in St Martin's Cathedral. Bratislava flourished during the reign of Maria Theresa of Austria (1740-80) and some imposing Baroque palaces were built. In 1918 the city was included in the newly formed Republic of Czechoslovakia and since 1969 it's been the capital of the Slovak Republic.

Many beautiful monuments survive in the old town to tell of this glorious past, and Bratislava's numerous museums are surprisingly rich. Franz Liszt visited Bratislava 15 times, and the opera productions of the Slovak National Theatre rival anything in Europe. Bear in mind, however, that Bratislava is expensive and overcrowded, so don't visit at the expense of the quieter sights farther east.

## Orientation

Bratislava's main railway station, Hlavná stanica, is several km north of town. Tram No 13 runs from this station to námestie L Štúra near the centre of town. A few trains also use stanica Bratislava-Nové Mesto, less conveniently located on the north-eastern side of the city.

Hviezdoslavovo námestie is a convenient reference point, with the old town to the north, the Danube to the south, Bratislava Castle to the west and Štúrova ulica to the east. The main bus station (autobusová stanica) is in a convenient modern building on Mlynské nivy, a little over one km east of Štúrova ulica.

## Information

General information about the city is supplied by BIPS (Bratislava Information & Publicity Service), Rybárska brána at the corner of Laurinská, off Hviezdoslavovo námestie (open weekdays from 8 am to 4 pm, Saturday from 8 am to 1 pm).

Knihkupectvo, Rybárska brána 1 near

BIPS, has books in English and German, maps and guidebooks.

CKM Student Travel is at Hviezdoslavovo námestie 16.

Staff at Slovakoterma, Radlinského 13, can arrange stays at health spas throughout Slovakia (from US$50/80 single/double all-inclusive).

**Money** To exchange money, go to Čedok at Štúrova 13.

**Post & Telecommunications** You can make international telephone calls at the office on Kolárska ulice 12. The rates are posted on the wall and the calls go right through.

**Consulates** Bratislava is a good alternative to Prague for collecting visas. The Hungarian Consulate General is at Palisády ulice 54, off Mierové námestie (open Monday, Wednesday and Friday from 9 am to noon). Nearby are the consulates general of Germany, at Palisády ulice 47 (open weekdays from 8 am to noon), and Bulgaria, at Kuzmányho 1 off Palisády ulice (open Monday, Wednesday and Friday from 9 am to noon).

The consulates of Austria, Holubyho 11 (tram No 214; open weekdays from 8 am to noon), and Poland, Hummelova 4, are in the residential area north-west of Bratislava Castle. To get to the Polish Consulate (open Monday to Friday from 8 am to 2 pm), where you can get a visa issued on the spot for US$25, take trolley bus No 213 or 217 from Mierové námestie to 'Hummelova'. The Romanian and Yugoslav consulates have closed.

### Things to See

Begin your visit with the **Slovak National Museum** (1928) opposite the hydrofoil terminal on the river. The museum features anthropology, archaeology, natural history and geology exhibits – notice the large relief map of Slovakia. A little farther up the riverfront is the ultramodern **Slovak National Gallery**, Bratislava's major art col-

lection with a good Gothic section. The gallery building itself is interesting because of the daring incorporation of an 18th century palace into the design.

Backtrack slightly to námestie L Štúra at the corner of Mostová to visit the Art-Nouveau **Reduta Palace** (1914), now the Reduta Air Terminal. It's worth going inside to see the architecture. Go north down Mostová and east down Jesenského to the neo-Baroque **Slovak National Theatre** (1886) with Ganymede's Fountain (1888) in front.

Crowded, narrow Rybárska brána penetrates the old town to Hlavní námestie, at the centre of which is Roland's Fountain (1572). To one side is the old town hall (1421), now the **Municipal Museum** with an extensive collection housed in finely decorated rooms and torture chambers in the casemates. You can enter from the picturesque inner courtyard where concerts are held in summer.

Leave the courtyard through the east gate and you'll be on a square before the **Primatial Palace** (1781). Enter to see the Hall of Mirrors where Napoleon and the Austrian emperor Franz I signed a peace treaty in 1805. In the municipal gallery on the 2nd floor are rare English tapestries (1632). St George's Fountain stands in the courtyard. On Saturdays the palace is crowded with couples being married, but is still open to visitors. Just beyond this palace is the **Hummel Music Museum**, Klobučnícka 2, in the former home of the German composer and pianist Johann Hummel (1778-1837).

Return through the old town hall courtyard and turn left into Radničná 1 to get to the **Museum of Wine Production** (closed Tuesday) in the Apponyi Palace (1762). Next head north on Dibrovovo námestie to the **Franciscan Church** (1297). The original Gothic chapel (1297) with the skeleton of a saint enclosed in glass is accessible through a door on the left near the front. Opposite this church is **Mirbach Palace** (built in 1770), Dibrovovo námestie 11, a beautiful Rococo building housing a good art collection.

From the palace continue around on narrow Zámočnícka ulica to the **Michael**

**Tower** (closed Tuesday), which has a collection of antique arms. There's a great view from the tower. Go north through the tower arch into the old barbican with the extensive **Pharmaceutical Museum** on the right. If you go out the north gate and across the street, you'll see the **Church of the Holy Trinity** (1725), an oval edifice with fine frescoes.

Return to the Michael Tower and stroll down Michalská to the **Palace of the Royal Chamber** (1756) at Michalská 1. Now the university library, this building was once the seat of the Hungarian parliament. In 1848 serfdom was abolished here, marking the end of feudalism in Hungary.

Take the passage west through the palace to the Gothic **Church of the Clarissine Order** with a unique pentagonal tower (1360) supported on buttresses. Continue west on Farská, then turn left into Kapitulská and go straight ahead to the 15th century coronation church, **St Martin's Cathedral**. Inside you'll find the bronze statue (1734) of St Martin cutting off half his robe for a beggar.

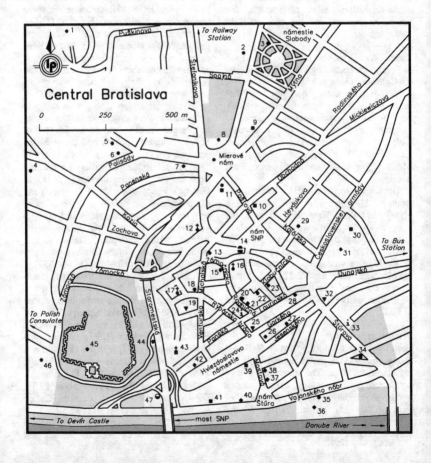

Central Bratislava

**Castles on the Danube** The busy motorway in front of St Martin's follows the moat of the former city walls. Construction of this route and the adjacent bridge was rather controversial as several historic structures had to be pulled down and vibrations from the traffic have structurally weakened the cathedral. Find the passage under the motorway and head up towards Bratislava Castle, built above the Danube on the southernmost spur of the Little Carpathian Mountains. At the foot of the hill is the **Decorative Arts Museum** (closed Tuesday).

Since the 9th century, **Bratislava Castle** has been rebuilt several times; it served as the seat of Hungarian royalty until it finally burnt down in 1811. Reconstructed from 1953 to 1962, the castle now houses a large historical museum. Climb up to the castle for a great view. The Slovak National Parliament meets in the modern complex that overlooks the river, just beyond the castle.

As you return from the castle, take a stroll on one of the pedestrian walkways across the sweeping new **most SNP** (SNP Bridge) (1972) over the Danube. On the far side you can take a lift up one of the pylons to a café that sits 80 metres above the river. Even the toilets have a view!

Below the Bratislava end of most SNP is a city bus terminal where you can catch city bus No 29 west along the Danube to the Gothic ruins of **Devín Castle** (open from May to October, closed Monday), which is on a hill where the Morava and Danube rivers meet. The castle withstood the Turks but was blown up in 1809 by the French. Stay on the bus to the end of the line and walk back to the castle. Austria is just across the rivers from Devín.

---

■ PLACES TO STAY

9 Hotel Tatra
10 Palace Hotel
11 Hotel Forum
30 Hotel Kyjev
34 Krym Hotel
39 Carlton Hotel
41 Hotel Devín

▼ PLACES TO EAT

19 U Zlatého Kapra Restaurant
25 Mliečne Speciality
32 Slovenská Restaurant

OTHER

1 Slavín War Memorial
2 Archbishop's Summer Palace
3 Site of the Klement Gottwald Monument
4 Austrian Consulate
5 Bulgarian Consulate
6 German Consulate
7 Hungarian Consulate
8 Grassalkovich Palace
11 Casino
12 Church of the Holy Trinity

13 Michael Tower
14 Main Post Office
15 Mirbach Palace
16 Franciscan Church
17 Church of the Clarissine Order
18 Palace of the Royal Chamber
20 Old Town Hall
21 Museum of Wine Production
22 Primatial Palace
23 Hummel Music Museum
24 BIPS Information Bureau
26 Slovak National Theatre
27 Předprodej (theatre ticket office)
28 PO Hviezdoslava Theatre
29 International Telephone Office
31 Prior Department Store
33 Čedok
35 Slovak National Museum
36 Hydrofoil Terminal
37 Reduta Air Terminal
38 Slovenská Filharmonia
40 Slovak National Gallery
42 CKM Student Travel
43 St Martin's Cathedral
44 Decorative Arts Museum
45 Bratislava Castle
46 Slovak National Parliament
47 Bus to Devín Castle

From the 1st to 5th centuries AD, Devín and Bratislava castles were frontier posts of the Roman Empire, manned by the 14th Legion. In the 9th century Devín Castle was a major stronghold of the Great Moravian Empire, and today both castles are regarded as symbols of the Slavonic peoples who maintained their identity despite centuries of foreign rule.

**Post-Socialist Bratislava** To see a bit of the Bratislava built by the Communists, head north from the Michael Tower across Mierové námestie to the Baroque **Grassalkovich Palace** (1760), previously the House of Pioneers. Continue north-east towards námestie Slobody, previously known as Gottwaldovo námestie. An impressive **monument to Klement Gottwald** (1980), the man instrumental in implanting socialism in Czechoslovakia, once stood in the north-west corner of the square but the massive marble figures of Gottwald and the others were decapitated during the political upheaval of late 1989. Some of the new buildings on the square belong to the **Technical University**. On the western side of námestie Slobody is what used to be the **archbishop's summer palace** (1765), now the seat of the Government of the Slovak Republic.

If you go west down Spojná and north down Štefanikova ulica 25, you'll come to the former **Lenin Museum**, now closed. Continue north a little, then head west up Puškinova towards the **Slavín War Memorial** (1965). This is where 6847 Soviet soldiers who died in the battle for Bratislava in 1945 are buried. There's a good view of modern Bratislava from here.

Unless otherwise noted, all of Bratislava's galleries and museums are closed on Mondays.

## Activities

To get out of the city and onto some hiking trails, take bus No 33 from the city bus terminal below the Bratislava end of the most SNP to the end of the line at Železná studienka in the forested Little Carpathian Mountains north of the city. Here a road and chair lift climb from the Snežienka Restaurant to the TV tower and Koliba EXPO Restaurant on Kamzík Hill (440 metres). You may manage to sample wine from the local vineyards at one of these restaurants.

**Organised Tours** Čedok, Štúrova 13, can arrange private guides for sightseeing around Bratislava (US$6 for three hours).

## Places to Stay

There's a severe shortage of budget hotels in Bratislava, and to make matters worse visitors from nearby Vienna swarm into Bratislava for cheap mini-holidays on weekends. In July and August all hotel rates are substantially increased.

**Hostels** Staff at CKM Student Travel, Hviezdoslavovo námestie 16 (open weekdays from 1 to 4 pm), may be able to tell you about summer youth hostels and perhaps reserve a room for you at the *Juniorhotel Sputnik* (☎ 23 4340) at Drieňová 14 in the eastern suburbs (tram No 8, 9 or 12 or bus No 34, 38 or 54). The Juniorhotel Sputnik, a large, modern hotel beside a large pond, is open all year and only costs US$5 for IYHF or student-card holders (it costs several times that for others). It's often full up with groups.

In July and August your best bet is the new *Studentský Domov Jura Hronca*, Benolakova ulice 1, about five blocks east of the main railway station. Holders of IYHF and student cards can rent beds here. The loud partying often lasts through the night. Ask CKM about this gigantic 12-storey student residence.

**Pensions** Čedok, at Štúrova 13, doesn't arrange private room accommodation but it does handle private 'pensions', which are basically the same thing. The staff will reserve a room for you in one of these for about US$11/12 single/double. Ask BIPS (see the Information section in this chapter) for the addresses of newly opened pensions.

Small private guesthouses only began to

appear in Bratislava in 1990 and one of the first was *Pension u Rudolfa*, Sláviče Údolie 36 in the residential area north-west of the castle (take trolley bus No 213 or 217 from Mierove námestie to 'Červený Kríž'). This luxurious pension is a 10-minute walk downhill from the trolley bus stop. Double rooms cost US$35 (no singles) including a large breakfast, but there are only four of them, so telephone 31 6894 for reservations. The facilities are clean and new. Owner Rudolf Benko is a local TV and movie director who speaks English and German.

**Hotels** The cheapest is the unappealing and usually full B-category *Palace Hotel*, Poštová 1, at US$14/22 single/double with shared bath. Noisy trams rattle on the street below.

If you're alone and all the Palace Hotel's singles are full, you'll do better for less at the higher class *Carlton Hotel*, Hviezdoslavovo námestie 2. This huge hotel has 149 single-bed B-category singles/doubles at US$17/36 without bath, US$31/47 with bath, but you have to request them specifically or you'll get an A*-category suite. Be aware that the door attendants are on the watch for guests who try to smuggle friends into their room to crash on the floor. A room at the Carlton includes a good cooked breakfast in the elegant dining room.

The only other moderately priced hotel is the *Krym Hotel*, Šafárikovo námestie 7 (US$18/25 single/double without bath), but it's noisy and usually full.

The B-category *Športhotel Trnavka*, Nerudova 2, north-east of town on the way to Zlaté piesky (bus No 214 from Mierove námestie), isn't luxurious and the rooms are small but at US$17 double it's good value.

**Zlaté piesky** There are bungalows, a motel, a hotel and two camping grounds at Zlaté

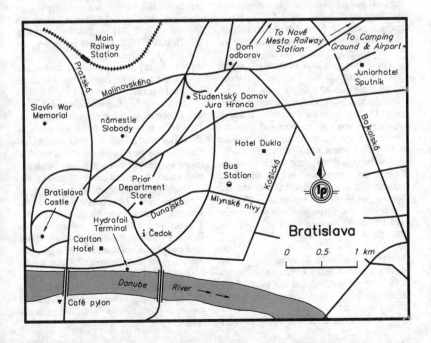

piesky (Golden Sands), which is near a clear blue lake seven km north-east of Bratislava. Trams No 2 (from the main railway station) and No 4 (from the city centre) terminate right at Zlaté piesky. You can hire rowing boats and sailboards here in summer and there are also tennis courts.

Rooms at the *Zlaté piesky Motel* cost US$21 double (no singles). The motel reception rents bungalows (US$12 double), but only from mid-May to mid-September when camping is also available (the toilet is dirty but the showers are hot). Nearby is the *Hotel Flora* with double rooms for US$12 (no singles). There's a restaurant in the hotel. Near the hotel is the reception of a second camping ground which may be preferable as it's right on the lake. Aircraft noise in the middle of the night is sometimes a problem.

## Places to Eat

Bratislava has a good range of excellent inexpensive restaurants, many offering regional dishes. The fastest and cheapest is the stand-up *Mliečne Speciality*, Rybárska brána 9 near the Slovak National Theatre. Here you can get real Slovakian peasant food – a rare paradise for vegetarians.

The *Dietna Jedalen Restaurant*, which you enter through the door just inside the passage at Laurinská 8, is a great place for lunch (closed Sunday). Ask the person in line behind you to translate the menu. It's self-service but you can get beer and there are flowers on the tables in the very pleasant dining room where you sit down to eat.

Another good place for lunch on weekdays is the inexpensive *Michalská Dietna reštaurácia*, ulica Michalská 2 in the old town (open Monday to Friday from 10 am to 5 pm only). You get regular table service here and the line of locals waiting to get in is proof that it's OK.

**Better Restaurants** You can enjoy local dishes at the *Slovenská Restaurant*, an excellent folkloric restaurant at the back of the arcade on Štúrova (not the basic self-service facing the street).

A wine restaurant worth trying is *Veľký*

*Františkáni Vináreň*, in the old monastery beside the Mirbach Palace. Other typical smoky wine-cellars, known as *pod viechou*, where Gypsy music is often played, are found in Baštová and Zámočnícka alleys near the Michael Tower.

For a leisurely meal also try the *U Zlatého Kapra Restaurant* (closed Sunday), ulica Prepoštská 6 off Venturska, which specialises in fish. The menu is in German.

*Stará Sladovňa*, Cintorínska 32, between the Prior Department Store and the bus station, is a huge, modern restaurant complex-cum-beer hall with live music in the evening.

If all else fails, the upstairs restaurant in the *Palace Hotel* is quite good and stays open until 11 pm.

## Entertainment

Opera and ballet are presented at the *Slovak National Theatre* (1836), Hviezdoslavovo námestie. The local opera company is outstanding. For classical drama in Slovak, go to the *Divadlo P O Hviezdoslava*, Laurinská 20. Tickets to these theatres are sold in the 'předprodej' office (open weekdays from noon to 8 pm) on the corner of Jesenského ulica and Komenského námestie, behind the National Theatre.

The *Slovenská filharmonia* is based in the neo-Rococo Reduta Palace (built in 1914) on Palackého at the corner of Mostová, across the park from the National Theatre. For concerts look for the office marked *'pokladnica'* (open weekdays from 1 to 5 pm) inside the gate across the street from the public toilets.

There's always something happening at the white-marble *Dom odborov* on námestie Františka Zupku (trams No 2, 4, 6, 8, 9, 10, 12 and 14). This major cultural centre includes a cinema, a restaurant, a bar and two theatres, plus exhibition areas, and is a good place to experience the type of entertainment many Czechoslovaks appreciate. Tickets to major events at Dom odborov go on sale at the centre's box office at 3 pm. Ask the people at BIPS to explain what's on at the centre.

## Getting There & Away

**Bus** If you're travelling between Banská Bystrica or Nitra and Bratislava, take a bus. At Bratislava's main bus station you usually buy the ticket from the driver, but check first at the information counter.

Four buses a day connect Vienna (Mitte Busbahnhof) to Bratislava (80 Austrian schillings). In Bratislava buy your ticket for this bus at the ticket window inside the bus station.

**Trains** All express trains between Budapest and Prague stop at Bratislava. Train services from Košice to Bratislava (via Poprad-Tatry, Žilina and Trenčín) are fairly frequent and couchettes are available on the night train.

There are two local trains a day between Vienna (Südbahnhof) and Bratislava (1½ hours, 64 km). Čedok, Štúrova 13, sells international railway tickets.

If you can't find a reasonable place to stay at in Bratislava, go to Čedok, námestie SNP 14 beside the Slovan Cinema, and try to book a couchette (US$2) or sleeper (US$4) to Košice or Prague for that night. Prices are lower than the cheapest room and you'll wake up at the next city on your itinerary. This Čedok office, which has railway timetables in the window, closes at 5 pm on weekdays and noon on Saturday. Ticketing is computerised. Don't forget that you'll need a regular train ticket along with the couchette ticket.

**Hitchhiking to Hungary or Austria** If you don't want to bother getting an international train ticket, take a local train or bus to Komárno and walk across the bridge in Komarom in Hungary. You could also take city bus No 116 to Čunovo from the city bus terminal below the Bratislava end of the most SNP and try to walk or hitchhike into Hungary.

Vienna is only 64 km west of Bratislava. The Austrian border is about two km across the most SNP and along Viedenská cesta, which is within walking distance of Bratislava. Hitchhiking into Austria is much easier than it is into Hungary.

**Boat** From mid-April to mid-September, Raketa hydrofoils ply the Danube between Bratislava and Budapest (3½ hours) but tickets are ridiculously expensive: in 1991 the one-way fare was increased to US$65 from the US$11 charged in 1990! You can also travel from Bratislava to Vienna several times a day from April to October for US$22 one-way (one hour). Children aged 15 and under pay half-price. Tickets and information are available at the hydrofoil terminal in Bratislava. In late summer the service can be interrupted because of low water levels.

## Getting Around

Public transport around Bratislava is based on an extensive tram network that is complemented by buses and trolley buses. Orange automats at tram and trolley bus stops sell tickets, but make sure that the green light is on before inserting any coins.

**To/From the Airport** The ČSA Reduta Air Terminal, Mostová 1-3, is just around the corner from the Carlton Hotel. Airport buses leave from here. You can also get to Ivanka International Airport on city bus No 24 from the railway station (eight km). Direct ČSA flights leave Bratislava for Kiev, Košice, Leningrad, Montreal, Moscow, New York, Poprad-Tatry, Prague and Sofia.

# West & Central Slovakia

Slovakia is the least touristy part of Czechoslovakia. Bratislava is on the beaten track between Budapest and Prague, but few visitors make the long detour out to see the magnificent Fatra or Tatra mountain ranges or the unspoiled medieval towns of East Slovakia. The Carpathian Mountains take up much of the Slovak Republic, and south of Nitra is the fertile Danube Plain. Two-thirds of Czechoslovakia's vineyards are on the southern and eastern slopes of the Little Carpathian Mountains north of Bratislava.

There are 180 quaint castles and castle ruins in Slovakia, the largest of which are

Spišský hrad, east of Levoča; Orava Castle, above the village of Oravský Podzámok, 81 km north of Banská Bystrica; and Trenčín Castle in West Slovakia.

The rural Slovaks are a people apart from the urbane Czechs. The peasant traditions of Slovakia are a clear transition from the Ukraine to the more Germanised culture of Bohemia and Moravia. This background is evident in the folk costumes you'll see in remote Slovak villages on Sundays, the traditional meal of roast goose with potato pancakes, and the area's colourful handicrafts. For 1000 years Slovakia was Hungarian and many ethnic Magyars still reside in the republic. Slovakia's 100,000 Gypsies managed to escape Nazi extermination because the Germans only occupied Slovakia in late 1944, after the collapse of their clero-fascist puppet state.

Important political events here include the declaration of the Slovak Soviet Republic at Prešov in 1919, the Slovak National Uprising (SNP) centred at Banská Bystrica in 1944, and the Košice Programme of 1945 (see the Košice section in this chapter). For centuries Slovakia was a backward agricultural area from which people sought to escape through emigration. After WW II the Communists developed industry in Slovakia almost from scratch and in 1969 the Czech and Slovak republics became equal partners in federal Czechoslovakia. Now Slovak nationalism is on the rise with lots of slightly scary flag-waving. Slovakia east of Bratislava has more to offer the adventurous budget traveller than any other part of Czechoslovakia.

## TRENČÍN
Here where the Váh River Valley begins to narrow between the White Carpathians and the Strážov Hills, Trenčín Castle guarded the south-west gateway to Slovakia and one of the routes from the Danube to the Baltic for centuries. Laugaricio, a Roman military post that was also the northernmost Roman camp in central Europe, was established here in the 2nd century AD. A rock inscription at Trenčín dated 179 AD mentions the stay of the Roman 2nd Legion here and its victory over the Germanic Kvad tribes.

The mighty castle which now towers above the town was first mentioned in 1069 in a Viennese illustrated chronicle. In the 13th century the castle's master, Matúš Čák, held sway over much of Slovakia. In 1412 Trenčín obtained the rights of a free royal city and the present castle dates from that period. Both castle and town were destroyed by fire in 1790 but much has been restored. Today Trenčín is a centre of the textile industry.

### Orientation & Information
From the adjacent bus and train stations walk west through the park and take the underpass under the highway to Mierové námestie, the main square.

Information is available from Čedok, Mierové námestie 35, and CKM Student Travel, Hviezdoslavova 10, a block from the Prior Department Store.

### Things to See
At the south-western end of Mierové námestie are the Baroque **Piarist Church** and the 16th century **town gate**. The **art gallery** in the former Piarist convent next to this church features works by local artists, especially the realist painter M A Bazovský.

A covered stairway from the corner of the square opposite the Piarist Church leads up to the Gothic **parish church** and the entrance to **Trenčín Castle** (open daily all year). The so-called 'Well of Love' on the first terrace is a fantastic construction that is 70 metres deep. Above is the castle's great central tower which provides a sweeping view of the whole area.

The famous Roman inscription of 179 AD is behind the Tatra Hotel at the north-eastern end of Mierové námestie and not directly accessible from the castle. The **Trenčín Museum**, Mierové námestie 46, is next to the Tatra Hotel.

**Near Trenčín** Hiking trails lead into the green hills that flank **Trenčianske Teplice**, a spa 14 km north-east of Trenčín. To get

Trenčín

0        250        500 m

| | |
|---|---|
| 1 | Camping Ground |
| 2 | Sports Stadium |
| 3 | Swimming Pool |
| 4 | Car Parking Lot |
| 5 | Prior Department Store |
| 6 | Hotel Laugaricio |
| 7 | Trenčín Hotel |
| 8 | Cultural Centre |
| 9 | CKM Student Travel |
| 10 | Town Gate |
| 11 | Piarist Church |
| 12 | Parish Church |
| 13 | Trenčín Castle |
| 14 | Čedok |
| 15 | Trenčín Museum |
| 16 | Tatra Hotel |
| 17 | Railway Station |
| 18 | Bus Station |

žába Restaurant on the hillside just above the spa is a **thermal pool** that is open to the public! Also visit the 'hamman', an exotic 19th century neo-Moorish bathhouse in the middle of town. From June to September a varied cycle of musical programmes is presented at the spa.

### Places to Stay

Rooms at the high-rise *Hotel Laugaricio*, Vajanského námestie, next to the Prior Department Store on the edge of the old town, a 10-minute walk from the railway station, cost US$8 single without bath, US$14 double with bath. The basic old *Trenčín Hotel* just around the corner from the Hotel Laugaricio costs US$8 triple (no singles or doubles).

A rather cramped *camping ground* with bungalows is on Ostrov, an island in the Váh River, opposite the large sports stadium near the city centre (open from June to September).

there by train from Trenčín, you must change at Trenčianska Teplá. The five hot sulphur springs at the spa are used to treat rheumatic and nervous system diseases. At the Zelená

At nearby Trenčianske Teplice are the B*-category *Jalta*, a modern five-storey hotel near the railway station, and the C-category *Miramare-Corfu*, Volgogradská 14, also nearby.

## Getting There & Away

All express trains on the main railway line from Bratislava to Košice via Žilina stop here. The Bathory and Bem express trains from Poland stop at Trenčín in the middle of the night. Take a bus to go to/from Brno (134 km) or Banská Bystrica (138 km).

## ŽILINA

Žilina, midway between Bratislava and Košice, at the junction of the Váh and Kysuca rivers, is the gateway to the Malá Fatra Mountains. Since its foundation in the 13th century at a crossing of medieval trade routes, Žilina has been an important transportation hub, a status that was confirmed with the arrival of railways from Košice in 1871 and Bratislava in 1883. It's a pleasant, untouristy town with an attractive main square and many interesting shops.

## Orientation

The adjacent bus and train stations are near the Váh River on the north-eastern side of town, a five-minute walk from námestie Dukla, Žilina's old town square. Another five minutes south from námestie Dukla is námestie Ľudovíta Štúra, with the Cultural Centre and the luxurious Interhotel Slovakia.

## Information

Čedok is at námestie Ľudovíta Štúra and CKM Student Travel is at námestie Dukla 24.

If you need a Polish visa there's a Polish consulate general (☎ 22 2822) at ulice Blahoslavova 4 in Ostrava, 102 km north-west of Žilina.

## Things to See

Other than Žilina's old town square, the only sight worth seeking out is the **Regional Museum** (closed Monday) in the Renaissance castle (*zámok*) across the river in Budatín, a 15-minute walk north-west from the railway station. As you come out of the railway station, turn left and go straight ahead for a few minutes, then go left under the railway tracks and straight again till you reach the bridge over the river. The white castle tower is visible from there.

## Places to Stay

Žilina has five older budget hotels, so getting an inexpensive room should not be difficult. The *Metropol Hotel* right opposite the railway station is the least expensive at US$5/7 single/double without bath. The rooms have a sink and double doors which keep out corridor noise. Also opposite the train station is the somewhat better *Hotel Polom*, at Olomoucká 1, which charges US$12/18 for singles/doubles with private bath.

Two less appealing old hotels just off námestie Dukla are the *Grand Hotel*, Sládkovičova 1 (US$5/8 single/double without bath), and the C-category *Hotel Dukla*, Dimitrovova ulica (US$8 double without bath). If all of these are full, look for the *Hotel Slovan*, Šmeralova 2, behind the Prior Department Store, back towards the railway station (US$5/8 single/double).

Žilina's finest hotel is the pretentious A*-category *Interhotel Slovakia*, a modern six-storey hotel on námestie Ľudovíta Štúra, on the opposite side of the old town from the railway station.

## Places to Eat

*Korzo Self-Service* (closed Sunday), on the corner below Hotel Polom, opposite the railway station, is a cheap, easy place for breakfast or a quick snack.

## Getting There & Away

Žilina is on the main railway line from Bratislava to Košice via Trenčín and Poprad-Tatry, and is served by with fairly frequent express trains. Most trains between Prague and Košice stop at Žilina. Express trains from Žilina take six hours to reach Prague (466 km), 1½ hours to Trenčín (80 km), three hours to Bratislava (203 km), two hours to Poprad-Tatry (141 km) and three hours to Košice (242 km).

The daily Polonia Express which travels between Budapest and Warsaw via Katowice stops here, but an easier way to get to Poland is to take a local train from Žilina to Český Těšín (69 km) and walk across the border.

To go to Banská Bystrica (90 km) you're better off taking a bus. Buses to Vrátna leave from platform No 10 at the bus station.

## THE MALÁ FATRA

The Malá Fatra (Little Fatra) Mountains stretch 50 km across north-western Slovakia; Veľký Kriváň (1709 metres) is the highest peak. Two hundred sq km of this scenic range, north of the Váh River and east of Žilina, are included in the Malá Fatra National Park. At the heart of the park is Vrátna, a beautiful mountain valley enclosed by forested slopes on all sides.

Noted for its rich flora, Vrátna Valley has something for everyone. The hiking possibilities vary between easy tourist tracks and rugged ridge walks. There are plenty of places to stay and eat, though in midsummer accommodation is tight. The valley is an easy day trip from Žilina. In winter Vrátna becomes a popular ski resort and has many lifts operating.

### Things to See & Do

The bus from Žilina enters the Vrátna Valley just south of Terchová where it runs through the **Tiesňavy Pass** which has rocky crags on both sides. One rock resembles a person praying (look back after you've gone through the pass).

Stay on the bus until **Chata Vrátna** (750 metres) where detailed maps of the area are posted. From just above Chata Vrátna, a **chair lift** climbs 770 metres to the Snilovské sedlo (1520 metres), a saddle midway between Chleb (1647 metres) and Veľký Kriváň (1709 metres). The chair lift (US$1 return) only runs if at least 20 people are present – no problem in summer when there may be a queue. In rain the chair lift doesn't

operate at all as there's no protection. You can also hike the green trail up the chair-lift route in two hours.

From Snilovské sedlo it's possible to continue right across the mountains to Šútovo (five hours from Chata Vrátna) where there are trains and buses going back to Žilina (many more trains stop at Kralovany, four km east of Šútovo). Otherwise follow the red trail south-east along the mountain ridges past Hromové (1636 metres), then north-east to Poludňový grúň (1460 metres) and Stoh (1608 metres) to the **Medziholie Pass** right below the bare summit of **Veľký Rozsutec** (1610 metres). From there it's easy to descend another green trail to **Štefanová**, a picturesque village of log houses with private rooms available (ask around). Allow a full day for this rather strenuous hike. Other possible hikes from Snilovské sedlo are the blue trail to Starý Dvor via the ridges (three hours) and the red trail west to Strečno Railway Station via the Starý hrad castle ruins (6½ hours).

A good alternative if the chair lift isn't operating, or you don't have much time, is to take the yellow trail from Chata Vrátna to **Chata na Grúni** at 970 metres (45 minutes). This mountain chalet has 30 beds and a restaurant but it's often closed or full. From Chata na Grúni the blue trail descends to Štefanová, where you can get buses back to Žilina (45 minutes).

### Places to Stay & Eat

*Chata Vrátna* (750 metres), a large wooden chalet with 88 beds (US$5 per person), is usually full up with hikers in summer and skiers in winter. In late autumn groups of school children occupy the whole building. A good self-service restaurant faces the bus stop below the hotel.

The *Hotel Boboty*, a fairly luxurious B*-category mountain hotel a five-minute walk up from a bus stop near Štefanová, costs US$24/35 single/double with shared bath, US$69 double for a suite with bath (cheaper in spring and autumn). The hotel also has a sauna and restaurant.

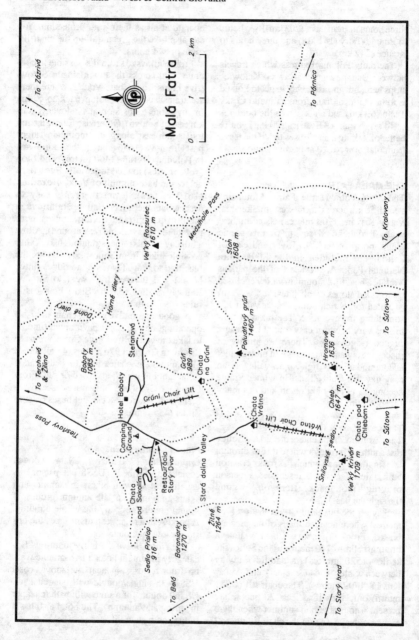

There's a large *camping ground* (open from mid-May to September) with a few bungalows near *Reštaurácia Starý Dvor* in the centre of the valley. *Chata pod Sokolím* on the hillside above the Starý Dvor has 60 beds and a large restaurant.

## Getting There & Away

A bus going from Žilina to Chata Vrátna, 32 km east, leaves about once an hour from platform No 10 at the Žilina Bus Station. The bus travels via Krasňany, which has a natural history museum, and Terchová, where a folk festival is held in July.

## BANSKÁ BYSTRICA

Banská Bystrica (Neusohl) on the main road from Budapest to Kraków sits on a bend of the Hron River near the centre of Slovakia. The Nízke Tatry (Low Tatra) and Slovenské rudohorie (Slovak Ore Mountains) flank this scenic valley. The town grew rich in medieval times from nearby silver and copper mines. Mining declined in the 17th century and only since WW II has the town boomed again.

On 29 August 1944 a liberated radio station at Banská Bystrica announced the beginning of the Slovak National Uprising (SNP). Until this time 'independent' Slovakia had been a German ally. The plan was to overthrow the puppet regime, switch sides in the war (as Romania had done) and establish a new government that would be friendly to the advancing Soviets. Though the local fascists quickly fell, the Germans invaded Slovakia and brutally re-established control of the towns. Banská Bystrica, the centre of the uprising, held out until 27 October 1944. At the Dukla Pass north-east of Bardejov, the Germans managed to slow the Soviet advance in one of the bloodiest battles of the war, which lasted from 8 September to 27 November 1944. Hundreds of monuments and plaques now recall the events of the uprising and a dramatic new museum at Banská Bystrica tells the story (if you read Slovak).

## Orientation

The adjacent bus and train stations are a little over a km east of námestie SNP, the city centre. City buses leave frequently from in front of the train station or you can walk into town. Čedok is at trieda SNP 4.

## Information

If you want information on events or anything else, try the Cultural Information Office in the barbican of the old city gate near the parish church. CKM Student Travel is at Horná 65.

## Things to See

Begin with the **Slovak National Uprising Museum** (closed Monday), the town's main sight. The museum's twin concrete pods are poised spectacularly on a ridge above the Lux Hotel, with towers from the old city walls on each side. Inside, groups are shown a film on the uprising (groups form quite frequently, so you may be lucky). This is one of the only remaining 'political' museums set up during the Communist era. New exhibits portraying the activities of Czechs and Slovaks who fought alongside the British forces during the war have now been added to give a more balanced picture. Unfortunately, there are no captions in English or German, so the presentation is rather confusing.

From this museum find your way west to námestie SNP, the attractive central square. On this square are the **Central Slovak Museum**, No 4 (closed Saturday), art galleries, Nos 7 and 16, the **bishop's palace**, No 19, the **municipal clock tower** (1567), No 24, and the **Jesuit Church**, No 26. A **Soviet War Memorial** graces the centre of the square.

Just north-east you'll see a cluster of churches and towers, site of the original 13th century mining settlement. The first tower belongs to the barbican of an **old city gate**. Beyond is another art gallery in the Renaissance **town hall** (1565) with arcades. The Gothic **parish church** is behind this and just beyond it, near the entrance to the cemetery, is a house of the Hungarian Renaissance

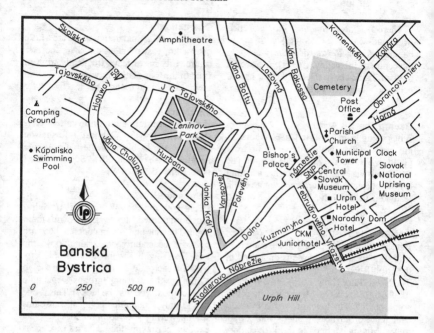

Banská Bystrica

0    250    500 m

king Matthias Corvinas (1479) and the **Church of the Holy Cross** (1452). If you enter the cemetery you'll be able to see the remaining walls and towers of the **town castle** (1510).

**Zvolen** Only 20 km south of Banská Bystrica and with frequent bus connections is the intact medieval castle of Zvolen (Altsohl), which was built between 1370 and 1382 as a summer residence for King Louis the Great of Hungary. In the 15th century Zvolen was held by the Hussites, and in 1548 it was rebuilt in the Renaissance style as a bulwark against the Turks. In the 18th century the Esterházys decorated the ceiling of a hall in the castle's western wing with the portraits of 78 Roman emperors. Today, exhibitions of the Slovak National Gallery are held at Zvolen Castle. Zvolen is famous for its embroidery and lace. Between Banská Bystrica and Zvolen is the health spa Sliač.

**Places to Stay**

The cheapest accommodation is the *CKM Juniorhotel*, Februárového víťazstva 12 (US$7/10 single/double with shared bath). Most of the rooms are doubles. People with a YHA or student card receive a discount but the place is usually full.

Nearby are two B*-category hotels: the *Národný Dom Hotel*, at Februárového víťazstva 7-9, an older hotel next to the J G Tajovského Theatre, which costs US$12/18 single/double with bath and breakfast; and the modern five-storey *Urpín Hotel*, at Nejedlého 5, which costs US$11 single without bath, US$18 double with bath.

Your most expensive choice would be the 16-storey, appropriately named *Lux Hotel*, ulica ČSA, at US$20/22 single/double with bath and breakfast.

The camping ground is near the *Hotel Turist*, Tajovského 9 beyond Leninov Park, within walking distance of the town (take bus No 7 from the city bus stop in front of

the railway station). It's open from mid-May to September.

### Getting There & Away
**Bus** Buses from Bratislava (208 km) run via Nitra and Zvolen. There's no direct railway line between the Vysoké Tatry and Banská Bystrica, making bus travel mandatory. The bus service to/from Žilina (90 km) is fairly frequent. Bus departure times are posted at the bus station, a few minutes' walk from the main railway station.

**Train** An overnight train with couchettes comes to Banská Bystrica from Prague, and the Polonia Express which travels from Warsaw to Budapest also stops here (reservations are required). Čedok, trieda SNP 4, has train tickets and times. There are direct trains to Banská Bystrica from Košice (4½ hours, 214 km), but within Slovakia you're usually better off travelling by bus.

# East Slovakia

East Slovakia is one of the most attractive touring areas in Eastern Europe. In one compact region you can enjoy superb hiking in the Tatra Mountains, white-water rafting on the Dunajec River, historic towns such as Levoča and Bardejov, the great medieval castle at Spišské Podhradie, the lovely spa of Bardejovské Kúpele and city life in the capital Košice. The proximity of the Ukraine gives the region an exotic air. Getting around is easy with frequent trains and buses to all these sights plus easy access to Poland and Hungary. In spite of all these advantages, exciting East Slovakia, the open back door to Czechoslovakia, is still well off the beaten track.

## THE VYSOKÉ TATRY
The Vysoké Tatry (High Tatra) are the only truly alpine mountains in Czechoslovakia. This 27-km-long granite massif covers 260 sq km, forming the northernmost portion of the Carpathian Mountains. The narrow, rocky crests soar above wide glacial valleys with precipitous walls. At 2655 metres, Gerlachovský štít (Mt Gerlach) is the highest mountain in the entire 1200-km Carpathian Mountains, and several dozen other peaks exceed 2500 metres. Enhancing the natural beauty packed into this relatively small area are 30 valleys, almost 100 glacial lakes and bubbling streams. The lower reaches are covered by dense coniferous forests. From 1500 to 1800 metres altitude, there's a belt of brushwood and knee pines, and above this are alpine flora and bare peaks.

Since 1949 most of the Slovak portion of this jagged range has been included in the Tatra National Park (TANAP), which complements a similar park in Poland. A network of 350 km of hiking trails reaches all the alpine valleys and many peaks. The famous red-marked Tatranská Magistrála Trail follows the southern crest of the Vysoké Tatry for 65 km through a striking variety of landscapes. The routes are colour-coded and

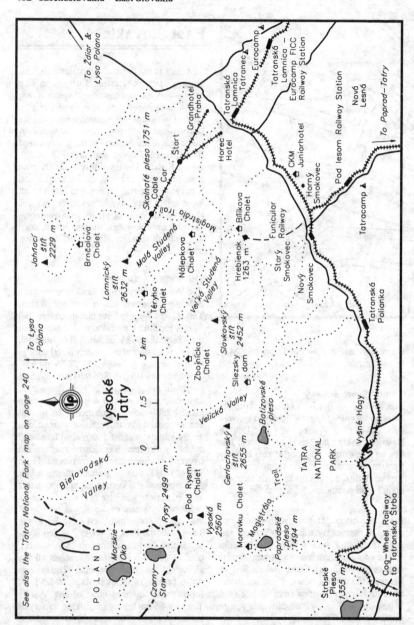

easy to follow. Park regulations require you to keep to the marked trails and refrain from picking flowers.

## Orientation

The best centre for visitors is Starý Smokovec, a turn-of-the-century resort that is well connected to the rest of the country by road and rail. Tram-style electric trains run frequently between the three main tourist centres in the park: Štrbské Pleso (1320 metres), Starý Smokovec (990 metres) and Tatranská Lomnica (850 metres). At Poprad-Tatry these trains link up with the national railway system. Buses also run frequently between the resorts. Cable cars, chair lifts and a funicular railway carry you up the slopes to hiking trails which soon lead you away from the throng. During winter, skiers flock to this area which offers excellent facilities.

## Information

The Čedok office is just above the railway station at Starý Smokovec. Another main Čedok office is at the Hotel Lomnica near the Tatranská Lomnica Railway Station.

The Vysoké Tatry map is intended for initial orientation only. Ask for the *Vysoké Tatry 21* map at bookshops as soon as you arrive in Czechoslovakia. Good maps are sometimes available at hotels or newsstands inside the park.

There's a bank in the commercial centre above the bus station in Starý Smokovec.

**Climate** When planning your trip, keep the altitude in mind. At 750 metres the camping grounds will be too cold for a tent from October to mid-May. By November there's snow, and avalanches are a danger from November to June when the higher trails will be closed (ask someone to translate the *achtung* notices at the head of the trails for you). Beware of sudden thunderstorms, especially in the alpine areas where there's no protection, and avoid getting lost if clouds set in. It's worth noting that the assistance of the Mountain Rescue Service is not free. July and August are the warmest (and most crowded) months, and August and September are the best for high-altitude hiking.

## Things to See

**Above Starý Smokovec** From Starý Smokovec a funicular railway (at 1025 metres) carries you up to **Hrebienok** (1280 metres), a ski resort with a view of the Veľká Studená Valley. The funicular railway (built in 1908) is closed in late autumn and early spring and every Friday morning, but if it's not running it takes less than an hour to walk up to Hrebienok (green trail). The Bílikova Chalet is a five-minute walk from Hrebienok and there are several waterfalls just below, such as Studenovodské vodopády and Obrovský vodopád.

For great scenery follow the blue trail from Hrebienok to Zbojnícka Chalet in the Veľká Studená Valley (three hours). Beyond Zbojnícka the blue trail climbs over a 2428-metre pass and descends to the Polish border.

The green trail leads north from Hrebienok to Téryho Chalet in the Malá Studená Valley (three hours). The Nálepkova Chalet is only an hour from Hrebienok up the same trail. The round trip from Hrebienok to Nálepkova, Téryho and Zbojnícka back to Hrebienok would take about eight hours.

If it's a cloudy day, you may want to follow the red Tatranská Magistrála Trail through the forest from Hrebienok to Sliezský dom (two hours).

**Via Štrbské Pleso** An all-day circle hike begins with a morning train to the famous ski resort Štrbské Pleso and its glacial lake (at 1355 metres). Swimming is possible in summer. After a look around this smart health and ski resort, take the Magistrála Trail up to Popradské Pleso (1494 metres). The trail continues east all the way to Hrebienok via Sliezsky dom. Food may be available at the chalets along the way, but pack your own supplies to be sure.

**Via Tatranská Lomnica** A shorter round trip would begin with a morning train from Starý Smokovec to Tatranská Lomnica. In 1937 a **cable car** able to carry 30 people at a time began operating, going from the resort up to **Skalnaté Pleso** (1751 metres); an extension to Lomnický štít (2632 metres) was completed in 1941. As soon as you arrive, visit the cable-car station near the Grandhotel Praha in Tatranská Lomnica to pick up tickets for the ride to Skalnaté Pleso. The cable car (closed Tuesday) is very popular with tourists, so you have to get to the office early to book the trip.

In 1973 a second, smaller cable-car line (closed Monday) with four-seat cabins was built to Skalnaté Pleso via Štart from above the Horec Hotel in Tatranská Lomnica. It doesn't operate when there's too much wind.

While you're waiting for your departure time to roll around, visit the **Museum of Tatra National Park**, a few hundred metres from the bus station at Tatranská Lomnica (open weekdays from 8.30 am to 5 pm, weekends from 8 am to noon). The exhibition on the natural and human histories of this area is excellent.

There's a large observatory at Skalnaté Pleso and the cable car to the summit of Lomnický štít. If you're lucky the service will be running, the sky will be clear and you won't have to wait too long to go. From Skalnaté Pleso it's only two hours down the Magistrála Trail to Hrebienok and the funicular railway back to Starý Smokovec.

If you visit the Tatra Mountains during a peak period when the place is overflowing with tourists, you can do the Skalnaté Pleso-Hrebienok trip in reverse. It's a lot easier to get in the cable car at the Skalnaté Pleso for a ride down than at Tatranská Lomnica for a ride up. Hundreds may be waiting to get on at Tatranská Lomnica.

### Activities

In summer Čedok offers several interesting bus excursions from the Vysoké Tatry resorts. The weekly trip to the Demänovská jaskyňa Caves near Liptovský Mikuláš also includes a chair-lift ride to Chopok Peak (2024 metres) in the Nízke Tatry which costs US$20. White-water rafting on the Dunajec River is offered four times a week from June to September (US$25). You can make bookings at Čedok offices in any of the three Tatra resorts.

**Mountain Climbing** You can reach the summit of Slavkovský štít (2452 metres) in nine hours on a round trip on the blue trail from Starý Smokovec. Rysy Peak (2499 metres), right on the Polish border, is about nine hours away on a round trip from Štrbské Pleso (via Popradské Pleso and Pod Rysmi Chalet). To scale the peaks without marked hiking trails (Gerlachovský štít included) you must hire a mountain guide. Members of recognised climbing clubs are exempt.

Staff at the Šport Centrum next to the Slovakoturist office in Horný Smokovec can arrange mountain guides with as little as 24 hours' notice. The price depends on weather conditions and the difficulty of the climb, but US$20 is about average. This private company also sells top-quality sporting equipment such as hiking boots, jackets, sleeping bags, skis, mountain-climbing gear, etc. The staff speak perfect English and are very helpful.

### Places to Stay

**Camping** There's no camping within the Tatra National Park. The nearest commercial camping ground to Starý Smokovec is the *Tatracamp* (☎ 2406) near the Pod lesom Railway Station, three km down the road to Poprad-Tatry. Six-person bungalows cost US$30 (open from June to September). There's also a camping ground at Tatranská Štrba (open from May to September) below Štrbské Pleso and three camping grounds a couple of km from Tatranská Lomnica (near the Tatranská Lomnica Railway Station on the line to Studený Potok).

The largest of these three is the *Eurocamp FICC* (open all year) with restaurants, bars, shops, a supermarket, a swimming pool, luxury bungalows, hot water and row upon row of parked caravans. The 1975 rally of the International Camping and Caravaneering Federation was held here. The smaller and more personal *Tatranec Campground*, where bungalows are available, is halfway between the Eurocamp and Tatranská

Lomnica. In the opposite direction, just down from the Eurocamp, is the *Športcamp* (open from mid-June to mid-September).

**Chalets** Up on the hiking trails are about eight mountain chalets *(chata)*. Signs at the trail heads usually indicate whether the chalets are open. Given the popularity and limited capacity of this area, the chalets could all be full. Staff at the TANAP horská služba (mountain rescue) office next to Čedok in Starý Smokovec will be able to tell you if a certain chalet is open and may even telephone ahead to see if there's a place for you. Many of the chalets close for maintenance in November and May. Although food is available at the chalets, you should take some of your own supplies.

The chalets basically come in three varieties as explained in the following examples. The *Moravku Chalet* (1500 metres, 82 dorm beds) on Popradské Pleso and *Sliezsky dom* (1670 metres, 79 dorm beds) are large mountain hotels with both dormitories and private rooms. *Bílikova* (1255 metres, 68 beds), *Nálepkova* (1475 metres, 20 beds) and *Brnčalova* (1551 metres, 52 beds) are rustic wooden buildings on the Magistrála Trail. *Pod Rysmi* (2250 metres, 13 beds), *Zbojnícka* (1960 metres, 18 beds) and *Téryho* (2015 metres, 21 beds) are high mountain chalets built of stone. These three make perfect bases for alpine exploration, but make sure they're open and available before you set out.

Čedok in Starý Smokovec handles chalet bookings at Bílikova, Sliezsky dom and Moravku (Popradské Pleso). The price is US$5 per person in a six-bed dorm in all three places. Sliezsky dom also has double rooms at US$12 double. Breakfast is included in all rates. Slovakoturist just above the Pekná vyhliadka Railway Station in Horný Smokovec, a 10-minute walk east from Čedok in Starý Smokovec, can reserve beds at Nálepkova, Brnčalova, Pod Rysmi, Zbojnícka and Téryho chalets for about US$3 per person.

**Hotels** Hotels in the Tatra, even the luxury-class hotels, are far more relaxed than those in lowland cities. Many of the hotels you see in this area are owned by the trade unions and are only open to their members. Other hotels are reserved for groups. Hotel prices are almost double in the high seasons (mid-December to March and June to September) as compared to the low season (April, May, and October to mid-December).

Staff at the Čedok office (closed on Saturday afternoon and Sunday) near the railway station at Starý Smokovec will help you to find a room. Čedok controls many hotel rooms around Smokovec, so it's sometimes easier to go there for a booking than to tramp around looking on your own. The staff can arrange rooms in all categories from low budget to deluxe. Čedok doesn't have any private rooms at Smokovec but can arrange rooms with families in the village of Nová Lesná for US$8/10 single/double (five-night minimum stay). Unless you have a car this is not convenient.

**Smokovec** The *Park Hotel*, a circular five-storey B*-category hotel that opened in 1970 just above the Nový Smokovec Railway Station, charges US$12/26 single/double, including breakfast in the low season, and US$21/30 without breakfast in the high season. All rooms have private bath.

The only C-category hotel is the *Bystrina* between the Park Hotel and the Grandhotel at Nový Smokovec. Rooms cost US$13/20 double/triple with shared bath (no singles) and you're supposed to book through the Čedok office. It's clean, has a good (if slow) restaurant and the cascading stream alongside creates nice sound effects.

If the price doesn't bother you, you'll like the A*-category *Grandhotel* at Starý Smokovec. This majestic building has a certain elegance that the high-rise hotels lack. Since many of the rooms (both single and double) have shared bath, it's not as expensive as you might think: US$16/20 single/double without bath; US$25/35 with bath in the low season, or US$23/36 without bath; US$40/58 with bath in the high season. In the high season breakfast is included, but in the low season it's not.

Cheaper rooms are available at the nearby B-category *Hotel Tatra* (also known as Hotel Úderník) just above the train station at Starý Smokovec (US$7/10 single/double without bath). However, it's often full.

Another inexpensive hotel at Starý Smokovec is the four-storey, B-category *Hotel Šport* (US$8/13 single/double with shared bath), a five-minute walk from the Starý Smokovec Čedok office. Čedok will book you in there.

The cheapest place to stay at if you have a YHA card is the *CKM Juniorhotel Vysoké Tatry*, just below the Horný Smokovec Railway Station. The charge will be around US$5 and the hotel is open all year, but it's 'always' full so make reservations at a CKM Student Travel office. Guests are accommodated in a half-dozen single-storey pavilions spread around the hotel grounds.

**Tatranská Lomnica** *Hotel Lomnica*, an older two-star hotel with quaint folk architecture just down from the railway station in Tatranská Lomnica, costs US$10 double without bath. One or two rooms with bath are available at US$14 double. The Lomnica reception also handles rooms at the *Hotel Mier*, a couple of blocks away (US$8 with shared bath).

Also try the newer, B-category *Hotel Horec*, a five-minute walk up the hill from the railway station.

Tatranská Lomnica's best hotel is the *Grandhotel Praha* (built in 1905) up the hill beside the cable-car terminal. In the high season singles/doubles with bath cost US$26/40, and US$22/34 in the off season. By all means stay there if price isn't a big consideration and you like a little style.

**Štrbské Pleso** The 11-storey *Hotel Panorama* next to the Prior Department Store, above the Štrbské Pleso Railway Station, costs US$20/28 single/double with bath.

The *Hotel Patria*, a huge new A*-category A-frame hotel overlooking the lake, a 10-minute walk uphill from the railway station, costs US$30 double (no singles).

*Hotel FIS* opposite the huge ski jumps, five minutes beyond the Patria Hotel, is US$10/14 single/double with bath. The FIS is a modern sports hotel and by far the best value at Štrbské Pleso. Both the hotel and ski jumps were built for the 1970 International Ski Federation world championships.

The old wooden *Sokolovo Hotel* on the highway, just above the railway station at Tatranská Štrba, charges US$8 double (no singles).

**Places to Eat**
Almost all the hotels and chalets of this region have their own restaurants.

The *Zbojnícka koliba* (usually only open for dinner from 4 to 11 pm) is a folk-style restaurant just below the Grandhotel Praha in Tatranská Lomnica. *Pizza Piccola*, right beside the Tatranská Lomnica Railway Station, has cold white wine and a great variety of pizzas.

**Getting There & Away**
**Bus** There are regular express buses from Bratislava to Tatranská Lomnica via Nitra, Banská Bystrica and Starý Smokovec. Bus services to and from Prešov are fairly frequent.

**Train** If you want to go by train, take one of the express trains running between Prague or Bratislava and Košice and change at Poprad-Tatry (couchettes are available). There are frequent narrow-gauge electric trains between Poprad-Tatry and Starý Smokovec (13 km). Alternatively, get off the express train at Tatranská Štrba, a station on the main line from Prague to Košice, and take the **cogwheel railway** up to Štrbské Pleso (there are over 20 services daily), which climbs 430 metres over a distance of five km. Also known as the 'rack railway', this service opened in 1896.

**To/From Poland** There's a highway border crossing between Czechoslovakia and Poland near Javorina, 30 km from Tatranská

Lomnica via Ždiar by bus. You'll find a bank at Lysa Polana on the Polish side where you can change money, but there is no Czechoslovak bank at Javorina. If you're unable to change money on either side of the border, the bus driver will probably take your smallest banknote in hard currency to cover the fare into town. The buses are less crowded on the Czechoslovak side. (See the Tatra Mountains section in the Poland chapter of this book for information on conditions on the Polish side.)

In perfect weather it would be possible to hike north to Javorina from the Téryho Chalet in half a day. This green trail crosses a 2372-metre pass, so it's only for experienced hikers with light packs. There's also a blue trail from Zbojnícka to Javorina, which runs right along the border itself. If you're really young, strong and foolish, you could hike right across from Starý Smokovec to Javorina on a fine summer day.

### Getting Around
You can experience virtually every type of mountain transport here: funicular railway, cog-wheel or rack railway, narrow-gauge electric trains, cable cars and chair lifts. The most used are the electric trains which run from Poprad-Tatry to Starý Smokovec (13 km) and Štrbské Pleso (29 km) about every half-hour. Trains also travel from Starý Smokovec to Tatranská Lomnica (six km) every 30 minutes. These trains make frequent stops along their routes; when there isn't a ticket window at the station, go immediately to the conductors upon boarding and buy your ticket from them.

### POPRAD-TATRY
Poprad-Tatry is a modern industrial city with little to interest visitors. It's an important transportation hub that you'll pass through at least once. The electric railway from here to Starý Smokovec was built in 1908 and was extended to Štrbské Pleso in 1912. The oldest section of Poprad-Tatry is Spišská Sobota, about three km from the station across the Poprad River, off the road to Kežmarok.

### Places to Stay & Eat
If you arrive too late to go on to somewhere nicer, you could stay at the old *Hotel Europa* (US$8/12 single/double with shared bath) just outside the Poprad-Tatry Railway Station. The hotel restaurant is quite good (the menu is in German).

*Gerlach Hotel*, Hviezdoslavovo námestie, is a more expensive B*-category high-rise establishment across the park in front of the station.

### Getting There & Away
**Air** Poprad-Tatry has a domestic airport that serves this part of the country, and the airline office is right beside the Gerlach Hotel.

**Bus** There are buses to almost everywhere else in Slovakia from the large bus station next to the railway station. Banská Bystrica (124 km), Bardejov and Prešov (84 km) are most easily reached by bus.

**Train** Poprad-Tatry is a major junction on the main railway line from Bratislava or Prague to Košice. Express trains run to Žilina (two hours, 141 km) and Košice (1½ hours, 101 km) every couple of hours. Electric trains climb 13 km to Starý Smokovec, the main Vysoké Tatry resort, every half-hour or so. A feeder railway line runs north-east to Plavec (two hours by local train, 61 km) where you can get a connection to Muszyna, Poland (check the times at the information window).

### DUNAJEC GORGE
**Pieniny National Park** (21 sq km) combines with a similar park in Poland to protect the nine-km Dunajec River gorge between the Slovak village of Červený Kláštor and Szczawnica, Poland. The river here forms the boundary between the two countries and the 500-metre limestone cliffs are impressive.

Although Čedok organises raft trips through the gorge, this activity is more common on the Polish side. If you can't manage to get on a raft, you can at least hike into the gorge on a trail that follows the river on the Slovak side and perhaps even have a swim. In a valley beyond the gorge is the village of Lesnica, from which you could return to Červený Kláštor over the mountains. This area is a favourite with canoeists.

Červený Kláštor is right beside the river at the entrance to the gorge. At the head of the trail into the gorge is a 14th century fortified **Carthusian monastery**, now an ethnological museum and park administrative centre. The lime trees on the riverbank were planted by monks who lived in small hermitages around the monastery courtyard.

### Places to Stay

No hotel exists at Červený Kláštor but just down from the monastery is a riverside camp site (**☎** 408) that is open from mid-June to mid-September. No bungalows are available. A basic inn *(Ubytovací hostinec)* with a few rooms without bath is at Lesnica. The nearest regular hotel is at the B*-category *Vrchovina* at Stará Ľubovňa.

### Getting There & Away

Direct buses go to Červený Kláštor from Poprad-Tatry. Though Poland is just across the river, there's no official border crossing here, so you must take a bus from Červený Kláštor to Stará Ľubovňa (25 km), and then a train to Plavec (16 km), where another train goes to Muszyna, Poland (16 km) twice a day. From Muszyna there are Polish trains to Nowy Sącz (50 km). Check connecting train times in the station at Stará Ľubovňa or beforehand. There are also buses from Stará Ľubovňa to Bardejov or Prešov.

## SPIŠSKÁ NOVÁ VES

Spišská Nová Ves is the administrative centre of the Spiš region. This modern city with a history dating back to 1268 is a good base from which to visit Levoča and Spišské Podhradie.

Just south-west of Spišská Nová Ves is Slovenský raj (the Slovak Paradise), a newly created **national park** with cliffs, caves, canyons, waterfalls and 1896 species of butterflies. This mountainous karst area is accessible via Čingov (eight km west) where

a 12½-km path up a canyon to Kláštorisko begins.

### Places to Stay

The modern, 10-storey *Metropol Hotel* (B*-category), at Dukelská 1, charges US$15 double with bath. You can also try the *Športhotel* at the stadium and the *Flora Hotel* at Čingov, both B-category. Chalets and hostels are available at Slovenský raj National Park.

### Getting There & Away

Spišská Nová Ves is on the main railway line from Žilina to Košice with trains from Poprad-Tatry (26 km) every hour or so. A feeder line runs 13 km north to Levoča with services every two or three hours.

Buses to Levoča and Spišské Podhradie leave from the bus station next to the Spišská Nová Ves Railway Station.

## LEVOČA

In the 13th century the king of Hungary invited Saxon Germans to colonise the Spiš region on the eastern borderlands of his kingdom as a protection against Tatar incursions and to develop mining. One of the towns founded at this time was Levoča (Leutschau), 26 km east of Poprad-Tatry. Granted urban privileges in 1271, the merchants of Levoča grew rich in the 14th century.

To this day the medieval walls, street plan and central square of Levoča have survived, unspoiled by modern developments. The town is an easy stop on the way from Poprad-Tatry to either Prešov or Košice. A large community of Gypsies resides here.

### Orientation & Information

The railway station is a km south of town down the road beside the Družba Hotel. Čedok is at Mierové námestie 46.

### Things to See

Bastions and 15th century walls greet the traveller arriving by bus at námestie Slobody. The old town begins just through **Košice Gate** with the **New Minorite Church** (1750) on the left.

Mierové námestie, Levoča's central square, is full of things to see. In the 15th century **St James Church** is a gigantic Gothic high altar (1517) by Master Pavol, one of the largest and finest of its kind in Europe. Next to St James is the Gothic **town hall**, enlivened by Renaissance arcades, today the **Museum of the Spiš Region** (closed Monday). Beside the old town hall is a 16th century cage where prisoners were once exhibited.

There's an **Art Museum** (closed Monday) in the 15th century house at Mierové námestie 40. While you're there have a peek in the courtyard of Mierové námestie 43. The **Evangelical Church** (1837), which once served the German community, is in the Empire style, as is the former **district council** (1826), Mierové námestie 59. Thurzov dom (1532), Mierové námestie 7, now the **State Archives**, is another fine building. At Mierové námestie 20 is the **Master Pavol Museum** (closed Monday).

From October to April, St James Church and all the museums of Levoča are open on Saturday and Sunday only.

## Places to Stay

Staff at Čedok, Mierové námestie 46, arrange private rooms. Levoča has only one hotel, the B-category *Družba Hotel*, Cesta Slobody 22, which is just outside the town walls. The Družba has only 25 rooms (US$5/7 single/double with shared bath), but as Levoča is off the beaten track you'll probably get one. On the outside the Družba looks very run-down, but the staff are friendly, the rooms are clean and comfortable and the hotel restaurant is good.

*Levočská Dolina Autocamp* (open from mid-June to August only) is three km north of námestie Slobody. Bungalows are available.

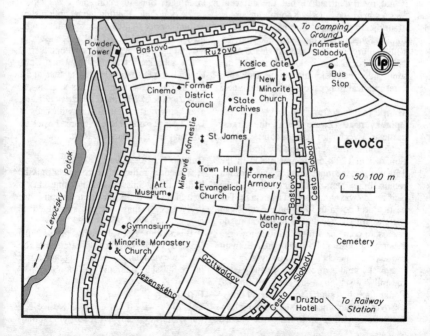

## Places to Eat
Levoča's best restaurant is the *Restaurant u 3 Apostolov*, Mierové námestie 11. For coffee and cakes go to *Mliečne Lahodky*, Mierové námestie 9.

## Getting There & Away
Levoča is connected by local train to Spišská Nová Ves, a station 13 km south on the Prague-Košice main line. Bus travel is more practical as there are frequent services to Poprad-Tatry, Spišské Podhradie and Prešov. All buses stop at námestie Slobody and some local buses stop at the railway station at the southern end of town.

## SPIŠSKÉ PODHRADIE
Spišské Podhradie, 10 km east of Levoča, is midway between Poprad-Tatry and Prešov in the centre of East Slovakia. In the 12th century a settlement appeared below the neighbouring castle, developing into an artisan's town in the 13th century. The town is not overly attractive but the adjacent Spišský hrad and Spišská Kapitula are sights of prime importance. The nearby Spišská Kapitula was built by the clergy and from the 13th century an abbot resided there. After 1776 a bishop also resided there. On the south side of Spišský hrad is the Dreveník karst area featuring caves, cliffs and ravines.

## Things to See & Do
**Spišský hrad** (Zipser Burg), the largest castle in Czechoslovakia, occupies a long ridge 180 metres above Spišské Podhradie. Founded in 1209 and reconstructed in the 15th century, the inhabitants of Spišský hrad repulsed the Tatars in 1241. Until 1710 the Spiš region was administered from here. The castle burnt down in 1780 but the ruins and the site are spectacular. The highest castle enclosure contains a round Gothic tower, a cistern, a chapel and a rectangular Romanesque palace perched over the abyss.

Spišský hrad is directly above and east of the railway station, a km south of Spišské Podhradie's bus stop. Cross the level crossing over the tracks near the station and follow the yellow markers up to the castle (closed

Monday and from November to April). If the first gate is locked, try the second one higher up. Even if both are closed, the exterior still justifies a stop. In winter Spišský hrad is often shrouded in mist and invisible from the train station it rises above.

On another ridge a km north of Spišské Podhradie, out on the road to Levoča, is the 13th century ecclesiastical settlement of **Spišská Kapitula** completely encircled by a 16th century wall. A single street lined with Gothic houses runs between two medieval gates. At the upper end of this street is the magnificent **St Martin's Cathedral** (1273) with twin Romanesque towers and a Gothic sanctuary. Inside are three folding Gothic altars (1499) and near the door a Romanesque white lion. On opposite sides of the cathedral are the old seminary and the Renaissance bishop's palace.

## Places to Stay
The *Spiš Hotel* near the bus stop in the middle of Spišské Podhradie costs US$6 single or double. Finding the receptionist or getting service in the hotel restaurant can be hit or miss, though you can always stick your head in the kitchen and ask someone there.

On a backstreet behind the Hotel Spiš, beyond some apartment blocks that are a five-minute walk from the bus stop, is the new *Turistická Ubytovna Družstevný Klub*, also known as the Hotel Raj, with beds at US$2 per person. This is a 'tourist hostel' so you may have to share the room.

## Getting There & Away
A secondary railway line connects Spišské Podhradie to Spišské Vlachy (nine km), a station on the main line from Poprad-Tatry to Košice. Departures are scheduled to connect with the Košice trains.

Buses from Prešov, Levoča, Spišská Nová Ves and Poprad-Tatry are quite frequent. You can leave your bags at the left-luggage office in the Spišské Podhradie Railway Station.

## PREŠOV
This old town 36 km north of Košice is a busy market centre. Prešov (Preschau)

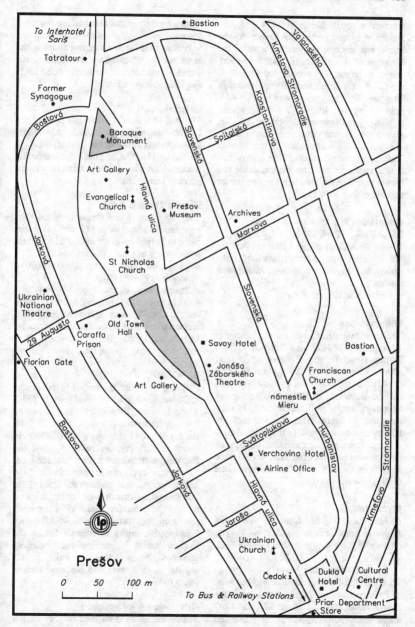

Prešov

0    50    100 m

received a royal charter in 1374 and, like Bardejov to the north and Košice to the south, was once an eastern bulwark of the Kingdom of Hungary. In June 1919 a Slovak Soviet Republic was proclaimed at Prešov, the result of a larger socialist revolution in Hungary. This movement was quickly suppressed by the big landowners, whose holdings were threatened, and in 1920 the region was incorporated into Czechoslovakia. Prešov is the centre of the Slovak Ukraine, the breadbasket of Czechoslovakia. It is a more central base for exploring the region than Košice, although there are fewer cultural offerings.

### Orientation & Information
Hlavná ulica, Prešov's central square, is a 15-minute walk north up Masarykova from the adjacent bus and train stations (take trolley bus No 4 or 6 to/from 'železničná stanica').

Čedok is at Hlavná ulica 1.

### Things to See
The most imposing structure in the city is 14th century **St Nicholas Church** with its Gothic structure and Baroque organ and altars. Behind it is the **Evangelical Church** (1642). To one side is the **Prešov Museum** (closed on weekend afternoons and every Monday), inside Rákóczi House, Hlavná ulica 86. In addition to the archaeology, history and natural history displays, there's a large fire-fighting exhibit. The Slovak Soviet Republic was declared on 16 June 1919 from the balcony of the **old town hall** (1533), Hlavná ulica 73.

### Places to Stay
*Dukla Hotel*, Hlavná ulica 2, a five-storey high-rise hotel next to the Cultural Centre, charges US$6/8 single/double without bath, US$8/12 with bath, or US$21 for a suite.

The old *Verchovina Hotel*, Hlavná ulica 26, costs US$4/6 single/double without bath.

Perhaps the best place to stay at is the *Savoy Hotel*, Hlavná ulica 50 (US$4/6/7 single/double/triple or US$9 for a five-bed

room), an elegant old hotel facing the main square.

Prešov's tallest and fanciest hotel is the eight-storey, B*-category *Interhotel Šariš*, which is just north of the centre (US$11/21 single/double with bath).

### Entertainment
The new *Cultural Centre* is opposite the Dukla Hotel, and the *Divadlo Jonáša Záborského* (Jonáša Záborského Theatre) is beside the Savoy Hotel. Also check the *Ukrainian National Theatre* (1894), Jarková 77, for plays in Ukrainian.

### Getting There & Away
The daily Cracovia Express between Kraków and Budapest stops at Prešov. Another route to Poland involves taking a local train from Prešov to Plavec (54 km) on the Polish border, and then a connecting train to Muszyna in Poland itself.

Trains north to Bardejov (45 km) and south to Košice (33 km) are frequent enough, but bus travel is faster on these routes. You'll want to take a bus to go to Spišské Podhradie, Levoča and Vysoké Tatry.

## BARDEJOV
Bardejov received municipal privileges in 1320 and became a free royal town in 1376. Trade between Poland and Russia passed through the town and in the 15th century the Bardejov merchants grew rich. After an abortive 17th century revolt against the Habsburgs, Bardejov's fortunes declined, but the medieval town survived. In late 1944 heavy fighting took place at the Dukla Pass into Poland, 54 km north-east of Bardejov on the road to Rzeszów. Since 1954 the town plan and the former Gothic-Renaissance houses of wealthy merchants lining the sloping central square have been carefully preserved. Much of the town walls, including the moat, towers and bastions, remain intact today.

### Orientation & Information
The new combined bus and railway station

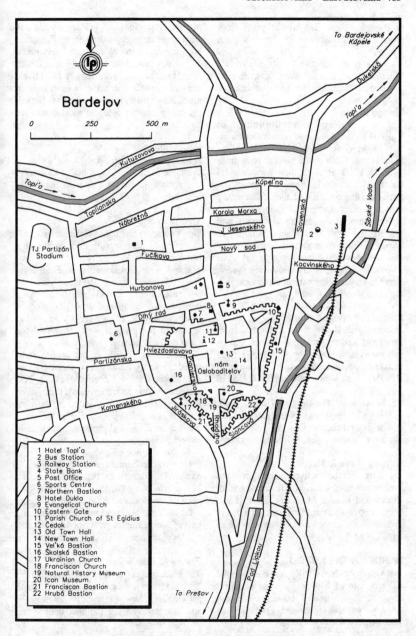

**Bardejov**

0      250      500 m

1 Hotel Topl'a
2 Bus Station
3 Railway Station
4 State Bank
5 Post Office
6 Sports Centre
7 Northern Bastion
8 Hotel Dukla
9 Evangelical Church
10 Eastern Gate
11 Parish Church of St Egidius
12 Čedok
13 Old Town Hall
14 New Town Hall
15 Vel'ká Bastion
16 Školská Bastion
17 Ukrainian Church
18 Franciscan Church
19 Natural History Museum
20 Icon Museum
21 Franciscan Bastion
22 Hrubá Bastion

at Bardejov is a five-minute walk from námestie Osloboditeľov, the town's main square.

Čedok is at námestie Osloboditeľov 46. The post office and the State Bank are both on the street running north from Hotel Dukla.

## Things to See

The 14th century **Parish Church of St Egidius** is one of the most remarkable buildings in the country, complete with no less than 11 tall Gothic altarpieces, built from 1460 to 1510, all with their own original paintings and sculptures! The structural purity of the church and the 15th century bronze baptismal font are striking.

Near this church is the **old town hall** (1509), the first Renaissance building in Slovakia. Two **museums** (closed Sunday and Monday) face one another on ulica Rhodyho at the southern end of the square. One has an excellent natural history exhibit, the other a collection of icons.

## Places to Stay

You can visit Bardejov on a day trip from Prešov or Košice, though the functional B-category *Hotel Dukla* (built in 1947), right next to the parish church, is OK for one night (US$5/7 single/double without bath, US$10 with bath).

The smaller C-category *Hotel Topla*, Fučíkova 25, about six blocks west of the bus station, is a bit cheaper than the Hotel Dukla, but there's a rowdy beer hall just downstairs.

## Getting There & Away

Local trains run between Bardejov and Prešov (45 km), but if you're coming from Prešov and Košice, buses are faster. If you want to go to Vysoké Tatry, look for a bus to Poprad-Tatry; some buses continue as far as Bratislava.

## BARDEJOVSKÉ KÚPELE

Just six km north of Bardejov is Bardejovské Kúpele, one of Slovakia's most beautiful spas, where diseases of the alimentary and respiratory tracts are treated. From the late 18th century, Bardejovské Kúpele was one of the most popular spas in Hungary and was frequented throughout the year by European high society. After WW II the Communist authorities rebuilt the spa, and, since health resorts such as this were heavily subsidised, the stores, cafés and services here are still much better than those of most other Slovak towns. In summer many musical events are held here.

## Information

A local map showing hiking trails is usually available at the bookshop below Čedok, in the shopping arcade opposite the Hotel Mineral.

## Things to See & Do

Don't come to Bardejovské Kúpele expecting to enjoy a hot-spring bath because it's impossible unless you've booked a programme with Slovakoterma in Bratislava. Everyone is welcome to partake of the drinking cure, however, and crowds of locals constantly pace up and down the modern **colonnade** (1972), where an unending supply of hot mineral water streams from eight different springs (bring your own cup).

Near the colonnade is a **museum** dedicated to local history and ethnography. Alongside this is Czechoslovakia's best **skanzen**, a fine collection of old farm buildings, rustic houses and wooden churches brought here from villages all over Slovakia. Both museum and skanzen are open daily except Monday all year.

In the absence of public baths, the best reason to spend a night or two at the spa is to explore the hiking paths through the forested hills surrounding Bardejovské Kúpele. One marked trail leads to the summit of Magura (900 metres). Walks along these paths are part of the treatment prescribed for patients but they're a delight for the healthy too.

## Places to Stay & Eat

The modern eight-storey *Hotel Minerál* near the bus station has singles/doubles with bath for US$7/11. Most of the other hotels at the spa are reserved for patients undergoing medical treatment.

## Getting There & Away

There's no train station, but Bardejovské Kúpele is connected to Bardejov by the city buses No 1, 2, 6, 7 and 10. Some long-distance buses for places as far away as Bratislava begin here.

## KOŠICE

Košice (Kaschau) is the second-largest city in Slovakia and capital of the eastern portion of the republic. Thousands of Gypsies live in Košice and the historic and ethnic influence of nearby Hungary is strong. The Transylvanian prince Ferenc Rákóczi II had his head quarters at Košice during the Hungarian War of Independence against the Habsburgs from 1703 to 1711. From 21 February to 21 April 1945, Košice was the capital of liberated Czechoslovakia, and on 5 April 1945 the Košice Government Programme was announced, outlining the future socialist development of the country.

Although now a major steel-making city with vast new residential districts built by the Communists, there is much in the old town to interest visitors. Churches and museums abound, and there's an active State Theatre. The city is a good base for excursions to other East Slovak towns. Daily trains between Kraków and Budapest stop here, making Košice the perfect beginning or end to a visit to Czechoslovakia.

## Orientation

The adjacent bus and train stations are just east of the old town, a five-minute walk down Mlynská ulica. This street will bring you into námestie Slobody, which becomes Hlavná ulica both north and south of the square. Much of your time in Košice will be spent on this colourful street.

## Information

Čedok is in the Slovan Hotel, Rooseveltova 1, and CKM Student Travel is at Hlavná ulica 82. There is a municipal information office at Hlavná ulica 105 next to the Prior Department Store.

There's no Hungarian or Polish consulate

in Košice, so be sure to get your onward visa beforehand in Prague or Bratislava.

## Things to See

One of the major sights is the **Cathedral of St Elizabeth** (1345-1508), a magnificent late-Gothic edifice a five-minute walk west of the railway station. In a crypt on the left side of the nave is the tomb of Ferenc Rákóczi (tickets are sold at the adjacent Urban Tower).

Beside the cathedral is the 14th century **Urban tower**, now a museum of metalwork. On the opposite side of the cathedral is the 14th century **St Michael's Chapel** and the **Košice Programme House**, Hlavná ulica 27, where the 1945 National Front programme was proclaimed. The building dates from 1779 and is still an active political centre.

Most of Košice's other historic sites are north along Hlavná ulica. The **Art History Museum** at Hlavná ulica 40 has a small but outstanding collection of artworks from the Romanesque to the contemporary, with large photos of corresponding architectural monuments tastefully mounted alongside the exhibits. In the centre of the nearby square is the ornate **State Theatre** (1899). Beside it at Hlavná ulica 59 is the Rococo former **town hall** (1780), now a cinema.

In the square to the north of the theatre is a large **plague column** (1723) and nearby at Hlavná ulica 72, the **East Slovak Gallery**, which has changing art shows. The Jesuit and Franciscan churches are on the opposite side of the square. Farther north at Hlavná ulica 88 is the **Slovak Technical Museum** (closed weekends).

The **East Slovak Museum** (1912) is on námestie Maratónu mieru at the northern end of Hlavná ulica. The 1st and 2nd floors are dedicated to archaeology and prehistory. Don't miss the Košice Gold Treasure in the basement, a hoard of over 3000 gold coins dating from the 15th to the 18th centuries and discovered by chance in 1935. In the park behind the museum building is an old wooden church.

Walk back along Hlavná ulica to the State

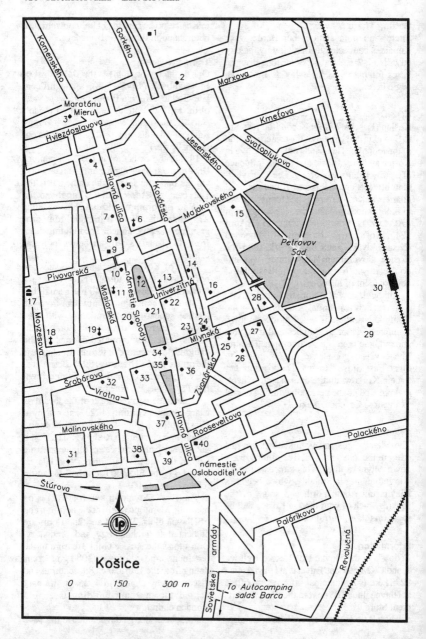

Košice

0    150    300 m

■ **PLACES TO STAY**

1 Hutník Hotel
9 Tatra Hotel
24 Imperial Hotel
27 Hotel Europa
40 Slovan Hotel

▼ **PLACES TO EAT**

23 Grill Dětva

**OTHER**

2 Dom kultúry VSZ
3 East Slovak Museum
4 State Bank
5 Prior Department Store
6 Franciscan Church
7 Slovak Technical Museum
8 CKM Student Travel
10 East Slovak Gallery
11 Ursuline Convent
12 Plague Column
13 Jesuit Church

14 Miklušova Väznica
15 Swimming Pool
16 Executioner's Bastion
17 Post Office
18 Ukrainian Church
19 Dominican Church
20 Art History Museum
21 State Theatre
22 Former Town Hall
25 Evangelical Church
26 Former Synagogue
28 Jakub's Palace
29 Bus Station
30 Railway Station
31 Dom Umenia Concert Hall
32 Art Gallery
33 Tatratour
34 Urban Tower
35 Cathedral of St Elizabeth
36 Košice Programme House
37 Forgach Palace
38 Thália Hungarian Theatre
39 ČSA Airline Office
40 Čedok

Theatre and take the narrow Univerzitná ulica beside the Jesuit church east to the **Miklušova Väznica**, ulica Pri Miklušovej Väznici 10. This connected pair of 16th century houses once served as a prison equipped with medieval torture chambers and cells. If the houses are closed, ask for the keys at the **Zoology Museum** beside the nearby church. The Zoology Museum is housed in the Executioner's Bastion, part of Košice's 15th century fortifications. The old maps and small model of Košice upstairs in the Miklušova Väznica will bring the town's history to life.

A large street market operates along ulica Cyrilometodejská from the Ukrainian to the Dominican churches.

Most museums and galleries in Košice are closed on Sunday afternoon and Monday.

**Places to Stay**

Because Košice is not a big tourist centre, hotel prices are much lower than those in Bratislava. Čedok in the *Slovan Hotel* will find a hotel room for you but has no private rooms.

CKM Student Travel, Hlavná ulica 82, is the place to enquire about summer youth hostels.

**Camping** South of the city is the *Autocamping salaš Barca* (☎ 58309). Take a tram south on trieda Sovietskej armády from the Slovan Hotel to the overpass, then walk west on Alejová (the Rožňava Highway) for about 500 metres till you see the camping ground on the left. It is open from 15 April to 30 September and there are bungalows (US$8) and tent space (US$1 per person, US$1 per tent).

**Hotels** The recently renovated *Hotel Europa*, a grand old three-storey building just across the park from the railway station, costs US$6/9 single/double with shared bath.

The B*-category *Imperiál Hotel*, Mlynská ulica 16, is close to the station (US$8/12 single/double with shared bath). Bright lights in the corridors shine into the rooms through windows above the doors.

The old C-category *Hotel Tatra*, at Pivovarská 1, has singles/doubles without bath for US$8/11, which is not good value compared to the other hotels.

Apart from these places there are two high-rise beauties: the 12-storey, B*-category *Hutník Hotel* at Tyršovo nábr 6 (US$8/11 single/ double with bath), and the 14-storey, A*-category *Slovan Hotel* at Hlavná ulica 1 (US$17/27 single/double with bath).

### Places to Eat

One of the cheapest and best places to eat at is *Grill Dětva*, Mlynská ulica 6. You'll be served good wholesome meals promptly. Something similar is available at the *Dietná Restaurant*, Hlavná ulica 74, and the draught beer compensates for this place's scruffier appearance and erratic service.

The *Zdroj Grill*, Hlavná ulica 81, offers succulent barbecued chicken which you eat standing up. The *Veverická Grill*, Hlavná ulica 95, is good for grilled meats.

Better restaurants for more leisurely dining include the *Zlatý ducat*, Hlavná ulica 16, and the *Yalta*, Hlavná ulica 69 (both upstairs). The *Miškolc Hungarian Restaurant*, Hlavná ulica 65, features a bright, attractive décor, an extensive menu, good food and a relaxed atmosphere – recommended. It's in Levoča House, a 16th century warehouse reconditioned into a restaurant, café and nightclub.

*Aida Espresso* on Pivovarská ulica, behind the East Slovak Gallery, has the best ice cream in town. On Sunday all but the Dietná and hotel restaurants may be shut.

### Entertainment

The *State Theatre* on námestie Slobody is currently closed for renovations; in the meantime performances are being held at *Dom kultúry VSŽ* near the Hutník Hotel.

The *Thália Hungarian Theatre* and the *State Philharmonic Dom Umenia* are both in the south-west corner of the old town, but performances are only held once or twice a week.

You can buy theatre tickets from the office in the passage at Hlavná ulica 76, opposite the Zlatá Hus Restaurant and the Cultural Information Office, Mlynská 21.

### Getting There & Away

Košice receives all trains between Moscow and Prague. Daily express trains between Budapest and Kraków pass through Košice, making access to Hungary and Poland easy. For information about local trains to Poland, see the section on Prešov.

Local trains run the 88 km from Košice to Miskolc, Hungary, via Hidasnémeti every morning and afternoon. This is an easy way to cross the border as no reservations are required. If you take the morning train, get a ticket right through to Budapest (if you're going there!) as you will only have five minutes to change trains at Miskolc and no time to buy another ticket.

You could also walk into Hungary by taking a local train from Košice to Slovenské Nové Mesto (one hour, 62 km). Here the Slovak Railway Station is right at the highway border crossing into Satoraljaujhely, Hungary, where you can catch a Hungarian train to Sarospatak or Miskolc.

Overnight sleepers are available to/from Košice and Prague (708 km), Brno (493 km), Bratislava (445 km), Děčín (807 km) and Karlovy Vary (897 km). Daytime express trains connect Košice to Prague (via Poprad-Tatry and Žilina) and Bratislava (via Banská Bystrica and Žilina). Čedok reserves sleepers and couchettes and sells international train tickets.

For shorter trips to Prešov (36 km), Bardejov and Spišské Podhradie, you're better off taking a bus.

# Hungary

Though until recently a Communist state, Hungary has long been the gateway to Eastern Europe. Only a short hop from Vienna, this romantic land of Franz Liszt, Béla Bartók, Gypsy music and the blue Danube welcomes visitors. You'll be enchanted by Budapest, once a great imperial city, and Pécs, the warm heart of the south. The fine wines, fiery paprika, sweet violins, good theatre and colourful folklore will induce you to extend your stay. The friendly Magyars are as inviting as delicious goulash soup.

The booming European Hungary of the 1990s comes as a bit of a shock to English-speakers whose image of Hungary often dates back to the repression and bleak poverty of 1956. Today's prosperous modern cities bustling with well-dressed, purposeful inhabitants are a far cry from the grey façades and the leaden-faced peasants queuing for bread in old newsreels. Here you can have all the glamour and excitement of Western Europe at prices you can still afford. It's just the place to kick off an Eastern European trip.

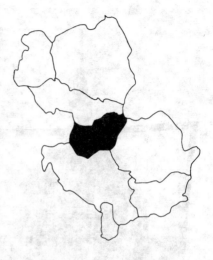

## Facts about the Country

### HISTORY

The Celts occupied Hungary in the final centuries BC but were themselves conquered by the Romans in 10 AD. From the 1st to the 5th centuries all of Hungary west and south of the Danube (the area today known as Transdanubia) was included in the Roman province of Pannonia. The Roman legion stationed at Aquincum (Budapest) guarded the north-eastern frontier of the Empire. The epicurean Romans planted the first vineyards in Hungary and developed the thermal baths. In 408 the West Goths invaded the area, followed in 451 by Attila's Huns, then by the Lombards and Avars. From 795 Pannonia was part of the Carolingian empire.

In 896 seven Magyar tribes under Khan Árpád swept in from beyond the Volga River and occupied the Danube Basin. They terrorised Europe with raids as far as France and Italy until they converted to Roman Catholicism in the late 10th century. Hungary's first king and patron saint, Stephen I (Szent István), was crowned on Christmas Day in the year 1000, marking the foundation of the Hungarian state. After the Tatars sacked Hungary in 1241, many cities were fortified.

Feudal Hungary was a large and powerful state which included Transylvania (now in Romania) and Croatia (now in Yugoslavia). The medieval capital shifted from Székes-fehérvár to Esztergom, Buda and Visegrád. Hungary's Golden Bull (1222) enumerating the rights of the nobility is just seven years younger than the Magna Carta. Universities were founded in Pécs (1367) and Buda (1389).

In 1456 at Nándorfehérvár (present-day Belgrade) Hungarians under János Hunyadi

The parliament building on the bank of the Danube in Budapest is one of Europe's most stunning works of neo-Gothic architecture

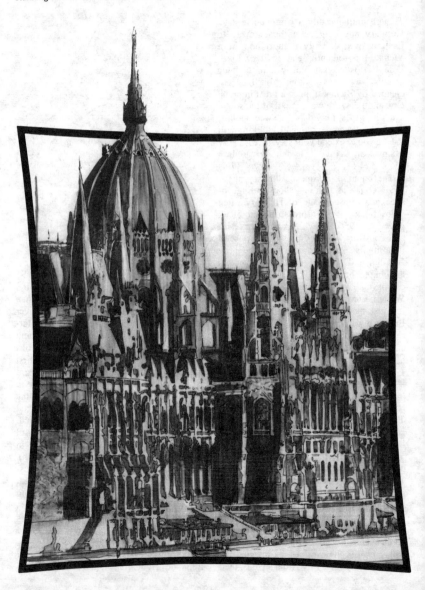

stopped a Turkish advance into Hungary. Hungary experienced a brief flowering of the Renaissance during a Golden Age under Hunyadi's son, Matthias Corvinus, who ruled from 1458 to 1490. In 1514 a peasant army that had assembled for a crusade against the Turks turned on the landowners. The serfs were eventually suppressed and their leader, György Dózsa, was executed, but Hungary was seriously weakened. In 1526 the Hungarian army was defeated by the Turks at Mohács and by 1541 the Turks had occupied Buda.

For the next century the Kingdom of Hungary was reduced to a Habsburg-dominated buffer strip between Balaton Lake and Vienna with its seat at Pozsony (Bratislava). Continued Hungarian resistance to the Turks resulted in heroic battles at Kőszeg (1532), Eger (1552) and Szigetvár (1566). Though a Turkish vassal, the Principality of Transylvania was never fully integrated into the Ottoman Empire. When the Turks were finally evicted in 1686 through the combined efforts of the Austrian and Polish armies, Hungary was subjected to Habsburg domination.

From 1703 to 1711 Ferenc Rákóczi II, Prince of Transylvania, led the War of Independence against the Austrians, which was eventually overcome through force of numbers. During and after this war, the Habsburgs demolished any medieval fortifications which had survived the Turkish period in order to deny their use to Hungarian rebels. Apart from the destruction they wrought, all the Turks created were a few bath houses in Buda and a couple of mosques in Pécs.

Hungary never fully recovered from these disasters. Most of the country's medieval monuments had been destroyed, and from the 18th century onwards Hungary had to be rebuilt almost from scratch.

The liberal-democratic revolution of 1848 led by Lajos Kossuth and the poet Sándor Petőfi against the Habsburgs demanded freedom for the serfs and independence. Although defeated in 1849, the uprising shook the oligarchy. In 1867 a compromise was struck between the Austrian capitalists and Hungarian landowners and the dual Austro-Hungarian monarchy was formed. Although this partnership stimulated industrial development, it proved unfortunate in the long run as Hungary came to be viewed by its neighbours as a tool of Habsburg oppression. After WW I Hungary became independent from Austria but lost two-thirds of its territory and 60% of its population to Czechoslovakia, Romania and Yugoslavia. The loss of Transylvania fuels resentment against neighbouring Romania to this day.

In August 1919, a brief 133-day socialist government led by Béla Kun was overthrown by counter-revolutionary elements and thousands were killed, imprisoned or forced to flee the country. In March 1920, Admiral Miklós Horthy established a reactionary regime which lasted 25 years. Before WW II Hungary was an agricultural country with a third of the farmland owned by a thousand magnates while two million peasants had no land at all.

In 1941 the Hungarians' desire to recover their country's 'lost territories' drew them into war alongside the Nazis. Nearly 500,000 Jewish Hungarians were murdered during this senseless conflict. When Horthy tried to make a separate peace with the Allies in October 1944, the occupying Germans ousted him and put the fascist Arrow Cross Party in power. (Horthy died in exile in Portugal in 1957.) In December 1944 a provisional government was established at Debrecen and by 4 April 1945 all of Hungary had been liberated by the Soviet army.

## Post WW II

After the fighting died down, the large estates were divided among the peasantry and the means of production nationalised. In 1948 the Communist and Social Democratic parties merged to become the Hungarian Workers' Party. During the early 1950s, Hungary followed the Stalinist line of collectivised agriculture and heavy industry. In February 1956 Nikita Khrushchev denounced Stalin at a closed session of the 20th

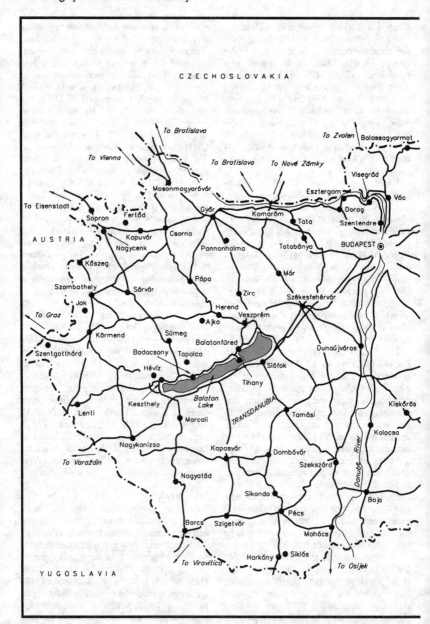

Hungary

0    25    50 km

Party Congress in Moscow and, amid increasing expectations of wide-sweeping reform and democratisation, the hardline party leader Mátyás Rákosi was forced to resign in July.

On 23 October 1956 Soviet troops participated in the suppression of student demonstrations in Budapest, leading to a general rebellion. That evening Imre Nagy, a reform-minded Communist, was made prime minister. The disorders spread and on 1 November Nagy announced that Hungary would leave the Warsaw Pact and become neutral. This led to a full-scale Soviet invasion on 4 November. Fighting continued until 11 November and 200,000 Hungarians fled to neighbouring Austria. The American CIA and Radio Free Europe openly encouraged the uprising, then stood by as it was crushed. Britain and France were in no position to object as their troops were intervening at Suez at that very moment. Nagy was arrested and deported to Romania where he was executed two years later. Most of the other prisoners were released from 1961 onwards. In 1989 Nagy was officially rehabilitated and reburied in Budapest.

After the revolt, the Hungarian Socialist Workers' Party was reorganised and János Kádár took over as president. In 1961 Kádár turned an old Stalinist slogan around to become, 'He who is not against us is with us,' to symbolise the new social unity. After 1968 Hungary abandoned strict central economic planning and control for a limited market system based on incentives and efficiency. In a way Kádár was the grandfather of *perestroika* and the one who initiated the reform process sweeping Eastern Europe today. His innovative 'goulash Communism' is discussed in the Economy section in this chapter.

In the 1970s and 1980s Hungary balanced its free-wheeling economic programme with a foreign policy which consistently reflected that of the Soviet Union. This was the exact opposite of neighbouring Romania, where an independent foreign policy was combined with orthodox 1950s internal central planning. By remaining a dependable Soviet ally during those years, Hungary was able to lay quietly the groundwork for the market economy of today.

In June 1987 Károly Grósz took over as premier and in May 1988 as party secretary general after Kádár retired. Under Grósz Hungary began moving towards full democracy, and beginning in January 1988 Hungarians were allowed to travel abroad freely, wherever and whenever they desired. Change accelerated under the impetus of reformers such as Imre Pozsgay and Rezso Nyers.

At a Party congress in October 1989 the Communists agreed to give up their monopoly on power, paving the way for free elections on 25 March 1990. The Party's name was changed from the Hungarian Socialist Workers' Party to simply the Hungarian Socialist Party and a new programme advocated democracy and a free-market economy. This was not enough to shake off the legacy of four decades of autocratic rule, however, and the 1990 elections were won by the centrist Democratic Forum, which advocated a gradual transition towards capitalism. The right-wing Alliance of Free Democrats which had called for much faster change came second and the Socialist Party (which had 870,992 members in 1985) trailed far behind. As Gorbachev looked on, Hungary changed political systems with scarcely a murmur.

## GEOGRAPHY

Hungary occupies the Carpathian Basin in the very centre of Eastern Europe and is not part of the Balkans. The 417-km Hungarian reach of the Danube River cuts through a southern extension of the Carpathian Mountains at the majestic Danube Bend north of Budapest. The Danube divides Hungary's 93,030 sq km in two: to the east is the Great Plain (Nagyalföld), to the west, Transdanubia (Dunántúl). The 579 km of the Hungarian portion of the Tisza River crosses the Great Plain about 100 km east of the Danube.

Two-thirds of Hungary is less than 200 metres above sea level. The almost treeless Hungarian *puszta* (another name for the

Great Plain) between the Danube and Romania is a harbinger of the steppes of the Ukraine. Balaton Lake (598 sq km) between the Danube and Austria reaches only 11½ metres at its deepest point. The lake's average depth is three to four metres and the waters warm quickly in summer. The 'mountains' of Hungary are actually hills as they seldom reach 1000 metres (whereas mountains in Czechoslovakia and Romania pass 2000 metres). The highest peak is Kékes (1015 metres) in the Mátra Range north-east of Budapest.

There are four national parks. The two on the Great Plain, Hortobágy and Kiskunság, preserve the environment of the open puszta while Bükk National Park north of Eger protects the Bükk Mountains, Hungary's largest continuous mountain range. North again is Aggtelek National Park with the country's largest caves.

## ECONOMY

In a way Hungary was lucky not to have had the natural resources of Poland and Czechoslovakia, because without vast reserves of hard coal and iron ore the Communists were never able to concentrate industrial development in heavy industry. The only metallic ore found here in significant quantities is bauxite. After the 1956 debacle, the emphasis shifted to light industry which produced consumer goods, the results of which can be seen today.

Hungary was the first Eastern European country to move successfully towards an open marketplace. The economic reforms proposed by Mikhail Gorbachev in the late 1980s bear a certain resemblance to those initiated by János Kádár two decades earlier. Kádár's 'New Economic Mechanism' combined central government planning with a market economy. Industrial plants and companies remained under state ownership but management was allowed wide discretionary power. The decentralised enterprises were required to compete and make a profit and those which consistently lost money were required to declare bankruptcy.

The competition resulted in an abundance of quality consumer goods. Prices were determined by actual costs or supply and demand rather than by state edicts. Numerous small, privately owned businesses, many of them bakeries, boutiques and restaurants, have functioned for years. Many Hungarians hold after-hours jobs to supplement their incomes and taxation of this 'second economy' is an important source of government income. In 1988 Hungary became the first Eastern European country to institute income tax. Just over 30% of the labour force is employed in government and services, 31.4% in industry, 18.9% in agriculture, 10.5% in trade and 7.1% in construction.

Agriculture was collectivised in Hungary from 1959 to 1961. Farming is cooperative and the country is a world leader in per capita grain and meat production. Hungary is self-sufficient in food, the main crops being barley, corn, potatoes, sugar beets and wheat. Fifty-four per cent of the land is arable, 18% is forest and woodland, 3% is taken up with permanent crops, and 14% with meadows and pastures. Only 2% of the land is irrigated.

Half of Hungary's industry is in Budapest and since 1945 industrial production has increased 12-fold. Almost half the national income is now obtained from exports. Ten per cent of the buses exported worldwide are produced in Hungary. Some famous Hungarian products include Ikarus buses, Herend and Zsolnay porcelain, Fabulon and Helia-D cosmetics, Elegant trademark clothing, Elzett locks and padlocks, Gamma nuclear instruments, Ganz electric current meters and cranes, Ganz-Mavag locomotives, Raba articulated vehicles, Lehel refrigerators, Tokay Aszú wine, Herz and Pick salami, Mino shoes, Taurus rubber mattresses, Pálma rubber products, Tungsram lamps, Biogal pharmaceutical products, Medicor medical instruments and Videoton electronic devices. Since 1990 the stocks of some of these companies have been traded on the new Hungarian stock market.

The economy is not all sunshine, however. Problems facing Hungary include shrinking foreign markets for the country's goods, a US$20 billion hard-currency debt to Western creditors and 30% inflation. The economic changes of the past few years have resulted in declining living standards. The first homeless tramps have already appeared on the streets of Budapest and public drunkenness has increased sharply. Pornography, which was previously banned, has become readily available.

## POPULATION & PEOPLE

Neither a Slavonic nor a Germanic people, the Finno-Ugrian Hungarians were the last major ethnic group to arrive in Europe during the period of the great migrations. Some 10.7 million Hungarians live within their country, another five million abroad. The 1.7 million Hungarians in Transylvania constitute the largest national minority in Europe and large numbers of Hungarians live in Czechoslovakia, Yugoslavia, the Soviet Union, the USA and Canada. Minorities within Hungary include Germans (1.6%), Slovaks (1.1%), South Slavs (0.3%) and Romanians (0.2%). Hungarian Gypsies live mostly in the north-eastern corner of the country.

Religion-wise, 67.5% of the population is Catholic, 20% Calvinist and 5% Lutheran. Half of the people live in cities, a fifth of them in Budapest. Hungary has the world's highest rate of abortion and the second highest rate of suicide. Yet Hungary also has more poets per head than any country in Europe; 99% of the population is literate.

Hungary is in a difficult position as regards the thousands of Romanian refugees flooding into the country. The Romanians selling handicrafts on the street in Budapest are quite obvious from their colourful peasant attire. Unlike Czechoslovakia and Austria which try to stop the Romanians at their borders, Hungary must treat them with care out of consideration for the large Hungarian minority in Romania. Now that Hungary has drastically reduced its border surveillance, neighbouring Austria has been forced to add thousands of troops to its border controls to stem the tidal wave of Arabs, Turks and Romanians trying to enter Austria illegally from Hungary.

## ARTS

Although the Renaissance flourished briefly in the late 15th century, Hungary was isolated from the mainstream of European cultural development during the century and a half of Turkish rule which began in the middle of the 15th century. Then came domination by the Austrian Habsburgs until 1918 and, more recently, external interference from Nazi Germany and the USSR. Against this background, it's not surprising that Hungarian writers have struggled against oppression.

Hungary's greatest poet, Sándor Petőfi (1823-49), castigated both the privileges of the nobility and the plight of the common people. His poem *Talpra magyar* (Rise, Hungarian) became the anthem of the 1848 revolution in which he actively fought and died. Petőfi used the simple style of Hungarian folk songs to express subtle feelings and ideals.

An early colleague of Petőfi, novelist Mór Jókai (1825-1904), wrote historical works like *The Golden Age of Transylvania* (1852) and *Turkish World in Hungary* (1853) which are still widely read. The visual equivalent of Jókai's writings are the realist paintings of village life by the artist Mihály Munkácsy (1844-1900).

Hungary's finest 20th century lyric poet, Endre Ady (1877-1919), attacked the narrow materialism of the Hungary of his time provoking a storm of reaction from right-wing nationalists. Later Ady went on to describe the pain and suffering of war. The work of novelist Zsigmond Móricz (1879-1942) portrays the human conflicts of provincial life, and that of poet Attila József (1905-37) expresses the torments faced by people in the technological age. A leading contemporary Hungarian writer is the novelist György Konrád (1933- ). Anything from his pen which you can find in English would be worth picking up.

## Music

Hungarian music has absorbed influences as diverse as German religious and classical music and Turkish fife and drum. The famous Hungarian pianist and composer Franz Liszt (Ferenc Liszt in Hungarian) (1811-86) was fascinated by the music of the Gypsies and even wrote a book on the subject. His *Hungarian Rhapsodies* pulse with the wild rhythms of Hungarian Gypsy music.

Franz Liszt

Opera composer Ferenc Erkel (1810-93) attempted to transform Italian opera into a Hungarian operatic style through the use of the *verbunkos*, a Gypsy dance based on Western European dance music which he thought was Hungarian. In his opera *Hunyadi László* (1844), Erkel utilised the *csárdás*, the national dance of Hungary, which begins slowly but soon picks up as the couples whirl to syncopated rhythms. Erkel's 1861 opera *Bánk bán* captured the fiery nationalism of his time by portraying a 13th century revolt against the queen's hated foreign court.

Like Liszt and Erkel, many of today's tourists in Hungary incorrectly assume that the romantic Gypsy violinists heard in local restaurants are playing Hungarian folk songs or have a music of their own when in fact they play mostly 19th century ballads and art songs written by Hungarian nobles. Béla Bartók (1881-1945) and his colleague Zoltán Kodály (1882-1967) went beyond this urban 'Gypsy music' to collect genuine folk music in remote villages. Bartók's writings on Hungarian, Romanian, Slovakian and Serbo-Croatian folk music are basic works of musical ethnology and both Kodály and Bartók integrated Hungarian folk songs and melodies into their own compositions.

One professional Gypsy group which does perform authentic Gypsy songs in the Gypsy dialect is Kalyi Jag ('Black Fire') from Szabolcs-Szatmár county in north-east Hungary. They use nonconventional instruments such as the water can and spoons alongside the double bass, oral bass, guitar and percussion in their stick dances and lyric songs.

Hungarian folk music is played on instruments such as bagpipes, the hurdy-gurdy, bombard, tamboura (lute), flute and zither. In times gone by villages which were too poor to buy an organ often used bagpipes during church services. Today this music has largely disappeared in its place of origin as the lives of the peasants have been irrevocably changed. In Transylvania, however, Hungarian folk music has partly survived as the Hungarian minority sought to preserve its identity by clinging to its traditional folk culture.

The revival of folk music in Hungary in the 1970s drew inspiration from Transylvania and a journey there became *de rigueur* for all aspiring Hungarian folk musicians who later played at *táncház* (dance houses). A recent album, *Blues for Transylvania*, by Hungary's top folk group, Muzsikas, includes songs about conditions in Romania and the insecure position of the Hungarians living there.

## LANGUAGE

The Hungarians speak Magyar, a language that only they understand. Of the languages of Europe only Finnish and Estonian are related. Though many Hungarians understand German, it is less common for them to understand English. As usual, if you have trouble making yourself understood, try writing it out. Some useful words to learn are: *utca* (street), *körút* (boulevard), *út* (road), *tér* (square), *útja* (avenue), *sétány* (promenade) and *híd* (bridge). Hungarians put surnames before given names.

The Hungarian alphabet has 40 letters or combinations of letters. In addition the Roman letters 'q', 'w', 'x' and 'y' are used in foreign words. Hungarian words are pronounced as they're written, with each letter pronounced separately; there are no silent letters or diphthongs. An acute accent lengthens an unaccented vowel, and a double acute accent lengthens a vowel with a dieresis (for example, ű is a long version of ü). A plural is indicated by a final 'k' rather than an 's'. *Nem* indicates a negative. The stress is always on the first syllable.

Spoken Hungarian contains sounds that don't exist in English and it's beyond the scope of this book to attempt to cover them. What you do need to do is pronounce c as the ts in hats, cs as the ch in chair, dz as the ds in roads, dzs as the j in jump, gy as the d in duty, ny as the n in onion, s as the sh in shoe, sz as the s in see, ty as the first t in student, zs as the s in usual and both j and ly as the y in yet.

### Greetings & Civilities

hello
  *jó napot kivánok* (formal)
hello
  *szia* (informal)
goodbye
  *viszontlátásra*
good morning
  *jó reggelt*
good evening
  *jó estét*
please
  *kérem*
thank you
  *köszönöm*
I am sorry/Forgive me.
  *Bocsánat.*

excuse me
  *elnézést*
You are very kind.
  *Nagyon kedves.*
yes
  *igen*
no
  *nem*

### Small Talk

Do you speak English?
  *Beszél angolul?*
I don't understand.
  *Nem értem.*
Could you write it down?
  *Kérem, irja le.*
Where do you live?
  *Hol lakik ön?*
What work do you do?
  *Mi a foglalkozása?*
I am a student.
  *Diák vagyok.*
I am very happy.
  *Nagyon boldog vagyok.*

### Accommodation

youth hostel
  *ifjúsági szálló*
camping ground
  *kemping*
private room
  *fizetővendégszoba*
How much is it?
  *Mibe kerül?*
Is that the price per person?
  *Ez az ára személyenként?*
Is that the total price?
  *Ez a teljes ár?*
Are there any extra charges?
  *Kell ezért plusszt fizetnem?*
Can I pay with local currency?
  *Fizethetek helyi pénznemben?*
Where is there a cheaper hotel?
  *Hol van egy olcsóbb szálloda?*
Should I make a reservation?
  *Szükséges a helyfoglalás?*
single room
  *egyágyas szoba*
double room
  *kétágyas szoba*

It is very noisy.
*Nagyon zajos.*
Where is the toilet?
*Hol van a mosdó?*

## Getting Around

What time does it leave?
*Mikor indul?*
When is the first bus?
*Mikor indul az első autóbusz?*
When is the last bus?
*Mikor van az utolsó autóbusz?*
When is the next bus?
*Mikor indul a következő autóbusz?*
That's too soon.
*Az túl korai.*
When is the next one after that?
*Mikor van a következő azután?*
How long does the trip take?
*Mennyi ideig tart a kirándulás?*
arrival
*érkezés*
departure
*indulás*
timetable
*menetrend*
Where is the bus stop?
*Hol van az autóbuszmegálló?*
Where is the railway station?
*Hol van a pályaudvar?*
Where is the taxi stand?
*Hol van a taxiállomás?*
Where is the left-luggage room?
*Hol van a csomagmegőrző?*

## Around Town

Just a minute.
*Rögtön.*
Where is...?
*Hol van...?*
the bank
*bank*
the post office
*posta*
the telephone centre
*telefon központ*
the tourist information office
*túrista információs iroda*
the museum
*múzeum*

the palace
*palota*
the castle
*vár*
the concert hall
*koncertterem*
the opera house
*operaház*
the musical theatre
*zenés szinház*
Where are you going?
*Hová megy?*
I am going to...
*Megyek...*
Where is it?
*Hol van ez?*
I can't find it.
*Nem találom.*
Is it far?
*Messze van?*
Please show me on the map.
*Kérem, mutassa meg a térképen.*
left
*bal*
right
*jobb*
straight ahead
*előre*
I want...
*Akarok...*
Do I need permission?
*Szükségem van engedélyre?*
May I?
*Szabad?*

## Entertainment

Where can I hear live music?
*Hol hallgathatok élő zenét?*
Where can I buy a ticket?
*Hol vehetek jegyet?*
I'm looking for a ticket.
*Én keresem a jegyet.*
I want to refund this ticket.
*Vissza akarom váltani ezt a jegyet.*
Is this a good seat?
*Ez jó hely?*
at the front
*elöl*
ticket
*jegyet*

## Food

I am hungry.
*Éhes vagyok.*
I do not eat meat.
*Nem eszem húst.*
self-service cafeteria
*önkiszolgáló étterem*
grocery store
*élelmiszerbolt*
fish
*hal*
soup
*leves*
salad
*saláta*
fresh vegetables
*friss zöldség*
milk
*tej*
bread
*kenyér*
sugar
*cukor*
ice cream
*fagylalt*
hot coffee
*forró kávé*
mineral water
*ásványvíz*
beer
*sör*
wine
*bor*

## Shopping

Where can I buy one?
*Hol vehetem meg ezt?*
How much does it cost?
*Mennyibe kerül?*
That's (much) too expensive.
*Az túl drága.*
Is there a cheaper one?
*Van ennél olcsóbb?*

## Time & Dates

today
*ma*
tonight
*ma este*

tomorrow
*holnap*
the day after tomorrow
*holnap után*
What time does it open?
*Mikor nyit?*
What time does it close?
*Mikor zár?*
open
*nyitva*
closed
*zárva*
in the morning
*reggel*
in the evening
*este*
every day
*naponta*
At what time?
*Mikor?*
when?
*Hányadikán?*

| | |
|---|---|
| Monday | *hétfő* |
| Tuesday | *kedd* |
| Wednesday | *szerda* |
| Thursday | *csütörtök* |
| Friday | *péntek* |
| Saturday | *szombat* |
| Sunday | *vasárnap* |

| | |
|---|---|
| January | *január* |
| February | *február* |
| March | *március* |
| April | *április* |
| May | *május* |
| June | *június* |
| July | *július* |
| August | *augusztus* |
| September | *szeptember* |
| October | *október* |
| November | *november* |
| December | *december* |

## Numbers

| | |
|---|---|
| 1 | *egy* |
| 2 | *kettő* |
| 3 | *három* |
| 4 | *négy* |
| 5 | *öt* |

| 6 | *hat* |
|---|---|
| 7 | *hét* |
| 8 | *nyolc* |
| 9 | *kilenc* |
| 10 | *tiz* |
| 11 | *tizenegy* |
| 12 | *tizenkettő* |
| 13 | *tizenhárom* |
| 14 | *tizennégy* |
| 15 | *tizenöt* |
| 16 | *tizenhat* |
| 17 | *tizenhét* |
| 18 | *tizennyolc* |
| 19 | *tizenkilenc* |
| 20 | *húsz* |
| 21 | *huszonegy* |
| 22 | *huszonkettő* |
| 23 | *huszonhárom* |
| 30 | *harminc* |
| 40 | *negyven* |
| 50 | *ötven* |
| 60 | *hatvan* |
| 70 | *hetven* |
| 80 | *nyolcvan* |
| 90 | *kilencven* |
| 100 | *száz* |

# Facts for the Visitor

## VISAS & EMBASSIES

Everyone entering Hungary must have a passport that is valid for at least nine months and in some cases must also have a visa. Nationals of the USA, Canada and most European countries do not require visas to visit Hungary and need read no further. Citizens of Australia, Greece, Japan, New Zealand and Portugal still require visas though this could change. If you hold a passport from one of these countries, check current visa requirements at a consulate or any Malév Hungarian Airlines office.

Visas are issued on the spot at Hungarian consulates upon receipt of US$20 to US$25 and two photos. A double-entry tourist visa costs between US$30 and US$40 and you must have four photos. (If you know you'll be visiting Hungary twice, get a double-

entry visa to avoid having to apply again somewhere else.) Some consulates charge US$5 extra for express service (10 minutes as opposed to 24 hours). Be sure to get a tourist rather than a transit visa. A tourist visa allows a stay of up to 30 days and can be used any time within three or six months. A transit visa is only good for a stay of 48 hours, cannot be extended and costs the same price. On a transit visa you must enter and leave through different border crossings and must have a visa for the next country you visit. Visas are only issued at highway border crossings in exceptional circumstances, so get your visa in advance at a diplomatic office. Visas are never issued on trains.

A notice on the visa form instructs you to report to police within 48 hours of arrival. If you're staying in a private room arranged by a Hungarian travel agency, or at a hotel or camping ground, this formality will be taken care of for you. The agency or hotel will stamp your visa form and write in the nights you stayed with them. If you're staying with friends, you're supposed to report to the police in person. Upon departure from Hungary, an immigration officer will scrutinise the stamps. If too many nights are unaccounted for, you'll have some explaining to do. Your visa serves as an exit permit and you can leave Hungary any time within the 30-day validity period. Those not needing a visa only have to register with the police and get a stamp if they stay longer than 30 days.

### Hungarian Embassies

Hungarian embassies around the world include the following:

Australia
    79 Hopetown Circuit, Yarralumla, ACT 2600
    (☎ 282 3226)
    Unit 6, 351/a Edgecliff Rd, Edgecliff, Sydney,
    NSW 2027 (☎ 328 7859)
Canada
    7 Delaware Ave, Ottawa, ON K2P OZ2
    (☎ 613-232 1549)
Greece
    16 Kalvou St, Paleo Psihiko, Athens
    (☎ 671 4889)

Japan
3-1, Aobadai 2-chome, Meguro-ku, Tokyo
(☎ 476 6061)
Portugal
Calcada de Santo Amaro 85, 1300 Lisbon
(☎ 363 0395)

## MONEY

Travel agencies charge 1% commission to change money. Main post offices often cash travellers' cheques at the same rate without commission. Only change as much as you intend to spend, as changing excess forints back into hard currency is difficult. Some Ibusz and National Bank branches will do it but only up to half the amount you changed originally, if this is verified by receipts, and will deduct 7% commission. To convert US dollar travellers' cheques into dollars cash also costs 7% commission.

You're only allowed to import or export 100 forints. Customs will confiscate 500 or 1000 forint notes if they find them. Upon departure you could deposit Hungarian currency exceeding 100 forints with customs against a receipt allowing you to pick it up at a savings bank on your next visit, less a 3% service charge. It's a good idea to bring the permitted 100 forints with you as the queues at exchange counters in Budapest railway stations are horrendous. Western banks, or Hungarian tourists you meet elsewhere, may be able to sell you a small bill. Banks in Vienna sell Hungarian currency at a nice discount.

The black market rate for cash (never travellers' cheques) is about 25% higher than the official bank rate. Take care, however, as most of the people offering to change money on the street in Budapest are thieves. They switch the counted money for paper, small bills or worthless Yugoslav banknotes at the last minute and will rush off exclaiming that the police are coming if you object. These operators usually work in pairs. The second man will appear just as you're completing the transaction to cover the escape of the first by distracting you, perhaps by asking if you want to change more money with him. Anyone who tries to pay you with 50 or 100 forint notes or offers more than 25% above the official rate is almost certainly a thief. There is less risk in dealing with someone who can't run away such as a waiter, taxi driver, landlord or vendor at a street market.

With any luck, by the time you read this Hungary will have finally made its currency convertible, ending these fun and games.

### Currency

At last report US$1 = 75 forints (Ft). The Hungarian forint is divided into 100 fillér. There are coins of 10, 20 and 50 fillér and 1,

2, 5, 10 and 20 Ft. Banknotes come in denominations of of 20, 50, 100, 500 and 1000 Ft.

Hungarian notes must be the most picturesque in Eastern Europe. The 50 Ft note bears the likeness of the 18th century independence leader Ferenc Rákóczi II on the front and has mounted horsemen on the back. The 100 Ft note depicts the 19th century revolutionary Lajos Kossuth and a horse cart, and for 500 Ft you get the poet Endre Ady and a nice view of Budapest. The 1000 Ft note features the composer Béla Bartók and a mother nursing a baby.

### Costs
Hungary is experiencing double-digit inflation. Food prices are going up fast, while accommodation and transport costs are increasing more slowly. However, you should be able to get by on under US$25 a day by staying in private rooms, eating in unpretentious restaurants and travelling 2nd class by train. Two or more people travelling together or those camping and eating only at self-services can spend less.

Hungary is still reasonable because it doesn't discriminate against Western tourists with a two or three-price system, as is the case in some other Eastern European countries. What you pay for a hotel room will be about the same as a Hungarian would pay. Average Hungarian workers earn only about US$150 a month so inflation has hit them hardest of all.

### Tipping
Hungarians routinely tip doctors, dentists, waiters, hairdressers and taxi drivers about 10%. In restaurants do this directly as you pay by rounding up the bill – don't wait to leave money on the table. If you feel you've been overcharged, you can make your point by paying exactly the amount asked and not a forint more.

### CLIMATE & WHEN TO GO
Hungary has a temperate continental climate with Mediterranean and Atlantic influences. The winters can be cold, cloudy and humid, the summers warm. May, June and November are the rainiest months, although more rain falls in the west than in the east. Of the 2054 hours of sunshine a year at Budapest, 1526 occur in the period from April to September. July is the hottest month and January the coldest. The average annual temperature is 10°C.

### WHAT TO BRING
The most important thing to bring is hard currency in small notes which will allow you to bargain with private operators for all manner of things, including accommodation. Travellers' cheques are easily changed into forints but Hungarian currency just doesn't have the impact of US dollars or Deutschmarks; in fact, even government-owned travel agencies insist on it as payment for all international tickets.

### TOURIST OFFICES
Every Hungarian town has a travel agency which doubles as an accommodation service and tourist information centre. The largest travel agency is Ibusz, which has 120 offices in Hungary plus representatives overseas (see the following list). Other national travel agencies with offices around the country include Cooptourist and Volántourist. Regional travel agencies in provincial centres (Dunatours, Siótour, Mecsek Tourist, etc) are often more familiar with their own local area. There's almost always someone in the office who speaks either English or German and you'll find them very helpful.

### Ibusz Offices Abroad
Ibusz offices in countries outside Hungary include:

Austria
    Karntnerstrasse 26, 1010 Vienna 1 (☎ 51555)
Belgium
    rue du Luxembourg 6, 1040 Brussels
    (☎ 511 6484)
Bulgaria
    Bulevard Georgi Dimitrov 44, Sofia 6
Czechoslovakia
    ulice Kaprova 5, 11000 Prague 1
    Hviezdoslavovo námestie 7, 81101 Bratislava

Finland
    Isorobertinkatu 48-50/B,
    00120 Helsinki (☎ 17 9859)
France
    27 rue du Quatre-Septembre,
    75002 Paris (☎ 4742 5025)
Germany
    Karl Liebknechtstrasse 9, 102 Berlin
    Mauritiussteinweg 114-116,
    5000 Cologne 1  (☎ 2191 0204)
    Baselerstrasse 46/48,
    Frankfurt am Main (☎ 25 2018)
    Grosser Burstah 53,
    2000 Hamburg 11 (☎ 37 3078)
    Dachauerstrasse 5, 8000 Munich 2 (☎ 55 7217)
    Kronprinzstrasse 6, 7000 Stuttgart (☎ 29 6233)
Italy
    Via V E Orlando 75, 00185 Rome (☎ 48 3441)
Japan
    No 13, Togensha Building, 3rd floor, 12-10,
    Roppongi 4-chome Minato-ku, Tokyo 106
    (☎ 404 8089)
Netherlands
    World Trade Centre, Toren B, 14e Etage,
    Strawinskylaan 1425, 1077 XX Amsterdam
    (☎ 664 9851)
Poland
    ulica Marszalkowska 80, 00517 Warsaw
Spain
    Juan Alvarez Mendizabal 136, 28008 Madrid
    (☎ 241 2544)
Sweden
    Beridarebanan 1, Stockholm 10326 (☎ 23 2030)
UK
    6 Conduit St, London W1R 9TG
    (☎ 071-493 0263)
USA
    One Parker Plaza, Suite 1104, Fort Lee, NJ 07024
    (☎ 592 8585)
Yugoslavia
    Strahinjica Bana 47, Belgrade 11 000

## Tourist Literature

One publication to get hold of as soon as possible after you arrive is the monthly *Programme in Ungarn/in Hungary* which lists concerts, opera and ballet performances, musicals, puppet shows, circuses, sporting events, exhibitions, museums and many other events and attractions not only in Budapest but around the country. Equally valuable are the *Hotel* and *Camping* brochures published annually by the Ministry of Tourism. These list almost every official accommodation possibility in the country complete with telephone numbers so you can

try ringing up for reservations. The hotels are categorised according to the star system so you have an idea of how much each should charge. Finally, a brochure entitled simply *Hungary – Tourist Information* provides general facts about how to visit Hungary. These free publications are often available at the Ibusz offices abroad listed in this chapter, at the Malév Hungarian Airlines' offices and at luxury hotels and tourist offices inside Hungary itself. Otherwise go to Tourinform, Sütő utca 2, Budapest (Metro: Deák tér), which will have all four of these publications.

## BUSINESS HOURS & HOLIDAYS

Grocery stores open weekdays from 7 am to 7 pm, department stores from 10 am to 6 pm. Most shops stay open until 8 pm on Thursday but on Saturday they close at 1 pm. Post offices open on weekdays from 8 am to 6 pm, and on Saturday from 8 am to 2 pm. In Hungarian the word for 'open' is *nyitva* and that for 'closed' is *zárva*. Most museums are closed on Monday and the days following public holidays (and a few also on Tuesday) and are free on Saturday (on Wednesday in Szentendre). Museum admission fees have doubled and tripled in the last few years though the vast majority are still well under US$1. Card-carrying students get into most museums for free and pay half-price for many cultural events.

The public holidays are 1 January (New Year's Day), 15 March (Day of the 1848 Revolution), Easter Monday, 1 May (Labour Day), 20 August (St Stephen's Day), 23 October (Republic Day) and 25 and 26 December (Christmas).

## CULTURAL EVENTS

Among Hungary's most outstanding annual events are the Budapest Spring Festival (held in the last third of March), Hortobágy Equestrian Days (late June), Sopron Early Music Days (mid-June to mid-July), Pécs Summer Theatre Festival (June and July), Szentendre Summer Festival (July), Kőszeg Street Theatre Festival (July), Szombathely Bartók Festival (July), Debrecen Jazz Days (July),

Szeged Open-Air Festival (mid-July to mid-August), Eger 'Agria' Folk Dance Meeting and Wine Harvest Days (September), Budapest Arts Weeks (September) and Budapest Contemporary Music Festival (September). The first Sunday in June there's a Folk Art Fair in Győr. St Stephen's Day (20 August) is celebrated with sporting events, parades and fireworks. On the same day there's a Floral Festival in Debrecen and a Bridge Fair in nearby Hortobágy. Formula 1 car races are held at the Hungaroring near Mogyoród, just north-east of Budapest.

The Budapest Spring Fair held in the second half of May features industrial products and the Autumn Fair in the middle of September focuses on consumer goods. Every March there's a Touristic Exhibition at Budapest's Hungexpo Fair Centre. In 1995 Vienna and Budapest will cohost a World's Fair with the theme 'Bridges To The Future' celebrating the links between Austria and Hungary, past and present. Twenty million visitors are expected to attend the six-month event with a new Metro line built out to the site.

## POST & TELECOMMUNICATIONS
Postage costs are low and the service is comparatively reliable, if slow. Letters take 20 days to go from Western Europe to Budapest and 10 days to go from Budapest to Western Europe.

### Telephone
International telephone calls can be made from any red public telephone in Hungary. Dial the international access code 00, the two-digit country code, the city or area code and the local number. For domestic calls within Hungary, dial the inland access code 06, the city or area code and the local number. Have lots of 10 and 20 Ft coins ready.

To call Hungary from Western Europe dial the international access code, 36 (the country code for Hungary), the area code and the number. Important area codes include 1 (Budapest), 46 (Miskolc), 52 (Debrecen), 72 (Pécs), 84 (Siófok) and 96 (Győr).

### TIME
GMT/UTC plus one hour. The clock is put an hour forward at the end of March and an hour back at the end of September.

### WEIGHTS & MEASURES
The electric current is 220 volts, 50 Hz AC.

### BOOKS & MAPS
Books are good value in Hungary and many titles are available in English. While visiting Budapest be sure to pick up an indexed city map at a bookshop.

*Hungary, A Comprehensive Guide* (Corvina, Budapest) is strong on maps and description. An American edition of the same book is published by Hippocrene Books, 171 Madison Ave, New York, NY 10016. Another local publication, *Budapest, A Critical Guide* by Andras Torok, is also highly recommended.

*Nagel's Encyclopedia-Guide Hungary* (Nagel Publishers, Geneva) is a precise, traditional guidebook useful for sightseeing and background reading. *Hungary: The Rough Guide* by Dan Richardson (Harrap-Columbus, London) is much better for practical information and covers a wide range of contemporary topics.

The yellow-covered *Magyarország Autóatlasza* (Cartographia, Budapest) contains twenty-three 1:360,000 road maps of Hungary plus small street maps of almost every village and town in the country. The complete index makes this a valuable reference for motorists or anyone spending much time in the country. Cartographia also publishes a yellow *Budapest Guide* with 38 maps of the city, a street index and descriptive information in English.

*Hungary* by Paul Ignotus (Ernest Benn, London, 1972) is a good modern history of the country which is often available at libraries. Paul Ignotus presents the country's history in a very personal way by constantly referring to Hungarian literature.

*A History of Modern Hungary* by Jörg K Hoensch (Longman, London, 1988) covers the period from 1867 to 1986 in a balanced way. Like almost every other observer, Hoensch failed to foresee the fall of Communism in Hungary.

In his amusing little book *Do It Yourself, Hungary's Hidden Economy* (Pluto Press, London, 1981), János Kenedi describes the machinations he employed to build himself a house outside Budapest. Kenedi's gentle exposé of the foibles of human nature provides a delightful glimpse of everyday life as it was in Communist Hungary.

## MEDIA

The *Daily News/Neueste Nachrichten* is available at newsstands from Tuesday to Saturday in English and German. The *News* has a section listing forthcoming events around the country and films in English showing at Budapest cinemas.

Two English-language magazines are the *Hungarian Digest* and *The New Hungarian Quarterly* (Box 3, Budapest H-1426). The *Budapester Rundschau* is weekly paper in German. Western magazines are sold at the luxury hotels.

## HEALTH

Tourists receive free first-aid treatment at clinics and hospitals. Hospital emergency and outpatient attention, free for Hungarians, is available to visitors at reasonable rates. Prescription drugs and all locally made medicines are inexpensive. In Budapest call your embassy for the name of a doctor or dentist

accustomed to treating foreigners. Otherwise ask a local tourist office for a reference. Telephone the doctor or dentist to make an appointment before going in for treatment.

If you want to have some dental work done in Budapest and don't mind paying Western European prices, there's a modern dental clinic at the Thermal Hotel on Margaret Island which specialises in treating foreigners.

## Thermal Baths

There are 154 thermal baths in Hungary, most of them open to the public. The Romans first developed the baths of Budapest, and the Turks and Habsburgs followed suit. The thermal lake at Hévíz is probably Hungary's most impressive spa, though public thermal pools at Debrecen, Eger, Győr, Harkány, Komárom and Lepence (Visegrád) are covered in this book.

In Budapest, Danubius Travels beneath the elevated car park on Martinelli tér can provide information about medical programmes at the spas and make reservations on the spot. For example, a stay at the Thermál Hotel in Hévíz begins at around US$80/120 single/double a day on a weekly basis, including half-pension, medical examination, massage, sauna, use of thermal baths, fitness room, etc. From mid-October to March prices are 25% lower.

## FILM & PHOTOGRAPHY

You can purchase Kodak film and have it developed at a dozen locations in Budapest, including Fotex Limited on Váci utca near Vörösmarty tér.

## ACTIVITIES

Watersports are concentrated around Balaton Lake, especially windsurfing at Balatonszemes and Killiántelep, and sailing at Balatonalmádi and Balatonboglár. Sailing boats and surfing boards can be hired at many points around the lake. For information on sailing courses, enquire at Budapest Tourist, Roosevelt tér 5, Budapest H-1052. Motorboats are banned on the lake, so waterskiing is only possible at the FICC Rally

Campground, Balatonfüred, where skiers are towed around a course by a moving cable.

## Canoeing

There are many possibilities for canoeing or kayaking on the rivers of Hungary. The journey down the Danube from Rajka to Mohács (386 km) is fairly obvious but there are smaller, less congested waterways. For example, you can go down the 205 km of the Rába River from Szentgotthárd (on the Austrian border) to Győr. From Csenger near the far-eastern tip of Hungary, you can paddle down the Szamos and Tisza rivers to Szeged (570 km). A shorter trip would be from Gyula or Békés to Szeged (210 km) via the Körös and Tisza rivers. All of these places have railway stations, making it easy to get there and easy to leave, and there are many other possibilities. For information on organised canoe trips, try Flotta Tours (☎ 117 7217), Práter utca 60, Budapest H-1083 (Metro: Ferenc körút).

## Cycling

The possibilities for cyclists are many. The slopes of northern Hungary can be steep, whereas Transdanubia is much gentler and the Great Plain completely flat. When planning your route, be aware that cycling is forbidden on motorways and main highways with a single-digit route number. Cycling is allowed on highways with two-digit numbers, although three-digit highways are preferable, as traffic is much lighter there.

Some railway stations rent bicycles, including the following ones along the south-eastern shore of Balaton Lake listed from east to west: Balatonaliga, Siófok, Zamárdi, Szántód-Kőröshegy, Balatonföldvár, Balatonszemes, Balatonlelle and Balatonmáriafürdő.

## Hiking

Though Hungary doesn't have high mountains, you can enjoy good hiking in the forests around Aggtelek, Visegrád and Badacsony. North of Eger are the Bükk Mountains and south of Kecskemét the Bugac puszta, both national parks with marked hiking trails. Before you go, pick up detailed hiking maps in Budapest as these are not always available locally.

## Horse Riding

The Hungarians have a passion for horses that goes back over 1000 years and the sandy puszta seems almost made for horse riding. To get in some horse riding yourself, contact Pegazus Tours (☎ 117 1644), Károlyi Mihály utca 5, H-1053 Budapest. This office is near Felszabadulás tér Metro Station and the staff speak English. Pegazus works with several ranches and can make advance reservations for rooms (about US$45/65 single/double with half-board in midsummer, less in the off season) and horses (US$10 an hour). Ask about the three-star Nagycenk *Kastélyszálló* near Sopron, in north-western Hungary.

Going through Pegazus is the sure way to arrange some riding because if you simply show up at a ranch in summer you may be told that it's fully booked. It's cheaper, however, to ask staff at provincial tourist offices about riding possibilities in their area and then try to get them to call ahead to make reservations. Few of the ranches are on bus or train routes, so unless you have your own transport be prepared for some long taxi rides.

## Courses

Each July and August, the Debrecen Kyati Egyetem Tilkatsaga (Debrecen University) organises a three-week international summer school featuring lectures on the Hungarian language, history, literature, folklore, music and politics. A programme of related cultural events accompanies the course. Write to Box 35, Debrecen, Hungary 4010 for information.

## HIGHLIGHTS
### Museums & Galleries

Budapest's Museum of Fine Arts shelters a huge collection of old master paintings. The Museum of Contemporary History in Budapest Castle mounts informative exhibitions on recent issues. Two galleries of note dedicated to individual Hungarian artists are the

Kovács Margit Museum in Szentendre and the Csontváry Museum in Pécs.

### Castles

Hungary's most famous castles are those which resisted overwhelming Turkish armies: Eger, Kőszeg, Siklós and Szigetvár. Though in ruins, Visegrád Citadel symbolises the power of medieval Hungary.

Among Hungary's finest palaces are the Esterházy Palace at Fertőd, the Festetics Palace at Keszthely and the Széchenyi Mansion at Nagycenk.

### Historic Towns

Many of Hungary's historic towns, including Eger, Győr, Sopron, Székesfehérvár and Veszprém, were rebuilt in the Baroque style during the 18th century. Kőszeg is one of the few towns which retain a strong medieval flavour, and Szentendre on the Danube has an air of the Balkans. The greatest monuments of the Turkish period are in Pécs.

### Hotels

Two fine old hotels still offering inexpensive lodging are the Park in Kőszeg and the Amazon in Keszthely. The Kastélyszálló in Fertőd provides the chance to stay in Hungary's finest palace for a reasonable price, and the tourist hostel at the Aggtelek Caves is a good cheap dormitory. In Budapest all of the hotels belonging to the Eravis chain are good value, especially the 11-storey Hotel Bekas north-west of the city.

### Restaurants

Two old traditional restaurants worth visiting are the Régiposta Étterem in Debrecen and the Bárczy Fogadó in Szentendre. The restaurant in the Minaret Hotel in Pécs offers substantial meals and the Korzo Söröző in Székesfehérvár is always excellent. Unfortunately, tourism has spoiled a good many Hungarian restaurants so just to spite them I'll list an Italian restaurant as one of Hungary's five best places to eat: Pizzeria da Francesco in Keszthely.

## ACCOMMODATION
### Camping

Hungary has 140 to 150 camping grounds and these are the cheapest places to stay. They're often in attractive locations and offer the opportunity to meet local people. Small private camping grounds accommodating as few as six tents are preferable to the large, noisy, 'official' camping grounds. Prices vary from $4 to US$12 for two adults at one, two and three-star camp sites. The sites around Balaton Lake are more expensive. An additional US$0.50 per person 'resort tax' is levied in some areas. Most camping grounds open from mid-May to mid-September and rent small bungalows (from US$7) to visitors without tents. In midsummer the bungalows may all be taken, so it pays to check with the local tourist office before making the trip. Members of the International Camping & Caravanning Club (FICC) and holders of student cards usually get a 10% discount, although this varies. Freelance camping is prohibited.

### Youth Hostels

Despite the 35 hostels listed in the IYHF handbook, a YHA (Youth Hostels Association) card doesn't get you very far in Hungary. Some of the places listed in the handbook are medium-priced hotels which do not recognise the card, others are closed or permanently full with 'groups', and the rest are converted student dormitories that only open for six to seven weeks in midsummer.

Express is the Hungarian travel agency officially responsible for youth hostels; it's best to check with staff there before going to a hostel, as they'll be able to call ahead and reserve your bed. Be persistent! Considering the unreliability of the listings in the IYHF handbook this is important. Though some hostels will admit you without the mediation of Express, it often seems to be at the discretion of the person holding the keys.

Hostel beds cost about US$6 in Budapest and less elsewhere. A YHA card is not required although you occasionally get US$0.50 off with one. Some hostels give an additional 25% discount if you show a student card. Camping is not allowed. There's no age limit at the hostels, they remain open all day and are often good places to meet young Eastern Europeans.

## Tourist Hostels

There's another class of accommodation which is similar to Western youth hostels but not included in the IYHF handbook. A tourist hostel *(turistaszálló)* offers beds in separate dormitories for men and women. There are no rules (ie, no curfew, smoking and drinking allowed in the room, etc). Tourist hostels are found in many cities and most stay open all year. The overnight fee will be under US$3, but as the people there are not accustomed to receiving Western visitors you may have to ask the local tourist office or Express to call ahead in order to gain admission. In winter you'll probably have a whole room to yourself.

## Private Rooms

There are beds for 100,000 people in private rooms in Hungary, costing US$3 to US$12 single, US$5 to US$22 double depending on whether the room is 1st, 2nd or 3rd class. Private rooms at Balaton Lake are slightly more expensive. Single rooms are sometimes hard to come by, but even the double room rate is reasonable. You have to pay a linen supplement if you stay only one or two nights.

This is your best accommodation bet by far. You share a house or flat with a Hungarian family. The toilet facilities are usually communal but otherwise you can close your door and enjoy as much privacy as you please. All 1st and some 2nd and 3rd-class rooms have shared kitchen facilities.

In Budapest you may have to take a room far from the centre of town, but public transport is good and cheap. Unless you buy a good city map or are very serious about saving money, take a taxi to your room the first time as the places can often be hard to find, especially if you're toting a lot of luggage.

The rooms are assigned by travel agencies which take your money and give you a voucher bearing the address. The offices close at 4 pm on weekdays and 1 pm on Saturday, so you must arrive early in the town you want to stay in. Longer hours are common in summer. If the first room you're offered seems too expensive, ask if there is a cheaper one. There are usually several agencies offering private rooms, so ask around if the price is higher than usual or the location inconvenient. The rooms only become available after 5 pm, so leave your bags at the station.

In Budapest private individuals at the railway stations or on the street in front of Ibusz offices may offer you an unofficial private room *(szoba)*. Their prices are often higher than those asked at the agencies and you have nowhere to complain in case of problems.

## Pensions

Small, privately owned pensions are popular with German-speaking visitors who like the personalised service and homy atmosphere. Most pensions have less than seven rooms and the restaurant that goes with them is their real moneymaker. Always ask to see the room first and ask if there is another if you're not completely satisfied as the rooms can vary considerably. Prices are about twice what you'd pay for a comparable private room (from US$20 double) but you can go straight there without wasting time at a travel agency and waiting until 5 pm. You'll find pensions in main tourist areas like the Danube Bend, Balaton Lake, Sopron, and so on.

## Hotels

Hungarian hotel rooms are significantly more expensive than private rooms, but cheap by international standards (from US$12 single, US$15 double). A hotel may be the answer if you're only staying one night or arrive too late to get a private room. Two-star hotels usually have rooms with a private bathroom, whereas at one-star hotels the bathroom is usually down the hall.

If you want to be sure of finding accommodation in another Hungarian city, have a travel agency (such as Ibusz, Express, Cooptourist, Dunatours, Volántourist) reserve a hotel room for you. The staff will need a couple of days' notice, and in addition to the regular room rate you must pay the telex charges and a 10% commission. Still, if you're there in the busy summer season, it may be worth it.

A 15% turnover tax is added to all accommodation charges in Hungary. This tax will already have been included in any price you're quoted.

## FOOD

Hungary has a tasty national cuisine all its own. Many dishes are seasoned with paprika, a red spice made from a sweet variety of red pepper which appears on restaurant tables beside the salt and pepper. Although paprika originated in Central America, the peasants of Szeged have been growing it since the early 18th century and it's now as important to Hungarian cuisine as the tomato is to Italian cuisine.

Hungarian goulash (gulyás) is a thick beef soup cooked with onions and potatoes. Pörkölt is meat stewed in lard with onions and paprika. If sour cream is added to pörkölt it becomes paprikás. Pork is the most common meat dish. Cabbage is an important vegetable in Hungary, either stuffed in the Turkish fashion (töltött káposzta) or made into a thick cabbage soup (káposzta leves) that is popular among late diners. Other delicacies include goose-liver sandwiches and paprika chicken (paprikás csirke) served with tiny dumplings.

Fisherman's soup (halászlé) is a rich mixture of several kinds of boiled fish, tomatoes, green peppers and paprika. Balaton Lake pike perch (süllő) is generally served breaded and grilled.

Noodles with cottage cheese and tiny cubes of crisp fried bacon (túrós csusza) goes well with fish dishes. Hungarian cream cheese (körözött) is a mixture of sheep cheese, paprika and caraway seeds. Strudel (rétes) is a typical layered pastry filled with apple, cherry, cabbage, curd or cheese. Look out for langos, a huge Hungarian doughnut of deep-fried dough eaten with salt, cheese and yoghurt. Unfortunately, vegetarians will have a hard time in Hungary as almost every dish contains some meat.

## Restaurants

Hungarian restaurants (étterem or véndeglő) are relatively cheap. Meal prices begin at around US$2 in a self-service restaurant, US$3 in a local restaurant and US$5 in a tourist restaurant. Lunch is the main meal of the day. Some restaurants offer a set lunch or menu on weekdays and this is always good value. It usually consists of soup, a side salad, a main course and occasionally dessert. Printed menus are often translated into German and sometimes into English.

Occasionally, a sharp waiter will bring you a side salad or something else you didn't order with the intention of inflating your bill. If you don't really want it, just say nem ezt rendeltem! (I didn't order that!) and send it back. At other times you'll be charged extra for unsolicited pommes frites (chips), some dish you never got or a special brand of imported beer when all you wanted was a draught beer. If you're sure they're overcharging but it's only by 15% to 20%, just pay the exact amount without a tip and try not to let it spoil your meal. The following is one reader's comment:

The waiters in Budapest frequently tried to rip us off, we felt, regardless of the poshness of the place. When we reached that conclusion (after more than a week in Budapest) we went back eating at büfés (cheap restaurants) and buying groceries at stores, both of which had invariably honest clerks.

Many restaurants feature Gypsy music after 6 pm and the musicians are accustomed to receiving tips. Give them a small amount and they'll move on to the next table. At better restaurants it's obligatory to check your coat (US$0.10). If you're on a strict budget, have a soft drink with your meal as most restaurants stock only the more expensive brands of beer and wine. If the prices of the drinks aren't listed on the menu they'll be higher than you expect.

A *csárda* is a traditional inn or tavern offering spicy fare and fiery wine. *Borozó* denotes a wine cellar, *söröző* a pub offering draught beer and sometimes meals. A *bisztró* is an inexpensive restaurant that is often self-service *(ökiszolgáló)*. *Büfés* are the cheapest places, although you may have to eat standing at a counter. Pastries, cakes and coffee are served at a *cukrászda*, while an *eszpresszó* is a café. A *bár* is a nightclub with music and dancing. In Hungary the ice cream is worth lining up for.

## DRINKS

Hungarian wines match the cuisine admirably. The best wines have a Hungarian flag around the top of the bottle. The finest are those produced in the volcanic soils of Badacsony, Eger, Sopron and Tokaj. Southern Hungary (Pécs, Villány and Szekszárd) is also noted. One of the best Hungarian red wines is Egri Bikavér, and Tokaji Aszú is a very sweet golden-white wine of an almost liqueur consistency. Louis XIV of France called Tokaji Aszú 'the king of wines and wine of kings'. Medoc Noir is a strong, sweet, red dessert wine. Others to watch for are Tihany Cabernet, Villány Pinot Noir, Soproni Kékfrankos, Badacsony Kéknyelű, Csopak Riesling and Móri Ezerjó (white). You can pick up a bottle of any of these at a local supermarket.

Also try the apricot, cherry or plum brandy *(pálinka)* which is to the Hungarians what schnapps is to the Germans. A shot before breakfast or dinner is in order. Mecseki and Hubertus are two Hungarian liqueurs. The beer served in Hungary is often imported and thus not as good value as wine.

Unicum, a bitter liqueur made from natural herbs, roots and spices, has been the national drink of Hungary since 1790. Occasionally you will see imitation versions of Unicum, but the real thing comes in a round bottle and bears the brand name Zwack. It's not cheap: a 700 ml bottle costs US$10.

## ENTERTAINMENT

Hungary is a paradise for culture vultures. In Budapest there are several musical events to choose from each evening and the best opera tickets never go over US$5. Under the Communists culture was heavily subsidised by the state and many of the benefits of this still remain. Unlike Prague, tickets are available and the friendly Hungarians usually go out of their way to help foreign visitors get seats. Aside from the traditional opera, operetta and concerts, there are rock and jazz concerts, folk dancing, pantomime, planetarium presentations, literary evenings, movies, floor shows and circuses to keep you smiling.

Excellent performances can also be seen in provincial towns such as Szombathely, Győr, Pécs, Kecskemét, Szeged, Eger and Debrecen, all of which have fine modern theatres. Information about events is readily available at tourist offices or in the *Daily News*. Some useful words to remember are *színház* (theatre), *pénztár* (ticket office) and *elkelt* (sold out). It's worth spending an extra week in Hungary just to take full advantage of this wonderful opportunity while it lasts.

## THINGS TO BUY

Shops in Hungary are well stocked. Prices are reasonable for almost everything a traveller would wish to buy and the quality of the products is high. Food, alcohol, books and folk-music records are affordable and there is an excellent selection. On the other hand, clothing and footwear are better value in Czechoslovakia and Bulgaria. Traditional products include folk-art embroidery and ceramics, bone lace, dolls, and Herend, Kalocsa or Zsolnay porcelain. You can often get a 25% discount from small private shops and street vendors if you offer to pay in cash hard currency though you'll need small bills. In theory, visitors are only allowed to export US$50 worth of goods without receipts and not in commercial quantities. In practice, it's unlikely that you'll be asked to open your bags at the border.

# Getting There & Away

## AIR

Malév Hungarian Airlines has direct flights to Budapest from Abu Dhabi, Algiers, Baghdad, Cairo, Damascus, Doha, Dubai, Istanbul, Kiev, Kuwait, Larnaca, Leningrad, Moscow, New York, Tel Aviv and many European cities. The cheapest return flight from London to Budapest costs US$575 on fixed dates with a heavy penalty if you change reservations. There are no domestic flights in Hungary and no airport departure tax.

## LAND

Budapest is connected to all surrounding countries by air, road, rail and river. Trains arrive from every neighbouring capital and in summer there's a hydrofoil service between Vienna and Budapest. Other major entry points by train are Sopron (from Vienna), Szombathely (from Graz, Austria), Pécs (from Osijek, Yugoslavia) and Miskolc (from Košice, Czechoslovakia). By road there's a bus service from Szeged to Subotica, from Pécs to Osijek, from Barcs to Zagreb and from Nagykanizsa to Zagreb, all in Yugoslavia.

## Bus

There's a weekly Eurolines bus service throughout the year from The Hague to Siófok via Amsterdam, Düsseldorf, Frankfurt/Main and Budapest (24 hours, US$100 one-way, US$160 return, with a 10% discount for those under 26 or over 60 years of age). From mid-June to September, the Amsterdam bus runs twice a week. In Amsterdam tickets are sold by Budget Bus (☎ 627 5151), Rokin 10. In Budapest you can buy them at the Erzsébet tér Bus Station. This bus is often full, so book well ahead.

A similar service from Antwerp to Siófok via Brussels and Budapest with a change of buses in Frankfurt/Main, also operates on a weekly basis from mid-May to September for a similar fare. Ask for information from the Europabus office (☎ 217 0025), Place de Brouckère 50, Brussels 1000.

Two buses travel daily between Vienna's Autobusbahnhof Mitte and Budapest's Erzsébet tér Bus Station, departing from each end at 7 am and 5 pm daily. Tickets (US$21 one-way, US$29 return) are available at both bus stations. In Budapest you can make enquiries at the Erzsébet tér Bus Station and in Vienna at Blaguss Reisen (☎ 0222-50 1800), Wiedner Hauptstrasse 15, or at Autobusbahnhof Wien-Mitte.

**From Budapest** On Wednesday and Saturday there's a bus from the Erzsébet tér Bus Station to Zakopane, Poland (US$9 one-way, nine hours). There is a daily bus from the Erzsébet tér Bus Station to Subotica, Yugoslavia (US$7).

Other buses leave about once a week from Erzsébet tér Bus Station to Banská Bystrica, Bratislava, Cluj-Napoca, Istanbul, Munich, Oradea and Tatranská Lomnica. In Hungary all international bus and train tickets must be purchased with cash hard currency.

## Train

Unless otherwise stated, the express trains listed here operate daily throughout the year and reservations are usually required. You'll find information is more easily obtained if you ask for the trains by name. Second-class couchettes and 1st-class sleepers are almost always available. Though most have dining cars, take along some food and drink. Trains which terminate or begin in Hungary are less likely to be delayed. Local unreserved trains are cheaper and easier if you just want to get across the border.

**Tickets** Railway tickets between Eastern European countries are cheap, especially when purchased in Hungary. For example, to go from Budapest to Berlin costs only US$25 (1st class), US$17 (2nd class), and US$36 extra for a sleeper. Budapest-Prague costs US$8 (1st class), US$5 (2nd class). Tickets are cheap because MÁV Hungarian Railways gives a 50% discount to tourists who pay in Western currency and the fares are low to begin with. You don't get the reduction on tickets to Yugoslavia, however. Budapest-Belgrade will cost US$20 (2nd class), although it's closer than Prague. A ticket to Sofia is four times as expensive via Belgrade (US$41) as it is via Bucharest (US$9), although the Romanian visa fee (US$30) cancels out this saving.

Tickets to Western Europe cost the same in Hungary as they would in the West, which is about five times as much as tickets for comparable distances in Eastern Europe. For example, Budapest to Amsterdam is US$185 one-way 2nd class. People under 26 years of age can get a reduction on all railway tickets, domestic or international, by showing a student or youth hostel card issued by the IUS, ISTC or IYHF. All student-card holders regardless of age are eligible for a 25% discount on tickets to other Eastern European countries. International train tickets are valid for two months one-way or four months return and stopovers are allowed.

Interrail passes (available only to those under 26) and Eurail passes are accepted in Hungary. It's almost impossible to use the train enough in Hungary to get your per diem Eurail cost out of it, so keep that part of your trip for before or after your Eurail pass comes into effect. MÁV Hungarian Railways, Andrassy út 34, Budapest, can sell you a Eurail pass but the cheapest one (for those over 26) is US$381 for 15 days! You must pay for the pass with cash dollars, not travellers' cheques.

**To/From Western Europe** From Vienna there are four trains a day to Budapest via Hegyeshalom. These include the Liszt Ferenc Express from Dortmund (15 hours) via Nuremberg, the Orient Express from Paris (21 hours) via Munich and the Wiener Walzer from Basel (17 hours) via Innsbruck, all from Vienna Westbahnhof. The Lehár Express arrives from Vienna Südbahnhof (three hours). The Orient Express goes on to Romania while the others terminate in Budapest. Seat reservations may (or may not) be required but they're highly recommended unless you want to stand. In Vienna ask about

special half-price return tickets between Vienna and Budapest on the Lehár.

Several unreserved local trains travel between Vienna-Südbahnhof and Sopron (1½ hours) via Wiener Neustadt or Ebenfurth. Sometimes you must change trains in these places. One local train runs between Graz, Austria, and Szombathely (146 km, four hours) though there are other trains if you change at Szentgotthárd, the Hungarian border station.

**To/From Prague & Berlin** From Berlin-Lichtenberg (15 hours) to Budapest via Prague, Bratislava and Štúrovo there are the daily Hungária and Metropol express trains which terminate in Hungary. The Pannónia, Balt-Orient and Meridian express trains also travel to Budapest from Berlin-Lichtenberg, carrying on to Romania or Bulgaria. From Prague to Budapest (nine hours) there's the Amicus Express.

**To/From Slovakia & Poland** The Bathory Express runs daily from Warsaw to Budapest (13 hours) via Katowice and Trenčín. The Polonia Express travels between Warsaw and Budapest via Zilina and Banská Bystrica. From Kraków to Budapest (13 hours) via Košice and Miskolc you can take the Cracovia Express. The Rákóczi Express also runs from Košice to Budapest (four hours) with an extension to/from Poprad-Tatry in summer. From western Poland there's the Bem Express to Budapest from Szczecin, Poznań and Wrocław via Trenčín. The Varsovia Express arrives from Gdynia/Gdańsk.

The two local trains a day between Košice and Miskolc (88 km, three hours) require no reservations.

**To/From Romania & Bulgaria** From Bucharest to Budapest you have a choice of the Balt-Orient Express via Oradea (15 hours) or the Orient Express via Arad (14 hours). The Pannónia Express to Budapest from Sofia (25 hours) also travels via Arad. The Karpaty Express passes Arad, Hatvan, Miskolc and Košice on its way to Warsaw. One seasonal train of interest is the Varna Express from

Varna, Bulgaria, to Warsaw via Oradea, Debrecen and Miskolc (mid-June to mid-October only).

Two local Hungarian trains a day also run between Oradea and Budapest-Nyugati (249 km, five hours) and these are useful as no reservations are required. At last report their departure times were from Budapest-Nyugati at 6.10 am and 1.30 pm and Oradea at 12.10 and 6.10 pm. If coming from Romania, buy your open ticket Oradea-Budapest at a CFR railway ticket office well ahead (but not in Bucharest), as Oradea Railway Station is as chaotic as ever. If you're visiting Romania as a side trip from Hungary, be sure to get a return ticket for these trains, as railway ticketing in Romania is a disaster. This is the easiest way to travel between these countries.

### To/From Yugoslavia & Bulgaria
From Yugoslavia to Budapest the possibilities are the Drava and Maestral express trains from Zagreb (seven hours) via Siófok, or the Avala and Polonia express trains from Belgrade (seven hours) via Subotica. The Drava conveys carriages from Rome (25 hours). There's also the Meridian Express to Budapest from Sofia (15 hours) via Belgrade. The Puskin Express from Belgrade to Moscow travels via Kecskemét and Debrecen.

Two unreserved local trains a day shuttle between Osijek and Pécs (82 km, two hours).

### To/From Moscow & China
In late 1990 MÁV Hungarian Railways, Andrássy út 34, Budapest, was selling Budapest-Beijing tickets for an unbelievable US$90 one-way 1st class with a sleeper. The catch was that you couldn't get a seat reservation for the Moscow-Beijing portion and without such a booking you couldn't get a Soviet transit visa. If MÁV still has these tickets, you could buy only the open return portion (valid for four months), fly to Hong Kong and come back by train. Also check the price of a flight from Budapest to Ulan Bator, Mongolia, where you could pick up the train.

Pannónia-Intourist, József körút 45, Budapest, can get you a ticket for the Trans-Siberian Railway from Budapest to Beijing *with* seat reservations, but it won't be cheap. Until the end of 1990, they were charging US$280 one-way for this trip but on 1 January 1991 the price jumped to around US$1000 one-way! Pannónia-Intourist can also reserve hotel rooms in Moscow but these cost US$180/200 single/double a night, payable in advance, which makes it cheaper to visit the USSR on a package tour from Britain.

### Car & Motorbike
Some highway border crossings are only open to citizens of Hungary, Czechoslovakia, Romania and Yugoslavia, though this could change. The crossings mentioned here (listed clockwise around the country) are open to everyone. In each case the name of the Hungarian border post is provided.

The border crossings to/from Czechoslovakia are at Rajka (16 km south-east of Bratislava), Vámosszabadi (13 km north of Győr), Komárom (opposite Komárno), Parassapuszta (80 km north of Budapest via Vác), Balassagyarmat, Somoskőújfalu (just north of Salgótarján), Bánréve (45 km north-west of Miskolc), Tornyosnémeti (21 km south of Košice) and Sátoraljaújhely (opposite Slovenské Nové Mesto). To/from the USSR you may cross at Záhony (opposite Cop).

To go to/from Romania you have a choice of Csengersima (11 km north-west of Satu Mare), Ártánd (14 km north-west of Oradea), Gyula (66 km north of Arad) and Nagylak (between Szeged and Arad).

To/from Yugoslavia there are border crossings at Roszke (between Szeged and Subotica), Tompa (11 km north-west of Subotica), Hercegszántó (32 km south of Baja), Udvar (48 km north of Osijek), Drávaszabolcs (eight km south of Harkany), Barcs (right on the Dráva River), Berzence (23 km west of Koprivnica), Letenye (between Nagykanizsa and Varazdin), Rédics (eight km south-west of Lenti) and Bajánsenye (west of Zalaegerszeg).

If you're going to/from Austria, you can cross at Rábafüzes (five km north of

Szentgotthárd), Bucsu (13 km west of Szombathely), Kőszeg, Kópháza (just south of Sopron), Sopron (61 km south of Vienna) and Hegyeshalom (70 km south-west of Vienna).

### On Foot

If you want to avoid the hassle or expense of getting an international train ticket, you can easily walk across the Danube bridge on the Czechoslovak/Hungarian border at Komárno/Komárom, 100 km south-east of Bratislava. See the Komárom section in this chapter for details.

Similarly you can cross on foot from Sátoraljaújhely near Sárospatak in north-eastern Hungary to Slovenské Nové Mesto, Czechoslovakia. The Czechoslovak and Hungarian railway stations are only two km apart with a highway border crossing between them.

### RIVER
#### Hydrofoil

Hydrofoil service on the Danube from Budapest to Vienna operates daily from April to September, twice daily in May and three times a day from June to mid-September. Fares are US$55 one-way, US$90 return. The hydrofoil takes about five hours to cover the 282 km between the two cities. Take along something to eat and drink and arrive early to get a good seat. In Vienna tickets are available from the Mahart Agency (☎ 505 5644 or 505 3844), Karlsplatz 2/8, A-1010 Vienna. In Budapest tickets are sold at the hydrofoil terminal on the river between the Erzsébet (Elizabeth) and Szabadság bridges or at Ibusz, Tanács körút 3.

# Getting Around

### BUS

Hungary's bright yellow Volánbuses are a good alternative to the trains and only a little more expensive. They're essential for crossing the southern part of the country, for instance, to go through Szombathely,

Keszthely, Kaposvár, Pécs and Szeged. For short trips in the Danube Bend or Balaton Lake areas, buses are recommended. If you have a front seat, you'll see more from the bus than you would from the train, though you may be a little cramped. Seats on Volán buses are spaced far enough apart for you to be able to fit your pack between your knees. Tickets are usually available from the driver, but ask at the station to be sure. There are sometimes queues for intercity buses so it's wise to arrive at the bus stop early.

Bus timetables are clearly posted at stations and stops. Some footnotes you could see include: *naponta* (daily), *hétköznap* (weekdays), *munkanapokon* (on workdays), *munkaszuneti napok kivetelevel naponta* (daily except holidays), *szabadnap kivetelevel naponta* (daily except Saturdays), *szabad es munkaszuneti napokon* (on Saturdays and holidays), *munkaszuneti napokan* (on holidays), *iskolai napokan* (on school days) and *szabadnap* (on Saturdays).

### TRAIN

The MÁV (Magyar Államvasutak) operates comfortable, reliable and not overcrowded railway services on 7769 km of track. Express trains are twice as expensive as local trains. When purchasing a ticket for an express train, make sure it has a red strip across the middle. If you buy a ticket on the train rather than in the station, there's a US$2 surcharge. Some express trains are fully reserved. Seat reservations for these cost US$0.35 in the station or US$2 from the conductor.

An unlimited travel pass for all trains in Hungary is available at US$22/32 2nd/1st class for seven days, US$32/48 for 10 days. Reservation charges are additional, and since reservations are required on most express trains, the pass doesn't give you the flexibility you might expect.

If you'll be using trains extensively, you can buy a complete Hungarian timetable with an explanation of the symbols in a number of languages, including English, for US$2. Large black-and-white schedules are plastered all over railway station walls. To

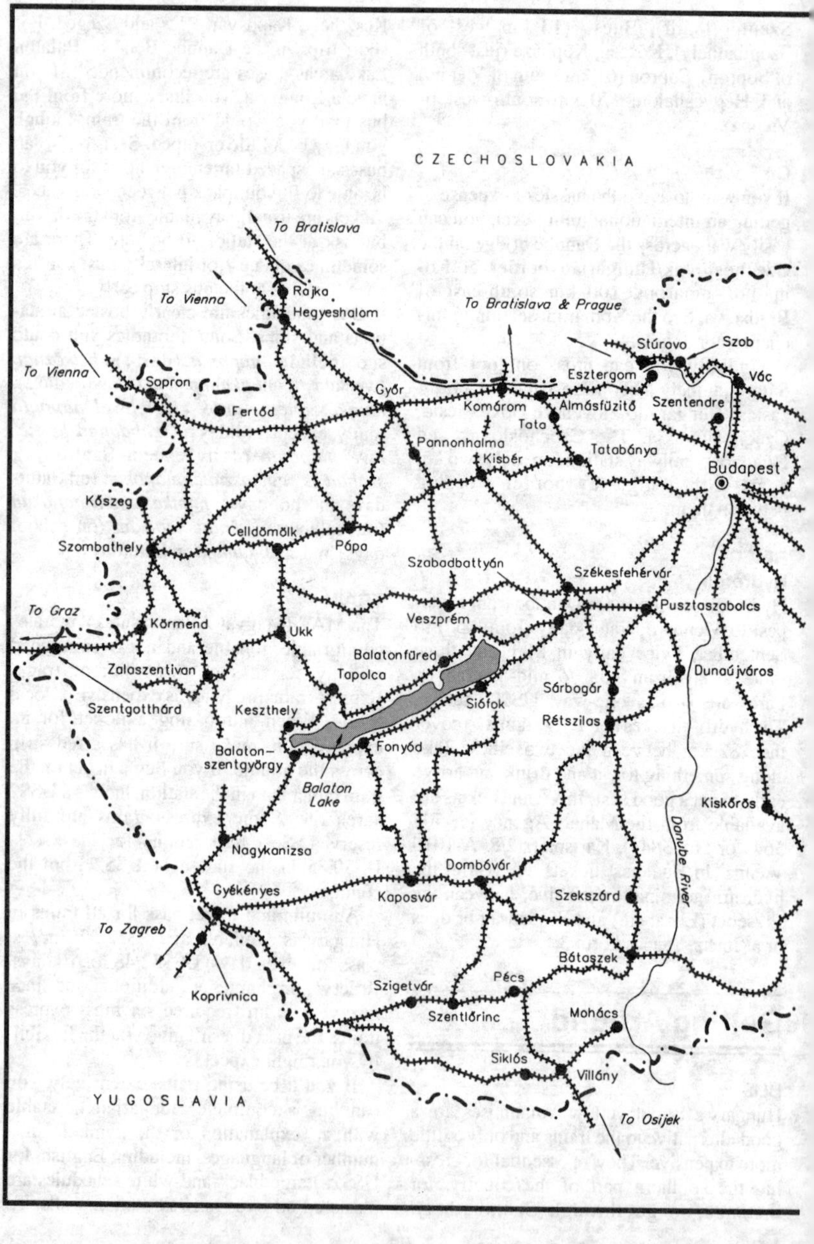
CZECHOSLOVAKIA
To Bratislava
Rajka
To Vienna
Hegyeshalom
To Bratislava & Prague
To Vienna
Sopron
Fertőd
Győr
Komárom
Almásfüzitő
Štúrovo
Szob
Esztergom
Vác
Szentendre
Tata
Pannonhalma
Kisbér
Tatabánya
Budapest
Kőszeg
Celldömölk
Pápa
Szombathely
Szabadbattyán
Székesfehérvár
To Graz
Veszprém
Pusztaszabolcs
Körmend
Ukk
Balatonfüred
Zalaszentivan
Tapolca
Dunaújváros
Szentgotthárd
Siófok
Sárbogár
Keszthely
Rétszilas
Balaton-
szentgyörgy
Fonyód
Balaton
Lake
Kiskőrös
Danube River
Nagykanizsa
Dombóvár
Gyékényes
Kaposvár
Szekszárd
To Zagreb
Bátaszek
Koprivnica
Szigetvár
Pécs
Szentlőrinc
Mohács
Siklós
Villány
YUGOSLAVIA
To Osijek

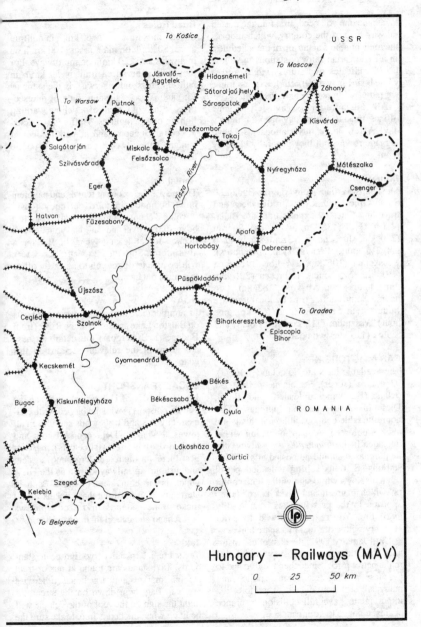

Hungary – Railways (MÁV)

0    25    50 km

locate the one you need, first find the posted railway map of the country, which indexes the route numbers at the top of the schedules. In all Hungarian railway stations, a yellow board indicates departures (indul) and a white board arrivals (érkezik). Express trains are indicated in red, local trains in black.

All railway stations have left-luggage offices, most of which stay open 24 hours a day. A few large bus stations also have luggage rooms, but they generally close by 6 pm.

### Routes
Most railway lines converge on Budapest. Some typical journeys with distances and travelling times by express train are Budapest to Győr (138 km, two hours), Sopron (210 km, three hours), Szombathely (236 km, 3½ hours), Pécs (229 km, three hours), Kecskemét (106 km, 1½ hours), Szeged (191 km, 2½ hours), Debrecen (221 km, three hours) and Miskolc (182 km, two hours). Some shorter trips by local train are Budapest to Székesfehérvár (67 km, one hour), Veszprém (112 km, two hours) and Siófok (115 km, two hours).

### CAR & MOTORBIKE
The available fuels are 86 octane (normal), 92 octane (super), 98 octane (extra), 95 octane (Eurosuper unleaded) and diesel. Diesel fuel is supposed to be purchased with nonrefundable coupons although this is not always enforced. A map indicating where unleaded fuel (olommentes uzemanyag) can be purchased should be posted at all filling stations. Stations selling unleaded petrol often display a white sign with a blue border on which a green and black petrol pump appears. In the past fuel has been readily available. You're not allowed to enter Hungary with extra fuel in a spare tank.

Until January 1991, the cost of car insurance for Hungarian motorists was included in the petrol price. Since then they've had to purchase a separate insurance policy and many are still not covered. Therefore, it's important to have full collision insurance against damage to your car.

### Road Rules
Speed limits for cars are 60 km/h in built-up areas, 80 km/h on main roads, 100 km/h on highways and 120 km/h on motorways. For motorbikes the speed limit is 50 km/h in built-up areas but otherwise is the same as for cars. A green flashing light at intersections is the equivalent of a yellow warning light in other countries. Traffic is restricted in central Budapest and as parking fees at garages in the city centre are high, use public transport.

### Rental
There's a 25% tax on car rentals and payment must be made in hard currency (cash, travellers' cheques or credit card). You must be aged 21 or over and have had your driver's licence for at least a year. In Budapest, Tourinform, Sütő utca 2 (Metro: Deák tér), will be able to direct you to a nearby office that hires out cars.

### BOAT
In summer there are regular passenger boats on Balaton Lake and the Danube River (from Budapest to Esztergom). Full details on these are given in the relevant sections in this chapter.

### LOCAL TRANSPORT
Less than 10% of Hungarians own cars so public transport is well developed, with efficient city bus and trolley bus services in all towns. Budapest, Debrecen, Miskolc and Szeged also have trams (streetcars). In Budapest there's a metro (underground) system and a suburban railway known as the HÉV, which is the equivalent of the S-Bahn in Germany. You must purchase tickets for all these at newsstands or ticket windows beforehand and cancel them once aboard.

### Taxi
Taxis are inexpensive by European standards. Taxi stands are found at bus or train stations, markets and large hotels, otherwise you can flag them down on the street. At night the sign on the roof of the vehicle will be lit up when the taxi is free. Make sure the

meter is operational and give the driver a 10% tip if all goes well.

## TOURS

Ibusz has package tours to Hungary that cater to special interests, such as cycling or stays at health spas. For those interested in horse riding there are many options. One-week hiking or 'tracking' tours in Northern Hungary are offered monthly, and twice a year there's a special one-week ornithologist tour to Hortobágy National Park, which costs US$700/1200 single/double, including room and half-board. On these Ibusz programmes you join the group at Budapest, allowing you to combine the advantages of organised and individual travel. Details are available from any Ibusz office abroad.

# Budapest

Hungary's capital, Budapest, straddles a curve of the Danube River where Transdanubia meets the Great Plain. One Hungarian in five lives here and Miskolc, the next largest Hungarian city, is only a 10th the size of Budapest. More romantic than Warsaw, more easy-going than Prague, Budapest is the Paris of Eastern Europe. The Romans built the town of Aquincum here and you can see their aqueduct and amphitheatres just north of Óbuda. Layer upon layer of history blankets Buda's castle district, and Pest's Váci utca is the city's Bond St (London) for its fine shops and fashionable clientele. Add to this a big city park brimming with attractions, a chair lift and cog-wheel railway in the nearby Buda Hills, riverboats plying upriver to the scenic Danube Bend, and hot thermal baths in authentic Turkish bathhouses and you have Budapest.

The city has many fascinating aspects. Eastern Europeans come here to make money or get a taste of the West, while Westerners revel in the nightlife, theatres, museums, restaurants and cafés. It's hard to get enough of Budapest. As the river descends from the Black Forest to the Black Sea, few cities are more striking than this 'Queen of the Danube'. Kick back for a week or two, and when you leave there'll be one more person in love with Budapest.

## Orientation

Budapest is 249 km south-east of Vienna, exactly halfway between Sofia and Berlin. The Danube is Budapest's main street dividing historic Buda from commercial Pest. All eight bridges which cross the Danube at Budapest were destroyed in the war and later rebuilt. Most visitors will arrive at one of the three main railway stations, Keleti (east), Nyugati (west) and Déli (south), all on the metro lines which converge at Deák tér on the northern edge of the city centre's shopping area.

From Deák tér, Andrássy út, Budapest's Broadway for its many theatres, runs northeast to City Park, while Tanács körút, Múzeum körút and Vamház körút swing around to the Szabadság híd (bridge) and Gellért Hill. Important crossroads in the city are Baross tér before Keleti pu Railway Station, Blaha Lujza tér where Rákóczi út meets Teréz körút, and Moszkva tér just north of Delí pu Railway Station and Castle Hill. Óbuda is at the western end of the Árpád híd north of Buda, and Aquincum is north of the Árpád híd.

**Arrival** Upon arrival in Budapest avoid the staggering queues in the railway stations by taking the metro direct to Deák tér. If you don't have any Hungarian money, you could take a chance and ride 'black' without a ticket this time. You can leave your luggage at the Erzsébet tér Bus Station on Deák tér and pay the fee later when you collect the bags. Be aware, however, that this luggage room sometimes fills up. Tourinform, the tourist information office, is nearby at Sütő utca 2, (a narrow street above Deák tér Metro Station), and although the people there don't rent private rooms or change money, they'll direct you to nearby offices which do both. The Ibusz office at Petőfi tér 3, only a short walk away, offers both services round the clock.

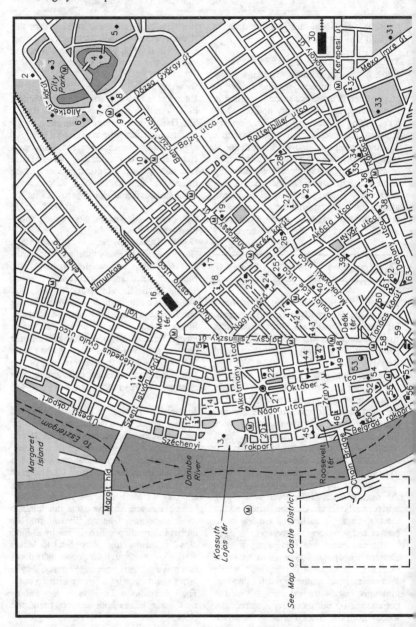

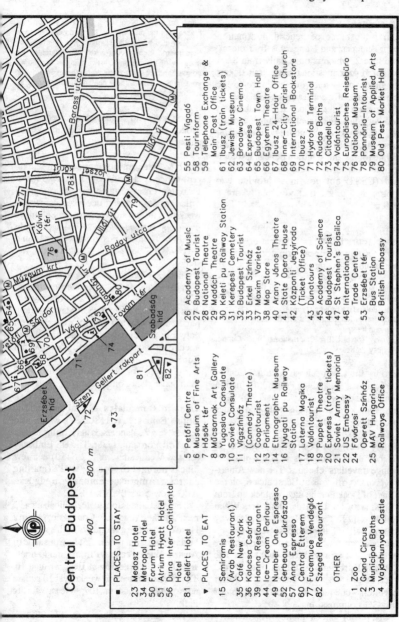

# Central Budapest

0     400     800 m

■ PLACES TO STAY

23  Medosz Hotel
34  Metropol Hotel
50  Forum Hotel
51  Atrium Hyatt Hotel
56  Duna Inter–Continental
    Hotel
81  Gellért Hotel

▼ PLACES TO EAT

15  Semiramis
    (Arab Restaurant)
35  Café New York
36  Kalocsa Csárda
39  Hanna Restaurant
44  Ice–Cream Parlour
49  Number One Espresso
52  Gerbeaud Cukrászda
57  Anna Espresso
60  Central Étterem
77  Fucemuce Vendéglő
82  Szeged Restaurant

OTHER

1  Zoo
2  Grand Circus
3  Municipal Baths
4  Vajdahunyad Castle

5  Petőfi Centre
6  Museum of Fine Arts
7  Hősök tér
8  Műcsarnok Art Gallery
9  Yugoslav Consulate
10  Soviet Consulate
11  Vígszínház
    (Comedy Theatre)
12  Cooptourist
13  Parliament
14  Ethnographic Museum
16  Nyugati pu Railway
    Station
17  Laterna Magika
18  Volántourist
19  Puppet Theatre
20  Express (train tickets)
21  Soviet Army Memorial
22  US Embassy
24  Fővárosi
25  MAV Hungarian
    Railways Office

26  Academy of Music
27  Budapest Tourist
28  National Theatre
29  Madách Theatre
30  Keleti pu Railway Station
31  Kerepesi Cemetery
32  Budapest Tourist
33  Erkel Színház
37  Maxim Varieté
38  Map Store
40  Arany János Theatre
41  State Opera House
42  Központi Jegyiroda
    (Ticket Office)
43  Dunatours
45  Academy of Science
46  Budapest Tourist
47  St Stephen's Basilica
48  International
    Trade Centre
53  Erzsébet tér
    Bus Station
54  British Embassy

55  Pesti Vigadó
58  Tourinform
59  Telephone Exchange &
    Main Post Office
61  Ibusz (train tickets)
62  Jewish Museum
63  Broadway Cinema
64  Express
65  Budapest Town Hall
66  Egyetemi Theatre
67  Ibusz 24–Hour Office
68  Inner–City Parish Church
69  International Bookstore
70  Ibusz
71  Hydrofoil Terminal
72  Rudas Baths
73  Citadella
74  Volántourist
75  Europäisches Reisebüro
76  National Museum
78  Pannónia–Intourist
79  Museum of Applied Arts
80  Old Pest Market Hall

**Information**
Your best source of general information about Budapest and Hungary is Tourinform, Sütő utca 2, which is open daily from 8 am to 8 pm. If your question is about train tickets and times, however, you should go to the nearby Ibusz office at Tanács körút 3/c.

The main Ibusz office, at Felszabadulás tér 5, supplies free travel brochures and the staff are very good about answering general questions. They also change money, rent private rooms and sell train tickets. Express, Semmelweis utca 4, sells the IUS student card (US$3) but you must provide two photos and proof that you really are a student.

**Other Tourist Offices** Information on the other Eastern European countries is available at the following offices:

Balkantourist (Bulgaria), Andrássy út 14/16
Čedok (Czechoslovakia), Kossuth Lajos tér 18
Orbis (Poland), Vörösmarty tér 6
Europäisches Reisebüro (Eastern Germany), Fovam tér 2/3
Yugoslav Travel Office, International Trade Centre, Bajcsy-Zsilinszky út 12.

Also try the Czechoslovak Cultural Centre, Rákóczi utca 15, and the Polish Information Centre, Andrássy út 32. Csehszlovak Kultura, Tanács körút 11, sells maps and guides to Czechoslovakia.

**Money** The main post office (see Post & Telecommunications) is a good place to change travellers' cheques. The new American Express office is at Bécsi utca 6, on the corner of Deák Ferenc utca, a block up from Vörösmarty tér towards Deák tér. When you leave, Ibusz at Keleti pu Railway Station will change excess forints back into hard currency if you have exchange receipts, but you will lose about 7%. The Central-European International Bank, Váci utca 16/B, will change US dollar travellers' cheques into dollars cash for only 3% commission.

One reader sent us the following letter:

The black market is not to be ignored as you get 25% higher than the official rate. If you do change do so on Váci utca where the changers are controlled by 'underworld elements' of sorts who guarantee the integrity of the changers. Always count the money yourself and put it in your pocket *before* even showing your money. This is the accepted practice among all legitimate changers.

If you do follow this advice, reread the Money section in the Facts for the Visitor chapter.

**Post & Telecommunications** The main post office is at Petőfi Sándor utca 13 near Deák tér. Poste restante is held in a small office beside the post office boxes here (open weekdays from 8 am to 8 pm). On Saturdays try asking at window No 21 inside the main building. There are post offices open around the clock at Keleti pu and Nyugati pu railway stations.

The best place to make international telephone calls is at the telephone exchange, upstairs at Petőfi Sándor utca 17 (open weekdays from 7 am to 9 pm, Saturday 7 am to 8 pm, Sunday 8 am to 1 pm). Ask the clerks on duty for the area code, then use the red coin telephones against the wall. Calls within Europe go through immediately and are fairly cheap. For North America and Australia have plenty of coins ready.

**Western Consulates & Embassies** The British Embassy (☎ 118 2888), which also serves New Zealanders, is at Harmincad utca 6 just off Vörösmarty tér. The US Embassy (closed Wednesday, ☎ 112 6450) is a few blocks north at Szabadság tér 12 (mailing address: American Embassy Budapest, APO New York 09213, USA).

The Australian Consulate, Délibáb utca 92 next to the Yugoslav Consulate (Metro: Hősök tér) is open Monday, Wednesday and Friday from 9 am to noon). The Consulate of Austria (open weekdays from 9 am to noon, ☎ 121 3213) is nearby at Benczúr utca 16. The Swiss Embassy (weekdays 10 am to noon), Népstadion út 107, is east of City Park.

The Canadian Embassy (☎ 176 7711 or

176 7686), Budakeszi út 30, is below the Buda Hills (take bus No 22 or 158 from Moszkva tér Metro Station). The German Consulate (open weekdays from 9 am to noon, ☎ 155 9366) is at Nógrádi utca 8 in the Buda Hills (bus No 21 from Moszkva tér Metro Station to Orbán tér, then ask).

**Eastern European Consulates** Budapest is a good place to pick up visas for other Eastern European countries. The most conveniently located consulate is that of Yugoslavia, Dózsa György út 92/a on Hősök tér, opposite the Műcsarnok Art Gallery.

The Romanian and Czechoslovak consulates are both south-east of City Park. The Czechoslovak Consulate, Népstadion út 24 (open weekdays from 8.30 am to 1 pm, visas US$8) is extremely crowded on Mondays with everyone who has been waiting all weekend to apply for a visa. Beware of arriving here to find over a hundred Turks or Arabs who have just got off trans-European buses waiting ahead of you in line for Czechoslovak transit visas to Germany.

The Romanian Consulate, Thököly út 72, is open Monday, Tuesday and Wednesday from 8.30 am to 12.30 pm and Friday from 8.30 to 11.30 am. The entrance is off Izsó utca around the corner, and is difficult to miss because of the huge crowd of Romanians waiting outside for new passports and so on. Don't be intimidated, they're trying to stay out of Romania, not get in. Just put US$30 in your passport, get in the middle of the crowd and, when the guard appears at the gate, wave it in the air shouting 'tourist visa' as loud as you can. That way he'll be sure to see you, will take your passport and within 30 minutes you'll have your visa. While you're waiting, have a chat with the people at the gate, some of whom may have been waiting in Budapest for as long as three years to get the visa they need to go to another country.

The Polish Consulate (open weekdays from 9 am to 3 pm) is at Törökvész út 15 in the Buda Hills (bus No 11 from Batthyány tér Metro). Tourist visas cost US$20 (US$30 for British citizens) and are issued in 24

hours, or one hour if you pay a 50% supplement. The interesting assortment of Third World nationals applying for Polish tourist visas here are people who have been refused German visas and need the onward Polish visa to get into Czechoslovakia, from whence they'll try again to enter Germany.

The Bulgarian Consulate (open Monday, Tuesday, Thursday and Friday from 9 am to 1 pm) is at Levendula utca 15/17 in the Buda Hills. Take bus No 21 from Moszkva tér Metro Station to Orbán tér, then ask. Unless you pay double for same-day express service, you must wait seven working days to get a Bulgarian tourist visa (US$19). Transit visas are always issued on the same day (US$12 for a single transit visa, US$19 for a double transit).

**Trans-Siberian Consulates** If you take the Trans-Siberian Railway east from Budapest to China or Japan, you'll need a Soviet transit visa. The Soviet Consulate, Andrássy út 104 (open Monday, Wednesday and Friday from 10 am to 1 pm), takes a week or more to issue visas. You must have confirmed transportation reservations right through the USSR, plus accommodation vouchers for each night to be spent in a Soviet city. The Chinese Embassy, Benczúr utca 17 corner of Bajza utca (Monday, Wednesday and Friday from 8 to 11.30 am), is only a block from the Soviet Consulate.

If you take the Chinese train from Moscow to Beijing, you'll also need to visit the Mongolian Embassy at Istenhegyi út 59-61 in the Buda Hills (take bus No 21 from Moszkva tér Metro Station). At last report, it was open Monday to Thursday from 10 am to noon and charged US$16 for transit visas. (The Soviet train to Beijing doesn't pass through Mongolia.)

**Bookshops** The International Bookstore, Váci utca 32, has travel guidebooks and maps, plus Hungarian and foreign art books. You can buy this book and other Lonely Planet titles there. For general reading material in English, try the Antikvárium, Károlyi Mihály utca 3 just off Felszabadulás tér.

In the arcade at Petőfi Sándor utca 2 is a bookshop which stocks maps of cities all across Europe. The newsstand at Petőfi Sándor utca 17 has English newspapers.

There's a self-service map shop at Nyár utca 1 (Metro: Blaha Lujza tér). Another map shop with different maps is at Bajcsy-Zsilinszky út 37. If you're planning to go on to Romania, be sure to pick up a map of Bucharest.

**Police** If you need to register with the police or want to report an accident, crime or theft (for insurance purposes) go to the foreigners' police (English is spoken) at Andrássy út 12 (Metro: Opera). It's open on Monday from 8.30 am to noon and 2 to 6 pm, Tuesday, Wednesday and Friday from 8.30 am to noon and Thursday from 2 to 6 pm. Ask about visa extensions here.

### Things to See

**Buda** Most of Budapest's medieval vestiges are in Castle Hill (Várhegy), the castle district of Buda. The easiest way to get there is to take the metro to Moszkva tér, cross the bridge above the square and continue straight up Várfok utca to Várhegy's **Vienna Gate**. A minibus marked 'Budavari Sikló' follows this same route from the bridge, shuttling every few minutes from Moszkva tér to Budapest Castle. Get off at the stop just after the Vienna Gate. Once through the gate, take a sharp right on Petermann biró utca past the National Archives to Kapisztrán tér. The **Magdalen Tower** is all that's left of a Gothic church destroyed in the last war. The yellow neoclassical building facing the square is the **Museum of Military History**, which you enter from the ramparts side straight ahead.

Walk south-east along Tóth Árpád sétány, the ramparts promenade, enjoying the views of the Buda Hills. The long black-and-white building below you is Budapest's Déli pu Railway Station. Halfway along the ramparts you'll be able to catch a glimpse of the neo-Gothic tower of **Matthias Church** up Szentháromság utca. The church (rebuilt in 1896) has a colourful tile roof outside, colourful murals inside and a museum which

you enter through the crypt. Franz Liszt wrote the *Hungarian Coronation Mass* for the 1867 coronation here of the Austrian king Franz Josef and his wife Elizabeth as king and queen of Hungary. Ask about organ concerts in the church. Behind the Matthias Church is an equestrian statue of St Stephen (977-1038), Hungary's first king. Alongside the statue is the **Fisherman's Bastion**, a late 19th century structure which offers great views of the parliament building and the Danube River.

From the **plague column** (1713) in front of Matthias Church, Tárnok utca runs southeast to the gate of the **Palace of Buda Castle**. The palace enjoyed its greatest splendour under King Matthias in the second half of the 15th century. Since then it has been destroyed and rebuilt three times, the last after WW II. Today the palace contains three important museums. The **National Gallery** has a huge collection of Hungarian works of art from Gothic to contemporary. The historical paintings by Mihály Munkácsy are worth noting. The **Historical Museum** shelters objects discovered during the recent reconstruction of the palace, plus a good overall display on Budapest through the ages. The **Museum of Contemporary History** often mounts penetrating exhibitions on political events in Hungary since WW II. An explanation in English is usually available at the ticket counter.

From the castle terrace take the **funicular railway** (US$0.50) down to the vehicular tunnel under Castle Hill at the Buda end of the **Chain Bridge** (Lánchíd), which was opened in 1849 and was the first bridge to be built across the Hungarian section of the Danube. In the park in front of the lower funicular station is the **Zero Kilometre Stone** for all highway distances in Hungary.

Go through the pedestrian tunnel under the end of the Chain Bridge and take tram No 19 south along the right bank of the Danube. Get off at Móricz Zsigmond körtér, the second stop beyond the Gellért Hotel (1918). Walk back a little, round the corner to the left and board bus No 27 at Villányi út 5. This bus will take you right up to the **Citadella**.

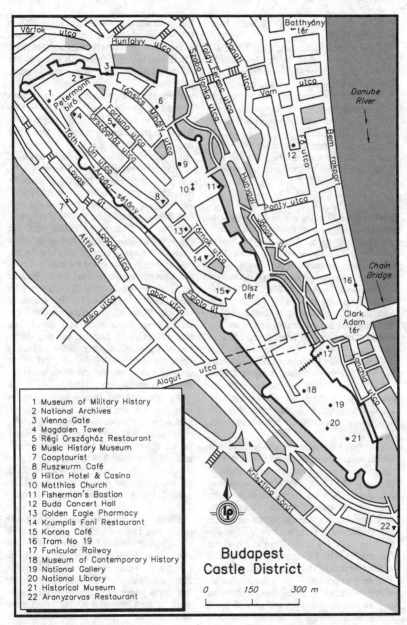

Budapest
Castle District

0    150    300 m

1 Museum of Military History
2 National Archives
3 Vienna Gate
4 Magdalen Tower
5 Régi Országház Restaurant
6 Music History Museum
7 Cooptourist
8 Ruszwurm Café
9 Hilton Hotel & Casino
10 Matthias Church
11 Fisherman's Bastion
12 Buda Concert Hall
13 Golden Eagle Pharmacy
14 Krumplis Fani Restaurant
15 Korona Café
16 Tram No 19
17 Funicular Railway
18 Museum of Contemporary History
19 National Gallery
20 National Library
21 Historical Museum
22 Aranyzarvas Restaurant

You can also walk up to the Citadella from beside the Gellért Hotel.

A commanding fortress, the Citadella (now a hotel) was built by the Austrians in 1854 to control the rebellious Hungarians. The **Statue of Liberty** at the southern end of the Citadella commemorates the Soviet soldiers who died to liberate Hungary in 1945. The bronze soldier statue was pulled down during the 1956 uprising but replaced a year later. You'll see your most memorable views of Budapest and the Danube from this hill. Walk back down to the river through the park.

**Pest** Industrialisation allowed Budapest to develop rapidly during the late 19th century and one of the nicest places to get a feeling for this period is **City Park**, north-east of the centre. Take the metro to Széchenyi Fürdő. This line, the oldest underground railway on the continent, opened in 1896. You'll come out of the station right in the middle of the park beside the **Municipal Baths** (1913), behind which are an **amusement park**, the **Grand Circus** and the **zoo** (closed Monday in winter).

Cross the busy boulevard to the south-east and you'll come to **Vajdahunyad Castle** (1896), a fascinating hodge-podge of replicas of actual buildings, many of them in what is now Romania. The **Agricultural Museum** is housed in the castle (there's also a snack bar inside).

City Park's dominant feature is **Hősök tér** with a great monument erected in 1896 for the millennium of the Magyar conquest of Hungary. The Tomb of the Unknown Soldier is also here. On the south-east side of the square is the **Műcsarnok Art Gallery**, the most prestigious in the city, where important contemporary art shows are held (open Monday to Friday from 10 am to 1 pm). On the other side of the square is the **Museum of Fine Arts** (1895), one of the richest of its kind in Europe. Here you'll see Hungary's major collection of foreign art with prints and ancient sculpture on the ground floor, European paintings on the 1st floor and

European sculpture on the 2nd floor. It's best to begin with the Spanish paintings to the left at the top of the stairs, then see the 2nd floor. These tend to close temporarily as the guards go to lunch, etc, and you can always come back later.

From Hősök tér stately Andrássy út runs straight into the heart of Pest. To save yourself a long walk, take the metro to Opera. The **State Opera House** was built in the Italian neo-Renaissance style in 1884. Many of the other great buildings along this section of Andrássy út also date from this time.

Proceed south-west on this fashionable avenue and round the corner onto Bajcsy-Zsilinszky út. You'll find the 96-metre-high neo-Renaissance dome of **St Stephen's Basilica** (1905) looming before you. The right hand of King St Stephen, founder of the Hungarian state, is kept in the chapel at the rear of the church, behind the altar.

Cross the square in front of the basilica and continue straight ahead for a block on Zrinyi utca, then right on Október 6 utca. At Október 6 utca 15 you can get a great ice-cream cone. Proceed straight ahead onto Szabadság tér with the National Bank (1905) to the right and the Television Company (also 1905) to the left. At the end of the square in front of the US Embassy is the **Soviet Army Memorial** (1945).

As you look up Vécsey utca from the memorial you see the great neo-Gothic silhouette of the **parliament building** (1904) on Kossuth Lajos tér. The exterior is impressive but individual tourists are not allowed inside. On 23 October 1956 Soviet troops fired on demonstrators here, touching off the Hungarian Revolution. The **Ethnographic Museum** (1896) also faces Kossuth Lajos tér.

There's a metro station on the south side of Kossuth Lajos tér. For a good long view of the parliament building, take the metro for one stop to Batthyány tér, where you'll also find a large public market hall and some old churches. Note the very deep tunnel as the line dives under the Danube at this point. Built by the Communists with Soviet assistance, this metro line opened in 1973.

**Óbuda & Aquincum** In 1872 three towns – Buda, Pest and Óbuda – united to form Budapest as the Austro-Hungarian Emperor Franz Josef sought to create a rival to Napoleon III's Paris. Óbuda is most easily reached by taking the HÉV suburban railway from Batthyány tér Metro Station to Árpád híd mh. The **Vasarely Museum** greets you right outside the HÉV station. Go round the corner onto Szentlélek tér, which takes you to Fő tér, the beautifully restored centre of old Óbuda. **Óbuda Town Hall** is at Fő tér 3, but the most interesting building is the Baroque **Zichy Mansion** (1752), Fő tér 1. At the back of the courtyard is an art gallery and the unique **Kassák Museum**, a tiny three-room exhibition with some real gems of early 20th century avant-garde art.

Return to the HÉV and take a train three stops farther north to Aquincum vm. Aquincum was the key military garrison of the Roman province of Pannonia. A **Roman aqueduct** used to pass this way from a spring in the nearby park and remains have been preserved in the median strip of the modern highway alongside the HÉV railway line. The 2nd century civilian **amphitheatre** is right beside the station. A few hundred metres away is a large excavated area and the **Aquincum Museum** (open from May to October, closed Monday). Don't miss the ancient musical organ with bronze pipes.

From Aquincum you have a choice of returning to Budapest or taking the HÉV on to Szentendre (see the Szentendre section). You can use regular yellow metro tickets as far as Aquincum or Rómaifürdő on the HÉV, but to go to Szentendre you have to buy a special ticket which is checked by a conductor.

**Other Museums** Two museums on the south side of Pest are worthy of special attention. The twin-towered synagogue (1859) on Dohány utca, the largest functioning synagogue in Europe, contains the **Jewish Museum** (open weekdays from mid-April to mid-October). In summer there's a service every Saturday at 10 am with a sermon and organ music. The former Jewish ghetto extends behind this synagogue.

The **National Museum**, Múzeum körút 14-16 (Metro: Kálvin tér), has Hungary's main collection of historical relics in a large neoclassical building (1847). Begin with the section on the ground floor, behind the cloakroom, which covers the period up to the Magyar conquest. Upstairs is a continuation of Hungarian history and, in place of honour before the entrance, the coronation regalia. These precious relics fell into the hands of the US troops in Germany in 1945 and were only restored to Hungary in 1978. In the opposite wing is a large natural history exhibit with dioramas to show the fauna in natural settings.

Most Budapest museums are closed on Monday and free on Saturday, though the National Museum is free on Wednesday.

**The Buda Hills** If you have children with you, the Buda Hills are the place to take them. The variety of transportation opportunities makes visiting fun. Begin with a ride on the **cog railway** (fogaskerekű), which has been winding through pleasant wooded suburbs into the Buda Hills since 1874. The lower terminus of the cog railway is on Szilágyi Erzsébet fasor, opposite the circular high-rise Hotel Budapest and within walking distance from Moszkva tér Metro Station. The fare is one yellow metro ticket (daily, all year).

Near the upper terminus of the cog railway is Széchenyi-hegy Station of the **Pioneer Railway**, a 12-km scenic route opened in 1950 (no service on Monday). Excepting the engineer, this line is completely staffed by children to interest them in transportation careers. Catch a train to János-hegy Station and walk up through the forest to the lookout tower on János-hegy (529 metres) with its 360° view. The **János-hegy chair lift** (operates daily, all year from 10 am to 4 pm, US$0.50) will take you down to Zugligeti út where you can catch bus No 158 back to Moszkva tér Metro Station.

If instead of getting out at János-hegy you stay on the Pioneer Railway to Hűvösvölgy

Station, the northern terminus, you can catch tram No 56 back to Moszkva tér.

**Margaret Island** When your head begins to spin from all the sights, take a walk from one end to the other of Margaret Island (Margit sziget). Bus No 26 from beside Nyugati pu Railway Station covers the island or you can get there on trams No 4 or 6, which stop halfway across the unusual three-way bridge leading to Margaret Island. As you stroll among the trees and statues, you'll come across the ruins of two medieval monasteries, a small zoo, a rose garden, an open-air theatre, swimming pools, cafés and a pseudo-Japanese garden with hot spring pools (beside the Hotel Thermál). The island is such a relaxing, restful place you'll seem ages away from the busy city.

**Cemeteries** Budapest's most offbeat sight is **Kerepesi Cemetery** on Mező Imre út near Keleti pu Railway Station. Beginning a century ago, it was the final resting place of Hungary's wealthiest and most prominent inhabitants. The evocative sculptured monuments scattered among the trees give Kerepesi Cemetery a unique, almost classical air which will enchant the wanderer. The most notable personages built themselves huge mausoleums which go well with the memorials to Communists of yesteryear. Half the streets in Hungary are named after people buried here.

The graves of Communists who died during the 1956 uprising are on the left side of the main avenue straight ahead from the entrance. The tombs of more recent Communist leaders, János Kádár (1912-89) among them, are a block or two over to the right. All are marked only by their name, the dates of their birth and death and a red star. Farther back are the 19th century mausoleums, including that of Ferenc Deák (1803-76), the politician who engineered the 1867 Austro-Hungarian 'compromise'.

Imre Nagy (1896-1958), the man most closely associated with the 1956 revolution, is buried in **Uj koztemeto**, Budapest's huge municipal cemetery on the far eastern side of town. Access to the municipal cemetery from Kerepesi Cemetery is fairly easy. As you leave Kerepesi, turn left on Mező Imre út and walk south-east along the cemetery wall to the next tram stop (not the one near the cemetery entrance). Take tram No 28 south-west to the end of the line right at Uj koztemeto's gate. When you want to return to town, take bus No 95 from the cemetery gate direct to Keleti pu Railway Station.

Nagy and many other prominent figures in 1956, plus some of the 2000 people who were executed between 1945 and 1956, lie in *parcelláz* 300 and 301 in the far north-east of the cemetery, a 30-minute walk from the entrance. A map of the Uj koztemeto stands near the gate and the way is clearly signposted. At peak periods you can take a microbus around the cemetery or hire a taxi at the gate. The site is still being developed but it's already something of a pilgrimage point for those interested in 1956.

### Places to Stay

**Camping** The largest camping ground in Budapest is *Rómaifürdő*, with room for 1300 guests, in a large park north of the city. To get there take the HÉV suburban railway from Batthyány tér Metro Station to Rómaifürdő vm Station, which is within sight of the camping ground. The facility is open all year so it's up to you to decide if it's warm enough for camping. From mid-April to mid-October bungalows are available from US$9/14 single/double. Use of the adjacent swimming pool, with lots of green grass on which to stretch out, is included, and nearby are a disco and several places to eat. In summer Rómaifürdő is overcrowded and buffeted by exhaust fumes from the nearby highway.

A somewhat better camping ground up in the Buda Hills is *Hárshegy Camping* (open from May to mid-October). Take bus No 22 from Moszkva tér Metro Station and watch for the signs on the right. Camping here costs US$2 per person, US$2 per tent; bungalows are from US$9/13 double/triple without shower. Both camping grounds are operated by Budapest Tourist, Roosevelt tér 5, so that would be the place to ask about on-site bungalows, etc.

There's also *Zugligeti Camping* at the bottom station of the Buda Hills chair lift (take bus No 158 from Moszkva tér Metro Station).

**Youth Hostels** Budapest doesn't have a regular year-round, dormitory-style youth hostel. In July and August three big student dormitories (US$7) are thrown open to YHA members. The main Express office at Semmelweis utca 4 (Metro: Astoria) will have information during business hours. There's also an Express office at Keleti pu Railway Station, but chances are the staff will be too busy changing money for tourists to bother about youth hostels. Try asking anyway if there's no line. Outside the two summer months, all the Express offices have to offer are some rather expensive private rooms.

One of the summer hostels is the *Schönherz Zoltán Kollégiuma Student Residence*, Irinyi József utca 42 (tram No 4 from Ferenc körút Metro Station to the second stop west of the Danube). In July and August only this 22-storey skyscraper operates as a youth hostel with a disco on the premises.

*Hotel Express* (☎ 175 3082), Beethoven utca 7/9, several blocks south-west of Déli pu Railway Station (take tram No 59 for two stops), is US$23/27 double/triple or US$31 for four with a 20% discount if you pay in hard currency. The toilet and shower are down the hall and breakfast costs extra. Although this place is listed in the IYHF handbook, there's no discount for YHA card holders. Staff at the main Express office will say this hotel is full even when it isn't.

**Private Rooms** The best value for accommodation in Budapest is the private rooms assigned by local travel agencies. They generally cost US$7/11 single/double or more plus US$1 to US$2 tax, with a 10% supplement if you stay less than four nights. To get a single or a room in the centre of town, you may have to try several offices. There are lots

of rooms available and even in July and August you'll be able to find something.

Following is a list of various agencies, beginning with those closest to the transportation terminals. Most are open only during normal business hours. If you arrive late or on a weekend, try the Ibusz Accommodation Centre at Petőfi tér 3 (Metro: Deák tér) which never closes. The centre's prices are slightly higher than those of the following agencies, however, so only go there when the others are closed. Individuals on the street outside this Ibusz office will offer you an unofficial private room, but their prices are higher than those asked inside and there is no quality control.

***Near Keleti pu Railway Station*** The Ibusz office in Keleti pu Railway Station (open daily) has private rooms but in summer they go quickly. The UTAS Tours office, next to the international booking office, across the foyer from Ibusz and Express, takes a minute to locate and is thus far less crowded. Staff there change money and rent private rooms (when there are any). Also look for Orient Tours, a tiny kiosk built into the foyer entrance off platform No 6, which also has rooms.

Budapest Tourist at Baross tér 3, just beyond the overpass on the opposite side of the square from Keleti pu Railway Station, also arranges private rooms and changes money. The lines are much shorter here. Another branch of Budapest Tourist, a 10-minute walk away at Teréz körút 41, is open from 8 am to 8 pm Monday to Saturday. Ibusz, Teréz körút 55, also has private rooms.

***Near Nyugati pu Railway Station*** Ibusz at Nyugati pu Railway Station does not arrange private rooms. Instead, try Cooptourist or Budapest Tourist in the underground concourse at the entrance to the metro below Nyugati pu Railway Station. Cooptourist has no singles though it does have rooms in the centre of town. Volántourist, Teréz körút 96, quite near Nyugati, is open till 5 pm on weekdays. Cooptourist is in the opposite

■ PLACES TO STAY

2　Sporthotel Lidó
15　Hotel Thermál
19　Hotel Express
40　Eben Hotel
43　Hotel Platanus
44　Schönherz Zoltán
　　Kollégiuma Student Residence

▼ PLACES TO EAT

16　Casino Etterem

OTHER

1　Rómaifürdő Camping Ground
3　Civilian Amphitheatre
4　Aquincum Museum
5　Hűvösvolgy Station
6　János-hegy Station
7　János-hegy Lookout Tower
8　Hárshegy Camping
9　Chair Lift
10　Canadian Embassy
11　Kiscelli Museum
12　Fő tér, Óbuda
13　Polish Consulate
14　Military Amphitheatre
17　Széchenyi-hegy Railway Station
18　Cog Railway Upper Terminus
20　German Consulate & Mongolian
　　Embassy
21　Cog Railway Lower Terminus
22　Király Baths
23　Parliament
24　Nyugati pu Railway Station
25　Déli pu Railway Station
26　Matthias Church
27　Budapest Castle
28　Rácz Baths
29　Citadella
30　Petőfi Centre
31　Transportation Museum
32　Swiss Embassy
33　Romanian Consulate
34　Czechoslovak Consulate
35　Keleti pu Railway Station
36　Kerepesi Trotting Track
37　People's Stadium
38　Budapest Sports Hall
39　Népstadion Bus Station
41　Race Track & Hungarexpo
42　Planetarium
45　Buda Park Theatre

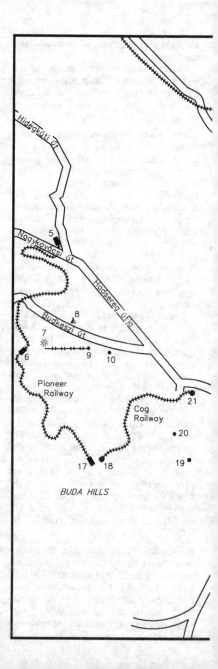

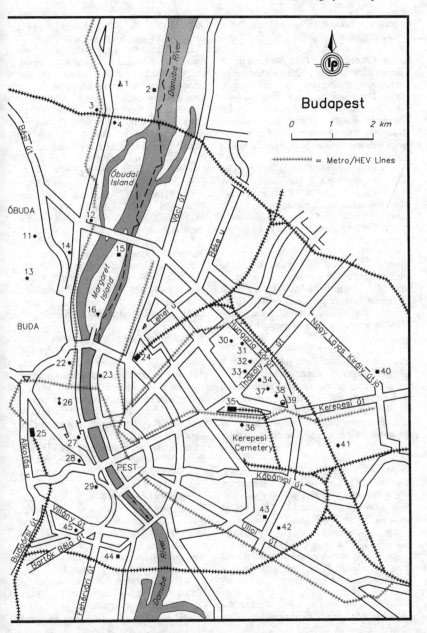

# Budapest

0        1        2 km

++++++++++ = Metro/HEV Lines

Danube River

Óbudai Island

ÓBUDA

Margaret Island

BUDA

Bécsi út

Váci út

Béke u

Lehel u

Hungária körút

Nagy Lajos Király útja

Mexikói

Thököly

Kerepesi út

Kerepesi Cemetery

Kőbányai út

Üllői út

Alkotás u

Villányi út

Budaörsi út

Bartók Béla út

Fehérvári út

Danube River

PEST

1 2 3 4 11 12 13 14 15 16 22 23 24 25 26 27 28 29 30 31 32 33 34 35 36 37 38 39 40 41 42 43 44 45

direction at Kossuth Lajos tér 13 near Parliament.

**Near Erzsébet tér Bus Station** Ibusz, Tanács körút 21 right at Deák tér has private rooms (open during business hours on weekdays). Dunatours and Cooptourist, are side by side at Bajcsy-Zsilinszky út 17 behind St Stephen's Basilica. (Apart from rooms in Budapest, Dunatours rents holiday cottages with cooking facilities in resort areas outside the city.)

One of the largest offices in the city offering private rooms is Budapest Tourist, Roosevelt tér 5 (open until 7.30 pm on weekdays and Saturday and Sunday mornings). It has lots of rooms and gives a 5% discount if you pay in hard currency (cash or travellers' cheques).

**Near Déli pu Railway Station** At Déli pu Railway Station private rooms are arranged by Ibusz, at the entrance to the metro, or Budapest Tourist, in the mall in front of the station. Also try Cooptourist, Attila út 107, directly across the park in front of Déli pu Railway Station.

**Near the Hydrofoil Terminal** Volántourist, Belgrád rakpart 6, is near the hydrofoil terminal. Also in the vicinity is Ibusz, at Felszabadulás tér 5, one of the largest travel agencies in the city. Coophotels, Váci utca 33, has private rooms in the very centre of town for a bit more than the other agencies charge.

**Hotels – Cheaper Hotels** A hotel room will cost more than a private room, though management doesn't mind if you stay only one night. The *Citadella Hotel* (☎ 166 5794) in a castle above the Danube is cheap and romantic but 'always' full. The 11 rooms go for only US$14 double and there's also a cheap US$2 dormitory *(turistaszallas)* but everything is usually booked by groups. Try calling several weeks in advance for a reservation.

Upriver beside the Danube, near the Rómaifürdő Camping Ground, is the *Sport-*

*hotel Lidó* (☎ 188 6865), Nánát 67 north of the city. Singles/doubles are available all year at US$10/16 with shared bath. Show your YHA card here for a possible discount. The Sporthotel Lidó has a sauna, solarium, fitness room and tennis courts which are available to guests, and from May to September there's a ferry service on the Danube from Római *part* (embankment) near the hotel to Margaret Island. Though the Sporthotel Lidó could be full in summer, it's a good choice during the rest of the year if you're only staying a few nights.

Also worth trying is the one-star *Hotel Polo* (☎ 180 3022), Mozaik utca 1-3 near the Filatorigat mh HÉV Station between the Hotel Békás and Budapest. You can't see the hotel from the station, but it's beside a BP service station, behind a long white building which runs along the east side of the tracks. Singles/doubles with shared bath are US$24/25, while the one room with private bath is US$28/29, breakfast included. It's a new hotel built in 1987 and is in the same building as the local Volkswagen dealer.

**Eravis Hotel Chain** The big news on the Budapest hotel scene is the Eravis chain of budget hotels in huge converted workers' hostels. These come in two varieties: regular two-star hotels, like the Eben and Platanus, which offer comfortable rooms with private bath, and the fully renovated 'tourist hostels', the Békás, Flandria and Poscher, which have only rooms with shared bath. For advance reservations, contact Eravis Utazasi Iroda (☎ 361-185 1188 or 185 1126; fax 361 186 9320; telex H 22 6089), Bartók Béla út 152, H-1113 Budapest XI.

The *Eben Hotel* (☎ 184 0677), Nagy Lajos király útja 15, is a modern six-storey hotel with singles/doubles at US$18/21 without bath, US$24/26 with bath, breakfast included. These prices apply only from November to mid-March. In summer prices at Eben Hotel more than double, so it's only a good deal in winter. Also known as the 'ESZV Hotel,' it's a five-minute walk from Ors vezér tér Metro Station.

Similarly, the two-star *Hotel Platanus*

(☎ 133 6057), Konyves Kálmán körút 44, a renovated four-storey hotel opposite the planetarium (Metro: Nepliget), is only reasonable from November to mid-March (US$14 double without bath, US$14/21 single/double with bath). Prices are more than double that during the rest of the year.

*Hotel Flandria* (☎ 129 6689), Szegedi út 27, is easily accessible on trams No 12 and 14 from Élmunkás tér Metro Station. From November to mid-March, rooms with shared bath in this five-storey tourist hotel cost US$12 for up to three people, plus US$2 per person for breakfast. Two blocks away is the *Poscher Hotel* (☎ 149 0321), Kerekes utca 12-20, a huge 11-storey block which still houses workers, as well as tourists. The Poscher is slightly cheaper than the Flandria, and even cheaper in summer when the Flandria doubles its prices while the Poscher only increases them by 50%. The atmosphere in the Poscher can be a little rough-and-ready at times because of the large numbers of Hungarian workers present, whereas the Flandria is only for regular tourists. There's a very cheap self-service restaurant in the Poscher – recommended for those who want to experience proletarian Budapest.

The *Hotel Békás* (☎ 180 3184), at Pünkösdfürdő utca 38, at the north-west end of Budapest, is an 11-storey workers' residence which now also serves as a pleasant 65-room tourist hotel. From November to mid-March, a four-bed room with shared bath costs US$14 for the room (for up to four people) and about US$23 the rest of the year. Breakfast is US$1.50 per person extra. The Hotel Békás is a 10-minute walk from Békásmegyar HÉV Station on the line to Szentendre (ask directions from the station). Though a little out of the way, it's good value if there are a few of you.

**Expensive Hotels** A couple of noisy old two-star hotels near Keleti pu Railway Station are the *Hotel Park* (☎ 113 1420), Baross tér 10 directly across from the station, and the *Metropol Hotel* (☎ 142 1175), Rákóczi út 58 (Metro: Blaha Lujza tér). Singles/doubles at either of these will cost you US$35/50 without bath, US$45/60 with bath, breakfast included. That may be fine for one night, but look elsewhere if you're staying longer.

A much better medium-priced hotel is the *Medosz Hotel* (☎ 153 1700), Jókai tér 9 in the theatre district (US$45/63 single/double with private bath and breakfast). There's no sign outside, so look for the modern building marked 'haza' beside the 'Babszinház' (Metro: Oktogon).

Moving up in price and altitude is the chalet-style, four-star *Hotel Panoráma* (☎ 175 0522) at the upper terminus of the Buda Hills cog railway. From April to October, singles/doubles with bath and breakfast are US$56/76, going down to US$35/54 in winter. During a few peak periods in the year, the price jumps to US$69/92 single/double, so ask. The Hotel Panoráma has only 36 hotel rooms so advance reservations are advisable, although the 54 slightly more expensive bungalows (breakfast not included) are often available. The bungalows are good for families with small children. The hotel has a sauna, outdoor swimming pool, restaurant and bar on the premises.

Where to stay if the price doesn't matter at all? Perhaps the modern five-star *Hotel Thermal* (☎ 132 1100) on Margaret Island (US$125/180 single/double, including breakfast and use of the thermal baths). It's quiet and you have all the facilities of a luxury spa right there on the premises.

### Places to Eat

**Cafeterias** The cheapest places to eat are the big self-service cafeterias, and one of the most convenient of these is *Centrál Étterem*, Tanács körút 7 near Deák tér (open daily from 8.30 am to 7 pm). In summer some tables are moved out onto the pavement. The meat dishes here cost double everything else and beware of getting cold food. Just stand and observe what the locals are taking for a while – don't let anyone rush you. Watch the price of the beer as it could cost more than your meal!

Another such is the *Unio Étterem*, Népszínház utca 7 facing Blaha Lujza tér. Notice the multilingual pictorial menu just where you pick up your tray. Far across the square is the *Emke Bisztró* on Akácfa utca, on the corner of Rákóczi út (Metro: Blaha Lujza tér). It's actually a Western-style fast-food place but the barbecued chicken and draught beer are OK.

*Önkiszolgáló Étterem*, Alkotás utca 7/B, beside Déli pu Railway Station, is a cheap cafeteria with big omelettes in the morning and grilled chicken all day. If you want barbecued chicken and beer, don't line up but just walk around to the special counter beyond the cashier. It's open daily from 8 am to 8 pm.

The *Halló Étterem*, Teréz körút 53, is a real proletarian self-service restaurant near the theatre district.

**Central Pest** *Paprika Aranybárány*, at Harmincad utca 4 right next to the British Embassy, is a glorified fast-food restaurant with colour photos of the dishes displayed outside (Metro: Vörösmarty tér).

The *Városház Snack*, Városház utca 16, opposite the town hall at the back exit of the main post office, serves good food at reasonable prices. Don't come at lunch time as the place will be jammed with local office workers.

*Pepita Oroszlán Vendéglő*, Váci utca 40, on the corner of Irányi utca, has the menu posted outside in English and German. Though not cheap, it has a pleasant open atmosphere, good pork and beef dishes and cold beer.

There are two unpretentious kosher restaurants in what was the Jewish ghetto, north-east of Tanács körút. The *Hanna Restaurant*, Dob utca 35 (open weekdays from 11.30 am to 4 pm only), is part of an active Jewish community centre occupying buildings which survived the war. A block or two away at Klauzál tér 2 is the more commercial *Salom Restaurant*.

Real Arab food is served at *Semiramis*, Alkotmány utca 20 near Nyugati pu Railway Station (there is additional seating upstairs). It's rather hidden halfway down the block.

Just a block from Nyugati pu Railway

Station is the *Szlovak Söröző*, Bihari utca 17 off Szent István körút, where you'll get big plates of Slovak or Hungarian food at reasonable prices, although the waiter may overcharge you slightly. You have a choice of eating at the bar and watching videos, or occupying one of the large tables which give the place its beer-hall atmosphere. It's open daily from 10 am to midnight.

The *Bohemtanya Vendéglő*, Paulay Ede utca 6 between Deák tér and the State Opera, is an unpretentious but OK eatery that serves large portions. You could even have to line up to get in. The menu is in English and German. Back on the beaten tourist track is the *Kalocsa Csárda*, upstairs at Teréz körút 2, on the corner of Rákóczi út (Metro: Blaha Lujza tér). Its saving grace is the folk dancing which is presented daily in summer except Sunday at 8 pm to diners who pay only for the meal and drinks (no cover charge). Expect to pay at least US$7 per person.

A good neighbourhood restaurant offering Gypsy music (in the evening), a German menu, good food and moderate prices at *Fucemüce Vendéglő* (open daily from 11 am to 11 pm), Kofarago utca 5 on a backstreet behind the National Museum.

The clean and attractive *Saláta Bar*, in a corner of the Grand Hotel Hungária, on Baross tér facing the overpass across the square from Keleti pu Railway Station, has fresh salad (!) although the attendant fills your plate and you have to eat standing up.

**Castle District** Expensive restaurants that are popular among tourists abound in the castle district. One worth mentioning is the rather expensive *Régi Országház*, Országház utca 17, which combines good wine with a medieval atmosphere. *Krumplis Fani*, Dísz tér 8, is one of the few places where you can get an inexpensive meal.

The perfect place for coffee and cakes is the crowded *Ruszwurm Café*, Szentháromság utca 7 near Matthias Church (closed Wednesday). The castle district's most illustrious café is *Korona Café*, Dísz tér 16, opposite the palace gate. Try the pastries and

Viennese coffee. Literary evenings in Hungarian are held here on certain weekdays at 7 pm (tickets cost US$2).

**Below Castle Hill** The *Aranyszarvas Restaurant*, Szarvas tér below Castle Hill, offers game food such as wild pig, pheasant and venison daily until midnight. It is expensive yet unpretentious. The *Szeged Restaurant*, Bartók Béla út 3 beside the Gellért Hotel, specialises in fish dishes.

There's a good little büfé (cheap restaurant) with regular table service which serves lunch on weekdays from 8 am to 3 pm in the Buda Concert Hall, Corvin tér 8, directly below the Fisherman's Bastion on Castle Hill. It's worth the slight detour as the tourists up on the hill don't know this place.

**Óbuda** There are a number of good restaurants around Fő tér, Óbuda (HÉV suburban railway from Batthyány tér Metro to Árpád híd mh). The *Postakocsi Restaurant*, Fő tér 2, is one; *Sipos*, Szentlelek tér 8, is less expensive (try the fish soup). Although tourist-oriented, it doesn't attract nearly as many foreigners as the places on Castle Hill. Menus are posted outside.

**Cafés** Like Vienna, Budapest is famous for its cafés and the most famous of the famous is the *Gerbeaud Cukrászda*, on the west side of Vörösmarty tér, a fashionable meeting place of the city's elite since 1870. *Anna Espresso*, nearby at Váci utca 7, is full of black-market operators. Its large green sign beckons.

The *Café New York*, Teréz körút 9-11 (Metro: Blaha Lujza tér), has been a Budapest institution since 1895. The elegant, turn-of-the-century décor glitters around the literary world which still meets there. At least one visit must be made to the Café New York!

*Number One Espresso*, Guszev utca 9 off Erzsébet tér, is a good local pub with draught beer but no food.

**Markets** The old Pest market hall (closed Sunday) is on Fovam tér (Metro: Kálvin tér).

A large open-air street market (open Sunday) unfolds behind the large church above Élmunkás tér Metro Station.

A large supermarket (open Monday, Tuesday, Thursday and Friday from 6 am to 8 pm, Wednesday and Saturday from 7 am to 4.30 pm, Sunday from 7 am to 1 pm) is in the old market hall on the south side of Batthyány tér near the metro station. Stock up.

## Entertainment
**Opera & Operetta** You should pay at least one visit to the *State Opera House* (1884), Andrássy út 22 (Metro: Opera), to see the frescoes and incredibly rich gilded decoration in the Italian Renaissance style. The box office is on the left-hand side of the building (closed Monday). Tickets are more expensive for Friday and Saturday nights.

Budapest has a second opera house, the modern *Erkel Színház* at Köztársaság tér 30 near Keleti pu Railway Station. Tickets are sold just inside the main doors.

Operettas are presented at the *Fővárosi Operett Színház*, Nagy-mező utca 17, a block from the State Opera House. Tickets are sold inside. The *National Theatre* on Hevesi Sándor tér, four blocks from Keleti pu Railway Station, also offers musical programmes, including rock operas such as *Stephen, the King*.

The musical *Cats* has been performed at the *Madách Theatre*, Teréz körút 31/33, for years. The Madách presents an interesting mix of rock operas, musicals and straight drama in Hungarian – it's worth checking.

**Concerts** A monthly *Koncert Kalendarium* lists all concerts in Budapest that month. Most nights you'll have two or three to choose from. The motto of the Budapest Spring Festival in late March is '10 days, 100 venues, 1000 events.' Budapest's main concert hall is the *Pesti Vigadó*, Vigadó tér 2 (Metro: Vörösmarty tér). Other concerts are held at the *Academy of Music*, Majakovszkij utca 64, on the corner of Liszt Ferenc tér (Metro: Oktogon).

Jazz concerts are often held at the

*Egyetemi Theatre*, Pesti Barnabás utca 1 off Március 15 tér (Metro: Felszabadulás tér). The Egyetemi Theatre ticket office nearby at Váci utca 33 also sells tickets to special events such as rock spectaculars.

Folk dancing is performed every week or two in the *Buda Concert Hall*, Corvin tér 8 (Metro: Batthyáni tér).

**Youth Scene**  The youth scene revolves around the *Petőfi Centre* in City Park (Metro: Széchenyi fürdő) where rock and blues concerts are held several nights a week. There are also a restaurant and cinema (open in summer only) in the complex. Ask at the information counter about events.

**Theatre**  The *Nulladik Színház* (Theatre No 0), Csengery utca 68 (Metro: Oktogon), presents Laterna Magika (magic lantern) performances featuring a combination of film and movement, usually on Saturdays at 7.30 pm. Check with Tourinform, a ticket agency or the theatre itself (☎ 133 0512) beforehand as performances at Nulladik Színház listed in the publication *Programme in Ungarn/in Hungary* are often cancelled.

The *Puppet Theatre*, Andrássy út 69 (Metro: Vörösmarty utca), presents afternoon shows designed for children and evening programmes for adults. There's a special adult performance on Monday at 6 pm. The shows are generally held at 3 pm on weekdays and at 11 am and 4 pm on weekends. They'll usually make room for foreign tourists.

**Circus**  The *Grand Circus*, Állatkerti körút 7 (Metro: Széchenyi Fürdő), appears on Wednesday to Sunday with afternoon performances at 3 pm on Wednesday to Sunday and evening performances at 7 pm Wednesday, Friday and Saturday. There are also morning shows on the weekend. Although the matinées are occasionally booked out by school groups, there's almost always space in the evening. Advance tickets (US$3) are sold at the circus itself.

**Other Events**  Budapest's *Planetarium*

(Metro: Nepliget) features exciting laser light shows to the accompaniment of rock music. There are usually shows held on Monday, Thursday, Friday and Saturday at 6.30 and 8 pm. You can purchase tickets (US$4) at the door or from any Budapest ticket agency.

The *Broadway Cinema*, Tanács körút 3 (Metro: Astoria), offers four sessions daily in the films' original languages. Most of the films are of the sex or violence variety, although occasionally something of value is shown.

**Nightlife**  Budapest has an active nightlife with numerous discos and cabarets. Perhaps the swankiest nightclub is *Maxim Variete* in the Emke Hotel, Akácfa utca 3 (Metro: Blaha Lujza tér). The club's chorus line consists of 12 scantily dressed Maxim girls, and magicians, acrobats, singers and dancers appear in a Las Vegas-style extravaganza. Performances are at 7.30 and 11 pm daily except Sunday and cost US$29 per person for dinner (including half a bottle of Hungarian champagne) and a show. It's also possible to enter without having dinner by paying US$21, which includes a US$9 voucher towards snacks and drinks. Reserve your table at the 'cassa' next to the hotel reception (☎ 122 7858, open from noon to 1 am).

You'll find more of the same at the *Moulin Rouge Cabaret* (☎ 112 4492) beside the Fővárosi Operett Színház (Metro: Opera). The erotic show at 9.30 pm is followed by international shows at 10 pm and midnight. The cabaret then functions as a disco until 5 am.

**Summertime Entertainment**  In July and August most of the theatres are closed for holidays. The cabarets remain open and folk dancing is performed at several locations. From mid-April to mid-October the Folklor Centrum offers traditional Hungarian dancing to Gypsy band music at the *Arany János Theatre*, Paulay Ede utca 35 (Metro: Opera). There's also an evening variety show at the *Casino Étterem*, an open-air restaurant on Margaret Island (closed in winter).

Tourinform on Sütő utca will have up-to-date information on programmes and times.

**Ticket Agencies** The busiest theatre ticket agency is the Központi Jegyiroda, Andrássy út 18 (Metro: Opera). You can get tickets there to numerous theatres and events, although the best are gone a couple of days in advance.

For concert tickets try Jegyiroda Országos Filharmonia, Vörösmarty tér 1. Check out the zany elevator next to this office.

As you pursue your quest for tickets, you'll sometimes be told that everything is sold out. You often get better seats by going directly to the theatre box office than you would by dealing with a ticket agency. Theatre tickets cost anywhere from US$1 to US$5.

**Horse Races** It should come as no surprise that the descendants of the nomadic Magyar tribes love horse racing. Races are held at the *Kerepesi Trotting Track*, Kerepesi út 9 near Keleti pu Railway Station (bus No 95), throughout the year, beginning at 2 pm on Saturday (10 races) and 4.30 pm on Wednesday (eight races). Admission is US$0.50 and there's a large section where food and drink are sold.

From mid-March to November regular horse races are held at the *Galopp Loversenypálya Race Track* on Dobó István út, next to Hungarexpo, every Sunday beginning at 10.30 in winter, 2 pm in summer. From May to September horse races are also held at Galopp Loversenypálya on Tuesday beginning at 4 pm. Each session lasts for about four hours (10 races). You can see the track from Pillangó utca Metro Station but the entrance is a 15-minute walk away (as you leave the station turn left, then left again onto Dobó István út).

**Thermal Baths** Budapest is a major spa with numerous bathing establishments that are open to the public. There are 140 thermal springs in Budapest gushing forth over 40 million litres of warm mineral water daily.

Begin your bathhouse tour with the *Gellért Baths* (enter through the side entrance of the eclectic hotel of the same name below Gellért Hill). The thermal pools there maintain a constant temperature of 44°C and a large outdoor pool is open in summer. The price list is posted in English and German beside the ticket booth (a thermal bath costs US$1, tub bath for two people US$4, 30-minute massage US$4, outdoor swimming pool US$2 for three hours, etc). You must wear a bathing cap (US$0.25 to hire) in the swimming pool. Therapeutical services such as traction cure, ultrasonic, inhalation and short-wave treatments are available. They're closed in the afternoon on weekends.

There are two famous bathing establishments near the Buda end of Erzsébet híd (Elizabeth Bridge). The *Rudas Baths* beside the river were built by the Turks in 1566 and retain a strong Islamic flavour. The Rudas Baths are open daily for men only (closed on weekend afternoons). Women should make for the *Rácz Baths* at the foot of the hill, on the opposite side of the bridge. The Rácz Baths are reserved for women on Monday, Wednesday and Friday and for men on Tuesday, Thursday and Saturday.

Everyone passing this way should seek out the *ivocsarnok*, or well room (closed Sunday), which is below the bridge, within sight of the Rudas Baths. Here you can indulge in the drinking cure for only 1 Ft. Give the coin to the cashier who will give you a ticket which entitles you to a big mug of hot radioactive water.

The *Király Baths*, Fő utca 84 (Metro: Batthyány tér), are genuine Turkish baths erected in 1566. Like the Rácz Baths there are alternate days for males (Monday, Wednesday and Friday) and females (Tuesday, Thursday and Saturday).

If you would rather bathe in ultramodern surroundings, try the *Hotel Thermal* on Margaret Island. The baths there are open to the public daily from 7 am to 7 pm. This includes the use of the three hot thermal pools and the sauna. A massage costs US$9. This is Budapest's most luxurious bathing establishment by far.

The easiest way to get to the baths is to take the metro to Batthyány tér, then tram No 19 south to Rácz, Rudas and Gellért, or walk north to Király. To go to Hotel Thermal, take bus No 26 from Nyugati pu Railway Station. All of these establishments offer massage, manicure, hairdressing and similar services. Admission is rarely over US$2 (except at the Hotel Thermal, where it's US$5). There are lockers where you can leave your valuables. Tip the staff a little and you'll soon make good friends. Most of the public baths hire out bathing suits and towels if you don't have your own. It's all part of the Budapest experience, so give it a try.

### Things to Buy

Before you do any shopping for handicrafts at street markets, have a look in the Folkart Centrum, Váci utca 14, a large government store where prices are clearly marked. When you know what you want and are familiar with the prices, you'll be in a better position to bargain with street vendors.

In the far back corner of the Pest Market on Fovam tér (Metro: Kálvin tér), past the strings of paprika and garlic, are a couple of stands where vendors sell genuine Hungarian folk costumes, dolls, painted eggs, embroidered tablecloths, etc. You can also get *langos* (big flat Hungarian doughnuts) or hot sausages here.

### Getting There & Away

**Bus** There are three important bus stations in Budapest. For buses to most points west of the Danube and outside Hungary, try the Erzsébet tér Bus Station (Metro: Deák tér). Some buses for places east of the Danube depart from the Népstadion Bus Station (Metro: Népstadion). Buses to the Danube Bend, including Esztergom, Visegrád and Vác leave from the bus station next to Árpád híd Metro Station.

It's usually possible to reserve seats on long-distance buses the day before, otherwise you can pay the driver and take a chance on getting a seat. There's a left-luggage office at Erzsébet tér Bus Station which is open till 6 pm. For details of international bus services see the general Getting There & Away section in this chapter.

**Train** Budapest has three main railway stations, all connected by metro. Keleti pu Railway Station (east) receives trains from Vienna Westbahnhof, Bratislava, Bucharest (via Arad), Belgrade, Poland, Košice, and northern Hungary.

Services from Bratislava (via Štúrovo), Bucharest (via Oradea), the Great Plain and the Danube Bend arrive at Nyugati pu Railway Station (west), also on the left bank of the Danube.

Trains from Vienna Südbahnhof, Zagreb, Pécs, Balaton Lake and western Transdanubia generally use Déli pu Railway Station (south) on the Buda side of the city. There are exceptions, however, so be sure to check carefully which station you'll be using.

If you arrive in Budapest on a special summer train that continues through to another destination (Berlin to Bulgaria, for example), beware of missing the stop as the trains often don't go in to a main station, stopping instead at Köbánya-Kispest.

*Railway Stations* Nyugati pu Railway Station is a historic iron structure built in 1877 by the engineer Alexandre Gustave Eiffel of Paris. When Keleti pu Railway Station opened in 1884 it was the most modern station in central Europe. Keleti has somewhat better facilities than Nyugati, but there can be a long queue at the luggage storage area (*poggyászmegőrző*). Although coin lockers are available, they're confusing to operate and often full. The left-luggage office at Nyugati is well hidden inside the main waiting room beside platform No 13. Few people know it so there probably won't be much of a queue. The atmosphere in both stations is unpleasant, so don't hang around.

There are often very long queues to change money at both Express and Ibusz in Keleti pu Railway Station and neither opens until 8 am. If the queues to change money are impossibly long in Keleti, try the Orszagos Takarékpenztár (National Savings Bank), Rákóczi út 84 a block from the station

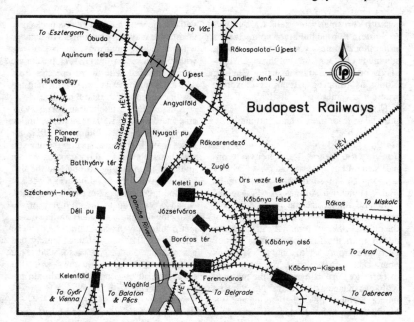

To Esztergom
Óbuda
To Vác
Rákospalota–Újpest
Aquincum felső
Hűvösvölgy
Újpest
Landler Jenő Jjv
Angyalföld
Budapest Railways
Pioneer Railway
Nyugati pu
Rákosrendező
Batthyány tér
Zugló
Örs vezér tér
Széchenyi-hegy
Keleti pu
Kőbánya felső
Rákos
To Miskolc
Déli pu
Józsefváros
Boráros tér
Kőbánya alsó
To Arad
Kelenföld
Vágóhíd
Ferencváros
Kőbánya–Kispest
To Győr & Vienna
To Balaton & Pécs
To Belgrade
To Debrecen
Szentendre HÉV
Danube River

(open Monday 8.15 am to 7 pm, Tuesday, Wednesday and Thursday 8.15 am to 3 pm, Friday 8.15 am to 1 pm).

Don't try to change money at the Ibusz office beside platform No 10 in Nyugati pu Railway Station, as the wide, disorderly queue is full of pickpockets and black marketeers. Instead, go down into the nearby metro arcade where there are two travel agencies which change money at the same rate and have no thieves or hustlers. If they're closed, follow the advice given in the Arrival section under Budapest.

There's generally no problem about stretching out a sleeping bag in either station but put your pack in the luggage room first. The police will wake you and the hundreds of Romanian Gypsies around you at about 5.30 am.

**Tickets** The MÁV Hungarian Railways office, Andrássy út 35 (Metro: Opera), is the place to purchase international train tickets or to make advance seat reservations for Hungarian express trains. The two international ticket queues here are long and slow throughout the year as each ticket is individually calculated and written out by hand, then the compulsory reservation made by phone. Save time by coming early, because around mid-afternoon the place is jammed.

Skip the long queue at MÁV by going to Ibusz, Tanács körút 3/c (Metro: Astoria or Deák tér), which sells the same tickets and can make seat reservations. Payment in Western currency is required. Staff at the Ibusz office in Keleti pu Railway Station will sell you a ticket to Arad or Oradea, Romania, for about US$2, or to other points in Eastern Europe.

If you want discounted youth or student train tickets go to Express, Beloiannisz utca 10 (Metro: Kossuth tér), open Monday to Thursday from 8.30 am to 6 pm, Friday from 8 am to 3 pm.

Wagons-lits Tourisme, Dorottya utca 3,

just off Vörösmarty tér, sells train tickets to Western Europe but brace yourself for a price shock. Unless you're in a real hurry, it's much cheaper to travel through Yugoslavia or Czechoslovakia, using Cheb or Koper as jumping-off points closer to where you want to go.

Keep in mind that all international tickets must be paid for in cash hard currency.

## Getting Around

**To/From the Airport** There are two terminals several km apart at Budapest Ferihegy Airport, 16 km south-east of the centre. Malév Hungarian Airlines, Air France and Lufthansa flights use the new Ferihegy 2 terminal, while most other airlines fly out of the older Ferihegy 1 terminal. Airport buses depart from the Erzsébet tér Bus Station every hour from 5 am to 9 pm (US$1) – buy your ticket from the driver. You can also get to Ferihegy Airport by taking the metro to Kóbánya-Kispest, then bus No 93 (red number) which stops at both terminals. Bus No 93 (black number) stops at Ferihegy 1 only.

**Public Transport** Budapest has three underground metro lines intersecting at Deák tér: line M1, the 'yellow' line from Vörösmarty tér to Mexikoi út, line M2, the 'red' line from Déli pu to Örs Vezér tér, and line M3, the 'blue' line from Árpád híd to Kóbánya-Kispest. A possible source of confusion on M2 is that one stop is called Vörösmarty tér and another is Vörösmarty utca. The HÉV suburban railway, which runs north from Batthyány tér Metro Station, is in effect a fourth metro line. There's also a very extensive network of tram, trolley bus and bus services. An invaluable transit map detailing all services is available at all metro ticket booths.

To use public transport you must buy tickets at a kiosk, newsstand, or metro entrance. Tickets for metro, trams, trolley buses and HÉV (as far as the city limits) are yellow and cost US$0.20 each. Bus tickets are blue and US$0.30 each. You have to validate your ticket once aboard. Every time

you change vehicles, you must cancel a new ticket. You may carry two pieces of luggage without paying an extra fare. Never ride without a ticket on the HÉV as tickets are always checked. The metro operates from 4.30 am till just after 11 pm. Certain tram and bus lines operate throughout the night.

A day ticket for public transport is available and costs US$1.50 for all trams, trolley buses, HÉV and metro lines, and US$2 for buses as well. You must specify the day you wish to use the pass and it's good only from midnight to midnight, so buy one the day before. If you'll be spending over a week in Budapest, consider getting a monthly pass, which is valid up to the fifth day of the following month on all trams, trolley buses, metro and HÉV lines within the city. The price is US$12, but you must supply one passport-size photo. This pass is sold at the main metro stations. You must write the serial number of your photo card onto the monthly ticket.

**Boats to the Danube Bend** Mahart riverboats operate on the Danube daily from May to mid-September between Budapest and Esztergom. Some boats go via Szentendre, others via Vác, making it possible to do a round trip on different arms of the Danube. The Szentendre route is the more scenic. All services stop at Visegrád, Nagymaros and Dömös.

In Budapest the boats leave from near Vigadó tér (Metro: Vörösmarty tér) on the left bank. Ask at the yellow ticket office on the riverside which is below the Duna Inter-Continental Hotel. They all stop first at Bem József tér on the right bank, near Margit híd HÉV Station, a 10-minute walk upriver from Batthyány tér Metro Station.

This five-hour scenic cruise is highly recommended for a running view of Budapest and the river. There's an open deck upstairs where you can sit. The fare is about US$1 for the full one-way trip.

**Local Ferries** From May to September passenger ferries run every 15 minutes from 7 am to 7 pm between Boráros tér, beside

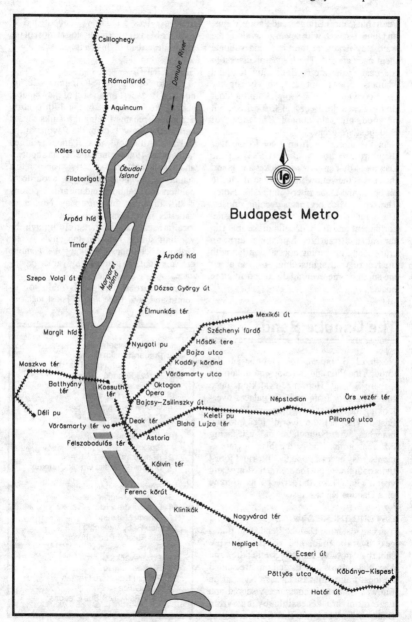

## Budapest Metro

Petőfi híd (Petőfi Bridge), and Park 9 Május, on Óbudai-sziget, with seven stops along the way. Buy tickets at the kiosk and validate them once aboard. The ferry stop closest to the castle district is Batthyány tér, and Március 15 tér is not far from Vörösmarty tér, a convenient place to pick up the boat on the Pest side. Beer and soft drinks, but no food, are sold aboard. The views of Budapest are great.

In the afternoon from May to October there are 1½ hour cruises (US$3) on the Danube. You can buy your ticket and board the boat at the yellow ticket office at Vigadó tér below the Duna Inter-Continental Hotel. The same office organises evening cruises. The night lights of the city rising to the castle, parliament and the Citadella make this trip far more attractive than the afternoon cruises, and the timing doesn't conflict with the rest of your sightseeing. Ask too about the summertime evening disco and folklore boats.

# The Danube Bend

North of Budapest, the Danube breaks through the Pilis and Börzsöny mountains in a sharp S-bend. Here medieval kings once ruled Hungary from majestic palaces overlooking the river at Esztergom and Visegrád. East of Visegrád, the river divides into two branches, with Szentendre and Vác facing different arms. Today the historic monuments, easy access, good facilities and forest trails combine to put the area at the top of any visitor's list. This is the perfect place to come on a Danube River cruise.

## GETTING THERE & AWAY

You can reach the Danube Bend from Budapest by rail, road, and river. The HÉV suburban railway runs to Szentendre, and Vác, Nagymaros and Esztergom are served by local trains from Budapest's Nyugati pu Railway Station. Szentendre, Visegrád and Esztergom are accessible by bus from Budapest's Árpád híd Bus Station. All of these services are fairly frequent and in summer Mahart riverboats stop at most of the places described in this chapter.

## SZENTENDRE

A trip to Szentendre (St Andrew), 20 km north of Budapest on an arm of the Danube, should not be missed. In the 17th century Serbian merchants fleeing the Turks settled here, bringing with them the flavour of the Balkans. Although most of them returned home in the 19th century, the Serbian appearance remained. In the early years of this century, Szentendre became a favourite of painters and sculptors, and the artists' colony is still alive and thriving today. Numerous galleries have been established to exhibit local artists' work, and a stroll through the winding streets between the city's exotic Orthodox churches, or along the Danube embankment, is a most enjoyable experience.

Szentendre is Hungary's main tourist centre and you'll see all the latest fashions

1 Kerényi Museum
2 Preobraženska Church
3 Ferry to Szentendre Island
4 Bárczy Fogadó
5 Belgrade Church
6 Serbian Art Museum
7 Czóbel Béla Museum
8 Catholic Parish Church
9 Vajda Lajos Museum
10 Amos-Anna Museum
11 Ibusz
12 Dunatours
13 Blagovesztenska Greek Orthodox Church
14 Görög Kancsó Vendéglő
15 Kováks Margit Museum
16 Szentendre Picture Gallery
17 Kmetty Museum
18 Rab-Ráby Vendéglő
19 Sts Peter & Paul Church
20 Barcsay Collection
21 Požarevačka Church
22 Bükkös Panzió
23 Roman Sculpture Garden
24 Post Office
25 HÉV Railway & Bus Stations

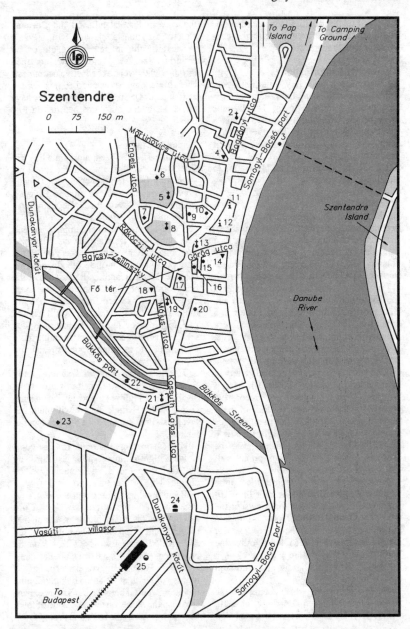

Szentendre

0    75    150 m

displayed in front of the thousand and one boutiques and on the trendy tourists parading up and down the streets.

## Orientation & Information

From the Szentendre HÉV station, it's only a short walk up Kossuth Lajos utca to Fő tér, the centre of the old town. The Danube embankment (Somogyi-Bacsó part) is a block east of this square. The riverboat terminal and camping ground are a couple of km farther north.

Dunatours (Idegenforgalmi Hivatal) is in Bogdányi utca 1.

## Things to See

Begin with Fő tér, which on July evenings becomes a stage for theatrical performances. Most of the buildings around the square date from the 18th century, as does the plague column (1763) in the centre and the **Blagovesztenska Greek Orthodox Church** (1752) in one corner. Also worth visiting are the **Kmetty Museum**, Fő tér 21, and the **Szentendre Picture Gallery**, Fő tér 2-5 (enter from the alley at the rear). The gallery mounts changing exhibitions by local artists.

Directly opposite the gallery entrance is the **Kovács Margit Museum** at Vastagh György utca 1, the most delightful gallery in Szentendre (admission US$0.50). Margit Kovács (1902-77) based her decorative ceramic objects on Hungarian folk art traditions to create a style all her own. Also be sure to see the **Ferenczy Museum**, Fő tér 6 beside the Greek Church, which displays the artworks of the Ferenczy clan, pioneers of the Szentendre artists' colony.

Narrow lanes lead up from Fő tér to the Catholic **Parish Church** (rebuilt in 1710) from where you get splendid views of the town. The **Czóbel Béla Museum** is opposite the church. Just north is the tall red tower of **Belgrade Church** (1756), the finest of the Serbian churches. Beside the church is a museum of Serbian religious art (admission US$0.75).

Other art galleries worth seeing are the **Amos-Anna Museum**, Bogdányi utca 10, the **Kerényi Museum**, Ady Endre utca 6 on the way to Pap Island, and the **Barcsay Collection**, Dumsta Jenő utca 10 near Fő tér.

Most of the museums are closed on Monday, free on Wednesday and open throughout the year. A collective ticket/postcard *(bérletjegy)* for entry to 10 museums is available for US$0.75, though you may have to ask at several museums before you find one.

## Places to Stay

You can easily see Szentendre on a day trip from Budapest. If you would like to use the town as a base for exploring the Danube Bend, Dunatours (Idegenforgalmi Hivatal), Bogdányi utca 1, and Ibusz, Bogdányi utca 11, arrange private rooms.

There's an expensive camping ground with bungalows (that are always full) open from mid-May to September on Pap Island, a couple of km north of Szentendre near the Danube riverboat landing. It's just across the bridge from the Hotel Danubius bus stop. The reception is open from 8 am to 4 pm only. Check out by 10 am or you'll have to pay for another night. The camping fee includes admission to the swimming pool alongside. The camping ground's restaurant is pricey but good.

The 48 rooms at *Hotel Danubius*, Ady Endre utca 28, a two-star, four-storey hotel on the main highway opposite Pap Island, cost US$38/41 single/double with bath and breakfast. Prices are about a third cheaper in winter.

*Villa Castra*, Ady Endre utca 54, is a comfortable eight-room pension, just north up the road from the Hotel Danubius, which charges US$34 a double (no singles) with bath and breakfast throughout the year.

Similar are the attractive *Coca Cola Pension* on the main highway, about 500 metres south of the Hotel Danubius, and the *El Dorádó Panzió*, Egressy út 22, left on the next street south of the Coca Cola Pension.

*Bükkös Panzió*, Bükkös-part 16, has 16 rooms with bath at US$43/51 single/double including a buffet breakfast. It's more expensive than the places on the north side of town but much closer to the HÉV and the old town.

## Places to Eat

The *Görög Kancsó Vendéglő*, Görög utca 1, is touristy but has reasonable fish dishes. The most colourful place in town to eat is *Bárczy Fogadó*, an old inn at Bogdányi utca 30 which is well worth the extra money.

Check to see if the langos stall is open. These hot Hungarian doughnuts are the best deal in Szentendre but in winter the stall is only open on weekends. The stall is halfway up Váralja Lépcsö, a tiny alley between Fő tér 8 and 9.

## Getting There & Away

Access to Szentendre couldn't be easier. Take the HÉV from Budapest's Batthyány tér Metro Station to the end of the line. There are several trains an hour. Buses from Budapest's Árpád híd Bus Station also run to Szentendre frequently. Hourly buses depart from stand No 3 at the Szentendre HÉV station to the ferry wharf opposite Vác (Váci rev).

From May to September, Danube riverboats between Budapest and Esztergom stop at Szentendre a couple of times daily. The landing is near Pap Island, a km north of the centre.

## VÁC

Vác (Wartzen), on the left bank of the Danube, 34 km north of Budapest, is far less touristy than the places on the right bank. Medieval Vác was destroyed by the Turks and much had to be rebuilt by the Catholic bishops in the 18th century. There are several beautiful churches and squares, but Vác's chief attraction is a chance to see a little more of the romantic Danube and experience Hungarian small-town life.

## Information

Dunatours is at Széchenyi utca 14.

## Things to See

As you leave the railway station, proceed straight ahead on Széchenyi utca and you'll soon reach Március 15 tér (Fő tér) which contains some of Vác's most beautiful buildings. Notice especially the Baroque **town**
hall (1731) at No 11 and the Gothic palace at No 6 opposite, now the **Institute for the Deaf & Dumb**. At the back of the courtyard at Március 15 tér 19 is an **art gallery** (closed Monday and in winter) housed in what used to be a church (1792). On the south side of the square is the lovely Rococo **Dominican Church** (1699), behind which is a **market** that is also well worth a visit.

Follow Köztársaság út south past the Baroque **Statue of the Trinity** (1750) and the **public swimming pool** to Konstantin tér, which is dominated by the massive neoclassical **cathedral** (1762). This building with its huge Corinthian columns outside and extensive frescoes inside is one of the most overpowering in Hungary (usually closed).

On Múzeum utca, which begins near the **bishop's palace** (1768) at the western end of Konstantin tér, is the **Tragor Ignác Museum** (closed Monday) with a small but select local history exhibit and a lapidarium in the basement. Continue going down Múzeum utca until you see the **Franciscan Church** (1721) before you. The Baroque pulpit, altars and organ in this church are splendid.

A lane beside the church leads down to the Danube embankment. If you follow this north, beyond the ferry terminal, you'll find the 15th century **round tower** that remains from the old city walls. Farther north along the river is a sinister-looking **prison**. Both the prewar fascist and postwar Communist regimes kept political prisoners here. Follow the prison wall around onto Köztársaság út where you'll find Hungary's only **triumphal arch**, erected in 1764 for Queen Maria Theresa.

If you have some spare time, take the ferry across the Danube to **Szentendre Island** for the views. It's possible to cross the island on foot or by hourly bus and return to Budapest via Tahitótfalu and Szentendre.

## Places to Stay

Dunatours, Széchenyi utca 14, and Ibusz, Széchenyi utca 6, can find you a private room.

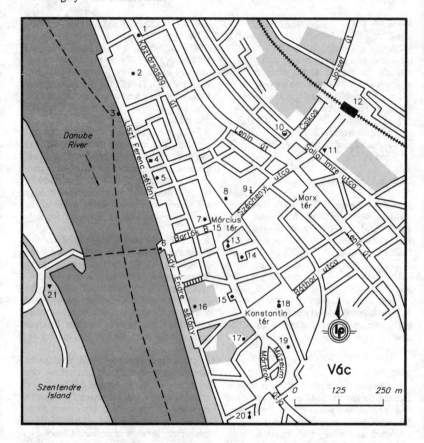

Vác

0    125    250 m

If all the private rooms are full, two small private pensions at Liszt Ferenc sétány 13 near the ferry terminal, the *Trio* and *Tabán*, rent doubles for about US$25 (no singles), breakfast included. The Trio (☎ 06-271 2638) has only five rooms so call ahead. The people there speak German.

**Places to Eat**
The *Pokol Csárda* (closed Tuesday) just across the river on Szentendre Island serves good fish soup. There's also the *Halászkert Vendéglő*, Liszt Ferenc sétány 9, opposite the ferry terminal.

In the centre of Március 15 tér, below ground level, is the *Révkapu Borozó*, a medieval wine cellar.

A good unpretentious place to enjoy a substantial meal is the *Széchenyi étélbár* (closed Sunday) on the corner of Széchenyi utca and Sallai Imre utca near the train station.

**Getting There & Away**
Getting to Vác is easy on hourly trains from Budapest's Nyugati pu Railway Station (look for the train to Szob). The first railway

| | |
|---|---|
| 1 | Triumphal Arch |
| 2 | Prison |
| 3 | Riverboat Terminal |
| 4 | Trio & Tabán Pensions |
| 5 | Round Tower |
| 6 | Ferry Terminal |
| 7 | Town Hall |
| 8 | Institute for the Deaf & Dumb |
| 9 | Dunatours |
| 10 | Bus Station |
| 11 | Széchenyi étélbár |
| 12 | Railway Station |
| 13 | Dominican Church |
| 14 | Market |
| 15 | Statue of the Trinity |
| 16 | Public Swimming Pool |
| 17 | Bishop's Palace |
| 18 | Cathedral |
| 19 | Tragor Ignác Museum |
| 20 | Franciscan Church |
| 21 | Pokol Csárda |

line built out of Budapest reached Vác in 1846.

If you want to go to Visegrád from Vác, catch a Szob train west to Nagymaros (see the Getting There & Away section under Visegrád).

## VISEGRÁD

Visegrád is superbly situated on a horseshoe bend of the Danube, between the Pilis and Börzsöny mountains. For hundreds of years the river was the border of the Roman Empire. After Tatar invasions in the 13th century, the Hungarian kings built a mighty citadel on a hilltop with a wall running down to a lower castle near the river. In the 14th century a royal palace was built on the flood plain at the foot of the hills and the Angevin court moved here in 1323. For nearly two centuries Hungarian kings and queens alternated between Visegrád and Buda. The reign of the Renaissance monarch Matthias Corvinus in the 15th century was the period of greatest glory for Visegrád.

The destruction of Visegrád came with the Turks and later in 1702 when the Habsburgs blew up the citadel to prevent Hungarian independence fighters from using it as a

base. All trace of the palace was lost until 1934 when archaeologists following descriptions in literary sources uncovered the ruins that you can visit today.

Communist central planners with financial backing from energy-hungry Austria had intended to build a barrage across the river here but work on the project has stopped. The partially completed barrage is visible just upstream from Visegrád. It all comes back to modern society's insatiable thirst for energy. Coal and nuclear-powered generators aren't very attractive either, and the problems created by acid rain or nuclear wastes and disasters are just as serious as the ecological havoc a barrage would wreak. Perhaps an idyllically beautiful yet threatened spot like Visegrád is just the place to sit and ponder these problems.

### Information

Dunatours is at Fő utca 3/a.

### Things to See & Do

You can visit the **palace ruins** at Fő utca 27 daily except Monday throughout the year from 9 am to 4 pm. Some of the highlights are a red-marble fountain bearing the coat of arms of King Matthias in the Gothic courtyard and, on an upper terrace, a copy of the lion wall fountain, which is covered in winter. The original fountains are kept in the museum at **Solomon's Tower**, which is next on the list of sights to visit. The tower is on a low hill above the Danube, a few hundred metres from the palace ruins. This was part of a lower castle that was intended to control river traffic. The 13th century walls are up to eight metres thick! The tower museum is only open from May to October daily except Monday, but visitors can enjoy the exterior any time.

**Visegrád Citadel** (1259) is on a high hill directly above Solomon's Tower, and is accessible on hiking trails (it is signposted as 'Fellegvár'). From June to August a local bus runs up to the citadel from the side street in front of the King Matthias statue near the Danube riverboat wharf. You can also hike up to the citadel in 40 minutes along a

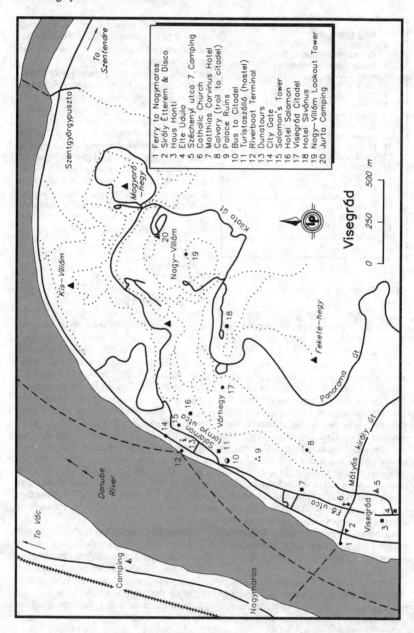

**Visegrád**

1 Ferry to Nagymaros
2 Sirály Étterem & Disco
3 Haus Honti
4 Elte Üdülő
5 Széchenyi utca 7 Camping
6 Catholic Church
7 Matthias Corvinus Hotel
8 Calvary (trail to citadel)
9 Palace Ruins
10 Bus to Citadel
11 Turistaszálló (hostel)
12 Riverboat Terminal
13 Dunatours
14 City Gate
15 Solomon's Tower
16 Hotel Salamon
17 Visegrád Citadel
18 Hotel Silvánus
19 Nagy–Villám Lookout Tower
20 Jurta Camping

0   250   500 m

marked trail behind the Catholic church in town (see the Visegrád map). Restoration work on the three defensive levels of the citadel will continue for many years, but the view of the Danube Bend from the walls is absolutely stunning, making this one of the most scenic spots in Europe. On another hill nearby is the **Nagy-Villám Lookout Tower** which offers another fabulous view.

Numerous opportunities exist for hiking in the mountainous forest behind Visegrád. One trail marked with blue strips leads 11.6 km from Nagy-Villám to Pilisszentlászló via Papret. If markers stop appearing, you're off the track. Hikers should buy the 1:40,000 *A Pilis* topographical map of the area at a tourist office or bookstore. New roads which cut across the trails at several points are not marked on this map!

**Near Visegrád** There's a new open-air thermal swimming pool at **Lepence** beside the road halfway between Visegrád and Dömös. An excellent half-day hike from **Dömös** is the climb to the village of Dobogókő via the Rám-szakadék Gorge, which takes about three hours. There are sweeping views of the river and mountains through openings in the forest along the way. From Dobogókő you can catch a bus to Esztergom or Pomáz va HÉV station, but it's an easy downhill walk back to Dömös via Kortvelyes or Lukács-arok for a circle trip. These trails through the **Pilis Nature Reserve** are clearly marked, and in early summer you will find raspberries along the way.

Alternatively, you can take a small ferry across the Danube from Dömös to Dömösi átkéles, then climb to the caves that are visible on the hillside and back into the hills behind Nagymaros.

## Places to Stay

Dunatours, Fő utca 3/a on the main highway opposite the riverboat terminal, arranges private rooms or turistaszálló (hostel) accommodation. One turistaszálló is nearby at Salamon tornya utca 5 and another is at Széchenyi utca 7. Both are closed from mid-

October to April. From June to August the Széchenyi utca 7 hostel, which is by the small stream back behind the church with the green tower, is a good place to try since you are also allowed to camp there.

Many houses along Fő utca have signs advertising *zimmer frei* (room available). One such is *Haus Honti*, Fő utca 66 next to a picturesque little stream. Also try the house at Fő utca 107 across the street. Nearby at Fő utca 117 is the *Elte Udulo*, a new four-storey hotel which closes in winter. In July and August room prices jump sharply in Visegrád.

*Jurta Camping* (open from May to September) is high up on a hillside north of the Nagy-Villám Tower. There is a bus service from June to August only, otherwise you face a stiff 40-minute uphill hike. You can rent bungalows and there is a small, expensive restaurant. The nearest grocery store is back down in Visegrád. It's a quiet camping ground but is crowded with cars and mobile homes.

A third camping ground is at Nagymaros, across the Danube by ferry. It's near the river up the busy highway beyond the petrol station, two km north of the ferry. Open from May to September this one has the advantage of hot showers and direct trains to Budapest. Bungalows are available and it's highway and railway-noise free. There's a restaurant on the premises.

Perhaps the best camping ground at the Danube Bend is at Dömös, six km west of Visegrád. It's behind a meadow with a lovely view of the river only a few minutes' walk from the riverboat landing and bus stop. Open from June to mid-September, there are two-bed cabins (often full). It can get crowded in midsummer but the facilities are excellent: clean washrooms, hot water, burners for cooking and a small bar. There's a grocery store and a large restaurant in the village a 10-minute walk away. The most appealing aspect is that the hills behind Dömös are among the best hiking areas in Hungary, and the monuments of Visegrád and Esztergom are only a short hop away by bus or boat.

## Places to Eat

The *Fekete Holló*, a fish restaurant opposite the Nagymaros ferry on the Visegrád side, is touristy, so you're better off crossing the river to the *Maros Vendéglő* (closed Monday but open all year), near the Nagymaros ferry wharf on the Nagymaros side. It's just enough off the beaten tourist track to remain unspoiled. The food is good, prices are moderate and in summer you can dine on a terrace overlooking the river. Check the ferry times carefully if you want to return late to Visegrád.

In summer the disco at *Sirály Étterem* opposite the Nagymaros ferry on the Visegrád side cranks up from 8 pm to 2 am on Friday and Saturday.

## Getting There & Away

Buses between Budapest's Árpád híd Bus Station and Esztergom sometimes go via Visegrád. Bus service is more frequent from stand No 1 or 2 at the Szentendre HÉV station. In summer some buses from the HÉV go all the way up to Nagy-Villám, so ask.

Hourly ferries cross the Danube to Nagymaros. Don't panic if the large car ferry closes down early for the night. A smaller passenger launch usually takes its place. The Nagymaros-Visegrád ferry operates all year except when the Danube freezes over, but service is also suspended when fog descends, a common occurrence in winter.

Trains between Budapest-Nyugati and Szob run along the left (north) bank of the Danube about every hour with stops at Vác, Nagymaros, Zebegény, and so on. Nagymaros Railway Station is just inland from the ferry wharf across the river from Visegrád. From May to September Danube riverboats between Budapest and Esztergom stop at Visegrád.

## ESZTERGOM

Esztergom, opposite Štúrovo in Czechoslovakia, at the western entrance to the Danube Bend, is one of Hungary's most historic cities. The 2nd century Roman emperor-to-be Marcus Aurelius wrote his famous *Meditations* while he was camped here. Stephen I, founder of the Hungarian state, was born and crowned at Esztergom, which was capital of Hungary from the 10th to the 13th centuries. After the Tatar invasion of 1241, the king and court moved to Buda but Esztergom remained the ecclesiastical centre of Hungary, as it is today. Originally the clerics lived by the riverbank and royalty on the hilltop above. When the king departed, the archbishop moved up and occupied the palace, maintaining Esztergom's prominence. In 1543 the Turks ravaged the town and much had to be rebuilt in the 18th and 19th centuries.

## Information

The three information offices are Komturist, Mártirok utca 6; Gran Tours, Széchenyi tér 25; and Express, Széchenyi tér 7.

## Things to See

The bus station is a couple of blocks southeast of Széchenyi tér, the medieval market place, where the **town hall** (1773) is found. A block south is the **Inner City Parish Church** (1757), near a branch of the Danube that is lined by delightful little houseboats. Cross the footbridge to Primas Island and follow Gózhajó utca directly across to the riverboat landing on the main Danube channel. Nearby stand the ruins of the only bridge across the Danube between Budapest and Komárom, destroyed in WW II.

Continue north along the river and cross the bridge to **Víziváros Parish Church** (1738). Esztergom's famous **Christian Museum** (closed Monday) is in the adjacent **Primate's Palace** (1882) at Berényi Zsigmond utca 2. This is one of the best art collections in Hungary so don't miss it. A plaque on the side of the Primate's Palace bears the name 'József Mindszenty' and is dated 26 December 1948. Cardinal Mindszenty was arrested on that day for refusing to allow the Catholic schools of Hungary to be secularised; in 1949 he was sentenced to life imprisonment for treason. Freed in the 1956 uprising, Mindszenty was soon forced to seek refuge in the US embassy in Budapest

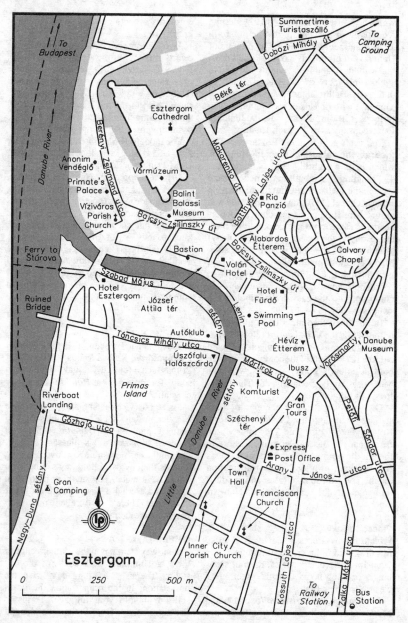

To Budapest

Danube River

Ferry to Štúrovo

Ruined Bridge

Summertime Turistaszálló

To Camping Ground

Dobozi Mihály út

Béké tér

Esztergom Cathedral

Berényi

Zsigmond utca

Makarenko út

Anonim Vendéglő

Vármúzeum

Primate's Palace

Balint Balassi Museum

Víziváros Parish Church

Ria Panzió

Bajcsy-Zsilinszky út

Batthyány Lajos utca

Bastion

Alabardos Étterem

Calvary Chapel

Bajcsy-Zsilinszky út

Volán Hotel

Szabad Május 1

Hotel Esztergom

József Attila tér

Hotel Fürdő

Lenin

Swimming Pool

Autóklub

Tánscsics Mihály utca

sétány

Úszófalu Halászcárda

Hévíz Étterem

Danube Museum

Vörösmarty

Mártírok útja

Ibusz

Primas Island

Riverboat Landing

Gőzhgjó utca

Danube River sétány

Komturist

Széchenyi tér

Gran Tours

Express

Post Office

Petőfi Sándor utca

Nagy-Duna sétány

Gran Camping

Arany

János utca

Town Hall

Franciscan Church

Little Danube

Inner City Parish Church

Esztergom

Kossuth Lajos utca

Zalka Máté utca

To Railway Station

Bus Station

0        250        500 m

which he refused to leave until 1971, despite requests from the Vatican that he do so. In 1974 Mindszenty was retired as primate of Hungary for his criticism of the Pope's dealings with the Communist regime. He died in Vienna in 1975. Nearby at Bajcsy-Zsilinszky út 63 is the **Bálint Balassi Museum** (closed Monday) with objects of local interest. The lyric poet Bálint Balassi died defending Esztergom from the Turks in 1594.

You can't help noticing **Esztergom Cathedral**, the largest church in Hungary, which is on a high hill above the Danube. The building was rebuilt in the neoclassical style in the 19th century, but the red-marble Bakócz chapel (1510) on the south side was moved here from an earlier church. Underneath the cathedral is a large crypt, but most interesting is the treasury (closed Monday) at the front of the church behind the altar. Many priceless medieval objects are kept here, including the 13th century Hungarian coronation cross. In summer you can even climb up onto the cathedral's cupola for a sweeping view.

Beside the cathedral, at the southern end of the hill, is the **Vármúzeum** (closed Monday) with remnants of the medieval royal palace (1215). Parts of the complex that were built in an early French Gothic style have been masterfully reconstructed. The views from this hill are great.

On your way back to the bus or train stations, drop into the **Danube Museum**, Kölcsey Ferenc utca 2 up Vörösmarty utca from near the Bástya Department Store in the middle of town (closed Tuesday). This fine museum provides much information on the river through photos and models, though most of the captions are in Hungarian.

### Places to Stay

Private rooms are assigned by Komturist, Mártirok utca 6, Ibusz, Mártirok útja 1, and Gran Tours, Széchenyi tér 25. Komturist has longer opening hours than the other agencies, so try there first.

In summer the *turistaszálló* at Dobozi Mihály út 8, near the cathedral, offers cheap dormitory accommodation. Ask Komtourist to refer you.

Two inexpensive hotels are found in the centre of town. At the stately *Hotel Fürdő*, Bajcsy-Zsilinszky út 14, you have the choice of a room with bath in the new section (US$28/34 single/double) or a room with shared bath in the old section (US$14/17), all including breakfast. There's a public swimming pool behind the hotel.

The modern *Volán Hotel*, József Attila tér 2, is US$11 single or double without bath, US$17 single or double with bath.

*Gran Camping* on Nagy-Duna sétány, Primas Island, offers convenient camping with riverside views (open from May to mid-October). Apart from tent space, there are luxurious bungalows complete with shower, kitchen and TV for US$26 (four beds) or US$31 (six beds). Three double rooms are available at US$10. In July and August all the rooms will be full, so get ready to unroll the tent. This site is one of the best in Hungary.

### Places to Eat

A recommended restaurant is the *Úszófalu Halászcsárda*, Szabad Május 1 sétány 4 on Primas Island (closed Tuesday). Try the fish soup. The restaurant in *Hotel Fürdő* is very elegant.

As self-service restaurants go, the *Hévíz Étterem*, upstairs at the back of the shopping centre behind Bástya Department Store on Bajcsy-Zsilinszky út, is pleasant enough, though the cashier isn't above overcharging tourists thereby cancelling any savings you might have made. For anything more than bread and a bowl of soup, you'll do better elsewhere. There's an excellent map shop beside this restaurant.

### Getting There & Away

The railway station is at the southern edge of town, a 10-minute walk south of the bus station. There's no left-luggage office at the bus station; in the train station the ticket seller will hold your luggage. Trains to Esztergom arrive from Budapest's Nyugati pu Railway Station. To go to western Transdanubia or Czechoslovakia and see something of the Danube above Esztergom in the process, take a local train to Komárom.

Bus services from Budapest's Árpád híd Bus Station are frequent. Buses from Budapest to Esztergom may travel either via Pilisvörösvár, which is the faster, more direct route, or via Visegrád, which is long, slow and scenic. Mahart riverboats travel to/from Budapest several times a day from May to September.

A ferry crosses the Danube to Štúrovo, Czechoslovakia, eight times a day from mid-February to December. Only citizens of Czechoslovakia and Hungary may use this border crossing. The nearest border crossing open to international tourists is at Komárom.

# Western Transdanubia

Beyond the Bakony Mountains, north-west of Balaton Lake, lies the Kisalföld, or Little Plain, which is bounded by the Danube and the Alps. Conquered by the Romans but never occupied by the Turks, this enchanting corner of Transdanubia is surrounded by a string of picturesque small towns with a decidedly European air. The old quarters of Sopron and Győr are brimming with what were once the residences of prosperous burghers and clerics, while Kőszeg offers an intact medieval castle, Szombathely has Roman relics, Fertőd a magnificent Baroque palace and Pannonhalma a functioning Benedictine monastery.

## GETTING THERE & AWAY

Sopron, only 69 km south of Vienna (and connected by bus and train), is a convenient gateway to/from Austria, and via Komárom you can walk to/from Czechoslovakia. From Budapest's Déli pu Railway Station you can catch trains to Tata, Komárom, Győr, Sopron and Szombathely. Rail links to/from the Danube Bend (Esztergom-Komárom) and Balaton Lake (Székesfehérvár to Komárom and Veszprém to Győr or Szombathely) are

also good, though travelling south-east from Sopron and Szombathely is often easier by bus.

## TATA

In summer it might be worth stopping at Tata (Totis), a pleasant town between Budapest and Győr. Tata's main attraction is its lakes: the large Lake Öreg-tó, with a ruined castle at one end, and the smaller Lake Cseke-tó, embraced by an enchanting English-style park with a walkway right around it. During the Middle Ages there used to be a royal hunting reserve here and there are still thermal baths and a riding school for the sports-minded. Hungary's Olympic team has its main training facility on the southern side of Cseke-tó.

### Orientation

Tata Railway Station is a couple of km north of town, so take a city bus to the main bus station (Autóbuszállómás), which is near Öregvár Castle. There's no left-luggage facility at this bus station. Between the lakes is the main street of Tata, Ady Endre utca, a busy four-lane highway lined by modern constructions. Don't worry – everything beyond this ugly strip is fine.

### Information

Komturist is at Ady Endre utca 9.

### Things to See

The moated **Öregvár Castle** sits right on the edge of Öreg-tó (Old Lake). The original Gothic structure was destroyed in wars long ago, and during the 19th century part of the castle was rebuilt in a neo-Gothic style. This now houses the **Kuny Domokos Museum** (open Tuesday to Sunday from 10 am to 2 pm). Nearby is a former country estate of the Esterházy family (1765), which has now been transformed into a hospital.

German speakers and anyone interested in the role of ethnic Germans in central Europe will want to visit the **German Nationality Museum** (closed Monday), Alkotmány utca 1, housed in an old mill (1758) just off Ady Endre utca. This ethnographical exhibit consists mostly of old folk costumes, furniture,

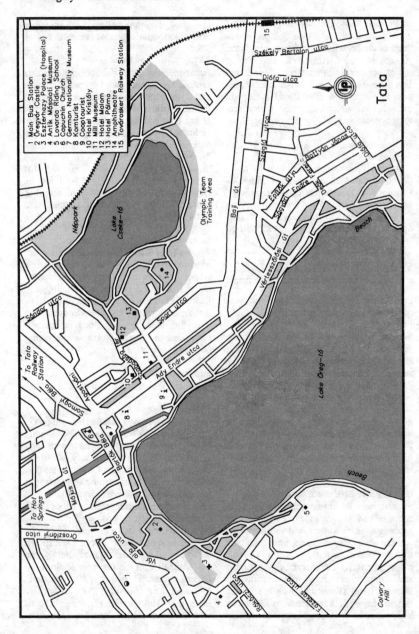

1 Main Bus Station
2 Öregvár Castle
3 Esztérházy Palace (Hospital)
4 Antik Másolati Museum
5 Lovarda Riding School
6 Capuchin Church
7 German Nationality Museum
8 Komturist
9 Cooptourist
10 Hotel Kristály
11 Mill Museum
12 Hotel Malom
13 Hotel Pálma
14 Amphitheatre
15 Tóvároskert Railway Station

Székely Bertalon utca

Diófa utca

Tata

Néppark

Lake Cseke-tó

Olympic Team Training Area

Szegái utca

Baji út

Batthyán János u

Eötvös Endre

Sógári Endre

Vértesszőlősi út

Beach

Sándor utca

Sport utca

To Tata Railway Station

Somogyi Béla

Apostoini

Ady Endre utca

Lake Öreg-tó

Bartók Béla

To Hot Springs

Mikus I út

Oroszlány utca

Vár alja utca

Beach

Calvary Hill

Rákóczi utca

Fazekas utca

farm implements and photos of local German communities of yesteryear. All captions are in German and Hungarian.

## Places to Stay

**Camping** Tata has two camping grounds, both with bungalows. The *Fényesfürdő Camping* near the hot springs north of Tata is about a km from Tata Railway Station. The *Öreg-tó Camping*, on Fáklya út south-east of Öreg-tó, is closer to Tóvároskert Railway Station if you're arriving by local train. Aside from camping, Öreg-tó also has motel rooms (open in summer only). Both camping grounds are open from May to September.

**Private Rooms** For private rooms, try Komturist, Ady Endre utca 9, and Cooptourist, Tópart sétány 18, two blocks apart in the centre of town.

**Hotels** There are three small hotels close to one another between Ady Endre utca and Lake Cseke-tó. The scruffy old *Hotel Kristály*, Ady Endre utca 22, is overpriced at US$28/30 single/double with bath and breakfast. You can get them to knock a couple of dollars off if you say you want a room with a shower instead of a bathtub.

Just up Szabadság tér from the Kristály is the much nicer *Hotel Malom*, a three-storey, one-star hotel in a resort style on a quiet road near the end of Cseke-tó. It's closed in winter.

Nearby is the *Hotel Pálma* with 19 rooms. Doubles with shared bath cost US$19 with breakfast (no singles). The Pálma has a great location right inside Néppark itself and a wonderful aristocratic air you don't expect from the low price. In summer it may be full but in the off season it's excellent value (open all year). A large public swimming pool has been set up between the Malom and Pálma hotels.

The three-star *Hotel Diana*, five km south of Tata at Remeteségpuszta (bus No 4), is another former Esterházy mansion. Rooms in the two-star 'touring' annexe are about half the price of those in the main building

but even so are still much more expensive than rooms at the Malom or Pálma hotels.

## Getting There & Away

Tata is on the main railway line between Budapest-Déli and Győr or Sopron. Trains are more frequent than buses and most express trains stop here. To go from Tata to Esztergom by train, change at Almásfüzitő or Komárom.

## KOMÁROM

Komárom is the gateway to Hungary for visitors arriving from Komárno, Czechoslovakia. Until 1920 these two towns were one. In antiquity the Romans had a military post called Brigetio here and the Habsburgs also fortified the area, although their fortresses ended up being used against themselves by Hungarian rebels during the 1848-49 War of Independence.

Komárom's position behind a large bridge across the Danube is of passing interest, but most tourists breeze straight through, so you'll find people very friendly if you stop here. There's a good camping ground next to the public thermal baths, within walking distance of the railway station and border crossing. If you arrive in the afternoon, this is a good place to stop for the night.

## Information

Komtourist is at Mártírok útja 19a in the centre of town.

## Things to See & Do

Right next to Hotel Thermál is a **thermal bathing complex** (open all year, closed Monday). To get to the thermal baths from the Danube Bridge, go south for two blocks and then turn left on Táncsics Mihály utca, a 10-minute walk. A sauna and massage are available in addition to the big thermal pool.

Among the sights of Komárom are two large 19th century fortifications that were built by the Habsburgs. The **Csillag Fortress** is near the river just north of the Thermál Hotel. You can see it from the train as you arrive from Budapest. The **Igmándi Fortress** is on the south side of town, less than 15 minutes on foot from the hotel. Today it houses the **Klapka György Museum** and an open-air theatre.

### Places to Stay & Eat
The 40 rooms with bath at *Hotel Thermál*, Táncsics Mihály utca 38, cost US$9/17 single/double in winter and US$24/34 in summer, breakfast included. Next to this attractive resort hotel is a camping ground that is open throughout the year.

The modern three-storey *Hotel Juno* across the street from the Hotel Thermál has singles/doubles for US$10/12 in winter.

### Getting There & Away
Train services from Komárom to Budapest-Déli (110 km), Tata, Győr (37 km) and Sopron are fairly frequent. For the Danube Bend, catch a train to Esztergom, and for Balaton Lake take a train to Székesfehérvár.

Komárom is a convenient entry or exit point between Hungary and Czechoslovakia. The highway bridge to Komárno, Czechoslovakia, is just a five-minute walk from Komárom Railway Station and you can easily join the throngs of locals crossing between the two countries on foot. Both Hungarian and Czechoslovak passport controls are at the Slovak end of the bridge. Komárno is a much larger town than Komárom and the Slovak railway station is a couple of km from the bridge. Though travellers with backpacks will probably enjoy the walk, there's a Slovak bus between the two stations every couple of hours. Ask at the information counter in the stations for the departure time of the next bus and pay the driver.

On the Slovak side you can easily catch a connecting local train to Bratislava (100 km), eliminating the need to buy an international train ticket. International trains usually cross the border here in the middle of the night and require compulsory seat reservations, so forget them.

### GYŐR
Győr (Raab) is a historic city midway between Budapest and Vienna, in the heart of the Kisalföld, at the point where the Mosoni-Danube, Rábca and Rába rivers meet. Győr-Sopron County is administered from here. In the 11th century, Stephen I established a bishopric here on what was the site of a Roman town named Arrabona. In the mid-16th century a strong fortress was erected at Győr to hold back the Turks.

Győr is Hungary's third-largest industrial centre, home to the Rába Engineering Works, which produces trucks and railway

---

■ PLACES TO STAY

15  Hotel Klastrom
26  Rába Hotel

▼ PLACES TO EAT

7   Halász Csárda
11  Vaskakas Taverna
12  Várkapu Restaurant
17  Szürkebarát Borozó
18  Korzo Restaurant
29  Magyar Büfé

OTHER

1   Thermal Baths
2   Bishop's Palace
3   Cathedral
4   Borsos Miklós Collection
5   Arc of the Covenant Monument
6   Margit Kováks Collection
8   Xantus János Museum
9   Former Charity Hospital
10  Casemates Museum
13  Napoleon House
14  Carmelite Church
16  Volántourist
19  Széchenyi Pharmacy
20  St Ignatius Church
21  Széchenyi Cultural Centre
22  Express
23  Kisfaludy Theatre
24  Post Office
25  Bartók Cultural Centre
27  Ibusz
28  Ciklámen Tourist
30  City Hall
31  Railway Station
32  Bus Station

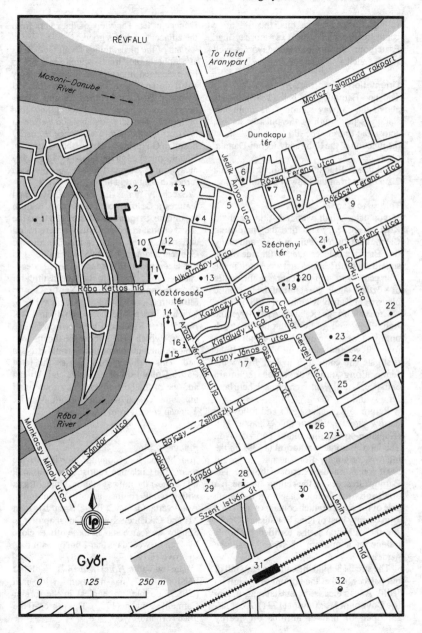

RÉVFALU

To Hotel
Aranypart

Mosoni–Danube
River

Dunakapu
tér

Móricz Zsigmond rakpart

Jedlik Ányos utca

Rózsa Ferenc utca

6

7

8

9

Rákóczi Ferenc utca

2

3

5

4

1

10

12

11

Alkotmány utca

Róba Kettos híd

13

Köztársaság
tér

14

Kazinczy utca

18

Kisfaludy utca

15

16

17

Arany János utca

Aradi Vértanúk útja

Czuczor Gergely utca

Bajcsy – Zsilinszky út

Bross Gábor út

Gorkij utca

Liszt Ferenc utca

Széchenyi
tér

21

20

19

22

23

24

25

26

27

Róba
River

Munkácsy Mihály utca

Fürst Sándor utca

Jókai utca

Árpád út

28

29

Szent István út

30

Lenin híd

31

32

Győr

0      125      250 m

rolling stock. Despite this, the old town centre retains its charm. Less touristy than Esztergom, Sopron or Eger, Győr is well worth a visit.

## Orientation & Information

The neo-Baroque city hall (1898) towers above the railway station. The main bus station is just south of the railway station, across the tracks. The old town is north, at the junction of the Rába and Mosoni-Danube rivers.

Ciklámen Tourist is at Aradi vértanúk útja 22, a block from the railway station.

## Things to See

If you take Aradi vértanúk útja north to Köztársaság tér, you'll find the enchanting **Carmelite Church** (built in 1725) and many fine Baroque palaces. On the far side of the square are fortifications that were built in the 16th century to stop the Turks. In the centre of Köztársaság tér is a statue of the Romantic playwright Károly Kisfaludy (1788-1830).

Cross the bridge (Rába kettős híd) over the Rába River and go north through the park until you locate the open-air **thermal baths** (open all year but closed on Monday). If the first gate you come to is locked, follow the fence along until you reach the main entrance. You'll want to come back here later for a swim!

Return to Köztársaság tér and follow the narrow street north up onto Chapter Hill (Káptalan-domb), the oldest part of Győr. The large Baroque **cathedral** (1639) on the hill was originally Romanesque, as you'll see if you look at the exterior of the apse. The Baroque frescoes on the ceiling are fine, but don't miss the Gothic chapel on the south side of the church which contains a glittering 14th century bust of King St Ladislas. Opposite the cathedral is the fortified **bishop's palace** in a mixture of styles. Visit the garden.

The streets behind the cathedral are full of old palaces, and at the bottom of the hill on Jedlik Ányos utca is the outstanding **Arc of the Covenant Monument** (1731). A colourful open-air market unfolds on nearby

Dunakapu tér. The view of the rivers from the adjacent bridge is good.

One of the nicest things about Győr is its atmospheric old streets, which seem not to have changed in centuries. Take a leisurely stroll down Rózsa Ferenc utca, Rákóczi Ferenc utca, Liszt Ferenc utca and Alkotmány utca where you'll see many fine buildings. The late Renaissance palace at Rákóczi Ferenc utca 6 was once a charity hospital. Go inside to admire the courtyards. Napoleon stayed in the house at Alkotmány utca 4 on 13 August 1809. It has now been turned into an art gallery.

Széchenyi tér is the heart of Győr and features a **Column of the Virgin** (1686) in the middle. **St Ignatius Church** (1641) is the finest church in the city with a superb pulpit and pews. Next door is the Benedictine Convent and next to it, at Széchenyi tér 9, is the **Széchenyi Pharmacy** (closed weekends) – a fully operating Baroque institution! Cross the square to visit the **Xantus János Museum** (closed Monday), Széchenyi tér 5, which is in a palace that was built in 1743. Beside it at Széchenyi tér 4 is Iron Stump House, which still sports the beam into which itinerant journeymen would drive a nail. This building now houses the **Imre Patkó Collection** of paintings and African art, one of the best of Győr's various small museums (closed November to mid-March). You can enter it from the alley.

## Places to Stay

Your best bet for accommodation is a private room from Ciklámen Tourist, Aradi vértanúk útja 22 near the railway station. Other offices with private rooms include Volántourist, Aradi vértanúk útja 2; Ibusz, Szent István út 31; and Ciklámen Tourist, Dunakapu tér 1. Singles are scarce and all these offices close by 4 pm on weekdays and 1 pm on Saturday, so arrive early.

The two-star *Hotel Klastrom*, ... Fürst Sándor utca 1, has 42 rooms with bath (US$35 double, no singles) in the former Carmelite convent (1720). This is great if the price is right for you.

In July and August ask about youth hostels at Express, Bajcsy-Zsilinszky út 41. The staff will know about the huge student dormitories at Ságvári Endre utca 3 north of the river.

Győr's only budget hotel is north in Révfalu, beyond the student dormitories. *Hotel Aranypart* (☎ 962 6033), Áldozat utca 12, is a modern one-star sport hotel that charges US$10/20 single/double without bath, US$15/30 with bath. To get there, cross the bridge from Dunakapu tér, then continue straight ahead for about four blocks till you see the *Revesz Panzió*, Ságvári Endre utca 22, on the right. The Hotel Aranypart is down the next street on the left. Bus No 16 passes near the Hotel Aranypart from beside the city hall.

*Kiskút-liget Camping* (open from mid-April to mid-October) is three km north-east of Győr, near the stadium. Take bus No 8 from beside the city hall. The camping ground has bungalows and a motel.

## Places to Eat

You will find the cheapest meals in Győr at the *Korzo Restaurant*, Baross Gábor út 13, which has juicy barbecued chicken. It's self-service, but there are tables where you can sit down.

A pair of typical inns near the market are the *Matróz Csárda*, Dunakapu tér 3, and the *Halász Csárda*, Rózsa Ferenc utca 4.

One of Győr's finest wine cellars is the *Szürkebarát Borozó*, Arany János utca 20. A stairway in the courtyard leads down into this vaulted restaurant. Only cold dishes are available at lunch.

The *Várkapu Restaurant*, Köztársaság tér 7, has its dishes listed on a blackboard outside.

The *Magyar Büfé*, Árpád út 18, is a good neighbourhood wine cellar that serves Hungarian fish soup and Balaton wine (closed Sunday).

For coffee and cakes go to the *Cukrászda*, Baross Gábor út 30.

## Entertainment

Győr has one of Hungary's most striking new theatres, the *Kisfaludy Theatre* on Czuczor Gergely utca. You can't miss the Vasarely mosaics covering the exterior walls! The box office is just inside. Győr's ballet company which performs here is internationally recognised.

At Kisfaludy utca 25, behind the Korzo Restaurant, is the Országos Filharmonia, where you can enquire about concerts. Also try the *Széchenyi Cultural Centre*, Széchenyi tér 7.

Other events are staged at the *Bartók Cultural Centre*, Czuczor Gergely utca 17.

## Getting There & Away

Győr is well connected by express train to Budapest's Déli pu Railway Station (138 km) and Sopron. Other trains run to Szombathely via Pápa. To go to Balaton Lake there's a secondary line with local trains going south to Veszprém via Pannonhalma.

To go to/from Vienna's Westbahnhof (126 km), you may have to change trains at Hegyeshalom since trains like the Wiener Walzer and Orient Express don't stop at Győr. A better route to Vienna is through Sopron. To go to/from Czechoslovakia, change at Komárom.

## PANNONHALMA

Pannonhalma Abbey, currently a Benedictine monastery, 18 km south of Győr, stands at the top of a 282-metre hill at the southern edge of the Kisalföld. Founded in 996, Pannonhalma has been restored and extended numerous times, so today you can see quite a patchwork of styles.

The view of the surrounding area from this hill is excellent and Pannonhalma is a good excuse to get out of the city and see an attractive slice of Hungarian country life.

### Things to See & Do

You can only gain admission to the **abbey** (closed Monday) with a group. You must wait at the entrance for a group to form, so it's best to come on a weekend or holiday when there will be lots of other visitors. The rather rushed tour takes you through the Gothic cloister (1486), into the Romanesque basilica (1225) and down to the 11th century crypt. The 55-metre-high tower was erected in 1830 and the impressive Empire-style library (also on the tour) dates from the same period. The visit concludes with a look in the one-room 'picture gallery'. Organ recitals are held in the church on Saturday afternoons about once a month.

## Places to Stay & Eat

There are several restaurants in the village below the abbey and from mid-May to mid-September a camping ground is open.

## Getting There & Away

Local trains between Győr and Veszprém stop at Pannonhalma every couple of hours. An easy day trip from Győr, Pannonhalma is best approached by bus, however, as the train station is a couple of km south-west of the abbey.

## SOPRON

Sopron (Ödenburg) sits right on the Austrian border, 217 km west of Budapest. In 1921 the town's residents voted to remain part of Hungary, while the rest of Bürgenland (the

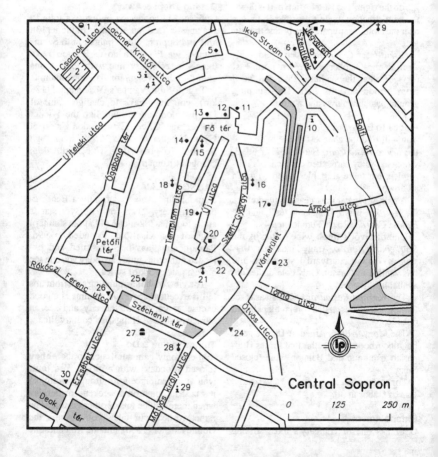

Central Sopron

region which Sopron used to belong to) went to Austria, thus explaining the town's location in a narrow neck of land between Lake Fertő and the green eastern ridges of the Alps.

Sopron (the ancient Scarbantia) has been an important centre since Roman times. The Tatars and Turks never got this far, so numerous medieval structures have come down to the present day intact. In the horseshoe-shaped old quarter, still partially enclosed by medieval walls built on Roman foundations, almost every building is historic. This is

Sopron's principal charm and wanderers among the Gothic and Baroque houses are rewarded at every turn. Some of the buildings are now museums and you can peek into the courtyards of many others.

## Orientation

From the main railway station, walk north on Mátyás király utca, which becomes Várkerület after a few blocks. Várkerület and Ógabona tér form a loop right around the old town, following the line of the former city walls. Sopron's Fire Tower is between the northern end of Várkerület and Fő tér, the old town square. The bus station is on Lackner Kristóf utca off Ógabona tér.

## Information

Ciklámen Tourist is at Ógabona tér 8 on the corner of Lackner Kristóf utca. Express is at Mátyás király utca 7.

## Things to See

The 61-metre-high **Fire Tower** above Sopron's north gate, erected after the fire of 1676, is the city symbol. You can climb up to the Renaissance loggia for a marvellous view of the city (closed Monday). What appears to be a Nazi bunker directly beside the Fire Tower is actually a museum (closed Monday and from November to mid-March) where you'll see the excavated remains of a Roman gate which stood here long ago.

Fő tér, just beyond the tower, is the heart of the old town. In the centre of the square is the magnificent **Holy Trinity Column** (1701) and beyond this the **Goat Church** (1300), built by a goatherd with gold uncovered by his herd! In the adjoining building is the Gothic Chapter House of the former Benedictine monastery, now a museum (closed Monday) with stone carvings of the seven deadly sins.

Across the street from the Goat Church is the Esterházy City Palace, which is now a most interesting **Mining Museum** (closed Wednesday). Unfortunately, this museum is experiencing serious budgetary problems and may no longer exist by the time you get there. Go inside anyway to see the courtyard.

### ■ PLACES TO STAY

7 Jegverem Fogadó
20 Palatinus Hotel
23 Hotel Pannónia

### ▼ PLACES TO EAT

22 Cesar-Pince Borozó
24 Várkerület Söröző
26 Ónkiszolgáló Étterem
30 Deák Restaurant

### OTHER

1 Bus Station
2 Market
3 Volántourist
4 Ciklámen Tourist
5 Rejpal House
6 Poncichter Borozó (Wine Cellar)
8 Church of the Holy Spirit
9 St Michael's Church
10 Ibusz
11 Fire Tower
12 Storno House
13 Fabricius House
14 Mining Museum
15 Goat Church
16 St George's Church
17 City Walls
18 Evangelical Church
19 Synagogue
21 Orsolya Church & Museum
25 Liszt Cultural Centre & Casino
27 Post Office
28 Dominican Church
29 Express

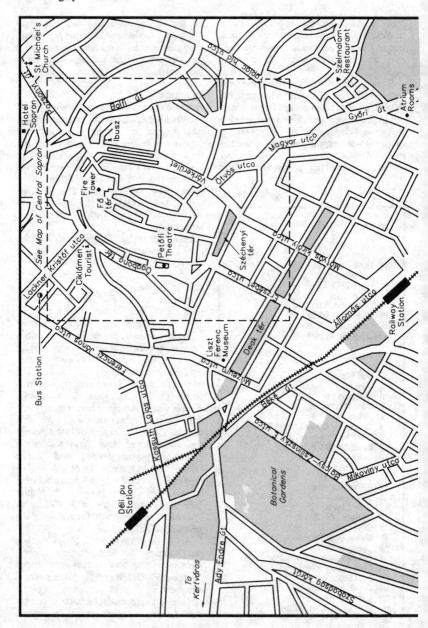

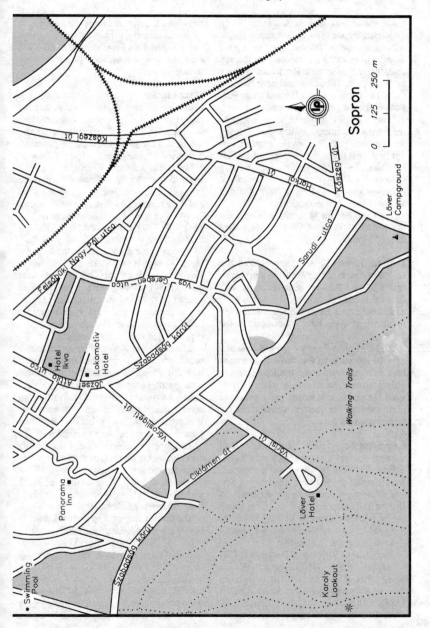

There are several other museums on Fő tér. **Fabricius House** at No 6 is a comprehensive historical museum (closed from November to mid-March) with impressive Roman sculpture in the Gothic cellar. **Storno House** at No 8 is a famous Renaissance palace (1560) that is now a museum and art gallery. Both houses are closed on Monday.

Sopron's most unique museum is housed in the 14th century **synagogue** (closed Tuesday) at Új utca 22. Jews were an important part of the community until their expulsion in 1526. Next to the **Orsolya Church** on Orsolya tér is a collection of religious art (open Monday, Thursday and Sunday from April to October).

The **Liszt Ferenc Museum** is in a villa at the corner of Deák tér and Múzeum utca (closed Monday).

**Around Sopron** To see some of Sopron's surroundings, take bus No 10 to **Kertváros** and climb the Baroque stairway to the Hill Church. Better yet, you could take bus No 1 or 2 to the Lövér Hotel and hike up through the fir forest to the **Károly Lookout** for the view.

An hourly bus from the main bus station runs 10 km north to **Fertőrákos** where the mammoth halls and corridors of the old stone quarry are an impressive sight (open daily all year). In summer, concerts and operas are performed in the theatre which is in the largest chamber.

**Nagycenk** Nagycenk, 13 km south-east of Sopron, was once the seat of Count István Széchenyi (1791-1860), a notable reformer who founded the National Academy of Sciences, improved communications (the Chain Bridge in Budapest was one of his many projects) and wrote a series of books intended to convince the nobility to lend a hand in modernising Hungary.

The Baroque **Széchenyi Mansion** (1758) contains a memorial museum to Count István. Part of the mansion has been made into a 19-room, three-star hotel (☎ 974 1586). Other attractions in Nagycenk include the park with its long avenue of linden trees, the Széchenyi family mausoleum in the local cemetery, a three-km narrow-gauge steam railway to Fertőboz and a 60-horse stud farm. Nagycenk is accessible by bus and train.

### Places to Stay

Ciklámen Tourist, Ógabona tér 8, has the largest number of private rooms, including some singles, so try there first. The staff also handle bookings at a few small pensions. You can arrange other private rooms at Volántourist, Lackner Kristóf utca 1, and Ibusz, Várkerület 41. The rooms are often full or expensive in summer. If it's a weekend and the agencies are closed or don't have an inexpensive room for you, consider catching the 3 pm bus to Kőszeg where budget accommodation is more plentiful.

Sopron's grand old hotel is the two-star *Hotel Pannónia*, at Várkerület 75, where singles/doubles go for US$29/31 without bath, US$41/43 with bath. The Pannónia opened in 1893 and the hotel café is highly recommended if you want to indulge in a coffee or tea break amid utter elegance, even if you're sleeping cheap elsewhere.

The *Jégverem Fogadó*, Jégverem utca 1 near the centre, is a renovated traditional inn with five rooms at US$26/28 single/double with bath, breakfast included. It caters mostly to visitors from nearby Austria who want a little class; the downstairs restaurant is expensive but good. If it's full, the *Royal Panzió* just down the street is similar.

The functional *Hotel Ikva*, József Attila utca 3-5, on the opposite side of the railway from the old town, charges US$18/19 for singles/doubles without bath, US$24/25 with bath, breakfast included. Only stay here in an emergency for one night.

The *Lövér Campground* is three km south of the station on Kőszegi út. Take bus No 12 going to 'Lövérek fele' from either the bus or train stations right to the camping ground, or buses No 1 or 2 to the *Lövér Hotel*, then walk a km through the forest. Camping is possible from mid-April to mid-October and in summer there are small bungalows. In winter heated rooms are available at the camping ground. You can make reservations from Ciklámen Tourist.

## Places to Eat & Drink

For a cheap lunch go to *Önkiszolgáló Étterem* at the western end of Széchenyi tér (open from 7 am to 3 pm daily). Note what all the regulars with meal tickets are having, then choose the same thing. This will cost less than US$1.

An inexpensive local restaurant with Hungarian flavour is the *Várkerület Söröző*, Várkerület 83. *Cesar-Pince Borozó*, Hátsókapu 2, is more touristy and though a wine cellar it does serve meals. *Corvinus Pizzeria* on Fő tér, right in front of the Fire Tower, is only reasonable if you stick to the pizza.

The *Deák Restaurant*, Deák tér, on the corner of Erzsébet utca, specialises in game dishes like wild boar or venison, though fish is also on the menu. In the evening there's live music and the place is popular with Austrian border jumpers who drop over to Sopron for the evening.

Wine tasters repair to the *Gyógygödör Borozó*, Fő tér 4, opposite the Goat Church (closed Monday), or the *Poncichter Borozó*, Szentlélek utca 13, both great little wine cellars. Try the local Kékfrankos wine.

## Entertainment

If you want to take in some local events, try the *Liszt Cultural Centre* on Széchenyi tér. Posters in the window announce what's coming up. Entry to Sopron's gambling casino is from the Széchenyi tér side of the Liszt Cultural Centre building (open after 4 pm). Just around the corner on Petőfi tér is the *Petőfi Theatre*.

## Getting There & Away

Express trains run to Budapest's Déli pu Railway Station via Győr and Komárom, and local trains run to Szombathely. Take a bus to go to Fertőd, Kőszeg, Keszthely or Veszprém.

There's a bus to Vienna from Monday to Saturday; tickets are sold by Ibusz. Several local trains also travel to/from Vienna's Südbahnhof every day, sometimes with a change at Wiener Neustadt or Ebenfurth. Other trains go to Deutschkreuz and Lackenbach in Austria fairly frequently. When boarding for Austria at Sopron, be at the station an hour early to clear customs, which is in a separate hall to one side.

## FERTŐD

Don't miss the 126-room **Esterházy Palace** (1766) at Fertőd, 28 km east of Sopron and readily accessible by bus. This magnificent Versailles-style Baroque palace, easily the finest in Hungary, is open from 8 am to 4 pm all year (closed Monday). You must visit the palace with a guide. On Sundays there's a lunchtime Haydn or Mozart concert (US$1) in the music room.

Joseph Haydn was court musician to the princely Esterházy family from 1761 to 1790 and his *Farewell* symphony was first performed in the palace concert hall. A Haydn exhibition is included in the visit. The famous Habsburg queen Maria Theresa stayed in the palace in 1773 and three rooms are dedicated to her. Fertőd was the summer residence of the Esterházys (their winter residence was at Eisenstadt, Austria) and the large French Park behind the palace will help you to visualise the bygone splendour.

## Places to Stay & Eat

You can spend the night in the palace. Clean, simple rooms in the *Kastélyszálló* on the 3rd floor are US$13/14 double/triple, US$18 for four, open all year. To find the hostel, look for the arrow near the ticket office that points up to the *szálloda*. For advance reservations, write to Kastélyszálló, Bartók Béla utca 2, 9421 Fertőd, or have someone who speaks Hungarian telephone 994 5971 for you. Only in Hungary could you enjoy a treat like this at such a low price!

In the *Grenadier House* opposite the palace's Rococo wrought-iron gate is a pleasant café (closed Monday). There are several good restaurants in the village.

## KŐSZEG

Kőszeg (Guns) is a lovely medieval town on the Austrian frontier among verdant hills between Sopron and Szombathely. Mt Írottkő (882 metres) right on the border south-west of Kőszeg is the highest point in Transdanubia. In 1532 the garrison of Kőszeg's 13th century Jurisich Castle held off a Turkish army of 200,000. This delay gave the Habsburgs time to mount a successful defence of Vienna, ensuring Kőszeg's place in European history. The houses along the street in front of the castle were erected in a saw-toothed design in order to give defenders a better shot at the enemy. Jurisich tér, Kőszeg's jewel-box main square, hasn't changed much since the 18th century. It's a pleasant place where fruit and vegetables are left out on the street with little honesty boxes to collect the money.

## Information

Try Savaria Tourist, Várkör 69, or Kőszeg Tourist, Kossuth Lajos utca 4, behind Hotel Írottkő.

## Things to See

The **City Gate** (1932) bears an exterior relief depicting the 1532 siege. In the 'General's

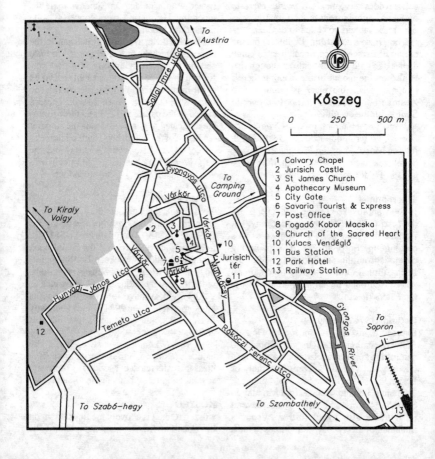

Kőszeg

0    250    500 m

1 Calvary Chapel
2 Jurisich Castle
3 St James Church
4 Apothecary Museum
5 City Gate
6 Savaria Tourist & Express
7 Post Office
8 Fogadó Kobor Macska
9 Church of the Sacred Heart
10 Kulacs Vendéglő
11 Bus Station
12 Park Hotel
13 Railway Station

To Austria

To Kiraly Volgy

To Camping Ground

To Sopron

To Szabó-hegy

To Szombathely

Sallai Imre utca

Gyongyos utca

Várkör

Hunyadi-János utca

Temeto utca

Rákóczi Ferenc utca

Munkácsy

Jurisich tér

Gyongyos River

House' next to the gate is a branch of the **Miklós Jurisich Museum** (closed Monday). The gate leads into Jurisich tér with the painted Renaissance façade of the **old town hall** at No 8. In the middle of the square a Statue of the Virgin (1739) and the town fountain (1766) adjoin two fine churches. The **Church of St Emerich** (1615) is closer to the gate. Behind it is **St James Church** (1403), a splendid Gothic building with medieval frescoes. At Jurisich tér 11 is a Baroque **apothecary**.

The other highlight of Kőszeg is **Jurisich Castle** (1263), now a historical museum (closed Monday). The courtyard and towers of this Gothic bastion have an almost fairy-tale air about them.

Other sights include the neo-Gothic **Church of the Sacred Heart** on Várkör (you can't miss it) and the Baroque chapel on **Calvary Hill**, a 25-minute hike away.

### Activities

Ask about bicycle rentals at the railway station.

### Places to Stay

Savaria Tourist, at Várkör 69, Ibusz on Városház utca near the city gate, and Kőszeg Tourist, at Kossuth Lajos utca 4, all arrange private rooms.

The cheapest accommodation is the *turistaszálló* in Jurisich Castle (open from April to mid-October). A bed in the 18-bed dorm costs US$3 and the attendants are usually helpful.

From mid-April to mid-October you can stay at the *Express Hotel Panoráma*, also known as the Napsugár Turistaszálló, on Szabó-hegy Hill (take bus No 2 from the railway station). Ask about this place at the Express office next to Savaria Tourist.

The *Park Hotel* on Felszabadulás Park, just west of Kőszeg, is excellent value at US$8/9 for singles/doubles without bath, US$14/15 with shower, breakfast included. If you have a YHA card you'll get a discount of US$0.50. This large Victorian hotel in a quiet location by a park is highly recommended to all travellers passing this way. It's

owned by the student travel agency Express, and any Express office can book a room for you here (it's only necessary to book in summer). It's open all year and there's a restaurant on the premises.

The *Fogadó Kóbor Macska*, Várkör 100, is a small seven-room pension overlooking the city walls, where a room with shared bath will cost US$11/21 single/double, breakfast included. Reserve well ahead in summer. Even if you don't stay here, the cosy little restaurant is well worth a visit.

The *Hotel Strucc*, Várkör 124 directly across the square from Savaria Tourist, is another fine old hotel with rooms at US$12/21 single/double with bath, breakfast included. With all these inexpensive places to stay at, there's no reason at all to pay US$38 for a double room (no singles) at the modern *Hotel Írottkő*, also a one-minute walk from Savaria Tourist.

A convenient camping ground is next to a public swimming pool (*strand/fürdő*) just across the river from the old town, a five-minute walk east on Kiss János utca from Várkör (open from mid-May to September).

### Places to Eat

A good restaurant at Kőszeg is the *Kulacs Vendéglő*, Várkör 14. Coffee and cakes are served next door. Also try the *Bécsikapu Söröző* on Rájnis utca, almost opposite St James Church.

### Getting There & Away

There are frequent trains and buses from Szombathely and less frequent buses from Sopron.

### SZOMBATHELY

Szombathely (Steinamanger), pronounced 'som-bat-eye', the seat of Vas County and a major crossroads in western Hungary, was founded as Savaria by the Roman emperor Claudius in 43 AD. It soon became capital of Upper Pannonia and an important stage on the Amber Road from Italy to the Baltic. Destroyed by an earthquake in 455 and pillaged by the Tatars, Turks and Habsburgs, Szombathely only regained its former stature when a bishopric was established here in 1777.

In 1945, just a month before the end of the war, US bombers levelled the town and it's a credit to Hungary that so much has been restored. Although off the beaten tourist track, Szombathely has all the facilities you could ask for, making it an ideal stop on your way around the country.

## Orientation & Information

The railway station is five blocks east of Mártírok tere along Szell Kálmán út. The bus station is on Petőfi Sándor utca, behind the cathedral. Szombathely's busiest square is Köztársaság tér, a long block south of Mártírok tere.

Savaria Tourist is at Mártírok tere 1.

## Things to See

One of the most interesting things to see is

the rebuilt neoclassical **cathedral** (1791) on Berzsenyi Dániel tér. Beside the cathedral are the excavated 4th century **remains of Roman Savaria** (Romkert), including mosaics, roads and a medieval castle. On the other side of the cathedral is the Baroque **bishop's palace** (1783), and beyond this on Hollán Ernő utca is the **Smidt Museum** (closed Monday), a fascinating assortment of small treasures collected by a local doctor before his death in 1975.

Head south to Rákóczi Ferenc utca to see the reconstructed 2nd century **temple of the Egyptian goddess Isis**. A festival is held here in August. The **Szombathely Gallery** overlooking the temple is the best modern art gallery in Hungary (closed Monday and Tuesday).

Also worth visiting is the **Savaria Museum** (closed Monday) on Szell Kálmán út, which is especially strong on archaeology and natural history. There's a large Roman

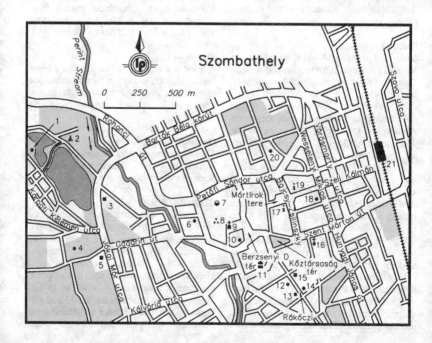

lapidarium (a collection of architectural fragments) in the basement.

On the western side of Szombathely is a major open-air **ethnographic museum**, or skansen (open from 10 am to 4 pm, closed Monday), with 50 reconstructed folk buildings. It's on a lake near the camping ground (bus No 7 from the railway station to the terminus).

### Places to Stay

Private rooms are assigned by staff at Savaria Tourist, Mártírok tere 1, and Ibusz, Szell Kálman út 3. In summer, Express, Bajcsy-Zsilinszky utca 12, may know of youth hostels. These tourist offices are next to one another.

The *Liget Hotel* in Szent István Park, west of the city centre, offers motel-style accommodation at US$25 double with bath and breakfast (no singles). The hotel reception staff may also help you to find a private room for about US$10 double. You can get there on bus No 7 from the railway station.

From May to September you can stay at a camping ground with bungalows on Kondics István utca 4 by a lake west of town (bus No 7 from the railway station to the end of the line). There's a swimming pool nearby.

Szombathely's nicest hotel is the turn-of-the-century *Hotel Savaria*, Mártírok tere 4 in the very centre of town. It's open all year but not cheap: double rooms with a bathtub cost US$59, US$54 with shower, US$40 without bath, breakfast included (no singles).

Other expensive hotels in Szombathely include the modern eight-storey *Isis Hotel*, Rákóczi utca 1, and the luxurious four-star *Hotel Claudius*, Bartók Béla körút 39.

Actually, Szombathely, unlike Rome, can be seen in a day and it may be better to go on to Kőszeg to spend the night.

### Places to Eat

Szombathely's most elegant restaurant is in the *Savaria Hotel* on Mártírok tere. They don't sully their menu with prices. For a less pretentious meal, try the *Gyöngyös Étterem*, Szell Kálmán út 8 nearby. It has a cheap 'menu' at lunchtime, but the food and service are always good (closed Monday).

The restaurant in the railway station (not the stand-up 'bisztró') is also good.

### Entertainment

If you're lucky, something will be happening in *Bartók Hall*, a former synagogue (1881) opposite the Szombathely Gallery, on Rákóczi Ferenc utca, now used as a concert hall. Also visit the *Cultural & Sports Centre* and a second cultural centre, the *Megyei Müvelődési es Ifjusagi Központ* opposite the bus station, which has an excellent café just inside. The friendly people at Savaria Tourist may also know of events.

1  Skansen
2  Camping Ground
3  Hotel Claudius
4  Liberation Memorial
5  Liget Hotel
6  Cultural Centre
7  Bus Station
8  Roman Ruins (Romkert)
9  Cathedral
10  Smidt Museum
11  Post Office
12  Temple of Isis
13  Szombathely Gallery
14  Bartók Concert Hall
15  Isis Hotel
16  Franciscan Church
17  Savaria Tourist
18  Savaria Museum
19  Ibusz
20  Cultural & Sports Centre
21  Railway Station

### Getting There & Away

Szombathely is only 13 km from the Austrian border and there are direct trains to/from Graz (146 km). Some of the Graz services involve a change of trains at the border (Szentgotthárd).

Express trains to Budapest-Déli (236 km) go via Veszprém and Székesfehérvár. Other express trains run to Győr via Pápa. There are frequent local trains to Kőszeg and Sopron. To go to southern Transdanubia or

Balaton Lake, take a bus to Keszthely via Hévíz. There's also an early morning express train to/from Pécs.

Railway information and tickets are available from MÁV Tours, Thököly utca 39 near the Isis Hotel.

# Balaton Lake

In the very heart of Transdanubia, the 77-km-long Balaton Lake (Plattensee) is the largest freshwater lake in central and Western Europe. The south-eastern shore of this 'Hungarian sea' is shallow and in summer the warm sandy beaches are a favourite family vacation spot. Better scenery and more historic sites are found on the deeper north-western side of the lake.

North of the lake are the Bakony Hills and the extinct volcanoes of the Tapolca Basin. Several ruined castles, such as that at Sümeg, remind visitors that during the Turkish period the border between the Ottoman and Habsburg empires ran down the middle of the lake. The Turks maintained a lake fleet that was based at Siófok. Székesfehérvár and Veszprém, just north of the lake, are old historic towns full of monuments and one of Hungary's finest palaces is at Keszthely. The Benedictine crypt in Tihany Abbey is the oldest existing church in Hungary.

The many towns and villages along both shores have an organic connection to this ancient lake. This is wine-making country. Scenic railway lines encircle the lake and there are no less than 39 camping grounds on its shores. 'Zimmer frei' signs are everywhere. Balaton's very popularity is perhaps its main drawback, though the north-western shore is quieter than the south-eastern one.

To avoid pollution and public nuisances, the use of private motorboats is prohibited, making Balaton a favourite yachting centre. Continuous breezes from the north speed sailors and windsurfers along. Other common activities here are tennis, horse riding and cycling. Any local tourist office will be able to provide information on these. The thermal baths of Hévíz are nearby. If you want to spend some time in the area, get hold of the *A Balaton* 1:40,000 topographical map available at Budapest bookshops which illustrates the many hiking possibilities.

### GETTING THERE & AWAY
Trains to Balaton Lake leave from Déli pu Railway Station and buses leave from the Erzsébet tér Bus Station in Budapest. If you're travelling north and south from the lake to/from towns in western and southern Transdanubia, buses are often preferable to trains.

### GETTING AROUND
Railway service around the lake is fairly frequent. A better way to see Balaton Lake is by Mahart passenger ferry. These ferries operate the Siófok-Balatonfüred-Tihany-Tihanyi-rév-Balatonföldvár route from mid-April to mid-October. During July and August there is a ferry every couple of hours. During the main summer season, which is from June to mid-September, ferries ply the entire length of the lake from Balatonkenese to Keszthely (five hours) with frequent stops on both shores. There are also car ferries across the lake between Tihanyi-rév and Szántódrév (from April to November), Révfülöp and Balatonboglár, and Badacsony and Fonyód (the last two operate from mid-April to mid-October). Fares are cheap: US$1 will take you anywhere. Of course, in winter there are no boats on the lake.

### SZÉKESFEHÉRVÁR
Traditionally, Székesfehérvár (Stuhlweissenburg) is known as the place where the Magyar chieftain Árpád set up camp, therefore it's considered the oldest town in Hungary. In 972 the Grand Duke of Geza established his seat here and his son, Stephen I (later St Stephen), founded a basilica which became the symbol of royal power. Thirty-eight kings of early medieval Hungary were crowned at Székesfehérvár and 18 were buried in the basilica's crypt. It was here in 1222 that Andrew II proclaimed the Golden Bull, Hungary's first constitution.

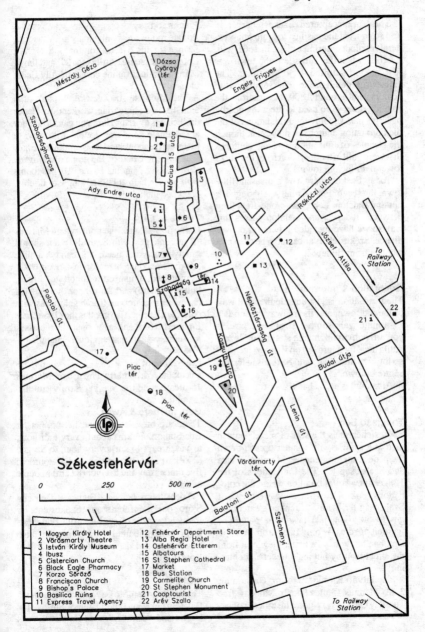

### Székesfehérvár

0        250        500 m

1 Magyar Király Hotel
2 Vörösmarty Theatre
3 István Király Museum
4 Ibusz
5 Cistercian Church
6 Black Eagle Pharmacy
7 Korzo Söröző
8 Franciscan Church
9 Bishop's Palace
10 Basilica Ruins
11 Express Travel Agency
12 Fehérvár Department Store
13 Alba Regia Hotel
14 Osfehérvár Étterem
15 Albatours
16 St Stephen Cathedral
17 Market
18 Bus Station
19 Carmelite Church
20 St Stephen Monument
21 Cooptourist
22 Arév Szallo

The Turks captured Székesfehérvár in 1543 and used the basilica to store gunpowder. It exploded during a siege in 1601, and, by 1688 when the Turks left, the town was just an uninhabited field of ruins. The Habsburgs rebuilt Székesfehérvár in the 18th century, and around 1800, stones from the basilica ruins were used to erect the nearby bishop's palace. Only the foundations of the old coronation church are now seen, though the steeples of four huge Baroque churches that were built after liberation from the Turks tower over the old town.

Today Székesfehérvár is a pleasant little town, the seat of Fejér County. Although it's not on Balaton Lake, everyone travelling between Budapest and Balaton passes this way so we have included it here for convenience. Székesfehérvár can also be seen as a day trip from Budapest.

## Orientation & Information

The bus station is just outside the west wall of the old town, and the railway station is a 15-minute walk south-east of the centre. If you arrive by train, march straight up József Attila utca, then turn left on Rákóczi utca and go through the city gate to Szabadság tér, the centre of town.

Albatours is at Szabadság tér 6.

## Things to See

Székesfehérvár is the sort of place you can visit at leisure as you wander up and down the pedestrian promenades, Március 15 utca and Szabadság tér. The foundations of the 12th century **royal basilica** where the coronations took place is at the eastern end of Szabadság tér, with St Stephen's sarcophagus to the right, just inside the gate. The 'garden of ruins' is only open from April to October, but you get a better view of it from the street than by buying a ticket and entering!

The **István Király Museum**, Gagarin tér 3, off Március 15 utca (closed Monday, free Tuesday), has a very good historical collection.

## Places to Stay

Private rooms are available from Albatours, Szabadság tér 6 (but not for one night!); Cooptourist, József Attila utca 37; and Ibusz, Március 15 utca on the corner of Ady Endre utca.

The high-rise *Arev Szálló*, József Attila utca 42, is a Hungarian workers' residence that accepts tourists. Here you pay US$13 for an adequate single or double with a wash basin, but the shower and toilet are down the hall.

If you crave luxury, the grand old *Magyar Király Hotel*, Március 15 utca 10, has rooms with private bath at US$43 single or double, breakfast included.

## Places to Eat

*Korzo Söröző*, near the point where Március 15 utca merges with Szabadság tér, should satisfy your every need. You can get a huge cooked breakfast here for just over US$1 (lemon tea, mushroom omelette, bread, butter and jam) and for dinner there's fried cheese or mushrooms (for vegetarians) with cold Czech beer. Also good is the *Osfehérvár Étterem* on Szabadság tér, opposite the basilica ruins, which has a set lunch 'menu'.

## Entertaiment

Check the Vörösmarty Theatre on Március 15 utca beside the Magyar Király Hotel.

## Getting There & Away

There are buses to Budapest (Erzsébet tér Bus Station, 66 km) about every half-hour, to Veszprém (44 km) every hour, to Szeged (206 km) four times a day, to Balatonfüred five times a day and to Győr (87 km) a couple of times a day.

Local trains between Budapest-Déli and Siófok or Baltonfüred stop at Székesfehérvár frequently. An express line from Budapest-Déli to Szombathely via Veszprém also passes here and there's a local line north to Komárom.

## SIÓFOK

The milky-green Sió River at Siófok drains Balaton Lake into the Danube. Siófok, the largest and busiest town on Balaton Lake's south-eastern shore, is the main gateway to the lake for people coming from Budapest. There are six huge camping grounds, plus workers' hostels, holiday cottages, and lots of expensive hotels. Siófok is the place to come to if you like big crowds of German and Austrian tourists, discos and a lively, even seamy nightlife. In summer this Hungarian (or German!) Riviera can get extremely overcrowded.

### Orientation & Information

Siófok stretches for several km along the south-eastern shore of Balaton Lake. The train and bus stations and the lake boat terminal are near the Sió River. Many travel agencies and large stores are near Fő tér, between the bus station and the river. Dimitrov Park between the train tracks and the lake is surrounded by tree-lined streets of old mansions, and east along the lakeside is a strip of pricey high-rise tourist hotels.

Siotour is at Szabadság tér 6.

### Things to See

A lock at the mouth of the river controls the

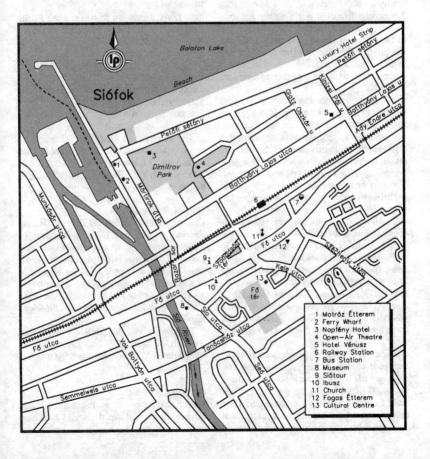

1 Matróz Étterem
2 Ferry Wharf
3 Napfény Hotel
4 Open—Air Theatre
5 Hotel Vénusz
6 Railway Station
7 Bus Station
8 Museum
9 Siótour
10 Ibusz
11 Church
12 Fogas Étterem
13 Cultural Centre

flow of water from Balaton Lake. Almost 2000 years ago the Romans dredged the riverbed here in order to lower the level of the lake. There's a fairly interesting **museum** that presents the history of the Balaton area at Sió utca 2, near the highway bridge over the river. Summaries in English and German are displayed.

## Places to Stay

For private rooms try Siotour, Szabadság tér 6, a few minutes' walk from the bus and railway stations. In midsummer, bedlam reigns at Siotour and the confused staff seem totally unable to cope with the golden hordes descending from the north. Other agencies with private rooms include MÁV Tours in the railway station, Ibusz, Fő utca 174, and Cooptourist, Fő utca 148 (but never for one night). Stafeta Tours, Fő utca 216, sometimes has rooms when the other agencies are sold out.

Siófok is one of the few places in Hungary where you may not be able to find a private room in summer. Singles are not welcome, nor are those staying only one or two nights (30% surcharge in this case). Prices here are much higher than elsewhere in Hungary, beginning at US$10 a single and rising fast. You may be offered a room in some distant suburb at twice the price you've been paying everywhere else.

The hotels of Siófok are very expensive – for example, the *Hotel Vénusz*, Kinizsi Pál utca 6, costs US$60/70 single/double. On Petőfi sétány nearby are four three-star high-rises, the *Balaton, Európa, Hungária* and *Lidó* hotels which are even more expensive than the Hotel Vénusz. The nondescript five-storey *Napfény Hotel* opposite the ferry wharf is also US$60/70 single/double. All these hotels are closed from mid-October to April.

None of the camping grounds are near the centre. If you're coming from Budapest by train, get off at Balatonszabadi vm Station, only 200 metres from the gate of *Golden Lake Camping* (U$3 per person, US$2 per tent). Golden Lake has an excellent location on a good bathing beach with ample shade

and a casual atmosphere. A large grocery store and several snack bars are nearby. Golden Lake is also open longer than the other Siófok camping grounds (from mid-May to September) and there's usually lots of space. Also near Batatonszabadi vm Station is a Siotour office offering private rooms, currency exchange, and so on. Bus No 2 runs the four km from Golden Lake to Siófok Bus Station or you can walk along the lakeshore most of the way. The only drawback is the washing facilities, which are cramped for such a big place.

## Places to Eat

Two fairly expensive restaurants are *Fogas Étterem*, Fő utca 184, opposite the train station, and *Matróz Étterem*, Mártírok útja 13, beside the lake boat terminal.

## Entertainment

On summer evenings folklore programmes are sometimes presented at the *Kálmán Imre Szabadteri* open-air theatre in Dimitrov Park, or in the *Cultural Centre*, Fő tér 2.

The *Tengerszem Disco Bar*, Tanácskoztarsaság útja on the corner of Glatz Oszkár utca, has a striptease at midnight and 1 am, a live sex show at 1.30 am and an erotic show at 2.30 am.

## Getting There & Away

Express trains between Budapest's Déli pu Railway Station and Nagykanizsa stop at Siófok every couple of hours, and local trains a couple of times an hour. To go to Veszprém, change trains at Lepsény and for Keszthely change at Balatonszentgyörgy. Some trains go straight through to Keszthely from Siófok. A branch line runs south from Siófok to Kaposvár.

The Dráva and Maestral express trains between Budapest-Déli and Zagreb stop at Siófok daily. You can buy tickets from Ibusz, Fő utca 174.

## Getting Around

Mahart ferries travel to Balatonfüred and Tihany from mid-April to mid-October. From June to mid-September the ferries continue as far as Badacsony. In midsummer one early morning ferry runs from Siófok to Keszthely, leaving Siófok at around 7 am, and departing from Keszthely for the return journey at 2 pm.

## BALATONFÜRED

Balatonfüred, an elegant spa with the easy-going grace that Siófok lacks, is called the 'Mecca of cardiacs' for its curative waters. Located on the northern shore of Balaton Lake between Tihany and Veszprém, it has been the most fashionable bathing resort on the lake since 1772, when a medicinal bathing establishment was set up here. During the early 19th century it became an important meeting place for Hungarian intellectuals. The town still bears an aristocratic air, although the once private sanatoriums are now open to the public and the clientele is more likely to be trade unionists than affluent bourgeois (for now).

Although Balatonfüred is a major spa, the mineral baths are reserved for patients being treated for heart disease, so casual tourists are out of luck. Yet because it's a health resort much is open throughout the year, so it's the best place to visit around the lake in the off season.

### Orientation & Information

The adjacent bus and train stations are a km north-west of the town centre. Some buses stop near the ferry landing below the Round Church on Jókai Mór utca. Blaha Lujza utca runs from in front of the church directly into Gyógy tér where the visit begins.

Balatontourist is at Blaha Lujza utca 5.

### Things to See

The heart of the spa is Gyógy tér with its **well house** (Kossuth Well), where budget travellers may freely fill their canteens with radioactive mineral water.

The park along the nearby lakeshore is worth a promenade. Near the wharf you'll encounter the bust of the Bengali poet **Rabindranath Tagore** before a lime tree that he planted in 1926 to mark his recovery from illness here. The poem 'Tagore' which

he wrote for the occasion is reproduced on a plaque in English.

A little inland, diagonally opposite the **Round Church** (1841), is the **Jókay Museum**, formerly the house of novelist Mór Jókai (closed from November to February and Monday).

### Places to Stay

MÁV Tours and Balaton Volán have offices in the railway station. Staff there may be able to find you a private room (summer only). Ibusz, Petőfi Sándor utca 4/a, is the office nearest the stations with private rooms; Balatontourist, Blaha Lujza utca 5, has more rooms than any of the others, so it's your best bet. Cooptourist, Jókai Mór utca 23, has private rooms in summer only.

Across the street from Ibusz is the *Ring Pension*, Vörösmarty utca 7, where neat, clean singles/doubles with shared bath cost US\$17/26, breakfast included (open all year). The larger *Krone Pension*, Vörösmarty utca 4, is similar.

The *Aranycsillag Hotel*, Zsigmond utca 1, costs US\$16/19 single/double with shared bath, breakfast included. Part of the Hungar Hotels chain, the Aranycsillag is a grand old hotel which has seen better days. The rooms are large and although you have to walk down the hall to take a shower the door isn't locked.

A cheaper hotel than the Aranycsillag is the *Hotel Blaha Lujza* behind the Blaha Lujza Restaurant, Blaja Lujza utca 4, opposite Balatontourist. Singles/doubles with shared bath are US\$9/17 or US\$14/27 with private bath. Breakfast is US\$1.50 extra. This hotel closes in January and February.

*Hotel UNI (BME)*, Széchenyi utca 10, is a modern four-storey hotel near the lake that offers singles/doubles with private bath at US\$29/37 in summer, US\$14/20 in winter, breakfast included, which is good value. It's just past the large ship/bar *Helka* (a large lake boat converted into a restaurant and bar) in the middle of the road as you're coming from the centre of town.

There's only one camping ground at Balatonfüred but it has a capacity for 3000

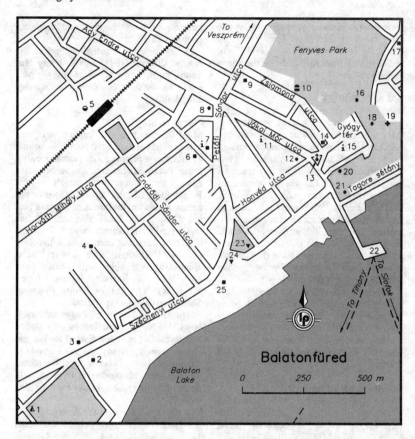

Balatonfüred

Balaton Lake

0        250        500 m

To Veszprém

Fenyves Park

To Tihany

To Siófok

| | |
|---|---|
| 1 | FICC Rally Camping |
| 2 | Hotel Marina |
| 3 | Hotel Margaréta |
| 4 | Baricska Csárda |
| 5 | Bus & Railway Station |
| 6 | Ring Pension |
| 7 | Ibusz & Krone Pension |
| 8 | Supermarket |
| 9 | Aranycsillag Hotel |
| 10 | Post Office |
| 11 | Cooptourist |
| 12 | Jókai Museum |
| 13 | Round Church |
| 14 | Hotel Blaha Lujza |
| 15 | Balatontourist |
| 16 | Balaton Pantheon |
| 17 | Hotel Éden |
| 18 | Kossuth Well |
| 19 | State Hospital |
| 20 | Cinema |
| 21 | Tagore Statue |
| 22 | Ferry Wharf |
| 23 | Halászkert Étterem |
| 24 | Ship/Bar Helka |
| 25 | Hotel UNI (BME) |

people. The *FICC Rally Camping* (open from mid-April to mid-October) is beside *Hotel Marina* on the lake, three km from the train station. The only water-skiing on Balaton Lake is practised here using an electric-powered cable to tow skiers.

### Places to Eat

The *Halászkert Étterem* on Széchenyi utca next to the ship/bar *Helka*, is a good place to sample local fish dishes. The menu is in English and German. The *Blaha Lujza Restaurant* mentioned before is an excellent place to eat.

### Getting There & Away

Balatonfüred is two hours from Budapest-Déli (132 km) by express train and three hours by local train. The line continues to Tapolca via Badacsony. Bus services to Tihany and Veszprém are frequent. There are Mahart ferries to Siófok from mid-April to mid-October.

## TIHANY

The Tihany Peninsula almost bisects the northern end of Balaton Lake. Consensus has it that this is the most beautiful place around and in summer Tihany gets more than its fair share of tourists. After a visit to the famous Benedictine Tihany Abbey, you can easily shake the hordes by hiking out past the hilly peninsula's inner lake, Belsó Lake, with its rare flora, fish and bird life. Külsó Lake has almost dried up.

### Orientation

Tihany Abbey sits on a ridge above the Tihany ferry landing on the eastern side of the peninsula's high plateau. The village of Tihany is perched above Belsó Lake, just below the abbey. Lake boats also stop at Tihanyi-rév, the car ferry landing at the southern end of the peninsula.

### Things to See & Do

Tihany's magnificent twin-towered **abbey church** (1754) is outstanding for its Baroque altars, pulpit and organ, but pride of place goes to the 11th century crypt at the front of

the church. Here is found the tomb (1060) of the abbey's founder, King Andrew I. The earliest written relic of the Hungarian language, dating from 1085, was found here. In summer, organ concerts are given in the church.

The monastery beside the church has been converted into the **Tihany Museum** (open from 9 am to 5 pm from March to October, closed Monday). An extensive lapidarium is in the museum basement.

The promenade Pisky sétány runs along the ridge north from the church to the Echo Restaurant, passing a cluster of folk houses which have now been turned into an open-air museum (closed from November to April and every Tuesday). From the restaurant you can descend to the harbour or continue up on to green and red-marked hiking trails which pass this way. The red trail crosses the peninsula between the two lakes to **Csúcs Hill**, which offers fine views (two hours).

### Places to Stay & Eat

The Balatontourist office opposite the bus stop, below Rege Presso, arranges private rooms in summer only. Many houses around Tihany have 'zimmer frei' signs, so in the off season you could try there.

The touristy *Rege Presso* beside the abbey offers a panoramic view from its terrace, but you would do better to eat at *Kecskeköröm Csárda*, Kossuth Lajos utca 19, a few hundred metres north-west on the main road, or just beyond at the *Fogas Csárda*, Kossuth Lajos utca 9.

### Getting There & Away

Buses cover the 11 km from Balatonfüred Railway Station regularly. The bus stops at both ferry landings before climbing to the village of Tihany.

The Balaton Lake ferries stop at Tihany from mid-April to mid-October. Catch them at the harbour below the abbey or at Tihanyi-rév, the car ferry terminal at the southern end of the peninsula. From April to November the car ferry crosses the narrow neck of Balaton Lake from Tihanyi-rév to Szántód-

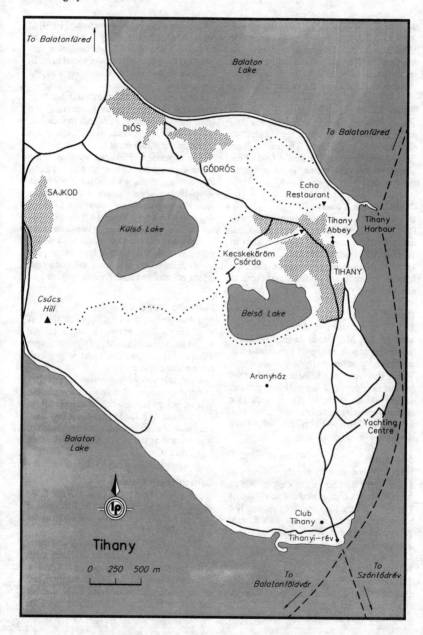

To Balatonfüred

Balaton Lake

DIÓS

GÓDRÓS

To Balatonfüred

SAJKOD

Echo Restaurant

Tihany Abbey

Tihany Harbour

Külső Lake

Kecskekörom Csárda

TIHANY

Csúcs Hill

Belső Lake

Aranyház

Yachting Centre

Balaton Lake

Club Tihany

Tihanyi-rév

Tihany

0   250   500 m

To Balatonföldvár

To Szántódrév

rév frequently (passengers on foot pay US$0.25).

## VESZPRÉM

Veszprém in the Bakony Hills, 20 km north of Balaton Lake, is built on five hills. The old town stands on an abrupt headland overlooking a gorge. At the end of the 10th century, Prince Geza founded the first Hungarian bishopric here. A century later Veszprém belonged to Hungary's queen. Much was destroyed during fighting between Turks, Hungarians and Habsburgs, and in 1702 the castle was demolished. In the 18th century the town was rebuilt by the feudal landowning bishops.

Today it's the seat of Veszprém County and the University of Chemistry. Off the beaten track, the picturesque buildings and scenery make Veszprém worth a visit any time. It's also a good base from which to visit the Balaton resorts without having to stay there.

**Veszprém**

0      250      500 m

### Orientation

The train station is on the far north side of town, so take a city bus to the bus station (which also has a left-luggage service), conveniently located near Kossuth Lajos utca.

Travel agencies, supermarkets and department stores are all on Kossuth Lajos utca, a modern shopping mall behind the Hotel Veszprém. From the crossroads at the lower end of this mall, turn left to reach the Bakony Museum, or right for Ovaros tér at the entrance to historic Veszprém.

### Information

Balatontourist is in the mall behind Hotel Veszprém.

### Things to See

The Baroque **Fire Tower** (1815) rises above Ovaros tér at the southern end of the old town. Only one street, Vár utca, runs the length of this easily defendable hill. The medieval buildings of Veszprém were later ravaged by the Turks and Habsburgs, so many of the imposing palaces seen today are Baroque. As you go up Vár utca, you'll pass under the **city gate**, reconstructed in 1936 and containing a small museum. There are other museums on Vár utca at Nos 3, 14, 29 and 35, but all are closed from November to April.

**Veszprém Cathedral** dominates a square near the end of Vár utca, behind the Baroque

| | |
|---|---|
| 1 | Benedek Hill |
| 2 | Cathedral |
| 3 | Bishop's Palace |
| 4 | Fire Tower |
| 5 | City Gate & Museum |
| 6 | Cooptourist |
| 7 | Petőfi Theatre |
| 8 | County Hall |
| 9 | Bakony Museum |
| 10 | Ibusz & Express |
| 11 | Hotel Veszprém |
| 12 | Balatontourist |
| 13 | Bus Station |
| 14 | Student Dormitory |

Holy Trinity Column (1750). The cathedral was completely rebuilt in a neo-Romanesque style in 1910 but the original Gothic crypt remains. The other massive building on the square is the **bishop's palace** (1776). At Vár utca 18 next to this palace is the **Gizella Chapel** (named after St Stephen's wife) with 13th century frescoes. The ruins of the Romanesque **St George's Chapel** next to the cathedral may be visited in summer. There's a spectacular view over the gorge from the end of Vár utca. A broad stairway behind the cathedral leads down to **Benedek Hill**, where a sweeping 360° panorama of the Séd Valley awaits you.

You should also visit the **Bakony Museum**, Megyeház tér 5, beyond the massive County Hall (1887). The museum (open all year, closed Monday) presents a comprehensive historical picture of the Bakony Hills and uplands from prehistory to the present time.

### Places to Stay

The main office offering private rooms is Balatontourist on the mall behind *Hotel Veszprém*. Also try Ibusz, Kossuth Lajos utca 6, or Cooptourist, Ovaros tér 2 (closed Saturday). The Express office is upstairs beside the restaurant above Ibusz.

Express (closed Saturday) doesn't have private rooms but the staff can usually fix you up with a bed at the student dormitory at Egyetem utca 12 in the university district, just south of the centre (US$4 all year). If Express is closed, you could try going directly to the dormitory, though it's much better to have the staff call ahead for you.

From mid-April to mid-October, Balatontourist operates the *Erdei Motel*, a camping ground with bungalows (US$4 double) on a hilltop above Vezprém's zoo, on the west side of town. The route to get there is very complicated by car, so if you're driving get precise directions from the Balatontourist office before heading out that way. On foot, find your way to the zoo parking lot, just beyond the huge highway overpass that is visible from the end of Vár utca, and climb the stairway through the forest. With any luck the motel's back gate will be open. You may be able to arrange some horse riding at the ranch next to the motel.

Singles/doubles at the modern two-star *Hotel Veszprém* cost US$13/15 without bath, US$26/28 with bath, breakfast included. Ask for a room at the back, which is quiet, and not one facing the busy highway.

### Getting There & Away

Veszprém is on the railway line between Budapest-Déli and Szombathely. There are also local trains from Győr via Pannonhalma, and Balatonfüred and Veszprém are connected by frequent bus service (30 minutes). Other useful buses run to Pécs (via Siófok, 166 km), Keszthely and Budapest (Erzsébet tér Bus Station, 110 km).

## BADACSONY

Badacsony lies between Balatonfüred and Keszthely in a picturesque region of basalt peaks among some of the best hiking country in Hungary. Vineyards hug the sides of Badacsony's extinct volcanic cone (elevation 437 metres). The benign climate and rich volcanic soils make this an ideal wine-making area, and in summer drunken Austrian devotees of Bacchus cavort here. If you like your wine, Badacsony is for you.

From mid-October to mid-April all of the travel agencies, pensions and restaurants mentioned in this section are *closed*. You should still be able to find a room by looking for 'zimmer frei' signs or asking around, but bring some food with you.

### Information

Balatontourist (closed from mid-October to mid-April) is at Park utca 10 behind the railway station.

### Things to See & Do

An **art gallery** (open from May to October, closed Monday) near the railway station displays the works of local painter József Egry (1883-1951), who lived here from 1918 onwards. Egry skilfully captured the beauty of Balaton at different times of day.

The beaten tourist track at Badacsony

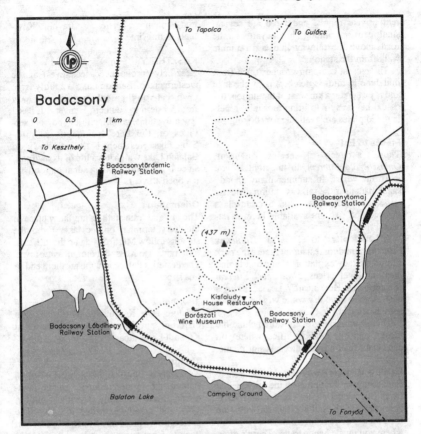

## Badacsony

0    0.5    1 km

To Keszthely

To Tapolca

To Gulács

Badacsonytördemic Railway Station

Badacsonytomaj Railway Station

(437 m)

Kisfaludy House Restaurant

Borászati Wine Museum

Badacsony Railway Station

Badacsony Lábdihegy Railway Station

Balaton Lake

Camping Ground

To Fonyód

leads up through the vineyards to the **Borászati Wine Museum** (open from mid-May to mid-October, closed Monday). You will pass some garish wine restaurants on the way, including one misleadingly labelled 'Bormúzeum'. The genuine museum isn't very interesting (captions are in Hungarian, German and Russian only) but the views of the mountain and lake are good.

The flat-topped forested massif overlooking the lake is just the place to escape the tipsy herd. If you'd like a running start on your hiking, catch the 'Badacsony Taxi', a topless jeep which leaves Badacsony post

office daily from 9 am to 7 pm from mid-May to mid-September (ask the price per seat before you get in). The jeep driver will drop you off at the Kisfaludy House Restaurant, where a large map outlining the well-marked trails is posted by the parking lot. There are numerous lookouts as well as a tall wooden tower that offers splendid views to the hiker.

### Places to Stay

If you want a private room, look for the Balatontourist office on Park utca, behind the railway station. Ibusz and Cooptourist also have offices near the post office which rent private rooms, and there are several small pensions among the vineyards on the road above the railway line, a 10-minute walk from the station.

The closest camping ground (open from mid-June to mid-September) is by the lake and is just under a km west of the station. It's casual but be sure to bring mosquito repellent. Hotplates are available for cooking.

### Places to Eat

There's a cheap self-service restaurant, *Ónkiszolgáló Étterem*, to the right as you leave the wharf. In summer many shoddy snack bars near the railway station dispense wine to rowdy Austrians. Second-class sausage and fish are available here at 1st-class prices.

A better place to eat is the *Hableány Étterem*, a modern restaurant facing the park behind the railway station. If you don't mind Austrian-level prices, *Halászkert Étterem* (Fisherman's Hut) nearby is Badacsony's best. A good local dry white wine is Badacsony Kéknyelű.

There's an ABC grocery store behind the kiosks, opposite the post office, where you can get the makings of a nice lakeside picnic.

### Getting There & Away

Badacsony vm Station is on the railway line from Budapest-Déli to Tapolca and Zala-egerszeg. To Keszthely the railway line follows a roundabout route via Tapolca, where you must change trains. There's often an immediate connection, however. If not, take a bus on to Kesthely, which would be a lot faster anyway.

If you want to swim in the lake, take a ferry across to Fonyód. Ferries between Badacsony and Fonyód are fairly frequent (from mid-April to mid-October). In Fonyód you can get a connection to southern Transdanubia by taking a train direct to Kaposvár, then a bus on to Pécs from there.

### Getting Around

A boat ride to Badacsony from Siófok or Balatonfüred is the best way to get the feel of Balaton Lake. Boats operate from June to

mid-September. Ferries also travel to Keszthely at this time.

## KESZTHELY

Keszthely (pronounced 'cast-eye') at the western end of Balaton Lake is a fairly large town that you'll pass through on your way from western to southern Hungary. It has a few attractions, good facilities and boat services on the lake from June to mid-September. Keszthely is the only town on Balaton Lake which has a life of its own and, since it isn't entirely dependent on tourism, it's open all year.

### Orientation

The bus and train stations are fairly close to the ferry terminal on the lake. From the stations follow Mártirok útja up the hill, then turn right on to Kossuth Lajos utca into town. The Festetics Palace is at the northern end of this street.

### Information

Zalatour is at Kossuth Lajos utca 32. An efficient public telephone office is at Kossuth Lajos utca 1.

### Things to See

Keszthely's finest sight is the **Festetics Palace**, the former residence of the landowning Festetics family, which was built in 1745 and greatly extended in 1887. The palace, now a museum, is open all year from 9 am to 5 pm except Mondays. A highlight of the 101-room palace is the Helikon Library, but the entire complex is richly appointed and well worth seeing.

In 1797 Count Festetics founded Europe's first agricultural institute here and even today Keszthely is noted for its large Agricultural University. Part of the original school, the **Georgikon Manor**, Bercsényi Miklós utca 67, is now a museum (open from April to October, closed Monday) with antique farming equipment, and so on. It's only a couple of blocks from the palace. The **Balaton Museum** (closed Monday) is on Kossuth Lajos utca, towards the railway station.

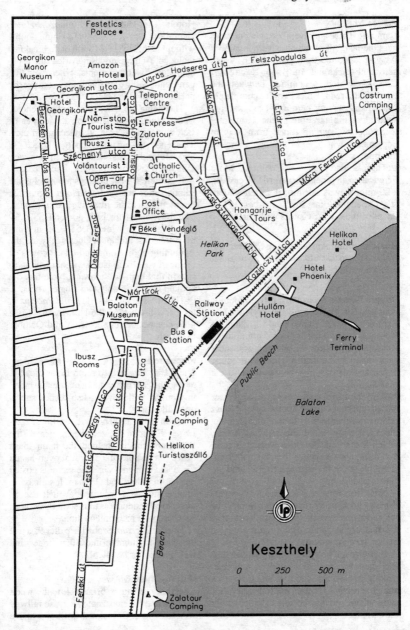

Festetics
Palace •

Georgikon
Manor
Museum

Amazon
Hotel ■

Vörös Hadsereg útja

Felszabadulás út

Castrum
Camping

Georgikon utca

Hotel
Georgikon ■

Telephone
Centre

Non-stop
Tourist i

Express i

Zalatour

Ady Endre utca

Móra Ferenc utca

Ibusz i

Széchenyi utca

Volántourist i

Catholic
Church

Open-air
Cinema

Tandestóztaroasság útja

Post
Office

Béke Vendéglő

Hongarije
Tours

Helikon
Park

Kazinczy utca

Helikon
Hotel ■

Hotel
Phoenix •

Mártírok útja

Balaton
Museum ■

Railway
Station

Hullám
Hotel ■

Ferry
Terminal

Bus
Station

Ibusz
Rooms i

Public Beach

Balaton
Lake

Honvéd utca

György utca

Római utca

Sport
Camping

Festetics út

Helikon
Turistaszálló

Beach

Feneki út

Keszthely

0    250    500 m

Zalatour
Camping

## Places to Stay

**Camping** There are several camping grounds near the lake, all of which have bungalows. As you leave the train station, head south across the tracks and you'll soon reach *Sport Camping* which is hemmed between the tracks and a road. Unless you're completely beat, avoid staying here and keep walking south along the lakeshore another 10 minutes to *Zalatour Camping* (open from May to September) which is in a more attractive location.

There's also *Castrum Camping*, Móra Ferenc utca 48 (open from April to October), a 20-minute walk north of the train station. It's expensive, far from the beach and intended mostly for visitors with cars.

**Hostels** From April to mid-October the *Helikon Turistaszálló*, at Honvéd utca 22, offers dormitory beds.

**Private Rooms** As usual, a private room is your best bet. Try Ibusz, Széchenyi utca 1-3, Express, Kossuth Lajos utca 22, Zalatour, Kossuth Lajos utca 32, or Volántourist, Kossuth Lajos utca 43, which are all near each other in the centre. Hongarije Tours, Tanácskoztarsaság útja 26, is closer to the train station.

If all the travel agencies in the centre are closed when you arrive, try the special Ibusz private room agency at Római utca 2, a few blocks south-west of the railway station, which is theoretically open weekdays from 5 to 8 pm, and weekends from 8 am to 8 pm. Continue south on Múzeum utca behind the Balaton Museum.

Non-Stop Tourist, Bakacs utca 12, advertises 24-hour-a-day service, but in practice it's only open when lots of room-hungry tourists are around. The prices are also higher, so go there last.

If you're only staying one night, some of the agencies levy exorbitant surcharges, making it worthwhile to forgo their services and go directly to houses with 'zimmer frei' signs where you may be able to bargain with the owners.

**Hotels** The 18th century *Amazon Hotel*, Georgikon utca 1, is US$9/18 single/double without bath, US$16/31 with bath, breakfast included. At these prices it's often full, especially on Saturday nights, when wedding parties attending gala functions in the nearby palace occupy the place.

This being the case, your next best choice is the *Hotel Georgikon*, on the corner of Bercsény Miklós utca and Georgikon utca. This renovated old manor charges US$26/38 for singles/doubles with bath in summer, US$14/28 in winter, breakfast included.

Keszthely's most picturesque hotel is the palatial three-star *Hullám Hotel* facing the ferry terminal in the attractive lakefront park. The 30 rooms with bath go for US$25/37 single/double in winter, US$38/50 in summer, breakfast included. Guests may use the swimming pool, sauna and tennis courts of the nearby Helikon Hotel without having to stay in that high-rise monster. Note that the Hullám Hotel has only two single rooms.

The two-star motel-style *Hotel Phoenix* in the park just behind the Hullám Hotel is a little cheaper but closed from mid-October to March.

## Places to Eat

The *Béke Vendéglő*, Kossuth Lajos utca 50, next to the post office, has a reasonable menu in German with several fish dishes and is open all year.

If you haven't had pizza for a while, *Pizzeria da Francesco*, Szabad nép utca 4 (the backstreet directly behind the main Ibusz office), is just the place for real oven-baked pizza and draught beer. The menu is posted outside in Italian and German. It's pleasant, inexpensive and informal. You'll see as many local residents as tourists at Pizzeria da Francesco – a recommendation.

The *Bár Piccolo*, Szabad nép utca 9, is just the place to stumble into after dinner, but watch the killer last step!

## Getting There & Away

Keszthely is on a branch line between Tapolca and Balatonszentgyörgy, so railway service is poor. Occasional fast trains arrive from Budapest-Déli (190 km) via Siófok. For Pécs take a train to Kaposvár, then change to a bus.

The morning service from Keszthely to Szombathely involves changing trains at Tapolca and Celldömölk but the connections are good. At Tapolca you must go to the ticket window to get a compulsory seat reservation for the Celldömölk-Szombathely leg. Ask about direct buses from Keszthely to Szombathely.

A bus station with services to most of western Transdanubia adjoins the railway station. Some buses for southern Transdanubia leave from opposite the Catholic church in the centre of town, so check carefully. Volántourist, Kossuth Lajos utca 43, has information on buses.

### Getting Around

Mahart ferries travel to Badacsony from June to mid-September. In July and August these boats continue on to Siófok.

### HÉVÍZ

In a country with 1500 thermal baths there just had to be a real thermal *lake*. Lake Gyógy, the second-largest warm-water lake in the world (one in New Zealand is the largest), averages 30°C at the surface and red Indian water lilies blossom in it in summer. Eighty million litres of thermal water gush daily from a depth of one km at a rate of 1000 litres, or one cubic metre, a second, flushing the lake completely every two days. Radioactive mud from the lake bed is effective in the treatment of locomotor disorders. In winter the steaming waters, which never fall below 24°C, seem almost surreal.

Wooden catwalks have been built over the lake, allowing you to swim in comfort. The **lake baths** *(tófürdő)* are open all year from 9 am to 4 pm (admission US$1). A massage costs US$6 and a cabin US$2. The indoor **thermal baths** next to the lake function all year from 7 am to 4 pm daily. If you're addicted to the drinking cure, you can get a free fill-up here, but bring a cup.

### Places to Stay & Eat

Only six km west of Keszthely, Hévíz is within easy commuting distance by bus, or you can get a private room right at the spa. Cooptourist and Zalatour, both on Rákóczi

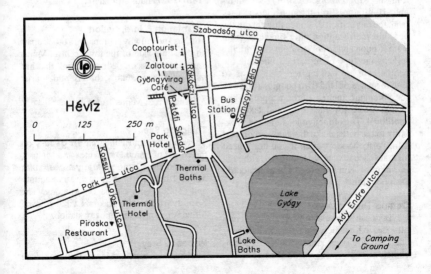

utca, or Zala Volántourist in the bus station can help you find one. You'll see 'zimmer frei' signs near the Piroska Restaurant on Kossuth Lajos utca 10.

From mid-April to mid-October a tourist dormitory (turistaszálló) operates above the *Gyöngyvirag Café*, Rákóczi utca 12.

The *Park Hotel*, Petőfi Sándor utca 26, is an elegant old three-star hotel erected in 1927, just a one-minute walk from the thermal baths. The five single rooms cost US$34 in winter, US$43 in summer, and the 11 doubles cost US$54 in winter, US$69 in summer, breakfast included. Guests may use the sauna, solarium, fitness room and tennis courts of the nearby Thermál Hotel. If you don't mind those prices you're certain to like the Park Hotel very much. Considering the small size, advance reservations are recommended (☎ 13243).

The new *Hotel Napsugár (Sonnenschein)*, Tavirózsa utca 3-5, among the apartment blocks a few blocks south-west of Hotel Thermál, is US$32/36 single/double with bath and breakfast. It's the least expensive of Hévíz's various high-rise tourist hotels.

Flanking the thermal river (!) at the southern end of Lake Gyógy is the luxurious four-star *Kurcamping 'Castrum'*, an enjoyable 10-minute stroll through the spa park from the bus station. It's open throughout the year but the reception only functions from 9 am to noon and from 5 to 7 pm. The pricing reflects the type of motorised clientele the people here are looking for: US$10 for 40 square metres of land (two people) or US$15 for 80 square metres (three people). They charge US$2 for each dog, and taxes are additional. The attractive location and proximity to the baths make this camping ground a fine place to stop, even if you don't need all that space to park your caravan, although in summer Kurcamping 'Castrum' could easily be full.

### Getting There & Away

Hévíz doesn't have a railway station, but a bus goes to Keszthely almost every half-hour and there are occasional services to Szombathely.

# Southern Transdanubia

Southern Hungary is close to Yugoslavia and is characterised by rolling, forested hills and an almost Mediterranean climate. Near Mohács on the Danube in 1526 the Hungarian armies under King Louis II were routed by a vastly superior Ottoman force. As a result the gracious southern city of Pécs still bears the imprint of 150 years of Turkish rule. The good facilities in Pécs make it a perfect base for day trips to the castles of Siklós and Szigetvár, the spas of Harkány and Sikonda, and hiking trails through the Meksek Hills. It's also a gateway to Osijek in Yugoslavia.

## KAPOSVÁR

Kaposvár, a large town on the Kapos River between Balaton Lake and Pécs, probably doesn't warrant a visit on its own, though it's a convenient stepping stone between western and southern Transdanubia. This pleasant Hungarian town off the beaten track is the seat of Somogy County, and the post-impressionist painter József Rippl-Rónai (1861-1927) hails from here.

### Orientation & Information

The bus and railway stations are a block apart on the south side of the town centre. Május 1 utca is a pleasant pedestrian mall that has most of the museums, hotels and tourist offices.

Siótour is at Május 1 utca 1.

### Things to See

There are two museums: an **art gallery** on the corner of Irányi Dániel utca and Május 1 utca, and the **Somogy Megyei Museum**, Május 1 utca 10, in the neoclassical county hall (1828), both closed on Monday. The **Kaposvári Galeria**, Rákóczi tér 4 (closed Monday), is near the railway station.

### Places to Stay

The Siotour office, Május 1 utca 1, can

arrange private rooms, or try Ibusz, Tanácsház utca 3.

The *Csokonai Fogadó*, Május 1 utca 1, is a wonderful 21-room country inn, but all summer it's full with tour groups. Small wonder, the rooms are only US$8/13 single/double.

The big old *Dorottya Hotel*, Széchenyi tér 8, on the corner of Május 1 utca, has been closed for renovations for several years but it may have been reopened by the time you get there.

The *Pálma Panzió*, Széchenyi tér 6, is a pleasant six-room guesthouse (US$23/28 single/double) but it's usually full in summer. Even if you don't stay there, the cake and ice-cream shop downstairs is well worth visiting.

Kaposvár's ugliest hotel is the modern *Kapos Hotel* on Kossuth tér, near the Csokonai Fogadó. As singles/doubles with private bath and breakfast cost US$24/26, you'll probably get a room.

*Deseda Camping* at Toponár, six km north-east of Kaposvár, is accessible on bus No 8 from the bus station. Toponár vm

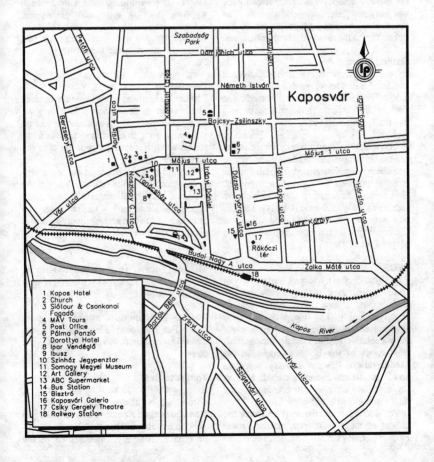

1 Kapos Hotel
2 Church
3 Siótour & Csonkonai Fogadó
4 MÁV Tours
5 Post Office
6 Pálma Panzió
7 Dorottya Hotel
8 Ipar Vendéglő
9 Ibusz
10 Szinház Jegypenztar
11 Somogy Megyei Museum
12 Art Gallery
13 ABC Supermarket
14 Bus Station
15 Bisztró
16 Kaposvári Galeria
17 Csiky Gergely Theatre
18 Railway Station

Railway Station on the line from Siófok to Kaposvár is within walking distance of the camping ground.

## Places to Eat

The *Bisztró*, Rákóczi tér 2 near the railway station, is a cheap cafeteria. An inexpensive restaurant offering large portions is *Ipar Vendéglő*, Tanácsház utca 8 (closed Sunday).

## Entertainment

Kaposvár's best theatre is the *Csiky Gergely Szinhaz* in the centre of Rákóczi tér, opposite the railway station. The resident company has attracted international attention. The Szinhaz Jegypénztár, Május 1 utca 8, has tickets for the theatres and all cultural events.

## Getting There & Away

Express trains arrive from Budapest-Déli and local trains travel north to Fonyód and Siófok. Bus service between Kaposvár and Pécs (67 km) is fairly frequent. Five buses a day run to Szigetvár but only occasionally to Keszthely.

You can get to Yugoslavia by taking a local train to Gyékényes, the border station, where you change for Koprivnica. Yugoslav trains from Koprivnica to Zagreb are frequent. Otherwise, take a bus to Barcs, which has four buses a day to Zagreb (US$11). You can buy advance train tickets at MÁV Tours, Csokonai vm utca (through the passage from Május 1 utca 21).

## PÉCS

Pécs (Fünfkirchen), a large historical city in southern Hungary that lies between the Danube and Drava rivers, is the seat of Baranya County. The fine position on the southern slopes of the Mecsek Hills gives Pécs a relatively mild climate and the red-tiled roofs of the houses accentuate its Mediterranean flavour. Zsolnay porcelain and Pannonia champagne are made here. A less appealing activity is the uranium mining on the slopes just north-east of town.

For 400 years Sopianae (Pécs) was the capital of the Roman province of Lower Pannonia. Early Christianity flourished here in the 4th century and by the 9th century the town was known as 'Quinque Ecclesiae' for its five churches. In 1009 Stephen I, Hungary's first king, made Pécs a bishopric. The first Hungarian university (and the fifth in Europe) was founded here in 1367 and the city's humanistic traditions climaxed with the poet Janus Pannonius. City walls were erected after the Tatar invasion of 1241, but 1543 marked the start of 150 years of Turkish rule. The Turks left their greatest monuments in Pécs and these, together with imposing churches and a synagogue, over a dozen museums, possibilities for hiking through the Mecsek Hills, and varied excursions, make Pécs the perfect place to spend a couple of days. If you only have time for two Hungarian cities, make them Budapest and Pécs.

## Orientation

The bus and railway stations are about three blocks apart on the southern side of the town centre. Use the maps provided here to find your way north to Széchenyi tér where 12 streets meet. Numerous city buses also run up this way (ask).

The left-luggage office in the main railway station is in an obscure building at the far west end of platform one. The left-luggage office at the bus station closes at 6 pm whereas the one at the railway station is open around the clock.

## Information

Mecsek Tourist is at Széchenyi tér 9. Express, Bajcsy-Zsilinszky utca 6, is near the bus station.

**Post & Telecommunications** The main post office is at Jókai Mór utca 10. You can make international telephone calls from there.

## Things to See

Széchenyi tér is the bustling heart of Pécs, dominated on the north by the former **Mosque of Gazi Kassim Pasha**, the largest Turkish building in Hungary. Now a Catholic church, Islamic elements such as the

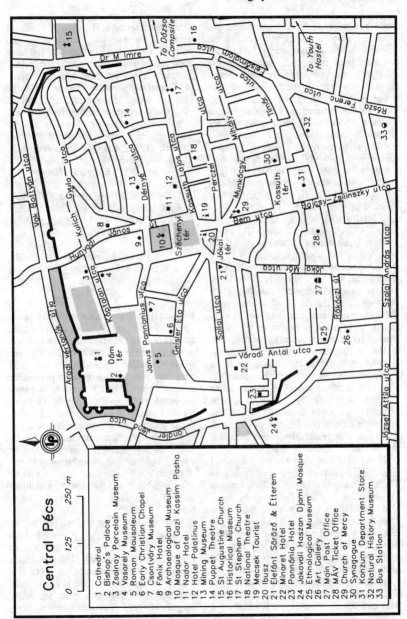

**Central Pécs**

0    125    250 m

1 Cathedral
2 Bishop's Palace
3 Zsolnay Porcelain Museum
4 Vasarely Museum
5 Roman Mausoleum
6 Early Christian Chapel
7 Csontváry Museum
8 Fönix Hotel
9 Archaeological Museum
10 Mosque of Gazi Kassim Pasha
11 Nador Hotel
12 Hotel Palatinus
13 Mining Museum
14 Puppet Theatre
15 St Augustine Church
16 Historical Museum
17 St Stephen Church
18 National Theatre
19 Mecsek Tourist
20 Ibusz
21 Elefánt Söröző & Étterem
22 Minaret Hotel
23 Pannónia Hotel
24 Jakovali Haszan Djami Mosque
25 Ethnological Museum
26 Art Gallery
27 Main Post Office
28 MÁV Ticket Office
29 Church of Mercy
30 Synagogue
31 Konzum Department Store
32 Natural History Museum
33 Bus Station

mihrab, a prayer niche on the south-eastern side, are easy to distinguish. Behind the mosque is the **Archaeological Museum** with exhibits from prehistory up to the Magyar conquest. Informative summaries in English and German are displayed in each room.

From this museum go west along Janus Pannonius utca for a block to the **Csontváry Museum**, Janus Pannonius utca 11, dedicated to the early 20th century painter-philosopher Tivadar Csontváry. His painting of the ruins of Baalbek, Lebanon (1905), is a masterpiece. On the corner opposite this museum is a good little wine cellar that is in front of the men's toilets.

Káptalan utca, which climbs east from here, is lined with museums. The most famous is the **Vasarely Museum**, Káptalan utca 3, with 150 original examples of op art. Victor Vasarely, a longtime resident of southern France, was born in this house in 1908. Across the street is the **Zsolnay Porcelain Museum**, Káptalan utca 2, which has mostly Art-Nouveau pieces (captions are in German). A room downstairs in the same building contains sculptures by Amerigo Tot.

Return to Dóm tér and the tremendous four-towered **cathedral** (admission costs US$0.50). The oldest part of the building is the 11th century crypt, but the entire complex was heavily rebuilt in a neo-Romanesque style in 1881. Behind the **bishop's palace** (1770), next to the cathedral, is a 15th century **barbican gate** that remains from the old city walls.

In the centre of the southern portion of Dóm tér is an excavated 4th century Roman Christian **mausoleum** with striking frescoes of Adam and Eve, and Daniel in the lion's den, certainly a remarkable sight that is unique in central Europe. Nearby at Geisler Eta utca 14 are the ruins of a 4th century Early Christian chapel. It's only open in summer but you can enter the courtyard and peek in through the windows any time.

Follow your map south-west a few blocks from Dóm tér to the 16th century **Jakovali Haszan Djami Mosque**, at Rákóczi út 2 (closed Wednesday), the best preserved Turkish monument in Hungary. Also known as the Little Mosque, the building and minaret are perfectly preserved and now form part of a museum of Turkish culture.

After seeing the Little Mosque, follow Péc's most enjoyable pedestrian malls, Sallai utca and Kossuth Lajos utca, east across the city. You'll pass three beautiful old churches and the ornate National Theatre (check for performances). Just beyond the **St Stephen Church** (1741), Kossuth Lajos utca 44/a, turn right to Felsőmalom utca 9, where you'll find an excellent **Historical Museum** that will sum up all you've seen.

Visitors to the **synagogue** (1869) on Kossuth tér are offered an informative text on the Jewish faith in a choice of languages (open from May to October, closed Saturday).

All of Pécs's museums except for the Little Mosque and the synagogue are closed on Mondays.

**Mecsek Hills** Every visitor should take a trip up into the Mecsek Hills. Bus No 35 from stand 2 in front of the railway station climbs to the 194-metre TV tower on Misina Peak (534 metres). You could also take bus No 35 from the Kossuth statue on Kossuth tér in the centre of town. There's a restaurant below the viewing balcony high up in the TV tower (open Tuesday to Sunday from 11 am to 6pm) which offers panoramic views. If you order something there, check the prices on the menu beforehand or you could end up paying double. The observation platform offers an unobstructed view as there is no glass. Bus No 35 also goes past Pécs' delightful **zoo** (open daily all year from 9 am to 6 pm).

There are numerous, well-marked hiking trails that fan out from the TV tower. Pick up the 1:40,000 *A Mecsek* topographical map which shows them all. Armed with this map, you could also take a bus from Pécs Bus Station to Orfű or Abaliget and hike back over the hills. The back parts are pretty logged over but don't attract nearly as many visitors and you might even see some deer.

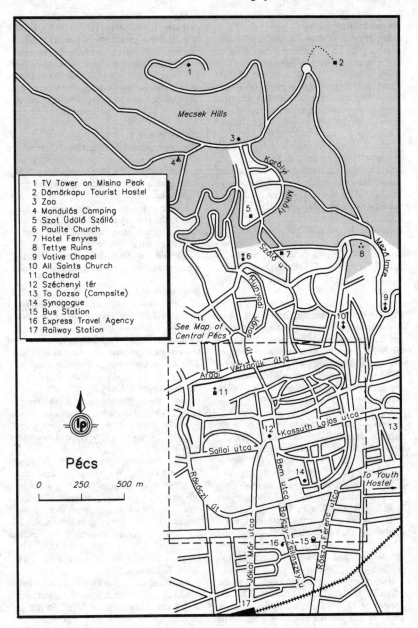

1 TV Tower on Misina Peak
2 Dömörkapu Tourist Hostel
3 Zoo
4 Mandulás Camping
5 Szot Üdülő Szálló
6 Paulite Church
7 Hotel Fenyves
8 Tettye Ruins
9 Votive Chapel
10 All Saints Church
11 Cathedral
12 Széchenyi tér
13 To Dozso (Campsite)
14 Synagogue
15 Bus Station
16 Express Travel Agency
17 Railway Station

Mecsek Hills

Károlyi Mihály

Mecsek Imre

Szőlő u.

See Map of
Central Pécs

Hunyadi János út

Aradi Vértanúk útja

Kossuth Lajos utca

Széchenyi tér

Sallai utca

Bem utca

Bajcsy Zsilinszky u.

Rózsa Ferenc utca

To Youth
Hostel

Rákóczi út

Jókai Mór utca

Pécs

0        250        500 m

## Places to Stay

**Camping** The *Dózso Campsite*, at Felső-vámház utca 72, is within walking distance of the centre. Go east on Kossuth Lajos utca from Szécheyi tér and continue straight ahead for 10 minutes. It costs US$4 per person to pitch a tent or US$3 per person to sleep in a six-bed dormitory in the historic mansion on the grounds (open from June to August only).

*Mandulás Camping* (open from mid-April to mid-October) near the zoo, up in the Mecsek Hills, has bungalows as well as tent space. Take bus No 34 right to the door or bus No 35 to the zoo and then walk five minutes to the camping ground.

**Hostel** In July and August, Szalay László Kivalo College, Universitas út 2, accommodates YHA members in three-bed dorms at US$3 per person. Go straight to the hostel, a 10-minute walk north-east of the bus station.

**Private Rooms** Mecsek Tourist and Ibusz, two offices that arrange private rooms, face one another at the southern end of Széchenyi tér. MÁV Tours in the railway station (open Monday to Thursday till 3.30 pm, Friday till 2.30 pm) also arranges private rooms. It's in the main building at the eastern end of the station but you have to look for it.

**Hotels** The cheapest hotel in town is the *Minaret Hotel*, Sallai utca 35 (US$14/17 double/triple with shared bath, no singles), in the old Franciscan monastery (1738), but it's often full. The hotel restaurant is good.

The *Főnix Hotel*, Hunyadi János út 2, is a small, modern hotel; singles/doubles/triples with bath cost US$29/39/48.

If you want to stay at the best hotel in Pécs, choose the fine old *Hotel Palatinus*, Kossuth Lajos utca 5, where a double room with private bath and breakfast will cost US$58 (no singles).

Two other places to stay at are up in the Mecsek Hills. The *Dömörkapu Tourist Hostel* (☎ 721 5987) is below Vidam Park (bus No 35), but it's closed in winter. The

two-star *Hotel Fenyves* (☎ 721 5996), Szőlő utca 65, has a great view of the city (US$23 double with bath and breakfast). The hotel restaurant is clean and reasonable. Take bus No 34 or 35 to Szot Udulo Szálló (a trade union hostel), then walk down to the hotel. Try calling these two places before you go up.

## Places to Eat

The medium-priced *Elefánt Söröző* on Jókai tér has two sections, the Elefánt Étterem upstairs and the Elefánt Söröző downstairs. Both post menus outside in German and Hungarian.

*Fiaker Vendéglő*, Felsőmalom utca 7 next door to the Historical Museum, is an unpretentious wine cellar with a good fixed 'menu' in German – recommended.

It's said Hungarian beer is not good; try the local Szalon beer and see what you think.

## Entertainment

Pécs has famous opera and ballet companies. If you're told that tickets to the *National Theatre* on Kossuth Lajos utca are sold out, try for a cancellation at the box office an hour before the performance. Ask at Mecsek Tourist about concerts and other events.

## Getting There & Away

Express trains run regularly to Budapest-Déli (229 km) and one early morning express goes to Szombathely (via Gyékényes). Some trains to Budapest carry compulsory seat reservations.

There are two local trains a day between Pécs and Osijek, Yugoslavia (82 km). You must buy your ticket to Osijek at a special office near the station restaurant which is only open weekdays from 8 am to 5 pm and Saturdays from 8 am to noon. You can only buy tickets as far as the border at the regular ticket window. Train reservations and tickets are more easily available at the MÁV ticket office, Rákóczi út 39/c.

There are also buses from Pécs to Osijek (US$3 or DM 5 in cash – pay the driver) and from Barcs to Zagreb (four daily, US$11). To go to Kaposvár, Siklós, Szeged or Veszprém, take a bus. The bus from Pécs to Szeged takes four hours (189 km).

## SZIGETVÁR

Szigetvár, 33 km west of Pécs, is famous in Hungarian history as the place where 2482 Hungarians held off 207,000 Turks for 33 days in 1566. As the moated 'island castle' was about to fall, the remaining defenders sallied out under Miklós Zrínyi to meet their end in bloody hand-to-hand combat. The Turks suffered tremendous losses, including Sultan Süleyman I, and their march on Vienna was halted. Almost a century later, a second Miklós Zrínyi (1620-64), great-grandson and namesake of the hero of Szigetvár, wrote an epic poem about the battle which still inspires Hungarians today.

Though an easy day trip from Pécs, you might want to linger at Szigetvár to enjoy the thermal baths near the fortress (open all year).

## Things to See & Do

Szigetvár's **fortress** (1420) with its four corner bastions contains a museum that

focuses on the 1566 battle (open all year from 10 am to 3 pm, closed Monday). Inside the museum is a mosque built soon after the fall of Szigetvár in honour of the sultan. Of the minaret only the base remains.

A second mosque, the **Ali Pasha Mosque** (1569), now a Catholic church, is in the centre of town.

### Places to Stay & Eat

A scowling lion on Zrínyi tér faces the modern *Oroszlán Hotel*, where you will find singles/doubles for US$23/32 with private bath and breakfast. Staff at Mecsek Tourist in the hotel can find you a room in a private home.

From mid-April to mid-October there's a turistaszálló (dormitory) in the fortress, but you must make advance reservations at Mecsek Tourist.

### Getting There & Away

Szigetvár is on the railway line from Pécs to Gyékényes, though buses are more frequent than trains. Buses go to Kaposvár five times a day.

For Yugoslavia catch a bus or train to Barcs, 32 km south-west of Szigetvár, where there are onward buses to Zagreb.

### SIKLÓS

Siklós, 32 km south of Pécs, beyond the red-wine-producing Villány Hills, is the southernmost town in Hungary. On a hilltop overlooking the surrounding farmland stands a well-preserved 15th century **castle**, the only one in Hungary continuously in use since the Middle Ages. Today it functions as part hotel, hostel, cellar restaurant and museum (open all year Tuesday to Sunday from 9 am to 4 pm). A section of the museum is dedicated to the 1848 Revolution and especially to the progressive lord of Siklós Castle, Casimir Batthyány, who freed his serfs in 1847. The tomb of this gentleman may be seen in the castle's Gothic chapel. There's also a small but excellent collection of 19th century costumes.

Harkány village, six km east of Siklós on the road to Pécs, has well-known **hot spring** baths and a good camping ground (open from mid-April to mid-September). The medicinal waters here have the richest sulphuric content in Hungary.

### Places to Stay & Eat

If you'd like to stay in the castle, you may choose between the somewhat expensive two-star *Tenkes Hotel* and a hostel (turistaszálló). You must make advance hostel reservations at Mecsek Tourist in Pécs.

The restaurant in the castle casemates is often reserved for groups, in which case repair to the *Központi Étterem*, Kossuth tér 5, in town, below the castle.

### Getting There & Away

Siklós is connected to Pécs by hourly bus (via Harkány), which makes it an easy day trip from Pécs.

# The Great Plain

South-eastern Hungary, the Great Plain (Nagyalföld), is a wide expanse of level puszta (prairie) drained by the Tisza River. This rich farming area bears barley, corn, oats, potatoes, rye, sugar beets and wheat. Perhaps no other region of Hungary has a place in Hungarian folklore like the Great Plain. The poet Sándor Petőfi wrote of the puszta: *Börtönéből szabadult sas lelkem, Ha a rónak végtelenjét látom* (that his soul soars like an eagle released from a cage, every time he sees this endless plain). In the blazing heat of summer many have witnessed mirages shimmering over the blonde plains.

Visitors to the region are introduced to the lore of the Hungarian cowboy and his long-horned, grey cattle or the nomadic shepherds and their tiny sheepdogs. Two national parks, Kiskunság in the Bugac puszta and Hortobágy in the Hortobágy puszta, preserve this unique environment. Kecskemét, Szeged and Debrecen are centres of the western, southern and eastern puszta.

## KECSKEMÉT

Exactly halfway between Budapest and Szeged, near the geographical centre of Hungary, Kecskemét is a clean, healthy city famous for its potent *barack pálinka* (apricot brandy) and level puszta. It's known as the garden city of Hungary for the million fruit trees in the surrounding area; wine is also produced. Bács-Kiskun County is administered from here. Among Kecskemét's most renowned native sons are József Katona (1791-1830), author of the historical play *Bank ban*, and the composer Zoltán Kodály (1882-1967).

### Orientation & Information

The adjacent bus and railway stations are on the north-eastern side of town, a 10-minute walk along Nagykőrösi utca or Rákóczi út to Szabadság tér and Kossuth tér, the centre of town.

Pusztatourist is between Szabadság tér and Kossuth tér.

### Things to See

Kossuth tér is surrounded by historic buildings. Dominating the square is a massive Art-Nouveau **town hall** (1897) with a carillon that gives concerts every hour on the hour. In front of the town hall is a statue of the 19th century politician Lajos Kossuth, who led the struggle for independence from Austria, and a monument bearing the distances to towns everywhere in Hungary.

Flanking the town hall are two fine churches: the neoclassical **Old Church** (1806) and the earlier **St Miklós Church** with a Baroque calvary (1790) before the door. Close by on Katona József tér is the magnificent **Katona József Theatre** (1896) with a Baroque statue of the Trinity (1742) standing in front of it.

### Places to Stay

Private rooms are arranged by staff at Pusztatourist (closed weekends), opposite the town hall on Kossuth tér; Budapest Tourist (open Saturday morning), Hornyik János körút; Volántourist, Ket templom köz 5; and Cooptourist, Ket templom köz 9. The people at Volántourist are especially helpful and will reserve rooms for you in other cities, if you want. Ibusz and Express are side by side upstairs at Dobó István körút 11.

The *Hotel Három Gúnár*, Batthyány utca 3, is expensive at US$37/43 single/double with bath and breakfast, but it has a certain charm and is minutes from the centre of town. A bowling alley and bar are in the hotel basement.

The 111 rooms at the modern *Aranyhomok Hotel*, Széchenyi tér 3, are somewhat more expensive that those at the Három Gúnár.

The camping ground (open from mid-April to mid-October) is on Sport utca, on the south-western side of Kecskemét, nearly five km from the railway station. Bus service there is lousy. It's clean and has bungalows but the adjacent swimming pool is often empty.

### Places to Eat

If all you want is a cheap, fast meal the *Szalag étélbár*, Petőfi Sándor utca 1, can provide it. The tables there are pleasant.

The *Jalta Borozó*, Batthyány utca 2, right opposite the Hotel Három Gúnár, is a rather homy wine cellar with a menu in English (!) and German. If this fails to please you, the restaurant in the *Hotel Három Gúnár* across the street won't.

Meals at *Pilseni Pince*, a beer cellar on Katona tér, just off Ket templom köz, are cheaper from 10 am to 4 pm than from 4 pm to midnight, but are never unreasonable.

A place not to miss is *Café Liberty*, next to Pusztatourist on Kossuth tér. In summer you can sit on the terrace and nurse your drink as people pass by, or indulge in an excellent meal. For classic elegance this fine old café ranks as one of the best in Hungary.

### Getting There & Away

Kecskemét is on the railway line that goes from Budapest-Nyugati to Szeged. To go to Romania, change to the local train from Budapest-Nyugati to Oradea at Cegléd.

There are almost hourly buses to Budapest (85 km), every couple of hours to Szeged (86 km) and three a day to Pécs (176 km).

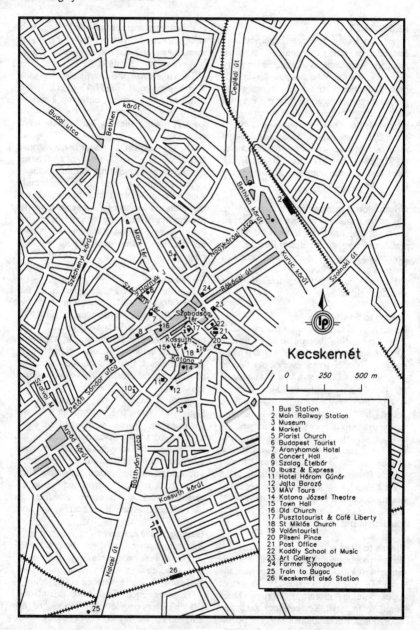

Kecskemét

0        250        500 m

1  Bus Station
2  Main Railway Station
3  Museum
4  Market
5  Piarist Church
6  Budapest Tourist
7  Aranyhomok Hotel
8  Concert Hall
9  Szalag Ételbár
10  Ibusz & Express
11  Hotel Három Gúnár
12  Jalta Borozó
13  MÁV Tours
14  Katona József Theatre
15  Town Hall
16  Old Church
17  Pusztatourist & Café Liberty
18  St Miklós Church
19  Volántourist
20  Pilseni Pince
21  Post Office
22  Kodály School of Music
23  Art Gallery
24  Former Synagogue
25  Train to Bugac
26  Kecskemét alsó Station

## BUGAC

Bugac, an accessible corner of the 306-sq-km Kiskunság National Park south-west of Kecskemét, is a good place to get close to the Great Plain. Great herds of fork-horned Hungarian grey cattle and flocks of twisted-horned sheep (*racka*), some black, some white, roam across the sandy puszta, while the adjacent juniper forest invites hikers.

### Orientation & Information

The *Bugaci Csárda*, an eight-minute walk from Bugac-Felső Railway Station, is a large folkloric restaurant where there's also a camping ground.

It's three km from the Csárda to Kiskunság National Park and the **Shepherd Museum** (closed from November to March and Monday). The real reason to come is the **horse shows** which are performed daily at 1 pm in summer and more often when tour groups are present. You'll see real whip-snapping Hungarian cowboys working their horses and exciting 'five-in-hand' riding during which one man makes five horses gallop around a field at full speed while standing on the backs of the rear two horses!

You can see many fine animals in the nearby stables, so Bugac is a must for horse lovers. Unfortunately, it's difficult to arrange any riding for yourself.

Admission to the park and horse shows is US$1. Avoid the 30-minute horse-cart rides which are certainly not worth US$5 per person!

### Getting There & Away

The fun way to get to Bugac is on the narrow-gauge railway from Kecskemét which rumbles 40 km south between vineyards, sunflower fields and apple orchards. The little carriages have hard wooden seats and a stove for heating in winter. This train departs from Kecskemét KK Railway Station, not the main station. To get there, walk south on Batthyány utca from the Három Gúnár Hotel and continue straight across a large bridge until you see the small station on the right. Get the 7.45 am train which reaches Bugac at around 9 am, but don't get off at Bugac-puszta or Bugac – you want Bugac-Felső.

If the return train times are inconvenient, catch a bus from the highway near the Bugaci Csárda to Kiskunfélegyháza, where there are frequent buses back to Kecskemét.

## SZEGED

Szeged (Segedin), the paprika and 'pick' salami capital of Hungary, straddles the Tisza River just before it enters Yugoslavia. The Maros River from Arad, Romania, enters the Tisza just east of the centre. In March 1879 a great flood burst upon Szeged, damaging almost every building in the city. Afterwards, the city was redesigned with concentric boulevards and radial avenues. Sections of the outer boulevard are named for cities which provided aid after the flood: Vienna, Moscow, London, Paris, Berlin, Brussels and Rome. Szeged is larger and livelier than Debrecen and in midsummer the city really comes to life for the famous Szeged Festival. It's the seat of Csongrád County and an important gateway to/from Yugoslavia.

### Orientation

The railway station is a 15-minute walk south of the centre, and the bus station is 10 minutes west of Széchenyi tér. Tram No 1 connects the railway station to town.

### Information

Szeged Tourist is at Klauzál tér 7.

### Things to See

The one sight of Szeged not to be missed is the neo-Byzantine **Votive Church**, built between 1913 and 1930 in remembrance of the 1879 flood. The dome of this huge red-brick structure is 53 metres high, and the twin neo-Romanesque towers soar 92 metres. The church's cavernous interior is covered with frescoes and the organ (1930) has 11,500 pipes.

Beside the church is the 13th century **Demetrius Tower** remaining from the previous church, which was demolished to make room for the present one. The old

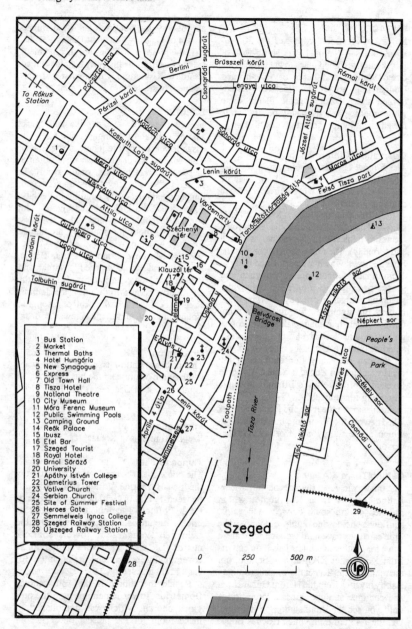

1 Bus Station
2 Market
3 Thermal Baths
4 Hotel Hungária
5 New Synagogue
6 Express
7 Old Town Hall
8 Tisza Hotel
9 National Theatre
10 City Museum
11 Móra Ferenc Museum
12 Public Swimming Pools
13 Camping Ground
14 Reők Palace
15 Ibusz
16 Etel Bar
17 Szeged Tourist
18 Royal Hotel
19 Brnol Söröző
20 University
21 Apáthy István College
22 Demetrius Tower
23 Votive Church
24 Serbian Church
25 Site of Summer Festival
26 Heroes Gate
27 Semmelweis Ignac College
28 Szeged Railway Station
29 Újszeged Railway Station

Szeged

0       250       500 m

Serbian Church (1745) behind the Votive Church provides a good contrast.

By the Belvárosi Bridge over the Tisza River is the **Móra Ferenc Museum** (closed Monday) in a huge neoclassical building (1896). The collection of Hungarian painting is good but the upper floor has been closed for rearrangement for years. Behind this museum in an **old gate** that remains from Szeged's 18th century fortress with a very informative city historical museum.

There are many fine buildings around Széchenyi tér in the centre of town, including the **old town hall** (1883). In summer this park is Szeged's prettiest place.

Surprisingly, Szeged's most compelling sight is the **New Synagogue** (1903), a few blocks west of Széchenyi tér. The names of the many Jewish victims of Nazi terror in this area are inscribed in stone on the synagogue walls. This building with its great blue dome has a wonderful oriental atmosphere.

### Places to Stay

If you want a private room, your best bet is Szeged Tourist, Klauzál tér 7. During the Summer Festival it's open from 9 am to 7 pm daily and rooms are available. Ibusz, Klauzál tér 2, also has private rooms, but not as many.

There's a camping ground on Közép kikötő sor in Partfürdő, right beside the river, opposite the city centre. You can see the tents from the Belvárosi Bridge. A second camping ground, *Napfeny Camping*, Dorozsmai út 2, with motel rooms (US$10 double), is near Rokus Railway Station on the west side of town (open from April to mid-October). Tram No 1 from the main railway station terminates there.

In July and August the student dormitories of Apáthy István College, Eutvös utca 4 right next to the Votive Church, and Semmelweis Ignac College, Semmelweis utca 4 between the train station and town, are opened as youth hostels. Go directly to the hostels or ask for information at Express, Kígyó utca 3.

If you want to stay in a hotel, consider the fine old two-star *Tisza Hotel*, Wesselényi utca 1 at Széchenyi tér. It costs US$20/37 for singles/doubles without bath and about 50% more with bath.

### Places to Eat

The *Boszorkanykonyha étélbár*, Híd utca 8, just off Széchenyi tér, is a cheap self-service. It's a little complicated because you have to pay first and get a ticket. Hang around until you see someone getting a plate you fancy and then point to it. The toilet here is free.

Two good inexpensive restaurants that are side by side are the *Brnoi Söröző* and *Hagi étterem*, both at Kelemen utca 3, opposite the Royal Hotel. The Hagi has a cheap set 'menu', and the Brnoi is a Czech-style beer hall. Both open daily.

The *Virág Cukrsázda*, Klauzál tér 1, opposite Szeged Tourist, serves great cakes and pastries.

### Entertainment

The *National Theatre* (built in 1883) is on Tanácsköztársaság útja on the corner of Vörösmarty utca.

The Szeged Summer Festival (held from mid-July to mid-August) unfolds on Dóm tér with the two great towers of the Votive Church as a backdrop. The open-air theatre here seats 6000 people. Main events include an opera, an operetta, a play, folk dancing, classical music, ballet and a rock opera. Festival tickets are sold in a yellow kiosk that opens from 5 to 9 pm and is labelled *szabadteri jegypénztár*. It's on the corner just behind the Votive Church.

Organ concerts are given in the Votive Church during July and August on weekends at 3 pm (US$1).

### Getting There & Away

Direct express trains travel from Budapest-Nyugati (191 km) via Kecskemét. Two local trains a day run to Subotica in Yugoslavia (US$2). Buy your ticket at the station.

Six buses travel daily to Pécs (189 km) and two daily to Gyula and Debrecen (224 km). Several buses run daily to Subotica. For buses to Yugoslavia you must reserve your seat in advance at the ticket window and pay for it in hard currency (US$1). On domestic buses you pay the driver.

Getting to Romania by train is complicated, as you must change at Békéscsaba (seven local trains a day go from Szeged to Békéscsaba, 94 km). This connection is not good. If you are adventurous and don't mind walking or hitching, you could take a local train from Ujszeged Station (across the Tisza River from central Szeged) to Nagylak, which is right on the Romanian border, halfway to Arad. The highway border crossing is near Nagylak Station and it's only a four-km walk from there to the first Romanian town, Nadlac, which has trains to Arad six times a day.

## DEBRECEN

Debrecen (Debrezin), Hungary's third-largest city and the capital of Hajdú-Bihar County, sits on a flat plain at the centre of a rich agricultural area, 230 km east of Budapest. In 1540 the inhabitants converted to Calvinism, and Debrecen is still the most strait-laced Protestant city in Hungary. In the 17th century Debrecen was right on the border of territories that were controlled by the Turks, Habsburgs and princes of Transylvania. By paying tribute to all three, it gained a measure of independence and became a great trading centre. Plundered by the Catholic Habsburgs more than once in the early 18th century, revolutionary governments that challenged the autocratic regimes in Vienna and Budapest were established in Debrecen in 1849 and 1944.

All trains between Moscow and Budapest stop here, and Debrecen is just the place to terminate a trans-Siberian odyssey and ease into Hungarian life without encountering the tourists in line in Budapest. Although it's also a major gateway to/from Romania, friendly Debrecen is still well off the beaten track.

### Orientation

Debrecen has only one tram line and this runs north up Vörös Hadsereg útja from the railway station to Kálvin tér in the centre of town, then continues north again into Nagyerdő Forest Park which has camping and recreation facilities.

### Information

Hajdú Tourist is at Kálvin tér 2/a, right next to the Great Reformed Church.

### Things to See

You can't miss the **Great Reformed Church** (1823) on Kálvin tér in the heart of the city. This huge neoclassical building is the largest Protestant church in Hungary. Near the church is the **Reformed College** (1816), which contains a historical museum (closed Monday) and the largest church-operated library in Hungary. The library, which is worth seeing, and the oratory are upstairs.

A couple of blocks away at Péterfia utca 28 is the **Déri Museum** (closed Monday), which was opened in 1928 and houses a diverse collection, the highlight of which is Mihály Munkácsy's *Ecce Homo* painting, which fills an entire wall. The folklore section is also good. The four recumbent statues in front of the museum are by Ferenc Medgyessy, a Debrecen sculptor who merits a museum of his own.

If you have some time to spare, take the tram north to **Nagyerdő Forest Park** where there are small lakes where you can rent a boat. You can also go for walks in the verdant surroundings and visit the monuments, zoo, amusement park and even the thermal swimming pools.

### Places to Stay

For private rooms go to Hajdú Tourist, at Kálvin tér 2/a, or Ibusz, at the Aranybika Hotel.

In July and August several student hostels in the northern section of the city are open to YHA members. They're a little out of the way so check first with Express, Vörös Hadsereg útja 77 (open weekdays from 8 am to 4.30 pm), about available places before going there.

A double room at the *Hotel Debrecen* opposite the train station costs US$19 without bath, US$27 with bath (no singles),

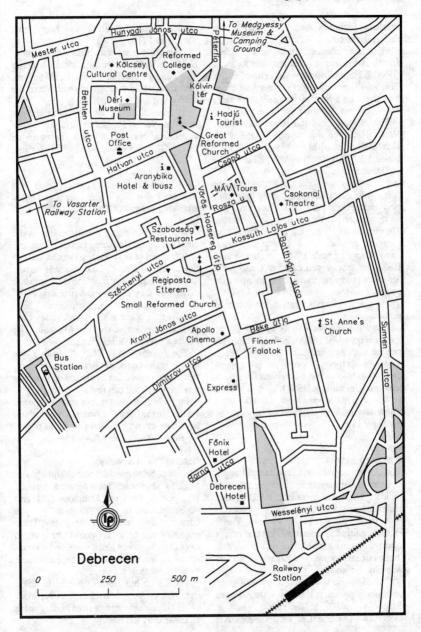

**Debrecen**

0      250      500 m

breakfast included. Avoid the noisy rooms facing the street.

A quieter choice would be the *Főnix Hotel*, Barna utca 17 just two blocks away (US$12/21 single/double with shared bath). This small modern hotel is your best bet if you arrive on a Sunday when all the offices arranging private rooms are closed.

The elegant three-star *Aranybika Hotel*, Vörös Hadsereg útja 11-15, is US$50/63 single/double with bath and breakfast. Since 1915 this has been *the* place to stay in Debrecen.

From May to September campers are taken good care of at the camping ground in Nagyerdő Forest Park, about five km north of the station. Take the tram as far as the Thermál Hotel, then ask for directions to the camping ground. It's a five-minute walk away. Camping costs US$2 per person plus US$3 per tent or you can pay US$8 for a 3rd-class bungalow that accommodates four people (1st-class bungalows cost US$40). There's a good restaurant at the camping ground.

The *Hotel Thermál* in Nagyerdő Forest Park charges US$18/28 single/double with private bath and breakfast (open all year). The open-air thermal pool at the hotel opens daily from May to mid-September from 6 am to 6 pm (admission is US$1). There's also an indoor pool that's open throughout the year. Those staying at Hotel Thermál may use the pools for free.

## Places to Eat

You can get an easy self-service meal in the *Debrecen Restaurant* upstairs in the new building across the street from the Debrecen Hotel. It's not very appetising, however.

A cheaper place is *Finom-Falatok*, Vörös Hadsereg útja 69, a meat market that offers stand-up meals to colourful regulars. Peek in the pots and point. The bar attached sells wine by the glass.

One of the best restaurants, yet still quite reasonably priced, is the *Régiposta Étterem*, Széchenyi utca 6, in the oldest house in Debrecen. The Swedish king Charles XII

spent a night here on his way home from Turkey in 1714.

Also fairly good is the *Szabadság Restaurant*, Vörös Hadsereg útja 29. In summer you can eat outside on the back terrace. Just go straight through to the back of the restaurant and turn left.

The nameless *étterem* down in the basement at Vörös Hadsereg útja 12 serves substantial Hungarian meals at reasonable prices. The menu is in German and Italian.

## Entertainment

Visit the *Csokonai Theatre* (1861) on Kossuth Lajos utca where operas and operettas are performed. The ticket office is just inside.

Also ask at Országos Filharmonia in the city hall, Vörös Hadsereg útja 20. Concerts only happen every couple of weeks and the tickets are sold out. Make yourself known to the friendly staff of the Filharmonia office and they'll sell you a rush seat at the door just before the performance. These usually take place at the new *Kölcsey Cultural Centre* behind the Déri Museum. The centre also has a mini cinema.

The *Ifjuszpolitikai Klub*, Kossuth Lajos utca 1, is the venue of alternative and countercultural events. Go inside and up the stairs and see what you can find.

From May to November organ concerts are held in the Great Reformed Church about once a month on Sundays at 6 pm as part of the religious service.

## Getting There & Away

All trains between Budapest, Belgrade and Moscow stop here. Train services between Budapest-Nyugati and Debrecen (221 km) via Szolnok are frequent. To go to Eger you have to change trains at Füzesabony. There are also direct buses between Debrecen and Eger (130 km). For Košice in Czechoslovakia take a bus to Miskolc (98 km) and catch a train from there.

There's no bus from Debrecen to Tokaj and by train you must change at Nyíregyháza. There's also no bus from Nyíregyháza to Tokaj, only the train.

For Szeged (224 km) take one of the two daily buses direct from Debrecen or a bus from Debrecen to Békéscsaba and then catch one of the seven daily trains from there to Szeged.

**To/From Romania** If you want to go to Oradea, you can connect with one of the two daily local trains from Budapest-Nyugati at Püspökladány. No reservations are required, but pick up an advance ticket at MÁV Tours, Rózsa utca 4. From mid-June to September the Varna Express passes through Debrecen on its way from Warsaw to Bulgaria via Košice and Oradea (reservations required).

### HORTOBÁGY

Between Debrecen and Eger, the railway line crosses the famous Hungarian puszta, a vast flat plain of damp grasslands. The centre of this eastern puszta is Hortobágy. The area was depopulated during the Turkish period, and from the 18th century it was used to breed horses, cattle and sheep. In 1973 a 520-sq-km national park was created here.

### Things to See & Do

A km south of the train station is the **Nine-Arched Bridge** (1833), the longest stone bridge in Hungary. Next to the bridge is the **Herdsman Museum** (closed Monday and from November to March). The museum is housed in an old wagon shed (1780) and contains shepherds' clothing, tools and folk art. A circular thatched building alongside (closed from November to mid-May and Monday) displays the flora and fauna of Hortobágy National Park.

Hortobágy is best visited in summer when fairs and horse shows are held near the bridge, the most important on St Stephen's Day (20 August). You will sometimes see real Hungarian cowboys and colourful five-in-hand riding. A large *camping ground* (open from May to September) is beside the museum, and nearby the *Hortobágy Csárda* is a typical restaurant which opens at noon.

### Getting There & Away

Hortobágy is on the secondary railway line from Debrecen to Füzesabony. An afternoon bus passes Hortobágy on its way to Eger.

# Northern Hungary

Northern Hungary is the most mountainous part of the country. The southern ranges of the Carpathian Mountains stretch east along the Czech border in a 1000-metre-high chain of woody hills from the Danube Bend almost to the Soviet border. Miskolc is heavily industrialised but historic Eger offers an ideal base for sightseers and wine tasters. Day trips to the nearby Mátra and Bükk mountains are possible. Farther north, right beside Czechoslovakia, are the caves near Aggtelek, Hungary's most extensive caves. To the east are the famous wine-growing centres of Tokaj and Sárospatak, a potential gateway to/from East Slovakia in Czechoslovakia.

### EGER

Eger (Erlau), the seat of Heves County, is a lovely Baroque city full of historic buildings. It was at Eger Castle in 1552 that 2000 Hungarian defenders temporarily stopped the Turkish advance into Europe and helped to preserve the Hungarian identity. The Turks returned in 1596 and captured the

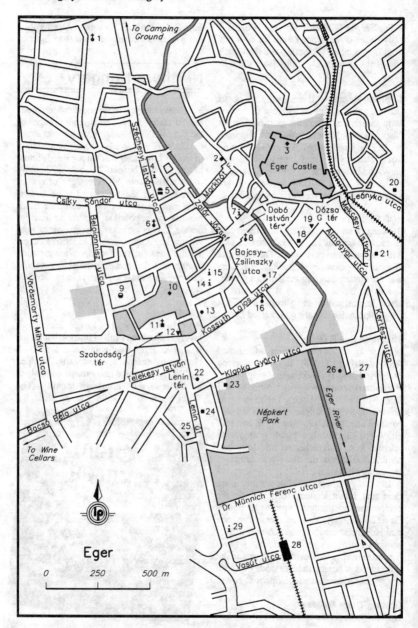

To Camping Ground

Széchenyi István utca

To Camping
Ground

1

2

Eger Castle

3

20

Leányka utca

Csíky Sándor utca

Markhot

Zalár József

Belojannisz utca

4

5

6

7

Dobó
István
tér

Dózsa
G tér

19

18

Mekcsey István

8

Bajcsy-
Zsilinszky
utca

21

15

17

9

10

14

Almagyar utca

13

16

Kossuth Lajos utca

11

12

Szabadság
tér

Telekesy István

Lenin
tér

22

Klapka György utca

26

27

Vörösmarty Mihály utca

23

24

Népkert
Park

Eger River

Kertész utca

Bacsó Béla utca

25

To Wine
Cellars

Dr Münnich Ferenc utca

29

28

Vasút utca

**Eger**

0      250      500 m

1 Serbian Church
2 Turkish Minaret
3 Eger Castle & Dobó István Museum
4 Express Travel Agency
5 Post Office
6 Former Jesuit Church
7 Cooptourist
8 Minorite Church
9 Bus Station
10 Archbishop's Palace
11 Cathedral
12 Kazamata Borozó Étterem
13 College
14 Eger Tourist
15 Ibusz
16 Franciscan Church
17 County Hall
18 Hotel Unicornis
19 Talizmán Vendéglő
20 'Ho Shi Minh' Student Residence
21 Tourist Motel
22 Gárdonyi Theatre
23 Park Hotel
24 Mini Motel
25 Három Farkas Restaurant
26 Thermal Pool & Turkish Baths
27 Hotel Flora
28 Railway Station
29 Villa Tours

castle but were themselves thrown out by the Austrians in 1687. Later Eger was a centre for Ferenc Rákóczi's unsuccessful 1703-11 War of Independence against the Habsburgs.

It was the bishops and later the archbishops of Eger who built the town you see today. The many handsome 18th century palaces and churches along Kossuth Lajos and Széchenyi streets deserve special attention. Eger possesses some of Hungary's finest examples of Zopf architecture, a late Baroque-Rococo style found only in Central Europe. Nineteenth-century railway builders left Eger to one side, so it retained its historic form and character.

Today Eger is more famous for its potent Egri Bikavér (Bull's Blood) red wine. Literally hundreds of wine cellars are to be seen in Szépasszonyvölgy (the Valley of Beautiful Women), just a 20-minute walk west of the cathedral.

## Information
Eger Tourist is at Bajcsy-Zsilinszky utca 9.

## Things to See
The first thing you see as you come into Eger from the bus or railway station is the huge neoclassical **cathedral** (1836) on Szabadság tér. Opposite this is the Rococo **college** (1785). Buy a ticket just inside the college door to see the frescoed library in room No 48 on the 1st floor and the **Museum of Astronomy** (open Tuesday to Sunday from 9.30 am to 12.30 pm) on the 6th floor of the tower at the back of the building. On the 9th floor of the tower is the periscope (use the same ticket for this), a unique apparatus which allows you to spy on all of Eger unobserved. Along Kossuth Lajos utca is the Baroque **county hall** at No 9, which has elegant wrought-iron gates and an old prison in the courtyard.

At the eastern end of Kossuth Lajos utca, across Dózsa György tér, is **Eger Castle**, erected after the Tatar invasion of 1242. Inside this great fortress are the foundations of St John's Cathedral, which was destroyed by the Turks. Models and drawings in the castle's **Dobó István Museum** (open daily in summer) give a clear idea of how the cathedral once looked. This museum, housed in the Gothic bishop's palace (1470), is named after the Hungarian national hero who led the resistance to the Turks in 1552. Below the castle are underground chambers *(kazamata)* hewn from solid rock, which you may tour with a guide. As soon as you arrive at the castle, ask the person at the ticket window when the next tour (in Hungarian) of the casemates will begin. The tour is included in the price of the ticket. A special tour in another language will cost US$4.

The Baroque **Minorite Church** (1771) on Dobó István tér was designed by the famous Prague architect Dientzenhofer. In front of the church is a statue of Dobó István and sculptures that depict a battle against the Turks. In the shadow of the castle in the old town is a climbable 35-metre **Turkish minaret** – the northernmost Turkish monument in Europe.

After so much history, you may like to clear your head in **Népkert Park**, once the private reserve of bishops. The 17th century **Turkish baths** (*török fürdö*) beside the park are open from noon to 6 pm. They are open to men on Tuesday, Thursday and Saturday, and to women on Monday, Wednesday and Friday. There are also open-air thermal baths here – enjoy them!

**Near Eger** Just to the north of Eger are the Bükk Mountains, much of which fall within the 388-sq-km **Bükk National Park**Bükk National Park. A good place to begin a visit to the forests of Bükk is the village of Szilvásvárad, which is connected to Eger by trains or, more frequently, by buses. Horse shows are put on here. Eger Tourist runs a camping ground (open from May to September) with bungalows one km from Szilvásvárad-Szalajkavolgy vm Railway Station. From here a road runs up the Szalajka Valley to hiking trails into the hills. Istállós-kö (958 metres), the highest peak in the Bükk Mountains, and the Istállóskoi Cave are up that way. Eger Tourist in Eger sells a detailed map of this area.

## Places to Stay

On summer weekends, accommodation is tight, so arrive early. For private rooms visit Eger Tourist, Bajcsy-Zsilinszky utca 9 in the centre of town (closed Sunday). Ibusz, in the alley behind Eger Tourist, and Cooptourist, Dobó István tér 3, also have private rooms.

Villa Tours, Lenin út 55, a four-minute walk from the railway station, is a private travel agency that arranges private rooms. It's open daily in summer from 9.30 am to 9 pm – convenient hours!

Express, Széchenyi István utca 28 (open weekdays from 8 am to 5 pm and Saturday from 7 am to 1 pm), may have information about summer youth hostels.

The centrally located *Mini Motel*, Lenin út 11, costs US$10 double. The modern *Hotel Unicornis* on Kossuth Lajos utca is US$21 double (no singles). And finally, the *Tourist Motel*, Mekcsey István utca 2, is US$11 double (no singles). All of these may be full.

If atmosphere is more important to you than the price, you will like the fine old *Park Hotel*, Klapka utca 8, where singles/doubles with private facilities are US$53/60. The modern *Eger Hotel* next door charges about the same.

The *camping ground* is at Rákóczi utca 79, four km north of Eger (take bus No 10, 11, 12 or 13 from the train station). From May to September, there are bungalows (US$6 double), a restaurant and tennis courts.

## Places to Eat

A good place to eat is the *Kazamata Borozó Étterem* on Szabadság tér, below the cathedral steps. Beer and wine restaurants are found in this attractive complex which features Gypsy music in the evening. You can get a cheap stand-up lunch at *Kondi Saláta Bár*, Széchenyi utca 2.

The *Talizman Vendéglő*, Kossuth Lajos utca 19, is a good wine cellar that's always packed with European tourists. The menu is in German (closed Monday).

Less touristy is the *Három Farkas Restaurant*, Lenin út 18, an unpretentious modern establishment that offers good, no-frills meals.

Eger's finest restaurant is the *Fehérszarvas Vadásztanya*, Klapka utca 8, below the Park Hotel. Here you can dine on game dishes by candlelight. It is open for dinner only and is closed on Monday; the menu is in German.

Many wine restaurants haunt the cellars of Szépasszony-völgy utca. The most famous is the *Ködmön Csárda*, where live Hungarian folk music accompanies dinner. The menu is in Hungarian, but ask to see it anyway to get an idea of the prices. There are many other similar places, such as the one at No 38. To get there, locate the Gárdonyi Theatre on Lenin tér, near the cathedral, then walk west on Telekesy István and Bacsó Béla streets. When you come to a fork in the road, go left down the incline and straight ahead.

## Getting There & Away

Eger is connected to Budapest's Keleti pu Railway Station by express train. It's sometimes quicker to take a local train to Füze-sabony, where you can catch a connecting express train to Budapest or a local train to Debrecen. There are also buses to Budapest from Eger's bus station (128 km).

## AGGTELEK

Hungary's largest and most famous scenic caves are the **Baradla Caves** in Aggtelek National Park on the Czech border, north of Eger and Miskolc. The caves stretch 22 km underground, 18 km of which is in Hungary and seven km in Czechoslovakia. The easiest way to get there is to take the morning Volán bus from Eger to Aggtelek (three hours). The same bus returns to Eger in the afternoon, allowing you plenty of time to see the Aggtelek caves. It doesn't, however, give you time to see the Jósvafö Caves. Alternatively, spend the night at Aggtelek and visit several different sections of the caves.

### Things to See & Do

The short tour at **Aggtelek** (one hour, US$1) includes recorded music in the 'concert hall'. Boat trips are offered on the underground lake when the water is high enough. There you will see beautiful karst formations. There's another entrance to the Baradla Caves near **Jósvafö**, six km east of Agg-telek, where you can go on different short tours. Two-hour trips (US$1.50) begin at **Vöröstó** between Aggtelek and Jósvafö, and in summer there's even an epic six-hour cave tour (US$5) during which visitors must carry lamps. All tours are led by guides who only set out when five tickets have been sold, so you may have to buy the extra tickets when things are slow.

Next to the Aggtelek entrance to the Baradla Caves is a small **museum** on the flora and fauna of the area, featuring the skeleton of a prehistoric bear that was found in the cave. **Hiking trails** begin behind this museum and even on a brief visit it's well worth climbing the hill for a view of the countryside. A trail marked with a green pine tree on a white base leads from here to the Jósvafö entrance (7½ km).

### Places to Stay & Eat

The bus from Eger stops in front of the modern *Cseppkö Hotel* at Aggtelek, where double rooms cost US$27 (no singles), including breakfast. The hotel has a restaurant which offers a good set 'menu' at lunchtime.

Also at the Aggtelek entrance is a very clean, pleasant *camping ground* (open from mid-April to September) with 3rd-class bungalows at US$9 (two beds). Camping for two people is US$5, including a tent. The camping ground reception also controls the *tourist hostel* above the natural history museum at the entrance to the caves. It has beds in eight-bed dorms at US$3; no discounts are offered to YHA members. The check-out time at the hostel is 10 am.

The *Tengerszem Szálló* is a rustic 22-room lodge at the Jósvafö Caves, a km or so west of Jósvafö village. All the buses stop here.

### Getting There & Away

Only one bus a day travels between Budapest, Eger and Aggtelek, leaving Budapest or Eger in the morning and Aggtelek in the afternoon. Buses travel from Aggtelek to Jósvafö every couple of hours and a morning bus goes from Miskolc to Aggtelek, returning to Miskolc in the afternoon.

You can also come by train from Miskolc to Jósvafö-Aggtelek Railway Station where a bus is usually waiting to carry you the 22 km on to the caves at Aggtelek. At Miskolc look for one of the seven daily trains bearing the sign 'Tornanádaska'.

Though the caves in Aggtelek are only a five-minute walk from the Slovak border, only Hungarians and Czechoslovaks may cross here. There's a morning bus from Aggtelek to Rožňava in Czechoslovakia, but Westerners are not allowed to take it.

## TOKAJ

Tokaj, at the junction of the Bodrog and Tisza rivers, sits below Tokaji-hegy, a rounded 515-metre extension of the Carpathian Mountains which is mostly covered by vineyards. The volcanic soils, protective mountains, sunny climate and long, dry autumns are ideal for wine-making and the vineyards here date back to Celtic times. Since the Middle Ages, large quantities of Tokaj wines have been exported to Poland. In the 17th century they attracted international attention when Ferenc Rákóczi II, lord of the region, introduced them to King Louis XIV of France. Since then the Empress Maria Theresa, Frederick the Great, Voltaire, Goethe, Anatole France and many others have sung its praises. Connoisseurs of fine wines will certainly want to visit Tokaj in summer, especially during the harvest, which begins in October.

### Orientation

There's a left-luggage office in the railway station and a large map of Tokaj by the road on the way into town. On leaving the station, turn left and follow the tracks north, down towards the river. Turn left on Ady Endre utca, go under the tracks and straight ahead and in 10 minutes you'll be in town.

### Things to See & Do

The **Tokaj Museum** (closed Monday), at Bethlen Gábor utca 7, is near the two large churches in the middle of the village. Another small museum is at Bethlen Gábor utca 18; the church across the street from it has been made into an art gallery. The former synagogue is on the next street behind the art gallery.

### Places to Stay & Eat

Many *privat zimmer* (private room) signs are seen around town. The *Tokaj Hotel*, a modern building near the river, costs US$17 double with shower (no singles).

*Tisza Camping* is right beside the river just across the bridge from town, a 15-minute walk from the railway station. Two-person bungalows cost US$8 and four-person units cost US$13. There's always lots of camping space but the bungalows fill up. It's very nice with plenty of shade (open from mid-April to September).

You can taste glasses of the local wines to your heart's content in the *Borkos Tolo*, Kossuth tér 15, next to the large church.

Tokaji Aszú, a sweet dessert wine, is a favourite and there's also a local cognac. You can purchase bottles of the different varieties of Tokaj wine here.

### Getting There & Away

Tokaj is on the railway line from Miskolc to Nyíregyháza. To go to Sárospatak, change at Mezözombor. To go to Debrecen change at Nyíregyháza.

## SÁROSPATAK

Sárospatak is on the Bodrog River, near the Slovak border, in upper northern Hungary. The Calvinist College established here in 1531 counted the great Moravian educational reformer Jan Amos Comenius (Jan Amos Komensky) among its teachers for five years from 1650. The present neoclassical college building was built in 1806 and its notable library was built in 1834. The names of many 19th century Sárospatak students will be familiar to anyone who has delved into modern Hungarian history or literature. However, Sárospatak is best remembered as the seat of the illustrious Rákóczi family. It's an attractive little town that is well worth spending a night in and is also a potential gateway to/from Czechoslovakia.

### Orientation

The adjacent train and bus stations are just north-west of the centre. Walk straight ahead through the park to Rákóczi út where you'll find Ibusz. If you go south on Rákóczi to the post office, then left on Szabadság tér for a block, you will reach Borsod Tourist and the back side of the Castle Church.

### Information

Borsod Tourist is at Kossuth Lajos út 50.

### Things to See

The 15th century **Castle Church** on Szent Erzsébet tér was transferred back and forth between Catholics and Protestants several times during Sárospatak's stormy history. Alongside the church are the foundations of an 11th century rotunda that was erected by King Andrew I. Next to this is a statue of St

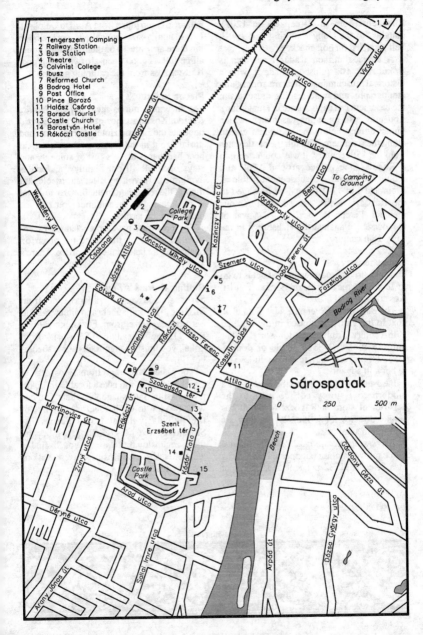

1 Tengerszem Camping
2 Railway Station
3 Bus Station
4 Theatre
5 Calvinist College
6 Ibusz
7 Reformed Church
8 Bodrog Hotel
9 Post Office
10 Pince Borozó
11 Halász Csárda
12 Borsod Tourist
13 Castle Church
14 Borostyán Hotel
15 Rákóczi Castle

Sárospatak

0          250          500 m

Elizabeth (born in Sárospatak in 1207), daughter of the Hungarian king Andrew II, being carried on horseback.

A block south on Kádár Kata utca is **Rákóczi Castle** (closed Monday), with a historical museum in the upstairs rooms, and ethnography and wine-making museums in the basement (all captions are in Hungarian). You may also enter the casemates, which tunnel around below the walls that extend along the river here. Though the castle dates from the 15th century, it was converted into a Renaissance palace around 1540 and rebuilt and extended in subsequent centuries. From 1616 to 1711 the palace belonged to the Rákóczi family, whose most famous member, Ferenc Rákóczi II, led a war of independence against the Habsburgs in the early 18th century.

### Places to Stay

To find a private room, your best bet is to go to Ibusz, Rákóczi út 3, or Borsod Tourist, Kossuth Lajos ut 50.

The *Borostyán Hotel* on Kádár Kata utca, next to the castle, is housed in the restored 17th century Trinitarian Monastery. It has only 13 rooms (US$16 single or double, US$22 triple) and they're usually full, so try to book in advance.

Sárospatak's other hotel, the *Bodrog*, is a modern four-storey edifice next to the department store at Rákóczi út 58. It has singles/doubles for US$22/29 but they are also full in summer.

*Tengerszem Camping*, 2½ km north-east of the railway station (signposted) at Herceg utca 2, costs US$2 per tent and US$1 per person to camp (open from April to October). Large family-size bungalows cost US$16 but there are only 10 of them and they could all be full. A good open-air swimming pool is just across from the camping ground.

### Places to Eat

For an unpretentious meal, try the *Halász Csárda*, Kossuth Lajos ut 57. *Pince Borozó* opposite the Bodrog Hotel has only fast food upstairs, but in the basement there's a great beer bar that is always full of students and stays open till 10 pm nightly (no food is available). If you're after more elegant dining, the restaurant in the *Borostyán Hotel* is recommended. In summer you can eat outside on the terrace.

For breakfast have some langos (deep-fried pastries) at the stand-up place on Szabadság tér behind the post office. There's always a line of savvy locals here.

### Getting There & Away

Sárospatak is on the railway line from Miskolc to Sátoraljaúhely and direct trains to Sárospatak arrive from Füzesabony (near Eger). If you're heading to Sárospatak from Tokaj, you must change trains at Mezözombor.

The easiest way to go from Sárospatak to Czechoslovakia is to take a local train 12 km north-east to Sátoraljaúhely, where you can walk two km to the border, or catch one of the two daily local trains across. At Slovenské Nové Mesto Station, just beyond the Czechoslovak customs, you'll find a local Slovak train to Košice. No reservations are required.

# Romania

Romania, a little known Balkan country straddling the Carpathian Mountains, offers surprising variety, ranging from alpine peaks and Black Sea beaches to the mighty Danube River. The towns of Transylvania are straight out of medieval Hungary or Germany, whereas the exotic Orthodox monasteries of Moldavia and Bukovina suggest Byzantium. Western Romania bears the imprint of the Austro-Hungarian empire whereas Constanţa is heavily Roman and Turkish, and Bucharest has a Franco-Romanian character all its own. Fine museums and churches are scattered throughout the country – few Eastern European countries feature such a kaleidoscope of cultures as Romania.

There is another side to Romania, however: one of economic hardship and political confusion. Here independent travellers share the everyday problems of the people as nowhere else. Tourist facilities exist everywhere, but they're geared to the big spender. For shoestring travellers, Romania can be the adventure of a lifetime, but only in summer, when it's possible to camp. Even the food is better then! In the cold, dark Romanian winter, which lasts from October to April, add about US$25 to your daily budget and shorten your stay.

If you come to Romania expecting fast efficiency and the conveniences of home, you will be disappointed. You'll often be thoroughly exasperated by the level of service you receive but you'll have experiences that would be inconceivable in the West. Romania chastises the unwary and rewards the intrepid. Because lots of things are unavailable, you're forced to be resourceful. By sharing some of the hardships, you stand a better chance of capturing part of the essence of this colourful, perplexing land.

Reader Andrew Warmington of Middlesex, England, sent us the following letter:

Any Hungarian or Bulgarian – and quite a lot of travellers – will tell you not to go, that it's dirty,

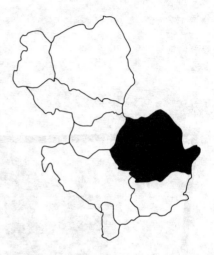

unsafe, hell on earth, etc, etc. Don't believe it. Easy it isn't and inexperienced travellers may find it too much (hope that doesn't sound snobbish!) but Romania is a real experience. More happened there in five days than during three times as long in twee little Hungary. Romania hides nothing from you and the people are mostly friendly and curious – remember it's not that long that they've been allowed to talk to foreigners, and many travellers find themselves given a bed and treated like kings.

# Facts about the Country

### HISTORY

Ancient Romania was inhabited by Thracian tribes. The Greeks called them the Getae, the Romans called them Dacians, but they were actually a single Geto-Dacian people. From the 7th century BC the Greeks established trading colonies along the Black Sea at Callatis (Mangalia), Tomis (Constanţa) and Histria. In the 1st century BC, a Dacian state was established to meet the Roman threat. The last king, Decebalus, consolidated this

The 16th century Bishop's Church in Curtea de Argeş

state but was unable to prevent the Roman conquest in 105-6 AD.

The Romans recorded their expansion north of the Danube on two famous monuments: Trajan's Column in Rome and the 'Tropaeum Trajani' on the site of their victory at Adamclisi in Dobruja. Most of present Romania, including the Transylvanian plateau, came under their rule. The slave-owning Romans brought with them a superior civilisation and mixed with the conquered tribes to form a Daco-Roman people speaking a Latin tongue. A noted visitor during the Roman period was the Latin poet Ovid, who was exiled to the Black Sea by the Emperor Augustus.

Faced with Goth attacks in 271, Emperor Aurelian decided to withdraw the Roman legions and administration south of the Danube, but the Romanised Vlach peasants remained in Dacia. Waves of migrating peoples, including the Goths, Huns, Avars, Slavs, Bulgars and Hungarians, swept across this territory from the 4th to 10th centuries. The Romanians survived in village communities and gradually assimilated the Slavs and other peoples who settled there. By the 10th century a fragmented feudal system ruled by a military class had appeared.

From the 10th century the Hungarians expanded into Transylvania, north and west of the Carpathian Mountains. By the 13th century all of Transylvania was an autonomous principality under the Hungarian crown, although Romanians remained a majority of the population. After devastating Tatar raids in 1241 and 1242, King Bela IV of Hungary invited Saxon Germans to settle in Transylvania as a buffer against further attacks.

When the Turks conquered Hungary in the 16th century, Transylvania became a vassal of the Ottoman Empire, retaining its autonomy by paying tribute to the sultan. This semi-independence meant that Catholicism was not reimposed as it was in the areas under Habsburg control and many of the Hungarians and Germans in Transylvania converted from Catholicism to Protestantism in the 16th century. The Austrian Habsburgs conquered Transylvania at the end of the 17th century and suppressed an independence struggle led by the Transylvanian prince Ferenc Rákóczi II from 1703-11.

The Romanian-speaking feudal principalities of Wallachia and Moldavia appeared south and east of the Carpathian Mountains in the 14th century. Throughout the 15th century they offered strong resistance to Turkish expansion north. Mircea the Old, Vlad Țepeș and Stefan the Great became legendary figures in this struggle. Vlad Țepeș 'the Impaler', ruling prince of Wallachia from 1456-62 and 1476-77, inspired the tale of Count Dracula by his habit of impaling his enemies on stakes. (The vampires originated in the imagination of 19th century Irish novelist Bram Stoker.)

After the Hungarian defeat, Wallachia and Moldavia also paid tribute to the Turks but maintained their autonomy. This indirect control explains why no Turkish buildings are seen in Romania today, except in Dobruja, the area between the Danube and the Black Sea. In 1600 the three Romanian states were briefly united under Michael the Brave (Mihai Viteazul) at Alba Iulia. There were major peasant uprisings in 1437, 1514 and 1784. In 1812 Russia took Bessarabia, the eastern half of Moldavia, from the Turks.

Turkish suzerainty persisted in Wallachia and the rest of Moldavia well into the 19th century despite unsuccessful revolutions in 1821 and 1848. After the Russian defeat in the Crimean War (1853-56), Romanian nationalism grew, and in 1859, with French support, Alexandru Ioan Cuza was elected to the thrones of Moldavia and Wallachia, creating a national state which took the name Romania in 1862. The reform-minded Cuza was forced to abdicate in 1866 and his place was taken by the Prussian Prince Carol I. With Russian assistance, Romania declared independence from the Ottoman Empire in 1877. After the 1877-78 War of Independence, Dobruja became part of Romania.

In 1916 Romania entered WW I on the side of the Triple Entente (Britain, France and Russia). The objective was to take Transylvania, where two-thirds of the population

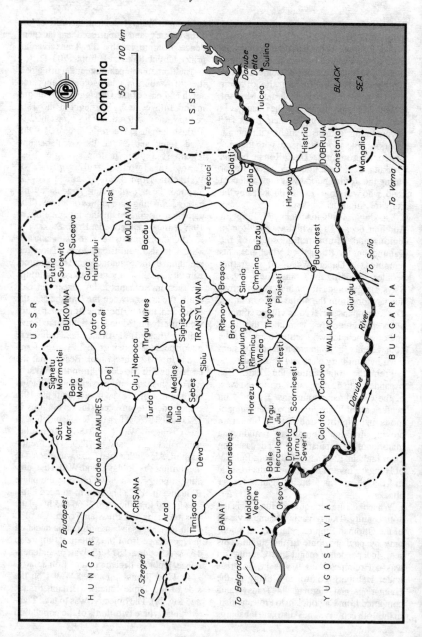

was Romanian, from Austria-Hungary. During the fighting, the Central Powers occupied Wallachia but Moldavia was staunchly defended by Romanian and Russian troops. With the defeat of Austria-Hungary in 1918, the unification of Banat, Transylvania and Bukovina with Romania was finally achieved.

In the years leading up to WW II, Romania, under the able guidance of foreign minister Nicolae Titulescu, sought security in an alliance with France, Britain and the Little Entente (Romania, Yugoslavia and Czechoslovakia). It signed a Balkan Pact with Yugoslavia, Turkey and Greece, and established diplomatic relations with the USSR. These efforts were weakened by the Western powers' appeasement of Hitler and by King Carol II, who declared a personal dictatorship in February 1938. After the fall of France in May 1940, Romania was isolated. In June 1940 the USSR occupied Bessarabia, which had been taken from Russia after WW I. Then, on 30 August 1940, Romania was forced to cede northern Transylvania, which covers 43,500 sq km, and 2,600,000 inhabitants to Hungary by order of Nazi Germany and Fascist Italy. In September 1940 southern Dobruja was given to Bulgaria.

These setbacks sparked widespread popular demonstrations. To defend the interests of the ruling classes, General Ion Antonescu forced Carol II to abdicate in favour of his son Michael and imposed a fascist dictatorship with himself as *conducǎtór*. German troops were allowed to enter Romania in October 1940. In June 1941 Antonescu joined Hitler's anti-Soviet war.

Deep-seated anti-Nazi resentment smouldered among the Romanian soldiers and people. As the war went badly and the Soviet army approached Romania's borders, a rare national consensus was achieved. On 23 August 1944 Romania suddenly changed sides, captured 53,159 German soldiers who were in Romania at the time, and declared war on Nazi Germany. By this dramatic act, Romania salvaged its independence and shortened the war. By 25 October the Romanian and Soviet armies had driven the Hungarian and German forces from Transylvania. The Romanian army went on to fight in Hungary and Czechoslovakia. Appalling losses were sustained: half a million Romanian soldiers died while their country was on the Axis side (Nazi Germany, Fascist Italy and Japan) and another 170,000 died after it joined the Allies.

## Post World War II

After national liberation, the government of Dr Petru Groza launched Romania's social liberation. Parliamentary elections held in November 1946 were won by the progressive parties. A year later the monarchy was abolished and a Romanian People's Republic proclaimed. The Communist and Social Democratic parties united as the Romanian Workers' Party in 1948, the name being changed back to Romanian Communist Party in 1965. In June 1948 the means of production (the raw materials and tools or machines used in the production process) were nationalised and a planned economy was instituted. Emphasis was placed on industrialisation, the formation of agricultural cooperatives, education and culture.

Throughout the Communist period, Romania was unique in Eastern Europe for its independent foreign policy which was based on disarmament, détente and peaceful coexistence with all countries. At the basis of this was a belief in equality and respect for national sovereignty, mutual advantage and noninterference. While a member of the Warsaw Pact, Romania did not participate in the Warsaw Pact's military manoeuvres, and the last Soviet troops were withdrawn in 1958. Although Romania never broke with the Soviet Union, as did Tito's Yugoslavia and Mao's China, it refused to assist in the intervention in Czechoslovakia in 1968 and President Ceaușescu publicly condemned the invasion. It's said that after the 1984 Los Angeles Olympic Games, in which Romania participated despite a Soviet bloc boycott, Romania received a telegram from the USSR reading, 'Congratulations for the following:

gold – stop, silver – stop, bronze – stop, oil – stop, coal – stop, gas – stop, etc.'

In contrast to its skilful foreign policy. Romania suffered from increasingly inept government at home during the 25-year reign of Nicolae Ceauşescu (1965-89). In 1974 the post of president was created for Ceauşescu, who placed members of his immediate family in high office during the 1980s. Thus his wife, Elena, became first deputy prime minister, his son, Nicu, became head of the Communist youth organisation and later political boss of Transylvania, and three brothers were assigned to key posts in Bucharest.

Ceauşescu's megalomania is illustrated by the various grandiose projects that he initiated: the functionless Danube Canal opened in 1984; the Transfăgărăşan Highway; the disruptive redevelopment of south Bucharest into a new political centre (1983-89); the building of the Bucharest Metro (opened in 1985); the destruction of the Danube Delta through agricultural development; and the unrealised plans to 'systematise' Romanian agriculture by transferring the inhabitants of 7000 of the country's 13,000 villages into thin, hastily constructed concrete apartment blocks, despite the cultural and social upheaval this would have caused. In March 1989 Ceauşescu arranged lavish public celebrations to mark the paying off of Romania's US$10 billion foreign debt. His greatest blunder, however, was the decision to export Romania's food to help pay the debt, as this created food shortages within Romania.

By the late 1980s, with the Soviet bloc quickly disintegrating, the USA no longer required an independent Romania and withdrew the 'most favoured nation' trading status that it had previously granted the country. Ethnic tensions continued to simmer and the population continued to suffer from prolonged scarcities of almost everything. In November 1987, 10,000 workers rioted in Braşov in support of better conditions. In late 1989 as the world watched one Communist regime after another tumble, it seemed only a matter of time before Romania's turn would come. However, on 20 November 1989, during a six-hour address to the 14th Congress of the Romanian Communist Party, Ceauşescu denounced the political changes in the other Eastern European countries and vowed to resist them. His speech was interrupted by 60 standing ovations and the congress re-elected him as general secretary.

**Revolution** The spark that ignited Romania came on 15 December 1989 when Father László Tökés spoke out publicly against the dictator from his small Hungarian church in Timişoara. The following evening people gathered outside Father Tökés' home to protest the decision of the Reformed Church of Romania to remove him from his post. By 9 pm this had turned into a noisy demonstration, and when the police began making arrests, the unrest spread to other parts of the city and armoured cars began patrolling the streets.

At noon on 17 December a huge crowd on Timişoara's Bulevardul 30 decembrie, between the Opera House and the Orthodox Cathedral, was confronted by Securitate (secret police) units and regular army troops. When demonstrators broke into the Communist Party's district headquarters and threw portraits of Ceauşescu out of the windows, the army used tanks and armoured cars to clear the vast square. Despite this, further clashes, took place in nearby Piaţa Libertăţii.

Back in Bucharest later that afternoon, the Executive Political Committee condemned the 'mild' action taken by the army and ordered that real bullets be used – the start of civilian casualties. The Securitate continued mopping-up operations all night and the dead were collected and buried in mass graves or sent to Bucharest to be cremated. The resistance continued, however, and on 19 December the army in Timişoara went over to the side of the demonstrators.

On 20 December negotiators from Bucharest arrived in Timişoara to buy time until fresh troops could be sent to the city, and newly arrived Securitate units began firing on the demonstrators once again. At 6 pm

Ceauşescu arrived back in Romania from a state visit to Iran and proclaimed martial law in Timiş County. Trainloads of elite troops were dispatched to the city with orders to crush the rebellion.

On 21 December a remarkable thing happened. Ceauşescu decided that he would address a mass rally in front of the Central Committee building in Bucharest to show the world that the workers of Romania supported him and approved his action against the 'hooligan' demonstrators in Timişoara. What went on behind the scenes may never be known but it's possible that Ceauşescu was set up by conspirators within the Communist Party who wanted to engineer his downfall. Factories around Bucharest dutifully sent their most trusted cadres to applaud Ceauşescu as they had done so many times before, but upon their arrival early in the morning at Piaţa Gheorge Gheorgiu-Dej, they were told that Ceauşescu had changed his mind about the speech and that they could go home. A few hours later the word went out again that the speech would in fact be held at noon and that the workers should reassemble. However, the reliable Party supporters had already left and the factory bosses were forced to be less selective as they scrambled to send the required number of people to the square.

At 12.30 pm as Ceauşescu began to speak to the assembly from the balcony of the Central Committee building, youths who were being held back by three cordons of police a block away started booing. Tension mounted in the silent crowd and suddenly there was a strange crack of sound and Ceauşescu was cut off in mid-sentence by shouts of disapproval. For a second the dictator faltered, amazement written across his face as recorded on live TV. Pandemonium broke loose as the youths attempted to break through the police lines and the assembled workers tried to escape. Urged on by his wife, Ceauşescu attempted to continue his speech even as police cleared the square, finally ending as the tape with prerecorded applause and cheers was switched off.

Meanwhile, the anti-Ceauşescu demonstrators retreated to the wide boulevard between Piaţa Universtăţii and Piaţa Romană. At about 2.30 pm reinforcements of special riot police with clubs and shields arrived down Calea Victoriei and plain-clothes police began making arrests. As more police and armoured cars arrived, the growing number of demonstrators became concentrated in the two piaţas (squares) just mentioned. Around 5 pm, when the crowds still refused to disperse, the police at Piaţa Romană first fired warning shots and then used gunfire and armoured cars to brutally crush the demonstration.

In front of the Inter-Continental Hotel on Piaţa Universităţii armoured cars also drove into the crowd. Drenched by ice-cold water from fire hoses, the demonstrators there refused to submit and began erecting barricades under the eyes of Western journalists in the adjacent hotel. At 11 pm the police began their assault on Piaţa Universităţii, using a tank to smash the barricades. By dawn the square had been cleared and the bodies of those killed removed.

At 7 am on 22 December, demonstrators began assembling in Piaţa Romană and Piaţa Universităţii once more. By 11 am huge crowds faced the phalanx of army troops in their tanks with Securitate behind them blocking the way to the Central Committee building where Ceauşescu was still believed to be. Rumours then began circulating about General Milea, the then minister of defence, who allegedly had been forced to commit suicide by Ceauşescu because he had refused to order his troops to fire on the people. Gradually the crowd began to chant 'The army is with us!' and to mix with the troops arrayed against them, offering the soldiers flowers and cigarettes.

As the demonstrators swarmed up onto the unresisting tanks and fraternised with the crews, the Securitate forces withdrew towards the site of the previous day's speech. At 11.30 am Bucharest Radio announced the 'suicide' of the 'traitor' Milea and the proclamation of a state of emergency. As thousands of people moved towards the Central Committee building, the Securitate continued to draw back. Around noon Ceauşescu again appeared on the same balcony and attempted to speak, but people began booing and throwing objects at him, forcing him to duck back quickly inside the building. At this point the crowd surged in through the main doors past unresisting police, but, with the crowd just a few dozen metres away, Ceauşescu, his wife and several others managed to escape by helicopter from the roof. Soon after, the radio and TV stations were taken by the rebels, who did not meet any resistance.

The helicopter took the Ceauşescus to their villa at Snagov, just north of Bucharest. The plan was that they would proceed to an air base near Piteşti, where a waiting jet would take them into exile outside Romania. Halfway to Piteşti, however, the helicopter pilot feigned engine trouble and set the chopper down beside a highway where the two Securitate officers present commandeered a passing private car. The party then drove on to Tîrgovişte, where the Ceauşescus were arrested and taken to a military base.

On 23 December Nicolae and Elena Ceauşescu were tried together by an anonymous court, condemned and summarily executed by a firing squad. The next day their bodies were exhibited on TV, allegedly to stifle resistance by die-hard Securitate units attempting to rescue them. News reports at the time told of fierce resistance by the Securitate, but anyone who visited Bucharest during the months immediately following the revolution would have seen that virtually all the buildings pockmarked with bullet holes were Securitate strongholds around the Central Committee building and TV station. This indicates that they were mostly on the receiving end of fire from young army conscripts who opened up at the slightest provocation. (This damage has now been repaired.) With their modern weapons, the Securitate officers could have caused tens of thousands of casualties had they so desired.

It is now believed that the Ceauşescus' speedy trial had much more to do with braking the revolution and saving former Party members than in stopping the Securitate. Clearly, Nicolae and Elena knew too much and many people still in high office today might have been dragged down with them had they been given an open trial. Among the charges brought against the Ceauşescus by the kangaroo court was that they had deposited US$470 million in Swiss banks, yet none of this mysterious treasure has ever been located.

Evidently, reformers in the Communist Party had been preparing a coup d'état against Ceauşescu and his family for at least six months, when the December 1989 demonstrations forced them to move their schedule forward. When Ceauşescu fell, therefore, the National Salvation Front was ready to take over. Most of its leaders, including President Ion Iliescu and Prime Minister Petre Roman, were former Party members.

Reports of casualties in the revolution were wildly exaggerated. At the Ceauşescus' trial it was claimed that 64,000 people died in the revolution; a few days later it was changed to 64,000 deaths in the entire 25-year Ceauşescu epoch. After a week the number of victims had been reduced to 7000 and the final count was around 750. In Timişoara 115 people died, not the 4000 reported.

**The Sequel** When the National Salvation Front (FSN) took over, it claimed to be only a caretaker government until elections could be held and that it would not field candidates. However, on 25 January 1990, the FSN announced that it would in fact run. This prompted mass demonstrations both for and against the Front amid accusations of neo-Communism.

The 20 May 1990 elections were contested by 88 political parties. In the presidential race Ion Iliescu of the FSN won 85% of the vote, Radu Câmpeanu of the National Liberal Party won 10.6% and Ion Ratiu of the National Peasant Party won 4.3%. The FSN also won control of the national assembly and senate. The next elections will take place in 1992 under a new constitution.

In the meantime, students had occupied Piaţa Universităţii to protest the FSN's ex-Communist leadership. On 13 June 1990, after police cleared demonstrators from the square, extremist youths burned police headquarters and attacked the Ministry of the Interior in what the government called a 'fascist coup attempt'. This prompted coal miners from Jiu River near Tîrgu Jiu to travel to Bucharest for a counter-riot in which many student and opposition heads were broken.

The present government has won the support of the miners by giving them more food, higher wages, longer holidays, and so on. There is strong opposition to the FSN among students and intellectuals, whereas many peasants, workers and elderly people seem satisfied with the present government. In 1984 the Communist Party had 3,400,000 members – obviously these people are still around.

**Romania Today** Since the revolution, Romanians have been allowed to have more contact with foreigners, to accommodate them in their homes, to hold foreign currency and to speak fairly freely. For travellers, the general atmosphere of increased personal freedom certainly makes travel much more pleasant, though as yet there has been no improvement in the austerity of local restaurants, and train tickets have become even more difficult to obtain than before as Romanians stream abroad.

The black market is much larger now but less oriented towards obtaining dollars from tourists for use in hard-currency shops; instead, Romanian marketeers now buy low-priced local goods in local stores, sell them abroad for hard currency while on 'tourist' trips, and then bring back scarce items for sale inside Romania itself. Previously, there were only government stores with empty shelves, but now flourishing street markets have sprung up where small farmers sell their produce and Gypsies (and others) peddle contraband. Travellers now have far less to

fear from the police when changing money on the street, but are at an even higher risk of being cheated by the moneychangers.

On the negative side, there has been a general relaxing of discipline, and scenes of public drunkenness, unthinkable under Ceauşescu, are now commonplace. The drunks are usually no problem for foreigners, however, and there's no antiforeign sentiment in Romania. On the contrary, many individual Romanians and occasionally even the bureaucracy (!) will treat you like someone special.

## GEOGRAPHY
Covering 237,500 sq km, oval-shaped Romania is larger than Hungary and Bulgaria combined (it is about half the size of France). The Danube River drains the whole of Romania except the Black Sea coast and completes its 2850-km course through eight countries here in Romania's Danube Delta. South of the delta is the Black Sea coast and west of it, along the Bulgarian border, stretch the Danube lowlands.

Most of central and northern Romania is taken up by the U-shaped Carpathian Mountains. The highest point in the Romanian Carpathians is Mt Moldoveanu at 2544 metres in the Făgăraş Mountains south-east of Sibiu. The Transylvanian plateau occupies the centre of the U, and the Moldavian plateau lies to the east. Earthquakes are common in the south and south-west.

The Carpathian Mountains account for about a third of the country's area with alpine pastures above and thick forests below. Another third of Romania is covered by hills and tablelands full of orchards and vineyards. The final third is a fertile plain where cereals, vegetables, herbs and other crops are grown. Forty-three per cent of the land is arable, 28% is forest and woodland, 19% meadows and pastures, 3% permanent crops and 7% is devoted to other uses. Eleven per cent of the land is irrigated.

## ECONOMY
Under the Communists the economy was

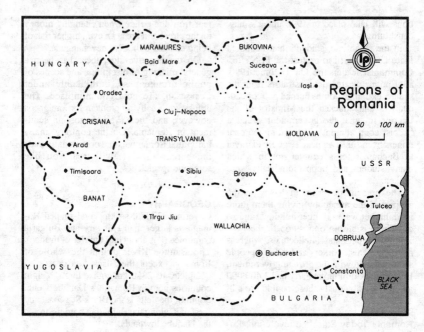

Regions of Romania

HUNGARY

MARAMUREŞ
Baia Mare

BUKOVINA
Suceava

Iaşi

Oradea

Cluj-Napoca

CRIŞANA

TRANSYLVANIA

MOLDAVIA

Arad

Timişoara

Sibiu

Braşov

BANAT

USSR

Tîrgu Jiu

WALLACHIA

Tulcea

DOBRUJA

Bucharest

YUGOSLAVIA

Constanţa

BLACK SEA

BULGARIA

0    50    100 km

centrally planned, so the change to a market economy has been slow in coming. Agriculture accounts for 31% of the gross national product, industry for 55% and services for 14%. Of the labour force of 10,600,000, about 34% is employed in industry and 28% in agriculture. Romania exports minerals, chemicals, machinery and manufactured goods to Germany, the USSR and Italy. Under Ceauşescu, self-sufficiency became a major goal, and beginning in 1980 every effort was made to eliminate Romania's foreign debt of US$10 billion. This was partly done by exporting food at the expense of domestic consumption, creating hunger in what had once been the granary of Europe. Although this policy has now ceased, Romania still suffers the lowest living standards in Europe.

The Communists promoted heavy industry and infrastructure projects, such as the Danube Canal, which runs from Agigea to Cernavodă, and the Bucharest Metro. The huge Iron Gate Hydropower Project at Drobeta-Turnu Severin on the Danube River which was opened in 1972 is one of the largest in Europe. The Ploieşti oilfields north of Bucharest have been pumping oil for over a century, but the giant iron and steel works at Galaţi has only been established since WW II. Other energy resources include natural gas from Transylvania, lignite coal from Tîrgu Jiu and the nuclear power station at Cernavodă, at the mouth of the Danube Canal. Three-quarters of Romania's electricity comes from thermal power stations, over half of which are powered by natural gas.

Romania is still a developing country. The emphasis on heavy industry was in line with Romania's long-range goal of self-reliance but it led to shortages of food and consumer goods. Queues are still long at shops and petrol stations. Only two types of cars are manufactured in Romania. The popular Oltcit is a homegrown Citroën put together at Craiova, and the more upmarket Dacia is in fact a Renault 12 built at Piteşti.

## POPULATION & PEOPLE

Romania has a population of 23,000,000, 43% of whom live in towns and cities. Bucharest (2,298,000) is by far the largest city, followed by Braşov, Constanţa, Iaşi, Timişoara, Cluj-Napoca, Galaţi and Craiova, in that order. The main educational centres are in Bucharest, Iaşi, Cluj-Napoca and Timişoara.

Romania is the only country with a Romance language that does not have a Roman Catholic background. Seventy per cent of the population is Romanian Orthodox, 10% is Greek Orthodox and 6% is Catholic. Baptists, Calvinists, Jews and Lutherans are also present.

The country's largest ethnic minorities are Hungarians (7.8%) and Germans (1.5%). The presence of the 1.7 million Hungarians in Romania continues to sour relations with neighbouring Hungary. Under Ceauşescu, all Hungarian-language newspapers and magazines in Romania were closed down, and official plans to relocate 7000 Romanian villages, many of them in Transylvania, threatened Romania's Hungarians with cultural assimilation. Most accounts of this problem published in the West show quite justified concern for the Hungarian minority, yet tend to forget that the Romanian majority in Transylvania was subjected to forced 'Magyarisation' under Hungarian rule prior to WW I. Romanians generally regard Hungary as an aggressive nation, and much anti-Gypsy sentiment also exists as these people offer a convenient scapegoat for Romania's economic problems.

## ARTS

The Romantic poet Mihail Eminescu (1850-89) captured the spirituality of the Romanian people in his work. The painter Nicolae Grigourescu (1838-1907) absorbed French impressionism and created canvases alive with the colour of the Romanian peasantry. You can see Grigourescu's work in art galleries in Bucharest and Constanţa. In his plays, satirist Ion Luca Caragiale (1852-1912) decried the impact of precipitous modernisation on city life and showed the comic irony of social and political change.

Though primarily a resident of France after 1904, abstract sculptor Constantin Brâncuşi (1876-1957) endowed his native Tîrgu Jiu with some of his finest works in 1937. Brâncuşi revolutionised sculpture by emphasising essential forms and the beauty of the material itself. Internationally, perhaps the best known Romanian writer is playwright Eugene Ionesco (born in 1912), a leading exponent of the 'theatre of the absurd', who has lived in France since 1938.

Novelist Paul Goma (1935- ) is Romania's best known contemporary writer. His *My Childhood at the Gate of Unrest* recently appeared in Britain in an English translation but all of his books are worth reading.

### Music

Romanian folk music is sung and played in the villages at annual celebrations, Sunday get-togethers or whenever; in the cities, professional groups such as the Romanian Radio Folk Music Orchestra perform the same music in a more sophisticated style. Couples may dance in a circle, semicircle or line. In the belt dance, the dancers form a chain by grasping their neighbour's belt, whereas in the waist dance the line of dancers have their arms around each other's waist.

The *doină* is an individual, improvised love song, a sort of Romanian blues with a social or romantic theme. The *baladă* on the other hand is a collective narrative song which reflects the conditions or feelings of the people, often with some historic content. Many group songs are vestiges of archaic rites, such as weddings, funerals or harvest festivals. Flute and bagpipe music originated with shepherds.

Traditional folk instruments include the *bucium* (alphorn), *cimpoi* (bagpipe), *cobză* (a pear-shaped string instrument with eight to 12 strings), *nai* (a pan pipe of about 20 cane tubes), many kinds of flutes, including the *ocarina* (a ceramic flute) and the *tilinca* (a flute without finger holes). The violin, though of more recent origin, is today the most common folk instrument. Romania's best known composer, George Enescu (1881-1955), himself a virtuoso violinist, used Romanian folk themes in his work.

## LANGUAGE

English and French are the first foreign languages taught in Romanian schools and German is useful in Transylvania. Romanian is much closer to classical Latin than the other Romance languages. The grammatical structure and basic word stock of the mother tongue are well preserved. Some Slavonic words were incorporated in the 7th to 10th centuries, as the Romanian language took definite shape. Speakers of French, Italian and Spanish won't be able to understand much spoken Romanian but will find written Romanian more or less comprehensible.

Until the mid-19th century, Romanian was written in the Cyrillic script. Today Romanian employs 28 Latin letters, some of which bear accents. It is spelt phonetically, so once you learn a few simple rules you'll be able to read aloud the expressions that follow. Pronounce ă as the ea in pearl, â and î as the i in river, c as ch, ch before e and i as k, g as the g in gentle, gh as the g in good, ş as sh and ţ as tz. Vowels without accents are pronounced as they are in Spanish or Italian. In Romanian there are no long and short vowels, but e, i, o and u form a diphthong or triphthong with adjacent vowels. There are no silent letters and the stress is usually on the penultimate syllable.

## Greetings & Civilities

hello
  *bună*
goodbye
  *la revedere*
good morning
  *bună dimineaţa*
good evening
  *bună seara*
please
  *vă rog*

thank you
  *mulţumesc*
I am sorry/Forgive me.
  *Lertaţi-mă.*
Excuse me.
  *Scuzaţi-mă.*
You are very kind.
  *Sînteţi foarte amabil.*
yes
  *da*
no
  *nu*

## Small Talk

Do you speak English?
  *Vorbiti englezeste?*
I don't understand.
  *Nu înţeleg.*
Could you write it down?
  *Puteţi să notaţi?*
Where do you live?
  *De unde sînteţi?*
What work do you do?
  *Cu ce vă ocupaţi?*
I am a student.
  *Sînt student.*
I am very happy.
  *Sînt foarte fericit.*

## Accommodation

youth hostel
  *camin studentesc*
camping ground
  *camping*
private room
  *camere particulare*
How much is it?
  *Cît costă?*
Is that the price per person?
  *Este pretul pentru o persoană?*
Is that the total price?
  *Acesta este preţul total?*
Are there any extra charges?
  *Mai este ceva de plătit?*
Can I pay with local currency?
  *Pot plăti în monedă locală?*
Where is there a cheaper hotel?
  *Unde este un hotel mai ieftin?*
Should I make a reservation?
  *Pot face o rezervare?*

single room
*o cameră pentru o persoană*
double room
*o cameră pentru două persoane*
It is very noisy.
*Este foarte zgomotos.*
Where is the toilet?
*Unde este toaleta?*

## Getting Around

What time does it leave?
*La ce oră este plecarea?*
When is the first bus?
*Cînd este primul autobuz?*
When is the last bus?
*Cînd este ultimul autobuz?*
When is the next bus?
*Cînd este următorul autobuz?*
That's too soon.
*Foarte curînd.*
When is the next one after that?
*Cînd este următorul după acesta?*
How long does the trip take?
*Cît timp durează excursia?*
arrival
*sosire*
departure
*plecare*
timetable
*mersul*
Where is the bus stop?
*Unde este stația de autobuz?*
Where is the railway station?
*Unde este gara?*
Where is the taxi stand?
*Unde este o stație taxi?*
Where is the left-luggage room?
*Unde este biroul pentru bagaje de mînă?*

## Around Town

Just a minute.
*Un moment.*
Where is...?
*Unde este...?*
the bank
*banca*
the post office
*poșta*
the telephone centre
*centrala telefonicâ*

the tourist information office
*birou de informatii turistice*
the museum
*muzeu*
the palace
*palat*
the castle
*castel*
the concert hall
*sala de concerte*
the opera house
*opera*
the musical theatre
*teatru muzical*
Where are you going?
*Unde mergeti?*
I am going to...
*Merg la..,*
Where is it?
*Unde este?*
I can't find it.
*Nu pot să găsesc.*
Is it far?
*Este departe?*
Please show me on the map.
*Vă rog arătați-mi pe hartă.*
left
*stînga*
right
*dreapta*
straight ahead
*drept înainte*
I want...
*Vreau...*
Do I need permission?
*Am nevoie de aprobare?*
May I?
*Pot să?*

## Entertainment

Where can I hear live music?
*Unde pot asculta muzică?*
Where can I buy a ticket?
*Unde pot cumpăra un bilet?*
I'm looking for a ticket.
*Nu aveți un bilet în plus?*
I want to refund this ticket.
*Aș vrea să renunț la acest bilet.*
Is this a good seat?
*Este un loc bun?*

at the front
  *în primele rînduri*
ticket
  *bilet*

## Food

I am hungry.
  *Îmi este foame.*
I do not eat meat.
  *Nu consum carne.*
self-service cafeteria
  *autoservire*
grocery store
  *băcănie*
fish
  *peşte*
soup
  *supă*
salad
  *salată*
fresh vegetables
  *legume proaspete*
milk
  *lapte*
bread
  *pîine*
sugar
  *zahăr*
ice cream
  *îngheţată*
hot coffee
  *cafea caldă*
mineral water
  *apă minerală*
beer
  *bere*
wine
  *vin*

## Shopping

Where can I buy one?
  *Unde aş putea cumpăra?*
How much does it cost?
  *Cît costă?*
That's (much) too expensive.
  *Este prea scump.*
Is there a cheaper one?
  *Pot găsi ceva mai ieftin?*
there is
  *există*

there isn't
  *nu există*

## Time & Dates

today
  *astăzi*
tonight
  *la noapte*
tomorrow
  *mîine*
the day after tomorrow
  *poimîine*
What time does it open?
  *La ce oră se deschide?*
What time does it close?
  *La ce oră se închide?*
open
  *deschis*
closed
  *închis*
in the morning
  *dimineaţa*
in the evening
  *deseară*
every day
  *în fiecare zi*
At what time?
  *La ce oră?*
when?
  *cînd?*

| | |
|---|---|
| Monday | *luni* |
| Tuesday | *marţi* |
| Wednesday | *miercuri* |
| Thursday | *joi* |
| Friday | *vineri* |
| Saturday | *sîmbătă* |
| Sunday | *duminică* |

| | |
|---|---|
| January | *ianuarie* |
| February | *februarie* |
| March | *martie* |
| April | *aprilie* |
| May | *mai* |
| June | *iunie* |
| July | *iulie* |
| August | *august* |
| September | *septembrie* |
| October | *octombrie* |

| November | *noiembrie* |
| December | *decembrie* |

## Numbers

| 1 | *unu* |
| 2 | *doi* |
| 3 | *trei* |
| 4 | *patru* |
| 5 | *cinci* |
| 6 | *şase* |
| 7 | *şapte* |
| 8 | *opt* |
| 9 | *nouă* |
| 10 | *zece* |
| 11 | *unsprezece* |
| 12 | *doisprezece* |
| 13 | *treisprezece* |
| 14 | *patrusprezece* |
| 15 | *cincisprezece* |
| 16 | *şaisprezece* |
| 17 | *şaptesprezece* |
| 18 | *optsprezece* |
| 19 | *nouăsprezece* |
| 20 | *douăzeci* |
| 21 | *douăzeci şi unu* |
| 22 | *douăzeci şi doi* |
| 23 | *douăzeci şi trei* |
| 30 | *treizeci* |
| 40 | *patruzeci* |
| 50 | *cincizeci* |
| 60 | *şaizeci* |
| 70 | *şaptezeci* |
| 80 | *optzeci* |
| 90 | *nouăzeci* |
| 100 | *o sută* |

# Facts for the Visitor

## VISAS & EMBASSIES

Most Western visitors require a tourist or transit visa to enter Romania. Some Romanian tourist publications claim that nationals of Austria, Denmark, Finland, Iceland, Norway, Portugal and Sweden don't require visas, whereas other sources say they do. Since visas are easily available at the border anyway, nationals of these countries should just check on entering Romania. Nationals of other countries should pick up their visa at a Romanian consulate beforehand, if possible.

Romanian visas are expensive but easily obtained. You can get one on the train, at the border crossing upon arrival or in advance at a Romanian consulate. The price will be about US$30, regardless of how long you intend to stay, and no photos are required. The best way to compensate for this high admission fee is to stay longer in the country. The exact price varies according to nationality, with citizens of countries that charge Romanians high visa fees paying the most.

When you receive your visa, you'll have to specify exactly how many days you wish to remain in Romania. Since there's no compulsory exchange in Romania, always ask for a 30-day visa, even if you intend to stay less. That way you won't need to worry about an extension should you decide to stay longer. You may use the visa any time within three months of the date of issue.

Once inside Romania, it's possible to extend your stay by reporting to police. Any ONT (the government tourist agency) office will be able to advise you on the procedure. However, you would be better off asking for enough time in the first place.

## Romanian Embassies

Romanian embassies around the world include the following:

Canada
    655 Rideau St, Ottawa, ON K1N 683
    (☎ 613-232 5345)
Netherlands
    Catsheuvel 55, 2517 KA The Hague
    (☎ 070-355 7369)
UK
    4 Palace Green, London W8 4QD
    (☎ 071-937 9666)
USA
    1607 23rd St NW, Washington, DC 20008
    (☎ 202-232 4749)

## MONEY

At last report, the Romanian leu was officially worth US$1.67, or 60 lei to the US dollar. One leu consists of 100 bani. There are coins of 25 bani, 1 leu, 3 lei and 5 lei and notes of 10, 25, 50 and 100 lei. The largest note is 100 lei, the equivalent of US$3 at the official rate, which is an attempt to control the black market. (All US dollar prices in this chapter were obtained by converting to lei at the official rate.) At present, Romanian currency is overvalued and most prices are based on the official rate. The cheapest Bucharest hotel room will cost US$25/45 single/double and a self-service meal will cost US$2. Romanians only earn around US$125 a month, so it's expensive for them, too.

When you change money at a tourist office, you're given a receipt which allows you to use the money to pay for hotel rooms. Without the receipt, your lei are worthless to pay for accommodation at hotels and camping grounds. You must pay directly in hard currency for international train tickets, ONT sightseeing tours and luxury goods purchased at hotel 'shops'. Be sure to have plenty of US$1 or DM 5 notes to cover these small expenditures, otherwise you'll be forced to accept change in lei. Everything else, such as domestic transportation tickets, taxis, restaurant meals, theatre and museum admissions and local goods, may be paid for in lei without any receipts. If in doubt about

a price, offer the vendors a pen and paper and ask them to write it down. Always count your change.

There's a 1% commission charged on official exchanges. It's impossible to change Romanian lei back into hard currency, even if the exchange receipt assures you it can be done. (Some readers have reported success in reconverting lei at Bucharest Airport, though receipts were required.) It's forbidden to import or export Romanian currency, but you may deposit excess lei with customs upon departure and pick it up again on your next visit.

There's a black market in Romania which offers five times the official rate for cash dollars or Deutschmarks. Be aware that this is extremely dangerous, as most of the individuals who offer to change money on the street are professional thieves who only want to trick you out of your cash. The amount of money you will be given the first time will always be 'short' and in the process of correcting the 'error' the real money disappears. The moneychangers flash a thick wad of 100 lei notes, count out the agreed price for your dollars or Marks, roll the money up into a tight little roll, then switch rolls at the last instant. Later, when you take the money out to count it again, you discover a roll of

newsprint or worthless Yugoslav banknotes with a 100 lei note plastered on top. These operators will insist that you change at least US$50 or DM 100 (even in lei, US$10 doesn't make much of a roll), so that's one way to recognise them. Another favourite trick is to take your dollars and give you the correct amount, then just as you're walking off, they will rush back shouting, 'Not good, not good.' The operators will then insist on giving you 'your' money back in exchange for theirs. As soon as they have the lei in hand again, they'll quickly disappear and you'll find that your US$20 and US$50 bills have been swapped for US$ 1 bills. Gangs of Arab students in Bucharest get rich this way, but you must be careful everywhere in Romania.

If you're set on cutting your costs by 500%, deal with people you meet in camping grounds or hotels rather than on the street. Polish businessmen who come to Romania to sell jeans and coffee are often eager to convert their lei into dollars. Waiters in expensive restaurants will often change money. Take the money from them, re-examine it carefully, put it away and only then show your money. Don't be in a hurry. Wait till you meet someone who can't run away, then change enough to cover your entire remaining stay, avoiding the need to take this serious risk a second time. If you have to change money officially to keep travelling while you're waiting for the right opportunity to come along, don't worry as you'll get receipts allowing you to use the lei to pay hotel bills.

Even if you don't decide to change money on the black market, you can always enjoy some of the benefits of the dual exchange rate by bargaining for taxis and hotel rooms with cash dollars. Since Romanians are now allowed to possess foreign currency, it's no longer illegal to pay taxi drivers in dollars instead of lei and this always works to your advantage. Keep in mind that when you pay for a service with cash dollars or DM your money is worth five times what it would be if you had changed it into lei at the bank. This is good reason to bring plenty of Western currency in small bills with you.

## Tipping

The two favourite tips in Romania are a packet of Kent cigarettes and a crisp US$1 note (bring a large supply of these). Packets of Kent are almost a second currency in Romania, serving the same function as a folded $20 bill in North America so bring a few packets with you. Hard-currency shops inside Romania sell Kent by the carton and you can use packets of them to pay taxi fares and to trade for all sorts of things which would be more expensive if you purchased them with lei obtained at the bank rate.

At restaurants, if the service charge is included, there's no need to tip extra though you should always round the bill up a little. If you are completely delighted by the excellent food and service, you could give a US$1 note to the waiter as you're paying (do not leave it on the table). A dollar bill should get you into almost any restaurant, bar or disco without a reservation. If you do give such a tip for preferential treatment somewhere, don't let the Romanians who are also waiting see you do it, otherwise you could provoke an irate response. While working wonders with service industry personnel, such tips should not be offered to officials, including railway conductors, as this could create a serious nuisance for future travellers.

## CLIMATE & WHEN TO GO

Romania has a variable continental climate. It can be cold in the mountains, even in midsummer. The average annual temperature is 11°C in the south and on the coast, but only 2°C in the mountains. Romanian winters can be extremely cold and foggy. In summer there's usually hot sunny weather on the Black Sea coast. Annual rainfall is 600 to 700 mm, much of it in spring. The mountains get the most rain and the Danube Delta the least.

## WHAT TO BRING

Romanian customs regulations are complicated but not often enforced. Gifts worth up to a total of US$100 may be imported duty-free. Duty-free allowances are four litres of wine, one litre of spirits, 200 cigarettes and

200 grams each of coffee and cocoa, but only for personal use, not for resale. If you're coming from Bulgaria, bring BT cigarettes, which are also greatly appreciated by Romanians. Bring some matches, too, as the Romanian variety is hopeless.

If you're coming from Hungary, bring some food with you, especially chocolate bars. Motorists intending to camp would be wise to stock up on canned foods, powdered soups, tea bags, cooking oil, sugar and salt, as these are almost unobtainable in Romania. You are not allowed to bring in uncanned meats and dairy products, however. What you can occasionally find in Romania are tomatoes, peppers, onions, potatoes, carrots, apples, dusty bottles of pickled beets and excellent dark bread. That's all, folks.

Most important of all, bring Western currency in small bills (100 US$1 notes would not be too many). Travellers' cheques are accepted at banks, tourist offices and large hotels but not at hard-currency shops. If you have to pay a hotel bill or buy petrol coupons with travellers' cheques or a large banknote, you'll receive change in lei at the official rate. Cash dollars or marks are like gold in Romania and the smaller the denominations, the further they'll go.

Finally, bring all the camera film with you that you'll need.

## TOURIST OFFICES

The Carpaţi-Bucureşti National Tourist Office (*Oficiul Naţional de Turism* – ONT) is the government agency that controls tourism in Romania. Everything that staff there arrange, from accommodation to railway tickets or sightseeing tours, must be paid for in Western currency. Visit the ONT offices for free travel brochures, but don't expect the staff to help you to save money, as their function is exactly the opposite. It's usually better to go directly to hotels, rather than have ONT make accommodation bookings for you.

County tourist offices called *Oficiul Judeţean de Turism* (OJT) are sometimes more helpful than ONT, although they cater mostly to Romanian tourists. They'll often just refer you to the tour desk at the nearest 1st-class hotel. It's always worth trying them, however, as some will provide information if they're not too busy. Romania's student travel organisation, the BTT, has little to offer individual foreign students. You'll often have to fend for yourself in Romania.

## Travel Agencies

An important feature of Romania's tourism *perestroika* is the appearance of private travel agencies. Some are listed in this book and many more will have mushroomed by the time you get there. Their main business is organising packaged holidays for Romanians, but most of them will happily arrange private rooms, transportation and sightseeing tours with an English-speaking guide in a private car, either in the city or surrounding countryside, for less than ONT would charge in a bus. To get this kind of service, you must pay in Western currency in cash – that's free enterprise for you!

## ONT Offices Abroad

The main ONT information office addresses abroad include:

Austria
    Währingerstrasse 6-8, 1090 Vienna (☎ 34 3157)
Belgium
    Place de Brouckère 46, Brussels 1000
    (☎ 218 0079)
Czechoslovakia
    Pářížská 20, Prague 11000 (☎ 231 7578)
Denmark
    Vesterbrogade 55-A, 1620 Copenhagen
    (☎ 24 6219)
France
    38 avenue de l'Opéra, Paris 75002
    (☎ 4742 2714)
Germany
    Corneliusstrasse 16, 4000 Düsseldorf
    (☎ 37 1047)
    Neue Mainzerstrasse 1, 6000 Frankfurt/Main
    (☎ 23 6941)
    Frankfurter Tor 5, 1034 Berlin (☎ 589 2684)
Israel
    1 Ben-Yehuda, Tel Aviv (☎ 66 3536)
Italy
    100 Via Torino, 00184 Rome (☎ 474 2983)

Netherlands
    Weteringschans 165, 1017 XD Amsterdam
    (☎ 623 9044)
Spain
    Avenida Alfonso XIII 157, Madrid 16
    (☎ 458 7895)
Sweden
    Vasahuset, Gamla Brogatan 33,
    11120 Stockholm (☎ 21 0253)
Switzerland
    Schweizergasse 10, 8001 Zürich
    (☎ 211 1730)
UK
    17 Nottingham St, London W1M 3RD
    (☎ 071-224 3692)
USA
    573 Third Ave at East 38th St, New York,
    NY 10016 (☎ 697 6971)

## BUSINESS HOURS & HOLIDAYS

Banking hours are weekdays from 8 am to noon. Some shops close for a mid-afternoon siesta – after all, this is a Latin country! Set both your clocks back when you come to Romania: the one on your wrist (see the Time section) and the one that tells you when to have a good time. Many bars and restaurants in Romania are closed by 10 pm. Although erratic, beer service tends to end a little before 8 pm. Theatrical performances and concerts usually begin at 7 pm, except on Mondays, when most theatres are closed. Sporting events are usually on Wednesday, Saturday and Sunday. Almost all museums in Romania are closed on Monday.

The public holidays in Romania are 1 and 2 January (New Year), 1 and 2 May (Labour Days), and 23 and 24 August (Liberation Days).

## CULTURAL EVENTS

In June the Hercules Festival is held at Băile Herculane. Many folklore festivals unfold along the coast in summer, including one in Tulcea in August and another in Brăila in September. Autumn is the time for musical festivals in Transylvania, such as Sibiu's Cibinium in September and Cluj-Napoca's Musical Autumn in October. In December the Days of Bihor Culture takes place in Oradea. The Bucharest International Fair in October is Romania's main trade fair.

## POST & TELECOMMUNICATIONS

Main post offices are open Monday to Saturday until 8 pm, Sunday until noon. Mail boxes are yellow and labelled *poşta*. When mailing purchases home from Romania, you may be asked to pay an export duty of 20% of their value in hard currency, calculated at the official rate. The Romanian postal service is slow and unreliable: mail your things from another country.

Romanian postal clerks are often confused about the postal rates to places outside Romania, so buy your stamps at a main post office in a large city. If you must receive mail here, have it sent care of your embassy, not to poste restante.

### Telephone & Telegraph

To call Western Europe from Romania involves waiting about five hours to get a line. Instead, try sending your party a telegram with a number where you can be reached, as incoming calls go through much more easily. It's very easy to send a telegram from any main post office and you can pay for it in lei.

If you do manage to place an international call at a main post office, the operator will ask you to put up a large deposit. If you are owed any change and haven't asked for a receipt for the deposit or don't ask for your change afterwards, you won't be given any.

To call Romania from Western Europe dial the international access code, 40 (the country code for Romania), the area code and the number. Important area codes in Romania include 0 (Bucharest), 16 (Constanţa), 51 (Cluj-Napoca) and 66 (Arad).

### TIME

GMT/UTC plus two hours, which means there's a one-hour difference between Romania and Hungary or Yugoslavia, but no difference from Bulgaria. Romania goes on summer time at the end of March, so clocks are turned an hour forward. At the end of September, they're turned an hour back. To save electricity, the streets are dimly lit in Romania, which is another good reason to visit in summer, when it stays light later.

## WEIGHTS & MEASURES

The electric current is 220 volts, 50 Hz AC.

## BOOKS & MAPS

The most detailed individual guide to Romania is *Nagel's Encyclopedia-Guide* (Nagel Publishers, Geneva) which is strong on background information but of limited practical use.

*The Rough Guide to Eastern Europe* by Dan Richardson & Jill Denton (Harrap Columbus, London) is something of a misnomer as it includes only Hungary, Romania and Bulgaria, though it does cover these countries in admirable detail. If you're looking for a second travel guidebook, this is it.

A recommended German guide to Romania is Evi Melas's *DuMont Kunst-Reiseführer Rumänien*, published by DuMont Buchverlag, Cologne.

## MEDIA

More than 1000 newspapers appeared after the revolution, precipitating a newsprint crisis. Important daily papers are *Adevârul* and *Tineretul Libera*, both of which favour the FSN, and *România Libera*, an opposition voice.

*Romania News* (Piaţa Presei Libere 1, 71341 Bucharest) is a weekly newspaper in English. Newsstands don't usually have it, but you can often pick up a free copy at the desk of luxury hotels. *Holidays in Romania* (Strada Gabriel Péri 8, Bucharest) is a monthly magazine published in English, French and German by the Ministry of Commerce and Tourism.

## HEALTH

Foreigners must pay for medical treatment in Romania. Diarrhoea can be a problem, so take extra care of what you eat and drink, and bring a remedy, just in case.

One-third of all European sources of mineral or thermal waters are concentrated in Romania. There are 160 spas. The mud baths on Lake Techirghiol at Eforie Nord go well with the salty lake water and nearby Black Sea. Other important spas are Băile Felix (near Oradea) and Băile Herculane (known since Roman times). Ask for the brochure *Health Sources & Original Treatments in Romania* at ONT offices abroad. Take care, however, with unchlorinated, poorly maintained public swimming pools, as diseases of the eyes, and so on, can be very contagious.

Some of the spas offer special treatments using the unique Romanian products Gerovital H3, Aslavital, Boicil Forte, Pellamar, Covalitin and Ulcosilvanil. Gerovital H3 and Aslavital are drugs used against ageing effects; Pell-amar, extracted from sapropel mud treats rheumatism; Covalitin dissolves kidney stones; Boicil Forte, which is extracted from medicinal herbs, relieves ankylosis and rheumatic pains; and Ulcosilvanil is used for the treatment of gastroduodenal ulcers. Gerovital H3 beauty cream, sold at hard-currency shops in Romania, rejuvenates the body.

## DANGERS & ANNOYANCES

More than anywhere else in Eastern Europe, be aware of theft in Romania. This is a poor country, so it's unwise to display your wealth. Apart from the possibility of being ripped off while camping or changing money on the street, you also have to take care in hotels by locking your things in your pack or suitcase when you go out. It's better not to leave your key at the hotel reception if it looks as though it would be easy for anyone to pick it up. Use the hotel safe if you're staying at a beach hotel. If you have a car, it's safer to carry your valuables into your hotel room rather than to leave them in the car overnight. (The Black Sea coast and Braşov are said to be the worst areas in this regard.) Always check that your car doors and windows are properly closed. Don't get paranoid, though. With a little care, nothing at all will be lost.

## ACTIVITIES

### Skiing

Romania's most famous ski resorts are Sinaia, Buşteni, Predeal and Poiana Braşov in the Carpathian Mountains, between

Bucharest and Braşov. All are fully developed with cable cars, chair lifts and modern resort hotels. The ski slopes at Sinaia vary in altitude from 400 to 2800 metres, with level differences up to 585 metres. Atop the Bucegi Plateau above the Sinaia resort is an eight-km cross-country route, and there is also a 13-bend bob track.

Poiana Braşov boasts 20 km of ski slopes and sledging runs at varying degrees of difficulty. As this resort is off the main railway line, it's less crowded and preferable for serious skiers. Other less well-known Romanian ski resorts include Păltiniş south-west of Sibiu, Borşa, between Suceava and Baia Mare, and Semenic near Reşita, south-east of Timişoara.

The ski season runs from December to March and you can hire gear at the main hotels. Courses at the ski school at Poiana Braşov last from four to six days and run for four hours a day, with about 12 students in each class. Special courses for children are available.

### Hiking

Romania's Carpathians offer endless opportunities for hikers, with the Bucegi and Făgăraş ranges south and west of Braşov being the most popular areas. Other choice Carpathian hiking zones include the Retezat National Park, north-west of Tîrgu Jiu, the Şureanu Mountains, between Alba Iulia and Tîrgu Jiu, the Apuseni Mountains, southwest of Cluj-Napoca, and the Ceahlău Massif, between Braşov and Suceava. Good hiking maps are hard to come by, so buy them when you see them.

### HIGHLIGHTS

#### Museums & Galleries

Constanţa's Archaeological Museum has one of the best collections of Greek and Roman artifacts in Eastern Europe. The Ethnographical Museum in Cluj-Napoca and Bucharest's Village Museum will be appreciated by anyone interested in Romanian folklore. Romania's oldest and finest art gallery is the Brukenthal Museum in Sibiu. Finally, the Danube Museum in Drobeta-

Turnu Severin is outstanding for history and natural history with the added bonus of an aquarium of fish from the Danube.

### Castles

Bran Castle near Braşov is everyone's idea of a fairy-tale castle, but Rîşnov Castle nearby is more the real thing. Hunedoara Castle is easily the finest Gothic castle in Romania, but it's rather spoiled by the ugly steel mill that's right next door. Alba Iulia Citadel has deep significance to Romanians as the place where the country was finally reunited. Peleş Castle at Sinaia is actually a royal palace but what a palace!

### Historic Towns

It may come as no surprise that Romania's best preserved medieval towns, Sighişoara, Sibiu, Braşov and Cluj-Napoca, are all in Transylvania. Oradea is an elegant 19th century Habsburg town.

### Hotels

Over the past 30 years, the Communists built scores of modern hotels around the country, but for atmosphere these can't compete with the hotels that were there before. Sibiu's Hotel Bulevard maintains the tradition of Transylvania's grand old hotels. The Steaua Hotel in Sighişoara is just fine, but as it's the only hotel in town, you may not get a room. The Hotel Marmaţia in Sighetu Marmaţiei has the feel of a mountain lodge, and the Vulturul Negru in Oradea and Mareşul in Arad are inexpensive but full of dusty old-world flavour.

### Restaurants

Foreign cuisine is rarely available in Romania but there are a few excellent (and expensive) Chinese restaurants, especially the Nan Jing in Bucharest and the Chinezesc in Braşov. Mamaia's Hanul Piraţilor is actually a nightclub, but dinner is served before the show and the nautical décor is fun. The restaurant in Dracula's house in Sighişoara is pleasantly uncommercial. The Restaurantul Intim in Cluj-Napoca is perhaps the only women-only restaurant in Eastern Europe and it's listed here for that reason alone.

## ACCOMMODATION

You may pay for official accommodation charges in lei, but you must present the receipt you got when you changed money at a bank or ONT tourist office. The amount spent is deducted from the back of the exchange receipt and you can go on using the same receipt until you have exhausted your credit, at which time you'll have to change more hard currency to pay for accommodation. Aside from this, there's no bureaucratic requirement to register with the police, get hotel stamps on a visa form or account for every night spent in the country.

### Camping

As there are no youth hostels in Romania, camping is one of the few ways to see the country on a low budget. Of course you'll need a tent and will have to come in summer. Dozens of official camping grounds have been set up along the Black Sea coast, the perfect place to relax for a few days and meet young Romanians. Some of the 154 camping grounds on the official *Popasuri Turistice* map and list are described in this chapter. Camping grounds with bungalows are called *popas turisticas*. Many Romanian camping grounds are in bad condition, some without toilets and showers, and most only open from June to mid-September.

Freelance camping is prohibited in cities and along the Black Sea coast, but not necessarily elsewhere. If you see Romanian tourists camping in an open field, there's nothing to prevent your joining them. If you're camping alone, try to keep out of sight of the road. If you wish to sleep in your car or van, it's safer to go to a camping ground or park near a hotel, as vehicles parked along roads can attract unwelcome attention. If anyone hints that there could be a problem about camping somewhere, believe them and go elsewhere. Wherever you camp, take care of your gear. Don't go off and leave valuable objects unattended, as there are lots of stories about rip-offs.

### Mountain Hostels

Although you can pitch a tent anywhere you like in the mountains, you may find it too cold to do so. In most mountain areas there's a network of cabins or chalets with restaurants and dormitories where hikers can put up for the night. The official *Cabane Turistice* map lists 148 *cabane*. Prices are much lower than hotels and no reservations are required, but arrive early if the *cabana* is in a popular location, for example, next to a cable car terminus, etc. Expect to find good companionship rather than cleanliness or comfort at these hostels.

### Private Rooms

Only since 1990 have Romanians been allowed to rent rooms in their homes to foreigners. This type of accommodation is so new that it's not fully organised yet, but always ask about private rooms at tourist offices. You may be lucky and get in on something which only started last week. A few agencies offering private rooms are mentioned in this chapter. As you get off the beaten track, you'll sometimes be invited to stay with local people you meet on trains or elsewhere.

### Hotels

Hotels are expensive in Romania. You will be very lucky if you can find a room for US$20/30 single/double, even in the most run-down places. Rooms in a good modern hotel will only cost about US$10 more than a flea bag, so this is one country where the cheapest isn't always the best value. Some hotels charge extra to use the communal shower. Ask first as it may be better value in the long run to take a room with a private bathroom. Most 1st-class hotels in Romania will call ahead to the next hotel on your itinerary and make a reservation for you for free or at a minimal expense.

Many Romanian hotels have been reclassified as 1st-class hotels simply to increase the prices, so a 1st-class hotel in no way ensures a 1st-class room. To boot, the lowest category of hotel is 2nd class, so all 3rd and 4th-class hotels are listed as 2nd class automatically. Some of the cheapest 2nd-class hotels have instructions not to admit foreign tourists.

On the positive side, Romanian hotel keepers will go out of their way to find you a room, even in hotels with large 'no vacancy' (nu avem locuri) notices on the door. This is partly because Western tourists must pay four times more than Romanians for the same rooms. Still, it's comforting to know that you'll almost always be able to find something. Breakfast is usually included in the price.

Some hotel receptionists will gladly give you a room for a US$20 bill with no questions asked, even though their official tariff may be higher. The desk clerk will put it through the books as if a Romanian had paid for the room in lei and just pocket your hard currency. Such a ploy might also get you a room in a supposedly 'full' hotel. It's not strictly legal to do this, however, so you'll have to be discrete.

**Hotel Coupons** If you want to visit Romania in reasonable comfort, the hotel coupons issued by the Romanian Automobile Club (Automobil Clubul Român) are highly recommended. You can only purchase these at ONT offices abroad, some foreign travel agencies, highway border crossings and the Automobil Clubul Român (Hertz), Strada Mihail Eminescu 7, just off Piaţa Romană, Bucharest (travellers' cheques are accepted). Since the Bucharest office could stop selling these coupons any day, and they may be out of stock at the border crossing, you should buy them before you come to Romania.

Each coupon guarantees you a room at a 1st-class hotel with bath, breakfast and five litres of petrol included. Reservations are not required as the participating hotels are required to hold a certain number of rooms free until 7 pm every day for coupon holders who may just show up. Almost every 1st-class hotel in Romania is on the official coupon list – the best ones are identified in this chapter. Until recently the price was US$31/43 single/double per coupon, which

is much less than what you would pay for the same rooms without coupons. Once purchased, the coupons are valid until March the next year.

Luxury category hotels, such as the Hanul Manuc in Bucharest, are not included. Hotel coupons will get you rooms in hotels, especially along the Black Sea coast, which are otherwise 'full', but be aware that a few hotels don't like the coupons and may claim that all the rooms are full. It's sometimes best to ask if they have a room before you present the coupon, whereas at other times the reverse works. Before turning over your coupon, ask how much it would be if you paid cash, as in a few cases it's slightly cheaper.

Even if you decide to use the coupons as your main means of acquiring accommodation around the country, don't buy too many as there are other places where you can stay. If you are left with any unused coupons, however, they will be refunded in lei. As a rule of thumb, buy one coupon for every two nights you plan to spend in Romania. Camping coupons are also available, but they are expensive and of no use.

## FOOD

Food is a problem in Romania. The cheaper restaurants have very little of it and there are formidable queues at any place serving beer. Coffee is usually unavailable and drinks of any kind are almost nonexistent at street stalls. The service in restaurants is usually poor. Dining at places with table service involves some waiting, so patronise the cafeterias if you don't have time for a leisurely meal. Most of the cheaper restaurants close shortly before 8 pm.

One way to make things easier for everyone in restaurants is to order only things you see on other tables. Just get the waiter's attention and point. This will eliminate language problems and unwelcome surprises. Otherwise, ask the waiter which dish is available and take it; only the finest restaurants serve more than one or two things. In any case it's always a good idea to have a look at the menu to get an idea of the price range, even if most of the things on it won't be available. Most restaurants do have soup and it's usually very good. Vegetarians are going to have a problem, as almost every restaurant dish is based on meat and there aren't many alternatives.

The price difference between 1st and 3rd-class restaurants is not great, so splash out now and then. Better restaurants with proper menus are less likely to cheat you than basic places without a menu. If you have trouble finding a decent place where you can eat, try the dining room of a major hotel. However, you really do need 'black' money to eat there, otherwise it's very expensive. Since foreigners tend to offer better tips, waiters in good restaurants will try to seat you. Except at the Inter-Continental Hotel in Bucharest, all restaurant meals, including those in hotel restaurants, can be paid for in lei without exchange receipts. If waiters ask you to pay in hard currency, they are trying to cheat you.

At the hotels along the Black Sea coast, the meals are served at 7.30 am, 12.30 and 6 pm. If you want to eat something, don't just sit down and wait to be served, because you won't be. Instead, try going into the kitchen and asking the chef what's available. Then, if necessary, carry your own food out to the table. Some beach hotels that provide full board try to make foreigners pay for the meal plan in hard currency, which makes it very expensive.

Take care what you eat in Romania or you could end up with Ceauşescu's Revenge!

### Romanian Specialities

Romanian favourites include *ciorbă de perişoare* (a spicy soup made with meat balls and vegetables), *ghiveciu* (vegetable stew), *tocană* (onion and meat stew), *ardei umpluti* (stuffed peppers), *mititei* (highly seasoned grilled meatballs), *sarmală* (cabbage or vine leaves stuffed with spiced meat and rice) and *pastramă* (smoked goat meat). *Mămăligă* is a maize porridge that goes well with everything. Typical desserts include *plăcintă* (turnovers) and *cozonac* (a brioche). Turkish sweets such as *baclavă*, *cataif* and *halva* are common. Unfortunately, it's extremely rare

for any of these dishes to be available at Romanian restaurants. Usually, all they will have will be a pork or beef cutlet served with chips (French fries) and a Balkan salad (cucumbers and tomatoes dusted with white cheese).

### DRINKS

Among the best Romanian wines are Cotnari, Murfatlar, Odobesti, Tirnave and Valea Calugareasca. Red wines are called *negru* in Romanian. When ordering wine at a restaurant, compare the price of a glass with that of a bottle, as it's usually much better value to order the whole bottle. *Must* is a fresh, unfermented wine available during the wine harvest. *Tuica* (plum brandy) is taken at the beginning of a meal. *Palinca* is a stronger variety of *tuica*. Romanians drink Russian-style tea and Turkish coffee. Often it's hard to find anything at all to drink. A couple of toasts are *poftă bună* (bon appétit) and *noroc!* (cheers!).

### ENTERTAINMENT

There isn't a lot to do after dark. Most Western-style nightlife takes place in the bars, discos and cabarets of the luxury hotels, and since these are not accessible to a majority of Romanians, the atmosphere can be stuffy and pretentious. The drinking places of average Romanians will be far too rough for most travellers, who may soon give up on ever being served.

Ask instead at tourist offices about local festivals or cultural events. Ask too about local events at the main theatre and concert hall of the town you're in, and visit any theatre ticket offices you can find. Opera companies exist in Bucharest, Cluj-Napoca, Iaşi and Timişoara. In summer, open-air cinemas operate in the Black Sea resorts. In large towns buy the local paper and try to decipher the entertainment listings. If nothing at all seems to be happening, just go to bed and get an earlier start the next day.

### THINGS TO BUY

Because of the scarcity of nearly all consumer goods, it may be better to do your shopping with Western currency in hotel or Comturist 'shops'. Wine purchased at hotel shops is excellent quality. The shops also carry plum brandy, Gerovital H3 and Pellamar cosmetics, embroidered blouses and Romanian handicrafts. At hard-currency shops you'll be assured top quality at reasonable prices and you'll have no problem taking the items out of Romania. Make sure you are given an itemised receipt to show to customs, otherwise you could be charged export duty if the total value is over US$100. Hard-currency shops accept only Western currency in cash – no travellers' cheques.

Shops in luxury hotels often sell coffee and Western cigarettes that are not available in local stores. Arab and African students make profits by purchasing these items with hard currency and then reselling them to Romanians at inflated prices in lei. You'll sometimes be asked if you have anything of this nature to sell.

People who befriend you on the street may end up asking for gifts or favours, such as requests for you to make purchases at these hard-currency shops. This is often the case with young men who say they wish to 'practise their English'.

Romarta stores sell glassware, textiles, women's clothing and ceramics, and Muzică stores sell Romanian records. You can pay with lei at these stores.

Consumer scarcities have developed a hunter instinct among Romanian consumers. Sometimes you'll notice a shop with no-one in it which looks marginally interesting and stop to go in for a look. Immediately a dozen passers-by, sensing that you've spotted something, will crowd in behind you and stand peering at what's behind the counter. Often people will suddenly change direction and try to beat you to the counter, queue or seat. When a scarce item does become available, the hoarding instinct takes over and huge crowds gather to buy as much of the item as they can possibly carry. Romanians often carry a small cloth shopping bag around with them everywhere for just such emergencies.

# Getting There & Away

## AIR

TAROM (Transporturile Aeriene Romane) Romanian Air Transport has flights to Bucharest from Abu Dhabi, Amman, Bangkok, Baghdad, Belgrade, Beijing, Cairo, Damascus, Dubai, Istanbul, Karachi, Larnaca, London, New York, Singapore and Tel Aviv. The flights between Bucharest and New York have been operating since 1974. From Western Europe and the USA, a package tour to Romania with flights, hotels and all meals included may be cheaper than a regular return plane ticket. Bucket shops in Asia sell TAROM tickets at a discount. There's no airport departure tax in Romania.

## LAND
### Bus

Walter Kessler (☎ 71581), Am Kornberg 84, 5900 Siegen, Germany, operates a regular year-round bus service from Cologne, Germany, to Sibiu.

Mihail Tours (☎ 5245 762), 12 Ag Konstantinou St, Athens, has a weekly bus from Athens to Bucharest, departing on Saturday at 7 am (US$50 one-way). You will need a Bulgarian transit visa.

Pan Istanbul (Intertrans Romania) at Piaţa Natiunile Unite, Bucharest, has a bus from Bucharest to Istanbul at 4 pm daily except Sunday (US$15 one-way).

### Train

Most budget travellers arrive in Romania by train. Fares to/from Hungary and Bulgaria are cheap. A one-way ticket from Arad or Oradea-Budapest costs only US$6, and Bucharest-Ruse costs US$4, or only half that if you're coming in instead of going out! You can save a little money by going across Romania on a domestic ticket purchased with lei, although Bucharest-Budapest is only US$15 one-way and Bucharest-Sofia US$11, which is still cheap.

International railway tickets must be purchased at a CFR (Romanian State Railways) travel agency or an ONT tourist office with Western currency. Only since 1990 have Romanians been allowed to go abroad and millions have already done so. The monolithic state railway ticketing bureaucracy just can't cope with the demand, so you can have problems buying international train tickets in Romania. Since the Bucharest ticket offices are impossibly overcrowded, try picking up an open international train ticket to get you out of the country at a provincial CFR travel agency (many are listed in this chapter). If you're coming from Hungary, buy your ticket right through to Bulgaria.

Most of the daily, year-round trains listed here have compulsory seat reservations. If you already have your ticket, you may be able to make reservations at the station an hour before departure, though it's preferable to do so at a CFR travel agency in advance.

**To/From Hungary & Beyond** To go to/from Budapest you have a choice of the Balt-Orient Express via Oradea or the Orient Express via Arad, both taking about 15 hours to travel Budapest-Bucharest. The Orient Express conveys carriages originating in Paris Est and Vienna West stations. The Pannonia Express from Berlin-Lichtenberg to Sofia also travels via Budapest, Arad and Bucharest.

The Carpaţi Express goes past Košice (Czechoslovakia), Miskolc, Hatvan (both in Hungary) and Arad on its way from Warsaw to Bucharest. One seasonal train of interest is the Varna Express from Warsaw to Varna, Bulgaria, via Miskolc, Debrecen and Oradea (from mid-June to mid-October only).

The easiest way to enter or leave Romania to/from Hungary by train is on one of the two daily local Hungarian trains which shuttle between Oradea and Budapest-Nyugati (249 km, five hours). At last report these trains left Oradea at 12.10 and 6.10 pm, and Budapest-Nyugati at 6.10 am and 1.30 pm. No reservations are required, but in Romania try to buy an open Oradea-Budapest ticket at a CFR travel agency well ahead. If this is impossible and you can't buy a ticket to Hungary in Oradea Station, just buy a ticket

to Episcopia Bihor, the border station, and pay the Hungarian conductor on the other side. If you're making a return trip to Romania from Hungary on this train, be sure to buy a return ticket, as all ticketing in Romania is chaotic.

From Arad you can go to Békéscsaba in Hungary by unreserved morning and afternoon trains with a change at Curtici.

**To/From Yugoslavia** The Bucureşti Express shuttles daily between Beograd-Dunav Railway Station and Bucharest via Timişoara, leaving both cities in the evening and travelling overnight.

If you can't get a ticket or reservation for this train, you can get an unreserved early morning train from Timişoara-Nord to Jimbolia, where you change to another local train to go to Kikinda, Yugoslavia.

**To/From Bulgaria** Train service between Romania and Bulgaria is poor. From Sofia to Bucharest there's the daily Pannonia Express, which passes Ruse in the very early morning. From mid-June to mid-October the Varna Express operates daily from Varna to Warsaw via Negru Vodă and Bucharest.

### Car & Motorbike

If you're crossing the Romanian border by car, expect long lines of Romanian cars at the Romanian checkpoint. There are fewer cars on Monday, Tuesday and Wednesday than on weekends. It is an accepted practice that foreigners in foreign cars may cut to the front of the line. Roll down your window and show your passport to the guards if they try to send you back.

The Romanian highway border crossings listed here in an anticlockwise direction around Romania are open to all nationalities. All are open 24 hours a day, except those to/from the USSR, which are open from 8 am to 8 pm.

To go to/from Hungary there are border crossings at Petea (11 km north-west of Satu Mare), Borş (14 km north-west of Oradea), Vărşand (66 km north of Arad) and Nădlac (between Szeged, Hungary, and Arad).

To/from Yugoslavia you may cross at Jimbolia (45 km west of Timişoara), Stamora Moraviţa (between Timişoara and Belgrade), Naidăş (120 km east of Belgrade) and Porţile de Fier (Iron Gate) (10 km west of Drobeta-Turnu Severin).

To/from Bulgaria you can cross at Calafat (opposite Vidin, Bulgaria), Giurgiu (opposite Ruse), Călăraşi (opposite Silistra), Negru Vodă (37 km north-east of Tolbuhin) and Vama Veche (10 km south of Mangalia). If you're going to/from the USSR, you may choose from Albiţa (65 km south-east of Iaşi) and Siret (46 km north of Suceava).

### Hitchhiking

If you don't have time to pick up an international train ticket, you could try walking out of Romania. At Borş, 14 km north-west of Oradea, the Hungarian and Romanian border posts are adjacent and it should be possible to hitchhike to Debrecen or Budapest.

It might be easier to take one of the six daily local trains from Arad to Nădlac, then walk or take a taxi the last four km to the Hungarian border. In Hungary there are local trains from Nagylak to Szeged.

To travel to/from Bulgaria, you could take a local bus, a taxi or hitchhike 10 km south from Mangalia to Vama Veche. There you can cross into Bulgaria and look for onward transport to Balchik, 62 km south-west.

### RIVER
### Ferry

A regular passenger ferry between Calafat, Romania, and Vidin, Bulgaria, crosses the Danube River several times a day throughout the year (US$1, 30 minutes). Both these towns are well connected to the rest of their countries by rail, so this route is practicable for travellers without vehicles. Westerners seldom pass this way, however, so it might be wise to have your onward Bulgarian or Romanian visa already and not expect to get one at the border.

From Craiova to Calafat by local train it takes 2½ hours (five daily). It's only 300 metres from Calafat Railway Station to the Romanian ferry terminal, where you can

easily obtain ferry tickets. You can pay in lei, though you must show a currency exchange paper and passport.

# Getting Around

## AIR

TAROM has an extensive network of domestic flights based in Bucharest and Constanţa. Many of the Constanţa flights operate only in July and August, but you can fly out of Bucharest's Băneasa Airport to every part of the country all year. Very few TAROM flights operate on Sundays.

Fares are reasonable and may be paid for in lei. Sample one-way fares from Bucharest are: Arad US$17, Cluj-Napoca US$15, Constanţa US$10, Iaşi US$14, Oradea US$17, Satu Mare US$18, Sibiu US$10, Suceava US$15, Timişoara US$17 and Tulcea US$20. From Constanţa it costs US$24 to Arad, US$19 to Cluj-Napoca, US$14 to Iaşi, US$25 to Oradea, US$16 to Sibiu, US$16 to Suceava and US$22 to Timişoara. Only 10 kilos of luggage is carried free but overweight charges are minimal.

## BUS

Romanian buses (ITA) are less reliable and more crowded than the trains. On rural routes only one or two jam-packed buses may run a day. You usually have to purchase your ticket before boarding and if you haven't done so at a bus station (autogară), you could have problems with the driver. If the bus is the only way to get there, try to reserve a seat by buying a ticket the day before. Arrive early at the stop.

## TRAIN

The CFR (Căilor Ferate Române) (Romanian State Railways) runs two types of trains: local (persoane or cursă), and express (accelerat or rapid), over 11,106 km of track. The express trains charge a supplement of US$0.75 to US$1.50 and have reserved seats only. First class costs about 50% more than 2nd class. Express train tickets with automatic seat reservations should be purchased the day before at the CFR travel agency *(agenţie de voiaj)* in town. These agencies can't provide reservations for trains leaving on the same day, however. In summer you may encounter tremendous queues at these offices and in Bucharest it's almost impossible to get a reservation.

Express tickets become available at railway stations *(gară)* just one hour before the train departs, but you're not guaranteed a seat or even a ticket if the queue is too long. Tickets for journeys between two Romanian cities on international express trains passing through the country can usually only be purchased in the railway station an hour before departure. In fact, the times for such tickets to go on sale are rounded off, so you could obtain them 1½ and even two hours in advance. Make sure you're in the right ticket line and avoid boarding a train without a ticket as you'll be charged a US$8 to US$11 supplement and might even be put off at the next station.

If you have a through international ticket, you're allowed to make stops along the route but must purchase a reservation ticket each time you reboard an *accelerat* or *rapid* train. If the international ticket was issued in Romania, you must also pay the express train supplement each time. Interrail passes (sold to those under 26) are accepted in Romania, but Eurail passes are not. Even with such a pass you must buy a reservation in the station every time you reboard an express. No fees or supplements are payable on local trains. The CFR has been known to sell a reservation for the same seat several times, so try to take it in your stride if you become a victim.

You can buy tickets for local trains at the station on the same day. Think about taking a local train whenever you encounter difficulties in obtaining an express train ticket. Since the local trains have no reservations, you don't have to worry about being kicked out of your seat once you find one. Local trains take twice as long, but often they're less crowded than the express trains. Since people are constantly getting on and off, you

will eventually get a seat, and the passengers on local trains are invariably more interesting – real Romanian country folk. First-class travel on local trains is quite comfortable and costs about the same as 2nd class on an express. Bring along a good book and enjoy a leisurely trip. You'll never find a restaurant car on a local train and only occasionally on an express, so bring food and water with you.

Sleepers *(vagon de dormit)* are available between Bucharest and Arad, Cluj-Napoca, Timişoara, Tulcea and other points and are a good way to cut hotel expenses. Book these well in advance at a CFR travel agency in town. Overnight trips on unreserved local trains are also good if you buy a 1st-class ticket and board the train early at the originating station. You can travel Braşov-Iaşi this way.

If you'll be travelling much in Romania, look out for the railway timetable booklet, the *Mersul Trenurilor*, which is sometimes sold at CFR travel agencies. On posted timetables, *sosire* means arrivals and *plecare* means departures.

### Important Railway Routes

Most visitors use one of the two main railway routes across Transylvania from Bucharest to Hungary or vice versa. The two routes are in fact one as far as Braşov (166 km and three hours from Bucharest by express). Here one line branches off west towards Arad (621 km and 10 hours from Bucharest by express) via Sibiu. A more important line continues north-west past Sighişoara and Cluj-Napoca to Oradea (651 km and 13 hours from Bucharest by express). At Teiuş a few of the Sighişoara trains swing south towards Arad.

Other main lines are from Bucharest to Mangalia (268 km, five hours by express), Bucharest to Suceava (450 km, seven hours by express) and Bucharest to Timişoara (533 km, eight hours by express). A useful route across the top of the country is Iaşi to Timişoara via Suceava and Cluj-Napoca. Beyond Cluj-Napoca some trains on this route go via Oradea and Arad, others via Simeria.

Some important domestic trains that leave

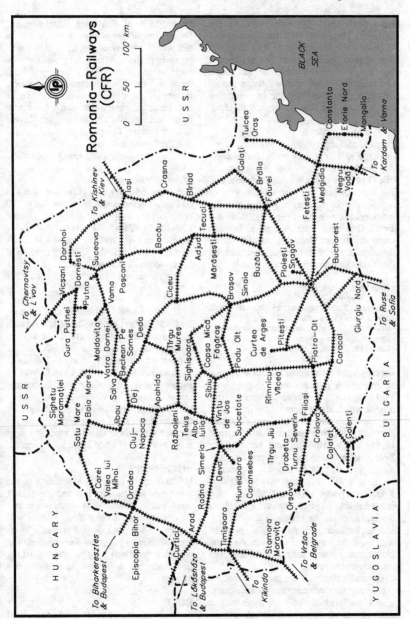

Romania – Railways (CFR)

from Bucharest's Gara de Nord are the Traian to Timişoara-Nord, the Transilvania to Oradea, the Maramureş to Baia Mare, the Bucovina to Suceava-Nord, the Moldava to Iaşi, the Dunărea to Galaţi and the Callatis to Mangalia. These first-rate trains are all classed as rapid and are the best that Romania has to offer. Reservations are required.

## CAR & MOTORBIKE

Petrol is no longer rationed in Romania but there are still long lines at the fuel pumps. Always try to keep your tank full as petrol at PECO petrol stations is sometimes sold out. The types of petrol available are normal or regular (88-90 octane), unleaded (95 octane), premium or super (96-98 octane) and diesel. Don't use normal petrol as this can damage your car. Unleaded petrol *(benzina far plumb)* is hard to find but the following PECO stations are supposed to have it:

- Piaţa Vasile Roaltă, Arad
- Dîrste, Braşov
- Bulevardul Schitu Măgureanu 15, Bucharest
- Strada Aurel Vlaicu 140, Cluj-Napoca
- Bulevardul Alexandru Lăpuşneanu 32, Constanţa
- Strada 1 mai 27, Suceava
- Calea Dorobanţilor, Timişoara

Foreign motorists must purchase special nonrefundable *benzina auto* coupons with hard currency at border crossings or tourist offices which allow them to cut in front of the lines. Station attendants won't accept payment in lei from foreigners unless a tip of US$5 or DM 10 is offered between the Romanian notes. Bring an empty fuel container with you as you're not allowed to bring in a full container. If you befriend Romanian petrol station attendants, they may be able to fill your container at the lower Romanian price. As petrol stations are few and far between, Romanians always travel with an extra supply of petrol in the boot. Occasionally you'll find that water has been mixed with the petrol.

Generally the roads are in poor condition and secondary roads can become a dirt track. Check the pressure of your tyres before entering Romania because it's often impossible to do so at Romanian petrol stations. Drive carefully as roadwork warnings are not posted and vehicles tend to stop unexpectedly in the middle of the road. You will come across slow-moving tractors pulling wagons loaded with personnel, produce, factory output, cement and manure. Trucks and bicycles sometimes don't have any lights, and since the revolution many drivers lack discipline. On the other hand, you'll find the Romanians very friendly and helpful and always eager to meet foreign motorists.

### Road Rules

The speed limit for cars in built-up areas is 60 km/h. On the open road the limits are 70 km/h for cars with a cylinder capacity under 1100 sq cm, 80 km/h for cars with a cylinder capacity of 1100-1800 sq cm, and 90 km/h for cars with a cylinder capacity over 1800 sq cm. Motorcycles are limited to 40 km/h in built-up areas and 50 km/h on the open road.

### Rental

ONT rents Dacia 1300 and Oltcit Club cars for US$15 a day plus US$0.25 a km. Rentals with unlimited mileage are also available. You can rent cars at Bucharest's ONT office, Bulevardul Magheru 7, or at ONT desks in large tourist hotels, such as the Capitol in Braşov, the Transilvania in Cluj-Napoca, the Dacia in Oradea, the Continental in Sibiu and the Bucovina in Suceava. It's possible to pick up a car at one ONT office and drop it off at another with no additional charge. You must leave a deposit of US$125 on all car rentals.

## HITCHHIKING

Hitchhiking in Romania is difficult as the little cars are usually full and there isn't much traffic on secondary roads where you may really need a ride. Your chances will improve if it's obvious that you're a Westerner. Waving a packet of Kent cigarettes at motorists is the best thing you can do, so long as it doesn't look like you're trying to sell them.

## BOAT

Navrom offers regular passenger boat

service on the Danube River from Sulina on the Black Sea inland to Tulcea, Galaţi and Brăila, daily throughout the year. Another Navrom service passes through the Iron Gates of the Danube from Orşova to Moldova Veche four times a week throughout the year. Both trips are great fun – see the respective sections in this chapter for details.

## LOCAL TRANSPORT

Public transport within towns and cities is fairly good though often overcrowded. Service is usually from 5 am to 11 pm daily. Most routes have numbers and if you ask the best dressed person at the stop for advice on which number to take, you'll find that getting around is no problem. You must purchase tickets at kiosks and tobacconists, and then validate them once aboard. Two-trip public transport tickets cost about US$0.10 for trams, US$0.15 for trolley buses and US$0.18 for regular city buses. The Bucharest Metro takes two 1 leu coins which you insert in a turnstile.

### Taxi

Government taxis are distinguished by a chequered design on the side and have meters (you pay what the meter displays). Private taxis which have the letters P or PO on the roof and have no meters are more expensive but often easier to find. If there's no meter, always bargain for a price beforehand. If the sign on the roof of a taxi says 'parti' it means *particular*, or private, and not that it belongs to a certain political party! If you're not changing money on the black market, a fresh packet of Kent cigarettes should pay for all but the longest private taxi rides.

### TOURS

ONT sightseeing tours are sometimes useful if you want to visit out-of-the-way attractions, but they generally operate only in summer and you must pay in hard currency. Book ONT tours at ONT offices or at the reception of luxury hotels. Be aware that with tourism to Romania declining, most advertised sightseeing tours will be cancelled. Foreigners are not permitted to join tours intended for Romanians and which are paid for in lei. Take this problem into consideration, especially before booking a package tour to Romania's Black Sea coast.

Among the ONT programmes on offer from Bucharest are a two-day visit to Tulcea, with a boat excursion into the Danube Delta (US$89 per person), and a two-day tour of the monasteries of Bukovina (US$93 per person). Bus tours around the country from Bucharest are available for three days (US$103 per person), five days (US$158 per person) and seven days (US$221 per person). Included are dual-occupancy hotel rooms (if you can't or don't wish to share a room, you must pay a single supplement) and some meals. At least eight people are required for a tour to run, so check with the Bucharest ONT office at Bulevardul Magheru 7 to see what tours are coming up.

ONT offices abroad can arrange three-week stays at Romanian health resorts and offer package tours to ski resorts such as Sinaia, Buşteni, Predeal and Poiana Braşov.

# Bucharest

Bucharest (Bucureşti), on the plains between the Carpathian foothills and the Danube, was founded by a legendary shepherd named Bucur and became capital of Wallachia in 1459, during the reign of Vlad Ţepeş. Now a city of over two million people, roughly the size of Budapest, Bucharest is the metropolis of Romania and has been its capital since 1862.

The broad tree-lined boulevards, park-girdled lakes, pompous public buildings and imposing monuments give the city a smooth Parisian flavour. Aside from the usual complement of museums, Bucharest has a gentle Latin air which goes well with the mysticism of the Orthodox churches. In summer the parks are relaxing, but more interesting are the colourful city streets, such as Calea Victoriei, Strada Lipscani and Strada 30 decembrie.

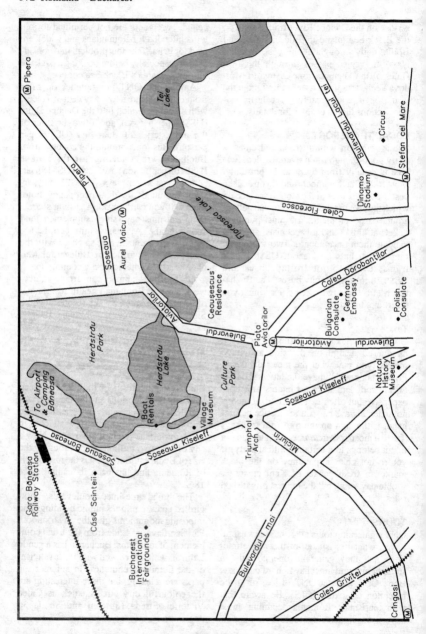

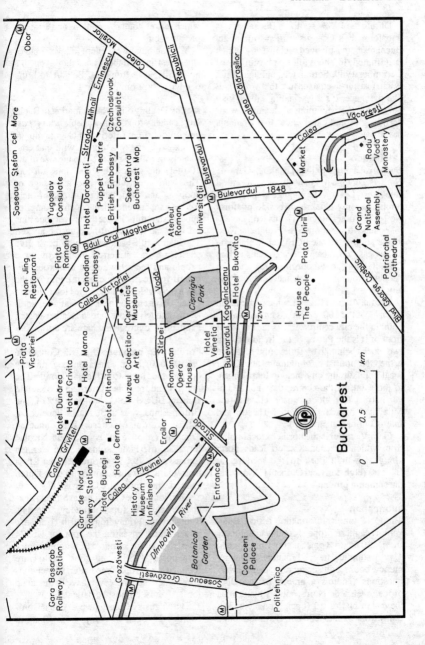

Bucharest

0    0.5    1 km

M Obor

Soseaua Stefan cel Mare
• Yugoslav Consulate
Calea Mosilor
Strada Mihail Eminescu
Calea Dorobanti
Puppet Theatre
■ Hotel Dorobanti
Czechoslovak Consulate
British Embassy
Calea Caldarasilor
Republicii

See Central Bucharest Map

Vacaresti
Calea
• Market
M
Radu Voda Monastery
Bulevardul 1848
Bdul Gral Magheru
M Piata Romana
Nan Jing Restaurant
• Canadian Embassy
Ateneul Roman
Universitatii
Bulevardul
M
M Piata Unirii
† Grand National Assembly
Patriarchal Cathedral
Bdul George Coșbuc

Calea Victoriei
Ceramics Museum
Vodă
Cismigiu Park
Hotel Bukovita
Hotel Venetia
House of The People

Muzeul Colectiilor de Arte
Stirbei
Romanian Opera House
Bulevardul Kogălniceanu
Izvor
M

M Piata Victoriei
Hotel Dunărea
Hotel Grivita
Hotel Marna
Hotel Oltenia
Calea Victoriei
Eroilor M

Calea Grivitei
Hotel Bucegi
Hotel Cerna
Calea Plevnei
History Museum (Unfinished)
Dîmbovita River
M
Entrance
Strada

Gara de Nord Railway Station M

Gara Basarab Railway Station

Grozăvesti
M
Soseaua Grozăvesti
Botanical Garden
Cotroceni Palace
M
Politehnica

During the 1980s, southern Bucharest was transformed as Ceauşescu tried to remodel Bucharest into a planned socialist city, which culminated in the violent revolution of December 1989. Fortunately, enough of old Bucharest survived to ensure that you'll still like the place. It's a fascinating city to visit but is only the beginning of the many wonderful sights and experiences that Romania has to offer.

## Orientation

Bucharest's main railway station, Gara de Nord, is a couple of km north-west of central Bucharest. Leave your luggage at the special foreigners-only cloakroom beside platform No 14. The other luggage rooms with incredible queues are not open to foreigners. Next to the station is Calea Griviţei, which you follow east to Calea Victoriei, then south to Piaţa Gheorghe Gheorghiu-Dej and the Ateneul Roman to reach the centre of the city.

Use the Ateneul Roman, which appears on the back of the 100 lei note, as an orientation point in the city centre. Across the square in front of it is the Palace of the Republic, and two blocks behind it on Bulevardul Magheru is the ONT tourist information office. Other focal points in the city include Piaţa Unirii, to the south of the centre, then Piaţa Universităţii a few blocks north, close to the Municipal Museum, National Theatre and Inter-Continental Hotel.

Piaţa Victoriei is the northern focal point, from which Şoseaua Kiseleff leads north along Herăstrău Park to the airports at Băneasa (eight km) and Otopeni (19 km) and the camping ground.

## Information

The ONT tourist information office, Bulevardul Magheru 7 (open Monday to Saturday from 7.30 am to 8 pm, Sunday from 8 am to 4 pm) supplies travel brochures, changes money, books sightseeing tours and answers questions. There's a branch of the ONT office in Gara de Nord (railway station), at the end of platform 1 (open Monday to Saturday from 9 am to 3.30 pm, closed Sunday), which makes hotel reservations and arranges private rooms.

You can buy an excellent indexed map of Bucharest in Budapest bookshops, but it's not available in Romania. Be sure to bring one with you from Hungary!

**Money** Dealing on the black market in Bucharest is dangerous. Many people who accost you on the street offering to change money are expert in tricking tourists with 'packets' – stacks or rolls of paper cut to the size of the 100 lei note with a few real notes on top. They lure their victim into a passage or doorway and then, the instant one of them has the hard currency in hand, an accomplice appears shouting 'Police!' and everyone runs off with the tourist left holding the packet. Travellers with backpacks, who can't give chase, are the preferred victims of these people and there have been numerous rip-offs. If you're still interested in exploring the Bucharest underworld, try the Hotel Nord in Calea Griviţei 143, near the Gara de Nord. It's hard to tell whose side the leather-coated gentlemen congregating here are on.

**Foreign Embassies** The US Consulate (☎ 10 4040) is on Strada Snagov, directly behind the Inter-Continental Hotel. The mailing address is American Consulate General BUCH, APO New York 09213. The British Embassy is at Strada J Michelet 24, off Bulevardul Magheru. The Canadian Embassy (☎ 506580) is at Strada Nicolae Iorga 36, off Piaţa Romană. The German Embassy (☎ 79 2580), Strada Rabat 21, is near Piaţa Dorobanţilor, with the Dutch Embassy nearby at Strada Atena 18.

The Hungarian Consulate, at Strada Alexandru Sahia 63 (open Monday, Tuesday, Thursday and Friday from 8.30 to 11.30 am), issues tourist visas on the spot for US$24 (two photos are required). A double-entry visa costs US$39 and four photos are required. You may encounter tremendous crowds here and may even have to queue up for the forms, but just be patient.

The Yugoslav Consulate is at Calea Dorobanţilor 34 (open weekdays from 10 am to

1pm). The Czechoslovak Consulate, at Strada Mihail Eminescu 124, 5th floor, apartment 12 (enter from Strada Drobeta), is open weekdays from 8 to 11.30 am.

North-east of Piaţa Victoriei Metro Station is the Polish Consulate, Aleea Alexandru 23 (open weekdays from 9 am to 2 pm). Visas cost US$30 for same-day service or US$20 for the next day. This is a good place to pick up a Polish visa.

The Bulgarian Consulate is at Strada Rabat 5 (open weekdays from 10 am to noon). Obtaining a Bulgarian tourist visa entails a 10-day wait unless you pay double the normal fee for same-day service.

## Things to See

**Southern Bucharest** In the last Ceauşescu years the southern section of Bucharest around Piaţa Unirii was 'systematised' to create a new Civic Centre. From Piaţa Unirii Metro Station walk over to the large (dry) ornamental fountain in the middle of the square to get your bearings. On the north-eastern side of the square is the **Unirea Department Store**; the main **city market** is behind it. South-west of the fountain, an older street, Aleea Marii Adunari Nationale, climbs to the **Patriarchal Cathedral** (1658) and **Patriarch's Palace** (1875). Surrounding the church are the **Grand National Assembly** (1907), a belfry (1698) and three 16th to 17th century stone crosses, a most impressive complex.

West from the fountain runs Calea Victoriei (Victory of Socialism), the widest street in Bucharest, directly towards the massive **House of the People**, an incredible Stalinist structure which was almost finished when Ceauşescu was overthrown. Some 20,000 workers and 400 architects toiled six years on this massive palace at a cost of 16 billion lei. Virtually all of the materials used were Romanian. Inside are two monumental neo-Baroque galleries that are 150 metres long and 18 metres high. At a height of 101 metres it's the tallest building in Bucharest and many historic structures had to be demolished to make way for it.

Nicolae Ceauşescu intended to house the Central Committee of the Communist Party, the State Council and the Government of Romania in his grandiose House of the People. On the converging streets surrounding it are great rows of apartment buildings to house the *nomenklatura* of privileged bureaucrats employed in nearby ministries. On the south side of the House of the People is the huge **National Institute for Science and Technology** of which Elena Ceauşescu was president. West is the new **Ministry of Defence**.

In the huge square facing the House of the People, huge mass rallies were to have been held with Ceauşescu himself addressing the throng from the first balcony. Ceauşescu intended to have the remodelling of Bucharest complete by the end of 1990 and literally hundreds of huge, almost finished buildings are seen around the city, especially in this southern part. Before work on this vast complex began, Ceauşescu had a smaller political-administrative centre similar to this built in each of Romania's district capitals!

**Central Bucharest** On the north-east side of Piaţa Unirii near the corner of Bulevardul 1848, is the CFR international railway ticket office. Penetrate the old city on the lane beside this office and veer left on Strada 30 decembrie. Enter the **Hanul Manuc** (1808), an old inn on the left, and peruse the nearby ruins of the **Old Princely Court** (Palatul Voievodal) and the oldest church (1546) in Bucharest on the right. In the 16th century, Prince Mircea Ciobanul ordered a palace to be built here. Continue west on Strada 30 decembrie a few blocks, and then, when you see a large white church, turn right on to Strada Poştei and continue to **Stavropoleos Church** (1724), one of the city's most typical churches.

Stavropoleos Church is almost behind Bucharest's most important museum, the **Museum of History** in the former Post Office Palace (1900) on Calea Victoriei. The 50 rooms on the 1st and 2nd floors tell the story of the country from prehistoric to recent times. The highlight of the museum is the fabulous treasury in the basement, which is full of objects of gold and precious stones created over the ages. There's also a complete plaster cast of Trajan's Column that depicts the conquest of Dacia by Rome. The 50 upstairs rooms were closed in 1990 as Romanian history was being rewritten, but the treasury could still be visited.

Proceed north on Calea Victoriei, Bucharest's main shopping street. After four or five blocks you will see **Crețulescu Church** (1722) on the left, then the massive **Palace of the Republic** (1937), formerly the king's palace and the seat of the State Council until 1989. The palace was the scene of heavy fighting during the revolution, and the extensive collection of European and Romanian art in the palace's four-storey **Fine Arts Museum** was damaged. Check the entrance on Strada Știrbei Vodă to see if it has been reopened. The large auditorium behind the building was once used for congresses of the Communist Party. Across Piața Gheorghe Gheorghiu-Dej from the palace is the neoclassical Ateneul Roman (1888), the city's main concert hall, with a statue of Romantic poet Mihail Eminescu in front.

Piața Gheorghe Gheorghiu-Dej was the very heart of the 1989 revolution. Ceaușescu made his last fateful speech from the balcony of the building of the **Central Committee of the Communist Party** (1950), the long white stone building across the square from Crețulescu Church. Underground passages connected the Central Committee building to the Palace of the Republic. The Securitate had occupied many of the buildings next to the Central Committee and these were pockmarked with bullet holes by fire from army troops. Most of the damage has now been repaired, but the greatest loss was the **University Library** (between the Central Committee and the Ateneul Roman), which was gutted.

North again at Calea Victoriei 107 is the nearby **Ceramics Museum**. The nearby **Muzeul Colecților de Arte**, Calea Victoriei 111 (closed Monday and Tuesday), was formed from several private art collections. Note the many fine works by the 19th century painter Nicolae Grigourescu.

**North of the Centre** A brisk walk north on Calea Victoriei will bring you to Piața Victoriei and the **Government of Romania** building, which is on the north-east side of the square. On the north-west side of Piața Victoriei is the **Natural History Museum**.

If you don't mind walking another km or so, Șoseaua Kiseleff will lead you north to the **Triumphal Arch** (1936), erected to commemorate the reunification of Romania in 1918. Alternatively, take the metro one station north to Piața Aviatorilor. Beyond this is **Herăstrău Park** and the **Village Museum** (closed Monday), with 297 rural Romanian buildings assembled here in a rich mixture of styles. First opened in 1936, the complex includes 42 houses and farms and three churches. This is one of Bucharest's most appealing attractions. In summer boats of all kinds ply the adjacent Herăstrău Lake. From the Village Museum walk back to Aviatorilor Metro Station through the park.

While you're in the area, you may wish to see the opulent former **personal residence of Nicolae and Elena Ceaușescu** not far from Piața Aviatorilor. To get there, walk north-east up Bulevardul Primăverii to the corner of Bulevardul Kalinin. The Ceaușescu mansion is the one on the south righthand corner – there may be a guard at the gate. Just across Bulevardul Kalinin from the entrance to the Ceaușescus' is the former residence of Gheorghe Gheorghiu-Dej, Romania's Communist ruler until Ceaușescu took over in 1965. Until late 1989 this entire area was reserved for the party elite and all nonresidents were kept out of the neighbourhood by police.

As you're returning to the city by metro, you may wish to get out at Piața Romană to see the plinth of an unfinished monument intended to glorify the Ceaușescu regime. In December 1989 student demonstrators clashed with police here and a year later there was talk of building a permanent memorial to the revolution on the site.

**Mad Dreams & Tragic Memories** Nicolae Ceaușescu was determined to leave an indelible mark on Bucharest and during his last decade in power he really succeeded. In order to make Bucharest a great capital city like Paris or Moscow, Ceauşescu decided that his new city needed a river, so he ordered that the **Dîmboviţa River** be rechannelled through southern Bucharest in a tremendous engineering project! To ensure a regular supply of water for the Dîmboviţa River, he had a massive dam built across the river on the west side of Bucharest, thereby creating **Dîmboviţa Lake**. Crîngaşi Metro Station is only about 500 metres from the dam, which is visible from the station. Notice how Ceauşescu's name has been chiselled out of the dedicatory inscription on the dam.

At Eroilor Metro Station, three stops south-east of Crîngaşi, is the unfinished **Museum of Romanian History**, a massive stone building with a long reviewing stand in the front where Ceauşescu used to take the salute during the annual Liberation Day Parade on 23 August. Ceauşescu intended that his tomb be placed in the centre of this museum amid the entire history of Romania! His actual burial place has been kept secret.

After seeing all these monuments to megalomania, you'll want to visit the **Heroes Cemetery**, where many of the victims of the December 1989 revolution are buried. As you come out of Pieptânari Metro Station, south of the city, you'll see the neat rows of white marble graves across Calea Şerban Vodă outside Cimitirul Şerban Vodă, the main cemetery. Romanians often bring flowers to leave at the tomb of a friend or family member or at the foot of the memorial cross. Photos of many of the dead are attached to their graves – a most moving sight.

Visible north of this cemetery are the high red marble arches of the **Memorial to the Heroes of the Struggle for the People's and the Homeland's Liberty, for Socialism** (1963) in Parcul Libertăţii. Gheorghe Gheorghiu-Dej and other early Romanian Communists are buried here. Walk along Calea Şerban Vodă towards the monument and keep going till you see the Adesga Factory on the left. The small street on the right which leads into the park opposite the

factory will bring you to Bucharest's main **crematorium** *(cenuşa)*. This is where the bodies of 40 people killed by the Securitate at Timişoara on 17 December 1989 were incinerated. Continue north-east on Calea Şerban Vodă to the next main intersection, where you'll find Tineretului Metro Station. If you don't feel quite up to returning directly to the city, **Parcul Tineretului** on the right offers an escape.

**Gardens** If you still have time to spare, hire a rowing boat in **Cişmigiu Park**, an enjoyable 19th century garden just west of the centre.

Walk west on Bulevardul M Kogălniceanu past the opera to the **Botanical Garden**, on Şoseaua Cotroceni in the eastern section of the city (Metro: Eroilor). The garden is divided into sections, with the flora of the different regions of the country in its own area. The garden opens from 7 am to 8 pm in summer and from 8 am to 5 pm in winter, but you may only visit the Botanical Museum and greenhouse on Tuesday, Friday and Sunday from 9 am to 1 pm.

The walled compound across the street from the Botanical Gardens is the 17th century **Cotroceni Palace**, restored by Ceauşescu as a personal residence but never occupied by him.

**Places to Stay**
**Camping** *Camping Băneasa*, in the forest beyond Băneasa Airport, north of the city, usually has plenty of space for campers (US$7 per person) and also has spacious bungalows with sink (US$25 single or double). In summer there's Romanian folk dancing in the adjacent restaurant daily except Monday around sunset (check). Bucharest's zoo adjoins the site. From Crîngasi Metro Station take trams No 41 and 42 to Piaţa Presei Libere (Piaţa Scinteii), the end of the line, then bus No 148 right to the camping ground. The last bus runs at around 10.30 pm from Monday to Saturday and at 8.30 pm on Sundays.

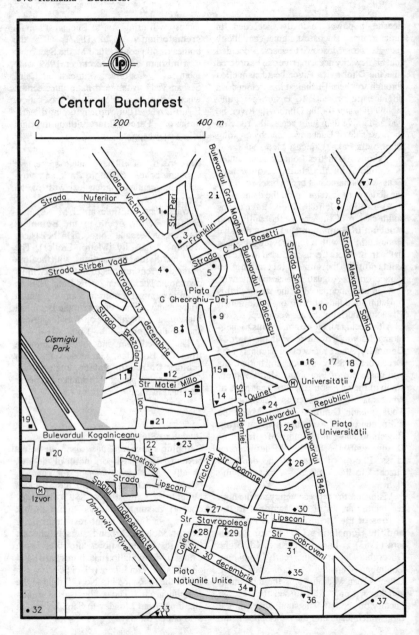

## Central Bucharest

0        200        400 m

**Private Rooms** The people at the ONT tourist office at Gara de Nord can arrange private rooms at US$10 per person in winter, US$12 per person in summer, breakfast included. This should be your first accommodation choice in Bucharest. The main ONT office, Bulevardul Magheru 7, also has

private rooms. If you're offered a private room by people at the station or on the street outside, evaluate them carefully and ask them to point out the location on a map. Make sure that you understand the price before you agree to take it.

**Hotels** There are lots of old 2nd-class hotels in Bucharest and it's usually no problem to find a room, even in midsummer. Prices average US$26/43 single/double, sometimes including breakfast (shared bath). Rates are slightly lower from November to mid-December. Staff at the ONT office at Gara de Nord will book a bed for you at one of the hotels listed in this section, or you can just set out on your own. Avoid accepting a room that faces onto a busy thoroughfare where the traffic could wake you at 5 am. Ask if breakfast is included. If you're not fully satisfied, compare prices and appearances at the next hotel before deciding. They all want to have you, because the official price you pay is many times higher than what locals pay for the same room. There are two clusters of inexpensive hotels: one around the train station and another in the city centre.

■ PLACES TO STAY

11  Hotel Opera
12  Hotel Carpați
15  Hotel Muntenia
16  Inter-Continental Hotel
19  Hotel Venetia
20  Hotel Dîmbovița
21  Hotel Cişmigiu
31  Hotel Universal
34  Hotel Rahova

▼ PLACES TO EAT

7   Restaurant Moldova
14  Casă Capşa
27  Caru cu Bere Beer Hall
33  Bucur Restaurant
34  Lacto Rahova
36  Hanul Manuc Inn

OTHER

1   Shop
2   ONT Tourist Information Office
3   Ateneul Roman
4   Palace of the Republic
5   Theodor Aman Museum
6   Hungarian Consulate
8   Crețulescu Church
9   Central Committee Building
10  US Consulate
13  Post Office
17  National & Operetta Theatres
18  American Library
22  CFR & TAROM Ticket Agency
23  Paralela 45 Travel Agency
24  University
25  Municipal Museum
26  Russian Church
28  Museum of History
29  Stavropoleos Church
30  Rapsodia Romana
32  House of the People
35  Old Princely Court
37  Market

**Hotels near Gara de Nord** The hotels closest to the railway station are the *Bucegi* and the *Cerna* and are on your right as you come out of the station's main entrance. To your left at Bulevardul G Duca 2 is the noisy and full *Hotel Dunărea*. Turn right on Calea Griviței and you'll pass the *Grivița* and *Oltenia* hotels at Nos 130 and 90 respectively. Around the corner to the left from the Hotel Oltenia is the *Hotel Marna*, Strada Buzeşti 3, one of the best of the lot. Get a room at the back to escape the noise of trams. The price at the Hotel Marna includes breakfast in the good little milk bar downstairs.

**Hotels in the Centre** There are quite a few hotels near Cişmigiu Park. The *Hotel Venetia*, Piața Mihail Kogălniceanu 2, and *Hotel Dîmbovița*, Bulevardul Schitu Măgureanu 6, are south-west of the park.

East of the park are the *Hotel Cişmigiu*,

Bulevardul Kogălniceanu 18; *Hotel Opera*, Strada Brezoianu 37; *Hotel Carpaţi*, Strada Matei Millo 16; and *Hotel Muntenia*, Strada Academiei 21. At the Hotel Cişmigiu, be sure to get a room at the back as it is quieter. The Hotel Muntenia is in a great location but is expensive at US$37/47 single/double. The *Hotel Opera* is also slightly more expensive than the others mentioned here.

South in the oldest part of the city are the *Hotel Rahova*, Calea Rahovei 2, and *Hotel Universal*, Strada Gabroveni 12.

**Expensive Hotels** If you have hotel coupons, you can stay at the *Hotel Capitol*, Calea Victoriei 29, *Hotel Majestic*, Strada Academiei 11, or *Hotel Negoiu*, Strada 13 decembrie 16, for only a few dollars more than you would pay at the 2nd-class hotels just listed.

If you don't already have the coupons, you must go first to the Automobil Clubul Român (Hertz), Strada Mihail Eminescu 7 (Metro: Piaţa Romană), to purchase them. Just showing up at these 1st-class hotels without coupons will mean that you pay prices 50% to 100% higher. All three hotels are within a block of each other in the centre of town.

**Places to Eat**
**Self-Service** There's a 'bufet express' (closes at 7 pm) between the Unirea Department Store and the main market, just off Piaţa Unirii. Otherwise try *Rapid Autoservire*, Bulevardul 1848 No 40, on the corner of Strada Lipscani, although it's very basic and you have to eat standing up.

At the *Simplon Restaurant Autoservire*, Calea Victoriei 31, next to Hotel Capitol, you can sit down to eat, but the line at the beer counter is formidable.

Also try the self-service restaurant in the *Hotel Dorobanţi* on Strada Mihail Eminescu (Metro: Piaţa Romană). If it's packed and you have lei to spare, you can eat at the regular restaurant upstairs in the hotel.

A self-service restaurant near Piaţa Victoriei is *Select*, Aleea Alexandru 18, near the Polish Consulate. The dining room upstairs, if open, is much better.

**Restaurants** The restaurant in Gara de Nord is always packed or closed, so if you want a meal while waiting for a train, cross the street to the *Bucegi Hotel*, to the right as you stand in front of the station. Service there is good.

*Lacto Marna* (closed Sunday) below Hotel Marna, Strada Buzeşti 3, serves simple meals quickly.

*Casă Capşa*, Calea Victoriei 36, is perhaps Bucharest's finest restaurant. A local institution since 1852, it will allow you to dine in style. If you can't get in for some reason, try the restaurant in *Hotel Continental*, at Calea Victoriei 56, which is also excellent.

Half a block from Casă Capsa, behind the Hotel Capitol, is the *Berlin Restaurant*, Strada Constantin Mille 4, which has an elegant restaurant downstairs and a German-style café upstairs where draught beer is served.

A typical Romanian restaurant in the southern section of old Bucharest is the *Hanul Manuc*, a historic old inn at Strada 30 decembrie 62, near Piaţa Unirii. Service in the beer garden is terrible and the indoor restaurant closes at 9 pm. Fried cheese is available for vegetarians. If you can't afford Hanul Manuc, try *Lacto Rahova*, nearby on the corner of Strada 30 decembrie and Calea Rahovie. Simple Romanian meals are served here at low prices. Since 1879 the *Caru cu Bere*, a large Munich-style beer hall on Strada Stavropoleos close to the History Museum, has served mititei (grilled meatballs) and other tasty treats along with big mugs of draught beer.

The *Restaurant Moldova*, Strada Icoanei 2, near the Hungarian Consulate, serves the cuisine of Moldavia.

The *Nan Jing Restaurant* in the Hotel Minerva on Bulevardul Ana Ipatescu, between Piaţa Romană and Piaţa Victoriei, serves exquisite Chinese food, and there's no smoking in the dining room!

The restaurants in the *Inter-Continental Hotel* on Piaţa Universităţii are about the only ones in the entire country which do have some of the things on the menu, though payment in cash dollars is required.

## Entertainment

**Theatres** The shiny new *National Theatre*, at Bulevardul N Bălcescu 2 (Metro: Universităţii), is opposite the Inter-Continental Hotel. The ticket office of the National Theatre is on the south side of the building, facing Bulevardul Republicii. Next to the National Theatre is the *Operetta Theatre*.

*Rapsodia Română*, Strada Lipscani 53 in the old town, is a folkloric theatre offering a programme that combines music, poetry and dancing – well worth visiting.

If at all possible, attend a performance at the *Ateneul Roman*, the main concert hall in Bucharest. Tickets are sold in the office on the north side of the building.

The *Teatrul Satiric Muzical 'C Tanase'*, Calea Victoriei 174 at Calea Griviţei, may have something on.

The *Teatrul de Marionete si Papusi 'Tandarica'*, (Puppet Theatre), just off Piaţa Cosmonautilor near the Dorobanţi Hotel (Metro: Piaţa Romană), presents innovative, amusing puppet shows, sometimes in the afternoon.

The *Romanian Opera House*, Bulevardul Kogălniceanu 70-72, is west of Cişmigiu Park, a little out of the way (Metro: Eroilor).

Bucharest's *circus* (closed in July and August) is on Aleea Circului, off Şoseaua Ştefan cel Mare (Metro: Ştefan cel Mare). The ticket office opens from 1 to 8 pm.

Theatre tickets are available at Casă Aria, Calea Victoriei 68-70. Check the daily papers for listings.

## Things to Buy

All of the luxury hotels have hard-currency shops where you'll find imported goods and high quality Romanian products that are not available in Romanian stores. The Comturist Magazin upstairs in the Hotel Dorobanţi is one of the largest.

Stock up on Kent cigarettes, coffee and imported liquor in the hard-currency shop at Strada Gabriel Peri 3, near the Ateneul Roman. It's often closed for inventory or some other unknown reason, but worth trying for laughs.

Muzica, Calea Victoriei 41-43, has the city's best selection of records and musical instruments.

To see what the average Romanian has to choose from, visit the Unirea Department Store on Piaţa Unirii.

Gypsies crowd along Strada Lipscani in the old town selling contraband in an impromptu free market.

## Getting There & Away

**Air** TAROM has flights several times a week throughout the year from Bucharest to Arad, Cluj-Napoca, Iaşi, Oradea, Satu Mare, Sibiu, Suceava and Timişoara. Fares are quoted in the introduction to this chapter. In summer there are also flights to Constanţa and Tulcea. (The address of the Bucharest TAROM office is given in the Train Tickets section later in this chapter.)

**Train** Almost all the express trains and many local trains use Bucharest's Gara de Nord. Many other unreserved local trains to/from Braşov, Craiova, Piteşti, Sibiu, Simeria, Suceava, Timişoara, and so on, arrive at or depart from Gara Basarab, which is a long block north-west of Gara de Nord.

Some local trains to/from Feteşti and Constanţa use Bucureşti-Obor Railway Station, which is east of the centre. Local trains to/from Snagov and a couple of accelerat trains to/from Mangalia use Gara Băneasa, on the north side of town. All local trains to/from Giurgiu arrive at Gara Progresul, on the far south side of Bucharest (take tram No 12 to Gara de Nord).

At Gara de Nord different windows sell tickets for different trains, as noted on small signs. There are separate ticket halls for 1st and 2nd class, but express train tickets are only sold an hour before departure at the station and then only if there happen to be unsold seats. One of the only posted railway timetables at Gara de Nord is in the ONT tourist office there.

The Railway Museum on Calea Griviţei, directly behind Gara de Nord, may provide some useful information for your trip.

**Tickets** The CFR travel agency (downstairs) and the TAROM airline office (upstairs) are in the same building on Strada Domniţa Anastasia, behind the Central Hotel, off Bulevardul Kogălniceanu. They are open Monday to Friday from 7.30 am to 7 pm and Saturday from 7.30 am to 1 pm. Come here to purchase tickets for planes, domestic trains or sleepers. You can also make reservations on domestic express trains here, but you must do this at least one day ahead. Visit the CFR office early in the day as it will be jammed by mid-afternoon.

Domestic train tickets are also sold by the CFR travel agency beside the Hotel Nord at Calea Griviţei 139, two blocks south of Gara de Nord. In summer you'll have to fight just to get in the door.

The CFR travel agency on the north side of Piaţa Unirii, near the corner of Bulevardul 1848, handles international train tickets. Railway fares are around US$4 to Ruse, US$11 to Sofia and US$15 to Budapest. A seat reservation costs an extra US$0.40. You must pay for international tickets in hard currency. The staff here are only required to serve 400 people a day (the 'quota') so the horrible queues hardly move. If at all possible, buy your international train tickets elsewhere!

**Train Travel in Summer** In summer you may find it impossible to get a seat reservation on an express train leaving Bucharest. One peek at the chaos in all of the offices just mentioned and you may regret having come to Romania at all. Wait a minute! Local trains (persoane and cursă) do not require reservations and getting a ticket is just a matter of spending a little time in a queue at the station. You will need to be there at least two hours early for this purpose. It's only a three-hour ride from Bucharest to Sinaia on the slowest local train and in 1st class it won't be so bad. After spending the night at Sinaia, you'll find that it's not that difficult to continue on into Transylvania by train. It takes five hours to reach Constanţa by local train, and three hours to reach Curtea de Argeş. This may be

less than perfect, but it's something you can put up with once.

## Getting Around

**To/From the Airport** Eighteen times a day (seven times on Sundays) a bus departs from the CFR/TAROM travel agency in the city centre for Otopeni International Airport (US$0.40). The times of this bus are posted at the stop outside the TAROM office – pay the driver. For transport to Băneasa Domestic Airport, ask the TAROM agent when you book your ticket.

**Public Transport** Bucharest has three flashy new metro lines offering rides for two 1 leu coins a trip. If you don't have the coins to put in the automat you must line up at a booth for change. Get into the habit of changing a bill for coins whenever you see a booth without a queue.

Purchase tickets for other forms of public transport at a kiosk. Each ticket is valid for two trips and you have to validate it once aboard. It costs US$0.10 for trams, US$0.15 for trolley buses and US$0.18 for regular buses. Tickets are checked on public transport, so be sure to validate them. All services can be extremely crowded, so hang onto your wallet.

**Underground** The Bucharest Metro, built during the last Ceauşescu years, has three lines. The present network is only half of what had been planned, but it is unlikely that it will be extended soon. Still, it is possible to get around to almost everywhere in Bucharest by metro if you don't mind walking a little.

Line M1 crosses the southern section of the city from east (Republica) to west (Industriilor). At Eroilor some M1 trains swing north to Gara de Nord, and the only way to know if a train will go to Industriilor or Gara de Nord is to read the sign on the front of the train. Many trains going from Eroilor to Gara de Nord continue east to Dristor via Piaţa Victoriei, the M3 line. The

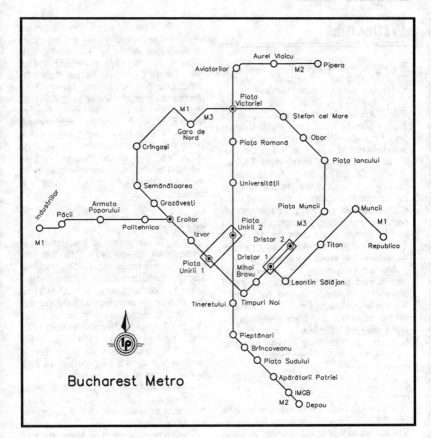

Bucharest Metro

third line is the north-south M2 line from Pipera to Depou.

The line from Gara de Nord to Piaţa Unirii takes a roundabout route through the western suburbs so it's faster to go to the centre from the train station by changing trains at Piaţa Victoriei. You can connect between lines without paying again at Piaţa Unirii, Piaţa Victoriei and Dristor.

The Bucharest Metro has modern carriages and stations but is fairly slow, with long waits between trains. Service is supposed to be every five minutes from 5 to 8 am and from 1 to 7 pm and every 10 minutes at other times, but it's often less frequent. The system closes down at around 11.30 pm. Smoking is prohibited.

The stations are poorly marked, so repeat the name of the line's end station to about three people to make sure that you're going in the right direction. At platform level, the name of the station you're at is the one with a box around it listed last on the sign. The others indicate in which direction the train is going. Few metro carriages have route maps displayed. There's usually a map at the entrance to the metro but seldom at platform level.

# Wallachia

Wallachia occupies the Danube plain north to the Carpathian Mountains' crest. The western part of Wallachia, west of the Olt River, is known as Oltenia, and the eastern half is known as Muntenia. Although the mighty Danube River flows right along the southern edge of Wallachia, the river is best seen between Moldova Veche and Drobeta-Turnu Severin in the west, where it breaks through the Carpathians at the legendary Iron Gate, a gorge of the Danube River on the Romanian-Yugoslav border. Calafat and Giurgiu are historic river ports that are connected to neighbouring Bulgaria by ferry or bridge. Towns like Curtea de Argeş and Tîrgu Jiu are jumping-off points for explorations into the Southern Carpathians.

Anyone intrigued by the Ceauşescu cult should visit his birthplace, the village of Scorniceşti, between Slatina and Piteşti. Nicolae's patronage brought facilities to Scorniceşti which few other Romanian villages enjoyed. There's no railway line, however, so it's probably only worth going there if you have your own transport.

## History

Prior to the formation of Romania in the 19th century, the Romanians were known as Vlachs, hence Wallachia. Founded by Radu Negru in 1290, the principality was subject to Hungarian rule until 1330, when Basarab I defeated the Hungarian king Charles I Robert and declared Wallachia independent. The Wallachian princes *(voivode)* built their first capitals, Cîmpulung, Curtea de Argeş, and Tîrgovişte, close to the protective mountains, but in the 15th century Bucharest gained the ascendancy, a role it has maintained to the present day. Medieval Wallachia prospered from agriculture and trade between Western Europe and the Black Sea.

After the fall of Bulgaria to the Turks in 1396, Wallachia faced a new threat, and in 1417 Mircea the Old was forced to acknowledge Turkish suzerainty. By paying tribute to the Turks, Wallachia remained largely autonomous, although trade and foreign policy were controlled by the Turks. By defying the Turks and refusing to pay tribute, Wallachian princes such as Vlad Ţepeş the Impaler and Michael the Brave became national heroes. In the 18th and early 19th century, Wallachia suffered instability first as the Turks placed Phanariote Greeks on the throne and then as the Russians dictated policy. The serfs were only freed in 1864, five years after Wallachia was united with Moldavia.

## SNAGOV

Snagov, 34 km north of Bucharest, is a favourite picnic spot with a famous 16th century church on an island in Snagov Lake. The first monastery was built on the island in the 11th century, and in 1456 Vlad Ţepeş the Impaler, the notorious 'Count Dracula', built fortifications and a prison near the church. The present church dates from 1521, with paintings done in 1563. Vlad Ţepeş himself is buried below the dome, just in front of the church's iconostasis (a high wooden partition that separates the public and private areas of an Orthodox church), so Snagov is included in all the 'Dracula' tours. A printing press was operating in the monastery as early as 1695.

The Snagov Palace, just across the lake from the island, was built by Prince Nicolae, the brother of King Carol II, in the Italian Renaissance style. During the Ceauşescu era it was used for meetings of high government officials and today it is a restaurant. Ceauşescu had a summer home on Snagov Lake, Villa No 10, which is now rented out to wealthy tourists at US$1000 a day. Villa No 1, the former abode of King Michael I, is now the summer residence of the Prime Minister, Petre Roman. Ceauşescu's two large yachts, both named *Snagov*, are used to take tourists around the lake at US$5 a head. There are two camping grounds in the lakeside oak forest.

## Getting There & Away

Three local trains a day travel between Bucharest's Gara Baneasa and Snagov. From June to September there's a train on Sunday from Gara de Nord (43 km).

ONT offers a six-hour coach excursion to Snagov (US$12) from Bucharest when there is a group of at least eight people wishing to go (a rare occurrence). For less than eight people the price jumps to US$30 per person.

## CURTEA DE ARGEŞ

Capital of Wallachia in the 14th century, the small town of Curtea de Argeş has two outstanding churches which make a visit worthwhile. The Patriarch of Constantinople recognised Curtea de Argeş as the Metropolitan of Wallachia's seat as early as 1359, and from 1793 until today the Bishop of Argeş has been based here.

As accommodation is poor, plan your departure as soon as you arrive. Three or four hours at Curtea de Argeş should be sufficient.

### Information

The tourist office, Filiala de turism, is in the Hotel Posada, Bulevardul Republicii 27-29.

### Things to See & Do

Coming from the adjacent bus and train stations, you first reach the **Prince's Church** (1352), every inch of its interior filled with striking 14th century frescoes. This church, next to the ruins of the medieval princely court, is the oldest well-preserved feudal monument in Wallachia.

A little over a km farther along the boulevard in the same direction is the famous monastery, which has the dazzling **Bishop's Church** at the centre of its courtyard. The frescoes were repainted late in the 19th century and don't compare with those in the Prince's Church. The church's architecture and exterior, however, are a unique blend of pseudo-Islamic decoration superimposed on a great Orthodox design. The tombs of the early 20th century royal family are just inside the door.

The Bishop's Church was built by Master Manole for Neagoe Basarab, prince of Wallachia from 1512 to 1517. It is said that just as the finishing touches were being added, the prince ordered that the scaffolding be removed, leaving the architect perched atop a tower. Neagoe's intention was to prevent Manole from building another church to rival this one in beauty. Manole made wings from the shingles and attempted to fly down. In the place where he crash-landed, a spring gushed forth, the **Fintina Mesterului Manole**, which you'll find in the park across the street from the monastery. Another story claims that Manole buried his wife alive beneath the church to ensure that it would never crumble.

### Places to Stay & Eat

The *Hotel Posada*, Bulevardul Republicii 27-29, near the monastery, is ultra expensive (hotel coupons are accepted), so try the *Hotel Cumpăna*, at Strada Negru Vodă 36.

North at Corbeni, on the way to Căpăţinenii (see Count Dracula's Castle) is the *Dumbrava campground*.

### Getting There & Away

Curtea de Argeş is linked to Piteşti by six local trains a day (38 km). At Piteşti you can get a connecting train to Bucharest's Gara Basarab (108 km) or Craiova (142 km).

Buses run every hour or two between Curtea de Argeş and Rîmnicu Vîlcea (35 km), where you can catch local trains north to Sibiu.

## COUNT DRACULA'S CASTLE

Twenty-three km north of Curtea de Argeş, close to the 165-metre-high Argeş Hydroelectric Dam, are the ruins of the 14th century **Poienari Citadel**. The castle's round towers are attributed to Vlad Ţepeş, Prince of Wallachia from 1456-62 and 1476-77. It's about an hour's climb up from the village and only ruined walls remain, but the views are spectacular. You can get there from Curtea de Argeş on the Căpăţinenii bus. Only one or two buses a day come this far.

North of the dam, the highway clings to

the side of Vidraru Lake and snakes up to *Cabana Bîlea Lac* in the Făgăraş Mountains. No buses go beyond Căpăţinenii and it might take a packet or two of Kent cigarettes to get a ride from a motorist. *Cabana Cumpăna* (920 metres, 138 beds) is on the west side of the lake, about three hours' walk from the castle.

## HOREZU

Horezu is a picturesque village noted for its orchards and pottery, midway between Curtea de Argeş and Tîrgu Jiu. The impressive **Hurezi Monastery** (1697) is three km north off the main road to Rîmnicu Vîlcea.

### Places to Stay

Horezu's *Stejarii campground*, Strada Vladimirescu 27, is a good alternative to the dismal accommodation in Curtea de Argeş and Tîrgu Jiu. The camp site is beside the road, right in Horezu itself, and there are bungalows, too (US$8). It's relatively clean and has a restaurant and even a toilet and cold shower (the shower is only for foreigners).

### Getting There & Away

There are buses to Horezu from Rîmnicu Vîlcea (43 km) every couple of hours, but from Tîrgu Jiu (70 km) they only run once or twice a day. Check the times carefully and try to purchase an advance ticket.

## TÎRGU JIU

Tîrgu Jiu, the seat of Gorj County, is associated with the famous Romanian sculptor **Constantin Brâncuşi** (1876-1957), whose best work may be seen in the town's parks and in the art museum at Craiova. Between 1937 and 1938, Brâncuşi, then at the peak of his career, created a stunning memorial in Tîrgu Jiu to those who fell in WW I. The Brâncuşi monuments are the only things to detain you in Tîrgu Jiu, however, so make it a quick stop on the way to somewhere else.

Brown coal from the Jiu Valley, north of Tîrgu Jiu, powers much of Romania's industry, and the miners there have long been a potent political force. In August 1977 President Ceauşescu was forced to intervene personally to end a strike by 35,000 Jiu Valley miners. The present FSN government has won support from the miners by granting them long-overdue benefits, and in June 1990 nearly a dozen trainloads of miners repaid the favour by travelling to Bucharest to beat student demonstrators whom they thought were attempting to overthrow President Iliescu by force. During the same visit, the miners took the opportunity to bash any 'profiteering Gypsies' they could lay their hands on.

### Information

The tourist office is at Strada Tudor Vladimirescu 17.

### Things to See & Do

The **Columna Infinita** (Endless Column), a towering brass-coated iron monument, is a few blocks north-east of the station. Calea Eroilor, the street with the Orthodox St Apostoli Church in the middle, runs west from the column. When you see the ornate Liceul (high school) just beyond the church, turn right and you'll soon reach the **County Museum** at Strada Griviţei 8 (closed Monday). Farther along Calea Eroilor is a park with Brâncuşi's **Poarta Sarutului** (Kissing Gate) straight ahead. Beyond it is the **Masa Tacerii** (Table of Silence), surrounded by 12 round chairs.

### Places to Stay & Eat

Tîrgu Jiu has only one expensive hotel, the *Gorjul*, Calea Eroilor 6, a block from the Kissing Gate (hotel coupons are accepted).

Both camping grounds are far from town. The one at Drăgoeni, 11 km east, has fairly frequent bus service from Piaţa Centrala but is officially for bungalow accommodation only. The *Castrul Roman Campground* is at Bumbeşti-Jiu, 18 km north of Tîrgu Jiu, which you can reach by bus or train.

### Getting There & Away

The adjacent bus and railway stations are within walking distance of the centre of town. There are no direct buses from Tîrgu

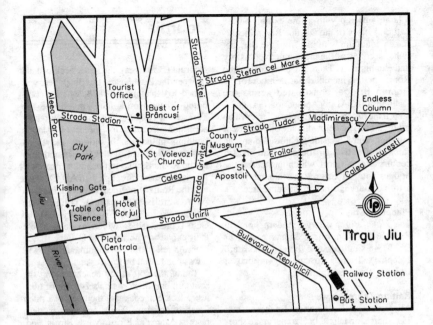

Tîrgu Jiu

Jiu to Drobeta-Turnu Severin. You have to go by train and change at Filiaşi. For Deva and Hunedoara, catch a train headed north to Simeria (130 km, four hours by local train). There are express trains to Bucharest via Craiova. The CFR travel agency is at Strada Unirii, Block 2.

For Curtea de Argeş you can take one of the infrequent buses to Rîmnicu Vîlcea via Horezu, and then another bus on to Curtea de Argeş. To reach **Retezat National Park**, take a Simeria-bound train north as far as Livezeni (45 km), where you change to one of the seven daily trains that travel the 17 km west to Bărbăteni. From here it's still a 12-km walk west along a road to the park boundary.

## DROBETA-TURNU SEVERIN

Drobeta-Turnu Severin, on the Danube between Bucharest and Timişoara, is the administrative centre of Mehedinţi County. Yugoslavia lies just across the river and a

road across the top of the huge Iron Gate Dam, just 10 km west, connects the two countries. Though of ancient origin, the present town was laid out in the 19th century and has a pleasant series of parks in the centre. A four-hour stop is enough to see the best of Drobeta-Turnu Severin.

### Orientation & Information

Drobeta-Turnu Severin Railway Station is in an ugly industrial area near the river, but the 19th century town centre is only a 10-minute walk up through the park and east down Bulevardul Republicii.

The tourist office and CFR travel agency are in the same building at Strada Decebal 43, beside the post office, not far from Hotel Parc.

### Things to See

Follow Bulevardul Republicii above the station all the way to the **Muzeul Porţile de Fier** (Iron Gate Museum) (closed Monday), a large museum with a fine exhibit on the natural history of the Danube River, including an aquarium with fish from the Danube. Other sections of the museum cover history and ethnography. There's a good deal on the Roman period, including a scale model of the **Roman bridge** constructed across the Danube in 103 AD by Apolodorus of Damascus on the orders of the Emperor Trajan. The bridge stood just below the site of the present museum, and alongside the museum are the ruins of **Castrul Drobeta**, a 2nd to 3rd century Roman fort which protected the bridge. You can also see the foundations of a 14th century basilica in the same area.

### Places to Stay

The *Hotel Parc*, a large modern hotel at Bulevardul Republicii 2, has rooms at US$31/46 single/double (hotel coupons are accepted). There's no camping ground at Drobeta-Turnu Severin.

### Getting There & Away

All express trains between Bucharest and Timişoara stop here. Local trains make shorter, more frequent trips in both directions.

### THE IRON GATE

West of Drobeta-Turnu Severin, the train runs along the north bank of the Danube through the famous Iron Gate, passing a huge concrete hydroelectric power station (1972), on top of which is a road that links Romania to Yugoslavia. You get a good view of everything from the train window. The dam has tamed the whirling Danube 'cauldrons' west of Orşova, once a major navigational hazard as the river raced through a narrow defile.

### Getting There & Away

Navrom boats travel on the Danube lake above the dam from Orşova Railway Station to Moldova Veche (99 km, 4½ hours), throughout the year on Monday, Wednesday, Friday and Saturday. Westbound the boat departs from Orşova in the afternoon at around 2.30 pm. Eastbound the boat leaves Moldova Veche at 7 am.

# Dobruja

Dobruja (Dobrogea), the squat neck of land between the Danube and the Black Sea, was joined to Romania in 1878, when a combined Russo-Romanian army drove the Turks from Bulgaria. This relatively recent accession accounts for the many Islamic buildings in the area. In antiquity the region was colonised first by the Greeks and then by the Romans, who left behind a great deal for visitors to admire. From 46 AD, Dobruja was the Roman province of Moesia Inferior. At Adamclisi (Tropaeum Traiani) the Romans scored a decisive victory over the Geto-Dacian tribes which made possible their expansion north of the Danube. Later, Dobruja fell under Byzantium, and in 1418 it was conquered by the Turks.

Today, the soft sandy beaches along the southern half of Romania's 245 km of tideless Black Sea coast are the country's main focus of tourism. There are nine modern resorts: Mamaia, Eforie Nord, Eforie Sud, Costineşti, Neptun-Olimp, Jupiter, Venus-Aurora, Saturn and Mangalia. Mamaia and Neptun-Olimp are popular among young people because of their varied entertainment possibilities, whereas Saturn, Venus, Aurora and Jupiter attract families. Eforie Nord is frequented by an older clientele attracted to the nearby spa, although lots of families and young people come here too. Costineşti is one gigantic students' playground, a real carnival if you're looking for action.

Each summer the trains are jammed with hordes of Romanians in search of fine white sand, warm water, 10 to 12 hours of sunshine and freedom from dangerous fish, sharks or undersea rocks. Far from being a nuisance, the crowds of vacationers have motivated the Romanian government to provide proper facilities, and in midsummer things become lively. You'll have interesting young neighbours in the camping grounds.

Keep in mind that the Black Sea beaches of neighbouring Bulgaria are even better and the crowds smaller. It's also cheaper farther south.

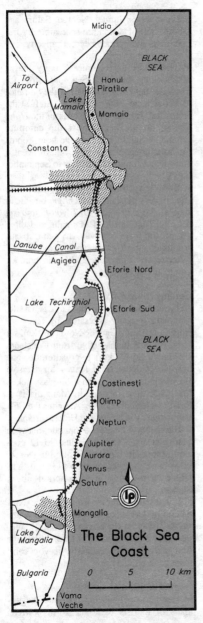

**The Black Sea Coast**

Midia

BLACK SEA

To Airport

Hanul Piratilor

Lake Mamaia

Mamaia

Constanţa

Danube Canal

Agigea

Eforie Nord

Lake Techirghiol

Eforie Sud

BLACK SEA

Costineşti

Olimp

Neptun

Jupiter

Aurora

Venus

Saturn

Mangalia

Lake Mangalia

Bulgaria

0    5    10 km

Vama Veche

## DANUBE CANAL

The train from Bucharest crosses the Danube at Cernavodă, on a great iron bridge erected in 1895. Romania's first nuclear power station, built with Canadian technology, is at Cernavodă. Between the Danube and Constanţa the train passes through the Murfatlar area, where Romania's best sweet dessert wines are produced. It then follows the new Danube Canal for almost its entire 64.2 km length. The canal, opened by President Ceauşescu in 1984, shortens the sea trip from Constanţa to Cernavodă by 400 km. There are two locks of 310 metres in length and water from the canal is used for irrigation. The canal took 30,000 people nine years to construct, but the one activity you probably won't see on it is shipping. It is hoped that eventually the Danube will be linked to the Main and Rhine rivers in Germany, making navigation possible between the North and Black seas, in which case the Danube Canal will come into its own.

## GETTING AROUND

The ONT tourist office offers various bus excursions from the beach resorts, for example, to the Roman ruins at Adamclisi (US$13) or Histria (US$11.50). There's also wine tasting at Murfatlar. The cost is US$25 for the trip, plus US$8.50 for lunch. Information should be available at any hotel or camping ground reception. Foreigners aren't allowed to go in the same tour groups as Romanians, so when there aren't enough foreign tourists around, the sightseeing tours for foreigners are cancelled.

## MANGALIA

Mangalia, at the southern end of the Romanian Black Sea strip, is a good place to go for starters. Founded by Dorians from Heraclea Pontica at the end of the 6th century BC, Callatis (now Mangalia) offers several archaeological sites. More of a draw are the workers' resorts along the Romanian Riviera to the north: Saturn, Venus, Aurora and Jupiter. Saturn is right next to Mangalia and thus is crowded with locals, with long queues at the food stalls. Beach hopping's the thing to do and on a hot summer's day it really becomes a zoo.

## Orientation & Information

There's an ONT tourist office in the Mangalia Hotel, Strada Costache Negri 2. The staff may know if any sightseeing tours are on offer.

## Things to See

The city of Mangalia doesn't have a lot to offer, yet it is worth a couple of hours. There are two Casăs de Cultura. Near the train station is a new white casă; an older casă with a large mural on the façade is a few hundred metres away in the centre of town. Cultural events take place in the older casă on most summer evenings and foreign tourists are welcome. Near the post office, not far from the old casă, is the Turkish **Sultan Esmahan Mosque** (1460) open from 9 am to noon and from 2 to 7 pm in summer.

Back near the new casă is the **Callatis Archaeological Museum** (open from 9 am to 8 pm in summer) which houses a good collection of Roman sculpture, and so on. Recently, a 4th century necropolis was destroyed to make way for a high-rise building next to the museum. Down on the beach, behind the Hotel Mangalia, are the ruins of a 6th century **palaeo-Christian basilica** and a fountain that dispenses sulphurous mineral water.

## Places to Stay

**Camping** One place to stay at is *Saturn Camping*, less than a km from Mangalia Railway Station (you can see the tents from the train window as you're coming in). You can get there from the station on foot or take bus No 14, 15, or 20 two stops north, right to the camping ground entrance. Though it does get very crowded, there's almost always space for people staying in tents (US$5 per person). This camping ground offers shady trees, snack and beer bars, occasional warm showers, and easy access to coastal buses and the beach.

Alternatively, there are similar camping grounds in the string of tourist resorts to the north – Venus, Jupiter, Neptun, Saturn and Olimp – all of which are accessible by frequent bus and operate beyond capacity.

**Hotels** There are countless luxury tourist hotels along the Black Sea coast strip, for example, the *Hotel Adriana* at the entrance to Venus, near *Venus Camping*. Staff at the Auto Club Roman (ACR) desk in the *Hotel Sirena*, on the beach near the camping ground in Saturn, can arrange hotel rooms for hotel coupon holders in Saturn, Venus, Aurora and Jupiter (from June to September only).

If you're aged 14 to 30, have a student card and are very persistent, you *might* be able to stay at the *Costineşti BTT youth tourism resort*, 17 km north of Mangalia and three km off the main highway. To avoid disappointment, try to have the people at the ONT office reserve one of the 5330 beds there for you in advance.

## Getting There & Away

At the end of the line on the Black Sea route, Mangalia is easily accessible by fast train from Bucharest's Gara de Nord (269 km, six hours). Local trains arrive from Constanţa six times a day (44 km). Every afternoon one unreserved local train leaves for Braşov. Board the train early with a 1st-class ticket. The CFR travel agency in Mangalia is at Strada Ştefan cel Mare 16. At Venus the CFR travel agency is beside the Hotel Adriana.

Buses No 12 and 20 operate between Mangalia and Constanţa. Bus No 12 goes along the main highway, while bus No 20 stops at all the beach resorts as far north as Olimp, terminating at Constanţa Railway Station.

If you're heading for Bulgaria, take a bus or taxi or hitchhike 10 km south to Vama Veche and cross the border on foot. Be prepared for a six-km walk to Durankulak, the first settlement in Bulgaria, if you can't manage to hitch a ride.

## Getting Around

In summer, open-sided jeeps haul wagonloads of tourists back and forth between

Mangalia and Olimp for US$0.20 a ride or US$0.60 for a complete trip, a fun way to familiarise yourself with what the area has to offer. The jeeps stop at all the beaches.

## NEPTUN-OLIMP

Before the 1989 revolution, Neptun and Olimp formed a separate tourist complex under the direct control of the Central Committee of the Communist Party of Romania. The resorts of Jupiter, Aurora, Venus and Saturn were administered separately from Mangalia and this administrative division still exists. Opened in 1960, Neptun-Olimp was formerly reserved for foreign tourists and important Romanians but the hotels are now open to everyone. Because of its unique history, Neptun-Olimp is perhaps the nicest and most chic of Romania's Black Sea resorts.

### Information

In Neptun there's a tourist information office upstairs in the shopping arcade, across the street from Hotel Decebal.

The CFR travel agency in Hotel Apollo, Neptun, sells train tickets (in summer only).

### Things to See

Ceauşescu had a summer residence at Neptun, the **Villa Nufar**, which you can now visit for US$9; the price includes a drink. All of the luxury villas in this area were reserved for members of the Ceauşescu family or for high party officials. Most are now rented out to tourists. Expect to pay US$160 a night for a double apartment in one of these units.

### Places to Stay

There are two camping grounds. *Camping Olimp* is at the northern end of the Olimp tourist strip, and *Neptun Camping* is by the lagoon, at the southern end of Neptun.

If you have hotel coupons, go directly to the ACR desk at *Hotel Belvedere*, Olimp (open from June to September only). The people there will find you a room at a 1st-class hotel in Neptun or you can pay an extra US$9.50 to upgrade your coupon and stay at the luxury category *Hotel Amfiteatru* in

Olimp. If you don't already have hotel coupons, the ACR representative at Hotel Belvedere may sell them to you.

### Getting There & Away

Halta Neptun Railway Station is within walking distance of the Neptun-Olimp hotels, midway between the two resorts. All of the trains that travel between Bucharest or Constanţa and Mangalia, local and express, stop here. Mangalia is nine km south of Neptun-Olimp by road and Constanţa 38 km north.

## EFORIE NORD

Eforie Nord, 17 km from Constanţa, is the first large resort south of the city and is within commuting distance. The beach is below 20-metre cliffs along the eastern side of the town, and walls built out into the sea trap additional sand. Tiny Lake Belona, just behind the sea beach at the southern end of town, is a favourite bathing place, as its water is much warmer than the Black Sea.

Just south-west of this is Techirghiol Lake, a former river mouth famous for its black sapropel mud baths, which are effective against rheumatism. The cold mud baths are the only place in Romania where mud-covered nudism is allowed (separate areas are designated for women and men). The lake's waters are four times as salty as the sea; the lake is in fact two metres below sea level.

### Places to Stay & Eat

*Camping Singai*, a few hundred metres west of Eforie Nord Railway Station, is right on Techirghiol Lake, but rather far from the Black Sea beaches. The shortest way to reach the camping ground is to walk west to the far end of the railway platform, cross the tracks and follow a path to a breach in the wall. Unfortunately, Singai is noisy and only recommended if you're arriving late from Bucharest and need a quick place to crash.

Better camping is available at *Camping Meduza* near the *Hotel Prahova* on the north side of Eforie Nord. It's closer to the beach but much farther from the train station.

If you have hotel coupons, ask for a room at the ACR desk in the *Europa Hotel*, Bulevardul Republicii 19 in the centre of town (open from June to September only). While you're at the Europa, sample the sirloin à la Europa in the hotel restaurant.

### Getting There & Away

All trains between Bucharest or Constanţa and Mangalia stop at Eforie Nord. The CFR travel agency next to the post office in Eforie Nord sells train tickets.

Buses No 10, 11, 12 and 20 leave for Eforie Nord from the street beyond the tram stop, just south of Constanţa Railway Station.

### CONSTANŢA

Constanţa, midway between Istanbul and Odessa, is Romania's largest port. Already in antiquity, the Greek town of Tomis, which the Romans renamed Constantiana, was the main port in these parts. After Küstendje (the name of the town under Turkish rule) was taken by Romania in 1877, Constanţa grew in importance, with a railway line being built to it from Bucharest.

Central Constanţa

0    100    200 m

Much remains today from every period of Constanța's colourful history. Despite ugly industrial development to the north and west, the picturesque old town has a charming Mediterranean air. The excellent museums are within easy reach of crowded city beaches. It's almost a world apart.

### Orientation

Constanța Railway Station is about two km west of the old town, and most of the trolley buses that leave from in front of the station go in that direction. The city beach is at the end of Bulevardul Republicii. From Hotel Continental, Bulevardul Tomis runs southeast to Piața Ovidiu, in the heart of old Constanța.

### Information

The ONT tourist information desk is inside the Hotel Continental, Bulevardul Republicii 20, on the corner of Bulevardul Tomis.

The Ziare Newsstand, Bulevardul Tomis 38, sometimes has foreign newspapers in English.

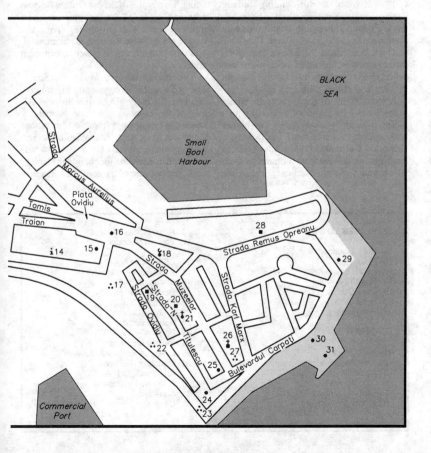

**Things to See**

Constanţa's most renowned attraction is the **Archaeological Museum** on Piaţa Ovidiu, with exhibits on three floors. Most of the cases bear captions in English and German. The most unusual objects are kept in the treasury downstairs. Don't miss the 2nd century AD sculpture of a Glykon, which is a serpent with the muzzle of an antelope and the eyes, ears and hair of a human. Also outstanding is the Goddess Fortuna, a horn of plenty in her arms, with Pontos, god of the Black Sea, leaning on a ship at her feet. The archaeological fragments of Roman Tomis spill over onto the surrounding square. Facing these is another museum, which shelters a gigantic 3rd century **Roman mosaic** discovered in 1959 and left *in situ*. The statue of Ovid, erected on Piaţa Ovidiu in 1887, commemorates the Latin poet, who was exiled to Constanţa in 8 AD and is thought to have been buried there.

A block south of this square on Strada Muzeelor is a large **mosque** (1910) with a 140-step minaret you may climb. Two blocks farther down the same street you'll find the **Orthodox Cathedral** (1885). One block to the right is the Saligny monument from which you'll get an excellent view of the modern harbour. Go east on the lovely waterfront promenade till you reach the **casino** (1904) and **aquarium**, which are face to face. Farther along the promenade is the **Genoese lighthouse** (1860) and the pier, with a fine view of old Constanţa.

The other worthwhile sights can be covered by returning to Piaţa Ovidiu and Bulevardul Tomis, which you follow northwest to the Hotel Continental. Halfway up Bulevardul Tomis you will pass another mosque and the **Folk Art Museum**, in an ornate building on the right. When you reach the hotel, turn left and explore Victoria Park, which has remains of the 3rd century **Roman city wall**, pieces of Roman sculpture and a modern **Victory Monument**. From the terrace across the street from the monument, you'll have another good view of the modern commercial port.

The **Naval History Museum**, Strada Traian 53, offers exceptionally informative exhibits on early Romanian history. Although the captions are all in Romanian, much can be garnered from the illustrations alone. As in all other Romanian museums, no mention is made of the 1941-44 war years, when Romania fought on the German side. The last year of the conflict, when they

| PLACES TO STAY | | |
|---|---|---|
| 4 | Hotel Continental | |
| 5 | Hotel Victoria | |
| 10 | Hotel Constanţa | |
| 13 | Hotel Tineretului | |
| 19 | Casă Cu Lei | |
| 20 | Hotel Intim | |
| 28 | Hotel Palace | |

| OTHER | |
|---|---|
| 1 | Post Office |
| 2 | TAROM Office |
| 3 | Art Gallery |
| 6 | Old City Wall |
| 7 | Fantasio Musical Theatre |
| 8 | Victory Monument |
| 9 | Naval History Museum |
| 11 | Folk Art Museum |
| 12 | Mosque |
| 14 | CFR Travel Agency |
| 15 | Archaeological Museum |
| 16 | Statue of Ovid |
| 17 | Roman Mosaic |
| 18 | Mosque |
| 21 | Catholic Church |
| 22 | Roman Baths |
| 23 | Basilica Ruins |
| 24 | Saligny Monument |
| 25 | Ion Jalea Sculpture Museum |
| 26 | Orthodox Cathedral |
| 27 | Archaeological Site |
| 29 | Genoese Lighthouse |
| 30 | Aquarium |
| 31 | Casino |

were on the 'right' side, receives full attention – an interesting approach to history.

Constanţa's **Art Gallery**, at Bulevardul Tomis 22, opposite the Hotel Continental, has a large collection of paintings by Nicolae Grigourescu and other well-known Romanian painters.

### Places to Stay

Singles/doubles at the *Hotel Continental*, Bulevardul Republicii 20, on the corner of Bulevardul Tomis, cost US$45/58. Ask about private rooms at the ONT tourist information desk in the hotel, though there's no guarantee that there will be any.

The *Hotel Victoria*, Bulevardul Republicii 7 across the street from the Hotel Continental, costs only half as much, and the *Hotel Constanţa*, Bulevardul Tomis 46, is an even better bet at US$15/24 single/double, but is usually 'full'. Try anyway.

*Hotel Palace*, Strada Remus Opreanu 5 in the old town, is in a beautiful location that overlooks the sea but it is overpriced at US$51/64 single/double.

A better top-end choice would be the *Casă Cu Lei*, or Lions' House, Strada Nicolae Titulescu 27, an 1898 building not far from the mosque in the old town (you might notice the sign while visiting the Mosaic Museum). It has only four nicely decorated rooms, so you don't have much hope without a reservation.

Another lovely old-world hotel is the *Hotel Intim*, Strada Nicolae Titulescu 9, just around the corner from the Casă Cu Lei. Singles/doubles cost US$63/93 and if those prices don't bother you, you'll be delighted with this place. This hotel has an elegant indoor dining room and a pleasant airy terrace.

None of these hotels accepts hotel coupons.

### Places to Eat

You will find many restaurants in every category, but the deluxe ones are along Bulevardul Tomis, between Hotel Continental and the Archaeological Museum. Take your pick. The *Lacto-Vegetarian Daina*, Bulevardul Tomis 78, is good and cheap, but

service is very slow and, despite the name, mostly meat dishes are served.

If the occasion calls for something better, try the *Casă Cu Lei* mentioned earlier. Even if you're not eating, the bar there is a pleasant oasis.

### Entertainment

The *Fantasio Musical Theatre*, Bulevardul Republicii 11, offers good programmes. The *State Dramatic Theatre* is in the park opposite the post office, Bulevardul Tomis, on the corner of Strada Ştefan cel Mare. The ticket office is at Bulevardul Tomis 97.

In summer, circuses are often set up by the lake near the Delfinarium between Constanţa and Mamaia.

### Things to Buy

Magazin Plafar, Strada Mircea cel Bătrîn 3, just off Piaţa Ovidiu, sells excellent, cheap herbal remedies for stomach problems, etc.

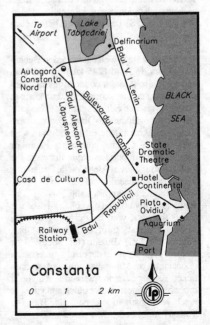

Constanţa

0    1    2 km

Black marketeers outside the Hotel Continental change money, but take care. There are Comturist hard-currency shops in the Continental and Palace hotels.

Perinita, Bulevardul Tomis 76, sells folk art souvenirs, including attractive clothing for women.

### Getting There & Away

**Air** TAROM, Strada Ştefan cel Mare 15, offers flights from Constanţa to Bucharest from April to October. In July and August there are flights several times a week to Arad, Cluj-Napoca, Iaşi, Oradea, Sibium, Suceava and Timişoara. Sample fares are provided in the introduction to this chapter.

If getting a train ticket out of Constanţa in mid-summer seems impossible, you may be amazed at how easy and inexpensive it is to book a TAROM flight to almost anywhere in the country. These direct flights don't stop at Bucharest and are an excellent way to avoid the transportation bottleneck in midsummer. TAROM runs a bus from its Constanţa office to Mihail Kogălniceanu International Airport (25 km, US$0.50) 1½ hours before each flight.

**Train** Constanţa is well connected to Bucharest's Gara de Nord (225 km) by fast train and there are through connections to Transylvania in summer. Local trains run north to Tulcea (via Medgidia), south to Mangalia and west to Bucureşti-Obor. For northern Romania take a Bucharest-bound train west to Feteşti (79 km) and change for Făurei or Buzău. You can purchase train tickets at the CFR travel agency at Aleea Vasile Canarache 4, near the Archaeological Museum.

In summer all express trains leaving Constanţa are fully booked a week in advance. If this is the case, your best escape may be a persoane (local) train to Bucureşti-Obor, Făurei (for Iaşi), Buzău (for Suceava) or Braşov. Try to board at the originating station (Constanţa or Mangalia) with a 1st-class ticket. As there are no reserved seats, you'll probably get one if you're quick and you will reach your destination eventually. Trains to Tulcea cannot be booked ahead.

From mid-June to mid-October, there's a daily local train from Medgidia to Kardam in Bulgaria, but it leaves Medgidia at 6 am and arrives back just after midnight!

### MAMAIA

Mamaia, a crowded eight-km strip of sand between Lake Mamaia (or Siutghiol) and the Black Sea, just north of Constanţa, is Romania's Miami, with 57 hotels and countless tourists. The abundant greenery and parklike environment makes Mamaia restful despite the crowds. The main thing to do here is swim and enjoy the sun, though historic Constanţa is just a bus ride away. Romania's first gambling casino was established here.

### Things to See & Do

An excursion boat ferries tourists across the freshwater Lake Mamaia from the wharf near Mamaia Casino to **Ovidiu Island** every hour or two during the summer season. Try the local seafood in the thatch-roofed restaurant on the island if you have time.

All kinds of activities such as windsurfing, water-skiing, yachting, rowing, pedal boats and tennis are laid on, but you must pay for these in hard currency.

### Places to Stay & Eat

The *camping ground* at Mamaia is at the northern end of the Black Sea coast six-km strip, 200 metres beyond the terminus of trolley buses No 41 and 50. However, it is small and always chock-a-block in summer.

The *Hanul Piraţilor Campground* is between the main road and the beach, three km north of the terminus of trolley buses No 41 and 50 (bus No 23 runs between this terminus and the camping ground). There's always tent space here (it costs US$5 to pitch your own tent) but no bungalows. Across the road is the *Hanul Piraţilor Restaurant*, where a band plays on a stage designed like a pirate ship (US$2.50 cover charge). You can enjoy a good mixed grill and plenty of wine. Book a table ahead if you can, though English speakers are usually admitted promptly without reservations. Ask what time the main show begins. There's another camping ground with less shade between Mamaia and this one, but just ask for the Hanul Piraţilor, which everyone knows.

For information on hotel rooms, ask at the tourist office in the *Perla Hotel*, at the southern end of the strip. The staff can organise singles/doubles from US$33/38, but in midsummer only more expensive rooms will be available, if you're lucky.

If you have hotel coupons, go directly to *Hotel Siret* at the northern end of Mamaia, near the trolley bus terminus (open from June to September only). A coupon should get you a room – there is no way you'll get a room here without a coupon. If the Siret doesn't have any rooms, the staff will place you in a similar hotel nearby.

### Getting There & Away
Travelling between Constanţa and Mamaia by trolley bus is easy. Catch No 41 from Constanţa Railway Station, or No 50 from the city centre.

### HISTRIA
The Graeco-Roman ruins at **Cetatea Histria**, the oldest ancient settlement in Romania, are on the coast, about 70 km north of Constanţa. Founded in 657 BC by Greek merchants from Miletus, Histria was protected by the Dacians and absorbed by the Romans. Beyond the **museum** (closed Monday) is a city wall complete with towers and gates, built at the end of the 3rd century AD with materials from buildings destroyed during the Gothic invasion of 248. You will also see the foundations of basilicas, residences and temples. By the end of the 7th century AD, Histria had been abandoned.

### Getting There & Away
Histria is difficult to reach unless you go on an ONT sightseeing tour (US$11.50). A crowded local bus runs a couple of times a day between Autogară Constanţa Nord (take tram No 100 from the train station) and Mihai Viteazu, which is on the railway line to Tulcea, but it will drop you 11 km from the site. There's a basic camping ground at Histria if you get stuck.

# The Danube Delta

The triangular 4340-sq-km Danube Delta on the Black Sea, just south of the Soviet border, is the youngest land in Europe. Here the mighty Danube splits into three arms, the Chilia, Sulina and Sfîntu Gheorghe channels. It's an ever-changing environment of marshes, reeds and sand bars, as the river carries over two tons of silt a second, making Romania 40 metres longer each year.

The flora and fauna are unique. The only large pelican colony in Europe is found here, along with another 250 species of birdlife. The converging migratory bird routes make this the richest area of its kind in Europe. Among the dazzling variety of insects are mosquitoes, which you'll encounter everywhere from May to July. Locals come to the delta to fish for carp and sturgeon. Small boats are required to see the wildlife, as the main channels are swept clean by hydrofoils.

About 10% of the delta is included in nature reserves, but these are poorly managed. In 1983 Ceauşescu approved plans to reclaim 38.4% of the Danube Delta for agriculture, fish farming and forestry. Six years later, with less than half the project complete, President Iliescu cancelled the plan, which would have seriously affected the ecological balance at the Danube mouth.

### GETTING AROUND
Passenger boats regularly ply the Danube Delta, making access relatively easy. 'Rapid' hydrofoils run from Tulcea to Sulina and Galaţi, but only 10 kg of luggage per person may be carried and departures are often cancelled without notice.

A better choice would be the 'classical' ferry boats from Brăila to Galaţi, Tulcea and Sulina. Eastbound these depart from Brăila for Tulcea at 7 am, and leave Tulcea for Sulina at around 1.30 pm, daily throughout the year (up to 30 kg luggage is allowed). Ferry tickets go on sale at the terminals about an hour before departure. In summer the queues are long, so get in the correct line early.

There are also Navrom ferries to Periprava (103 km) and Sfintu Gheorghe (113 km) on the north and south arms of the Danube, but foreign tourists aren't allowed on those services.

### Tours

There are ONT tours through the delta from Tulcea, which you can pay for in Western currency (US$27 or more, including lunch at Crişan, which is 43 km from Tulcea). Sign up for the tour at the Delta Hotel in Tulcea. The delta wildlife generally moves off quickly when it hears these noisy tourist boats coming.

### TULCEA

Tulcea, the seat of Tulcea County, which includes the Danube Delta, is a modern industrial city with little to detain you more than a couple of hours. Accommodation is a problem in Tulcea, so try to schedule your visit so that you don't have to stay there. Tulcea's position on the Danube at a crossing of transportation routes makes this difficult, but try to arrive before 1 pm so that you can catch an onward ferry on the same day. Central Tulcea was totally rebuilt during the 1980s and its setting against the river makes it rather attractive despite the polluting aluminium smelter.

### Orientation

Tulcea's bus and railway stations and Navrom ferry terminals are next to each other by the Danube. Lake Ciuperca near the railway station is completely surrounded by a park. Central Tulcea focuses on the riverfront promenade, where you will see boats and people constantly coming and going. The promenade stretches eastward along the river to the Delta Hotel, and inland a block

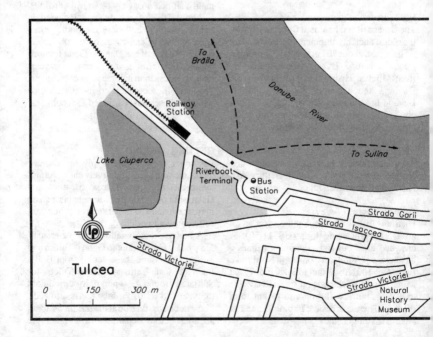

is Piaţa Civică, the modern centre of rebuilt Tulcea.

## Information

Try the tour desk of the Delta Hotel, Strada Isaccea 2. Ask for the excellent ONT tourist map *The Danube Delta*. Across the street from Union Restaurant is a bookshop (closed Thursday and Sunday) that sells detailed maps of the delta, when these are available.

## Things to See

As you stroll along the river, you'll see the **Independence Monument** (1904) on Citadel Hill at the far eastern end of town. You can reach this by following Strada Gloriei from behind the Egreta Hotel to its end. You'll find a fairly good **historical museum** just below the monument and the view is worth the trip. Some ruins of ancient Aegisos are seen here. On your way back, look out for the minaret of the Turkish **Azizie Mosque** (1863) down Strada Independenţei.

The **Natural History Museum and Aquarium**, Strada Progresului 32, west of Piaţa Civică, behind Patria Cinema, should certainly be visited if you have time. There is a good collection of Danube fish. In front of the Greek Orthodox church opposite the museum is a memorial to local victims of the 1989 revolution.

## Places to Stay

Of Tulcea's two high-rise hotels, the *Egreta Hotel*, at Strada Păcii 1, is the cheaper, but at US$35/40 for a single/double with shared bath it's no bargain. All the rooms at the *Delta Hotel*, Strada Isaccea 2, cost US$51 double (no singles). The Delta accepts hotel coupons.

A no-camping regulation within Tulcea's city limits is strictly enforced by police. At a pinch, take the hourly passenger ferry across

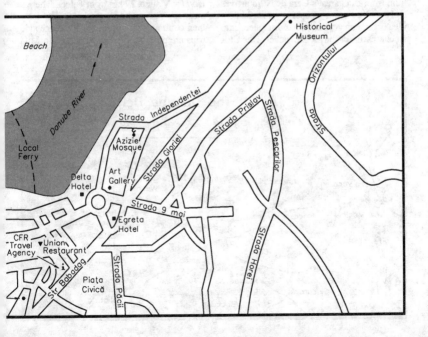

the Danube and follow the path downstream a little. There are places to pitch a tent along the river there.

The closest official camping ground is the *Pelicanul* near Murighiol (Independenta), 40 km south-east of Tulcea by bus, and then three km on foot. The facilities here are abysmal and the only return bus to Tulcea departs from Murighiol at 5 am! Give it a miss.

### Places to Eat

The easiest place to eat at is the cafeteria at the *Union Restaurant*, Strada 23 august, near the Delta Hotel. There's another good cafeteria on the back side of the *Egreta Hotel* (not the main hotel restaurant you see first).

### Getting There & Away

There are local trains from Constanţa via Medgidia (179 km, four hours). The daily express train from Bucharest's Gara de Nord takes five hours (335 km). An overnight local train from Bucharest's Gara de Nord arrives early and conveys sleepers – an excellent idea if you can get one. Book your sleeper to Bucharest or just buy a train ticket at the CFR

travel agency on Strada Babadag, opposite Piaţa Civică. Buses arrive in Tulcea from Constanţa, Brăila and Galaţi.

If you arrive in Tulcea around noon on a train from Bucharest or Constanţa, hurry to the nearby Navrom Riverboat Terminal and get right in line for a ticket on the Sulina ferry, which leaves around 1.30 pm. Ask the person in line behind you for Sulina, to make sure that you're in the right line. The Tulcea-Sulina ferry operates daily all year.

### ON THE DANUBE

The only part of the delta readily accessible to foreigners is the middle arm of the Danube, which cuts directly across from Tulcea to Sulina (71 km). Much river traffic uses the Sulina arm, which was straightened for this purpose in the 19th century. You pass huge ocean-going ships rising out of the water as well as kayakers in their diminutive craft.

The Sulina ferry's first stop is at the *Salcia Hotel* at Maliuc, 27 km from Tulcea. There's a camping ground near the hotel. The ferry then continues to Crişan, from whence side trips are possible on smaller ferries to Mila

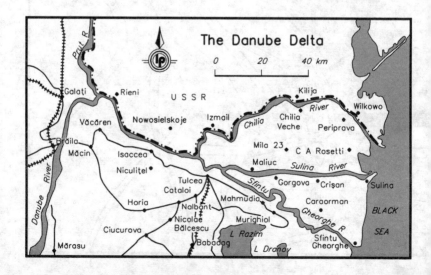

The Danube Delta

23 and Caraorman. The 1st-class *Lebăda Hotel* is on the opposite side of the Danube from the Crişan ferry landing and a km upstream (hotel coupons are accepted). Once again, you may camp in the vicinity of the hotel. Rowing boats to explore the side channels are sometimes available at Crişan and Maliuc. Take some food and water with you on your expedition into the delta.

## SULINA

Sulina is the highlight of the ferry trip from Tulcea and you get a great view of it as the ship sails through the middle of town on its way to the landing. You will pass derelict old dredges and ships. A canal dug from 1880 to 1902 shortened the length of the Sulina arm from 83.3 to 62.6 km. After WW I Sulina was declared a free port and trade boomed, a period that Jean Bart describes in his novel *Europolis*. Greek merchants dominated business here until their expulsion in 1951. Now the Sulina arm has been extended eight km out into the Black Sea by two lateral dykes.

Sulina's riverfront promenade is most evocative at sunset, as the pink fireball drops behind the Danube. Sulina is not connected to the European road network so there are few vehicles. Although not at all as good a base as Maliuc or Crişan for seeing the delta wildlife, Sulina is a romantic spot, palpably one of the extreme edges of Europe.

### Things to See & Do

The only specific attractions at Sulina are the old lighthouse you pass between the ferry landing and the hotel, and an overgrown 19th century British cemetery on the way to the beach. Carry on for one km to this beach where you'll see how the accumulation of Danube silt has required the creation of a channel far out into the Black Sea. You'll also see a long line of Romanian radar installations among the dunes, pointed at the Soviet Union. This broad beach continues 30 km south, all the way to Sfîntu Gheorghe.

### Places to Stay & Eat

You can stay at the expensive *Sulina Hotel*, Strada Deltei 207 (hotel coupons accepted), or you can camp for free in the cow pasture opposite. Aside from the hotel, there's nowhere decent to eat.

### Getting There & Away

It's possible to go straight through from Sulina to Brăila or vice versa on Navrom classical ferries which connect at Tulcea, an eight-hour trip. Through tickets are sold, saving you the major inconvenience of having to line up again in Tulcea. You sometimes change boats at Tulcea and may have a few hours to look around.

## UPRIVER FROM TULCEA

The ferry trip between Tulcea and Galaţi is especially interesting since the Danube here marks the boundary between Romania and the USSR. You'll sail along the electric fence which encloses this vast, enigmatic country. You get a fine continuous view of Rieni, the second most important Soviet Danube port (the most important port is Izmail, on the northern arm of the Danube), perhaps the best free peek possible into the USSR.

Galaţi is a large industrial city with a steel mill and docks and shipyards stretching for km along the riverside. Galaţi's massive housing complexes, which fill the city and cover entire hillsides, are best appreciated from aboard ship. It's strongly recommended that you continue to Brăila, the ferry's next port of call (you may have to change boats in Galaţi).

## BRĂILA

Brăila, the seat of Brăila County, is a sleepy 19th century Danube town full of charming turn-of-the-century mansions, tree-lined boulevards and restful parks. Piaţa Lenin, a lovely central square at the heart of the city, is complete with statues, fountain, tower, church and people sitting on benches under the trees. It's a perfect place to end your trip. You can get onward connections to Bucharest and northern Romania by train.

### Orientation & Information

From the Navrom ferry terminal, walk

straight up Strada Împăratul Traian to Piaţa Lenin, the central square. To reach Brăila Railway Station, about two km north-west at the end of Strada Victoriei, catch a city bus from in front of the CFR Agenţie de Voiaj (travel agency) on this square.

### Things to See

In the middle of Piaţa Lenin is a 17th century **mosque** that was converted into a Romanian Orthodox church in 1835, and a bust of the Emperor Trajan (1906). The **Historical Museum** (closed Monday) is on the north side of Piaţa Lenin. Check for performances at the Dramatic Theatre on the west side of the square. On the east side of Piaţa Lenin stands high-rise Hotel Traian, looking like grandma's last tooth. Behind this odd monstrosity, in a mansion on Strada Belvedere, is the local **art gallery** (closed Monday).

Walk north on Strada Belvedere for two blocks, then turn left on Strada Grădina Publică to reach a large **public park** with an **ethnographical museum** and a view of the industrial area beside the Danube. South of Piaţa Lenin, on the street beside Hotel Danubiu, is a huge **Greek Orthodox church** (1872).

### Places to Stay

There are three old 2nd-class hotels in Brăila, all offering spacious singles/doubles with shared bath for US$17/28, including breakfast. The nicest is the *Hotel Danubiu*, Piaţa Lenin 8, brimming with old-world flavour. Close by are the *Hotel Pescăruş*, Strada Republicii 17, and the *Hotel Delta*, Strada Republicii 58.

If these three hotels are full or still obeying orders not to accept foreigners, you may be forced into the sterile, unfriendly *Hotel Traian*, Piaţa Lenin 12, which wants US$36/52 single/double. Hotel coupons are grudgingly accepted.

An alternative is to take bus No 6 or a taxi eight km south to *Hotel Turist* on Sărat Lake where doubles cost US$8. It's open all year, there's a good restaurant and it's friendly. You can also camp here if the rooms are full.

Two km back towards Brăila near the city zoo is *Cabana Stejarilor*, where nice little cabins are US$7 double (only open in summer) and camping is possible. It's also accessible on city bus No 6. Since it would be hard to catch the 7 am boat to Sulina if you stayed at either of these places, they make Brăila a better place to end a Danube Delta trip than to begin one.

A final choice would be to take one of the eight ferries across the Danube to Smîrdan and camp freelance over there.

### Places to Eat

There's a self-service restaurant in the *Hotel Traian*. Avoid the main hotel restaurant upstairs in the Traian, where beer and wine

Brăila

0    150   300 m

| 1 | Hotel Delta |
|---|---|
| 2 | Hotel Pescarus |
| 3 | Historical Museum |
| 4 | Hotel Traian |
| 5 | Art Gallery |
| 6 | Public Park |
| 7 | Hotel Danubiu |
| 8 | Greek Orthodox Church |
| 9 | Ferry Terminal |

are exotic luxuries and the food and service are lousy.

Also try the *Restaurant Lacto-Vegetarian*, opposite Central Cinema, up Calea Galaţi from beside the museum. This closes early, however.

### Getting There & Away

The times of all the trains that depart from Brăila are posted in the window of the CFR Agenţie de Voiaj at Piaţa Lenin 11, in front of Hotel Danubiu. You can purchase tickets inside.

Direct morning express trains travel to Bucharest (199 km), Braşov and Suceava, but for Iaşi you must change at Galaţi and Bîrlad.

There are early morning Navrom ferries downriver on the Danube from Brăila to Tulcea and Sulina. Get a through ticket to Maliuc, Crişan or Sulina and avoid Tulcea, where you must change boats. Between Sulina and Tulcea, you must often change boats at Galaţi.

# Moldavia

Moldavia, one of the three original principalities of Romania, is a land rich with folklore and excellent horses. Some of Romania's best vineyards are at Cotnari, between Iaşi and Suceava. In 1859, Moldavia, where the empires of the tsars, Habsburgs and Ottomans met, became the birthplace of modern Romania when Prince Alexander Ioan Cuza united Moldavia and Wallachia for defence purposes against these three encroaching powers.

Prince Bogdan won Moldavian independence from Hungary in 1349, and the centre of the medieval principality became Bukovina (which means beech wood) in the easily defended Carpathian foothills. From Suceava, Ştefan cel Mare (Stefan the Great), called the 'athlete of Christ' by Pope Pius VI, led the resistance against the Turks for nearly half a century from 1457 to 1504. This prince

and his son, Petru Rareş, erected fortified monasteries throughout Bukovina. On the exteriors were stunning frescoes intended to educate the illiterate masses. Only with Petru Rareş' defeat by the Turks in 1538 did Moldavia's golden age wane, as the principality began paying tribute to the Ottoman Empire.

After Bukovina was ceded to Austria by the Turks in 1775, the emphasis shifted to the Moldavian Plateau, an inclined plain stretching north from Galaţi. Romanian Moldavia is only the western half of the medieval principality. Bessarabia, the portion east of the Prut River, was taken by Russia in 1812, at a time when Moldavia was a vassal state of the Ottoman Empire under Phanariote Greek rule (1711-1821). Although recovered by Romania from 1917 to 1940 and again from 1941 to 1944, Bessarabia is today a union republic of the USSR. Many Romanians on both banks of the Prut have never accepted the loss of Bessarabia to the USSR as one of the spoils of WW II, and in June 1990 the newly elected parliament of Soviet Moldavia switched its official language from Russian to Romanian and adopted the Romanian tricolour as the republic's official flag. For most of the nearly three million ethnic Romanians comprising 64% of Bessarabia's population, reunification with Romania is a cherished goal.

Although Bukovina attracts lots of tour groups, the rest of the region, Iaşi included, is well off the beaten track.

## IAŞI

Iaşi (Jassy) became capital of Moldavia in 1565. When the principalities of Moldavia and Wallachia were united in 1859, Iaşi served as the national capital until it was replaced by Bucharest in 1862. This illustrious history accounts for the city's great monasteries, churches, public buildings and museums which surprise visitors who have never heard of the place. Always a leading intellectual centre, Romania's first university was founded here in 1860. You'll need a full day at least to visit Iaşi.

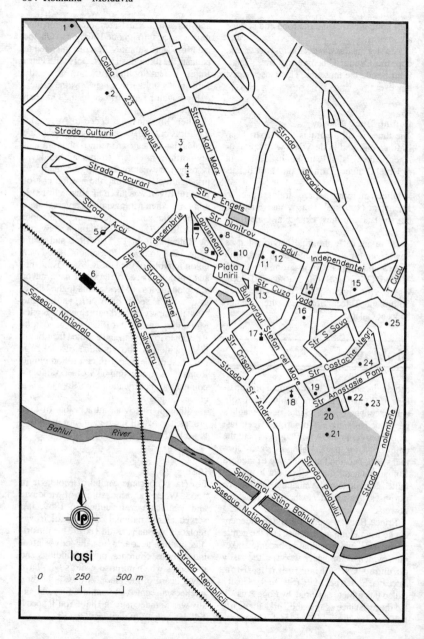

**Iași**

0    250    500 m

### Orientation

To reach Piaţa Unirii, the city's heart, from the railway station, walk north-east two blocks on Strada 30 decembrie, then turn right on to Strada Arcu. From Piaţa Unirii, Bulevardul Ştefan cel Mare runs south-east past the Moldavian Metropolitan Cathedral to the massive Palace of Culture, one of Romania's finest buildings. Calea 23 august runs north-west to the university and Copou Park.

### Information

The tourist office is in the alley beside Hotel Unirea, off Piaţa Unirii.

### Things to See

On Piaţa Unirii, in the centre of Iaşi, is a

■ PLACES TO STAY

9   Hotel Traian
10  Hotel Unirea
13  Hotel Continental
22  Hotel Moldova

▼ OTHER

1   Copou Park
2   University
3   Casă Pogor Literary Museum
4   Casă Studentilor
5   Bus Station
6   Railway Station
7   Post Office
8   Museum of the Union
11  Theatrical Museum
12  Natural History Museum
14  Filharmonia
15  Golia Monastery
16  National Theatre
17  Moldavian Metropolitan Cathedral
18  Church of the Three Hierarchs
19  Former Communist Party
    Headquarters
20  Dosoftei House
21  Palace of Culture
23  Luceafarul Theatre
24  Central Market
25  Bărboi Monastery

statue (1912) of Prince Alexander Ioan Cuza (1820-73), the founder of modern Romania, who achieved the union of Wallachia and Moldavia in 1859. Walk up the pedestrian street beside Hotel Traian to the residence of this man, a large Empire building (1806) that is now the **Museum of the Union**, Strada Lapusneanu 14.

The broad tree-lined Bulevardul Ştefan cel Mare leads directly south-east from Piaţa Unirii towards the monumental Palace of Culture. Along the way you'll pass two magnificent churches on the right: first the **Moldavian Metropolitan Cathedral** (1886) with four towers and a cavernous interior, and then the fabulous **Church of the Three Hierarchs** (1639), the exterior of which is completely covered with intricate decorative patterns in stone. Inside are the tombs of the church's founder, Prince Vasile Lupu, and the aforementioned Prince Alexander Ioan Cuza. The unmarked white stone building beside this church is a gallery of 17th century frescoes.

The giant neo-Gothic **Palace of Culture** (1906-25), formerly the administrative palace, contains four museums: historical, fine arts, ethnological and technical. In addition, special exhibitions are held here. Separate tickets are sold for each museum and exhibition, so you could end up with six or seven tickets if you visit everything. As with most of Iaşi's other museums, they're all closed on Mondays. You would probably have to be a specialist to appreciate the neolithic Cucuteni pottery in the Historical Museum, but it's worth noting for its importance to European prehistory.

On the square in front of the Palace of Culture is an old stone building (Dosoftei House) in which Metropolitan Dosoftei printed the first major work in verse to appear in the Romanian language (1673). Behind this is the former headquarters of the local Communist Party. Also on the square is **St Nicolae Domnesc Church** (1492), Iaşi's oldest building, and an equestrian statue of Stefan the Great (1883).

Find your way a few blocks north past the Central Market to **Golia Monastery** (1660) on Strada Cuza Vodă which overlooks Tîrgu Cucu. The monastery's walls and tower shelter a 17th century church that has twin domes, frescoes, intricate carved doorways and iconostasis.

If you have extra time, take a tram from Tîrgu Cucu up to **Copou Park**, which has monuments, gardens, and a literary museum, then walk back down Calea 23 august. You'll pass the huge neoclassical **university** (1897) on the way. Just before the statue in the middle of the street, turn left to the 1858 mansion which houses the **Casă Pogor Literary Museum**, Strada I C Frimu 4. Many well-known Romanian writers have lived in Iaşi, including the poet Vasile Alecsandri (1821-90). In the garden in front of the museum is a Soviet war cemetery.

## Places to Stay

Staff at the Tourism Agency of Moldavia, a private travel bureau in the Casă Studentilor, at the bottom of Calea 23 august, should be able to help you find a private room.

There are five hotels in Iaşi, all graded 1st class. The elegant but expensive old *Hotel Traian* is at Piaţa Unirii 1 (US$44/58 single/double). The modern 13-storey high-rise *Hotel Unirea*, Piaţa Unirii 5, is cheaper at US$35/49 single/double. This is a popular meeting place for Arab and African students. A block away at Strada Cuza Vodă 4 is the *Hotel Continental*, where singles/doubles begin at US$22/34. The people there will claim that all of the cheaper rooms are full. Both the Traian and Continental suffer from tram noise in the very early morning.

Behind the high-rise *Hotel Moldova*, Piaţa Palatului 1, near the Palace of Culture, is the smaller *Hotel Orizont* with overpriced rooms at US$30 per person. The Traian, Unirea and Moldova hotels all take hotel coupons.

There's a pleasant camping ground in the forest at Lake Ciric near Iaşi Airport, about six km north of town. The easiest way to get there is by taxi (US$5), or take a train to Tîrgu Cucu and then wait for the hourly bus. On the lake near the camping ground is a restaurant that specialises in Romanian cuisine.

## Places to Eat

The *Restaurant Iaşul* behind the Hotel Traian is one of the city's best dining rooms. The *Restaurant Select*, opposite the Hotel Continental, serves pizza and cakes downstairs, and full meals with wine upstairs. Next door to the Restaurant Select is the unpretentious *Restaurant Miorita*.

On the 13th floor of the Hotel Unirea is a café with an open terrace that overlooks the city. There's a special lift that goes directly up to the 13th floor, otherwise you can take the hotel lift to the 12th floor and go up the stairs.

## Entertainment

On the east side of Bulevardul Ştefan cel Mare, nearly opposite the Moldavian Metropolitan Cathedral, is the neo-Baroque *Vasile Alecsandri National Theatre* (1896), which was designed by the famous Viennese architects Fellner and Hellmer. If you want tickets for events held here and at the nearby *Filharmonia*, they are available from the Agenţia Teatrala on Bulevardul Ştefan cel Mare, near the Moldavian Metropolitan Cathedral.

## Getting There & Away

There are TAROM flights to Iaşi from Bucharest and Constanţa.

Iaşi is on the main line between Bucharest and Kiev which goes via Kishinev, the capital of Bessarabia. Express trains to Bucharest (406 km) and Suceava (138 km) leave several times a day. One accelerat train travels daily from Iaşi to Timişoara via Suceava and Cluj-Napoca – a good train to catch. For Brăila you may have to change trains at Bîrlad and Galaţi. The CFR travel agency is on Piaţa Unirii, across from the Hotel Traian.

There's a daily overnight persoane train in each direction between Iaşi and Braşov, which is quite acceptable if you go 1st class (US$6.50), and is a cheap, easy connection between these points. Just be on the platform an hour early to grab a seat as no reservations are accepted.

# Bukovina

The painted churches of Bukovina are among the greatest artistic monuments of Europe. Erected at a time when northern Moldavia was threatened by Turkish invaders, the monasteries were surrounded by strong defensive walls. Great popular armies would gather inside these walls, waiting to do battle. To educate, entertain and arouse the illiterate soldiers and peasants who were unable to enter the church or understand the Slavonic liturgy, well-known biblical stories were portrayed on the church walls in cartoon-style frescoes, a unique mass media. The exterior of the church at Suceviţa Monastery is almost completely covered with these magnificent 16th century frescoes.

What catches our attention is the realistic manner of painting human figures in vast compositions against a backdrop not unlike the local landscape of the forested Carpathian foothills. Over the centuries the colours have preserved their freshness, from the greens of Suceviţa to the blues of Voroneţ

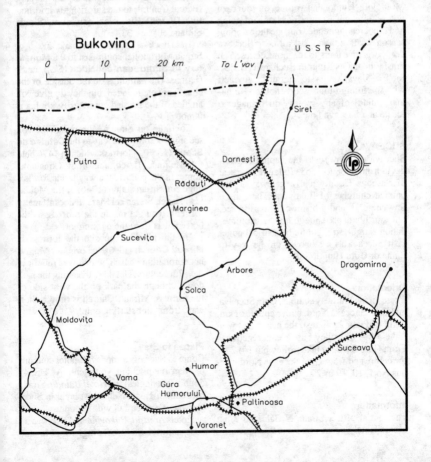

(famous because of the blue background on Voroneţ Monastery) and the reds of Humor. The church domes are a peculiar combination of Byzantine pendentives and Moorish crossed arches with larger-than-life paintings of Christ or the Virgin peering down from inside.

If your time is limited, the Voroneţ and Moldoviţa monasteries, both quite accessible by bus and train (see the Moldoviţa and Gura Humorului Getting There & Away sections), will give you a good cross section of what Bukovina has to offer. To do a complete circuit of Suceava, Putna, Rădăuţi, Suceviţa, Moldoviţa, Humor and Voroneţ on your own will require at least three days of hard going and is not recommended outside the camping season. Staff at the tourist office in Suceava don't organise tours to the monasteries. You must join an ONT tour in Bucharest (US$93 for two days) or try to ingratiate yourself with the foreign tour escort (not the Romanian guide) of any group you manage to locate at a Suceava hotel.

## SUCEAVA

Suceava (Soczow) was the capital of Moldavia from 1388 to 1565. Today it's the seat of Suceava County and a gateway to the painted churches of Bukovina. There are a few churches and a historic fortress to see, but four hours are enough here. Accommodation is tight, so if you're on a strict budget visit Suceava as a stopover on the way to Putna or Gura Humorului.

## Orientation

There are two railway stations, Gara Suceava and Gara Suceava Nord, both a couple of km north of Piaţa 23 august, the centre of town (take a bus or trolley bus to either station). From Gara Suceava take trolley bus No 2 to the centre and from Gara Suceava Nord take bus No 1, 10, 19 or 29.

## Information

The tourist office, Strada N Bălcescu 2, is beside Hotel Suceava on Piaţa 23 august.

## Things to See

The foundations of the 15th century **Princely Palace** are near the bus stop at Piaţa 23 august. The large church beyond is **St Dumitru** (1535) and nearby is the main Suceava vegetable market.

At Strada Ciprian Porumbescu 5, just west of Piaţa 23 august, is the **Hanul Domnesc**, a 16th century princely guesthouse that is now the Ethnographical Museum (closed Monday). Its collection of folk costumes and photos is quite good.

Return to Piaţa 23 august and follow Strada Ştefan cel Mare south past the park (Parcul Central) to the surprisingly informative **District Historical Museum**, Strada Ştefan cel Mare 33.

Backtrack a little to the park and take Strada Mitropoliei south-east to the **Monastery of Sfîntu Ioan cel Nou** (1522), or St George. The paintings on the outside of the church are badly faded, but they do give you an idea of the painted churches Bukovina is famous for.

Continue on Strada Mitropoliei till you see signs pointing the way to the **Cetatea de Scaun** (1388), a fortress which in 1476 held off Mehmed II, conqueror of Constantinople. In the park on the way to the fort is a huge equestrian statue (1966) of the Moldavian leader, Ştefan cel Mare. It doesn't really matter if you get inside the fortress, as the best view is from the parking lot.

On the hillside opposite the fortress is **Mirăuţi Church** (1390), the original Moravian coronation church, which was rebuilt in the 17th century. Get there by taking the path down through the park on the west side of the fortress. Mirăuţi Church is only a short walk from your starting point.

## Places to Stay

Come to Suceava armed with hotel coupons or plan on pitching your tent. At US$41 double (no singles) the *Hotel Balada*, Strada Mitropoliei 1, is the cheapest hotel in Suceava, but it's often full with groups.

Hotels *Arcaşul, Bukovina* and *Suceava* all cost about US$42/64 single/double and

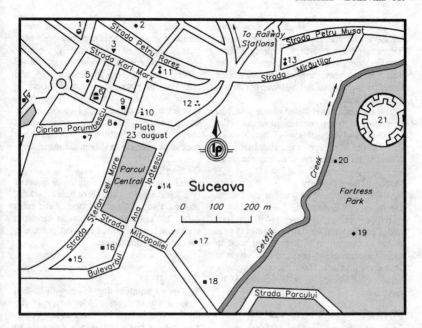

| | | | |
|---|---|---|---|
| 1 | Bus Station | 12 | Princely Palace Ruins |
| 2 | Market | 13 | Mirăuţi Church |
| 3 | Select Restaurant | 14 | Municipal Theatre |
| 4 | Hotel Arcasul | 15 | District Historical Museum |
| 5 | Synagogue | 16 | Hotel Bucovina |
| 6 | Post Office | 17 | Sfintu Ioan cel Nou Monastery |
| 7 | Hanul Domnesc | 18 | Hotel Balada |
| 8 | Casă de Cultura | 19 | Cemetery |
| 9 | Hotel Suceava | 20 | Statue of Ştefan cel Mare |
| 10 | Tourist Office | 21 | Cetatea de Scaun |
| 11 | St Dumitru Church | | |

accept hotel coupons. The high-rise *Hotel Bucovina*, Strada Ana Ipătescu 5, is your best bet if you have coupons. It's the most likely to have a room for you even in midsummer and it's right on the trolley bus line from the stations.

*Camping Ştrand* is near the Suceava River, between Gara Suceava Nord and Suceava. Bungalows cost about US$20 and

there's a swimming pool and pleasant market nearby.

### Places to Eat

An easy self-service restaurant is *Beraria Carpaţi*, opposite the bus station. The 'Bar de Zi' just upstairs from this restaurant serves a good cup of coffee.

One of Suceava's finest restaurants that is

not in a hotel is the *Select*, between Hotel Suceava and the main vegetable market. There are two exclusive dining rooms upstairs, but the main problem with the Select Restaurant is the thick cigarette smoke that fills the rooms. All of these places are open on Sunday.

If these restaurants fail to please you, you can choose from the restaurants in the Bukovina and Arcaşul hotels. There's also a disco in the basement at the Hotel Arcaşul, Strada Mihai Viteazul 4-6. Dress sharp to get in.

### Getting There & Away

TAROM flights operate to Suceava from Bucharest and Constanţa.

Express trains to Bucharest (450 km), Iaşi and Cluj-Napoca are fairly regular. Local trains of interest to visitors travel west to Gura Humorului (47 km) and north-west to Putna via Rădăuţi. The CFR travel agency, Strada N Bălcescu 8, is beside the Hotel Suceava.

### PUTNA

Putna Monastery, founded in 1466, is still home to a very active religious community. Groups of monks chant mass just before sunset. A text posted just inside Putna's church reads: 'The monastery of Putna, the first foundation of Stefan the Great, princely necropole and a real centre of Romanian culture through the centuries, represents a living testimony of the cultural and artistic traditions of the Romanian people and by that a remarkable school of patriotism.' Stefan the Great himself is buried in the church.

The large building behind the church contains a rich museum of medieval manuscripts and rare 15th century textiles. Place of honour goes to the *Tetraevanghel* of 1473, with a portrait of the prince offering the book to the Virgin.

### Places to Stay & Eat

Just outside the monastery gate is a large tourist complex with a medium-priced hotel that is open all year. Adequate meals are served in the hotel restaurant. Beside the

hotel are many small bungalows and a camping ground. These are open from May to mid-September. Unfortunately, the male receptionist here is said to be uncooperative.

Some people camp freelance in the field opposite the rock-hewn hermit's cave at Chilia near the train station. To get there, follow the river upstream to a wooden bridge which you cross, and then continue straight ahead. The spiritually inclined could ask special permission to stay in the monastery.

### Getting There & Away

Local trains travel to Putna from Suceava (via Rădăuţi) every couple of hours (70 km), making Putna Monastery one of the most accessible in Bukovina. The large monastic enclosure is at the end of the road, just under two km from the station.

### RĂDĂUŢI

This is an uninteresting town with several buses a day to Suceviţa Monastery. If you don't arrive in time for a convenient departure, take a bus to Marginea and walk or hitchhike the last nine km to the monastery. The bus station is two blocks from Rădăuţi Railway Station.

The *Hotel Bukovina* on Piaţa Republicii has inexpensive rooms, but it's often full. There's a **folk art museum** opposite the hotel which features local pottery and embroidered coats. A large market is held in Rădăuţi on Fridays.

### SUCEVIŢA

The church inside the fortified monastic enclosure at Suceviţa (1586) is almost completely covered in frescoes inside and out. As you enter you first see the *Virtuous Ladder* fresco covering most of the north exterior wall, which depicts the 30 steps from Hell to Paradise. On the south exterior wall is a tree symbolising the continuity of the Old and New Testaments. The tree grows from the reclining figure of Jesse, who is flanked by a row of ancient philosophers. To the left is the Virgin as a Byzantine princess, with angels holding a red veil over her head. Apart from the church, there's a small museum to visit at Suceviţa Monastery.

If you have time, climb the hill opposite the monastery to enjoy the view. Freelance camping is possible in the field at the foot of this hill, across the stream from the monastery. There's also the *Hanul Suceviţa*, a restaurant about a km back towards Rădăuţi, which also rents expensive rooms and inexpensive bungalows.

### Getting There & Away

Suceviţa is by far the most difficult monastery to reach on public transport. Service from Rădăuţi is infrequent and only one early morning bus a day runs the 36 km from Suceviţa to Moldoviţa. Hitchhiking is not easy, but try waving a packet of Kent cigarettes. The westbound highway winds up and over a high mountain pass, through forests which enclose both the Suceviţa and Moldoviţa monasteries.

### MOLDOVIŢA

As at Suceviţa, Moldoviţa Monastery (1532) consists of a strong fortified enclosure with towers and gates, and a magnificent painted church at its centre. Both monasteries are in the care of pious nuns and have undergone careful restoration in recent years.

Several of the paintings at Moldoviţa are unique. For example, on the south exterior wall of the church is a depiction of the defence of Constantinople in 626 against Persians dressed as Turks, and on the porch is a representation of the Last Judgment. Inside the sanctuary, on a wall facing the original carved iconostasis, is a portrait of Prince Petru Rareş (the founder) and his family offering the church to Christ. All of these works date from 1537. In the small museum at Moldoviţa Monastery is Petru Rareş' original throne.

### Places to Stay & Eat

There's a camping ground with bungalows (Popas Turistic) between the station and the monastery, and a satisfactory restaurant in the Complex Commercial nearby, on the road to Vama.

### Getting There & Away

Moldoviţa Monastery is much easier to reach than Suceviţa Monastery since it's right above Vatra Moldoviţei Railway Station, on a 14-km branch line from Vama off the Suceava-Cluj main line. There are three trains a day in each direction.

### GURA HUMORULUI

This small logging town, 36 km west of Suceava on the main railway line to Cluj-Napoca, is an ideal centre for visiting the monasteries. Most trains stop here. The adjacent train and bus stations are a seven-minute walk from the centre of town. The **Ethnographical Museum**, Strada 23 august 18, is on the main street, east of the post office.

There are 10 buses a day to the painted churches of Humor and Voroneţ, each about six km from Gura Humorului. On Sunday, however, bus service is greatly reduced. The walk back to town from Voroneţ is enjoyable, as you will pass many large farm houses. In summer both churches stay open until 8 pm.

### Things to See

**Humor** At Humor (1530) the best paintings are on the church's south exterior wall. There's a badly faded depiction of the siege of Constantinople, with the legend of the return of the prodigal son beside it to the right. Notice the feast scene and five dancers. Above this is the devil as a woman (the figure with wings but no halo). On the porch is a painting of the Last Judgment and, in the first chamber inside the church, scenes of martyrdom. In the middle chamber is the tomb of Toader Bubuiog, who ordered the church built, with his portrait (offering the church to Christ) just above and to the left of the tomb.

**Voroneţ** The Last Judgment, which fills the entire west wall at Voroneţ, is perhaps the most marvellous, unified composition of any of the frescoes on the Bukovina churches. At the top angels roll up the signs of the zodiac to indicate the end of time. The middle fresco shows humanity being brought to judgment. On the left St Paul escorts the believers, while on the right Moses brings forward the unbelievers. The latter are, from left to right: Jews, Turks, Tatars, Armenians and Negroes – a graphic representation of the prejudices of the time. Below is the resurrection. Even the wild animals give back pieces of bodies to complete those rising from the graves. The sea also gives forth its victims.

At the top of the north wall is Genesis, from Adam and Eve on the left to Cain and Abel on the right. The south wall features another tree of Jesse with the genealogy of Biblical personalities. In the vertical fresco to the left of this is the story of the martyrdom of St John of Suceava. This saint is buried in the Monastery of Sfîntu Ioan cel Nou in Suceava. Inside, facing the iconostasis, is the famous portrait of Stefan the Great offering Voroneţ Church to Christ. This prince ordered that Voroneţ be erected in 1470, although the paintings date from 1547.

### Places to Stay & Eat

The *Hotel Carpaţi*, Strada 9 mai 3, the street beside the post office, has singles or doubles for US$11.

Otherwise try the *Cabana Ariniş* at the foot of the wooded hill, two km south of town. You cross a bridge to the Parc Dendrologic and then a suspension bridge to the cabana, which has rooms at US$12 per person. You may also join the people camping upstream from the cabana. Meals are served at the cabana and in the large terrace restaurant by the suspension bridge. This is a very nice area in which to stay.

### Getting There & Away

Gura Humorului is on the main railway line between Suceava and Cluj-Napoca. If you're going to Sighetu Marmaţiei, change at Salva, and if you're going to Baia Mare, change at Dej.

# Transylvania

To most people, the name Transylvania conjures up haunted castles, werewolves and vampires. Certainly the 14th century castles of Bran and Hunedoara appear ready-made for a Count Dracula movie, but Vlad Tepeş (Vlad Dracul) was a real prince who led Romanian resistance to Ottoman expansion in the 15th century. His habit of impaling slain Turkish foes on stakes may seem extreme, but Transylvania has had a tumultuous past.

Vlad Tepeş

For 1000 years, right up to WW I, Transylvania was associated with Hungary. In the 10th century a Magyar tribe, the Szeklers, settled here 'beyond the forest', followed in the 12th century by Saxon merchant-knights. The seven towns they founded, Bistriţa (Bistritz), Braşov (Kronstadt), Cluj-Napoca (Klausenburg), Mediaş (Mediasch), Sebeş (Muhlbach), Sibiu (Hermannstadt) and Sighişoara (Schässburg), gave Transylvania its German name, Siebenbürgen. Although

Romanians have always constituted a majority, Hungarians still number 1,700,000 in Transylvania, and 250,000 ethnic Germans are also present. Scattered through the countryside around Sibiu and Sighişoara are many small villages which seem to have been lifted directly out of 19th century Germany.

Medieval Transylvania was an autonomous unit under the Hungarian crown. After the defeat of Hungary by the Turks in 1526, the region became independent in practice while recognising Turkish suzerainty after 1566. This independence was maintained in the 17th century by playing the Ottoman sultan off against the Habsburg emperor. In 1683 Turkish power was broken at the gates of Vienna and in 1687 Transylvania came under Habsburg rule. The Catholic Habsburg governors sought to control the territory by favouring first the Protestant Hungarians and Saxons and then the Orthodox Romanians. In 1848, when the Hungarians revolted against the Habsburgs, the local Romanian population sided with the Austrians. After 1867 Transylvania was fully absorbed into Hungary to the dismay of the increasingly nationalist Romanians, who massed at Alba Iulia in 1918 to demand Transylvania's union with Romania.

Although easily accessible from Hungary (daily trains and visas are issued at the border), the Transylvanian plateau is still one of the travel frontiers of Europe. Facilities such as camping grounds, hotels, restaurants, trains and buses do exist, however, and aside from the enchanting old towns there are rugged mountains to climb all round. For lovers of medieval art and history, it's an unparalleled chance to escape the hordes in Budapest and Prague and have an untamed corner of the old Austro-Hungarian empire all to themselves.

## SINAIA

This well-known winter ski resort snuggles at an altitude of 800 to 930 metres in the narrow Prahova Valley sliced between the fir-clad Bucegi Mountains. Sinaia and nearby Buşteni are perfect starting points for summer hikes into the Bucegi Carpathians. In winter the Bucegi Plateau is a favourite cross-country ski area. Cable cars carry you effortlessly up to the crest from points on the main railway line between Bucharest and Braşov.

Though a monastery had existed here since the 17th century, Sinaia only developed into a major resort after King Carol I selected it as his summer residence in 1870 and had a railway built from Bucharest in 1879. The local elite soon followed suit, constructing imposing residences and villas along the wooded slopes. Until 1920 the Hungarian-Romanian border ran along Predeal Pass just north of Sinaia; for convenience we have included this area with Transylvania even though it belongs with Wallachia.

### Information

The tourist office is just up the hill from the train station at Bulevardul Carpaţi 19, opposite the Hotel Sinaia. The staff there is usually very helpful.

### Things to See

Above the park and the Palace Hotel is **Sinaia Monastery**, named after Mt Sinai. The large Orthodox church you see as you enter the town dates from 1846, but an older church (1695) with its original frescoes is in the compound to the left. Beside the newer church is a museum.

Just behind the monastery begins the road to **Peleş Castle** (1883), the former royal palace and under Ceauşescu a private retreat for leading Communists. Today it's accessible to the general public as a museum (open Wednesday to Sunday from 9 am to 3 pm, admission US$1.50). The main palace, with its pointed towers and turrets, was built in the German Renaissance style, with oriental touches for the Prussian princeling Carol I, first king of Romania, who ruled from 1866 to 1914. In the garden outside the palace is a statue of the man. Imre Nagy, leader of the 1956 Hungarian Revolution, was held at Peleş before his execution in 1958. The huge park, thick with towering conifers, stretches up into the foothills. It has a number of

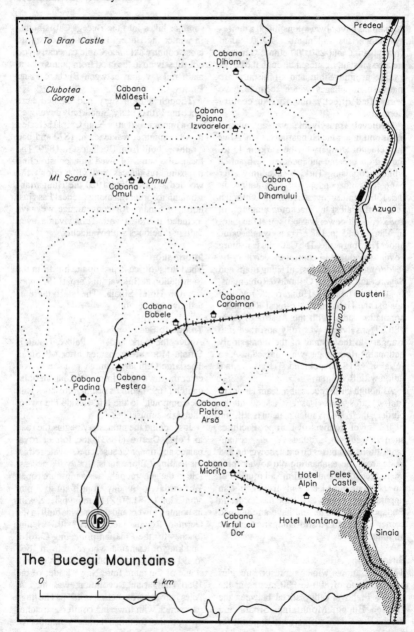

To Bran Castle

Predeal

*Clubotea Gorge*

Cabana Mălăeşti

Cabana Diham

Cabana Poiana Izvoarelor

*Mt Scara* ▲ ▲ *Omul*
Cabana Omul

Cabana Gura Dihamului

Azuga

Cabana Caraiman

Buşteni

Cabana Babele

*Prahova River*

Cabana Peştera

Cabana Padina

Cabana Piatra Arsă

Cabana Miorița

Hotel Alpin

Peleş Castle

Cabana Virful cu Dor

Hotel Montana

Sinaia

## The Bucegi Mountains

0        2        4 km

secondary buildings in mock medieval style that now serve as restaurants and cafés. The queue to enter the main palace can be long on summer weekends but it's worth waiting as the interior rooms are magnificent.

**From Sinaia to Babele** During summer, swarms of Romanian day-trippers take the cable car *(telecabină)* from Sinaia up to **Cabana Miorița** (2000 metres) in the Bucegi Mountains. From Miorița they walk north to **Cabana Piatra Arsă** (1½ hours) and on to **Cabana Babele** (another hour), where they catch a second cable car back down to the railway at Bușteni. The walk from Cabana Miorița to Cabana Babele is not difficult, involving a 50-metre drop to Piatra Arsă (1950 metres) and then a climb back up to Babele (2206 metres). This explains the route's tremendous popularity.

You catch the first cable car (US$0.55) just above Hotel Montana in Sinaia. This will take you up to Hotel Alpin at about 1400 metres. Here you change to a chair lift which carries you up another 557 metres to Cabana Miorița, near the crest. You can have meals and drinks at the Miorița, Piatra Arsă and Babele cabanas, but the rooms in these are usually full. It's a well-beaten track, so if you'd rather experience the Carpathian Mountains without the crowds, consider the following route: take the cable car from Bușteni to Babele, then hike north all the way to Bran Castle (see the following section).

**To Bran Castle** One of the easiest and most practical expeditions into the Carpathian Mountains involves a three-hour train ride from Bucharest to Sinaia or Bușteni, a cable car up to the mountain crest, and a hike north-west across the mountains all the way to Bran Castle, where there are buses to Brașov. You can do this in one very strenuous day if you get an early start from Babele, but it's preferable to take two days and spend a night at either Cabana Omul or the 'refuge' on Mt Scara.

As you look north from Babele, you'll see a red-and-white TV transmitter on a hilltop, which looks like a rocket about to take off.

To the right of this is a trail marked with a cross which leads to a large monument that offers a great view of Bușteni (45 minutes each way from Babele). To the left is a yellow-marked trail which leads to **Cabana Omul** (two hours). North of Babele the scenery gets better, with great drops into valleys on either side. Cabana Omul is right on the summit (2505 metres) in the Bucegi Carpathians. Accommodation is usually available on dormitory platforms with mattresses (US$4 per person), and simple meals are sometimes served, but it's best to bring your own food and water. There are good views on all sides from Omul, and the sunsets and sunrises are great.

To go from Omul to Bran Castle takes five hours or more and involves a tough 2000-metre drop. To climb up from Bran Castle to Omul would be murder. The trail is easy to follow, as it has yellow triangle markers, and chances are that you and the mountain goats will have this surprisingly beautiful landscape all to yourselves. From Omul you begin by crossing Mt Scara (2422 metres), where there's a plain empty hut with a hard wooden platform, popularly called the refuge. Stay here only if you have a warm sleeping bag and accommodation in Omul is full.

You then begin the descent down the Ciubotea Gorge. Your legs will remember this trip for many days! After a couple of hours you come out on a logging road beside a river (wash up!), which you follow right down to Bran Castle. If it's getting late, you can camp in the forest here. This invigorating hike combines sightseeing, adventure and transportation, a great way to experience the mountains with none of the logistical problems you'll encounter elsewhere.

### Places to Stay

Staff at the tourist office in Sinaia will direct you to a private room if someone on the street outside doesn't ask you if you want one. You should be able to pay in lei.

Hotel coupons are accepted at the *Sinaia* and *Montana* hotels, both near the tourist office. The regular tariff at these hotels is about US$43/67 single/double. Both are modern high-rise hotels with indoor swimming pools and saunas, though perhaps the Sinaia, Bulevardul Carpaţi 8, is preferable.

If you don't mind paying dearly for real old-world elegance, the luxury-category *Palace Hotel* (founded in 1911), Strada 30 decembrie 4, should fill the bill (US$52/95 single/double).

Hotel rates at Sinaia, Buşteni, Predeal and Braşov are slightly lower from mid-March to mid-May and from mid-October to mid-December.

**Camping** The *camping ground* is at Izvorul Rece, four km south of central Sinaia. Ask at the tourist office about bus service.

*Camping Fulg de Nea* at Predeal is a better option than the camping grounds at either Sinaia or Braşov. It's only a five-minute walk from Predeal Railway Station, and you can see the tents from the train on the right-hand side, just before Predeal as you arrive from Sinaia. The road to the chair lift up Mt Clăbucet begins here. Camping costs only US$2, but don't expect much in the way of facilities for that.

### Places to Eat
Before taking the cable car up the mountainside at Sinaia, indulge yourself at the self-service restaurant in *Hotel Montana*. Enter the restaurant from the road which leads up to the cable car station. Fill your water bottle here.

### Getting There & Away
Sinaia is on the main railway line from Bucharest to Braşov – 126 km from the former and 45 km from the latter. All trains between Bucharest and Transylvania stop here. Local trains to Buşteni, Predeal and Braşov are quite frequent.

The CFR travel agency is in the post office on the main street, between the Sinaia and Montana hotels.

### Getting Around
The cable cars at both Sinaia and Buşteni operate all year, but the one at Sinaia is closed Monday. At Buşteni they close on Tuesday. The Sinaia cable car has three times the capacity of that at Buşteni, but also attracts larger crowds. Both stop operating at 4 pm. In summer there can be quite a crowd waiting for a ride up the mountain, so get there early.

## RÎŞNOV & BRAN
Both Rîşnov and Bran, in the foothills southwest of Braşov, on the main road to Piteşti, are well known for their castles. Bran Castle is heavily promoted as a tourist attraction and it's hard to visit Romania without seeing it in travel brochures or on postcards. The tour buses rarely visit Rîşnov Castle, which is larger but less accessible than that at Bran.

### Rîşnov
A short 15-km train ride on the Zarnesti line from Braşov, Rîşnov offers the double attraction of a castle and a convenient camping ground. From the railway station, you'll see the large 14th century castle on a distant hilltop. To reach it climb up the stairs behind the Casă de Cultura on Piaţa 23 august, about a km from the station. The castle is open Tuesday to Sunday from 10 am to 4 pm.

The camping ground is in the forest just below the castle, near a restaurant and public swimming pool. You can stay in bungalows or camp in the camping ground. It's sometimes crowded with school groups but is usually OK. There are hiking trails in the vicinity for those not interested in downing big mugs of beer (when available) on the restaurant terrace overlooking the pool.

### Bran
The overpromoted Bran Castle (1378) originated as a toll station that was erected by the German merchants of Braşov to regulate trade between Transylvania and Wallachia. Beside the entrance to the castle is a park with a collection of Transylvanian farm buildings. You may visit these on the same admission ticket as that for the castle.

Though this 53-room fairy-tale castle (open from 9 am to 4 pm, closed Monday) is impressive in itself, don't be taken in by tales that Bran is **Count Dracula's castle** as it is unlikely that the real Vlad Țepeș ever stayed here. Despite this, plans exist to reconstruct 'Dracula's torture chamber' and stage Dracula light-and-sound shows at the castle. In his 1897 novel, Bram Stoker placed Dracula's castle far away on the Tihuta Pass in northern Romania, exactly halfway between Cluj-Napoca and Suceava (there is nothing to see there). True Dracula freaks can indulge their ghoulish hunger with less effort by dining in the Sighișoara house where Vlad himself was born (see the Sighișoara section).

### Getting There & Away
Bran Castle is easily accessible by bus from Rîșnov Railway Station and the buses usually connect with local trains to/from Brașov. Buy your bus ticket at the kiosk beside the bus stop at Rîșnov Station. In Bran you can pick up your return bus ticket at the *Cofetarie*, on the corner near the castle. The posted bus times are not always accurate, so ask. Avoid Bran on Sunday as there are fewer buses.

### BRAȘOV
Brașov is a pleasant medieval town flanked by verdant hills on either side. The original German mercantile colony was protected by the walls of old Kronstadt (now Brașov). The Romanians lived at Scheii, just outside the walls to the south-west of the town. Strategically situated at the meeting point of three principalities, Brașov was a major medieval trading centre.

Contemporary Brașov is Romania's second-largest city, although it's still only a sixth the size of Bucharest. Today the city's tractor, truck and textile factories are more important than commerce, and endless rows of concrete apartment blocks have risen to house the proletariat. Fortunately, these buildings are far enough away not to spoil the charm of Brașov's quaint old town.

### Orientation
The railway station is to the north-east, far from the centre of town, so take trolley bus No 4 (buy your ticket at the kiosk) to Parcul Central, if you're looking for a hotel, or to the Black Church, if you're sightseeing. Strada Republicii, Brașov's pedestrian promenade, is crowded with shops and cafés from Parcul Central to Piața 23 august. At the train station, the left-luggage office is in the underpass that leads out from the tracks.

### Information
The tourist information office is in the building attached to the east side of the Carpați Hotel, Bulevardul Gheorghe Gheorghiu-Dej 25, on Parcul Central.

For concerts and theatre, ask for details at the theatre ticket agency, Strada Republicii 4, just off Piața 23 august.

### Things to See
In the middle of Piața 23 august is the town hall (1420), now the **Historical Museum** (closed Monday). The 58-metre Trumpeter's Tower above the building dates from 1582. The Gothic **Black Church** (1384-1477), still used by German Lutherans, looms just south of the square. The church's name comes from its appearance after a fire in 1689. As you walk around the building to the entrance, you'll see statues on the exterior of the apse. The originals are now inside at the back of the church, and Turkish rugs hang from every balcony. In summer, recitals are given on the 1839 organ at 6 pm from Tuesday to Saturday (US$0.25).

Go south-west a little to the neoclassical **Schei Gate** (1828), then walk 500 metres up Strada 30 decembrie to Piața Unirii. Here you'll find the black-spired Greek Orthodox Church of **St Nicolae din Scheii** (1595). Beside the church is the **First Romanian School Museum** which houses a collection of icons, paintings on glass, old manuscripts, and so on. The clock tower (1751) was financed by Elizabeth, Empress of Russia; there's a picturesque cemetery opposite.

Go back as you came and turn right before Schei Gate to reach the 16th century **Weaver's Bastion**, which is a little hidden above the sports field. This corner fort on the old city walls has a museum with a fascinating

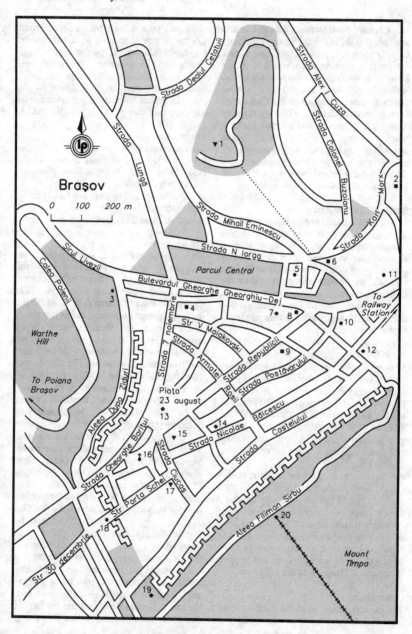

**Braşov**

0   100   200 m

scale model of Braşov as it was in the 17th century. The model itself was created in 1896. Above the bastion is a pleasant promenade through the forest overlooking the town. Halfway along you'll come to the **Tîmpa Cablecar** (open all year, closed Monday), which rises from 640 metres to 960 metres, which offers a stunning view of the entire area.

The **Art Gallery**, Bulevardul Gheorghe Gheorghiu-Dej 21, next to the Hotel Capitol, has a good Romanian collection upstairs with explanations of the different styles posted in English!

Take bus No 20 from the Biblioteca Judeteana (County Library) at the western end of Parcul Central, to the winter ski resort of Poiana Braşov, which is 13 km away. From Poiana Braşov you can get cable cars up to cabanas *Cristianul Mare* (1704 metres) and *Postăvarul* (1602 metres).

### Places to Stay

If you want a private room, go to the Biroul de Inchirieri EXO, Strada Postăvarului 6 (open weekdays from 5 to 9 pm and Saturday from 1 to 9 pm). On Sundays telephone 33060. Sometimes women on the street outside the Carpaţi Hotel also offer private rooms.

The only medium-priced hotels are the *Sport Hotel* (from US$20/32 single/double with shared bath), Strada V Maiakovski 3, behind the Carpaţi Hotel, and the *Hotel Turist*, Strada Karl Marx 32 (from US$21/35 single/double).

*Hotel Parc*, Strada N Iorga 2, is greatly overpriced at US$31/62 single/double but the desk clerk may agree to give you a room for less if you offer to pay in cash dollars with no questions asked.

Of the 1st-class hotels, the most characterful is the *Hotel Postăvarul*, Strada Republicii 62 (from US$41/56 single/double). The Postăvarul is often full in summer, in which case you'll be sent to the nearby high-rise *Hotel Capitol*, at Bulevardul Gheorghe Gheorghiu-Dej 19, with singles/doubles for US$52/67 (hotel coupons are accepted). Ask for a room on one of the top floors at the Capitol as it's rather noisy and smelly on the lower floors.

At nearby Poiana Braşov (1020 metres), hotel coupons are accepted at the huge *Ciucaş* and *Piatra Mare* hotels and the smaller *Hotel Bradul*, beside the cable-car station.

The nearest camping ground is at Dîrste, eight km south on the Bucharest Highway. Bungalows cost US$13/26 single/double and camping with your own tent costs US$6 per person. There's no bus service here but the Dîrste Railway Station is just behind the large brewery, only two km from the camping ground. Only local trains stop at Dîrste.

The camping ground at Rîşnov (see the Rîşnov section in this chapter) is in much more attractive surroundings than that at Dîrste and is easier to reach on public transport.

### Places to Eat

The easiest place to eat is *Autoservire Pioana* below Hotel Capital, Bulevardul Gheorghe Gheorghiu-Dej 19. *Crama Postăvarul* on Strada Republicii, opposite the Hotel Postăvarul, is a beer cellar that serves typical Romanian dishes.

| | |
|---|---|
| 1 | Citadel Restaurant Complex |
| 2 | Hotel Turist |
| 3 | Biblioteca Judeteana (County Library) |
| 4 | Carpaţi Hotel |
| 5 | Municipal Council |
| 6 | Hotel Parc |
| 7 | Folklore Museum & Art Gallery |
| 8 | Hotel Capitol |
| 9 | Hotel Postăvarul |
| 10 | District Council |
| 11 | Dramatic Theatre |
| 12 | Department Store |
| 13 | Historical Museum |
| 14 | Private Room Office |
| 15 | Cerbul Carpatin |
| 16 | Black Church |
| 17 | Restaurantul Pescarul |
| 18 | Schei Gate |
| 19 | Weaver's Bastion |
| 20 | Tîmpa Cablecar |

Vegetarians can try the *Lacto-Vegetarian Restaurant*, Strada Gheorghe Bariţui 1, and *Restaurantul Pescarul*, a seafood restaurant on the corner of Strada Porta Schei and Strada Ciucaş, though shortages of vegetables and fish often force both places to fall back on meat.

Braşov's most famous restaurant is the *Cerbul Carpaţin* in Hirscher House (1545), Piaţa 23 august 12. There's a wine cellar here that opens from 7 to 10 pm, and a large restaurant upstairs that serves meals from 10 am to 10 pm. It's usually crowded with men drinking cheap red wine.

The new *Restaurant Chinezesc* (closed Wednesday), also on Piaţa 23 august, is good for a change from the usual bland international cuisine often served up in Romania. Appealing features include the authentic oriental décor, excellent service, menus in English and German and the choice of wines. There is even a selection of fish and vegetable dishes. Be prepared to find several unexpected extras added to your bill, however, including a 12% service charge and a fee for the condiments on the table.

The Braşov Citadel (1817) has been converted into a restaurant complex (open from 11 am to 10 pm, closed Tuesday). There are beer gardens in the corner bastions, where you can get warm beer straight from the bottle, a disco and a medieval restaurant with an evening show (cover charge). Look for the signposted walkway opposite the Parc Hotel leading up to the *Restaurant Cetate*. Actually it's all a little forced and stuffy, with private parties in the inside rooms and hard plebeian drinking on the outside terraces.

### Getting There & Away
Braşov is well connected to Bucharest, Sibiu, Sighişoara and Cluj-Napoca by fast trains. Local trains to/from Sinaia (45 km) are fairly frequent. Local trains along the line from Braşov to Sibiu (149 km) drop off hikers headed for the Făgăraş Mountains. If you're bound for Bran Castle, take a Zarnesti train as far as Rîşnov (16 km). The tour desk at the Hotel Capitol can arrange a private taxi to take you to Bran Castle for US$15 cash.

The CFR travel agency is at Strada Republicii 53, opposite the Hotel Postăvarul.

## SIGHIŞOARA
Sighişoara (Schässburg), birthplace of Vlad Ţepeş, is a perfectly preserved medieval town in beautiful hilly countryside. No less than 11 towers remain on Sighişoara's intact city walls, inside which are sloping cobbled streets lined with 16th century burgher houses and untouched churches. All trains between Bucharest and Budapest (via Oradea) pass here, so watch for it from the window if you're foolish enough not to get off.

### Orientation
Follow Strada Gării south from the railway station to the Soviet war cemetery, where you turn left to the large Orthodox church. Cross the Tirnava Mare River on the footbridge here and take Strada Morii to the left, then keep going right, all the way up to Piaţa Lenin and the old town. Many of the facilities you'll want to use are found along a short stretch of Strada 1 decembrie to the left off Strada Morii.

### Information
The tourist office is at Strada 1 decembrie 10, beside the Steaua Hotel.

### Things to See
The first tower you reach above Piaţa Lenin

| | |
|---|---|
| 1 | Railway Station |
| 2 | Bus Station |
| 3 | Soviet War Cemetery |
| 4 | Orthodox Church |
| 5 | Piaţa Cetăţii |
| 6 | Vlad Dracul's House |
| 7 | Clock Tower & Museum |
| 8 | Bergkirche |
| 9 | Post Office |
| 10 | CFR Travel Agency |
| 11 | Steaua Hotel |

is the massive **clock tower** on Piața Muzeului. The 1648 clock still keeps time and the 14th century tower is now a **museum** (open Tuesday to Sunday from 9 am to 3.30 pm) with a very good collection of local artifacts, a scale model of the town and a superb view from the walkway on top. Next to the tower is the **monastery church** (1515), which has a collection of Oriental rugs hanging on each side of the nave (usually closed). Nearby on Piața Muzeului is the house in which **Vlad Dracul** lived from 1431 to 1435, and which now has a

good restaurant upstairs and wine cellar downstairs. Piața Cetății, complete with benches and fine old houses, is the heart of old Sighișoara. Go left up Strada Școlii from the square to the 172 steps of the **Covered Stairway** (1642). This leads to the Gothic **Bergkirche** (1345) with its frescoes of knights in armour rescuing damsels in distress. The old German tombstones in the church and adjacent **cemetery** are fascinating. The church opens daily from noon to 1 pm. Leave a donation if the caretaker opens for you at other times.

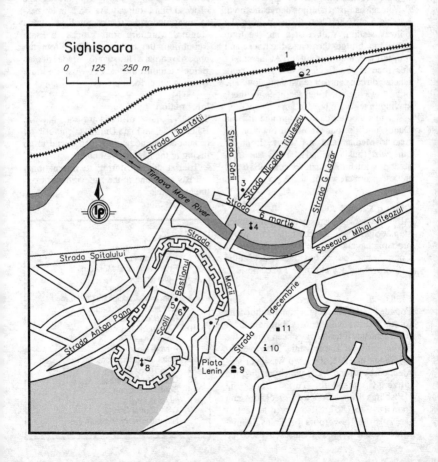

Sighișoara

0    125    250 m

## Places to Stay & Eat

The *Steaua Hotel*, Strada 1 decembrie 12 (from US$23/37 single/double with private bath), is Sighişoara's only hotel. This comfortable 1st-class hotel takes hotel coupons, but it's cheaper to pay in cash. The Steaua Hotel does fill up, so it might be wise to have your previous hotel call ahead for a reservation. If you show the staff there a coupon, however, they'll 'find' you a room even when the hotel is officially full. The TV sets in every room make for some noise. Rather than patronise their restaurant, have dinner in Vlad Dracul's house in the upper town.

You can camp on a hilltop above the town, but it's a stiff half-hour hike up from the railway station. Walk east along the train tracks to a bridge, then cross the tracks and turn left to a road leading up. At the end of this road is the *Dealul Gării Restaurant*, where you can camp or rent a bungalow. The bungalows are good, but facilities for those staying in tents are poor to nonexistent.

There's a better camping ground at Hula Daneş, but it's four km out of town on the road to Mediaş, and bus service from the *autogară* (bus terminal) beside the train station is lousy. Bungalows cost US$6 and the site is not crowded.

## Getting There & Away

All trains between Braşov and Cluj-Napoca stop at Sighişoara. For Sibiu (95 km) you'll probably have to change trains at Mediaş or Copşa Mică. You can buy train tickets at the CFR travel agency at Strada 1 decembrie 2.

## SIBIU

Founded in the 12th century on the site of the former Roman village of Cibinium, Sibiu (Hermannstadt) has always been one of the leading cities of Transylvania. Destroyed by the Tatars in 1241, the town was later surrounded by strong walls which enabled the citizens to resist the Turks. Under the Habsburgs from 1703 to 1791 and again from 1849 to 1867, Sibiu served as seat of the Austrian governors of Transylvania. More recently, Nicu Ceauşescu used the town as a power base until his family was overthrown in late 1989.

Much remains from this colourful history for visitors to see, and Sibiu is also a gateway to the Făgăraş Mountains, Romania's best hiking area. You can go camping and Sibiu is just far enough off the beaten track to be spared the tourist tide that occasionally engulfs Braşov. If you only visit one Romanian city, make it Sibiu.

## Orientation

The adjacent bus and railway stations are near the centre of town. The left-luggage office at Sibiu Railway Station is in the passageway under the tracks. Stroll up Strada General Magheru four blocks to Piaţa Republicii, the historic centre. From the opposite corner of the square, Strada Nicolae Bălcescu continues south-west to Piaţa Unirii, another focal point.

## Information

The ONT tourist office is at Strada Nicolae Bălcescu 53, on Piaţa Unirii. Ask here about cabana accommodation if you intend to go hiking in the Făgăraş Mountains.

Tourist desks catering to international tourists are found in the Bulevard and Continental hotels.

| | |
|---|---|
| 1 | Hat Shop |
| 2 | Ursuliens Church |
| 3 | Franciscan Church |
| 4 | Pharmaceutical Museum |
| 5 | Casă Artelor |
| 6 | Evangelcial Church |
| 7 | Primaria Municipiului Museum |
| 8 | City Historical Museum |
| 9 | Catholic Cathedral |
| 10 | Brukenthal Museum |
| 11 | Casă Haller |
| 12 | Private Room Office |
| 13 | Hotel Împăratul Romanilor |
| 14 | CFR Travel Agency |
| 15 | Orthodox Cathedral |
| 16 | Soldisch Bastion |
| 17 | Hotel Bulevard |
| 18 | ONT Tourist Office |
| 19 | Natural History Museum |

The Libreria Dacia Traian, Piaţa Republicii 7, often stocks useful Romanian maps and guidebooks.

## Things to See

Central Sibiu is a perfectly preserved medieval monument, and there's no better place to begin your visit than at the top of the council tower (1588) on Piaţa Republicii, now the **City Historical Museum**. The old maps and photos complement the view of red roofs, with the Făgăraş Mountains beckoning to the south. After this visual treat, walk along the square past the Baroque **Catholic Cathedral** (1728) to the **Brukenthal Museum** (closed Monday), the oldest and finest art gallery in Romania. Founded in 1817, the museum is in the aristocratic Baroque palace (1785) of Baron Samuel Brukenthal, former governor of Transylvania. Apart from the paintings, there are excellent archaeological and folk art collections housed in the same building. Note especially the folk paintings on glass.

Just west along Strada octombrie Roşu is the **Primaria Municipiului** (1470), now a

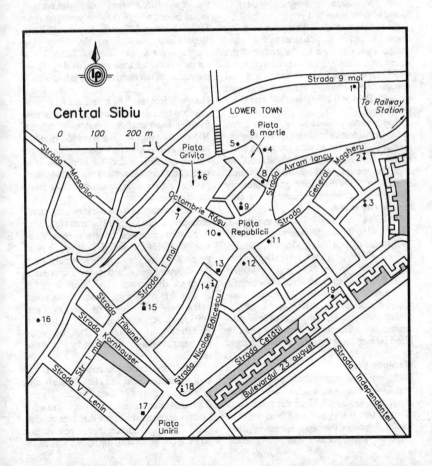

Central Sibiu

0    100    200 m

LOWER TOWN

To Railway Station

Strada 9 mai

Piaţa 6 martie

Piaţa Griviţa

Strada Masarilor

Octombrie Rôşu

Piaţa Republicii

Strada Avram Iancu

Strada General Magheru

Strada 1 mai

Strada Tribunei

Strada Kornhauser

Str. 1 mai

Strada V I Lenin

Strada Nicolae Bălcescu

Strada Cetăţii

Bulevardul 23 august

Strada Independentei

Piaţa Unirii

historical museum. Nearby on Piaţa Grivita is another of Sibiu's many highlights, the Gothic **Evangelical Church** (1300-1520), its great five-pointed tower visible from afar. As you enter, you will see four magnificent Baroque funerary monuments on the upper nave, and the organ of 6002 pipes (1772). In summer, organ concerts are held on Wednesdays at 6 pm. Don't miss the fresco of the Crucifixion (1445) up in the sanctuary – a splendid work. There's a large collection of old tombstones in the closed-off section behind the organ, but you have to ask to be let in. The church itself opens Monday to Saturday from 9 am to 1 pm.

From here you have the choice of going down the 13th century **Staircase Passage**, on the opposite side of the church from where you entered, into the lower town, which is thick with local characters and popular scenes. Nearby Piaţa 6 martie with its **Iron Bridge** (1859) is also extremely picturesque.

Continue south-west along Strada 1 mai to the **Orthodox Cathedral** (1906), a monumental building styled after the Hagia Sofia in Istanbul. Strada Tribunei, around the corner to the left, will lead to Piaţa Unirii, where you'll find the beginning of a pleasant walk north-east along a section of the 16th century **city walls**.

If you've got an extra afternoon, it's well worth taking in the **Museum of Popular Techniques** (open May to October, Tuesday to Sunday from 10 am to 6 pm) in **Dumbrava Park** (take trolley bus No 1 from the station to get there). A great number of authentic old rural buildings and houses have been reassembled around several lakes in the park to create an open-air **ethnographical museum**. At the Dumbrava **zoo** here you can hire a boat and row yourself around the lake.

### Places to Stay
**Camping** There are two camping grounds near Sibiu. The closest is beside the Hanul Dumbrava Restaurant, four km south-west of town (take trolley bus No 1 from the train station direct to the site). Camping costs US$6 per person, and a small cabin costs about US$20 double – expensive. There's plenty of space.

Fourteen km north of Sibiu on the railway line to Copşa Mică is Ocna Sibiului, with a large camping ground in the forest. The camping ground is very near the station and most trains stop here. The many natural pools and geological curiosities around Ocna Sibiului make it a popular bathing resort. The Lacul Fără Fund (Bottomless Lake) here is the flooded shaft of a former salt mine.

**Private Rooms** To find a private room, try the small office marked *'informatii cazare'* (open from 2 to 7 pm) in the passageway at Strada Nicolae Bălcescu 1, just off Piaţa Republicii. The sign on the street says *'rooms – camere de inchiriat'*. You'll pay about US$18 for a triple room (no singles) but it could work out cheaper if you pay in lei.

**Hotels & Hostels** The hotels are all expensive but the most colourful is the centrally located *Împăratul Romanilor*, at Strada Nicolae Bălcescu 4. This hotel has recently been upgraded to luxury category but some rooms are still graded 1st class and cost US$39/67 single/double. Personalities such as Franz Liszt and Johann Strauss have stayed here.

Another good place is the imposing *Hotel Bulevard*, at Piaţa Unirii 10 (from US$38/64 single/double). Avoid the nearby *Hotel Continental*, Calea Dumbrăvii 2-4, which is of the concrete and glass high-rise variety. Both the Bulevard and Continental accept hotel coupons. Though expensive, the Bulevard is an excellent hotel with unlimited quantities of hot water and a cosy room where a cooked breakfast is served to guests from 6.30 to 11 am. The high-rise Continental absorbs visiting groups, which leaves room for you at the Bulevard.

Sibiu's moderate accommodation is all concentrated around the *Hanul Dumbrava* four km south-west of town. You can stay in the Hanul Dumbrava itself, a rustic inn with several large restaurants downstairs, for US$21/46 single/double, though you can expect a lot of noise until the restaurants close

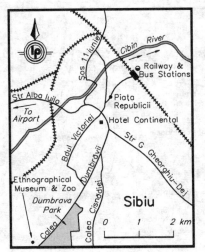

Sibiu

0    1    2 km

at around 9 pm. Behind the Hanul Dumbrava is the camping ground mentioned earlier. There's also a motel nearby at US$32/40 single/double and the facilities are much better than at the inn. The Hanul Dumbrava reception also handles accommodation at the motel.

### Places to Eat
*Autoservire Expres* has two locations: Strada General Magheru 42, between the railway station and Piaţa Republicii, and Strada 1 mai 7, not far from the Brukenthal Museum.

### Things to Buy
Perhaps the most distinctive souvenir of Romania you'll ever find is one of the hats at the men's hat shop (open weekdays from 8 am to 1 pm), Strada 9 mai 50, a couple of blocks from the stations. Good luck trying to get the colourful ones through customs!

### Getting There & Away
Sibiu is on the railway line from Braşov to Arad. Local trains bound for Braşov and Bucharest stop at the Făgăraş trailheads. For Sighişoara or Cluj-Napoca, you may have to change at Copşa Mică or Mediaş, although

some trains go direct, so ask. For Alba Iulia you must change at Vinţu de Jos.

The CFR travel agency is at Strada Nicolae Bălcescu 6, next to the Romanilor Împăratul Hotel.

There are direct Autotransport buses from opposite the Hotel Bulevard to Alba Iulia (ask about times at the hotel reception).

### THE FĂGĂRAŞ MOUNTAINS
In summer, hordes of backpackers descend on the Făgăraş Mountains, a section of the Carpathian Mountains in central Romania. Here they soon get lost in Alpine glory, for Făgăraş is the most popular hiking area in the country. First, get a good map at a bookshop, tourist office, or luxury hotel reception. Just keep looking until you find one.

To hike Făgăraş you must be in good physical shape and have warm clothing and sturdy boots. The trails are well marked, but keep the altitude in mind and be prepared for cold and rain at any time. From November to April these mountains are snow-covered, and August and September are the best months. Basic food is available at the cabanas mentioned in the Sinaia section, but carry a good supply of biscuits and keep your water bottle full. You'll meet lots of other hikers eager to tell you of their adventures, and with the help of a good map you'll soon know exactly where to go.

### Routes & Places to Stay
The easiest access is from Sibiu, and local trains on the Făgăraş line to Braşov pass many starting points. One of the best places to get off at is Gara Sebeş Olt, from where you can hike to *Cabana Suru* (1450 metres, 60 beds) in about five hours via Sebeşu de Sus (450 metres). *Cabana Negoiu* (1546 metres, 170 beds) is seven hours east of Suru across peaks up to 2306 metres high.

Alternatively, ask about the daily morning bus from Sibiu direct to *Cabana Poiana Neamţului* (706 metres, 39 beds). From here it's a three-hour climb to *Cabana Bîrcaciu* (1550 metres, 20 beds), then another two hours to Cabana Negoiu. From Porumbacu

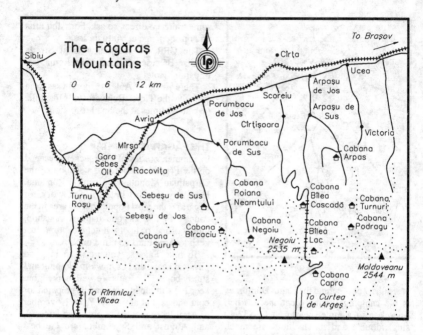

The Făgăraş Mountains

0    6    12 km

To Braşov

Sibiu

• Cîrţa

Ucea

Arpaşu de Jos

Scoreiu

Porumbacu de Jos

Arpaşu de Sus

Avrig

Cîrţişoara

Victoria

Mîrşa

Porumbacu de Sus

Cabana Arpaş

Gara Sebeş Olt

Racoviţa

Turnu Roşu

Sebeşu de Sus

Cabana Poiana Neamţului

Cabana Bîlea Cascadă

Cabana Turnuri

Sebeşu de Jos

Cabana Podragu

Cabana Bîrcaciu

Cabana Negoiu

Cabana Bîlea Lac

Cabana Suru

Negoiu 2535 m

Moldoveanu 2544 m

To Rîmnicu Vîlcea

Cabana Capra

To Curtea de Argeş

de Jos Railway Station, you can hike up to Cabana Negoiu in about seven hours. Eight strenuous hours east of Cabana Negoiu is *Cabana Bîlea Lac* (2034 metres, 170 beds), where there's a cable car down to *Cabana Bîlea Cascadă* (1234 metres, 63 beds) and to the road leading out of the mountains. On this section you will pass Mt Negoiu (2535 metres), the second-highest peak in Romania. *Cabana Capra*, south of Bîlea Lac, was Ceauşescu's private hunting lodge complete with two helicopter pads.

If you want to begin your trip at Bîlea Cascadă and use the cable car to avoid an 800-metre climb, take the afternoon bus from Sibiu to Cîrţişoara, a 22-km walk from Bîlea Cascadă. On Sundays there's a bus from Sibiu direct to Bîlea Cascadă. Another way to get to Bîlea Cascadă is to take a train to Halta Cîrta Railway Station, which will add about an hour to your walk. The ruins of a fortified 13th century Cistercian monastery are about a km north of Cîrta station. The cabanas near the cable car may well be full of tourists with cars, forcing you to camp.

A seven-hour walk east of Bîlea Lac is *Cabana Podragu* (2136 metres, 100 beds), which you can use as a base to climb Mt Moldoveanu (2544 metres), Romania's highest peak. From Cabana Podragu you can descend to the railway at Arpasu de Jos (420 metres) or Ucea in a day or continue east along the ridge. Other ways to get into this area include the road north from Curtea de Argeş to Bîlea Lac (there is no bus service beyond Căpăţinenii) or a train north from Rîmnicu Vîlcea to Turnu Roşu or Gara Podu Olt near Gara Sebeş Olt.

## CLUJ-NAPOCA

Cut in two by the Someşul Mic River, Cluj-Napoca is as Hungarian as it is Romanian. Its position near the middle of Transylvania made it a crossroads, which explains its present role as an educational and industrial centre. Known as Klausenburg to the

Germans and Kolozsvár to the Hungarians, the old Roman name of Napoca has been added to the city's official title to emphasise its Daco-Roman origin.

The history of Cluj-Napoca goes back to Dacian times. In 124 AD, during the reign of Emperor Hadrian, Napoca attained municipal status and Emperor Marcus Aurelius elevated it to a colony. Documented references of the medieval town date back to 1183. German merchants arrived in the 12th century and after the Tatar invasion of 1241 the medieval earthen walls of *castrenses de Clus* were rebuilt in stone. From 1791 to 1848 and again after the union with Hungary in 1867, Cluj-Napoca served as capital of Transylvania.

Though Cluj-Napoca has far fewer historical relics than Sibiu and is in a less picturesque location than Braşov, it has several good museums and a large botanical garden. To the south-west are the Munti Apuseni, or Western Carpathians, a favourite hiking area almost unknown to foreigners.

## Orientation

The railway station is some distance north of the centre, so catch a trolley bus or take any southbound bus on Strada Horea and get off at the first stop after crossing the river. From the bridge here, Strada Gheorghe Doja climbs slightly to Piaţa Libertăţii, the heart of the city.

## Information

The tourist office is on the corner of Strada 30 decembrie and Strada Şincai, three blocks west of Piaţa Libertăţii.

## Things to See

**St Michael's Church**, a 15th century Gothic hall church with a neo-Gothic tower (1859), sits in the centre of Piaţa Libertăţii. Flanking it on the south is a huge equestrian statue (1902) of the famous Hungarian king Matthias Corvinus (ruled 1458-90), son of János Hunyadi (Iancu de Hunedoara). On the east side of the square is the **Fine Arts Museum** in the Baroque Banffy Palace (1785). A **pharmaceutical museum** is diag-

onally across the street at Strada Gheorghe Doja 2 (open Monday to Saturday from 9 am to 1 pm), on the site of Cluj-Napoca's first apothecary (1573).

Strada Matei Corvin leads from the northwest corner of the square to **Corvinus' birthplace** (in 1440) at number 6. A block ahead is the beautifully decorated **Franciscan Church**. Left on Piaţa Muzeului is the **History Museum of Transylvania** (closed Monday) which has been open since 1859 and has an extensive collection on display. The **Ethnographical Museum**, with its Transylvanian folk costumes and farm implements, is at Strada 30 decembrie 21.

South at Strada Republicii 42 are the large and varied **Botanical Gardens**. These include greenhouses, a museum and a Japanese garden – in summer allow several hours to explore it. For an overall view of Cluj-Napoca, climb up the steps behind Hotel Astoria to the Transilvania Hotel in the **citadel** (1715).

## Places to Stay

**Camping** *Camping Făget* (open from May to mid-October) is up in the hills seven km south of Cluj-Napoca. Camping costs US$7 for one person with tent, and the 143 bungalows on the site go for US$24 single or double. The restaurant here closes at 9 pm. Bus No 46 from Piaţa Mihai Viteazul 29 goes about five km up Calea Turzii to within two km of the camp site, but you must still walk the last two km uphill. Ask the bus driver to let you know where to get off.

A rough dirt road leads one km up from the camping ground to the 24-bed *Cabana Făget Pădure* (open all year) where a four-bed room is US$29 for the room. There's a large restaurant here so it's a nice walk if you're staying at the camping ground.

**Hotels** Cluj-Napoca has one of the best selections of hotels in Romania. *Hotel Pax*, Strada Gării 2, opposite the railway station, is US$25 double (no singles). *The Hotel Vlădeasa*, Strada Gheorghe Doja 20, is Cluj-Napoca's cheapest at US$21 double (no

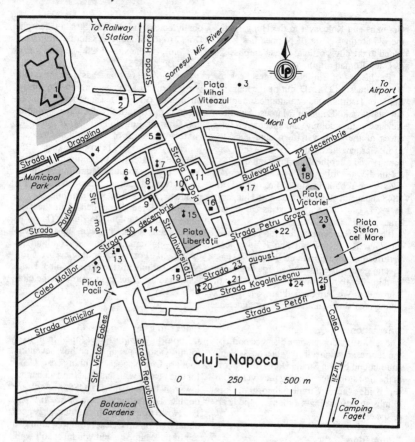

Cluj–Napoca

singles). The next cheapest hotel is the *Astoria*, Strada Horea 3, at US$17/29 single/double with shared bath and breakfast. In the same category is the *Hotel Central*, Piaţa Libertăţii 29 (US$18/31 single/double with shared bath). You are welcome here.

A step up in price is the elegant old *Continental Hotel* on the south-west corner of Piaţa Libertăţii, with singles/doubles from US$27/40 with shared bath. A hotel coupon will get you a better room at the Continental. The newer *Hotel Siesta*, Strada Şincai 4, behind the tourist office, is about the same

price as the Continental, though it also has some singles without bath for US$21.

Cluj-Napoca's finest hotel is the *Hotel Transilvania* on Citadel Hill, overlooking the city. This modern hotel is expensive at US$58/74 single/double but hotel coupons are accepted. The hard-currency shop in the hotel is well stocked.

### Places to Eat

The dining room at the *Continental Hotel* has great atmosphere and is frequented by some interesting underworld characters. If you like seafood, try the *Restaurantul Pescarul*

■ PLACES TO STAY

1 Hotel Transilvania
2 Astoria Hotel
11 Hotel Vlădeasa
13 Hotel Siesta
16 Hotel Central
19 Hotel Continental

▼ PLACES TO EAT

9 Restaurantul Intim
17 Hubertus Restaurant

OTHER

1 Citadel
3 Market
4 Hungarian State Theatre & Opera
5 Post Office
6 History Museum of Transylvania
7 Franciscan Church
8 Birthplace of Matthias Corvinus
10 Pharmaceutical Museum
12 Town Hall
13 Tourist Office
14 Ethnological Museum
15 St Michael's Church
16 Banffy Palace
18 Orthodox Cathedral
20 Piarist Church
21 State Philharmonic Orchestra
22 Agenție Teatrala (Theatre Ticket Office)
23 National Theatre
24 Reformed Church
25 Tailor's Bastion

(closed Monday) on Strada Universitătii, next to Cinema Arta, behind the Continental Hotel.

One of the cheapest places to eat at is the *Lacto-Vegetarian Restaurant*, at Piața Libertății 12, though most of the dishes are meat-based. *Berarie*, Piața Libertății 19, is a large beer garden with a good self-service restaurant at the back.

*Restaurantul Intim*, Strada Matei Corvin 2 (closed Sunday), is a rare beast: it's a women's restaurant and bar where (almost) no men are allowed. The *Dacia Restaurant*, Strada 30 decembrie 13, is the place to try for local specialities, but there's no guarantee

that you'll get them. If you want game meat go to *Hubertus*, Bulevardul 22 decembrie 22 (closed Sunday).

*Restaurant Metropol*, Strada Horea 7, has its menu displayed in the window.

### Entertainment

The Agenția Teatrala, Strada Dr Petru Groza 36, has tickets for most events. The neo-Baroque *National Theatre* (1906) on Piața Victoriei was designed by the famous Viennese architects Fellner and Hellmer. There's also the *Hungarian State Theatre & Opera* at the northern end of Strada 1 mai, near the river.

### Getting There & Away

There are express trains from Cluj-Napoca to Oradea, Sighişoara, Braşov, Timişoara, Baia Mare and Bucharest. Through trains run to Iaşi via Gura Humorului and Suceava. For Sibiu you may have to change at Copşa Mică. For Alba Iulia or Hunedoara you sometimes have to change at Teiuş. Sleepers are available to Bucharest.

You can buy train tickets at the CFR travel agency at Piața Libertății 9, opposite the Continental Hotel.

### ALBA IULIA

The imposing fortifications of Alba Iulia (also known as Karlsburg or Weissenburg) near the Mureş River, between Cluj-Napoca and Deva, dominate the south-western flank of Transylvania. It was here in 1600 and 1918 that the union of Transylvania to Romania was proclaimed. Today Alba Iulia is the seat of Alba County and since 1841 has been the source of some of Romania's best champagne. Three million bottles a year are produced.

Already in Roman times, Apulum (now Alba Iulia) was an important town and head-quarters of the 13th legion. From 1542 to 1690, Alba Iulia served as the capital of the Principality of Transylvania. Michael the Brave, ruler of Romania from 1593 to 1601, entered Alba Iulia on 1 November 1599, thus unifying the three Romanian principalities of Wallachia, Moldavia and Transylvania under his rule, a union that endured until he was assassinated a year later. The present Vauban-style citadel with its seven bastions and six gates was designed by the Italian architect Giovanni Visconti and was erected between 1714 and 1741. Previous fortifications on this site had been destroyed by the Tatars in 1241 and the Turks in 1661. Today Alba Iulia is best remembered by Romanians for the 'Great Assembly' which occurred here on 1 December 1918, when some 100,000 Romanians from Transylvania, Banat, Crişana and Maramureş gathered to express their wish to be united with Romania. In 1920 this wish was granted in the Treaty of Trianon.

### Orientation
The adjacent bus and train stations are two km south of the centre of town. Walk north on Strada Republicii as far as the main post office (PTTR), where you turn left up Strada Mihai Viteazul to go to the Alba Carolina Citadel. It's not a particularly pleasant walk, so consider taking a bus or taxi if you can. To go to the Hotel Transilvania, go straight ahead for another two blocks from the post office.

### Information
The tourist office is in the Hotel Transilvania, Piaţa 1 mai 22.

### Things to See & Do
Strada Mihai Viteazul leads up from the lower town to a ramp which brings you to the Baroque east gate of the **Alba Carolina Citadel** (1735). An obelisk opposite this gate commemorates the peasant uprising of 1784 led by Cloşca, Crişan and Horea, who were imprisoned here. (Crişan committed suicide and the other two were tortured to death.) Above the gate is Horea's cell.

Enter the citadel and continue straight ahead to the large equestrian statue of Mihai Viteazul (Michael the Brave). The statue faces **Unification Hall**, where the act of unification between Romania and Transylvania was signed on 1 December 1918. Across the street is the **Museum of the Unification**

(closed Monday), which opened in 1888 and has an extensive historical collection (all captions are in Romanian).

Just beyond the statue is the **Catholic Cathedral**. This impressive cathedral, built on the site of a Romanesque church that was destroyed during the Tatar invasion of 1241, was rebuilt in a transitional Romanesque-Gothic style in the late 13th century. Many famous Transylvanian princes are buried here, including János Hunyadi (Iancu de Hunedoara), who defeated the Turks at Belgrade in 1456. The cathedral is currently undergoing restoration and may still be closed, but try the western entrance below the towers.

The adjacent **Orthodox Cathedral** with its 52-metre bell tower was erected in 1922 in an attempt to overshadow the work of the Catholic Hungarians; Ferdinand and Marie were crowned king and queen of Romania in the cathedral that year. This massive yellow stone complex faces the impressive new city of Alba Iulia, which was built by the Communists in the 1980s.

### Places to Stay & Eat
Alba Iulia's two modern hotels, the *Transilvania*, Piaţa 1 mai 22, in the lower town, east of the citadel, and the high-rise *Cetate*, Bulevardul Horia 41, in the new town, west of the citadel, are both expensive, but hotel coupons are accepted. Both are about two km from the bus and train stations by different routes. The Transilvania is closer to local facilities, whereas the Cetate would be preferable if you're driving.

The basic *Hanul Dintre Sălcii* camping ground is just across the Mureş River, about three km south of the stations, in the opposite direction from town. You may be able to camp here but there are few facilities.

### Getting There & Away
The local train trip from Alba Iulia to Sibiu (92 km, three hours) involves a change at Vinţu de Jos and the connections are poor. To go to/from Sighişoara or Cluj-Napoca by local train, you'll have to change at Teiuş. Express trains with compulsory reservations

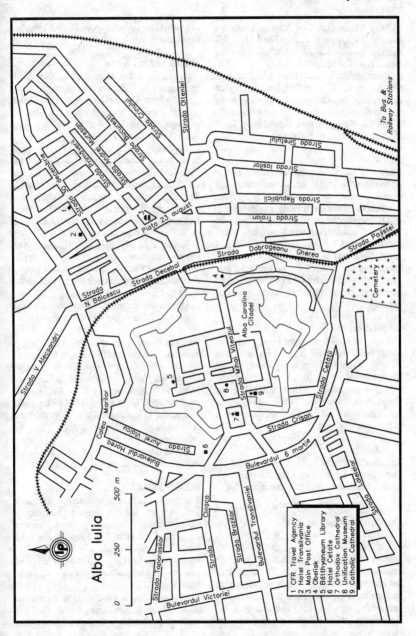

Alba Iulia

0    250    500 m

1  CFR Travel Agency
2  Hotel Transilvania
3  Main Post Office
4  Obelisk
5  Bdtithyaneum Library
6  Hotel Cetate
7  Orthodox Cathedral
8  Unification Museum
9  Catholic Cathedral

To Bus &
Railway Stations

Cemetery

Alba Carolina Citadel

Strada Olteniei
Strada Crinului
Strada Bucuresti
Strada Andrei Muresan
Strada Primaverii
Strada 30 decembrie
Piata 23 august
Strada Decebal
Strada N Balcescu
Strada V Alecsandri
Strada Siretului
Strada Iasilor
Strada Republicii
Strada Traian
Strada Dobrogeanu Gherea
Strada Pajistei
Strada Mihai Viteazul
Strada Cetatii
Strada Crisan
Calea Motilor
Strada Aurel Vlaicu
Bulevardul Horea
Bulevardul 6 martie
Bulevardul Victoriei
Strada Toporasilor
Strada Closca
Strada Brazilor
Bulevardul Transilvaniei
Strada Latelor

to/from Timişoara, Cluj-Napoca, Suceava and Iaşi do stop here, so ask. The CFR travel agency is on Strada 30 decembrie, near the Hotel Transilvania.

There are direct buses from Alba Iulia Bus Station to Sibiu (five daily), Cluj-Napoca (three daily) and Oradea (one daily). In addition to these, there are other direct buses to Sibiu via Sibiu Airport from Hotel Transilvania (ask at the hotel desk).

## DEVA

Deva, the administrative centre of Hunedoara County, might be a convenient first stop in Transylvania if you're arriving from Yugoslavia or southern Hungary. For centuries Deva guarded the western entrance to the Transylvanian plateau where the Mureş breaks through the encircling mountains and flows west into Hungary. Prior to WW II, Deva was the base of the opposition Farm Workers' Front led by Dr Petru Groza, who served as prime minister in the postwar period.

### Orientation

The bus and railway stations are adjacent. Go south on Bulevardul V I Lenin from the railway station for about 600 metres through the redeveloped city centre to the main post office, on the corner of Bulevardul Dr Petru Groza. From here the old town and museum are to the right and the modern city centre is to the left.

### Information

The local tourist office is at Bulevardul Dr Petru Groza 13. There's a special office for foreign tourists at the Hotel Sarmis.

### Things to See

The **County Museum**, Bulevardul Dr Petru Groza 29 (closed Monday), with archaeological exhibits on display, is in the 16th century Magna Curia Palace, directly below Deva's 13th century **citadel**. You can climb the extinct volcano (371 metres) on which the citadel is perched from the park beside the museum. At the eastern end of Bulevardul Dr Petru Groza is an **equestrian**

**statue** of Decebalus, the last Dacian king, by the sculptor Ion Jalea.

### Places to Stay & Eat

The nearest camping ground to Deva and Hunedoara is *P T Strei* by the Strei River, about three km east of Simeria. Halta Simeria Veche, the next station east of Simeria, is much closer to the camping ground than Simeria Station.

If you're looking for a budget room, your first choice should be the 3rd-class *Hotel Bulevard*, Bulevardul Dr Petru Groza 16 (US$14/23 single/double with shared bath). The old *Hotel Dacia*, nearby at Piaţa Unirii 11, isn't much better than the Hotel Bulevard but charges twice as much (US$29/42 single/double with private bath).

Rather than pay these rip-off rates, go to the modern *Hotel Sarmis*, Piaţa Victoriei 3. It is near the Decebalus statue, a few blocks east. Good singles/doubles cost US$35/49 and hotel coupons are accepted.

Unlike the rooms, meals in the restaurant at the *Hotel Dacia* are good and cheap.

### Getting There & Away

Simeria, nine km east of Deva, is an important railway junction with direct lines to Hunedoara, Arad (via Deva), Alba Iulia (via Vinţu de Jos), Sibiu and Tîrgu Jiu. A local train between Deva and Arad (149 km) will take about three hours. To go to/from Alba Iulia takes just under two hours (63 km) by local train.

Buses from Deva to Hunedoara leave every hour from 6 am to 11 pm.

## HUNEDOARA

The main attraction of this area is the intact 14th century Gothic castle at Hunedoara (Eisenmarkt), 13 km south of Deva. This was the seat of the Hunedoara family and both János Hunyadi and his son Matthias Corvinus (Matei Corvin), two famous kings of Hungary, made notable improvements to the building.

Iron ore has been extracted from this region since Roman times and in the 19th century a smelter was built here. After

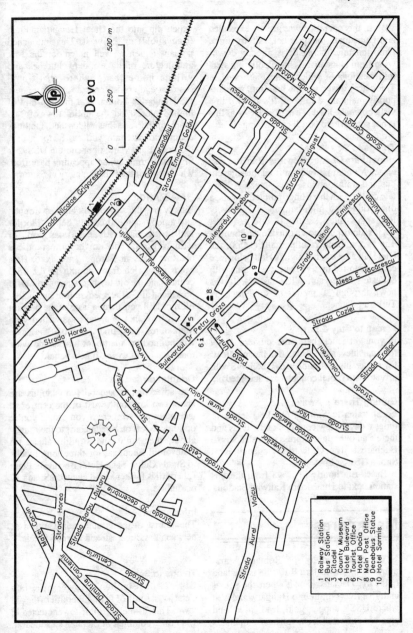

Deva

1 Railway Station
2 Bus Station
3 Citadel
4 County Museum
5 Hotel Buleyard
6 Tourist Office
7 Hotel Dacia
8 Main Post Office
9 Decebalus Statue
10 Hotel Sarmis

WW II, this operation was greatly expanded and Hunedoara today is not a pretty sight. Unfortunately, the castle is directly downwind from Hunedoara's huge polluting steel mill, sections of which almost surround it. Thick grey dust coats the building, which is poorly maintained to boot! It's still worth a visit, but make it a day trip from Deva, as this is not somewhere you'll care to linger.

### Things to See
**Hunedoara Castle** (open from 9 am to 5 pm, closed Monday) is two km from the adjacent bus and train stations. This amazing fairytale castle, with three huge pointed towers, a drawbridge and high battlements, is easily Romania's finest secular Gothic structure, yet it's almost unknown outside the country. The two authentic Gothic halls (1453), the Diet Hall above and Knight's Hall below, are each supported by five marble columns with delicate ribbed vaults. The castle well was hewn through 30 metres of solid rock by Turkish prisoners.

### Places to Stay & Eat
If you get stuck here, the modern *Hotel Rusca*, Bulevardul Dacia 10 in the middle of town, has singles/doubles for US$30/48 with private bath (hotel coupons are accepted).

### Getting There & Away
Local trains to Simeria (15 km) leave 11 times a day. A few continue on to Teiuş and there's an overnight express with sleepers to Bucharest. The CFR travel agency is at Strada George Enescu 3.

Buses run hourly to Deva from the bus station next to Hunedoara Railway Station.

# Maramureş

Never conquered by the Romans, Maramureş in north-western Romania is the land of the free Dacians. Here is where the Someş and Tisa rivers drain into Hungary, and also where USSR copper, gold, lead, silver and zinc are extracted from forested mountains which dip into the Great Hungarian Plain (Nagyalföld) in the west. This untouched peasant region is well noted for the folk architecture of its wooden churches and village homesteads where traditional customs and crafts persist. Satu Mare, near the Hungarian border, is a modern city of limited interest, but the mining town of Baia Mare farther east has sights and facilities enough to entertain you easily for a day. North of Baia Mare, opposite the USSR, is Sighetu Marmaţiei, an appealing base from which to visit the folk cemetery at Săpinţa.

## BAIA MARE
Baia Mare, the seat of Maramureş County, sits among apple orchards below Florilor Hill on the Săsar River, 151 km north of Cluj-Napoca. The northernmost edible chestnut trees in Europe grow here. Baia Mare grew rich from mining in the 15th century and the old town retains its colourful provincial air. In the open-air museum below Florilor Hill you'll get a taste of the peasant architecture that is always associated with Maramureş. Your first vision of Baia Mare will be modern apartment blocks and wide roads but don't worry, it gets better.

### Orientation
The adjacent bus and railway stations are about two km south-west of the centre, so take a bus or taxi there if you can. If you're on foot, go left on Strada Gării to the roundabout, then right and straight ahead on Bulevardul Bucureşti for three long blocks to Strada Culturii and Hotel Bucureşti. Piaţa Libertăţii is farther ahead again on Strada 17 octómbrie.

### Information
The tourist office is at Strada Culturii 1, between the Bucureşti and Carpaţi hotels.

### Things to See
Begin with **Stephen's Tower** on Piaţa Cetăţii just south of Piaţa Libertăţii in the old town. This 50-metre Gothic tower erected in 1347 once adjoined St Stephen's Cathedral.

Baia Mare

1 Chestnut Trees
2 Zoo
3 Open-Air Museum
4 Museum of Ethnography
5 Soldier Monument
6 County Museum
7 Piaţa Libertăţii
8 Hotel Minerul
9 Stephen's Tower
10 Butchers' Tower
11 Market
12 Hotel Maramures
13 Political-Administrative
   Centre
14 Hotel Bucureşti
15 Tourist Office
16 Carpaţi Hotel
17 Casă de Cultură
18 CFR Travel Agency
19 Department Store
20 Hotel Mara
21 Bus Station
22 Railway Station

However, it was struck by lightning in 1769 and finally demolished a century ago. Just across the square from the tower is the Baroque **Trinity Cathedral** (1720), and directly behind this, in a 1748 building, is the **County Art Museum**, Strada 1 mai 8, which houses 19th century works representative of the Baia Mare school of painting.

Go north across the pleasant Piaţa Libertăţii and north again on Strada 23 august to the large church at No 10. Here turn right to get to the **County Museum**, Strada Bicazului 1-3, which is in a Baroque palace dating from 1739. The medieval mint once stood on this site and the museum's emphasis is on mining and geology.

Continue north on Strada 23 august, and after crossing the bridge you will see the **Monument to the Romanian Soldier** in the park ahead and slightly to the left. Beyond the monument, up a road lined with chestnut trees, you'll see the **County Museum of Ethnography and Popular Art** in a massive 1950s structure. The paintings on glass are worth noting and you can purchase examples. On the hillside to the right of this museum is an **open-air museum** of Maramureşean traditional dwellings. Ask the attendant to open a few of the houses for you if they're closed. West of the cemetery beside these museums is a large park with many more chestnut trees.

### Places to Stay

There are no cheap hotels in Baia Mare. The characterful old *Hotel Minerul*, Piaţa Libertăţii 7, is overpriced at US$48 double (no singles). The schedule of when hot water is available is posted at the reception. A cheaper choice would be the newer four-storey *Hotel Bucureşti*, Strada Culturii 4 (US$28/36 single/double).

You're much better off using a hotel coupon at the *Carpaţi Hotel*, Bulevardul Independenţei 2, next to the Casă de Cultura and not too far from the centre. *Hotel Mara*, Bulevardul Unirii 11, between the railway station and the middle of town, also takes coupons. Both of these are standard high-rise hotels.

Camping is possible at the Baraj Firiza (Firiza Dam) 11 km north of Baia Mare (bus No 1). There's a restaurant at the *Cabana Păstrăvul* here.

### Places to Eat

*Hotel Minerul*, Piaţa Libertăţii 7, features a beer garden, restaurant, coffee shop and self-service, so you shouldn't go hungry there. There's even a cinema in the hotel.

A very pleasant pizza bar with an outdoor terrace is right next to Stephen's Tower. When the brew flows, *Prodas*, at Piaţa Libertăţii 15, has a great beer garden at the back with whole roast chickens available, if you're lucky.

### Entertainment

The *Dramatic Theatre*, Strada Crişan 4, is opposite Stephen's Tower. Most events take place during the 'Baia Mare in Autumn' festival during the first 10 days of October. Ask at the tourist office about performances by the Maramureşul Song and Dance Ensemble, which are usually held at the Casă de Cultura, Bulevardul Independenţei 4, next to the Carpaţi Hotel.

### Getting There & Away

Baia Mare is on the main line from Bucharest to Satu Mare via Braşov, Ciceu and Deda. The Maramureş Express departs from Baia Mare in the early morning for Cluj-Napoca and Bucharest. In the other direction it runs north from Cluj-Napoca to Baia Mare in the afternoon – a good connection if you get a ticket. To go to/from Oradea, change at Satu Mare; to/from Suceava change at Dej. The CFR travel agency, Strada Victoriei 57, is a long block from the Carpaţi Hotel.

There are two buses a day to Cluj-Napoca and six a day to Sighetu Marmaţiei.

### SIGHETU MARMAŢIEI

Sighetu Marmaţiei, at the junction of the Iza and Tisa rivers, is a centre for the woodworking industry. The area just north across the Tisa River is now part of the Soviet Union; however, it used to belong to Czechoslovakia until WW II and smugglers did brisk business. Today Sighetu Marmaţiei is an attractive little town unspoiled by modern developments, with fairly good shopping in the stores facing Piaţa Libertăţii.

## Orientation & Information

The adjacent bus and railway stations are on the north side of town. From the stations follow Strada Republicii south towards the large church, where you turn left to the city centre.

The tourist office, Piaţa Libertăţii 21, is directly across the square from the Tisa Hotel.

## Things to See

The **Art Gallery** at Strada Mara 17 features an enchanting collection of paintings of regional scenes by local artist Traian Biltiv Dancus. The **Maramureşean Museum** (closed Monday), Strada Bogdan Voda 1, in the centre of town, has a passable collection of ethnographical objects.

On Dobăieş Hill, four km east of Sighetu Marmaţiei off the road to Baia Mare, is an **open-air museum** with exhibits of popular Maramureşean architecture (closed Monday). Only a few of the houses are furnished and all are of the same style. It's not really worth the long walk, so either take a taxi or skip it.

**Săpînţa** By far the most interesting sight around Sighetu Marmaţiei is the Merry Cemetery by the church in Săpînţa, a village 18 km west. In 1935 Ioan Stan Pătras, a local artist, began carving wooden crosses complete with painted reliefs and epitaph verses and these now fill the cemetery in orderly rows. The largest tomb is that of Ioan himself, who died in 1977, directly opposite the church door. On the back of the cross you'll see the gentleman doing some carving. If you're lucky, someone will translate a few of the Romanian verses on the crosses for you, as these present the good and bad traits of the deceased in a most amusing way, which is why it's called the 'merry' cemetery. Ioan's house, now a museum, is a five-minute walk back behind the cemetery.

There's a thriving cottage industry in Săpînţa which makes the rugs and folk costumes that are for sale along the road.

Getting to Săpînţa is a problem as only two buses a day come here from Sighetu Marmaţiei, leaving Sighetu Marmaţiei at 5 am and 4 pm. They return to Sighetu Marmaţiei immediately, so it's difficult to use them to visit the cemetery. Consider hiring a taxi for the excursion if there are a few of you. Another option is to take a train from Sighetu Marmaţiei to Cîmpulung la Tisa (five daily, 12 km), and then walk or hitchhike the remaining six km to Săpînţa.

## Places to Stay

The *Ardealul Hotel*, Strada Republicii 78, opposite Sighetu Marmaţiei Railway Station, is US$16 double (no singles) for a simple room with a wash basin and shared bath.

The old *Tisa Hotel*, Piaţa Libertăţii 8, is poor value at US$23/45 single/double.

*Hotel Marmaţia*, Strada M Eminescu 74, is a charming old wooden lodge-style hotel on the bank of the Iza River on the southern side of town, about two km from the railway station. Singles/doubles without bath are US$23/35, with bath US$32/49, and hotel coupons are accepted. Grădina Morii Park next to the hotel is full of huge poplar trees.

At a pinch you could cross the suspension bridge behind Hotel Marmaţia, turn left and look for a hidden camp site in the nearby hills.

## Getting There & Away

Sighetu Marmaţiei is most easily approached from the south by train (from Cluj-Napoca or Suceava) or bus (from Baia Mare). Unless you have your own car, do not try coming from the west (from Satu Mare via Negreşti Oaş) as buses are rare, there is no train, and there's not much to see along the way. The CFR travel agency is at Piaţa Libertăţii 6 in the centre of town.

Coming from Cluj-Napoca or Suceava, you may have to change trains at Salva, though some trains from Cluj-Napoca and Bucharest go right through to Sighetu Marmaţiei. An overnight train with sleepers connects Sighetu Marmaţiei to Bucharest.

At Valea Vişeului, 25 km east of Sighetu Marmaţiei, locomotives must change to the other end of the train, as the line here points north towards a disused crossing into the USSR. The railway between Valea Vişeului and Sighetu Marmaţiei runs right along the Tisa River, which marks the Soviet border, and both sides look about the same. Notice how the single line of track along this stretch has four rails to accommodate the broader gauge trains from the USSR.

Seven buses a day run between Sighetu Marmaţiei and Baia Mare, three of them originating in Sighetu Marmaţiei and the rest in transit. Two buses go to Satu Mare.

# Crişana & Banat

The plains of Crişana and Banat merge imperceptibly into Yugoslavia's Vojvodina and the Great Hungarian Plain. In Romania the Mureş River roughly divides Crişana (to the north) from Banat (to the south). Until 1918 the whole region was one, and although Novi Sad (Yugoslavia), Szeged (Hungary) and Timişoara now belong to three different nations, all three cities bear the unmistakable imprint of the old Habsburg Empire, which is strongly felt in Arad and Oradea as well. The Hungarian element is strong throughout and in the Banat you'll see the influence of the Serbians.

It's logical that Romania's 1989 revolution should have begun in the west, where the country's ethnic mix has always been at the margin of socialist economic development. Drained of food and resources to finance Ceauşescu's great projects around Bucharest, facing increasing marginalisation of national minorities and bombarded with Hungarian and Yugoslav TV coverage of the political changes in East Germany, Czechoslovakia, etc, the west exploded in December 1989. Pilgrims following the 'freedom trail' will want to visit the little Hungarian church in Timişoara where it all began.

To be sure, western Romania is Romania's front door and all the trains from Hungary and Yugoslavia pass through the three gateway cities of Timişoara, Arad and Oradea. Each city offers a touch of fading imperial glory, easy accommodation and a place to stop and get your bearings. If you're leaving Romania and have spare lei and an extra hotel coupon or two, this is your last chance to use them.

## ORADEA
Oradea (Nagyvárad in Hungarian, Grosswardein in German), only a few km east of the Hungarian border and 153 km west of Cluj-Napoca, is the seat of Bihor County. It's the centre of the Crişana region, a fertile plain drained by the Crişul Alb, Crişul Negru and Crişul Repede rivers at the fringe of the Carpathian Mountains and the Great Hungarian Plain. Oradea's majestic city centre area straddles both banks of the Crişul Repede River. This town may be useful as a stopover if you're travelling to or from Budapest.

### Orientation
The railway station is a couple of km north of town, so take a tram to Piaţa Victoriei (ask to make sure that you're on the right one). Piaţa Republicii with the tourist office, hotels and State Theatre is just across the bridge over the Crişul Repede River. Calea Republicii, the main pedestrian mall, runs north-east from beside the State Theatre.

### Information
The Oficiul Judeţean de Turism (tourist office) is at Piaţa Republicii 4, and the theatre ticket agency is at Calea Republicii 6. The international branch of the tourist office is in the Hotel Dacia.

### Things to See
Oradea's most imposing sights are on the two city-centre squares, Piaţa Victoriei and Piaţa Republicii. The **Orthodox Church** (1792) on Piaţa Victoriei is also known as the 'Moon Church' for a three-metre sphere on the tower which shows the phases of the Moon. The other fine churches and palaces on this square are an interesting mix of

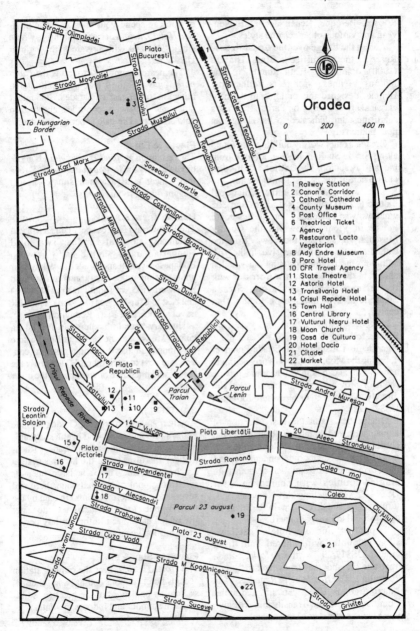

**Oradea**

0    200    400 m

1 Railway Station
2 Canon's Corridor
3 Catholic Cathedral
4 County Museum
5 Post Office
6 Theatrical Ticket
  Agency
7 Restaurant Lacto
  Vegetarian
8 Ady Endre Museum
9 Parc Hotel
10 CFR Travel Agency
11 State Theatre
12 Astoria Hotel
13 Transilvania Hotel
14 Crişul Repede Hotel
15 Town Hall
16 Central Library
17 Vulturul Negru Hotel
18 Moon Church
19 Casă de Cultura
20 Hotel Dacia
21 Citadel
22 Market

Rococo, Baroque, Renaissance, Art Nouveau and various other eclectic styles.

Across the bridge over the Crişul Repede River is the magnificent **State Theatre** (1900), dominating Piaţa Republicii. The famous Viennese architects Fellner and Hellmer designed this building in the neoclassical style. Nearby on Parcul Traian is a small museum dedicated to the Hungarian poet Endre Ady.

Oradea's other worthy buildings are found along Strada Stadionului, just a block from the railway station. The **Catholic Cathedral** (1780) here is the largest Baroque church in Romania. The adjacent former **episcopal palace** (1770) with its 100 rooms and 365 windows was modelled after the Belvedere Palace in Vienna. Now it's the County Museum. The side that faces away from the cathedral is the most impressive. In the park adjoining these buildings is an old wooden church (1785). The **Canon's Corridor** with its series of archways along Strada Stadionului also dates back to the 18th century.

## Places to Stay

Agenţie de Turism Lucon, Strada Prahovei 1, beside the Moon Church, is a private travel agency which can help you to find a private room or provide a special car to take you directly to Debrecen or elsewhere for about US$25 cash.

Oradea has about the best selection of atmospheric old hotels in Romania. First choices for the budget traveller are the *Vulturul Negru*, at Strada Independenţei 1, and the *Parc*, at Calea Republicii 5, both with singles/doubles with shared bath for US$14/22. The yellow Art-Nouveau Vulturul Negru Hotel, erected in 1908, is an architectural curiosity in itself.

Two other fine old hotels that have singles/doubles with shared bath from around US$17/29 are the *Astoria*, Strada Teatrului 1, and the *Transilvania*, Strada Teatrului 2. The *Hotel Crişul Repede*, Strada Libertăţii 6, is US$23/36 single/double. Both the Astoria and Transilvania will give you a better room if you have a hotel coupon,

or you can spend your coupon at the highrise *Hotel Dacia*, Aleea Ştrandului 1, where singles/doubles with private bath begin at US$42/65.

The nearest camping ground is the *Campare Venus* at Băile 1 mai, near Băile Felix, nine km south-east of Oradea. It's rather noisy and dirty with few toilets and broken cold showers. The gate is poorly guarded.

## Places to Eat

The restaurant at *Hotel Transilvania* is good, or you can try the *Restaurant Oradea*, Strada Iosif Vulcan 1, just across the square – a most elegant dining room.

## Getting There & Away

The Balt-Orient Express between Berlin and Bucharest stops at Oradea. Two local Hungarian trains shuttle daily between Budapest-Nyugati and Oradea (249 km, four hours). Many other local trains run north to Satu Mare (133 km), south to Arad (121 km) and east to Cluj-Napoca (153 km). The CFR travel agency is at Piaţa Republicii 2.

Hungary-bound travellers can also take a taxi 14 km west to the border at Bors, where the Hungarian and Romanian passport controls are next to each other. Walk across the border and hitchhike onwards from the other side.

## BĂILE FELIX

An alternative to staying in Oradea is Băile Felix, a famous year-round health spa that is only eight km south-east of Oradea. Rheumatism and diseases of the nervous system are treated here. There's a large open-air swimming pool of thermal water here and several smaller thermal pools covered by the rare *Nymphea lotus thermalis*, a white water lily which dates back to the Tertiary period three million years ago.

## Places to Stay & Eat

The *Hotel Thermal* near the railway station accepts hotel coupons and has a hot thermal swimming pool right in the hotel (it is outdoors in summer and indoors in winter).

Although officially prohibited, many

people camp freelance in the parking lot at Băile Felix; the official camping ground is three km away at Băile 1 mai.

## Getting There & Away

Several local trains a day run from Oradea to Băile Felix, or you can take bus No 14 from Cartierul Nufărul in southern Oradea.

## ARAD

Arad sits in wine-making country on the Mureş River, which drains much of central Transylvania. The city's streets are lined with huge turn-of-the-century buildings that were constructed while this was still part of the Austro-Hungarian empire. The river loops around Arad's 18th century citadel before flowing west to Szeged in Hungary. Arad Citadel itself is occupied by the military and can't be visited, but the surrounding parks are crowded all summer with bathers in the river and pools. After crushing the liberal revolution of 1848, the Habsburgs had 13 Hungarian generals executed outside the citadel.

Only 20 km south of the Hungarian border by rail, Arad is an entry point to Romania. Hunedoara Castle, Sibiu and Sighişoara are on the main line east of Arad and Timişoara is just south.

## Orientation

The railway station is a couple of km north of the centre. Take a tram (buy a ticket at the stop) down Bulevardul Revoluţiei into town.

## Information

The local tourist office is at Bulevardul Revoluţiei 72, opposite the impressive town hall (1876). A special ONT tourist office for foreigners is in the Astoria Hotel nearby.

## Things to See

On Piaţa George Enescu, behind the town hall, is the **History Museum** (closed Monday) in the Palace of Culture (1913). The museum's large display covers the entire history of the area, although the exhibits are difficult to see because of the low lighting.

Walk south on the attractive Bulevardul Revoluţiei to the neoclassical **State Theatre** (1874). On a corner at Piaţa Veche, two blocks beyond the theatre, is a stump (against the outside wall of the house) in which apprentice blacksmiths used to hammer a nail to symbolise their acceptance into the guild. You'll notice it by the large padlock alongside.

## Places to Stay

The *Ardealul Hotel*, Bulevardul Revoluţiei 98, beside the State Theatre (US$28 double with shared bath, no singles), is a fine old neoclassical building (1841) with a music room where Brahms, Liszt and Strauss once gave concerts.

The cheapest hotel in Arad is the 2nd-class *Mureşul*, Bulevardul Revoluţiei 88, which charges US$18/28 single/double for a spacious room with shared bath and breakfast.

If you have hotel coupons, go to the *Parc Hotel*, Strada Dragalina 25 (US$50/64 single/double without coupons). They're more likely to have a room for you than Arad's other high-rise tourist hotel, the *Astoria Hotel*, Bulevardul Revoluţiei 89 (US$42/65 single/double without coupons). The Parc Hotel's restaurant and location are much better than those at the Astoria.

Hotels in Arad are often crowded with Romanians coming from or going to Hungary. Since they get a very cheap rate at hotels inside Romania, most stop here for the night. Despite this, you should still find a room.

If you're going to the *Sub Cetate Campground*, Strada 13 Generali 13, cross the bridge near the *Parc Hotel*, turn right and follow the river downstream two km or so until you reach the Popas Turistic.

## Getting There & Away

The Orient and Pannonia express trains stop at Arad between Budapest and Bucharest. You can also get to Hungary by changing from a local train at Curtici (the border station) to a local Hungarian train twice a day. This should be used as a last resort, however, as the connections are uncertain. Other local trains run north to Oradea (121

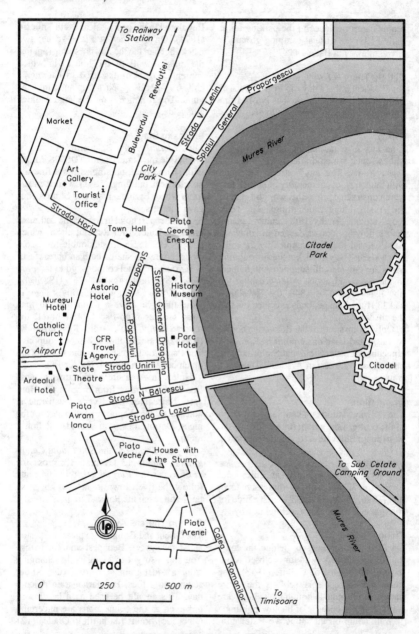

**Arad**

km), east to Deva (149 km) and, more frequently, south to Timişoara (57 km). There's an overnight train with sleepers between Bucharest and Arad. The CFR travel agency is at Bulevardul Revoluţiei 99, beside the State Theatre.

## TIMIŞOARA

The Banat plain around Timişoara (Temesvár in Hungarian, Temeschburg in German) is an eastward extension of Yugoslavia's Vojvodina, and the Bega Canal, which curves through the city, leads into the Tisa River in Yugoslavia. The Serbian influence is evident in a few of the churches, and the inhabitants are a mix of Romanians, Germans, Hungarians and Serbians. Although it is Romania's fourth-largest city, central Timişoara has a garden-like, Mediterranean air. Timiş County, of which Timişoara is the administrative centre, is the richest agricultural area in Romania. If you're coming from Yugoslavia, you'll probably enter Romania through Timişoara.

### Orientation

Timişoara-Nord Railway Station is just west of the city centre. If you're on foot, walk east on Bulevardul Republicii to the Opera House, then north a block to the verdant Piaţa Libertăţii. Piaţa Unirii, the old town square, is two blocks farther north.

If you'd rather ride, catch the tram with the black No 1 just outside the station, which does a great scenic loop through the centre of town. It doesn't matter if you're too enthralled to get off because they all come back the same way.

### Information

The tourist office is at Strada Piatra Craiului 3, behind the Hotel Banatul.

The Agenţia Teatrala (the theatre ticket office) is at Strada Maraşeşti 2, beside the Hotel Timişoara.

### Things to See

Piaţa Unirii is Timişoara's most picturesque square and features a Baroque **Catholic Cathedral** (1754), fountain and palace, as well as a **Serbian church** (1754). People come from afar to fill their water bottles at a spring which sometimes bubbles forth in front of the cathedral.

Take Strada V Alecsandri south from the Serbian church to Piaţa Libertăţii and the **old town hall** (1734). Continue straight ahead on Strada K Marx to the 15th century **Huniades Palace**, which houses the local history museum (closed Monday).

Go west a little to the opera house, which looks straight down Bulevardul 30 decembrie to the exotic domed Romanian Orthodox **Metropolitan Cathedral** (1936). Between the opera and the cathedral is a column with the figures of Romulus and Remus, a gift from the city of Rome. In front of the cathedral are a number of memorials to the people who died in the fighting here between 16 and 23 December 1989. (For an account of these events see the introduction to this chapter.) The parks along the Bega Canal, beside the cathedral, are worth an extended stroll.

The 1989 revolution began on 15 December 1989 at the **Biserica Reformata Tökés**, Strada Timotei Cipariu 1, just off Bulevardul 6 martie, a Reformed Protestant church which serves the local Hungarian community. The church itself is upstairs on the 1st floor and, although it's usually locked, someone in the office just inside the building may open it for you (offer a donation if they do). It was here that the words of Father Lászlo Tökés's condemning Ceauşescu set off the chain reaction that led to the dictator's fall.

### Places to Stay

**Camping** The camping ground is in the Pădurea Verde forest on the opposite side of town from the Timişoara-Nord Railway Station. The tram with the black No 1 outside the station will take you there. Ask to be let off at the 'camping'. Timişoara-Est Railway Station is much closer to the camping ground, but few trains stop there. From Timişoara-Est take any eastbound tram about four stops to the camping ground (ask). There's plenty of tent space at US$6 per

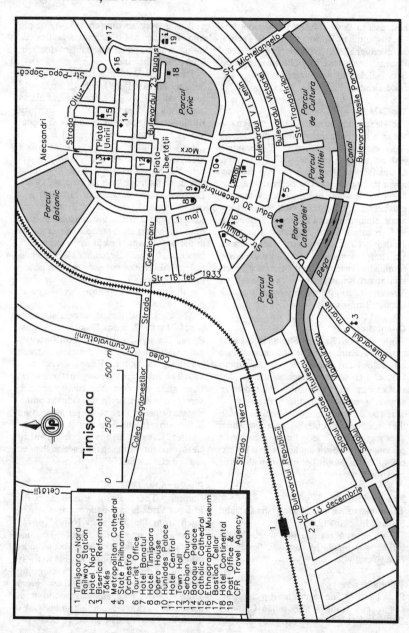

Timişoara

1 Timişoara–Nord
  Railway Station
2 Hotel Nord
3 Biserica Reformata
  Tökés
4 Metropolitan Cathedral
5 State Philharmonic
  Orchestra
6 Tourist Office
7 Hotel Banatul
8 Hotel Timişoara
9 Opera House
10 Huniades Palace
11 Hotel Central
12 Town Hall
13 Serbian Church
14 Baroque Palace
15 Catholic Cathedral
16 Ethnographical Museum
17 Bastion Cellar
18 Hotel Continental
19 Post Office &
  CFR Travel Agency

person or you can pay US$20 single or double for a small cabin. There's a good restaurant on the premises but it closes at 8 pm. If it's closed, try the restaurant at the nearby *Hotel Pecotim* (closed Monday) but it also closes before 9 pm.

**Hotels** The *Hotel Nord*, Strada 13 decembrie 47, around the corner from Timişoara-Nord Railway Station, is overpriced at US$24/40 single/double and run down, but is there if you need it.

*Hotel Banatul*, Bulevardul Republicii 5, is much better than the Hotel Nord yet charges similar prices (US$24/46 single/double). *Central Hotel*, Strada Lenau 6, doesn't have much going for it.

If you have hotel coupons, your choice should be the modern *Hotel Timişoara*, Strada 1 mai 2, next to the opera (US$52/67 single/double without coupons). You enter the hotel from the rear.

The high-rise *Hotel Continental*, at Bulevardul 23 august 2, was spoiled by Western journalists who flocked to Timişoara to cover the 1989 revolution, so now the hotel wants three hotel coupons for a double room – an utter rip-off! If you pay money, it costs US$57/74 single/double, which is far more than this shabby place is worth.

### Places to Eat

There's a good self-service restaurant in the *Hotel Central*, Strada Lenau 6. The *Cina Restaurant*, Strada Piatra Craiului 4, opposite the tourist office, is one of the best in the city. The *Bastion Cellar*, in a section of the city's 18th century defence system, is a wine restaurant.

### Getting There & Away

The daily Bucureşti Express from Belgrade (159 km) arrives at Timişoara around midnight and returns to Yugoslavia early the next morning. It's also possible to get to Yugoslavia by taking a local train to Jimbolia (39 km) and then a connecting train to Kikinda (twice daily).

Timişoara is 1½ hours south of Arad by local train (57 km). Service to Bucharest is fairly frequent via Băile Herculane, Orşova, Drobeta-Turnu Severin and Craiova. Sleepers are available to Bucharest. Through express trains link Timişoara to Iaşi via Cluj-Napoca and Suceava.

The CFR travel agency is at Bulevardul 23 august 2, in the main post office building. For international train tickets go to the CFR travel agency at Bulevardul Republicii 6.

Hitchhiking in Yugoslavia is much worse than in Romania but if you want to try it, take one of the six daily local trains 56 km south to the border station, Stamora Moraviţa, walk across and stick out your thumb – Belgrade is 98 km south-west. Take any ride offered as far as Vršac, 14 km south of the border, as there are six cheap local trains a day from there to Beograd-Dunav (84 km).

### Getting Around

Tram and trolley bus tickets are very difficult to find, so try to pick some up as soon as you arrive at the station.

One of the many Byzantine church ruins at
Nesebâr, featuring characteristic horizontal
strips and blind arches

# Bulgaria

Bulgaria has an enigmatic reputation. Tales of intrigue seem to be confirmed by stamp-happy border guards determined to separate you and your money. Tourism officials add to the fun by stacking the rules in their favour. The various rates of exchange, complicated visa regulations, segregated hotels and assorted paperwork speak of a Byzantine heritage.

This image is only partly justified. Economically, Bulgaria is better off than any of its neighbours and the people are far friendlier than the jaded Yugoslavs and Greeks. Since Bulgaria doesn't get nearly as many Western tourists as it deserves, you'll be assured of a warm welcome. It's a fairly safe country, there's plenty to see and prices are very reasonable. The Rila Mountains and Black Sea coast are natural attractions of European stature. Transport, public services, food, museums, monuments, climate, beaches – everything is good. Even the red tape is easy to comply with, if you manage to figure it all out.

The Cyrillic script and Turkish mosques are constant reminders that Bulgaria has one foot firmly in the east. Bulgaria has been liberated by Russia twice (in 1877 and 1944). This close historical relationship with Russia made Bulgaria one of the Soviet Union's most dependable allies. Even the Bulgarian custom of shaking the head to show agreement and nodding to say no is unique. A visit to such a remarkable country can be a memorable experience!

# Facts about the Country

### HISTORY

In antiquity, Bulgaria, the land of Orpheus and Spartacus, belonged to the Kingdom of Macedonia and the inhabitants were Thracians. By 46 BC the Romans had conquered the whole peninsula, which they divided into Moesia Inferior north of the Stara Planina (Balkan Mountains) and Thrace to the south. Slavonic tribes arrived in the mid-6th century and absorbed the Thraco-Illyrian population. The Slavs were peaceful farmers organised in democratic local communities.

In 679, the Bulgars, a fierce Turkic tribe ruled by khans (chiefs) and boyars (nobles), crossed the Danube River after a long migration which had brought them to Europe from their homelands between the Ural Mountains and the Volga. In 681 Khan Asparoukh founded the First Bulgarian Empire (681-1018) at Pliska in Moesia. In 1981 the 1300th anniversary of this foundation was passionately celebrated. The kingdom expanded south at the expense of Byzantium and in the 9th century extended into Macedonia. The Bulgars were eventually assimilated by the more numerous Slavs and adopted their language and way of life.

In 865 a Byzantine monk frightened Tsar Boris I into accepting Orthodox Christianity

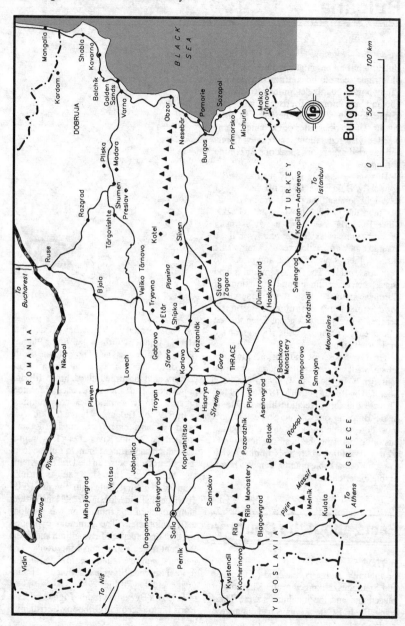

by painting a picture of hell on the palace walls, and in 870 the Bulgarian church became independent with its own patriarch. The kingdom attained its greatest power under Tsar Simeon (893-927), who moved the capital to Preslav and extended his empire as far west as the Adriatic. Even the Serbians were brought under his rule.

Simeon's attempts to gain the Byzantine crown for himself weakened the country, as did internal conflicts after his death. Serbia broke away in 933 and Byzantium took back eastern Bulgaria in 972. Tsar Samuel (980-1014) tried to reverse these losses but was defeated in 1014. After the Battle of Belasitsa in 1014, the Byzantine emperor Basil II had the eyes of 15,000 Bulgarian soldiers put out and it is said that Samuel died of a broken heart. Bulgaria passed under Byzantine rule four years later.

In 1185 two brothers named Asen and Peter led a general uprising against Byzantium and the Second Bulgarian Empire (1185-1396) was founded under the Asen dynasty, with Veliko Târnovo as capital. Tsar Ivan Asen II (1218-41) extended his control to all of Thrace, Macedonia and Albania. After Ivan's death in 1241, the power of the monarchy again declined. Tatars struck from the north and the Serbians took Macedonia. Turkish incursions began in 1340 and by 1371 the Bulgarian tsar Ivan Shishman had become a vassal of the sultan Murad I. In 1389 the Turks defeated the Serbians at the Battle of Kosovo and in 1393 they captured Veliko Târnovo. The last Bulgarian stronghold, Vidin, fell in 1396 and five centuries of Ottoman rule began.

The Turkish governor general resided at Sofia and Turkish colonists settled on the plains, forcing the Bulgarians into the mountains and less favourable areas. Although subjected to heavy taxation, no systematic attempt was made to convert the Bulgarians to Islam or to eradicate their language and customs. Bulgarian Christianity survived in isolated monasteries such as Rila, Troyan and Bachkovo. On a local level the Bulgarians were self-governing.

As Turkish power weakened in the 18th century, the country's inhabitants suffered the burden of Turkish wars against the Austrians and Russians. The Crimean War (1853-56), in which Britain and France sided with Turkey against Russia, delayed Bulgarian independence. The Turkish governor Midhat Pasha attempted to use this breathing space to introduce reforms aimed at assimilating the Bulgarians, but it was too late.

In the early 19th century popular customs and folklore blossomed forth in a National Revival of Bulgarian culture. Schools were opened and books printed in the Bulgarian language for the first time. There was also a struggle against Phanariote Greek domination of the Orthodox church.

Underground leaders such as Hristo Botev, Lyuben Karavelov and Vasil Levski had been preparing a revolution for years when the revolt against the Turks broke out prematurely at Koprivshtitsa in April 1876. The Turks suppressed the uprising with unprecedented brutality, spreading tales of 'Bulgarian atrocities' throughout Europe. About 15,000 Bulgarians were massacred at Plovdiv and 58 villages destroyed. Serbia soon declared war on Turkey, and in April 1877 it was joined by Russia and Romania. Decisive battles were fought at Pleven and Shipka. Russia suffered an appalling 200,000 casualties in the conflict. With the Russian army advancing to within 50 km of Istanbul, Turkey ceded 60% of the Balkan Peninsula to Bulgaria.

Fearing the creation of a powerful Russian satellite in the Balkans, the Western powers reversed these gains with the 1878 Treaty of Berlin. This dictate made southern Bulgaria an 'autonomous province', again nominally subject to the sultan, while Macedonia was to remain part of the Ottoman Empire. Northern Bulgaria adopted a liberal constitution in 1879, but this was suspended two years later by Prince Alexander of Battenberg, a German aristocrat whom the Bulgarians had elected as their prince. In 1885 southern Bulgaria was annexed to the new state, which had been created in 1878. Complete independence from Turkey was declared on 22 September 1908.

All three Balkan states – Bulgaria, Serbia and Greece – coveted Macedonia, which was still in Turkish hands, and the First Balkan War broke out in 1912. Turkey was quickly defeated but the three states could not agree on how to divide the spoils. On 29 June 1913 the Bulgarian army suddenly attacked its Serbian and Greek allies, probably on orders from the Bulgarian king Ferdinand (ruled 1908-18). The Second Balkan War soon resulted in Bulgaria's defeat by these countries together with Romania. Macedonia was divided between Serbia and Greece while Romania took southern Dobruja.

Bulgarian disenchantment with the loss of Macedonia, and the pro-German sympathies of the king, led Bulgaria to side with the Central Powers (Germany, Austria-Hungary and Turkey) against Serbia and Russia in WW I. There was widespread opposition to this policy within Bulgaria, and in September 1918 a mutiny among the troops led to the abdication of King Ferdinand and an armistice. Bulgaria lost additional territory to Greece and Serbia.

Elections in 1920 brought to office the antiwar leader Aleksander Stambolijski, whose government passed an agrarian reform bill dividing the large estates. Serious problems were caused by Macedonian refugees in Bulgaria and continuing terrorist activities within Macedonia itself. Stambolijski was killed during a right-wing coup in June 1923 and in September an armed uprising by Agrarians and Communists was suppressed. Thousands were killed in the ensuing reactionary terror. Georgi Dimitrov, the Communist leader, managed a narrow escape to Russia.

An amnesty in 1926 restored a degree of normality to the country and the League of Nations provided financial aid to resettle the Macedonian refugees. The 1930s world economic crisis led to an authoritarian trend across Eastern Europe and in 1935 King Boris III took personal control over Bulgaria. On 24 January 1937 Bulgaria signed a treaty of 'inviolable peace and sincere and perpetual friendship' with Yugoslavia.

Bulgarian claims to Macedonia again led the country to side with Germany. In September 1940 Romania was forced to return southern Dobruja to Bulgaria on orders from Hitler and in 1941 Bulgaria joined in the Nazi invasion of Yugoslavia. Fearing a popular uprising, however, King Boris rejected German demands to declare war on the USSR. In 1942 an underground Fatherland Front was formed to resist the pro-German government. King Boris mysteriously died in August 1943 and a Council of Regency was set up to govern until his six-year-old son, Prince Simeon, came of age. The Front planned an armed uprising for 2 September 1944.

In August 1944, with the Soviet army advancing across Romania, Bulgaria declared itself neutral and disarmed the German troops present. The USSR insisted that Bulgaria declare war on Germany, whereupon Soviet soldiers entered Bulgaria unopposed and Fatherland Front partisans took Sofia on 9 September 1944. After this the Bulgarian army fought alongside the Soviet army until the war's end.

### Post WW II

After a referendum in 1946, Bulgaria was proclaimed a republic and on 27 October 1946 Georgi Dimitrov was elected premier. Peace treaties were signed in 1947 and all Soviet troops left the country. In 1954 all outstanding disputes with Greece were settled and in 1955 Bulgaria was admitted to the United Nations. In the 1980s Bulgaria joined Greece in calls for a Balkan nuclear-free zone, but relations with Turkey remain strained.

Beginning in the late 1940s, industrialisation and the collectivisation of agriculture were carried out. Under Todor Zhivkov, Bulgaria's leader from 1954 to 1989, the country became one of the most prosperous in Eastern Europe. Within the framework of central planning, managers were allowed some flexibility and workers were given incentives to exceed their norms. Private-plot farming during the workers' spare time was allowed.

By late 1989, Gorbachev's *perestroika* was sending shock waves through Eastern

Europe as veteran Communists looked on uneasily. On 9 November 1989 the Berlin Wall fell and the next day an internal Communist Party coup put an end to the 35-year reign of 78-year-old Todor Zhivkov. In much the same way that Romanian Communists sacrificed Nicolae Ceauşescu, Zhivkov was placed under house arrest 43 days later and in February 1991 he became the first ex-Communist leader in Eastern Europe to stand trial for corruption during his period in office. Petar Mladenov, who took over as president on 10 November 1989, promised sweeping reforms.

With free elections planned for June 1990, new political forces emerged. The Communist Party, which had 932,055 members in 1986, agreed to relinquish its monopoly on power and changed its name to the Bulgarian Socialist Party (BSP). On 23 November 1989, at a meeting held at Sofia University, the Union of Democratic Forces (UDF), a coalition of 16 different opposition groups, was founded.

In the 10 June 1990 elections, which were monitored by international observers, the BSP won 211 parliamentary seats, the UDF won 144 seats, the Movement for Rights and Freedoms (a party oriented towards the Turkish minority) won 23 seats and the Agrarian Party won 16 seats. The results were not very different from the 1946 elections when the Communists captured 53.16% of the vote. A majority of city dwellers and the young voted for the opposition, whereas rural voters and older Bulgarians voted Socialist.

Many in the opposition were unwilling to accept the Socialist victory and staged protests to overturn the election results. In mid-1990 President Mladenov was forced to resign after a controversy over his advocacy of the use of force against student demonstrators. On 1 August 1990 Zhelyu Zhelev of the UDF was elected to replace him by the Socialist-dominated parliament as a compromise to quell tensions.

During the June 1990 elections, the Socialists had spoken out against 'shock therapy' reforms and advocated an easy transition to capitalism, but in October 1990, with the economy collapsing around them, they changed course and introduced a radical reform programme similar to that proposed by the opposition. This sparked nationwide strikes and demonstrations against threatened price hikes, and on 29 November 1990 Andrei Lukanov, the Socialist prime minister, resigned.

Lukanov was replaced by Dimiter Popov, an independent who formed a coalition Socialist/UDF government which agreed to fresh elections in 1991. Before then, a new constitution and land ownership law were to be written. Meanwhile, Bulgaria descended into economic chaos as Soviet oil supplies were interrupted, alternative oil supplies from Iraq were cut off by the Gulf War and food shortages occurred for the first time in decades. An independent trade union, Podkrepa, was formed and it has led the fight to dismantle the Communist system.

By mid-1991 the reforms were well advanced, with prices freed, the lev nearly convertible, a new banking system set up and thousands of businesses in the process of being privatised. Bulgaria seems to have caught everyone by surprise by passing the rest of Eastern Europe in the rush to a market economy.

## GEOGRAPHY

Bulgaria lies in the heart of the Balkan Peninsula, at the crossroads of Europe and Asia. An amazing variety of landforms are jammed into this relatively small area of 110,912 sq km. From the high banks of the Danube, a windswept plain slopes up to the rounded summits of the Stara Planina. This east-west range runs right across the northern half of the country from the Black Sea to Yugoslavia. The Sredna Gora branch is separated from the main range by a fault that is followed by the railway from Sliven to Sofia. Some 70% of the world's rose oil, which is used in the manufacture of cosmetics and perfumes, comes from the Valley of Roses near Kazanlâk in this fault.

Southern Bulgaria is even more mountainous. Musala Peak (2925 metres) in the Rila

Mountains south of Sofia is the highest mountain between the Alps and Transcaucasia and is almost equalled by Vihren Peak (2915 metres) in the Pirin Massif, which is farther south. These sharply glaciated massifs with their bare rocky peaks, steep forested valleys and glacial lakes are the geographical core of the Balkans – a paradise for hikers. Aside from the Rila Mountains, which are covered in this book, there's the Pirin National Park, just south of Bansko. Take a train from Pazardzhik to get there.

The Rodopi Mountains stretch west along the Greek border from Rila and Pirin, separating the Aegean from the Thracian Plain of central Bulgaria. This plain opens on to the Black Sea coast with great bays and coastal lakes at Burgas and Varna. The long sandy beaches that lie north, south and between these cities are among the finest in Europe.

Railways have been constructed along the great rivers of Bulgaria from Sofia: they follow the Iskâr River north-east towards the Danube, the Maritsa River south-east into Turkey and the Struma River south into Greece. About a third of Bulgaria is forested, with deciduous trees in the lowlands and conifers in the mountains.

## ECONOMY

During the Communist era, five-year plans were prepared and implemented by a Council of Ministers. Half the national budget was devoted to economic development, and industry grew dramatically until it contributed over half the gross national product. The Communists allotted about 30% of the national budget to social services – a substantial additional income for the people. Before 1989 Bulgaria was a prosperous country with adequate supplies of attractive consumer goods in the stores and food readily available. The contrast with the austerity of Romania was striking.

Bulgaria is largely self-sufficient in agriculture. Prior to WW II, agriculture suffered from the overdivision of the land, but today the large cooperative and state farms have increased production by using machinery and fertilisers, improving irrigation and employing agricultural specialists. Two-thirds of the land is devoted to cereals, including wheat, corn, barley, rye, oats and rice. Also important are industrial crops such as sunflowers, cotton, sugar beets and tobacco. The quality of Bulgarian fruits and vegetables is outstanding.

There are iron and steel works at Pernik and Kremikovci, on opposite sides of Sofia. A chemical plant at Dimitrovgrad produces fertilisers and a large petrochemical plant is at Burgas. Modern textile mills have been established in Plovdiv, Sliven and Sofia. Other important industries are machine-building, food processing and consumer goods production.

Brown coal found near Pernik is used by Bulgaria's iron industry, and lignite from Dimitrovgrad is burned in thermoelectric plants. There are hydroelectric projects in the Rodopi Mountains, but Bulgaria is the Eastern European country that most depends on nuclear power, with 32% of its electricity thus generated. The first nuclear power plant opened in 1974 at Kozloduj on the Danube. Some oil and gas is produced north-east of Varna and there are small oil refineries at Ruse and Burgas.

Exports include machinery, transportation equipment, chemicals, vegetables and fruit. Bulgaria is the world's second largest exporter of cigarettes. Until recently, about 75% of Bulgaria's foreign trade was conducted with the Warsaw Pact countries, the USSR alone accounting for over half of the trade. As the only dependable Soviet ally in the Balkans, Bulgaria benefited from substantial trade subsidies from the USSR. Now that these have been curtailed, Bulgaria is experiencing grave economic difficulties, including 50% annual inflation, a scarcity of basic foodstuffs, petrol rationing and electric power cuts.

## POPULATION & PEOPLE

About nine million people live in Bulgaria, over a million of them in the capital, Sofia. The other major cities are Plovdiv (367,195), Varna (295,038), Ruse (178,920), Burgas (178,239), Stara Zagora (141,722) and

Pleven (135,899). Dimitrovgrad and Pernik are major industrial centres.

The Bulgarians, like the Serbians, are South Slavs. Many ethnographers recognise the Macedonians as Bulgarians, an issue which has involved Bulgaria in four wars this century. Religion is only practised by a minority (30% Orthodox, 5% Muslim and 1% Catholic).

The largest national minorities are Turks (8.5%), Macedonians (2.5%) and Gypsies (2.5%). The 800,000 Turks live mostly in the north-east and in the eastern Rodopi foothills. Between 1912 and 1940 some 340,000 ethnic Turks left Bulgaria for Turkey, and after WW II another 200,000 left. In early 1985 the Communists mounted a programme to assimilate the remaining Turkish inhabitants, all of whom were required to take Bulgarian names.

## ARTS

After five centuries of Turkish rule, Bulgarian culture reappeared in the 19th century as writers and artists strove to reawaken national consciousness. Zahari Zograph (1810-53) painted magnificent frescoes in monasteries at Bachkovo, Preobrazhenski, Rila and Troyan, with scenes that were inspired by medieval Bulgarian art but were more human than divine. Zograph and his contemporaries also painted icons (wooden panels bearing sacred images) often exhibited on an intricately carved iconostasis (a high wooden partition separating the public and private areas of an Orthodox church).

It is sadly indicative of the troubled early history of the country that Bulgaria's three leading poets met with violent deaths around the age of 30. The folk poetry of Hristo Botev (1848-76) features rebels who struggled for independence or noble outlaws who robbed from the rich and gave to the poor. *Borba* is a poetic condemnation of injustice, and *Mehanata* satirises café politicians. In 1876 Botev returned from exile in Romania and was killed in the anti-Ottoman uprising.

The symbolist Dimcho Debelyanov (1887-1916) expresses the purity of human feelings in his melodious lyric poetry. His poem *Orden* (1910) criticises the court of King Ferdinand. Despite this, Debelyanov volunteered for military service in WW I and was killed in action in Macedonia.

Geo Milev (1895-1925), who lost an eye in WW I, wrote poetry dealing with social themes. His epic poem *Septemvri* about the September 1923 agrarian revolution is the high point of Bulgarian expressionism. The authorities confiscated the volume in which the poem appeared and Milev was arrested and fined. After the trial Milev was kidnapped by the police and murdered.

The grand old man of Bulgarian literature is Ivan Vazov (1850-1921) whose novel *Under the Yoke* (1893) describes the 1876 uprising of the entire nation against the Turks. Vazov's *Epic of the Forgotten* is a cycle of poems to the heroes of the Bulgarian National Revival. His plays, written in the early 20th century, bring medieval Bulgarian history to life. Vazov was also a noted travel writer who never tired of writing stories about his country.

In his novel *The Iron Candlestick*, Dimitur Talev (1898-1966) went beyond socialist realism to portray the complexity of human nature against the background of Macedonia's struggle for liberation from the Ottoman Empire in the 19th century.

## Music

An ancient Greek myth ascribed a Thracian origin to Orpheus and the Muses. The Bulgarians of today are still renowned singers, and to hear Orthodox chants sung by a choir of up to a hundred is a moving experience. The songs, cantatas and oratorios convey the mysticism of chronicles, fables and legends in unified artistic patterns. Bulgarian ecclesiastic music dates back to the 9th century and this antique manner of singing played a key role in the 19th century Bulgarian National Revival. The old Bulgarian chants with their Church-Slavonic texts are sometimes performed during mass at churches such as Sofia's Aleksander Nevski Memorial Church. Watch especially for concerts by the Gusla Male Choir.

Alongside the scholarly Byzantine traditions maintained in Orthodox church music is the Turkish influence that is evident in the spontaneous folk songs and dances of the unschooled village people. However, the Bulgarians' folk culture goes much deeper and held them together during five centuries of Ottoman rule. These love songs, working songs and *haiduk* (a romantic outlaw of the Robin Hood type) songs often employ the antiphonal, or responsive, technique in which one person or group echoes or answers another. Philip Koutev (1903-82), founder of the State Folk Ensemble, composed over 500 new songs of this kind.

In most peasant cultures of Eastern Europe, women were not given access to musical instruments so they performed the vocal parts. The remarkable use of voices by female choirs such as the State Radio/TV Folk Ensemble (*Le Mystère des Voix Bulgares*), Plovdiv's Trakia Ensemble, Trio Bulgarka and the Bisserov Sisters has gained great fame in Western Europe in the last few years. The singers are often accompanied by traditional instruments such as the *dajre*

(tambourine), *dvojanka* (double flute), *gadulka* (pear-shaped fiddle), *gajda* (bagpipes), *kaval* (long open flute), *tambura* (long-necked lute), *tarabuka* (vase drum) and *teppan* (large drum).

Bulgarian wedding band ('Stambolovo') music is traditional but employs modern instruments such as the electric guitar (instead of the tambura), clarinet (instead of the kaval), accordeon and saxophone (instead of the gajda) and drum battery (instead of the teppan). The singing is in modern Thracian style but has deliberate vibratory effects that differ from the open-throated singing of the traditional female choirs. As with jazz there's much improvisation and it's very popular as lively dance music at urban weddings, where the traditional circle dances are supplemented by youths doing break dances before the band. The most famous of these groups is led by Ivo Papasov. Stambolovo music developed outside official channels which feared that Gypsy and other foreign influences threatened to drown out the quieter national folk music just described.

### The Cyrillic Alphabet of Bulgaria

| Аа | Бб | Вв | Гг | Дд | Ее | Жж | Зз |
|----|----|----|----|----|----|----|----|
| a | b | v | g | d | e | zh | z |
| Ии | Йй | Кк | Лл | Мм | Нн | Оо | Пп |
| i | y | k | l | m | n | o | p |
| Рр | Сс | Тт | Уу | Фф | Хх | Цц | Чч |
| r | s | t | u | f | h | ts | ch |
| Шш | Щщ | Ъъ | Ьь | Юю | Яя | | |
| sh | sht | â | - | yu | ya | | |

## LANGUAGE

For most Bulgarians, Russian is the second language. There's always someone who speaks English, French or German at the reception of large hotels and at Balkantourist offices. Apart from this, only well-educated Bulgarians understand English.

The Cyrillic alphabet used in Bulgaria, the USSR and parts of Yugoslavia dates back to the 9th century, when Sts Cyril and Methodius translated the Bible into old Bulgarian. As almost everything in Bulgaria is written in Cyrillic, it's essential to learn the alphabet. Several systems exist for transcribing Cyrillic into Latin script and in this book we've used the one illustrated herein, which is almost phonetic. The Cyrillic y is transcribed as u and pronounced as the u in lute, and the Cyrillic ъ is transcribed as â and pronounced as the u in but. The Cyrillic letter ь has no sound but softens the preceding consonant.

To assist in deciphering street signs, buy one of the Cyrillic maps of Bulgaria which are available for a pittance at newsstands and bookshops. And keep in mind the Bulgarian idiosyncrasy of shaking the head to say 'yes' and nodding to say 'no'.

Some useful words to know are *ima* (there is), *neema* (there isn't), *kolko sstruwa?* (how much?), *dobar den* (good day), *dobre doshli* (welcome). *Dobre* (good) is a useful response in many situations.

### Greetings & Civilities

hello
    здравей
        zdravey
    здрасти (colloquial)
        zdrasti
goodbye
    довиждане
        dovizhdane
    чао (coll)
        chao
good morning
    добро утро
        dobro utro
good evening
    добър вечер
        dobâr vecher

please
    моля
        molya
thank you
    благодаря
        blagodarya
    мерси (coll)
        mersi
I am sorry (forgive me)
    съжалявам (*or* простете)
        sâzhalyavam (*or* prostete)
excuse me
    извинете ме
        izvinete me
you are very kind
    Вие сте много любезен
        Vie ste mnogo lyubezen
yes
    да
        da
no
    не
        ne

### Small Talk

Do you speak English?
    Вие говорите ли на английски език?
        Vie govorite li na angliyski?
    Говорите на английски? (coll)
        Govorite na angliyski?
I don't understand.
    Аз не Ви разбирам.
        Az ne vi razbiram.
    Не разбирам. (coll)
        Ne razbiram.
Could you write it down?
    Можете ли да то напишете?
        Mozhete li da to napishete?
Where do you live?
    Вие къде живеете?
        Vie kâde zhiveete?
    Къде живеете? (coll)
        Kâde zhiveete?
What work do you do?
    Вие с какво се занимавате?
        Vie s kakvo se zanimavate?
    С какво се занимавате? (coll)
        S kakvo se zanimavate?

I am a student.
>Аз съм студент.
>>Az sâm student.

I am very happy.
>Аз съм много щастлив.
>>Az sâm mnogo shtastliv.

>Много се радвам. (coll)
>>Mnogo se radvam.

## Accommodation

youth hostel
>младежки хотел (or хижа or
>общежитие)
>>mladezhki hotel (or hizha or
>>obshtezhitie)

camping ground
>място за лагеруване (or място за
>къмпингуване)
>>myasto za lageruvane (or myasto za
>>kâmpinguvane)

private room
>стоя в частна квартира
>>stoya v chastna kvartira

How much is it?
>Колко струва?
>>Kolko struva?

Is that the price per person?
>Това цената на човек ли е?
>>Tova tsenata na chovek li e?

Is that the total price?
>Това общата цена ли е?
>>Tova obshtata tsena li e?

Are there any extra charges?
>Трябва ли да се заплаща
>допълнително за нещо?
>>Tryabva li da se zaplashta
>>dopâlnitelno za neshto?

Can I pay with local currency?
>Мога ли да платя с местна валута?
>>Moga li da platya s mestna valuta?

Where is there a cheaper hotel?
>Къде мога да намеря по-евтин
>хотел?
>>Kâde moga da namerya po-evtin
>>hotel?

>Къде има по-евтин хотел? (coll)
>>Kâde ima po-evtin hotel?

Should I make a reservation?
>Трябва ли да направя резервация?
>>Tryabva li da napravya rezervatsiya?

single room
>единична стая
>>edinichna staya

double room
>двойна стая
>>dvoyna staya

It is very noisy.
>Много е шумно.
>>Mnogo e shumno.

Where is the toilet?
>Къде е тоалетната?
>>Kâde e toaletnata?

## Getting Around

What time does it leave?
>В колко часа тръгва?
>>V kolko chasa trâgva?

When is the first bus?
>Кога е първият автобус?
>>Koga e pârviyat avtobus?

When is the last bus?
>Кога е последният автобус?
>>Koga e posledniyat avtobus?

When is the next bus?
>Кога е следващият автобус?
>>Koga e sledvashtiyat avtobus?

That's too soon.
>Това е доста (or твърде) скоро.
>>Tova e dosta (or tvârde) skoro.

When is the next one after that?
>Кога е по-следващият автобус?
>>Koga e po-sledvashtiyat avtobus?

How long does the trip take?
>Колко време се пътува до там?
>>Kolko vreme se pâtuva do tam?

arrival
>пристигане
>>pristigane

departure
>заминаване
>>zaminavane

timetable
>разписание
>>razpisanie

Where is the bus stop?
>Къде е автобусната спирка?
>>Kâde e avtobusnata spirka?

Where is the railway station?
>Къде е железопътната гара?
>>Kâde e zhelezopâtnata gara?

Where is the taxi stand?
   Къде е стоянката за такси?
      Kâde e stoyankata za taksi?
Where is the left-luggage room?
   Къде е гардеробът?
      Kâde e garderobât?

## Around Town

Just a minute.
   Един момент
      Edin moment
Where is...?
   Къде е...?
      Kâde e...?
the bank
   банката
      bankata
the post office
   пощата
      poshtata
the telephone centre
   телефонна централа
      telefonna tsentrala
the tourist information office
   бюрото за туристическа
   информация
      byuroto za turisticheska informatsiya
the museum
   музея
      muzeya
the palace
   двореца
      dvoretsa
the castle
   замъка
      zamâka
the concert hall
   концертната зала
      kontsertnata zala
the opera house
   оперен театър
      operen teatâr
the musical theatre
   музикален театър
      muzikalen teatâr
Where are you going?
   Къде отивате?
      Kâde otivate?

I am going to...
   Аз отивам в...
      Az otivam v...
Where is it?
   Къде е това?
      Kâde e tova?
I can't find it.
   Аз не мога да го намеря.
      Az ne moga da go namerya.
Is it far?
   Далече ли е?
      Daleche li e?
Please show me on the map.
   Моля покажете ми на картата.
      Molya pokazhete mi na kartata.
left
   ляво
      lyavo
right
   дясно
      dyasno
straight ahead
   направо
      napravo
I want...
   Аз искам...
      Az iskam...
Do I need permission?
   Нуждая ли се от разрешение?
      Nuzhdaya li se ot razreshenie?
May I?
   Може ли? (or Позволяватели?)
      Mozhe li? (or Pozvolyavateli?)

## Entertainment

Where can I hear live music?
   Къде мога да слушам музика на
   живо?
      Kâde moga da slusham muzika na
      zhivo?
Where can I buy a ticket?
   Къде мога да си купя билет?
      Kâde moga da si kupya bilet?
I'm looking for a ticket.
   Аз търся билет.
      Az târsya bilet.
I want to refund this ticket.
   Аз искам да върна този билет.
      Az iskam da vârna tozi bilet.

Is this a good seat?
   Добро ли е това място?
      Dobro li e tova myasto?
at the front
   отпред
      otpred
ticket
   билет
      bilet

## Food

I am hungry.
   Аз съм гладен.
      Az sâm gladen.
I do not eat meat.
   Аз не ям месо.
      Az ne yam meso.
self-service cafeteria
   закусвалня на самообслужване
      zakusvalnya na samoobsluzhvane
grocery store
   зарзаватчийница
      zarzavatchiynitsa
fish
   риба
      riba
soup
   супа
      supa
salad
   салата
      salata
fresh vegetables
   пресни зеленчуци
      presni zelenchutsi
milk
   мляко
      mlyako
bread
   хляб
      hlyab
sugar
   захар
      zahar
ice cream
   сладолед
      sladoled
hot coffee
   горещо кафе
      goreshto kafe

mineral water
   минерална вода
      mineralna voda
beer
   бира
      bira
wine
   вино
      vino

## Shopping

Where can I buy one?
   Къде мога да купя...?
      Kâde moga da kudya...?
How much does it cost?
   Колко струва?
      Kolko struva?
That's (much) too expensive.
   Това е (много) прекалено скъпо.
      Tova e (mnogo) prekaleno skâpo.
Is there a cheaper one?
   Има ли по-евтино?
      Ima li po-evtino?
Can I pay with local currency?
   Мога ли да платя в левове?
      Moga li da platya v levove?

## Time & Dates

today
   днес
      dnes
tonight
   довечера
      dovechera
tomorrow
   утре
      utre
the day after tomorrow
   вдругиден
      vdrugiden
What time does it open?
   В колко часа отваря?
      V kolko chasa otvarya?
What time does it close?
   В колко часа затваря?
      V kolko chasa zatvarya?
open
   открит(о)
      otkrit(o)

closed
  закрит(о)
    zakrit(o)
in the morning
  сутринта
    sutrinta
in the evening
  вечерта
    vecherta
every day
  всеки ден
    vseki den
At what time?
  В колко часа?
    V kolko chasa?
when?
  кога?
    koga?

Monday
  понеделник
    ponedelnik
Tuesday
  вторник
    vtornik
Wednesday
  сряда
    sryada
Thursday
  четвъртък
    chetvârtâk
Friday
  петък
    petâk
Saturday
  събота
    sâbota
Sunday
  неделя
    nedelya

January
  януари
    yanuari
February
  февруари
    fevruari
March
  март
    mart

April
  април
    april
May
  май
    may
June
  юни
    yuni
July
  юли
    yuli
August
  август
    avgust
September
  септември
    septemvri
October
  октомври
    oktomvri
November
  ноември
    noemvri
December
  декември
    dekemvri

**Numbers**

| 1 | едно |
| | edno |
| 2 | две |
| | dve |
| 3 | три |
| | tri |
| 4 | четири |
| | chetiri |
| 5 | пет |
| | pet |
| 6 | шест |
| | shest |
| 7 | седем |
| | sedem |
| 8 | осем |
| | osem |
| 9 | девет |
| | devet |
| 10 | десет |
| | deset |

| 11 | единайсет |
| | edinayset |
| 12 | дванайсет |
| | dvanayset |
| 13 | тринайсет |
| | trinayset |
| 14 | четиринайсет |
| | chetirinayset |
| 15 | петнайсет |
| | petnayset |
| 16 | шестнайсет |
| | shestnayset |
| 17 | седемнайсет |
| | sedemnayset |
| 18 | осемнайсет |
| | osemnayset |
| 19 | деветнайсет |
| | devetnayset |
| 20 | двайсет |
| | dvayset |
| 21 | двайсет и едно |
| | dvayset i edno |
| 22 | двайсет и две |
| | dvayset i dve |
| 23 | двайсет и три |
| | dvayset i tri |
| 30 | трийсет |
| | triyset |
| 40 | четиридесет |
| | chetirideset |
| 50 | петдесет |
| | petdeset |
| 60 | шейсет |
| | sheyset |
| 70 | седемдесет |
| | sedemdeset |
| 80 | осемдесет |
| | osemdeset |
| 90 | деветдесет |
| | devetdeset |
| 100 | сто |
| | sto |

# Facts for the Visitor

## VISAS & EMBASSIES

Most visitors entering Bulgaria need a visa. Consulates require seven working days to process tourist visa applications, but they don't keep your passport while you're waiting and you only pay the visa fee (US$19 to US$30) after your application has been approved. Most consulates will issue the visa on the spot if you're willing to pay double the usual visa fee. Theoretically, you can also get a Bulgarian visa at the border. Sometimes this costs double and at other times it's cheaper.

You must specify the number of days you wish to stay in Bulgaria to a maximum of 90 days. Put down the longest possible period you might stay there, to avoid the hassle of having to get an extension. You may use a tourist visa any time within three months of the date of issue. Nationals of Austria and all Scandinavian countries do not require visas. If you arrive on a package tour, you don't need to get a visa, an advantage which the bureaucrats hope will convince you to come with a group.

Thirty-hour transit visas are issued at consulates on the spot and cost only half as much, but you must have an onward visa if one is required in the next country you're going to. Transit visas cannot be changed to tourist visas upon arrival. If you're in transit, you're not supposed to stay at a hotel and most places won't accept you if they see a transit visa.

At the border you may be told that it's obligatory to change enough money to cover the first two nights in Bulgaria at US$15 a night. They usually demand cash but will take travellers' cheques after an argument. Try to avoid changing money at customs if at all possible, as Bulgarian hotels demand payment in hard currency, not leva (the local currency). Some embassies want you to have a voucher for two nights of prepaid accommodation at a three-star hotel before they'll issue the visa, although you can usually get around this.

## Rubber Stamps

During the Communist era, everyone entering Bulgaria was given a white 'Statistical Card' by immigration. The card was to remain in the bearer's passport, and hotels, hostels, camping grounds and tourist offices arranging private accommodation would stamp the back of it each night and write in the number of days you spent there. When you left Bulgaria, immigration would scrutinise the card to make sure that you had a stamp to account for every night spent in the country. If one or two nights were missing, it was generally no problem, but if too many nights were unaccounted for, officials could levy an on-the-spot fine of US$100 or more.

Whether this system will still be in place by the time you get there is doubtful, but if it is, avoid losing the card and check that people stamp it as they should. The purpose of the card then was not to control your movements but simply to force you to stay in official accommodation where, it was hoped, you would spend a lot of money. If you camped in the mountains, stayed with friends or in a private room arranged on the street, you didn't get a stamp and were liable to get a fine. Of course it was petty bureaucratic controls of this kind that contributed to the collapse of Bulgarian Communism in 1989. However, it is best to take it seriously if you are given this small white card.

### Warning

Official policy on tourism in Bulgaria can be summed up in one word: unpredictable. They have brought in regulations overnight which reduced the exchange rate by 50%; imposed, withdrawn and imposed again compulsory currency exchange; tripled private room prices; required the purchase of luxury hotel vouchers; and made it necessary to pay all hotel bills directly in hard currency, all without notice either before or after. What will come next is anybody's guess, but consider everything in this chapter only as a description of the way things may have been and could still be.

### Bulgarian Embassies

Bulgarian embassies in foreign countries include the following:

Canada
    100 Adelaide St West, Suite 1410,
    Toronto ON M5H 1S3 (☎ 416-363 7307)
Netherlands
    Duinroosweg 9, 2597 KJ The Hague
    (☎ 70-350 3051)
UK
    188 Queen's Gate, London SW7 5HL
    (☎ 071-584 9400)
USA
    1621 22nd St NW, Washington, DC 20008
    (☎ 202-483 5885)

### MONEY

Bulgaria has been going through tremendous economic changes recently and future monetary policies are still uncertain. In the past there were three different rates of exchange: a low 'official rate' used for official purposes, a medium 'hotel payment rate' used to set hotel and international transportation prices, and a high 'tourist rate' applicable to almost everything else. In late 1990 the official rate was US$1 = 0.80 lev; the hotel payment rate was US$1 = 3 leva; and the tourist rate was US$1 = 7 leva. At this time the black market was paying 10 leva to the dollar.

Early in 1991, as the value of the lev was collapsing, it was announced that this system would be scrapped and a uniform exchange rate adopted. There was even speculation that the lev might be made interchangeable with Western currency! A late report indicates that there is no longer any compulsory exchange in Bulgaria, that you may pay for everything directly in leva and that the uniform exchange rate is now US$1 = 18 leva.

A whole list of Communist-era regulations depend on the outcome of this decision. If the lev is not fully convertible, you should hang onto the pink exchange receipt, or 'Bordereau', you get when you change money, as it might be required when you pay camping fees, leave the country, etc. In the past the amount spent at camping grounds and hostels was deducted from the back of the slip and you could go on using it until all your credit was exhausted. Until you're sure that you fully understand the system, don't change too much money, as you may still have to pay upmarket hotel bills and sight-seeing tours directly in hard currency, not in leva.

When you change money the first time, ask the people at the bank or travel agency if you can also change your Bulgarian leva back into hard currency. If they say you can't or that exchange receipts are required, then you can be sure that the black market will still be operating. If it is and you decide to participate, beware of receiving counterfeit leva or worthless banknotes issued before the 1962 monetary reform. Dealing on the street is always risky, so wait until you meet someone reliable and then change your money in private.

In late 1990, a compulsory exchange regulation of US$15 per day was still being sporadically enforced. Upon arrival, tourists were usually told they had to change US$30 cash per person, which was enough for the first two days. Upon departure, however, the border guards seldom bothered to mention compulsory exchange or ask to see any receipts to show how much money had been changed. Whether compulsory exchange ever really existed at all is one of the mysteries of Bulgaria.

One thing is certain, however: you're well advised to bring Western currency in small banknotes or small denomination travellers' cheques. If the hotels are still insisting upon payment in hard currency, you'll need small bills, otherwise you might be forced to accept change in leva. No currency declaration is required upon entry, but the importation or exportation of leva is prohibited. Balkantourist (government tourist agency) offices are usually quicker at changing money than banks.

All prices in this chapter were obtained by converting at the hotel payment rate and are only approximate, but even so, they should still be relative to each other.

### Currency

Bulgarian banknotes come in denominations of 1, 2, 5, 10 and 20 leva. One lev (plural – leva) is divided into 100 stotinki.

### Costs

In late 1990 all forms of transport (including taxis), souvenirs, admissions, food and drink were ridiculously cheap. Inflation is bound to take off as a market economy is introduced, but you'll probably still find Bulgaria a very inexpensive country.

## CLIMATE & WHEN TO GO

Bulgaria has a temperate climate with cold, damp winters and hot, dry summers. The Rodopi Mountains form a barrier to the moderating Mediterranean influence of the Aegean, while the Danube Plains are open to the extremes of central Europe. Sofia has average daily temperatures above 15°C from May to September, above 11°C in April and October, above 5°C in March and November, and below freezing point in December and January. The Black Sea moderates temperatures in the eastern part of the country. Rainfall is highest in the mountains.

## TOURIST OFFICES

Balkantourist is the official government travel agency that organises tourism in Bulgaria. It arranges accommodation, changes money, books sightseeing tours, and so on. Staff at Balkantourist offices abroad are often evasive about answering questions regarding individual tourism and may try to convince you to sign up for a package tour.

Student travellers are catered for by the Orbita Youth Travel Agency, and 'Pirin', the travel bureau of the Bulgarian Tourist Union. 'Rila' railway ticket offices are found in the city centres.

### Balkantourist Offices Abroad

Balkantourist offices in countries outside Bulgaria include:

Austria
    13 Rechte Wienzeile, 1040 Vienna (☎ 57 7762)
Belgium
    62 rue Ravenstein, 1000 Brussels (☎ 513 9610)
Czechoslovakia
    Pařížská 3, Prague 1 (☎ 232 4500)
Denmark
    6 Vester Farimagsgade, 1606 Copenhagen V
    (☎ 12 3510)
Finland
    9 Annankatu, 00120 Helsinki 12 (☎ 64 6044)
France
    45 Avenue de l'Opéra, 75002 Paris
    (☎ 4261 6968)

Germany
    Arko Reisen, Uhlandstrasse 20-25,
    D-1000 Berlin 12 (☎ 883 8041)
    Stefanstrasse 3, 6000 Frankfurt am Main 1
    (☎ 295 2846)
    Unter der Linden 40, 0-1080 Berlin (☎ 229 2072)
Greece
    12 Akademias St, Athens (☎ 363 4675)
Hungary
    Andrassy út 14/16, 1061 Budapest
Italy
    14 Viale Gorizia, 00198 Rome (☎ 85 6438)
Netherlands
    Leidsestraat 43, 1017 NV Amsterdam
    (☎ 620 9400)
Poland
    Marszalkowska 83, Warsaw (☎ 21 1278)
Romania
    Strada Batistei 9, Bucharest (☎ 14 8994)
Spain
    Calle Princesa 12, 28008 Madrid (☎ 242 0720)
Sweden
    30 Kungsgatan, 11135 Stockholm (☎ 11 5191)
Switzerland
    Schaffhauserstrasse 5, 8006 Zürich (☎ 362 8070)
Turkey
    8 Gumhuryet Cad, Taksim Gezisi, Istanbul
    (☎ 145 2456)
UK
    18 Princess St, London W1R 7RE
    (☎ 071-499 6988)
USA
    161 East 86th St, New York, NY 10028
    (☎ 212-722 1110)
Yugoslavia
    Ulica Nusiceva 3, 1st floor, 11000 Belgrade
    (☎ 34 1152)

## BUSINESS HOURS & HOLIDAYS

Many shops close for lunch from 1 to 2 pm. Some offices are closed from noon to 1 pm.

Public holidays include 1 January (New Year's Day), 1 and 2 May (Labour Days), 24 May (Day of Bulgarian Culture), 9 and 10 September (Liberation Days) and 7 November (Revolution Day).

## CULTURAL EVENTS

Bulgarians observe a number of traditional customs and folk festivals of interest. Trifon Zarezan on 14 February is the ancient festival of the wine growers. Vines are pruned and sprinkled with wine for a bounteous harvest. On 1 March Bulgarians give each other *martenitsi*, red-and-white tasselled threads worn for health and happiness at the coming of spring. Lazarouvane is a folk ritual associated with spring and youth. At noon on 2 June sirens announce a moment's silence as a tribute to those who fell for Bulgaria's freedom. Students' Day is on 8 December. Koledouvane is the ritual singing of Christmas carols and takes place on 24 and 25 December.

At the Koprivshtitsa Folk Festival, which is held every five years (the next perhaps in August, 1996), some 4000 finalists compete for awards in various fields. In Pernik at the National Festival of Koukeri and Sourvakari held every five years in the second half of January (the next will be in 1995), thousands of participants perform ancient dances in traditional masks and costumes to drive away evil spirits and ask the good spirits for fertility and a bountiful harvest. Annual folk festivals are held at Golden Sands during the second half of July, with Bulgarian groups participating, and at Burgas and Sunny Beach in August, with Bulgarian and foreign groups participating. The Festival of Roses is celebrated with folk songs and dances at Kazanlâk and Karlovo on the first Sunday in June.

The March Musical Days are held annually at Ruse, followed by the two-month Sofia Music Weeks International Festival beginning on 24 May. During the first week of June the Golden Orpheus International Pop Song Festival is held at Sunny Beach. Also in June are the Varna Summer Festival, the International Ballroom Dancing Competition at Burgas and the International Chamber Music Festival at Plovdiv. In late October or November the Katya Popova Laureate Festival takes place at Pleven with concerts and recitals. The New Year Music Festival is held in Sofia's Palace of Culture.

The Plovdiv International Trade Fair is dedicated to consumer goods in May and industrial products in September.

## POST & TELECOMMUNICATIONS

Only books printed in Bulgaria and written in Bulgarian may be mailed from Bulgaria. Keep this in mind if you see a coffee table

Soviet art book you fancy. Once purchased, you'll have to carry it out of the country in your luggage. Postage for postcards and letters is very cheap.

### Telephone

It's very easy and inexpensive to telephone Western Europe from Bulgaria. International telephones are found in most large post offices and the calls go right through. It's not possible to call North America in this way, however, as there's no automatic connection.

To call Bulgaria from Western Europe dial the international access code, 359 (the country code for Bulgaria), the area code and the number. Important area codes include 2 (Sofia), 32 (Plovdiv), 52 (Varna), 56 (Burgas), and 82 (Ruse).

### TIME

GMT/UTC plus two hours. At the end of March Bulgaria goes on summer time and clocks are turned forward an hour. At the end of September they're turned back an hour.

## WEIGHTS & MEASURES

The electric current is 220 volts AC, 50 Hz.

## BOOKS & MAPS

No serious books about Bulgaria or translations of Bulgarian literature are available in English at Bulgarian bookshops. All you'll find are official travel guidebooks, such as *Bulgaria, A Guide* and *Sofia, A Guide* (Sofia Press, Sofia), both by Dimiter Michailow & Pantscho Smolenow. These are handy for addresses and background information. Also watch for *With Automobile in Bulgaria* (Sofia Press, Sofia) by Dimiter Zhelev.

By far the most complete travel guidebook to Bulgaria is *Nagel's Encyclopedia-Guide Bulgaria* (Nagel Publishers, Geneva). Perhaps the best of Nagel's Eastern European series, the 526 pages of the Bulgaria volume are packed with history and description. *The Rough Guide to Eastern Europe* (Harrap Columbus, London) isn't really what it seems as only Hungary, Romania and Bulgaria are covered, but it does provide a lot more practical listings than Nagel's.

*The Bulgarians From Pagan Times to the Ottoman Conquest* by David Marshall Lang (Thames and Hudson, Britain, 1976) brings medieval Bulgaria to life. The maps, illustrations and lucid text make this book well worth looking for in your local library.

*A Short History of Modern Bulgaria* by R J Crampton (University Press, Cambridge, 1987) is also useful if you want to read up before coming. The book's last sentence is: 'The power of the Bulgarian Communist Party, however, is hardly likely to be challenged or to diminish.'

## MEDIA

The *Sofia News* is a weekly newspaper in English, French, German, Russian and Spanish which has theatre and concert listings in the back. You'll often find it on the counter at luxury hotels.

The monthly magazine *Bulgaria* offers an official picture of the country and *Discover Bulgaria* is a tourist-oriented magazine that is published bimonthly. *Welcome to Sofia* (ulitsa Triaditsa 4, 1000 Sofia) is a monthly tourist newspaper.

## HEALTH

Visitors receive free medical attention in case of accident or emergency. Longer treatments must be paid for but the rates are reasonable. Prescribed medicines are cheap unless they are imported from the West.

There are over 500 curative hot springs at 190 locations in Bulgaria, with a total daily output of 178,000 cubic metres of mineral water. Those of Bankya, Hisarya and Kyustendil have been known since antiquity. Other Bulgarian spas include Sandanski (23 km north of Kulata) and Velingrad.

## ACTIVITIES

### Skiing

Skiing is well developed in Bulgaria. Mt Vitosha, on the southern outskirts of Sofia, is the most accessible of Bulgaria's ski areas. International slalom and giant slalom competitions are held here in March. Bulgaria's largest ski resort is Borovets, 70 km south of Sofia, with the highest mountains in the Balkans as a backdrop. The 19 km of runs at Borovets are intended for advanced or very good skiers and international competitions are often held here. Skiers on a package tours are often sent to Pamporovo, 84 km south of Plovdiv, which has 17 km of ski runs in all categories serviced by several chair lifts. The 3800-metre Snezhanka 1 run is fit for beginners and there are steep competition runs and cross-country tracks as well.

### Hiking

Mountain climbing is a feasible activity in Bulgaria and it doesn't take Edmund Hillary to scale Musala Peak (2925 metres) in the Rila massif, the highest peak between the Alps and the Caucasus. Vihren Peak (2915 metres) in the Pirin Massif is almost as high and can be climbed from Bansko. The highest peak in the Stara Planina is Mt Botev (2376 metres), which you can climb via Troyan and Apriltsi. Those who appreciate less strenuous day hikes from the comfort of their lodgings will find possibilities at

Koprivshtitsa, Madara, Rila and Veliko Târnovo.

## HIGHLIGHTS
### Museums & Galleries
Many Bulgarian museums provide only Cyrillic captions in Bulgarian and cannot be recommended. This used to be the case at the Foreign Art Gallery in Sofia, but new English labels affixed by the staff make quite a difference. Also in Sofia is the Ivan Vazov Museum for a peek into Bulgarian literature. The Etâr Ethnographic Village Museum and all of the house museums at Koprivshtitsa will delight lovers of traditional culture. The 1877 Panorama in Pleven brings a pivotal moment in Bulgarian history to life.

### Castles
The Baba Vida Fortress in Vidin is the only intact medieval castle in Bulgaria. The Tsarevets Fortress in Veliko Târnovo was destroyed by the Turks but its historic significance emanates from its ruins. Even older are the ruined 9th century walls of the Inner City of Pliska and the Shumen Fortress, which are both of great historic importance to Bulgaria. Oldest of all and in much better shape are the 3rd century Roman walls of Hisarya.

### Historic Towns
Of Bulgaria's historic towns, Nesebâr and Veliko Târnovo are survivors from the Middle Ages, and Koprivshtitsa and Plovdiv are representative of the 19th century Bulgarian National Revival. Melnik is one of many picturesque provincial villages.

### Hotels & Restaurants
For one reason or another, it's difficult to single out any of Bulgaria's government-owned hotels as worthy of special mention, although the Odessa Hotel in Varna comes close. Two privately owned 'perestroika' hotels (see the Guesthouses section that follows) can be recommended without hesitation: the Hotel Constantin & Elena in Arbanasi, near Veliko Târnovo, and Hotel

Florina in Galata, near Varna. The Madara Camping at Madara is also very good.

Choosing the best restaurants is even harder but a good one is the Zlatno Pile Restaurant in Varna which has big servings of chicken. Plovdiv's Alafrangite Restaurant and the Vinarna Bourgaska srechta in Burgas have pleasant terraces where you can eat outside in summer. The Warszawa Restaurant in Sofia offers really elegant dining.

## ACCOMMODATION
### Camping
The hard-to-find Balkantourist *Camping-plätze* map lists 103 camping grounds in Bulgaria. Although the map claims that many of them are open from May to October, you can only rely upon them from June to early September. These are the months in which budget travellers should visit Bulgaria. The opening dates for camping grounds listed in this book are also approximations. It's no use asking the people at Balkantourist about camping because they really don't know.

Camping fees are an average of US$3 a night. Most camping grounds rent small bungalows, but these are sometimes full, so bring a tent if you're on a budget. Camping grounds along the coast tend to be very crowded, whereas those in the interior usually have bungalows available that cost just slightly more than camping. While all of the Balkantourist camping grounds accept foreigners, some of the others do not. Freelance camping is prohibited.

### Student Hotels
If you have a student card, the Orbita Youth Travel Agency, Stambolijski bulevard 45, Sofia, may be able to book rooms for you in student hotels around the country. You have to get through to the right person upstairs in the Orbita building because the woman in the currency exchange office on the main street can't help you. If the first person you get isn't helpful, go back a few hours later and try again. Once the reservations are made, you buy a voucher from Orbita to pay for the rooms for about US$13 a night. If you just

show up at an Orbita hotel without a reservation, you will have to pay about US$20/28 single/double, if the staff there accept you at all.

There are Orbita hotels in Rila village (about 22 km from the monastery), Batak (in the mountains south of Plovdiv), Lovech (between Troyan and Pleven), Veliko Târnovo, Shumen and Varna, as well as in the Kavarna and Primorsko resorts on the Black Sea. Reservations can also be made for similarly priced hotels in Koprivshtitsa and Kotel. Some student hotels are open only in summer. Unfortunately, singles/doubles in the Orbita Student Hotel in Sofia cost US$32/40.

## Youth Hostels

The IYHF handbook lists 52 youth hostels in Bulgaria. The hostels come in two varieties. A *Turisticheski dom* or a *Turisticheska spalnya* is a fairly comfortable hotel or hostel with double rooms usually located in or near a town. A *hizha* is a mountain hut offering dormitory beds. Most of the Bulgarian hostels display the standard YHA symbol outside.

Reservations for youth hostels are handled by Pirin, the travel bureau of the Bulgarian Tourist Union. Pirin offices in various cities around Bulgaria are listed under those cities in this chapter. A few years ago it was essential to go first to Pirin for a reservation, but now the hostels have become more accustomed to Westerners and it's often possible to go directly to a hostel and be accepted. Show your YHA membership card to the hostel clerks as soon as you arrive so they'll know you're a member and give you a reduced rate. Hostels in Bulgaria are about US$4 with a YHA card, US$9 without, and they're open all day.

## Private Rooms

Balkantourist claims to have 150,000 beds available in private houses and flats, 110,000 of them at the seaside. Along the Black Sea coast, private rooms are by far the cheapest and easiest way to go, but they're only available in the cities and towns as hotels have a monopoly at the resorts. There's usually a three-night minimum stay and people travelling alone often have to pay for double rooms. Always ask travel agencies about private rooms as your first accommodation preference.

## Guesthouses

Since November 1989, privately owned 'perestroika' hotels have appeared in Bulgaria and are the equivalent of guesthouses or pensions in other countries. All are fairly small with less than a dozen rooms and new ones are opening all the time, so it's hard to give specific information in this book. As yet these places are concentrated in the southern suburb of Simeonovo, outside Sofia, and along the Black Sea coast. One of the original perestroika hotels was Hotel Constantin & Elena in Arbanasi, near Veliko Târnovo. In future these establishments are sure to give the big Balkantourist hotels a tight run for their money.

## Hotels

Bulgaria would be a very inexpensive country if it weren't for the price of the hotels. You'll rarely find a hotel under US$15/25 single/double (with shared bath, breakfast usually included). Balkantourist tries to enforce its monopoly over foreign tourism by preventing Western visitors from staying at cheaper hotels that it does not own. As a result, you will sometimes be told a hotel or dormitory is reserved for Bulgarians only. On the positive side, rooms usually are available.

All hotel bills must be settled directly in Western currency. Even with receipts to prove the legal exchange of foreign currency, you can't pay in leva, so bring lots of hard currency in small bills and avoid changing money at the low hotel payment rate (see the Money section in this chapter). Camping grounds and private-room offices will sometimes accept leva, but only if verified by exchange receipts.

Hotels are classified from one to five stars. The most expensive are called Interhotels, which can have anything from three to five stars. During July and August most of the hotels along the Black Sea coast will be fully booked but private rooms will be available. Very few of the hotels in Bulgaria have air-conditioning.

Sometimes you can book a hotel room through a travel agency in Sofia or abroad at a cheaper rate than you would pay on the spot. For example, Wagons-lits Tourisme, Lege 10, Sofia, can book rooms in two and three-star hotels all around the country at big discounts on the regular 'rack rate' that you would be charged if you just showed up at the door. Average prices for a good two-star hotel are US$15/24 single/double, including a continental breakfast. Travellers' cheques are accepted but there's a 10% surcharge if you pay with a credit card. Give Wagons-lits about 24 hours to make the necessary reservations. Balkantourist offices in Sofia (try the one in the Palace of Culture) and abroad may offer these same discounts.

## FOOD

The food is good, plentiful and, by Western standards, extremely inexpensive in Bulgaria. The price difference between a good hotel restaurant and the cheapest self-service is only about three to one, so it's worth splashing out a little.

If you have difficulty finding a restaurant to suit your fancy, just go to any upmarket hotel and patronise its restaurant. Since you pay in local currency it's fairly cheap to eat there, even including a bottle of wine with the meal (except at the Sofia Sheraton where you must pay in dollars).

A folk-style tavern that serves traditional Bulgarian dishes is known as a *mehana*; these are often located in a basement and offer live music. At the better restaurants it makes things much easier to drop by earlier in the day to make reservations.

Don't waste too much time studying restaurant menus – they don't have the dishes or charge you the prices shown. If you aren't fussy about what you eat, ask for the speciality at restaurants. Waiters in Bulgaria routinely overcharge foreigners slightly. They still expect the bill to be rounded up to

the next round figure, however, and you can give a bit more if the service was efficient and honest. Tips should be given as you're paying, and not left on the table.

Restaurants usually charge extra for the garnishes (vegetables, etc) that accompany the meals. Lunch is the main meal of the day.

### Bulgarian Specialities

A *shopska* salad is made of fresh diced tomatoes, cucumbers, onions and peppers covered with grated white sheep's cheese (*siren*). *Cheese à la Shoppe* is cheese baked in an earthenware pot. Bulgarian yoghurt is famous and *tarator* is a refreshing cold soup of yoghurt, diced cucumber and onions. *Plakiya* and *gyuvech* are rich fish and meat stews.

Other popular Bulgarian dishes with a Turkish flavour include *kebabcheta* (grilled meat rolls), *kavarma* (meat and vegetable casserole), *drob sarma* (chopped lamb liver baked with rice and eggs), *sarmi* (stuffed vine or cabbage leaves) and *kebab* (meat on a spit). *Banitsa* is a baked cheese, spinach or boiled milk pastry like Yugoslav *burek*, while *mekitsas* is a batter of eggs and yoghurt fried in oil.

### DRINKS

In Bulgaria the production of wine is an ancient tradition dating back to the Empire of Thrace in the 9th century BC. Bulgaria today is one of the world's five leading exporters of wine in both red (Cabernet, Gamza, Mavrud, Melnik, Merlot, Otel, Pamid and Trakia) and white (Chardonnay, Euksinovgrad, Galatea, Misket, Riesling and Tamyanka) varieties.

Bulgarians swear by *slivova* (plum brandy). Bulgaria's finest beers are Sagorka from Stara Zagora and Shumensko pivo from Shumen. Beware of their potency! All alcoholic drinks are cheap.

Bulgarian fruit juices (apricot, peach, plum) are exported all over Eastern Europe. *Sok* is a sweet refreshing drink often served with coffee. Coffee and beer are readily available.

## ENTERTAINMENT

Go to the theatres, concert halls and ticket offices listed in this chapter to find out about events. If any of the festivals mentioned in the Cultural Events section coincide with your visit, ask staff at the local tourist office if they have a programme. They'll also know about discos. The easiest place to get a drink is in the lounge at any upmarket hotel. In Bulgaria movies are shown in the original language with Bulgarian subtitles.

## THINGS TO BUY

Typical souvenirs include embroidered dresses and blouses, linen, carpets, Valley of Roses perfume, pottery, leather goods, dolls in national costume, silver filigree jewellery, recordings of folk music and wrought copper and iron. Eyeglasses, clothes and shoes are very cheap and easily available in Bulgaria. If you're bound for Romania, take along a few packs of BT cigarettes as gifts. You're allowed to take out locally purchased souvenirs and articles for personal use worth up to a total of US$20. Beyond this, you could be charged an export tax of 100% or more.

Corecom shops that sell imported or other scarce goods for hard currency are often located in the luxury hotels. Items purchased there may be exported duty-free if receipts are shown. Some large Corecom stores selling consumer goods like colour TVs and vacuum cleaners are reserved for model workers with special bonus coupons.

# Getting There & Away

## AIR

Balkan Bulgarian Airlines has flights to Sofia from Abu Dhabi, Accra, Algiers, Bangkok, Beirut, Cairo, Casablanca, Colombo, Damascus, Dubai, Harare, Istanbul, Khartoum, Lagos, Larnaca, Malé, Malta, Nairobi, Tripoli, Tunis and many European cities. A return flight from Amsterdam to Sofia will cost about US$450. Bucket shops in Asia often sell Balkan Airlines tickets at cut rates,

so ask around the budget travel agencies in Bangkok, Penang, Singapore, etc.

Before buying a return air ticket from Western Europe or North America to Bulgaria, check the price of the cheapest package tour to the Black Sea resorts. This could be cheaper and you can just throw away the hotel vouchers if you don't care to sit on the beach for two weeks. There's no airport departure tax in Bulgaria.

## LAND

### Bus

One of the best ways to get to Bulgaria is on the regular overnight bus service between Athens and Sofia (US$23 one-way, 15 hours). A train ticket from Athens to Sofia costs US$50 one-way. The customs check tends to be stricter on the train.

In Athens the Sofia bus departs from Omonia Square at 8 pm a couple of nights a week (usually Tuesday and Friday). Book with Economy Travel (☎ 363 8033), 18 El Venizelou St (in the arcade), or Mihail Tours (☎ 524 5762), 12 Ag Konstantinou St or 10 Omonia Square (upstairs).

Appia Tours (☎ 22 2453), Mak Aminis 1, near Aristotelous Square, Thessaloniki, has daily morning buses to Sofia for US$10 one-way (313 km). Cheap package bus tours to Bulgaria are available from the same agencies, eliminating the need to apply for a visa.

In Sofia you'll find the Greek buses at the Novotel Europa Hotel, near the Central Railway Station. Make arrangements with the Greek drivers in the morning for a seat that afternoon. A Greek tour bus goes to Thessaloniki every afternoon, leaving from Sofia's Hotel Rodina. Book a seat (US$10) either with the Greek drivers or the tour guides inside the hotel.

Morning buses travel to Skopje, Yugoslavia (US$8, 216 km), daily except Sunday from Sofia's International Bus Station, Gen Hristo Mihailov 23. Twice a week (currently on Wednesday and Friday afternoons) a bus leaves from this station for Athens (US$22). You must pay cash in Western currency (no travellers' cheques).

From mid-May to mid-October, Budget

Bus (☎ 20-627 5151), Rokin 10, Amsterdam, has a weekly bus from Amsterdam to Sofia with a change at Munich (37 hours, US$160 one-way, US$270 return). Those aged 25 and under receive a 10% discount.

### Train

The main railway routes into Bulgaria are from Bucharest (Romania), Niš (Yugoslavia), Thessaloniki (Greece), and Edirne (Turkey). All these lines are served several times a day with through trains from Istanbul, Athens, Munich, Berlin (via Belgrade or Bucharest), Warsaw and Moscow.

Train travel between Romania and Bulgaria is problematic because of the difficulty of purchasing tickets or making reservations, whereas if you go to/from Greece the buses are much cheaper. If you want to go to/from Turkey, it's just as easy to walk across the border. Only to/from Yugoslavia is it as good to take the train.

**To/From Romania & Beyond** The daily Pannonia Express from Berlin to Sofia via Budapest, Bucharest and Ruse is the most reliable connection, travelling overnight between Bucharest and Sofia (545 km, 11 hours) in both directions.

From June to September there's also the Nesebâr Express from Budapest to Burgas via Ruse but this does not stop at Bucharest. The Varna Express from Poland to Varna via Miskolc, Debrecen, Oradea, Bucharest and Kardam runs from mid-June to mid-October. Reservations are required on all of these services.

**To/From Yugoslavia & Beyond** The Meridian Express runs daily from Berlin to Sofia via Prague, Budapest, Novi Sad and Belgrade. Reservations are required if you're going north, but not if you're going south. Between Belgrade and Sofia (417 km, nine hours) the train travels overnight in both directions.

The Istanbul Express runs daily from Munich to Istanbul (2152 km) via Salzburg, Zagreb, Belgrade, Sofia and Kapikule.

If you're coming from somewhere in Yugoslavia, only buy a ticket as far as Dimitrovgrad, the border station, then ride across into Bulgaria without a ticket and on the other side pay the Bulgarian conductor for the ticket on to Sofia (a couple of dollars should be enough). This is much cheaper than buying a through ticket in Yugoslavia.

**To/From Greece** The daily Transbalkan Express links Athens to Sofia (882 km, 18 hours) via Thessaloniki. If you're travelling from Bulgaria to Greece, don't take the train! Trying to get a railway ticket across the Bulgarian border is a nightmare, so take one of the relatively hassle-free buses described in the Bus section instead.

**To/From Turkey** The famous Orient Express route which opened in 1885 used to pass through Belgrade and Sofia on the way from Paris to Istanbul. Though this classic service no longer operates, the Istanbul Express still rolls through Sofia and Plovdiv daily on its way south-east from Munich.

A train ticket from Istanbul to Sofia will cost around US$32 (652 km, 15 hours). It's cheaper to buy a ticket only as far as the Turkish border town Kapikule and then pay the additional fare into Bulgaria on the train itself. At last report, conductors were charging DM 15 cash for a ticket from Kapikule right across Bulgaria to Dimitrovgrad in Yugoslavia.

**Train Tickets** International tickets should be purchased at Rila railway ticket offices. The Sofia Rila offices are incredibly crowded, so pick up your international train tickets at a Rila office in some other Bulgarian city. Ask about seat reservations when you buy the ticket.

You pay for international train tickets in leva, but you must have an exchange receipt at the hotel payment rate that is sufficient to cover the amount. They keep the receipt so only change the amount required to pay for the ticket. Most Rila offices don't have an exchange counter so come prepared. Theoretically, student-card holders get a 30%

discount on international train tickets between Eastern European countries.

It's cheaper to get tickets for the shortest possible distances across borders and then arrange an onward domestic ticket on the other side. For example, you could go from Dimitrovgrad (Yugoslavia) to Sofia, and from Bucharest (Romania) to Ruse.

Even though it's much farther to go from Sofia to Budapest via Romania than through Yugoslavia, it's less than half the price (US$11 versus US$35). Unfortunately, the savings are wiped out by the Romanian transit visa fee (US$30). This option is still worth considering as the Romanian route is far more scenic.

Traditionally, the Bulgarian government has made it difficult for its citizens to leave the country and this situation is reflected in the tremendous problems involved in getting an international railway ticket. You may have wait in several long, slow-moving queues to order the ticket, change money to pay for it and make your compulsory seat reservation – all for a ticket which may only cost a couple of dollars! Rather than hassle with this, try the other means of transport across borders.

## Car & Motorbike

Here is a list of highway border crossings clockwise around Bulgaria, with the Bulgarian port of entry named. To/from Turkey you may cross at Malko Târnovo (92 km south of Burgas) and Kapitan-Andreevo (20 km west of Edirne). To/from Greece you can cross Kulata (127 km north of Thessaloniki).

To/from Yugoslavia you can cross at Zlatarevo (37 km west of Kulata), Stanke Lisichkovo (26 km west of Blagoevgrad), Gjueshevo (between Sofia and Skopje), Strezimirovci (66 km west of Pernik), Kalotina (between Sofia and Niš), Vrâshka Chuka (45 km south-west of Vidin) and Bregovo (29 km north-west of Vidin).

To/from Romania you can cross at Vidin (opposite Calafat), Ruse (opposite Giurgiu), Silistra (opposite Călăraşi), Kardam (37 km north-east of Tolbuhin) and Durankulak (between Balchik and Mangalia).

In the past Western travellers have been hassled to buy expensive hotel vouchers by Bulgarian border guards at the smaller crossings. Though this may no longer be a problem, it probably still is easier to enter Bulgaria at the larger entry points (Kapitan-Andreevo, Kulata and Kalotina) where lots of wealthy 'capitalists' pass through. Motorists in transit from Yugoslavia to Turkey can only use Kalotina and Kapitan-Andreevo and must follow the autoroute (US$10 toll) between Sofia and Plovdiv.

### Hitchhiking

You can avoid the major hassle of getting an international railway ticket by walking out of Bulgaria. For Turkey take a local train to Svilengrad; if you can't easily get an onward train ticket for the 39-km Svilengrad-Edirne hop, take a bus or taxi or hitchhike the 14 km from Svilengrad to Kapitan-Andreevo, the border post, and walk across. Moneychangers and a Turkish *dolmus* (minibus) to Edirne wait on the other side, and there are lots of buses from Edirne to Istanbul (247 km). This will cost about US$6 in all as compared to US$17 for a Sofia-Istanbul train ticket (or US$35 for Istanbul- Sofia). It's also easy to enter Bulgaria this way, though the taxi drivers on the Bulgarian side will want hard currency.

Hitchhiking in Greece and Yugoslavia is pretty bad, so you're probably better off taking a bus (see the Bus section under Getting There & Away). If you do decide to hitchhike to Greece, take a local train to Kulata, walk across and stick out your thumb. If you're going to Yugoslavia, Belgrade is 278 km north-west of the Bregovo border crossing in north-west Bulgaria.

If you're heading for Romania, there's a regular ferry service between Vidin and Calafat, both of which are well connected to the rest of their respective countries by cheap local trains. On the Black Sea coast you can catch a bus to Durankulak, 62 km north-east of Balchik, then walk or hitchhike to the border, which is six km north. From there it should be easier to cover the last 10 km into Mangalia.

## RIVER
### Ferry
A regular passenger ferry across the Danube from Vidin to Calafat, Romania, operates several times a day throughout the year (US$1).

## PACKAGE TOURS
There are numerous all-inclusive tours to the Black Sea resorts. These are fairly cheap but you're tied to a beach hotel, and outside the peak season (from June to mid-September) facilities are limited. Though accommodation is included, these tours are often cheaper than a regular return plane ticket from northern Europe to Bulgaria. Another advantage of going in a tour group is that no visa is required.

More imaginative than the beach holidays, but three times as expensive, are the tours featuring a seven-country cruise along the Danube from Ruse to Passau, Germany. There are also bus tours around the country, cycle tours, stays at luxury health resorts such as Sandanski, skiing at Borovets or Pamporovo, and so on. Balkantourist offices abroad will have details of these.

### From Greece
Agelos Tours (☎ 522 1300), 12 Ag Konstantinou St, Athens, organises package bus tours to Bulgaria including transport, accommodation, meals, excursions and a Greek-speaking guide. A four-day tour to Sofia costs US$135 cash (no Greek currency or travellers' cheques) double occupancy (US$30 extra for single occupancy). A seven-day package to Sofia, Plovdiv and Varna costs US$250 cash (US$55 extra for single occupancy). Other variations are available. Assos Tours (☎ 523 2217) in the same building as Agelos has similar programmes. You stay at luxury hotels like Sofia's Novotel Europa Hotel.

Both companies allow you to travel on their buses as a passenger for about US$23 one-way. At last report departures were at 5.30 am on Wednesday and Saturday.

# Getting Around

## AIR
Balkan Airlines has five or six flights a day from Sofia to Varna and Burgas (US$20 one-way). You pay in Bulgarian currency backed up with exchange receipts at the hotel payment rate. Other daily flights operate from Sofia to Gorna Oryahovitsa, Ruse, Silistra and Vidin, if you're really in love with flying. The trouble involved in getting a domestic air ticket, however, may convince you that it's just as easy to take the train.

## BUS
Long-distance buses serve many points that are not directly connected by train. Take a bus to go from Sofia to Rila Monastery, from Pleven to Troyan, from Troyan to Plovdiv, from Burgas to Varna, etc. Only as many tickets are sold as there are seats, so it's important to arrive at the bus station (autogara) early to make sure you get one. You usually buy the ticket at the office rather than from the driver. At way stations, tickets for long-distance buses can only be purchased after the bus arrives and the driver tells the ticket clerk how many seats are available. Long-distance buses generally leave in the very early morning.

## TRAIN
There are 4278 km of railway in Bulgaria. Bulgarian trains are classified as *ekspresen* (express), *brzi* (fast) or *putnichki* (slow). Trains from Sofia to Burgas go via either Karlovo or Plovdiv. Trains from Sofia to Varna go via either Karlovo or Gorna Oryahovitsa. All trains from Sofia to Ruse go via Pleven and Gorna Oryahovitsa. Service between Sofia and Plovdiv is fairly frequent. Sleepers and couchettes are available between Sofia and Burgas or Varna.

Gorna Oryahovitsa is a main railway junction in northern Bulgaria where trains from Sofia, Ruse, Varna and Stara Zagora meet. The branch line south from Gorna Oryahovitsa to Stara Zagora via Veliko Târnovo

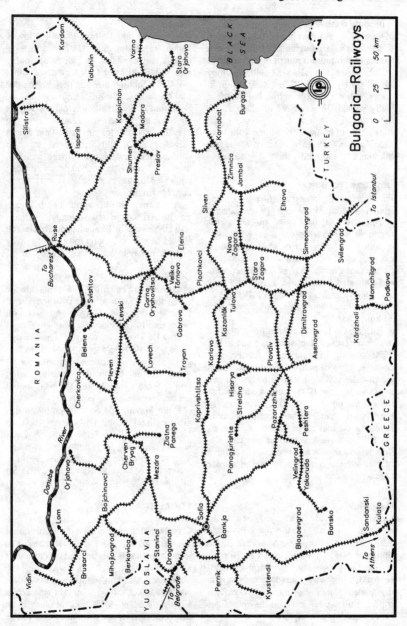

Bulgaria – Railways

is the only north-south line across the centre of the country. Another branch line runs from Ruse to Varna, although buses (via Shumen) are faster and more frequent on this route.

Take care not to miss your station as they are all poorly marked. Most have a sign in both Cyrillic and Latin script, but it's often badly placed. If you have to change at a minor junction or want to get off at a small station, try to know at what time your train should arrive there, then watch carefully and ask the people around you.

## CAR & MOTORBIKE

Fuel is available in normal (86 octane), unleaded (93 octane) and super (93-96 octane) and must be obtained using special nonrefundable vouchers purchased with hard currency at the border or at Balkantourist exchange offices. Normal petrol has an octane rating that is too low for Western cars and unleaded fuel is hard to find and only available from May to October. Petrol stations are found along main highways every 35 km or less.

Bulgaria's recent economic problems have led to severe fuel shortages and in late 1990 individual Bulgarians could only purchase 30 litres of petrol a month. Queues at petrol stations were one km long and for two weeks in January 1991 petrol wasn't sold to the general public at all. Of course Western tourists with fuel vouchers aren't subject to rationing and can cut in front of the queues, but fill up the tank whenever you can. Officially, you're only allowed to bring 20 litres of fuel into the country with you in a spare tank.

### Road Rules

Car speed limits are 60 km per hour in built-up areas, 80 km/h on the open road and 120 km/h on autoroutes. Motorcycles are limited to 50 km/h in built-up areas, 70 km/h on the open road and 100 km/h on autoroutes. On highways, cars may only stop at designated places. Beware of overzealous traffic police who levy on-the-spot fines (always ask for a receipt).

### Rental

Hertz has car rental offices in Sofia, Plovdiv and at the Black Sea. Unlimited-mileage rentals are available at prices beginning around US$40 daily for a Lada but with a two-day minimum hire stipulation. You can rent cars with a mileage charge for one day. Sometimes only much more expensive cars are available. If the car is returned late, you may be charged for an extra day. Prices include public liability insurance but a collision damage waiver is extra. To rent a car you must show your passport and put up a deposit equivalent to the rental fee. Payment must be in hard currency.

A cheaper option would be to hire a private taxi for the day, which will perhaps cost US$35 to Rila Monastery and back. You should be able to bargain for a lower rate by offering to pay in cash hard currency.

## BOAT

From May to September hydrofoils operate along the Black Sea coast between Varna, Nesebâr, Pomorie, Burgas and Sozopol. Fares are low (for example, Varna to Burgas is only US$4 plus a small additional charge for luggage) but there are big crowds. Tickets go on sale at the maritime terminal *(morska gara)* an hour before the departure, so if you're there a little before that you should get on. Have your passport ready.

From May to mid-September, hydrofoils zip up the Danube daily from Ruse to Nikopol and Vidin (US$4 one-way, six hours), departing from either end at 8 am. The schedule can be interrupted by low-water levels, so call Ruse (☎ 22791) for information.

## LOCAL TRANSPORT
### Bus

City bus tickets are sold at information counters in bus and railway stations. The same blue tickets can be used on city buses all over Bulgaria, except in Sofia, where the tickets are pink. You're supposed to validate an extra ticket for luggage. Always carry a supply of tickets with you, because if an inspector catches you without a ticket you're liable for a US$3 fine. Trams and trolley buses operate from 4 am to 1 am and buses operate until midnight.

### Taxi

Taxis are plentiful in Bulgaria and you can even flag them down on the street. They are most easily found in front of train stations. Taxi drivers in Bulgaria charge what the meter says and are not expensive. Always try to take a taxi with a meter that works, otherwise ask what the fare will be beforehand. The drivers don't usually charge you for the return journey, even if it's out of town. Fares are 50% higher from 10 pm to 5 am.

# Sofia (София)

Sofia (Sofiya) sits on a 550-metre-high plateau in western Bulgaria at the foot of Mt Vitosha, just west of the Iskâr River. Its position at the very centre of the Balkan Peninsula, midway between the Adriatic and Black seas, made Sofia a crossroads of trans-European routes. The present city centre is attractive with large traffic-free areas paved with yellow bricks. It's a remarkably clean, quiet city considering that much of Bulgaria's industry is concentrated here. If you can find reasonable accommodation, Sofia repays an unhurried stay.

### History

Under various names, Sofia has a history that goes back thousands of years. The Thracian Serdi tribe settled here in the 7th century BC, and in the 3rd century AD the Romans built strong walls around Serdica (Sofia), their capital of Inner Dacia. After the Hun invasion of 441, the town was rebuilt by the Byzantines. The Slavs gave Sredets (Sofia) a key role in the First Bulgarian Empire, then in 1018 the Byzantines retook Triaditsa (Sofia). At the end of the 12th century the Bulgarians returned and Sredets became a major trading centre of the Second Bulgarian Empire.

The Turks captured Sofia in 1382 and made it the centre of the Rumelian beylerbeyship. The city declined during the feudal unrest of the 19th century, but with the establishment of the Third Bulgarian Empire in 1879 Sofia again became capital. Between 1879 and 1939 the population grew from 20,000 to 300,000. Today, 1,208,000 people live in Sofia. The Yugoslav border at Dimitrovgrad is only 55 km north-west of Sofia, and the city's off-centre location in Bulgaria is a reminder of the loss of Macedonia to Serbia and Greece in 1913.

### Orientation

The central railway station is on the north side of the city centre. Upon arrival at the station, go down into the underpass and walk right through to the far end. From there catch tram No 1, 7 or 15 four stops to the centre of town. You should be able to buy tram tickets in the underpass.

From the station, bulevard Georgi Dimitrov curves around and runs south through ploschtad Lenin (Lenin Square). Beyond the Holy Sunday Cathedral this thoroughfare becomes Vitosha bulevard (formerly Stalin bulevard), the fashionable avenue of modern Sofia. Many travel agencies and airline offices are found along Stambolijski bulevard, which runs west from the Holy Sunday Cathedral.

Largo opens east from ploschtad Lenin and spills into ploschtad 9 Septemvri. The former Georgi Dimitrov mausoleum on ploschtad 9 Septemvri is the very heart of the city. Ruski bulevard continues south-east as far as the Clement of Ohrid University, then runs on and out of the city as bulevard V I Lenin.

### Information

**Tourist Offices** The main Balkantourist office that helps individual tourists is at Knyaz Dondukov 37, in the centre of town (open from 7 am to 10 pm). The people there reserve accommodation, change money and book sightseeing tours. They may also answer questions if they're not too busy.

For information on hostelling go to the

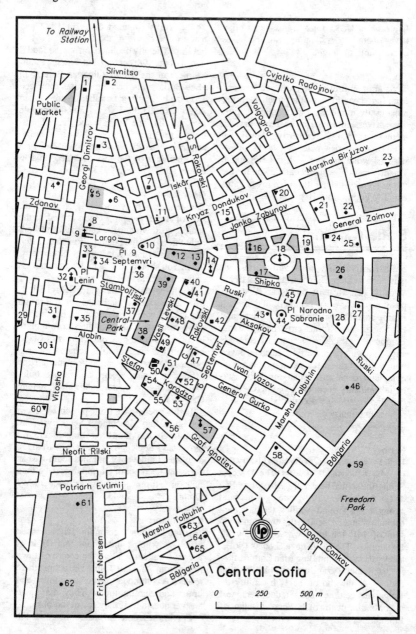

Central Sofia

0      250      500 m

■ PLACES TO STAY

1  Edelweis Hotel
2  Sredna Gora Hotel
3  Hotel Zdravec
7  Iskår Hotel
24  Serdika Hotel
33  Sheraton Balkan Hotel
42  Slavinska Beseda Hotel
55  Sevastopol Hotel

▼ PLACES TO EAT

20  Self-Service Restaurant
23  Warszawa Restaurant
29  Erma Restaurant
35  Mehana Koprivshtitsa Restaurant
52  Budapest Restaurant
56  Self-Service Restaurant
60  Bålgarska Gozba Restaurant

OTHER

4  Synagogue
5  Banya Bashi Mosque
6  Central Mineral Baths
8  Central Department Store
9  St Petra Semerdjuska Church
10  Party House
11  Balkantourist
12  National Art Gallery
13  Natural Science Museum
14  St Nicholas Russian Church
15  National Academic Theatre
    for Opera & Ballet
16  Church of St Sophia
17  Patriarch's Palace
18  Aleksander Nevski Church

19  Foreign Art Gallery
21  Makedonski State Musical Theatre
22  Czechoslovak Consulate
25  Albanian Consulate
26  National Library
27  Fine Art Sales Gallery
28  Clement of Ohrid University
30  Orbita Private Rooms Office
31  National Museum of History
32  Holy Sunday Cathedral
34  Church of St George's Rotunda
36  National Archaeological Museum
37  US Embassy
38  City Art Gallery
39  Georgi Dimitrov Mausoleum
40  Concert Bureau
41  Sala Bulgaria
43  Balkan Airlines
44  Monument to the Liberators
45  National Assembly
46  Soviet Army Monument
47  Ivan Vazov Museum
48  Ivan Vazov National Academic
    Theatre
49  Rila Railway Ticket Office
50  Main Post Office & Telephone Centre
51  Puppet Theatre
53  Satirical Theatre
54  Domestic Railway Ticket Office
57  Saints Sedmotchislenitsi Church
58  Turkish Embassy
59  Vasil Levski Stadium
61  1300th Anniversary Monument
62  NDK Palace of Culture
63  British Embassy
64  Polish Consulate
65  Hungarian Consulate

Pirin Travel Bureau at Stambolijski bulevard 30. The Orbita Youth Travel Agency, Stambolijski bulevard 45a, handles student travel.

**Tourist Offices of Other Countries** Along Stambolijski bulevard west of the Holy Sunday Cathedral are the tourist information offices of the USSR (No 24), Hungary (No 26), Czechoslovakia (No 29), Poland (No 29) and Eastern Germany (No 37).

**Money** The American Express representative is Balkantourist/Hertz, bulevard Vitosha 1, opposite the National Museum of History. You can convert 50% of the value of your travellers' cheques into cash dollars and you get the rest in leva.

The National Bank, beside the Georgi Dimitrov Mausoleum, will change large dollar notes into small bills (if they are available) but will not change dollar travellers' cheques into dollars cash.

**Western Embassies** The US Embassy (☎ 88 4801), Stambolijski bulevard 1, is near the Georgi Dimitrov Mausoleum. Its mailing address is American Embassy Sofia SOF,

APO New York 09213. The British Embassy (☎ 88 5361), Marshal Tolbuhin bulevard 65, east of the NDK Palace of Culture, serves all Commonwealth nationals.

**Eastern European Consulates** The Czechoslovak Consulate, General Zaimov 9, is open Monday to Wednesday and Friday from 10 to 11.30 am. A couple of blocks away is the Yugoslav Consulate, Shipka 7, which opens weekdays from 9 am to noon.

The Hungarian Consulate, 6 Septemvri 57, directly behind the British Embassy, opens Monday, Tuesday, Thursday and Friday from 9 am to 11 am. The Polish Consulate, Khan Kroum 46 (open Monday to Wednesday and Friday from 9 am to 1pm), is also behind the British Embassy (see the Central Sofia map).

The Romanian Consulate is on the east side of town, on the corner of Sipchenski Prohod and Sitnjakovo (take tram No 20 from General Zaimov). It opens Tuesday from 3 to 5 pm and Wednesday and Thursday from 10 am to noon. This ludicrous kitsch palace was one of Ceauşescu's last follies.

You shouldn't need visas for Greece or Turkey but it's better to check.

**Things to See**
Sightseeing in Sofia is centred mostly around museums, although there are a number of old churches and mosques to visit. Begin with the largest: the neo-Byzantine **Aleksander Nevski Church** (1912), a memorial to the 200,000 Russian soldiers who died for Bulgaria's independence. In the crypt is a museum of icons (closed Tuesday). The 6th century basilica across the square in front of the Aleksander Nevski Church is the **Church of St Sophia**, which gave its name to the city. By the church wall is the **Tomb of the Unknown Soldier**. The large building behind the Aleksander Nevski Church contains the **Foreign Art Gallery** (closed Tuesday), with an important collection of European paintings, as well as African, Japanese and Indian art.

The street that runs south from the Aleksander Nevski Church empties into ploschtad Narodno Sabranie where you'll find the **National Assembly** (1884) and an equestrian statue (1905) of Alexander II, the Russian tsar who freed Bulgaria from the Turks. Bulevard Ruski runs west into ploschtad 9 Septemvri, the heart of official Sofia. On the way, beyond the park, is **St Nicholas Russian Church** (1913) and then the **Natural Science Museum**, bulevard Ruski 1 (closed Monday and Tuesday), with flora and fauna exhibits on four floors.

You'll then reach ploschtad 9 Septemvri, which is dominated by the former **Georgi Dimitrov Mausoleum**. Dimitrov faced Hermann Göring at the Reichstag fire trail in 1933 (see Leipzig in the Eastern Germany chapter) and after spending the war years in the USSR was elected premier of Bulgaria in 1946. From his death in 1949 until mid-1990, when the wax-like body was cremated, the public was allowed to file reverently past the deified figure on Wednesday, Friday and Sunday afternoons as an honour guard looked on.

Opposite the mausoleum are the **National Art Gallery** (Bulgarian painting) and the **Ethnographical Museum** (closed Monday and Tuesday), housed in the former Royal Palace (1887). Before 1878 the residence of the Turkish governor occupied this same site. The park behind the mausoleum is dominated by the neoclassical **Ivan Vazov National Academic Theatre** (1907) which was designed by the Viennese architects Fellner and Hellmer.

Hidden behind the Bulgarian National Bank, at the western end of ploschtad 9 Septemvri, are the nine lead-covered domes of the Buyuk Djami, or the Great Mosque (1496), now the **National Archaeological Museum** (closed Monday). The museum's excellent collection of antique sculpture is accessible through an entrance on the Party House side. Largo is surrounded by **Party House** (1955) on the east, the Council of Ministers on the north and the State Council on the south – perhaps the greatest architectural achievements of Stalinism outside the USSR. In the courtyard formed by the State Council and the Sheraton Balkan Hotel

(1955) is an imposing 4th century Roman Rotunda that was converted into the **Church of St George** in the Middle Ages. On the dome inside are 11th to 14th century frescoes; outside, the ruins of Roman streets surround the church.

The western end of Largo opens on to ploschtad Lenin, with a huge statue of the man looking across the square. In the shopping mall below street level in the centre of ploschtad Lenin is the 14th century church of **St Petra Semerdjuska** with its frescoes (open Tuesday to Saturday from 10.30 am to 1 pm and from 3.30 to 6 pm). The church was built at the beginning of the Turkish period, which explains its low profile and inconspicuous exterior. The padlocked **Banya Bashi Mosque** (1576), with its majestic minaret, is north of Largo, and nearby behind the supermarket (1911) is Sofia's **synagogue** (1910), which has a huge chandelier. Two blocks beyond the synagogue is the teeming public market along ulitsa Georgi Kirkov.

South of ploschtad Lenin is the **Holy Sunday Cathedral** (1863), which was restored after a bomb attempt on King Boris III in 1925. Beyond it on Vitosha bulevard is the **National Museum of History** (closed Monday) in the building of the former Palace of Justice (1936). This huge museum takes up two floors of an entire city block. Don't miss the 4th century BC Panagjurishte gold treasure in room No 3. Some of the exhibits appear to be copies, but it's hard to tell since only Bulgarian labels are provided. Unfortunately, the lack of translated information makes much of the collection meaningless to foreigners.

**Other Sights** Sofia's other sights are rather scattered. Worth seeking out is the **Jewish Exhibition** on the 5th floor of the bank building on ploschtad Vazrazdane (west of the Holy Sunday Cathedral), where you'll learn how Bulgaria's Jews were saved from Nazi extermination. At the outbreak of WW II, there were 50,000 Jews in Bulgaria. After the war, most of them left for Israel and only about 5000 live in the country today. A recorded commentary in English is played upon request.

Vitosha, Sofia's most elegant boulevard, runs south from the Holy Sunday Cathedral to Sofia's modern **NDK Palace of Culture** (1981), often used for concerts and conferences. This ultramodern building was previously named after Lyudmila Zhivkova, daughter of Todor Zhivkov and Minister of Culture until her death in 1981. Lyudmila was extremely popular in Bulgaria for her vigourous cultural nationalism. Visit the underground arcade in front of the palace. On the square in front of the palace is the huge Monument to the 1300th Anniversary of Bulgaria.

**Saints Sedmotchislenitsi Church**, in what was originally the Black Mosque (1528), is on ulitsa Graf Ignatiev.

**Mt Vitosha** Mt Vitosha (2290 metres), the rounded mountain which looms just eight km south of Sofia, is a popular ski resort in winter. In summer the chair lift operates for the benefit of sightseers. If you have a little extra time, take a bus up Mt Vitosha to Hizha Aleko, where there's a chair lift approaching the summit. There are a number of tourist hotels on the mountain, but they're geared for package tourism and have little to offer the individual visitor. Everything can be seen in a couple of hours and you'll get the best view of the city during the bus ride up the mountain. The Vitosha bus departs from near the southern terminus of trams No 2 and 9.

### Places to Stay

**Camping** *Camping Vrana* (open from May to October) is nine km out of the city on the Plovdiv Highway. From the Central Railway Station take bus No 213 out onto bulevard V I Lenin, then change to bus No 5, 6, or 7, all of which pass the site. Alternatively, take tram No 20 south-east, then change to bus No 5 or 6. Camping costs US$6 and bungalows cost US$21/28 single/double, with payment in Western currency required. There's a restaurant on the premises – don't pitch your tent too close to it if you want to get any sleep.

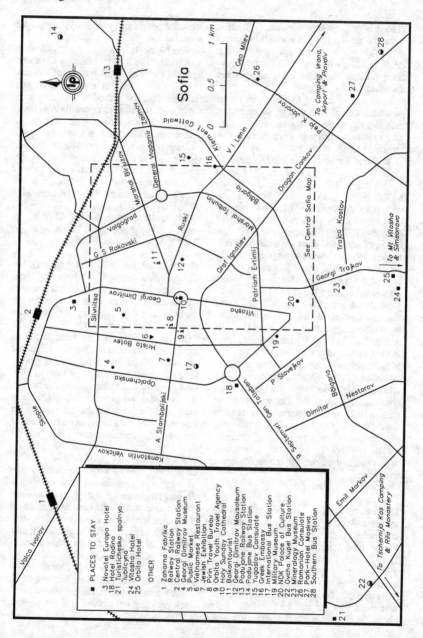

Sofia

0    0.5    1 km

**PLACES TO STAY**

3  Novotel Europa Hotel
18  Hotel Rodina
21  Turisticheska spalnya
24  Vitosha Hotel
25  Orbita Hotel

**OTHER**

1  Zaharna Fabrika
2  Railway Station
4  Central Railway Station
5  Georgi Dimitrov Museum
6  Public Market
7  Vietnamese Restaurant
8  Jewish Exhibition
9  Pirin Travel Bureau
10  Orbita Youth Travel Agency
11  Holy Sunday Cathedral
12  Balkantourist
13  Georgi Dimitrov Mausoleum
14  Poduiane Railway Station
15  Poduiane Bus Station
16  Yugo Bus Station
17  Greek Embassy
18  Romanian Consulate
19  International Bus Station
20  Military Museum
21  NDK Palace of Culture
22  Ovcha Kupel Bus Station
23  Mineralogy Museum
26  Romanian Consulate
27  Park-Hotel Moskva
28  Southern Bus Station

*Tschernija Kos Camping*, 11 km south-west of Sofia on the main highway to Greece, offers camping (US$3 per person) and bungalows (US$13/16 single/double, including breakfast). From the city centre take tram No 5 to the end of the line, then buses No 58 or 59 till you see a huge white statue on the left-hand side of the road. Though more difficult to reach on public transport than Camping Vrana, this site is friendlier and more attractive. It's convenient if you're travelling to or from Rila Monastery. Both these camping grounds have plenty of space for campers.

For a third camping possibility see the Bankya section in this chapter.

**Hostels** *Turisticheska spalnya 'lubilcyna'* at Komplex 'Krasma polyana' listed in the IYHF handbook offers beds in double rooms for US$4 with a YHA card or US$11 without a card. It's next to a large housing area for Vietnamese students, a km or two west of the Ovcha Kupel Bus Station. Trams No 4 and 11 pass within a few blocks of the hostel and you get out amid a cluster of high-rise apartments (ask). It may be easier to take a taxi the first time.

There are also several hostels on Mt Vitosha. *Hizha Aleko* is one. Staff at the Pirin Travel Bureau, Stambolijski bulevard 30, can make the necessary reservations for you.

**Private Rooms** Balkantourist, at Knyaz Dondukov 37 (open from 7 am to 10 pm), books hotels and private rooms, but only after noon, when the rooms become available. A one-star (2nd-class) hotel room with shared bath costs about US$28/31 single/double, including breakfast. Balkantourist also has private rooms for around US$10 double (no singles). If you arrive late in the day, you may be told that only the really expensive hotels still have rooms.

A better bet for a private room is the Orbita office at Vitosha 4, just near the National Museum of History. The staff there can't book rooms either until after noon, but they are friendly and helpful and should be able to tell you if something will be available (about US$10/12 double/triple).

**Hotels** The *Edelweis Hotel*, bulevard Georgi Dimitrov 79, *Sredna Gora Hotel*, bulevard Georgi Dimitrov 60, and the *Hotel Zdravec*, bulevard Georgi Dimitrov 30, are on a noisy tram route between the railway station and the centre of town. The *Iskâr Hotel*, ulitsa Iskâr 9, is also afflicted with tram noise, but it's in a better location, only a block from Balkantourist. A more central one-star hotel is the *Sevastopol Hotel* (☎ 87 5941), ulitsa Rakovski 116, on the corner of Graf Ignatiev. All five of these one-star hotels cost about US$28/31 single/double with breakfast and shared bath. The Sredna Gora Hotel is very basic and has no hot water.

If you want to stay at a more expensive hotel, it's cheaper to go first to Wagons-lits Tourisme, Lege 10, near the National Archaeological Museum (open weekdays from 8.30 am to 1 pm and from 2 to 4 pm). Ask how much they're charging for a room at the three-star *Grand Hotel Bulgaria*, bulevard Ruski 4.

A new phenomenon is the many small privately owned perestroika hotels in the suburb of Simeonovo on the south side of Sofia, at the foot of Mt Vitosha. A few of these include the *Bozhour, Delia, Edelweis, Kamenitsa* and *Korona* hotels. Any taxi driver will take you to one if Balkantourist is reluctant to provide information.

## Places to Eat

**Bottom End** There are three basic places to appease your stomach on Vitosha bulevard opposite the National Museum of History. The first is the very popular self-service restaurant in the yellow building near the Holy Sunday Cathedral at the beginning of the boulevard (open from 6.30 am to 9.30 pm daily except Sunday). You pay as you leave.

You will find a similar but slightly better establishment through the narrow doorway at Vitosha bulevard 5/7. Between these two is the *Mehana Koprivshtitsa Restaurant*, downstairs from the arcade at Vitosha bulevard 1/3, which offers Bulgarian specialities.

There's another self-service restaurant at Graf Ignatiev 32/34. If you need to get something fast to eat just before the opera or operetta, there's a basic self-service restaurant at Knyaz Dondukov 80.

**Middle** The *Bålgarska gozba Restaurant*, bulevard Vitosha 34, serves a good *mesena skara* (mixed grill) and other Bulgarian specialities with draught beer.

The *Erma Restaurant*, ulitsa Alabin 25, behind the National Museum of History, may not present itself as specialising in national dishes but it serves a mixed grill which is hard to beat. If you're lucky, you'll also get cold beer here.

**Top End** Among Sofia's finest restaurants are those dedicated to the cuisines of other countries. The *Vietnamese Restaurant* on Hristo Botev, just up from bulevard Stambolijski, may not serve beer but it does have a pictorial (!) menu and the atmosphere is informal. Reservations are not required.

The *Warszawa Restaurant*, General Zaimov 15 (across the park) is one of Sofia's most elegant restaurants, with fine food, excellent service and live music in the evening. Reservations are usually not required.

For Hungarian food, try the *Budapest Restaurant*, ulitsa Stefan Karadza 9, opposite the Satirical Theatre. The food and service aren't quite up to Hungarian standards, however, so make this place your last choice.

The *Cerveno Zname Restaurant* upstairs above Coop Café, bulevard Vitosha 16, may be Italian but it could end up being your favourite Sofia restaurant if you appreciate its many uses of cheese. A pianist plays as you dine. Reservations are recommended.

For a chilled bottle of white wine in plush surroundings, try *Rubin* opposite the Holy Sunday Cathedral, on the corner of bulevard Stambolijski. There's usually live music with lunch or dinner.

The restaurants and bars in the *Sheraton Balkan Hotel*, ploschtad Lenin 2, insist on payment in hard currency.

## Entertainment

Sofia's finest entertainment is the *National Academic Theatre for Opera & Ballet* on ulitsa Janko Zabunov, not far from the Aleksander Nevski Church. Tickets (US$2) are sold inside and you should be able to get one.

For lighter fare, visit the *Makedonski State Musical Theatre* on bulevard Volgograd, behind the Aleksaner Nevski Church. You'll enjoy the operettas put on here, even if they are in Bulgarian – highly recommended.

The *Puppet Theatre*, ulitsa Gurko 14, never fails to please. Nearby is the *Satirical Theatre*, ulitsa Stefan Karadza 26. You won't understand a word of it, but the acting is superb. The *Ivan Vazov National Academic Theatre*, ulitsa Vasil Levski 5, presents classical theatre in Bulgarian.

If you want concert tickets, visit the Concert Bureau beside Aeroflot, near the Georgi Dimitrov Mausoleum. Many concerts take place in the *Sala Bulgaria*, just around the corner from the bureau at ulitsa Aksakov 3. Others are performed in the *NDK Palace of Culture* and tickets for those are sold at the Palace of Culture itself.

At all of these theatres, performances begin at 7 pm, with matinées being held on weekends.

**Discos** The disco in the 'café-theatre' in the basement of the *NDK Palace of Culture* cranks up daily from 8 pm to 2 am with the dancing beginning at 10.30 pm (admission is US$1 plus US$3 compulsory consumption). Entry is from the lower arcade. This disco isn't really a pick-up place as it's mostly full of couples and groups of friends; if you're female you'll be able to dance and enjoy yourself without being unduly hassled.

## Things to Buy

The best shops for traditional handicrafts are along bulevard Ruski, near ploschtad Narodno Sabranie. If you're in the market for an original painting or sculpture by a Bulgarian artist, go to the Fine Art Sales Gallery, Shipka 6. Ask about export regulations before making a major purchase. Better shops for

Bulgarian consumers are along Vitosha bulevard and in the arcade below the NDK Palace of Culture. There you'll also find a shop that sells folk music records.

The locals shop on the five floors of the Central Department Store (ZUM) on Largo. Lots of clothing is available – even leather coats and fur hats – or you can buy fancy knives, compact discs, postage stamps and other souvenirs. Even if you're not buying anything, you'll be impressed by how much is available in comparison to Romania and how low the prices are in comparison to Yugoslavia. There's a supermarket in the basement.

## Getting There & Away

**Bus** Places that you can reach more easily by bus than by train include Rila Monastery, Troyan and Gabrovo. Direct services to the Rila Monastery and Melnik depart from the Ovcha Kupel Bus Station (trams No 5 or 19), and buses to Troyan and Gabrovo leave from the Podujane Bus Station near the Gerena Stadium, north-east of the centre.

*Bus Tickets* If you want information on all long-distance buses leaving Sofia and advance tickets, visit the ticket office in the arcade below the NDK Palace of Culture at least one day beforehand.

For information about buses to Thessaloniki and Athens, ask at the information desk in the Novotel Europa Hotel. The Athens bus departs from this hotel at around noon and you pay your fare directly to the driver in hard currency. Also check the bus information in the Getting There & Away section in this chapter.

**Train** All railway service in Bulgaria focuses on Sofia. There are international lines to Belgrade, Athens, Istanbul, Bucharest and beyond. You can reach the Greek border at Kulata, 225 km south of Sofia, by train.

Important domestic express trains run to Ruse (via Pleven), to Varna (via Pleven or Karlovo) and to Burgas (via Karlovo or Plovdiv). For Veliko Târnovo change at Stara Zagora, Tulovo or Gorna Oryahovitsa.

Plovdiv is only two hours from Sofia by express train. A local line east to Kazanlâk serves Koprivshtitsa, Karlovo (for Troyan) and Kazanlâk (for Shipka). Sleepers and couchettes are available to Burgas and Varna.

*Railway Station* Sofia's Central Railway Station can be a little confusing. In addition to the Cyrillic destination signs, the platforms are numbered in Roman numerals and the tracks in Arabic numerals! Allow an extra 10 minutes to find your train, then ask several people to ensure that it really is the right one!

Domestic tickets are sold on the lower level, with different queues for different destinations, so ask. (Tickets to the Black Sea may be sold upstairs.) The left-luggage office is also on the lower level, as is the entrance to the tracks.

On the upper level is a tourist service currency exchange and tourist information office, theoretically open from 7 am to 10 pm. In the event that this is closed, try the soaring white Novotel Europa Hotel, visible from in front of the station, which changes money on a similar schedule.

Near the tourist service office on the upper level is an office that sells international train tickets (US$4 to Dimitrovgrad, Yugoslavia). It's much easier to buy these tickets here than at Sofia's chaotic Rila office, so long as you don't need a reservation.

*Train Tickets* Domestic railway tickets and advance seat reservations can be easily obtained at the railway ticket office on ploschtad Slavejkov 8, around the corner from the Sevastopol Hotel. You can't book sleepers here, however.

The combined transportation ticket office in the lower level arcade at the NDK Palace of Culture sells domestic train tickets and books couchettes or sleepers to Varna and Burgas. You can also purchase international tickets at this office. The clerk at the counter marked *'Eisenbahnfahrkarten für Auslandsreisen'* can provide your international ticket and make any required seat or couchette reservations in the one operation. There's an exchange window opposite where you're supposed to be able to change money to pay for the ticket, but it's usually closed, so bring along some exchange receipts at the hotel payment rate. Come early as the queues are long and slow.

The Rila office, ulitsa General Gurko 5 (open weekdays from 8 am to 7 pm), also sells international tickets but it's incredibly crowded with slow, slow queues at every counter and enough red tape to tie up an army. Provided you have an acceptable exchange receipt, you must queue up for a ticket, queue up to pay, queue up to hand in the slip to get the ticket, then queue up again to make a reservation. The whole operation will take about six hours, so long as you're waiting at the door an hour before they open. If you've always wanted to experience Communist repression, here's your chance.

Rila offices in other Bulgarian cities are far less crowded than these, so wait to get your international train ticket somewhere else if possible.

### Getting Around

**To/From the Airport** Vrazdebna Airport, 12 km east of Sofia, is accessible on city buses No 84 and 284 from the stop on bulevard Ruski, opposite the university.

The main Balkan Airlines office is on ploschtad Narodno Sabranie, off Ruski bulevard, with a branch office in the arcade below the NDK Palace of Culture.

**Public Transport** Sofia's public transport system is based on trams and is supplemented by buses and trolley buses. You should purchase red tickets, which are valid on all vehicles, in advance at kiosks.

**Taxi** Government taxis have meters but private taxis don't and fares are based on the odometer reading per km. You can flag cabs down on the street and the drivers are usually honest, but make sure they understand your destination by naming a major landmark near it.

# Western Bulgaria

Western Bulgaria merges imperceptibly into Macedonia at the very heart of the Balkan Peninsula. Bulgaria's highest mountains are found in the Rila and Pirin massifs between Sofia and Greece. Medieval Bulgaria was ruled from towns in the north-east, but after independence in 1878 Sofia was chosen as the centrally located capital of 'Greater Bulgaria' (which would have included Macedonia).

The west has much to offer, from the excitement of Sofia to the thermal baths at Bankya and Sandanski, the history and natural beauty in the area around Rila and intact folklore in Pirin villages such as Bansko and Melnik. For travellers arriving from Western Europe, the west is the gateway to Bulgaria.

### BANKYA (БАНКЯ)

A good place to escape the crowds is Bankya spa, only 17 km west of Sofia. Few foreign tourists visit Bankya but it's popular among the Bulgarians, who fill the 40 sanatoriums and promenade through the well-kept parks. Unlike some Eastern European health resorts which are reserved for patients under medical supervision, everyone is welcome to bathe in these hot springs (36.5°C). When imbibed, the spa's mineral waters stimulate the digestive system.

### Things to See & Do

Bankya's **mineral baths** are in the yellow semicircular building on one side of the park, a few blocks west of the railway station. Men and women use facilities in separate wings of the building, and explanatory signs in French are posted. For US$1 you get a small private cubicle with an individual bathing tub.

A large open-air bathing pool (open in summer only) is on the opposite side of the park.

## Places to Stay & Eat

Bankya's camping ground is an excellent alternative to the two camping grounds near Sofia. Frequent buses running between Sofia and Bankya stop right at the gate, and Ivan-yane Railway Station, the last station before Bankya on the line from Sofia, is only a five-minute walk away, ensuring regular transport to or from the capital. Small rustic bungalows are only US$5 per person and camping is US$1 per person. The reception-ist on duty usually speaks English, and since Western tourists are a rarity here you should be well received.

Alternatively, try the *'Zimmernachweis'* office just across the small stream near the railway station. The people there arrange private rooms at US$3 per person; however, all the rooms could be taken if you arrive late in the day. There are no public hotels in Bankya.

*Biraria 'Bankya'* on ulitsa Mayor Petâr Budinov, the street running east from near the Zimmernachweis office, offers simple meals at the bar with beer.

## Getting There & Away

Local trains to the spa leave Sofia's Central Railway Station every half-hour from 5 am to midnight. There's also a bus service.

## THE RILA MOUNTAINS

The majestic Rila Mountains south of Sofia are *the* place to go hiking. Mountain hostels (hizhas) provide basic dormitory accommo-dation and although many serve meals you had best bring food. For current information on the hostels, enquire at the Pirin Travel Bureau, Stambolijski bulevard 30, Sofia.

The classic trip is across the mountains from Complex Malyovitsa to Rila Monas-tery (Rilski Manastir), which can be done in one day, or in two if you visit the Seven Lakes. A longer route to Rila Monastery begins at the ski resort of Borovets and includes a climb to the top of Musala Peak (2925 metres), the highest mountain in the Balkan Peninsula. You could also do both and make it a trip there and back in four or five days.

## Samokov

Almost everyone on their way to Complex Malyovitsa or Borovets passes through Samokov on the Iskâr River, 62 km south-east of Sofia. The town sprang up as an iron-mining centre in the 14th century and later devoted itself to trade. The 19th century Samokov school of icon painting and wood-carving was famous. Just above the bus station is the beautiful **Bairakli Mosque** (1840) with a wooden dome decorated in the National Revival style.

Buses to Samokov leave frequently from the bus station below the overpass beyond Sofia's Park-Hotel Moskva (take trams No 14 and 19). There's an onward bus from Samokov to Complex Malyovitsa (27 km) approximately seven times a day.

## Complex Malyovitsa

This mountain resort (elevation 1750 metres) at the foot of the Rila Mountains is the site of the Central School of Alpinism and an ideal starting point for anyone wishing to hike over the mountains to Rila Monastery. The large wooden hotel operated by the Pirin Travel Bureau (make reservations at the Sofia office) offers rooms (US$11 per per-son) and 14-bed dormitories (US$6 per person) and there's a good restaurant. In winter the complex functions as a ski resort.

From Complex Malyovitsa you get a stun-ning view straight up the valley to the jagged double peaks of Malyovitsa (2729 metres). You can hike to the peak from the complex in about four hours and a strong climber could make it right through to Rila Monas-tery in a day. Try to buy the Rila hiking map in Sofia before coming, although maps are sometimes sold at the complex reception.

There are two buses a day direct from Sofia to Complex Malyovitsa at 6 am and 2.30 pm. Buy tickets for the return bus trip at the hotel reception.

## To Rila via Malyovitsa

About an hour's hike above Complex Malyovitsa is the *Hizha Malyovitsa* (2050 metres), where a dorm bed and bowl of soup

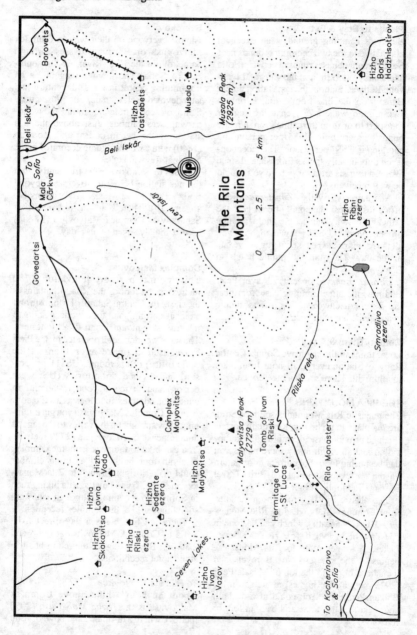

The Rila Mountains

are usually available (open all year). From Hizha Malyovitsa you can hike up to *Hizha Sedemte ezera* (no meals served, bring food) in about six hours. This hizha is right beside one of the legendary Seven Lakes on a mountain plateau at 2200 metres elevation. A notorious sun-worshipping cult was centred on these lakes before the war. From Hizha Sedemte ezera you can hike down to Rila Monastery (elevation 1147 metres) in five hours.

### To Rila via Borovets

From Sofia catch the bus to Samokov (as described in the Samokov section), where you'll find another bus every 30 minutes to Borovets (elevation 1300 metres, 72 km from Sofia). This popular ski resort founded by Prince Ferdinand in 1897 is upmarket, so arrive early enough to make the stiff four-hour hike up to *Hizha Musala* (2389 metres) the same day. Check to see if the 4827-metre cable car to *Hizha Yastrebets* (2363 metres) is operating from Borovets, as it would save you quite a climb.

Musala Peak is only two hours beyond Hizha Musala. Carry on for another five hours to *Hizha Boris Hadzhisotirov* (2185 metres) beside Granchar Lake. There's a restaurant here and a road south to Yakoruda on the railway to Bansko. The next day it will take you five hours to reach *Hizha Ribni ezera* (2230 metres), between the Fish Lakes. The Smradlivo ezero (Stinking Lake), the largest lake in the Rila Mountains, is only an hour from the hostel. Rila Monastery (1147 metres) is a six-hour walk from Hizha Ribni ezera.

### RILA MONASTERY (РИЛСКИ МАНАСТИР)

Rila, Bulgaria's largest and most famous monastery, blends into a narrow valley 119 km south of Sofia, three hours away by bus. Rila was founded by Ivan Rilski in 927 as a colony of hermits, and in 1335 the monastery was moved three km to its present location. **Hrelyu's Tower**, the clock tower beside the church, is all that remains from this early period.

By the end of the 14th century, Rila Monastery had become a powerful feudal fief owning many villages. Plundered in the 15th century, Rila was restored in 1469 after the relics of Ivan Rilski were brought here from Veliko Târnovo in a nationwide patriotic procession. Under adverse conditions, Rila Monastery helped to keep Bulgarian culture alive during the long dark age of Turkish rule, which lasted from the 15th to the 19th centuries. In 1833 a fire destroyed the monastery, but it was soon rebuilt on an even grander scale in the National Revival style.

### Things to See & Do

The monastery's forbidding exterior contrasts dramatically with the warmth and cosiness of the striped arcades inside. Four levels of balconies surround the large, irregular courtyard and three **museums** occupy some of the 300 rooms. One museum contains the monastery's original charter (1378), signed and stamped by Tsar Ivan Shishman, and Brother Raphael's wooden cross bearing 1500 human figures, each the size of a grain of rice. There are excellent views of the surrounding mountains from the uppermost verandah. Don't miss the **kitchen** (1816) at courtyard level in the northern wing, with a 24-metre chimney cutting through all storeys by means of 10 rows of arches crowned by a small dome. Food was once prepared in huge cauldrons for the pilgrim masses.

The present magnificent **church** with its three great domes was built between 1834 and 1837. The 1200 frescoes painted between 1840 and 1848 depict donors, Old Testament kings, apostles, angels, demons and martyrs, all with an extremely rich ornamentation of flowers, birds and stylised vines. The gilded iconostasis depicting 36 biblical scenes is a wonderful work of art by artists from Samokov and Bansko.

The monastery is open daily, but people wearing shorts are not admitted and backpacks must be left in a cloakroom outside. There's a fine view of the monastery from the cross on the hillside to the north-east.

A little over a km up the valley, beyond the turn-off to the camping ground, is the

**Hermitage of St Lucas**, hidden in the trees on the left. From there a well-marked trail leads up through the forest to the tomb of Ivan Rilski.

### Places to Stay & Eat

There are several restaurants behind the monastery. Dorm accommodation (US$2) is available at the *Turisticheski Spalnia*, behind and above the old bakery (1866) near the snack bars. *Camping Bor* is a km farther up the valley beyond the monastery (open from June to September), and the three-star *Hotel Rilets* is nearby.

### Getting There & Away

There's a small bus station on the west side of Rila Monastery. If you catch the early morning bus from Sofia, you can easily visit Rila on a day trip. Two buses a day depart from Sofia's Ovcha Kupel Bus Station (take trams No 5 and 19). The morning bus operates daily throughout the year. In winter, which lasts from October to March, the afternoon bus does the return trip from Rila to Sofia only from Friday to Sunday. Get tickets to go from Sofia to Rila the day before at the booking office in the arcade below the NDK Palace of Culture in Sofia.

In summer, on Sundays and holidays, the return afternoon bus from Rila to Sofia may be sold out a day in advance, in which case ask about buses from Rila Monastery to Kocherinovo Railway Station, 29 km west on the railway line from Sofia to Kulata.

# Thrace

The Thrace of Greek and Roman antiquity was much larger than modern Thrace, only two-thirds of which lies within Bulgaria. The Maritsa River (which passes Plovdiv) drains the region and flows south into the Aegean, forming the border between present-day Greek and Turkish Thrace. At Svilengrad, on the Maritsa River, the three nations meet. Bulgaria's Thracian Plain is squeezed between the Sredna Gora and Rodopi mountain

ranges and opens on to the Black Sea to the east.

Plovdiv is the capital of Bulgarian Thrace and has evocative vestiges of the Roman and Turkish periods. Some of the finest monuments of the Bulgarian National Revival are found in Plovdiv, the Bachkovo Monastery and Koprivshtitsa. Hisarya, north of Plovdiv, has been a major spa since Roman times.

## KOPRIVSHTITSA (КОПРИВЩИЦА)

This picturesque village (elevation 1030 metres) in the Sredna Gora Mountains, 113 km east of Sofia, has been carefully preserved as an open-air museum of the Bulgarian National Revival. Legend tells of a beautiful young Bulgarian woman who obtained a *firman* (decree) from the Ottoman sultan which exempted the Koprivshtitsa villagers from paying tribute and allowed them to ride horses and carry arms. It is known for certain that the town was founded at the end of the 14th century by refugees fleeing the Turkish conquerors.

Sacked by brigands in 1793, 1804 and 1809, Koprivshtitsa was rebuilt during the mid-19th century and was as big as Sofia at the time. It was here on 20 April 1876 that Todor Kableshkov proclaimed the uprising against the Turks which eventually led to the Russo-Turkish War of 1877-78. After independence in 1878, Bulgarian merchants and intellectuals abandoned their mountain retreats for the cities and Koprivshtitsa survived largely unchanged to this day.

These events are well documented in the various house-museums, but even without its place in history the village would be worth a visit for its cobbled streets winding between low-tiled red roofs and little stone bridges over trickling rivulets. Some 388 registered architectural monuments grace the town. Koprivshtitsa is a joy to wander through, but keep in mind that this is a living village. Try to avoid intruding and say *dobar den* (good day) to those you meet.

### Orientation & Information

Many of the house-museums and most of the facilities for visitors are found near the park

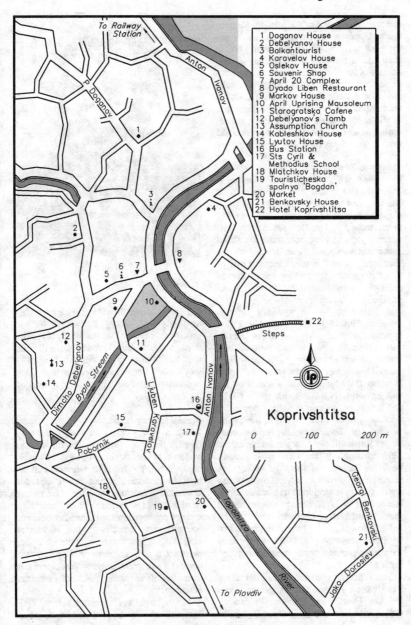

1 Doganov House
2 Debelyanov House
3 Balkantourist
4 Karavelov House
5 Oslekov House
6 Souvenir Shop
7 April 20 Complex
8 Dyado Liben Restaurant
9 Markov House
10 April Uprising Mausoleum
11 Starogratska Cafene
12 Debelyanov's Tomb
13 Assumption Church
14 Kableshkov House
15 Lyutov House
16 Bus Station
17 Sts Cyril &
   Methodius School
18 Mlatchkov House
19 Touristicheska
   spalnya 'Bogdan'
20 Market
21 Benkovsky House
22 Hotel Koprivshtitsa

Koprivshtitsa

0          100          200 m

that contains the **April Uprising Mausoleum**. Opposite the mausoleum you'll see the modern April 20 Complex, with a coffee shop and a self-service restaurant. A few doors west up the narrowing street is a souvenir shop with a ticket office that sells guidebooks, maps and postcards. It also sells the comprehensive ticket that will admit you to all the local museums. All of the house-museums are open from 7.30 am to noon and from 1.30 to 5 pm all year.

### Things to See

The houses of Koprivshtitsa are of two types. The early 19th century 'wooden house' was characterised by a stone ground floor and a wooden upper floor with two rooms in each. In the second half of the 19th century, this austerity gave way to a more richly decorated house that was strongly influenced by the 'Baroque' Plovdiv house. Characteristic of these later houses are the large salons, carved ceilings, sunny verandahs, multicoloured façades, and jutting eaves.

Almost next to the souvenir shop is **Oslekov House** (1856), formerly a rich merchant's home whose spacious interior and stylish furnishings are outstanding. Within the walled enclosure at the top of this street is a cemetery with the grave of the poet **Dimcho Debelyanov** and a statue of his mother anxiously awaiting his return ('I die and am yet born again in light.') Beyond is the **Assumption Church** (1817), which you pass to reach the house of the revolutionary **Todor Kableshkov**, now a museum of the 1876 uprising (all labels are in Bulgarian). Both this house and that of Oslekov are representative of the later Koprivshtitsa style. Continue south to the small stone bridge over the Byala Stream, where the first shot of the 1876 uprising was fired.

Walk downstream a little to the **house of Lyuben Karavelov** (1834-79), ideologue of the uprising, now a house-museum portraying his life.

The other museums on your ticket are **Debelyanov House** (1832), not far from Oslekov House, and **Benkovsky House** (1831), which is on the hillside in the south-

Lyuben Karavelov

eastern part of town. The Benkovsky and Karavelov houses date from the earlier architectural period. Georgi Benkovsky led the insurgent cavalry on legendary exploits through the Sredna Gora and Stara Planina until he fell in a Turkish ambush. The stairway beside his house leads up to a huge equestrian statue of the man and a view of the entire valley.

### Places to Stay & Eat

You can visit Koprivshtitsa on a day trip from Sofia or as a stopover on the way to somewhere else. Accommodation, however, is expensive. The *Hotel Koprivshtitsa* on the hillside just east of the centre charges US$20/22 single/double, plus a US$5 per person 'resort tax'. The hotel will also arrange private rooms with the Mavrodiev or Sapoundyiev families in the village at US$13/16 single/double, plus the US$5 per person tax. Balkantourist in Koprivshtitsa doesn't rent private rooms to Westerners nor does its staff speak any Western European language.

Youth hostellers should try the IYHF *Turisticheska spalnya 'Bogdan'*, Lyuben

Karavelov 24, though a reservation from a Pirin office may be required.

The nearest camping ground is at Mirkovo, between Koprivshtitsa and Sofia, about four km downhill from the Mirkovo Railway Station (there is a bus service from the station to the camping ground). The site is allegedly open all year; during the off season call Mirkovo 484 to check. When it's too cold for camping, you can stay in good little bungalows with private facilities. A restaurant adjoins the camping ground.

Just across the Topolnitza River from the April Uprising Mausoleum is the expensive *Dyado Liben Restaurant* (slow service) in another of the National Revival houses.

### Getting There & Away
The railway station is about 10 km from town, but connecting buses to Koprivshtitsa await every train. Train service to/from Sofia (93 km) is every couple of hours. If you're eastbound from Koprivshtitsa, change trains at Karlovo for Hisarya, Plovdiv or Burgas, and change at Tulovo for Veliko Târnovo.

To get to Koprivshtitsa from Plovdiv, take the early morning train to Strelcha on the Panagjurishte line. A waiting bus will take you from the station to the centre of Strelcha, where you shouldn't have to wait long for a bus to Koprivshtitsa. If you're going in the other direction, it's better to get a bus from Koprivshtitsa right through to Panagjurishte, where there are also buses to Plovdiv.

### HISARYA (ХИСАРЯ)
Even in antiquity, Hisarya, the Roman Augusta, was an important spa with fine marble baths, an aqueduct and paved streets. After the Gothic invasion of 251 AD, the Romans fortified their settlement with a strong city wall, and in the 5th and 6th centuries the town developed into an important episcopal centre with many churches. In the early Middle Ages, Toplitsa (as it was known under the Byzantines) continued to flourish, and later the Turks rebuilt the baths and renamed the town Hisar (fortress).

Hisarya's 22 hot springs spew forth 2800 litres of mineral water a minute at tempera-

tures ranging from 27°C to 51°C. Bathing in these alkaline waters is said to ease digestive problems, and the Momina Banya (Maiden's Bath) mineral water bottled at Hisarya soothes the stomach and kidneys. Despite these attractions, this remarkable place is almost unknown to Western tourists.

### Orientation
The adjacent bus and train stations are just outside the north-west city walls. Bulevard V I Lenin is the main north-south thoroughfare through the walled area passing the two cheaper hotels and the spa park. East across the ravine of Tekedere Stream are the Augusta Hotel and the main mineral baths.

### Things to See & Do
The rectangular **Roman wall**, which is ten metres high and 2315 metres long, was completed in the 4th century AD and originally had 43 towers and four gates. Much of the area inside and around the walls is now a park with the ruins of various Early Christian basilicas and tombs, a small amphitheatre and an **archaeological museum** scattered among the modern constructions.

You can wallow in warm mineral water at the large modern **bathhouse** near the modern theatre in Hisarya. Individual cabins and a large pool are available to the public, but they close at 4.30 pm. If you miss these, there are smaller public baths in the park near the Slaveev Dol Snack Bar which stay open until 7 pm.

Public fountains dispense unlimited quantities of mineral water to eager adherents of the drinking cure at various points in the park. Bring along your canteen or cup for a free fill-up.

### Places to Stay & Eat
There's no camping ground or youth hostel at Hisarya and one-star hotels like the *Balkan* or *Republika* in the centre of town are forbidden to accept Westerners, who must stay at the three-star *Hotel Augusta*. This will cost about US$22 per person if you book through Wagons-lits Tourisme or Balkantourist in Sofia but three times that if you just show up

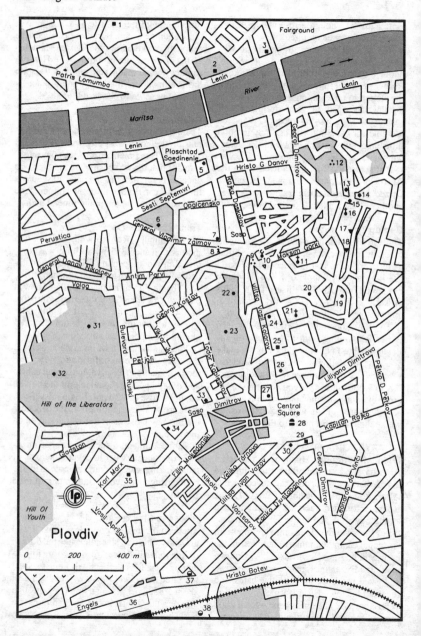

Plovdiv

■ PLACES TO STAY

1   Leningrad Hotel
2   Hotel Novotel
3   Hotel Maritsa
25  Hotel Bulgaria
29  Hotel Trimontium
35  Leipzig Hotel

▼ PLACES TO EAT

17  Alafrangite Restaurant
18  Restaurant Pudin

    OTHER

4   Imaret Mosque Museum
5   Archaeological Museum
6   Natural History Museum
7   Puppet Theatre
8   Pirin Travel Bureau
9   Roman Amphitheatre
10  Djoumaya Mosque
11  Church of the Holy Virgin
12  Ruins of Eumolpias
13  Ethnographical Museum
14  National Revival Museum
15  Hissar Kapi
16  Church of Constantin & Elena
19  Lamartine House
20  Roman Theatre
21  St Marina Church
22  Museum of the Revolution
23  Clock Tower
24  Art Gallery
26  Rila Railway Ticket Office
27  Bookstore
28  Post Office
30  Party House
31  Open-Air Theatre
32  Monument to the Soviet Army
33  Art Gallery
34  Opera House
36  Railway Station
37  Bus Station
38  Rodopi Bus Station

## Getting There & Away

About 10 local trains a day link Hisarya to both Karlovo and Plovdiv (41 km). There are also buses to Karlovo (26 km).

## PLOVDIV (ПЛОВДИВ)

Plovdiv, on the Upper Thracian Plain, is Bulgaria's second-largest city, occupying both banks of the Maritsa River. Two main communication corridors converge here: the route from Asia Minor to Europe, and the route from Central Asia to Greece via the Ukraine. This strategic position accounts for Plovdiv's pre-eminence, beginning in 341 BC when Philip II of Macedonia conquered Philipopolis (Plovdiv). The Romans left extensive remains in the city, which they called Trimontium, as did the Turks, who made Philibe (Plovdiv) the seat of the Bey of Roumelia; this was made up of Macedonia, Albania, Thrace and the autonomous province of Eastern Roumelia.

Yet it was the Bulgarian National Revival which gave Plovdiv's Three Hills the picturesque aspect that visitors can appreciate today. The 19th century Plovdiv 'Baroque' house shares the dynamism and passion of historic Baroque but is uniquely Bulgarian. Arranged around the oval or square central salon are the drawing rooms and bedrooms of the family. The carved or painted ceiling and wall decorations are in excellent taste, as are the brightly painted façades. Many of these charming buildings, which were built by prosperous traders, are now open to the public as museums, galleries or restaurants and make a visit to Plovdiv well worthwhile.

## Orientation

The railway station is south-west of the old town. Cross the square in front of the station and take ulitsa Ivan Vazov on the right straight ahead into Central Square, a five-minute walk away. Ulitsa Vasil Kolarov, Plovdiv's pedestrian mall, runs north from this square, and you can reach the old town from here through the narrow streets to the

at the hotel and ask for a room. If you haven't made reservations, it's best to see Hisarya on a day trip from Plovdiv. The Hotel Augusta has an excellent balneology section in the building where hotel guests can enjoy thermal baths, massage and other treatments at reasonable rates.

right. The area north of the river is a grey, modern suburb devoid of interest.

## Information

The Balkantourist office, Moskva bulevard 34 (open daily from 9 am to 6 pm), is near the fairground north of the river.

The Pirin Travel Bureau, General Vladimir Zaimov 3, has information on hiking and hostelling in the Rodopi Mountains.

## Things to See

Begin your sightseeing with the excavated remains of the **Roman Forum**, behind the modern post office on Central Square. Ulitsa Vasil Kolarov, a bustling pedestrian mall, runs north from this square to the 15th century Djoumaya, or **Friday Mosque**, which is still used for Islamic religious services. Below ploschtad 19 Noemvri, in front of the mosque, is a section of the **Roman amphitheatre** (2nd century AD).

Continue straight ahead on the mall (now ulitsa Rajko Daskalov) and through an underpass to the **Imaret Mosque** (1445), now a museum. Plovdiv's **Archaeological Museum** (closed Monday) is nearby on ploschtad Saedinenie, to the left. A copy of the 4th century BC gold treasure from Panagjurishte is on display (the original is now at the National Museum of History in Sofia). The monument in the square in front of the museum commemorates the union of Eastern Roumelia (of which Plovdiv was the capital) with Bulgaria in 1885.

Return to the Djoumaya Mosque and go east on ulitsa Maksim Gorki, up into the old city, which was named Trimontium (Three Hills) by the Romans. In recent years the **Church of Constantin & Elena** (1832) has been beautifully restored, and next to it is a very good icon gallery. In the National Revival mansion (1847) of the wealthy merchant Argir Koyumdjioglou, on ulitsa Doctor Tchomakov, just beyond the end of Maksim Gorki, is the **Ethnographical Museum** (closed Monday) which houses a collection of folk costumes. Up the street from this museum is a hilltop with the **ruins**

**of Eumolpias**, a 2nd millennium BC Thracian settlement excavated by Dr A Peykov. There is a good view from here.

The street beside the Ethnographical Museum leads down through **Hissar Kapi**, the Roman eastern city gate, to Georgiadi House (1848), another fine example of Plovdiv Baroque, now the **National Revival Museum**.

To the south of this museum is a quaint cobbled quarter, with colourful 19th century houses crowding the winding streets, so do a little exploring. At ulitsa Knyaz Ceretelev 19 is the Baroque house (1830) in which the French poet Alphonse de Lamartine stayed in 1833 during his *Voyage en Orient*.

Nearby to the west and directly above the southern entrance to a big highway tunnel is the 3000-seat **Roman theatre** (2nd century), now restored and once again in use at festival time. Below the theatre on the city centre side is **St Marina Church** (1854) with a photogenic wooden tower and intricate iconostasis. From here it's only five minutes back to your starting point at the Roman Forum.

## Places to Stay

**Camping** *Camping Trakia* (open from May to October) is at the Gorski Kat Restaurant, about four km out on the Sofia Highway, a continuation of Moskva bulevard, west of Plovdiv. Take bus No 4 or 18 to the end of the line and then walk one km along the highway. There's a good restaurant and the site is uncrowded (US$5/8 single/double in cash hard currency to camp, US$30 single for a bungalow). Bring mosquito repellent.

**Private Rooms & Hostels** Balkantourist, Moskva bulevard 34, can arrange private room accommodation at US$6 double (no singles). During the Plovdiv Trade Fair (a couple of weeks in May and September) the price for these same rooms skyrockets to US$29/35 single/double (including breakfast)! If you don't want to pay that much, check carefully that your visit doesn't coincide with the fair.

Ask about youth hostels at the Pirin Travel

Bureau (☎ 22 3958), General Vladimir Zaimov 3, although there isn't a hostel in Plovdiv itself. Many of the hostels in the Rodopi Mountains are permanently booked by youth groups, but the Pirin Bureau staff should be able to reserve a place for you at the *Anton Ivanovtzi Memorial Complex*, which overlooks a long reservoir south-west of Plovdiv (US$4 for YHA members, US$9 for others). To get there, take a bus bound for Devin via Kricim from Plovdiv's Rodopi Bus Station. This will drop you off very near the hostel.

**Hotels** The cheapest hotel is the one-star *Hotel Republica*, Vasil Kolarov 39, almost beside Hotel Bulgaria. A double room with a shared bath down the hall is US$18 (no singles).

Plovdiv's two-star hotels are the 10-storey *Hotel Leipzig*, Ruski bulevard 70, four blocks from the railway station (US$26/37 single/double), and the four-storey *Hotel Bulgaria* in the centre of town (US$25/34 single/double). The *Novotel, Trimontium* and *Maritsa* hotels are much dearer.

### Places to Eat
The *Alafrangite Restaurant*, ulitsa Cyril Nectariev 17, near the National Revival Museum, offers excellent Bulgarian meals on the outside patio.

### Entertainment
Opera tickets are available from offices on both sides of the cinema opposite Hotel Bulgaria. There's an office selling theatre tickets at ulitsa Vasil Kolarov 49.

### Getting There & Away
All trains between Istanbul and Belgrade pass through Plovdiv, and Sofia is only two hours away (156 km) by frequent fast train. To go from Plovdiv to Burgas (294 km) takes four hours with a few overnight services (there are couchettes from Sofia to Burgas). For Veliko Târnovo you may have to change trains at Stara Zagora. For Turkey take a local train to Svilengrad (161 km), a taxi to

the border (14 km) and walk across. Otherwise, board the Istanbul Express late at night. The Rila railway ticket office is at ulitsa Vasil Kolarov 45.

Plovdiv has several bus stations. Buses to Troyan (124 km) leave from the Northern Bus Station. Buses to Pazardzhik and Asenovgrad depart from the bus station near the main train station. Buses to Pamporovo and Smolyan (100 km) use the Rodopi Bus Station, which is across the train tracks.

## BACHKOVO MONASTERY
## (БАЧКОВСКИ МАНАСТИР)
Thirty km south of Plovdiv, beside the highway up the Tschepelarska Valley, is the Bachkovo Monastery (Bachkovski Manastir), founded in 1083 by two Byzantine aristocrats, the brothers Gregory and Abasius Bakuriani. This is the largest monastery of its kind in Bulgaria after Rila. Sacked by the Turks in the 15th century, the monastery underwent major reconstruction 200 years later.

In the high courtyard are two churches: the smaller 12th century **Archangel Church**, painted in 1841 by Zahari Zograph, and the large **Church of the Assumption of Our Lady** (1604). On the northern side of the courtyard is a small **museum**, while one corner of the southern side is occupied by the former **refectory** (1606), with a marvellous painting of the genealogy of Jesus on the ceiling which was painted between 1623 and 1643. The refectory is usually locked, so give a donation to anyone who takes the trouble to let you in.

Through the gate by the refectory is **St Nicholas Chapel** with a superb Last Judgment painted in 1840 by Zahari Zograph on the porch. Note the condemned Turks (without halos) on the right, and Zahari's self-portrait (no beard) in the upper left corner.

Just below the monastery is a restaurant, camping ground and bungalows. To get there, take a bus from Plovdiv to Asenovgrad (19 km) and then another bus on to Bachkovo.

# The Black Sea Coast

Every summer, Bulgaria's Black Sea beaches vie with those of neighbouring Romania to lure the masses of Eastern Europeans on holiday. Burgas and Varna take on a carnival atmosphere as camping grounds and hotels fill up, and small towns like Nesebâr and Sozopol become literally jammed with tourists. Fortunately, the hotel developments are concentrated in a few flashy resorts like Albena (38 hotels), Golden Sands (67 hotels), Druzhba (12 hotels) and Sunny Beach (112 hotels), all absolutely packed with Germans and Brits on package tours. The Georgi Dimitrov International Youth Centre at Primorsko is a programmed students' hang-out. But all along the 378-km coast it's fairly easy to escape the crowds and have a stretch of tideless golden beach to yourself.

The climate is warm and mild and in winter it rarely drops below freezing point. The average summer day temperature is a warm 23°C but sea breezes keep it cool. Summer is the best time to come here. Everything will be open, the restaurants will have their tables out on the street, the water will be warm and hydrofoils will carry you along the coast in comfort. The resorts are quite accustomed to receiving large numbers of visitors and they will find a place to squeeze you in somewhere. In the off season, which is from mid-September to the end of May, even the big hotels slash staff and services drastically.

Best of all, it's cheap. This is one part of Bulgaria where you won't have to search far for a place to camp. If you don't have a tent, ask Balkantourist to assign you a private room. Bulgaria offers better beach facilities than either Romania or Yugoslavia at far lower prices. To stay at one of the new resorts, however, you're better off coming on a package tour. Any way you do it, you'll have an exciting time and make lots of new friends.

## GETTING AROUND

From May to September, hydrofoils shuttle up and down the coast from Sozopol to Burgas, Pomorie, Nesebâr and Varna. Schedules are clearly posted at the stations. Advance booking is not possible. Tickets go on sale an hour before departure and sales end 15 minutes before the scheduled departure time. One person may buy four tickets and fares are reasonable. It's easier to get on the hydrofoils at Varna, Burgas and Sozopol because at Nesebâr you can only get on if there are enough seats.

A regular excursion boat known as a 'hydro bus' runs from Varna to Druzhba, Golden Sands and Balchik four times a day from mid-June to mid-September and three times a day from mid-May to the end of September.

## BURGAS (БУРГАС)

In the 17th century, a fishing community from Pomorie and Sozopol founded Burgas on a narrow spit between Burgasko Ezero and the sea. An ancient tower known as Pirgos gave the city its name. The town grew quickly after completion of the railway from Plovdiv in 1890 and the city's port in 1903. The Great Dockers Strike of 1923 led by Georgi Dimitrov, and the dramatic escape in 1925 of 43 Communists to the USSR from the prison on St Anastasia (now Bolshevik) Island in the bay, are notable episodes in the city's revolutionary history.

Smaller and less crowded than Varna, Burgas has less to offer. The north side of the city has row after row of concrete apartments with a big oil refinery west of it. The old town by the port is still nice, however, and Burgas makes a good base from which to explore the towns up and down the coast. Once you have a good place to stay at, it's a fairly relaxed town with good shopping and an abundance of restaurants. In summer Burgas still gets its share of mosquitoes, but they're no longer malarial.

### Orientation

The railway station and the bus and hydrofoil terminals are all adjacent in the old town. The

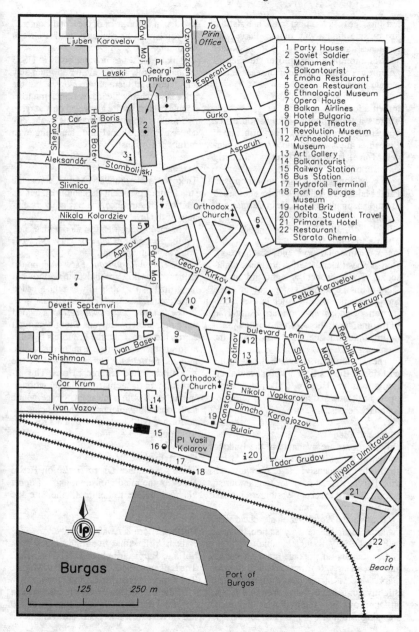

Burgas

0    125    250 m

To Pirin Office

1 Party House
2 Soviet Soldier Monument
3 Balkantourist
4 Emoha Restaurant
5 Ocean Restaurant
6 Ethnological Museum
7 Opera House
8 Balkan Airlines
9 Hotel Bulgaria
10 Puppet Theatre
11 Revolution Museum
12 Archaeological Museum
13 Art Gallery
14 Balkantourist
15 Railway Station
16 Bus Station
17 Hydrofoil Terminal
18 Port of Burgas Museum
19 Hotel Briz
20 Orbita Student Travel
21 Primorets Hotel
22 Restaurant Starata Ghemia

Ljuben Karavelov
Pârvi Maj
Ozvobozdenie
Esperanto
Levski
Pl Georgi Dimitrov
Gurko
Car Boris
Hristo Botev
Shenova
Asparuh
Aleksandâr
Stambolijski
Slivnica
Orthodox Church
Nikola Kolardziev
Aprilov
Pârvi Maj
Georgi Kirkov
Petko Karavelov
7 Fevruari
Deveti Septemvri
Ivan Basev
bulevard Lenin
Republikanska
Ivan Shishman
Fotinov
Slavjanska
Marsko
Car Krum
Orthodox Church
Nikola Vapkarov
Ivan Vazov
Konstantin
Dimcho Karagjozov
Bulair
Pl Vasil Kolarov
Todor Grudov
Liljana Dimitrova
To Beach

Port of Burgas

left-luggage office is next to the bus station, just outside the railway station. Pârvi Maj, the pedestrian mall, runs north to the Soviet soldier monument on ploschtad Georgi Dimitrov. The beach is along the east side of the old town.

## Information

There's a Balkantourist information office opposite the train station. The Pirin Travel Bureau is at Osvobozdenie 47. Orbita Student Travel is at Todor Grudov (formerly Filip Kutev) 2a.

A good foreign-language bookshop is at Pârvi Maj 36 and although there's not much in English, plenty is available in German and Spanish.

## Things to See

As a commercial port and beach resort, Burgas doesn't lend itself to organised sightseeing. The only specific sights are the **Art Gallery** in the former synagogue at ulitsa Sterju Vodenicarov 22, which houses a collection of icons and modern Bulgarian paintings, and the **Archaeological Museum**, bulevard Lenin 21, just around the block.

The **Maritime Park** above the beach on the east side of Burgas is well worth a late afternoon wander. Here you'll find a large open-air theatre and a mausoleum for revolutionary heroes.

## Places to Stay

Private rooms are available at the Balkantourist office near the train station. At last report, the inexpensive *Hotel Czechoslovakia*, Pârvi Maj 2, next to Balkantourist, wasn't allowed to accept Westerners, but you can always try.

The two-star *Hotel Briz* on ploschtad Vasil Kolarov, near the railway station, is poor value at US$20/28 single/double.

For tourists on package holidays there's the three-star, 20-storey *Hotel Bulgaria*, Pârvi Maj 21 in the centre of town. The slightly run-down two-star *Primorets Hotel*, at Dimitrova 1, in the park near the beach, has singles/doubles for US$11/15. This is less than half the price of the Hotel Bulgaria, but you have little chance of getting a room in summer.

Balkantourist has private rooms at US$5 double. There's a three-night minimum-stay stipulation and there are no singles, but the price is so reasonable it's worth paying for a double even if you're alone and only staying two nights. Rooms are available in the city centre and you should find something even in July and August.

## Places to Eat

There's a cafeteria at Pârvi Maj 11, across the street from Restaurant Balkantourist, but it's a bit of a hassle since you pay at the beginning of the line.

For cheap Bulgarian fast food with a beer, try the *Emoha Restaurant*, Pârvi Maj 87. Point at what you want.

The *Ocean Restaurant*, Pârvi Maj, on the corner of Aprilov, specialises in seafood but the grilled fish is rather oily and the breaded variety reminiscent of fish and chips.

The *Vinarna Bourgaska srechta* is a good wine restaurant on Liliyana Dimitrova, right across the street from the Primorets Hotel.

In summer the best place in Burgas to dine at is the *Restaurant Starata Ghemia* on the beach behind the Primorets Hotel. This establishment is actually a large wooden 'pirate' ship with a pleasant terrace where traditional Bulgarian music and dancing are performed (US$1 cover). Often it's reserved for groups.

## Entertainment

There's a modern *Opera House* on Hristo Botev in the middle of town and a *Puppet Theatre*, bulevard Lenin 8, opposite the Hotel Bulgaria.

## Getting There & Away

Balkan Airlines has five flights a day from Sofia to Burgas for about US$20 one-way. The Balkan Airlines office is at Pârvi Maj 24. The airport is eight km north of town.

There are through express trains between Sofia and Burgas (470 km via Plovdiv or 450 km via Karlovo). Couchettes are available on the overnight Sofia trains. By express train, Plovdiv is four hours and 297 km from Burgas. For Veliko Târnovo change trains at Stara Zagora or Tulovo. From June to September the Nesebâr Express runs between Budapest and Burgas but it doesn't stop at Bucharest. Reservations are necessary.

For all advance bus or railway tickets go to the Rila office, Pârvi Maj 106. Staff there can book couchettes to Sofia and you can also buy international railway tickets. The Burgas Rila office is amazingly efficient compared with the one in Sofia. If you want to take a bus to Varna (six daily, 132 km) be sure to visit the Rila office early as all buses can be fully booked 24 hours ahead.

Frequent local buses run late into the night as far north as Sunny Beach. Southbound from Burgas they can be fully booked several hours in advance, so get a ticket early.

From May to September, hydrofoils glide north to Pomorie, Nesebâr and Varna and south to Sozopol. On their way from Burgas to Pomorie the hydrofoils stop at tiny Bolshevik Island, the site of a museum of socialism.

If you're bound for Turkey, catch a bus to Malko Târnovo (82 km) from another bus station in the north-west corner of Burgas (ask). Take a taxi the last 10 km to the border and walk across. Alternatively, go via Svilengrad, a longer but perhaps easier route.

## SOZOPOL (СОЗОПОЛ)

Apollonia (Sozopol) was founded in 610 BC by Greeks from Miletus in Asia Minor. The settlement flourished as an independent trading state until sacked by the Romans in 72 BC, at which time the town's famous bronze statue of Apollo, measuring 13 metres high, was carted off to Rome as booty. Sozopol (which means 'town of salvation') never recovered from this calamity and remained a tiny fishing village until a revival in the early 19th century, when 150 houses were rebuilt in the traditional 'Black Sea' style.

Today, sturdy wooden dwellings built on lower floors made of stone choke the narrow cobbled streets of this picturesque little town

as women below sell lace to visitors. On the west side of the peninsula, a Bulgarian naval base flanks the local fishing port and on the east side are two good beaches. A bustling tourist colony is blossoming to the south. Yet the entire Bulgarian coast south of Burgas is much less impacted by high-rise resorts like Sunny Beach and Golden Sands, and the farther south you go, the fewer tourists on package holidays you see.

Because of this, Sozopol compares well with historic Nesebâr, its rival coastal town. Although the archaeological remains at

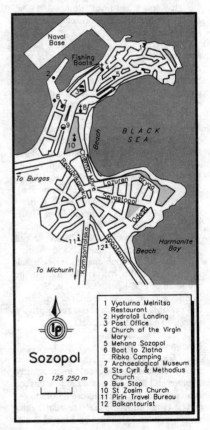

Sozopol

0    125  250 m

1 Vyaturna Melnitsa Restaurant
2 Hydrofoil Landing
3 Post Office
4 Church of the Virgin Mary
5 Mehana Sozopol
6 Boat to Zlatna Ribka Camping
7 Archaeological Museum
8 Sts Cyril & Methodius Church
9 Bus Stop
10 St Zosim Church
11 Pirin Travel Bureau
12 Balkantourist

Nesebâr are far more significant, Sozopol is more relaxed with a resident artistic community which migrates here every summer. It's nice to come for the arts festival during the first half of September, but Sozopol rates highly as an unstructured beach resort from May to early October.

### Things to See

Your best bet is just to wander around the old town, though there's an **Archaeological Museum** (captions are only in Bulgarian) in the modern complex between the bus stop and the fishing harbour. The tiny 18th century **Church of the Virgin Mary**, almost hidden below street level at ulitsa 1911 No 13, is worth a brief stop to see its wooden iconostasis.

### Places to Stay

*Zlatna Ribka Camping* is six km before Sozopol on the road from Burgas. No bungalows are available but there's plenty of camping space (US$5 per person, US$5 per tent) and several places where you can eat. The camping ground is at the southern end of the long beach you can see from Sozopol's harbour. In summer, small boats shuttle back and forth between Sozopol and Zlatna Ribka, leaving whenever there are 10 passengers waiting to go (US$0.25 per person).

If you want a bungalow, walk north a couple of km along the beach from Zlatna Ribka to *Camping Gradina*, where simple wooden bungalows cost US$26 double and more luxurious chalets cost US$56 double.

Balkantourist, Ropotamo 28, on the beach south of the centre, has private rooms in the old town at US$4 per person. The Sozopol Tourist Service, ulitsa Lazuren Bryag 1, also has private rooms. Ask about small private perestroika hotels at Sozopol.

### Places to Eat

The *Mehana Sozopol*, a large tavern on the main street leading into the old town, is fairly obvious and touristy but the outdoor terrace is nice. Local grilled meats are on offer.

The *Vyaturna Melnitsa Restaurant*, below an old wooden lighthouse on Morski Skala,

at the northern end of the old town, serves a good buffet breakfast in summer. You'll get a bird's-eye view of a small island just off Sozopol from the restaurant terrace.

### Getting There & Away

A crowded local bus travels to/from Burgas (34 km) every couple of hours. The hydrofoil from Sozopol to Burgas, Nesebâr and Varna operates three times a day from mid-June to mid-September and once a day in late May and early June.

### COASTAL CAMPING GROUNDS

Near the airport eight km north-east of Burgas is the *Sarafovo Hostel* (open from May to September) listed in the IYHF handbook. Set tents and bungalows are available at US$3 per person or you can pitch your own tent for less. The beach is about five minutes away. While perhaps not the most attractive or convenient hostel around, it usually has space, so it's good to fall back on if all the rooms in Burgas are full. You can register at the hostel itself (no need to visit the Pirin office in Burgas) but no English is spoken. Take the Sunny Beach bus as far as the airport roundabout at Sarafovo, then ask for 'Camping Pirin', about a 10-minute walk east through town.

Of the 45 Black Sea camping grounds in the Balkantourist list, *Europa Camping* (no bungalows), beside the busy highway just before Pomorie, is the first one north of Burgas.

North-east of Burgas, beyond Pomorie between the highway and the sea, is *Acheloj Camping* (open from mid-May to mid-October). There are bungalows but they're fully booked all summer by groups, so get ready to unroll the tent (US$2 per person, US$2 per tent). It's quieter than Europa Camping and is in a nice location on the beach, midway between Pomorie and Sunny Beach. Any Sunny Beach bus will drop you off at the gate.

On a fine beach near Obzor, halfway between Varna and Burgas, are the *Luna* and *Prostor* camping grounds, both with bungalows and both right between the main

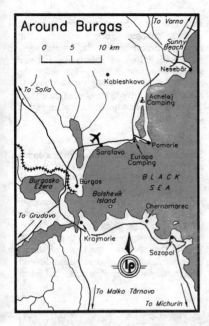

## Around Burgas

0　5　10 km

To Varna

Sunny Beach

Nesebâr

Kableshkovo

To Sofia

Achelo Camping

Sarafovo

Pomorie

Europa Camping

Burgasko Ezero

Burgas

Bolshevik Island

BLACK SEA

To Grudovo

Chernomorec

Krajmorie

Sozopol

To Malko Târnovo

To Michurin

highway, less than a km apart (open from June to September). Luna has lousy toilets but a very good restaurant with home cooking. Beware of camping at the huge *Kamchiya* complex farther north, as it's overrun by local families who stay in the rows of tiny bungalows lined up along the muddy slope, and there's no decent place for a tent.

All of these camping grounds are near the main highway between Burgas and Varna.

## SUNNY BEACH (СЛЪНУЕВ БРЯГ)

Sunny Beach, or Sonnenstrand (Slânchev Bryag), is Bulgaria's largest seaside resort, with 112 hotels (24,792 beds) stretching along a six-km sandy beach, 36 km north of Burgas. Sunny Beach caters especially to families with small children by providing playgrounds, children's pools, special menus, baby sitters and nurseries, and the gently sloping beach is safe for waders. Other attractions are sailing, windsurfing,

tennis and horse riding, although everything along this package-tourist strip is over-crowded in summer and closed all winter.

## Places to Stay & Eat

There are two camping grounds at the north-ern end of the strip, both open from May to mid-October. *Camp Emona* by the beach is US$2 per person and US$2 per tent (no bungalows). It's absolutely jammed with tents.

The *Slantchev Briag Campground*, on the inland side of the main highway a few hundred metres from Emona, has bungalows at US$8 per person, but you'd be very lucky to get one. Camping here is US$3 per person, US$3 per tent. It's crowded and the facilities are only so-so, but there's lots of space.

If you want to stay at one of the high-rise hotels in Sunny Beach, you would do better to come on a package tour or book a dis-counted room in advance from Sofia. The people at the Balkantourist accommodation office near Hotel Kuban, opposite the bus station in the centre of the complex, can sometimes arrange hotel rooms ranging from US$15 to US$25 per person, but they don't have any private rooms – you must go to Nesebâr for that. Nobody at the Sunny Beach Balkantourist office speaks much English.

Expect to be cheated at the restaurants in Sunny Beach and count your change care-fully elsewhere – there are too many tourists around here.

## Getting There & Away

Buses to Burgas and Varna leave from the bus station about 250 metres south of Bal-kantourist, on the inland side of the main highway. The Nesebâr-Sunny Beach bus stops right in front of Balkantourist.

A miniature road train runs from one end of the resort to the other every 15 minutes.

## NESEBÂR (НЕСЕБЪР)

Nesebâr, the ancient Mesembria, was founded by Greek Chalcedonians on the site of an earlier Thracian settlement in 510 BC. Mesembria prospered through trade with the Thracians of the interior, declining after the

Roman conquest in the 1st century BC. Under Byzantium, Mesembria regained its former importance and in the 5th and 6th centuries a number of imposing churches were erected, including the Metropolitan Church, the ruin of which you can still see. Byzantine nobles exiled here built more churches until the town had as many as 40. Beginning in the 9th century, Nesebâr (the Slavonic name now used) passed back and forth between Byzantium and Bulgaria many times but the town remained unscathed. Even the Turks left Nesebâr alone and allowed it to strengthen its fortifications to defend itself against Cossack pirates. Overshadowed by Varna, and later by Burgas, Nesebâr ceased to be an active trading town in the 18th century and today lives mostly from fishing and tourism.

The town sits on a small rocky peninsula connected to the mainland by a narrow isthmus. Remnants of the 2nd century city walls rise above the bus stop, and along the winding cobbled streets are picturesque stone and timber houses with wooden stairways and jutting 1st floors. In summer tourists from nearby Sunny Beach clog the narrow streets of Nesebâr and you have to run a zigzag course to stay out of their way. The crowds do thin out in the eastern part of town, however.

## Things to See

Scattered through the town are over a dozen surviving medieval churches, most of them in ruins. Characteristic of the Nesebâr style are the horizontal strips of white stone and red brick offset by striped blind arches resting on vertical pilasters, the façades highlighted by ceramic discs and rosettes.

Of special interest is the 11th century **St Stefan Church** above the hydrofoil terminal, almost completely covered inside with 16th century frescoes. The small but select

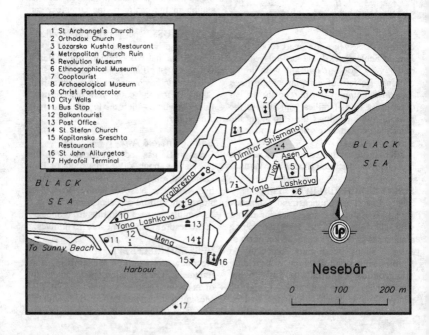

1  St Archangel's Church
2  Orthodox Church
3  Lozarska Kushta Restaurant
4  Metropolitan Church Ruin
5  Revolution Museum
6  Ethnographical Museum
7  Cooptourist
8  Archaeological Museum
9  Christ Pantocrator
10  City Walls
11  Bus Stop
12  Balkantourist
13  Post Office
14  St Stefan Church
15  Kapitanska Sreschta Restaurant
16  St John Aliturgetos
17  Hydrofoil Terminal

BLACK SEA

BLACK SEA

Nesebâr

To Sunny Beach

Harbour

0    100    200 m

collection of the **Archaeological Museum** is housed in the 10th century church of St John the Baptist. Ask at one of the travel agencies in town about evening concerts held in the 6th century Metropolitan Church ruin.

## Places to Stay

Balkantourist, between the bus stop and the harbour, and Cooptourist, Yana Lashkova 23, both have private rooms for about US$5 per person. Many of the rooms are in the new town near the beach, just west across the isthmus.

## Places to Eat

You'll find lots of nice places to eat and drink in Nesebâr. The *Kapitanska Sreschta Restaurant*, an old sea captain's house that overlooks the harbour, has lots of atmosphere. It's rather touristy (the waiters are dressed in sailor suits) but you should be able to get seafood here.

Farther off the beaten track is the *Lozarska Kushta Restaurant* near the east end of town, a typical Bulgarian tavern with local dishes.

## Getting There & Away

Jam-packed buses run regularly between Nesebâr and Sunny Beach (10 km), where you change buses for Burgas or Varna. There's also the more comfortable hydrofoil which connects Nesebâr to Burgas, Pomorie, Sozopol and Varna. The demand for seats usually outstrips supply, so get in line early.

## VARNA (BAPHA)

Varna, Bulgaria's largest Black Sea port, has become the summer capital of Bulgaria. The city's history began in 585 BC when Miletian Greeks founded ancient Odessos. Varna flourished under the Romans, who left extensive ruins. During the Middle Ages, Varna alternated between Byzantium and Bulgaria but remained prosperous. The Turks captured Varna in 1393 and made it a northern bastion of their empire. In 1444 the Polish-Hungarian king Vladislav III Jagiello was killed in battle here while leading a crusade against Ottoman expansion. After

the Crimean War (1853-56) Turkey allowed its allies Britain and France to sell their products throughout the Ottoman Empire and Varna became a great trading centre. In 1866 the railway arrived from Ruse, providing a direct route from the Danube to the Black Sea. Since WW II, much of Bulgaria's trade with the USSR has passed through the port of Varna.

In recent years Varna has developed into an ideal resort with excellent beaches, parks, museums, historic sites, accommodation, restaurants, theatres and teeming pedestrian malls. Even the street signs are in both Cyrillic and Latin script! It's an attractive city on a bay hemmed in by hills that offer scenic views. Industrial installations like the big chemical plant at Devnya and the Shipbuilding Combine are well west of town. If you don't have time to visit more of the coast, come and see the sea at Varna.

## Orientation

The bus and railway stations are on opposite sides of the city, but many local buses run between them (ask). The hydrofoil terminal is just south of the city centre, within walking distance from the railway station. Everything north-east of the hydrofoil terminal is beach and everything west of it is the commercial port. The left-luggage office at the train station is in a separate building labelled '*Gepäckaufbewahrung*' across the street.

From the train station, walk north up ulitsa Avram Gatchev into ploschtad 9 Septemvri, the centre of town. A broad pedestrian mall, ulitsa V I Lenin, runs east from here. Northwest of ploschtad 9 Septemvri is ploschtad Varnenska Komuna, a major crossroads. From here bulevard Karl Marx runs northwest to the bus station and the airport. The great Asparuh Bridge over the navigable channel between Varnensko Ezero and the Black Sea is just west of ploschtad Varnenska Komuna.

## Information

Staff at the Balkantourist office, Avram Gatchev 33, near the train station, are very helpful with maps and information. The Pirin

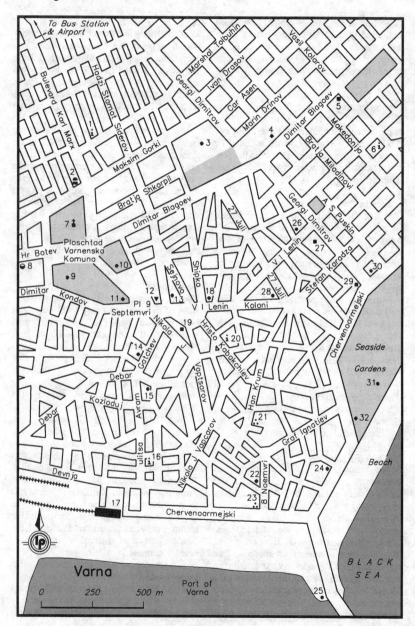

To Bus Station & Airport

Bulevard Karl Marx

Hadzi Stamat Siderov

Maksim Gorki

Bratja Shkorpil

Dimitar Blagoev

Georgi Dimitrov

Marshal Tolbuhin

Ivan Drasov

Car Asen

Marin Drinov

Vasil Kolarov

Dimitar Blagoev

Makedonija

Bratja Mladinovi

Georgi Dimitrov

A S Puskin

27 Juli

Lenin

Karadza

Stefan

27 Juli

Chervenoarmejski

Seaside

Gardens

Hr Botev

Ploschtad
Varnenska
Komuna

Dimitar

Kondov

Pl 9
Septemvri

Sejnova

Shipka

V I Lenin

Koloni

Nikola
J

Gatchev

Debar

Kozloduj

Avram

Debar

Hristo Kabakchiev

Voptsarov

Han Krum

Ulitsa

Devnja

Nikola J Vapcarov

8 Noemvri

Chervenoarmejski

Graf Ignatiev

Beach

BLACK
SEA

Varna

0       250       500 m

Port of
Varna

Travel Bureau, Hristo Kabakchiev 13, has information on youth hostels.

The Sofia Press Agency, ulitsa V I Lenin 51, offers political literature in English. For maps of Bulgaria, try the stationery shop at ulitsa V I Lenin 6. In Varna there are consulates of Poland, Chervenoarmejski 43 (see the Varna map), and Czechoslovakia, Chervenoarmejski 135, north-east of the Festival Complex.

**Post & Telecommunications** You can place long-distance telephone calls at the main post office, Maksim Gorki 36.

■ PLACES TO STAY

5  Orbita Hotel
19  Musala Hotel
27  Tcherno More Hotel
29  Odessa Hotel

OTHER

1  Balkantourist
2  Main Post Office
3  Museum of History & Art
4  Party House
6  Balkantourist
7  Assumption Cathedral
8  Bus to Camping Panorama & Albena
9  Dramatic Theatre
10  Town Hall
11  Opera House
12  Zlatno Pile Restaurant
13  Puppet Theatre
14  Railway Ticket Office
15  Ethnographic Museum
16  Balkantourist
17  Railway Station
18  Balkan Airlines
20  Pirin Travel Bureau
21  Roman Thermae
22  Worker's Museum
23  Roman Baths
24  Polish Consulate
25  Hydrofoil Terminal
26  Sofia Press Agency
28  National Revival Museum
30  Festival Complex
31  Aquarium
32  Maritime Museum

## Things to See

There are two sets of **Roman baths**. The newer baths are on Chervenoarmejski, just above the port between the train station and the hydrofoil terminal. There's a **Worker's Museum** at ulitsa 8 Noemvri 5, next to these baths. Much more interesting are the other baths, the 2nd century **Roman Thermae** on ulitsa Han Krum, north from the Worker's Museum and to the left. Aside from the large, well-preserved baths, there's the beautiful **St Anastasius Orthodox Church** (built in 1602) within the compound.

Go east on ulitsa Graf Ignatiev from the Roman Thermae to the south-west end of the **Seaside Gardens**. This attractive park contains the **Maritime Museum** and, nearby, the **Aquarium** (1911). There's a good beach below the Seaside Gardens, but it's body-to-body in summer.

Walk through the gardens to the Odessa Hotel, then north-west on bulevard Georgi Dimitrov to Varna's largest museum, the **Museum of History & Art** near Party House at ulitsa Dimitar Blagoev 41. The ground floor of this neo-Renaissance former girls' high school is dedicated to archaeology. Unfortunately, few of the exhibits are captioned in anything other than Bulgarian, and the excellent collection of icons which was once upstairs has been replaced by an industrial exhibit.

West of this museum, ulitsa Dimitar Blagoev cuts across ploschtad Varnenska Komuna where you'll find the **Assumption Cathedral** (1886), the town hall, the Opera House (1921) and other sights.

Cross ploschtad 9 Septemvri and stroll down the mall. Below street level on ulitsa V I Lenin, opposite Balkan Airlines, is a 2nd century **Roman tower** and wall of ancient Odessos. Beyond at ulitsa 27 Juli 9 is the **Museum of the Bulgarian National Revival**, housed in the first Bulgarian school (1862) in Varna. Between this museum and the train station is the **Ethnographic Museum**, ulitsa Panagjurishte 22, with a large collection of folk art and implements in a National Revival-style house that was erected in 1860.

Many of Varna's museums and archaeological sites are open Tuesday to Sunday from 10 am to 5 pm.

## Places to Stay

**Camping** The closest camping ground (open from June to September) is at Cape Galata, six km south-east across the bridge. Camping is US$2 per person, US$2 per tent (there is plenty of space), but no bungalows are available. Bus No 17 runs to Galata every 20 minutes from 5 am to 11.30 pm from just outside Varna Railway Station, and then it's a one-km walk downhill to the camping ground. A taxi to Galata will cost US$2 from Varna. There's a restaurant below the lighthouse near the camping ground which has a great view of Varna and the Black Sea. From here a footpath leads down to a place on the beach that serves fresh fish and chips.

**Hostels & Private Rooms** *Turisticheska spalnya 'Hans Asparuh'* listed in the IYHF handbook is hidden among the warehouses of the Port of Varna, almost directly below the gigantic Asparuh Bridge. It's on the Varna side of the waterway linking Varna Lake to the Black Sea. Before you go, check with staff at the Pirin Travel Bureau (☎ 22 2710), Hristo Kabakchiev 13, and have them write out the full address in Bulgarian, as this hostel is not well known and very hard to find. Its inconvenient, unappealing location and crowds of adolescents make it a poor choice.

Four Balkantourist offices in Varna rent private rooms from around US$4 per person, but singles are seldom available. The office at ulitsa Avram Gatchev 33 is near the train station and there's another beside the Musala Hotel. The Balkantourist office at ulitsa Marshal Tolbuhin 5, just off bulevard Karl Marx, is less well known and a good bet. Finally there's the Balkantourist office at ulitsa V I Lenin 73.

The three offices tend to have rooms in the section of town closest to them, so go first to the one in the area in which you wish to stay.

**Hotels** The cheapest hotel is the rather depressing *Hotel Musala*, Musala 3, off ulitsa V I Lenin near ploschtad 9 Septemvri (US$9/18 single/double, not including breakfast). You can't check in before 2 pm, but if you're in line by 1.30 pm you should get a room.

Of Varna's luxury hotels, the three-star *Tcherno More Hotel*, Georgi Dimitrov 35, boasts the tallest building and the highest prices, but the two-star *Odessa Hotel*, Georgi Dimitrov 1, with singles/doubles for US$20/28, is closer to the beach and more relaxed. This is also less than half the price of the Tcherno More Hotel, which means you may find it full.

Unless you have a reservation, just forget the *Orbita Hotel*, Vasil Kolarov 25 (US$28 double, no singles), which is packed all summer.

Some of Bulgaria's new, privately owned perestroika hotels are springing up in Galata, 10 km south-east of Varna. One of the best is the five-room *Hotel Florina* (US$7 double) run by English-speaking entrepreneur Nicolai Dimitrov. Some of Nicolai's relatives run *Hotel Zeravna* across the street. The meals at the Florina are great so it's well worth dropping in for a meal at the restaurant there, even if you choose to stay at the camping ground down the hill.

## Places to Eat

The *Zlatno Pile* (Golden Chicken) *Restaurant*, on the corner of ploschtad 9 Septemvri and ulitsa V I Lenin, serves half-chickens and beer in unpretentious surroundings. You can get coffee and ice cream in the café across the street.

Bulevard Georgi Dimitrov, between the Tcherno More and Odessa hotels, is solidly lined with restaurants serving meals to tourists at the outdoor tables. Stroll along till you see someone eating a dish you fancy. If these places fail to please, step up to Varna's finest, the 2nd-floor dining room at the *Tcherno More Hotel*, Georgi Dimitrov 35.

## Entertainment

Both the *Opera House* and the *Dramatic Theatre* are on ploschtad 9 Septemvri. The ultramodern *Festival Complex* (1986) on bulevard Georgi Dimitrov, opposite the Odessa Hotel, is used mainly for congresses, though in July and August there's nightly entertainment in the café-theatre downstairs.

A theatre ticket office is at Shipka 5 near Balkan Airlines. If you're in Varna between mid-June and mid-July, be sure to check the programme of the Varna Summer Festival, which features outstanding musical events. At this time you can enjoy opera and ballet in the open-air theatre in Seaside Gardens, chamber music in St Anastasius Church, theatre in the Roman Thermae and concerts in the Festival Complex.

### Getting There & Away

Balkan Airlines has six flights a day from Sofia to Varna for about US$20 one-way. Bus No 15 connects Varna Airport to town. The Balkan Airlines office is at ulitsa V I Lenin 15, on the corner of ulitsa Shipka.

From mid-June to mid-October the Varna Express runs between Poland and Varna via Debrecen, Oradea, Bucharest and Kardam. From June to September the Nesebâr Express runs between Budapest and Varna but it doesn't pass Bucharest. Other international trains operate during summer but reservations are required.

Express trains go to Sofia (543 km via Pleven or 553 km via Karlovo); couchettes are available on the overnight service. For Veliko Târnovo change trains at Gorna Oryahovitsa. Two trains a day go direct to Ruse. The daily local train between Varna and Burgas takes five hours.

You can buy advance domestic railway tickets and obtain information at ulitsa Avram Gatchev 10, just down from ploschtad 9 Septemvri. Make couchette bookings at ulitsa 27 Juli 13. The Rila office, Shipka 3, sells international train tickets.

Advance bus tickets can only be purchased at the bus station, bulevard Karl Marx 159. To go from Varna to Burgas (132 km) takes three hours by bus and reservations are essential. Southbound buses to Nesebâr, etc, stop running at around 6 pm.

Transportation to the beach resorts north

of Varna is good, continuing late into the night. Bus No 99 runs to Camping Panorama at Golden Sands, 17 km north-east of Varna, from the south side of Hristo Botev, west of Assumption Cathedral. The bus to Albena also leaves from this stop (the last bus leaves around 7 pm). Purchase tickets in advance at the kiosk.

From May to September hydrofoils run south to Nesebâr, Pomorie, Burgas and Sozopol.

### GOLDEN SANDS (ЗЛАТНИ ПЯСЪЦИ)

Golden Sands, or Goldstrand (Zlatni Pyasâtsi), is perhaps Bulgaria's most chic resort, the green wooded hills rising directly behind the four km of golden sands with some 67 hotels (14,230 beds) hidden among the trees. Aside from the beach life, Golden Sands offers all kinds of organised sports such as windsurfing, sailing, diving, water-skiing, archery, tennis and horse riding with qualified instructors available.

Other flashy resorts along this Bulgarian Riviera are Chalka, Druzhba and Albena, all of which feature high-rise hotels, jam-packed beaches and the sort of programmed holiday atmosphere that tourists on package holidays enjoy. Albena seems to attract a younger clientele than the others, so make it your choice if you're into nightlife. All of these places, Golden Sands included, cater mostly to tour groups and aren't really set up to receive individuals. The best plan is to stay in Varna or Balchik and catch a bus to one of the resorts for a day in the sun.

### Places to Stay

The Balkantourist accommodation service *(nastanjavane)* issuing hotel rooms is on the main highway, near the polyclinic, just above Hotel Diana at Golden Sands. Rooms are only issued after noon, and without a booking you may be told that only bungalows for US$70 a night are available. Don't expect any bargains and, best of all, come on a package tour or with reservations made in Sofia.

*Camping Panorama* is by the highway at the northern end of Golden Sands, about a

10-minute walk from the beach. Camping costs US$5 per person plus US$3 per tent and no bungalows are available. Buses No 53 and 99 from Varna stop here.

## BALCHIK (БАЛЧИК)

Balchik is a picturesque old town huddled below weathered white chalk bluffs, 47 km north-east of Varna. The Greek traders who settled here in the 5th century BC called the place 'Krunoi' for its springs and the Romans changed it to Dionysopolis in honour of the god of wine. From 1913 to 1940 Balchik and the rest of southern Dobruja belonged to Romania. It was here in 1931 that Queen Maria of Romania had an Oriental-style summer residence built overlooking the sea. It is said that the queen entertained many lovers in the building, and though it's easy to imagine such affairs in such a place, much of the romance has since worn off.

Balchik makes a good day trip from Varna by boat, otherwise it's easy to arrange a stay and patronise the beach at nearby Albena.

### Orientation & Information

The bus station is on ulitsa Lenin in the upper part of the old town, a 10-minute walk from the ferry wharf if you know the way. Balkantourist, Georgi Dimitrov 33, is between the two and it's worth entering the office to examine the town map displayed on the wall.

### Things to See

The local **museum** is near Balkantourist and there's an art gallery nearby.

Queen Maria's villa is about two km west of the ferry wharf (follow the shore) and it's possible to enter whenever local artists exhibit their wares inside for sale. This villa and several other buildings are now included in Balchik's **botanical gardens**, which allegedly contain more than 600 varieties of Mediterranean plants and cacti. Unfortunately, it's poorly maintained, so don't come expecting a lot and you won't be disappointed.

### Places to Stay

*Camping 'Bissar'* listed in the IYHF handbook is a couple of km west of Balchik on the road to Albena (any Albena bus will drop you off nearby). Nice little bungalows are US$5 per person (show your YHA card for a discount). You can also camp here should the bungalows all be full (open from May to September). This site is about a km above the botanical gardens.

Balkantourist, Georgi Dimitrov 33, a five-minute walk up from the ferry wharf, has private rooms at US$3/5 single/double, so try there first.

The one-star *Raketa Hotel*, on ulitsa Maksim Gorki adjoining Restaurant Dionysopolis near the ferry wharf, charges US$4 per person. The two-star *Hotel Balchik*, a modern three-storey hotel facing a park in the centre of town, charges US$8/16 single/double with bath.

### Getting There & Away

The boat ride to Balchik on the hydro bus is a nice two-hour trip with an open deck where you can sit outside to enjoy the great views of the coast. This enjoyable Black Sea cruise costs US$1 from Varna to Balchik.

It's fairly easy to make a circle trip of it by returning to Varna on local buses with a change at Albena and Golden Sands. In summer local buses travel from Balchik to Albena (18 km) every 20 minutes, and bus No 2 from Albena to Golden Sands (16 km) is about as frequent. From Golden Sands, bus No 109 runs to Varna frequently.

# Northern Bulgaria

Northern Bulgaria, between the Danube and the crest of the Stara Planina, corresponds to the ancient Roman province of Moesia Inferior. To the south was Roman Thrace and to the north, Dacia. Despite barbarian invasions in the 3rd century AD, Moesia remained part of the Eastern Roman Empire until the formation of Bulgaria in 681. Pliska and Preslav, historic capitals of the First Bulgarian Empire, and Veliko Târnovo, capital of the Second Bulgarian Empire, are all here.

During the long Turkish period, Ruse and Vidin served as northern bastions of the Ottoman Empire. Much later, during the Bulgarian National Revival, the renowned monasteries at Preobrazhenski and Troyan were erected. During the Russo-Turkish War of 1877-78, the great battles of Pleven and Shipka waged here decided the fate of modern Bulgaria. All this makes northern Bulgaria a region of special interest for historians.

Coming or going from Romania, northern Bulgaria is the gateway to both countries. Most travellers cross the 'Friendship Bridge' at Ruse, but the Calafat-Vidin ferry is a viable alternative. Hydrofoils cruise the Danube from Vidin to Ruse and there's good hiking in the Stara Planina. Northern Bulgaria is worth exploring.

## VIDIN (ВИДИН)

Vidin, the first major Bulgarian town on the Danube River below the famous Iron Gate, serves as a convenient entry or exit point to/from Romania and Yugoslavia or as an embarkation point for a hydrofoil ride on the Bulgarian Danube. Calafat, Romania, is just opposite.

### History

On the site of the 3rd century BC Celtic settlement of Dunonia, the Romans built a fortress they called Bononia to control the Danube crossing here. Medieval Vidin was an important north-western bastion and trading centre of the Second Bulgarian Empire. In 1371, as Bulgaria wavered before the Ottoman onslaught, the king's son, Ivan Sratsimir, declared the region the independent Kingdom of Vidin with himself as ruler.

The fall of the city to the Turks in 1396 marked the completion of their conquest of Bulgaria. The Turks built an extensive city wall around Vidin, the various gates of which have survived to this day. As their rule in turn weakened, a local pasha, Osman Pazvantoglu, declared his district independent of the sultan from 1792 to 1807. In 1878 Vidin was returned to Bulgaria by the Romanian Army

and in 1885 an attempt by Serbia to take the area was resisted.

### Orientation & Information

Central Vidin is very convenient, with the new hydrofoil/ferry terminal, railway station and bus station all a block apart in the middle of town. The Orbita office is opposite the high-rise Hotel Rovno, five minutes away on foot.

### Things to See

Vidin's main sight is the **Baba Vida Fortress** at the northern end of the park, overlooking the river. Baba Vida was built by the Bulgarians from the 10th to the 14th centuries on the ruined walls of 3rd century Roman Bononia. In the 17th century the Turks rebuilt the fortress and today it's the best preserved medieval stone fortress in Bulgaria.

In the riverside park between the fortress and the centre is the 18th century **Osman Pazvantoglu Mosque**, with a small religious library alongside. Nearby are the 17th century **Church of St Petka** and the 12th century **Church of St Panteleimon**. The former was partially sunk into the ground out of deference to the mosque.

### Places to Stay & Eat

The IYHF *Turisticheski dom 'Vidin'*, ulitsa Iskra 3, is just a few minutes' walk from the ferry terminal. Both Vidin's two-star hotels, the high-rise *Hotel Rovno*, at ulitsa Todor Petrov 4, and the older, run-down *Hotel Bononia*, are a five-minute walk from the terminal.

*Camping Nora* is just beyond the fairground, a couple of km west of town along bulevard V I Lenin. Older bungalows cost US$4 per person, new bungalows cost US$9 per person and camping costs US$2 per person.

For dinner it's worth trying the private *Naj Naj Najdenov Restaurant*, which you'll need a taxi to find.

### Getting There & Away

There are direct express trains between Vidin

and Sofia (211 km), two buses a day to Pleven (226 km) and 11 buses a day to Bregovo (29 km) on the Yugoslav border. It is possible to walk in and out.

The Vidin-Calafat ferry operates several times a day all year. The crossing takes half an hour (US$1). There are actually two services here: a car ferry which crosses about five km north of Vidin and a passenger launch which uses the Maritime Terminal right in the centre of town. If you're on foot, try to take the passenger boat.

**Hydrofoil** The hydrofoil between Vidin and Ruse operates from 30 May to 30 September leaving each end at 8 am daily. It takes six hours to go from Vidin to Ruse (US$4) and there are 12 stops between the two towns. The hydrofoil is used as public transport by the locals – this is not only a tourist trip.

If you're bound for Pleven, only get a ticket to Nikopol, four hours downriver from Vidin. Hourly buses cover the 53 km from Nikopol to Pleven and the bus station is very near the hydrofoil landing.

Getting a hydrofoil ticket is usually no problem, but try to buy one the day before. No passport or exchange receipts are required. There's very comfortable airline seating inside and you can stand in the open viewing area amidships. There's a snack bar and you can carry luggage aboard with no objections.

## PLEVEN (ПЛЕВЕН)
Pleven, between Ruse and Sofia, 35 km south of the Danube, is best known as the site of a five-month 1877 battle between the Turks, under Osman Pasha, and a Russo-Romanian army. An entire Turkish army of 11 pashas, 2000 officers and 37,000 men was encircled and captured in this decisive engagement. Aside from sites related to the battle, there are parks and an inviting city centre to see. Pleven doesn't receive many Western visitors, so you'll be assured of a warm welcome.

## Orientation
Pleven's adjacent bus and train stations are on the north side of town. Bulevard V I Lenin runs south towards the centre, passing many large shops. Ploschtad 9 Septemvri is the very heart of the city. Georgi Dimitrov, a pleasant pedestrian street, curves back towards the stations from this spacious square.

## Information
Balkantourist is at San Stefano 3 near the District Museum. The Pirin Travel Bureau, Tsvetan Spassov 21-23, has information on hostelling.

## Things to See
Begin your visit with Pleven's most unique sight, the **1877 Panorama** on a hilltop above the city. Bus No 2 runs directly there from the railway station via bulevard V I Lenin.

---

■ PLACES TO STAY

3  Hotel Pleven
11  Hotel Rostov na Don
16  Hotel Balkan

OTHER

1  Railway Station
2  Bus Station
4  St Paraskeva Church
5  Mehana Restaurant
6  Bookstore
7  St Nicholas Church
8  Dramatic Theatre
9  Railway Ticket Office
10  National Revival Park
12  Monument to the Soviet Army
13  Puppet Theatre
14  Party House
15  Pirin Travel Bureau
17  City Art Gallery
18  The Common Grave
19  Concert Hall
20  Mausoleum
21  Town Hall
22  Balkantourist
23  District Historical Museum
24  Ilya Beshkov Art Gallery
25  Freedom Monument
26  1877 Panorama

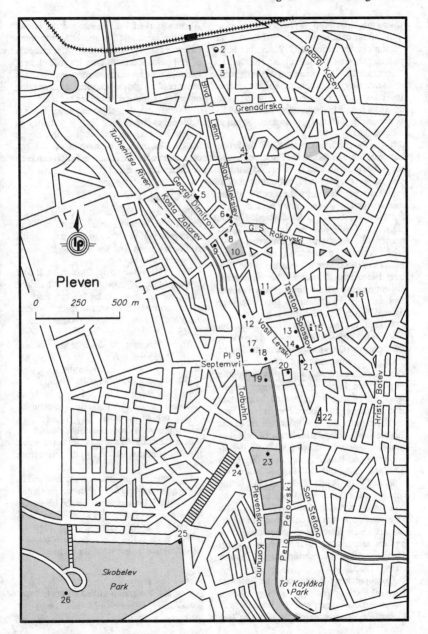

Pleven

0    250    500 m

Inside this large building (1977) is a fantastic 360° mural painting of the third assault on Pleven (11 September 1877). Another huge painting shows the final Turkish attempt (10 December 1877) to break out of their encirclement. Buy the brochure which explains the many details or request a guide who speaks a language you understand (no additional charge). Hand luggage must be left at a kiosk outside.

From the panorama, walk down the broad path east through **Skobelev Park**, veering to the left at the end. You'll see period artillery pieces, an ossuary and numerous monuments to the dead. In the centre of the monumental stairway leading back down to the city is a Freedom Monument. On the right at the bottom of the steps is the ultramodern **Ilia Beshkov Art Gallery** (1978), which is closed on Tuesday. In the old yellow barracks (1888) across the street is the **District Historical Museum**. This impressive collection covers the entire history of Pleven and vicinity and includes theatrical and natural history exhibits.

Go through the park north of the museum towards the high white marble pillar marking the **Common Grave** of those who died in the struggle against fascism. This memorial faces the monumental fountain in the middle of ploschtad 9 Septemvri, an attractive open space full of interest. In front of the fountain is a red flag flying above Party House, and the **town hall** (1922), with its musical clock. Beside this is the **Mausoleum of Russian and Romanian Soldiers** (1907), a red-and-white striped building commemorating the 31,000 Russian and 4500 Romanian soldiers who died in the Battle of Pleven. Back on the other side of the fountain, beyond the common grave, is the **City Art Gallery**, with an extensive permanent collection of Bulgarian art in an Oriental-style building. The square merges north into ulitsa Georgi Dimitrov at the **Monument to the Soviet Army** (1955).

Continue down this street to the **National Revival Park** on the right. This small park features old cannons and the house where Osman Pasha surrendered his sword to Tsar Alexander II of Russia. Around the corner from the Dramatic Theatre is **St Nicholas Church** (1834), now a good little museum of Bulgarian icons. In fact, it's half church, half museum, and in the early morning you'll see people lighting candles and praying before the captioned museum exhibits.

If you've still got some time, catch a trolley bus from bulevard V I Lenin to **Kaylâka Park**, six km south of the city at Mosta. This extensive park with very enjoyable walks between ponds and cliffs can keep you busy for hours.

### Places to Stay

Balkantourist, San Stefano 3, has private rooms at US$6 per person. If the people there seem reluctant to give you one, explain that you're not fussy and are looking for something cheaper than a hotel.

The IYHF youth hostel *'Turisticheski dom Tsvetan Spassov'* is on a hill a few hundred metres from the Mosta trolley bus stop. To get in you may have to make reservations at the Pirin Travel Bureau, Tsvetan Spassov 21-23.

You can camp (US$4/6 single/double) beside the two-star *Kaylâka Hotel* in lovely Kaylâka Park. A hotel room will cost US$20/44 single/double with private facilities. Get a room on the 3rd floor to avoid disco noise. There's a good restaurant on the terrace behind the hotel. To get there, take trolley bus No 1 from the railway station to Mosta, then bus No 4 or 23 right to the hotel. It's a 25-minute walk through the forest from Mosta to the hotel.

Overlooking the bus station is the 12-storey, three-star *Hotel Pleven*, ploschtad Republika 2. Less expensive is the 12-storey, two-star *Hotel Rostov Na Don*, ulitsa Slavi Aleksiev 2, in the centre of town. Pleven's newest hotel is the three-star *Hotel Balkan*, a five-minute walk east of the centre.

### Places to Eat

For typical Bulgarian grilled meats try *Mehana*, Georgi Dimitrov 123. Go through into the back courtyard.

The café at the *Hotel Rostov Na Don* prepares a good bacon-and-egg breakfast.

Pleven's most memorable meals are served at the *Peshterata Restaurant*, located in a natural cave in Kaylâka Park between Mosta and the hotel. It caters to groups and in summer it can be hard for individuals to get seats, but there are several other good folkloric restaurants in the park.

### Entertainment

Pleven's *Dramatic Theatre* is a fine old building (1869) on ulitsa Georgi Dimitrov, and the *Concert Hall* stands on ploschtad 9 Septemvri, beside the mausoleum. Tickets for events at either place are sold in the offices with posters in the windows beside the Monument to the Soviet Army. Also check the *Puppet Theatre* at ulitsa Tsvetan Spassov 14.

### Getting There & Away

Trains to Sofia (194 km), Ruse (211 km) and Varna (349 km) are fairly frequent. (For the last two-thirds of its journey from Pleven to Sofia, the train follows the fantastic Iskâr Gorge.) You can get the overnight Pannonia Express to Bucharest here around midnight (reservations required). For Veliko Târnovo change at Gorna Oryahovitsa. For Troyan take a bus (twice daily, 70 km). Domestic and international train tickets are available at Rila, Zamenhoff 2.

### THE STARA PLANINA (СТАРА ПЛАНИНА)

A good slice of the Stara Planina (Balkan Mountains) can be seen on a loop from Pleven to Veliko Târnovo going via Lovech, Troyan, Karlovo, Kazanlâk, Shipka, Etâr and Gabrovo, or vice versa. You'll visit old monasteries, war memorials, quaint villages and the forested peaks themselves.

It's not possible to do all this in one day, so you'll have to spend a night or two somewhere. There are camping grounds between Karlovo and Veliko Târnovo, all of them with bungalows for those without tents. From Karlovo to Pleven you'll have a choice of youth hostels or fairly expensive hotels.

It's quite an adventure to do this loop on public transport, but it calls for a hardy, rough-and-ready traveller willing to put up with occasional difficulties and delays. An amazing variety of attractions are packed into this little circuit.

### TROYAN (ТРОЯН)

Troyan, a small town by the Beli Osâm River, at the foot of 1525-metre Troyan Pass, is a base for visiting Troyan Monastery, 10 km east. An hourly bus from Troyan Bus Station runs right to the monastery door. Before you set out, however, leave your pack at the station and buy an onward bus ticket to Karlovo or Plovdiv. There's a good **Arts & Crafts Museum** on Troyan town's main square if you have time to see it.

**Troyan Monastery**, founded in 1600 and Bulgaria's third-largest monastery, is famous as a centre of the Bulgarian National Revival. The church was rebuilt in 1835 and covered with frescoes by Zahari Zograph in 1849. Look for his self-portrait, paint brush in hand, by one of the windows inside the church. The condemned in the *Last Judgment* on the church's exterior façade are Turks. Many of the frescoes in the church are blackened by candle soot but restoration work is underway. Noted anti-Ottoman revolutionaries such as Georgi Benkovski and Vasil Levski found shelter in the monastery, and the room up on the monastery's 3rd floor where Levski was lodged is now a small museum. There's also a guesthouse in the monastery, but, unfortunately, it's only open to Bulgarians. However, everyone is welcome to sample the local plum brandy and 'Troyanska' dry sausage. Folk art is sold at a nearby bazar.

### Places to Stay

The IYHF youth hostel *Turisticheski dom 'Nikola Gaberski'*, on the hill just east of Troyan Bus Station, is open all year and offers comfortable double rooms. If you arrive during office hours, go to 'Ambaritza', ulitsa Slaveikov 54, right beside the Hotel Troyan. Ask for Mr Gregor Topuzon (☎ 23311), who speaks French and will announce your arrival to the hostel. Otherwise, just hike straight up to the hostel itself (☎ 26017) and hope that there's space.

Hikers will prefer the *Hizha 'Zora'* (open in July and August only) at Apriltsi, 19 km east of Troyan Monastery, with a bus service from Troyan every two hours. Apriltsi is the base for climbing Mt Botev (2376 metres), the highest peak in the Stara Planina. *Hizha 'Pleven'* is up near the summit.

The basic *Hotel Edelweis*, just north of Troyan Bus Station, is about US$8 per person, but the staff are not very used to receiving Westerners. Just across the river from the Hotel Edelweis is the two-star *Hotel Troyan* with singles/doubles with private bath at US$14/22. Hotel Troyan is rather attractive with balconies facing the river.

### Getting There & Away
Troyan Railway Station is just above the bus station. There are three trains a day to Levski via Lovech.

Four buses a day go from Troyan to Sofia (174 km), two to Plovdiv (124 km), two to Pleven (70 km) and four to Sevlievo (45 km). Tickets should be purchased early. No direct buses link Troyan to Veliko Târnovo. You must change buses in Sevlievo and the connections are poor.

### KARLOVO (КАРЛОВО)
Karlovo, in the Valley of Roses, 58 km north of Plovdiv, is a transportation hub you may pass through at one time or another. Trains and buses from here to Kazanlâk (56 km) are frequent.

The nearest official camping ground is at Byala Reka (bungalows are available) on the road to Kazanlâk, about 15 km east of Karlovo. The *Sevtopolis Campground* is on the same highway, closer to Kazanlâk.

### KAZANLÂK (КАЗАНЛЪК)
Many trains from Sofia to Burgas or Varna stop at Kazanlâk, which is tucked between the Stara Planina and Sredna Gora mountains in the Valley of Roses. The bus and train stations in Kazanlâk are adjacent. This is not a particularly attractive town, but it is a

useful stopping point or base for visiting nearby attractions. The Festival of Roses, held on the first Sunday in June, features carnivals and parades in Kazanlâk and Karlovo.

### Things to See & Do
In Tjulbeto Park, just two km north-east of the stations, is a 4th century BC **Thracian tomb** with delicate frescoes that were discovered during the construction of a bomb shelter in 1944. The original brick tomb has been scrupulously protected since then and cannot be visited, but a full-scale replica has been created nearby. Along the vaulted entry corridor, or *dromos*, is a double frieze with battle scenes. The burial chamber itself is 12 metres in diameter and covered by a beehive dome showing a funeral feast and chariot race. This unique example of Thracian painting is well worth seeing.

The Valley of Roses is the source of 70% of the world's supply of rose attar. The roses bloom from late May to early June and must be picked before sunrise when still wet with dew if the fragrance is to be preserved. Two thousand petals are required for a single gram of attar of roses. Some of the finest perfumes originate here. A **rose museum** is at the edge of town by the road to Shipka.

### Places to Stay
To stay at the *Hizha 'Buzludzha'* (see the Shipka section) enquire at Pirin, ulitsa Akademik Stainov 10, a block from the Hotel Roza in Kazanlâk.

The two-star *Hotel Roza*, at bulevard Tolbuhin 1, is just four blocks up from the railway station, and the *Hotel Zornitsa* is just above the Thracian Tomb, a couple of km away. Both these hotels charge US$14/22 for singles/doubles with private bath and US$1 per person for breakfast.

The Shipka bus passes the *Kasanlaschka Rosa Campground* (open from May to mid-October) between Shipka and Kazanlâk. It's the highest category camping ground in this area and the most likely to have a bungalow (expensive) if you need it.

### Getting There & Away

Kazanlâk is on the main line from Sofia to Burgas via Karlovo. For Veliko Târnovo change at Tulovo or go by bus via Gabrovo, which is better. To go to Shipka (12 km) take bus No 6 (hourly) from in front of Kazanlâk Railway Station.

## SHIPKA (ШИПКА)

Shipka is a quaint little village below the Stara Planina. Poking through the trees above the village are the five golden onion-shaped domes of a huge **votive church** (1902) built after the Russo-Turkish War (1877-78). The church bells were cast from spent cartridges from the battle and in the crypt lie the remains of the Russian solders who perished. Ask the woman selling bus tickets about the times of buses over the Shipka Pass to Gabrovo (36 km), then go have a look at the church. You'll get a great view of the Valley of Roses from up there.

At the top of 1306-metre **Shipka Pass**, 13 km beyond the church, is a large monument (1934) commemorating the Russian troops and Bulgarian volunteers who, in August 1877, fought back numerous attacks by vastly superior Turkish forces intent on relieving the besieged Turks at Pleven. The *Stoletov Campground* (bungalows) is also up at the pass, but it gets cool at night.

The *Hizha 'Buzludzha'* is near a huge circular memorial pavilion, 12 km east of the pass along a side road. To stay there, you should make an advance reservation at a Pirin office.

## ETÂR (ЕТЪР)

Northbound from Shipka, get off the Gabrovo bus at the *Ljubovo Campground* (open from mid-May to September). Here you'll find nice little bungalows as well as tent space, but no restaurant. Ljubovo is only two km west of the **Etâr Ethnographic Village Museum** and bus service is frequent.

At the Etâr Village Museum (open daily from 8 am to 5 pm) you'll see Bulgarian craftspeople (baker, cartwright, cobbler, furrier, glass worker, hatter, jeweller, leather worker, miller, potter, smith, weaver, etc)

practising their age-old trades in typical 18th and 19th century Gabrovo houses that were reconstructed here in the 1960s. Some of the workshops on the right bank of the stream running through the wooded site are powered by water. The items produced by craftspeople along the arts and crafts street on the left bank may be purchased. At the far end of the village is a small tavern where you can sample the local brew or have lunch. Coffee and traditional pastries are also served. This is one of Bulgaria's most appealing attractions.

From Etâr you'll have no trouble finding a bus on to Gabrovo (nine km) and then another bus to Veliko Târnovo.

## VELIKO TÂRNOVO (ВЕЛИКО ТЪРНОВО)

Veliko Târnovo (Great Târnovo) is laced with history. The Yantra River winds through a gorge in the centre of this 'city of tsars' and picturesque houses cling to the cliffs. Almost encircled by the river, the ruined Tsarevets Citadel recalls the Second Bulgarian Empire (1185-1393), when Veliko Târnovo was the capital. North-west, across the abyss, is the now overgrown Trapezitsa Hill, residence of the nobles and courtiers, while below in the valley the artisans' and merchants' quarter (Asenova) is marked by medieval churches. Renowned monasteries once stood on Sveta Gora Hill, where the university is today. The narrow streets of old Veliko Târnovo bear the imprint of the Bulgarian National Revival; the modern city spreads west. This is one town you won't want to miss.

### History

Both the Thracians and Romans had settlements here and in the 5th century AD a Byzantine fortress was built on Tsarevets Hill by Emperor Justinian. The Slavs captured it in the 7th century and in 1185 the town was the main centre of the uprising against Byzantium led by the brothers Asen and Peter. With the foundation of the Second Bulgarian Empire in the 12th century, Veliko

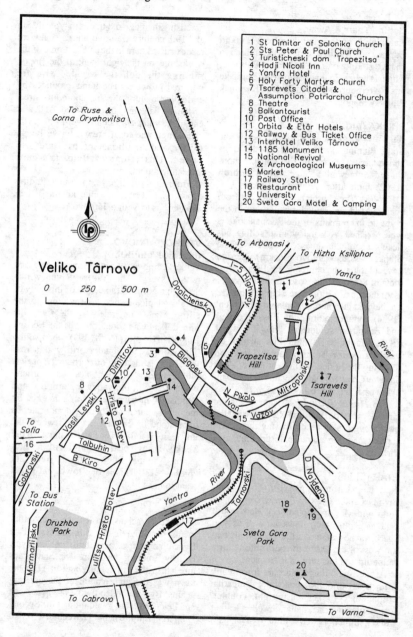

1  St Dimitar of Salonika Church
2  Sts Peter & Paul Church
3  Turisticheski dom 'Trapezitsa'
4  Hadji Nicoli Inn
5  Yantra Hotel
6  Holy Forty Martyrs Church
7  Tsarevets Citadel &
   Assumption Patriarchal Church
8  Theatre
9  Balkantourist
10 Post Office
11 Orbita & Etâr Hotels
12 Railway & Bus Ticket Office
13 Interhotel Veliko Târnovo
14 1185 Monument
15 National Revival
   & Archaeological Museums
16 Market
17 Railway Station
18 Restaurant
19 University
20 Sveta Gora Motel & Camping

**Veliko Târnovo**

0    250    500 m

To Ruse &
Gorna Oryahovitsa

To Arbanasi
To Hizha Ksiliphor

I-5 Highway

Opalchensko

Yantra

River

Trapezitsa
Hill

Tsarevets
Hill

D Blagoev

D Najdenov

Mitropolska

G Dimitrov

Hristo Botev

Vasil Levski

N Pikolo
Ivan  Vazov

To Sofia

Tolbuhin
B Kiro

Gabrovski

To Bus
Station

Marmarlijska

uiltsa Hristo Botev

Druzhba
Park

Yantra
River

T Tarnovski

Sveta Gora
Park

To Gabrovo

To Varna

Târnovo became an imperial city second only to Constantinople in this region. For the next two centuries, trade and culture flourished. The literary school founded here in 1350 by Theodosius of Târnovo attracted students from as far away as Serbia and Russia. On 17 July 1393, Târnovgrad Velico Târnovo fell to the Turks after a three-month siege. The fortress was destroyed, but in the 19th century Veliko Târnovo re-emerged as a crafts centre. Bulgarian culture gradually reasserted itself as part of the National Revival movement of the time and in 1877 the Russian general I V Gurko liberated the town. Today there is again a university at Veliko Târnovo. Nowhere else is the power of medieval Bulgaria experienced better.

## Orientation

The railway station is down by the river, far below the centre of town (catch buses No 4, 12 and 13). Ulitsa Hristo Botev ends at a T-intersection with ulitsa Vasil Levski and the modern city to the left, and ulitsa Georgi Dimitrov and its continuation, ulitsa Dimitar Blagoev, to the right.

The bus station is on Nikola Gabrovski, at the western edge of town (buses No 7 and 11). Bus No 10 begins at the bus station but passes through the middle of town. Many buses arriving in Veliko Târnovo stop near the market before going on to the bus station, so ask.

## Information

The Balkantourist office is at Vasil Levski 1, nearly opposite the theatre. For information on hostels, try the Pirin Travel Bureau, Dimitar Blagoev 79.

## Things to See

Opposite the Yantra Hotel on Dimitar Blagoev you'll see a stairway leading up into picturesque streets. Go up and veer left, then go down stone-surfaced ulitsa G S Rakovski, where Bulgarian artisans keep small shops. At number 17 is the **Hadji Nicoli Inn** (1858), one of the best known National Revival buildings in Bulgaria. The street above G S Rakovski is lined with quaint old houses and terminates at a church.

Return to the Yantra Hotel and walk east keeping right on Ivan Vazov until you reach the **Bulgarian National Revival Museum** (closed Monday). The museum is in the old Turkish town hall (1872), the large blue building you see straight ahead. Notice the stone building with six arches beside this museum. The **Archaeological Museum** is in the basement, down the stairway between the two buildings (same hours).

Follow the street on the left to the entrance to **Tsarevets Citadel**, which was sacked and burned by the Turks in 1393. This vast fortress offers great views from the rebuilt **Assumption Patriarchal Church** at the top of the hill. Just below, to the north, are the foundations of the extensive **Royal Palace** on three terraces. Twenty-two successive kings ruled Bulgaria from this palace. Continue north to a bluff directly above the large factory. This was **Execution Rock**, from which traitors were pushed into the Yantra River. At the southern end of the fortress is the **Baldwin Tower** (rebuilt in 1932) where Baldwin I of Flanders, the deposed Latin emperor of Byzantium, was imprisoned and finally executed after his defeat in 1205. In summer there's an incredible **light-and-sound show** here around 10 pm, with the whole of Tsarevets Hill lit in myriad colours.

From the entrance to Tsarevets Hill walk down the steep incline to the **Holy Forty Martyrs Church** by the river at the foot of the hill. The church was built by Tsar Ivan Asen II to commemorate his victory over the despot of Epirus, Teodor Komnin, at Klokotnitsa in 1230, as recorded on the Asen Column inside. Originally a royal mausoleum, the Holy Forty Martyrs Church was converted into a mosque by the Turks. There are murals to be seen, but the church has been closed for restoration for many years.

Turn right (don't cross the river) and continue two blocks to the 13th century **Sts Peter & Paul Church** with frescoes. Walk back a little, then cross the big wooden bridge and continue right up through the village till you see a church enclosed by a high stone wall. This is **St Dimitar of Salonika**, the town's oldest church. During the consecration of this church in 1185, the noblemen brothers Asen and Peter proclaimed an uprising against Byzantine rule. Later, St Dimitar of Salonika was used for royal coronations. From here you can return to the city centre on bus No 7 or 11.

**To Sveta Gora** Another memorable walk begins at the Interhotel Veliko Târnovo. Cross the footbridge behind the hotel to reach **Asenovtsi Park**, which has an art gallery and a great monument to the re-establishment of the Bulgarian Empire by Asen I in 1185. From here you'll get the classic view of the city's tiers of rustic houses hanging above the Yantra Gorge.

After an eyeful, walk south-east towards **Sveta Gora Park** and climb the stairs to the restaurant you can see protruding through the trees. From it you'll get a sweeping view of the city and its surroundings. The founders of the Târnovo schools of literature and painting were active in the monasteries of Sveta Gora, which have since disappeared. Return the way you came or ask directions to the university, where you can get a bus.

**Preobrazhenski Monastery** A recommended side trip or stop on the way north is Preobrazhenski (Transfiguration) Monastery, seven km north of Veliko Târnovo, on the road to Gorna Oryahovitsa. The location on a wooded hillside below the cliffs of the Yantra Gorge is lovely. The ruins of the 14th century monastery destroyed by the Turks are 500 metres south of the present monastery (rebuilt in 1825) with frescoes (1851) by Zahari Zograph and large icons (1864) by Stanislav Dospevski.

Get there on bus No 10, which runs frequently between Veliko Târnovo and Gorna Oryahovitsa. From the stop it's a two-km climb to the monastery with a *camping ground* halfway up. The **Holy Trinity Monastery** (1847) is below the cliffs on the opposite side of the gorge from Preobrazhenski and is only accessible on foot (1½ hours).

**Arbanasi** In summer another good side trip would be to the village of Arbanasi, 10 km north-west of Veliko Târnovo. Buses run from the main bus station every couple of hours, or just take a taxi and catch a bus back. Originally founded by Albanians, Arbanasi grew rich after Sultan Süleyman I gave it to one of his sons-in-law in 1538 thus exempting the town from the Ottoman Empire's ruinous taxation. The highlight of this typical Bulgarian village is the medieval **Birth of Christ Church**, the interior of which is completely covered with colourful frescoes painted between 1632 and 1649. Over 3500 figures are depicted in some 2000 scenes. The same ticket admits you to **Konstantzaliev House**, a 17th century residence converted into a museum of local life. There's much more to see along Arbanasi's winding lanes, but in winter and on Mondays everything could be closed.

### Places to Stay
**Camping** *Sveta Gora Camping* beside the two-star *Sveta Gora Motel* in Sveta Gora Park has small bungalows from May to October (US$6/19 single/double). Camping is US$2 per person, US$2 per tent. From the bus or train stations, take buses No 4, 12 or 13 towards the university at the end of the line and then ask.

**Youth Hostels** The *Turisticheski dom 'Trapezitsa'*, right in the centre of town at Dimitar Blagoev 79, offers beds in three-bed dorms with an en suite bathroom for US$8. You face an uncertain reception here, so it may be better to have Pirin in Sofia call ahead for a reservation. If the hostel receptionist says that the hostel is full, ask if the Pirin representative is working that day and he or she may be able to tell you about other hostels.

Youth hostel accommodation is available all year at *Turisticheski dom 'Momina Krepost'* (also known as *Hizha Ksiliphor*), in a forest north-east of Veliko Târnovo. Take bus No 7 or 11, bound for Mavrikov, to the end of the line. Walk straight ahead beside the river for a bit to a factory, then turn left up the hill and continue for another two km to a café where there are also bungalows for hostellers. You could also take a bus bound for Arbanasi to the access road, and then walk down to Hizha Ksiliphor. Make an advance reservation if you can.

**Private Rooms & Hotels** For private room accommodation ask at Balkantourist, Vasil Levski 1. *Hotel Orbita*, Hristo Botev 15, is inexpensive but usually full. Try anyway – the reception is up at the top of the stairs.

The two-star, 14-floor *Hotel Etâr*, ulitsa Ivailo 1 (US$14/17 single/double without bath, US$19/23 with private bath), is in the building directly behind the Hotel Orbita.

There's also the three-star *Yantra Hotel*, Velchova Zavera 4 on the corner of Dimitar Blagoev. The flashy four-star *Interhotel Veliko Târnovo*, at ulitsa Emil Popov 2, is double or triple the price of any of the places just mentioned.

A new private hotel has appeared in the village of Arbanasi. The *Hotel Constantin & Elena* (☎ 35370) is a traditional Bulgarian house just down from Birth of Jesus Church. There are only a few rooms (all with shared facilities, US$10 per person), so call before going. There's a bus to Arbanasi from Veliko Târnovo Bus Station every couple of hours, or you can take a taxi.

### Places to Eat

There is a good self-service restaurant at G Dimitrov 17, just up from the post office. The food in there may not be so hot, but at least you won't have to contend with the abysmal service in many of Veliko Târnovo's other restaurants.

On the back terrace restaurant of the *Hotel Yantra* you can feast on the view of the river as much as the food.

There's a good market west on Vasil Levski, on the corner of Dimitar Ivanov. Stock up on fresh vegetables and fruit here.

### Getting There & Away

To get a train to Pleven, Sofia, Ruse or Varna, take bus No 10, which runs frequently, to Gorna Oryahovitsa Railway Station. Some local trains from Dimitrovgrad direct to Ruse stop at Veliko Târnovo Railway Station. To go to/from Burgas or Plovdiv, change trains at Stara Zagora or Tulovo. You can reach Gabrovo and Etâr more easily by bus.

Check train times at the railway ticket office, Hristo Botev 12 opposite the Hotel Orbita. Bus tickets with seat reservations are also available here. There are two buses a day to Plovdiv (197 km) running over Shipka Pass and two a day to Sofia (247 km). For international train tickets, try the Rila office, Stambolijski 1, near the Etâr Hotel.

## RUSE (РУСЕ)

Ruse, the largest Bulgarian port on the Danube, is a gateway to the country. Soviet and Bulgarian riverboats stop here, as do twice daily trains from Bucharest. The double-decker highway/railway Friendship Bridge (1954), six km downstream, links Ruse to Giurgiu, Romania. This massive 2.8-km-long structure is the largest steel bridge in Europe; during high water the central section can be raised. Along the Bulgarian right bank of the Danube are parks and promenades full of mementos of the two liberations (1878 and 1944). This might be a nice place to break your journey if it weren't so hard to find inexpensive accommodation outside the camping season.

### History

A Roman fortress, Sexaginta Prista (60 ships), was established here in 70 AD as part of the defensive Danubian Lines (the Roman defensive line along the south bank of the Danube River). Although strengthened by Emperor Justinian in the 6th century, the fort was finally obliterated during the 'barbarian' invasions of the 7th century.

The Slavs forsook the site and in the 9th century built the town of Cherven 30 km south on an easily defensible loop of the Cherni Lom River. Six churches, city walls and a citadel have been excavated at Cherven. The rock-hewn cave churches of Ivanovo, between Cherven and present-day Ruse, are another reminder of this period.

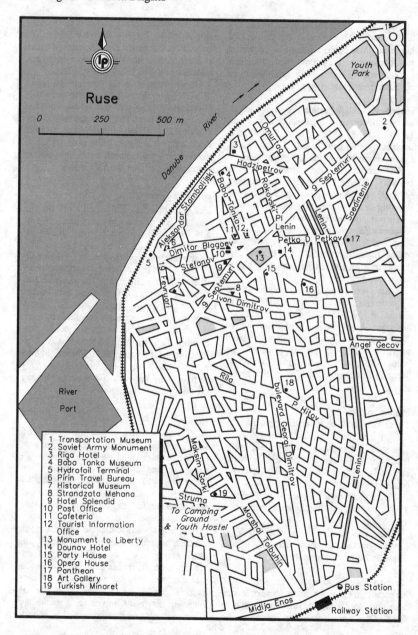

## Ruse

0     250     500 m

River

Danube

Youth
Park

River

Port

1   Transportation Museum
2   Soviet Army Monument
3   Riga Hotel
4   Baba Tonka Museum
5   Hydrofoil Terminal
6   Pirin Travel Bureau
7   Historical Museum
8   Strandzata Mehana
9   Hotel Splendid
10  Post Office
11  Cafeteria
12  Tourist Information
    Office
13  Monument to Liberty
14  Dounav Hotel
15  Party House
16  Opera House
17  Pantheon
18  Art Gallery
19  Turkish Minaret

Omurtag
Hadzipetrov
Rakovski
9 Septemvri
Lenin
Saedinenie
Aleksandar Stamboliiski
Baba Tonka
Pl
Lenin
Petko D Petkov
Dimitar Blagoev
Stefanov
19 Fevruari
Septemvri
S Ivan Dimitrov
Angel Gecov
Rila
buleverd Georgi Dimitrov
P Hitov
Maksim Gorki
Struma
To Camping
Ground
& Youth Hostel
Marshal Tolbuhin
Lenin
Midija Enos
Bus Station
Railway Station

After the Ottoman conquest in 1388, Cherven was abandoned.

The Turks rebuilt and strongly fortified Rouschouk (Ruse). The Russians captured the city in 1773 and 1811, but were forced to withdraw because of the Napoleonic attack on Moscow. In 1864, under the reforming Turkish *vali* (district governor) Midhat Pasha, founder of the Young Turks movement, Rouschouk was modernised and became capital of the Danubian Vilayet (including everything west to Niš, Yugoslavia). In 1866 a railway from Ruse to Varna linked the Danube directly to the Black Sea. The eclectic architecture of the city centre dates from the building boom which followed Ruse's liberation by Russian troops in 1878.

## Orientation

The adjacent bus and train stations are on the south side of town. There's luggage storage in the underground mall in front of the train station. From the stations walk or take a bus a km north up bulevard Georgi Dimitrov to ploschtad Lenin, the centre of town. Among the 18 streets which meet on this square is ulitsa 9 Septemvri, Ruse's pedestrian mall, which runs off in both directions. The hydrofoil terminal is straight down Dimitar Blagoev from ploschtad Lenin.

## Information

The tourist information office is on ploschtad Lenin on the corner of Dimitar Blagoev 45. Try the Balkantourist desks in the Riga and Dounav hotels for information and currency exchange.

For hostelling information, ask at the Pirin Travel Bureau, Dimitar Blagoev 1. Orbita Student Travel is at ulitsa G Rakovski 13.

## Things to See

Most of Ruse's monuments and museums open from 9 am to noon and from 3 to 6 pm, daily except Mondays. The **City Art Gallery** is at bulevard Georgi Dimitrov 45 between the train station and ploschtad Lenin. The **Monument to Liberty** created by the Italian

sculptor Arnoldo Zocchi in 1908 dominates ploschtad Lenin.

At the end of Petko D Petkov, east of the square, are the graves of Ruse's revolutionary heroes in the gold-domed **Pantheon** (1978). North-east of the Pantheon at the end of Saedinenie is the **Soviet army Monument** (1949) with **Park na mladezta** (Youth Park) and the Danube beyond.

Railway buffs won't want to miss the **Transportation Museum**, by the Danube below Youth Park, in what was the first railway station in Bulgaria (1866). It has a large collection of old equipment, including steam locomotive 148, the Sultanie, Bulgaria's first.

Proceed upstream along the Danube to the **Riga Hotel**, where there's an attractive terrace and promenade. The Panorama Bar (open from 5 pm to midnight) on the 20th floor of the Riga Hotel provides a sweeping view. Overlooking the Danube near this hotel is the **Baba Tonka Museum**, bulevard Aleksandar Stambolijski 6. Seven of Baba (Grannie) Tonka's children participated in the 1876 uprising against the Turks. One of them, Bilyana Raicheva, resided in what is now the museum building.

## Places to Stay

Ask about private rooms (US$4 per person) at the tourist information office at Dimitar Blagoev 45 on ploschtad Lenin.

There are several cheaper hotels, such as the *Balkan*, ulitsa 9 Septemvri 26, but these are closed to Western tourists, who are expected to stay at the low-rise two-star *Dounav Hotel*, on ploschtad Lenin, or the 16-storey three-star *Riga Hotel*, ulitsa Aleksander Stambolijski 22, overlooking the river, both very expensive. The Dounav Hotel looks forbidding from the outside, but the rooms are large and comfortable.

The *Hotel Splendid*, ulitsa 9 Septemvri 49, is US$12 double. It's a little hard to find, but just go up ulitsa Stefanov beside the post office and look for a four-storey concrete building on the left.

The *Ribarska Koliba Campground* (open from May to mid-October) is six km out of

Ruse on the road to Sofia (take bus No 6 or 16). It's US$2 per person plus US$2 per tent to camp or US$7 double (no singles) for a bungalow. There's a small bar by the gate of this pleasant wooded site above the Danube.

A km beyond the camping ground is the IYHF youth hostel, the *Hizha Prista*. Before going, try to make a reservation at the very helpful Pirin Travel Bureau, Dimitar Blagoev 1.

### Places to Eat

There's a cheap cafeteria in the building beside the post office at Dimitar Blagoev 35. The *Strandzhata Mehana*, ulitsa Ivan Dimitrov 5, has a huge dining room downstairs where traditional Bulgarian specialities are served. The 2nd-floor restaurant in the *Riga Hotel* should satisfy anyone.

Near the Danube, down the hill from the Ribarska Koliba Campground, is the *Fisherman's Lodge* restaurant. Live music and an outdoor terrace make this a pleasant place on a summer's evening. Take a sunset stroll along the riverside before dinner.

### Entertainment

Check the puppet theatre at Dimitar Blagoev 9. The theatrical booking office is at ulitsa 9 Septemvri 61, on the corner of ploschtad Lenin. Check the programme of the March Music Days Festival if you're in Ruse at that time.

### Getting There & Away

The daily Pannonia Express to/from Bucharest passes Ruse in the middle of the night or the very early morning. For international railway tickets and reservations, go to the Rila office, Dimitar Blagoev 33. The trains to Romania are inconvenient as they leave at the crack of dawn and are difficult to board. Try to reserve your seat, otherwise the conductor will demand additional payment. There's no bus from Ruse to Romania, but you could try taking a taxi to the Friendship Bridge and walking across the upper level.

Two trains a day go from Ruse to Varna (226 km) with others on this line stopping short at Kaspichan (142 km). Other direct express trains run to Sofia (404 km) via Pleven, including one overnight train. For Veliko Târnovo change trains at Gorna Oryahovitsa, although local trains from Ruse to Plachkovci and Momchilgrad go direct to Veliko Târnovo. Advance tickets for domestic railway services are available from the office on ulitsa Rakovski, directly behind the Dunav Hotel.

From May to mid-September, hydrofoils ply the Danube between Ruse and Vidin (US$4), departing from each end in the very early morning. Other hydrofoils connect Ruse to Svishtov daily. Low-water levels and technical problems sometimes interrupt these services.

Express buses run to Silistra and Varna (each twice daily, 200 km), and also to Shumen (three times daily, two hours, 116 km). The camping ground and youth hostel are in a perfect location if you want to hitchhike to Veliko Târnovo, Pleven, or Sofia.

### SHUMEN (ШУМЕН)

Shumen is a large city between Varna and Veliko Târnovo or Ruse, halfway from the Black Sea to the Danube. Both the Thracians and the Romans had settlements here, and, during the early Middle Ages, Shumen and nearby Preslav, Madara and Pliska became the birthplaces of medieval Bulgaria. Shumen was captured by the Turks in 1388. For the next five centuries, Chumla (Shumen) was an important market town with the largest mosque in Bulgaria. In the early 19th century, the Turks included it in their strategic quadrangle of fortified towns, along with Ruse, Silistra and Varna, as a defence against Russian advances.

Though the accommodation situation is not good, Shumen is a transportation hub that you will pass through once or twice while touring this part of the country, and there are several things to see if you have time. The gigantic hilltop monument that overlooks Shumen was built in 1981 to commemorate 13 centuries of Bulgarian history on the 1300th anniversary of the founding of the First Bulgarian Empire.

## Orientation & Information

The adjacent bus and train stations are on the east side of town. Follow boulevards Tolbuhin and Slavyanski west to the centre – a pleasant walk. The old Turkish town is to the west of Hotel Madara.

## Things to See

A half-day visit to Shumen is best organised by taking a taxi from the stations directly up to the **Shumen Fortress** (Shumenska Krepost), on a hilltop west of the modern city. The walls and foundations of the 12th to 14th century medieval settlement have been rebuilt and the site museum contains artifacts found during the excavations, as well as maps and photos. There's a tremendous view of Shumen from here.

Directly below the fortress is the famous **brewery** and it's fairly easy to walk or hitchhike back down. Shumensko pivo, the local beer, dates back to 1882 and the many prizes it has won are listed on the label. It has a nice bite. The wines of this region are also excellent.

In the western part of town below the fortress are a few scattered remnants of old Shumen that were not steamrolled by modern buildings. The **Tombul Mosque** (1744), visible from above, is the largest and most beautifully decorated in Bulgaria. The Turks built their mosque with stones torn from the ruins of earlier Bulgarian monuments. Beyond is the Turkish **covered market**.

Follow the pedestrian promenade back towards the stations. On the way you'll pass the **District Historical Museum**, bulevard Slavyanski, on the corner of ulitsa Dimitar Blagoev, in the centre of the modern city. It has a large collection, but the captions are only in Bulgarian.

## Places to Stay & Eat

Shumen's hotels are expensive and during the camping season you're much better off staying at nearby Madara. In winter there's the three-star, seven-floor *Hotel Madara* and the newer four-star *Hotel Shumen*, both near the centre of town. The two-star *Orbita Hotel*

in Kyoshkovete Park, beyond the brewery on the far west side of town, is no bargain. Private rooms are not available.

The *Popsheitanovata Kushta Restaurant*, halfway between the Madara and Shumen hotels, serves traditional Bulgarian food in a quaint 19th century building.

## Getting There & Away

Shumen is on the main line from Sofia to Varna via Pleven. For Veliko Târnovo change at Gorna Oryahovitsa. For Ruse (116 km) take a bus.

There's a bus service from Shumen to Preslav (20 km) about every hour till 10 pm, and it is a fairly easy connection. Bus service to Pliska and Madara, on the other hand, is infrequent and very overcrowded, so you may want to check the price of a taxi. The taxi dispatcher's office is just outside the railway station. Madara is accessible by local train on the line to Kaspichan.

## PRESLAV (ПРЕСЛАВ)

Preslav, 20 km south-west of Shumen, was founded in the year 821 by Khan Omourtag. Khan Simeon moved his seat here from Pliska in 893 and Preslav remained capital of the First Bulgarian Empire until it was conquered by Byzantium in 971. A notable school of literature existed here and even after the court left for Veliko Târnovo, Preslav remained an important town. The Turks sacked Preslav in 1388 and hauled away its stones to construct mosques elsewhere.

The ruins of Veliki Preslav are two km south of the present town of Preslav. The five-sq-km outer city was protected by a high stone wall and contained churches, monasteries and the residences of the nobles. An inner wall encircled the 1½ sq km citadel with the royal palace at its centre. The most famous building was the **Round Gold Church**, built by Khan Simeon in 908 and partially restored in recent times. It derived its name from the dome, which was gilded on the outside and covered with mosaics inside.

The **archaeological museum** at the ruins

contains architectural fragments and a model of the palace to help you visualise what it must have been like. Prize exhibits are a 10th century ceramic icon of St Theodore Stratilates from a nearby monastery and the 10th century silver goblet of Zhoupan Sivin.

The town of Preslav is easily accessible by local bus from Shumen. A good plan upon arrival is to take a taxi out to the site museum and walk back. If you want to stay there's the two-star *Hotel Preslav* in the middle of town which also serves meals.

## MADARA (МАДАРА)

Madara, 18 km east of Shumen, is a convenient stopover between Ruse and Varna. From the train station a wide stairway leads two km up towards the cliffs. Madara makes a perfect base for exploring the nearby capitals of the First Bulgarian Empire, Preslav and Pliska. There's plenty to see at Madara itself, so you could spend a couple of days here.

### Things to See & Do

Archaeological remains dating from the 8th to the 14th centuries are to be seen below the cliffs of Madara. Higher up are some caves, but more famous is the **Madara horseman**, a relief of a mounted figure spearing a lion which symbolises victories of Khan Tervel over his enemies. It was carved in the early 8th century, 25 metres up on the rock face, and the adjacent Greek inscriptions date from the years 705 to 831.

North of the horseman, a regular stairway leads up to the top of 100-metre cliffs where there are fortifications from the First Bulgarian Empire, part of a defensive ring intended to protect the nearby capitals of Pliska and Preslav.

### Places to Stay & Eat

*Camping Madara*, one of the nicest camp sites in Bulgaria, is a few hundred metres from the horseman. Open from May to October, it has bungalows (US$6 per person) and tent space (US$3 per person, US$4 per tent). The camping ground has a nice little restaurant of its own and there's a larger

restaurant on the main road nearby. This peaceful site is a good place to come for a rest.

There's a youth hostel at Madara, the *Hizha 'Madarski Konnik'*, near the ticket office for the horseman.

### Getting There & Away

Madara is on the main railway line between Sofia and Varna via Pleven though not all express trains stop here. Every morning there are several trains to Varna (2½ hours). Direct buses run from the archaeological area near the camping ground to Shumen and there are also local trains.

## PLISKA (ПЛИСКА)

Pliska squats on a level plain 23 km northeast of Shumen and 12 km north of Madara. Founded by Khan Asparoukh in 681, Pliska was the capital of the First Bulgarian Empire in the 8th and 9th centuries. Though destroyed by the Byzantines in 811, Khan Omourtag rebuilt the town, which remained important even after the court moved to Preslav in 893.

There were three walled circuits at Pliska. The outermost fortification enclosed 23 sq km (including the present village) with an embankment and a ditch. The common people and soldiers lived in this Outer City. The Inner City, three km north of the village, had a 10-metre-high stone wall with guard towers. The rebuilt 9th century Eastern Gate gives access to the foundations of the **Big Palace** with its throne room, the ceremonial centre of the city. Just west was the Court Church, originally a pagan temple. This inner fortress also enclosed the **citadel**, clearly distinguished by its brick walls, where the khan used to reside. Underground passages led from the citadel to various points in the Inner City.

The **museum** at the site contains a model of the 9th century, three-naved **Great Basilica**, which has been partly rebuilt a km north of the main archaeological area. This great building, 100 metres long by 30 metres wide, is linked to the adoption of Christianity in Bulgaria in 865.

## Getting There & Away

If you don't have your own vehicle, you will have trouble visiting Pliska as buses from Shumen come only every three hours and you still have to walk three km north to the ruins. There's no bus service to the ruins themselves and taxis are rare. Arrival by train is even worse, as the village of Pliska is six km north-west of Kaspichan, the nearest railway station.

If you're staying in Madara consider hiring a taxi for the trip. Ask the person who is selling the entry tickets to the Madara horseman if Rosan is around. He conducts private tours to Pliska in his own car for US$10 cash per group. He speaks no English but is cooperative.

The postcard-perfect Turkish Bridge over the
Neretva River in Mostar

# Yugoslavia

**IMPORTANT NOTE: See Stop Press on page 13.**

Yugoslavia, the land of the South Slavs, occupies much of the western half of the Balkan Peninsula. The country is a rich mosaic of mountains, rivers and seascapes, climates, cultures, customs, cuisines and peoples. Many disparate influences have shaped the Yugoslav Federal Republic: Venetian along the coast, Austrian in Slovenia, Hungarian in Vojvodina, and Turkish in Bosnia-Hercegovina, Kosovo and Macedonia. Serbia and Croatia have always been jealous leading actors in this decentralised state which is torn by ethnic tensions.

Tourism is focused along the Adriatic coast where the combination of history, natural beauty, good climate, clear water and easy access are unsurpassed. There are numerous seaside resorts and the swimming is good. The atmosphere is relaxed – there are few rules about behaviour and few formalities. Since 1960 nudism has been promoted and Yugoslavia is now *the* place to go in Europe to practise naturism. But the resorts are impersonal, artificial environments, out of touch with real Yugoslav life. It's a world built around tourists: you'll have few personal encounters with the people. Prices are much higher than elsewhere in Eastern Europe, yet it's possible to enjoy yourself for a reasonable amount if you plan carefully. Yugoslavia's not the sort of country you fall in love with right away, but it would be hard to find another with as much to offer.

## Facts about the Country

### HISTORY

Yugoslavia's history is complex as it's actually the history of many countries. The original inhabitants were the Illyrians, fol-

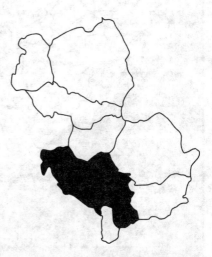

lowed by the Celts who arrived in the 4th century BC. In 229 BC the Romans began their conquest, establishing a colony at Salona (near Split) in Dalmatia. Under Augustus the empire extended to Singidunum (Belgrade) on the Danube, including the provinces of Illyricum (Dalmatia and Bosnia), Moesia Superior (Serbia) and Pannonia (Croatia). In 285 AD Emperor Diocletian decided to retire to his palace/fortress at Split, today the greatest Roman ruin in Eastern Europe. When the empire was divided in 395 what is now Slovenia, Croatia and Bosnia-Hercegovina stayed with the Latin Western Empire, while present Serbia, Kosovo and Macedonia went to Byzantium. Visigoth, Hun and Lombard invasions marked the fall of the Western Empire in the 5th century.

In the middle of the 6th century, Slavonic tribes (Serbians, Croats and Slovenes) crossed the Danube in the wake of the Great Migration of Nations and occupied most of what is now Yugoslavia. In the 9th century the Serbians were converted to the Orthodox

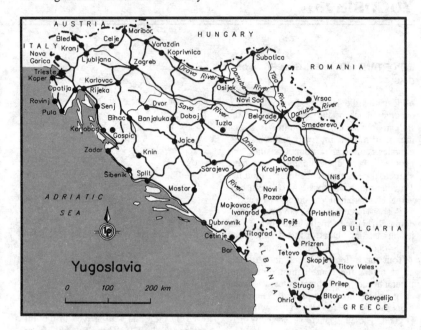

Church by Sts Cyril and Methodius. In 969 Serbia broke free from Byzantium and established an independent state. In the north the Croats picked up the legacy of Roman civilisation, forming a kingdom under Tomislav in 925. Slovenia came under the Germanic Holy Roman Empire in the 10th century. Byzantium re-established its authority over the South Slavs in the 11th century, but in 1102 Romanised Croatia united with Hungary to defend itself against Orthodox Byzantium. In 1242 a Tatar invasion devastated Hungary and Croatia.

An independent Serbian kingdom reappeared in 1217 and climaxed during the reign of Stefan Dušan (1346-55). Numerous frescoed Orthodox monasteries were erected during this Serbian 'Golden Age'. Then, at the Battle of Kosovo on 28 June 1389, the Serbian army was defeated by the Ottoman Turks, ushering in 500 years of Islamic rule. The Serbians were pushed north as the Turks advanced into Bosnia in the 15th century and

the city state of Venice occupied the coast. In 1526 the Turks defeated Hungary at the Battle of Mohács, adding territory north and west of the Danube to their realm. In 1527 Croatia turned to the Habsburgs of Austria for protection and remained under their control until 1918. The Adriatic coast was threatened but never fully conquered by the Turks. After the naval Battle of Lepanto in 1571 this threat was much reduced.

The first centuries of Turkish rule brought stability to the Balkans, but, as the power of the sultan declined, local Turkish officials and soldiers began to oppress the Slavs. During the 16th and 17th centuries the Turks strengthened their hold on Bosnia-Hercegovina as an advance bulwark of their empire. After their defeat at Vienna in 1683, the Turks began a steady retreat. By 1699 they had been driven out of Hungary and many Serbians moved north into Vojvodina where they enjoyed Habsburg protection.

After Venice was shattered by Napoleonic

France in 1797, Austria-Hungary moved in to pick up the pieces along the coast. Napoleon's merger of Dalmatia, Istria and Slovenia into the 'Illyrian Provinces' in 1805 stimulated the concept of South Slav unity. In 1848 a liberal democratic revolution against the old autocracy was suppressed, but serfdom was abolished. The brief Napoleonic experience and the national revival movements of the mid-19th century led to a reawakening among the South Slavs, and there were uprisings against the Turks in Bosnia and Bulgaria in 1875-76. In 1878 Turkey suffered a crushing defeat by Russia in a war over Bulgaria. At this point Austria-Hungary occupied Bosnia-Hercegovina, annexing it completely in 1908.

A revolt in 1815 had led to de facto Serbian independence in 1816. Serbia's autonomy was recognised in 1829, the last Turkish troops departed in 1867, and in 1878 complete independence was achieved. Montenegro also declared itself independent of Turkey in 1878.

Macedonia remained under Turkish rule right into the 20th century. In the First Balkan War (1912), Serbia, Greece and Bulgaria combined against Turkey for the liberation of Macedonia. The Second Balkan War (1913) saw Serbia and Greece join forces against Bulgaria, which had claimed all of Macedonia for itself. About this time Serbia wrested control of Kosovo from Albania with the help of the Western powers.

World War I was an extension of these conflicts as Austria-Hungary used the assassination of Archduke Ferdinand on 28 June 1914 as an excuse to overrun Serbia. Russia and France came to Serbia's aid. In the winter of 1915-16 a defeated Serbian army of 155,000 retreated across the mountains of Montenegro to the Adriatic where it was evacuated to Corfu. In 1918 these troops fought their way back up into Serbia from Thessaloniki, Greece.

After WW I, Croatia, Slovenia and Vojvodina were united with Serbia, Montenegro and Macedonia to form a kingdom of Serbians, Croats and Slovenes under the king of Serbia. In 1929 the name was changed to Yugoslavia. The Vidovdan constitution of 1921 created a centralised government dominated by Serbia. This was strongly opposed by the Croats and other minorities, forcing King Alexander to end the political turmoil by declaring a personal dictatorship in 1929. The assassination of the king by Croatian nationalists in 1934 led to a regency which continued the Serbian dictatorship. Corruption was rampant and the regent tilted towards friendship with Nazi Germany.

Under German pressure Yugoslavia joined the Tripartite Alliance, a fascist military pact, on 25 March 1941. This sparked mass protest demonstrations and a military coup which overthrew the profascist regency. Peter II was installed as king and Yugoslavia abruptly withdrew from the alliance. Livid with rage, Hitler ordered an immediate invasion and the country was carved up between Germany, Italy, Hungary and Bulgaria. A fascist Ustaše puppet government was set up in Croatia under Ante Pavelić (who fled to South America after the war).

Almost immediately the Communist Party under Josip Broz Tito declared an

Marshal Tito

armed uprising. There was also a monarchist resistance group, the Četniks, but they proved far less effective than Tito's partisans, and after 1943 the British gave full backing to the Communists. A 1943 meeting of the Antifascist Council of National Liberation of Yugoslavia (AVNOJ) at Jajce laid the basis for a future Communist-led Yugoslavia. The partisans played a major role in WW II by tying down huge German armies, but Yugoslavia suffered terrible losses. Almost a tenth of the population died in the war. The resistance did, however, guarantee Yugoslavia's postwar independence.

### Recent History

In 1945 the Communist Party (which had been officially banned since 1920) won control of the National Assembly which in November declared Yugoslavia a republic. Tito broke with Stalin in 1948 and, as a reward, received US$2.5 billion in economic aid from the US and UK between 1950 and 1960. After the break Yugoslavia followed its own 'road to socialism' based on a federal system, self-management, personal freedom and nonalignment. The decentralisation begun in 1951 was to lead to the eventual 'withering away of the state' of classical Marxism. Yugoslavia never became a member of either the Warsaw Pact or NATO, and in 1956 the country played a key role in the formation of the nonaligned movement.

The 1960s witnessed an economic boom in the north-west accompanied by liberalisation throughout the country, and in July 1966 Tito fired his hardline secret police chief Alexander Ranković. Yet the growing regional inequalities led to increased tension as Slovenia, Croatia and Kosovo demanded greater autonomy within the federation. In 1971 Tito responded with a 'return to Leninism', which included a purge of party reformers and a threat to use military force against Croatia.

With the most talented members of the leadership gone, Yugoslavia stagnated through the 1970s while borrowing billions of recycled petrodollars in the west. A 1970 constitutional amendment declared that the federal government would have control of foreign policy, defence, trade, the national economy and human rights, while all residual powers were vested in the six republics (Croatia, Bosnia-Hercegovina, Macedonia, Montenegro, Serbia and Slovenia) and two autonomous provinces of Serbia (Kosovo and Vojvodina). To limit Serbian hegemony, Tito (a Croat) had given republic status to Macedonia right after the war, and the 1974 constitution strengthened the powers of the autonomous provinces.

Tito died in 1980 and the state presidency became a collective post rotated annually among nine members elected every four years by the national assembly, the six republics and the two autonomous provinces. This cumbersome system proved unable to solve Yugoslavia's deepening economic problems or to control vested regional interests.

In 1987 Slobodan Milošević took over as party leader in Serbia by portraying himself as champion of the allegedly persecuted Serbian minority in Kosovo. Milošević hoped to restore the flagging popularity of the League of Communists by inciting the latent anti-Albanian sentiments of the Serbians. When moves by Serbia to limit Kosovo's autonomy led to massive protest demonstrations in the province in late 1988 and early 1989, the Serbian government unilaterally scrapped Kosovo's autonomy. Thousands of troops were sent to intimidate Kosovo's 85% Albanian majority, and in direct confrontations with the security forces 29 civilians were shot dead.

Milošević's vision of a 'Greater Serbia' horrified residents of Slovenia and Croatia, who elected non-Communist republican governments in the spring of 1990. These called for the creation of a loose Yugoslav 'confederation' which would allow them to retain most of their wealth for themselves, and threatened to secede from Yugoslavia if such reforms were not forthcoming. November 1990 elections in Bosnia-Hercegovina were won by three nationalist parties (the Communists got only 19 of 240 seats), but in the Serbian elections in December, Milošević's policies paid off when the Com-

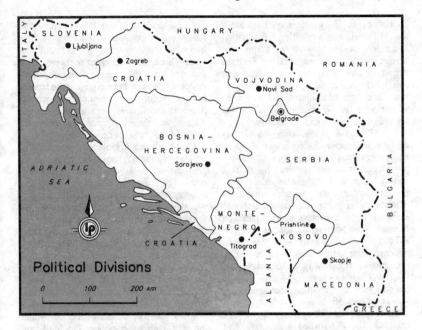

Political Divisions

0    100    200 km

**Political Divisions & Populations**

|  | Area (sq km) | Population (1988 estimate) |
|---|---|---|
| Yugoslavia | 255,804 | 23,512,000 |
| Bosnia-Hercegovina | 51,129 | 4,440,000 |
| Croatia | 56,538 | 4,680,000 |
| Kosovo | 10,887 | 1,850,000 |
| Macedonia | 25,713 | 2,090,000 |
| Montenegro | 13,812 | 632,000 |
| Serbia | 55,968 | 5,830,000 |
| Slovenia | 20,251 | 1,940,000 |
| Vojvodina | 21,506 | 2,050,000 |

munists won 194 of 260 seats (the Albanians boycotted the election). In the other republics the Communists held Montenegro but lost Macedonia.

Meanwhile the federal prime minister, Ante Marković (a Croat), tried to steer clear of the ethnic turmoil. In late 1989 Marković introduced major economic reforms to control inflation.

In early 1991 Serbian nationalists staged provocations in several Croatian towns in the hope of triggering a military coup or martial law which might halt separatist moves by Slovenia and Croatia and reimpose the authority of Serbia. In March 1991 Serbia's state-controlled media broadcast false reports of a massacre of ethnic Serbians in Croatia in an attempt to precipitate a crisis leading to a military takeover. This outraged prodemocratic Serbian students who massed outside the TV studios in Belgrade demanding that those responsible be sacked. Milošević sent in police to quell the demonstrations, but after two deaths and hundreds of brutal arrests the Communist leadership was forced to meet the students' demands.

During this crisis Serbia requested that the army be given emergency powers in order to bring the country back under control. The collective presidency refused on the grounds that Milošević was exploiting the situation as a means of diverting attention from economic problems, reasserting Serbian hegemony and perpetuating Communist rule, whereupon Serbia and its allies Montenegro and Vojvodina announced they were withdrawing from the presidency which was scheduled to pass to Croatia in May.

On 25 June 1991 Slovenia and Croatia declared themselves independent of Yugoslavia, and the Serbian enclave of Krajina proclaimed its autonomy from Croatia. This soon led to heavy fighting as the federal army moved into Slovenia to re-establish control of the border crossings into Austria, Italy and Hungary, and the airports of Ljubljana and Maribor were bombed by federal jets. The EC and the USA emphasised that they would not contribute to instability in the region by recognising breakaway states. Bulgaria, which has historic claims to Macedonia, was the only state to immediately recognise Slovenian independence.

Fearing the unleashing of a tidal wave of refugees, the EC rushed a delegation of foreign ministers to Yugoslavia to negotiate a compromise under which Serbia would allow Croatian leader Stipe Mesic to become head of the collective presidency, and Slovenia and Croatia would suspend their independence declarations for three months. The federal troops were to withdraw.

This fragile peace soon broke down when Slovenian militia forces surrounding Yugoslav army camps announced that they would only allow the federal troops safe conduct out of the area if they surrendered their weapons. In retaliation federal jets bombed Slovenian radio and TV stations on 2 July. The army staged massive troop movements in the centre of the country to intimidate the republics, as rumours of impending military coups in Slovenia and Croatia floated about and Bosnia-Hercegovina feared it would be partitioned between Serbia and Croatia. The EC imposed a weapons embargo on Yugoslavia and economic aid was frozen.

On 7 July federal and republican leaders met on Brioni Island in the hope of preventing a full-scale civil war. It was agreed that the federal troops would withdraw to their barracks, the Slovenian militia would be demobilised, and the border posts would be guarded by Slovenian police, although customs revenues were to go into the federal coffers. Negotiations on independence for Slovenia and Croatia were rescheduled for August, and the EC offered to send 50 observers to oversee the ceasefire.

On 14 July ethnic violence flared anew as Serbian nationalists known as Četniks began provocative attacks on Croatian police stations. The Yugoslav collective presidency announced on 18 July that all federal troops would be withdrawn from Slovenia within three months. But many Croatians viewed this as an attempt to isolate Croatia, and President Tudjman demanded that the army also withdraw from Croatia.

It's hard to predict what will happen next. Though the breakup of Yugoslavia into separate states is quite possible, the 180,000-member, 2000-tank federal army remains a potent force. The army's officer corps and the powerful secret police, the SDB, are dominated by Serbian Communists, and during the June/July crisis the army seemed beyond political control, intervening on its own authority. Both Slovenia and Croatia have built dedicated militias, and the use of force to hold the country together could easily convert Yugoslavia into another Lebanon. After further talks at Ohrid failed, Tudjman warned Croatians in an emotional TV speech in July to prepare for total war.

The crisis shook the already wobbly Yugoslav economy. In June 1991 alone, industrial production decreased 20% and there was 10% inflation. The federal government was forced to introduce severe austerity measures to avoid a total collapse. Even relatively developed Slovenia and Croatia face serious problems if they lose their markets in the rest of the country.

With the forced cohabitation imposed by Tito and the Communists for four decades collapsing on all sides, Yugoslavia seems poised to tear itself apart. Croatia, Serbia and Bosnia-Hercegovina all have within their present boundaries large minority groups fiercely opposed to being cut off in an independent state dominated by a rival ethnic group, and even neighbouring countries like Albania and Bulgaria could be drawn into a bloody civil war to settle old scores.

As this book goes to press, the fighting between Croatian militia forces and Serbian guerillas is developing into open conflict between Croatia and the Serbian-controlled national army, air force and navy, with ceasefires proving ineffective. Meanwhile, in a referendum Macedonians have voted overwhelmingly for independence, and the parliament in Bosnia-Hercegovina has done likewise – developments that add new dimensions to the conflict.

It appears that Serbia has resigned itself to independence for Slovenia. But there is little doubt that Milošević and his supporters hold fast to their dream of a 'Greater Serbia' consisting of Serbia proper, Vojvodina, Kosovo, the Serbian-populated parts of Croatia, large chunks of Bosnia-Hercegovina, and possibly Macedonia. Non-Serbians are unlikely to agree to this scenario, and unless pressure is brought to bear on Serbian hardliners (and their Montenegrin allies), the scene looks set for an old-fashioned Balkan war.

## GEOGRAPHY

It is said that Hernán Cortez described Mexico to the king of Spain by taking out a leaf of parchment, crinkling it up and dropping it onto a table with the words, 'That, Your Majesty, is the map of Mexico.' Yugoslavia is no less a mass of mountains. Mountains and plateaus account for three-quarters of this 255,804-sq-km country, the remainder being the Pannonian Plain on both sides of the Sava, Danube and Tisa rivers in the north-east. The mountains of Slovenia and the coastal range are part of the Alps, while most of Yugoslavia's interior and southern mountains belong to the Balkan range. The highest peak is Mt Triglav (2864 metres) in the Julian Alps near Austria, but Titov vrh (2748 metres) in Macedonia's Šar Planina is only slightly lower.

Most of the rivers flow north into the Danube, which runs through Yugoslavia for 588 km. Its tributary, the Sava, is 940 km long. Many smaller rivers have cut deep canyons in the plateau which make for memorable train rides. There are 300 lakes, but only five over 10 sq km in size. The largest are lakes Skadar, Ohrid and Prespan in the south on the Albanian border. Forests cover 34% of the land.

The Adriatic coast is only 628 km long as the crow flies, but it's so indented that the actual length is 2092 km. If the coastlines of the offshore islands are added to the total, the length becomes 6116 km. Most of the narrow coastal belt at the foot of the Dinaric Alps belongs to Croatia. Only a small southern section of seashore close to Albania is part of Montenegro, while Slovenia includes a little bit of northern Istria. The fantastic Bay of Kotor is the only real fjord in southern Europe. Most of the beaches along this jagged coast are rocky except for the 12-km sandy strip at Ulcinj. Officially there are no private beaches in Yugoslavia, although you must pay to use 'managed' beaches.

Yugoslavia's offshore islands are every bit as beautiful as those in Greece. There are 725 islands along this submerged Adriatic coastline, 66 of them inhabited. The largest islands are Cres, Krk, Lošinj, Pag and Rab in the north, and Brač, Hvar, Korčula and Mljet in the south. Many are barren with high mountains that drop right into the sea.

Yugoslavia has 22 national parks, each unique. On the coastal islands are three national parks: Brioni, Kornati and Mljet. Krka National Park near Šibenik and Plitvice National Park feature a series of cascades. Triglav National Park in the Julian Alps includes the country's highest peak, while Montenegro's Durmitor National Park has its largest canyon. A coastal gorge is seen at Paklenica National Park near Zadar. It would take several visits to see even a small part of all that this country has to offer.

## ECONOMY

Agriculture accounts for 40% of the gross national product, services 34% and industry only 26%. The importance of agriculture is indicative of a backwardness that is not immediately apparent to the casual tourist in developed areas like Slovenia and Croatia. After WWII, Yugoslavia was a war-torn land of peasants, but from 1948 to 1951 a concentrated attempt was made to form agricultural cooperatives. This failed, however, and 85% of the land is still worked privately by small farmers. In 1953 individual private holdings were reduced to 15 hectares maximum.

During the 1950s, state property was handed over to the workers in a reaction against Stalinist socialism. The economy was thus reorganised on the basis of 'self-management' and elected workers' councils began running the factories and businesses with coordination from producers' councils on a regional level. State control was limited to the broadest economic planning.

This system soon led to inefficiencies and an expensive duplication of services without the full benefits of open competition. Since socially owned property had no clear owner, it was impossible to enforce economic efficiency or to guarantee profits. Initiative was stifled and employees often used self-management to improve their own financial standing without feeling any responsibility towards their property. Income was spent on higher wages and, with little or no capital left for development, companies turned to the banks. The cycle of inefficiency and dependency deepened as companies borrowed with little hope of ever paying off the loans. The Central Bank now penalises banks which lend money to unprofitable companies to pay wages.

The crisis of 2000% inflation in 1989 shattered the self-management ideal and led reformers to consider as inevitable a return to private or state property. For the state to nationalise socially owned property would be a backward step, but where is the capital for privatisation to come from? Over 80% of Yugoslav property is socially owned, and with their savings individual Yugoslavs could not hope to purchase more than 10% of it. While privatisation is a top priority, moving too quickly might cause property values to tumble, and everyone wants to avoid selling social property off cheaply to foreigners. Any streamlining of companies will inevitably mean many people will lose their jobs, yet property reform is at the heart of Yugoslavia's economic problems. Already there are many privately owned small businesses.

Yugoslavia today is one of the most indebted countries on earth with about US$18 billion in hard-currency obligations, most of it accumulated in the 1970s. Borrowing from the West worked fine while Tito was alive, but the burden is now being felt. In 1989 there was 2000% inflation, so at the beginning of 1990 the government just stopped printing money and declared a wage freeze. Prices still jumped by 75% but by mid-1990 inflation had levelled off to 13% a year; however, the dinar is now substantially overvalued. Unless Yugoslavia can become more competitive in consumer production, the country faces economic collapse. Convince yourself of this by going into any department store and examining the goods and prices. People in Slovenia find it much cheaper to pop across into Austria and Italy to do their shopping. Yugoslavia's total imports are double the total exports.

The state is attempting to maintain social services in spite of rising unemployment, inflation, economic inefficiencies and bankruptcies by major firms. Strikes against falling real wages and the closure of uneconomic enterprises have become commonplace. Unemployment is running around 20% but there are big regional differences. The average income in Slovenia is twice that in Macedonia, and real incomes have declined 40% nationwide since 1980. In the meantime, city dwellers have been transformed into avid consumers and the inequalities are evident: you don't have to look far to find the nouveaux riches. Only tourism and remittances from the one million Yugoslavs working in the West (mostly in Germany) keep this country afloat.

## POPULATION & PEOPLE

Yugoslavia is one country with two alphabets, three religions, four languages, six republics and seven major nationalities. Most of the 24 million people in Yugoslavia are South Slavs, including Croats (19.8%), Macedonians (6%), Montenegrins (2.6%), Serbians (36.3%) and Slovenes (7.8%). Non-Slavonic nationalities include Albanians (7.7%) and Hungarians (1.9%), with a smattering of Bulgarians, Italians, Romanians, Turks, Slovaks and Ukrainians thrown in for the flavour.

Twenty per cent of the population of Vojvodina is Hungarian, and 85% of Kosovars are Albanian. Less visible internal minorities are the 800,000 Serbians in Croatia, 200,000 Serbians in Kosovo and 400,000 Albanians in Macedonia and Montenegro. In total there are 1,800,000 ethnic Albanians in Yugoslavia, a large number considering the population of Albania itself is only 3,200,000. The population of Bosnia-Hercegovina consists of 32% Serbians, 18% Croats and the balance are 'Muslims' (Slavonic converts to Islam).

The largest cities in descending order are Belgrade (1,500,000), Zagreb (1,200,000), Skopje (500,000), Sarajevo (450,000), Ljubljana (300,000), Novi Sad (250,000), Niš (230,000), Prishtinë (210,000) and Rijeka (200,000).

Half of the population is Orthodox, 30% Catholic and 10% Islamic. There has always been a degree of rivalry between the two largest groups: the Catholic, Romanised Croats and the Orthodox, Byzantine Serbians. The Macedonians and Montenegrins are also Orthodox, whereas the Slovenes and Hungarians are Roman Catholic. Bosnia-Hercegovina is a mixture of Catholic, Orthodox and Muslim while the Albanians are predominantly Muslim.

## ARTS

Yugoslavia's best known writer is Ivo Andrić (1892-1975), winner of the 1961 Nobel Prize for Literature. His novels *Travnik Chronicle* and *The Bridge on the Drina*, both of which were written during WW II, are fictional histories of the small Bosnian towns of Travnik and Višegrad which deal with the intermingling of Islamic and Orthodox civilisations there.

The work of sculptor Ivan Meštrović (1883-1962) is seen in town squares all around the country. Aside from creating public monuments, Meštrović was responsible for imposing buildings such as the Njegoš mausoleum near Cetinje. Both his sculpture and architecture display a powerful classical restraint he learned from Rodin. Meštrović's studio in Zagreb and his retirement home at Split have been made into galleries of his work.

## Music

'Blehmuzika' or brass music is the national music of Serbia. Though documented as far back as 1335, blehmuzika evolved under the influence of Turkish and later Serbian military music. During the early 20th century the trumpet became a symbol of Serbian resistance to foreign domination. In the 1920s, retired military men formed orchestras of eight to 10 musicians, but right up to the present, Serbian brass music is played mostly by village farmers in their spare time.

The heartland of blehmuzika is the area around Guča, a village south of the railway line between Kraljevo and Pozega. Each year around the end of August more than 100,000 people attend the three-day Guča trumpet festival to hear 20 competing bands. A second centre for Serbian brass music is the Niš region where Gypsy bands play wild Eastern-inspired dance music. An unfortunate side effect of the popularity of the bleh or *duvacki* orchestras is that groups using traditional folk instruments have been overpowered, and even the old combination of accordion and *frula* (a small flute) has lost ground.

## LANGUAGE

As a result of history, tourism and the number of returned 'guest workers' from Germany, German is the most commonly spoken second language in Yugoslavia. Many people in Istria understand Italian. In Kosovo and Serbia educated people often speak French, while throughout Slovenia and Croatia, along the coast and among the young English is more popular.

Serbo-Croatian, an amalgam of the two main Slavonic dialects, is the most common language in Yugoslavia, followed by Slovene and Macedonian. Serbian is spoken in Montenegro, while Albanian is spoken in Kosovo.

Both the Latin and Cyrillic alphabets are in common use. Albanian, Croatian, Hungarian and Slovene are written in the Latin alphabet, Serbian and Macedonian in Cyrillic. The Latin alphabet is used in Croatia, Bosnia-Hercegovina, Slovenia, Kosovo and Vojvodina. In Montenegro you'll encounter a mixture of Latin and Cyrillic but in Serbia and Macedonia most things are only in Cyrillic. It's worth spending an hour or two studying the Cyrillic alphabet if you'll be visiting eastern Yugoslavia; we provide one in the introduction to the Bulgaria chapter.

*Croatian Through Conversation* by Mladen Engelsfeld (Mladost, Zagreb, 1990) is useful if you want to study the language, though it lacks an English-Croatian vocabulary and is of limited practical use to travellers. For travel you're better off buying a cheap bilingual dictionary such as the white-covered *Engelsko Hrvatski ili Srpski* (Skolska Knjiga, Zagreb, 1989). Both of the above are available at Yugoslav bookshops.

Serbo-Croatian is written as it's pronounced and there are no silent letters or diphthongs. The stress is usually on the first syllable and only rarely on the last. There are 30 letters or combinations of letters (q, w, x and y don't exist). The vowels are pronounced as in Italian or Spanish and many of the consonants as in English. Pronounce the Serbo-Croatian c as ts, č as ch, ć as tch, dž as j, đ as dj, j as y, lj as ly, nj as ny, š as sh and ž as s (as in measure). You'll sometimes see lj written ļ. The letter r is trilled and can serve as a vowel between two consonants.

Two words everyone should know are *ima* (there is) and *nema* (there isn't). If you make just a small effort to learn a few words of Serbo-Croatian you'll distinguish yourself from the packaged tourists and be greatly appreciated by the local people. Here's a Serbo-Croatian vocabulary to get you started:

## Greetings & Civilities

hello
  *zdravo*
goodbye
  *doviđenja*
good morning
  *dobro jutro*
good evening
  *dobro večer*
please
  *molim*
thank you
  *hvala*
I am sorry.
  *Žao mi je.*
You are very kind.
  *Vrlo ste ljubazni.*
yes
  *da*
no
  *ne*

## Small Talk

Do you speak English?
  *Da li govorite engleski?*
I don't understand.
  *Ne razumijem.*
Could you write it down?
  *Dali bi mogli da to napišete?*
Where do you live?
  *Gdje živite?*
What work do you do?
  *Koja je vaša profesija?*
I am a student.
  *Ja sam student.*
I am very happy.
  *Ja sam veoma sretan.*

## Accommodation

youth hostel
  *omladinski dom*
camping ground
  *autokamp*
private room
  *privatna soba*

How much is it?
*Koliko to košta?*
Is that the price per person?
*Dali je to cena po osobi?*
Is that the total price?
*Dali je to ukupna cena?*
Are there any extra charges?
*Dali ima dodatnih troškova?*
Can I pay with local currency?
*Mogu li to platiti sa lokalnom valutom?*
Where is there a cheaper hotel?
*Gdje je jeftiniji hotel?*
Should I make a reservation?
*Dali bih mogao napraviti rezervaciju?*
single room
*jednokrevetna soba*
double room
*dvokrevetna soba*
It is very noisy.
*Veoma je bučno.*
Where is the toilet?
*Gdje je toilet?*

## Getting Around

What time does it leave?
*Kada odlazi?*
When is the first bus?
*Kada je prvi autobus?*
When is the last bus?
*Kada je posljednji autobus?*
When is the next bus?
*Kada je sljedeći autobus?*
That's too soon.
*Uskoro.*
When is the next one after that?
*Kada je sledeći?*
How long does the trip take?
*Kako dugo traje putovanje?*
arrival
*dolazak*
departure
*odlazak*
timetable
*vozni red*
Where is the bus stop?
*Gdje je autobuska stanica?*
Where is the railway station?
*Gdje je željeznička stanica?*
Where is the taxi stand?
*Gdje je taksi stanica?*

Where is the left-luggage room?
*Gdje je garderoba?*

## Around Town

Just a minute.
*Samo minut.*
Where is...?
*Gdje je...?*
the bank
*banka*
the post office
*pošta*
the telephone centre
*telefonska centrala*
the tourist information office
*turističke informacije*
the museum
*muzej*
the palace
*palača*
the castle
*dvorac*
the concert hall
*koncertna dvorana*
the opera house
*operna kuća*
the musical theatre
*muzičko kazalište*
Where are you going?
*Gdje idete?*
I am going to...
*Ja idem...*
Where is it?
*Gdje je to?*
I can't find it.
*Ja ne mogu pronaći to.*
Is it far?
*Je li to daleko?*
Please show me on the map.
*Molim vas, pokažite mi na mapi.*
left
*lijevo*
right
*desno*
straight ahead
*ravno naprijed*
I want...
*Ja želim...*
Do I need permission?
*Dali mi treba dozvola?*

May I?
*Smijem li?*

## Entertainment

Where can I hear live music?
*Gde mogu slušati živu muziku?*
Where can I buy a ticket?
*Gde mogu kupiti kartu?*
I'm looking for a ticket.
*Ja tražim kartu.*
I want to refund this ticket.
*Ja želim da vratim ovu kartu.*
Is this a good seat?
*Dali je ovo dobro mesto?*
at the front
*naprijed*
ticket
*karta*

## Food

I am hungry.
*Gladan sam.* (male)
*Gladna sam.* (female)
I do not eat meat.
*Ja ne jedem meso.*
self-service cafeteria
*restauracija sa samoposluživanjem*
grocery store
*trgovina mješovitom robom*
fish
*riba*
soup
*juha*
salad
*salata*
fresh vegetables
*sveže povrće*
milk
*mlijeko*
bread
*kruh*
sugar
*šećer*
ice cream
*sladoled*
hot coffee
*vruća kava*
mineral water
*mineralna voda*

beer
*pivo*
wine
*vino*

## Shopping

Where can I buy one?
*Gde mogu kupiti ovu stvar?*
How much does it cost?
*Kolko to košta?*
That's (much) too expensive.
*To ke preskupo.*
Is there a cheaper one?
*Ima li nešto jeftinije?*

## Time & Dates

today
*danas*
tonight
*večeras*
tomorrow
*sutra*
the day after tomorrow
*prekosutra*
What time does it open?
*Kada se otvara?*
What time does it close?
*Kada se zatvara?*
open
*otvoreno*
closed
*zatvoreno*
in the morning
*ujutro*
in the evening
*uveče*
every day
*svaki dan*
At what time?
*U koliko sati?*
when?
*kada?*

| | |
|---|---|
| Monday | *ponedjeljak* |
| Tuesday | *utorak* |
| Wednesday | *srijeda* |
| Thursday | *četvrtak* |
| Friday | *petak* |

| | |
|---|---|
| Saturday | *subota* |
| Sunday | *nedjelja* |
| | |
| January | *siječanj* |
| February | *veljača* |
| March | *ožujak* |
| April | *travanj* |
| May | *svibanj* |
| June | *lipanj* |
| July | *srpanj* |
| August | *kolovoz* |
| September | *rujan* |
| October | *listopad* |
| November | *studeni* |
| December | *prosinac* |

**Numbers**

| | |
|---|---|
| 1 | *jedan* |
| 2 | *dva* |
| 3 | *tri* |
| 4 | *četiri* |
| 5 | *pet* |
| 6 | *šest* |
| 7 | *sedam* |
| 8 | *osam* |
| 9 | *devet* |
| 10 | *deset* |
| 11 | *jedanaest* |
| 12 | *dvanaest* |
| 13 | *trinaest* |
| 14 | *četrnaest* |
| 15 | *petnaest* |
| 16 | *šesnaest* |
| 17 | *sedamnaest* |
| 18 | *osamnaest* |
| 19 | *devetnaest* |
| 20 | *dvadeset* |
| 21 | *dvadeset jedan* |
| 22 | *dvadeset dva* |
| 23 | *dvadeset tri* |
| 30 | *trideset* |
| 40 | *četrdeset* |
| 50 | *pedeset* |
| 60 | *šezdeset* |
| 70 | *sedamdeset* |
| 80 | *osamdeset* |
| 90 | *devedeset* |
| 100 | *sto* |

# Facts for the Visitor

## VISAS & EMBASSIES

Visas are not required by most Europeans, Americans, Canadians, Australians, New Zealanders and Japanese – in fact, about the only Westerners who still do need visas are Greeks! If you are a national of a Third World country, check the visa requirements at a consulate, although you also may not need one and even if you do, it's issued free of charge on the spot. The entry stamp in your passport allows you to stay in Yugoslavia for 90 days.

While in Yugoslavia you're supposed to have your passport with you at all times. If you're staying at a hotel or camping ground, they may keep your passport at the desk and give you a stamped card which serves the same purpose. You won't be able to cash travellers' cheques without a passport, though many camping grounds in Yugoslavia are perfectly happy if you give them your camping carnet instead.

Officially, if you stay somewhere other than organised accommodation (hotel, private room from an agency, camping ground, etc) you're supposed to report to the local authorities within 24 hours. It's unlikely you'll ever have to do such a thing, but the police can bring it up if you're caught camping freelance, staying with friends or in a private room arranged on the street. You don't need to get any stamps on a visa form to prove where you stayed (as you still do in Hungary or Bulgaria).

Yugoslavia does not recognise dual nationality, so anyone who has ever held Yugoslav citizenship will still be considered a citizen unless he/she has officially renounced his/her Yugoslav citizenship at a Yugoslav diplomatic office. For example, a person born in Yugoslavia but presently a citizen of Australia could be denied the right to communicate with the Australian Embassy in Belgrade if arrested or drafted into the Yugoslav army while on holiday here!

## Yugoslav Embassies

Yugoslav Embassies abroad include:

Australia
11 Nuyts St, Canberra, ACT 2603 (☎ 95 1458)
58 Lisson Grove, Hawthorn, Vic 3122
(Melbourne) (☎ 818 2254)
24 Colin St, West Perth, WA 6005 (☎ 321 4539)
12 Trelawney St, Woollahra, NSW 2025
(Sydney) (☎ 328 6455)
Canada
17 Blackburn Ave, Ottawa, Ont K1N 8A2
(☎ 233 6289)
377 Spadina Rd, Toronto, Ont M5P 2V7
(☎ 481 7279)
Holland
Groot Hertoginnelaan 30, 2517 EG The Hague
(☎ 363 6800)
Japan
7-24, 4-chome, Kitashinagawa, Shinagawa-ku,
Tokyo (☎ 447 3571)
UK
5-7, Lexham Gardens, London W8 5JU
(☎ 071-370 6105)
USA
307 North Michigan Ave, Suite 1600, Chicago,
IL 60601 (☎ 332 0169)
1700 E 13th St, Suite 4R, Cleveland, OH 44114
(☎ 612 2093)
767 Third Ave, 17th floor, New York, NY 10017
(☎ 212-838 2300)
625 Stanwix St, Suite 1605, Pittsburg, PA 15222
(☎ 471 6191)
1375 Sutter St, Suite 406, San Francisco,
CA 94709 (☎ 776 4941)
2410 California St NW, Washington, DC 20008
(☎ 202-462 6566)

## MONEY

All banks and travel agencies change hard currency into Yugoslav dinars at the same official rate of exchange minus 1.5% commission. Unlike Western Europe, you won't be given a worse rate at fancy hotels or on Sundays. A passport is required to change travellers' cheques but not for cash. Only change what you're sure you'll need, however, as it's *impossible* to change dinars back into hard currency. There's no compulsory exchange of currency in Yugoslavia and no black market. Anyone who offers to change money on the street intends to rip you off.

Early in 1990 the Marković government introduced a system to make the dinar a convertible currency. Henceforth Yugoslavs would be able to go to a bank and purchase foreign currency with their dinars without restrictions. Surprisingly the new regulations stipulated that foreigners could not change dinars back into hard currency, with or without exchange receipts. This wrinkle was intended to prevent other Eastern Europeans from converting dinars obtained by selling articles to Yugoslavs, but for legitimate visitors it meant that money was still 'convertible' only one way: into dinars that had to be spent. Check, as this may change.

In 1989 Yugoslavia suffered 2000% inflation and no one knows what will happen in future. For this reason we list prices in US dollars, to give you an idea of real costs. You pay for almost everything directly in dinars, however.

You're not supposed to import or export large quantities of dinars. There's no reason

to do either as the bank rate within Yugoslavia is as good as anything you'll find abroad and most foreign banks won't accept Yugoslav currency. You might want to bring along a small quantity of dinars to ease your entry, however.

## Currency

In 1990 four zeros were knocked off the Yugoslav dinar so 10,000 old dinars became one new dinar. The design and colour of the old and new bills in circulation are identical (the new 10 dinar note is red, the 100 note is yellow, etc) and some unscrupulous locals will try to shortchange you by giving you what seem to be large bills, for example 20,000 old dinars instead of 200,000 old dinars, so be careful. In January 1991 the Yugoslav dinar was devalued 25% and traded at 13 new dinars (or 130,000 old dinars) to the US dollar. In late 1991 the rate was US$1 = 22 dinars.

## Costs

Whether you love or hate Yugoslavia could well depend on where you were before. If you're coming directly from Western Europe, Yugoslavia will seem fairly reasonable, but if you've been travelling in the other Eastern European countries you'll find it very expensive. For this reason you'll enjoy your stay a lot more if you visit Yugoslavia *before* going to Hungary, Bulgaria or Czechoslovakia. That way you'll have the cheaper countries of the region to look forward to and your trip to Yugoslavia won't be completely spoiled.

Transportation, concert and theatre tickets are reasonable and food is averagely priced. Accommodation is increasingly expensive, partly because the rates are linked to hard currency, but more because of a two-price system in which foreigners pay several times more than locals for hotels, private rooms, camp sites, etc. Transportation and theatre tickets are inexpensive because everyone pays the same price.

Average prices per person are US$8 to US$20 for a private room, US$4 to US$5 for a meal at a self-service, US$2 for a museum admission and US$3 to US$5 for an average intercity bus fare. If you're on a strict budget you can do it on US$25 a day if you eschew all luxuries, even less if you camp and eat only groceries. A student card will get you half-price admission at some museums and galleries (though never in Dubrovnik). The east and far south of the country are cheaper than the north and west for food.

Your daily expenses will come way down if you can find a private room with cooking facilities to use as a base for exploring nearby areas. Coastal towns which lend themselves to this include Izola, Rovinj, Split, Korčula and Dubrovnik. You'll get more of a feel for your surroundings if you spend four nights in a place, and using a town as a base allows you to make day trips without hassles over luggage or worrying where you'll sleep. You also escape 50% surcharges on private rooms rented for under four nights.

If it still seems expensive, keep in mind that the average monthly income in Yugoslavia is US$400, so it's even more difficult for the Yugoslavs. Most only manage to make ends meet because they still receive subsidised housing, free health care and education, etc, and keep two or three jobs. Like people in the West, Yugoslavs buy most consumer goods on credit and they're sharp dressers. At first glance it's hard to realise the country is an economic basket case.

**Cheating** The official double pricing for accommodation has set a dangerous precedent. Waiters now feel it's OK to abuse foreigners who may not understand the currency or prices, aren't regular customers and can't complain anyway. Check your bill in any establishment which caters mostly to tourists as they *habitually* overcharge. Be careful in a place which doesn't have a menu with prices clearly stated. If the drinks aren't listed on the menu they'll be about double what you'd expect. Whenever ordering coffee always repeat the posted price with the order, otherwise you'll be served a larger cup for double price. Even ice-cream sellers and bartenders will cheat you unless you check the price before ordering. Also beware of being short-changed by railway station ticket clerks.

It's too bad that it's like this, but you're looked upon as an even greater fool if you let yourself be taken advantage of without protesting. If Yugoslavia wants to join Europe and have a hard currency, it had better start charging everyone the same price and end its official and unofficial policies of cheating tourists!

## Tipping

If you're served fairly and well at a restaurant, you can round the bill up slightly as you're paying (don't leave money on the table). If a service charge has been added to the bill no tip is necessary. Bar bills and taxi fares can also be 'rounded up'. Tour guides on day excursions expect to be tipped.

## CLIMATE & WHEN TO GO

The climate varies from Mediterranean along the Adriatic coast to continental inland and temperate in Slovenia. The high coastal mountains help shield the coast from the cold northerly winds, making for an early spring and late autumn. In spring and early summer a landward breeze called the *maestral* keeps the temperature down along the coast. Winter winds include the *bura* from the north and *široko* from the south.

The sunny coastal areas experience hot, dry summers and mild, rainy winters, while the interior regions are cold in winter, warm in summer. Due to a warm current flowing north up the Adriatic coast, sea temperatures never fall below 10°C in winter, and in August they go as high as 26°C. The resorts south of Split are the warmest. Belgrade has average daily temperatures above 17°C from May to September, above 13°C in April and October and above 7°C in March and November.

May is the best month to travel the Adriatic coast, with good weather and few tourists. June and September are also good but in July and August all Europe arrives and prices soar. April and October may be too cool for camping but the weather should still

be fine along the coast, and private rooms will be plentiful and inexpensive. Much the same is true for Slovenia, though winter will be longer. The rest of the interior is only easily accessible to low-budget travellers from May to September when the camping grounds are open. Hotels in the interior are very expensive and private rooms almost don't exist, so winter is a risky time to travel there, though the cultural life will be in full swing.

## TOURIST OFFICES

The Yugoslav National Tourist Office doesn't have any offices inside Yugoslavia itself, so visit one of its offices abroad. Ask for the *Tourist Map of Yugoslavia*, *Private Accommodation Rates*, *Camping* and the *Calendar of Events* brochures. The brochure *The Sunny Adriatic* describes every coastal town, while *Tourist Information Yugoslavia* has lots of practical information on the country. While you're there ask if they have the little booklet entitled *Jadrolinija, Carferry and Local Lines* which includes the schedules of most coastal ferries. Aside from these annually updated national publications, the offices abroad should have brochures on some of the towns and areas that you'll be visiting. All of these free publications are well worth having.

Inside Yugoslavia tourist information is dispensed by commercial travel agencies which also arrange private rooms, sightseeing tours, etc. Keep in mind that these are profit-making businesses so don't be put off if you're asked to pay for a town plan, etc. The agencies often sell local guidebooks which are excellent value if you'll be staying long in one place.

Municipal tourist offices have lots of free brochures and are good sources of information on local events. These are found in Belgrade, Dubrovnik, Ljubljana, Novi Sad, Pula, Rijeka, Sarajevo, Skopje, Split, Titograd and Zagreb. Most towns also have an office selling theatre and concert tickets. We've tried to list most of these offices in this chapter.

## Tourist Offices Abroad

Yugoslav tourist offices abroad include:

Austria
 Yugoslav National Tourist Office, Mahlerstrasse 3, 1010 Vienna (☎ 512 7174)
Belgium
 Yugoslav National Tourist Office, 103c rue Royale, 1000 Brussels (☎ 219 5828)
Denmark
 Yugoslav National Tourist Office, Trommesalen 2, 1614 Copenhagen V (☎ 11 6300)
France
 Yugoslav National Tourist Office, 31 Boulevard des Italiens, 75002 Paris (☎ 4268 0707)
Germany
 Yugoslav National Tourist Office, Graf Adolfstrasse 64, 4 Düsseldorf (☎ 16 1704)
 Yugoslav National Tourist Office, Goetheplatz 7, 6 Frankfurt/Main (☎ 20798)
 Yugoslav National Tourist Office, Sonnenstrasse 14, 8 Munich 2 (☎ 59 5545)
Greece
 Yugoslav National Tourist Office, 4 Voukourestiou St, 2nd floor, Athens (☎ 322 6889)
Hungary
 Yugoslav National Tourist Office, International Trade Centre, Bajcsy-Zsilinszky ut 12, Budapest (☎ 138 2372)
Italy
 Yugoslav National Tourist Office, Via Veneto 10, 00187 Rome (☎ 46 1455)
 Yugoslav National Tourist Office, Via Pantano 2, 20122 Milan (☎ 86 7607)
Netherlands
 Yugoslav National Tourist Office, Jan Luykenstraat 12, 1071 CM Amsterdam (☎ 675 0496)
Sweden
 Yugoslav National Tourist Office, Slöjdgatan 10, 10386 Stockholm 40 (☎ 10 1993)
Switzerland
 Yugoslav National Tourist Office, Limmatquai 70, 8001 Zürich (☎ 252 1270)
UK
 Yugoslav National Tourist Office, 143 Regent St, London W1 (☎ 071-734 5243)
USA
 Yugoslav National Tourist Office, Rockefeller Center, Suite 280, 630 Fifth Ave, New York, NY 10111 (☎ 212-757 2801)

## BUSINESS HOURS & HOLIDAYS

Banks in Yugoslavia keep long hours, often from 7 am to 7 pm weekdays, 7 am to noon Saturday. Most government offices are closed on Saturday though shops stay open Saturdays until 2 pm. Weekdays many shops close for lunch from noon to 4 pm but stay open until 8 pm. Department stores and self-services generally stay open throughout the day. Some self-services open Sunday mornings.

Public holidays throughout Yugoslavia include 1 and 2 January (New Year), 1 and 2 May (Labour days), 4 July (Partisan Day), and 29 and 30 November (Republic days). In addition, there are the following regional holidays: 7 July (Serbia), 13 July (Montenegro), 27 April, 22 July and 1 November (Slovenia), 27 July (Croatia, Bosnia-Hercegovina) and 2 August and 11 October (Macedonia). If any of these should fall on a Sunday then the following Monday or Tuesday is a holiday.

## CULTURAL EVENTS

In July and August there are summer festivals in Budva, Dubrovnik, Ljubljana, Ohrid, Opatija, Rovinj, Sarajevo, Split and Zagreb. The Balkan Festival of Original Folk Dances & Songs occurs in Ohrid in early July. That same month there's also an International Review of Original Folklore in Zagreb. Jazz festivals take place in Ljubljana (mid-June), Zagreb (October) and Belgrade (end of October). The Belgrade International Theatre Festival is in mid-September. Film festivals are held in Belgrade (February) and Pula (July).

Some noted international fairs include the Zagreb Spring (mid-April) and Autumn (mid-September) Grand Trade fairs, the Novi Sad Agricultural Fair (mid-May) and the Ljubljana Wine Fair (early September).

## POST & TELECOMMUNICATIONS

To mail a parcel from Yugoslavia take it unwrapped to a main post office where they will wrap and seal it. You then fill out six or seven forms, stand in line for a while and hopefully get it off. Not all post offices will do this, however. Allow several hours to complete the transaction.

The mail service is said to be reliable and

you can receive mail addressed to poste restante in all towns for a small charge.

## Telephones

To call Yugoslavia from western Europe dial the international access code (different from each country), 38 (the country code for Yugoslavia), the area code (without the initial zero) and the number. Important area codes include 11 (Belgrade), 41 (Zagreb), 51 (Rijeka), 58 (Split), 61 (Ljubljana) and 91 (Skopje).

To place a long-distance phone call in Yugoslavia you usually go to the main post office. Avoid doing this on weekends as the office may be jammed with military personnel waiting to call home. International calls placed from hotels are much more expensive.

## TIME

GMT (UTC) plus one. Yugoslavia goes on summer time at the end of March when clocks are turned an hour forward. At the end of September they're turned an hour back.

## WEIGHTS & MEASURES

The electric voltage is 220 volts AC, 50 Hz. Yugoslavia uses the metric system.

## BOOKS & MAPS

Books are expensive in Yugoslavia and there's little in English other than local travel guidebooks. Unfortunately, Yugoslav literature, even classics like *The Bridge on the Drina*, is unavailable in English in Yugoslavia.

*The Rough Guide to Yugoslavia* (Harrap-Columbus, London) covers a lot more ground in far greater detail than can be included here. In the US the same book appears as *The Real Guide Yugoslavia* (Prentice Hall, New York). If your main interest is hiking get hold of *Yugoslavia Mountain Walks & Historic Sites* by Piers Letcher (Bradt Publications, England). Letcher would do well to drop his city sections which contain information you can also find in the Rough Guide, and to provide more backwoods information and better maps.

Rebecca West's *Black Lamb & Grey Falcon* is a classic portrait of prewar Yugoslavia. Former partisan leader (and regime ideologist until purged in 1954) Milovan Djilas has written many fascinating books about history and politics in Yugoslavia, most of them published in English translations in the West. Any good library will have a couple. *Tito, A Biography* by Phyllis Auty (Longman, London, 1970) is also good background. One of the best contemporary Serbian writers is Danilo Kiš.

## MEDIA

The newspaper *Politika* has a weekly edition in English (six-month subscription US$30 from Politika, Makedonska 29, Belgrade). It's hard to find so grab it whenever you see it.

The *Review of International Affairs*, a magazine published 24 times a year (annual subscription by surface mail US$25 from Nemanjina 34, Belgrade), carries articles reflecting Yugoslavia's continuing interest in the Third World.

## HEALTH

Citizens of Austria, Belgium, Germany, the Netherlands, Italy, Luxembourg and Great Britain receive free medical treatment in Yugoslavia, provided they are covered by their national health programmes. British nationals need only show their passport for this purpose, but citizens of the other countries must have a certificate from their national medical insurance authority entitling them to free medical care in Yugoslavia.

This should be obtained before leaving home. All other nationalities must pay for medical treatment, though the charges are much lower than in North America, for example.

## DANGERS & ANNOYANCES

Personal security is not a problem in Yugoslavia although single women will be harassed by local men in the coastal resorts. It's important to firmly repulse all such approaches. Women should stay within sight of other people and not go off sunbathing or hiking alone.

Theft is rare and mostly practised by fellow travellers, so take care of your gear in youth hostels and on international trains.

## FILM & PHOTOGRAPHY

Bring all your own film as that sold locally is expensive and unreliable. You're only allowed to bring five rolls per person, and although this isn't enforced, distribute larger quantities through your luggage. Photographing soldiers or military facilities will cause problems if you're caught. The funny little signs with a camera crossed out should be taken seriously.

## ACTIVITIES
### Yachting

The long, rugged islands off Yugoslavia's mountainous coast all the way from Istria to Dubrovnik have created a yachting paradise. The fine, deep channels with abundant anchorages and steady winds attract yachties from around the world. Throughout the region there are quaint little ports for provisioning, and yachts can tie up right in the middle of everything. Some 30 modern marinas dot the coast. In the Mediterranean only the Greek islands are comparable.

Those arriving with their own boat can check in at any of the following ports: Koper, Izola, Piran, Umag, Novigrad, Poreč, Rovinj, Pula, Raša, Mali Lošinj, Rijeka, Senj, Zadar, Šibenik, Primošten, Split, Hvar, Korčula, Kardeljevo, Metković, Dubrovnik, Herceg-Novi, Zelenika, Kotor, Budva and Bar. Navigation permits are not required for unpowered boats and kayaks under three metres in length.

Yacht charter companies in North America and elsewhere arrange yacht rentals here. You can either hire a 'bareboat' for your party and set out on your own or join a flotilla of yachts sailing along a fixed route. Yacht tours begin from around US$100 a day all inclusive (airfare extra), while a yacht charter might go for US$1000 a week for four persons (food and skipper extra). The season runs from May to mid-October.

### Skiing

Yugoslavia has many well-equipped ski resorts. Not surprisingly, the most popular are in Slovenia's Julian Alps, especially Vogel (1923 metres) above Bohinj, Kranjska gora (810 metres), Krvavec (1853 metres) east of Kranj, and Pohorje (1543 metres) near Maribor. World Cup trials are held at Kranjska Gora, and the current world ski-jumping record (194 metres) was set at nearby Planica. Every fourth Slovene is an active skier!

Since the 1984 Winter Olympics, Sarajevo has been Yugoslavia's most famous winter sports centre and there are major ski resorts nearby at Jahorina (1913 metres) and Bjelašnica (2067 metres).

West of Skopje in Macedonia there's Popova šapka (1875 metres) on the southern slopes of the Šar Planina. On the north side of the same range is Brezovica, at 1750 metres, Kosovo's major ski resort. Serbia's largest ski centre is Kopaonik (2017 metres) south of Kraljevo.

All of the above have multiple chair lifts, cable cars and large resort hotels. Ski schools are found at Pokljuka west of Bled, Kranjska Gora, Pohorje and Jahorina. For information about special all-inclusive ski tours to Yugoslavia, consult a branch of the Yugoslav National Tourist Office abroad. This would be much cheaper and easier than trying to make your own arrangements. The season is roughly December to March (November to mid-May at the highest resorts).

## White-Water Rafting

Companies like Atlas Tours organise white-water rafting on wild and scenic rivers like the Tara in Montenegro's Durmitor National Park and the Soča in north-western Slovenia. For more information turn to Package Tours under the Getting There & Away section that follows and to the Durmitor National Park section.

## Hiking

The opportunities for hiking are endless, but for those with limited time four areas are recommended. You'll experience the full grandeur of the Julian Alps in Triglav National Park at Bohinj. The barren coastal mountains are an entirely different environment which you can get the feel of by climbing Mt Iliya (961 metres) above Orebić opposite Korčula, or hiking through the gorge at Paklenica National Park near Zadar. For high-altitude lakes and one of the world's deepest canyons, Montenegro's Durmitor National Park can't be beaten. All these are easily accessible on public transport.

## HIGHLIGHTS
### Museums & Galleries

It's significant that two of Yugoslavia's finest museums are in Zagreb: the Muzejski prostor, where special exhibitions are held, and the Museum Mimara, an impressive new gallery. The Museum of Church Art in Zadar and the Meštrović Gallery in Split display Yugoslav art old and new. Princess Ljubica's Palace in Belgrade is a fine example of a 19th century Balkan noble's house.

## Castles

Yugoslavia has a wealth of castles from fairytale Bled Castle in the Julian Alps to Smederevo Castle on the Danube, Serbia's last medieval fortress. Empty Hvar Fortress is perhaps the finest coastal fortress. Petrovaradin Citadel at Novi Sad is one of the great Baroque fortresses of Europe. Belgrade's Kalemegdan Citadel must be mentioned for its historic importance.

## Historic Towns

It would be easy to list a dozen picturesque old towns in this diverse country and each of these well-preserved urban complexes has a character of its own: Dubrovnik (medieval), Ohrid (Byzantine), Piran (Venetian), Sarajevo (Turkish) and Split (classical Roman).

## Hotels & Restaurants

Yugoslavia has lots of good hotels – if you've got lots of hard currency. The five listed here have been chosen with their off-season rates in mind. Three characterful old city hotels are the Hotel Riviera at Poreč, the Hotel Riviera at Pula and the Central Hotel at Sarajevo. The Hotel Mediteran at Ulcinj is reasonable for what you get and the Hotel Park in Ljubljana is about as close as you'll come to a cheap hotel around here.

Yugoslavia's restaurants won't break your budget quite as often. Restaurant Planjak in Korčula serves unpretentious grilled meats in appealing surroundings. The Pozorisni Klub in Mostar is rather elegant while at the Pivnica Pizzeria in Split you can let your hair down. Grill Danilo Godina in Izola is a nice little Italian-style place serving seafood. The Surf Bar in nearby Piran is a sort of English pub/pizzeria.

## ACCOMMODATION

Tourism in Yugoslavia is built around groups who arrive on cheap package holidays for a week or two at the beach. Motorists with camping gear are also catered for, but independent budget travel is becoming a real challenge. When the first edition of this book was researched a couple of years ago, Yugoslavia was already one of the most expensive countries in Eastern Europe. Since then accommodation prices have doubled in hard-currency terms. The government has levied high taxes on private rooms to make them less competitive with the government-owned hotels, and earns a tidy profit in the process.

Along the coast, accommodation is priced according to three seasons which vary from place to place. In July and August count on paying at least 50% more than the prices listed in this book. Prices for rooms in the interior regions are more constant. Add US$1 to US$2 per person per night 'residence tax' to all official accommodation rates. Yugoslavs get a 65% discount, which explains why all those expensive hotels were full.

## Camping

There are about 150 camping grounds in Yugoslavia, half of them along the coast. Tourist information offices can supply a complete list. Most operate from mid-May to September only, although a few are open in April and October. In May and late September check carefully to make sure the camping ground really is open before beginning the long trek out. Don't go by the opening and closing dates you read in travel brochures or this book, as these are only approximate. Even local tourist offices can be wrong.

Many camping grounds are expensive for backpackers because the prices are set in dollars or DM per person with no extra charge per tent, caravan, car, electric hook-up, etc. This is fine for people with mobile homes who occupy a large area but bad news for those with only a small tent. If you don't have a vehicle you're better off at camping grounds which have a much smaller fee per person and charge extra per tent, automobile, caravan, electric hook-up, etc. These prices are given in the official 'Camping' brochure.

Germans are the largest users of Yugoslav camping grounds. Unfortunately many of these are gigantic 'autocamps' with restaurants, shops and row upon row of caravans. Nudist camping grounds (marked FKK) are among the best because their secluded locations ensure peace and quiet. Freelance camping is officially prohibited everywhere.

## Youth Hostels

The Ferijalni savez Jugoslavije operates a couple of dozen IYHF youth hostels around the country. They're sometimes referred to as the 'mladost' or 'omladinski' hotel. Some are overpriced, others close during the winter and most are inconveniently located. There's usually a midnight curfew. Overnight charges range from US$8 to US$18. Although the hostels are open to anyone, persons under age 27 get priority. A Youth Hostel Association membership card is not necessary, although it does get you a lower rate.

The most convenient hostels are those in Bled, Sarajevo, Skopje and Zagreb, all of which are open throughout the year. Useful summer hostels include those in Dubrovnik, Korcula, Ohrid and Zadar. The Belgrade hostel is far from the centre, unfriendly, overcrowded and overpriced, but there if you need it. Some hostels have double rooms as well as the usual dormitories. In May and June the hostels can be crowded with local school groups and in midsummer all could be full. None are luxurious.

In July and August you can often rent vacant rooms in student dormitories. Ask tourist information offices about this, although these places are often as expensive as regular hotels.

## Private Rooms

The best accommodation in Yugoslavia is private rooms in local homes, the Yugoslav equivalent of small private guesthouses in other countries. Such rooms can be arranged by travel agencies but they add a lot of taxes to your bill, so you'll almost always do better dealing directly with proprietors you meet on the street or by knocking on the doors of houses with *sobe* or *zimmer* signs. This way you avoid the residence tax and four-night minimum stay, but forego the agency's quality control. The householder gets off without paying a commission to the agency and 30% tax on the income. Hang around coastal bus stations and ferry terminals, luggage in hand, looking lost, and someone will find you.

Except at the busiest times of midsummer you're fairly certain of being approached by women renting private rooms in Zadar, Split and Dubrovnik. When things are slow you'll also be approached in Rab, Korčula and Hvar. Elsewhere you may have to work through a travel agency or look for *sobe* signs, though in many interior towns no private rooms are available at all.

If the price asked is too high, bargain. Be sure to clarify whether the price agreed upon is per person or for the room. At the agencies, singles are expensive and hard to find, but on the street *sobe* prices are usually per person which favours the single traveller. Showers are always included. Although renting an unofficial room is common practice along the Adriatic coast, be discreet as technically you're breaking the law by not registering with the police. Don't brag to travel agencies about the low rate you got, for example.

Private rooms usually work out cheaper in the tourist resorts along the coast than in the interior where there isn't much competition and you're forced to work through an agency, some of which levy a US$3 booking fee. If you stay less than four nights the agencies add a 30% to 50% surcharge (see the Costs section in this chapter, for a way of coping with this problem). Travel agencies classify the rooms according to categories I, II or III. If you want the cheapest room always ask for category III. In the resort areas many category I rooms have cooking facilities, and private apartments are available.

Some rooms are excellent, other times the landlord is coming in every half-hour with only a brief knock on the door. Generally, what you pay for a private room won't be much more than camping or youth hostel charges. Also, in a country where people are often indifferent to foreigners, staying in a private room is a way of meeting a local family.

### Hotels

There are no cheap hotels in Yugoslavia. Very few cost less than US$40 double, even in the off season. Still, if you're only staying one night and the private room agency is going to levy a 50% surcharge you might consider getting a hotel room. In the off season when most rooms are empty you could try bargaining for a more realistic rate.

The staff at many of the state-run hotels have a couldn't-care-less attitude and just laugh at complaints. Maintenance isn't their concern and the level of service is often geared towards mass tours, not the individual who has to pay a lot more.

Most hotels include breakfast in the room price. This may consist of one cup of tea from the pot, two miserable pieces of bread and a bit of butter and jam, though some large beach hotels offer a good buffet breakfast.

### FOOD

Self-service cafeterias are quick, easy and inexpensive though the quality of the food varies. If the samples behind glass look cold or dried out, ask them to dish out a fresh plate for you. Better restaurants aren't that much more expensive if you choose carefully. In most the vegetables, salads and bread are charged extra and some deluxe restaurants add a 10% service charge to the menu prices (not mentioned on the menu). The fish dishes are often charged by weight which makes it difficult to know how much a certain dish will cost. Always check the menu and if the price of the drinks or something else isn't listed, ask. Ice cream cones are priced by the scoop.

Breakfast is difficult in Yugoslavia as all you can get easily is coffee. For eggs, toast and jam you'll have to go somewhere expensive, otherwise buy some bread, cheese and milk at a supermarket and picnic somewhere. The cheapest breakfast is Bosnian *burek*, a greasy layered pie made with cheese *(sir)* or meat *(meso)* available everywhere (US$1). *Krompirusa* is potato burek. A load of fruit and vegetables from the local market can go to make a healthy, cheap picnic lunch. There are plenty of supermarkets in Yugoslavia – cheese and milk are readily available and fairly cheap. Soup is sold in packets if you have access to a kitchen.

Food is cheaper in the interior than along the coast or in the north. National meat dishes can be very cheap in the Turkish-influenced areas. Though food *is* expensive you'll sometimes be served excellent meals at the better restaurants along the coast.

### Regional Dishes

Yugoslavia's regional cuisines reflect many

influences, including Austrian strudel in Slovenia, Italian pizza and pasta in Istria and Dalmatia, spicy Hungarian goulash in Vojvodina, and Turkish kebab in Bosnia, Serbia, Kosovo and Macedonia. Pizza is a good option everywhere along the coast, costing about half what you'd pay in Western Europe.

In Slovenia you'll taste the Germanic flavour in the sausages with sauerkraut, game dishes and meats with mushrooms. The Adriatic coast of Croatia excels in seafoods from sea fish to scampi (prawns), *prstaci* (shellfish) and Dalmatian *brodet* (mixed fish stewed with rice), all cooked in olive oil and served with boiled vegetables or *tartufe* (mushrooms) in Istria. In the Croatian interior watch for *manistra od bobića* (beans and fresh maize soup). A speciality of Vojvodina is *alaska čorba* (fiery river fish stew). In Montenegro try the pastoral fare such as boiled lamb or *kajmak* (cream from boiled milk, salted and turned into cheese).

Bosnia's Oriental background is savoured in its grilled meats, *bosanski lonac* (Bosnian stew of cabbage and meat), *baklava* (a Turkish sweet) and the ubiquitous *burek*. Serbia is famous for grilled meats such as *ćevapčići* (small patties of spiced, minced meat, grilled), *pljeskavica* (a large spicy hamburg steak) and *ražnjići* (a shish kebab of chunks of pork or veal with onions and peppers grilled on a skewer). If you want to try them all at once order a *mešano meso* (a mixed grill of pork cutlet, liver, sausage and minced meat patties with onions). Serbian *đuveč* is grilled pork cutlets with spiced stewed peppers, zucchinis and tomatoes in rice, cooked in an oven – delicious. Macedonia offers *gravče na tavče* (beans in a skillet) and Ohrid trout.

Other popular dishes are *musaka* (eggplant and potato baked in layers with minced meat), *sarma* (cabbage stuffed with minced meat and rice), *kapama* (stewed lamb, onions and spinach served with yoghurt), *punjena tikvica* (zucchini stuffed with minced meat and rice) and stuffed peppers (peppers stuffed with minced meat, rice and spices, cooked in tomato sauce).

Most traditional Yugoslav dishes are based on meat so vegetarians will have problems, although every restaurant menu will include a Serbian salad (*Srpska salata*) of raw peppers, onions and tomatoes, seasoned with oil, vinegar and chilli. Also ask for *gibanica* (a layered cheese pie) and *zeljanica* (cheese pie with spinach).

## DRINKS

It is customary to have a small glass of brandy before a meal, and to accompany the food with one of Yugoslavia's fine wines – red with the meat dishes, white with fish. Ask for the local, regional wine. Beer is always available – Nikšićko Pivo from Nikšić in Montenegro is imbibed all along the southern Adriatic coast. Yugoslavia is also famous for its plum brandies (*šljivovica*), herbal brandies (*travarica*), cognacs (*vinjak*) and liqueurs. Beer and liquor purchased at supermarkets are cheap. Italian-style espresso coffee (infused by a machine) is popular in the north-west while in the south-east you'll receive Turkish coffee (boiled in a small individual pot). Both are excellent and not expensive.

## ENTERTAINMENT

Culture was heavily subsidised by the Communists and admission to operas, operettas and concerts is still reasonable. The main theatres offering musical programmes are listed herein, so note the location and drop by some time during the day to check what's on and purchase tickets. Ask municipal tourist offices for a list of cultural events in their area. In the interior cities winter is the best time to enjoy the theatres and concert halls. These close for holidays in summer and the cultural scene shifts to the many summer festivals.

Discos operate in summer in the coastal resorts and all year in the interior cities. If you're male you'll find the local women aren't interested in meeting you, if you're female you'll find the local men are too interested in meeting you, so it's always a good idea to go accompanied. It doesn't cost anything at all to participate in the early evening *korzo*, a casual promenade enjoyed by great crowds in the town centres.

## Cinemas

The cheapest entertainment in Yugoslavia is a movie. Admissions are always low and the soundtracks in the original language. American sex-and-violence films are the standard fare, however, and the last film of the day is usually hard-core pornography. Check the time on your ticket carefully as admission is not allowed once the film has started.

## THINGS TO BUY

Among the traditional handicraft products of Yugoslavia are fine lace from the Dalmatian islands, hand-made embroidery, woodcarvings, woollen and leather items, Serbian knitware, carpets, filigree jewellery, ceramics, national costumes and tapestries. At regular department stores, clothing, footwear and most consumer goods are expensive and poor quality.

# Getting There & Away

## AIR

JAT Yugoslav Airlines operates direct flights to Belgrade from Algiers, Amman, Baghdad, Bangkok, Cairo, Chicago, Damascus, Dubai, Istanbul, Kuala Lumpur, Kuwait, Los Angeles, Malta, Melbourne, Montreal, New York, Singapore, Sydney, Toronto, Tripoli, Tunis and many European cities. To Zagreb there are direct JAT flights from Algiers, Cairo, Chicago, Istanbul, Los Angeles, Montreal, New York and Toronto.

Normal economy fares are expensive but there are excursion fare discounts up to 60% linked to advance purchase requirements, minimum/maximum stay, cancellation penalties, age limits and other restrictions. Bucket shops in Europe and Asia often sell unrestricted JAT tickets at deep discounts. For example, Amsterdam to Singapore with a free stop in Belgrade will be around US$600 one-way, US$1000 return trip, from budget travel agencies in Amsterdam,

Bangkok, Penang and Singapore. You must work through a travel agency specialising in discount airfares – JAT offices are required to charge full fare. From Britain check for cheap charter flights to Yugoslavia, and always ask about youth or student fares if you're eligible.

## Departure Tax

The airport departure tax on international flights is US$7 (US$3.50 on domestic flights).

## LAND

### Bus

From Italy there are 17 buses a day from Trieste to Koper (20 km, US$3). From Hungary you can catch a bus from Zalaegerszeg to Ljubljana twice a week (322 km, US$11), from Barcs to Zagreb four times a day (161 km, US$11), from Pécs to Osijek twice a day (98 km, US$3) and from Szeged to Subotica several times a day (46 km, US$2). From Bulgaria there's service daily except Sunday from Sofia to Skopje (216 km, US$8).

From Germany the buses of the Deutsche Touring GmbH are much cheaper than the train. Buses to Yugoslavia depart Berlin, Cologne, Dortmund, Frankfurt/Main, Mannheim, Munich, Nuremberg and Stuttgart. Baggage is DM 3 extra per piece. Service is usually only once or twice a week, but they operate all year. Information is available at bus stations in the above cities.

From Holland Budget Bus, Rokin 10, Amsterdam, offers service two or three times a week all year to Zagreb (US$95 one-way, US$165 return trip, 22 hours). Europabus operates a similar weekly service all year from Antwerp, Belgium, to Zagreb. On all of the Dutch and Belgian services you must change buses at Munich where you will be charged DM 3 per piece for luggage. Excessive luggage is DM 50 and on return services an advance reservation is recommended (US$3). This is still much cheaper than the train which is US$150 one-way 2nd class from Amsterdam to Ljubljana.

From Britain the cheapest way to Yugoslavia is on one of the transcontinental buses headed for Greece, as advertised in the weekly London entertainment magazines. These buses aren't supposed to accept passengers bound only for Yugoslavia. Of course they all will, but you could end up being dumped at a crossroads far from prying eyes in the town centres. The 48-hour journey and food costs are other disadvantages.

### Train

There are countless ways to come to Yugoslavia by train. Only buy a ticket as far as your first stop in Yugoslavia as domestic fares are much cheaper than international fares. Consider breaking your journey in Ljubljana or Skopje for this purpose alone. The same applies if you're going north through Hungary to a point beyond Budapest (to Prague or Warsaw, for example). It's much cheaper to buy a ticket only as far as Budapest, then another there. A student card will get you a reduction on railway fares from Yugoslavia to other Eastern European countries. Railway fares in Italy are also cheap, so if you can get across the Italian border from France or Switzerland it won't cost too much to take a train on to Trieste.

All of the international 'name trains' mentioned in this section run daily all year unless otherwise stated.

**To/From Italy & Austria** International express trains between Munich and Belgrade (1087 km via Villach) are fairly frequent, often continuing to Istanbul (via Sofia) or Athens. The Jugoslavija Express runs from Dortmund, Germany, to Belgrade via Frankfurt/Main, Stuttgart, Munich, Salzburg, Villach and Ljubljana. The Mostar-Dalmacija Express goes from Stuttgart to Kardeljevo via Munich, Salzburg, Ljubljana and Zagreb. The Zürich-Beograd Express is from Zürich to Belgrade via Villach.

The Ljubljana Express from Vienna to Rijeka (nine hours, 615 km) via Ljubljana, the Croatia Express from Graz to Zagreb (four hours, 258 km) and the Slavija Express from Vienna to Belgrade (13 hours, 888 km) and Athens all travel via Maribor.

The Simplon Express from Paris to Belgrade goes via Venice, Trieste, Ljubljana and Zagreb. From Venice there's also the Venezia Express to Athens via Ljubljana, Zagreb, Belgrade and Skopje.

**To/From Hungary** The Avala Express from Prague and the Polonia Express from Warsaw both run from Budapest to Belgrade (six hours, 354 km). The Meridian Express from Berlin passes Budapest-Keleti, Subotica, Novi Sad and Belgrade on its way to Sofia.

To go from Budapest to Zagreb via Siofok (seven hours, 412 km) you have a choice of the Drava Express bound for Rome or the Maestral Express to Split. From mid-June to August the Adriatica Express runs from Budapest-Deli to Rijeka (618 km).

Aside from these international expresses there are unreserved local trains between Gyékényes and Koprivnica, Pecs and Osijek (two hours, 82 km) and Szeged and Subotica (46 km, US$3), all two or three times a day.

**To/From Romania & Bulgaria** From Romania the overnight Bucureşti Express runs between Bucharest and Belgrade-Dunav (13 hours, 693 km) via Timişoara. Aside from this there's an unreserved local train from Jimbolia, Romania, to Kikinda, Yugoslavia, twice a day. From Kikinda there are four local trains a day to Belgrade-Dunav (3½ hours, 161 km).

The most reliable service to/from Bulgaria is the Meridian Express from Sofia to Berlin via Niš, Belgrade, Novi Sad and Budapest. If bound for Bulgaria you can easily board this overnight train in Novi Sad. Southbound reservations are not required, but only buy a ticket as far as the border station, Dimitrovgrad, and pay the Bulgarian conductor a couple of dollars for a ticket on to Sofia once inside Bulgaria.

There's also the Istanbul Express between Istanbul and Munich via Sofia, Belgrade, Zagreb, Ljubljana and Salzburg.

**To/From Greece** The southern main line between Belgrade and Athens (1267 km) is through Skopje and Thessaloniki. On this route you'll find the Venezia Express from Venice, the Attika/Hellas Express from Munich and the Akropolis Express also from Munich. You could also take a local train to the border station, Gevgelija, and change there.

For the slightly adventurous there's a local line with one train a day which takes all afternoon to cover the 39 km between Bitola, Yugoslavia, and Florina, Greece, with a change at Kremenica.

### Car & Motorbike

Here's a list of the main highway entry/exit points clockwise around Yugoslavia with the Yugoslav border post named. To/from Italy there's Škofije (between Trieste and Koper), Kozina (between Trieste and Rijeka), Fernetiči/Sežana (between Trieste and Ljubljana), Rožna dolina (between Gorizia and Nova Gorica), Robič (32 km north-east of Udine), Predel (13 km south of Tarvisio) and Rateče (12 km east of Tarvisio).

To/from Austria there's Korensko sedlo (20 km south-west of Villach), Ljubelj (between Klagenfurt and Kranj), Jezersko (35 km north-east of Kranj), Vič (between Klagenfurt and Maribor), Šentilj (17 km north of Maribor) and Gornja Radgona (41 km north-east of Maribor).

To/from Hungary there's Hodoš (west of Zalaegerszeg), Lendava (eight km south-west of Lenti), Goričan (between Nagykanizsa and Varazdin), Gola (23 km west of Koprivnica), Terezino Polje (opposite Barcs), Donji Miholjac (eight km south of Harkany), Kreževo (48 km north of Osijek), Bački Breg (32 km south of Baja), Kelebija (11 km north-west of Subotica) and Horgoš (between Szeged and Subotica).

To/from Romania you may cross at Sprska Crnja (45 km west of Timişoara), Vatin (between Timişoara and Belgrade), Kaluđerovo (120 km east of Belgrade) and Kladovo (10 km west of Drobeta-Turnu Severin).

To/from Bulgaria you have a choice of Negotin (29 km north-west of Vidin), Zaječar (45 km south-west of Vidin), Gradina (at Dimitrovgrad between Sofia and Niš), Klisura (66 km west of Pernik), Kriva Palanka (between Sofia and Skopje), Delčevo (26 km west of Blagoevgrad) and Novo Selo (37 km west of Kulata).

To/from Greece there's only Gevgelija (between Skopje and Thessaloniki) and Medžitlija (16 km south of Bitola).

To/from Albania you can try Ćafa San (16 km south-west of Struga), Vrbnica (18 km south-west of Prizren) and Božaj (24 km south-east of Titograd).

## SEA

### Ferries

Three companies offer ferry service to Yugoslavia. The Greek Strintzis Lines and the Yugoslav line Jadrolinija serve both Italy and Greece while the Italian company Adriatica Navigazione specialises in service to/from Italy.

International ferry tickets purchased in Yugoslavia must be paid in foreign currency and are more expensive than the same tickets purchased abroad. There are no student discounts on Jadrolinija ferries, while Adriatica gives students up to age 30 and everyone under 26 a 20% discount. Compare prices as Jadrolinija tickets may still be cheaper. Tickets for local ferry services are 50% cheaper when purchased abroad in conjunction with an international ticket!

Throughout Yugoslavia, when asking about ferry times beware of ticket agents who give incomplete or misleading information about departures. Study the posted Serbo-Croatian timetable carefully, *then* ask your questions.

**To/From Italy** Adriatica Navigazione car ferries cross the sea all year between most large Italian ports (Trieste, Venice, Ancona, Pescara, Bari) and Zadar, Split and Dubrovnik. Any travel agent will have times, frequencies and tickets. Fares range from US$41 to US$53 one-way and bicycles are carried free.

From mid-June to September Jadrolinija car ferries sail weekly from Venice to

Dubrovnik (20 hours, US$34), twice weekly from Venice to Split (13 hours, US$26). From June to September there's a Jadrolinija ferry several times a week between Ancona and Split (eight hours, US$26). Ancona to Zadar (6½ hours, US$23) is almost daily in July and August, four times a week in June and September. Dubrovnik-Bari (seven hours, US$26) is weekly from mid-June to mid-September.

All of the above deck fares are 25% to 50% higher in the peak season which is mid-July to mid-August eastbound, August to mid-September westbound.

**To/From Istria** One of the nicest ways to come is on the motor ship *Dionea*, a small Adriatica Navigazione passenger boat. Fares are low because Rome subsidises the service as a way of showing the flag up and down the formerly Italian Istrian coast. The *Dionea* departs from a wharf in central Trieste for Izola, Piran, Poreč, Rovinj and Pula at 8 am daily except Wednesday in summer. There are two sailings weekly in October and November, four weekly in May and six a week from June to mid-September.

Fares from Trieste on the *Dionea* run US$14 to Poreč or Rovinj, US$18 to Pula (4½ hours). If you're going from Yugoslavia towards Trieste it's less. In Trieste the agent is Adriatica di Navigazione, Piazza Duca degli Abruzzi 1/A. Since this is an Italian boat, Yugoslav travel agencies in Istria are sometimes reluctant to volunteer information about it and don't sell tickets. If the tourist office can't or won't tell you the schedule try asking at the local port captain's office. On our city maps of Istria we mark the pier where the *Dionea* ties up as the 'Custom's wharf' and you'll usually find the port captain somewhere around there. This service cannot be used for travel between two Yugoslav ports, only from Trieste to Istria or vice versa. In Yugoslavia you buy your ticket once aboard.

**To/From Greece** From April to mid-October Jadrolinija runs a weekly car ferry service from Corfu to Rijeka via Dubrovnik,

Korčula, Hvar, Split, Zadar and Rab. In July and August the boat runs twice a week and from mid-May to September the same ferry also calls at Patras (same fare). From Corfu to Dubrovnik is 15 hours.

In Greece a ticket from Corfu, Igoumenitsa or Patras to Dubrovnik, Korčula, Hvar or Split costs US$35 one-way deck plus US$6 port tax. A through ticket to Zadar or Rijeka is only about US$4 more (deck class). In Yugoslavia exactly the same ticket costs almost double so buy a through ticket before arriving in Yugoslavia! All fares are 25% higher during the peak season which is usually in July southbound and in August northbound. In Corfu ferry tickets to Yugoslavia are sold by Mancan Travel near the port.

When buying a Jadrolinija ticket from Greece to Yugoslavia, always ask for a ticket to Split which costs the same as Dubrovnik, Korčula or Hvar. The purser on board will stamp your ticket to permit free stopovers at intermediate points. After having the ticket so validated you can get off at any of the ports along the way and reboard a later schedule without having to buy another ticket (be sure to have the ticket stamped each time you want to get off). With a ticket to Rijeka (only about US$4 more) you can also get free stops at Zadar and Rab.

Deck passage is just that: airline-type seats are about US$8 extra and a cabin (if available) will be US$25 per person. Cabins can be arranged at the reservation counter aboard ship, but advance bookings are recommended if you want to be sure of a place (probably cheaper too). Deck is fine for passages during daylight hours and when you can stretch out a sleeping bag on the upper deck in good weather, but if it's rainy you could end up sitting in the smoky cafeteria which stays open all night. During the crowded midsummer season, deck class can be unpleasant in wet weather.

Large Greek car ferries of the Strintzis Lines also operate twice a week between Patras, Corfu and Dubrovnik from mid-June to September, sometimes carrying on to Ancona.

## PACKAGE TOURS

Companies like Yugotours offer cheap packaged holidays to beach hotels up and down the coast. Often the price isn't much more than a return plane or train ticket to Yugoslavia, and for Northern Europeans with only a week or two off work it's excellent value. If booked on a last-minute basis, packages from Britain to Yugoslavia are as low as £120 for a week at the beach with two meals a day, deluxe hotel and flight included. If you come as an individual you won't even get a basic hotel room for that!

More exciting are the sea kayaking, canoeing, bicycling and white-water rafting tours offered weekly by Atlas Tours from mid-May to mid-October. The one-week trips include kayaking in Kornati National Park, canoeing in Plitvice or Krka national parks, cycling in Triglav National Park and rafting in Durmitor National Park, all around US$500 per person (excluding airfare). Travel agents in North America book through Atlas Ambassador of Dubrovnik, 60 East 42nd St, New York, NY 10165 (☎ 212-697 6767). Elsewhere enquire at a Yugoslav National Tourist Office.

Keep in mind that tips are never included in package tours to Yugoslavia and that guides, drivers and other personnel will expect to be tipped.

# Getting Around

## AIR

Domestic airfares within Yugoslavia used to be cheap, but since the Yugoslav government ordered the airlines to charge foreigners 50% more than Yugoslavs for the same tickets they're no longer a good deal. Current fares for nonresidents on Yugoslav Airlines (JAT) are Pula-Zadar US$31, Belgrade-Dubrovnik US$65, Split-Skopje US$85 and Ohrid-Ljubljana US$141. A student card could get you a 10% discount. Only 15 kg of checked baggage is allowed on domestic flights. Some flights only operate once or twice a week, so check well in advance. In summer all flights are heavily booked. JAT runs inexpensive buses to the airports from city centres.

Adria Airways also operates many routes within Yugoslavia, including such unusual runs as Zagreb-Mali Lošinj (US$25). Especially useful are its direct flights between the Adriatic coast and Macedonia, which is badly covered by road and rail. Examples are Split-Skopje (US$68), Skopje-Pula (US$100), Skopje-Sarajevo (US$48), Skopje-Titograd (US$31) and Skopje-Dubrovnik (US$46). Adria also has many flights to and from main resort cities such as Split (to Sarajevo, Belgrade, Ljubljana and Osijek) and Dubrovnik (to Belgrade, Osijek and Ljubljana). Some flights only operate during the peak summer season, however. Since JAT and Adria compete on many routes, check both to determine which is more convenient before booking.

## BUS

Bus service in Yugoslavia is excellent. Fast express buses go everywhere, often many times a day. Along the Adriatic coast they are the main means of transport. They'll stop to pick up passengers at designated stops anywhere along their route. Buses charge about US$2 for each hour of travel and you can expect to cover about 40 km in that time. Checked luggage is extra, around US$0.50 to US$1 a piece which includes insurance. If your bag is small carry it onto the bus.

Bus tickets must be purchased at the office, not from drivers, and try to book ahead to be sure of a seat. Lists of departures over the various windows at the bus stations tell you which one has tickets for your bus. Your ticket will only be valid on buses of the issuing company and only for the departure specified on the ticket. If you miss your bus it's unlikely you'll get a refund, but without an advance ticket you'll only be allowed on if there happen to be vacant seats. The front seats on buses are often reserved for invalids.

In some places like Dubrovnik where supply doesn't always meet demand, trying to catch a bus can be quite an experience! Always check for overnight buses which get you where you're going for what you'd have to pay for a room anyway. Don't expect to get much sleep, however, as the inside lights will be on and music blasting the whole night. Take care not to be left behind at meal or rest stops and beware of buses leaving 10 minutes early.

## TRAIN

Railway service along the interior main line Ljubljana-Zagreb-Belgrade-Skopje is adequate and there are branch lines down to the coast at Split (from Zagreb), Kardeljevo (via Sarajevo) and Bar (from Belgrade). Some of the routes through the mountains are highly scenic, especially Jesenice to Nova Gorica, Sarajevo to Mostar and Kolašin to Bar. There are four classes of trains: *ekspresni* (express), *poslovni* (rapid), *brzi* (fast) and *putnicki* (slow). Make sure you have the right sort of ticket for your train.

The train is cheaper than the bus and you don't have to pay for luggage, though some of the express trains carry only 1st-class seats. It's usually only possible to make seat reservations in the originating station of the train, unless reservations are mandatory, in which case try to book the day before. Most trains have 'no smoking' compartments, though you'd hardly know it from all the locals you see puffing away in there. Interrail passes are valid in Yugoslavia, but not Eurail.

On posted timetables in Croatia the word for arrivals is *dolazak,* for departures it's *odlazak* or *polazak*; in Slovenia it's *prihodi* for arrivals, *odhodi* for departures. All railway stations (except in Kosovo) have left-luggage offices where you can dump your bag for about US$1. These are often more cooperative and open longer hours than the cloakrooms in bus stations, so use the railway facility if the bus and train stations are adjacent.

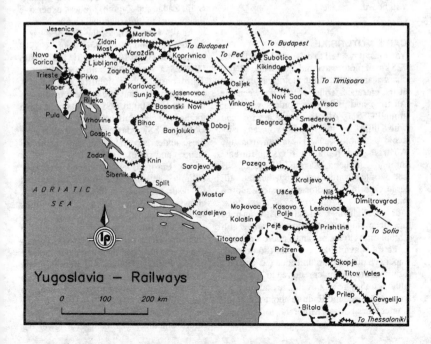

## Overnight Trains

Among the best travel bargains in Yugoslavia are 2nd-class couchettes, costing only about US$6 (2nd-class sleepers are US$12). If the clerk says flatly that no couchettes are available ask for a 2nd-class sleeper. Nearly all overnight trains to Belgrade carry couchettes, as do trains from Ljubljana to Bitola via Skopje. You arrive in the early morning and have the day to look around before taking another couchette on to somewhere else.

Couchettes are surprisingly easy to book in the originating city of the train. This is usually done at a specific travel agency rather than in the station itself. Staff at the information counter in the station will tell you where to go. Buying a ticket for couchette on the train itself is problematic as the attendants may claim everything's full until you offer a tip. Remember that even with a couchette or sleeper ticket you must also buy a train ticket in the station where you board.

## CAR & MOTORBIKE

You must pay a toll to drive on Yugoslavia's 725 km of motorways and it's not cheap. Toll charges are posted at the motorway exit, not at the entrance. Tolls to drive between the Austrian and Bulgarian borders will total around US$50. All other roads are free and with a little time and planning you can easily avoid the motorways. These run from the Austrian and Italian borders south-east through Ljubljana, Zagreb, Belgrade, Niš and Skopje towards Greece, but there are still large gaps in the motorway system and no motorways along the coast. The spectacular Adriatic Highway from Italy to Albania hugs the steep slopes of the coastal range with abrupt drops to the sea and a curve a minute.

Petrol is available in regular (86 octane), super (98 octane) and unleaded (95 octane). Coupons are no longer required to buy petrol although they're still available and may get you a 5% discount. Enquire about this at the border tourist office. Motorway toll coupons are also sold.

## Road Rules

The speed limits for cars and motorcycles are 60 km/h in built-up areas, 80 km/h on the open road, 100 km/h on main highways and 120 km/h on motorways. The police systematically fine motorists exceeding these limits and even confiscate driver's licences for serious offences. It's illegal to pass a whole line of cars caught behind a slow-moving truck or any military convoys on any of Yugoslavia's winding, two-lane highways. Passing is always prohibited on stretches signposted *Crna Tacka*. Drive defensively as local motorists lack discipline.

## Rental

The large car rental chains are represented in Yugoslavia by travel agencies such as Unis Tours (Europcar), Emona Globtour (Budget) and Kompas (Hertz), with Europcar the cheapest and Hertz the most expensive. Local companies such as Dubrovnik Rent-a-Car (offices in Belgrade, Dubrovnik, Opatija, Split, Zadar and Zagreb) are less expensive than any of the international chains.

At all of the agencies the cheapest car is the Renault 4 and prices begin around US$19 a day plus US$0.19 per km or US$200 to US$325 a week with unlimited mileage. Third party public liability insurance is included by law but you are responsible for the first US$500 to US$2000 damage done to the vehicle. Full collision insurance is US$5 to US$7 a day extra (compulsory for those under age 23). Add 15% tax to all charges and petrol is additional.

Ask Europcar about special three-day unlimited mileage rates including tax and full insurance. Budget offers one-way rentals allowing you to drop the car off at any of its stations in Yugoslavia free of charge.

The age limits vary from company to company. Hertz will rent to persons 18 years of age who have had their licence for at least a year while at Budget and Europcar you have to be 21. At Dubrovnik Rent-a-Car you must be 23 and have had your licence two years. A deposit of US$150 to US$250 must be posted unless you're paying by credit card. Sometimes you can get a lower car rental rate by booking your car from abroad. Tour companies in Britain and Western Europe often have fly-drive packages which include a flight to Yugoslavia and a car (two-person minimum).

One of the nicest parts of Yugoslavia to tour by rental car is Montenegro with a tremendous variety of attractions packed into a small area. The scenery is superb, the roads good and there's very little traffic. The best place to rent a car for a trip around Montenegro is Dubrovnik where all the car rental companies have offices.

## HITCHHIKING
The hitchhiking in Yugoslavia is lousy. There are lots of little cars but they're usually full and the local motorists are not noted for their courtesy. Tourists never stop. Unfortunately the image many Yugoslavs have of this activity is based on violent movies like *Hitchhiker*.

## BOAT
From April to mid-October big white Jadrolinija car ferries, each with a red star on the funnel, operate almost daily along the coastal route Rijeka-Rab-Zadar-Split-Hvar-Stari Grad-Korčula-Dubrovnik, with some continuing on to Greece. The most scenic section is Split to Dubrovnik, which all of the ferries cover during the day. Rijeka to Split (12½ hours, US$27 deck) is usually an overnight trip in either direction.

The ferries are a lot more comfortable than the buses, if several times more expensive. Fares are slightly higher from mid-June to September. Kvarner Express is the agent for these ferries, so enquire about departure times and prices at any of its offices throughout Yugoslavia. With a through ticket you can stop over at any port for up to a week, provided you notify the purser beforehand and have your ticket validated. This is much cheaper than buying individual tickets. About 25% cheaper again is to buy a through ticket from Rijeka to Dubrovnik or Greece at a travel agency outside Yugoslavia.

Meals in the restaurant aboard ship are about US$8 for lunch or dinner (drinks extra)

and all the cafeteria offers are ham and cheese sandwiches for US$1. Coffee is cheap in the cafeteria but wine and hard drinks tend to be expensive. Breakfast in the restaurant is good value at US$2 with bread, butter, jam, one hard boiled egg and a bottomless cup of coffee. It's best to bring some food and drink along with you.

## Local Ferries
A ferry connection between Pula and Zadar via Mali Lošinj operates six times a week from mid-June to mid-September, weekly the rest of the year, except February when there's no service.

Other local ferries connect the main offshore islands to the mainland. The most important of these are Brestova to Porozine on Cres Island (all year), Baška on Krk Island to Lopar on Rab Island (June to September), Jablanac to Mišnjak on Rab Island (all year), Zadar to Preko (all year), Split to Supetar on Brač Island (all year), Split to Stari Grad and Vira on Hvar Island (all year), Drvenik to Sućuraj on Hvar Island (all year), Split to Vela Luka on Korčula Island via Hvar (all year), Kardeljevo to Trpanj (all year), Orebic to Korčula Island (all year) and Dubrovnik to Polače on Mljet Island (all year). In the off season service is greatly reduced, so check.

To take a bicycle on these services is an extra fare. Some of the ferries operate only a couple of times a day, and once the vehicular capacity is reached, remaining motorists must wait for the next service. In summer the lines of waiting cars can be long so it's important to arrive early. Foot passengers and cyclists should have no problem getting on.

## LOCAL TRANSPORT
Public transport strip tickets or tokens are available from newsstands. If you pay a city bus or tram driver directly it will be about double fare. On city buses inspectors regularly control tickets.

### Taxi
Taxi fares are average, but make sure the meter is turned on.

# Slovenia

Slovenia (20,251 sq km) is clearly a transitional zone between Eastern and Western Europe. The cities bear the imprint of the Italian Counter-Reformation, while up in the Julian Alps you can feel the proximity of Austria. Slovenia was under Germanic rule from 743 to 1918, first as part of the Holy Roman Empire, then under the Habsburgs, yet the Slovene inhabitants of this northernmost region retained their Slavonic identity. The Slovene language diverged from Serbo-Croatian in the 8th century, and although the Bible was translated into Slovene during the Reformation, only in the 19th century did it come into common use as a written language.

The two million Slovenes of today have the highest standard of living in Yugoslavia. You sense the richness in the well-wooded slopes, fertile valleys and scenic rivers on this sunny side of the Alps. Mass tourism is exploited in resorts like Bled, Koper, Portorož and Piran, and foreign motorists jam the highways, yet the rugged Alps and vibrant Ljubljana retain their appeal. For convenience we've included the Slovene Riviera with our section on Croatian Istria. If you're arriving from Italy or Austria, Slovenia will be your gateway to Yugoslavia.

## LJUBLJANA

Foggy Ljubljana (Laibach), capital of Slovenia, is a pleasant small city a quarter the size of Zagreb, 135 km to the east. The most beautiful part is along the Ljubljanica River below the castle. Ljubljana began as the Roman town of Emona, and the Italian influence continued under the Catholic Habsburgs when many churches were built during the Counter-Reformation. From 1809 to 1814 Ljubljana was the capital of the 'Illyrian Provinces', a Napoleonic puppet state. Despite the Austrian imperial overtones, contemporary Ljubljana has a vibrant Slavonic air all its own. You can easily see the best of the city in a day – and don't worry, the fog usually clears up by mid-morning.

### Orientation

The bus and train stations are adjacent on the north side of town. Walk west a block or two to Titova cesta, a broad avenue which leads south into the centre. The old town and castle are south-east, just across the river.

■ PLACES TO STAY

34  Pension Pri Mraku

▼ PLACES TO EAT

11  Daj-Dam
14  Self-Service Restaurant
17  Pizzeria Parma
18  Maximarket
29  Pri Vitezu Restaurant

OTHER

1  Slovene Alpine Association
2  Slovenijatourist
3  Pošta Center
4  Bus Station
5  Railway Station
6  Serbian Orthodox Church
7  National Gallery
8  Modern Art Gallery
9  National Museum
10  Opera House
12  'Skyscraper'
13  Tourist Information Centre
15  Franciscan Church
16  Cultural and Congress Centre
19  Ursuline Church
20  University
21  Filharmonia
22  Municipal Gallery
23  Town Hall
24  Cathedral
25  Vegetable Market
26  Puppet Theatre
27  Castle
28  St James Church
30  Town Museum
31  Academy of Sciences
32  National Library
33  Ljubljana Festival Theatre
35  Roman City Wall

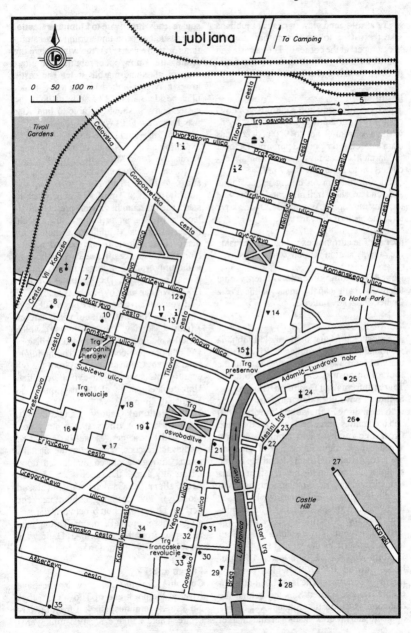

Ljubljana

For an all-round view of central Ljubljana take the lift up to the terrace bar atop the 'skyscraper' at the corner of Titova cesta and Kidričeva ulica (no admission fee, normal prices, closed Monday).

## Information
The Tourist Information Centre is at Titova cesta 11. From April to September it opens weekdays from 8 am to 9 pm, weekends 8 am to noon and 5 pm to 8 pm; from October to March it's weekdays 8 am to 7 pm, weekends 8 am to noon and 4 to 7 pm.

For information on hiking in the Julian Alps and excellent trail maps and guides visit the Slovene Alpine Association, Dvoržakova 9 (at the back of the yard).

**Money** The currency exchange office inside the railway station is open 24 hours a day.

**Post & Telecommunications** International telephone calls can be made at the Pošta Center, Pražakova ulica 3.

## Things to See
The most picturesque sights of old Ljubljana are found along the Ljubljanica River, a tributary of the Sava, which curves around the foot of imposing Castle Hill. From the Tourist Information Centre on Titova cesta, follow Copova ulica down to Prešernov trg with its inviting **Franciscan Church** (1660) and the famous 'three bridges' over the river. Cross one of these and continue straight ahead to the Baroque fountain (1751) in front of the **town hall** (1718) on Mestni trg. Italian sculptor Francesco Robba designed this fountain and numerous monumental altars in the city's churches. Enter the town hall to see the two courtyards, and then visit the **Municipal Gallery**, Mestni trg 5, which has changing exhibits. To the south of this is Stari trg, atmospheric by day or night.

North-west are the twin towers of **Ljubljana Cathedral** (1708) which contains impressive frescoes. The large open-air **vegetable market** (closed Sunday) behind the cathedral is colourful. Studentovska ulica opposite the Vodnik statue in the market square leads directly up to **Ljubljana Castle**. The castle has been undergoing reconstruction for many years, but the wing above the castle café is now open, rebuilt in an ultra-modern glass-and-marble style. The castle tower may be climbed for the view. Reber ulica beside Stari trg 17 also leads up to the castle, and you should be able to find your way back down this way.

There's a second interesting area worth exploring on the east side of the Ljubljanica River. The **Town Museum**, Gosposka ulica 15 (open Tuesday to Friday 10 am to 1 pm and 4 to 6 pm, Saturday 3 to 6 pm, and Sunday 10 am to 1 pm), is a good place to start. The museum has a well-presented collection of Roman artifacts, plus a scale model of Emona (Ljubljana) to help it all make sense. Upstairs are period rooms. North on Gosposka ulica at Trg osvoboditve is the **university** building, formerly the regional parliament. The **Ursuline Church** (1726) with an altar by Robba is nearby.

If you still have time, go east on Subiceva ulica to the **National Museum**, Trg herojev 1 (closed Monday, free on Saturday), which includes mediocre prehistory, natural history and ethnography collections. The highlight is an ancient Celtic situla (pot) from the 6th century BC sporting an evocative relief. Unfortunately none of the captions is in English or German.

The **National Gallery**, Cankarjeva 20 (closed Monday), offers 19th century portraits and landscapes, as well as copies of medieval frescoes. You enter the upstairs rooms through a closed, unmarked door. Diagonally across the street is the **Modern Art Gallery**, at Cankarjeva 15 (closed Monday), with changing exhibitions. The Serbian Orthodox church between the two art galleries is open afternoons. Through the underpass from the Modern Art Gallery are the relaxing **Tivoli Gardens**.

## Places to Stay
**Camping** *Camping Ježica* is by the Sava River at the north end of Titova cesta (bus No 8 to the terminus), six km from the city centre. There's a large, shady camping area

(US$5 per person, US$5 per tent) and new deluxe bungalows for those without tents (US$30/50 single/double). It's clean and quiet with hot water, a restaurant, currency exchange and some tourist information. This recommended site is open from mid-May to mid-September.

**Private Rooms** The Tourist Information Centre, Titova cesta 11 (hours listed in the information section), has private rooms for about US$10/18 single/double, but they aren't usually in the city centre and if you're staying too far outside town you won't be able to attend any of the wonderful theatrical presentations and concerts. During summer ask at the Tourist Information Centre about accommodation in vacant student dormitories.

**Hotels** The C-category *Hotel Park* (also known as 'Hotel Tabor'), Tabor 9 in a quiet residential area just east of the centre, offers 90 simple, functional rooms at US$22/35 single/double without bath, US$28/43 with bath, breakfast included.

The next-cheapest hotel is 30-room *Pension Pri Mraku*, Rimska cesta 4 to the south of the centre, with singles/doubles without bath from US$28/40.

The *Bellevue Hotel*, in an old yellow building above the north end of Tivoli Gardens with a terrace overlooking the city, used to be a good place to stay but in 1991 it closed for renovations and upgrading.

## Places to Eat

The *Samopostrezna Restauracija*, Mikloši-čeva cesta 10 at the back of the passage opposite the Holiday Inn, is a modern self-service restaurant open daily all year.

There's another self-service restaurant labelled 'Maximarket' downstairs in the shopping arcade on Trg revolucije. At the south end of the corridor from it is *Pizzeria Parma*, downstairs in the mall off Erjavčeva cesta. The pizza here is so good and cheap that you may have to stand around waiting for a seat (come at odd hours). It's open from

9 am to 9 pm, closed Sundays and has an English menu.

*Daj-Dam* (closed Sunday), around the corner from the tourist office at Cankarjeva cesta 4, offers a US$3 'menu' in the rear dining room.

The *Gostilna 'Pri Vitezu'*, 20 Breg facing the river, is slightly up-market but in summer you can eat on the pleasant pavement terrace. It offers many game dishes such as bear, turtle, deer and wild boar, and oddities you always wanted to try like pickled tongue, stuffed stomach, fried brains, etc. This is one of the few places open on Sunday (from 1 to 10 pm). A 10% service charge is added to the menu prices.

If you don't like the 'Pri Vitezu', check the nearby *Pizzeria Ljubljanski Dvor* on Dvorni trg facing the river just behind the Filharmonia.

## Entertainment

Ljubljana enjoys a rich cultural life, so ask the Tourist Information Centre for its monthly *Calendar of Events*. The ticket office of the neo-Rococo *Opera House* (1892), Zupančičeva ulica 1, opens weekdays from 11 am to 1 pm and an hour before the performance.

Ljubljana's ultramodern *Cultural & Congress Centre 'Cankarjev dom'* includes four theatres. The symphony orchestra often appears in the Big Hall. For tickets and information look for the office downstairs in the adjacent shopping mall (weekdays from 1 to 8 pm, Saturday 9 am to noon, and an hour before performances). Also check for concerts at the *Filharmonia* at Trg osvoboditve 9.

In summer, things happen in the *Ljubljana Festival Open Air Theatre* on Trg francoske revolucije opposite the Town Museum. The *Puppet Theatre* is at Krekov trg 2 near the vegetable market. In the evening check the bars and cafés on Prešernov trg and in the old town. It can get pretty lively.

## Things to Buy

The largest department store in town (with a

supermarket in the basement) is Maximarket on Trg revolucije.

## Getting There & Away

There are through trains to Trieste (165 km) and Venice. From Ljubljana to Koper (175 km) the train is cheaper, faster and more comfortable than a bus. To Rijeka (155 km), Zagreb (160 km) and Maribor (178 km) you're also better off by train. But be sure to take a bus if you're headed from Ljubljana to Bled or Bohinj in the Julian Alps, as Lesce-Bled Railway Station is far from the action.

There's a bus to Trieste, Italy, twice each morning (US$12). For Zalaegerszeg, Hungary, a bus (US$11) leaves Ljubljana on Tuesday and Thursday at 5.50 am. For Germany you have a choice of a bus to Munich at 7.30 pm on Tuesday, Wednesday, Thursday and Sunday (US$35) or Stuttgart on Tuesday and Sunday at 7.30 pm (US$54). Obtain details at the bus station. The airport bus also leaves from the bus station (US$1).

## Getting Around

Buy bus tokens in advance at a newsstand.

## POSTOJNA

The much-touted **Postojna Caves** (Adelsberger Grotten) between Ljubljana and Rijeka are a bit of a rip-off. For US$15 a head, hordes of tourists are taken on a miniature train ride between the colourfully lit karst formations. Of the 27 km of caves five km are visited, one km on foot, the rest on the miniature electric train. Near the exit, tourists gawk at blind salamanders in a pool.

Other sights of this area include a **Karst Museum** beside Kompas in the centre of town, and cliffside, Renaissance-style **Predjama Castle** (1570), nine km beyond the Postojna Caves (bus service every couple of hours, admission US$5).

## Orientation

The caves are within walking distance of Postojna bus or railway stations (both of which have left-luggage offices). The railway station is on the east side of town, one km from the centre. The bus station is right in the centre and the caves are another km west of it. Visits are at 9.30 am and 1.30 pm daily all year, with more frequent tours from April to October and on Sunday. Dress warmly as the cave is a constant 8°C all year.

The tour takes 1¼ hours and you'll hear a commentary in your own language. Don't worry if you see countless masses waiting impatiently to enter. Most will go around with their German or Slovene-speaking guides – the English groups are much smaller. There's no use joining in the pushing to be the first one in, as everyone is divided up inside anyway.

## Places to Stay & Eat

If you want to stay at Postojna, the Turist Biro on the main street just above the bus station has private rooms, as does Kompas Travel Service nearby.

Overcrowded *Autocamp Pivka Jama* (US$9 per person) is in a pine forest four km beyond the Postojna Caves. Right in the middle of the autocamp itself is the Pivka Cave (US$5 admission, open in summer only).

There's an overpriced self-service restaurant among the tourist shops at the entrance to the Postojna Caves.

## Getting There & Away

There are direct trains to Postojna from Ljubljana (76 km), Rijeka (79 km) and Koper (99 km). The bus station in Postojna is more conveniently located and buses also link these places.

## ŠKOCJAN CAVES

The Škocjan Caves, 10 km from Divača between Postojna and Koper, have been heavily promoted since 1986 when they were entered on UNESCO's 'world heritage' list. There's a visit at 10 am daily all year and more frequent visits in summer (US$15 per person). These caves are in far more natural surroundings than those at Postojna but they're really only feasible to visit if you have your own transport. It's over an hour's walk along a busy highway from Divača

Railway Station just to the access road to the caves.

## JULIAN ALPS

Yugoslavia shares with Italy the Julian Alps in the far north-west corner of Slovenia. Three-headed Mt Triglav (2864 metres), the country's highest peak, is scaled regularly by hundreds of summer weekend mountaineers, but there are countless less ambitious hikes. Lakes Bled and Bohinj make ideal starting points – Bled with its chic resort facilities, Bohinj right beneath the rocky crags themselves. Most of this spectacular area falls under **Triglav National Park** (admission free). A few of the many possible routes are mentioned in the following sections.

## BLED

Bled, a fashionable resort at 501 metres altitude, is set on an idyllic, two-km-long emerald lake which you can walk right around in under two hours. Trout and carp proliferate in the crystal-clear lake water which is surprisingly warm, a pleasure to swim in. The climate is also good: there's no fog at Bled during the summer. To the northeast the Karavanke Range forms a natural boundary with Austria. You'll hear a lot of English spoken around Bled as it's a favourite destination for packaged holiday-makers from Britain, but somehow you couldn't call it spoiled.

## Orientation

The village is at the east end of the lake below Castle Hill. The bus station is also here, but Lesce-Bled Railway Station is about five km east. In addition there's Bled-Jezero, a branch-line railway station above the west end of the lake, where the camping ground is also found.

## Information

The tourist office is on Ljubljanska cesta upstairs in the building right next to the post office. Tourist information is also dispensed by the very helpful Turistično Društvo souvenir stand in the casino building. Ask for the useful booklet *Bled Tourist News*. Kompas

at Hotel Krim sells good hiking maps. The Triglav National Park office is midway along the lake's north shore.

## Things to See

The neo-Gothic **Parish Church** (1904) with frescoes done in 1937 is just above the bus station. Follow the road north-west to the youth hostel where there's a trail up to the castle *(grad)*. **Bled Castle** (open daily, US$3 admission) was the seat of the bishops of Brixen (South Tyrol) for over 800 years. Set atop a steep cliff 100 metres above the lake, it offers magnificent views in clear weather. The castle museum presents the history of the area and allows a peep into the 16th century chapel. By the altar is a fresco of the Holy Roman emperor Henry II presenting the church to Christ in 1004. You get free admission to the castle if you eat at the restaurant (a US$5 deposit against your meal must be paid at the gate).

The other feature of Bled which immediately strikes the eye is a tiny **island** at the west end of the lake. From the massive red-and-white belfry rising above the dense vegetation the tolling 'bell of wishes' echoes across the lake. Underneath the present Baroque church are the foundations of a pre-Romanesque chapel, unique in Slovenia. Most people reach the island on one of the large hand-propelled gondolas, which let you off for a half-hour visit (US$7 return trip per person, admission to church and belfry included). If there are two or three of you it would be cheaper to hire a rowing boat from the bathing establishment below the castle (US$10 an hour for three people, US$14 for five people). Rowing boats are also available on the shore in front of Grand Hotel Toplice (US$8 an hour for three people) – compare prices, as they fluctuate a lot. It's also quite feasible to swim across to the island from the beach at Zaka Camping, although you might not feel comfortable visiting the church in your bathing suit. In winter you can skate across the ice to the island.

**Day Hike** An excellent half-day hike from Bled features a visit to the **Vintgar Gorge**

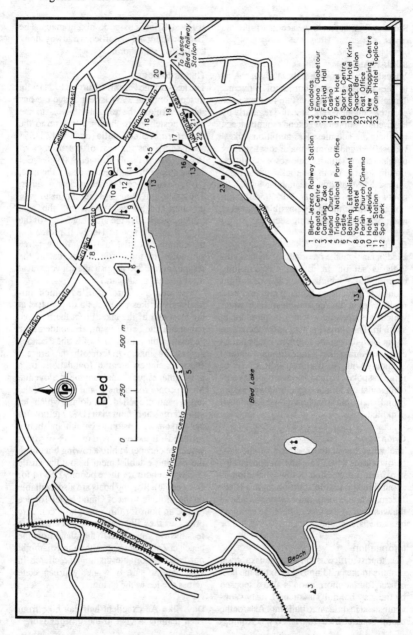

Bled

0   250   500 m

Bled Lake

To Lesce –
Bled Railway
Station

1  Bled–Jezero Railway Station
2  Regata Centre
3  Camping Zaka
4  Island Church
5  Triglav National Park Office
6  Castle
7  Bathing Establishment
8  Youth Hostel
9  Parish Church/Cinema
10  Hotel Jelovica
11  Bus Station
12  Spa Park
13  Gondolas
14  Emona Globetour
15  Festival Hall
16  Casino
17  Park Hotel
18  Sports Centre
19  Kompas/Hotel Krim
20  Snack Bar Union
21  Post Office
22  New Shopping Centre
23  Grand Hotel Toplice

Beach

(Soteska Vintgar). Begin by taking the Krnica bus from Bled to Zgornja-Gorje. From beside the 'Gostilna' opposite the church follow the signposted road through lovely alpine countryside to Vintgar (two km), where you pay US$2 to enter the gorge. The clear, trout-filled Radovna River roars below the wooden walkways and high cliffs. At the far end of the gorge a trail climbs over the hill to St Catherine's Chapel, from which you can walk down the road through Zasip straight back to Bled. In summer a 'tourist bus' runs direct from Bled Bus Station to Vintgar (US$1.50 one-way).

**Pokljuka** The easiest way to get into the mountains is to take the morning bus from Bled to the Sporthotel at Pokljuka. Since the hotel is at 1266 metres elevation it's a logical place from which to begin climbing Mt Triglav. The trail starts at Rudno Polje (1340 metres), 2.5 km west of the Sporthotel by road. It's three hours to the first hut, Vodnikov dom (1805 metres, 50 beds), seven or eight hours all the way to the summit. A round trip to the summit from Pokljuka in one day is only possible for Olympic athletes. Don't brag to us if you're crazy enough to do it! Bring a hiking map with you as none are available at the Sporthotel. You can stay at the hotel for US$22 per person for a bed and full board, US$16 per person with half-board (closed in April, May, October and November).

## Places to Stay
**Camping** *Camping Zaka* (open from May to September) is in a quiet valley at the west end of Bled Lake about two km from Bled Bus Station. The location is good and there's even a beach, supermarket and restaurant, but at US$9 per person it's not cheap.

**Hostels** The *Bled Youth Hostel*, Grajska cesta 17 (open all year), is conveniently situated just up the hill from the bus station. The surroundings are nice, but it's hard to justify the US$18 overnight charge (members, non-members and people under 27 all pay the same). Breakfast is US$4 extra.

**Private Rooms** Your best bet for accommodation in Bled is a private room. Kompas Tourist Service, in the new shopping mall and at *Hotel Krim*, rents private rooms for US$20/32 single/double, less 30% if you stay three or more nights. Also ask about private rooms at Emona Globtour just below the bus station near the lake which may be slightly cheaper. Forget Bled's hotels which start at US$56 single.

## Places to Eat
The only 'cheap' place to eat is the burek shop opposite the bus station but it's still no bargain (burek US$1.50). There's a vegetable market nearby. In the new shopping centre across the street from Hotel Park is a supermarket.

*Snack Bar Union* by the busy highway just beyond Hotel Krim has a US$5 'tourist menu', plus traditional meat dishes.

## Entertainment
Admission to the Bled Cinema beside the Parish Church is cheap. There's a beautiful 23°C **thermal pool** downstairs at the Grand Hotel Toplice which you can use all day for US$5. Information is available at the hotel desk. Bled also has Yugoslavia's first golf course!

The traditional rowing regatta on Bled Lake takes place around 1 May.

## Getting There & Away
Express trains between Munich and Belgrade stop at Lesce-Bled Station, about five km from Bled. Local trains from Ljubljana to Jesenice also pass this way. There are frequent buses from this railway station to Bled.

Bled-Jezero Station, above the west end of the lake, is on a secondary line between Jesenice and Nova Gorica, border stations for Austria and Italy. Six local trains a day in each direction follow this scenic route.

It's preferable to arrive in Bled by bus (frequent service from Ljubljana, 65 km). Bus service between Bled and Bohinj is good.

## BOHINJ

Bohinj, 28 km south-west of Bled, is a more nature-oriented place to stay than Bled. Bohinj Lake (475 metres elevation) is exceedingly beautiful as high mountains rise directly from the basin-shaped valley. Secluded beaches for nude swimming are encountered off the trail along the north shore. There are many hiking possibilities at Bohinj, including an ascent of Mt Triglav. Bohinj often has a morning fog which clears before noon.

### Orientation

The area's main tourist centre is Jezero at the east end of the lake. One km north across the Sava River sits the old town, Stara Fužina, at the mouth of the Mostnica Canyon. *Hotel Zlatorog* is at the west end of the lake near the camping ground and the Vogel cable car.

### Information

The Turist Biro is at Jezero.

### Things to See & Do

A footpath leads over the 'Devil's Bridge' and up the **Mostnica Canyon** into the Voje Valley just north of Stara Fužina. The *Dom bohinjskih prvoborcev*, an hour's hike up this deep gorge from Stara Fužina, is a beginning point for climbing Mt Triglav. It costs US$10 per person to stay at the Dom (open from late May until October).

The 'Zicnice Vogel' cable car, near the camping ground at the west end of Bohinj Lake, can carry you 1000 metres up into the mountains (US$6 one-way, US$9 return, closed in November). From the *Ski Hotel* (1540 metres) on top you can scale **Mt Vogel** (1922 metres) in a couple of hours for a sweeping view of everything. Be careful in fog!

### Places to Stay & Eat

**Camping** The *Zlatorog Campground* (open from May to September) is at the west end of the lake. At US$9 per person it's expensive, but the location right on a lake beach is lovely and it's a good base for hiking.

**Private Rooms** The Turist Biro and Globtour, both at Jezero, have private rooms for US$11 per person for one or two nights, US$9 per person for three or more nights. Ask if there's anything cheaper if the first room they offer seems too expensive. Many houses here and in Stara Fužina village bear *sobe* signs.

### Getting There & Away

Buses are fairly frequent between Bohinj and Ljubljana, covering the 83 km in two hours (US$5). These buses stop at Jezero then run right along the south shore of Bohinj Lake, terminating at the Hotel Zlatorog at the west end of the lake.

The closest railway station is Bohinjska Bistrica on the Jesenice-Nova Gorica line, six km east of Jezero.

## TREKKING MT TRIGLAV

The Julian Alps are one of the finest hiking areas in Eastern Europe. A mountain trip here is also an excellent way to meet young Yugoslavs, so take advantage of this opportunity if you're in the country during the hiking season. Mountain huts *(planinska koča)* are scattered throughout the range, normally less than five hours' walk apart. The huts in the higher regions are open from July to September, in the lower regions from June to October. No reservations are possible at the huts but the ones around Mt Triglav become crowded on Friday and Saturday nights. A bed for the night shouldn't be over US$10 per person. Meals are also sold, so you don't need to carry a lot of gear. Leave most of your things below.

Warm clothes, sturdy boots and good physical condition are indispensable. The best months to do it are August and September though above 1500 metres you could encounter true winter weather conditions any time. Keep to the trails well marked with red & white circles. Before you come, pick up the *Bohinj Bled in Okolica* 1:50,000 excursion map or something similar at a bookshop. These maps are *sometimes* also available locally.

The circular three-day route described

here is not the shortest nor the easiest way to climb Yugoslavia's highest mountain, but it is one of the most rewarding. Get hold of the booklet *How to Climb Triglav* or the brochure *An Alpine Guide* which provide infinitely more detail than can be included here.

## The Route

An hour's hike west of the Zlatorog Campground at Bohinj is the Savica Waterfall, source of the Sava River, which gushes from a limestone cave and falls 60 metres into a narrow gorge. From here a path zig-zags up the Komarča Crag. From the top of this cliff (1340 metres) there's an excellent view of the lake. Farther north, three hours from the falls, is the hut *Koča pri trigavskih jezerih* (1683 metres, 120 beds) at the south end of the fantastic Valley of the Seven Triglav Lakes. Spend the night here. If you're still keen and it's not too late, you can climb nearby Mt Tičarica (2091 metres, one hour from the hut) for a sweeping valley view. The Komna Plateau to the south was a major WW I battlefield (Hemingway described it

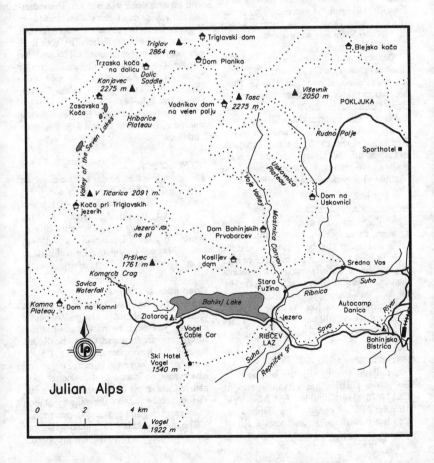

Julian Alps

in *A Farewell to Arms*). *Dom na Komni* there stays open all year.

The next morning you hike up the valley past the largest glacial lakes, then north-east to the desert-like Hribarice Plateau (2358 metres). You descend to the Dolič Saddle (2164 metres) where the hut *Trzaska koča na dolicu* (2120 metres, 60 beds, four hours from Koča pri trigavskih jezerih) offers a night's rest. You could well carry on to *Dom Planika* (2408 metres, 80 beds), 1½ hours beyond, although on weekends Dom Planika is packed. From this hut it's just over another hour to the summit of Triglav (2864 metres), a well-beaten path. If you decide to do the trip in reverse, Dom Planika is a seven-hour climb from Stara Fužina or about six hours from the Sporthotel, Pokljuka.

The way down passes the hut *Vodnikov dom na velem polju* (1805 metres, 50 beds), less than two hours from Dom Planika. There are two routes between Vodnikov dom and Stara Fužina: down the Voje Valley or over the Uskovnica pasture. Uskovnika is a little longer but allows better views. The way to Rudno Polje and the Sporthotel, Pokljuka, branches off the Uskovnika route. Stara Fužina (546 metres, four hours down from Vodnikov) is back near Bohinj Lake.

## BOHINJSKA BISTRICA

This village is a good place to stay if you're catching an early train towards Austria or Istria and it can also be used as a base for visiting Bled and Bohinj, as bus service here is good. Since it's between the main tourist centres, Bohinjska Bistrica is less affected by tourism, thus is cheaper and friendlier. It's a good choice if you'd like to escape the packaged tourists yet still be conveniently close to everything.

### Places to Stay & Eat

Slovenijaturist opposite the bus stop in Bohinjska Bistrica has private rooms at US$11/20 single/double. The Mladinski Turisticni Biro, nearby at Trg Svobode 1, also has private rooms and posts a list of these in the window in case it's closed. Ask

about youth hostel accommodation here. Both offices sell hiking maps.

*Autocamp Danica*, a few minutes' walk from the bus stop in Bohinjska Bistrica, is US$7 per person to camp. It's very convenient.

The *Almira Buffet* beside the Mladinski Turisticni Biro is cheap, but there are only two or three things to choose from and these are listed on a board by the bar.

### Getting There & Away

Six trains daily run Jesenice-Nova Gorica with a stop in Bohinjska Bistrica. This mountain railway is one of the most picturesque in Yugoslavia. To/from Austria you connect at Jesenice (32 km) for Villach. To/from Italy you connect at Nova Gorica (76 km) for Gorizia. Going from Bohinjska Bistrica to Nova Gorica sit on the right-hand side of the train to see the valley of the emerald-green Soča River at its best.

All the buses between Bled and Bohinj stop here, as do the Bohinj buses to/from Ljubljana.

## NOVA GORICA

This medium-sized border town has grown up since 1918 when the region was partitioned, with Italy getting the old town of Gorizia and Yugoslavia its hinterland to the east. Modern Nova Gorica contains little of interest to visitors but is a convenient way station between the Julian Alps and Istria or an entry/exit point to/from Italy.

### Orientation & Information

Nova Gorica Railway Station is right on the Italian border and there's a secondary border crossing just near the railway station, but foreigners on foot must use the Rožna dolina/Casa Rossa crossing about 1.5 km away. As you leave the railway station you look across the fence into Italy and the footpath to Casa Rossa follows the border south. The travel agency in the railway station changes money and provides information.

The bus station is a 15-minute walk from the railway station (turn left as you leave the railway station and left again at the secondary border crossing mentioned above).

## Getting There & Away

Six local trains a day run from Nova Gorica to Bohinjska Bistrica (76 km), Bled-Jezero (96 km) and Jesenice (108 km). Two trains a day link Nova Gorica to Gorizia Centrale, Italy. To go from Nova Gorica to Ljubljana you must change trains at Sežana, so take a bus instead.

There are frequent bus connections from Nova Gorica to Postojna and Ljubljana but fewer to Koper. For Istria change buses at Postojna. From Nova Gorica Bus Station you can catch a city bus to Gorizia, Italy.

# Croatia

Croatia (Hrvatska) extends in an arc from the Danube to Istria and south along the Adriatic coast to Dubrovnik. Roman Catholic since the 7th century, and under Hungary since 1102, Croatia only united with Orthodox Serbia in 1918. Croatia's centuries of resistance to Hungarian and Austrian domination continue today in its jealously guarded position within the Yugoslav federal system. Yet within Croatia itself cultural differences remain between the Habsburg-influenced Central European interior and the formerly Venetian Mediterranean coast.

This 56,538-sq-km republic has a near monopoly on tourism to Yugoslavia. The strikingly beautiful Mediterranean landscapes so close to central Europe draw nearly 10 million foreign visitors a year to the coastal areas, although the crowds are smaller in late spring and early autumn. The Croatian capital, Zagreb, is the cultural centre of Yugoslavia, and coastal Croatian towns like Poreč, Rovinj, Pula, Krk, Rab, Zadar, Šibenik, Trogir, Split, Hvar, Korčula and Dubrovnik all have well-preserved historic centres with lots to see and do.

In this heavily visited region, natural attractions are carefully packaged to resist the onslaught of mass tourism. Croatia's national parks include Plitvice (between Zagreb and Zadar), Brioni (near Pula), Paklenica and Kornati (near Zadar), Krka (near Šibenik) and Mljet (near Korčula). Brioni, Kornati and Mljet are day trips by boat on tours organised by travel agencies, while Plitvice, Palenica and Krka are accessible by bus.

## ZAGREB

Zagreb (Agram), a city of over a million inhabitants and capital of the Republic of Croatia, is a far more attractive, relaxed city than Belgrade. Spread out towards the Sava River, Zagreb sits on the southern slopes of Medvednica, the Zagreb uplands. Medieval Zagreb developed from the 11th to 13th centuries in the twin towns of Kaptol and Gradec, Kaptol with St Stephen's Cathedral and Gradec centred on St Mark's Church. The clerics established themselves in Kaptol as early as 1094, while Gradec was the craftsmen's quarter.

Much of medieval Zagreb remains today, although the stately 19th century city between it and the railway station is the present commercial centre. There are many fine parks, galleries and museums in both upper and lower towns. Zagreb is also Yugoslavia's main centre for primitive or naive art.

## Orientation

As you come out of the railway station you'll see a series of parks and pavilions directly in front of you. Many banks and travel agencies are along the street up the left side of these parks. Just up Praška from the north end of the parks is the tourist office on Trg Republike, the main city square. The bus station is one km east of the railway station. Tram No 6 runs from the bus station to the railway station and on up to Trg Republike.

## Information

The tourist office, Trg Republike 11, opens weekdays 8 am to 8 pm, weekends 9 am to 6 pm. The quality of service varies, so try another clerk if the first one isn't amenable. The tourist office has a second information

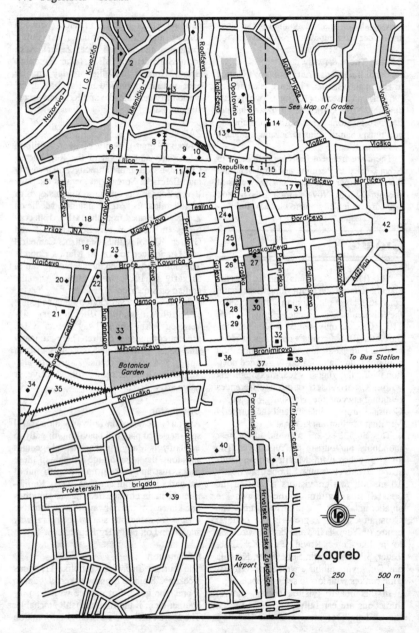

Zagreb

0      250      500 m

■ PLACES TO STAY

21 Inter-Continental Hotel
31 Youth Hostel &
   Beograd Hotel
32 Central Hotel
36 Hotel Esplanade

▼ PLACES TO EAT

5 Pizzeria Medulić
6 Express Restaurant
  'Cetvrti Lovac'
16 Mosor Cafeteria
17 Slavija Restaurant
35 Studentski Centar

OTHER

1 City Museum
2 Saloon Disco
3 St Mark's Church
4 Komedija Theatre
7 Academy of Music
8 Funicular Railway
9 British Consulate
10 Nama Department Store
11 Trg bratstva i jedinstva
12 Blagasija Oktogon
13 Dolac Market
14 St Stephen's Cathedral
15 Tourist Office
18 Czech Consulate
19 Arts & Crafts Museum
20 Museum Mimara
22 Ethnological Museum
23 Croatian National Theatre
24 Generalturist &
   Achaeological Museum
25 US Consulate
26 Gallery of Modern Art
27 Strossmayer Gallery
28 Puppet Theatre
29 Croatia Express & National
   Park Office
30 Exhibition Pavilion
33 National Library
34 Technical Museum
37 Railway Station
38 Post Office
39 German Consulate
40 City Hall
41 'Vatroslav Lisinski'
   Concert Hall
42 Museum of the Revolution

bureau at Trg Nikole Zrinjskog 14 next to the American Centre.

There's an information office for Plitvice National Park at Trg Tomislava 19 where you can buy a park map and find out about current accommodation rates.

**Money** There's a 24-hour exchange office in the railway station.

**Post** Poste restante is held in the post office on the east side of the railway station.

**Consulates** There's no Hungarian consulate in Zagreb so get your visa in Belgrade or elsewhere (if required). The Czech Consulate is at Prilaz JNA 10 (weekdays 9 am to noon).

The Austrian and British (☎ 42 4888) consulates are at Ilica 12 and the US Consulate General (☎ 44 4800) at Brace Kavurica 2. The German Consulate is at Proleterskih brigada 64, south of the railway station.

**Things to See**

**Kaptol** Zagreb's colourful Dolac **vegetable market** is just up the steps from Trg Republike and north along Opatovina. It functions daily with especially large markets Friday and Saturday. The twin neo-Gothic spires of **St Stephen's Cathedral** (1899) are nearby. Elements from the medieval cathedral on this site, destroyed by an earthquake in 1880, can be seen inside, including 13th century frescoes, Renaissance pews, marble altars and a Baroque pulpit. The Baroque **Archiepiscopal Palace** surrounds the cathedral, as do 16th century fortifications constructed when Zagreb was threatened by the Turks.

**Gradec** From ulica Radićeva 5 off Trg Republike a pedestrian walkway, stube Ivana Zakmardija, leads to the **Lotršćak Tower** and a funicular railway which connects the lower and upper towns. The tower may be climbed for a sweeping 360° view of the city (closed Sunday). A cannon in the tower is fired daily at noon. To the right is Baroque **St Catherine's Church** with Jezuitski trg beyond. The **Muzejski prostor**, Jezuitski trg

4, is Zagreb's premier exhibition hall where superb art shows are staged. Farther north and to the right is the 13th century **Stone Gate** with a miraculous painting of the Virgin which escaped the devastating fire of 1731.

The colourful painted-tile roof of Gothic **St Mark's Church** on Radićev trg marks the centre of Gradec. Inside are works by Ivan Meštrović, Yugoslavia's most famous modern sculptor. At Mletačka 8 nearby is former **Meštrović Studio**, now a museum (closed Monday). Other museums in this area include the **Historical Museum of Croatia**, Matoševa 9, and the **Natural History Museum**, Demetrova 1. More interesting is the **City Museum**, Opatićka 20 (Monday to Saturday 9 am to 1 pm, Tuesday and Thursday also 4 to 7 pm, Sunday 10 am to 1 pm), with a scale model of old Gradec. Summaries in English and German are in each room of this museum housed in the former Convent of St Claire (1650).

**The Lower Town** Zagreb is a city of museums. There are four on the parks between

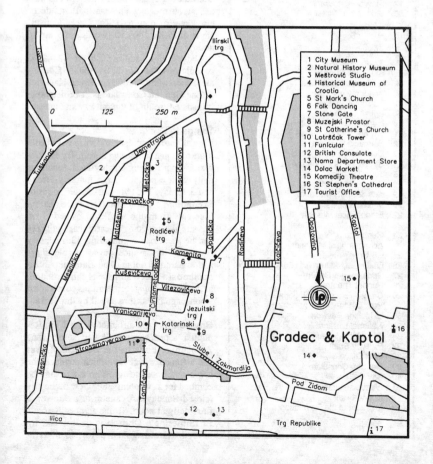

1 City Museum
2 Natural History Museum
3 Meštrović Studio
4 Historical Museum of Croatia
5 St Mark's Church
6 Folk Dancing
7 Stone Gate
8 Muzejski Prostor
9 St Catherine's Church
10 Lotrščak Tower
11 Funicular
12 British Consulate
13 Nama Department Store
14 Dolac Market
15 Komedija Theatre
16 St Stephen's Cathedral
17 Tourist Office

Gradec & Kaptol

the railway station and Trg Republike. The yellow pavilion (1897) across the park from the station presents changing contemporary art exhibitions. The second building north, also in the park, houses the **Strossmayer Gallery** of the Academy of Arts & Sciences with old master paintings (closed Monday). If the gallery's closed for reasons unknown, as it often is, enter the interior courtyard anyway to see the Baška Slab (1102) from the island of Krk, one of the oldest inscriptions in the Croatian language.

The **Gallery of Modern Art** (closed Monday), adjacent at Braće Kavurića 1, has a large collection of rather uninspiring paintings. The **Archaeological Museum** (closed Saturday), nearby at Trg Nikole Zrinjskog 19, displays prehistoric to medieval artifacts, plus Egyptian mummies. There's a garden of Roman sculpture behind.

**West of the Centre** The **Museum Mimara**, Rooseveltov trg 5 (open daily from 10 am to 8 pm, Monday 2 to 8 pm only, US$2, free Monday), is one of the finest art galleries in Europe. Housed in a neo-Renaissance former school building (1883), this diverse collection shows the loving hand of Ante Topić Mimara, a private collector who donated over 3750 priceless objects to his native Zagreb, although he spent much of his life in Salzburg, Austria. The Spanish, Italian and Dutch paintings are the highlight, but there are also large sections of glassware, sculpture and Oriental art. Don't miss it.

Nearby on Trg Maršala Tita is the neo-Baroque **Croatian National Theatre** (1895) with Ivan Meštrović's *Fountain of Life* (1905) in front. The **Ethnographic Museum**, Trg Mažuranića 14 (open Tuesday, Wednesday, Thursday 9 am to 1 pm and 5 to 7 pm, Friday, Saturday, Sunday 9 am to 1 pm) has a large collection of Croatian folk costumes with English explanations. South of here is the Art-Nouveau **National Library** (1907). The **Botanical Garden** on ulica Mihanovićeva (open April to October, closed Monday, free) is attractive with the plants and landscaping as well as its restful corners.

**Sljeme** A cable car *(žičara)* runs up Sljeme, the forested mountain (1035 metres) behind Zagreb (also known as Mt Medvednica). To get there take tram No 14 to Mihaljevac (the end of the line), then tram No 15 to its terminus at Dolje. Go through a tunnel and follow a footpath 10 minutes to the lower terminal. The cable car operates every hour on the hour and climbs 669 metres over its four-km route. On top is a TV tower (no entry) and pleasant trails through the forest. You can walk back down on a broad trail marked with red-and-white circles in under two hours.

If you'd like to spend the night on Sljeme the *Dom 'Izviđača'* (☎ 44 5226) has beds for US$20 per person. The bar is worth seeking out even if you're only day tripping.

**Places to Stay**

**Camping** There's a camping area at *Motel 'Plitvice'* (☎ 52 2230) 10 km west of the city on the main highway to Ljubljana and Maribor (US$5 per person, US$4 per tent, open April to September). Take trams No 4, 14 or 17 to Savski Most, then bus No 112 or 167 to Lučko, then walk three km. This may be OK for one night at a pinch or if you have transport, but for others bus fares, commuting time, traffic noise and the lack of shade make it unappealing. Evenings there's often live music in the motel restaurant.

There's another camping ground east of Zagreb at Sesvete, equally inconvenient.

**Hostels** Budget accommodation is in short supply in Zagreb. The only cheap option is the 215-bed *Omladinski Hotel/Youth Hostel* at Petrinjska 77 near the railway station (open all year). Its prices are US$8 for those under age 27, US$12 for those over 27, both in one of the six-bed dormitories. The few double rooms cost US$45, but they're usually booked solid by Yugoslavs who pay a lot less. Sheets and blankets are provided and there are hot showers. You don't have to be a YHA member to stay in the hostel, so it's a good last resort if nothing else turns up. It's central and a good place to meet people.

Ask about accommodation in other youth

hostels and at *Dom 'Izviđača'* on Mt Sljeme, at the Youth Tourist Centre, Petrinjska 73 beside the hostel.

The Turist Biro at the Studentski Centar, Savska cesta 25, rents rooms in student dormitories in summer at US$30 per person. A valid student card might net you a lower rate, but don't count on it. The dorms are usually far from the city centre.

**Private Rooms** The only place in town with private rooms is Generalturist, Trg Nikole Zrinjskog 18. Category II rooms are US$17/28 single/double a night for one to three nights, US$13/23 a night for four nights or more, plus US$1 per person per night tax. Regardless of whether you stay three or four nights the price is about the same, so you may as well relax and plan on a leisurely four-night stay. Singles are seldom available and all of the rooms are often full.

**Hotels** Most of the older hotels in Zagreb have been renovated and the prices raised to B category (around US$40/50 single/double with bath). *Hotel Beograd*, Petrinjska 71 near the youth hostel, is US$40/55 single/double for a room with private bath.

The 110-room *Central Hotel*, Branimirova 3 opposite the train station, is US$36/56 single/double with bath and breakfast. High rollers will delight in the palatial *Hotel Esplanade* near the railway station (US$141/171 single/double with bath).

## Places to Eat

*Restaurant 'Jana' Samoposluga*, Petrinjska 79, is a self-service cafeteria near the youth hostel. There's a super cheap dining hall at the *Studentski Centar*, Savska cesta 25, but student ID is checked at the door.

*Mosor*, Jurišićeva 2 across from the tourist office, has coffee and cakes in front and a self-service cafeteria at the back. Soup and salad with bread makes a cheap lunch. The *Slavija Restaurant*, Jurišićeva 18, is an informal lunch counter.

In summer the *Express Restaurant 'Četvrti Lovac'*, Dezmanova 2 through the underpass marked 'Kino Sloboda', moves its tables out onto the street and dispenses real pizza at reasonable prices in a friendly atmosphere.

*Pizzeria Medulić*, Medulićeva 2 at Ilica, serves vegetarian food in the back dining room and the menu is in English. The pizza is also good.

For regional dishes and lots of local colour with your meal, dine in one of the outdoor restaurants up ulica Tkalčićeva from Trg Republike on summer evenings.

## Entertainment

Much more happens in Zagreb than in Belgrade. Its theatres and concert halls present a great variety of programmes throughout the year. Many (but not all) are listed in the monthly brochure *Zagreb events & performances,* usually available from the tourist office. The daily paper *Vecernji list* carries cinema, concert, exhibition and museum listings. Even if you don't read Serbo-Croatian the information isn't hard to decipher.

It's also worth making the rounds of the theatres in person to check the calendars. Tickets are usually available, even for the best shows. A small office marked 'Kazalište Komedija' (look for the posters) in the Blagasija Oktogon, a passage connecting Trg bratstva i jedinstva to Ilica near Trg Republike, also sells theatre tickets. On odd years in April there's the 'Zagreb Biennale of Contemporary Music', since 1961 Yugoslavia's most important musical event. Many free outdoor performances are offered during the 'International Review of Original Folklore' in the last week of July. The 900th anniversary of the city in 1994 promises to herald major celebrations!

The neo-Baroque *Croatian National Theatre* (1895), Trg Maršala Tita 15, presents opera and ballet performances (box office Monday to Saturday from 10 am to 1 pm and 6 to 7 pm, tickets US$6). The *Komedija Theatre*, Kaptol 9 near the cathedral, stages operettas and musicals. The ticket office of the *'Vatroslav Lisinski' Concert Hall*, just south of the railway station, is open weekdays from 10 am to 1 pm, 5.30 to 7.30 pm, Saturday 10 am to 1 pm. Concerts also take place at the *Academy of Music*, Gundulićeva 6a near Trg Republike. There are performances at the *Puppet Theatre*, ulica 8 maja 35, Sundays at 10 am. On summer Wednesdays at 6 pm there's folk dancing in the courtyard at Kamenita 15 near St Mark's Church.

The *Omladinski Kulturni Centar*, ulica Teslina 7, is a popular hangout for counter-culture youth. Zagreb's most popular disco is *Saloon*, Tuškanac 1a (open after 9 pm daily). Weekends it's packed. In the evening the cafés along Tkalčićeva north off Trg

Republike buzz with activity as overflow crowds spill out onto the street, drinks in hand. Farther up on Kozarska ulica the city youth clusters shoulder to shoulder. Trg bratstva i jedinstva also has more interesting street life than Trg Republike. A late stroll through these areas will demonstrate that Zagreb isn't as staid as you thought!

### Things to Buy

Ilica is Zagreb's main shopping street. Get in touch with Yugoslav consumerism at the Nama Department Store on Ilica near Trg

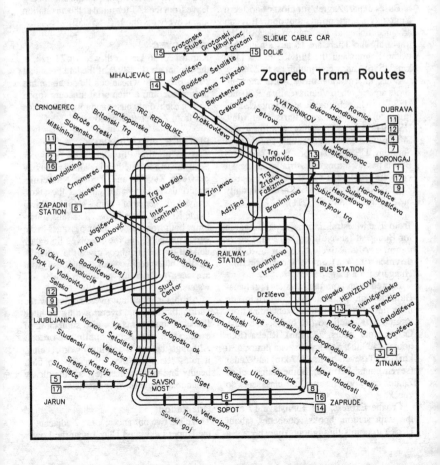

Republike. The shops and grocery stores in the passage under the tracks beside the railway station stay open long hours.

## Getting There & Away
**Bus** Zagreb's big modern bus station has a large enclosed waiting room where you can stretch out while waiting for your bus. The signs posted in English at the station are reassuring and the people at Information speak English too! Buy international tickets at window No 2, change money at window No 1. The left-luggage office is open non-stop 24 hours a day.

Buses depart Zagreb for most of northern Yugoslavia and points beyond. Buy an advance ticket at the station if you'll be travelling far. There are 15 buses a day between Zagreb and the Plitvice Lakes (130 km, US$6), many continuing on to Zadar.

Some international buses worth knowing about are Zagreb to Vienna (daily at 9.30 pm, US$37), Munich (daily at 7 pm, US$45, luggage US$2 apiece), Paris (Saturday, US$99), Berlin (Tuesday, Saturday and Sunday, DM 130) and Istanbul (Tuesday and Saturday, US$53). The bus from Zagreb to Berlin passes through Austria so no transit visas are required. To go to Hungary there's Zagreb-Nagykanizsa (US$7) or four daily buses Zagreb-Barcs (US$11).

**Train** The Maestral Express departs Zagreb for Budapest (seven hours, 412 km) every morning. Alternatively take a train to Koprivnica (92 km) and a local train into Hungary from there.

Zagreb is on both the Munich-Ljubljana-Belgrade and Vienna-Maribor-Belgrade main lines. There are other direct trains from Zagreb to Kardeljevo (11 hours, 758 km), Osijek (four hours, 277 km), Rijeka (four hours, 243 km), Sarajevo (seven hours, 530 km), Split (seven hours, 727 km) and Zadar (seven hours, 720 km). Some trains out of Zagreb carry only reserved 1st-class seats, so check.

Croatia Express, Trg Tomislava 17 near the train station, books couchettes (about US$6) to points throughout Yugoslavia – a perfect way to beat Zagreb's high hotel prices. Couchettes are available to Belgrade, Bitola, Kardeljevo, Pula, Sarajevo, Šibenik, Skopje, Split and Zadar.

## Getting Around
Public transport is based on an efficient network of trams, although the city centre is compact enough to make them unnecessary. Enter trams through the rear doors to pay your fare or buy tickets at newspaper kiosks. You can use your ticket for transfers within 90 minutes.

Buses to Pleso Airport, 17 km south-east, leave from the JAT terminal at the bus station about every half-hour (US$2.50).

## KUMROVEC
Kumrovec, 56 km north-west of Zagreb, is the birthplace (in 1892) of the late President Josip Broz Tito whose childhood home has been made into a memorial museum (open daily). Eight daily buses and four daily trains run from Zagreb to Kumrovec.

## PLITVICE NATIONAL PARK
The 16 pristine Plitvice Lakes (Plitvicer Seen) lie in a forested valley almost midway between Zagreb and Zadar. Numerous waterfalls and cascades connect the lakes, arrayed in a series of terraces stepping down to the Korana River Gorge. The falls sometimes pour from subterranean passages in the karst landscape, and the dissolved lime they deposit on the lake beds gives the water its unique blue-green colour. Countless trout are seen swimming in the crystal clear waters.

All this is great, but overcharging by the park authorities and overcrowding by huge flocks of tourists make a visit something of a sacrifice and occasionally an ordeal. Although the area is definitely worth seeing, it rates second to the Julian Alps in both beauty and variety, despite what the glossy brochures would have you believe.

## Orientation
There are two entrances: Ulaz 2 adjacent to the Upper Lakes and Ulaz 1 near the Lower

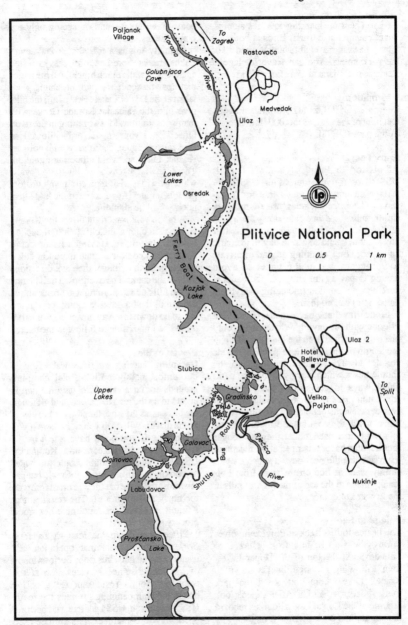

Plitvice National Park

Lakes. There are parking lots, restaurants, ticket counters and Turist Biros at both, but Ulaz 2 has a more reliable bus stop and all of the park hotels. You can leave luggage at Restaurant Poljana at Ulaz 2 for US$1.

## Information
There are Turist Biros at both park entrances. Get hold of the useful 1:50,000 'tourist map' of the park (US$2).

## Entry Fee
Admission to Plitvice National Park is US$16 for foreign tourists or US$10 for foreign students and much less for Yugoslavs. The price includes use of the park shuttle buses and one ride along the length of Kozjak Lake on the park tourist boat. If you want to spend a second day in the park, have your hotel, camping ground or private room agency stamp the ticket to avoid having to pay again. Only official national park accommodation (including everything listed here) can do this.

Some travellers have managed to visit Plitvice without buying a ticket as the only place it's punched is on the tourist boat along the length of the lake (from A to Z). Tickets are not always strictly controlled on the shuttle buses which carry you into the park. Other ways to get around the exorbitant admission price are to share a single ticket between several people, taking turns visiting, or to ask someone at the camping ground to give you a used ticket they no longer require, then have it stamped at the reception for free entry the next day. It's also easy to simply walk in free on the road from Poljanak village to the top of the highest falls in the Lower Lakes area.

## Things to See
The beaten tourist track at Plitvice involves taking the shuttle bus from Ulaz 2 to Labudovac at the top of the Upper Lakes, then following the boardwalks down to Kozjak Lake where you board the park tourist boat from A to Z. After a quick look at some of the Lower Lakes, tourists reboard the shuttle bus back to Ulaz 2 or return by boat. Many people end up seeing only the Upper Lakes.

Actually this is a mistake as the Lower Lakes area is more beautiful, less crowded and the waterfalls much higher. All the pretty pictures you see in the park brochures were taken at the Lower Lakes. Best of all, the falls give into the fantastic Korana Gorge with many possibilities for swimming in the river. Officially, swimming is only allowed in Prošćansko Lake and the west shore of Kozjak Lake, so avoid attracting attention. There are large caves in the gorge walls which you may visit free. Not many visitors get this far and if you come in the late afternoon you'll be all alone.

A boardwalk runs right down the Korana Gorge then climbs the cliff to a trail back to Ulaz 1. If you're staying at Autocamp Korana you could continue three km down the gorge to the village, then ask directions back to the camp. The overgrown trail begins on the hillside at the first switchback above the end of the boardwalk. Don't leave it too late to go down this way however, as the trail would be impossible to follow in the dark.

## Places to Stay
**Camping** Camping is the cheapest way to go but unfortunately both official camping grounds are far away. *Autocamp Korana* is eight km up the road to Zagreb, and although the bus passes the gate, the stop is a km away. Some drivers will drop you right there if you ask nicely. If you don't have a tent or it's raining, you can rent a caravan at Korana for US$15/21/24 single/double/triple (no water or cooking facilities inside). Small bungalows cost the same but they're often reserved for noisy school groups. The restaurant at Korana is expensive but there's a good grocery store.

Fifteen km down the road to Zadar is *Borje Autocamp*, a similar operation. It's usually easy to get a bus from Borje as many of the long-distance services stop at the camping ground restaurant for a coffee break. At both camping grounds the fee is US$5 per person, US$4 per tent, and both are open May to September. The altitude (580 metres) can mean cool camping. Officially there's no camping within the park itself but you'll find plenty of unofficial places to pitch a tent. Keep in mind this is against the rules.

**Private Rooms** Private rooms are available from the Turist Biro at Ulaz 1 and Ulaz 2, beginning around US$15/25 single/double, breakfast not included. The rooms are three to 15 km from the park with the closer ones being the most expensive. If you stay four nights or more there's a 20% discount but in winter you may simply be told there are no private rooms. Take food to your room as there probably won't be anywhere to eat in the vicinity.

**Hotels** The hotels at Ulaz 2 are not cheap. *Hotel Bellevue* is US$50/75 single/double for a room with bath, breakfast included. *Villa Poljana* nearby is only a dollar or two more expensive. The reception at Hotel Plitvice, which is next to Hotel Bellevue, handles bookings for 14-room Villa Poljana. Both hotels have cheaper rooms with shared facilities but they don't like giving them to foreigners. From November to March these hotels are closed, though A-category *Hotel Jezero* nearby remains open and offers discount rates during this low season.

### Places to Eat
The 'market' beside the Turist Biro at Ulaz 2 sells such basic backwoods necessities as liquor, sweets and cheap souvenirs. It does not carry a great deal of food. You may get bread, milk and cheese, if you're lucky. *Restaurant Poljana* at Ulaz 2 has a reasonable self-service section (lunch only).

### Getting There & Away
It's easy to get to Plitvice by bus. There are 15 buses daily from Zagreb (three hours, 130 km, US$6) and about nine from Zadar (four hours, 156 km, US$8). Catching a bus out of Plitvice in the late afternoon can be difficult on weekends or in midsummer when they whiz past full. Some drivers are also reluctant to pick up foreigners with large backpacks though most buses do stop at Ulaz

2. Shout out your destination as you board to avoid taking the wrong bus. The Turist Biro at Ulaz 2 has a list of bus times.

### Getting Around
The shuttle buses and boats operate every 30 to 40 minutes throughout the day. In winter all services (but not entry fees) are greatly reduced.

## OSIJEK
As this book goes to press, Osijek (Esseg), on the right bank of the Drava River near its confluence with the Danube, is the scene of fierce clashes between Croatian and Serbian forces. In normal times, it is a useful exit/entry point for those travelling between Yugoslavia and Hungary. There's nothing special to see here and accommodation is much cheaper in Hungary, so you may as well breeze straight through Osijek.

### Places to Stay & Eat
*Hotel Turist* opposite Osijek Railway Station is expensive. For private rooms (US$35 double) try the tourist office at A Cesarca 2 in the centre of town. You may camp near the *Copacabana Restaurant* just across the river from the centre.

### Getting There & Away
There are two Hungarian trains a day between Osijek and Pecs, Hungary, a pleasant two-hour trip. Tickets for this journey (82 km, US$3) can be purchased at the Croatia Express office in Osijek Railway Station, which also changes money.

If you miss the train take one of the three daily buses between Osijek and Pecs (US$3). In Osijek the bus and train stations are adjacent.

Other direct trains leave Osijek for Zagreb (288 km via Koprivnica, three trains daily), Strizivojna-Vrpolje (51 km, four daily) and Vinkovci (36 km, 12 daily). The last two stations are on the main railway line from Belgrade to Zagreb with connections to much of Yugoslavia.

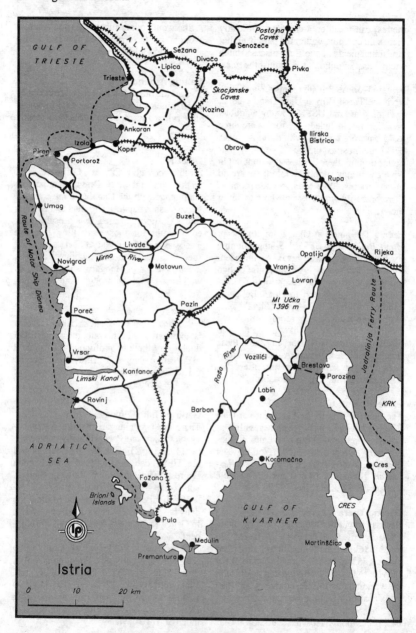

Istria

0          10          20 km

# Istria

Istria, the heart-shaped, 3600-sq-km peninsula just south of Trieste, Italy, is named for the Illyrian Histri tribe conquered by the Romans in 177 BC. In the 20th century Istria has been a political basketball. Italy got Istria from Austria in 1919, then had to give it to Yugoslavia in 1947. A large Italian minority is found in Istria and Italian is widely spoken. There's even an Italian daily paper, *La Voce del Popolo*, published in Rijeka. Marshal Tito wanted Trieste (Trst) as part of Yugoslavia too, but in 1954 the Anglo-American occupiers returned the city to Italy so it wouldn't fall into the hands of the 'Communists'. Today the Koper-Piran strip belongs to Slovenia, the rest to Croatia.

The 430-km Istrian Riviera basks in the Mediterranean landscapes and climate for which the Yugoslav coast is famous. The long summer season from May to October attracts big crowds. This and the proximity to Central Europe are its main drawbacks. Hordes of motorists from Austria, Italy, Yugoslavia, etc, vie with swarms of holiday-makers on cheap package tours from Britain. In midsummer all accommodation will be jammed and the police come down heavily on freelance campers. Industry and heavy shipping along the north side of Istria around Koper and Izola mean polluted waters. The farther south you go in Istria the quieter it gets with cleaner water, fewer cars, less industry and fewer tourists. See Piran quickly, then move south to Rovinj, a perfect base from which to explore Poreč and Pula.

## GETTING AROUND

From May to mid-December the motor ship *Dionea* connects many Istrian towns to Trieste, but cannot be used to travel between two Yugoslav ports (for more information on the *Dionea* see the general Getting There & Away section in this chapter). Railway service is limited in Istria, so plan on getting around by bus.

## KOPER

Koper (Capodistria), only 21 km south of Trieste, is the first of the three quaint old Italian towns along the north side of the Istrian Peninsula. Once an island but now firmly connected to the mainland, the medieval flavour of the old town lingers, but contemporary Koper is surrounded by industry, container ports, high-rise buildings, noisy super-highways and developments. Only the old part is still beautiful, so it's best to stay at Izola or Piran and see this administrative centre and largest town on the Slovene Riviera as a day trip. With frequent bus service from nearby Trieste, Koper is an easy gateway to Yugoslavia.

### Orientation

The bus and train stations are adjacent about two km south of the old town. You can change money at the Slovenijaturist window inside the railway station, otherwise change at the large post office beside the stations.

### Information

Slovenijaturist is at Ukmarjev trg 7 opposite the small boat harbour.

### Things to See

From the stations you enter Presernov trg through the **Muda Gate** (1516). Follow the crowd past the **Bridge Fountain** (1666) and up into Čevljarska ulica (Shoemaker's St), a narrow pedestrian street that opens onto Titov trg, Koper's historic central square.

Most of the things to see in Koper are clustered around the **Town Tower** (1480) on Titov trg, which is visible from afar. The 15th century **cathedral**, the **loggia** (1464) and the **Praetor's Palace** (1452) all belong to the Venetian Gothic style. The lower portion of the cathedral façade is Gothic, the upper part Renaissance. On the narrow lane beside the cathedral is an earlier building, the Romanesque **Carmin Rotunda** (1317). Trg Revolucije behind the cathedral contains several more old Venetian palaces.

The excellent **Provincial Museum** (open Tuesday to Sunday 9 am to noon) is in the Belgramoni-Tacco Palace on Kidričeva ulica between Titov trg and the small boat harbour. The museum features old maps and photos of the area, Italianate sculpture and copies of medieval frescoes.

## Places to Stay

Slovenijaturist, Ukmarjev trg 7 opposite the small boat harbour, has private rooms, but insist on something in the old town. Private rooms are also available from Kompas, opposite the vegetable market. There's no camping ground in Koper (see the Piran section).

## Places to Eat

The *Buffet 'Istrska klet'*, Župančićeva ulica 39 just up from the Bridge Fountain (closed Saturday), offers a filling US$5 set lunch weekdays, and glasses of wine straight from the barrel any time. Try Refosk, the hearty local red wine.

## Getting There & Away

There are 17 daily buses from Trieste to Koper (US$3). To Ljubljana (2½ hours, 175 km) the train is more comfortable than the bus. There's an overnight train to Belgrade

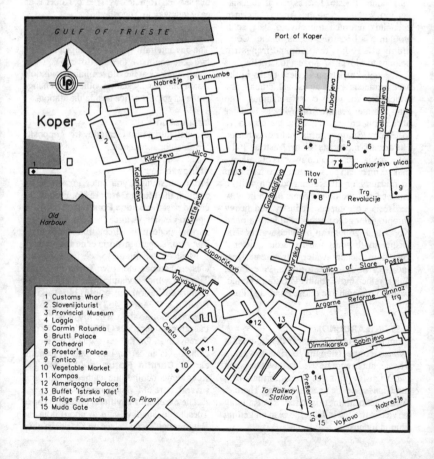

Koper

**Old Harbour**

1 Customs Wharf
2 Slovenijaturist
3 Provincial Museum
4 Loggia
5 Carmin Rotunda
6 Brutti Palace
7 Cathedral
8 Praetor's Palace
9 Fontico
10 Vegetable Market
11 Kompas
12 Almerigogna Palace
13 Buffet 'Istrska Klet'
14 Bridge Fountain
15 Muda Gate

To Piran

To Railway Station

with couchettes available. Buses connect Koper to Pula (104 km), Postojna (63 km) and Rijeka (86 km).

## Getting Around

There's a bus about every half-hour between Koper and Piran (16 km), calling at Izola and Portorož. This bus begins at Koper Railway Station and you can also catch it beside the vegetable market in Koper. Enter through the rear doors to pay the conductor.

## IZOLA

Izola, between Koper and Piran, is an active fishing town with its own cannery. The area of the old town was once an island, hence the name. Izola makes an excellent base for exploring the Slovene Riviera because it's midway between the hot spots and all the coastal buses stop there. Izola doesn't live only from tourism, so it's friendlier and more natural than Portorož or Piran, as long as you don't mind a slightly fishy smell.

## Orientation & Information

The bus from Koper/Piran stops on the edge of the old town, just around the corner from the Turist Biro, Kidricevo nabrezje 4.

## Places to Stay

*Autocamp Jadranka* (open from June to September) is conveniently located on the waterfront one km west of Izola (coming from Koper get off at the next stop after you see the caravans). It costs US$7 per person. Unfortunately it's unbelievably noisy because of the adjacent highway so you're much better off going on to the camping grounds in Portorož or Piran.

The Turist Biro, Kidricevo nabrezje 4 facing the waterfront, has private rooms. There's a 50% surcharge if you stay only one or two nights and the office closes from 1 to 5 pm daily.

In July and August the C-category *Hotel Riviera* near the Turist Biro offers hotel rooms at US$30/50 single/double. During other months this hotel is closed.

## Places to Eat

There's a very poor but cheap self-service cafeteria, the *Samopostrezna Restauracija*, at Cankarjev Drevored 17 just east of the post office on the road to Koper.

*Grill Danilo Godima*, Verdijeva ulica 10 behind the Azienda Comunale just off the harbour, specialises in seafood (as the nautical décor suggests) but it also does grilled meat dishes. For such a tourist area it's surprisingly unpretentious.

*Pizzeria Palma*, about 100 metres along the road to Piran, is also good.

## PORTOROŽ

Portorož (Port of Roses) is a bloated resort on a sandy bay five km south-east of Piran. While Koper, Izola and Piran have history going back hundreds of years, Portorož is a recent creation. Obala, the main drag, is a solid strip of high-rise hotels, restaurants, bars, travel agencies, shops, discos, parked cars, tourists and the occasional tree. There's even a casino for those with spare money. If you liked Surfers Paradise or Miami Beach, Portorož is for you.

## Information

The Turist Biro is at Obala 16 near the bus station.

## Things to See

The beaches of Portorož are 'managed' so you'll pay about US$2 (US$1.50 after 1 pm) to use them.

The **Terme Palace** behind the Grand Palace Hotel at Portorož offers warm seawater baths (US$6 per half-hour), brine baths (US$16) and mud baths (US$16) Monday to Saturday from 7 am to 2 pm. Reservations are necessary.

## Places to Stay & Eat

From mid-May to mid-September there's *Autocamp Lucija*, beyond the marina at the south end of Portorož. It's on the Seca Peninsula beside the Forma Viva Sculpture Park (ask for the 'marina' bus stop). Not only is it cramped but you can expect to pay US$9 per person to pitch a tent. In July and August it could be full. Messages over the public address system of the adjacent marina could make you believe you were sleeping in a railway station.

Many travel agencies along Obala offer private rooms, including Generalturist, Globtour, Kompas, Kvarner Express, Slovenijaturist and the Turist Biro. Just stroll along until you find one that meets your fancy. Many of the rooms are up on the hillside quite a walk from the beach.

There's a self-service restaurant behind the Montenegro Express office at Plaza Beach (open only in summer). Another 'Self-Service Grill' faces the beach behind the Generalturist office.

### Getting There & Away

The Portorož bus station is in the middle of things just off the strip. There are about 10 direct daily buses from Portorož to Trieste (35 km) and seven daily to Zagreb (284 km). Buses to Piran, Izola and Koper run every half-hour.

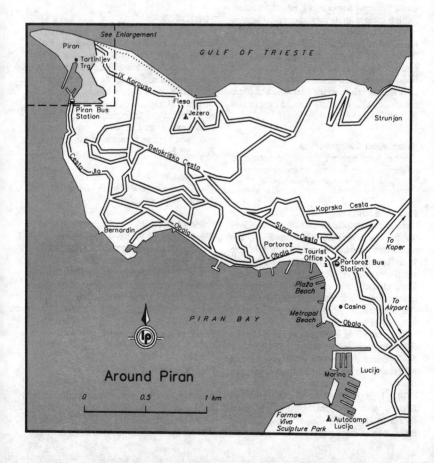

## PIRAN

Set on a point at one extreme of the Istrian Peninsula three km beyond Portorož, picturesque Piran (Pireos) is the pearl of Istria, a gem of Venetian architecture. The name derives from the Greek word 'pyr' (fire), referring to fires on the ancient lighthouse here. Piran has a long history dating from the time of the ancient Greeks, and town walls still protect it to the east.

Because it's at the end of the peninsula, tourists tend to pile up in Piran, though fortunately traffic is restricted. All cars entering the town for over an hour must pay a stiff parking fee. If you can put up with a little bustle, the tiny lanes and squares of the old town are well worth exploring.

### Orientation

The bus station is just south of the small boat harbour, an easy walk from town. Tartinijev trg, Piran's heart, opens off the top of this harbour.

### Information

The Turist Biro is at Tartinijev trg 44.

### Things to See

The **Maritime Museum** (closed Monday, US$1) in a 17th century palace on the harbour is an excellent museum with detailed descriptions of the salt-collecting basins near Piran, antique model ships, paintings and photos. The captions are in Italian and Slovene. Piran's **aquarium** (US$1.50 per person) on the other side of the small boat harbour may be small but there's a tremendous variety of life packed into the 25 tanks.

The **town hall** and **Court House** stand on Tartinijev trg, in the centre of which is a statue of the violinist and composer Giuseppe Tartini who was born here in 1692. Deeper in the medieval town is Trg 1 Maja with a Baroque fountain.

The compact old town is dominated by the tall tower of the **Parish Church of St George** on a hill overlooking the sea. This church was founded in 1344 and rebuilt in the Baroque style in 1637. It's wonderfully decorated with frescoes, marble altars and a large statue of St George killing the dragon over one door. The freestanding bell tower (1609) is modelled on the tower of San Marco in Venice, and the 17th century octagonal **baptistry** next door contains a wooden medieval crucifix (1300).

The town walls to the east can be climbed for a superb view of Piran and the sea.

### Places to Stay

**Camping** Perhaps the best place to stay is *Camping Jezero* at Fiesa, one km east of the old town. It's in a quiet valley by a small lake just a few minutes' walk from a pebble beach. A lovely path below the bluffs on the north side of the peninsula brings you into town. Camping is US$8 per person and there are also regular hotel rooms in the building above the restaurant at US$22 per person with breakfast (no supplement if you stay only one night). It's open May to September.

**Private Rooms** Because of its popularity, accommodation in Piran is always tight. The Turist Biro, Tartinijev trg 44, the pink building in the far corner of the square, has private rooms for US$11/17 single/double, with a 50% surcharge if you only stay one or two nights. The price is always 50% higher in July and August.

Kompas Tourist Service, Tartinijev trg 10, has self-contained apartments for US$20 double, but they're fully booked all summer. There's a 100% surcharge for less than three nights.

**Hotels** The cheapest hotel is the C-category *Sidro*, at Tartinijev trg 14 (US$24/34 single/double with breakfast), overpriced but full anyway. Open May to October only, it's worth considering if you're only staying one night.

Remember that US$1.25 per person per night tax will be added to all accommodation charges in Piran or Portorož.

### Places to Eat

Have a look at the affluent European tourists consuming conspicuously at the waterfront

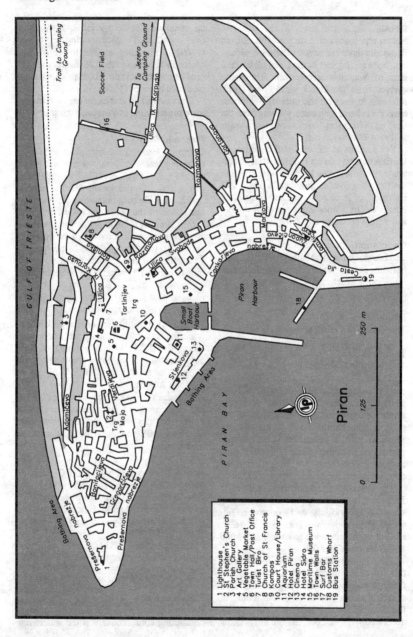

GULF OF TRIESTE

Trail to Camping Ground

Soccer Field

To Jezero Camping Ground

Ulica IX Korpusa

Razmanova

Marxova

Župančičevo

Tomšičevo nabrežje

Cesta Jla

Cankarjevo nabrežje

Ulica Svoboda

Tartinijevo

Bonifiko

Ulica IX Korpusa

Tartinijev trg

Verdijevo

Trg 1 Maja

Bonifiko

Gregorčičevo nabrežje

Prešernovo nabrežje

Adamičevo nabrežje

Prešernovo nabrežje

Stjenkova

Bathing Area

Bathing Area

Piran Harbour

Small Boat Harbour

PIRAN BAY

Piran

0    125    250 m

1 Lighthouse
2 St Stephen's Church
3 Parish Church
4 Art Gallery
5 Vegetable Market
6 Town Hall/Post Office
7 Turist Biro
8 Church of St Francis
9 Kompos
10 Court House/Library
11 Aquarium
12 Hotel Piran
13 Cinema
14 Hotel Sidro
15 Maritime Museum
16 Town Walls
17 Surf Bar
18 Customs Wharf
19 Bus Station

seafood restaurants along Presernova nabrezje.

A better bet is the *Surf Bar* on a backstreet not far from the bus station (watch for the signs). Its unique album menu contains colour photos of all its dishes. The pizza is excellent and draught beer is served in big glass mugs. In the morning you can get ham and eggs. You'll enjoy the pub-like atmosphere, and the polyglot staff will speak to you in any language you like, so it's worth stopping by for a drink at the bar even if you're not hungry.

### Getting There & Away

Local buses between Piran, Portorož, Izola and Koper are frequent. Tickets are sold on the bus (back doors). Only a few of the long-distance buses from Koper to southern Istria call at Piran Bus Station. Many more pass through Portorož Bus Station nearby.

### POREČ

Poreč (Parenzo), the Roman Parentium, sits on a low, narrow peninsula about halfway down the west coast of Istria. The ancient Dekumanus with its polished stones is still the main street of town. Even after the fall of Rome, Poreč remained important as a centre of early Christianity with a bishop and famous basilica. Though it's now the largest tourist resort in Istria, the vestiges of earlier times and the small-town atmosphere make it well worth a stop today. There are many places to swim in the clear water off the rocks on the north side of the old town.

### Orientation

The bus station is directly opposite the small boat harbour just outside the old town. There's a left-luggage room *(garderoba)* in the bus station.

### Information

Adriatikturist is at Trg Slobode 3.

### Things to See

There are many historic sites in the old town. The ruins of two **Roman temples** lie between Trg Marafor and the south end of the

peninsula. Archaeology and history are featured in the four-floor **Regional Museum** in an old Baroque palace at Dekumanus 9 (captions in German and Italian).

The main reason to visit Poreč however is to see the 6th century **Euphrasian Basilica** with its wonderfully preserved Byzantine gold mosaics. The capitals, sculpture and architecture are remarkable survivors of that distant period. Entry to the church is free and for a small fee you may visit the adjacent 4th century mosaic floor of an Early Christian basilica.

There are passenger boats (US$1.50 return) every half-hour 24 hours a day to **Sveti Nikola**, the small island opposite Poreč harbour, but it's crowded with expensive hotels and is a bore.

### Places to Stay

Accommodation in Poreč is tight and the camping grounds are far from the centre, so you might want only to stop off for the day on your way south.

**Camping** There are two camping grounds at Zelena Lacuna, six km south of Poreč. Both *Autocamp Zelena Lacuna* and *Autocamp Bijela Uvala* are open May to September and charge around US$4 per person, US$3 per tent. There are buses to Zelena Lacuna from Poreč bus station every hour or two, or catch the hourly boat from beside the Hotel Riviera in the old town. The boat landing at the Parentium Hotel is nearly two km from Autocamp Zelena Lacuna, however, and even farther from Bijela Uvala. Ask if the boat will go on to Hotel Delfin, which is closer.

**Private Rooms & Hotel** Adriatikturist, Trg Slobode 3 (and a second Adriatikturist office near the market), rents private rooms for US$8 per person. If you only stay one to three nights there's a 30% surcharge.

Slovenijaturist, Bratstva i jedinstva 12, and Kompas, Partizanska 2 beside the market, also have private rooms for similar prices. To all accommodation add US$1.50 per person per night 'residence tax'.

Rooms at the elegant old C-category *Hotel Riviera* on the waterfront are a bargain at US$19/32 single/double without bath or US$43 double with bath, breakfast included (50% more in midsummer). It's almost as cheap as a private room if you're only staying a few nights, but it's closed November to March.

## Places to Eat

In summer you can dine on an open terrace at *Self-Service Restaurant 'Peškera'* just outside the north-west corner of the old city wall. The posted menu is in English and German, and there's a free toilet at the entrance.

## Getting There & Away

The motor ship *Dionea* arrives from Trieste, Italy, one to three times a week from May to mid-December. For information ask the port captain at Obala M Tita 17 beside Kvarner Express. Tickets are sold aboard and there's a US$1.50 embarkation tax.

The nearest railway station is at Pazin, 30 km east. There are direct buses to Rijeka via

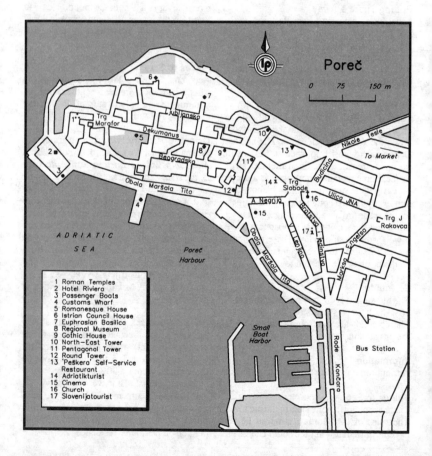

Poreč

0    75    150 m

1  Roman Temples
2  Hotel Riviera
3  Passenger Boats
4  Customs Wharf
5  Romanesque House
6  Istrian Council House
7  Euphrasian Basilica
8  Regional Museum
9  Gothic House
10 North–East Tower
11 Pentagonal Tower
12 Round Tower
13 'Peškera' Self–Service Restaurant
14 Adriatikturist
15 Cinema
16 Church
17 Slovenijatourist

Buzet or Pazin. Buses run hourly to Rovinj (39 km) and Pula (55 km). Between Poreč and Rovinj the bus runs along the Lim Channel, a drowned valley. To see it, sit on the right-hand side southbound, the left-hand side northbound.

## ROVINJ

Relaxed Rovinj (Rovigno), its high peninsula topped by the great 57-metre-high tower of massive St Euphemia Cathedral, is perhaps the best place to go in all of Istria. Wooded hills punctuated with low-rise luxury hotels surround the town, while the 13 green offshore islands of the Rovinj archipelago make for varied views. The charming atmosphere of cobbled, inclined streets in the old town is charmingly picturesque. Still an active fishing port, you actually see local people leading normal lives! There's a large Italian community here.

Private rooms are expensive and the hotels prohibitive (unless you're on a cheap package tour) but there are many quiet camping grounds on the beaches north and south of the town. Friendly Rovinj is just the place to rest up for your island-hopping journey farther south.

### Orientation

The bus station is just south-west of the old town. Go down to the waterfront and follow it around to Trg Maršala Tita.

### Information

The tourist office is at Obala Pina Budicina 12 just off Trg Maršala Tita.

### Things to See

The only sight of Rovinj worth special attention is the **Cathedral of St Euphemia** (1736), which completely dominates the town from its hilltop location. This, the largest Baroque building in Istria, reflects the period during the 18th century when Rovinj was the most populous town in Istria, an important fishing centre and the bulwark of the Venetian fleet. Inside the cathedral don't miss the tomb of St Euphemia (martyred in 304 AD) behind the right-hand altar. The

remains were brought here from Constantinople in 800. On the anniversary of her martyrdom (16 September) devotees congregate here. A copper statue of the saint tops the cathedral's mighty tower.

Take a wander along the winding narrow backstreets below the cathedral, such as ulica Grisia where local artists sell their work. Rovinj has developed into an important art centre and each year in mid-August Rovinj's painters stage a big open-air art show in the town.

The **Regional Museum** on Trg Maršala Tita (closed Sunday, US$1.50 admission) contains an unexciting collection of paintings and a few Etruscan artifacts found in Istria. These might harbour some interest if the captions were in something more than Serbo-Croatian and Italian. The **Franciscan Convent**, up the hill at E de Amicis 36, also has a small museum.

Better than either of these is the **Rovinj Aquarium** (established 1891), Obala Giordano Paliaga 5 (open daily, US$1.50), which exhibits a good collection of local marine life from poisonous scorpion fish to colourful anemones.

When you've seen enough of town, follow the waterfront south past the Park Hotel to **Punta Corrente Forest Park**. Here you can swim off the rocks, climb a cliff, or just sit and admire the offshore islands.

### Activities

Excursion boats take tourists on half-day scenic cruises to **Crveni otok** (US$5) or the **Lim Channel** (US$12), with an hour ashore at the turn-around points. It's better to go to Crveni otok (Red Island) on the hourly ferry (US$1.50 return). There's a frequent ferry to nearby **Katarina Island** (US$1 return) from the same landing.

### Places to Stay

**Camping** The closest camping ground to Rovinj is *Porton Biondi* on a wooded hill two km north of the old town. If it's closed there's *FKK Monsena Camping* three km farther north, a nudist camp. Both these are served by the Monsena bus, which terminates right

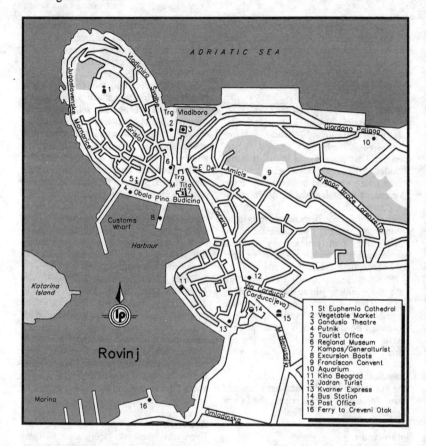

1 St Euphemia Cathedral
2 Vegetable Market
3 Gandusio Theatre
4 Putnik
5 Tourist Office
6 Regional Museum
7 Kompas/Generalturist
8 Excursion Boats
9 Franciscan Convent
10 Aquarium
11 Kino Beograd
12 Jadran Turist
13 Kvarner Express
14 Bus Station
15 Post Office
16 Ferry to Creveni Otak

in front of the reception of Monsena Camping. Five km south of Rovinj is *Villas Rubin Camping* with *FKK Polari Camping* just beyond (Villas Rubin bus). All of the above charge about US$4 per person, plus US$3 per tent, and open from May to September. Polari tends to be the first to open and last to close each season.

**Private Rooms** Many offices in Rovinj offer private rooms beginning at US$10 per person with a 30% surcharge for a stay of less than four nights. Pula and Poreč are easy commuting distance from Rovinj, so having

to stay four nights may not be such a problem. Try Jadran Turist, ulica Via Carducci 4 opposite the bus station, Kvarner Express on the harbour near the bus station, Generalturist and Kompas both on Trg Maršala Tita in the centre, or Putnik opposite the tourist office nearby. If you're told the cheaper rooms are full, try another agency. An additional US$1.50 daily per person 'residence tax' is added to all accommodation bills.

**Hotel** The 192-room *Hotel Monte Mulin*, on the wooded hillside overlooking the bay just beyond Hotel Park, is about a 15-minute walk south of the bus station. Open May to October only, bed and breakfast is US$24/46 single/double (higher in midsummer).

## Entertainment

Check the *Gandusio Theatre* on Trg Valdibora or *Kino Beograd* on the harbour.

## Getting There & Away

The motor ship *Dionea* shuttles between Rovinj and Trieste once or twice a week from May to mid-December. For information try asking at the port captain's office behind Putnik. You buy your ticket on the boat.

The closest railway station is Kanfanar, 19 km away on the Pula-Divaca line. There's a bus from Rovinj to Pula (34 km) every hour.

## Getting Around

Local buses run every two hours from the bus station, north to Monsena and south to Villas Rubin.

## PULA

Pula (the ancient Polensium) is a large regional centre with some industry, a big naval base and a busy commercial harbour. It's a noisy, crowded city, but the old town with its museums and well-preserved Roman ruins is certainly worth a visit. Near Pula are rocky wooded peninsulas overlooking the clear Adriatic waters, which may explain the many resort hotels and camping grounds concentrated there.

## Orientation

The bus station is on ulica Mate Balote in the centre of town. One block south is Trg bratstva i jedinstva, the central hub, while the harbour is just north. The railway station is near the water about one km north of town.

## Information

The Tourist Association of Pula is on ulica Jugoslavenske Narodne Armije 13.

## Things to See

Pula's most imposing sight is the 1st century AD **Roman amphitheatre** overlooking the harbour north-east of the old town. At US$6 admission (students US$2) the amphitheatre is a rip-off, but you can see plenty for free from outside. Around the end of July a Yugoslav film festival is held in the amphitheatre.

Also grossly overpriced is the US$5 **Archaeological Museum** (closed Sunday) on the hill opposite the bus station. All the captions are in Serbo-Croatian only, so content yourself with a free visit to the large sculpture garden around the museum and the **Roman Theatre** behind it. The garden is entered through 2nd century AD twin gates.

Along the street facing the bus station are **Roman walls** which mark the east boundary of old Pula. Follow these walls south and continue down Trg bratstva i jedinstva to the **Triumphal Arch of Sergius** (27 BC). The street beyond the arch winds right around old Pula, changing names several times as it goes. Follow it to Trg Republike where you'll find the ancient **Temple of Augustus** and the **Old Town Hall** (1296). Above this square is the **Franciscan Church** (1314) with a museum in the cloister (entry from around the other side) containing paintings, medieval frescoes, a Roman mosaic, etc.

Better is the **National Revolution Museum** (US$1) in the 17th century Venetian citadel on a high hill in the centre of the old town. Aside from the exhibits, which deal mostly with the partisan struggle in WW II, the views of Pula from the citadel walls are unsurpassed.

## Places to Stay

**Camping** The closest camping ground to Pula is *Autocamp Stoja* (open mid-April to mid-October) three km south-west of the centre (bus No 1 Stoja to the terminus). Camping is US$4 per person, plus US$2 per tent, plus US$1.50 per person tax. There's lots of space on the shady promontory with swimming possible off the rocks. The two restaurants at this camping ground are good. There are more camping grounds at Medulin and Premantura, beach resorts south-east of Pula.

**Hostels** The *Letovalište Ferijalnog Saveza Youth Hostel*, Zaliv Valsalina 4 (open May to

September), is three km south of central Pula in a great location overlooking a clean pebble beach open to the sea. Take the Verudela bus (about every 10 minutes) to the 'Piramida' stop and walk back to the first street, turn right and look for the sign. Beds are US$9 per person and camping is allowed at the hostel (US$3). You can sit and sip cold beer on the hostel's terrace where a rock band plays some summer evenings. If the youth hostel is full and you have a tent it's only a 10-minute walk from there to *Autocamp Ribarska Koliba* (open from mid-June to mid-September).

**Private Rooms** Arenaturist, Trg bratstva i jedinstva 4 a block from the bus station, has private rooms for US$10 per person with an additional 30% surcharge if you stay less than four nights. Other offices offering similar rooms at similar rates are Brioni Turist Biro, Ulica Jugoslavenske Narodne Armije 3 beside the bus station, and Kompas, Premanturska 6 near the main market.

**Hotels** The cheapest hotel is 112-room *Pension Ribarska Koliba* near the camping ground of the same name, towards Verudela about three km south of Pula (Verudela bus).

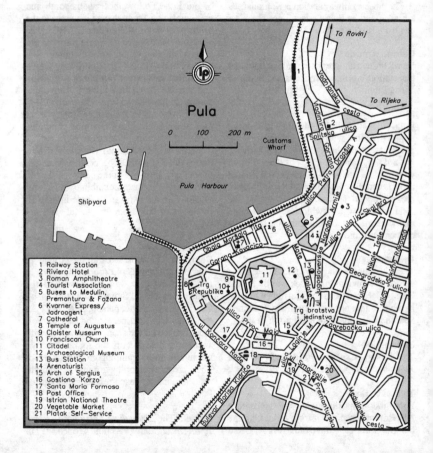

Pula

0    100    200 m

1  Railway Station
2  Riviera Hotel
3  Roman Amphitheatre
4  Tourist Association
5  Buses to Medulin,
   Premantura & Fazana
6  Kvarner Express/
   Jadroagent
7  Cathedral
8  Temple of Augustus
9  Cloister Museum
10 Franciscan Church
11 Citadel
12 Archaeological Museum
13 Bus Station
14 Arenaturist
15 Arch of Sergius
16 Gostiona 'Korzo'
17 Santa Maria Formosa
18 Post Office
19 Istrian National Theatre
20 Vegetable Market
21 Platak Self-Service

Rooms with shared bath are US$20/33 single/double (plus 25% in midsummer) but it's often full with groups. The pension has a nice terrace overlooking a bay full of small boats.

Treat yourself to a little luxury at the B-category *Hotel Riviera*, Splitska ulica 1 overlooking the harbour. Comfortable rooms in this elegant old hotel erected in 1908 run US$33/41 single/double with shared bath, US$40/53 with private bath, breakfast included.

### Places to Eat

There's a self-service restaurant in the back of *Snack Express Gorica*, Trg bratstva i jedinstva 21, but it's a little complicated as you must pay first and get a ticket from the cashier. *Platak Self-Service* opposite the city market is larger, cheaper and easier since you see what you're getting and pay as you leave. The good food and attractive décor make this one of the best of its kind in Yugoslavia.

For grilled meats and local dishes such as goulash, smoked ham and squid risotto try *Gostiona 'Korzo'*, ulica Prvog maja 34. Despite the plain exterior it's moderately expensive so check the menus in the window carefully before entering. Beware, there are two menus here – a reasonable lunch menu and a relatively expensive dinner menu. Both are posted outside in English, German and Italian. You can eat inexpensively if you order carefully.

### Getting There & Away

**Bus** Buses to Rijeka (104 km) are sometimes crowded, especially those continuing on to Zagreb, so reserve a seat a day in advance if you can. Going from Pula to Rijeka be sure to sit on the right-hand side of the bus for a stunning view of Kvarner Bay. There are also direct buses to Split and Dubrovnik, some travelling overnight. Other buses run north to Koper (104 km) via Rovinj and Poreč.

**Train** Ever since the days when Pula was the main port of the Austro-Hungarian empire the railway line in Istria has run north towards Italy and Austria instead of east into what is now Yugoslavia. Most local trains terminate at Divača (140 km) near Trieste, where you connect for Ljubljana. Couchettes are available between Pula and Belgrade all year, between Pula and Zagreb in summer, saving you a night's accommodation.

**Boat** For the ferry to Mali Lošinj (US$10 one-way), Silba (US$15 one-way) and Zadar (US$18 one-way) ask at Kvarner Express on the harbour. They leave daily except Friday from mid-June to mid-September and only on Friday the rest of the year. In February there's no service. Departure time may be at 5 am! You can fly from Pula to Zadar for US$31.

Get information about the motor ship *Dionea* to Trieste, Italy, from Jadroagent on the harbour. There's service once a week from May to mid-December.

### Getting Around

Catch city buses on Trg bratstva i jedinstva. Tokens for these are sold at newsstands. The JAT airport bus (US$2) leaves from the main bus station.

### BRIONI

The Brioni Group consists of two main, pine-covered islands and 12 islets off the coast of Istria just north-west of Pula. Each year from 1949 until his death in 1980 Marshal Tito spent six months at his summer residences on Brioni in a style any western capitalist would admire. Tito received 90 heads of state here, and at a meeting on Veliki Brioni in 1956 Tito, Nasser and Nehru laid the foundations of the Non-Aligned Movement.

Tito had three palaces on Veliki Brioni: the main island, Vila Jadranka, Bijela Vila and Vila Brionka. The famous 1956 Brioni Declaration was signed in Bijela Vila, Tito's 'White House'. Tourists are driven past these three, but Tito's private retreat on the tiny islet of Vanga cannot be visited. Some 680 species of plants grow on the islands, including many exotic subtropical species planted at Tito's request.

In 1984 Brioni was proclaimed a national

park but there's still a heavy military presence on the islands. As you arrive after a half-hour boat ride from Fažana on the mainland, you'll see Tito's two private yachts still tied up in the harbour, and four luxury hotels near the landing where his guests once stayed.

The four-hour tour of Veliki Brioni begins with a visit to **St German Church**, now a gallery of copies of medieval frescoes in Istrian churches. The **'Tito on Brioni'** exhibit in another building includes large photos of Tito with film stars such as Gina Lollobrigida, Sophia Loren, Elizabeth Taylor and Richard Burton, all of whom visited Tito here.

Then you're driven around the island in a small train, past the palaces and through a **safari park**. The fenced area was Tito's private hunting ground, and the exotic animals presently there were given to Tito by world leaders. Deer wander wild across the island. You go past the ruins of a 1st century AD **Roman villa** without stopping, and then have a walk around an unexciting zoo. Towards the end of the tour you're herded quickly through the excellent **ethnographical museum** with Yugoslav folk costumes.

### Getting There & Away

You may only visit Brioni National Park with a group. Take a public bus from Pula to Fažana (eight km), then sign up for a tour (US$27) at the Brioni Tourist Service office near the wharf.

You can book the same tour through Arenaturist or another travel agency in Pula for US$31, thus ensuring transport to/from Fažana and a tour in a language you understand (if you just show up at Fažana you'll take pot luck which language your guide will speak). Also check along the Pula waterfront for excursion boats to Brioni.

If you can spare the cash, a far better possibility is to stay at the 58-room *Hotel Jurina* (US$50 double with bath, no singles) on Veliki Brioni itself and see the island at leisure. It's open May to October only and advance bookings (☎ 052-22455) are essential, otherwise you'll be put in one of the

three A-category hotels, the *Istra, Karmen* and *Neptun*, all of which cost double the B-category Jurina. Check the price with half and full board when you call.

# Gulf of Kvarner

The Gulf of Kvarner (Quarnero) stretches 100 km south from Rijeka between the Istrian Peninsula and the Croatian littoral. The many elongated islands are the peaks of a submerged branch of the Dinaric Alps, the range which follows the coast south all the way to Albania. Krk, Cres and Pag are among the largest islands in Yugoslavia. Rijeka, an ugly commercial port and communications hub at the north end of the gulf, is well connected to Italy and Austria by road and rail, which explains the heavy tourist traffic. Big crowds also funnel into nearby Opatija, one-time bathing resort of the Habsburg elite, and Krk Island, now linked to the mainland by bridge. Historic Rab is the jewel of the Gulf of Kvarner but it's hard to reach and expensive. To get slightly off the beaten track and see the best of the gulf into the bargain, consider Mali Lošinj, easily accessible from Rijeka by bus and boat.

### RIJEKA

Rijeka, 126 km south of Ljubljana, is the sort of place you try to avoid but sometimes can't. Although the city does have a few saving graces, such as the pedestrian mall, Korzo narodne revolucije, and a colourful market, it seems to have lost its soul under a hail of wartime bombs. You don't have to dive far into the old town off Korzo to sense the confusion and decay. The belching industry, automobiles, shipyards, refineries, cranes and container ships jammed into the narrow coastal strip aren't beautiful. This largest of all Yugoslav ports does have a sort of crude energy, however, and if you like punishment Rijeka will give it to you.

### Orientation

The bus station is on Trg Žabica below the

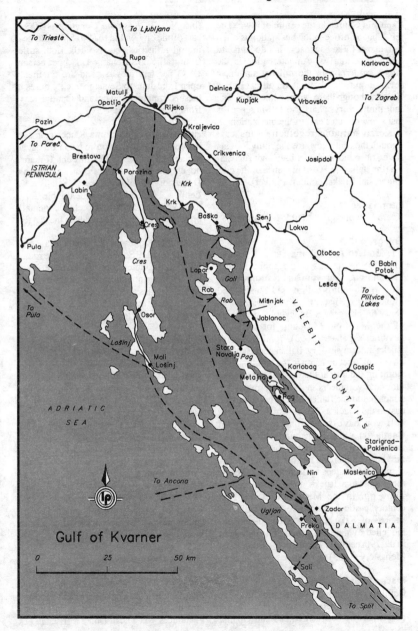

Gulf of Kvarner

0    25    50 km

Capuchin Church in the centre of town. The left-luggage office in the bus station is often full, doesn't like backpacks but does like to overcharge tourists. An alternative is the larger *garderoba* in the railway station, a seven-minute walk west on ulica Borisa Kidriča, though there can be a line there. The Jadrolinija ferry wharf (no left-luggage) is just a few minutes east of the bus station.

Korzo narodne revolucije runs east through the centre towards the filthy Rječina River, once the border of Italy and Yugoslavia (the Italian and current names of the city, Fiume and Rijeka, both mean river).

## Information

Kvarner Express is on Trg P Togliattija 3.

## Things to See

The **Modern Art Gallery**, Dolac 1 (closed Monday), is upstairs in the public library. The **Maritime Museum** and **National Revolution Museum** (both closed Sunday and Monday) are adjacent at Žrtava fašizma 18 above the city centre. Bullet holes in the side of the Maritime Museum, formerly the governor's palace (1893), remind one of Rijeka's stormy history. Italian poet Gabriele d'Annunzio set up camp in the building after storming the city at the head of a couple of thousand volunteers in 1919, a provocation which led to the Italian border being moved east to the Rječina.

If you have some time to kill, **Trsat Castle**, on a high ridge overlooking Rijeka and the canyon of the River Rječina, is your best bet. Get there on bus No 1 from town or climb the 559 steps up from the arch beside the Jugobanka Rijeka at the north end of Titov trg. In the Middle Ages the 13th century castle belonged to the Frankopan princes of Krk, but it was completely remodelled by the Irish general Laval Nugent in the 19th century. There's also a Franciscan Monastery (1453) at Trsat.

## Places to Stay

**Camping** There are two camping grounds outside Rijeka. *Preluk Camping* is beside the busy highway between Rijeka and Opatija

(bus No 32). *Kostrena Camping* is 10 km east of the city on the road to Split, out near the oil refineries (bus No 10). Both suffer from traffic noise, charge US$4 per person, US$3 per tent plus tax and are unreliably open from June to September. City buses to these camping grounds and Opatija leave from Beogradski trg.

**Hotels & Private Rooms** Rather than stay in depressing Rijeka you're better off catching an onward bus to Krk or Pula. If there's no choice the 'cheapest' hotel is the old D-category *Hotel Kontinental*, Šetalište V I Lenjina 1 (US$47/62 single/double for a room with shared bath). Hotel Kontinental's prices have more than doubled in the last few years.

Kvarner Express, Trg P Togliattija 3, and Generalturist, F Supila 2, have private rooms for US$20 double with a 30% discount if you like Rijeka enough to stay four or more nights. Singles are seldom available and all rooms are often full. Add US$1.50 tax per person per night to all accommodation.

## Places to Eat

*Restoran Index*, ulica Borisa Kidriča 18 between the bus and railway stations, has a good self-service section *(samoposluzi)* with set 'menus' for breakfast, lunch and dinner (under US$2). It's cheap, clean and straightforward.

A quick stand-up snack bar is *Pecenjara*, Titov trg 6 across the river from Hotel Kontinental.

## Entertainment

Performances at the *'Ivan Zajc' National Theatre* (1885) are mostly drama in Serbo-Croatian, although opera and ballet are sometimes offered. The ticket office is open weekdays and Saturday mornings.

## Getting There & Away

**Bus** There are 13 buses a day between Rijeka and Krk (53 km, 1½ hours, US$3) using the huge Tito Bridge. The buses to Krk are overcrowded and a seat reservation in no way guarantees you a seat. Don't worry, the bus

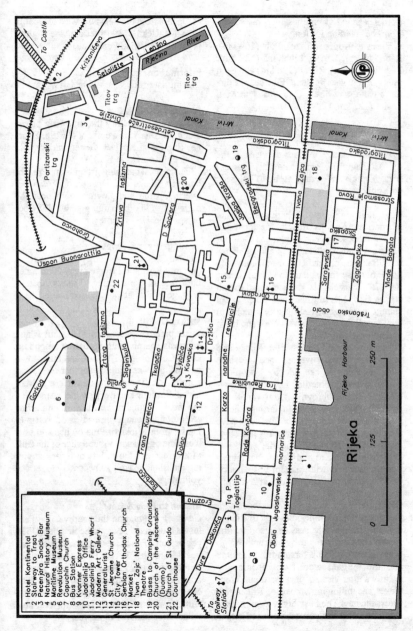

Rijeka

1 Hotel Kontinental
2 Stairway to Trsat
3 Pecenjara Snack Bar
4 Natural History Museum
5 Maritime Museum
6 Revolution Museum
7 Capuchin Church
8 Bus Station
9 Kvarner Express
10 Jadrolinija Office
11 Jadrolinija Ferry Wharf
12 Modern Art Gallery
13 Generalturist
14 St Jerome Church
15 City Tower
16 Serbian Orthodox Church
17 Market
18 'Ivan Zajc' National
   Theatre
19 Buses to Camping Grounds
20 Church of the Ascension
   (Duomo)
21 Church of St Guido
22 Courthouse

from Rijeka to Krk empties fairly fast so you won't be standing for long.

Buses to Koper (86 km), Pula (104 km), Rab (115 km, US$9), Ljubljana (128 km), Zagreb (184 km), Zadar (228 km) and Split (404 km) are also frequent. Five buses a day run all the way down Cres Island to Mali Lošinj (122 km, US$9).

**Train** Trains run from Rijeka to Ljubljana (155 km via Postojna) with a change of trains at Pivka necessary on many services. Some trains to Zagreb (243 km) have only 1st-class seats. There's an overnight train to Belgrade with couchettes.

**Boat** Jadrolinija, at Obala jugoslovenske mornarice 16, sells tickets for the large coastal ferries between Rijeka and Dubrovnik from mid-April to mid-October. Fares run US$27 to Split and US$35 to Dubrovnik. Some of these ships go on to Corfu, Greece (US$70). This ship is also supposed to call at Rab (US$13), but if there's 'fog' (ie not enough passengers to drop off or pick up) they cancel the stop without notice and leave you holding your bags.

The southbound ferries leave Rijeka at 6 pm several times a week. Since the ships travel between Rijeka and Split at night, you're better off boarding in Split and travelling south to Dubrovnik if you want to see anything. Otherwise buy a through ticket from Rijeka to Dubrovnik or Corfu and have the purser validate your ticket for free stopovers at Split, Hvar and Korčula.

From mid-June to mid-September there's a daily ferry to Mali Lošinj (6½ hours, US$14), departing from Rijeka at 2.15 pm.

## OPATIJA

Opatija, just a few km south-west of Rijeka, was the fashionable seaside resort of the Austro-Hungarian empire right up until WW I. Many grand old hotels remain from this time and the elegant waterfront promenade affords a fine view of the apartment complexes and billowing smoke of Rijeka just across the bay. The busy highway runs right along the coast and you get a passing glance of Opatija from the Pula bus. West of Opatija rises Mt Učka (1396 metres), the highest point on the Istrian Peninsula.

### Information
The tourist office is at Maršala Tita 183.

### Places to Stay & Eat
For private rooms, try the following places along Maršala Tita: Putnik at No 196, Kvarner Express at No 183, Generalturist at No 178, and Kompas at No 170.

The nearest camping grounds are *Preluka* between Rijeka and Opatija, and *Ičići* between Opatija and Lovran, both near the highway and both charging about US$4 per person plus US$3 per tent.

### Getting There & Away
Bus No 32 runs right along the Opatija Riviera from Rijeka to Lovran every 20 minutes until late in the evening. There's no left-luggage facility at Opatija Bus Station.

## MALI LOŠINJ
Lush, pine-covered Lošinj (Lussino) Island contrasts sharply with its barren neighbour Cres (Cherso). Mali Lošinj, the main town on Lošinj's west side, is another old Habsburg retreat. There's not a lot to see in Mali Lošinj but four km away on the east side of the island is smaller Veli Lošinj with a few old buildings and a pleasant park. A trip to Lošinj from Rijeka or Pula by bus and boat would be a good way to see a slice of the Gulf of Kvarner, and the variety of ferries servicing the island make it unnecessary to retrace your steps.

### Places to Stay & Eat
*Camping Poljana* on the nearby Čikat Peninsula is open from May to September (US$8 per person). Private rooms are available all year from the Turist Biro and Kvarner Express in Mali Lošinj. The Turist Biro in nearby Veli Lošinj also has rooms. The cheapest hotel is the D-category *Istra* in town with 23 rooms for US$22/40 single/double with shared bath (open all year).

## Getting There & Away

Mali Lošinj is connected by ferry to Pula (3½ hours, US$10 one-way) and Zadar (four hours) six times a week from mid-June to mid-September but only once a week the rest of the year. In February there's no service. The timings of this ferry are more convenient southbound than northbound. Another ferry links Mali Lošinj to Rijeka daily from mid-June to mid-September (US$14), departing from Mali Lošinj at 4.30 am and Rijeka at 2.15 pm with two to four stops along the way. Tourist boats sometimes cross to Rab Island. A local ferry links Mali Lošinj to the offshore islands of Srakane Vele, Unije, Ilovik and Susak daily, a four-hour return cruise.

Five buses a day run from Rijeka to Mali Lošinj (122 km, US$9). The bus uses the Brestova-Porozina ferry and drives down the entire length of Cres and Lošinj islands, a very scenic trip.

## KRK

Krk (Veglia), Yugoslavia's largest island (409 sq km), is barren and rocky with little vegetation. It's the first main Adriatic island you come to on the way south and it's *on* the beaten tourist track. Since completion of the Tito Bridge in 1980 Krk has suffered too rapid a development – Rijeka Airport and some industry are at the north end of Krk, big tourist hotels are in the middle and far south. Still, the main town (also called Krk) is rather picturesque and the camping facilities are good. You can easily stop at Krk town for a few hours of sightseeing, then catch a later bus to Baška and Krk's longest beach.

From the 12th to the 15th centuries Krk and the surrounding region remained semi-independent under the Frankopan Dukes of Krk, an indigenous Croatian dynasty, at a time when much of the Adriatic was controlled by Venice. This history explains the various medieval sights you'll see in Krk town, the ducal seat.

## Orientation

The bus from Baška and Rijeka stops by the harbour, a few minutes' walk from the old town of Krk. There's no left-luggage facility at Krk Bus Station.

## Information

The Turist Biro is in the unmarked white building on the waterfront between the bus station and the old town (enter from the side facing the road).

## Things to See

The 14th century **Frankopan Castle** and lovely 12th century Romanesque **cathedral** are in the lower town near the harbour. In the upper part of Krk are three old monastic churches. The narrow streets of Krk are worth exploring.

## Places to Stay

**Camping** There are three camping grounds. The closest is *Autocamp Ježevac* on the coast, 10 minutes' walk south-west of town. The rocky soil makes it nearly impossible to use tent pegs, but there are lots of stones to anchor your lines. There's good shade and places to swim. *Camping Bor* is on a hill inland from Ježevac, while *Camp Politin FKK* is a naturist camp south-east of Krk just beyond the large resort hotels.

**Private Rooms** Kvarner Express on the harbour has private rooms for US$18 double plus a 30% surcharge for less than four nights. Similar rooms can be had from the Turist Biro.

## Getting There & Away

Thirteen buses a day to/from Rijeka (53 km) make Krk the perfect escape from that city. En route the bus crosses the massive Tito Bridge. Bus service from Krk to Baška (20 km, one hour) is also good.

## BAŠKA

Baška, at the south end of Krk Island, is a popular resort with a long sandy beach set below a high ridge. Most of the buses from Rijeka to Krk go on to Baška and you might consider going all the way if swimming and scenery are your main interests. These are better at Baška than at Krk.

## Orientation

The bus from Krk stops at the edge of the old town between the beach and the harbour. To reach the Lopar ferry, follow the street closest to the water through the old town, heading south-east for less than a km.

## Things to See & Do

Climb up to the **Chapel of Sveti Ivan** on the hillside above Baška for the view.

## Places to Stay & Eat

**Camping** There are two camping possibilities. *Camping Zablaće* (open from May to September) is on the beach visible south-west of the bus stop (look for the rows of caravans). In heavy rain you risk getting flooded here. A better bet is *FKK Camp Bunculuka* (open from May to September) over the hill east of the harbour (a 15-minute walk). It's quiet, shady and conveniently close to the ferries and town.

**Private Rooms** The tourist office, Zvonimirova 114 just up the street from the bus stop, has private rooms for US$20 double (plus 30% if you stay less than four nights) but it won't rent rooms for one night. Kvarner Express at the Corinthia Hotel has no such problems and Kompas nearby also has private rooms, so try there first.

**Hotels** Small, basic rooms without private bath are available at the hotels *Velebit* and *Baška* right on the main beach for US$15/25 single/double including breakfast (25% higher in midsummer, open from May to October only). Bookings must be made at the reception of the *Hotel Corinthia* nearby where you'll take breakfast. You must insist on these rooms – the Corinthia staff will try to steer you into much more expensive rooms in the main hotel.

## Getting There & Away

From June to August there are car ferries from Baška to Senj (US$5) on the mainland between Rijeka and Zadar twice a day. Buses run from Senj to the Plitvice Lakes. The ferry from Baška to Lopar on Rab Island operates about three times a day from June to September (US$5). The rest of the year you could be forced to backtrack to Rijeka to get farther south.

## RAB

Rab (Arbe) Island, near the centre of the Kvarner Island Group, is one of the most enticing in the Adriatic. The north-east side of Rab is barren and rocky, the south-west side fairly green with pine forests. High mountains protect Rab from the colder northern and eastern winds.

Medieval Rab town is built on a narrow peninsula pointing south which encloses a sheltered harbour. The old stone buildings climb from the harbour to a cliff overlooking the sea. For hundreds of years Rab was an outpost of Venice until the Austrians took over in the 19th century.

Even today you'll hear as much German as Serbo-Croatian on Rab and you'll find that transport, accommodation and food – virtually everything connected with a visit – is very expensive. Even so, it's a convenient stepping stone between Krk and Zadar and one of the prettiest little towns on the Adriatic.

## Orientation

The bus station is opposite the Merkur department store near the harbour, a five-minute walk from the old town. The large Jadrolinija ferries tie up near the Beograd Hotel in the old town.

## Information

The Turist Biro has two branches, one between the bus station and the harbour (open all day) and another on Maršala Tita in the old town.

## Things to See

Four tall church towers rise above the red-roofed mass of houses on Rab's high peninsula. If you follow Rade Končara north from the **Monastery of St Anthony** (1175) you soon reach the Romanesque **cathedral**, alongside a pleasant belvedere overlooking the sea. Farther along, beyond a tall Romanesque tower and another convent, is a second belvedere and **St Justine Church**, now a small museum of religious art. Just past the next chapel look for a small gate giving access to a park with the foundations of Rab's oldest church and the fourth tower.

Rade Končara ends at the north city wall, which you should try to climb for a splendid view of the town, harbour, sea and hill, although the gate is often locked. The scene is especially beautiful just after sunset. North of the wall is the extensive **city park** with many shady walkways.

## Places to Stay

**Camping** To sleep cheap, carry your tent south along the waterfront about 25 minutes to *Autocamp Padova* (US$4 per person, US$3 per tent) at Banjol. If you're arriving by bus ask the driver to drop you off at the Restaurant St Lucia on the hill above. There's a wooded ridge by the camping ground where you can pitch a tent away from the noise and caravans. The beach is just below.

**Private Rooms** Private rooms are dispensed

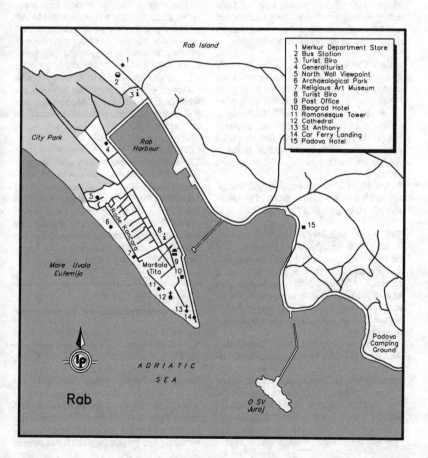

1 Merkur Department Store
2 Bus Station
3 Turist Biro
4 Generalturist
5 North Wall Viewpoint
6 Archaeological Park
7 Religious Art Museum
8 Turist Biro
9 Post Office
10 Beograd Hotel
11 Romanesque Tower
12 Cathedral
13 St Anthony
14 Car Ferry Landing
15 Padova Hotel

Rab Island

City Park

Rab Harbour

Rade Končara

More Uvala Eufemija

Maršala Tita

Padova Camping Ground

ADRIATIC SEA

Rab

O SV Juraj

by the Turist Biro at two locations: one near the bus station and another on Maršala Tita in the old town. Prices start at US$12/20 single/double plus tax, but you pay 30% more if you only stay one or two nights. The Turist Biro near the bus station has only 1st-category private rooms in the newer section of town. For 2nd and 3rd-category rooms in the old town go to the Turist Biro on Maršala Tita. The Kompas kiosk at the bus station and Generalturist on the harbour may also have private rooms.

You could be approached by women at the bus station offering *sobes*. They've been rather spoiled by overspending tourists and the high rates charged by hotels, tourist offices, etc, so expect to have to bargain.

**Hotels** The cheapest hotel is the 54-room, D-category *Beograd* on the harbour in the old town. The second-rate orchestra playing in the restaurant could keep you awake but the rooms are reasonable, US$19/33 single/double with breakfast in June and September, US$24/43 in July and August (hotel closed during other months). Full board at the Beograd is only about US$4 per person extra!

Add US$1.50 per person per night 'tourist tax' to all accommodation rates. In midsummer all the hotels of Rab are full.

### Getting There & Away

**Bus** The most reliable way to come or go is on one of the two daily buses between Rab and Rijeka (115 km, US$9). In the tourist season there's also a direct bus from Zagreb to Rab (215 km). These services can fill up so book ahead if possible. If you're bound for the Plitvice Lakes from Rab you change buses at Senj.

There's no direct bus from Rab to Zadar. You must take the Rijeka or Zagreb bus up to the main highway at Jablanac and wait there. This is fairly easy as there are lots of connecting buses to Zadar running down the main coastal highway. Going from Zadar to Rab by bus is much more difficult as you probably won't find a bus from Jablanac to Rab and may have to walk or hitchhike.

**Boat** Getting to Rab by boat is not easy. The ferry from Baška on Krk Island to Lopar at the north end of Rab operates thrice daily from June to September only (US$5). From June to August there are two daily ferries from Senj on the mainland to Lopar. Unless you're on a through bus to/from Rijeka or Zagreb, the more frequent year-round ferry from Jablanac on the mainland to Mišnjak on Rab Island is problematic. Jablanac is four km off the main Rijeka-Split highway (downhill all the way) and there are no local buses from Mišnjak into Rab town (11 km).

The large Jadrolinija coastal ferries between Zadar and Rijeka are supposed to call at Rab a few times a week and this would certainly be the best, if not the cheapest way to come, *except* that northbound they arrive in the middle of the night and don't stop at all if the captain decides there aren't enough passengers waiting to make it worth his while (ie if there's 'fog'). The ships' agent at Rab shares an office with the tourist office on Maršala Tita.

### LOPAR

The bus from Lopar to Rab town stops in front of Pizzeria Aloha opposite the small boat harbour about 300 metres ahead of the Lopar ferry landing. The stop is unmarked so ask. There's a bus every hour or two to Rab town (12 km). Several houses around here have *sobe* signs. *Camping Rajska Plaza* (San Marino) is about three km south of the Lopar ferry landing, across the peninsula.

# Dalmatia

Dalmatia (Dalmacija) occupies the central 375 km of Yugoslavia's Adriatic coast from the Gulf of Kvarner to the Bay of Kotor, offshore islands included. Except for Bosnia-Hercegovina's tiny opening to the sea at Kardeljevo, this entire coastal region belongs to the Republic of Croatia. The rugged Dinaric Alps form a 1500-metre-high barrier separating Dalmatia from Bosnia with only two breaks: the Krka River canyon at Krin and the Neretva Valley at Mostar, both with railways. After the last ice age, part of the coastal mountains were flooded, creating the same sort of long, high islands seen in the Gulf of Kvarner. The deep, protected passages between these islands are a paradise for sailors and cruisers.

Historical relics abound in towns like Zadar, Šibenik, Trogir, Split, Hvar, Korčula and Dubrovnik, framed by a striking natural beauty of barren slopes, green valleys and clear water. The vineyards of Dalmatia supply a third of Yugoslavia's wine. A warm current flowing north up the coast keeps the climate mild, dry in summer, damp in winter. Although not unexplored, much of Dalmatia is less touristed than Istria, Krk, Dubrovnik and Budva. This is the Mediterranean at its best.

## HISTORY

The Illyrians settled here around 1000 BC, followed in the 4th century BC by the Greeks who established colonies at Korčula, Hvar and Salona. When Greek and Illyrian interests collided, the Romans intervened and after 74 years of wars they succeeded in subjugating the province of Dalmatia in 155 BC. Major Roman ruins are still seen in Zadar, Salona and Split. After the Western Roman Empire fell in the 5th century AD, the region became a battleground for barbarians, Byzantines and countless other conquerors. The present inhabitants are descended from Slavonic tribes which arrived in the 6th century.

Medieval Dalmatia was ruled at different times by Venice and Croatia. In 1409 Venice purchased Dalmatia from Louis of Naples, the Hungaro-Croatian king, and held it until Napoleon captured Venice itself in 1797. Most of the coastal towns still bear a deep Italian imprint, quite a contrast to the Turkish influence just a few dozen km inland. Through diplomatic deals Dalmatia was eventually handed to Austria which held it until 1918.

In 1915 Britain and France promised northern Dalmatia to Italy if that country would enter WW I on their side. After

postwar wranglings it was finally agreed that Italy could have Istria, Cres, Lošinj, Zadar and Lastovo while Yugoslavia got the rest. In 1941 Mussolini annexed the whole of Dalmatia to Italy but in 1947 everything was formally given back to Yugoslavia, including the territory Italy got from Austria in 1920.

## PAKLENICA NATIONAL PARK

A good place to get in touch with the environment of Yugoslavia's Dinaric Alps is Paklenica National Park, 50 km north-east of Zadar near Starigrad-Paklenica village. All the coastal buses pass this way. Get out at Hotel Alan, one hour from Zadar by bus, where there's a large camping ground, private rooms, supermarket, etc. The three-km park access road up the Velika Paklenica Gorge begins near the hotel, and the person charging admission (US$4) usually has hiking maps for sale. It's a three-hour hike on a beaten track up the gorge to the refuge, Borisov Dom (550 metres). From here you can climb Vaganski Vrh (1758 metres), the highest peak in the Velebit Mountains, in a full-day return trip. Excellent half-day side trips off the main trail to Borisov Dom are to Aniča Kuk (712 metres) to the right and Manita Cave (bring a torch) and Vidakov Kuk (866 metres) to the left. There are lots of other hiking possibilities of varying degrees of difficulty.

## ZADAR

Zadar (Zara), the main city of northern Dalmatia, occupies a long peninsula between the harbour and the Zadar Channel. The city of Iader was laid out by the Romans, who left behind considerable ruins. Later the area fell under Byzantium which explains the centrally planned Orthodox churches. In 1409 Venice took Zadar from Croatia and held it for four centuries. Dalmatia was included in the Austro-Hungarian empire during most of the 19th century, with Italy exercising control from 1918 to 1943.

Badly damaged by Anglo-American bombing raids in 1943-44, much of the city had to be rebuilt. Luckily the original street plan was respected and an effort made to harmonise the new with what remained of old Zadar. Although the scars of war are still visible, the narrow, traffic-free stone streets are full of life, and Zadar can be a fascinating place in which to wander. Tremendous 16th century fortifications still shield the city on the landward side and high walls run along the harbour. None of the various museums is exceptional and the monuments show signs of wear, but Zadar is surprising for its variety of sights. It's also famous for its Maraska cherry liqueur.

## Orientation

The train and bus stations are adjacent, a 15-minute walk south-east of the harbour and old town. The left-luggage office is in the railway station, not the bus station. From here, 8 korpusa and Rade Končara lead north-west past the main post office to the harbour. Either walk or take a local bus into town as the unmetered taxis here want US$6 for the trip. Narodni trg is the heart of Zadar.

## Information

Sunturist is on Narodni trg, though it's not good on transport times.

## Things to See

The main things to see are near the circular **St Donatus Church**, a 9th century Byzantine structure built over the Roman forum. In summer ask about musical evenings here (Renaissance and early Baroque music). The outstanding **Museum of Church Art** (closed Monday) in the Benedictine Monastery opposite offers a substantial display of reliquaries and religious paintings. The obscure lighting deliberately recreates the environment in which the objects were originally kept.

The 13th century Romanesque **Cathedral of St Anastasia** nearby never really recovered from wartime destruction, and the **Franciscan Monastery** a few blocks away is more cheerful. The large Romanesque cross in the treasury behind the sacristy is worth seeing.

Other museums include the **Archaeological Museum** (closed Monday) across from St Donatus, and the **Ethnological Museum** in the Town Watchtower (1562) on Narodni trg. More interesting is the **National Museum** on Poljana V Gortana just inside the Sea Gate. This excellent historical museum features scale models of Zadar from different periods, and old paintings and engravings of many coastal cities. Upstairs there's a display on the activities of the partisans. The same admission ticket will get you into the local **Art Gallery**. Unfortunately, the captions in all of Zadar's museums are in Serbo-Croatian only.

## Activities

Any of the many travel agencies around town can supply information on the daily tourist cruise to the beautiful **Kornati Islands** (US$42, including lunch and a swim in the sea or a salt lake). As this is about the only way to see these 101 barren, uninhabited islands, islets and cliffs it's worthwhile if you can spare the cash, but the trips are cancelled during bad weather and throughout winter. Check with Kvarner Express on Omladinska, and with Sunturist. The Kornati boats leave from the wharf near Hotel Zagreb.

## Places to Stay

**Camping** *Autocamp Borik* (open from May to September, US$4 per person, US$3 per tent) is near a large hotel complex four km north-west of Zadar. There's even a beach! Buses No 5 and 8 pass the autocamp.

*Autocamp Punta Bajlo* is on a quiet shady headland overlooking the sea 2.5 km south-east of the old town (bus No 2). It's within walking distance of the railway station: turn left towards the sea and ask for directions after a block or two. Camping is US$4 per person, US$3 per tent (open from May to September).

**Hostels** The 330-bed *Borik Youth Hostel*, Obala oktobarske revolucije 76 (open from May to September), is near the beach on the coast a few km north-west (ask for 'Ferjalni savez Hevatake', the official name of the

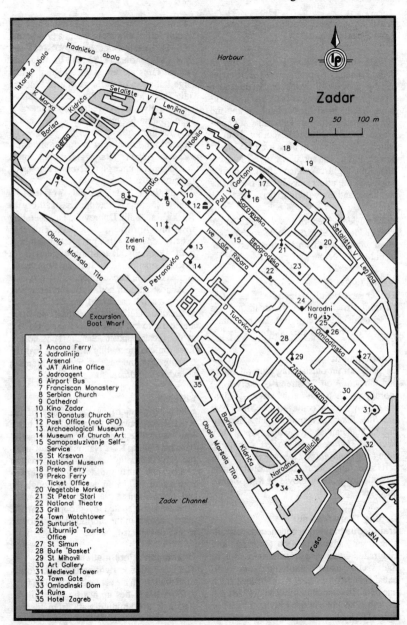

## Zadar

0    50    100 m

1  Ancona Ferry
2  Jadrolinija
3  Arsenal
4  JAT Airline Office
5  Jadroagent
6  Airport Bus
7  Franciscan Monastery
8  Serbian Church
9  Cathedral
10 Kino Zadar
11 St Donatus Church
12 Post Office (not GPO)
13 Archaeological Museum
14 Museum of Church Art
15 Samoposluzivanje Self-
   Service
16 St Krsevan
17 National Museum
18 Preko Ferry
19 Preko Ferry
   Ticket Office
20 Vegetable Market
21 St Petar Stari
22 National Theatre
23 Grill
24 Town Watchtower
25 Sunturist
26 'Liburnija' Tourist
   Office
27 St Simun
28 Bufe 'Basket'
29 St Mihovil
30 Art Gallery
31 Medieval Tower
32 Town Gate
33 Omladinski Dom
34 Ruins
35 Hotel Zagreb

Croatian youth hostel association). Buses No 5 and 8 pass the hostel.

**Private Rooms** Finding a place to stay in Zadar is usually no problem. If you're arriving by bus you'll probably be offered a private room before your pack hits the pavement. If not, head for Narodni trg and the Sunturist office, or for 'Liburnija' at Omladinska ulica 1 around the corner, both of which offer private rooms for US$10 per person plus a 30% surcharge if you stay less than four nights. Women offering private rooms on the street outside don't levy this surcharge and are willing to bargain.

**Hotels** The B-category *Hotel Zagreb* on the promenade is US$35/56 single/double for a room with private bath and breakfast (open from May to October only).

### Places to Eat

The cheapest and easiest place to eat is *Samoposluzivanje* self-service in the passage at Beogradska 9 (open daily). The restaurant in the train station is also good.

### Entertainment

Zadar is not an outstanding cultural centre and the action on the streets is likely to be more lively than that on the stage. At night the old town really comes to life! Small bars like *Bufe Basket*, Tucovića 4, buzz till midnight. You can always check the shabby *National Theatre* to see if there's anything doing and *Omladinski Dom* where rock concerts sometimes occur. You'll probably have to settle for a lousy movie at *Kino Zadar*, however.

### Getting There & Away

**Train & Bus** In summer couchettes are available from Zadar to Zagreb (442 km) and Belgrade. Otherwise train service out of Zadar is bad, usually involving an uncoordinated change of trains at Krin. Instead catch one of the frequent buses to Rijeka (228 km), Zagreb (286 km via the Plitvice Lakes) or Split (164 km).

**Boat** Lots of ferries call at Zadar. There are weekly ferries all year to Ancona (7½ hours, US$41), Trieste (nine hours, US$41) and Bari (22½ hours, US$42). In July and August fares are up to 50% higher. These large Italian ships of the Adriatica Line are quite luxurious. The Pula ferry (US$18) leaves daily except Wednesday from mid-June to mid-September, then Wednesday only for most of the rest of the year, with a stop at Mali Lošinj. For information on services to Ancona (Italy) and Pula contact Jadroagent on ulica Natka Nodila just inside the city walls.

Jadrolinija, Radnička obala 7 on the harbour, sells tickets for the coastal ferry to Rijeka, Rab, Split, Dubrovnik, etc, operating from mid-April to mid-October. This ship usually departs Zagreb just after midnight in both directions. Jadrolinija car ferries to Ancona operate from June to September, almost daily in midsummer.

Almost once an hour throughout the year there's a small car ferry from Pier 7, Zadar, to Preko on Ugljan Island (US$2 one-way), a nice trip to kill some time. Tickets are sold at the kiosk opposite Pier 7. The shortest ferry route is the rowing boat ride across the harbour from the bus station to the Maraska sea wall (US$0.20).

## ŠIBENIK

Šibenik (Sebenico) on the estuary of the Krka River between Zadar and Split has a few worthwhile things to see and is a useful base for visiting Krka National Park. Unfortunately the polluting aluminium smelter nearby and surrounding high-rise apartments give the city an ugly face, though the old town around the cathedral is nice. Šibenik is inundated by groups from the nearby resorts in the morning but otherwise almost untouristed.

### Orientation & Information

The bus station is right on the waterfront a short walk from the centre of town. The ferry to Žirje Island ties up nearby. The railway station is a 10-minute walk from the bus station along a complicated route (ask for directions). The left-luggage office is in the bus station.

The Turist Biro is just above Kavana Medulić off ulica 12 kolovoza 1941, the pedestrian street behind the cathedral.

## Things to See

From the **theatre** (1870) on Poljana Maršala Tita in the centre of town go down ulica 12 kolovoza 1941 towards the Italianate **Cathedral of St Jacob**, built between 1431 and 1536 in a transitional Gothic-Renaissance style. The great stone slabs used in the con-

struction are impressive. On the apse exterior are 71 human heads, portraits of contemporaries of the cathedral's architect Juraj Matejev Dalmatinac. In front of the cathedral is a bronze statue (1961) of Dalmatinac himself by Ivan Meštrović.

On the opposite side of Trg Republike from the cathedral is the Renaissance **town hall**. Inside the Rector's Palace just behind the cathedral is the **Šibenik City Museum** (closed Monday) which offers a complete historical exhibit from the first archaeological remains until WW II. All captions are in

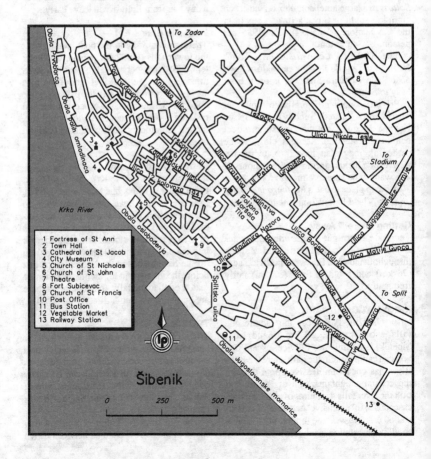

1  Fortress of St Ann
2  Town Hall
3  Cathedral of St Jacob
4  City Museum
5  Church of St Nicholas
6  Church of St John
7  Theatre
8  Fort Subicevac
9  Church of St Francis
10 Post Office
11 Bus Station
12 Vegetable Market
13 Railway Station

Šibenik

0          250          500 m

Serbo-Croatian. For a superb view of everything, find your way up to the nearby **Fortress of St Ann**, the 11th century Croat military garrison below which Šibenik developed.

### Activities

Dalmacijaturist (☎ 059-23580), on Trg Republike 4 near Šibenik Cathedral, offers weekly cruises to the **Kornati Islands** for US$32 per person, lunch and wine included.

### Places to Stay & Eat

The nearest camping ground is *Autocamp Solaris* in a large hotel complex on the beach eight km south of Šibenik (take a bus from the bus station or market). It's US$5 per person, US$4 per tent.

The 180-bed *Letovalište FSH Youth Hostel*, Put Luguša 1 on the east side of town near Rade Končara Stadium, is open from May to September.

Private rooms are available from the Turist Biro (closed Sunday), just above Kavana Medulić on the pedestrian street behind the cathedral. Kompas, closer to the cathedral, may also have private rooms. Arrive in Šibenik during business hours if you want to be sure of a private room.

A cheap place to eat is *Restaurant Mornar* on ulica Vlade Perana opposite the market.

### Getting There & Away

There are overnight trains with couchettes from Šibenik to Belgrade and Zagreb throughout the year. Buses run north to Zadar (76 km) and south to Split (82 km) fairly frequently.

## KRKA NATIONAL PARK

Krka National Park near the picturesque village of Skradin, 20 km inland from Šibenik, is a miniature Plitvice, except that you can camp right in the park. Here the Krka River has cut an impressive gorge through the coastal mountains, and at **Skradinski buk** the river falls 45 metres over 17 separate cascades. An extensive network of boardwalks crisscrosses the upper falls, and a small power station is adjacent.

Admission to the park is US$7, a lot of money to see a pretty waterfall in a pleasant wooded location, and Yugoslavs pay a pittance to get in. There are no hiking trails around Visovac Lake above the falls. Boat trips to Visovac Monastery on a lake island, and to **Roški Falls** at the lake's north end, are charged extra (US$10 per person to the first, US$14 per person to the second). Be prepared too for a stiff additional entry fee to get into the monastery, and for a lack of water going over all the falls at the end of summer. Even so, the lower falls make a nice excursion from the coast and can even be done as a day trip from Split if you leave early.

### Places to Stay & Eat

There's a camp site at the boat landing near the lower falls (US$2 per person, US$2 per tent, US$1 per person tax). It's open from mid-May to mid-October and if you're staying there you only pay the park entry fee once for the duration. A grocery store and restaurant are adjacent to the camp site, though the grocery store is usually sold out of bread.

### Getting There & Away

It's fairly easy to get to Krka National Park. From Šibenik take a bus to Skradin (US$1), then the hourly boat (30-minute ride) up Lake Prokljan to the lower falls (fare included in park admission). The boat operates from May to mid-October. You can also walk into the park in about 30 minutes by getting off the Skradin bus at the bridge (*most*) just before the village and following the riverside road around to the falls. In midsummer there are buses from Šibenik directly to the falls.

## TROGIR

Trogir (Trau), a lovely medieval town on the coast just 20 km west of Split, is well worth a stop if you're coming down from Zadar. A day trip to Trogir from Split can be easily combined with a visit to the Roman ruins of Salona (see the section on Salona in this chapter).

The old town of Trogir occupies a tiny island in the narrow channel between Čiovo

Island and the mainland, just off the coastal highway. Many sights are seen on a 15-minute walk around this island.

## Orientation

The heart of the old town is a few minutes' walk from the bus station. After crossing the small bridge near the station go through the North Gate. Trogir's finest sights are around Narodni trg, slightly left and ahead.

There's no left-luggage office in Trogir Bus Station, so you'll end up toting your bags around town if you only visit the town as a stopover.

## Information

The Turist Biro opposite the cathedral sells a map of the area.

## Things to See

The glory of the three-naved Venetian **Cathedral of St Lovro** on Narodni trg is the Romanesque portal of Adam and Eve (1240) by Master Radovan, which you can admire for free any time. Enter the building through an obscure back door to see the perfect Renaissance Chapel of St Ivan, choir, pulpit, ciborium and treasury. You can even climb the cathedral tower for a delightful view. Also on Narodni trg are the **town hall** with an excellent Gothic staircase and the Renaissance loggia.

## Places to Stay

**Camping** *Camping Rožac* is on Čiovo Island (connected to Trogir by a bridge). It's a half-hour walk from Trogir Bus Station, or take the Okrug bus. *Medena Camping* is just off the highway to Zadar about four km west of Trogir. *Seget Camping* is between Medina and Trogir. All these charge US$4 per person, US$3 per tent.

**Private Rooms** If you'd like to stay at Trogir, the Turist Biro opposite the cathedral has private rooms for US$14/18 single/double, less 30% if you stay longer than four nights.

## Getting There & Away

Southbound buses from Šibenik and Zadar will drop you off here. Getting buses north from Trogir can be more difficult, as they often arrive full from Split.

City bus No 37 runs between Trogir and Split (28 km) every 20 minutes throughout the day, with a stop at Split Airport en route. If making a day trip to Trogir on bus No 37, also buy your ticket back to Split as the ticket window at Trogir Bus Station is often closed (drivers also sell tickets if you're stuck).

## SPLIT

Split (Spalato), the largest Yugoslav city on the Adriatic coast, is the heart of Dalmatia. The old town is built around the harbour on the south side of a high peninsula sheltered from the open sea by many islands. Ferries to these islands are constantly coming and going. The entire west end of the peninsula is a vast wooded mountain park, while industry, shipyards, limestone quarries and the ugly commercial/military port are mercifully far enough away, inland and on the north side of the peninsula. The high coastal mountains set against the blue Adriatic provide a striking frame to the scene.

Split attained fame when the Roman emperor Diocletian (245-313), noted for his persecution of early Christians, had his retirement palace built here from 295 to 305. After his death the great stone palace continued to be used as a retreat by Roman rulers. When the nearby colony Salona was abandoned in the 7th century, many of the Romanised inhabitants fled to Split and barricaded themselves behind the high palace walls where their descendants live to this day.

First Byzantium and then Croatia controlled the area, but from the 12th to 14th centuries medieval Split enjoyed a large measure of autonomy which favoured its development. The western portion of the old town around Narodni trg dates from this time and became the focus of municipal life, while the area within the palace walls proper continued as the ecclesiastical centre.

In 1420 the Venetians conquered Split

which led to a slow decline. During the 17th century, strong walls were built around the city as a defence against the Turks. In 1797 the Austrians arrived, and with only a brief interruption during the Napoleonic wars, they remained until 1918.

Since 1945 Split has grown into a major industrial city with large apartment-block housing areas. Much of old Split remains, however, and combined with its exuberant nature makes it one of the most fascinating cities in Europe. It's also the perfect base for excursions to Solin, Trogir, Šibenik, Krka National Park, Brač and Hvar, so settle in for a few days. Brač (Brazza), the island directly opposite Split, is the easiest day trip by boat.

## Orientation

The bus, train and ferry terminals are adjacent on the east side of the harbour, a short walk from the old town. Don't leave your pack in the left-luggage office at the bus station where they charge foreigners double. Instead walk 100 metres towards town and patronise the railway station garderoba, at the end of the platform farthest away from the bus station, which has fixed prices and is open nonstop. Titova obala, the waterfront promenade, is your best central reference point in Split.

## Information

The tourist office is at Titova obala 12. The British Consulate (☎ 41464) is at Titova obala 10.

Znanstvena Knjižara on Trg Preporoda has a large selection of imported books in English but nothing in English by Yugoslav writers – only cheap adventure and romance. Knjižara, Titova obala 20, sells foreign newspapers.

## Things to See

There's much more to see than can be mentioned here so pick up a local guidebook if you're staying longer than a day or two. The old town is a vast open-air museum made all the more interesting by the everyday life still going on throughout. Be aware, however, that the historic centre of Split is literally jammed with tour groups in the morning, so visit in the afternoon. Many shops are closed in the afternoon so the narrow streets are also not crowded with shoppers at this time.

**Diocletian's Palace** facing the harbour is one of the most imposing extant Roman ruins anywhere. It was built as a strong rectangular fortress with walls 215 by 180 metres long and reinforced by towers. The imperial residence, temples and mausoleum were south of the main street connecting the east and west gates.

Enter through the central ground floor of the palace at Titova obala 22. On the left you'll see the excavated basement halls (US$0.70), empty but impressive. Continue through the passage to the **Peristyle**, a picturesque colonnaded square, with the neo-Romanesque cathedral tower rising above. The **vestibule**, an open dome above the ground-floor passageway at the south end of the Peristyle, is overpowering. A lane off the Peristyle opposite the cathedral leads to the **Temple of Jupiter**, now a baptistry.

On the east side of the Peristyle is the **cathedral**, originally Diocletian's mausoleum. The only reminder of Diocletian in the cathedral is a sculpture of his head in a circular stone wreath below the dome directly above the Baroque white marble altar. The Romanesque wooden doors (1214) and stone pulpit are worth noting but forget the cathedral treasury, entered from the choir behind the main altar, which is hardly worth the US$1 fee. You may also climb the tower for a small fee.

The west palace gate opens onto medieval Narodni trg, dominated by the 15th century Gothic old town hall, now the **Ethnological Museum** (closed Sunday). Trg Preporoda between Narodni trg and the harbour contains the surviving north tower of the 15th century Venetian garrison castle which once extended to the water's edge. The east palace gate leads into the market area.

In the Middle Ages the noblility and rich merchants built residences within the old palace walls, one of which, the Papalic Palace, Papalićeva or 'Zarkova' ulica 5, is now the **town museum**. Go through the

1 Croatian National Theatre
2 Bastion Self-Service Restaurant
3 Dalmacija Concert Hall
4 Ero Restaurant
5 Fish Market
6 Dalmacijaturist
7 JAT Office
8 Tourist Office
9 Central Hotel
10 Ethnological Museum
11 Main Post Office
12 National Revolution Museum
13 Statue of Gregorius of Nin
14 North Palace Gate

15 Town Museum
16 West Palace Gate
17 Temple of Jupiter
18 Prenoćište Slavija
19 Basement Halls of Palace
20 Vestibule
21 Cathedral
22 East Palace Gate
23 Vegetable Market
24 Bus No 17 to Camping Ground
25 Airport Bus Stop
26 Adria Airlines
27 Bus & Train Stations

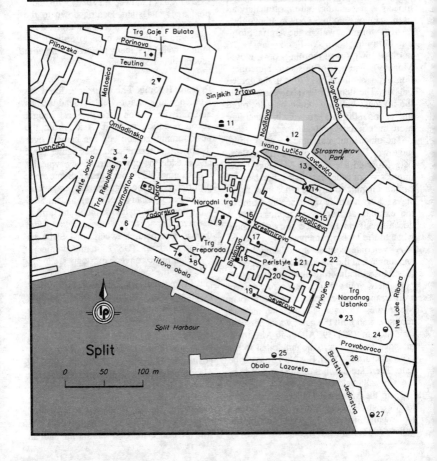

northern palace gate to see the powerful statue of 10th century Slavonic religious leader Gregorius of Nin by Ivan Meštrović (1929). The **National Revolution Museum**, housed in the nearby former city hospital (1872) at I L Lavčevića 15, recalls wartime partisan activities through photos.

**Museums & Galleries** Split's least known yet most interesting museum is the **Naval Museum** (open from 9 am to noon, closed Monday, free) in Gripe Fortress (1657) on a hilltop east of the old town. The large exhibit of wartime maps, photos, artifacts and scale models is fascinating, but unfortunately all of the captions are in Serbo-Croatian only.

Also worth the walk is the **Archaeological Museum**, Zrinjsko-Frankopanska 25 north of town (open mornings only, closed Monday). The best of this valuable collection first assembled in 1820 is in the garden outside. The items in the showcases inside the museum building would be a lot more interesting if the captions were in something more than Serbo-Croatian.

The other Split museums are west of the old town. The **Museum of Croatia** on Šetalište Moše Pijade (closed Monday) looks impressive outside but inside the lack of captions legible to anyone other than Yugoslavs makes it hardly worth seeing. Some of the exhibits appear to be replicas, but it doesn't really matter since you don't know what you're looking at anyway!

A welcome contrast to this neglect is encountered at the **Meštrović Gallery**, Šetalište Moše Pijade 46 (daily from 9 am to 6 pm). Here you will see a comprehensive, well-arranged collection of works by Ivan Meštrović, Yugoslavia's premier modern sculptor, who built the gallery as a personal residence in 1931-39. Although Meštrović intended to retire here, he emigrated to the USA soon after WW II. Bus No 12 passes the gate. There are beaches on the south side of the peninsula below the gallery.

From the Meštrović Gallery it's possible to hike straight up **Marjan Hill**. Go up Keršovani ulica on the west side of the gallery and continue straight up the stairway

to Put Meja ulica. Turn left and walk west to Put Meja 76. The trail begins on the west side of this building. Marjan Hill offers trails through the forest, viewpoints, old chapels and the local zoo.

### Places to Stay

**Camping** The nearest camping ground is at Trstenik, five km east near the beach (bus No 17 from the east side of the market). *Autocamp Trstenik*, just beyond the last stop of bus No 17 on a cliff overlooking the sea, charges US$5 per person, US$1.50 per tent, US$1 for a hot shower. It's shady with many pine trees and stairs leading down to the beach. From here a concrete path runs along the shore all the way back to Split (a 45-minute walk) past many places to swim with several public showers.

**Private Rooms** The *zimmer* offered by women who look for clients around the bus and railway stations are the best budget accommodation in Split. Aside from the peak summer season you can bargain over the price but rooms tend to be rather basic and outside the city centre. They typically cost around US$8 per person. Some *sobe* proprietors at the stations ask exorbitant prices and you can often get an instant 50% reduction by saying it's too much and turning to leave. Try not to pay more for your room than you've paid elsewhere, or US$10 per person maximum (US$15 in midsummer).

Better, more convenient rooms are available from the tourist office, Titova obala 12, and Dalmacijaturist, Titova obala 5. Prices begin at US$13/20 single/double, less 30% if you stay four nights or more.

**Hotels** The 'cheapest' hotel is the ageing D-category *Central Hotel*, Narodni trg 1 opposite the Ethnological Museum (US$28/41/54 single/double/triple with breakfast but shared bath, US$37/52/63 in midsummer). Slightly better is the quieter 32-room *Prenoćište Slavija*, Buvinova 3 (US$30/42 single/double with shared bath, US$33/48 with private bath, US$42/58 with bath in

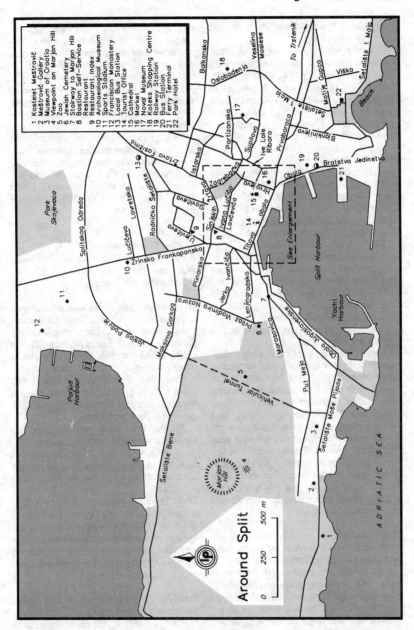

**Around Split**

0    250    500 m

Legend:

1 Kaštelet Meštrović
2 Meštrović Gallery
3 Museum of Croatia
4 Viewpoint on Marjan Hill
5 Zoo
6 Jewish Cemetery
7 Stairway to Marjan Hill
8 Bastion Self-Service
9 Restaurant Index
10 Archaeological Museum
11 Sports Stadium
12 Franciscan Monastery
13 Local Bus Station
14 Tourist Office
15 Cathedral
16 Market
17 Naval Museum
18 Koteks Shopping Centre
19 Railway Station
20 Bus Station
21 Ferry Terminal
22 Park Hotel

Park Skojevaca

Poljud Harbour

Šetalište Bene

Marjan Hill

Vehicular Tunnel

ADRIATIC SEA

Yacht Harbour

Split Harbour

See Enlargement

Beach

To Trstenik

Balkanska
Oslobodenja
Veselina Masleše
Matije Gupca
Viška
Šetalište 1 Maja
Bjankinijeva
Prvoboraca
Bratstva Jedinstva
Obala
Ive Lole Ribara
Supilova
Partizanska
Zrtava Fašizma
Istarska
Zagrebačka
Sin Skim
Slavičeva
Ivana Lučića Lavčevića
Tilovo
Tkalčićeva
Lovretska
Radničko Šetalište
Zrinsko Frankopanska
Plinarska
Vladimira Nazora
Jerka Ivančića
Lenjingradsko
Put Meja
Marasovića
Obala Jugoslavenske
Obala Mose Pijade
Šetalište Mose Pijade
Maksima Gorkog
Josipa Poduje
Lučićeva
Splitskog Odreda

midsummer). Both of these are in the old town and open all year.

If you're willing to pay that, however, you're better off at the B-category *Park Hotel*, Šetalište 1 Maja 15 (US$46/65 single/ double with private bath). This attractive 58-room resort hotel is a 10-minute walk from the old town, but more conveniently located to the bus and railway stations and the beach.

## Places to Eat

The cheapest place in town is *Restaurant Index*, a self-service student eatery at Ujevićeva 8. Vegetarians should avoid this place. Better fare for only a little more is available at the *Bastion Self-Service*, Marmontova 9 (open daily). It's clean and inexpensive.

The unpretentious *Ero Restaurant*, Marmontova 3, offers local specialities. It's more expensive but good value, has a nice atmosphere and the regional wine is reasonable.

*Prenoćište Srebrena Vrata*, hidden in a corner just inside the east palace gate, is one of the cheapest regular restaurants in Split. It's also a great place to sit on the terrace and enjoy a coffee or beer.

The *Koteks Shopping Centre*, a huge white complex 10 minutes' walk east of the old town beyond the Naval Museum, is the largest of its kind in Dalmatia. It includes a supermarket, department store, boutiques, restaurants, bars, banks, post office, two bowling alleys, sports centre, etc. If you want a slice of suburban Yugoslav life with your dinner, the *Pivnica Pizzeria* upstairs in the centre has spaghetti, pizza and national meat dishes, plus draught beer. The menu is in Serbo-Croatian only but it's a modern, friendly place. Many travellers stay in private rooms in this area.

## Entertainment

In summer you'll probably find the best evening entertainment in the small streets of the old town or along the waterfront promenade. During winter, opera and ballet are presented at the *Croatian National Theatre*, Trg Gaje Bulata. The best seats are about US$10 and tickets for the same night are

usually available. It's worth attending a performance for the architecture alone. This century-old theatre erected in 1891 was fully restored in 1979 in the original style. At intermission, head upstairs to see the foyer.

For concerts check the *Dalmacija Concert Hall*, Trg Republike 1 beside Kino Marjan (the box office is through the door and upstairs).

The Split Summer Festival from mid-July to mid-August features opera, drama, ballet and concerts on open-air stages. From June to September there's a variety of entertainment in the old town in the evening. Check for folk dancing in Trg Republike on Sunday nights.

## Getting There & Away

**Air** The Adria Airlines office faces the waterfront near the railway station, while JAT Airlines is at Titova obala 9.

**Bus** Advance bus tickets with seat reservations are recommended. There are through buses almost hourly to Dubrovnik (235 km), Sarajevo (331 km), Rijeka (404 km), Zagreb (412 km) and Titograd (429 km). Two buses a day run from Split to Međugorje (US$7).

Every Sunday morning in summer there's a bus from Split to Cologne, Germany, via Munich, Ulm and Frankfurt/Main (US$90 one-way). Book well ahead.

All the above leave from the main bus station beside the harbour, but bus No 37 to Solin, Split Airport and Trogir leaves from a local bus station on Žrtava Fašizma one km north-east of the centre (see the map).

**Train** There are overnight trains from Split to Ljubljana (576 km), Zagreb (416 km) and Belgrade (727 km). Some of the day trains to Zagreb have only 1st-class seats. For railway tickets and couchette reservations go to Croatia Express beside the train station. Couchettes are inexpensive.

**Boat** Two offices in the large Marine Terminal opposite the bus station sell ferry tickets. Jadrolinija handles year-round services to

Supetar on Brač Island (US$5), with frequent daily departures. There are also daily ferries all year to Hvar, Vira or Stari Grad on Hvar Island (US$6), Rogač on Šolta Island and Vela Luka on Korčula Island (US$10).

Jadrolinija also runs the big coastal ferry from Rijeka to Dubrovnik calling at Rab, Hvar and Korčula (from mid-April to mid-October). The southbound ferry trip to Dubrovnik (eight hours) is highly recommended, although it's several times more expensive than the bus. This ship usually leaves Split at 8 am southbound and 7 pm northbound, but it's not always daily so check the schedule at a travel agency beforehand. Some services go on to Greece.

Large Italian ferryboats of the Adriatica Line connect Split to Pescara, Ancona, Trieste, Venice and Bari weekly (all US$42). Fares are up to 50% higher in July and August. Tickets for these are available from Jadroagent in the Marine Terminal.

### Getting Around

**To/From the Airport** The bus to Split Airport (US$3) leaves from Obala Lazareta 3, a five-minute walk from the aforementioned terminals. This bus departs 80 minutes before flight times.

**Public Transport** Line up for city bus tickets at one of the very few kiosks around town which sell them. Newsstands don't have these tickets. For Trogir buy a zone 3 ticket. Solin and Trstenik are zone 1. Validate the ticket once aboard. Split bus tickets with an arrow at each end are good for two trips – you cancel one end at a time. You can also pay the driver but that costs double. There's a US$10 fine if you're caught without a ticket.

### SALONA

The ruins of the ancient city of Salona (Solin), among the vineyards at the foot of

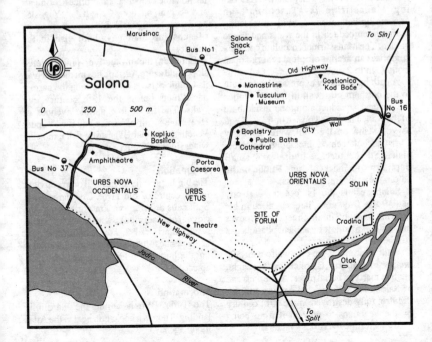

the mountains just north-east of Split, are about the most interesting archaeological site in Yugoslavia. Surrounded by noisy highways and industry today, Salona was the capital of the Roman province of Dalmatia from the time Julius Caesar elevated it to the status of colony. Salona held out against the barbarians and was only evacuated in 614 AD when the inhabitants fled to Split and neighbouring islands in the face of Avar and Slav attacks.

### Things to See
A good place to begin your visit is at the large parking lot near the Snack Bar Salona. **Manastirine**, the fenced area behind the parking lot, was a burial place for early Christian martyrs prior to the legalisation of Christianity. Excavated remains of the subsequent cemetery and the 5th century basilica are highlights, although this area was outside the ancient city itself. Overlooking Manastirine is 'Tusculum', an archaeological museum, with interesting sculpture embedded in the walls and in the garden. The Manastirine/Tusculum complex comprises an **archaeological reserve** open from 7 am to 2 pm.

A path bordered by cypresses leads south to the northern **city wall** of Salona. Notice the covered aqueduct along the inside base of the wall. The ruins you see in front of you as you stand on the wall were the Early Christian cult centre, including the three-aisled 5th century **cathedral** and small **baptistry** with inner columns. **Public baths** adjoin the cathedral on the east.

South-west is the 1st century east city gate, **Porta Caesarea**, later engulfed in the growth of Salona in all directions. Grooves in the stone road left by ancient chariots can still be seen at this gate.

Walk west along the city wall about 500 metres to **Kapljuc Basilica** on the right, another martyrs' burial place. At the west end of Salona is the huge 2nd century **amphitheatre**, only destroyed in the 17th century by the Venetians to prevent it from being used as a refuge by Turkish raiders.

### Getting There & Away
The ruins are easily accessible on city bus No 1 direct to Snack Bar Salona every half-hour from opposite Dalmacijaturist, Titova obala 5 in Split. Bus No 16 will also bring you to Solin, but you have to get out where the Sinj highway and city wall meet and then walk west along the old highway one km to the snack bar.

From the amphitheatre at Solin it's easy to continue on to Trogir by catching a west-bound bus No 37 from the nearby stop on the adjacent highway (buy a three-zone ticket in Split if you plan to do this). If, on the other hand, you want to return to Split, use the underpass to cross the highway and catch an eastbound bus No 37 (one-zone ticket).

### HVAR
Hvar town on Hvar (Lesina) Island cherishes its reputation as one of the most exclusive, chic resorts on the Dalmatian coast, and the fashionable crowd sets the prices for meals and accommodation. Called the 'Yugoslav Madeira', Hvar is said to receive more hours of sunshine than anywhere else in the country.

Between the protective, pine-covered slopes and azure Adriatic lies medieval Hvar, its Gothic palaces hidden among the narrow backstreets below the 13th century city walls. The traffic-free marble avenues of Hvar have an air of Venice and it was under Venetian rule that Hvar grew rich exporting wine, figs and fish.

### Orientation
The big Jadrolinija ferries will drop you right in the centre of old Hvar. The barge from Split calls at Vira, four km north across the ridge (bus service), while other ferries service Stari Grad, 20 km east. The attendant at the public toilets beside the market adjoining the bus station holds luggage for US$1 apiece.

### Information
The Turist Biro is beside the Jadrolinija landing. There's a bookshop next to the Atlas travel agency.

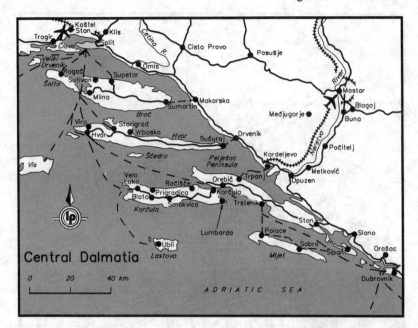

Central Dalmatia

0    20    40 km

ADRIATIC SEA

## Things to See

The full flavour of medieval Hvar is best savoured gently on the backstreets of the old town. At each end of town is a monastery with a prominent tower. The **Dominican Monastery** at the head of the bay was destroyed by the Turks in the 16th century and the local archaeological museum is now housed among the ruins. If the museum is closed you'll still get a good view of the ruins from the road just above which leads up to a stone cross on a hilltop offering a picture-postcard view of Hvar.

At the south-east end of Hvar is the 15th century Renaissance **Franciscan Monastery** with a fine collection of Venetian painting in the church and adjacent museum, including *The Last Supper* by Matteo Ingoli.

Smack in the middle of Hvar is the imposing Gothic **arsenal**, its great arch visible from afar. The communal war galley was once kept here. Upstairs off the arsenal terrace is Hvar's prize, the first **municipal**

theatre in Europe (1612), rebuilt in the 19th century. Try to get into the theatre (not sex-and-violence Kino Madeira downstairs!) to appreciate its delightful human proportions (admission US$1).

On the hilltop high above Hvar town is a **Venetian fortress** (1551), well worth the climb for the sweeping panoramic views (US$1). Inside is a tiny collection of ancient amphoras recovered from the seabed. The fort was built to defend Hvar from the Turks who sacked the town in 1539 and 1571.

## Activities

Beaches are scarce at Hvar so everyone ends up taking a launch (US$3) to the naturist (FKK) islands of Jerolim and Stipanska, just offshore. Stipanska is much larger than Jerolim.

## Places to Stay

**Camping** *Camping Vira* is just above the

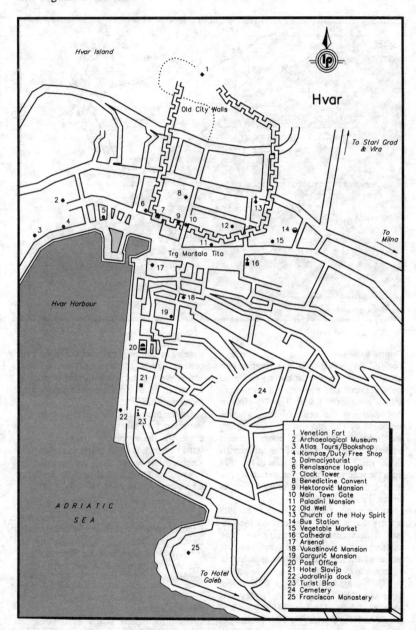

Hvar Island

To Stari Grad
& Vira

Hvar

Old City Walls

To Milna

Trg Maršala Tita

Hvar Harbour

ADRIATIC
SEA

To Hotel
Galeb

1 Venetian Fort
2 Archaeological Museum
3 Atlas Tours/Bookshop
4 Kompas/Duty Free Shop
5 Dalmacijaturist
6 Renaissance loggia
7 Clock Tower
8 Benedictine Convent
9 Hektorović Mansion
10 Main Town Gate
11 Paladini Mansion
12 Old Well
13 Church of the Holy Spirit
14 Bus Station
15 Vegetable Market
16 Cathedral
17 Arsenal
18 Vukašinović Mansion
19 Gargurić Mansion
20 Post Office
21 Hotel Slavija
22 Jadrolinija dock
23 Turist Biro
24 Cemetery
25 Franciscan Monastery

port where the smaller car ferry from Split ties up, four km north of Hvar town.

**Private Rooms** The Turist Biro on the waterfront beside the Jadrolinija landing will find you a private room for US$10/16 single/double in the cheapest category. More private rooms at the same rates are available at Dalmacijaturist beyond the small boat harbour, at the Privatni Smjestaj office in the passage leading in to the Duty Free Shop beside the Kompas office a little farther along, and at an office in the bus station. You can bargain for a lower rate with proprietors who approach you at the ferry landing. In midsummer everything could be full so try coming in spring or autumn.

**Hotels** The cheapest hotel is the *Galeb* on a quiet bay past the Franciscan Monastery just beyond Hotel Bodul. The 30 rooms, each with a balcony overlooking Hvar, go for US$15/24 single/double in April, May and October, US$21/39 single/double in June and September, 50% more in July and August. From November to March the place is closed. The Galeb caters mostly to Germans.

### Places to Eat

Carefully check prices before eating or drinking anything in Hvar, otherwise you'll end up paying double or triple. Especially avoid the grubby buffet at the bus station where they're sure to rip you off. *Cafe Barba* at the Turist Biro is one of the few places on Hvar that posts its prices.

The many pizzerias of Hvar offer the most predictable inexpensive eating, for example *Pizza Miko* up the small street beside the arsenal.

The two supermarkets on the main square are your best alternative to hassling with the restaurants, and there's a nice park in front of the Dalmacijaturist office just made for picnics. A nice breakfast of bread, cheese and cold milk will cost less than a coffee at the various flash cafés.

Staunch beer drinkers will be disappointed to hear that their favourite brew is a lot more expensive here than at Korčula or Split.

### Entertainment

Hvar has a very lively nightlife. In the evening the town comes alive with crowds of locals and tourists promenading along the waterfront and up the huge town square as music drifts across the water from the pavement cafés. On summer evenings a live band plays on the terrace of the *Hotel Slavija* next to the Turist Biro, just like in Venice. From 10 pm to 4 am at this magical time of year the fortress above Hvar functions as a disco.

### Getting There & Away

From mid-April to mid-October the Jadrolinija ferries between Rijeka and Dubrovnik call at Hvar almost daily, by far the nicest if not the cheapest way to come. Northbound they leave around 4 pm, southbound at 10 am. The Turist Biro beside the Jadrolinija landing sells ferry tickets.

There's a daily local ferry from Hvar town direct to Split, leaving Hvar at the crack of dawn and returning in the afternoon. The barges from Vira and Starigrad to Split operate several times daily throughout the year at more convenient times. Ask at the bus station about connecting buses to Vira and Starigrad.

Five times a week all year the ferry from Split to Hvar town carries on to Vela Luka on Korčula Island, a convenient interisland connection.

### STARIGRAD

Hvar gets its name from Pharos, Greek for lighthouse, after an ancient beacon which once stood at the east end of the long inlet which bisects western Hvar. The present town of Starigrad on this site is rather picturesque though somewhat of a disappointment after Hvar town, 20 km across the island. Starigrad was the capital of the island until 1331 when the Venetians shifted the administration to Hvar. This explains the extensive medieval quarter you still see at Starigrad. The palace of the Croatian poet Petar

Hektorović (1487-1572) is worth a visit to see the fish pond and garden.

## Places to Stay

*Kamp 'Jurjevac'* is just off the harbour right in the centre of Starigrad (open June to early September). There's no sign so ask directions.

Private room proprietors are less likely to meet the buses and ferries here than in Hvar town, so you may have to work through an agency. Dalmacijaturist opposite the bus stand arranges private rooms but probably won't have any cheap 3rd-category rooms.

## Getting There & Away

The ferry landing at Starigrad is about two km from town along a pleasant path by the pine-fringed bay. Buses also meet the ferries at Starigrad.

Once or twice a week from mid-April to mid-October the big coastal ferries between Rijeka and Dubrovnik call at Starigrad. Smaller local ferries run from Split to Starigrad (US$6) a couple of times a day. It's possible to do Hvar as a day trip from Split by catching the morning ferry to Starigrad, a bus to Hvar town, then the 4 pm ferry from Hvar town directly back to Split.

Though a ferry operates from Drvenik on the mainland to Sućuraj at the east end of Hvar Island every couple of hours, the connecting bus to Starigrad only runs on Monday, Wednesday and Friday.

The bus from Starigrad to Jelsa is almost hourly and there are five buses a day from Starigrad to Hvar town (US$1 plus US$1 per piece of baggage).

## KORČULA

Korčula (Curzola) hugs a small hilly peninsula jutting into the Adriatic Sea. With its round defensive towers and compact cluster of red-roofed houses, Korčula is a typical medieval Dalmatian town. In contrast to Turkish cities like Mostar and Sarajevo, Korčula was controlled by Venice from the 14th to 18th centuries. Venetian rule left its mark, especially on Cathedral Square which could have dropped out of Italy. It's a peace-ful little place, the grey stone houses nestling between the deep-green hills and gunmetal-blue sea with rustling palms all around.

Korčula is noticeably cheaper than Hvar and there's lots to see and do, so it's worth planning a relaxed four-night stay to avoid the 30% surcharge on private rooms. Day trips are possible to Orebić, Mljet, Lumbarda and Vela Luka.

## Orientation

If you arrive on the big Jadrolinija car ferry, no problem – it will drop you below the walls of the old town of Korčula on Korčula Island. The passenger launch from Orebić is also convenient, terminating at the old harbour, but the barge from Orebić goes to Bon Repos in Dominče, several km south-east of the centre.

## Information

The Turist Biro is near the old town.

## Things to See

Other than following the circuit of the former city walls or walking along the shore, sightseeing in Korčula centres on Cathedral

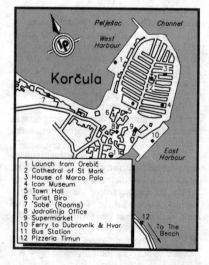

1 Launch from Orebić
2 Cathedral of St Mark
3 House of Marco Polo
4 Icon Museum
5 Town Hall
6 Turist Biro
7 'Sobe' (Rooms)
8 Jadrolinija Office
9 Supermarket
10 Ferry to Dubrovnik & Hvar
11 Bus Station
12 Pizzeria Timun

Square. The Gothic **Cathedral of St Mark** features two paintings by Tintoretto (the *Three Saints* on the altar and the *Annunciation* to one side).

The **Treasury** in the 14th century Abbey Palace next to the cathedral is worth a look, and even better is the **Town Museum** in the 15th century Gabriellis Palace opposite. It's said Marco Polo was born in Korčula in 1254 and you climb the tower of his alleged house for a fee. There's also an **Icon Museum** in the old town. It isn't much of a museum but visitors are let into the beautiful old Church of All Saints as a bonus.

### Activities

In the high summer season ask about shuttle boats from Korčula to **Badija Island**, which features a 15th century Franciscan monastery (now a D-category hotel) and a nudist beach.

### Places to Stay

**Camping** *Autocamp 'Kalac'* is behind Hotel Bon Repos, not far from the Orebić car ferry. There are no bungalows, but tenting is around US$6 per person, US$4 per tent, and the beach is close by. The facilities were recently renovated.

**Hostels** The *Letovalište FSH Youth Hostel* (open June to mid-September only) is near the junction of the Trajekt, Lumbarda and Korčula roads (one km from the Orebić car ferry, two km from Korčula). If the hostel is closed or full there are many houses nearby bearing *sobe/zimmer* signs. To get to the hostel from town take the Lumbarda bus as far as the hospital; for Autocamp 'Kalac' get out of the same bus at Hotel Bon Repos.

**Private Rooms** The Turist Biro and Kompas beside the Hotel Korčula arrange private rooms in town (US$12/16 single/double). Some of the private operators who meet the boats ask exorbitant rates for private rooms, so if their price is more than you're accustomed to paying check the agencies (which charge a 30% supplement if you stay under four nights).

There are numerous *sobe* and *zimmer* signs around town, so you could try knocking on doors. The houses on the road along the waterfront north-west from the old town are a good bet.

**Hotels** B-category *Hotel Korčula* facing Pelješac Channel on the edge of the old town is about US$28/42 single/double with breakfast (50% higher in July and August). The 24 rooms are often full.

The four large beach hotels just east of town cater mostly to packaged tourists from Britain – you're welcome to join them for a swim. These hotels do have the advantage of staying open all year, and from October to May you can get a discount of over 50% on the summer rates. In winter a room with all meals at the A-category *Liburna Hotel* will be US$45/70 single/double.

### Places to Eat

One of the best places to eat is *Pizzeria Timun* on the bay between the tourist hotels and town. It posts its menu outside (stick to the pizzas), but you may have difficulty finding a table. Don't confuse this place with another pizzeria near the bus station: you want the one with the tables right down beside the beach.

Alternatively try the *Restaurant Grill Planjak* between the supermarket and the Jadrolinija office in town. It's good for chicken or steaks, national specialities like *raznjici*, *čevapčiči* and *pljeskavica*, and huge mugs of draught beer. You can also get morning coffee here.

Two trendier, more expensive restaurants in the old town are the *Gradski Podrum* opposite the old town hall and the *Adio Mare* near Marco Polo's house. The terrace at *Hotel Korčula* is a nice place to nurse a coffee.

### Entertainment

From May to September there's *moreška* sword dancing by the old town gate every Thursday evening at 9 pm (US$7 – tickets from the Turist Biro). *Cinema Liburna* is in the building marked 'kino' behind the Liburna Restaurant near the bus station.

## Getting There & Away

**Ferry** Getting to Korčula is easy since all the big Jadrolinija coastal ferries between Split and Dubrovnik tie up at the landing adjacent to the old town. If it's too windy in the east harbour, this ferry lands at the west harbour in front of Hotel Korčula. If you didn't plan a stop here, your glimpse of Korčula from the railing will make you regret it. Car ferry tickets may be purchased at the Jadrolinija office or the Turist Biro (same prices).

Another approach is on the daily ferry from Split to Vela Luka at the west end of Korčula Island. Some of these services call at Hvar town en route.

Coming from Belgrade, Sarajevo or Mostar, take the train to Kardeljevo and then a ferry to Trpanj on the Pelješac Peninsula. A waiting bus will carry you across Pelješac to Orebić, from where ferries to Korčula are frequent.

Instead of the barge-type car ferry between Orebić and Korčula which lands at Bon Repos a couple of km from town, look for the passenger launch (seven times a day, 15 minutes, US$1 one-way) which will drop you at the Hotel Korčula right below the old town's towers. This is best if you're looking for a private room but if you want to camp or stay at the youth hostel be sure to take the auto barge to Bon Repos in Domince.

**Bus** There's also a twice-daily bus service from Dubrovnik to Orebić and Korčula (113 km, US$7). Three times a week there's a Zagreb-Korčula bus (US$24).

Six daily buses link Korčula town to Vela Luka (48 km). Most of the Vela Luka buses cost US$1 but some (which come from or continue to Dubrovnik) are US$2, so ask. Buses to Lumbarda run hourly (seven km, US$0.50).

## LUMBARDA

Just 15 minutes from Korčula town by bus, Lumbarda is a picturesque small settlement near the east end of the island. A good ocean beach (Plaza Pržina) is on the other side of the vineyards beyond the supermarket, but the area around the lighthouse at the eastern tip of Korčula is a secret military installation closed to foreigners.

The reception at *Hotel Lumbarda* arranges private rooms and there are a couple of camping grounds just up the road beside the hotel. 'Grk', a dry white wine originating in the vineyards around Lumbarda, is named for the Greek settlers who colonised Korkyra Melania (Korčula) in the 4th century BC.

## VELA LUKA

Vela Luka at the west end of Korčula is the centre of the island's fishing industry because of its large sheltered harbour. Tiny, wooded, button-shaped Ošjak Island in the bay just off Vela Luka is a national park visited in summer by tour groups. There isn't a lot to see at Vela Luka and no real beaches, so if you're arriving by ferry from Split or Hvar it's probably a good idea to jump on the waiting bus to Korčula town and look for a room there.

## Places to Stay & Eat

The Turist Biro (open summer only) beside the Jadran Hotel on the waterfront a hundred metres from the ferry landing arranges private rooms. *Camping Mindel* is six km north-west of Vela Luka (no bus service).

## Getting There & Away

The ferries from Split land at the west end of the harbour and buses to Korčula town meet all arrivals. There's at least one boat a day from Vela Luka to Ubli on Lastovo Island and Split. Ferry service from Vela Luka to Hvar is five times a week throughout the year.

## OREBIĆ

Orebić on the south coast of the Pelješac Peninsula between Korčula and Kardeljevo offers better beaches than are found at Korčula. The easy access by ferry from Korčula makes it the perfect place to go for the day, and a good alternative place to stay if all the rooms on Korčula are full or too expensive. All bus passengers bound for Dubrovnik, Mostar or Zagreb will transit the town.

## Things to See & Do

The small **Maritime Museum** in Orebić is hardly worth the US$1 admission. There's a good beach to the east of the port, two km along a peaceful waterfront road.

A trail leads up from Hotel Bellevue to an old **Franciscan monastery** on a ridge high above the sea. The monastery is worth seeing and the view from above makes the climb worthwhile.

A more daring climb is to the top of **Mt Ilija** (961 metres), the bare grey massif that hangs above Orebić. The three-hour hike through thick vegetation begins beside the cathedral near the port and is marked with red-and-white circles or red arrows. A second, more difficult route up Mt Ilija departs from the Franciscan monastery. The last half-hour is very steep and the final bit is a scramble over the rocks. The trail is safe and well marked, but avoid getting lost near the top as there's no rescue service. You'll get a sweeping view of the entire coast from up there.

## Places to Stay & Eat

The Turistički ured Orebić near the ferry landings rents private rooms and can provide a town map.

*Autokamp Videla* high up on the hillside above the port is jammed with row after row of parked caravans. A better bet is *Autokamp Hauptstrand*, a pleasant 15-minute walk east along the shore from the port. It overlooks an excellent long beach and has recently been upgraded to a 1st-class facility. There are several other camping grounds near Orebić but in the off season check first at the tourist office to make sure they're open.

## Getting There & Away

In Orebić the passenger and car ferry terminals and bus station are all adjacent. See the Korčula section for bus and ferry information.

## MLJET ISLAND

**Mljet National Park**, created in 1960, occupies the western third of the island of Mljet (Melita) between Korčula and Dubrovnik. The park centres around two saltwater lakes cradled by pine-clad slopes. Most people visit on day trips from Korčula or Dubrovnik but it's also possible to come by regular ferry and spend a few days here. If you do you'll have Mljet almost to yourself!

## Orientation

The tour boats from Korčula and Dubrovnik arrive at Pomena wharf at Mljet's west end where a good map of the island is posted. From Pomena it's a 15-minute walk to a jetty on Veliko jezero, the larger of the two lakes. Here the groups board a boat to a small lake islet where lunch is served at a 12th century **Benedictine monastery**, now a hotel.

Those who don't want to spend the rest of the afternoon swimming and sunning on the monastery island can catch an early boat back to the main island, allowing a couple of hours to walk along the lakeshore before catching the late-afternoon boat back to Korčula or Dubrovnik. There's a small landing opposite the monastery where the boatman drops passengers upon request. It's not possible to walk right around the larger lake as there's no bridge over the channel connecting the lakes to the sea.

## Getting There & Away

Atlas Tours in Korčula offers a day trip to Mljet Island twice a week from mid-April to mid-October. The tour lasts from 8.30 am to 6 pm, and at US$20 per person including the US$6 park entry fee it's good value. The boat takes two hours to motor south-east from Korčula to Pomena. Other tourist cruises depart Dubrovnik. Lunch isn't included in the tour prices and meals at the hotels on Mljet are very expensive, so it's best to bring the makings of a picnic.

You can come on your own by taking the regular ferry from Trstenik on the Pelješac Peninsula across to Polače on the north-west side of Mljet (several times daily). Another ferry to Polače leaves Dubrovnik at 1 pm daily except Sunday (US$7), returning to Dubrovnik around 4 am (!). There are private rooms on Mljet, and just east of Pomena is *Autokamp Sikjerica*. Mljet is a good island for cycling and the hotels rent bicycles at US$2 an hour.

# Dubrovnik

Founded 1300 years ago by refugees from Epidaurus, Greece, medieval Dubrovnik (Ragusa) was the most important independent city state on the Adriatic after Venice. Until the Napoleonic invasion of 1806 it remained an independent republic of merchants and sailors. Like Venice, Dubrovnik now lives mostly from tourism. Conspicuous consumption by the hordes of affluent visitors has converted the city into something of a tourist trap, and at peak periods, a circus. Yet Stari Grad, the perfectly preserved old town, is unique for its marble-paved squares, steep cobbled streets, tall houses, convents, churches, palaces, fountains and museums, all cut from the same light-coloured stone. The intact city walls keep motorists at bay and the southerly position between Split and Albania makes for an agreeable climate and lush vegetation. Dubrovnik is well worth a couple of days.

### Orientation

The Jadrolinija ferry terminal and bus station are a few hundred metres apart at Gruž, several km north-west of the old town. Left-luggage at the bus station is open from 5 am to 10 pm. Bus service into town is fairly frequent. The camping ground and most of the luxury tourist hotels are on the Lapad Peninsula, west of the bus station.

### Information

The tourist information centre is on Placa opposite the Franciscan Monastery in the old town.

### Things to See

You'll probably begin your visit at the city bus stop outside **Pile Gate**. As you enter the city, Placa, Dubrovnik's wonderful pedestrian promenade, extends before you all the way to the clock tower at the other end of town. Just inside Pile Gate is the huge **Onofrio Fountain** (1438) and the **Franciscan Monastery** with the third-oldest functioning pharmacy in Europe by the cloister (operating since 1391). The church may be entered free but the cloister museum is not worth the US$2 admission.

The urge to continue down Placa should prove irresistible. In front of the clock tower at the other end of the street you'll find the **Orlando Column** (1419), a favourite meeting place. On opposite sides of Orlando are the 16th century **Sponza Palace** (now the State Archives) and **St Blaise's Church**, a lovely Italian Baroque building you may enter free.

At the end of the broad street beside St Blaise is the Baroque **cathedral** (don't pay US$2 to peep into the tiny treasury behind the altar) and, between the two churches, the Gothic **Rector's Palace** (1441), now a museum (US$2, closed Sunday in winter) with furnished rooms, Baroque paintings and historical exhibits. The elected Rector was not permitted to leave the building during his one-month term without the permission of the Senate. The narrow street opposite this palace opens onto Gundulićeva Poljana, a bustling morning market. Up the stairway at the south end of the square is the imposing **Jesuit Monastery** (1725).

Return to the cathedral and take the narrow street in front to the **Aquarium** (US$3.50) in Fort St John. Through an obscure entrance off the city walls, above the aquarium, is the **Maritime Museum** (US$2). If you're museumed out you can safely give both these overpriced sights a miss.

By this time you'll be ready for a leisurely walk around the **city walls** themselves (US$1). These powerful walls, built between the 13th and 16th centuries and intact today, are the finest in the world and Dubrovnik's main claim to fame. They enclose the entire city in a curtain of stone over two km long

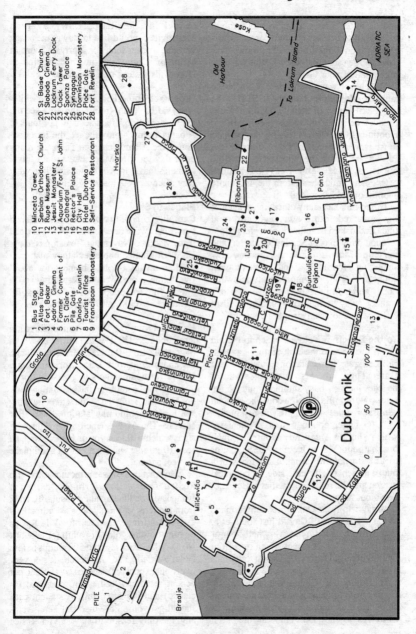

1 Bus Stop
2 Atlas Tours
3 Fort Bokar
4 Jadran Cinema
5 Former Convent of
  St Claire
6 Pile Gate
7 Onofrio Fountain
8 Tourist Office
9 Franciscan Monastery
10 Mineeta Tower
11 Serbian Orthodox Church
12 Rupe Museum
13 Jesuit Monastery
14 Aquarium/Fort St John
15 Cathedral
16 Rector's Palace
17 City Hall
18 Hotel Dubravka
19 Self-Service Restaurant
20 St Blaise Church
21 Sloboda Cinema
22 Lockrum Ferry Dock
23 Clock Tower
24 Sponza Palace
25 Synagogue
26 Dominican Monastery
27 Ploce Gate
28 Fort Revelin

Dubrovnik

and up to 25 metres high, with two round towers, 14 square towers, two corner fortifications and a large fortress. The views over town and sea are great, so make this walk the high point of your visit.

Whichever way you go you'll notice the large **Dominican Monastery** (US$2) in the north-east corner of the city. Of all of Dubrovnik's religious museums the one in the Dominican Monastery is the largest and most worth paying to enter. Outside the Ploče Gate behind the monastery and up the hill is the **Atlas Cable Car** (US$5) which offers panoramic views from the 412-metre summit of Srđ Mountain.

Dubrovnik has many other sights, such as the unmarked 16th century **synagogue** at ulica Žudioska 5 near the clock tower (10 am to noon daily except Sunday, donation) and the **Rupe Museum**, a former granary now sheltering ethnological and archaeological collections. The uppermost streets below the north and south walls are also worth a wander, away from the crass commercialism of Placa and adjacent streets.

**To the Beach** The closest beach to the old city is just beyond the 17th century **Lazareti** (former quarantine station) outside Ploče Gate. There are also 'managed' hotel beaches facing a busy shipping route on the **Lapad Peninsula**, but you could be charged admission unless they think you're a guest.

A far better option is to take the ferry which shuttles frequently from the small boat harbour (May to October, US$3 return) to **Lokrum Island**, a national park with a nudist beach on its east side, a botanical garden and the ruins of a medieval Benedictine monastery.

A day trip from Dubrovnik can be made to the resort town of **Cavtat** just south-east. Bus No 10 runs to Cavtat every half-hour or catch the regular tour boat which runs from Dubrovnik's old harbour to Cavtat four times a day from May to October (US$3 one-way). Like Dubrovnik, Cavtat was founded by Greeks from Epidaurus and there are several churches, museums and historic monuments as well as beaches. Don't miss the memorial

chapel for the Račič family by Ivan Meštrović. If you'd like to stay at the beach you could even look for a private room in Mlini or Cavtat and make day trips to Dubrovnik instead of the reverse!

**Organised Tours** For information on whitewater rafting tours from Dubrovnik see the Durmitor National Park section. For tours to Albania from Dubrovnik see the introduction to the Albania chapter. There are many other day tours to Mljet, etc, and all travel agencies have brochures describing what they offer.

**Places to Stay**
**Camping** *Camping Solitude* on the Lapad Peninsula (walk or catch bus No 6) is open from March to November. To camp is about US$9/15 single/double and they also rent small caravans (mobile homes) for about five dollars more. Weather permitting you'll always find tent space, but the caravans fill up so phone 050-20247 for reservations.

**Hostels** From May to September there's a large, modern IYHF *youth hostel* up Vinka Sagrestana from Put Oktobarske revolucije 17 charging about US$8 for members, US$12 for nonmembers in a six-bed dorm. To reach the hostel from the bus station walk up Maršala Tita, the main street leading south-east behind the station. Just after Maršala Tita 61 is a lane on the right with signs which will lead you on to the hostel, an easy 10-minute walk in all. It's a good place to meet people.

Also open in these same months is the *Vila Rašica International Youth Centre* at Ivanjska 14 on the Lapad Peninsula. To walk from the ferry or bus stations ask directions to Hotel Adriatic, then ask for Vila Rašica before you start going downhill (or take bus No 4). Vila Rašica is about 500 metres before Hotel Adriatic and the beach. It's a very lively but expensive place to stay (US$30 per person in a three-bed dorm, breakfast included) and it's often full. A student card should get you a 25% discount here. Actually, the only reason to stay at Vila Rašica

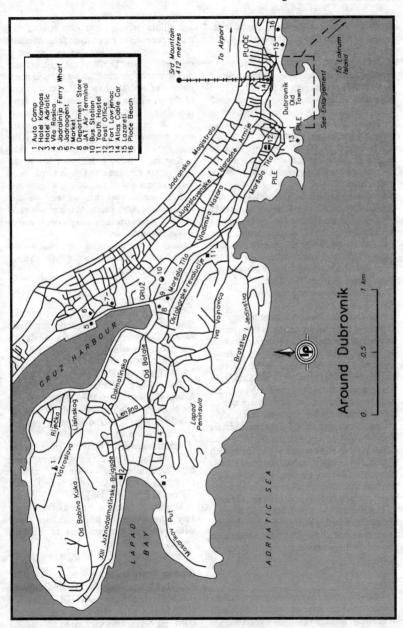

**Around Dubrovnik**

1 Auto Camp
2 Hotel Kompas
3 Hotel Adriatic
4 Vila Rosica
5 Jadrolinijp Ferry Wharf
6 Jadroagent
7 Market
8 Department Store
9 JAT Air Terminal
10 Bus Station
11 Youth Hostel
12 Post Office
13 Fort Lovrijenac
14 Atlas Cable Car
15 Lazareti
16 Ploce Beach

Srd Mountain
412 metres

To Airport

PLOCE

To Lokrum Island

Dubrovnik Old Town

See Enlargement

PILE

PILE

Jadranska Magistrala

Jugoslavenske

Narodne Armije

Vladimira Nazora

Marsala Tita

Marsala Tita

Oktobarske revolucije

Iva Vojnovica

Bratstva i Jedinstva

GRUZ

GRUZ HARBOUR

Dalmatinska

Od Batale

Lenjino

Rijecka

Lisinskog

Vatroslava

Od Babina Kuka

XIII Juznodalmatinske Brigade

Lapad Peninsula

Masarikov Put

LAPAD BAY

ADRIATIC SEA

0     0.5     1 km

would be a serious determination to meet groups of young Yugoslavs (who pay a lot less for their rooms than you do).

**Private Rooms** The easiest way to find a place to stay is to accept the offer of a *sobe* from one of the women who will approach you at the bus or ferry terminals. Their prices are lower than those charged by the room-finding agencies and are open to bargaining (from around US$9 per person). Because there's so much competition among private room proprietors, Dubrovnik can actually be quite cheap.

Opposite the harbour, Dalmacija-Turist at Gruška Obala 30 and Kompas at Gruška Obala 26 arrange 1st-category private rooms for about US$21/32 single/double. They levy a 30% surcharge if you stay less than three nights. The tourist office opposite the Franciscan Monastery in the old town, and Atlas Tours, Maršala Tita 2 just outside Pile Gate, also charge these prices.

**Hotels** Dubrovnik's hotels are so much more expensive than private rooms as to be hardly worth considering. The only hotel inside the old town walls is the C-category *Hotel Dubravka*, ulica od Puča 1 beside the vegetable market in the old town. It's US$28/46 single/double for a room with shared bath including breakfast, but in summer the 22 rooms are usually full (open all year).

The C-category *Hotel Stadion*, Maršala Tita 96 right behind the bus station (same building), has basic rooms with private bath at US$30/42 single/double. The hotel is built around an Olympic swimming pool and the 74 rooms are often all taken by noisy student groups. It's closed from November to March.

The quieter 33-room *Hotel Gruž* directly above the Jadrolinija ferry landing charges about the same as the Stadion but there's no shower in the rooms and no pool (open all year).

**Places to Eat**

At US$4.50 a plate *Express Self-service Restaurant* on ulica Lučarica behind the Church of St Blaise is neither cheap nor good and for just a little more you can get a much better meal at one of the expensive seafood restaurants along ulica Prijeko, a narrow street parallel to Placa. Don't let the waiters there hustle you – just stroll along till you see a place you like. The ones at the far west end of the street are slightly cheaper. We can't recommend any of them, however, so use your own judgment. The cheapest way to fill your stomach in Dubrovnik is to buy the makings of a picnic at a local supermarket.

*Konoba Primorka*, Nikole Tesle 8 just west of the department store in Gruž, has a good selection of seafood and national dishes at medium prices. In summer you dine below the trees on a lamp-lit terrace – a good choice for an extravagant night out if you're staying near the bus station.

At all Dubrovnik restaurants beware of the price of the drinks, especially if they're not listed on the menu.

**Entertainment**

For entertainment go see a movie – cheaper than any of Dubrovnik's museums. The *Jadran Cinema* is just off Paska Miličevića near the tourist office.

*Bakhos Disco* is downstairs in the old Lazareti just outside the Ploče Gate.

The majestic 19th century *Marin Drzic National Theatre* is on Pred Dvorom beside the Rector's Palace. Performances here are mostly drama in Serbo-Croatian and it's closed all summer.

Ask at the tourist office about concerts and folk dancing. Every Monday at 9 pm from May to October the Dubrovnik Chamber Orchestra plays in the Franciscan Church beside the Pile Gate (US$10).

The Ohrid Summer Festival from mid-July to mid-August is a major cultural event with over 100 performances at different venues in the old city.

**Getting There & Away**

**Air** There are JAT flights to Belgrade (US$68), Ljubljana (US$101), Maribor (US$99), Ohrid (US$60) and Zagreb (US$79). Some only operate in summer.

**Bus** During the busy summer season and on weekends, buses out of Dubrovnik can be crowded, so it's important to get in line for a ticket well before the scheduled departure time. Southbound buses to Kotor and Bar arrive from the north, so seats cannot be reserved in advance. If you're in line an hour before the departure you should get on.

**Train** The closest railway stations are at Kardeljevo, 110 km north-west, and Bar, 130 km south-east. Atlas Tours, Maršala Tita 2 just outside Pile Gate of the old town, can reserve couchettes on trains from Kardeljevo to Zagreb or Bar to Belgrade (about US$7 for the couchette, ticket extra).

**Boat** There are weekly Adriatica Line or Jadrolinija car ferries all year from Dubrovnik to Bari (nine hours, US$42), Ancona (14½ hours, US$42) and Venice (21 hours, US$65). In July and August fares are up to 50% higher. Tickets for international ferries are sold by Jadroagent, Gruška Obala 26 at the port. Payment must be in hard currency, cash or travellers' cheques.

The Jadrolinija coastal ferry north to Korčula, Hvar and Split (mid-April to mid-October) is far more comfortable than the bus, if several times more expensive. Still, it's well worth the extra money. The ferry to Korčula, Hvar and Split leaves at 10 am several times a week; to Greece at 5 pm once or twice a week. Sample fares from Dubrovnik are US$13 to Korčula, US$16 to Hvar or Split and US$50 to Corfu or Igoumenitsa.

A local ferry leaves Dubrovnik for Mljet Island (US$7) at 1 pm daily except Sunday throughout the year. Tickets for these lines can be bought from travel agencies or Jadrolinija opposite the port.

### Getting Around

**To/From the Airport** Čilipi International Airport is 24 km south-east of Dubrovnik. The airport bus (US$1.50) leaves from the JAT Air Terminal near the bus station 90 minutes prior to all JAT flights.

**Public Transport** Buy tickets for city buses at a kiosk.

**Car Rental** Dubrovnik Rent-a-Car (☎ 24922), Put Republike 5a, is the cheapest, followed in ascending order of price by Europcar (☎ 25593), Masarikova 9, Budget (☎ 26541), Gruška Obala 25, and Hertz (☎ 27387) at Hotel Kompas, I L Ribara 50.

# Montenegro

The Republic of Montenegro (Crna Gora), the smallest republic in the Yugoslav Federation, occupies a corner of south-central Yugoslavia directly above Albania near where the Dinaric Alps merge with the Balkan range. The republic's Adriatic coastline attracts masses of visitors, but there are also the spectacular Morača and Tara canyons in the interior. Between Titograd and Kolašin a scenic railway runs right up the Morača Canyon with fantastic views between the countless tunnels. West of Mojkovac, the next station after Kolašin, is the 100-km-long Tara Canyon, the second-largest in the world. Other dominant features of this compact, 13,812-sq-km republic are the winding Bay of Kotor and Skadar Lake, the largest in the Balkans, which Montenegro shares with Albania. There are no major islands off the Montenegrin coast but the sandy beaches here are far longer than those farther north.

### HISTORY

Only tiny Montenegro kept above the Turkish tide which engulfed the Balkans for over four centuries. Medieval Montenegro was part of Serbia, and after the Serbian defeat in 1389 the inhabitants of this mountainous region continued to resist the Turks. In 1482 Ivan Crnojević established an independent principality at Cetinje ruled by *vladike* (bishops) who were popularly elected after 1516. Beginning in 1697 the succession was limited to the Petrović Njegoš family (each bishop being succeeded by his nephew) which forged an alliance with Russia in 1711.

The strangest *vladike* of all was the monk Stephen the Small who claimed to be the murdered Russian emperor Peter III, husband of Catherine the Great. The trusting Montenegrins accepted this and followed Stephen on raids against Turks and Venetians alike. In 1769 Catherine herself sent an ambassador to Montenegro to denounce the little monk and remove him from office. Stephen so impressed the emissary, however, that he was given a Russian staff uniform and promises of support against the Turks. Later, an explosion during road-building work blinded the monk. He retired to a monastery where in 1773 he was murdered by his barber who cut his throat for Turkish gold.

The wars with the Turks and Albanians continued until 1878, when the European portion of the Ottoman Empire largely collapsed and Montenegrin independence was recognised by the Congress of Berlin. Nicola I Petrović, Montenegro's ruler from 1860, declared himself king in 1910. In 1916 the Austrians evicted the bishop-king and in 1918 Montenegro was incorporated into Serbia. During WW II Montenegrins fought valiantly in Tito's partisan army and after the war the region was rewarded with republic status within Yugoslavia. In 1946 the administration shifted from Cetinje to Titograd (formerly Podgorica), a modern city with little to interest the visitor.

## GETTING AROUND

Apart from the coastal strip and Morača Canyon, much of the best of Montenegro is most easily accessible by car. If you can get a few people together consider sharing the cost of renting a car. You'll find the scenery breathtaking, the roads not bad at all and very little traffic. You'll be able to tour the mountains, lakes, bays, canyons, gorges, wild

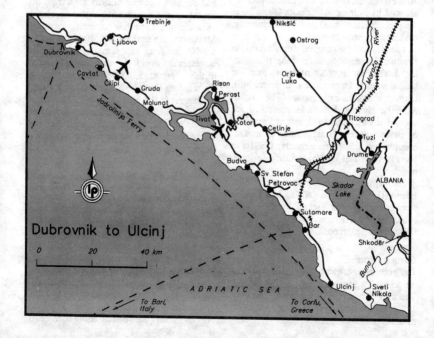

Dubrovnik to Ulcinj

rivers and national parks at leisure, dine at roadside restaurants serving fresh trout fried with garlic, and stay in out-of-the-way places. This compact, diverse region really lends itself to exploration by rental car, so if you only rent once in Yugoslavia do it here. Rental cars are most easily available at Dubrovnik (see above), though you can get one at any of the beach resorts.

## KOTOR

The Bay of Kotor (Cattaro), south-east of Dubrovnik halfway to Bar, is the longest and deepest fjord in southern Europe. For centuries this bay formed a boundary between the empires of the Ottomans and Venetians and later the Habsburgs and Serbians. The secure anchorage made the towns of Perast and Kotor important maritime centres and both had their own navies. Like most of Dalmatia this area was under Venice until 1797, only being finally incorporated into Montenegro after WW II.

A ferry crosses the mouth of the Bay of Kotor but most buses take the scenic one-hour drive right around the back of the fjord. Just off picturesque Perast on the north side of the bay are two small cypress-clad islands, one bearing a former Benedictine monastery, the other a church. Gripped by steep slopes, the town of Kotor was badly shaken by two earthquakes in 1979 but it's now largely rebuilt. This is a good place to stop.

### Orientation & Information

Kotor Bus Station is convenient to the old town and has a left-luggage office. To walk to town (five minutes), head for the modern Hotel Fjord and turn right along the waterfront.

The tourist information office in the kiosk just outside the main town gate provides information but no rooms.

### Things to See & Do

Just through the town gate is a square with a 17th century **clock tower**, and on another square a few blocks back are the twin towers of the 12th century **Cathedral of St Tryphon**. North of the cathedral and still within the old walled quarter are the **Naval Museum** (US$2) and the Serbian Orthodox **Church of St Lucas** (1195) with a larger Orthodox church opposite.

Some 4.5 km of 15th century **city walls** built by the Venetians zigzag up the mountainside behind Kotor, and you can climb to the **Fortress of St Ivan** on top for a superb view (leave the town by the north gate beyond the Orthodox churches, cross the footbridge and turn right).

### Places to Stay & Eat

For a private room (around US$11 per person) contact Montenegro Express in the plush Hotel Fjord at the head of the bay, a few hundred metres from Kotor Bus Station. Intours beside the clock tower just inside the city gate also has private rooms, but only doubles. Another Montenegro Express office across the square from Intours is a third place to try. Most of the rooms are in the modern suburbs around Kotor.

### Getting There & Away

Buses depart Kotor for Dubrovnik (89 km), Cetinje (45 km), Budva (24 km), Ulcinj (85 km) and Titograd (95 km). Service is good.

## CETINJE

Cetinje, atop a high plateau between the Bay of Kotor and Skadar Lake, is the old capital of Montenegro, subject of song and epic poem. The open, easily defended slopes help explain Montenegro's independence, and much remains of old Cetinje from museums to palaces and monasteries. At the turn of the century all the large states of Europe had embassies here. Unfortunately the numerous tour buses which arrive around midday throw cold water on the romance.

### Things to See & Do

The most imposing building in Cetinje is the **State Museum**, the former palace (1871) of Nicola I Petrović, the last king. Looted during WW II, only a portion of the original furnishings remain but the many portraits and period weapons give a representative picture of the times. Nearly opposite this is the older 1832 residence of the prince-bishop Petar II Petrović Njegoš, who ruled from 1830 to 1851. This building, now a museum, is also known as **Biljarda Hall** for a billiard table installed in 1840, the first in Yugoslavia.

Around the side of Biljarda Hall is a large, glass-enclosed pavilion containing a fascinating relief map of Montenegro created by the Austrians in 1917 for tactical planning purposes. Ask one of the Njegos Museum attendants to let you in. Beyond the map is **Cetinje Monastery**, founded in 1484 but rebuilt in 1785. The monastery treasury contains a copy of the *Oktoih* or 'Oktoechos' printed near here in 1494, one of the oldest collections of liturgical songs in a Slavonic language. Vladin Dom, the former Government House (1910) and now the **National Gallery**, is not far away. A collective ticket to all the museums is available for US$6.

Back towards the bus station is 15th century **Vlach Church** (rebuilt in 1864), surrounded by a fence formed from the barrels of 2000 captured Turkish rifles.

Twenty km away at the summit of **Mt Lovćen** (1749 metres), the 'Black Mountain' which gave Montenegro its name, is the mausoleum of Petar II Petrović Njegoš, a revered poet as well as a ruler. The masterful statue of Njegoš inside is by Croatian sculptor Ivan Meštrović. There are no buses up Lovćen and taxis want US$30 return; the building is visible in the distance from Cetinje. From the parking lot one must climb 461 steps to the mausoleum and its sweeping view of the Bay of Kotor, mountains and coast. The whole of Mt Lovćen has been declared a national park.

### Places to Stay & Eat

If you're looking for a private room try Intours near the State Museum. The only hotel, the A-category *Grand*, is very expensive so if all the private rooms are full you'll have a problem.

### Getting There & Away

Some buses between Dubrovnik and Titograd pass through Cetinje. There's also bus service to Kotor and Budva. The 45-km ride over Lovćen Pass direct from Kotor is spectacular.

## BUDVA

Budva, the largest tourist resort on the Montenegrin coast, caters mostly to people on cheap packages. If you're on your own you'll be expected to pay higher than usual prices for lower than usual service.

Budva's big attraction is its glorious beach which curves around the bay. The old walled town of Budva was levelled by the same 1979 earthquake which struck Kotor, and after the quakes the residents were permanently evacuated. Since then the old town has been completely rebuilt as a tourist centre. It's possible to walk three-quarters of the way around the top of the town wall.

Only a few km south-east of Budva is the former village of **Sveti Stefan**, an island now linked to the mainland. During the 1960s the entire village was converted into a luxury hotel but unlike Budva, which you may enter free, to set foot on the hallowed soil of Sveti Stefan costs US$6. Settle for the long-range, picture-postcard view and keep your money.

### Orientation & Information

The new bus station is a 10-minute walk inland from the beach. Ask directions to the Turist Biro at ulica Maršala Tita 23. The old town is five minutes beyond there.

### Places to Stay & Eat

There are many fancy hotels around Budva filled with packaged holiday-makers from Britain but you're better off in a private room arranged by an agency such as the Turist Biro, ulica Maršala Tita 23, Emona Globetour next door, Kompas Tours, Maršala Tita 7, or Montenegro Express across the parking lot from Kompas. Single rooms are not available and they don't like renting doubles for one night. Hotels begin at US$40 single and all accommodation is tight.

If you have a tent, *Autocamp Avala* is behind Hotel Bellevue, two km east along the shore (through a small tunnel). It costs

US$3 per person, US$4 per tent, and is crowded with caravans but at least near the beach.

There's an express self-service restaurant beside the supermarket above the vegetable market, just inland from the post office.

### Getting There & Away
There's good bus service to Dubrovnik (113 km), Kotor (24 km), Cetinje (31 km), Bar (38 km) and Ulcinj (64 km).

### BAR
Bar (Antivari) is an uninteresting port city, terminus of the railway from Belgrade and a ferry line to/from Bari, Italy. You won't want to linger here. Unless your train or ferry comes in too late, catch a bus to Ulcinj right away, a far better place to stay.

### Orientation
The ferry terminal in Bar is only a few hundred metres from the centre of town, but the adjacent bus and train stations are about two km south-east of the centre and ferry landing.

### Places to Stay & Eat
*Autocamp Susanj* is two km north of the ferry landing along the beach. Putnik Turist Biro opposite the ferry landing arranges private room accommodation.

There's a good restaurant in the railway station.

### Getting There & Away
There are four trains a day to Belgrade (two with couchettes, 524 km) and buses to Dubrovnik and Ulcinj. The ferry from Bar to Bari operates from March to December. In midsummer all transport to/from Bar is very crowded.

### ULCINJ
A broad military highway tunnels through the hills between olive groves for 26 km from Bar to Ulcinj (Ulqin in Albanian, Dulcigno in Italian) near the Albanian border, the only Muslim town on the Yugoslav coast. The Turks held Bar and Ulcinj for over 300 years,

and today most of the inhabitants are ethnic Albanians. You'll notice the difference in people right away from the curious direct looks you get and the lively bazar atmosphere in the many small shops lining the streets. Many older women at Ulcinj still wear traditional Islamic dress, especially on market day (Friday).

Ulcinj is unlike any other place on the Yugoslav coast. People actually stop to talk to you even when they're not interested in selling anything! It's not as swamped with packaged tourists as the other resorts and there are lots of places to stay for budget travellers. You couldn't call Ulcinj a hippie hang-out like Bali's Kuta Beach or Lamu Island in Kenya but of all the Yugoslav beach towns it certainly comes closest. It's also a popular holiday resort for Serbians who seem to arrive en masse on the Belgrade-Bar railway to join the Germanic hordes flowing down the coast. In July and August it can get very crowded!

### Orientation
You'll arrive at Ulcinj Bus Station about two km from Mala Plaža, the small beach below the old town. It's an interesting walk to Mala Plaža and you'll pass several buildings with *sobe* and *zimmer* signs where you can rent a room.

Velika Plaža (Great Beach), Ulcinj's famous 12-km stretch of unbroken sand, begins about five km south-east of town (bus service).

### Information
Yumototours is about 500 metres from the bus station on the way into town.

### Things to See
Founded by the Greeks, Ulcinj gained notoriety as a base for North African pirates from 1571 to 1878. There was even a slave market from which the few present black families are descended. The ancient ramparts of old Ulcinj overlook the sea, but most of the buildings inside were shattered by the 1979 earthquakes, though reconstruction is well advanced. The **museum** (closed Monday)

by the upper gate is now open and you can walk among the houses and along the wall.

### Activities
Montenegroturist in Hotel Mediteran offers Tara River rafting and other organised excursions.

### Places to Stay
**Camping** There are two camping grounds on Velika Plaža, *Milena* and *Neptun*. On Ada Island, just across the Bojana River from Albania, is *Camping Ada Bojana FKK*, a nudist camping ground accessible by boat from Mala Plaža or by bus.

**Hostels** The IYHF *'Bratstvo-Jedinstvo'* Youth Hostel is on Velika Plaža, five km south-east of town, but it's only open during the summer. The hostel has a seven-night minimum stay and costs US$15 with no discount for YHA members! A better bet is *Autocamp Neptun* across the road which has caravans for US$11 per person if you don't have a tent.

**Private Rooms** The Yumototours tourist information office on the road into town from the bus station can give you a map of the town or rent you a private room. Just around the corner to the right is Adriatours with more private rooms. Several houses around here have *sobe* signs. Their prices are reasonable and the location convenient for buses to Velika Plaža and elsewhere. If you continue into town towards Mala Plaža you'll pass Olcinium Travel Agency (more private rooms) nearly opposite Kino Basta (Basta Cinema). Facing Mala Plaža itself is Turist Biro 'Neptun' (Montenegroturist) with another selection of private rooms.

**Hotel** The least expensive hotel is the 202-room **Mediteran**, a pleasant modern hotel a five-minute walk uphill from Mala Plaža. Rooms with private bath and breakfast are US$22/35 single/double (25% more or less in midsummer or winter). Most rooms have a balcony overlooking the sea. It's open all year.

### Places to Eat
There are numerous inexpensive restaurants around Robna Kuca Ulcinj between the bus station and Mala Plaža offering cheap grilled meat or more expensive seafood.

### Getting There & Away
Buses from Bar (26 km) are fairly frequent. In Bar you can connect with the train to Belgrade (524 km, US$13), a bus to Dubrovnik or a ferry to Italy.

## BIOGRADSKA GORA NATIONAL PARK
This national park between Kolašin and Mojkovac just east of the Bar-Belgrade railway protects one of the last remaining virgin forests in Europe. The park facilities are at Biogradsko jezero, a lake four km east of the main highway, where you'll find a camping ground, bungalows and a restaurant. Buses will drop you at the turn-off, seven km south of Mojkovac, or if you're arriving by local train from Bar or Titograd (three daily) get off at Štitarička Rijeka (the expresses only stop in Mojkovac four km north).

With a park map you can explore the varied flora and fauna of these primeval woods at about 1100 metres elevation. To walk around the lake takes only an hour, or do the four-hour, eight-km hike to the source of the Biograd River, climbing 600 metres as you go. The rowing boats for rent on Biograd Lake are also fine. Most visitors arrive on package bus tours and don't get far beyond the restaurant, so you'll have the place to yourself most of the time.

## DURMITOR NATIONAL PARK
Montenegro's Durmitor National Park is a popular hiking and mountaineering area just west of Žabljak, a ski resort which is also the highest town in Yugoslavia (1450 metres). Žabljak was a major partisan stronghold during WW II, changing hands four times at great cost to the inhabitants.

Some 20 mountain lakes dot the slopes of the Durmitor Range (2523 metres) just south-west of Žabljak. You can walk right around the largest lake, **Crno jezero** or 'Black Lake', three km from Žabljak, in an hour or two and from it climb Savin Kuk (2313 metres) in an eight-hour trip there and back.

Durmitor's main claim to fame is the 1067-metre-deep **Tara Canyon** which cuts dramatically into the mountain slopes and plateau for about 100 km. The edge of the Tara Canyon is about 12 km north of Žabljak, a three-hour walk. Yugoslav tourist brochures claim that this is the second-largest canyon in the world after the Grand Canyon in the USA, though any Mexican will tell you their Barranca del Cobre is bigger. Any way you look at it, it's one of the top sights of Eastern Europe.

### White-Water Tours

Several local travel agencies offer raft excursions on the clean, green water down the high forested gorge over countless foaming rapids. From June to mid-September Atlas Tours in Dubrovnik runs a day trip down the wide, lower 20 km of the Tara in 12-person rubber rafts. The US$65-per-person price includes transfers, lunch and rafting equipment (helmet, life jacket, windcheater and rubber boots – bring your bathing suit), but it's a five-hour bus ride each way from Dubrovnik and you're only on the river for about two hours.

Preferable are the two-day raft excursions offered from mid-June to mid-September by Montenegroturist at Budva and Ulcinj. These put in at Đurđevića Tara near Žabljak and are on the narrower upper Tara River. The US$120 per person includes meals and a night at a hotel in Durmitor National Park.

Better still are the special three-day rubber raft expeditions right down the Tara River from the bridge at Đurđevića Tara to the junction with the Piva River at Šcepan Polje (88 km). These are only offered occasionally (about US$175 per person including tent accommodation and food). For information call Vera Drobnic at Atlas Tours (☎ 050-23743), Dubrovnik, as far in advance as possible.

### Places to Stay

Žabljak's cheapest hotel is the wretched, C-category *Durmitor* which has only dismal rooms with shared bath at US$15/21 single/double. Instead try the B-category *Žabljak*, which costs US$19/25 single/double with bath. The centrally located Žabljak also arranges private rooms though there's a 30% surcharge if you stay less than four nights. There's also a camping ground but keep in mind the elevation. For information on mountain huts enquire at the national park office near Hotel Durmitor.

### Getting There & Away

The easiest way to get to Žabljac is to take a bus from Mojkovac Railway Station on the Belgrade-Titograd line (three trains daily, 71 km). To come from Sarajevo involves two changes of buses (at Foča and Pljevlja). The two routes meet at Đurđevića Tara where there's a spectacular bridge over the canyon. Šcepan Polje on the lower Tara is on the Sarajevo-Nikšić bus route.

# Bosnia-Hercegovina

Bosnia-Hercegovina is a mountainous, 51,129-sq-km region in the very middle of Yugoslavia, almost cut off from the sea by Croatia. Most of the rivers of the republic flow north into the Sava and only the Neretva cuts south from Mostar through the Dinaric chain to Kardeljevo on the Adriatic. The republic contains over 30 peaks from 1700 to 2386 metres high.

## HISTORY

The region's ancient inhabitants were Illyrians, followed by the Romans who settled by the mineral springs at Ilidža near Sarajevo. The Slavs arrived in the 7th century and in 960 became independent of Serbia. Beginning in the mid-12th century the Hungarians exercised some control. The first Turkish raids came in 1383 and by 1463 Bosnia was a Turkish province with Sarajevo as capital. Hercegovina is named for Herceg

(Duke) Stjepan Vukcic who ruled the southern portion of the present republic from his mountaintop castle at Blagaj near Mostar until the Turkish conquest in 1468.

During the 400-year Turkish period, Bosnia-Hercegovina was completely assimilated and became the boundary of the Islamic and Christian worlds. Wars with Venice and Austria were frequent. Forty per cent of the local Serbian population is still Muslim today and Jajce, Mostar and Sarajevo are historic towns with an authentic oriental air. When it was decided at the 1878 Congress of Berlin that Bosnia-Hercegovina would be occupied by Austria-Hungary, the population, which desired autonomy, had to be brought under Habsburg rule by force.

Resentment that one foreign occupation had been replaced by another became more intense when Austria annexed Bosnia-Hercegovina outright in 1908. The assassination of the Habsburg heir, Archduke Franz Ferdinand, by a Serbian nationalist at Sarajevo on 28 June 1914 (the 525th anniversary of the Battle of Kosovo) led Austria to declare war on Serbia. When Russia supported Serbia and Germany came to the aid of Austria, the world was soon at war.

After WW I, Bosnia-Hercegovina was annexed to Serbia, and during WW II this rugged area became a partisan stronghold. The foundations of postwar Yugoslavia were laid at Jajce in 1943, and after the war Bosnia-Hercegovina was granted republic status within Yugoslavia.

## MOSTAR

Mostar, a medium-sized city among vineyards between Dubrovnik and Sarajevo, is the main centre of Hercegovina. Founded by the Turks in the 15th century at a strategic river crossing, Kujundžiluk, the old quarter, has all the carefully groomed attractions required to satisfy the thousands of daily visitors in search of instant Islamic virtue. The postcard-perfect Turkish Bridge (*most*) arches 20 metres above the green water in the Neretva River gorge, a guard tower at each end and mosques on all sides. The packaged

tourists mill in the nearby sales strips and it's possible to join them and see the sights in a stopover of three hours or less. If you spend the night at Mostar, however, you'll get the bonus of being able to visit the bridge in relative peace as the groups all head back to the coast around mid-afternoon.

## Orientation

As you leave the adjacent bus and train stations, head west towards the new bridge but don't cross it. Turn left onto ulica Mladena Balorde which, with continuations, will take you south into the Kujundžiluk bazar.

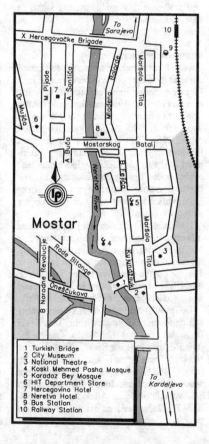

1 Turkish Bridge
2 City Museum
3 National Theatre
4 Koski Mehmed Pasha Mosque
5 Karadoz Bey Mosque
6 HIT Department Store
7 Hercegovina Hotel
8 Neretva Hotel
9 Bus Station
10 Railway Station

## Information

Hetmos Turist is below the Neretva Hotel on Trg Republike.

## Things to See

Before reaching the **Turkish Bridge** (1566) you'll pass two mosques of note. The larger of the two is the **Karadoz Bey Mosque** (1557) opposite ulica Braće Fejića 54, but the **Koski Mehmed Pasha Mosque** (1619) beside the market offers a chance to climb the minaret for a stunning view of everything in return for your ticket.

After 'doing' the bridge look for the **City Museum**, which is right beside the eastern guard tower but entered off Maršala Tita, the main road above the museum. This museum has two parts: a signposted revolutionary museum and an archaeological section in the old mosque alongside. Be sure to ask the attendant to open the mosque if it's closed. The scale model of Mostar inside is a highlight. The **New Orthodox Church** (1873) on the hillside above the museum is the largest in the republic and the seat of a Serbian Orthodox bishop.

**Počitelj** South of Mostar by the highway to Metković are the castle and mosque of the old Turkish village of Počitelj, now an 'artists' colony' where all the tour groups from the coast stop on their way to/from Mostar. It's not worth a special trip, but do try to get a glimpse of it as you zip past on the bus.

## Places to Stay

The nearest camping ground is at Buna, 12 km south near the main road. It's US$2 per person, US$2 per tent.

Hetmos Turist, below the Neretva Hotel on Trg Republike, can place you in a private home (US$13 per person). Several houses along ulica Mladena Balorde have *sobe* signs.

The 18-room *Hercegovina Hotel*, Moše Pijade 18 near HIT Department Store, used to be the cheapest in Mostar but a recent face-lift has boosted prices.

The B-category *Neretva Hotel*, a charac-

terful old hotel overlooking the river, is US$40/50 single/double with private bath, not such a bad deal considering how much such rooms are these days, though this hotel is due for renovations soon and prices may skyrocket. It's open all year.

## Places to Eat

Rather than eat at the touristy places around the Turkish Bridge, splurge at the elegant *Pozorisni Klub* downstairs in the National Theatre, Maršala Tita 119. Prices are about the same as in the tourist traps but the service is impeccable and the portions are large. Try the mixed grill *(mješano meso)* for a sampling of all the country's traditional meat dishes in one go, or the fresh river trout *(pastrmka)*. Add a 10% service charge and US$1 cover to the menu prices (not mentioned) and don't be surprised if they add a little to the price of the salad ('out of season'). You should still get away for under US$10 per person with drinks.

*Restoran Lovac*, Braće Fejića 21, is a good local beer garden with inexpensive grilled meats listed on the wall beside the kitchen window.

## Getting There & Away

There are trains to Kardeljevo (76 km), Sarajevo (152 km), Belgrade (648 km) and Zagreb (688 km). Train service to/from Sarajevo is frequent enough but some express trains have only 1st-class seats and levy a US$1 compulsory reservation fee which gets you a small cup of coffee or juice from the hostess. Beware of being cheated by the ticket clerk at Mostar Railway Station.

It's a wonderfully picturesque train ride north from Mostar. The line runs along the Neretva Valley between high cliffs, loops up around a lake, and snakes through the mountains to Sarajevo.

Carefully check the times of buses to Split (179 km) or Dubrovnik (139 km) and try for an advance ticket. In case of difficulty take a train to Kardeljevo and look for a bus there. For Korčula connect with the year-round ferry to Trpanj at Kardeljevo.

## MEÐUGORJE

Meðugorje is one of Europe's most remarkable sights. On 24 June 1981 six teenagers in this dirt-poor mountain village between Mostar and the coast saw a miraculous apparition of the Virgin Mary, and Meðugorje's instant economic boom began. A decade later Meðugorje is flush with tour buses, duty-free shops, souvenir stands, car rental offices, travel agencies, furnished apartments, restaurants, traffic jams and shiny Mercedes taxis. 'Religious tourism' is being developed Yugoslav-style as if this were a beach resort. Shops sell postcards of Christ and the Virgin. It's become *the* trendy place to go and you'll even see Japanese groups, although most of the packaged pilgrims come from Britain and the USA.

### Orientation

Meðugorje is in the hills between Čitluk and Ljubuški, 23 km south-west of Mostar. It's an easy day trip from Mostar or you can stop here on your way from Split to Mostar. There's no place to leave luggage at Meðugorje although the travel agencies will sometimes hold it for you if you ask nicely. Don't worry about communicating as this is one of the only places in Yugoslavia where everybody speaks English! There's a map of the area posted in front of the Church of St James.

### Things to See & Do

As soon as you arrive, head towards the twin towers of the **Parish Church of St James** (1969) to check the daily programme for pilgrims. This includes Holy Mass in English at 10 am, an information meeting at 3 pm, recitation of the rosary at 6 pm and Serbo-Croatian evening mass at 7 pm, followed by the blessing of religious articles, prayers for the sick and a final recitation of the Glorious Mysteries which finishes around 9 pm. In winter the schedule is moved an hour forward.

A long row of confessionals (open just before and after mass) flanks the church, and the circular pavilion behind St James allows mass to be celebrated before the countless multitudes at major feasts such as June 24 (the anniversary of the first apparition), 15 August (Assumption of the Virgin) and 8 September (Nativity of the Virgin). **Videos** about Meðugorje are shown in a hall near the church.

The highlight of any visit to Meðugorje is an **apparition** and these are usually on Monday and Friday. Thousands of people jam the side of Podbrdo, the **Hill of Apparitions**, whenever one is scheduled. **Miracles** also occur. It's about a one-hour walk to this rocky hill from St James. At the foot of the hill are the houses where the visionaries were born.

A more ambitious hike is to Križevac, the **Hill of the Cross** (448 metres), another hour away. The 14-metre-tall cross on this high hill visible from the entire area was erected in 1933.

It's possible to arrange **audiences** with the original visionaries who saw the Virgin in 1981, when they aren't off touring Europe or North America. The visionaries still receive daily messages from the Virgin and on the 25th of each month a message to the world is passed on through them. (It must be noted that the Catholic Church has not yet officially acknowledged the Meðugorje apparitions, the first in Europe since those of Lourdes, France, in 1858 and Fatima, Portugal, in 1917.)

### Places to Stay & Eat

There are dozens of travel agencies along the road to the church and most arrange private rooms for about US$13/25 single/double. Many houses have signs in English advertising apartments for rent. The *autocamp* is on the main highway about three km from the Church of St James.

There are rows of pizzerias and ice-cream stands in front of the church.

### Getting There & Away

Bus No 48 runs from Mostar to Meðugorje fairly frequently (US$1). In Meðugorje catch the bus to Mostar from the post office by the bridge, about 500 metres from St James (check this, as Meðugorje is developing fast). Buy your bus ticket at the kiosk and validate it once aboard.

If you arrive on one of two daily buses from Split (US$7) you'll be dropped off on the main highway about two km from town.

### Getting Around
The Unis Tours 'Peace Train', a tractor or jeep pulling a couple of wagons loaded with pilgrims, shuttles around town and out to the trailheads whenever there are enough paying passengers.

## SARAJEVO
Sarajevo, near the geographical centre of Yugoslavia, is the capital of the Republic of Bosnia-Hercegovina. Set in hilly, broken countryside by the Miljacka River, Sarajevo's 73 mosques give it the strongest Turkish flavour of any city in the Balkans. Aside from being the seat of the head of all of Yugoslavia's Muslims, this city of nearly half a million has an Orthodox metropolitan and a Catholic archbishop.

From the mid-15th century till 1878 Turkish governors ruled Bosnia from Sarajevo. The name comes from *saraj*, Turkish for 'palace'. When the Turks finally withdrew, half a century of Austro-Hungarian domination began, culminating in the assassination of Archduke Franz Ferdinand and his wife, Sophie, by conspirators desiring a South Slav republic.

Sarajevo, the only oriental city in Europe, retains the essence of this rich history in Baščaršija, the picturesque old Turkish bazar full of mosques, markets and local colour, and along a riverfront largely unchanged since that fateful day in 1914 when history was irrevocably changed here. Seventy years later Sarajevo again attracted world attention by hosting the 14th Winter Olympic Games (1984). Luckily the major sporting facilities and hotels built for this event blend harmoniously with old Sarajevo.

### Orientation
The bus and train stations are adjacent, a couple of km west of the old town. A detailed city map is posted near the tram stop in front of the railway station. Tram No 1 loops east by the river directly into town. Buy a ticket at the kiosk and punch it once aboard.

### Information
The tourist office at Jugoslovenske narodne armije (JNA) 50, provides maps and brochures.

### Things to See
Begin your visit at **Baščaršija**, the old Turkish marketplace. This medieval square still pulses with life as artisans ply their trades, ćevapčići sizzles on the grills and believers hurry to any of the ubiquitous mosques for prayer. The **Brusa Bezistan** (1551), a former silk market, now caters to tourism, but you'll see more locals than visitors in Baščaršija – it's for real, not show.

Stroll along ulica Sarači which soon becomes ulica Vase Miskina, Sarajevo's throbbing pedestrian corridor. At Sarači 77 is the **Marića Han**, a 17th century caravanserai where traders once rested. A little farther along you'll reach the **Gazi Husrev-bey Mosque** (1531), Yugoslavia's largest, which you may enter outside of prayer times for a fee. Notice the fountain in the courtyard, the clock tower, and the **Kuršumli Medresa** (1537), a former Islamic school across the street. At the start of ulica Vase Miskina is the 16th century **covered market** *(bezistan)* on the left.

Continue along to the **Catholic Cathedral**. Behind this on Maršala Tita are the **Gazi Husrev-bey Baths**, now a casino. Walk east to the **Jewish Museum** (closed Monday), Maršala Tita 98, which is housed in the old Sephardic Synagogue erected in the 16th century by refugees from Spain. At Maršala Tita 87 is **St Michael the Archangel Serbian Orthodox Church**, rebuilt in 1730 after a fire. There's an icon museum in the adjacent building. Return to Baščaršija Square, then go north up Remzije Omanovića to the **City Museum** (closed Sunday) where you'll see an informative scale model of the city centre you just wandered through

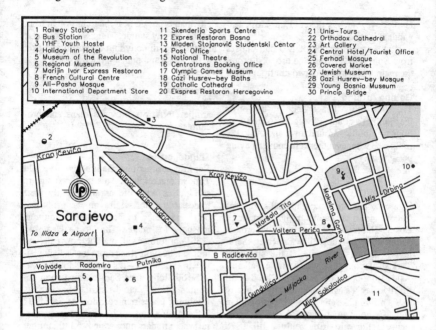

1 Railway Station
2 Bus Station
3 IYHF Youth Hostel
4 Holiday Inn Hotel
5 Museum of the Revolution
6 Regional Museum
7 Marijin Ivor Express Restoran
8 French Cultural Centre
9 Ali-Pasha Mosque
10 International Department Store
11 Skenderija Sports Centre
12 Expres Restoran Bosna
13 Mladen Stojanović Studentski Centar
14 Post Office
15 National Theatre
16 Centrotrans Booking Office
17 Olympic Games Museum
18 Gazi Husrev-bey Baths
19 Catholic Cathedral
20 Ekspres Restoran Hercegovina
21 Unis-Tours
22 Orthodox Cathedral
23 Art Gallery
24 Central Hotel/Tourist Office
25 Ferhadi Mosque
26 Covered Market
27 Jewish Museum
28 Gazi Husrev-bey Mosque
29 Young Bosnia Museum
30 Princip Bridge

– ask to borrow the typewritten museum guide in English.

Go back to Baščaršija again and follow the tram tracks east till they loop around Sarajevo's **old town hall** (now the university library), erected in pseudo-Moorish form in 1895. On 28 June 1914 Austrian Archduke Franz Ferdinand and his wife, Sophie, paid a courtesy call here and then rode west along the riverside in an open car to the second bridge, where they met assassin's bullets. Retrace their route where trams rattle today and see the story in the **Young Bosnia Museum** on the corner at Obala vojvode Stepe 36. On the pavement (sidewalk) beside the museum are footprints where the Serbian nationalist Gavrilo Princip stood and fired the first shots of WW I.

Cross the Miljacka River on the 18th century Princip Bridge and follow the river east a block to the Careva or the **Sultan's Mosque** (1566), which adjoins an important Islamic library usually open only to groups.

The court *(seraglio)* of the Bosnian governors was once here. Continue east by the river to the market opposite the old town hall. Signs point the way south a few hundred metres to the cable car up **Mt Trebević** (US$1 return), departing every hour on the hour. Don't miss it. The bobsleigh course from the 1984 Winter Olympics is just below the upper station.

After (or before) your ride up Mt Trebević, jump on any tram and get out at the first stop after the Holiday Inn. The large building across the road is the **Regional Museum** (closed Monday) with extensive archaeology, ethnography and natural history collections, plus a compact botanical garden and some unusual funerary monuments in the courtyard. The modern building alongside is the **Museum of the Revolution** (closed Monday). Both museums close at 5 pm weekdays and 1 pm weekends, so don't leave it too late.

Ilidža, 10 km west of Sarajevo, is a famous

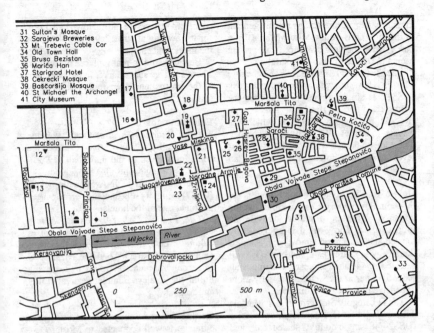

31 Sultan's Mosque
32 Sarajevo Breweries
33 Mt Trebevic Cable Car
34 Old Town Hall
35 Brusa Bezistan
36 Marića Han
37 Starigrad Hotel
38 Cekrecki Mosque
39 Baščaršija Mosque
40 St Michael the Archangel
41 City Museum

spa dating back to Roman times. It's possible to bathe in the warm sulphuric waters of the **thermal pool** at the Hotel Terme here daily (except Sunday) from 8 am to 7 pm for US$5 a half-hour (not recommended for those with heart conditions). Get there by taking tram No 3, 4 or 6 west to the terminus, then ask.

### Places to Stay

**Camping** Campers may stay at *Autocamp Ilidža* (☎ 62 1432), 10 km west of Sarajevo, for US$4 per person, US$4 per tent, US$2 per person tax (open from May to September). Bungalows here are US$39/58 double/triple. Take tram No 3, 4 or 6 west to the terminus, then walk along Džemala Bijedića to the bridge. The information office at the end of this bridge will direct you to the camping ground and provide other assistance.

**Hostels** The 90-bed IYHF *'Dom Firijalaca'* Youth Hostel, Zadrugina 17, is only a short walk uphill from the train station. The route is a little confusing so unless you have a detailed map you'll have to ask directions and watch for signs pointing the way to the 'Omladinski Hotel'. Registration begins at 2 pm, doors shut at 11 pm, and it costs US$10 for members, US$13 for nonmembers (open all year).

Up on Mt Trebević, a 20-minute walk from the upper cable car station, is the *Dom Odmora Mladost* (☎ 53 5921) with rooms for US$8. Bus No 38 from Princip Bridge goes close to this hostel – buy your ticket at a kiosk. Do call before going up, as it fills and is often closed.

In July and August young travellers may find a bed at *Mladen Stojanović Studentski Centar*, ulica Radićeva 4d, for about US$20 per person, breakfast included.

**Private Rooms** The Olimpik Tours office in the railway station arranges private rooms (US$15/30 single/double), but its prices are higher than those charged by travel agencies in the city. Unis-Tours, Vase Miskina 16, a block from the tourist office, has private rooms at US$25 double (few singles).

The Tourist Office, Sarači 81 beside Marića Han, has cheaper 2nd-category (US$12/24 single/double) and 1st-category rooms (US$19/32). If all else fails try the 'Recepcija', Maršala Tita 108, which has private rooms at US$18/30 single/double. There are no houses with *sobe* signs in Sarajevo, thus you're forced to go through an agency.

**Hotels** Your best bet for a hotel room is the 50-room, D-category *Central Hotel*, on the corner of Zrinjskog 8 and JNA beside the tourist office. The Central is conveniently located and has a good atmosphere. Singles/doubles with shared bath and breakfast will run US$30/44 (open all year). The imposing red velvet bar at the Central isn't any more expensive than the cafés outside.

The D-category *Starigrad Hotel*, Maršala Tita 126 just off Baščaršija, is noisier (US$24/48 single/double, shared bath and breakfast).

**Places to Eat**

Two self-service restaurants to know about are *Ekspres Hercegovina*, on Vase Miskina beside the Catholic Cathedral, and *Expres Marijin Ivor*, Maršala Tita 1 between the station and town. *Expres Restoran Bosna*, Maršala Tita 36 (go back behind the snack bar), is another self-service.

*Aščinica 'Sebilj'*, Maršala Tita 95, is an easy place to eat since you pick what you want from the pots near the window. Regional dishes are served at *Marića Han*, an old Baščaršija caravanserai at Sarači 77. In summer you can dine in the courtyard. The *Taverna Ragusa*, Vase Miskina 10, is good for seafood, though smoky and slightly up-market.

Beer lovers repair to *Restoran Brodac*, a menuless local hang-out where small bottles of excellent Zlatorog Pivo and portions of fresh roast goat are the standard fare. It's in a ramshackle subterranean building on the riverfront just west of the old town hall. Look for the awning at street level and listen for the music and shouts.

Burek is sold in many places by weight. There's a large supermarket in the basement of the International Department Store, Maršala Tita 26.

**Entertainment**

Try the *National Theatre*, Obala vojvode Stepe 9 nearby, beside the river. Concerts are sometimes given in the main hall at *Skenderija*. Sporting events also happen here.

The tourist office, JNA 50, sells tickets (US$7) to nightly folk dancing performances put on at one of the hotels.

The *French Cultural Centre*, Valtera Perića 11, shows free videos and organises cultural events. In summer check the open-air cinema at Sarači 42 in the bazar area. Many cultural events take place in Baščaršija during the Sarajevo Summer Festival in July and August.

**Getting There & Away**

Sarajevo is well connected to Mostar (152 km), Kardeljevo (228 km), Banja Luka (315 km), Belgrade (496 km) and Zagreb (536 km) by train. Couchettes are available to/from Belgrade, Ljubljana and Zagreb. Some express trains departing from Sarajevo are all 1st class (no 2nd-class carriages), so make sure you get the right ticket. Olimpik Tours, Maršala Tita 20 or Vase Miskina 2, makes train reservations and books couchettes on trains leaving Sarajevo. Make sure they fill in your ticket clearly, otherwise you could have problems with the conductor.

Centrotrans, Maršala Tita 39, sells advance bus tickets with seat reservations.

The JAT airport bus leaves from the Holiday Inn Hotel.

## TRAVNIK

From 1699 to 1851 the Turkish vizier of Bosnia resided at Travnik, 90 km north-west of Sarajevo, as the 16 mosques, Islamic tombs and other remains attest. It all looks picturesque as you arrive from Sarajevo, but the lower town is being rapidly transformed by mushrooming apartment blocks, and the house-museum of Nobel Prize winner **Ivo Andrić** (author of the novel *Travnik Chronicle*) is now completely engulfed in modern constructions. Travnik may still be worth a brief stop to climb up to the medieval fortress for a view of the old town and the verdant hills all round, though it actually looks much better from the bus than it does up close.

### Places to Stay & Eat

The Turist Biro next to the high-rise *Orient Hotel* on ulica Maršala Tita, a five-minute walk from the bus station, doesn't arrange private rooms and there are no camping facilities at Travnik. Don't plan on spending the night here unless you're willing to shell out US$65 for a very ordinary room at the Orient.

### JAJCE

Jajce (pronounced 'Yitse' with a long i as in white) is a medieval walled city of cobbled streets and old houses in hilly country on the main highway from Sarajevo to Zagreb. Prior to the 15th century Turkish conquest, Jajce was the seat of the Christian kings of Bosnia and for a short period in 1943 it was the capital of liberated Yugoslavia.

It's a very friendly town, a pleasure to stroll around, and one of the largest waterfalls in Europe is here. Even the heavy smell of coal in the air from ugly polluting factories just outside the town doesn't detract too much from its appeal, and it's far enough from the coast not to be spoiled by tour groups. The weekly market is on Wednesday.

### Orientation & Information

The bus station is just south of the centre, near where the Pliva and Vrbas rivers meet. The tourist office is through the tunnel beside the station and straight ahead a block.

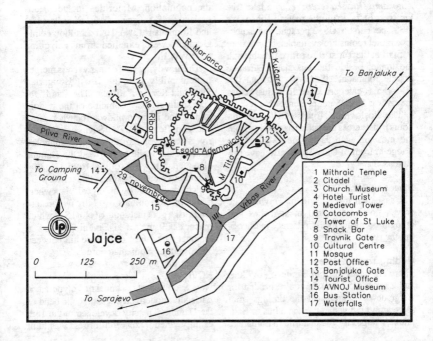

**Jajce**

0    125    250 m

1 Mithraic Temple
2 Citadel
3 Church Museum
4 Hotel Turist
5 Medieval Tower
6 Catacombs
7 Tower of St Luke
8 Snack Bar
9 Travnik Gate
10 Cultural Centre
11 Mosque
12 Post Office
13 Banjaluka Gate
14 Tourist Office
15 AVNOJ Museum
16 Bus Station
17 Waterfalls

## Things to See

If you avoid the tunnel and walk north from the bus station through the park, you'll soon reach an attractive series of **waterfalls** on the Pliva River just outside the old town walls. A little above the falls near the bridge leading towards town is the **AVNOJ Museum** in a hall where the 142 delegates to the second session of the Antifascist Council for the National Liberation of Yugoslavia (AVNOJ) gathered on 29 November 1943. It was at this historic meeting that a new constitution was proclaimed and Marshal Tito officially replaced the deposed King Peter II as Yugoslavia's legitimate leader.

Cross the bridge and enter the walled city through the **Travnik Gate** on the right. Aside from a mosque and several old towers there's a 15th century **citadel** at the highest point in the old town, though all these sights could be locked.

## Places to Stay

*Autokamp 'Plivska jezera'* is by a lake five km west of Jajce on the road to Bihac. It's US$2 per person, US$2 per tent, and expensive motel rooms are available.

Staff at the Turist Biro office just through the tunnel beside the bus station arrange private rooms at US$10 per person. The 40-room, B-category *Hotel Turist* just across the river is US$25 per person.

The Poslovnica Tourist Office (Unis-Tours), just across the pedestrian bridge from the museum, and Jajce Tours, below the bridge in front of Unis-Tours, also have private rooms.

## Places to Eat

The snack bar just outside the Travnik Gate serves good traditional meat dishes and draught beer on a pleasant terrace overlooking the river.

## Getting There & Away

There are buses to/from Sarajevo (189 km) and Zagreb (259 km). If you're headed for Belgrade or Zagreb and the timings from Jajce aren't convenient, catch a bus to Banjaluka, a large city 76 km north. In Banjaluka

the bus from Jajce first lets off passengers in the centre of town, but stay on until you reach the main bus station next to Banjaluka Railway Station.

# Vojvodina

Vojvodina (21,506 sq km) forms part of the Republic of Serbia, an 'autonomous province' until Serbia scrapped this arrangement in 1990. Slavs settled here in the 6th century, followed by Hungarians in the 10th. Vojvodina became depopulated after the 16th century Turkish conquest, but when the Habsburgs drove back the Turks in the late 17th century the region reverted to Hungary, where it was to remain until 1918. In the 18th century large numbers of Serbians fled to this Hungarian-controlled area to escape Ottoman rule in the lands farther south, and today ethnic Serbians comprise a 55% majority of the population. Minorities include Hungarians (24%), Croats (8%), Slovaks (4%) and Romanians (3%). Half a million ethnic Germans were expelled from Vojvodina after WW II.

This low-lying land of many rivers merges imperceptibly into the Great Hungarian Plain and Romania's Banat. The Tisa River cuts south across the middle of the region, joining the Danube midway between Novi Sad and Belgrade. The Sava and Danube rivers mark Vojvodina's southern boundary with Serbia, while to the west the Danube also separates Vojvodina from Croatia. Numerous canals crisscross this fertile plain which provides much of Yugoslavia's wheat and corn. Vojvodina's two hilly regions are the Fruška gora just south of Novi Sad which reaches 539 metres at Crveni čot, now a national park, and a 641-metre hill between Vršac and the Romanian border.

## NOVI SAD

Novi Sad (Neusatz), capital of Vojvodina, is a friendly modern city at a strategic bend of the Danube. The city developed in the 18th century when a powerful fortress was built on a hilltop overlooking the river to hold the area for the Habsburgs. Novi Sad remained part of the Austro-Hungarian empire until 1918 and still has a Hungarian air about it today. The main sights can be covered in a couple of hours or made into a leisurely day. Provided you aren't forced to stay at an expensive hotel it's a good escape from Belgrade.

## Orientation & Information
The adjacent train and bus stations are at the end of Bulevar 23 oktobra, several km northwest of the city centre. Catch a bus to Trg slobode, then ask directions to the tourist office at Dunavska 27, in a quaint old part of town. This office has brochures on many parts of Yugoslavia besides Novi Sad.

## Things to See
There are three **museums** on Dunavska near the tourist office: paintings at No 29 (closed Monday and Tuesday), archaeology at No 35 (closed Monday) and the history of the Revolution at No 37. This latter museum is very near the Danube.

Walk across the old bridge to majestic **Petrovaradin Citadel** (built in 1699-1780), the 'Gibraltar of the Danube' designed by the French architect Vauban. The stairs beside the large church in the lower town lead up to the fortress. Today the citadel contains a hotel, restaurant and two small museums (closed Monday), but the chief pleasure is simply to walk along the walls enjoying the splendid free view of the city, river and surrounding countryside. There are as many as 16 km of underground galleries and halls below the citadel, but these can only be visited by groups.

Other sights of Novi Sad include three substantial **art galleries** (closed Monday and Tuesday) side by side in a row on Vase Stajića, not far from Trg slobode, and the ultramodern **Serbian National Theatre**, also close by.

## Places to Stay
**Camping** There's a large *Autocamp* near the Danube at Ribarsko Ostrvo, with bungalows (US$42 double) available all year. Camping is US$4 per person and US$3 per tent plus US$1 per person tax. Take the Liman bus to the end of the line, then walk two km towards

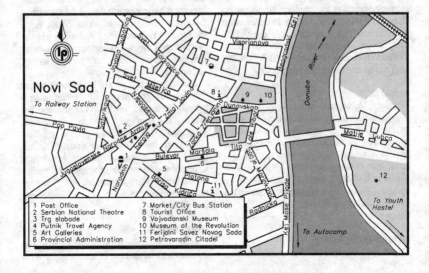

| | |
|---|---|
| 1 Post Office | 7 Market/City Bus Station |
| 2 Serbian National Theatre | 8 Tourist Office |
| 3 Trg slobode | 9 Vojvodanski Museum |
| 4 Putnik Travel Agency | 10 Museum of the Revolution |
| 5 Art Galleries | 11 Ferijalni Savez Novog Sada |
| 6 Provincial Administration | 12 Petrovaradin Citadel |

the river. If you walk all the way from the centre of town it will take one hour.

**Hostels** If you arrive during business hours and want IYHF youth hostel accommodation, visit the Ferijalni Savez Novog Sada, Borisa Kidriča 11 (open weekdays from 8 am to 3 pm, ☎ 021-57474). They'll let you know if any beds are free at the hostel (open from April to September), which is quite a distance out on the south side of the river. To get to the hostel take the Paragovo, Beočin or Ledinci buses from the market as far as Ribnjak, then ask for *Ferijalni dom* (☎ 021-43 4846), Donji put 79. It's down near the river about a km from the bus stop.

**Private Rooms** All of Novi Sad's hotels are characterless and expensive so ask about private rooms at Putnik, Narodnih heroja 8 just off Trg slobode.

### Places to Eat
If you're thirsty on your way to/from the fortress there's a good beer bar at ulica Matije Gubca 10 in the lower town. A self-service restaurant is at Narodnih heroja 1.

### Getting There & Away
Novi Sad is on the main railway line between Belgrade, Budapest and Sofia. In the evening you can easily pick up the overnight Meridian Express to Sofia (12 hours, 485 km). Trains to Subotica (99 km) and Belgrade (80 km) run every couple of hours.

### SUBOTICA
Subotica, Vojvodina's second city, is a large Hungarian-speaking town up near the Hungarian border. Though the Art-Nouveau town hall tends towards the exotic, there's no reason to spend the night here and the one hotel, the B-category *Patria*, is way overpriced at US$40/70 single/double. There's a camping ground by a lake at Palić, seven km east of Subotica on the railway line to Szeged.

### Getting There & Away
There are two local trains a day to/from Szeged, Hungary (46 km, US$3). Several daily buses also shuttle between Szeged and Subotica (US$2).

Three express trains a day run north to Budapest (six hours, 274 km) and there are 12 trains a day to Novi Sad (99 km).

# Serbia

The dominant role of Serbia (Srbija) in the Yugoslav Federation is suggested by the inclusion within its boundaries of two formerly 'autonomous provinces', Vojvodina and Kosovo, and the national capital, Belgrade. At 88,361 sq km it's by far the largest of Yugoslavia's six republics, though if you subtract the two former provinces it's only 55,968 sq km, slightly smaller than 56,538-sq-km Croatia.

Northern Serbia along the Danube is an extension of the lowland plains of Hungary, while the mountainous centre and south merge into Montenegro, Kosovo, Macedonia and Bulgaria. East of Belgrade the Danube River passes the medieval castles of Smederevo and Golubac, then flows through the famous Iron Gate along the Romanian border. A hydroelectric dam has now tamed this once wild stretch of water. South along the roads to Bulgaria and Kosovo are a string of medieval Orthodox monasteries rich in frescoes and icons, symbols of the glory of old Serbia.

Serbia is the one part of Yugoslavia where you can still get well off the beaten track – outside Belgrade you'll never see another tourist. Transport and food are cheap and, away from Belgrade, the people are less jaded than those along the coast. The big problem is accommodation as hotels are expensive and scarce and private rooms unavailable. If you have a tent and a taste for adventure you can really get lost-and-found out there.

### HISTORY
The Serbians arrived in the Balkans in the 7th century and accepted Christianity in 879.

Under the 14th century ruler Stefan Dušan, Serbia was a great power including much of present Albania and northern Greece within its boundaries. After Stefan's death in 1355 Serbia declined, and on 28 June 1389 the Serbian army was defeated by the Ottoman Turks at the Battle of Kosovo. By 1459 Serbia was a Turkish *pashalik* (province) and the inhabitants had become mere serfs.

As the Turkish tide receded in the 18th century, Austria began encroaching on historic Serbian territory from the north, holding Vojvodina and Belgrade from 1718 to 1739. Through diplomacy the sultan regained northern Serbia for another century, but after a war between Turkey and Russia in 1829 Serbian autonomy was obtained. The utter defeat of Turkey by Russia in 1878 led to Serbian independence and in 1882 it became a kingdom.

Tensions mounted after Austria's annexation of Bosnia-Hercegovina in 1908 with Russia backing Serbia. The Balkan Wars of 1912 and 1913 gave much of Turkish-held Macedonia to Serbia. Austria's invasion of Serbia in 1914 sparked WW I. After 1918 the King of Serbia ruled a territory corresponding largely to present Yugoslavia. Serbia's size was reduced after WW II when Bosnia-Hercegovina, Montenegro and Macedonia were granted republic status within the Yugoslav Federation.

## BELGRADE (БЕОГРАД)

Belgrade (Beograd) is strategically situated on the southern edge of the Carpathian Basin where the Sava River joins the Danube. Just east of the city is the Morava Valley, route of the famous 'Stamboul Road' from Turkey to Central Europe. At this major crossroads a city developed which has long been the flash point of the Balkans. It might be an interesting place to poke around for a few days if accommodation weren't so absurdly expensive.

Until WW I Belgrade was right on the border of Serbia and Austria-Hungary and its citadel has seen too many battles for a lot to have survived. Destroyed and rebuilt 40 times in its 2300-year history, socialist Belgrade never managed to pick up all the pieces. Swarms of polluting vehicles and transiting travellers will test your nerves. Do your business and have a look round, then move on to better things.

### History

The Celtic settlement of Singidunum was founded in the 3rd century BC on a bluff overlooking the confluence of the Sava and Danube rivers. The Romans arrived in the 1st century AD and stayed till the 5th century. The present Slavonic name Beograd ('White City') first appeared in a Papal letter dated 16 April 878. Belgrade became the capital of Serbia in 1403, as the Serbians were pushed north by the Turks. In 1456 the Hungarians under János Hunyadi succeeded in defeating a Turkish advance in this direction but in 1521 the Turks finally took Belgrade. In 1842 the city again became the capital of Serbia and in 1918, the capital of all Yugoslavia. In April 1941, 17,000 lives were lost in a Nazi bombing raid on Belgrade. Soon after, on 4 July 1941, Tito and the Communist Party's Central Committee meeting at Belgrade decided to launch an armed uprising. Since Belgrade was liberated on 20 October 1944, the population has grown sixfold to about a million and a half.

### Orientation

You'll probably arrive at the railway station on the south side of the city centre or at the adjacent bus station. In the railway station you can get train information at window 25, tourist information at window 32, change money at window 35, book a couchette at window 34 and buy international tickets at window 3. Window 36 may help you find a room.

The regular train information window in the railway station dispenses information in Serbo-Croatian only. For train information in English you'll be directed to tourist information in the next building.

Backpacks can only be left in the railway station left-luggage office (not at the bus

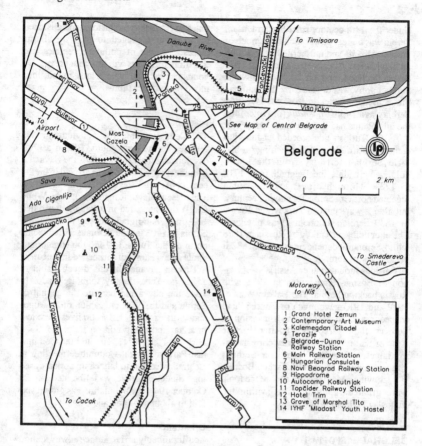

1 Grand Hotel Zemun
2 Contemporary Art Museum
3 Kalemegdan Citadel
4 Terazije
5 Belgrade–Dunav
  Railway Station
6 Main Railway Station
7 Hungarian Consulate
8 Novi Beograd Railway Station
9 Hippodrome
10 Autocamp Kosutnjak
11 Topčider Railway Station
12 Hotel Trim
13 Grave of Marshal Tito
14 IYHF 'Mladost' Youth Hostel

station). Putnik Garderoba across the street from the railway station is also good. Allow plenty of time to pick up your bag.

To walk into town take Milovanovića east a block, then go straight up Balkanska to Terazije, the heart of modern Belgrade. Kneza Mihaila, Belgrade's lively pedestrian boulevard, runs north-west through Stari Grad (the old town) from Terazije to Kalemegdan Park, where you'll find the citadel.

### Information

The tourist office (open daily from 8 am to 8 pm) is in the underpass in front of the bookshop at the beginning of Terazije, on the corner of Kneza Mihaila. The bookshop has English books.

**Money** If the exchange window in the railway station is closed, try the JIK Banka across the park in front of the station (open from 8 am to 8 pm weekdays, and from 8 am to 3 pm Saturdays).

The large post office on the right side of the railway station changes money on weekdays from 7 am to 8 pm and the lines are much shorter than in the station or at the bank.

**Post & Telecommunications** The main post office, Takovska 2, holds poste restante. International telephone calls can also be made here.

**Foreign Embassies** Most of the consulates and embassies are on or near Kneza Miloša, a 10-minute walk south-east from the railway station. The Polish Consulate is at Kneza Miloša 38 (weekdays from 8 am to noon, visas US$20 cash dollars, 24-hour service). The American Embassy (☎ 64 5655) is at Kneza Miloša 50. The Albanian Embassy is at Kneza Miloša 56. The Romanian Consulate is at Kneza Miloša 70 (weekdays from 9 am to 11 am, visas US$30 in dinars, issued on the spot). The German Embassy is at Kneza Miloša 74-76. The Canadian Embassy (☎ 64 4666) is at Kneza Miloša 75.

The British Embassy (☎ 64 5055) is at Generala Ždanova 46. The Bulgarian Consulate is at Birčaninova 26 (weekdays from 9 am to noon, visas US$30 in dinars).

The Hungarian Consulate, Ivana Milutinovića 74 (weekdays from 9 am to noon), is a few blocks east, while the Czechoslovak Consulate, Bulevar Revolucije 22 (weekdays from 9 am to noon), is near the main post office. As usual the Australian Embassy is in an odd location at Čika Ljubina 13 in Stari Grad.

### Things to See

From the railway station take tram No 2 north-west to **Kalemegdan Citadel**, a strategic hilltop fortress at the junction of the Sava and Danube rivers. The Roman settlement of Singidunum was on the flood plain at the foot of the citadel. Although much of what is seen today dates from the 17th century, this area has been fortified since Celtic times. Medieval gates, Orthodox churches, Muslim tombs and Turkish baths are among the varied remnants to be seen. Ivan Meštrović's *Monument of Gratitude to France* (1930) is also here. The large **Military Museum** on the battlements of the citadel presents a complete history of Yugoslavia in 53 rooms. The benches in the park around the citadel are relaxing and on summer evenings lots of people come strolling here.

Adjacent to Kalemegdan is Stari Grad, the oldest part of Belgrade. The best museums are here, especially the **National Museum**, Trg Republike, which has archaeology downstairs, paintings upstairs. The collection of European art is quite good. A few blocks away at Studentski trg 13 is the **Ethnographical Museum** with an excellent collection of Serbian costumes and folk art. Detailed explanations are provided in English. Not far away is the **Gallery of Frescoes**, Cara Uroša 20, with full-size replicas of paintings in remote churches of Serbia and Macedonia. Belgrade's most memorable museum is the **Palace of Princess Ljubice**, on the corner of Svetozara Markovića and 7 jula, an authentic Balkan-style palace (1831) complete with period furnishings.

Among the things to see in the modern city east of Terazije is the **Museum of the Revolution**, Trg Marksa i Engelsa 11, with interesting photos but no explanations in English or German. The imposing edifice just east of this museum is **Skupština**, the Yugoslav parliament (built in 1907-32). East again behind the main post office is **St Marks Serbian Orthodox Church** (built in 1932-39) with four tremendous pillars supporting a towering dome. There's a small Russian Orthodox church behind it.

If you'd like to visit the flowery **grave of Marshal Tito** (open from 9 am to 4 pm), it's within the grounds of his former residence on Bulevar Oktobarske Revolucije a few km south of the city centre (trolley buses No 40 or 41 from Kneza Miloša). This tomb and all of the museums are closed on Mondays.

Escape the bustle of Belgrade on **Ada Ciganlija**, an island park in the Sava River just upstream from the city. In summer you can swim in the river (naturists walk a km upstream from the others), rent a bicycle (US$2.50 an hour) or just stroll among the trees. Many small cafés overlooking the beach dispense cold beer at reasonable rates.

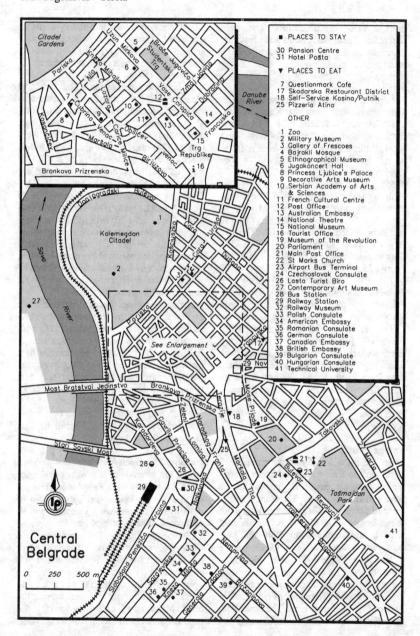

**PLACES TO STAY**

30 Pansion Centre
31 Hotel Pošta

**PLACES TO EAT**

7 Questionmark Cafe
17 Skadarska Restaurant District
18 Self-Service Kasina/Putnik
25 Pizzeria Atina

**OTHER**

1 Zoo
2 Military Museum
3 Gallery of Frescoes
4 Bajakli Mosque
5 Ethnographical Museum
6 Jugokoncert Hall
7 Princess Ljubice's Palace
8 Decorative Arts Museum
9 Serbian Academy of Arts
  & Sciences
11 French Cultural Centre
12 Post Office
13 Australian Embassy
14 National Theatre
15 National Museum
16 Tourist Office
19 Museum of the Revolution
20 Parliament
21 Main Post Office
22 St Marks Church
23 Airport Bus Terminal
24 Czechoslovak Consulate
26 Lasta Turist Biro
27 Contemporary Art Museum
28 Bus Station
29 Railway Station
32 Railway Museum
33 Polish Consulate
34 American Embassy
35 Romanian Consulate
36 German Consulate
37 Canadian Embassy
38 British Embassy
39 Bulgarian Consulate
40 Hungarian Consulate
41 Technical University

Central
Belgrade

0    250    500 m

## Places to Stay

Accommodation in Belgrade is the most expensive in Yugoslavia with places in the budget category both inconvenient and overpriced. Try to arrange an early-morning arrival and a late-evening departure.

**Camping** *Autocamp Košutnjak*, Kneza Višeslava 17, is about eight km south-west of the city centre. The camping ground is open for campers (US$4 per person, US$3 per tent, US$5 tax) from May to September only, but there are expensive new bungalows all year (US$32 per person with private bath). The older, cheaper bungalows are permanently occupied by locals. It's a fairly pleasant wooded site with lots of shade, but pitch your tent far from the noisy restaurant. To get there take trams No 12 or 13 from beside the railway station to Kneza Višeslava, the next stop after you see the horse-racing track *(Hippodrome)* on the left.

**Youth Hostel** The rather unpleasant IYHF *'Mladost' Hotel* is in a modern three-storey building opposite Bulevar JNA 253 on the south side of the city. At US$13 for a bed in a six-bed dorm it's expensive though breakfast is included. Those without a YHA card pay US$2 more. Individual rooms at the hostel are US$50/68 single/double. It's open all day (check in from noon) and there's no curfew or rules. This hostel was recently remodelled into a fancy B-category hotel full of middle-aged Yugoslav 'youth' – YHA members toting backpacks are only reluctantly received. It is a good place to meet other travellers, though. From Beograd-Dunav Railway Station take bus No 47 directly to the hostel. From the main railway station take tram No 9 from outside the station to Vojvode Stepe 274, then walk back to Vojvode Stepe 266, turn left and go straight ahead.

**Private Rooms** Turist Biro Lasta (closed Sunday) on Milovanovića below the Astorija Hotel in front of the station sometimes has private rooms at US$20/40 single/double but this cannot be relied upon. There are only two (!) single rooms, for example, and neither are in the city centre. Also, they won't reserve private rooms for future return visits. You must take your chances, which aren't good. If you're lucky, someone on the street outside Lasta will offer you an unofficial private room.

**Hotels** The cheapest hotel is the *Hotel Pošta*, Slobodana Penezića-Krcuna 3 right beside the railway station (US$22 per person). The main problem here is the 24-hour traffic roar outside.

*Pansion Centre*, Trg bratstva i jedinstva 7 opposite the train station, is overpriced at US$25 per person. If you're alone you'll have to pay that for a bed in its dorm! It's usually full of locals who pay half-price.

The C-category *Hotel Trim* (☎ 55 8128), Kneza Višeslava 72, one km south of Autocamp Košutnjak, has 41 rooms at US$30/44 single/double with private bath. Take bus No 53 from Kneza Miloša 42 and get out at the next stop after you see a large park on the right with a swimming pool at the bottom of the hill. Call first as it could be full.

**A Valuable Tip** Save a day's travelling time, a night's hotel bill and a lot of aggravation by booking a couchette out of Belgrade at window 34 in the train station. This is easily done and costs only around US$6. There's no way you'll get a room for that! There are overnight trains to most large cities in Yugoslavia. If you arrive in Belgrade in the morning, you'll have all day to look around before boarding the train late that evening. The main sights can be seen in a busy day. Don't forget that a train ticket (purchased at another window) is required in addition to the couchette ticket.

If for some reason you can't get a couchette, consider an overnight bus with a seat reservation to your next destination. It's cheaper than the train and advance tickets are easily purchased at the bus station, but it's much more tiring.

## Places to Eat

*Expres Restoran Luksor*, Balkanska 7 on the

street leading down to the railway station from Hotel Moskva, is the cheapest of all the self-services. Another self-service is *Kasina*, Terazije 25 beside Putnik. Nearby on the opposite side of the boulevard is *Pizzeria Atina*, Terazije 28.

A great breakfast place near the railway station is the burek counter at Nemanjina 5 just below Hotel Beograd (open weekdays from 5 am to 1 pm, Saturday from 5 to 11 am). Prices are clearly marked and if you don't care to eat your burek and yoghurt standing up you can carry the food up to the nice park diagonally opposite the hotel. Avoid the food kiosks right opposite the railway station which overcharge.

The *Questionmark Cafe*, 7 jula 6 opposite the Orthodox church, is unpretentious. It has an English/German menu, traditional meat dishes, side salads and draught beer at reasonable prices.

Around the corner beside Princess Ljubice's Palace is the *Knez Restaurant*, Svetozara Markovića 10, a wine bar serving spaghetti and pizza. It's so popular among local yuppies that you could have difficulty getting a table.

For local colour, check the more expensive folkloric restaurants near the fountain on ulica Skadarska, a street full of summer strollers. In the evening, open-air folkloric, musical and theatrical performances are often staged here.

## Entertainment

Concerts are held at the *Jugokoncert Hall* of Kolarac University, Studentski trg 5. Folk dancing can be seen here on Tuesdays at 8 pm. Concerts also take place in the hall of the *Serbian Academy of Arts & Sciences*, Kneza Mihaila 35.

The French Cultural Centre, Kneza Mihaila 31, often shows free films and videos. In the evening throngs of street musicians play along Kneza Mihaila.

From May to October there's horse racing at the hippodrome *(Trkalište)* every Sunday afternoon (trams No 12 and 13 from the railway station).

## Getting There & Away

**Air** There are JAT flights from Belgrade to Dubrovnik (US$65), Ohrid (US$76), Pula (US$94), Sarajevo (US$42), Skopje (US$62), Split (US$65) and Zadar (US$75).

**Bus** The office with the JAT sticker on the window between the bus and railway stations sells international bus tickets to Vienna (daily, US$42) and Munich (twice a week, US$63).

Bus ticketing is computerised at Belgrade and there are overnight buses to places all around the country. Buy your ticket as far ahead as you can to be assured of a good seat.

**Train** Belgrade is the hub of the railway service in Yugoslavia. There are international trains to Athens (via Skopje), Berlin (via Budapest), Bucharest (via Timişoara), Istanbul (via Sofia), Moscow (via Kecskemét), Munich (via Ljubljana), Paris (via Venice) and Vienna (via Maribor). Overnight domestic trains with couchettes or sleepers run from Belgrade to Bar, Bitola, Kardeljevo, Koper, Ljubljana, Maribor, Pula, Rijeka, Sarajevo, Skopje, Split, Zadar and Zagreb. Most of the above depart the main station on Trg bratstva i jedinstva. Trains to Romania depart from Beograd-Dunav Station, Đure Đakovića 39.

Putnik Travel Agency, Terazije 27, sells train tickets and makes advance reservations at the same prices charged in the station, but without the crowds. International tickets can be purchased with Yugoslav dinars.

## Getting Around

**To/From the Airport** The JAT bus (US$3) departs frequently from the JAT City Terminal on Bulevar Revolucije in front of St Mark's Church. Surčin Airport is 18 km west of the city.

**Public Transport** Twelve-strip public transport tickets are sold at kiosks. You validate your own ticket once aboard – two strips for the first zone then one more for each additional zone. If you're going far, ask someone how many strips to use. Tickets purchased from the driver are more expensive. Night buses between midnight and 4 am charge double fare. A *dnebna karta* allows you to ride all city buses for one day (US$1).

## SOUTHERN SERBIA

Among the most outstanding monuments of the old Serbian state are the many Orthodox monasteries with 13th and 14th century frescoes. It's an elevating experience to visit these imposing sacred monuments, but most are in remote locations difficult to reach without your own transport.

On the east side of the Morava River valley between Belgrade and Niš are a pair of old Serbian monasteries built just before or soon after the Battle of Kosovo (1389). Near the village of Despotovac is **Manasija Monastery** (1418), completely enclosed in defensive walls and towers. Also outstanding is **Ravanica Monastery** (1381), 33 km south of Manasija by a little-travelled road. Ravanica is accessible by bus from Ćuprija on the main railway line from Belgrade to Niš but both monasteries are very inconvenient to reach by public transport. They're worth the slight detour if you're driving between Belgrade and Bulgaria or Greece, however.

South of Kraljevo both the road and railway to Kosovo follow the 'valley of lilacs' along the Ibar River where another cluster of monasteries is found. Eleven km west of Ušće Station on the railway line to Kosovo Polje is **Studentica Monastery**, the oldest of the great monasteries of medieval Serbia. Inside the main church within the monastery's circular compound is buried King Stefan Nemanja, the founder, below his likeness and other frescoes dating back to 1209. Two adjacent churches also contain wonderful 13th and 14th century frescoes. Getting to Studentica is fairly easy as the early morning Kosovo Express from Belgrade covers the 238 km to Ušće in 4½ hours (reservations required) and bus service up to the monastery is good. Near the monastery is the 60-bed *Studentica Hotel* (☎ 036-83 6222).

To reach **Sopoćani Monastery** take a bus from Ušće to **Novi Pazar**, 55 km south, then another bus 15 km west to the monastery. The Stari Ras region around Sopoćani was the heartland of medieval Serbia and contemporary Serbians look upon it as their spiritual homeland. Sopoćani Monastery was built during the reign of King Stefan Uroš I (1242-76) with an exterior narthex and tower added in the 14th century. The frescoes (1265) here mark the apogee of the Byzantine-influenced Raška school and are probably the finest medieval paintings in Yugoslavia. Nearby Novi Pazar is a Muslim town with a couple of old Turkish mosques, inns and bathhouses now quite ruined by adjacent modern constructions.

From Novi Pazar you have a choice of proceeding 67 km south-west to **Rožaj** by bus (for bus connections from Rožaj to Kosovo see the Getting There & Away information in the Kosovo section) or backtracking 21 km to **Raška** where you could pick up a train to Kosovo Polje and points south. The 31-room *Motel Putnik* (☎ 036-76115) at Raška is said to be cheap.

# Kosovo

A visit to Kosovo is a little like visiting the West Bank or Gaza Strip: you feel you've entered an occupied territory. The locals have an uninhibited Third World friendliness and curiosity which sets them apart from other Yugoslavs. The poverty and backwardness are also apparent, as is the watchful eye of the central government. Police posts have taken the place of left-luggage facilities in the region's bus and train stations. Your presence won't go unnoticed.

Until recently an 'autonomous province', Kosovo is now an integral part of the Republic of Serbia. Isolated medieval Serbian monasteries tell of an early period which ended in 1389 with the Battle of Kosovo just outside Prishtinë (Priština in Serbian). After this disaster the Serbians moved north, abandoning the region to the Albanians, the descendants of the ancient Illyrians who had inhabited this land for thousands of years. In the late 19th century the ethnic Albanians, who today comprise 85% of the population of Kosovo, fought to free themselves of Ottoman rule. Yet in 1913 when the Turkish government finally pulled out, Kosovo was handed over to Serbia instead of remaining with the rest of Albania.

After WW II Tito wanted Albania itself included in the Yugoslav Federation as a seventh republic with Kosovo united to it. This never came to pass and thus began two decades of neglect. After serious rioting broke out in Kosovo in 1968, the 'autonomous province' was created (in 1974) and economic aid increased. These changes brought only cosmetic improvements, and in 1981 fresh disturbances were put down by military force. At the time, unemployment stood at 27.5% and, despite some of the most fertile land in the Balkans, the standard of living in Kosovo was a quarter the Yugoslav average.

Trouble began anew in 1988 as Albanian demonstrators protested the sacking of local officials by Belgrade. A Kosovo coal miners' strike in February 1989 was followed by new limits imposed by Serbia on Kosovo's autonomy, a curfew and a state of emergency. This resulted in serious rioting, and 29 unarmed Albanian civilians were shot dead by the Yugoslav security forces. On 5 July 1990 the Serbian parliament cancelled Kosovo's political autonomy and dissolved its parliament and government. All Albanian police officers were fired and TV and radio broadcasts in Albanian terminated.

The local Albanians say all they want is republic status like Montenegro or Macedonia, but many Serbians feel they have a historic right to Kosovo as part of Serbia. So Kosovo stays poor, solutions seem remote and it's impossible not to feel the resentment. Some Serbian politicians have even threatened to colonise Kosovo with Serbians – the parallels with Palestine are obvious.

Just under two million people occupy Kosovo's 10,887 sq km, the most densely populated portion of Yugoslavia with the highest birth rate. The inhabitants adopted Islam after the Turkish conquest and today the region has a definite Muslim air, from the inhabitants' food and dress to the ubiquitous mosques. The capital, Prishtinë, is a depressing, redeveloped city with showplace banks and hotels juxtaposed against squalor, but in the west the Metohija Valley between Pejë and Prizren offers a useful transit route from the Adriatic to Macedonia, plus a chance to see another side of this perplexing country.

## GETTING THERE & AWAY

Getting through from the Adriatic coast to Kosovo takes a full night or day. The simplest way is to catch a bus to **Titograd** and look for another bus direct to Pejë from there. Seven buses a day run between Titograd and Pejë (244 km), crossing the 1849-metre Čakor Pass. Alternatively take one of the 16 daily buses between Titograd and **Ivangrad** (152 km) and look for an onward bus to Pejë. If you're leaving from Ulcinj take an early bus to Bar, then the train 186 km to Bijelo Polje (this scenic ride takes you across Skadar Lake and up the Morača Canyon). Minibuses to Ivangrad await the trains at Bijelo Polje.

From Ivangrad to Pejë is the most difficult part of the trip, possibly involving a wait of a few hours for an onward bus. *Autocamp Berane* is less than one km from Ivangrad Bus Station if you get stuck. Otherwise go on to **Rožaj** (32 km) and spend the night at the comfortable *Rožaje Hotel* (US$18/34 single/double) near the Rožaj Bus Station. An early bus will carry you the 37 km from Rožaj to Pejë the next morning. There's nothing much to see in Rožaj other than the view of the mountains from the white war memorial but it's a friendly, untouristed place.

Getting to Kosovo from Serbia and Macedonia is much easier as there are direct trains to Kosovo Polje (near Prishtinë) from Belgrade (359 km) and lots of buses from Skopje to Prizren.

## PEJË

Pejë (Peć in Serbian), below high mountains between Titograd and Prishtinë, is a friendly, untouristed town of picturesque dwellings slowly being ruined by uncontrolled development. Ethnic Albanians with their white felt skullcaps and Muslim women in traditional dress crowd the streets, especially on Saturday market day. The horse wagons carrying goods around Pejë share the streets with lots of beggars.

## Orientation

The bus and train stations are about 500 metres apart, both in the east part of Pejë about a km from the centre. Neither station has a left-luggage room. Follow Rruga Marshall Tito west from the bus station into the centre of town.

## Information

Try Turist Kosova Agency, Marshall Tito 100, Aurora Travel Agency, Marshall Tito 48, and Metohija Turist, Marshall Tito 20.

## Things to See

There are eight well-preserved, functioning mosques in Pejë, the most imposing of which is the 15th century **Bajrakli Mosque**, its high dome rising out of the colourful **bazar** (*čaršija*) giving Pejë an authentic Oriental air.

By the river two km west of Pejë is the **Patrijaršija Monastery**, seat of the Serbian Orthodox patriarchate in the 14th century, from 1557 to 1766 and again after 1920. The restoration of the patriarchate in 1557 allowed the Serbians to maintain their identity during the darkest moments of Ottoman domination, so this monastery is of deep significance to contemporary Serbians. Inside the high-walled compound are three mid-13th century churches, each of which has a high dome and glorious medieval frescoes. There is a detailed explanation in English in the common narthex. Two km west of the monastery along the main highway is the **Rugovo Gorge**, an excellent hiking area.

Pejë's most impressive sight, however, is 15 km south, past the large military base, accessible by frequent local bus. The Visoki Dečani Monastery (1335) with its marvellous 14th century frescoes is a two-km walk from the bus stop in Deçan (Dečani in Serbian) through beautifully wooded countryside. This royal monastery built under kings Decanski and Dušan survived the long Turkish period intact. From Deçan you can pick up an onward bus to Prizren.

## Places to Stay

**Camping** The only inexpensive place to stay is *Kamp Karagač* over the bridge and a km up the hill from the Metohija Hotel. It charges US$15 for two people to camp, but it's quiet and rather pleasant with lots of shade. There's a restaurant at the camping ground. Kamp Karagač has two nice little bungalows available at US$20 per person. Ask about youth hostel accommodation here. The B-category *Hotel Karagač* just beyond the Kamp is fully occupied by police!

**Hotels** Accommodation in Pejë is problematic as none of the travel agencies in town offer private rooms. The A-category *Metohija Hotel*, Marshall Tito 60, is a budget breaker at US$35/58 single/double with private bath and breakfast. The 50-room *Hotel Korzo*, Marshall Tito 55, was recently renovated and is a little cheaper than the Metohija across the square.

## Getting There & Away

**Bus** Bus service from Prizren (73 km) and Skopje is good and there's a night bus to/from Belgrade. In July and August direct buses run to Pejë from Herceg Novi and Ulcinj.

**Train** The Akropolis Express running between Munich and Athens stops at Kosovo Polje, a junction eight km west of Prishtinë, from where there are branch lines to Pejë (82 km) and Prizren. There's an overnight train to Belgrade with couchettes.

## PRIZREN

Prizren, the most Albanian-looking city in Yugoslavia, is midway between Pejë and Skopje. The closed road to Shkodër reaches the Albanian border 18 km west of Prizren. A big military base with lots of armoured vehicles is just outside Prizren on the way to Skopje.

Prizren was the medieval capital of 'Old Serbia' but much of what we see today is Turkish. Houses climb colourfully up the hillside to the ruined citadel *(kaljaja)* from which the 15th century Turkish bridge and 19 minarets are visible.

The Bistrica River emerges from a gorge behind the citadel and cuts Prizren in two on its way into Albania. East up this gorge is the Bistrica Pass (2640 metres), once the main route to Macedonia. Wednesday is market day when the city really comes alive.

### Orientation
The bus and train stations are adjacent on the west side of town, but there's no left-luggage facility in either. A private garderoba operates in a house behind the bus station charging US$2 apiece (expensive).

### Information
Putnik is on Trg 17 Novembar in the centre of town.

### Things to See
On the way into town from the bus station you'll see the huge white-marble Bankkos Prizren building facing the river. On a backstreet behind the bank is the 14th century **Church of Bogorodica Ljeviška** with an open bell tower above and frescoes inside. Nearby, a tall square tower rises above some Turkish baths, now the **Archaeological Museum** (usually closed).

The **Sinan Pasha Mosque** (1561) beside the river in the centre is closed, as are the **Gazi Mehmed Pasha Baths** (1563) beyond the Theranda Hotel. A little back from these is the large dome of the beautifully appointed 16th century **Bajrakli (Gazi Mehmed) Mosque**, which is still in use. Behind this mosque on the side facing the river is the **Museum of the Prizren League**, a popular movement which struggled for Albanian independence from the Ottoman Empire in 1878-81.

The largest Orthodox church in Prizren is **Sveti Georgi** (1856) in the old town near the Sinan Pasha Mosque. Higher up on the way to the **citadel** is **Sveti Spas** with the ruins of an Orthodox monastery.

### Places to Stay & Eat
Unfortunately no private rooms are available in Prizren. The B-category *Theranda Hotel*, in the centre of town by the river, is overpriced at US$54/72 single/double with private bath. Also try *Motel Putnik* three blocks from the bus station (US$30/50 single/double). There's supposed to be a camping ground in the area behind the Putnik but it's seldom open.

Several good ćevapčići places lie between Sveti and Sinan Pasha.

### Getting There & Away
Bus service from Prishtinë (75 km), Pejë (73 km) and Skopje (150 km) is good. An overnight train with couchettes runs to/from Belgrade.

---

# Macedonia

Macedonia's volatile position in the centre of the Balkan Peninsula between Albania, Bulgaria, Greece and Serbia has often made it a political powder keg. From here Alexander the Great set out to conquer the ancient world. Alternating Islamic and Orthodox overtones tell of a later struggle which ended in 1913 when the Treaty of Bucharest divided Macedonia among its four neighbours. Serbia got the biggest chunk; the southern half went to Greece. Bulgaria and Albania each received much smaller slices.

The Internal Macedonian Revolutionary Organization (IMRO) which had been fighting the Turks since 1893 was unsatisfied with this result and continued the struggle against royalist Serbia. The interwar government responded by banning the Macedonian language and even the name Macedonia. Though some IMRO elements supported the Bulgarian occupation of Macedonia during

WW II, many more joined Tito's partisans, and after the war 25,713-sq-km Serbian Macedonia got republic status within the Yugoslav Federation.

The Macedonians of today are South Slavs who bear no relation whatever to the Greek-speaking Macedonians of antiquity. The Macedonian language is much closer to Bulgarian than to Serbo-Croatian and many ethnographers consider the Macedonians to be ethnic Bulgarians. A high proportion of the population is Muslim.

Much of Yugoslav Macedonia is a plateau between 600 and 900 metres high. The Vardar River cuts across the middle of this southernmost republic, passing the capital, Skopje, on its way to Greece. Lakes Ohrid and Prespan in the south-west drain into Albania. To the north-west the 2748-metre-high Šar Planina forms the border with Kosovo. Macedonia is a land of contrasts including space-age Skopje with its ultramodern shopping centre and antique bazaar, Ohrid with its many medieval monasteries, and thoroughly Turkish Bitola.

## SKOPJE (СКОПЈЕ)

Skopje, the third-largest city in Yugoslavia and capital of the Yugoslav portion of Macedonia, is strategically set on the Vardar River at a crossroads of Balkan routes almost exactly midway between Tiranë and Sofia, capitals of neighbouring Albania and Bulgaria. Thessaloniki, Greece, is 260 km south-east, near the point where the Vardar flows into the Aegean.

The Romans recognised the location's importance long ago when they made Scupi the centre of the Dardania region. Later conquerors included the Slavs, Byzantines, Bulgarians, Normans and Serbians, until the Turks arrived in 1392 and managed to hold onto Uskup (Skopje) until 1912. Since then the city has belonged to what is now Yugoslavia, although the Bulgarians occupied the area during both world wars.

If any city in the world is disaster-prone it must be Skopje. There were devastating earthquakes in 518 and 1555 and in 1689 the Austrians burned the city. In November 1962 the Vardar River suddenly flooded 5000 homes. But the date no one in Skopje will ever forget is Friday 26 July 1963 when an earthquake almost levelled the city, killing 1066 people in the process.

After this disaster massive outside aid poured in to create the modern urban landscape we see today. It's evident that many of the planners got carried away by the money being thrown their way, and they erected some oversized, irrelevant structures which are now crumbling for lack of maintenance and function. Fortunately, much of the old town survived so Skopje offers the chance to see the whole history of the Balkans in one shot, almost as if it had been cut in half with a knife. It's not a city you will easily forget, nor will you care to linger, but one hectic day is sure to teach you something if you keep your eyes open.

### Orientation

Most of central Skopje is a pedestrian zone. The 15th century Turkish stone bridge over the Vardar River links the old and new towns. South of the bridge is Ploštad Maršal Tito which gives into ulica Maršal Tito leading south. The new elevated railway station is a 15-minute walk east of the stone bridge. The bus station is a few minutes' walk north of the bridge, although plans exist to move it east to a new location near the railway station. Farther north is Čaršija, the old Turkish bazar.

### Information

The tourist information office is opposite the Daut Pasha Baths on the viaduct between the Turkish bridge and Čaršija.

**Post** Poste restante is at the railway station post office, not the main post office.

### Things to See & Do

As you walk north from the Turkish bridge you'll see the **Daud Pasha Baths** (1466) on the right, the largest Turkish baths in the Balkans. The **City Art Gallery** (US$1.50) now occupies its six domed rooms. Almost

PLACES TO STAY
2 Camping Park
24 Hotel Turist
25 Bristol Hotel
28 Grand Hotel
32 Youth Hostel

PLACES TO EAT
23 Self-Service Restaurant

OTHER
1 Stadium
3 Museum of Contemporary Art
4 Theatre of the Minorities
5 Vegetable Market
6 Museum of Macedonia
7 Mustafa Pasha Mosque
8 Castle Hill
9 Communist Party HQ
10 Church of Sveti Spas
11 Suli Han
12 Sultan Murat Mosque & Clock Tower
13 University
14 Tourist Information
15 Turkish Bath House
16 Orthodox Church
17 Turkish Stone Bridge
18 Bus Station
19 Main Post Office
20 Cathedral
21 JAT Airline Office
22 Adria Airways
26 City Museum
27 Shopping Centre
29 Cultural Centre
30 Bus to Matka
31 Academy of Sciences
33 Railway Station

Skopje

0    250    500 m

opposite this building is a functioning Orthodox church.

North again is Čaršija, the old market area, which is well worth exploring. Steps up on the left lead to the tiny **Church of Sveti Spas** with a finely carved iconostasis done in 1824 (US$1.20). It's half buried because at the time of construction in the 17th century no church was allowed to be higher than a mosque. In the courtyard at Sveti Spas is the tomb of Goce Delčev, an IMRO freedom fighter killed by the Turks in 1903.

Beyond the church is the **Mustafa Pasha Mosque** (1492), now popular among tour-

ists who come to see the earthquake-cracked dome. The US$1 ticket includes the right to ascend the 124 steps of the minaret. In the park across the street from this mosque are the ruins of the castle, **Fort Kale**, with an 11th century Cyclopean wall and good views of Skopje. Higher up the same hill is the lacklustre **Museum of Contemporary Art** (closed Monday) where special exhibitions are presented.

The lane on the north side of Mustafa Pasha Mosque leads back down into Čaršija and the **Museum of Macedonia**. This large collection covers the history of the region fairly well, but much is lost on visitors unable to read the Cyrillic captions and explanations, though the periods are identified in English at the top of some of the showcases. The museum is housed in the modern white building behind the **Kuršumli Han** (1550), a caravanserai or inn used by traders during the Turkish period. In the 19th century it was turned into a notorious prison. Two more caravanserais distinguished by their two-storey interior courtyards, the Suli Han and the Kapan Han, are hidden among the streets of old Čaršija.

You don't really need a guide to modern Skopje as its interest is more sociological than architectural. Don't miss the huge **shopping centre** however, just south-east of the Turkish stone bridge, the biggest in the country. Finally, take the time to go to the former train station, now the **City Museum** at the south end of ulica Maršal Tito, where the clock stopped at 5.17 am on 26 July 1963. There's a little too much politicising inside to make you take it very seriously but it certainly does tell you what today's Skopje is all about.

**Hiking** If you appreciate nature and have an afternoon to spare, take bus No 60 (every two hours – pay the conductor on the bus) from the local bus stand on the north side of the river just east of the Cultural Centre to the end of the line at **Matka**. Here a huge concrete dam on the Treska River has created an artificial lake winding up a canyon below high cliffs. Just above the dam is the **Church of Sveti Andreja** (1389) with period frescoes.

Right beside the church is *Planinski Dom Matika*, a mountain hut that's used by rock climbers who train on the sheer cliff opposite. It's possible to sleep in the hut daily in summer or on weekends all year for US$10 per person, but reservations must be made at least a day in advance by calling Saso Andonov (☎ 091-25 3706 – call in the evenings; Saso speaks perfect English). The hut bar serves refreshments on the terrace to locals who come to swim in the lake, but bring your own food.

It's possible to follow a narrow trail two km up the lakeside from the hut, but the area beyond this is a military zone that is closed to foreigners. Also cross the river just below the dam and climb to the **Church of Sveti Nikola** (closed). Other hikes through this beautiful area are possible.

### Places to Stay

**Camping** From April to mid-October you can pitch a tent at *Feroturist Autocamp Park* for US$3 per person, US$2.50 per tent. Basic camping caravans are for hire at US$10 per person (mosquitoes free). Late-night music from the restaurant can be a problem. This camping ground is between the river and the stadium, a 15-minute walk upstream from the Turkish stone bridge along the right (south) bank. It could be crowded in July and August, otherwise it's a good bet.

**Hostels** The *Dom 'Blagoj Šošolčev' Youth Hostel* (IYHF), Prolet 25, is near the railway station. Open all year, the charge including breakfast is US$10 for members, US$15 for nonmembers in a six-bed dorm, breakfast included. The hostel is open 24 hours a day.

**Private Rooms** The tourist information office on the viaduct two blocks north of the Turkish stone bridge has private rooms beginning at US$19/33 single/double, but they're in short supply and there's no reduction for stays longer than one night. In July and August ask at the tourist information office about accommodation in student hostels.

**Hotels** There are no cheap or even moderately priced hotels in Skopje. The cheapest of the expensive is the old 33-room *Bristol Hotel* opposite the City Museum which charges US$59/95 single/double with breakfast. The newer 91-room *Hotel Turist* just up ulica Maršal Tito is US$64/94 single/double. At these prices both hotels are usually empty so you needn't worry about getting a room, though neither is worth anywhere near that.

## Places to Eat

Colourful small restaurants in Čaršija serving kebab and ćevapčići reflect a Turkish culinary heritage still dear to the stomachs of many Macedonians.

For more prosaic fare there are two self-service restaurants in the modern city centre beyond Ploštad Maršal Tito at the south side of the Turkish stone bridge. *Pelister Self-Service* is fairly obvious across the square at the beginning of ulica Maršal Tito, on the left as you come from the bridge. *Ishrana Self-Service* is half a block away down the next street over to the right. Look for the vertical sign reading 'restaurant' in large blue letters. Because it takes a few minutes to locate, Ishrana gets far fewer tourists than Pelister. Neither place is exceptional but they do fill your stomach without a hassle to order or a fight over the price.

## Getting There & Away

**Bus** There are buses to Ohrid, Bitola, Prishtinë, Prizren, Pejë, Titograd and Belgrade. Book a seat on the bus of your choice the day before, especially if you're headed for Lake Ohrid. There are two bus routes to Lake Ohrid. The one through Tetovo is much faster and more direct than the bus that goes via Titov Veles and Bitola. If you just want to get to the Adriatic from Skopje catch a through bus to Titograd (382 km, two daily).

There's a daily bus to Sofia, Bulgaria (US$8, 216 km).

**Train** All three daily trains between Central Europe and Greece pass through Skopje. There are many daily trains from Athens to Skopje (795 km, US$36 one-way). A slower, cheaper route from Athens to Yugoslavia is via Florina and Bitola.

Fast trains run to Belgrade (465 km), local trains to Bitola (229 km). Couchettes are available to Belgrade and Zagreb. There's a travel agency in Skopje Railway Station which sells international tickets and books couchettes and sleepers. It will even change money.

## Getting Around

City buses in Skopje use tokens (*getone*) which you must buy at a tobacco kiosk.

## OHRID (ОХРИД)

Lake Ohrid, a natural tectonic lake in the south-west corner of Macedonia, is the deepest lake in Europe (294 metres) and one of the oldest in the world. A third of its 15-by-30-km surface belongs to Albania. Nestled amid mountains at an altitude of 695 metres, the Macedonian section of the lake is the more beautiful and accessible with striking vistas of the open waters from beach and hill.

The town of Ohrid is the Yugoslav tourist mecca of the south. Signs in the windows of market cafés offer *hollandse koffie*. Some 30 'cultural monuments' in the area keep the droves of visitors busy. Predictably, the oldest ruins readily seen today are Roman. Lihnidos (Ohrid) was on the Via Egnatia which connected the Adriatic to the Aegean, and part of a Roman amphitheatre has been uncovered in the old town.

Under Byzantium Ohrid became the episcopal centre of Macedonia. The first Slavonic university was founded here in 893 by Bishop Clement of Ohrid, a disciple of Cyril and Methodius, and from the 10th century until 1767 the patriarchate of Ohrid held sway. Many of the small Orthodox churches with intact medieval frescoes have now been adapted to the needs of ticketed tourists. Nice little signs in Latin script direct you to the sights, but even the cellophane wrapping doesn't completely spoil the flavour of enchanting Lake Ohrid.

## Orientation

Ohrid Bus Station is next to the post office in the centre of town. West is the old town, south is the lake.

## Information

'Biljana' Tourist Office is at Partizanska 3 beside the bus station.

## Things to See

The picturesque old town of Ohrid rises from

Moša Pijade, the main pedestrian mall, up towards Sveti Kliment Church and the citadel. A medieval town wall still isolates this hill from the surrounding valley. Near the North Gate is 13th century **Sveti Kliment**, almost covered inside with vivid frescoes of biblical scenes. Below is 11th century **Sveti Sofija**, also worth the US$1.50 admission price. Aside from the frescoes there's an unusual Turkish *mimbar* (pulpit) from the days when the church was used as a mosque, and an upstairs portico of real architectural interest.

From here signs direct you on to the tiny 13th century **Church of Sveti Jovan**, a very pleasant spot even if you don't pay to go inside. There's a beach at the foot of the cliffs. In the park above Sveti Jovan on the way to the citadel is the shell of **Sveti Pantelejmon**, now a small museum, and nearby the ruins of an Early Christian **basilica** with 5th century mosaics covered by protective sand. The many splendid views from the walls of the 10th century **citadel** make it all worthwhile.

The better part of a second day at Ohrid

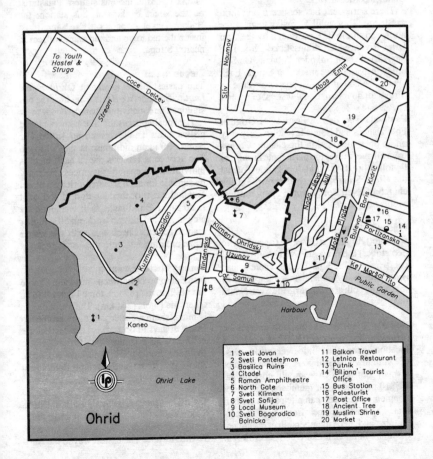

To Youth Hostel & Struga

Goce Delčev

Stream

Stiv Naumov

Aboš Ermin

• 20

• 19

18 •

Nada Hexo

4 Juli

• 4

5

• 6

7

Kuzman Kapidan

Kliment Ohridski

Ilindenska

H. Uzunov

9

Car Samuil

• 3

• 16

17 15

14

Bulevar Partizanska

Boris Kidrič

13

Moša Pijade

12

11

• 2

8

10

Kej Maršal Tito

Public Garden

1

Kaneo

Harbour

Ohrid Lake

**Ohrid**

| | |
|---|---|
| 1 Sveti Jovan | 11 Balkan Travel |
| 2 Sveti Pantelejmon | 12 Letnica Restaurant |
| 3 Basilica Ruins | 13 Putnik |
| 4 Citadel | 14 'Biljana' Tourist |
| 5 Roman Amphitheatre | Office |
| 6 North Gate | 15 Bus Station |
| 7 Sveti Kliment | 16 Palasturist |
| 8 Sveti Sofija | 17 Post Office |
| 9 Local Museum | 18 Ancient Tree |
| 10 Sveti Bogorodica | 19 Muslim Shrine |
| Bolnicka | 20 Market |

could be spent on a pilgrimage to the Albanian border to see the 17th century **Church of Sveti Naum** on a hill above the lake, 29 km south of Ohrid by bus. You have to walk the last km or so and there's no guarantee the church will be open but you do get a view of the Albanian town of Pogradec across the lake. Inside the church is a finely carved iconostasis. In summer you can also come by boat (ask at the Putnik office opposite the bus station about times and tickets – US$4 return). The mountains east of Ohrid Lake, between it and Prespan Lake, are included in Galičica National Park.

There's frequent bus service from Ohrid to **Struga**. This small Yugoslav town at the north end of the lake is divided by the Crni Drim River, which drains Lake Ohrid into the Adriatic near Shkoder, Albania. On Saturday there's a large market at Struga. Each year at the end of August poets converge on Struga for an international festival of poetry.

**Festivals** The Balkan Festival of Original Folk Dances and Songs is held in early July on an open-air stage in the citadel. Groups from all over the region participate in authentic folk attire. From mid-July to mid-August the Ohrid Summer Festival centres on the church of Sveti Sofija where many musical events take place.

### Places to Stay

**Camping** *Autocamp Gradište* (open May to September) is halfway to Sveti Naum (US$3 per person, US$3 per tent). There's also *Autocamp Sveti Naum* near the monastery of that name, both accessible on the Sveti Naum bus.

**Hostels & Hotels** Alternatively there's the *'Mladost' Youth Hostel* (IYHF) in a pleasant location on the lake a little over two km west of Ohrid towards Struga. A bed in a dorm or a small four-berth caravan will cost around US$10 per person for members, US$12 for nonmembers, or you can pitch a tent for half that. The hostel is open from April to mid-October and YHA membership cards are not essential. In midsummer it can get crowded.

If you're walking to the hostel turn left at the fifth minaret counting from the one opposite the old tree at the top of Moša Pijade.

The *Mladinski Centar*, a modern hotel next to the youth hostel, is US$36 per person in a three-bed room, including three meals daily (open all year).

**Private Rooms** Private rooms from the 'Biljana' Tourist Office, Partizanska 3 beside the bus station, cost US$9 per person (three nights or less) plus US$1 per person per day tax. Other private rooms are available from Putnik opposite the bus station, Palasturist on the street behind the bus station, the Balkan Travel Agency on Car Samuil just inside the old town and the tourist offices in nearby Struga.

### Places to Eat

The easiest place to eat at Ohrid is the *Letnica Self-Service Restaurant* near the bus station. The food is surprisingly good.

For local specialities like lake trout and grilled meats it's the *Restaurant Antiko*, Car Samuil 30 in an old house in the old town. The service is rather slow as each meal is individually prepared but prices are fairly reasonable for such a tourist-oriented place. Watch the cost of the lake trout if you want it prepared Ohrid-style as it's charged by weight and the bill can work out 50% higher than expected. Check this with the waiter when ordering.

### Getting There & Away

**Bus** Some buses between Ohrid and Skopje run via Tetovo (167 km, three hours, US$5), others via Bitola (261 km). The former route is much shorter, faster and more scenic, so check. It pays to book a seat the day before.

There's an overnight bus from Ohrid to Belgrade leaving Ohrid around 3.30 pm, Bitola at 5.20 pm, and reaching Belgrade at 5.28 am.

**Train** The nearest railway station is at Bitola, 80 km east.

**To the Adriatic** The easiest way to the Adriatic is a direct flight to Dubrovnik (US$60). Book with Putnik opposite the bus station. Alternatively take a bus to Skopje, then another to Titograd, then another to Ulcinj or Dubrovnik.

## BITOLA (БИТОЛА)

Bitola, the southernmost city in Yugoslavia and second-largest in Yugoslav Macedonia, sits on a 660-metre-high plateau between the mountains 16 km north of the Greek border. It's a friendly, untouristed town with lots of Turkish architecture and a colourful old bazar area (Stara Čaršija).

Most travellers only spend a few hours in Bitola on their way to/from Greece but the city is worth a stop for its own sake. The Roman ruins at Heraclea are among the most beautifully situated and peaceful in Europe.

## Orientation

The adjacent bus and train stations are on the south side of town, a 15-minute walk from the centre via City Park and Bitola's pedestrian promenade, ulica Maršal Tito.

## Information

Palasturist is on ulica Rooseveltova around the corner from Putnik.

## Things to See

The **Heraclea ruins** beyond the old cemetery one km south of the railway station should be at the top of your list (admission US$1.20, photos US$6 extra). Founded in the 4th century BC by Philip II of Macedonia, Heraclea was conquered by the Romans two centuries later and became an important stage on the Via Egnatia. From the 4th to 6th centuries AD it was an episcopal seat. Excavations continue but the Roman baths, portico and theatre can now be seen. More interesting are the two Early Christian basilicas and the episcopal palace complete with splendid mosaics. There's also a small museum through the refreshment stand, and a nice terrace on which to have a Coke or beer.

The other sights of Bitola are two km north of Heraclea via the City Park and ulica

Maršal Tito. On the square at the north end of Maršal Tito are the 17th century **clock tower**, a symbol of Bitola, the **Jeni Dzami Mosque** (now the Moša Pijade Art Gallery), the **Isak Mosque** and the **Bezistan**, a 16th century covered market. The **Church of St Dimitrius** on ulica 11 Oktomvri just south of the clock tower contains a large wooden iconostasis (1830).

**Stara Čaršija**, the 19th century old bazar district, is just east of the Bezistan, north of the river. Here artisans pursue their age-old trades, while the bustling **city market** is beyond (busiest on Tuesday).

## Places to Stay

There's a basic camping ground near the Bonanza Restaurant in New Bitola three km out on the road to Ohrid. The travel agencies of Bitola don't handle private rooms but you may get one by enquiring at ulica Maršal Tito 78 just behind the Epinal Hotel.

There are two hotels: the high-rise *Epinal Hotel* (US$30/50 single/double) and the *Macedonia Hotel* beside Putnik nearby (US$18 per person).

## Places to Eat

Bitola's self-service restaurant is next to Putnik. Also try *Lav Pizzeria*, Maršal Tito 115.

## Getting There & Away

The bus and train stations are adjacent with left-luggage in the bus station. Bus service to Ohrid (80 km) and Skopje (181 km) is good. There are local trains to Skopje.

An overnight express train runs north to Ljubljana via Zagreb. For tickets and couchettes go to Feroturist in the Epinal Hotel as the ticket office in the railway station is hopeless.

**To/From Greece** There's a daily afternoon train at around 3.30 pm between Bitola and the Greek border (Kremenica). There you change to a connecting Greek train which carries you slowly into Florina, Greece. The ticket office at Bitola Railway Station will only sell you a ticket as far as the border

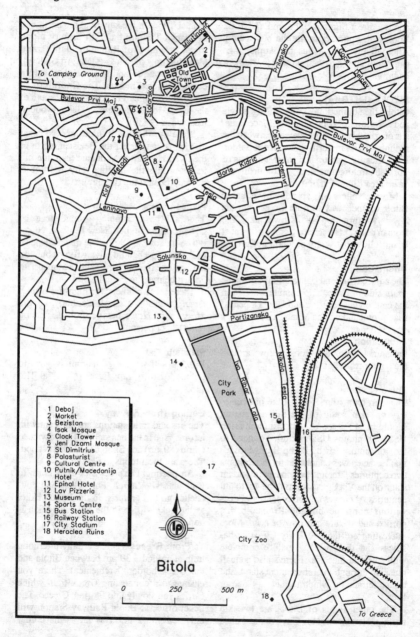

1 Deboj
2 Market
3 Bezisten
4 Isak Mosque
5 Clock Tower
6 Jeni Dzami Mosque
7 St Dimitrius
8 Palasturist
9 Cultural Centre
10 Putnik/Macedonija
   Hotel
11 Epinal Hotel
12 Lav Pizzeria
13 Museum
14 Sports Centre
15 Bus Station
16 Railway Station
17 City Stadium
18 Heraclea Ruins

Bitola

0    250    500 m

To Greece

(US$0.50). Putnik or Feroturist can sell you a through ticket right to Florina for about US$5 or you can buy the onward ticket directly from the Greek conductor at the border itself (about US$2). The ticket Florina-Athens is about US$15 (631 km).

By the time you get to Florina all the banks will be closed (there's a one-hour time difference) so plan ahead and bring some drachma from Western Europe. Northbound when you arrive in Bitola from Greece in the late afternoon you'll find no exchange facilities at the bus or train stations. Walk into town and change at Putnik, Feroturist, Palasturist, a bank or the Epinal Hotel.

The clock tower in Tiranë

# Albania

Until recently considered a closed Communist country, Albania caught world attention in late 1990 as the last Stalinist domino to tumble in Eastern Europe's sudden series of democratic revolutions. Yet the current changes date back to 1985 and the death of Enver Hoxha, who was Albania's Marxist-Leninist leader since 1944. The statues of Stalin and Hoxha have toppled and economic and political reforms are proceeding, putting Albania at a crossroads.

Long considered fair prey by every imperialist power, Albania chose a curious form of isolation. Backwardness, blood vendettas and illiteracy were replaced by what some claimed was the purest form of Communism. Right up until December 1990, monuments, factories, boulevards and towns were dedicated to the memory of Joseph Stalin. Hoxha's iron-fisted rule saved Albania from annexation by Yugoslavia in 1948. Albanian folk songs and dances express passionate feelings of freedom and independence – still keen issues today.

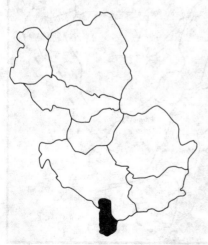

Few European countries have the allure of the mysterious Republika Popullore e Shqipërisë, or 'Land of the Eagle', as the Albanians call it. Albania is Europe's last unknown, with enchanting classical ruins at Durrës, Apolonia and Butrint, the charming 'museum towns' of Gjirokastër and Berat, vibrant cities like Tiranë, Shkodër, Korçë and Durrës, colourful folklore and majestic landscapes of mountains, forests, lakes and the sea. You can see a great number of things in a pocket-sized area and, compared to over-visited Yugoslavia and Greece, tourism is minimal. The absence of motor cars and blatant advertising is another refreshing change, while it lasts. Come and see Albania now the way it will never be again.

# Facts about the Country

### HISTORY
In the 2nd millennium BC, the Illyrians, ancestors of today's Albanians, occupied the western Balkans. The Greeks arrived in the 7th century BC to establish self-governing colonies at Epidamnos (Durrës), Apolonia and Butrint. They traded peacefully with the Illyrians, who formed tribal states in the 4th century BC. The south became part of Greek Epirus.

In the second half of the 3rd century BC, an expanding Illyrian kingdom based at Shkodër came into conflict with Rome, which sent a fleet of 200 vessels against Queen Teuta in 228 BC. After a second Roman naval expedition in 219 BC, Philip V of Macedonia came to the aid of his Illyrian allies in 214 BC. This led to a long war which resulted in the extension of Roman control over the entire Balkans by 167 BC.

Like the Greeks, the Illyrians preserved their own language and traditions despite centuries of Roman rule. Under the Romans Illyria enjoyed peace and prosperity, though

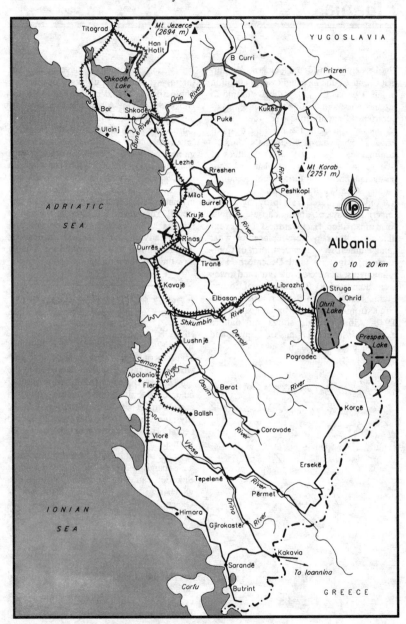

the large agricultural estates were worked by slave labour. The main trade route between Rome and Constantinople, the Via Egnatia, ran from Durrës to Thessaloniki.

When the empire was divided in 395 AD, Illyria was included in the Eastern Roman Empire, later known as Byzantium. Invasions by migrating peoples – the Visigoths, Huns, Ostrogoths and Slavs – continued through the 5th and 6th centuries and only in the south did the ethnic Illyrians survive (prior to the Roman conquest, Illyria stretched north to the Danube). In the 11th century, control of this region passed back and forth between the Byzantines, the Bulgarians and the Normans.

The feudal principality of Arberit was established at Krujë in 1190. Other independent feudal states appeared in the 14th century and the towns developed. After the defeat of Serbia by the Turks in 1389, Albania was open to Ottoman attack. The Venetians occupied some coastal towns, and from 1443 to 1468 the national hero Skanderbeg (George Kastrioti) led Albanian resistance to the Turks from his castle at Krujë. Skanderbeg (Skënderbeg in Albanian) won all 25 battles he fought against the Turks, and even Sultan Mehmet-Fatih, conqueror of Constantinople, could not take Krujë.

Albania was not definitively incorporated into the Ottoman Empire until 1479 and remained there until 1912, the most backward corner of Europe. In the late 18th century, the Albanian nobles Karamahmut Pasha Bushatlli of Shkodër and Ali Pasha Tepelenë of Ioannina (Janinë) established semi-independent pashaliks, but Ottoman despotism was reimposed in the early 19th century.

In 1878 the Albanian League at Prizren (in present-day Yugoslavia) began a liberation struggle that was put down by the Turkish army in 1881. Uprisings between 1910 and 1912 culminated in a proclamation of independence and the formation of a provisional government led by Ismail Qemali at Vlorë in 1912. These achievements were severely compromised by the London ambassadors'

conference, which handed nearly half of Albania (Kosovo) over to Serbia in 1913. In 1914 the Great Powers imposed a German aristocrat named Wilhelm von Wied on Albania as head of state but an uprising soon forced his departure. With the outbreak of WW I, Albania was occupied by the armies of Greece, Serbia, France, Italy and Austria-Hungary in succession.

In 1920 the Congress of Lushnje denounced foreign intervention and moved the capital from Durrës to the less vulnerable Tiranë. Thousands of Albanian volunteers converged on Vlorë and forced the occupying Italians to withdraw. In May 1924 Bishop Fan Noli established a fairly liberal government which was overthrown on Christmas Eve that year by Ahmet Zogu, a brutal reactionary. Ahmet Zogu represented the landed aristocracy of the lowlands and the tribal chieftains of the highlands and ruled with Italian support, declaring himself King Zog in 1928. Zog's close collaboration with Italy backfired in April 1939 when Mussolini ordered an invasion of Albania. Zog fled to Britain and used gold looted from the Albanian treasury to rent a floor at London's Ritz Hotel.

On 8 November 1941 the Albanian Communist Party was founded with Enver Hoxha (pronounced Hodja) as First Secretary, a position he held until his death in April 1985. The Communists led the resistance to the Italians and, after 1943, to the Germans. A provisional government was formed at Berat in October 1944, and by 29 November the Albanian National Liberation Army had crushed tribal quislings in the north and pursued the last Nazi troops from the country. Albania was the only Eastern European country where the Soviet army was not involved in these operations.

## Post WW II

After the fighting died down, the National Liberation Front transformed itself into the Democratic Front, which won 92% of the vote in the December 1945 elections. In January 1946 the People's Republic of Albania was proclaimed with Enver Hoxha as

RPS E SHQIPËRISE

Enver Hoxha

president. In February a programme of socialist construction was adopted and all large economic enterprises were nationalised. By 1952 seven years of elementary education had become mandatory (this was raised to eight years in 1963) and literacy was increased from just 15% before WW II to 75% today.

In October 1946 two British warships struck mines in the Corfu Channel with the loss of 44 lives. The British government blamed Albania and demanded £843,947 compensation. To back their claim they impounded 7100 kg of gold (now worth £50 million) which had been stolen from Albania by the Fascists. Albania has never accepted responsibility for the incident nor agreed to pay damages but the stubborn British are still holding Albania's gold. Because of this the two countries have no diplomatic relations. It is now widely believed that Yugoslavia placed the mines. Good relations with Tito were always important to the British, whereas Albania was expendable.

In September 1948 Albania broke relations with Yugoslavia, which had hoped to incorporate the country into the Yugoslav Federation. Instead, Albania allied itself with Stalin's USSR and put into effect a series of Soviet-style economic plans, the first a two-year plan, and then five-year plans beginning in 1951. In the early 1950s, there were British and US-backed landings in Albania by right-wing émigrés. One British attempt in 1949 was thwarted when Stalin passed along to Hoxha a warning he had received from double agent Kim Philby.

Albania collaborated closely with the USSR until 1960, when a heavy-handed Khrushchev demanded a submarine base at Vlorë. With the Soviet alliance becoming a liability, Albania broke diplomatic relations with the USSR in 1961 and reoriented itself towards the People's Republic of China.

From 1966 to 1967 Albania experienced a Chinese-style cultural revolution. Administrative workers were suddenly transferred to remote areas and younger cadres were placed in leading positions. The collectivisation of agriculture was completed and organised religion banned. Western literary works were withdrawn from circulation and replaced by a strong national culture firmly rooted in socialist ideals.

After the Soviet invasion of Czechoslovakia in 1968, Albania left the Warsaw Pact and began building concrete bunkers. Today literally thousands of igloo-shaped bunkers and pillboxes with narrow gun slits are strung along all borders, both terrestrial and maritime, as well as the approaches to all towns. The highway from Durrës to Tiranë is one bunker after another for 35 km.

With the death of Mao Zedong in 1976 and the changes in China after 1978, Albania's unique relationship with China came to an end. In 1981 there was a power struggle within the Albanian Party of Labour (as the Communist Party has been called since November 1948) and former partisan hero and prime minister Mehmet Shehu 'committed suicide' after being accused of being a Yugoslav spy.

Shehu had wanted to expand Albania's foreign contacts, an orientation which brought him into direct conflict with Hoxha. Until 1978 Albania thrived on massive

Yugoslav, Soviet and Chinese aid in succession. Building socialism alone without credits or foreign loans meant Albania couldn't import essential equipment if its exports didn't earn sufficient hard currency, and the country began falling far behind.

Hoxha died after a long illness in April 1985 and longtime associate Ramiz Alia assumed leadership of the 147,000-member Party of Labour. Aware of the economic decay caused by Albania's isolation, Alia began a liberalisation programme within Albania in 1986 and broadened Albania's ties with foreign countries.

In late 1989 reports on Italian and Yugoslav television of political upheavals in the other Eastern European countries created a sense of expectation in Albania. In May 1990 UN Secretary-General Javier Pérez de Cuellar visited Tiranë and obtained safe passage out of the country for a six-member Albanian family that had been living in the Italian Embassy since 1985. This triggered a rush by some 4500 Albanians who took refuge in Western embassies in Tiranë in June 1990. After a brief confrontation, Alia announced that they and anyone else were free to leave. Most boarded ships across the Adriatic to Brindisi in Italy, where they were held in an abandoned army camp.

In early December 1990, after three days of student demonstrations in Tiranë, the Alia government agreed to allow the formation of opposition political parties. The Democratic Party formed on 12 December with Tiranë University professors Sali Berisha and Gramoz Pashko (both ex-Communists) as leaders. Elections were scheduled to take place on 10 February 1991, but after protests that the opposition had no time to prepare, these were rescheduled for 31 March. The situation changed dramatically as fear of the Sigurimi (secret police) vanished and people began talking freely for the first time in decades. Violent antigovernment rioting followed in several Albanian cities but this was denounced by the leaders of the newly founded Democratic Party.

On 22 December Radio Tiranë announced that factories and streets bearing the name

Joseph Stalin would be renamed and statues of Stalin removed. The next day Radio Tiranë announced 'many changes in the Council of Ministers...to build a spirit of national reconciliation...to solve economic problems as soon as possible.'

On 26 December Alia told an extraordinary Party congress that the Party might have to 'distance itself from many socialist principles' but that it had no intention of abandoning its Marxist ideology. Alia presented delegates with a grim picture of the economic situation, such as the unfulfilled economic plan and rising unemployment. He called for more collaboration with the West and did not exclude the possibility of Albanians leaving the country to seek work abroad. A new constitutional law giving Albanians freedom of religion, the right to private property, political pluralism and the right to strike was accelerated. Alia's *senderrim* (perestroika) would also allow Albanians to set up private businesses.

Between Christmas and early January 1991, the government relaxed controls along its border with Greece, and some 6000 ethnic Greeks from southern Albania poured into Greece without luggage. Greek officials accused the Albanian government of encouraging the exodus in order to rid itself of its Greek minority and political opponents. Also in early January, 1000 coal miners near Tiranë staged a one-day strike demanding an independent trade union. This demand was granted a month later.

After three days of violent demonstrations in Tiranë in February 1991, during which a 10-metre-high statue of Enver Hoxha was knocked down, President Alia sacked hardline Prime Minister Adil Carcani and his cabinet and replaced them with a presidential council of younger members led by economist Fatos Nano, aged 39. The opposition refused an offer to join the government.

In early March 1991, another 20,000 Albanians fled to Brindisi by ship, attracted by the glitz and glamour on Italian TV. President Alia imposed martial law on Durrës to stop the flow of migrants and the Italian government announced that the new arrivals had come for economic rather than political reasons and would not qualify for political asylum. On 10 March some 1500 embittered Albanians arrived back in Durrës complaining of the poor reception they had been given in Italy. Some 500 political prisoners were freed in the first months of 1991.

As the election date approached, Alia granted rural inhabitants the right to own land and livestock and to sell their produce at markets. This quickly paid off as the country people, fearing disorder and the loss of their land, voted overwhelmingly for the Communists. Yet the Democratic Party won in the cities and even Ramiz Alia himself lost his Tiranë seat to a Democratic Party candidate. The final results left the Party of Labour with 68% of the vote and 162 seats in the 250-member parliament, and the Democratic Party with 25% of the vote and 60 seats. Foreign observers reported that the elections were fair and free, and even the presence of a large delegation of US legislators who promised massive US aid if the opposition won, didn't greatly influence the results.

Unwilling to accept the election results, the Democratic Party called for a general strike throughout the country, but this got little response. On 2 April a tragedy occurred when a mob attacked the Party of Labour offices in Shkodër and three people were killed. Soon after the election, the daily *Zëri i popullit* (The People's Voice) announced that the government intended to privatise state enterprises and allow joint ventures with foreign companies. A committee was founded to reorganise the economy.

In mid-May 1991, the independent trade union called for a general strike demanding a 50% pay increase and a 36-hour work week (down from 48 hours). In June the government and opposition reached agreement on an interim administration in which all parties would be represented, but the opposition insisted on new elections within eight months.

By meeting almost all of the demands of the strikers and demonstrators, Alia had bought time for both the Party of Labour and

his own economic reforms in an impressive display of political skill. Interestingly, Enver Hoxha's 70-year-old widow, Nexhmije Hoxha, has emerged as a leader of hardliners demanding a crackdown on dissent. The parallel with Chairman Mao's now deceased widow, Jiang Qing, is obvious. What the outcome will be is anyone's guess, but by mid-1991 only two pre-1989 Eastern European presidents remained on the scene: Ramiz Alia and Mikhail Gorbachev – certainly no small achievement for them both.

## GEOGRAPHY

Albania's strategic position between Greece, Yugoslavia and Italy, just west of Bulgaria and Turkey, has been decisive throughout its history. Vlorë watches over the narrow Strait of Otranto, which links the Adriatic to the Ionian Sea. For decades Albania has been something of a barrier separating Greece from the rest of Europe. The Greek island of Corfu is only a few km from Sarandë across the Ionian Sea.

Over three-quarters of this 28,748-sq-km country (the size of Belgium) consists of mountains and hills. There are three zones: a coastal plain, mountains and an interior plain. The coastal plain extends over 200 km from north to south and up to 50 km inland. The 2000-metre-high forested mountain spine that stretches along the entire length of Albania culminates at Mt Jezerce (2694 metres) in the north. Although Mt Jezerce is the highest mountain entirely within the country, Albania's highest peak is Mt Korab (2751 metres) on the border with Macedonia. The country is subject to destructive earthquakes, such as the one in 1979 which left 100,000 people homeless.

The longest river is the Drin River (283 km), which drains Ohrit Lake. In the north the Drin flows into the Bunë, Albania's only navigable river, which connects Shkodër Lake to the sea. Albania shares three large tectonic lakes with Yugoslavia: Shkodër, Ohrit and Prespes. Ohrit is the deepest lake in the Balkans. The Ionian littoral, especially the unspoiled 'Riviera of Flowers' from Vlorë to Sarandë, offers magnificent scenery. Forty per cent of the land is forested, and the many olive trees, citrus plantations and vineyards give Albania a true Mediterranean air.

## ECONOMY

Albania stuck to strict Stalin-era central planning and wage and price controls longer than any other Eastern European country. Two-thirds of the national income was directed towards consumption and social benefits, and the rest used for capital investment. Industrial development was spread out with factories in all regions. Before WW II, 90% of the population worked in agriculture and there was little or no industry. Today 60% work in agriculture, 24% in industry and 16% in services.

Albania is one of the few countries in the world with no foreign debt. In 1976 Albania even included a provision in its constitution forbidding any overseas loans. Considering the country's small size, self-sufficiency was an even greater challenge.

Albania is rich in natural resources such as crude oil, natural gas, coal, copper, iron nickel and timber and is the world's third-largest producer of chrome. The Central Mountains yield minerals such as copper in the north-east around Kukës, chromium farther south near the Drin River, and iron nickel closer to Ohrit Lake. The new railway to Pogradec carries ore down to the steel mill at Elbasan (the major source of air and water pollution in central Albania). Textiles are made at Berat, Korçë and Tiranë.

Albania supplies all its own petroleum requirements and Fier's oil and gas have also permitted the production of chemical fertilisers. There are several huge hydroelectric dams on the Drin River in the north. Albania obtains 80% of its electricity from such dams and since 1972 has exported power to Yugoslavia and Greece. Electricity had reached every village in the country by 1970. Both the steel mill and dams were built with Chinese technical assistance before 1978.

There's a good deal of foreign trade. After the breaks with the Soviet Union and China,

Albania's trade had to be completely redirected and Albania's main trading partners are now Czechoslovakia, Italy and Yugoslavia, which purchase Albanian food products, asphalt, bitumen, chromium, crude oil and tobacco. Trade with the West is increasing and Albania has always had a favourable balance of trade.

Once an importer, Albania now grows all its own food on collective farms, with surpluses available for export. About 20% of these farms are state farms run directly by the government, and the rest are cooperatives. The main crops are corn, cotton, potatoes, sugar beets, tobacco, vegetables and wheat. The average monthly wage is just 650 lekë (US$93) but there's no income tax, rent is only 10% of this and all basic necessities are subsidised. Until recently, problems like inflation and unemployment were unknown. There's a serious shortage of consumer goods, milk products and meat, but Albania has the advantage of varied natural resources and no foreign debt, factors which bode well for the future.

## POPULATION & PEOPLE

The Albanians are an olive-skinned Mediterranean people, physically different from the more nordic Slavs. While the Slavs and Greeks look down on the Albanians, the Albanians themselves have a sense of racial superiority based on their descent from the ancient Illyrians who inhabited this region before the coming of the Romans. The country's name comes from the Albanoi, an ancient Illyrian tribe.

Three million Albanians live in Albania and another two million suffer Serbian oppression in Kosovo (Greater Albania), in Yugoslavia, a situation which continues to sour relations with Yugoslavia. Harsh economic conditions in Albania have unleashed successive waves of emigration: to Serbia in the 15th century, to Greece and Italy in the 16th century and to the USA in the 19th and 20th centuries. The longtime Albanian residents of 50 scattered villages in southern Italy are known as Arbereshi. Minorities inside Albania include Greeks (2%), Romanians (1%) and Macedonians (1%). Some 50,000 ethnic Greeks reside in southern Albania (the Greek government, however, claims that the number is 350,000).

Albania is one of the most densely populated states of Europe, with 35% of the people living in urban areas (compared to only 15% before WW II). Despite genuine Communist concern for women's rights, birth control was forbidden and since liberation the population growth rate has been 2.5% per annum. Part of this growth can be ascribed to an increase in life expectancy from 38 years in 1938 to 71.3 years today. Tiranë, the capital, is the largest city, with 202,000 inhabitants, followed by Durrës, Shkodër, Elbasan, Vlorë and Korçë. Albania is divided into 26 administrative districts *(rrethi)* and one municipality *(qytet)*.

The Shkumbin River forms a boundary between the Gheg cultural region of the north and the Tosk region in the south. The people in these regions still vary in dialect, musical culture and traditional dress (the Ghegs are also said to have larger noses), even though the Communists worked hard to level regional differences by building a modern industrial society in the Durrës-Tiranë-Elbasan triangle, well away from the old tribal centres of Shkodër and Korçë.

Traditional dress is still commonly seen in rural areas, however, especially on Sundays and holidays. The men wear an embroidered white shirt and knee trousers, the Ghegs with a white felt skullcap, the Tosks with a flat-topped white fez. Women's clothes are brighter than those of the men. Along with the standard white blouse with wide sleeves, women from Christian areas wear a red vest, and Muslim women have baggy pants tied at the ankles and a coloured scarf around the head. Married women wear a white scarf around the neck.

## ARTS

Prior to the adoption of a standardised orthography in 1909, very little literature was produced in Albania, though Albanians resident elsewhere in the Ottoman Empire or in Italy did write works. The noted poet Naim Frashëri (1846-1900) lived in Istanbul. About the time of independence (1912), a group of romantic patriotic writers at Shkodër wrote epics and historical novels.

Several notable poets and short-story writers worked during the interwar period, including Mitrush Kuteli (1903- ), whose *Netë shqipëtari*, or Albanian Nights, (1937) is a collection of evocative stories about his native Pogradec. Perhaps the most interesting writer during this period was Fan Noli (1880-1965). Educated as and ordained a priest in the USA, Fan Noli returned there to head the Albanian Orthodox Church in America after the democratic government in which he served as premier was overthrown in 1924. Although many of his books are based on religious subjects, the introductions he wrote to his own translations of Cervantes, Ibsen, Omar Khayyám and Shakespeare established him as Albania's foremost literary critic.

Albania's best known contemporary writer is Ismail Kadare (1936- ), whose novels have been published abroad in many languages, as well as in Albania. His *Kronikë në gur* (1971), or *Chronicle in Stone* (Serpent's Tail, London, 1987), relates wartime experiences at Gjirokastër as seen through the eyes of a boy. *Broken April* (New Amsterdam Books, New York) deals with the blood vendettas of the northern highlands before the Italian invasion of 1939. Among Kadare's other novels available in English are *The General of the Dead Army* (1963), *The Castle* (1970), *The Great Winter* (1972) and *Doruntine*. Despite living in Tiranë throughout the Hoxha years, Kadare sought political asylum in Paris in October 1990 (his latest book, *Albanian Spring*, tells why). Other notable Albanian writers whose books have appeared in English translations are Dritëro Agolli, Teodore Laço and Naum Prifti.

As for the visual arts, the 16th century religious painter Onufri and his son Nikola left behind many dramatic icons, some of which are now preserved at museums in Berat and Korçë.

## Music

Polyphony, the blending of several independent vocal or instrumental parts, is a southern Albanian tradition that dates back to ancient Illyrian times. The peasant choirs perform in a variety of styles, and the songs, usually with epic-lyrical or historical themes, may be dramatic to the point of yodelling or slow and sober, with alternate male or female voices combining in harmonies of unexpected beauty. Instrumental polyphonic 'kabas' are played by small Gypsy ensembles usually led by a clarinet. Improvisation gives way to dancing at colourful village weddings. Albanian popular music climaxes every five years at Gjirokastër's National Folk Festival (the next will be in 1993) when thousands of singers, dancers and musicians meet for a full week.

## RELIGION

From 1967 to 1990 Albania was the only officially atheist state in the world. Public religious services were banned and many churches were converted to theatres and cinemas. This situation has now ended and in 1991 Nobel Prize-winner Mother Teresa of Calcutta, an ethnic Albanian from Kosovo, attended Easter Mass at Tiranë. Traditionally Albania has been 70% Muslim, 10% Catholic (mostly in the north) and 17% Albanian Orthodox (mostly in the south).

## LANGUAGE

Until the break with the Soviet Union in 1961, Russian was the most taught foreign language. Now English is more important, with French rating a distant second. Italian is sometimes a useful language in Albania, as some of the older people will have learned it in school before 1943. Others may have picked it up by watching Italian television stations.

Albanian (Shqiptimi) is an Indo-European dialect of ancient Illyrian with many Latin, Slavonic and (modern) Greek words. The two main dialects of Albanian diverged over the past 1000 years. In 1909 a standardised form of the Gheg dialect of Elbasan was adopted as the official language, but since WW II a modified version of the Tosk dialect of southern Albania has been used. Outside the country, Albanians resident in Yugoslavia speak Gheg, whereas those in Greece and Italy speak Tosk. With practice you can sometimes differentiate between the dialects by listening for the nasalised vowels of Gheg. A Congress of Orthography at Tiranë in 1972 established a unified written language which is now universally accepted.

Pronunciation of the Albanian language follows regular rules and only two of the 36 letters are accented: the ç which is pronounced ch, and the ë, which sounds like the er in sister but is silent when at the end of a word. Other variations from English include c (which is pronounced as the English ts), dh (as th), j (as y), q (as ky), x (as dz), xh (as j), y (as the ue in glue) and zh (as the s in pleasure). The Albanian rr is trilled and each vowel in a diphthong is pronounced.

Different spellings exist for place names but in this book we use the version given on official Albanian maps. On signs at archaeological sites, *pe sonë* means BC, and *e sonë* means AD. Public toilets may be marked *burra* or simply 'B' for men, *gra* or 'G' for women. Albanians, like Bulgarians, shake their heads to say yes and nod to say no.

## Greetings & Civilities

hello
*tungjatjeta*
goodbye
*mirupafshim*
good morning
*mirëmengjes*
good evening
*mirëmbrëma*
please
*ju lutem*
thank you
*falem nderit*
I am sorry/Forgive me.
*Më falni.*
excuse me
*ju lutem*

You are very kind.
*Jam shum mirënjohës.*
yes
*po*
no
*jo*

## Small Talk
Do you speak English?
*A folni Anglisht?*
I don't understand.
*Nuk kuptoj.*
Could you write it down?
*A mund t'ma shkrueni?*
Where do you live?
*Ku banoni?*
What work do you do?
*Ç'far pune bëni?*
I am a student.
*Unë jam student.*
I am very happy.
*Jam shum i gëzueshëm.* (male)
*Jam shum e gëzueshmë.* (female)

## Accommodation
youth hostel
*bujtinë të rijsh*
camping ground
*kamp*
private room
*dhomë private*
How much is it?
*Sa kushton?*
Is that the price per person?
*Është ky çmim për një persón?*
Is that the total price?
*A është ky çmimi i plotë?*
Are there any extra charges?
*A ka ndonjë shtesë shpenzimesh?*
Can I pay with local currency?
*A mund të paguaj me Lek?*
Where is there a cheaper hotel?
*Ku gjënden hotele jo të kushtueshëm?*
Should I make a reservation?
*A më duhet t'a rezervoj?*
single room
*dhomë për një*
double room
*dhomë për dy*

It is very noisy.
*Është shum me zhurmë.*
Where is the toilet?
*Ku është nevojtorja?*

## Getting Around
What time does it leave?
*Në ç'orë niset?*
When is the first bus?
*Kur vjen autobuzi i parë?*
When is the last bus?
*Kur vjen autobuzi i fundit?*
When is the next bus?
*Kur vjen autobuzi i tjetër?*
That's too soon.
*Shum herët.*
When is the next one after that?
*Cili tjetër vjen mbas atij?*
How long does the trip take?
*Sa larg është udha?*
arrival
*arritje*
departure
*t'ikur*
timetable
*orari*
Where is the bus stop?
*Ku është stacjoni i autobuzit?*
Where is the railway station?
*Ku është stacjoni i hekurudhës?*
Where is the taxi stand?
*Ku është vendi i taksive?*
Where is the left-luggage room?
*Ku është vendi i bagazheve?*

## Around Town
Just a minute.
*Një minut, ju lutem.*
Where is...?
*Ku është...?*
the bank
*bankë*
the post office
*zyra e postës*
the telephone centre
*qendra telefonike*
the tourist information office
*zyra e informacjonit turistik*
the museum
*muze*

the palace
*pallat*
the castle
*kështjellë*
the concert hall
*dhoma e koncertit*
the opera house
*shtëpia e operës*
the musical theatre
*opereta*
Where are you going?
*Ku po shkoni?*
I am going to...
*Po shkoj në...*
Where is it?
*Ku është?*
I can't find it.
*Nuk e gjej dot.*
Is it far?
*A është larg?*
Please show me on the map.
*Ju lutem m'a tregoni nëharte.*
left
*majtas*
right
*djathtas*
straight ahead
*drejte-për-drejtë*
I want...
*Unë dua...*
Do I need permission?
*A më duhet lejë?*
May I?
*A mundem?*

## Entertainment

Where can I hear live music?
*Ku mund të ndëgjoj muzikë të gjallë?*
Where can I buy a ticket?
*Ku mund te blejë një biletë?*
I'm looking for a ticket.
*Po kërkoj për një biletë.*
I want to refund this ticket.
*Dua t'a kthej këtë biletë.*
Is this a good seat?
*A është vend i mirë ky?*
at the front
*në rradhën përballë*
ticket
*biletë*

## Food

I am hungry.
*Jam i uritur.*
I do not eat meat.
*Unë nuk haj mish.*
self-service cafeteria
*kafeteri vetëshërbimi*
grocery store
*dyqan ushqimor*
fish
*peshk*
soup
*supë*
salad
*sallatë*
fresh vegetables
*zarzavate të freskëta*
milk
*qumësht*
bread
*bukë*
sugar
*sheqer*
ice cream
*akullore*
hot coffee
*kafe*
mineral water
*ujë mineral*
beer
*birrë*
wine
*verë*

## Shopping

Where can I buy one?
*Ku mund të blej një?*
How much does it cost?
*Sa kushton?*
That's (much) too expensive.
*Është shum e shtrënjtë.*
Is there a cheaper one?
*A ka më të lira?*

## Time & Dates

today
*sot*
tonight
*sonde*

tomorrow
*nesër*
the day after tomorrow
*pasnesër*
What time does it open?
*Në ç'far ore çilet?*
What time does it close?
*Në c'far ore Mbyllet?*
open
*celë*
closed
*mbyll*
in the morning
*në mëngjes*
in the evening
*në mbrëmje*
every day
*përditë*
At what time?
*Në ç'orë?*
when?
*kur?*

| Monday | E Hënë |
| Tuesday | E Martë |
| Wednesday | E Mërkurë |
| Thursday | E Ejte |
| Friday | E Prëmte |
| Saturday | E Shtunë |
| Sunday | E Dielë |

| January | Janar |
| February | Shkurt |
| March | Mars |
| April | Prill |
| May | Maj |
| June | Qershor |
| July | Korrik |
| August | Gusht |
| September | Shtator |
| October | Tetor |
| November | Nëndor |
| December | Dhjetor |

**Numbers**

| 1 | Një |
| 2 | Dy |
| 3 | Tre |
| 4 | Katër |
| 5 | Pesë |
| 6 | Gjashtë |
| 7 | Shtatë |
| 8 | Tetë |
| 9 | Nëndë |
| 10 | Dhjetë |
| 11 | Njëmbëdhjetë |
| 12 | Dymbëdhjetë |
| 13 | Trembëdhjetë |
| 14 | Katërmbëdhjetë |
| 15 | Pesëmbëdhjetë |
| 16 | Gjashtëmbëdhjetë |
| 17 | Shtatëmbëdhjetë |
| 18 | Tetëmbëdhjetë |
| 19 | Nëndëmbëdhjetë |
| 20 | Njëzet |
| 21 | Njëzetëenjë |
| 22 | Njëzetedy |
| 23 | Njëzetetre |
| 30 | Tridhjetë |
| 40 | Dyzet |
| 50 | Pesëdhjetë |
| 60 | Gjashtëdhjetë |
| 70 | Shtatëdhjetë |
| 80 | Tetëdhjetë |
| 90 | Nëndëdhjetë |
| 100 | Njëqind |

# Facts for the Visitor

### VISAS & EMBASSIES

Entry into Albania used to be possible only as a member of a package tour on a group visa (US$25 per person), but individuals are now admitted so long as they prebook a personalised guided tour through a travel agency. Once your accommodation and guide services in Albania have been confirmed, the agency will arrange for an Albanian visa to be stamped into your passport at an embassy. It will take six weeks to complete these requirements.

Group visa applications are submitted two months in advance by the tour company, not the individual tourist. Four identical photos are required, but not your passport. Details on the visa application must correspond to your passport exactly. If your passport is subsequently replaced prior to your arrival in Albania, contact the tour operator immediately. Journalists could have visa problems, so just list another occupation – they don't check. Throughout your stay in Albania, the group visa is held by the tour leader and you must travel with the group. There is, however, no problem about walking around towns on your own.

Since 1989, US nationals have been admitted to Albania, but not as individuals, only with groups. At last report South African and Israeli nationals were still not being granted visas. Long hair and beards are no longer a problem.

Visa regulations may be further relaxed in the near future so check with an Albanian embassy for the latest information.

### Albanian Embassies
Albanian embassies in foreign countries include the following:

Bulgaria
    Dimitar Poljanov 10, Sofia
Czechoslovakia
    Pod kaštany 22, Prague 6 (☎ 37 9329)
France
    131 rue de la Pompe, 75116 Paris (☎ 4553 5132)

Germany
    Dürenstrasse 35, D-5300 Bonn 2
    (☎ 228 35 1044)
Hungary
    Munkácsy Mihály utca 6, Budapest VI
    (☎ 22 9278)
Yugoslavia
    Kneza Miloša 56, Belgrade

### CUSTOMS
As recently as 1990 bibles and publications considered hostile to Albania (including certain travel guidebooks) were confiscated by Albanian customs. How strictly these rules are being followed today is uncertain, but only take to Albania what you really need for your trip.

Upon entry into Yugoslavia, all materials printed in Albania are confiscated by Yugoslav customs (this stupid policy says more about Yugoslavia than anything the Albanian booklets ever could). Overlanders should mail all Albanian publications home from Tiranë.

### MONEY
One lek is divided into 100 qindarkës and US$1 gets you 5.8 lekë. Cash US dollars are the second currency in Albania and are used

in hard-currency shops and to pay for Albturist excursions, etc. Commission charges for changing travellers' cheques vary anywhere from two to seven lekë, depending on the whim of the person making the transaction. Less commission is charged for changing cash.

Upon arrival you'll have to list all your money and valuables on a declaration form which you return to customs as you leave. There's no compulsory exchange, but the import and export of Albanian currency is prohibited. You probably won't be aware of a black market. Until 1991 local prices in Albania hadn't changed since the 1950s and you'll probably still find almost everything cheap. Bring travellers' cheques in small denominations and cash in small bills.

## Tipping

Tipping in lekë isn't done in Albania but a small souvenir of your country would be welcome. You're allowed to import 200 cigarettes and a litre of alcohol duty-free and these make excellent tips for guides, drivers, waiters or anyone else who has been especially helpful. Albanian women appreciate Western cosmetics.

Some discretion should be used in tipping in order to avoid spoiling Albania. Tourists who hand out chewing gum or pens to children on the street are creating a nuisance (would they behave that way at home?).

## CLIMATE & WHEN TO GO

Albania has a warm Mediterranean climate. The summers are hot, clear and dry, and the winters, when 40% of the rain falls, are cool, cloudy and moist. In winter the high interior plateau can be very cold and wet as continental air masses move in. Along the coast the climate is moderated by sea winds. July is the hottest month, but even May and October are quite pleasant.

## TOURIST OFFICES

Albturist is the government agency responsible for tourism in Albania. Albturist guides accompany all tour groups and individuals on package tours and they will be your initial source of information. There are no tourist information offices, but hotel receptionists will sometimes give you directions. Both guides and hotel staff are liable to give misleading information on cultural events and sightseeing attractions not included in the tour, usually because of a lack of knowledge. You must personally check theatre and museum times on the spot to be sure.

Not only are city maps unobtainable in Albania, but the streets don't bear name plates nor the houses numbers! Most of the towns are small enough that you can do without such things.

In Britain information is available from Steve Day, the Secretary, Albanian Society, 76 Simonside Terrace, Newcastle-upon-Tyne NE6 5JY. The Society's journal, *Albanian Life*, is published three times a year and a subscription costs £5. Albanian books are readily available from The Albanian Shop (☎ 071-836 0976), 3 Betterton St, London WC2H 9BP.

Your best information source in the USA is Jack Shulman, PO Box 912, Church Street Station, New York, NY 10008. Jack is a one-man, nonprofit, unpaid organisation who sells Albanian books and periodicals. Send him a contribution and he'll put you on the list for his bulletin, the *Albania Report*, which comes out twice a year.

In Australasia write to F G Clements, The Albanian Society, PO Box 14074, Wellington, New Zealand. For a donation Fred will send you the Society's quarterly magazine, *Albania Old & New*.

In Germany you can contact the Deutsch-Albanische Freundschaftsgesellschaft e.V., Postfach 203137, D-2000 Hamburg 20 (☎ 040-850 2736).

## BUSINESS HOURS & HOLIDAYS

Most shops open at 7 am and then close for a siesta from noon to 4 pm. They open again until 7 pm and some also open on Sunday. Banks open only in the morning. Concerts and theatrical performances invariably begin at 6 pm, usually on weekends only.

Albanian museums don't seem to follow any pattern as far as opening hours go and museums in small towns may only open for a couple of hours a week. You may find them inexplicably closed during the posted hours or simply closed with no hours posted. Museums are often unprepared for individual visitors and remain closed even during visiting hours unless a group has made an appointment. Individuals sometimes meet with surprise at museums and may even be told that they're closed for cleaning, renovations, holidays, or any other reason, as an excuse for not letting you in. At other times you'll be admitted at odd hours as a special guest, so it's always worth trying to get in. Museum admission is free everywhere except in Tiranë.

Public holidays include 1 January (New Year), 11 January (Republic Day), 7 March (Teachers' Day), 8 March (International Women's Day), 1 May (Labour Day), 7 November (October Revolution Day), 28 November (Independence Day) and 29 November (Liberation Day).

## CULTURAL EVENTS

A National Folk Festival is held at Gjirokastër every five years (the next is to be held in 1993). This spectacular event attracts folk singers and dancers in full traditional costume from all over Albania to the open-air theatre at Gjirokastër Citadel. For reservations contact one of the tour operators mentioned in this chapter about a year in advance.

## POST & TELECOMMUNICATIONS

Hotel receptions sell postcards and stamps and you can also post mail with them, though it's better to do so at a post office. Mail your parcels from Tiranë to reduce the amount of handling. The main post office near Hotel Tiranë is open until 10 pm daily. Postage is inexpensive and the service surprisingly reliable, but always use air mail.

## TIME

GMT/UTC plus one hour, the same as Yugoslavia and Italy, but one hour behind Greece. Albania goes on summer time at the end of March when clocks are turned an hour

forward. At the end of September they're turned back an hour.

## WEIGHTS & MEASURES

The electric current is 220 volts AC. Albania uses the metric system.

## BOOKS & MAPS

Every town has a bookshop where you'll find some interesting works in English on Albanian history and culture. Since the Yugoslav border guards confiscate all books printed in Albania, you'll have to mail them home if you'll be transiting that country. Postage is cheap and the mail service reliable, but bring some Jiffy bags or wrapping paper and string. Always use air mail.

*Albania – A Travel Guide* by Philip Ward (Oleander Press, Cambridge, England, 1983) is a rambling survey full of confusing, irrelevant digressions which mixes anecdotes and trivia with practical information. *Albania, A Guide and Illustrated Journal* by Peter and Andrea Dawson (Bradt Publications, Britain, 1989) is a more sympathetic introduction to the country. A better guidebook than either of these is *Albanien: Reise-Handbuch und Länderkunde* by Ralph-Raymond Braun (available only in German).

The weighty 295-page *Albania, General Information* ('8 Nëntori' Publishing House, Tiranë, 1984) provides a sleepy official view of the country complete with 40 pages on state organisation, 46 pages on the people's economy, and 63 pages on education, culture, art and science. It's sold at most Albanian hotels and only costs eight lekë, so you can't go wrong.

A more exciting book about the country is *The Artful Albanian, The Memoirs of Enver Hoxha* (Chatto & Windus, London, 1986), edited by Jon Halliday. Halliday has selected the most revealing passages from the 3400 pages of Hoxha's six volumes of memoirs. Some chapters, such as 'Decoding China' and 'Battling Khrushchev' are classics.

## MEDIA
### Newspapers & Magazines

*Zëri i popullit* (The People's Voice) is the

daily organ of the Central Committee of the Party of Labour of Albania. *Bashkimi*, organ of the Democratic Front, is also published daily.

*New Albania* is a bimonthly illustrated magazine which covers various aspects of Albanian life, and *Albania Today* is a bimonthly political magazine. Both are published in English, French, German and Spanish editions; subscriptions (US$4.25 per annum each) are available from Jack Shulman, PO Box 912, Church Street Station, New York, NY 10008, USA. Both publications are air-mailed directly from Tiranë.

## HEALTH
Medical care is free for everyone, visitors included. Prescription medicines must be paid for but the price is right. Most tourists drink bottled mineral water, although tap water is usually safe.

## FILM & PHOTOGRAPHY
Bring all the film you'll need. It's considered rude to take pictures of people without asking permission. You're not supposed to take pictures of military installations, but you'll have lots of opportunities to sneak shots of bunkers, if that interests you.

## HIGHLIGHTS
### Museums & Galleries
Albanian museums and galleries vary in quality but all are well worth visiting. Two little-known galleries housing masterpieces of medieval icon painting are the Museum of Albanian Medieval Art in Korçë and the Onufri Museum in Berat Citadel. Two political museums you should try to visit (though perhaps they no longer exist) are the Atheist Museum in Shkodër and the ultramodern Enver Hoxha Museum in Tiranë. If these are gone, the National Museum of History in Tiranë and the historical museum in Krujë Citadel make excellent substitutes.

### Castles & Historic Towns
Albania's two 'museum towns', Berat and Gjirokastër, both have remarkable citadels.

Earthquakes, such as the one in 1979, have damaged many of the country's other historic towns, though Skanderbeg's Krujë Citadel has been carefully restored. The Rozafa Fortress at Shkodër is perhaps Albania's most evocative castle, as much for its location and the Rozafa legend (see the Rozafa Fortress section under Shkodër) as for what's there now.

## ACCOMMODATION
Since all hotel accommodation and meals are included in your package, you won't have any choice and even if you did there's only one tourist hotel in most towns anyway. Tour prices are based on double occupancy, which means that singles must share a double room with a stranger of the same sex. It's sometimes possible to arrange a single room upon arrival at a hotel for an extra payment of US$10 or less per night, but not always.

When you arrive at your hotel, check that the room has the correct number of towels. Otherwise you could be charged for the 'missing' ones when you try to leave.

## FOOD
All meals will be included in your package, but you ought to miss a couple to try the local Albanian restaurants and taste what the people really eat. Generally you should be able to find places where the food is good and prices reasonable. Just walk into any bar or restaurant you see, sit down and order. There are no restrictions. Lunch is the main meal of the day and in the evening restaurants close early, usually by 9 pm.

Albanian cuisine, like that of Serbia, was strongly influenced by Turkey. Grilled meats like *shishqebap* (shish kebab) and *qofte* (meat balls) are served all across the Balkans. Some local dishes include *mëmëligë* (corn-meal porridge), *qomlek* (rabbit and onion stew) and *tavllë kosi* (roast mutton with yoghurt). Lake Shkodër carp and Lake Ohrit trout are the most common fish dishes. For dessert there's *oshaf* (figs with cinnamon and sheep's milk). Try the ice cream *(akullore)*, which has a peculiar burnt taste.

## DRINKS

Coffee is readily available, both *kafe turke* (Turkish coffee) and *kafe ekspres* (espresso). Albanian white wine is better than the vinegary red. Raki (a spirit distilled from grapes) is taken as an aperitif or combined with cocoa to create a cocktail known as a *Lumumba*. There's also cognac *(konjak)* and various fruit liqueurs.

## ENTERTAINMENT

Hotel bars are surprisingly pleasant (the low prices help a lot) and public bars and cafés patronised mostly by local men are also very sociable. Just go into any place that takes your fancy and order what you see on other people's tables or behind the counter. It's very unlikely that you'll have trouble with drunks.

Check the local theatre for performances. These are usually advertised on painted boards either in front of the theatre or on main streets. Ask someone to direct you to the venue if it's not clear, but be there before 6 pm as that's when the programs usually begin. Soccer games take place at local stadiums on Saturday and Sunday afternoons. As a foreigner, you will need to ask someone to help you obtain tickets.

Later on at hotel bars there's often a band pumping out 1960s rock and roll. Folk music and dancing is sometimes presented there too, so ask your guide or the hotel receptionist.

## THINGS TO BUY

Most of the hotels have hard-currency shops where you can buy Albanian handicrafts, such as carpets, silk, items made from silver, copper and wood, embroidery, shoulder bags, picture books, musical instruments, records and tapes of folk music. Bring foreign currency in small bills and even coins, as the clerks usually don't have change.

To see what the Albanians have to choose from, visit a MAPO (Magazinë Popullore) department store in any town.

Bargaining is not done in Albania.

# Getting There & Away

## AIR

Rinas Airport is 25 km north-west of Tiranë. All tourists are met at the airport by their designated Albturist guide and driven to their hotel.

There's no Albanian national airline, but Air France arrives from Paris, JAT Yugoslav Airlines from Belgrade, Lufthansa from Frankfurt/Main, Malév Hungarian Airlines from Budapest, Olympic Airlines from Athens, TAROM Romanian Air Transport from Bucharest and Rome, and Swissair from Zürich. Groups originating from elsewhere must change planes in one of these cities. Most of the flights are twice a week.

## LAND

Although Shkodër is linked to Titograd by freight train, there's no passenger service. Bus service also doesn't exist and all of the border crossings are far from the main cities. As long as you're forced to come on a prearranged group or individual package tour, this is irrelevant.

### Car & Motorbike

The highway border crossings to/from Yugoslavia are at Han i Hotit (24 km south-east of Titograd), Kukës (18 km south-west of Prizren) and Ćafa San (between Struga and Pogradec). To/from Greece the border crossing is Kakavia, which is between Ioannina (Greece) and Gjirokastër.

At present, entry by private vehicle is not allowed.

### PACKAGE TOURS

Until recently all tourists had to arrive on a package tour, but this has now been changed slightly to allow individuals to come provided that they prebook accommodation and are accompanied throughout their stay by a personal guide and driver. This is more expensive than group travel but not unreasonably so; however, it can take six weeks to arrange. At last report, US citizens were not permitted to travel as individuals, only with groups.

For group travel, call or write the companies mentioned in this section two months in advance. You can often book over the phone and then forward the visa photos, a photocopy of your passport and full payment by mail. All tour prices include transportation, accommodation, meals, admissions and guides, but they don't include visa fees, airport taxes, or alcohol with the meals. Single hotel rooms also cost extra.

Tours with Greek and Yugoslav companies can often be arranged in less than a week, but although these are also cheaper, they're rushed and less carefully planned than the British, Dutch, German and French tours. Keep in mind that British groups will have English-speaking guides, Greek groups Greek-speaking guides, etc.

The main problem with group travel is that you have no control over the itinerary and you do a lot of waiting around. You're required to sleep and travel with the group, but aren't obliged to eat and sightsee with them. To Albania, tourism is sort of political, with visits to hospitals, schools, kindergartens, farms and factories, which is a refreshing change of pace.

Because of the limited capacity at Tiranë's airport, many groups fly to Titograd or Ohrid in Yugoslavia and board a bus to Albania there. It's far better, however, to take a tour that flies direct to Tiranë, as transiting Yugoslavia will cost you at least two days and expose you to tiresome luggage searches by Yugoslav border guards. Also beware of tours which require you to sleep in Durrës for more than two nights, because the town's sightseeing and entertainment possibilities are soon exhausted and you have to pay extra for excursions to other areas.

### Tours from Greece & Yugoslavia

Since 1986 Greek tour groups have been entering Albania. In Athens tours to Albania are organised by Albturist near Syntagma Square. Its one-week trips cost US$300 in dollars cash (no drachmas or travellers'

cheques are accepted) but you only get four full days in Albania. The Athens tours are often fully booked, but if space is available all the arrangements can be completed in a week to 10 days. Be persistent as the Athens Albturist staff only keep office hours when they feel like it. Day trips from Corfu to Sarandë by boat can be arranged five days in advance.

Kompas Travel in Dubrovnik organises a weekly day trip to Albania for US$150, including a bus from Dubrovnik to Budva, a hydrofoil from Budva to Durrës, a bus from Durrës to Tiranë and return, all in one day. This is fine for those who just want to say they've been there. Bookings must be made with Kompas Travel, Gruska obala 26, Dubrovnik, at least three days in advance. If you book with Kompas Tours, Maršala Tita 7, Budva, and join the group in Budva, the same trip costs US$145 per person.

From mid-April to October, the Yugoslav company Atlas Tours has a two-day bus tour to Albania for US$175. You spend the night in Tiranë and have free time in Shkodër after lunch the next day. Putnik Travel Agency may also soon have tours to Albania from Yugoslavia. Ask tourist offices in Yugoslavia about other agencies offering these trips.

Interimpex Travel Agency (☎ 091-22 8572 or 22 8644) in the shopping centre just off Plostad Marsala Tito, Skopje, offers two-day trips from Yugoslavia to Albania twice a week. From June to September, Interimpex also has 10-day bus tours (US$440) which include a week at the beach at Durrës.

### Tours from Britain

English-speaking visitors will want to join a British tour and there are two companies that offer them. Regent Holidays (☎ 0272-21 1711), 13 Small St, Bristol BS1 1DE, England, pioneered tourism to Albania. Its 12-day bus tour visits 11 Albanian towns for £689. Shorter eight-day trips based in Tiranë with a four-day excursion to the south are £534. Five-day trips (£418) are also available. Regent Holidays tour groups fly direct to Tiranë via Zürich. This company also specialises in individual prearranged travel to Albania. It costs from £770 per person for seven nights, including the flight from London.

The second company offering these trips is Voyages Jules Verne (☎ 071-486 8080), 10 Glentworth St, London NW1 5PG, England. It offers a 'Classical' nine-day bus trip (£385) which operates 15 times a year and enters Albania from Titograd. It also has a five-day 'Albanian Weekend' throughout the year for £305, including the flight to Titograd.

### Other Tours

The specialist for German-speaking tours to Albania is Skanderbeg-Reisen GmbH (☎ 0203-76 7986), Zum Walkmüller 8, D-4100 Duisburg 29. It runs 23 trips a year (DM 1595 to DM 2535), with the groups flying direct from Frankfurt/Main to Tiranë.

Several companies offer tours from the Netherlands. Kontakt International (☎ 020-623 4771), Prins Hendrikkade 104, NL-1011 AJ Amsterdam, has eight-day (1395 guilders) and 15-day (2095 guilders) bus tours around the country with the groups flying from Amsterdam to Ohrid. Delta Reizen (☎ 050-14 6200), Postbus 1577, NL-9701 BN Groningen, also travels via Ohrid (1795 guilders for 10 days). Scope Reizen (☎ 077-73 5533), Spoorstraat 41, NL-5931 PS Tegelen, is slightly different in that its nine-day trips (1695 guilders) enter Albania from Titograd and depart via Ohrid, whereas the 15-day tours (2390 guilders) are direct from Amsterdam to Tiranë.

If you want to go on a French-speaking tour, Transtours (☎ 1-4261 5828), 49 Avenue de l'Opéra, 75002 Paris, arranges five-night weekends in Tiranë or Durrës for FF10,490, including the return flight to Paris. Excursions to Krujë, Berat or Gjirokastër cost extra.

From North America, Exotik Tours (☎ 416-736 9669), 1179 Finch Avenue West, Suite 201, Downsview, Ontario, Canada M3J 2G1, offers 10-day tours of Albania from Toronto and Montreal for C$1800 all-inclusive.

# Getting Around

## TRAIN

Before 1948 Albania had no railways, but there's now a fairly comprehensive network based on the port of Durrës, with daily passenger trains leaving Tiranë for Shkodër (98 km), Fier (121 km), Ballsh (146 km), Vlorë (155 km) and Pogradec (189 km). In August 1986 a railway was completed from Shkodër to Titograd, but as yet this is for freight only. The most scenic route by far is that to Pogradec.

Officially, foreign tourists are only allowed to travel around the country in an Albturist vehicle accompanied by a guide, but how strictly this is being enforced these days is questionable. If you have a day to spare and want to find out, just go to the railway station in Durrës or Tiranë and try to buy a ticket. It's only about a one-hour ride between these cities (36 km) and there are nine trains a day, so if you manage to go, you should be able to get back. You'll be an object of considerable curiosity for the other passengers.

## OTHER

You can sometimes hire private taxis for day trips or excursions. Car rentals are not available but individuals on package tours will have a car and driver included. Hitchhiking may be possible on trucks, but truck drivers expect to be paid for lifts.

## LOCAL TRANSPORT

Once you arrive in a town, the guides don't try to force you to stick with the group and you can do as much exploring on your own as you please. No one will bother you. Between towns, foreign tourists used to be required to travel as a group and there was no opportunity to take local trains, though this may have changed. It always was OK to use city buses in Tiranë and Durrës, however. Buy a ticket at a kiosk or from another passenger.

# Tiranë

Tiranë (Tirana), a pleasant city of 300,000 (compared to 30,000 before WW II), is almost exactly midway between Rome and Istanbul. Founded by a Turkish pasha in 1614, Tiranë became a crafts centre with a lively bazar. In 1920 the city was made capital of Albania and bulky Italianate government buildings went up in the 1930s; only in recent years have larger-than-life 'palaces of the people' blossomed around Skanderbeg Square and along Bulevardi Deshmoret e Kombit (Martyrs of the Nation Boulevard).

Tiranë is one of the quietest capital cities in the world. Motor traffic is minimal and nowhere is too far to walk. You'll see Italian parks and a Turkish mosque, but there's no mistaking the pride of this small country. Break loose from your tour and explore the older, eastern side of the city. You can see it all during a two-day stay.

## Information

**Bookshops** The International Bookstore on Rruga Puntoret e Rilindjes east of the park is Tiranë's best. The Libraria Arsimore, a few blocks north on the same street, has school textbooks.

## Things to See

Most visits to Tiranë begin on **Skanderbeg Square**, a great open space in the heart of the city. Tourists stay at the 13-storey Hotel Tiranë on the north side of the square. Beside the hotel is the new **National Museum of History** (1981), the largest and finest of its kind in Albania (open Tuesday to Sunday from 9 am to noon and 4 to 7 pm, Friday from 8 am to 1 pm only). A huge mosaic mural entitled *Albania* covers one side of the museum building.

To the east is another massive building, the **Palace of Culture**, with a theatre, library, restaurant, galleries and so on. Construction of the palace began as a gift of the Soviet people in 1960 and was completed by the Albanian people in 1966 after the 1961 Soviet-Albanian split. Beside this is the cupola and minaret of the **Mosque of Ethem Bey** (1823), one of the most distinctive buildings in the city. Tiranë's **clock tower** (1830) stands beside the mosque.

On the west side of Skanderbeg Square is the National Bank with the main post office behind, while the south side is taken up by the massive yellow-and-red buildings of various government ministries. In the middle of the square is an equestrian statue (1968) of Skanderbeg himself looking straight up Bulevardi Stalin, north towards the railway station.

Behind Skanderbeg's statue extends Bulevardi Deshmoret e Kombit, directly south to the three arches of **Tiranë University** (1957). As you stroll down this largely traffic-free boulevard, you'll see Tiranë's **Art Gallery** (open Tuesday to Sunday from 9 am to noon, and Wednesday, Saturday and Sunday from 4 to 7 pm also), a stronghold of socialist realism with a significant permanent collection exhibited here since 1976. Nearby is the Italian-built **Hotel Dajti** which you should enter to see the dramatic painting of Gjirokastër in the lobby.

When you reach the river, go west a few blocks to the **Ekspozita 'Shqipëria sot'** (Albania Today), a mammoth exhibition of Albanian industrial products, which is well worth seeing if you can get in.

Return to Bulevardi Deshmoret e Kombit and continue south across the bridge over the Lana River. Beyond is **Party House** (1955), the well-guarded four-storey building on the right, and the ultramodern **Congress Hall** (1986) and **Enver Hoxha Museum** (1988) on the left. The boulevard terminates at the university, with the Faculty of Music on the right and the **Archaeological Museum** on the left. Behind the museum is **'Qemal Stafë' Stadium** (1946) where football matches are held every Saturday and Sunday afternoon, except during July and August.

Beyond the university is Parku kombëtar, a large park with an open-air theatre (Teatrin Veror) and an artificial lake. The view across the lake to the olive-coloured hills is superb. Cross the dam retaining the lake to **Tiranë**

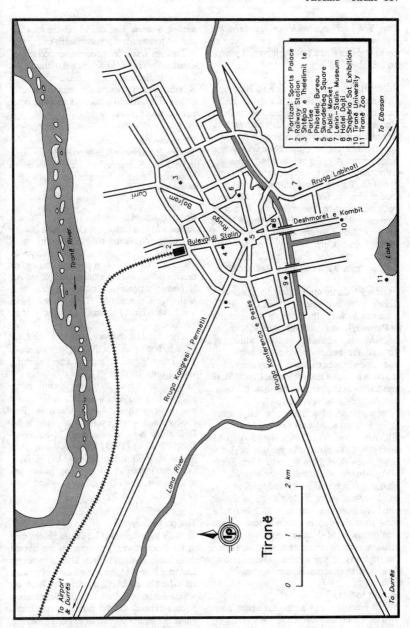

1 'Partizan' Sports Palace
2 Railway Station
3 Shtëpia e Thelellimit te Partise
4 Philatelic Bureau
5 Skanderbeg Square
6 Public Market
7 Lenin–Stalin Museum
8 Hotel Dajti
9 Shqipëria Sot Exhibition
10 Tiranë University
11 Tiranë Zoo

To Elbasan

Rruga Labinoti

Deshmoret e Kombit

Rruga Currit

Rruga Bajram

Bulevardi Stalin

Tiranë River

Rruga Kongresi I Permetit

Rruga Konferenca e Pezes

Lana River

Lake

To Airport & Durrës

To Durrës

Tiranë

0      1      2 km

**Zoo.** The excellent **botanical gardens** are just west of the zoo (ask directions). If you're keen, you can rent a rowing boat and paddle on the lake.

**Political Sights** As you return up Bulevardi Deshmoret e Kombit from the university, turn right onto the street just before Party House to the **Lenin-Stalin Museum** (1954), Rruga Labinoti 100 (open Sunday to Tuesday from 9 am to 1 pm, Wednesday and Friday from 4 to 6 pm), with a fascinating collection of photos and political paintings.

Seven illegal partisan hide-outs in Tiranë, used against the Fascists during WW II, have been made into 'house-museums'. The most conveniently located to Hotel Tiranë is the **Shtëpia Muze e Emine Ketes** in an alley off Rruga Bajram Curri (open Wednesday from 9 am to 1 pm and 5 to 9 pm, Friday and Sunday from 9 am to 1 pm). Ask for directions.

To reach the most significant of the house-museums, follow Rruga Bajram Curri about a km north-east to the **Shtëpia e Thelelimit te Partise**, Rruga Formimi i Partise 60 (same opening hours as the Emine Ketes Museum). To find the building, write the name and address on a piece of paper. Everyone knows it. It was here that Enver Hoxha, Qemal Stafë and 13 others founded the Albanian Communist Party on 8 November 1941.

You should also make the pilgrimage about five km south-east on Rruga Labinoti, which becomes the Elbasan Highway, to the **Martyr's Graveyard** (Varrezat e dëshmorëve), open daily from 8 am to 6 pm. Some 900 partisans who died during the War of National Liberation are buried here, as well as important party leaders such as Enver Hoxha. The hilltop setting with a beautiful view over the city is subdued and a great white figure of Mother Albania (1972) stands watch. Nearby, on the opposite side of the highway, is the former palace of King Zog, now a government guesthouse.

**Places to Stay**

You'll probably stay at the high-rise *Hotel Tiranë*, which was erected in 1979 on Skan-derbeg Square. You can't beat the location and all rooms have private facilities.

Foreign business people are accommodated at the *Hotel Dajti*, erected in the 1930s by the Italians on Bulevardi Deshmoret e Kombit. The hard-currency shop in the hotel is less scrutinised by tourists and the hotel bar has atmosphere.

**Places to Eat**

Try the *Restaurant Donika*, which is beside the old 'Ali Kelmendi' Palace of Culture on Bulevardi Stalin, a few minutes' walk from Hotel Tiranë.

**Entertainment**

As soon as you arrive, check the new *Palace of Culture* on Skanderbeg Square for opera or ballet performances. Most events in Tiranë are advertised on placards in front of this building. There's also the older *'Ali Kelmendi' Palace of Culture* on Bulevardi Stalin, just behind the Hotel Tiranë. Here you'll see variety shows or circus performances.

The *Teatri i Kukallave*, beside the bank on Skanderbeg Square, is the children's theatre. The *Teatri Popullar*, on the street running south from the Palace of Culture between the mosque and the clock tower, features more serious drama in Albanian. Across the square east of the mosque is *Kinema Partizani*. Pop concerts and sports events take place in the *Pallatin e Sportit 'Partizan'* ('Partizan' Sports Palace) (1963) about two km from Skanderbeg Square on the road to Durrës.

Performances at all of these places are most frequent on Friday, Saturday and Sunday, usually at 6 pm.

**Things to Buy**

Tiranë's public market is several blocks east of the clock tower, just north of the Sheshi Avni Rustemi roundabout. The Ekspozita e Kulturës Popullore here has a display of folk art. There's a MAPO department store on Rruga Kongresi i Permetit, off Skanderbeg Square. The Philatelic Bureau is on Bulevardi Stalin, north-west of Hotel Tiranë.

## Getting There & Away

The railway station is at the northern end of Bulevardi Stalin. There are nine trains a day to Durrës, a one-hour journey away (one class only). Trains also depart for Fier (121 km, four hours), Pogradec (189 km, six hours) and Shkodër (98 km, 3½ hours).

## DURRËS

Unlike Tiranë, Durrës (Durazzo) is an ancient city. In the 7th century BC the Greeks founded Epidamnos (Durrës) which the Romans changed to Dyrrhachium, the largest port on the eastern Adriatic and the start of the Via Egnatia to Constantinople. The famous Via Appia to Rome began 150 km north-west at Brindisi, Italy.

Durrës changed hands frequently before being taken in 1501 by the Turks under whom the port dwindled to insignificance. A slow revival began in the 17th century and from 1914 to 1920 Durrës was the capital of Albania. Landings here on 7 April 1939 by Mussolini's troops met fierce though brief resistance and those who fell are regarded as the first martyrs of the War of National Liberation.

Today Roman ruins and Byzantine fortifications embellish this major industrial city and commercial port which lies 38 km west of Tiranë. Durrës is Albania's second-largest city, with 72,000 inhabitants. On a bay south of the city are long sandy beaches where all of the tourist hotels are concentrated. There's really no reason to spend more than one or two nights in Durrës and even confirmed beach people will find more exciting resorts elsewhere.

## Things to See

A good place to begin your visit to Durrës is the **Archaeological Museum** (open from 10 am to 1 pm) which faces the waterfront park near the port. The two rooms are small but each object is unique and there's a large sculpture garden outside. Behind the museum are the 6th century AD Byzantine **city walls** built after the Visigoth invasion of 481 and supplemented by round Venetian towers in the 14th century.

The town's impressive **Roman amphitheatre** (built between the 1st and 2nd centuries AD) is on the hillside just inside the walls. Much of the amphitheatre has been

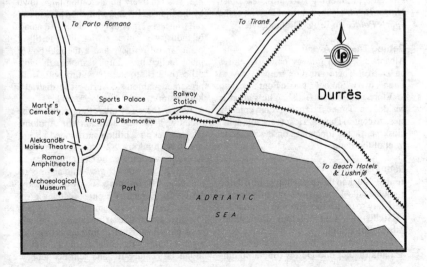

excavated and you can see a small built-in 10th century Byzantine church with wall mosaics. Follow the road just inside the walls down towards the port and you'll find the **Moisiut Ekspozita e Kulturës Popullore** with ethnographic displays.

The **Museum of the National Liberation War** (open from 10 am to 1 pm) is on the other side of town, above the **Martyr's Cemetery** at the west end of Rruga Dëshmorevë. East on Rruga Dëshmorevë, across the square from the train station, is an **Ekspozita Industrial** (Industrial Exhibition) with local products.

### Places to Stay

Foreign tourists stay at the *Adriatiku Hotel* or a neighbouring hotel on the long sandy beach five km south-east of Durrës. This four-storey building is the highest along the entire Albanian coast, a good indication of just how charmingly undeveloped tourism is here. Occasionally the quality of the water lapping the Adriatiku's beach is somewhat less charming, so have a look before plunging in.

### Entertainment

For entertainment go to the *Aleksandër Moisiu Theatre* in the centre of Durrës, or the *Sports Palace* on Rruga Dëshmorevë.

### Getting There & Away

Albania's 437-km railway network centres on Durrës. There are nine trains a day to Tiranë, two to Shkodër, two to Pogradec, two to Vlorë and one to Ballsh. The station is beside the Tiranë Highway, conveniently close to central Durrës. Tickets are sold at the kiosk below the timetables on the square in front of the station.

### Getting Around

Tourists stuck in the beach hotels are offered a choice of 44 excursions ranging from a half-day trip to the Pioneer Camp for US$0.80 to a four-day tour of southern Albania for US$60.

There's frequent bus service from the Adriatiku Hotel into Durrës (buy a 30 qin-

darkës ticket at a kiosk). For the return journey look for the bus near the new post office in Durrës.

# Southern Albania

The south of the country is rich in historical and natural beauty. Apolonia and Butrint are renowned classical ruins, and Berat and Gjirokastër are museum towns and strongholds of Tosk traditions. Korçë is the cultural capital of the south whereas Pogradec and Sarandë, on Lake Ohrit and the Ionian Sea respectively, are undeveloped resort towns.

South-east of the industrialised Elbasan-Vlorë plain, the land becomes extremely mountainous with lovely valleys such as those of the Osum and Drino rivers where Berat and Gjirokastër are found. The Ionian Coast north from Sarandë to Vlorë is stunningly beautiful, with 2000-metre mountains falling directly towards the sea and not a hotel in sight. See it now before the land developers get there.

## FIER & APOLONIA

Fier is a relatively uninteresting large town by the Gjanica River at a junction of road and rail routes 89 km south of Durrës. Albania's oil industry is centred at Fier with a fertiliser plant, an oil refinery and a thermal power plant fuelled by natural gas. Near the post office is a **Historical Museum** with well-presented exhibits covering the district's long history.

By far the most interesting sight in the vicinity is the ruins of ancient Apolonia (Pojan), set on a hilltop surrounded by impressive bunkers 12 km west of Fier. Apolonia was founded by Corinthian Greeks in 588 BC and quickly grew into an important city state minting its own currency. Under the Romans the city became a great cultural centre with a famous school of philosophy. Julius Caesar rewarded Apolonia with the title 'free city' for supporting him against Pompey the Great during a civil war in the 1st century BC and sent his nephew

Octavius, the future Emperor Augustus, to complete his studies there. After a series of disasters, the population moved south to present-day Vlorë (the ancient Avlon) and by the 5th century AD only a small village with a bishop remained at Apolonia.

Visitors first reach the imposing 13th century Orthodox **Monastery of St Mary**. Aside from the icons in the church, the capitals in the narthex and the Byzantine murals in the adjacent refectory are outstanding. The monastery now houses an extremely rich archaeological museum with a large collection of ceramics and statuary from the site.

Only a small part of ancient Apolonia has yet been uncovered. The first ruin to catch the eye is the roughly restored 2nd century AD **Bouleterion**, or Hall of the Agonothetes. In front of it is the 2nd century AD **Odeon** (a small theatre). To the west of this is a long 3rd century BC **portico** with niches that once contained statues. Apolonia's **defensive walls** are nearby. The lower portion of these massive walls, which are four km long and up to 6.5 metres high, dates back to the 4th century BC.

## GJIROKASTËR

This historic museum town in the hills, midway between Fier and Ioannina, is strikingly picturesque. A mighty citadel surveys the Drino Valley above the three or four-storey stone-roofed tower houses clinging to the mountainside. For defence purposes, during blood feuds these unique houses (*kullë*) had no windows on the ground floor, which was used for storage, and the living quarters above were reached by an exterior stairway. The town's Greek name, Argyrokastron, is said to refer to a Princess Argyro, who chose to throw herself from a tower rather than fall into the hands of enemies, though it's more likely to come from the Illyrian Argyres tribe which inhabited these parts.

Gjirokastër (also Gjirokastra) was well established by the 13th century, but the arrival of the Turks in 1417 brought on a decline. By the 17th century Gjirokastër was thriving again with a flourishing bazar where

embroidery, felt, silk and the still famous white cheese were traded. Ali Pasha Tepelenë took the town in the early 19th century and strengthened the citadel. Today all new buildings must conform to a historical preservation plan.

### Things to See

For the classic view of Gjirokastër, climb up to the **Muzeu Historik Çerçis Topulli** in a large traditional house at the highest point of the town, up above the castle. If the museum is open, you'll see displays on the Topulli brothers, who led an anti-Ottoman uprising in 1908.

From here you'll easily find your way down into the 14th century **citadel** (*kalaja*) itself, now a Museum of Armaments, with an excellent collection, including a two-seater US reconnaissance plane intercepted over Albania in 1957. In 1812 Ali Pasha had a 10-km aqueduct built to supply the citadel with water but this was demolished in 1932. During the 1920s the fortress was converted into a prison and the Nazis made full use of it during their stay in 1943-44. Every five years the National Folk Festival is held in the open-air theatre beside the citadel.

Enver Hoxha was born at Gjirokastër in 1908, and since 1966 his house, which is among the narrow cobbled streets of the Palorto quarter, has been a **Museum of the National Liberation War**. Apart from the exhibits, this is a good chance to see inside one of the distinctive Gjirokastër houses which are noted for their carved wooden ceilings, decorated fireplaces, divans and carpets.

In the centre of Gjirokastër is the **Bazar Mosque**. The 17th century **Turkish baths** (*hamam*) are below the hotel in the lower town, near the polyclinic. The remnants of the **Mecate Mosque** are nearby. Gjirokastër also has a lively Sunday market.

### Places to Stay

If possible, spend a night in Gjirokastër to allow yourself ample free time to wander. However, the *Hotel Çayupi* has only 80 beds and is often full.

## SARANDË

Sarandë (Saranda) is a relatively uninteresting town on the Gulf of Sarandë, between the mountains and the Ionian Sea. An early Christian monastery here dedicated to 40 saints (Santi Quaranta) gave Sarandë its name. This southernmost harbour of Albania was once the ancient port of Onchesmos but Sarandë's main attraction today is its sunny climate and the nearby ruins of Butrint. It's traditional for Albanians to spend their honeymoons here, perhaps while staring at the Greek island of Corfu, which is visible from the shore.

### Things to See

Sarandë's waterfront promenade is attractive but lacks the street life of nearby Greece. In front of the cinema in the centre of town are some ancient ruins with a large mosaic exposed to the open air. At Rruga 8 Nëntori, near the corner of Rruga Qazim Pali, is the **Muzeu Historik**, but no hours are posted and you would be lucky to get in. A more reliable local sight is the sun setting in the west behind Corfu and the searchlights sweeping the bay later on.

### Places to Stay

Tourists in Sarandë stay at the modern *Hotel Butrinti* overlooking the harbour just south of town. Beware of rooms without balconies.

## BUTRINT

The ancient ruins of Butrint, 15 km south of Sarandë, are surprisingly extensive and interesting. Virgil claimed the Trojans had founded Buthroton (Butrint) but no evidence of this has been found. Though the site had been inhabited long before, Greeks from Corfu settled on the hill here in the 6th century BC and within a century Butrint had become a fortified trading city with an acropolis. The lower town began developing in the 3rd century BC and many large stone buildings existed when the Romans took over in 167 BC. Butrint's prosperity continued throughout the Roman period and the Byzantines made it an ecclesiastical centre. Then the city declined and was almost abandoned when Italian archaeologists arrived in 1927 and began carting off any relics of value to Italy until WW II interrupted their work. In recent years the Italian government has returned some important Butrint sculptures to Albania and these are now in the National Museum of History in Tiranë.

### Things to See

The site (open daily from 7 am to 2 pm) lies by a channel connecting salty Butrint Lake to the sea. A triangular **fortress** erected by warlord Ali Pasha Tepelenë in the early 19th century watches over the modern vehicular ferry.

In the forest below the acropolis is Butrint's 3rd century BC **Greek theatre**, also in use during the Roman period. The small **public baths** with geometrical mosaics are close by. Deeper in the forest is a wall covered with crisp Greek inscriptions, and a 6th century palaeo-Christian **baptistry** with colourful mosaics of animals and birds, which are covered by protective sand. Beyond a 6th century basilica stands a massive **Cyclopean wall** dating from the 4th century BC. Over one gate is a splendid relief of a lion killing a bull, symbolic of a protective force vanquishing assailants.

In a crenellated brick building atop the acropolis is a **museum** full of statuary from the site. There are good views from the terrace.

## BERAT

Although not quite as enchanting as Gjirokastër, Berat deserves its status as Albania's second museum town. Berat is sometimes called the 'city of a thousand eyes' for the many windows in the white-plastered, red-roofed houses on terraces overlooking the Osum River. Along a ridge high above the gorge is a 14th century citadel that shelters small Greek Orthodox churches. On the slope below this, all the way down to the river, is Mangalem, the old Muslim quarter. A seven-arched stone bridge (1780) leads to Gorica, the Christian quarter.

In the 3rd century BC an Illyrian fortress called Antipatria was built here on the site of an earlier settlement. The Byzantines strengthened the hilltop fortifications in the 5th and 6th centuries, as did the Bulgarians 400 years later. The Serbians renamed it Beligrad, or 'White City', which has become today's Berat. The Serbians occupied the citadel in 1345, but in 1450 the Ottoman Turks took Berat. The town revived in the 18th and 19th centuries as a Turkish crafts centre specialising in woodcarving. For a brief time in 1944, Berat was the capital of liberated Albania. Today most of Albania's crude oil is extracted from wells just northwest of the city, but Berat itself is a textile town with a mill once known as 'Mao Zedong'.

### Things to See

On the square in front of Hotel Tomori is a white hall where the National Liberation Council met from 20 to 23 October 1944 and formed a provisional government of Albania with Enver Hoxha as prime minister. Beyond this is the **Leaden Mosque** (1555), named for the material covering its great dome. Today the mosque is an interesting Museum of Architecture with photos of historic buildings from all over Albania.

Follow the busy street towards the citadel from here and after a few blocks you'll reach the former **Dervishes Mosque** (1791), now the **Archaeological Museum**. The modern **Ekspozita Galeria** beside the mosque complex contains an exhibition of regional products and a good art gallery featuring the realistic paintings of local artist Sotir Capo. By the nearby river is the 'Margarita Tutulani' Palace of Culture, a theatre worth visiting shortly before 6 pm, when most events begin. Beyond this is the **Bachelor's Mosque** (1827), now a folk art museum.

Carry on towards the old stone bridge and you'll see the 14th century **Church of St Michael** high up on the hillside, below the citadel. In Mangalem, behind the Bachelor's Mosque, is the **Muzeu i Luftes**, which is as worth seeing for its old Berati house as for its exhibits on the partisan struggle during WW II. Beyond the Savings Bank on the stone road leading up towards the citadel is

the **Muzeu Etnografik** in another fine old building.

After entering the **citadel** through its massive gate, continue straight ahead on the main street and ask anyone to direct you to the **Muzeu Onufri**. This museum and the Greek Orthodox Cathedral of Our Lady (1797) are both within the monastery walls. The wooden iconostasis (1850) and pulpit in the cathedral are splendid and the museum has a large collection of icons, especially those of the famous mid-16th century artist after whom the museum is named. Onufri's paintings are more realistic, dramatic and colourful than those of his predecessors.

It's unlikely you'll get into any of the other churches in the citadel, although the 14th century **Church of the Holy Trinity** *(Shen Triadhes* in Albanian) on the west side near the walls has an impressive exterior. The 16th century **Church of the Evangelists** is most easily found by following the eastern citadel wall.

The various museums in Berat open irregularly from 9 am to noon and from 4 to 6 pm a couple of days a week.

### Places to Stay

All tourists stay at the *Hotel Tomori*, named after Mt Tomori (2416 metres), which overlooks Berat to the east. The hotel has no lift but the balcony-front views of the riverside park compensate for the climb.

### ELBASAN

Elbasan, on the Shkumbin River, midway between Durrës and Pogradec and 43 km south-east of Tiranë, has been prominent since 1974, when the Chinese built Albania's mammoth 'Steel of the Party' metallurgical combine. There's also a cement factory and burgeoning pollution, though the old town retains a certain charm.

The Romans founded Skampa (Elbasan) in the 1st century AD as a way station on the Via Egnatia. Stout stone walls with 26 towers were added in the 4th century to greet invading barbarians and the Byzantines continued this trend, also making Skampa the seat of a bishopric. In 1466 Sultan Mohammed II rebuilt the walls as a check against Skanderbeg at Krujë and renamed the town El Basan ('The Fortress' in Turkish). Elbasan was an import trade and handicrafts centre throughout the Turkish period.

### Things to See

Tour parties often stop for lunch at the Hotel Skampa beside the former **Turkish baths**. Opposite the hotel are the **city walls** which were erected by the Turks and are still relatively intact on the south and west sides. Go through the south gate and look for the **Shtëpia Muze e Aresimit**, a museum that's in among the houses and has two old churches alongside. On the west city wall is a museum dedicated to the partisan war.

If you have extra time, ask someone to point the way to the **Shtëpia Muze e Qemal Stafë**, a museum on Rruga Rinia in the newer part of the city. Qemal was a Communist youth leader killed by the Fascists in 1942 at the age of 22.

### POGRADEC

Pogradec is a pleasant beach resort at the southern end of Ohrit Lake, 140 km southeast of Tiranë. The 650-metre elevation gives the area a brisk, healthy climate and the scenery here is fine. Pogradec is much quieter and more relaxing than the Yugoslav lake towns of Ohrid and Struga.

### Things to See & Do

Tourists are allowed to walk east along the beach about two km to a barrier which marks the beginning of the four-km-wide **border zone** with Yugoslavia. There's little else to do except visit the local **museum** (with archaeology exhibits downstairs, partisan mementos upstairs) near the modern theatre on the waterfront, go to the movies, or take a swim.

### Places to Stay & Eat

The only place to stay is the *Guri i Kug Hotel*, named after the 'red-stone' mountain on the west side of the lake where nickel and

chrome ore are extracted. Ohrit Lake trout *(koran)* is a speciality.

### Getting There & Away

The railway station, with service to Durrës and Tiranë, is near the mineral-processing factory, about four km from the Guri i Kug Hotel.

### KORÇË

Korçë (Koritsa in Greek), the main city of the south-eastern interior, sits on a high plateau west of Florina, Greece, 39 km south of Lake Ohrit. Under the Turks, Korçë was a major trading post and carpet-making town (it is still Albania's biggest carpet and rug-producing centre). Though at the heart of a rich agricultural area, Korçë saw hard times in the late 19th and early 20th centuries and became a centre of emigration from the country. Albanians abroad often regard Korçë as home and quite a few still come back to retire here.

The first school in the Balkans that taught in the Albanian language opened at Korçë on 7 March 1887, a date now celebrated as Teachers' Day. In 1891 the first Albanian school for girls opened here. The French occupied Korçë from 1916 to 1920 and set up a *lycée* in 1917. Enver Hoxha studied at the school and later taught French there. Korçë's educational connection continues today in the Higher Institute of Agriculture.

At first you may wonder why you've been brought to Korçë. Much of the old city centre was gouged out by urban renewal after devastating earthquakes in 1931 and 1960 which toppled the minarets and flattened the churches. The city has a rich cultural life but finding it can be hit or miss and even the museums are hard to visit. Korçë isn't as neatly packaged as some other towns but it does have substance all the same.

### Things to See

Tourists are taken to the Hotel Iliria. Behind it on Bulevardi Lenin is the **Muzeu Historik**, which seems always to be closed. As you continue up Bulevardi Lenin, you will pass the **'Ali Kelmendi' Palace of Culture** on the left and a large café on the right. At the top of the boulevard is the *National Warrior* statue (1932) by Odhise Paskali and, nearby, the **Muzeu i Arsimit Kombëtar**, or Education Museum, housed in the first school to teach in the Albanian language. Across the boulevard is the **Themistokli Gërmenji House Museum**.

To the left of the National Warrior statue is **Party House**. Plunge into the small streets behind this building and you should be able to find the **Muzeu i Artet Mesjetar Shqiptar** (Museum of Albanian Medieval Art), by far the most important of Korçë's museums. There are several icons by Onufri among other wonders, so fall to your knees and beg entry if they tell you it's only for groups (theoretically, it's open daily from 10 am to 1 pm and from 4 to 7 pm). Even if you do arrive by tour bus, accompanied by your Albturist guide, some rooms may remain inexplicably closed. The museum director takes being an Albanian seriously!

Return to Party House and follow the main street east to Kinema Morava. Up the small street beside the cinema is the **Shtëpia Muze ku ka Banuar Shoku Enver Hoxha**, where the gentleman lived while working as a teacher in Korçë from 1937 to 1939 (open Wednesday, Friday and Sunday from 3 to 5 pm). You may be shown around by Aunt Poliksene, one of Enver's early associates.

As you stroll down Bulevardi Republik from Kinema Morava, you'll pass two museums dedicated to the War of National Liberation in large mansions on the left. High on the hillside above here is the **Martyr's Graveyard** (Varrezat e dëshmorëve) from which you can enjoy a fine view.

As you return to the hotel, you may still wonder why you're in Korçë, so delve into the cobbled streets lined with quaint old shops beyond the bus station, west of the hotel. The **Ekspozita e Kulturës Materiale Popullare** is on the main square here. There's a popular restaurant at the back of a courtyard between this exhibition and the bus station. Continue south through this

quarter to the **Mirahorit Mosque** (1485), the oldest of its kind in Albania.

### Entertainment
The *A Z Cajupi Theatre* is beside the post office opposite the hotel. Live variety shows sometimes take place in the *Kinema Morava*.

# Northern Albania

A visit to northern Albania usually means only the coastal strip, as tourism in the interior is undeveloped. Many groups fly to Titograd and cross by coach to Shkodër, the old Gheg capital near the lake of the same name. It's a pleasant introduction to Albania and the change of pace from Yugoslavia, or almost anywhere else in Europe, is striking. Southbound the groups have lunch at Lezhë and see Skanderbeg's tomb. Krujë is off the main road but is usually included for its crucial historical importance to Albania. From Krujë it's only 32 km to Tiranë.

### KRUJË
In the 12th century, Krujë (Kruja) was already the capital of the Principality of Arberit, but this hilltop town attained its greatest fame between 1443 and 1468, when the national hero George Kastrioti (Skanderbeg) (1405-68) made Krujë his seat.

At a young age, George Kastrioti, son of an Albanian prince, was handed over as a hostage to the Turks, who converted him to Islam and gave him a military education at Edirne. There he became known as Iskander (after Alexander the Great) and Sultan Murat II promoted him to the rank of bey, thus the name Skanderbeg. In 1443 Skanderbeg abandoned Islam and the Ottoman army and rallied his fellow Albanians against the Turks. Among the 13 Turkish invasions he subsequently repulsed was that in 1450 led by Murat II himself. Pope Calixtus III named Skanderbeg 'captain general of the Holy See' and Venice formed an alliance with him. The Turks besieged Krujë four times and though beaten back in 1450, 1466 and 1467, they took control of Krujë in 1478 (after Skanderbeg's death) and Albanian resistance was snuffed out.

## Things to See

Set below towering mountains, the **citadel** that Skanderbeg defended still stands on an abrupt ridge above the modern town. In 1982 an excellent new museum opened in the citadel and the saga of the Albanian struggle against the Ottoman Empire is richly told with models, maps and statuary. (The museum was designed by Pranvera Hoxha, Enver's daughter, and the attempt to associate Hoxha and Skanderbeg as parallel champions of Albanian independence is obvious.) Among the old houses in the citadel are the 18th century **Bektashi tekke**, place of worship of a mystical Islamic sect, and the 16th century **Turkish baths**, which are just below the tekke.

Between the citadel and the bus station is Krujë's 18th century **Turkish bazar**, which was later destroyed but has now been fully restored and made into an ethnographical museum and workplace for local artisans and craftspeople.

## LEZHË

It was at Lezhë (Alessio) in March 1444 that Skanderbeg succeeded in convincing the Albanian feudal lords to unite in a League of Lezhë to resist the Turks. Skanderbeg died of fever here in 1468 and today his tomb may be visited among the ruins of the Franciscan **Church of St Nicolas**. Reproductions of his helmet and sword grace the gravestone and along the walls are 25 shields bearing the names and dates of battles he fought against the Turks.

Near the tomb beside the grey apartment blocks is the **Ethnographical Museum**, and on the hilltop above is the medieval **Lezhë Citadel**. Much of old Lezhë was destroyed by an earthquake on 15 April 1979.

## Places to Eat

Tour groups in transit along the coast often have lunch in the former hunting lodge of Count Galeazzo Ciano, Mussolini's son-in-law and foreign minister, seven km south of Lezhë. (To please Hitler, Mussolini had Ciano executed at Verona on 11 January 1944.) Enjoy your lunch.

## SHKODËR

Shkodër (also Shkodra and in Italian, Scutari), the traditional centre of the Gheg cultural region in northern Albania, is one of the oldest cities in Europe. In 500 BC an Illyrian fortress already guarded the strategic crossing just west of the city where the Bunë and Drin rivers meet and all traffic moving up the coast from Greece to Montenegro must pass. These rivers drain two of the Balkan's largest lakes: Shkodër, just to the north-west of the city, and Ohrit, far up the Drin River, beyond several massive hydroelectric dams. The route inland to Kosovo also begins in Shkodër. North of Shkodër, line after line of cement bunkers point the way to the Han i Hotit border crossing into Yugoslavia (33 km); Tiranë is 116 km south.

In the 3rd century BC, Queen Teuta's Illyrian kingdom was centred here and despite wars with Rome in 228 and 219 BC Shkodër was not taken by the Romans until 168 BC. Later the region passed to Byzantium before becoming the capital of the feudal realm of the Balshas in 1350. In 1396 the Venetians occupied Shkodër's Rozafa Fortress, which they held against Suleiman Pasha in 1473 but lost to Mehmet Pasha in 1479. The Turks lost 14,000 men in the first siege and 30,000 in the second.

As the Ottoman Empire declined in the late 18th century, Shkodër became the centre of a semi-independent Pashalik, which led to a blossoming of commerce and crafts. In 1913 Montenegro attempted to annex Shkodër (they succeeded in taking Ulcinj), but this was not recognised by the international community and the town changed hands often during WW I. Badly damaged by a 1979 earthquake, Shkodër was subsequently repaired and is now Albania's third-largest city, with a population of 70,000.

Shkodër was formerly the most influential Catholic city of Albania, with a large cathedral, and Jesuit and Franciscan monasteries, seminaries and religious libraries, but under the Communists it was better known for its Muzeu Ateist (see the Things to See section that follows).

## Orientation & Information

On the same roundabout as the Rozafa Hotel is the Migjenit Theatre and, from opposite it, Bulevardi Stalin runs south-east past the hotel and post office. The post office looks north-east up Rruga Enver Hoxha, a delightful street lit by antique lamps in the evening and lined with harmonious old buildings.

## Things to See

The **Muzeu popullor** in the former mosque opposite the hotel contains objects related to ethnography and the partisan campaign of WW II. On Rruga Enver Hoxha, across the park beside this museum, is the **Muzeu Ateist** (Atheist Museum), which opened in 1973. The exhibits attempt to show how organised religion was an obstacle to scientific progress, how religious leaders sided with reactionary forces, how women were exploited as a result of religion, and so on, but foreigners have difficulty gaining entry to the museum.

On the backstreet behind the Muzeu Ateist, between it and the ex-church (now an auditorium), is the house-museum of the poet Migjeni, whose *Vargjet e lira* (1936) sought to dispel the magic of the old myths and awaken the reader to present injustices.

A couple of blocks north-east up Rruga Enver Hoxha, near the corner of Rruga Branko Kadija, is the **Ekspozita e Kulturës Popullore** with displays of Albanian handicrafts in several buildings. You may like to do some window-shopping here. The exhibition and museums listed here open irregularly, although in theory it's open daily from 10 am to noon and 6 to 8 pm, so check during those hours if you can.

**The Rozafa Fortress** Two km south-west of Shkodër, near the southern end of Shkodër Lake, is the Rozafa Fortress, founded by the Illyrians in antiquity but rebuilt much later by the Venetians and Turks. Upon entering the second enclosure you pass a ruined church which was first converted into a mosque and then into a restored stone palace. From the highest point there's a marvellous view on all sides.

The fortress derived its name from a woman named Rozafa, who was allegedly walled into the ramparts as an offering to the gods so the construction would stand. The story goes that Rozafa asked that two holes be left in the stonework so that she could continue to suckle her baby. Nursing women still come to the fortress to smear their breasts with milky water taken from a spring here.

Below the fortress, but difficult to reach, is the many-domed **Leaden Mosque** (1774). The view from above must suffice.

## Places to Stay

You'll stay, either for lunch or the night, at the *Rozafa Hotel*, a nine-storey building on the Five Heroes roundabout.

## Places to Eat

The *Shkodra Restaurant*, on Rruga Enver Hoxha, a few blocks north of the Muzeu Ateist, serves excellent Albanian dishes at very reasonable prices.

## Entertainment

The *Pallatin te Kulturës Vasil Shanto*, on a backstreet behind the Muzeu Ateist, is a former church that has been converted into an auditorium. South-east on Bulevardi Stalin, beyond the post office, is *Kinema Republika* on the left.

# Alternative Place Names

The following abbreviations are used:
(A) Albanian
(B) Bulgarian
(C) Czech
(Ce) Celtic
(Cr) Croatian
(D) Dutch
(E) English
(G) German
(Gk) Greek
(H) Hungarian
(I) Italian
(L) Latin
(M) Macedonian
(MGk) Medieval Greek (Byzantine)
(P) Polish
(R) Romanian
(Rus) Russian
(Se) Serbian
(Slav) Slav
(Slk) Slovak
(Sle) Slovene
(T) Turkish

## ALBANIA
*Shqipëri (A), Illyria (L)*

Apolonia (L) – Pojan (A)
Berat (A) – Antipatria (L)
Butrint (A) – Buthroton (Gk)
Durrës (A) – Durazzo (I), Epidamnos (Gk), Dyrrhachium (L)
Elbasan (A) – Skampa (L), El Basan (T)
Gjirokastër (A) – Gjirokastra (A), Argyrokastron (Gk)
Ioannina (Gk) – Janinë (A)
Korçë (A) – Koritsa (Gk)
Krujë (A) – Kruja (E)
Lezhë (A) – Alessio (I)
Sarandë (A) – Saranda (E), Onchesmos (Gk)
Tiranë (A) – Tirana (E)
Vlorë (A) – Avlon (L)

## BULGARIA
*Bâlgariya*

Bachkovo Monastery (E) – Bachkovski Manastir (B)
Balchik (B) – Krunoi (Gk), Dionysopolis (L)
Golden Sands (E) – Zlatni Pyasâtsi (B), Goldstrand (G)
Hisarya (B) – Augusta (L), Hisar (T), Toplitsa (MGk)
Nesebâr (B) – Mesembria (Gk)
Plovdiv (B) – Philipopolis (Gk), Philibe (T)
Rila Monastery (E) – Rilski Manastir (B)
Ruse (B) – Rouschouk (T)
Shumen (B) – Chumla (T)
Sofia (E) – Sofiya (B), Serdica (L), Sredets (Slav), Triaditsa (MGk)
Sozopol (B) – Apollonia (Gk)
Stara Planina (B) – Balkan Mountains (E)
Sunny Beach (E) – Slânchev Bryag (B), Sonnenstrand (G)
Varna (B) – Odessos (Gk)
Vidin (B) – Dunonia (Ce), Bononia (L)

## CZECHOSLOVAKIA
*Československo*

Banská Bystrica (Slk) – Neusohl (G)
Bratislava (C) – Pressburg (G), Pozsony (H)
Brno (C) – Brünn (G)
Česke Budějovice (C) – Budweis (G)
Český Krumlov (C) – Krumau (G)
Cheb (C) – Eger (G)
Danube (River) (E) – Dunáj (C)
Františkovy Lázně (C) – Franzensbad (G)
Gerlachovský štít (Slk) – Mt Gerlach (E)
Hluboká nad Vltavou (C) – Frauenberg (G)
Karlovy Vary (C) – Karlsbad (G)
Košice (Slk) – Kaschau (G)
Krkonoše (C) – Giant Mountains (E)
Krusne Hory (C) – Ore Mountains
Labe (River) (C) – Elbe (G)
Levoča (Slk) – Leutschau (G)
Mala Fatra (Slk) – Little Fatra (E)
Mariánské Lázně (C) – Marienbad (G)
Nizke Tatry (Slk) – Low Tatra (E)
Plzeň (C) – Pilsen (G)
Prague (E) – Praha (C), Prag (G)
Prešov (Slk) – Preschau (G)

Slavkov u Brna (C) – Austerlitz (G)
Slovenské rudohorie (Slk) – Slovak Ore
  Mountains (E)
Slovenský raj (Slk) – Slovak Paradise (E)
Spišsky hrad (Castle) (Slk) – Zipser Burg (G)
Telč (C) – Teltsch (G)
Vltava (River) (C) – Moldau (G)
Vysoké Tatry (Slk) – High Tatra (E)
Zlaté piesky (C) Golden Sands (E)
Znojmo (C) – Znaim (G)
Zvolen (Slk) – Altsohl (G)

## (EASTERN) GERMANY
*Deutschland (Ost)*

Baltic Sea (E) – Ostsee (G)
Chemnitz (G) – formerly: Karl Marx
  Stadt (G)
Federal Republic of Germany (FRG) (E) –
  Bundesrepublik Deutschland (BRD) (G)
German Democratic Republic (GDR) (E) –
  Deutsche Demokratische Republik
  (DDR) (G)
Mecklenburg-Pomerania (E) –
  Mecklenburg-Vorpommern (G)
Pomerania (E) – Pommern (G)
Prussia (E) – Preussen (G)
Saxony (E) – Sachsen (G)
Saxony-Anhalt (E) – Sachsen-Anhalt (G)
Thuringia (E) – Thüringen (G)
Thuringian Forest (E) – Thüringer Wald (G)

## HUNGARY
*Magyarország*

Balaton (Lake) (H) – Plattensee (G)
Debrecen (H) – Debrezin (G)
Eger (H) – Erlau (G)
Great Plain (E) – Nagyalföld (H)
Győr (H) – Raab (G), Arrabona (L)
Kisalföld (H) – Little Plain (E)
Komárom (H) – Brigetio (L)
Köszeg (H) – Guns (G)
Pécs (H) – Fünfkirchen (G), Sopianae (L)
Sopron (H) – Ödenburg (G), Scarbantia (L)
Szeged (H) – Segedin (G)
Székesfehérvár (H) – Stuhlweissenburg (G)
Szombathely (H) – Steinamanger (G),
  Savaria (L)
Tata (H) – Totis (G)

Vác (H) – Wartzen (G)
Transdanubia (E) – Dunántúl (H)

## POLAND
*Polska*

Brzezinka (P) – Birkenau (G)
Bydgoszcz (P) – Bromberg (G)
Częstochowa (P) – Tschenstochau (G)
Frombork (P) – Frawenburg (G)
Gdańsk (P) – Danzig (G)
Gdynia (P) – Gdingen (G)
Gniezno (P) – Gnesen (G)
Kołobrzeg (P)- Kolberg (G)
Giżycko (P) – Lötzen (G)
Gniezno (P) – Gnesen (G)
Kętrzyn (P) – Rastenburg (G)
Kraków (P) – Krakau (G), Cracow (E)
Lidzmark Warmiński (P) – Heilsberg (G)
Lvov (E) – Lwów (P), Lemberg (G)
Malbork (P) – Marienburg (G)
Małopolska (P) – 'Little Poland' (E)
Mikołajki (P) – Nikolaiken (G)
Nowy Sącz (P) – Neusandez (G)
Nysa (River) (P) – Neisse (G)
Odra (River) (P) – Oder (G)
Olsztyn (P) – Allenstein (G)
Opole (P) – Oppeln (G)
Oświęcim (P) – Auschwitz (G)
Poznań (P) – Posen (G)
Ruciane-Nida (P) – Rudschanny (G)
Silesia (E) – Śląsk (P), Silesien (G)
Świnoujście (P) – Swinemünde (G)
Szczecin (P) – Stettin (G)
Sopot (P) – Zoppot (G)
Tannenberg (G) – Stębark (P)
Toruń (P) – Thorn (G)
Vistula (River) (E) – Wisła (P), Weichsel (G)
Warsaw (E) – Warszawa (P), Warschau (G)
Węgorzewo (P) – Angerburg (G)
Wielkopolska (P) – 'Great Poland' (E)
Wilczy Szaniec (P) – Wolfschanze (G),
  Wolf's Lair (E)
Wrocław (P) – Breslau (G)

## ROMANIA
*Romania*

Adamclisi (R) – Tropaeum Traiani (L)

Alba Iulia (R) – Karlsburg (G), Weissenburg (G), Apulum (L)
Bistriţa (R) – Bistritz (G)
Braşov (R) – Kronstadt (G)
Bucharest (E) – Bucureşti (R)
Chernovtsy (Rus) – Cernăuţi (R), Czernowitz (G)
Cluj-Napoca (R) – Klausenburg (G), Kolozsvár (H), Napoca (L)
Constanţa (R) – Constantiana (L), Tomis (Gk), Küstendje (T)
Dobruja (E) – Dobrogea (R), Moesia Inferior (L)
Hunedoara (R) – Eisenmarkt (G)
Iaşi (R) – Jassy (G)
Mangalia (R) – Callatis (L)
Mediaş (R) – Mediasch (G)
Oradea (R) – Grosswardein (G), Nagyvárad (H)
Sebeş (R) – Muhlbach (G)
Sibiu (R) – Hermannstadt (G), Cibinium (L)
Sighişoara (R) – Schässburg (G)
Suceava (R) – Soczow (G)
Timişoara (R) – Temeschburg (G), Temesvár (H)
Transylvania (R) – Siebenbürgen (G)

**YUGOSLAVIA**
*Jugoslavija*

Bar (Se) – Antivari (I)
Belgrade (E) – Beograd (Se)
Brač (Cr) – Brazza (I)
Cres (Cr) – Cherso (I)
Croatia (E) – Hrvatska (Cr)
Dalmatia (E) – Dalmacija (Cr)
Danube (River) (E) – Dunav (Cr)
Decçan (A) – Dečani (Se)
Dubrovnik (Cr) – Ragusa (I)
Hvar (Island) (Cr) – Lesina (I)
Koper (Sle) – Capodistria (I)
Korčula (Cr) – Curzola (I)

Kotor (Se) – Cattaro (I)
Krk (Island) (Cr) – Veglia (I)
Kvarner (Gulf of) (E) – Quarnero (I)
Ljubljana (Sle) – Laibach (G), Emona (L)
Lošinj (Island) (Cr) – Lussino (I)
Mljet (Island) (Cr) – Melita (I)
Montenegro (E) – Crna Gora (Se)
Novi Sad (Se) – Neusatz (G)
Ohrid (M) – Lihnidos (L)
Osijek (Cr) – Esseg (G)
Pejë (A) – Peć (Se)
Piran (Sle) – Pireos (Gk)
Plitvice Lakes (E) – Plitvicer Seen (G)
Porec (Cr) – Parenzo (I), Parentium (L)
Postojna Caves (E) – Adelsberger Grotten (G)
Prishtinë (A) – Priština (Se)
Pula (Cr) – Polensium (L)
Rab (Island) (Cr) – Arbe (G)
Rijeka (Cr) – Fiume (I)
Rovinj (Cr) – Rovigno (I)
Salona (L) – Solin
Serbia (E) – Srbija (Se)
Šibenik (Cr) – Sebenico (I)
Skopje (M) – Uskup (T), Scupi (L)
Split (Cr) – Spalato (I)
Titograd (Se) – Podgorica (Se)
Trieste (I, E) – Trst (Cr)
Trogir (Cr) – Trau (G)
Ulcinj (Se) – Ulqin (A), Dulcigno (I)
Vintgar Gorge (E) – Soteska Vintgar (Sle)
Zadar (Cr) – Zara (I), Iader (L)
Zagreb (Cr) – Agram (G)

**Miscellaneous**
Cologne (E) – Köln (G)
Hoek van Holland (D) – Hook of Holland (E)
Munich (E) – München (G)
Nuremberg (E) – Nürnberg (G)
Switzerland (E) – Schweiz (G)
Vienna (E) – Wien (G)

# International Automobile Signs

The following is a list of official country abbreviations that you may encounter on vehicles in Eastern Europe. Other abbreviations are likely to be unofficial, and often refer to a particular region, province or city. A motorised vehicle entering a foreign country must carry a sticker identifying its country of registration, though this rule is not always enforced.

A – Austria
AL – Albania
AND – Andorra
AUS – Australia
B – Belgium
BG – Bulgaria
CC – Consular Corps
CD – Diplomatic Corps
CDN – Canada
CH – Switzerland
CS – Czechoslovakia
CY – Cyprus
D – Germany
DDR – German Democratic Republic (the former East Germany)
DK – Denmark
DZ – Algeria
E – Spain
ET – Egypt
F – France
FL – Liechtenstein
GB – Great Britain
GR – Greece

H – Hungary
HKJ – Jordan
I – Italy
IL – Israel
IR – Iran
IRL – Ireland
IRQ – Iraq
IS – Iceland
J – Japan
L – Luxembourg
LAR – Libya
M – Malta
MA – Morocco
MC – Monaco
N – Norway
NL – Netherlands
NZ – New Zealand
P – Portugal
PL – Poland
RL – Lebanon
RO – Romania
RSM – San Marino
S – Sweden
SF – Finland
SU – Soviet Union
SYR – Syria
TN – Tunisia
TR – Turkey
USA – United States
V – Vatican
VN – Vietnam
YU – Yugoslavia
ZA – South Africa

# Index

## ABBREVIATIONS

AL – Albania
BG – Bulgaria
CS – Czechoslovakia

D – Germany
H – Hungary
PL – Poland

RO – Romania
YU – Yugoslavia

## MAPS

Alba Iulia (RO) 631
Albania 868
Arad (RO) 642
Badacsony (H) 511
Baia Mare (RO) 635
Balatonfüred (H) 506
Banská Bystrica (CS) 400-401
Bardejov (CS) 413
Belgrade (YU) 848
  Central Belgrade 850
Berlin (D)
  Around Berlin 108-109
  Around Köpenick 105
  Berlin Rapid Transit 124-125
  Central East Berlin 94-95
  Downtown West Berlin 102
  South of Tiergarten 98
  West Berlin 90-91
Bitola (YU) 864
Black Sea Coast (RO) 589
Bled (YU) 764
Braşov (RO) 618
Bratislava (CS) 391
  Central Bratislava 388
Brăila (RO) 602
Brno (CS) 382
Bucegi Mountains (RO) 614
Bucharest (RO) 572-573
  Bucharest Metro 583
  Central Bucharest 578
Budapest (H)
  Around Budapest 460-461
  Budapest Castle District 455
  Budapest Metro 471
  Budapest Railways 469
  Central Budapest 450-451
Bukovina (RO) 607
Bulgaria 648
  Bulgaria Railways 673
Burgas (BG) 697
  Around Burgas 701
České Budějovice (CS) 372
Český Krumlov (CS) 375
Cheb (CS) 365
Cluj-Napoca (RO) 628

Constanţa (RO) 595
  Central Constanţa 592-593
Czechoslovakia 308-309
  Czechoslovakia Railways 332-333
  Regions of Czechoslovakia 312
Częstochowa (PL) 255
Dalmatia, Central (YU) 817
Danube Delta (RO) 600
Debrecen (H) 531
Deva (RO) 633
Dresden (D) 134
Dubrovnik (YU) 825
  Around Dubrovnik 827
  Dubrovnik to Ulcinj 830
Durrës (AL) 889
Eastern Europe
  Eastern Europe Railways 15
  Eastern Europe Roads 14
Eastern Germany 55
  Eastern Germany Railways 84
Eger (H) 534
Eisenach (D) 154
Esztergom (H) 481
Făgăraş Mountains (RO) 626
Gdańsk (PL) 290
  Tri-City Area (PL) 287
Gdynia (PL) 286
Gniezno (PL) 272
Great Mazurian Lakes (PL) 301
Győr (H) 487
Halle (D) 160
Hévíz (H) 515
Hungary 422-423
  Hungary Railways 446-447
Hvar (YU) 818
Istria (YU) 780
Jajce (YU) 843
Julian Alps (YU) 767
Kaposvár (H) 517
Karlovy Vary (CS) 361
Kecskemét (H) 526
Keszthely (H) 513

Koper (YU) 782
Koprivshtitsa (BG) 689
Korčula (YU) 820
Košice (CS) 416
Kőszeg (H) 496
Kraków (PL) 246
  Around Kraków 249
Kutná Hora (CS) 358
Kvarner, Gulf of (YU) 795
Leipzig (D) 142
Levoča (CS) 409
Ljubljana (YU) 759
Lublin (PL) 225
Lutherstadt Wittenberg (D) 163
Malá Fatra (CS) 398
Mariánské Lázně (CS) 368
Moritzburg (D) 139
Mostar (YU) 836
Nesebâr (BG) 702
Novi Sad (YU) 845
Ohrid (YU) 861
Olsztyn (PL) 297
Opole (PL) 258
Oradea (RO) 639
Oświęcim (PL) 253
Pécs (H) 521
  Central Pécs 519
Piran (YU) 786
  Around Piran 784
Pleven (BG) 711
Plitvice National Park (YU) 777
Plovdiv (BG) 692
Plzeň (CS) 370
Poland 178-179
  Poland Railways 208-209
Poreč (YU) 788
Potsdam (D) 128
Poznań (PL) 266
Prague (CS) 344
  Central Prague 338-339
  Prague Castle 342
  Prague Metro 355
  Prague Railways 354
Prešov (CS) 411
Przemyśl (PL) 231

Pula (YU) 792
Rab (YU) 801
Rijeka (YU) 797
Rila Mountains (BG) 686
Romania 544
    Romania Railways 569
    Regions of Romania 550
Rostock (D) 170
Rovinj (YU) 790
Ruse (BG) 720
Rzeszów (PL) 234
Salona (YU) 815
Sarajevo (YU) 840-841
Sárospatak (H) 539
Schwerin (D) 166
Šibenik (YU) 807
Sibiu (RO) 625
    Central Sibiu 623
Sighişoara (RO) 621
Siófok (H) 503
Skopje (YU) 858
Sofia (BG) 680
    Central Sofia 676

Sopron (H) 492-493
    Central Sopron 490
Sozopol (BG) 699
Split (YU) 811
    Around Split 813
Stralsund (D) 173
Suceava (RO) 609
Świnoujście (PL) 281
Szczecin (PL) 278
Szeged (H) 528
Székesfehérvár (H) 501
Szentendre (H) 473
Szigetvár (H) 523
Szombathely (H) 498
Tata (H) 484
Tatra National Park (PL)
    240-241
Telč (CS) 378
Tihany (H) 508
Timişoara (RO) 644
Tiranë (AL) 887
Tîrgu Jiu (RO) 587
Toruń (PL) 274
Trenčín (CS) 395

Tulcea (RO) 598-599
Vác (H) 476
Varna (BG) 704
Veliko Târnovo (BG) 716
Veszprém (H) 509
Visegrád (H) 478
Vysoké Tatry (CS) 402
Warsaw (PL) 214
    Around Warsaw 218
Weimar (D) 148
Wismar (D) 169
Wrocław (PL) 260
    East of Wrocław 263
Yugoslavia 728
    Yugoslavia Political
        Divisions 731
    Yugoslavia Railways 755
Zadar (YU) 805
Zagreb (YU) 770
    Gradec & Kaptol 772
    Zagreb Tram Routes 775
Zakopane (PL) 237
Zamość (PL) 229
Znojmo (CS) 380

---

## TEXT

Map references are in **bold** type

Ada Island (YU) 834
Adamclisi (RO) 543, 588, 589
Aggtelek (H) 537
Alba Iulia (RO) 629-632, **631**
Albania 867-897, **868**
Albena (BG) 707, 708
Alia, Ramiz (AL) 871-872
Altefähr (D) 174
Amerika (CS) 364
Apolonia (AL) 890-891
Apriltsi (BG) 714
Aquincum (H) 457
Arad (RO) 641-643, **642**
Arbanasi (BG) 718
Arberit (AL) 869, 895
Auschwitz, see Oświęcim

Babele (RO) 615
Bachkovo Monastery (BG) 695
Bad Bibra (D) 162
Bad Schandau (D) 136
Badacsony (H) 510-512, **511**
Badija Island (YU) 821
Baia Mare (RO) 634-636, **635**
Băile Felix (RO) 640-641
Bakony Hills (H) 500
Balaton Lake (H) 500-516
Balatonfüred (H) 505-507, **506**

Balchik (BG) 708
Baltic Sea (D) 165, 171
Banat (RO) 638-645
Bankya (BG) 684-685
Banská Bystrica (CS) 399-401,
    **400-401**
Bar (YU) 833
Baradla Caves (H) 537
Baraj Firiza (RO) 636
Bardejov (CS) 412-414, **413**
Bardejovské Kúpele (CS)
    414-415
Baška (YU) 799-800
Bay of Kotor, see Kotor, Bay of
Belgrade (YU) 847-853, **848,**
    **850**
Belsó Lake, Tihany (H) 507
Berat (AL) 892-893
Bergen (D) 175
Berlin (D) 86-126, **90-91, 94-95,**
    **108-109, 124-125**
Bessarabia (RO) 603
Bieszczady Mountains (PL) 232
Binz (D) 175
Biogradska Gora National Park
    (YU) 834
Biogradsko jezero (YU) 834
Birkenau, see Brzezinka
Bismarck, Chancellor Otto von
    (D) 54, 88, 165

Bistrica Pass (YU) 856
Bistrica River (YU) 856
Bitola (YU) 863-865, **864**
Black Sea Coast (BG) 696-708
    (RO) **589**
Bled (YU) 763-765, **764**
Bode Valley (D) 157
Bohemia (CS) 307-310, see also
    Central Bohemia, South
    Bohemia, West Bohemia
Bohinj (YU) 766
Bohinjska Bistrica (YU) 768
Borovets (BG) 665, 685, 687
Börzsöny Mountains (H) 472
Bosnia-Hercegovina (YU)
    835-844
Břeclav (CS) 385-386
Bran (RO) 616-617
Bran Castle (RO) 615, 616
Brandenburg (D) 126-132
Braşov (RO) 617-620, **618**
Bratislava (CS) 386-393, **388,**
    **391**
Brioni (YU) 793-794
Brioni National Park (YU) 794
Brno (CS) 381-385, **382**
Brzezinka (PL) 252-254
Bucegi Carpathians, see Bucegi
    Mountains
Bucegi Mountains (RO) 615, **614**

Bucharest (RO) 571-583,
 **572-573, 578, 583**
Buchenwald (D) 150
Buda (H) 454-456
Buda Hills (H) 457-458
Budapest (H) 449-472, **450-451,
 455, 460-461, 469, 471**
Budva (YU) 832-833
Bugac (H) 527
Bükk National Park (H) 536
Bukovina (RO) 607-612, **607**
Bulgaria 647-725, **648, 673**
Bumbeşti-Jiu (RO) 586
Buna (YU) 837
Bunë River (AL) 896
Burgas (BG) 696-699, **697, 701**
Buşteni (RO) 613, 615
Butrint (AL) 892
Byala Reka (BG) 714
Bydgoszcz (PL) 275-276

Cape Galata (BG) 706
Carpathian Mountains 21 (CS)
 313 (RO) 560, 561
Castle District (H) 464
Castle Hill (H) 454-456, 465
Cavtat (YU) 826
Ceauşescu, Nicolae 19 (RO)
 546-548, 576
Central Bohemia (CS) 356-359
Central Slovakia (CS) 393-401
Cernavodă (RO) 589
Červený Kláštor (CS) 408
České Budějovice (CS) 371-374,
 **372**
Český Krumlov (CS) 374-376,
 **375**
Cetatea Histria (RO) 597
Cetinje (YU) 831-832
Chalka (BG) 707
Charlottenburg (D) 106
Cheb (CS) 364-366, **365**
Chochołów (PL) 239
Čingov (CS) 408
Cluj-Napoca (RO) 626-629, **628**
Colditz (D) 133
Comecon 18, 20-21
Complex Malyovitsa (BG) 685-
 687
Constanţa (RO) 592-596, **592-
 593, 595**
Corbeni (RO) 585
Costineşti (RO) 590
Cottbus (D) 61
Count Dracula's Castle (RO)
 585-586
Count Dracula's Citadel (RO)
 585
Crişan (RO) 600

Crişana (RO) 638-645
Croatia (YU) 769-780
Crveni otok (YU) 789
Curtea de Argeş (RO) 585
Czarny Staw Lake (PL) 239
Czechoslovakia 307-418, **308-
 309, 312, 332-334**
Częstochowa (PL) 254-256, **255**

Dalmatia (YU) 802-824, **817**
Dalmatian Coast 22
Danube Bend (H) 470-483
Danube Canal (RO) 550, 589
Danube Delta (RO) 597-603, **600**
Danube River 16, 22, 50
Debrecen (H) 530-533, **531**
Dečan, see Visoki Dečani
 Monastery
Deva (RO) 632, **633**
Dimitrovgrad (BG) 653
Dinaric Alps (YU) 803
Dîrste (RO) 619
Dobogókő (H) 479
Dobruja (RO) 588-597
Domažlice (CS) 322, 360
Dömös (H) 479
Dřenice (CS) 364
Drăgoeni (RO) 586
Dresden (D) 133-139, **134**
Drin River (AL) 896
Drobeta-Turnu Severin (RO)
 587-588
Druzhba (BG) 707
Dubrovnik (YU) 824-829, **825,
 827, 830**
Dunajec Gorge (CS) 407-408
Dunajec River (CS) 404
Đurđevića Tara (YU) 835
Durmitor National Park (YU)
 834-835
Durrës (AL) 889-890, **889**

East Slovakia (CS) 401-418
Eastern Germany 53-175
Eforie Nord (RO) 591-592
Eger (H) 533-537, **534**
Eisenach (D) 153, **154**
Elbasan (AL) 893-894
Elbe River (D) 89, 132, 136,
 156, 158
Elbląg Canal (PL) 298
Erfurt (D) 151-152
Esterházy Palace, Fertőd (H) 495
Esztergom (H) 480-483, **481**
Etăr (BG) 715
Eumolpias (BG) 694

Făgăraş Mountains (RO) 586,
 625, **626**

Fertőd (H) 495
Fertőrákos (H) 494
Fier (AL) 890-891
Fonyód (H) 512
Františkovy Lázně (CS) 366
Freyburg (D) 162
Frombork (PL) 299-300

Galata (BG) 706
Galaţi (RO) 601
Gdańsk (PL) 289-294, **290**
Gdynia (PL) 285-286, **285**
Gellért Hill (H) 467
Gerlachovský štít (CS) 313, 401
Giżycko (PL) 302-303
Gjirokastër (AL) 891
Gniezno (PL) 271-272, **272**
Göhren (D) 175
Golden Sands (BG) 707-708
Gorna Oryahovitsa (BG) 672
Granchar Lake (BG) 687
Great Plain (H) 524-533
Grosser Müggelsee (D) 89, 104,
 110
Grünewald (D) 89
Grunwald (PL) 298-299
Gulf of Kvarner, see Kvarner,
 Gulf of
Gura Humorului (RO) 611-612
Győr (H) 486-489, **487**
Gypsies 20

Habsburg Dynasty 17 (CS) 308
 (H) 421
Halle (D) 159-162, **160**
Halta Cirta (RO) 626
Han i Hotit (AL) 896
Harkány (H) 524
Harz Mountains (D) 156
Havel River (D) 89, 107
Havel, Václav (CS) 311
Hel (PL) 286-288
Heraclea (YU) 863
Hévíz (H) 515-516, **515**
Hiddensee Island (D) 174, 175
Hisarya (BG) 691-693
Histria (RO) 597
Hluboká nad Vltavou (CS) 373
Horezu (RO) 586
Horný Smokovec (CS) 404, 406
Hortobágy (H) 533
Hoxha, Enver (AL) 869, 871
Hradčany (CS) 336, 341-343
Hrebienok (CS) 403
Hula Daneş (RO) 622
Humor (RO) 611
Hunedoara (RO) 632-634
Hungary 419-540, **422-423, 446-
 447**

Hvar (YU) 816-819, **818**

Iaşi (RO) 603-606, **604**
Ilfeld (D) 155
Ilidža (YU) 840
Illyria (AL) 867
Illyrians (AL) 867
Ilm River (D) 147
Iron Gate (RO) 584, 588 (YU) 846
Istria (YU) 781-794, **780**
Ivangrad (YU) 854
Izola (YU) 783
Izvorul Rece (RO) 616

Jagiello Dynasty (PL) 179-180
Jajce (YU) 843-844, **843**
János-hegy (H) 457
Jaruzelski, General Wojciech (PL) 182-183
Javorina (CS) 407
Jerolim Island (YU) 817
Jezero, see Bohinj
Jósvafő Caves (H) 537
Julian Alps (YU) 763, 766, **767**
Jupiter (RO) 590

Kádár, János (H) 424, 425
Kaposvár (H) 516-518, **517**
Kardeljevo (YU) 802
Karlovo (BG) 714
Karlovy Vary (CS) 360-364, **361**
Karlštejn (CS) 356
Karlshorst (D) 104-106
Kastrioti, George (AL) 895
Kaylâka Park (BG) 712, 713
Kazanlâk (BG) 714-715
Kazimierz Dolny (PL) 228
Kecskemét (H) 525, **526**
Keszthely (H) 512-515, **513**
Kętrzyn (PL) 303
King Zog, see Zogu, Ahmet
Kirchdorf (D) 168
Kiskunság National Park (H) 527
Kladow (D) 107
Kloster (D) 175
Kołobrzeg (PL) 283
Kolín (CS) 359
Komárom (H) 485-486
Königstein (D) 136
Konopiště (CS) 356-357
Köpenick (D) 104-106, **105**
Koper (YU) 781-783, **782**
Koprivshtitsa (BG) 688-691, **689**
Korana Gorge (YU) 778
Korčula (YU) 820-822, **820**
Korçë (AL) 894-895
Kornati Islands (YU) 808
Kórnik (PL) 268-269

Košice (CS) 415-418, **416**
Kosovo (YU) 853-856
Kőszeg (H) 495-497, **496**
Kotor (YU) 831
Kotor, Bay of (YU) 733, 802
Kraków (PL) 244-252, **246, 249**
Kreuzberg (D) 89
Krk (YU) 799
Krka National Park (YU) 808
Krujë (AL) 895-896
Kumrovec (YU) 776
Kutná Hora (CS) 357-359, **358**
Kuźnice (PL) 238, 239
Kvarner, Gulf of (YU) 794-802, **795**

Lake Łuknajno (PL) 304
Lake Belona (RO) 591
Lake Ciric (RO) 606
Lake Cseke-tó (H) 483
Lake Gyógy (H) 515, 516
Lake Mamaia (RO) 596
Lake Nidzkie (PL) 305
Lake Öreg-tó (H) 483, 485
Łańcut (PL) 232-233
Lapad Peninsula (YU) 826
Łeba (PL) 283-285
Leipzig (D) 141-146, **142**
Lepence (H) 479
Lesnica (CS) 408
Levoča (CS) 408-410, **409**
Lezhë (AL) 896
Lidice (CS) 310
Lidzbark Warmiński (PL) 299
Little Carpathian Mountains (CS) 389, 390
Ljubljana (YU) 758-762, **759**
Ljubovo (BG) 715
Łódź (PL) 184, 224
Loket (CS) 362
Lokrum Island National Park (YU) 826
Lomnický štít (CS) 404
Lopar (YU) 802
Lošinj Island (YU) 798
Loschwitz (D) 136
Lower Silesia (PL) 257
Lublin (PL) 224-228, **225**
Lumbarda (YU) 822
Luther, Martin 16 (D) 64, 151, 153, 162-164
Lutherstadt Wittenberg (D) 162-165, **163**
Łysa Polana (PL) 244

Macedonia (YU) 856-865
Macocha Abyss (CS) 312, 384
Madara (BG) 723-724
Magdeburg (D) 158-159

Magistrála Trail (CS) 401, 403, 405
Majdanek (PL) 226
Malá Fatra (CS) 397-399, **398**
Malá Fatra National Park (CS) 397
Malá Studená Valley (CS) 403
Malbork (PL) 294-295
Mali Lošinj (YU) 798-799
Maliuc (RO) 600
Małopolska (PL) 224-256
Mamaia (RO) 596-597
Manasija Monastery, Serbia (YU) 853
Mangalia (RO) 589-591
Maramureş (RO) 634-638
Margaret Island (H) 458, 463, 467
Mariánské Lázně (CS) 366-369, **368**
Maritsa River (BG) 688
Matka (YU) 859
Mazuria (PL) 294-305
Mazurian Lakes (PL) 300-305, **301**
Mecklenburg-Pomerania (D) 165-175
Mecsek Hills (H) 520, 522
Međugorje (YU) 838-839
Meissen (D) 140-141
Mělník (CS) 356
Międzyzdroje (PL) 282-283
Mikołajki (PL) 303-304
Milošević, Slobodan (YU) 730-732
Mirkovo (BG) 691
Misina Peak (H) 520
Miskolc (H) 449, 533, 537
Mittel Teich (D) 137, 140
Mljet Island (YU) 823-824
Mljet National Park (YU) 823
Mohács (H) 421, 437
Moldavia (RO) 603-606
Moldoviţa (RO) 611
Montenegro (YU) 829-835
Moravia (CS) 377-386
Moravian Karst, see Moravský Kras
Moravský Kras (CS) 311, 384
Moritzburg (D) 137, 139-140, **139**
Morskie Oko Lake (PL) 238
Mosta (BG) 712
Mostar (YU) 836-837, **836**
Mt Botev (BG) 714
Mt Gerlach, see Gerlachovský štít
Mt Giewont (PL) 238
Mt Gubałówka (PL) 238

Mt Ilija (YU) 823
Mt Kasprowy Wierch (PL) 238
Mt Lovćen National Park (YU) 832
Mt Moldoveanu (RO) 626
Mt Negoiu (RO) 626
Mt Rysy (PL) 239
Mt Sljeme (YU) 773
Mt Trebević (YU) 840, 841
Mt Triglav (YU) 765, 766-768
Mt Vitosha (BG) 679
Murfatlar (RO) 589
Murighiol (RO) 600
Musala Peak (BG) 651
Museum Island (D) 96-97, 106

Nagy, Imre (H) 424 (H) 458
Nagyalföld, see Great Plain
Nagycenk (H) 494
Nagyerdő Forest Park (H) 530, 532
Nagymaros (H) 479, 480
Nagy-Villám (H) 479
National Parks
  Biogradska Gora National Park (YU) 834
  Brioni National Park (YU) 794
  Bükk National Park (H) 536
  Durmitor National Park (YU) 834-835
  Kiskunság National Park (H) 527
  Krka National Park (YU) 808
  Lokrum Island National Park (YU) 826
  Malá Fatra National Park (CS) 397
  Mljet National Park (YU) 823
  Mt Lovćen National Park (YU) 832
  Ojców National Park (PL) 248
  Paklenica National Park (YU) 803
  Pieniny National Park (CS) 407
  Plitvice National Park (YU) 776-779, 777
  Retezat National Park (RO) 587
  Slovenský raj National Park (CS) 408
  Słowiński National Park (PL) 284
  Tatra National Park (PL) 242, 240-241 (CS) 401
  Wolin National Park (PL) 283
Naumburg (D) 162
Neptun (RO) 590, 591, see also Neptun-Olimp
Neptun-Olimp (RO) 591
Nesebâr (BG) 701-703, 702
Neuendorf (D) 175

New Bitola (YU) 863
Nordhausen (D) 155
Northern Hungary (H) 533-540
Nova Gorica (YU) 768-769
Nová Lesná (CS) 405
Novi Pazar (YU) 853
Novi Sad (YU) 844-846, 845
Nový Smokovec (CS) 405
Nowa Huta (PL) 248
Nowy Sącz (PL) 234-236

Óbuda (H) 457, 465
Obzor (BG) 700
Ocna Sibiului (RO) 624
Ohrid (YU) 860-863, 861
Ohrit Lake (AL) 872
Ojców National Park (PL) 248
Olimp (RO) 590, 591, see also Neptun-Olimp
Olsztyn (PL) 295-298, 297
Omul (RO) 615
Opatija (YU) 798
Opole (PL) 257-259
Oradea (RO) 638-640, 639
Orebić (YU) 822-823
Öregvár Castle, Tata (H) 483
Osijek (YU) 779
Oświęcim (PL) 252-254, 253
Ovidiu Island (RO) 596

Paklenica National Park (YU) 803
Pamporovo (BG) 665
Pannonhalma (H) 489-490
Pannonia (H) 420, 457 (YU) 727
Pap Island (H) 474
Pasieka Island (PL) 257, 258
Patrijaršija Monastery, Pejë (YU) 855
Pécs (H) 518-523, 519, 521
Pejë (YU) 854-855
Peleş Castle (RO) 613
Pernik (BG) 653 (BG) 664
Pest (H) 456
Pfaueninsel (D) 107
Pieniny National Park (CS) 407
Pilis Mountains (H) 472
Pilis Nature Reserve (H) 479
Pillnitz (D) 136
Piran (YU) 785-787, 784, 786
Pirin Massif (BG) 652
Pleven (BG) 710-713, 711
Pliska (BG) 724-725
Plitvice National Park (YU) 776-779, 777
Plovdiv (BG) 688, 693-695, 692
Plzeň (CS) 369-371, 370
Počitelj (YU) 837
Poel Island (D) 168

Pogradec (AL) 894
Poiana Braşov (RO) 619
Poienari Citadel, see Count Dracula's Citadel
Pokljuka (YU) 765
Poland 177-305, 178-179, 208-209
Pomerania (PL) 276-294
Pomorie (BG) 700
Poprad-tatry (CS) 407
Popradské Pleso (CS) 405
Poreč (YU) 787-789, 788
Portorož (YU) 783-784
Postojna (YU) 762
Postojna Caves (YU) 762
Potsdam (D) 89, 127-132, 128
Poznań (PL) 265-271, 266
Pracký Kopec (CS) 384
Prague (CS) 336-356, 338-339, 342, 344, 354, 355
Predeal (RO) 616
Preobrazhenski Monastery (BG) 718
Preslav (BG) 723-724
Prešov (CS) 410-412, 412
Primas Island (H) 482
Prizren (YU) 855-856
Przemyśl (PL) 230-232, 231
Pszczyna (PL) 253
Pula (YU) 791-793, 792
Punkevní (CS) 384
Punta Corrente Forest Park (YU) 789
Putbus (D) 175
Putna (RO) 610

Quedlinburg (D) 157-158

Rab (YU) 800-802, 801
Rába River (H) 437
Rădăuţi (RO) 610
Rákóczi Castle, Sárospatak (H) 540
Raška (YU) 853
Ravanica Monastery, Serbia (YU) 853
Reinberg (D) 174
Remeteségpuszta (H) 485
Retezat National Park (RO) 587
Rijeka (YU) 794-798, 797
Rila Monastery (BG) 687-688
Rila Mountains (BG) 685-687, 686
Rîşnov (RO) 616-617, 619
Rodopi Mountains (BG) 694, 695
Rogalin (PL) 268-269
Romania 541-645, 544, 550, 569
Rostock (D) 170, 170

Rovinj (YU) 789-791, **790**
Rožaj (YU) 854
Rozafa Fortress (AL) 897
Ruciane-nida (PL) 305
Rügen Island (D) 174 (D) 175
Rugovo Gorge (YU) 855
Ruse (BG) 719-722, **720**
Rysy Peak (CS) 404
Rzeszów (PL) 233-234, **234**

Sachsenhausen (D) 107
Salona (YU) 815-816, **815**
Samokov (BG) 685
Săpînța (RO) 637
Sarajevo (YU) 839-842, **840-841**
Sarandë (AL) 872, 892
Sărat Lake (RO) 602
Sárospatak (H) 538-540, **539**
Sassnitz (D) 175
Saturn (RO) 589, 590
Saxony (D) 132-146
Saxony-Anhalt (D) 156-165
Schmarl-Dorf (D) 171
Schwerin (D) 165-168, **166**
Schweriner See (D) 167
Seaside Gardens (BG) 705, 707
Seeburg (D) 161
Sellin (D) 175
Serbia (YU) 846-853
Seven Lakes (BG) 687
Shipka (BG) 715
Shkodër (AL) 896-897
Shumen (BG) 722-723
Šibenik (YU) 806-808, **807**
Sibiu (RO) 622-625, **623, 625**
Sighetu Marmației (RO) 636-638
Sighișoara (RO) 620-622, **621**
Siklós (H) 524
Sikonda (H) 516
Silesia (PL) 257-265
Sinaia (RO) 613-616
Siófok (H) 502-505, **503**
Skalnaté Pleso (CS) 404
Skanderbeg, see Kastrioti, George
Škocjan Caves (YU) 762-763
Skopje (YU) 857-860, **858**
Slavkov u Brna (CS) 384
Slavkovský štít (CS) 404
Sljeme, see Mt Sljeme
Slovak National Uprising (CS) 310, 399
Slovak Paradise, see Slovenský raj
Slovakia (CS) 309-310, 311
Slovenia (YU) 758-769
Slovenský raj (CS) 312
Slovenský raj National Park (CS) 408

Słowiński National Park (PL) 284
Smradlivo ezero (BG) 687
Snagov (RO) 584-585
Snilovské sedlo (CS) 397
Sofia (BG) 675-684, **676, 680**
Solidarity Trade Union 18, 182-183, 292
Solidarność, see Solidarity Trade Union
Sömmerda (D) 150
Sopoćani Monastery (YU) 853
Sopot (PL) 288-289
Sopron (H) 490-495, **490, 492-493**
South Bohemia (CS) 371-377
Southern Transdanubia (H) 516-524
Sozopol (BG) 699-701, **699**
Spandau (D) 89 (D) 107
Spišská Kapitula (CS) 410
Spišská Nová Ves (CS) 408
Spišské Podhradie (CS) 410
Spišský hrad (CS) 410
Split (YU) 809-815, **811, 813**
Spree River (D) 89, 110
Stahlbrode (D) 174
Stara Fužina (YU) 766
Stará Ľubovňa (CS) 408
Stara Planina (BG) 651, 713
Starigrad (YU) 819-820
Stary Sącz (PL) 236
Starý Dvor (CS) 399
Starý Smokovec (CS) 403-407
Štefanová (CS) 397
Stipanska Island (YU) 817
Stralsund (D) 172-175, **173**
Strážnice (CS) 385
Štrbské Pleso (CS) 403, 406
Struga (YU) 862
Stubnitz (D) 175
Studentica Monastery (YU) 853
Subotica (YU) 846
Suceava (RO) 608-610, **609**
Sulina (RO) 601
Sunny Beach (BG) 701
Süsser See (D) 161
Sveta Gora (BG) 718
Sveta Gora Park (BG) 718
Sveti Nikola (YU) 787
Sveti Stefan (YU) 832
Świnoujście (PL) 280-282, **281**
Szamos River (H) 437
Szczecin (PL) 277-280, **278**
Szeged (H) 527-530, **528**
Székesfehérvár (H) 500-502, **501**
Szentendre (H) 472-475, **473**
Szentendre Island (H) 475, 476
Szépasszonyvölgy (H) 535

Szigetvár (H) 523-524, **523**
Szombathely (H) 497-500, **498**

Tábor (CS) 376-377
Tapolca Basin (H) 500
Tara Canyon (YU) 835
Tara River (YU) 835
Tata (H) 483-485, 484
Tatra Mountains (PL) 236-244
Tatra National Park (PL) 242, **240-241** (CS) 401
Tatranská Lomnica (CS) 403-404, 406
Tatranská Štrba (CS) 404, 406
Techirghiol Lake (RO) 591
Tegel (D) 89
Telč (CS) 377-379, **378**
Țepeș, Vlad (RO) 543, 584
Teutonic Knights (PL) 276, 294-295, 298, see also Malbork and Grunwald
Thale (D) 157
Thrace (BG) 688-695
Thuringia (D) 147-155
Tiergarten (D) 89, 97-100, **98**
Tihany (H) 507-508, 509, **508**
Timișoara (RO) 643-645, **644**
Tiranë (AL) 886-889, **887**
Tîrgu Jiu (RO) 586-587, **587**
Tisza River (H) 437
Tito, Josip Broz (YU) 729-730, 793
Titograd (YU) 830, 854
Tjulbeto Park (BG) 714
Tokaj (H) 537-538
Toponár (H) 517
Torgau (D) 57
Toruń (PL) 272-275, **274**
Transdanubia (H) 483-524, see also Western Transdanubia and Southern Transdanubia
Transylvania (RO) 612-634
Travnik (YU) 842-843
Trenčín (CS) 394-396, **395**
Trenčianske Teplice (CS) 394, 396
Triglav, see Mt Triglav
Trogir (YU) 808-809
Troyan (BG) 713-714
Trstenik (YU) 812
Tsarevets Hill (BG) 717
Tulcea (RO) 598-600, 601, **598-599**

Ucevița (RO) 610-611
Ulcinj (YU) 833-834, **830**
Unstrut Valley (D) 162
Upper Silesia (PL) 184, 257

Vác (H) 475-477, **476**
Valley of Roses (BG) 714
Várhegy, see Castle Hill
Varna (BG) 703-707, **704**
Vela Luka (YU) 822
Veľká Studená Valley (CS) 403
Veli Lošinj (YU) 798
Velika Plaža (YU) 833
Veliki Brioni (YU) 793, 794
Veliko Tărnovo (BG) 715-719,
    **716**
Venus (RO) 590
Veszprém (H) 509-510, **509**
Vidin (BG) 709-710
Vintgar Gorge (YU) 763
Visegrád (H) 477-480,**478**
Visoki Dečani Monastery,
    Dečan (YU) 855
Vitte (D) 175
Vlorë (AL) 869, 870, 872, 891
Vltava River (CS) 312, 336,
    347, 350
Vojvodina (YU) 844-846
Voroneţ (RO) 611

Vöröstó (H) 537
Vrátna Valley (CS) 397
Vyšehrad (CS) 345
Vysoké Tatry (CS) 401-407, **402**

Wałęsa, Lech (PL) 182-183
Wallachia (RO) 584-588
Wannsee (D) 107
Warnemünde (D) 171-172
Warnow River (D) 170, 171
Warsaw (PL) 213-224, **214, 218**
Warsaw Pact 18
Weimar (D) 147-151, **148**
Weissensee (D) 150
Weisser Hirsch (D) 137
Wernigerode (D) 156-157
West Bohemia (CS) 359-371
West Slovaca (CS) 393-401
Western Transdanubia (H) 483-
    500
Westerplatte, Gdańsk (PL) 180,
    289, 292
Wieliczka Salt Mines (PL) 248
Wielkopolska (PL) 265-276

Wilczy Szaniec (PL) 303
Wismar (D) 168-169, **169**
Wittenberg, see Lutherstadt
    Wittenberg
Wolin National Park (PL) 283
Wrocław (PL) 259-265, **260, 263**

Yugoslavia 727-865, **728, 731,
    755**

Žabljak (YU) 834, 835
Zadar (YU) 803-806, **805**
Zagreb (YU) 769-776, **770, 775**
Zakopane (PL) 236-244, **237**
Zamosć (PL) 228-230, **229**
Zelena Lacuna (YU) 787
Zhivkov, Todor (BG) 650-651
Zierow (D) 169
Žilina (CS) 396-397
Zlaté piesky (CS) 391-392
Znojmo (CS) 379-381, **380**
Zogu, Ahmet (AL) 869
Zvolen (CS) 400

# Where Can You Find Out...

HOW to save money on a flight?

WHERE to get bicycles in RAC?

WHAT to expect from the harbour boat people in Peru?

WHEN and where to see the newest mansion?

# Where Can You Find Out.........

*HOW to get a Laotian visa in Bangkok?*

*WHERE to go birdwatching in PNG?*

*WHAT to expect from the police if you're robbed in Peru?*

*WHEN you can go to see cow races in Australia?*

## In the Lonely Planet Newsletter!

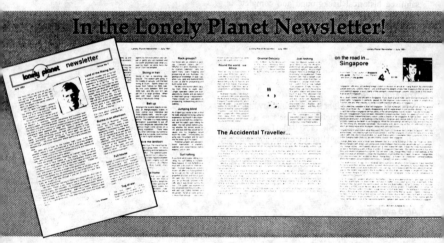

## Every issue includes:

- *a letter from Lonely Planet founders Tony and Maureen Wheeler*
- *a letter from an author 'on the road'*
- *the most entertaining or informative reader's letter we've received*
- *the latest news on new and forthcoming releases from Lonely Planet*
- *and all the latest travel news from all over the world*

# Guides to Europe

### Iceland, Greenland & the Faroe Islands - a travel survival kit
Iceland, Greenland and the Faroes contain some of the most beautiful
wilderness areas in the world. This practical guidebook will help travellers
discover the dramatic beauty of this region, no matter what their budget.

### USSR - a travel survival kit
Invaluable advice on getting around and beating red tape for individual
and group travellers alike. This comprehensive guide includes an un-
sanitised historical background and complete information on arts and
culture. It has over 130 reliable maps, and all place names are given in
Cyrillic script.

### Trekking in Spain
Aimed at both overnight trekkers and day hikers, this guidebook includes
useful maps and full details on hikes in some of Spain's most beautiful
wilderness areas – the Sierra Nevada, Las Alpujarras, Western and Central
Gredos in Castilla, the High Pyrenees, Picos de Europa and Mallorca.

*Also available:*
*Russian* phrasebook

# Lonely Planet Guidebooks

Lonely Planet guidebooks cover every accessible part of Asia as well as Australia, the Pacific, South America, Africa, the Middle East and parts of North America and Europe. There are four series: *travel survival kits*, covering a single country for a range of budgets; *shoestring guides* with compact information for low-budget travel in a major region; *walking guides*; and *phrasebooks*.

## Australia & the Pacific
Australia
Bushwalking in Australia
Islands of Australia's Great Barrier Reef
Fiji
Micronesia
New Caledonia
New Zealand
Tramping in New Zealand
Papua New Guinea
Papua New Guinea phrasebook
Rarotonga & the Cook Islands
Samoa
Solomon Islands
Sydney
Tahiti & French Polynesia
Tonga
Vanuatu

## South-East Asia
Bali & Lombok
Burma
Burmese phrasebook
Indonesia
Indonesia phrasebook
Malaysia, Singapore & Brunei
Philippines
Pilipino phrasebook
Singapore
South-East Asia on a shoestring
Thai Hill Tribes phrasebook
Thailand
Thai phrasebook
Vietnam, Laos & Cambodia

## North-East Asia
China
Hong Kong, Macau & Canton
Japan
Japanese phrasebook
Korea
Korean phrasebook
Mandarin Chinese phrasebook
North-East Asia on a shoestring
Taiwan
Tibet
Tibet phrasebook

## West Asia
Trekking in Turkey
Turkey
Turkish phrasebook
West Asia on a shoestring

**Indian Ocean**
Madagascar & Comoros
Maldives & Islands of the East Indian Ocean
Mauritius, Réunion & Seychelles

# Mail Order

Lonely Planet guidebooks are distributed worldwide and are sold by good bookshops everywhere. They are also available by mail order from Lonely Planet, so if you have difficulty finding a title please write to us. US and Canadian residents should write to Embarcadero West, 112 Linden St, Oakland CA 94607, USA and residents of other countries to PO Box 617, Hawthorn, Victoria 3122, Australia.

## Europe
Eastern Europe on a shoestring
Iceland, Greenland & the Faroe Islands
Russian phrasebook
Trekking in Spain
USSR

## Indian Subcontinent
Bangladesh
India
Hindi/Urdu phrasebook
Trekking in the Indian Himalaya
Karakoram Highway
Kashmir, Ladakh & Zanskar
Nepal
Trekking in the Nepal Himalaya
Nepal phrasebook
Pakistan
Sri Lanka
Sri Lanka phrasebook

## Africa
Africa on a shoestring
Central Africa
East Africa
Kenya
Swahili phrasebook
Morocco, Algeria & Tunisia
Moroccan Arabic phrasebook
West Africa

## North America
Alaska
Canada
Hawaii

## Mexico
Baja California
Mexico

## South America
Argentina
Bolivia
Brazil
Brazilian phrasebook
Chile & Easter Island
Colombia
Ecuador & the Galápagos Islands
Latin American Spanish phrasebook
Peru
Quechua phrasebook
South America on a shoestring

## Central America
Costa Rica
La Ruta Maya

## Middle East
Egypt & the Sudan
Egyptian Arabic phrasebook
Israel
Jordan & Syria
Yemen

## The Lonely Planet Story

Lonely Planet published its first book in 1973 in response to the numerous 'How did you do it?' questions Maureen and Tony Wheeler were asked after driving, bussing, hitching, sailing and railing their way from England to Australia.

Written at a kitchen table and hand collated, trimmed and stapled, *Across Asia on the Cheap* became an instant local bestseller, inspiring thoughts of another book.

Eighteen months in South-East Asia resulted in their second guide, *South-East Asia on a shoestring*, which they put together in a backstreet Chinese hotel in Singapore in 1975. The 'yellow bible' as it quickly became known to backpackers around the world, soon became *the* guide to the region. It has sold well over ½ million copies and is now in its 6th edition, still retaining its familiar yellow cover.

Today there are over 80 Lonely Planet titles – books that have that same adventurous approach to travel as those early guides; books that 'assume you know how to get your luggage off the carousel' as one reviewer put it.

Although Lonely Planet initially specialised in guides to Asia, they now cover most regions of the world, including the Pacific, South America, Africa, the Middle East and Eastern Europe. The list of *walking guides* and *phrasebooks* (for 'unusual' languages such as Quechua, Swahili, Nepalese and Egyptian Arabic) is also growing rapidly.

The emphasis continues to be on travel for independent travellers. Tony and Maureen still travel for several months of each year and play an active part in the writing, updating and quality control of Lonely Planet's guides.

They have been joined by over 50 authors, 40 staff – mainly editors, cartographers, & designers – at our office in Melbourne, Australia, and another 10 at our US office in Oakland, California. Travellers themselves also make a valuable contribution to the guides through the feedback we receive in thousands of letters each year.

The people at Lonely Planet strongly believe that travellers can make a positive contribution to the countries they visit, both through their appreciation of the countries' culture, wildlife and natural features, and through the money they spend. In addition, the company makes a direct contribution to the countries and regions it covers. Since 1986 a percentage of the income from each book has been donated to ventures such as famine relief in Africa; aid projects in India; agricultural projects in Central America; Greenpeace's efforts to halt French nuclear testing in the Pacific and Amnesty International. In 1991 $68,000 was donated to these causes.

Lonely Planet's basic travel philosophy is summed up in Tony Wheeler's comment, 'Don't worry about whether your trip will work out. Just go!'